Introduction to Federal Income Taxation in Canada

26th edition, 2005-2006

By

Robert E. Beam, F.C.A.
Professor Emeritus, University of Waterloo
Stanley N. Laiken, Ph.D.
Deloitte Professor, University of Waterloo
James J. Barnett, F.C.A.
Director, Master of Taxation Program, University of Waterloo

Contributors
Kenneth J. Klassen, Ph.D., C.A.
Deloitte Professor, University of Waterloo
Joan A. Kitunen, BBM, C.A.
University of Toronto
Joanne E. Magee, MBA, F.C.A.
York University
Barbara Rockx, M.ACC., C.A.
University of Toronto and University of Waterloo
Michael Zender, B.Comm., LLB
Ernst & Young, Chartered Accountants, Toronto

www.cch.ca
A WoltersKluwer Company

CCH CANADIAN LIMITED
90 Sheppard Avenue East, Suite 300
Toronto, ON M2N 6X1
Telephone: (416) 224-2248 Toll Free: 1-800-268-4522
Fax: (416) 224-2243 Toll Free: 1-800-461-4131
www.cch.ca

Published by CCH Canadian Limited

By

Robert E. Beam, F.C.A.
Professor Emeritus, University of Waterloo

Stanley N. Laiken, Ph.D.
Deloitte Professor, University of Waterloo

James J. Barnett, F.C.A.
Director, Master of Taxation Program, University of Waterloo

Contributors

Ling Chu
Wilfred Laurier University

Kenneth J. Klassen, Ph.D., F.C.A.
Deloitte Professor, University of Waterloo

Joan A. Kitunen, BBM, C.A.
University of Toronto

Joanne E. Magee, LLM, F.C.A.
York University

Barbara Rockx, M.Acc., C.A.
University of Toronto and University of Waterloo

Michael Zender, B. Comm, LLB
Ernst & Young, Chartered Accountants, Toronto

Typeset by CCH Canadian Limited.
Printed in Canada.

About This Book

The study of Canadian federal income taxation is made more complex, particularly at the introductory level, not because of the lack of good interpretive materials to guide the student, but, in the authors' opinion, because of the lack of organization in the presentation of these materials for systematic study. While the *Income Tax Act* (the Act), the statute governing the federal taxation of income in Canada, is organized generally by source of income, interpretive material available to students at the introductory level is often organized by topics which may cover elements of several sources.

Since the authors of these materials feel that it is important to the understanding of the Act that the student generally studies the major provisions of the statute in sequence, the chapters of this book generally follow the organization of the Act. The purpose of these materials is to guide the student in the study at the introductory level of the major provisions of the Act and some of the related provisions in the *Excise Tax Act* (the ETA) pertaining to the Goods and Services Tax. A copy of the Act plus the Canada Revenue Agency's (CRA's) Interpretation Bulletins, Information Circulars and Advance Tax Rulings are considered to be essential materials for the course. The purpose is to organize the student's reference to interpretive material in the order of presentation in the Act. This book is designed to encourage students to refer to the Act, case law and the CRA's publications; it is not written to be used as a completely independent text.

The commentary presented in this book highlights key areas of the Act. The textbook provides additional interpretation of particularly difficult provisions of the Act or elements of the common law or case law in the area. The basic concepts and principles underlying the rules of the legislation are emphasized throughout these materials. Most important for the study of income taxation, it provides fact situations or example problems which demonstrate the application of the provisions of the Act to realistic situations. In fact, the primary teaching approach used in this commentary is the presentation of example problems and exercises with solutions. These solutions demonstrate various methods of approaching actual problems in income taxation. The solutions also provide explanatory and interpretive notes which are an important component of these materials, often expanding a topic beyond the confines of the particular facts under discussion.

The authors must emphasize that these materials are in no way intended to be a substitute for the Act. It is essential that students obtain practice in reading the Act not only for the purpose of becoming familiar with a particular provision under study, but also for the purpose of learning how to read and interpret the legislation in general. These materials are designed to present situations which will help students to focus their attention on the reading and understanding of a particular provision or set of provisions with the objective of developing more generalized skills to be used in the interpretation of the Act.

At the outset of each major heading in the chapter, a list of references for the material under the heading is provided. These references are to the following sources:

(1) ITA refers to the sections of the *Income Tax Act* to be discussed in the chapter;

(2) ITAR refers to the *Income Tax Application Rules, 1971*, which are found in the volume containing the Act immediately following the provisions of the Act;

(3) ITR refers to the Income Tax Regulations which are also found in the volume containing the Act;

(4) ETA refers to sections of the *Excise Tax Act* in which provisions of the Goods and Services Tax (GST) can be found; and

(5) IT, IC, TR and ATR refer, respectively, to Interpretation Bulletins, Information Circulars, Tax Rulings and Advance Tax Rulings — Second Series and are available in a one-volume softcover edition published by CCH Canadian Limited.

An explanation of all of these references is provided at the beginning of Chapter 1. References to sections of the Act are provided for all exercises and assignment problems. It should also be understood that in the course of discussion all the references preceded by such specific terms as "section," "subsection," "paragraph," "subparagraph," etc. without any indication of the pertinent statute, refer to the provisions of the *Income Tax Act*. Similarly the provisions of the Income Tax Regulations are preceded by the term "Regulation" without specifying the relevant legislation.

References to the *Excise Tax Act* are usually confined to the GST part of a chapter and are specifically indicated as being to that legislation. An attempt has been made to integrate GST with relevant transactions discussed under the *Income Tax Act* in the chapters where these transactions are discussed.

A copy of the CD, containing the CCH *TaxWorks* Electronic Research Library, is enclosed with student editions of this book. Thorough and accurate tax research is an important part of tax practice. To help students learn how to perform this type of research, Chapter 19 of this book provides a self-study guide to tax research using electronic products. Exercises are provided with solutions in Appendix III, to facilitate the self-study process.

A set of review questions is provided at the end of each chapter. These short-answer questions attempt to review key points made in the text or points that are not integrated into the example problems, multiple choice questions, exercises or assignment problems in the chapter. Discussion notes on the review questions are provided in Appendix I at the end of the text.

Since multiple choice questions are common in professional examinations, this textbook provides six or seven such questions covering the material in Chapters 2 to 18 at the end of each of those chapters, for a total of over 100 questions. Annotated solutions are provided in Appendix II at the end of the book to enhance learning through self-study.

Exercises have been provided at the end of each chapter. These usually consist of short problems to highlight particular areas of the chapter. They are designed to be fairly narrow in scope, to provide the student with an opportunity to apply the material in the chapter to a specific problem situation. Solutions to these exercises have been provided in Appendix III.

Assignment problems are provided for each chapter of these materials. These problems are designed to have the student apply the material discussed in each chapter to an actual fact or problem situation. While these problems focus on the key elements of the chapter in much the same way that the solved example problems in the commentary do, the problems are not identical in their coverage or presentation. As a result, it will be necessary for the student to read the assignment problems very carefully in preparing a solution. Solutions to these problems are not available. However, similar additional problems with solutions are provided on the accompanying CD, as discussed below.

Students often request additional problems with solutions that they can use on a self-study basis for preparation for tests and examinations. For this purpose, a comprehensive compilation of problems similar to the assignment problems in this book and multiple choice questions are provided on the CD accompanying this book. There are over 150 problems and solutions on the CD, classified by coverage of chapters in this textbook. The problems, most of which have been used as examination questions, will provide students with an opportunity to deal with problems of a comprehensive nature. Since these supplemental problems may cover material from several chapters, as examination questions often do, they provide an excellent source for review in preparation for examinations.

The authors suggest the following approach to the use of these materials. First, the student should read the references for each major heading of the commentary. Thus, the student should scan for coverage and content of the particular sections of the Act under discussion, any Income Tax Application Rules or Regulations applicable to these sections, and any Interpretation Bulletins, Information Circulars or Advance Tax Rulings applicable to these sections. Then, the student should read the commentary in this book, including the example problems. The solutions provided for these problems will demonstrate the approach that can be taken for the type of example problem under consideration. The solutions can also be used as a check on the student's understanding as well as a means of providing further interpretation and explanation of the material covered. The exercises at the end of the chapter can be used in a similar manner with the solutions provided on the accompanying CD being used as a means of self-study and reinforcement. Once the parts of a chapter have been completed in this manner, the student should be sufficiently prepared to attempt the assignment problems relevant to a particular part or to the whole chapter. When reviewing material for examination or other purposes, the multiple choice questions at the end of each chapter and the problems on the accompanying CD can be attempted. The solutions in Appendix II and on the CD can then be checked. Review might also focus on the approaches used to address the various types of problems presented.

Materials at the introductory level on Canadian income tax legislation are not easy to study. A conscientious effort to do the work and, particularly, to do problems and apply what has been read is essential to a good understanding of this material. The authors have attempted to meet the challenge of presenting the material by setting out the work that must be done and by explaining, as best they can, the major provisions of the legislation. The challenge of learning the material is, of course, left to the student.

Toronto, Ontario   Robert E. Beam

Waterloo, Ontario   Stanley N. Laiken

Waterloo, Ontario   James J. Barnett

July 2005

Acknowledgement

Over the years, many people have participated in the preparation, revision and improvement of these materials. The authors would like to acknowledge their indebtedness to all who have helped in this undertaking. The Institute of Chartered Accountants of Ontario funded the initial concept and application of these materials through its correspondence course. The Chartered Accountants Students' Association of Ontario permitted the inclusion of some of its material in the area of advanced corporate taxation in Chapters 15, 16 and 17. Miss Kathy Matthews, Secretary to the Finance and Business Economics area of the Faculty of Business at McMaster University, diligently prepared the original version of the manuscript and the revision in the first edition. The business students of both McMaster University and Ryerson Polytechnical University when we were faculty members there, the students in the accountancy and the tax programs of the University of Waterloo and C.A. finalist students in the preparation program of the Chartered Accountants Students' Association of Ontario and in the School of Accountancy of the Institute of Chartered Accountants of Ontario have constantly given invaluable assistance in revising and polishing the final manuscript for each edition. In addition, a number of our colleagues teaching either full-time or part-time at various universities and colleges and teaching at the Institute of Chartered Accountants of Ontario School of Accountancy have made most helpful comments for the improvement of this book.

In particular we are greatly indebted and most grateful to the following individuals for their efforts in making contributions of materials, in providing their comments or views on various aspects of the book and in reviewing and revising these materials.

The following past major contributors have provided text materials or problems, which were added to the book and helped with annual revisions and updates. Some provided materials on specialized areas of taxation.

Greg Boehmer	Linda Hyatt	Michael Robillard
Catherine Brayley	Gena Katz	Wayne Rudson
Mariann Coward	John MacCulloch	Karen Wensley
Irene David	Alan Macnaughton	Susan Whitney
Kass Ebrahim	Debbie Lee Mailling	Karen Wilkinson
Nancy Harley	D.L. (Del) McLennan	Brian Wilson
	Jane Ritchie	

The following individuals have provided detailed and valuable comments for improvements and revisions from various perspectives of practice and education.

Bill Chan	Paul Jarvis	Annalee Richler
Richard Colden	David Lam	Rick Robertson
Brian Cookson	Michelle Ma	Julie Robson
Austin Davey	Thomas Matthews	Martin Schwartz
Jonathan Eckler	Alastair Murdoch	Ian Simpson
Thomas Haddrath	Ian Niven	Tari Lee Vaughan
Ken Hurdle	David Palamar	Dorothy Wright
		Allister Young

The following individuals have provided extensive reviews of the manuscript and ably provided detailed comments on readability of the text. Some participated in a painstaking proofreading of the text and methodical checking of calculations.

Rayna (Laiken) Baker	Janna (Laiken) Krieger	Rob Law
Howard Bergman	Jonathan Kreiger	Terry McDowell
Tom Kingissepp	Adam Laiken	Robert Montgomery
		Kirsten Richter

As a result of the continuous change in materials on taxation, all editions required extensive revisions. A considerable burden was placed, as usual, on the Editorial Department of CCH Canadian Limited and, in particular, Kee-Hyung Kim who was a great help in the preparation of the first 19 editions before his retirement in 1998. He, also, was enticed out of retirement, briefly, to do a thorough editorial review of the 22nd edition. We are very happy that he was willing to do so. His work in converting very messy manuscripts into final copy on all those editions has been tremendous and greatly appreciated. His editorial thoroughness has held us to high standards of writing and presentation. His pleasant manner of keeping us on schedule to ensure timely production of the materials has been a major and invaluable contribution to the work for which we are very grateful. We hope that he continues to enjoy a healthy and happy retirement. For subsequent editions, the considerable editorial work was ably continued by Ann Choi, Douglas Robb, and James McColl. The tradition of invaluable editorial work was meticulously provided by Jerry D'Souza for this and the previous edition.

The authors have benefited tremendously from their respective associations with Ernst & Young, Chartered Accountants, Toronto (Beam), RSM Richter, Chartered Accountants, Toronto (Laiken) and Deloitte Chartered Accountants, Toronto and London (Barnett). Our experiences with these firms have provided a practical perspective which we feel is essential as academics working in the field of income taxation.

In an undertaking of this nature our wives, Karen, Elaine and Fay, and children have had to bear a burden that is often unrecognized and certainly unrewarded. We greatly appreciate their contribution of patience and understanding to the preparation of this book, because without them there would be nothing!

July 2005   Robert E. Beam

                                                                          Stanley N. Laiken

                                                                          James. J. Barnett

Note on Legislation for
Twenty-sixth Edition

This edition refers to proposed amendments released on October 31, 2003 pertaining to the deductibility of interest and other expenses and other proposals contained in the Revised Draft Legislation and Explanatory Notes for Technical Amendments to the *Income Tax Act* dated February 27, 2004. Neither set of proposals was legislated by July 2005.

However, by the end of June 2005, Bill C-33 which implemented the 2004 federal budget and Bill C-43 which implemented the 2005 federal budget had received Royal Assent. This edition incorporates the relevant provisions of both bills as law. Several proposals made in the 2005 federal budget were not included in Bill C-43 and, hence, are referred to as proposals in this edition.

Table of Contents

		Page
About This Book		iii
Acknowledgement		vii
Chapter 1	Introduction	1
	Exercises	35
	Assignment Problems	37
Chapter 2	Liability for Tax	39
	Review Questions	62
	Multiple Choice Questions	63
	Exercises	65
	Assignment Problems	68
Chapter 3	Employment Income	75
	Review Questions	129
	Multiple Choice Questions	130
	Exercises	132
	Assignment Problems	137
Chapter 4	Income from Business: General Concepts and Rules	149
	Review Questions	200
	Multiple Choice Questions	201
	Exercises	203
	Assignment Problems	206
Chapter 5	Depreciable Capital Property and Eligible Capital Property	219
	Review Questions	247
	Multiple Choice Questions	248
	Exercises	249
	Assignment Problems	252
Chapter 6	Income from Property	263
	Review Questions	300
	Multiple Choice Questions	301
	Exercises	303
	Assignment Problems	306
Chapter 7	Capital Gains: An Introduction	315
	Review Questions	343
	Multiple Choice Questions	344
	Exercises	346
	Assignment Problems	348

  Page

Chapter 8   Capital Gains: The Finer Points......................   365
             Review Questions   400
             Multiple Choice Questions   402
             Exercises   404
             Assignment Problems...................................   407

Chapter 9   Other Sources of Income and Deductions in Computing
             Income...   419
             Review Questions   456
             Multiple Choice Questions   458
             Exercises   460
             Assignment Problems...................................   463

Chapter 10   Computation of Taxable Income and Taxes Payable for
             Individuals   471
             Review Questions   527
             Multiple Choice Questions   527
             Exercises   529
             Assignment Problems...................................   532

Chapter 11   Computation of Taxable Income and Tax after General
             Reductions for Corporations..........................   537
             Review Questions   600
             Multiple Choice Questions   600
             Exercises   602
             Assignment Problems...................................   608

Chapter 12   Integration for Business and Investment Income of the
             Private Corporation   619
             Review Questions   677
             Multiple Choice Questions   678
             Exercises   680
             Assignment Problems...................................   685

Chapter 13   Planning the Use of a Corporation and
             Shareholder-manager
             Remuneration   697
             Review Questions   738
             Multiple Choice Questions   739
             Exercises   740
             Assignment Problems...................................   744

Chapter 14   Rights and Obligations under the Income Tax Act.........   755
             Review Questions   784
             Multiple Choice Questions   785
             Exercises   786
             Assignment Problems...................................   789

Page

Chapter 15 Corporate Distributions, Windings-up and Sales 801

      Review Questions 832

      Multiple Choice Questions 833

      Exercises 835

      Assignment Problems................................... 839

Chapter 16 Income Deferral: Rollover on Transfers to a Corporation
      and Pitfalls 849

      Review Questions 904

      Multiple Choice Questions 905

      Exercises 906

      Assignment Problems................................... 911

Chapter 17 Income Deferral: Other Rollovers and Use of Rollovers
      in Estate Planning 919

      Review Questions 943

      Multiple Choice Questions 944

      Exercises 945

      Assignment Problems................................... 947

Chapter 18 Partnerships and Trusts 953

      Review Questions 976

      Multiple Choice Questions 977

      Exercises 979

      Assignment Problems................................... 981

Chapter 19 Computer-Assisted Tax Research 999

      Part II Exercises 1027
      Part III Exercises 1044
      Part IV Exercises 1051

	Page
Appendix I : Discussion Notes for Review Questions	1053
Appendix II : Solutions to Multiple Choice Questions	1079
Appendix III : Solutions to Exercises	1111
Topical Index	1207

Chapter 1

Introduction

TOPICS DISCUSSED

	Page
HISTORICAL, LEGAL AND THEORETICAL BACKGROUND	2
Brief History of the Income Tax Act	2
Constitutional Basis for Income Taxation	3
Some Theoretical Concepts of Taxation	3
INTRODUCTION TO INCOME TAX LEGISLATION	6
Note on Organization of Legislation and Availability of Interpretive Sources	6
Structure of the Income Tax Act	11
Approaches to Defining Income	14
Income vs. Capital	16
Computation of Income	16
Determination of Income and Taxable Income	18
Interpretation of Tax Legislation	22

	Page
The Role of the Professional Accountant in Tax Matters	25
GENERAL BACKGROUND ON ADMINISTRATION AND ENFORCEMENT OF THE ACT	26
Onus of Proof	26
Appeals	26
Administration and Enforcement	27
Tax Evasion, Avoidance and Planning	27
INTRODUCTION TO THE GOODS AND SERVICES TAX	28
Note on Organization of Legislation and Availability of Interpretive Sources	28
Overview and Basic Concepts	32
Supplies	32
Input Tax Credits	34
Reform of the GST and Provincial Harmonization	35

This chapter covers three basic areas of income taxation in Canada. First, it provides a historical, legal and theoretical perspective. Second, it introduces the *Income Tax Act* (ITA or the Act),[a] the legal statute governing income taxation in Canada, by providing an overview of the structure of the legislation. Third, the materials present an overview of the administration and enforcement of the legislation.

This chapter also introduces, on a conceptual basis, the Goods and Services Tax (GST). Subsequent chapters will discuss the related GST implications of the topics described in those chapters. This chapter first describes the organization of the GST in

[a] Unless otherwise stated, all statutory references are to the *Income Tax Act*, RSC 1985, c.1 (5th Supplement) as amended (referred to as "the Act").

the context of its legislative authority, the *Excise Tax Act* (ETA),[b] and various interpretive sources. The balance of this material then gives an overview of the GST system and, in particular, certain basic concepts such as taxable transactions, exempt transactions and GST refunds.

I. HISTORICAL, LEGAL AND THEORETICAL BACKGROUND

A. Brief History of the Income Tax Act

From Confederation in 1867 through to World War I, the major sources of federal government revenue were customs and excise taxes comprising about 80% of all revenue. Remaining requirements were met largely by the issue of debt. Income tax was first imposed federally in 1917 as a temporary measure to help finance World War I. The legislation was embodied in the *Income War Tax Act* which was a relatively simple document of some ten pages in length. In 1948 the *Income Tax Act* was passed. Although it involved a rewording and codification of the old law, there were few changes in policy.

A major reform of federal income tax legislation began in 1962 with the setting up of the Royal Commission on Taxation under the chairmanship of the late Kenneth Carter. The Carter Commission presented its seven-volume report in 1967 recommending fundamental changes in tax legislation which would use a comprehensive tax base including capital gains. Next, the government issued a White Paper on tax reform in 1969, drawing on the Carter recommendations, but modifying them. Public hearings were held by two parliamentary committees on the White Paper proposals. This process culminated in the budget address of June 18, 1971 which proposed Bill C-259 to amend the *Income Tax Act*. This bill was given Royal Assent on December 23, 1971, effective January 1, 1972. Since that date, every budget address has presented a considerable number of amendments to the tax legislation to both "fine-tune" the existing legislation and introduce new fiscal policy.

Sixteen years later, on June 18, 1987, the government released a White Paper on Tax Reform which was to be implemented in two phases. Phase One, implemented in 1988, included changes to the personal and corporate income tax systems and interim changes to the existing federal sales tax. After consultation and recommendations made by the House of Commons Committee on Finance and Economic Affairs and the Senate Committee on Banking, Trade and Commerce, the resultant legislation was introduced as Bill C-139 which was passed on September 13, 1988. Phase Two replaced the existing federal sales tax with a broad-based multi-stage sales tax referred to as the Goods and Services Tax (GST), effective January 1, 1991.

The Statutes of Canada, of which the *Income Tax Act* is one, are revised periodically to reflect amendments to the legislation. The most recent revision referred to as the *Fifth Supplement to the Revised Statutes of Canada, 1985*, proclaimed in force on March 1, 1994, contains major revisions to the structure of sections of the Act. In particular, changes were made in definition sections and in sections which contain algebraic formulae. Even this version of the Act has been amended many times since its proclamation.

Currently, income taxes comprise about 60% of total federal government revenues, with personal income taxes raising about 3.5 times the amount of revenue as corporate

---

[b] Unless otherwise stated, the *Excise Tax Act* will be referred to as "the ETA".

income taxes. Sales and excise taxes, including the GST, represent about 20% of total federal government revenues. Exhibit 1-1 gives some indication of the relative importance of various taxes.

EXHIBIT 1-1
Government of Canada Budgetary Revenues
(2005-2006 Forecast)

Revenue item	Billions of dollars*	Percentage
Personal income tax	94.3	47.0
Corporate income taxes	29.2	14.6
Employment insurance contributions	17.2	8.6
Goods and services tax	31.5	15.7
Customs import duties	3.1	1.5
Other tax revenue	13.8	6.9
Non-tax revenue	11.4	5.7
Total budgetary revenues	200.5	100.0

* Source: Table 7.7, "The Revenue Outlook" in Chapter 7 "Sound Financial Management", *The Budget Plan 2005*, Department of Finance Canada, February 23, 2005.

B. Constitutional Basis for Income Taxation

The *British North America Act, 1867*, renamed the *Constitution Act, 1867* in the process of the repatriation of the Constitution, granted authority for all taxation in Canada, separating federal and provincial powers to impose income taxes. Subsection 91(3) of the *Constitution Act, 1867* provides the federal government with unlimited powers of taxation by permitting "the raising of money by any mode or system of taxation". On the other hand, subsection 92(2) limits provincial powers to direct taxation of income earned in the province and of income of persons resident in the province. Of course, income taxation falls within both sets of these government powers. Even with a fairly liberal interpretation of the provincial powers of direct taxation, to meet increasing provincial requirements over the years, there has been a constant trading of tax points through federal–provincial taxation agreements. Nevertheless, intergovernmental problems of raising revenues through taxation persist.

C. Some Theoretical Concepts of Taxation

1. Classification of taxes

Taxes can be classified in a number of different ways. One such method is the basis of the tax, with the name of the tax reflecting to some extent the tax base or what is to be taxed. A head tax is, in essence, a tax on the existence of a particular type of taxpayer such as a tax of $X paid by all individuals over the age of 18. An income tax, as the title implies, is a tax on the income of the taxpayer and is exemplified by a tax on the income of individuals or corporations. A wealth tax, such as a tax on capital gains or succession duties, is a tax on the accumulated capital of a taxpayer. A commodity tax is, essentially, a tax on the consumption of the commodity subject to tax as is the case of a provincial sales tax. A user tax, such as a toll for a bridge or road, is a tax on the use of a facility or service. A tariff is a tax or duty usually imposed on imported goods to increase the price of such goods relative to domestic goods. A transfer tax is a tax on the value of property transferred from one owner to another as is the case on the transfer of land under certain conditions. Finally, a business transfer tax, a value-added tax or a multi-stage sales tax, such as the goods and services tax, is a tax on the increase in value of a commodity created by the taxpayer in moving it from one stage of production or distribution to another.

Another method of classifying taxes is by the incidence of the tax, which determines the taxpayer who ultimately bears the tax. The incidence of a direct tax is likely to be on the initial payer of the tax. For example, the burden of the individual income tax is generally considered to be on the individual who pays the tax. On the other hand, the incidence of an indirect tax is usually not on the initial payer of the tax, but is on someone else. A sales tax imposed at the manufacturer's level is an example of such an indirect tax. While an income tax may be paid by a corporation, the incidence of the tax may be on customers, suppliers, employees or shareholders of the corporation, depending on its economic ability to pass the tax on to the others.

Finally, taxes can be classified by the nature of the tax levy. A proportional or flat tax is levied at a constant percentage of the income of the payer of the tax. Under certain conditions, the corporate income tax can be considered as such a tax. A progressive tax is levied at an increasing percentage of the income of the payer as is the case of the personal income tax. Similarly, a regressive tax is levied at a decreasing percentage of the income of the payer. A sales tax is considered to be a regressive tax to the extent that those with higher income may spend a lower proportion of that income on the item subject to the sales tax.

2. Desirable characteristics of an income tax

An income tax should be equitable on two dimensions. It should be equitable horizontally so that persons at the same economic level are affected by the tax to the same degree in terms of the amount of tax irrespective of the form of income generated. An income tax should also be equitable vertically so that persons at a higher economic level pay a greater share of the tax based on their greater ability to pay than those at a lower economic level.

An income tax should be neutral so that the tax does not affect economic decisions. Thus, for the tax system to be considered neutral, a decision based on the after-tax results of an economic opportunity should not be any different than it would have been in the absence of taxation. At the same time, the income tax system must be sufficiently flexible to permit its use as an instrument of economic policy to achieve specified economic objectives. Of course, what might be considered economically desirable may not be politically feasible. For example, the Carter Commission recommendation to achieve horizontal equity by taxing all sources of economic gain equally, because "a buck is a buck", was apparently rejected for political reasons.

The position of the taxpayer with respect to a tax should be certain. The taxpayer must be in a position to understand and determine with some certainty the payer of the tax, the base of the tax, the amount of the tax, the deadline for payment of the tax and the method of payment.

Administration of the tax must be feasible and efficient. Thus, the total costs, including those of the taxpayer, of administering and collecting the tax should be as low as possible. The relative costs of administration and collection of the Canadian income tax are very low when compared with those of other countries.

Familiarity with the specifics of the Canadian income tax legislation will facilitate an evaluation of its characteristics relative to these ideal characteristics.

At the outset of its report on tax simplification,[c] the House of Commons Standing Committee on Finance and Economic Affairs made the following general observations on the current Canadian tax system.

> In addition to raising revenue efficiently, the ideal tax system is equitable and simple, and it assists the promotion of economic growth. Unfortunately, the goals of the ideal tax system often conflict. Changes made to make the system more equitable or to increase economic growth may make the system less simple. In fact since the early 1970s the tradeoffs between equity and simplicity and between growth and simplicity have been quite one-sided: if one of the goals had to give, it was always simplicity. The result, of course, is a Tax Act that even experts find confusing and a tax form for the average taxpayer that is daunting in length and complexity.
>
> Any tax system is defined by six characteristics:
>
> 1. who pays the tax,
>
> 2. the base to be taxed,
>
> 3. the rates to be applied to the base,
>
> 4. general exemptions,
>
> 5. general deductions, and
>
> 6. other selective measures [including how and when the tax is to be paid].
>
> The nature of the six characteristics determines how much revenue is produced by the tax system, as well as the equity of the system and its ability to promote growth. It is the exemptions, deductions and other selective tax measures that make modern tax systems so complicated. There are in Canada, for example, over one hundred selective tax measures dealing with personal income tax. There are even more measures dealing with corporate tax.
>
> The Income Tax Act includes the tax measures, and the tax forms must allow for them. Too often the tax system is changed — the changes rationalized in terms of improved equity or economic growth — with no attention to the possible increased complexity of the Tax Act and tax forms. The Act and forms are treated as matters that can take care of themselves — an attitude that provides no check on the ever-increasing complexity of the Tax Act and tax forms. The Committee believes that the analysis of the tax system must be realigned with attention devoted to simplifying both the Act and the forms.

3. Tax Reform guidelines

Guidelines for comprehensive tax reform announced by the Minister of Finance in 1986 in a speech to the House of Commons are summarized below. These guidelines can be used as a basis for evaluating the legislation as it exists at any time.

> *Fairness:* The tax system should ensure fair sharing of the tax burden among taxpayers. People in similar circumstances should receive the same tax treatment; all high-income individuals and corporations should pay their fair share of tax; and similar products should bear the same rate of sales tax.
>
> *Simplicity and Compliance:* Tax compliance should be made easier by making the system simpler and more readily understood.

---

[c] This report was released on June 19, 1986.

Balance: Tax reform would redress the too-heavy share of tax revenues raised through the personal income tax, by requiring more of profitable corporations and by broadening the sales tax base.

Stability: Stability and dependability of tax revenues are essential for government budgeting. Raising more total tax revenues is not an objective of tax reform, but it should increase the certainty of achieving the revenue goals that the government sets itself.

International Competitiveness: The tax system should reinforce the ability of Canadians to compete internationally.

Economic Growth: The tax system should encourage growth through lower tax rates on a broader tax base. Business opportunities, rather than tax planning, should be the driving force behind business decisions.

Canadian Priorities: The tax system should help meet national social and economic needs, including regional needs, in keeping with Canadian priorities and values.

Transitional Implementation: Changes should be implemented with appropriate transitional provisions, to avoid leaving Canadians in doubt about tax rules.

Consultation: The government will consult broadly before making its final legislative proposals for tax reform.

II. INTRODUCTION TO INCOME TAX LEGISLATION

A. Note on Organization of Legislation and Availability of Interpretive Sources

1. The *Income Tax Act*

It is very important to the study of income taxation that one becomes thoroughly familiar with the organization, structure and coverage of the *Income Tax Act* (Act). When a tax problem arises, knowing where to find the provisions in the Act which are most likely to deal with the problem will save a considerable amount of time in the resolution of the problem. An overview of the Act can best be obtained from an inspection of the Table of Contents to the Act. A detailed sectional list of the Act is provided at the beginning of the CCH edition of the Act. References to the Act in court cases, for example, may have been changed in the *Fifth Supplement to the Revised Statutes of Canada, 1985.* A Table of Concordance is provided in the current CCH edition of the Act to relate revised provisions in the current Act to the equivalent provisions in the former Act.

CCH editions, which contain the Act, also contain several other important pieces of Canadian tax legislation, such as the Income Tax Regulations which support the Act, and the U.K. and U.S. tax treaties with Canada. The Act is divided into over 30 Parts, most of which represent specific types of tax, other than income tax. Of course, the largest Part deals with income tax and, because of its size, requires further classification into Divisions and Subdivisions. Exhibit 1-2 illustrates this structure of the Act with selected categories of provisions.

EXHIBIT 1-2
Structure of the *Income Tax Act*

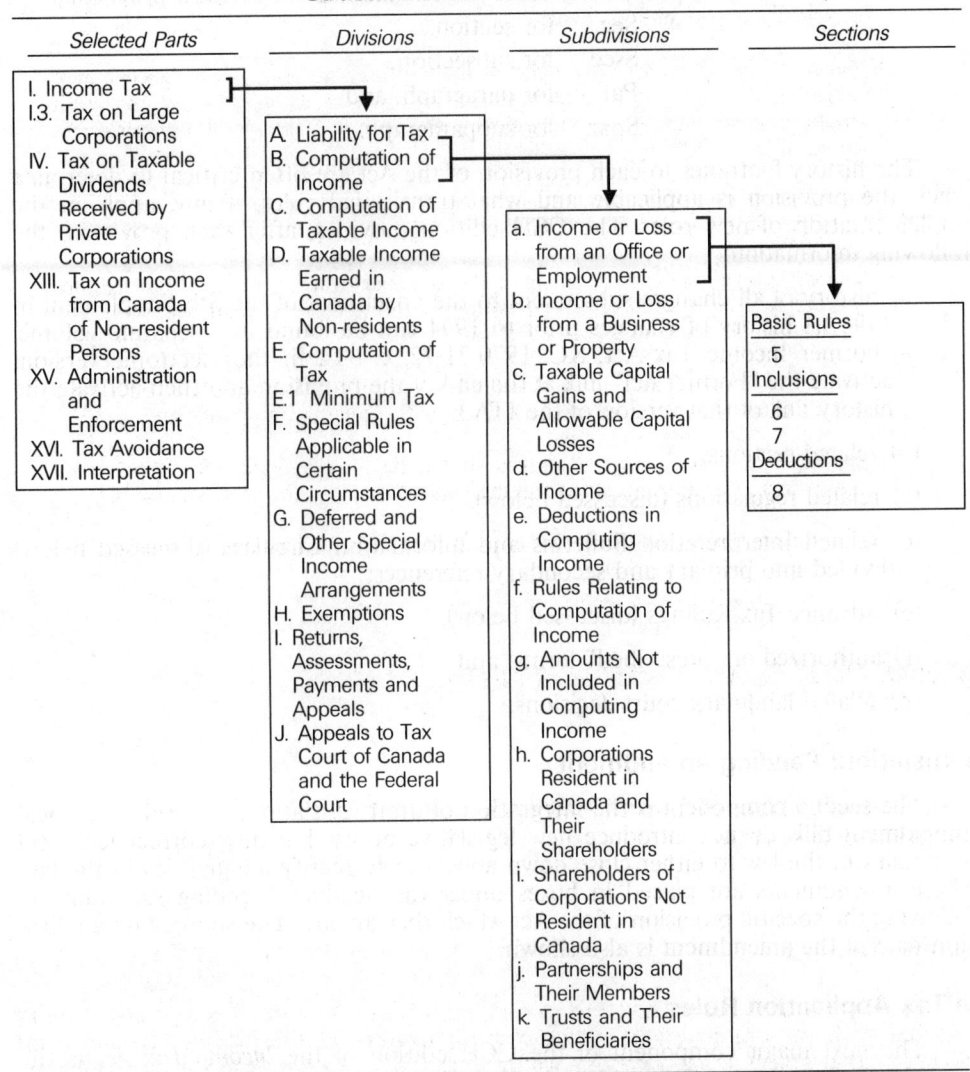

Selected Parts	Divisions	Subdivisions	Sections

I. Income Tax
I.3. Tax on Large Corporations
IV. Tax on Taxable Dividends Received by Private Corporations
XIII. Tax on Income from Canada of Non-resident Persons
XV. Administration and Enforcement
XVI. Tax Avoidance
XVII. Interpretation

A. Liability for Tax
B. Computation of Income
C. Computation of Taxable Income
D. Taxable Income Earned in Canada by Non-residents
E. Computation of Tax
E.1 Minimum Tax
F. Special Rules Applicable in Certain Circumstances
G. Deferred and Other Special Income Arrangements
H. Exemptions
I. Returns, Assessments, Payments and Appeals
J. Appeals to Tax Court of Canada and the Federal Court

a. Income or Loss from an Office or Employment
b. Income or Loss from a Business or Property
c. Taxable Capital Gains and Allowable Capital Losses
d. Other Sources of Income
e. Deductions in Computing Income
f. Rules Relating to Computation of Income
g. Amounts Not Included in Computing Income
h. Corporations Resident in Canada and Their Shareholders
i. Shareholders of Corporations Not Resident in Canada
j. Partnerships and Their Members
k. Trusts and Their Beneficiaries

Basic Rules
5
Inclusions
6
7
Deductions
8

For ease of reference, provisions are numbered, separating various elements of the provision. For example, consider the following reference:

$$6(1)(b)(i)(A)$$

The first number refers to the section of the Act and the second number refers to the subsection. Notice that section 6 subsection (1) is a fairly lengthy sentence covering several pages of text. The letter (*b*) refers to what is called a paragraph and the lower case Roman numeral (i) refers to a subparagraph. The upper case letter (A) refers to a clause. If necessary, a subclause would be referred to with an upper case Roman numeral and a sub-subclause would be referred to with an Arabic numeral. The above reference would be called "clause 6(1)(*b*)(i)(A)", stating the numerals and letters in order, in normal speech. From time to time an amendment is made to the Act and it is necessary to insert it between existing provisions without renumbering the whole Act. In such a case a reference such as section 6 subsection (2.1) will be entered between subsections 6(2) and 6(3). Some sections, like section 3, have no subsections. Hence, references skip directly to paragraphs as is the case in paragraph 3(*a*). As a short-form reference in this book, the following abbreviations may be used with a provision:

>   Sec.   for section,
>   Ssec. for subsection,
>   Par.   for paragraph, and
>   Spar. for subparagraph.

The history footnotes to each provision of the Act are often critical to determine when the provision is applicable and what transitional rules, if any, apply in the implementation of new rules. The CCH edition provides, after each provision, the following information:

(a) history of all changes subsequent to the enactment of the 5th Supplement in 1994 (A history of changes prior to 1994 can be found in a separate volume, "Former Income Tax Act, S.C. 1970-71-72, c. 63". In the electronic version, activate the "Former Act" link at the end of the provision and then activate the history link of that version of the ITA.);

(b) related sections;

(c) related regulations (discussed below);

(d) related Interpretation Bulletins and Information Circulars (discussed below) divided into primary and secondary references;

(e) Advance Tax Rulings (discussed below);

(f) authorized or "prescribed" forms; and

(g) related landmark court decisions.

2. Draft legislation: Pending amendment

The second component is the integration of draft legislation. As a rule, technical amendment bills do not introduce new legislative policy, but only correct technical anomalies in the law to either close down abuses or to rectify inequalities in the law. These amendments are placed in boxes under the heading "Pending Amendment" following the specific provision of the Act which they amend. The source and application date of the amendment is also shown.

3. Income Tax Application Rules

The next major component of the CCH edition of the *Income Tax Act* is the provisions of the *Income Tax Application Rules, 1971* (ITARs). Technically, these rules appear in Part I of Chapter 2 of the *Fifth Supplement to the Revised Statutes of Canada, 1985*. These rules provide largely for the transition from the pre-1972 Act and its system of taxation to the current Act and its system of taxation including the introduction of the taxation of capital gains. These transitional rules are an important part of the law of income taxation and reference will be made to them throughout this book.

4. International tax conventions or treaties

The Act must be interpreted in light of International Tax Conventions which Canada has negotiated with many countries in order to reduce the impact of potential double taxation and tax avoidance. Both the Canada–United States Tax Convention (1980) and the Canada–U.K. Income Tax Convention (1978) are reproduced in the CCH edition of the Act. Over 80 others have been or are being negotiated. It is important to note that tax conventions override the provisions of the *Income Tax Act* and, hence, should be the first reference source when examining the tax implications of cross-border transactions.

5. Income Tax Regulations

The *Income Tax Regulations* (Regulations) are set out to handle various specific situations and to carry on the general purposes and provisions of the Act. Unlike the Act itself, these regulations, which are part of the law, may be passed by Order-in-Council without ratification by Parliament. However, regulations must be written within the authority of a particular section of the Act and cannot be independent of the Act. Reference will also be made frequently in this book to the regulations which are part of the law and have assumed increasing importance in recent years.

6. Other interpretive sources

(a) *Judicial Decisions*

Although not part of the statute itself, a number of sources have importance in the interpretation of the Act over the years of income taxation in Canada.

- Judicial decisions, which form the common law, on income tax matters may be appealed up to the Supreme Court of Canada (S.C.C.).

- The middle level of court hearing tax cases is the Federal Court. Prior to 1990, income tax cases went to the Federal Court–Trial Division (F.C.T.D.) and then to the Federal Court of Appeal (F.C.A.). Now, only the Federal Court of Appeal is used for income tax cases, except for some administrative matters pertaining to income tax, which are heard by the F.C.T.D. Prior to 1972, this middle level of court was called the Exchequer Court (Ex. Ct.).

- The lowest level of court hearing tax cases is now called the Tax Court of Canada (T.C.C.). Prior to 1984, the lowest level was the Tax Review Board (T.R.B.), called the Tax Appeal Board (T.A.B.) prior to 1972.

- Court decisions, which are almost always based on particular sets of facts, interpret the application of the law to these facts. Most tax cases heard in Canada are published by CCH in the DOMINION TAX CASES. These cases are referred to using the name of the taxpayer and a reference such as 83 DTC 5041, as seen in the next paragraph. The numeral 83 refers to the 1983 volume and the letters DTC refer to the DOMINION TAX CASES set. The numeral 5041 refers to the first page of the 1983 volume on which the case report begins. The CCH electronic version of the court cases also refers to the hard copy pages — just click on the page icon in the electronic text and a popup box will indicate the hard copy page.

While the court's decisions represent the law, as interpreted for a specific set of facts, and may be useful as a guide in interpreting the law more generally, it must be remembered that each set of facts differs from the previous cases in some degree and that a slight difference in the facts of a given case may materially affect the outcome.

Often a Canadian court will refer to a decision of a court outside Canada, such as a U.S. court or a court in a country with legislation and common law rooted in the British system. These decisions, at any level, made outside Canada are not binding on a Canadian court, but they may be referred to as persuasive, particularly, where principles of taxation or tax legislation are similar.

The part of a decided case that provides a binding precedent is referred to as the *ratio decidendi* or reasons for judgement. The application of principles of law or the interpretation of the law in a fact situation presented to a court is the basis for generalizing from decided cases which establish a precedent.

Often, a judicial decision will contain comments that are not necessary for the decision in the fact situation under consideration. These comments are known as *obiter dicta* or comments made in passing. While these comments are not part of the precedent established by the case under consideration and, hence, not necessarily binding on other courts, they may provide insights to the interpretation of the law in different fact situations that might arise in subsequent cases.

(b) *Forms*

Forms issued by the Canada Revenue Agency (CRA) and officially prescribed by the legislation may provide some insights to the interpretation of a provision in the legislation.

All of these forms can be obtained from the district taxation offices, the CRA's web site (www.cra.gc.ca), or from commercial publishers either in print or electronic form.

(c) *CRA Publications*

The CRA releases some explanatory information on the official position in various taxation matters through a series of publications which are available on its web site. The series of publications include: Information Circulars (ICs) which deal mainly with administrative and procedural matters and Interpretation Bulletins (ITs) which outline the CRA's interpretation of specific sections of the tax law.

Advance Tax Rulings (ATRs) contain disguised summaries of certain advance income tax rulings given by the CRA and selected for publication. The last ruling published in the initial series was TR-101 dated December 9, 1980. Since many of the rulings in that initial series have become obsolete due to changes in the law, the CRA began with ATR-1 dated November 29, 1985, to reissue as part of a Second Series those former rulings that are still valid. The last published ATR was March 1996. The ATRs have been replaced by published technical interpretations discussed below.

Through the *Access to Information Act* and advance income tax rulings, the CRA's responses to taxpayers' requests for technical interpretations on specific tax issues are published by commercial tax publishers. For example, CCH publishes in print form and electronically a summary, called WINDOW ON CANADIAN TAX, of the more significant interpretations. In addition, CCH publishes the *full* text of every one of these interpretations, referred to as TAX WINDOW FILES, but only in electronic form.

In addition, the CRA publishes a number of non-technical information pamphlets for the general public and technical guides on specific topics all of which are available at the district taxation offices, the CRA's web site, or through the commercial tax services either in hard copy or electronically.

The CRA, also, issues a periodic newsletter, *Income Tax Technical News*, which provides timely commentary on recent tax issues and which can be found in the aforementioned sources, in particular, CCH's CANADIAN TAX REPORTER in print or electronic form.

The above publications, representing what is known as "departmental practice", or "administrative practice" are not the law, although in the case of *Nowegijick v. The Queen*, 83 DTC 5041, Mr. Justice Dickson of the Supreme Court of Canada stated at page 5044 that "administrative policy and interpretation are not determinative, but are entitled to weight and can be an 'important factor' in case of doubt about the meaning of legislation". In the case of *The Queen v. Royal Trust Corporation of Canada*, (F.C.A.) 83 DTC 5172, it was noted that an Interpretation Bulletin interpreted a provision in a manner which Mr. Justice Urie of the Federal Court of Appeal concluded was correct.

(d) *Technical Notes and Explanations*

Technical notes are issued by the Department of Finance to explain new legislation when it is introduced. Although the impact of the technical notes on judicial decisions has yet to be determined, they should at least establish the general or broad intention of Parliament in respect of a particular issue.

In these Technical Notes, the Department of Finance generally indicates that:

> These explanatory notes are provided to assist in an understanding of amendments to the Income Tax Act, the Income Tax Application Rules and related statutes. These notes are intended for information purposes only and should not be construed as an official interpretation of the provisions they describe.

(e) *Generally Accepted Accounting Principles*

Generally accepted accounting principles have been important guides in the interpretation of the Act where the statutory law was silent on a particular point. Also, an authoritative book, article or tax service may provide a helpful source of interpretive material.

B. Structure of the Income Tax Act

Since the transitional rules, tax conventions and regulations typically relate to specific provisions of the Act, this introduction will focus on the table of contents to the Act itself. The reader is advised to become familiar with the headings for specific sections of the Act as listed in the table of contents mentioned previously. Refer to the table of contents for the following discussion.

1. Parts I, I.2, and I.3 — Income Tax, Tax on OAS Benefits, and Tax on Large Corporations

[ITA: 2–181.71]

Part I, income tax, is the longest of the Parts of the *Income Tax Act*. This Part deals with income tax as opposed to the variety of special transaction taxes handled in most of the other Parts. There are eleven divisions in Part I of the Act.

Division A — Liability for Tax [Sec. 2]

This short Division charges the taxpayer with the responsibility for paying the tax and, hence, is known as the "charging" provision. It answers the question: who is liable to pay the tax? Income tax is payable by "every person resident in Canada at any time in the year" and by a non-resident person who meets certain specified conditions.

Division B — Computation of Income [Secs. 3–108]

Division B is the longest of the divisions in Part I. This division provides a partial answer to the question: on what base is the tax levied? Income for tax purposes (as computed under the rules set out in Division B) is the major part of the tax base. The first five subdivisions deal with the major sources of income and deductions in the computation of net income. These are:

Subdivision a — Income or Loss from an Office or Employment [Secs. 5–8]

Subdivision b — Income or Loss from a Business or Property [Secs. 9–37]

Subdivision c — Taxable Capital Gains and Allowable Capital Losses [Secs. 38–55]

Subdivision d — Other Sources of Income [Secs. 56–59.1]

Subdivision e — Deductions in Computing Income [Secs. 60–66.8]

The first three of these subdivisions contain rules for both inclusions and deductions, whereas the final two subdivisions separate inclusions from miscellaneous sources and miscellaneous deductions not attributable to a particular source of income.

The remaining subdivisions in Division B provide rules which expand on the rules set out in the first five subdivisions listed above. They do not provide for new sources of income or deductions. These additional rules are classified in the following subdivisions:

Subdivision f — Rules Relating to Computation of Income [Secs. 67–80.5]

Subdivision g — Amounts Not Included in Computing Income [Sec. 81]

Subdivision h — Corporations Resident in Canada and Their Shareholders [Secs. 82–89]

Subdivision i — Shareholders of Corporations Not Resident in Canada [Secs. 90–95]

Subdivision j — Partnerships and Their Members [Secs. 96–103]

Subdivision k — Trusts and Their Beneficiaries [Secs. 104–108]

Divisions C and D — Computation of Taxable Income [Secs. 110–114.2] and *Taxable Income Earned in Canada by Non-Residents* [Secs. 115–116]

These divisions complete the computation of the tax base. Division C contains deductions from net income to arrive at taxable income which is the actual tax base. Division D contains some special rules for non-residents.

Divisions E and E.1 — Computation of Tax [Secs. 117–127.41] and *Minimum Tax* [Secs. 127.5–127.55]

Division E sets out the rates of tax applicable to individuals and to corporations. It also sets out a variety of tax credits applicable to all taxpayers. This is accomplished in the following four subdivisions:

Subdivision a — Rules Applicable to Individuals [Secs. 117–122.51]

Subdivision a.1 — Child Tax Benefit [Secs. 122.6–122.64]

Subdivision b — Rules Applicable to Corporations [Secs. 123–125.5]

Subdivision c — Rules Applicable to All Taxpayers [Secs. 126–127.41]

Division E.1 contains the rules for the Minimum Tax. [Secs. 127.5–127.55]

Other Divisions in Part I [Secs. 128–180]

The remaining divisions of Part I deal with a variety of special situations and with procedural matters and appeals under the Act. These divisions include:

Division F — Special Rules Applicable in Certain Circumstances [Secs. 128–143.2]

Division G — Deferred and Other Special Income Arrangements [Secs. 144–148.1]

Division H — Exemptions [Secs. 149–149.1]

Division I — Returns, Assessments, Payment and Appeals [Secs. 150–168]

Division J — Appeals to the Tax Court of Canada and the Federal Court [Secs. 169–180]

Part I.2 — Tax on Old Age Security Benefits [Sec. 180.2]

Part I.3 — Tax on Large Corporations [Secs. 181–181.71]

2. Special transaction taxes

[ITA: 182–211.91]

The following special transaction taxes currently remain in effect. Each of these taxes is found in a separate part of the Act as follows:

Part II	— Tobacco Manufacturers' Surtax [Secs. 182–183]
Part II.1	— Tax on Corporate Distributions [Secs. 183.1–183.2]
Part III	— Additional Tax on Excessive Election [Secs. 184–185]
Part IV	— Tax on Taxable Dividends Received by Private Corporations [Secs. 186–187]
Part IV.1	— Taxes on Dividends on Certain Preferred Shares Received by Corporations [Secs. 187.1–187.61]
Part V	— Tax in Respect of Registered Charities [Secs. 187.7–189]
Part VI	— Tax on Capital of Financial Institutions [Secs. 190–190.211]
Part VI.1	— Tax on Corporation Paying Dividends on Taxable Preferred Shares [Secs. 191–191.4]
Part VII	— Refundable Tax on Corporations Issuing Qualifying Shares [Secs. 192–193]
Part VIII	— Refundable Tax on Corporations in Respect of Scientific Research and Experimental Development Tax Credit [Secs. 194–195]
Part IX	— Tax on Deduction under Section 66.5 [Sec. 196]
Part X	— Taxes on Deferred Profit Sharing Plans and Revoked Plans [Secs. 198–204]
Part X.1	— Tax in Respect of Over-Contributions to Deferred Income Plans [Secs. 204.1–204.3]
Part X.2	— Tax in Respect of Registered Investments [Secs. 204.4–204.7]
Part X.3	— Registered Labour-Sponsored Venture Capital Corporations [Secs. 204.8–204.87]
Part X.4	— Tax in Respect of Over-Payments to Registered Education Savings Plans [Secs. 204.9–204.93]
Part X.5	— Payment Under a Registered Education Savings Plan [Sec. 204.94]
Part XI	— Tax in Respect of Certain Property Acquired by Trusts, etc. Governed by Deferred Income Plans [Secs. 205–207]
Part XI.1	— Tax in Respect of Certain Property Held by Trusts Governed by Deferred Income Plans [Secs. 207.1–207.2]
Part XI.2	— Tax in Respect of Certain Property Disposed of by Certain Public Authorities or Institutions [Secs. 207.3–207.4]
Part XI.3	— Tax in Respect of Retirement Compensation Arrangements [Secs. 207.5–207.7]
Part XII	— Tax in Respect of Certain Royalties, Taxes, Lease Rentals, etc. Paid to a Government by a Tax Exempt Person [Sec. 208]
Part XII.1	— Tax on Carved-out Income [Sec. 209]

Part XII.2 — Tax on Designated Income of Certain Trusts [Secs. 210–210.3]

Part XII.3 — Tax on Investment Income of Life Insurers [Secs. 211–211.5]

Part XII.4 — Tax on Mining Reclamation Trusts [Sec. 211.6]

Part XII.5 — Recovery of Labour-Sponsored Funds Tax Credit [Secs. 211.7–211.9]

Part XII.6 — Tax on Flow-Through Shares [Sec. 211.91]

This book will deal with several of these Parts as the need arises.

3. Non-residents

[ITA: 212–219.3]

Two parts of the Act are devoted to the taxation of non-residents. These are:

Part XIII — Tax on Income from Canada of Non-Resident Persons [Secs. 212–218.1]

Part XIII.1 — Additional Tax on Authorized Foreign Banks [Sec. 218.2]

Part XIII.2 — Non-Resident investors in Canadian Mutual Funds [Sec. 218.3]

Part XIV — Additional Tax on Non-Resident Corporations [Secs. 219–219.3]

4. Administration and interpretation

[ITA: 220–260]

The final three parts of the Act deal with matters of administering the Act, outlining tax evasion and interpreting the Act. These parts are:

Part XV — Administration and Enforcement [Secs. 220–244]

Part XVI — Tax Avoidance [Secs. 245–246]

Part XVI.I — Transfer Pricing [Sec. 247]

Part XVII — Interpretation [Secs. 248–260]

C. Approaches to Defining Income

[ITA: 3]

There is no statutory definition of the word "income" in the Act. While section 3 might be considered as such a definition, it really provides a set of rules for aggregating a taxpayer's income from various sources once these amounts have been identified as income either by a statutory provision of the Act or by judicial decisions. In the absence of a statutory definition, it is customary to refer to prior judicial decisions which may define the term and which, in turn, may have referred to a standard dictionary to establish the ordinary meaning of the word. *The Concise Oxford Dictionary* defines "income" as "the money or other assets received, esp. periodically or in a year, from one's business, lands, work, investments, etc.". While income is usually thought of as a monetary receipt or currency, it may take the form of money's worth, that is, something of commercial value such as gold, shares, wheat, etc.

1. The economist's perspective

Adam Smith's concept of income was limited to the three sources of rent, profit and wages. Excluded from income would be capital gains, windfalls and gifts. Nevertheless, income was considered to be "net" income, that is, gross revenues less expenses incurred to produce revenues. This is a basic principle of the Canadian income tax system. In more recent years, the economist's concept of income has been broadened to include all net increases in economic power between two points in time. This would include gains of all kinds and imputed income such as the value of a tax professor's labour in preparing his or her own tax return. Obviously, there are considerable valuation and administrative problems in collecting taxes on such imputed income. However, the comprehensive tax base concept of the Carter Commission came close to this broader concept of income.

2. The role of generally accepted accounting principles

It will be seen in subsection 9(1) that income from a business is the "profit" therefrom and the computation of profit is not completely specified by provisions in the Act. Until the early 1990s, the courts have been inconsistent in their reference to generally accepted accounting principles (GAAP) as an authoritative source for interpretation of profit under the *Income Tax Act*. The Supreme Court decision in *Symes v. The Queen et al.*, 94 DTC 6001 appears to have cleared the air by the following statement:

> ... Any reference to G.A.A.P. connotes a degree of control by professional accountants which is inconsistent with a legal test for "profit" under s. 9(1). Further, whereas an accountant questioning the propriety of a deduction may be motivated by a desire to present an appropriately conservative picture of current profitability, the *Income Tax Act* is motivated by a different purpose: the raising of public revenues. For these reasons, it is more appropriate in considering the s. 9(1) business test to speak of "well accepted principles of business (or accounting) practice" or "well accepted principles of commercial trading".

Therefore, GAAP is still to be considered but should be put into the context of overall business practices and should not stand alone. In the case of *Canderel Limited v. Her Majesty the Queen*, 98 DTC 6100, the Supreme Court of Canada stated, as a principle, that:

> well-accepted business principles, which include but are not limited to the formal codification found in G.A.A.P, are not rules of law but are interpretative aids. To the extent that they may influence the calculation of income, they will do so only in a case-by-case basis, depending on the facts of the taxpayer's financial situation.

It must be emphasized that the existence of specific statutory provisions, which are used in the computation of income for tax purposes, results in an income computation that will vary widely from income for financial accounting purposes. A major cause of this variance is the use of the capital cost allowance system for tax purposes based on a declining balance method of capital cost write-off in lieu of depreciation for financial accounting purposes often based on a straight-line method.

3. The doctrine of constructive receipt

The "constructive receipt" of income involves the inclusion of amounts which may not actually be received but are beneficially received or receivable. For example, subsection 153(3) deems the taxpayer to have received amounts withheld as tax by his or her employer. Although the taxpayer does not receive these amounts, they are included in his or her income subject to tax. The use of the accrual system is another example of the use of the concept of constructive receipt. While amounts in accounts receivable have not actually been received they result in amounts being included in income.

In applying the doctrine of constructive receipt, one of the key determinants is that the amounts must be beneficially received or receivable by the taxpayer so that his or her use of the amounts is free and unrestricted. The test was set out in the early Canadian case of *Kenneth B. S. Robertson Ltd. v. M.N.R.*, (Ex. Ct.) 2 DTC 655, in the form of the following questions:

> ... Is his right to it (the amount) absolute and under no restriction, contractual or otherwise, as to its disposition, use or enjoyment? To put it another way, can an amount in a taxpayer's hands be regarded as an item of profit or gain from his business as long as he holds it subject to specific and unfulfilled conditions and his right to retain it and apply it to his own use has not yet accrued and may never accrue? ...

As an example of an amount that is not constructively or beneficially received, consider retail sales taxes collected by retailers and passed on to the provincial government. In this case, the retailer simply acts as a conduit or transmitter of the amount and, therefore, is not taxed on it.[d]

D. Income vs. Capital

Receipts can be classified as either income or capital. As long as taxation has existed in Canada receipts of capital have received more favourable tax consequences than receipts of income. This situation continues to exist since only $\frac{1}{2}$ of capital gains is included in income.

The problem of determining whether a given receipt is one of capital or one of income has been the subject of countless court cases. In subsequent chapters, the major factors used by the courts in their determination will be examined and a number of cases will be used to illustrate these factors. One factor is the nature of the asset which is determined from its use or intended use. The classic capital asset is one which produces income from holding it or using it. A common analogy used by the courts likens a capital asset to a tree which produces income during the period of ownership in the form of fruit. Sale of the tree results in a receipt of capital and capital gains treatment whereas sale of the fruit results in a receipt of income.

E. Computation of Income

[ITA: 3; 4]

1. Aggregation formula

For Canadian taxpayers, both income and capital receipts, resulting in income subject to tax, are aggregated by the rules of section 3 irrespective of geographic source. The computation of income, that is, net income for tax purposes, is illustrated by the flow chart presented in Exhibit 1-3. A subsequent chapter will return to the rules in section 3 after all of the sources of income have been considered so that the terminology used in section 3 is more meaningful. Until then a cursory examination of section 3 will provide an overview of the coverage of subsequent chapters.

---

[d] For two Canadian cases which illustrate situations in which constructive receipt was at issue, see *Cliffe v. M.N.R.*, (T.A.B.) 57 DTC 305, dealing with unpaid salaries left in a corporation and *Green v. M.N.R.*, (T.A.B.) 50 DTC 320, dealing with unpaid interest left in a corporation. For an application of the concept of constructive receipt to a third-party payment in a marital breakdown situation, see the case of *The Queen v. Arsenault* (FCA), 96 DTC 6131, in which the "free and unrestricted use" test was at issue. For an example of a fact situation in which it was concluded that the test that an amount must have been received by someone for the benefit of the payee was not met, see *Markman v. MNR* (TCC), 89 DTC 253.

EXHIBIT 1-3
Simplified Computation of Income under Section 3
Division B

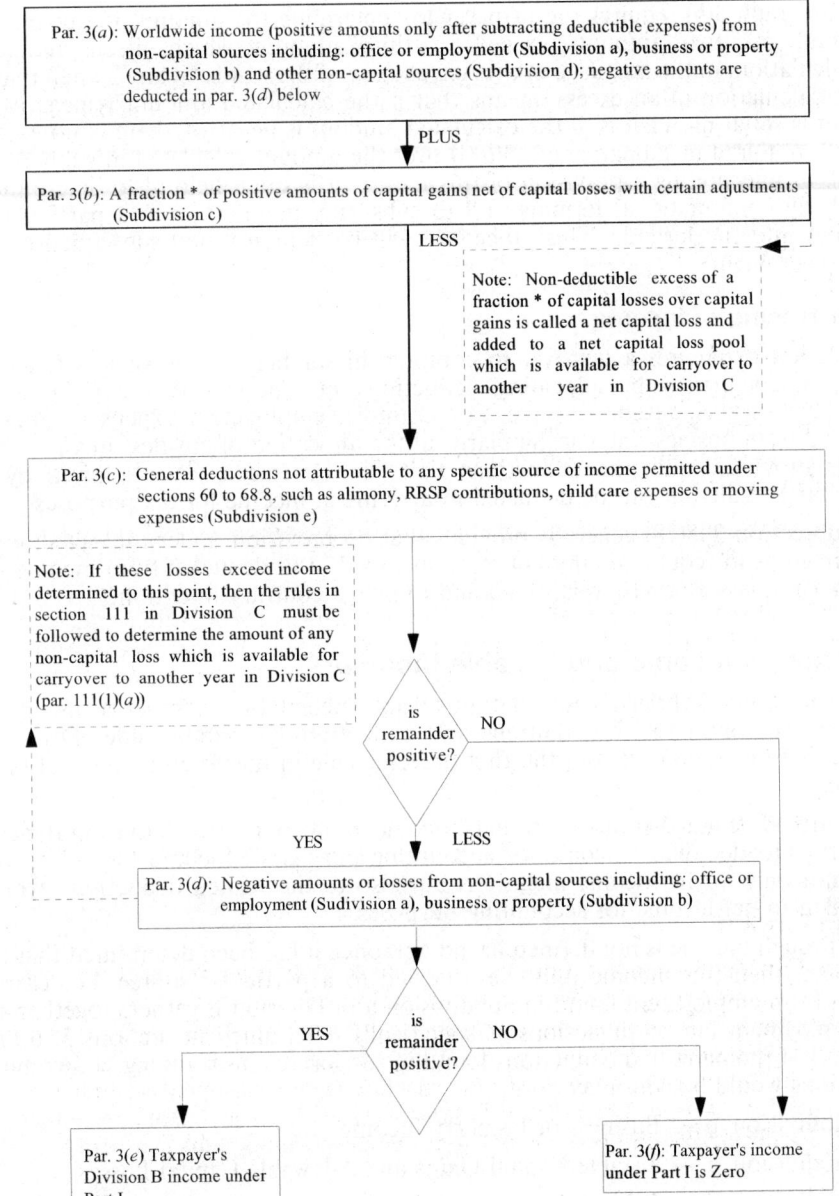

Note how section 3 represents the expression of a complex formula in words contained in one very long sentence. For example, paragraph 3(*a*) requires the taxpayer

---

* ¹/₂ for years prior to 1988; ²/₃ for 1988 and 1989; ³/₄ for years after 1989 and before February 28, 2000; ²/₃ after February 27, 2000, and before October 18, 2000; and ¹/₂ after October 18, 2000.

to "determine the total of all amounts" of income from all of the non-capital sources, e.g., employment income, business income and sundry receipts. In fact, this aggregate includes only positive amounts, i.e., an excess of inclusions over deductions, from these sources. However, it is only evident that these amounts must be positive when paragraph 3(*d*), referring to losses from the same non-capital sources, is read.

Paragraph 3(*b*) requires the taxpayer to "determine the amount, if any, by which the total of" two amounts exceeds a third amount which, itself, requires a sub-calculation. In the language of the Act, the use of the words "if any", when referring to the calculation of an excess, means that if the calculated amount is negative, the amount is set at nil. That is, if the calculated amount is negative, there is no excess of the sum required in subparagraph 3(*b*)(i) over the amount calculated in subparagraph 3(*b*)(ii). In interpreting a provision of this nature, it is often helpful to determine the underlying computational formula and to substitute numbers from a particular fact situation into the formula. This procedure will be demonstrated subsequently in an example problem.

2. Sourcing or tracing of income

Section 4 requires a taxpayer to compute his or her income or loss from each source independently by allocating deductions in amounts that can be applied reasonably to each revenue source. For example, employment expenses cannot be deducted from business income. Similarly, in the allocation of business income among various provinces only the deductions that can be traced to or allowed by that particular jurisdiction can be deducted in arriving at income for tax purposes.

Subsection 248(28) generally provides that no provision under the Act should be interpreted as to require an amount to be included in or deducted from income more than once unless a provision is so worded to give a contrary intention.[e]

F. Determination of Income and Taxable Income

Subsection 2(2) briefly states that the taxable income of a taxpayer is "income" for the year plus or minus the additions and deductions permitted under Division C. Hence, this subsection sets out the first ordering rule in the determination of taxable income.

It should be noted at this point that "income for tax purposes" (Division B income) is a term broader than "income for accounting purposes". Income for tax purposes refers not only to the income inclusions but also to the related deductions, which is more akin to net income for accounting purposes.

Although income is not defined in the Act, once it has been determined that there is income, then this income must be attached to a particular source. For example, income from employment found in Subdivision a of Division B gathers together all of the employment income inclusions as specifically determined in sections 5, 6 and 7 minus all of the permitted deductions found in section 8. This sourcing of income and deductions would be continued for:

Subdivision b — Business or Property Income

Subdivision c — Taxable Capital Gains and Allowable Capital Losses

Subdivision d — Other Income

Once the sourcing of income has been completed, then the ordering rules for Division B, which are found in section 3 of the Act, can be applied. These ordering rules are quite complex and would require extensive knowledge of the following chapters. Hence, these rules have been simplified at this introductory stage (see Exhibit 1-3).

---

[e] For example, see *Joel Attis v. M.N.R.*, (T.C.C.) 92 DTC 1128, involving the repayment of shareholder loans.

Once income for tax purposes (Division B income) has been determined, adjustments are made to this amount by the Division C additions and deductions according to the ordering rules (applicable to individuals) for this division as set out in section 111.1 (see Exhibit 1-4 which highlights some of these deductions).

Tax credits reduce the tax computed in Division E. The ordering rule for these tax credits is provided in section 118.92 (see Exhibit 1-5). All of these tax credits are often referred to as non-refundable tax credits, because any excess of these credits over tax payable is not available for refund.

EXHIBIT 1-4

Ordering Rules Applicable to Individuals for Division C
Section 111.1

Sec. 110	—Sundry deductions such as employee stock options and home relocation loan deductions
Sec. 110.2	—Lump-sum payments
Sec. 111	—Various loss carryovers arising from Division B calculations for another year such as non-capital losses and net capital losses
Sec. 110.6	—Capital gains deduction
Sec. 110.7	—Residing in prescribed zone

EXHIBIT 1-5

Ordering Rules Applicable to Individuals for Non-Refundable
Tax Credits in Division E
Section 118.92

Ssec. 118(1)	—Personal credits
Ssec. 118(2)	—Age credit
Sec. 118.7	—Employment Insurance premium and Canada Pension Plan contribution credits
Ssec. 118(3)	—Pension credit
Sec. 118.3	—Mental or physical impairment credit
Sec. 118.61	—Unused tuition and education credits
Sec. 118.5	—Tuition credit
Sec. 118.6	—Education tax credit
Sec. 118.9	—Transfers to supporting person
Sec. 118.8	—Transfer of unused credits to spouse
Sec. 118.2	—Medical expenses credit
Sec. 118.1	—Charitable gifts of individuals
Sec. 118.62	—Credit for interest on student loan
Sec. 121	—Dividend tax credit

Example Problem

The following list of income inclusions and deductions or tax credits has been determined correctly by a junior staff accountant prior to the preparation of the tax return for Ms Ichbina Blintz.

Inclusions

Salary	$50,000
Canadian bank interest	1,200
Standby charge for company car	745
Taxable capital gains	7,500
Taxable benefits from employment	1,035
Pension income	5,000
Taxable amount of dividends from taxable Canadian corporations	750

Deductions, Losses or Tax Credits:

Non-capital losses claimed	$2,000
Net capital losses carried forward	6,000
Basic personal and spousal tax credits	2,411
Registered pension plan contributions	1,000
Medical expenses tax credit	68
Interest expense to acquire Canadian shares	300
Moving expenses	600
Charitable donations tax credit	202
Pension tax credit	160
Canada Pension Plan contributions tax credit	298
Employment Insurance premiums tax credit	122
Dividend tax credit	100
Allowable capital losses	650
Business loss	3,080

— REQUIRED

(A) From the structural outlines and exhibits on the preceding pages, determine the income, taxable income and basic federal tax net of non-refundable tax credits based upon the above correct information using the ordering rules in sections 3, 111.1 and 118.92 for 2005. Assume federal tax before credits is $9,436 in 2005. Try to determine with logic where an item might be found.

(B) Cross-reference each amount to the appropriate section of the Act. (Refer to Sectional List of the Act.)

—SOLUTION

Division B — Section 3

Par. 3(*a*) *Subdivision a*

Sec. 5	Salary	$ 50,000		
Par. 6(1)(*a*)	Fringe benefits	1,035		
Par. 6(1)(*e*), ssec. 6(2)	Standby charge	745		
			$ 51,780	

Less

Par. 8(1)(*m*)	Registered pension plan contributions	(1,000)	
		$ 50,780	

Subdivision b

Business .... Nil

Property

Par. 12(1)(*c*)	Canadian bank interest	$ 1,200	
Par. 12(1)(*j*)	Dividends (taxable amount)	$ 750	
		$ 1,950	
Par. 20(1)(*c*)	Interest expense	(300)	$ 1,650

Subdivision d

Ssec. 56(1)	Pension income	5,000	
		$ 57,430	

Par. 3(*b*) *Subdivision c*

Sec. 38	Taxable capital gains	$ 7,500	
Sec. 38	Allowable capital losses	(650)	6,850
		$ 64,280	

Par. 3(*c*) *Subdivision e*

Sec. 62	Moving expenses	(600)	
		$ 63,680	

Par. 3(*d*)	Sec. 9	Business loss	(3,080)	
		Division B income	$ 60,600	

Division C — Section 111.1

Par. 111(1)(*a*)	Non-capital losses	$ (2,000)	
Par. 111(1)(*b*)	Net capital losses	(6,000)	(8,000)

Taxable income .... $ 52,600

Division E — Section 118.92

Federal tax before credits .... $ 9,436

Less tax credits:

Sec. 118	Personal tax credits	$ 2,411	
Sec. 118.7	CPP tax credit	298	
Sec. 118.7	EI premium tax credit	122	
Ssec. 118(3)	Pension tax credit	160	
Sec. 118.2	Medical expense credit	68	
Sec. 118.1	Donation tax credit	202	
Sec. 121	Dividend tax credit	100	(3,361)

Basic federal tax .... $ 6,075

Several other non-refundable tax credits are available in Subdivision c of Division E, but these are deductible from basic federal tax as computed in the above example. These additional non-refundable tax credits include: foreign tax credits [sec. 126], political contribution tax credits [ssec. 127(3)] and investment tax credits [ssec. 127(5)].

The goods and services tax (GST) credit [sec. 122.5] is a type of refundable tax credit available to individuals. This credit is actually paid separately in instalments to qualifying taxpayers.

G. Interpretation of Tax Legislation

The development of tax legislation over the years has included the acceptance of rules of interpretation or construction of the income tax law. First, every attempt is made to achieve precision in the language of tax legislation so that it is clearly understood, thereby providing the taxpayer with some degree of certainty about his or her tax liability. (To see how the drafters of the Act have succeeded in this respect, try to read subsection 256(3) as an example of such language!) To quote a famous British decision heard in 1891 on the question of the drafting of legislation:

> . . . it is not enough to attain a degree of precision which a person reading in good faith can understand, but it is necessary to attain if possible to a degree of precision which a person reading in bad faith cannot misunderstand (and) it is all the better if he cannot pretend to misunderstand it . . .

It has long been held that the words used in a taxing statute must be given their plain and obvious meaning, unless there is a specific definition contained in the statute or unless another meaning is required in the context of the remainder of the Act. This has become known as the "Golden Rule" of interpretation and it was expressed by a member of the British House of Lords as follows:

> In the construction of statutes their words must be interpreted in their ordinary grammatical sense, unless there be something in the context, or in the object of the statute in which they occur, or in the circumstances with reference to which they are used, to show that they were used in a special sense different from their ordinary grammatical sense . . .

In an elaboration of this principle, another Lord stated:

> . . . the grammatical and ordinary sense of the word is to be adhered to, unless that would lead to some absurdity or some repugnance or inconsistency with the rest of the [statute], in which case the grammatical and ordinary sense of the words may be modified so as to avoid that absurdity and inconsistency but no farther.

Again, this principle is intended to help increase the taxpayer's certainty of his or her position.

In interpreting a taxing statute, inferences about the intention of Parliament are often made. As indicated previously, the Department of Finance now often publishes detailed explanatory notes to accompany draft legislation. These notes may be helpful in determining intention but are not binding on a court. No interpretation is allowed to defeat the plain intention of the legislation. The courts assume that what is stated in the Act is what was meant by Parliament.[f] Thus, a meaning that is consistent with the intention of Parliament is allowed to prevail.

The meaning of a provision cannot be extended by an interpretation which is not clear from the words used. A British judge expanded on this point in an 1869 case by stating:

> . . . if the person sought to be taxed comes within the letter of the law he must be taxed, however great the hardship may appear to the judicial mind to be. On the other hand, if the Crown, seeking to recover the tax, cannot bring the subject within the letter of the law, the subject is free, however apparently within the spirit of the law the case might otherwise appear to be. In other words, if there be admissible in statute, what is called an equitable construction, certainly such a

---

[f] This is illustrated by the case of *M.N.R. v. MacInnes*, (Ex. Ct.) 54 DTC 1031, on the meaning of "property substituted". The intention of Parliament as a means of interpretation was also raised in the case of *Duha Printers (Western) Ltd. v. The Queen* (SCC), 98 DTC 6334.

construction is not admissible in a taxing statute, where you can simply adhere to the words of the statute.

To illustrate this point, the reader should refer to the case of *Witthuhn v. M.N.R.*, (T.A.B.) 57 DTC 174, in which a taxpayer was denied a deduction for certain medical expenses because the patient was confined to bed or a special type of rocking chair rather than "to a bed or wheelchair" as required at the time of the facts in the case and, in fact, until the provision was amended in 1986.

In more recent years, however, this approach appears to have been softened to some extent. For example, in the case of *Overdyck v. M.N.R.*, (T.R.B.) 83 DTC 307, where the taxpayer used a leg brace to go to work and a chair with castor-like wheels while at work, the same wording was given a much more liberal interpretation on the basis that if the taxpayer had been left completely alone without external aid or assistance, he would have been in bed at all times as a result of paralysis in one leg. In fact, it has been stated in another British case that:

> . . . the Court's task is merely one of construction of the words used, although, in the case of ambiguity, that construction will be favoured, which seems to the Court more consonant with fairness in the circumstances . . .

Thus, while taxing statutes were to be interpreted strictly, according to early rules of interpretation, in the case of doubt the construction of the statute was to be resolved in favour of the taxpayer in the case of a charging provision and in favour of the Crown in the case of an exemption provision. Furthermore, while it was not possible for the Courts to render what they would consider to be an equitable decision in a particular case, relief for the taxpayer could be found under the *Financial Administration Act*. Subsection 17(1) of that Act provides for the remission of taxes and penalties when it is considered in the public interest.[g]

More recently, the Supreme Court of Canada has suggested that the strict interpretation rule is still applicable where the plain meaning of the words is straightforward. Where the provision is vague and/or confusing, it is to be interpreted within its context in the Act on a basis consistent with the object of the Act and the intention of Parliament, which may reflect political, economic, social or technological objectives. This "object and spirit" test of interpretation was used in the case of *Stubart Investments Ltd. v. The Queen*, 84 DTC 6305 by the Supreme Court of Canada and, at least to some extent, has been codified in subsection 245(4) of the Act.[h] The Supreme Court has often quoted the authority on the interpretation of statutes, E.E. Driedger in *Construction of Statutes* as follows:

> Today, there is only one principle or approach, namely, the words of an Act are to be read in their entire context and in their grammatical and ordinary sense harmoniously with the scheme of the Act, the object of the Act, and the intention of Parliament.

In the case of *Corporation Notre-Dame de Bon-Secours v. Communauté Urbaine de Québec*, 95 DTC 5017, the Supreme Court of Canada again rejected the strict rule of interpretation in cases of doubt, as outlined above, and established the following rules of interpretation:

  (a) tax legislation should be interpreted according to ordinary rules of statutory interpretation;

  (b) a legislative provision should be given a strict or liberal interpretation depending on the purpose underlying it and that purpose must be identified in

---

[g] For a case which refers a taxpayer to the *Financial Administration Act*, see *Bayraktaroglu v. M.N.R.*, (T.R.B.) 73 DTC 27.

[h] See *Antosko et al. v. The Queen*, (S.C.C.) 94 DTC 6314 and *Friesen v. The Queen*, (S.C.C.) 95 DTC 5551.

the light of the context of the statute, its objective and the legislative intent (i.e., the "teleological" approach);[i]

(c) the teleological approach will favour the taxpayer or the tax department depending solely on the legislative provision in question and not on predetermined presumptions;

(d) substance will prevail over form (see discussion below) where this is consistent with the wording and objective of the statute; and

(e) only a reasonable doubt, not resolved by ordinary rules of interpretation, will be settled by recourse to the residual presumption in favour of the taxpayer.

The issue of form versus substance has long posed a problem in the application of the tax legislation to a taxpayer's situation. It was addressed in the often cited 1935 British case of the *Duke of Westminster* in which a member of the House of Lords stated that:

> Every man is entitled if he can to order his affairs so that the tax attaching under the appropriate Acts is less than it would otherwise be. If he succeeds in ordering them so as to secure this result, then, however unappreciative the Commissioners of Inland Revenue or his fellow taxpayers may be of his ingenuity, he cannot be compelled to pay an increased tax. This so-called doctrine of "the substance" seems to me to be nothing more than an attempt to make a man pay notwithstanding that he has so ordered his affairs that the amount of tax sought from him is not legally claimable . . .

> . . . There may be, of course, cases where documents are not *bona fide* nor intended to be acted upon but are only used as a cloak to conceal a different transaction . . .

Thus, the form or legal effect of a transaction must prevail in attempting to determine the tax effects, unless the taxing statute requires that such form be disregarded in cases where form is inconsistent with the wording and objective of the Act, or unless the form is considered to be a "sham" which misrepresents the true form, based on the facts of the case.[j] Another British case has described a "sham" as:

> . . . acts done or documents executed by the parties to the sham which were intended by them to give to third parties and to the Courts the appearance of creating between the parties legal rights and obligations different from the actual legal rights and obligations (if any) which the parties intended to create.

> . . . For acts and documents to be a sham, with whatever legal consequence falls from this, all the parties thereto must have a common intention that the acts or documents are not to create the legal rights and obligations which they give the appearance of creating . . .

Furthermore, the Courts have even applied what has come to be known as a "repugnancy" or "smell" test in certain situations where substance was at considerable variance with the form of a transaction.

The Act contains a number of statements of general principle followed by an exception or series of exceptions to that rule. An exception or other specific provision of the legislation will override the general provision, but the former must be given a strict interpretation. This rule was followed in a Canadian case, which will be discussed in a subsequent chapter, when the judge stated that:

> . . . the subsection must in my opinion be regarded as an exception to the general rule, and while it must be given its full effect so far as it goes, it is to be strictly construed and not extended to anything beyond the scope of the natural meaning

---

[i] This approach was applied in the case of *Harvey C. Smith Drugs Limited v. The Queen*, (F.C.A.) 95 DTC 5026.

[j] This was confirmed by the Supreme Court of Canada in the case of *Stubart Investments Ltd. v. The Queen*, 84 DTC 6305.

of the language used, regardless again of how much a particular case may seem to fall within its supposed spirit of intendment . . .

Thus, a taxpayer cannot obtain an exemption from tax unless the circumstances fall squarely within the wording of the provision.

Two other principles have been important in the interpretation of the Act over the years. One is the *ejusdem generis* rule for enumerations of similar items. According to this rule, when a series of specific words in a statute is followed by general words, the general words are confined to the same scope as the specific words. This rule could be involved in the interpretation of the words "other remuneration" as used in subsection 5(1) which states that ". . . a taxpayer's income for a taxation year from an office or employment is the salary, wages and other remuneration, including gratuities, received by him in the year". The scope of the meaning of the specific words "salary", "wages" and "gratuities" might be used to constrain the meaning of the words "other remuneration".

The other principle deals with the role of court decisions as precedents often referred to as the concept of *stare decisis*. This principle establishes that decisions on similar facts are to be similar. The precedent value of a case is determined by the seniority of the court. A decision of a higher Canadian court is binding on a lower Canadian court in a subsequent decision. At a given level of court, consistency in decisions on similar facts is usually attempted. If a decided case is not to apply to a given situation, the facts of the decided case must be distinguished or differentiated sufficiently from the case under consideration to justify a different decision. In the case of *B. B. Fast & Sons Distributors Ltd. v. M.N.R.*, 82 DTC 1017, a member of the Tax Review Board, as it was then, invoked the "judicial comity rule" indicating that judgments of courts of equal or co-ordinate jurisdiction should be followed in the absence of strong reasons to the contrary. However, it has been recognized that too rigid adherence to precedent might lead to injustice in a particular case and also unduly restrict the proper development of the law.

Finally, the effects of the *Interpretation Act* which deals with the interpretation of Canadian statutes should be considered. In subsection 3(3) it recognizes rules of construction such as those discussed to the extent that they are not inconsistent with a provision of this Act. In section 14, it sets out some rules of construction of its own regarding the use of definitions and the interpretation of exceptions to rules. Section 27 deals with the interpretation of time limits specified in a statute. For example, if such a deadline falls on a holiday, the deadline is extended to the following day that is not a holiday. Section 32 provides that deviations from a prescribed form which do not affect the substance do not invalidate a form used. Gender is dealt with in subsection 33(1) which states that "words importing female persons include male persons and corporations and words importing male persons include female persons and corporations".

H. The Role of the Professional Accountant in Tax Matters[k]

Professional accountants and others who are not qualified as lawyers very frequently play a major role in providing tax-related services to taxpayers. The basis of these services is, of course, tax law embodied in the legislation and jurisprudence discussed previously. It must be recognized that the practice of law by non-lawyers is an offence under certain provincial legislation which regulates that practice by lawyers. Often, there is a very fine and ill-defined line between an activity that constitutes the practice of law and services provided to clients by non-lawyers in the tax area. In addition to committing the foregoing offence, an adviser may be liable for the civil consequences of negligence in providing services for which the adviser is not qualified, such as drafting a will, incorporating a company, etc.

---

[k] For a more detailed examination of this area, see James Rossiter, "Surviving in the twilight zone", *CA Magazine*, Vol. 126, No. 2, February, 1993, pp. 37–41.

Often, the complementary nature of financial services and tax law makes the combination of the two by a single adviser most practical in providing service to clients. In these situations, the role of non-lawyers is generally recognized in most provinces and conflicts can be avoided if the non-lawyer is careful not to provide advice that can be construed as a legal opinion and not to prepare documents of a purely legal, non-tax nature arising from more general laws such as contract law and corporate law.

III. GENERAL BACKGROUND ON ADMINISTRATION AND ENFORCEMENT OF THE ACT

The purpose of this section of the chapter is to provide a broad overview of how the tax legislation is administered and enforced. A discussion of the specific details of provisions dealing with these aspects of the law is deferred until Chapter 14 where it can be related more meaningfully to material covered in the intervening chapters.

A. Onus of Proof

In tax matters, it has been established by the Supreme Court of Canada in the case of *Johnston v. M.N.R.*, [1948] 3 DTC 1182, that the taxpayer always has the burden of proving that an assessment is incorrect. Placing the burden of proof on the taxpayer is often referred to as a "reverse onus", because the usual burden of proof is on the Crown. In tax matters, the reverse onus is justified, since it is assumed that under our self-assessment system the taxpayer has all of the basic data under his or her own control.[1] This reverse onus may be challenged someday with a Supreme Court of Canada interpretation of the Charter of Rights and Freedoms. In the case of *M.N.R. v. Taylor*, (Ex. Ct.) 61 DTC 1139, it was established that the standard of proof in cases dealing with the Act need only be that of the "balance of probabilities" used in civil cases rather than the more rigorous standard of "beyond reasonable doubt" used in criminal proceedings. Where penalties are assessed, the burden of proof of the facts justifying the assessment of the penalties is transferred to the Minister [ssec. 163(3)]. The standard of proof that the Minister must demonstrate is that of the "balance of probabilities".

B. Appeals

Prior to taking any formal steps in the appeal procedure, the taxpayer may consult with officials responsible for his or her file in the appropriate Tax Services Office. Many differences can be resolved in this less formal manner. If, however, they cannot be resolved in this manner to the taxpayer's satisfaction, a notice of objection may be filed as the first formal step. There is no prescribed form at the present time. The notice of objection simply contains a statement of the facts and the reasons for objection. In the case of corporations or certain trusts, the notice of objection must be received by the CRA on or before the 90th day subsequent to the date of mailing of the notice of assessment. In the case of individuals or testamentary trusts, the deadline is the later of one year after the day the taxpayer is required to pay the balance of tax due for a year (i.e., April 30th) and 90 days after the mailing of the notice of assessment for the year.

Next, the taxpayer can appeal to the Tax Court of Canada (T.C.C.) (formerly the Tax Appeal Board (T.A.B.) or the Tax Review Board (T.R.B.)). It is highly accessible, meeting in 20 cities across Canada.

The Tax Court of Canada now has exclusive jurisdiction to hear appeals under the Act and certain other federal statutes. On appeal to the Tax Court, the taxpayer is given the option of an "informal procedure" or a "general procedure". The informal procedure may be elected when the amount of federal tax and penalties in issue for one taxation year is $12,000 or less or when the amount of the losses is $24,000 or less. The only requirement of the informal procedure is that the appeal is submitted in writing. Court rules of evidence are flexible and hence, the taxpayer can represent himself or herself or be represented by an agent (i.e., any individual) who may be a lawyer. However, the taxpayer cannot appeal on questions of fact from a Tax Court decision reached through the informal procedure and the decision cannot be used as a precedent in subsequent cases. Judicial review of a judgment under the informal procedure lies with

---

[1] This onus of proof was applied in the case of *Violi v. M.N.R.*, (T.R.B.) 80 DTC 1191.

the Federal Court of Appeal (F.C.A.) on errors of law or erroneous findings of fact made in a perverse or capricious manner.

Where the general procedure is chosen in the Tax Court of Canada, the Court will be bound by strict rules of evidence. The taxpayer can only represent himself or herself or be represented by legal counsel. In this general procedure, the taxpayer can appeal the decision of the Tax Court to the Federal Court of Appeal and the Tax Court decision can be used as a precedent in other cases.

The ultimate court of appeal for tax cases in Canada is the Supreme Court of Canada (S.C.C.). According to subsections 31(2) and (3) of the *Federal Court Act*, an appeal can be made to the Supreme Court only if the Federal Court decides that the issue should be referred to the Supreme Court, or if the Supreme Court authorizes the appeal. At this level, questions of legal interpretation are raised rather than questions of fact alone. Not many cases on tax matters are given leave to appeal to the Supreme Court of Canada.

C. Administration and Enforcement

While the Department of Finance formulates tax policy, the CRA controls, regulates, manages and supervises the income tax system. Direct contact between the taxpayer and the CRA is generally made through one of the almost 30 Tax Services Offices. Trained assessors and special investigators who conduct desk audits of an individual's return or field audits of business returns are located in these offices.

The Head Office in Ottawa serves to maintain efficiency and uniformity of treatment across Canada, by supervising and directing the activities of the Tax Services Offices. In addition, a number of regional Taxation Centres are maintained to do routine operations and the initial processing of all individual income tax returns among other things.

D. Tax Evasion, Avoidance and Planning

[IC 73-10R3]

It is important to distinguish the terms "tax evasion", "tax avoidance" and "tax planning". Generally, tax evasion involves knowingly reporting tax that is less than the tax payable under the law with an attempt to deceive by omitting revenue, fraudulently claiming deductions or failing to use all of the true facts of a situation. This is clearly illegal and can be prosecuted as such. See IC 73-10R3 for a description of the consequences of tax evasion.

Tax avoidance is generally considered to arise in cases in which the taxpayer has legally circumvented the law resulting in the reduction or elimination of tax through a scheme or series of transactions which do not truly reflect the real facts. While not illegal, the CRA will challenge such tax avoidance by various means available to it.

Finally, the CRA suggests that tax planning involves cases of tax reduction or elimination that are clearly provided for or not specifically prohibited in the law in a manner that is genuine and open within the framework of the law.

Despite these statements which attempt to distinguish the terms, there are undoubtedly judgments that must be made in distinguishing between cases of tax evasion and tax avoidance and between cases of tax avoidance and tax planning.

Section 245 of the Act contains a general anti-avoidance rule (GAAR). In the words of the explanatory notes accompanying Bill C-139 which introduced the GAAR, issued on June 30, 1988, the rule is:

> intended to prevent abusive tax avoidance transactions or arrangements, but at the same time is not intended to interfere with legitimate commercial and family transactions. Consequently, the new rule seeks to distinguish between legitimate tax planning and abusive tax avoidance and to establish a reasonable balance between the protection of the tax base and the need for certainty for taxpayers in planning their affairs.[m]

---

[m] Reproduced in *Technical Notes to Bill C-139*, Special Report No. 851, Extra Edition, CCH Canadian Limited, June 30, 1988, p. 313.

IV. INTRODUCTION TO THE GOODS AND SERVICES TAX

A. Note on Organization of Legislation and Availability of Interpretive Sources

It is important in the study of the Goods and Services Tax (GST) to become thoroughly familiar with the organization, structure and coverage of the *Excise Tax Act* (ETA). This knowledge is vital to the resolution of GST problems.

The ETA is divided into twelve Parts, most of which represent specific types of tax, including the GST, and twelve Schedules.[n] As in the *Income Tax Act*, for ease of reference, provisions are numbered, separating various elements of the provision. The history footnotes to each provision of the ETA are important to determine when the provision is applicable and what transitional rules, if any, apply.

As noted above, the ETA also contains twelve Schedules, which must be read in conjunction with the other provisions of the ETA. References to the provisions of the Schedules are read somewhat differently than references to the other provisions of the ETA. For example, consider the following reference:

V, VI, 20(e)(ii)

The first upper case Roman numeral refers to a Schedule and the second upper case Roman numeral refers to a Part. The number 20 refers to a section and the letter (*e*) refers to a paragraph. The lower case Roman numeral (ii) refers to a subparagraph. The above reference would be called Schedule V, Part VI, subparagraph 20(*e*)(ii).

In addition to the ETA, the GST Regulations form part of the law and are set out to handle various specific situations and to carry on the general purposes and provisions of the ETA. Unlike the ETA, though, these regulations may be passed by Order-in-Council without ratification by Parliament. Forms issued by the CRA and officially prescribed by legislation may provide some insights to the interpretation of a provision in the legislation.

Additional sources also exist to provide assistance in interpreting the legislation. First, the CRA provides some explanatory information through a series of publications. These publications include GST Memoranda, which are grouped under various topic headings and contain the CRA's interpretations of specific provisions of the ETA and outline its administrative practices. In addition, the CRA issues Technical Information Bulletins (TIBs) and Policy Statements, which are intended to provide current information on new policy or policy changes on a timely basis. Draft Policy Statements are also issued by the CRA, although these statements are subject to further review before being adopted as the CRA's policy. As well, various pamphlets, booklets and guides which provide general information, often targeted for specific groups of taxpayers, are issued from time to time. Based on the income tax jurisprudence referred to earlier in this chapter, publications of this nature, although not legally binding, may be considered by the courts. As taxpayers have begun to appeal decisions of the CRA through the court system, case law which provides an additional important source of interpretation for the GST is developing.

The Department of Finance issued explanatory notes to explain the new GST provisions when the legislation was first introduced as well as when amendments to the legislation have been introduced in the House of Commons. Finally, an authoritative book, article or tax service may also provide interpretive assistance.

---

[n] The ETA also contains the legislation for the Harmonized Sales Tax (HST) which was implemented by the provinces of Nova Scotia, New Brunswick and Newfoundland and Labrador on April 1, 1997. Under the HST, those provinces that are referred to as the "participating provinces" have harmonized their provincial sales tax systems with the federal GST. The HST applies at a combined rate of 15% and includes a federal component (the 7% GST) and a provincial component (8%).

The following discussion will focus on the structure of the ETA itself.

1. Excise Tax Act structure — Parts

Part I	—	Insurance Premiums other than Marine [Secs. 3–7]
Part II	—	Air Transportation Tax [Secs. 8–21]
Part II.1	—	Telecommunication Programming Services Tax [Secs. 21.1–21.21]
Part II.2	—	Telecommunication Services Tax [Secs. 21.22–21.34]
Part III	—	Excise Taxes on Cosmetics, Jewellery, Radios, etc. [Secs. 22–24]
Part IV	—	Excise Taxes on Playing Cards and Wines [Secs. 25–28.1]
Part V	—	Tobacco Products Inventory Tax [Secs. 29–34]
Part V.1	—	Tax on Split-Run Periodicals [Secs. 35–41.3]
Part VI	—	Consumption or Sales Tax [Secs. 42–58]
Part VII	—	General [Secs. 58.1–116]
Part VIII	—	Transitional [Secs. 117–121.1]
Part IX	—	Goods and Services Tax [Secs. 122–368]

As can be seen from the titles of the various Parts set out above, the ETA imposes a number of taxes other than GST. This text will concentrate on the GST rules which are set out in Part IX of the ETA and will not examine the other taxes imposed under the ETA. The structure of Part IX of the ETA is set out below.

2. Structure of Part IX of the Excise Tax Act — GST legislation

Division I — Interpretation [Secs. 123–164.2]

This Division contains a number of definitions and basic interpretive rules that are important to an overall understanding of the GST.

Division II — Goods and Services Tax [Secs. 165–211]

Division II is the longest of the Divisions in Part IX. It contains rules which set out the rate of tax, the liability for tax, and the circumstances in which tax paid on inputs used in the supply of goods and services may be recovered. This Division contains the following four subdivisions:

Subdivision a — Imposition of Tax [Secs. 165–168]

Subdivision b — Input Tax Credits [Secs. 169–170]

Subdivision c — Special Cases [Secs. 171–194]

Subdivision d — Capital Property [Secs. 195–211]

Division III — Tax on Importation of Goods [Secs. 212–216]

As the title suggests, Division III sets out the rules relating to the liability for GST on the importation of goods.

Division IV — Tax on Imported Taxable Supplies other than Goods [Secs. 217–220]

This Division sets out rules for determining when GST is payable in respect of imported services and intellectual property.

Division IV.1 — Tax on Property and Services Brought into a Participating Province [Secs. 220.01–220.09]

This Division sets out rules for the self-assessment of the provincial component of the Harmonized Sales Tax (HST) in certain circumstances, where property or services are brought into a participating HST province.

Division V — Collection and Remittance of Division II Tax [Secs. 221–251]

Division V sets out the various requirements in respect of the collection and remittance of tax. The rules relating to the requirement to register are also contained in this Division. Division V contains the following five subdivisions:

Subdivision a — Collection [Secs. 221–224]

Subdivision b — Remittance of Tax [Secs. 225–237]

Subdivision c — Returns [Secs. 238–239]

Subdivision d — Registration [Secs. 240–242]

Subdivision e — Fiscal Periods and Reporting Periods [Secs. 243–251]

Division VI — Rebates [Secs. 252–264]

Division VI sets out the rules for claiming rebates of GST paid on purchases in a variety of circumstances.

Division VII — Miscellaneous [Secs. 265–274]

Division VII sets out a number of miscellaneous provisions, including a general anti-avoidance provision. The three subdivisions in Division VII are as follows:

Subdivision a — Trustees, Receivers and Personal Representatives [Secs. 265–270]

Subdivision b — Amalgamations and Windings-up [Secs. 271–272]

Subdivision b.1 — Partnerships and Joint Ventures [Secs. 272.1 –273]

Subdivision b.2 — Export Distribution Centres [Secs. 273.1]

Subdivision c — Anti-Avoidance [Sec. 274]

Division VIII — Administration and Enforcement [Secs. 275–335]

Division VIII sets out various rules for administering the Act and enforcing its provisions. The seven subdivisions in Division VIII are as follows:

Subdivision a — Administration [Secs. 275–277.1]

Subdivision b — Returns, Penalties and Interest [Secs. 278–285.1]

Subdivision c — General [Secs. 286–295]

Subdivision d — Assessments, Objections and Appeals [Secs. 296–312]

Subdivision e — Collection [Secs. 313–325]

Subdivision f — Offences [Secs. 326–332]

Subdivision g — Evidence and Procedure [Secs. 333–335]

Division IX — Transition [Secs. 336–347]

The GST came into effect on January 1, 1991. This Division contains a number of transitional rules intended to ensure an orderly transition from the federal sales tax system to the GST.

Division X — Transitional Provisions for Participating Provinces [Secs. 348–363.2]

The Harmonized Sales Tax (HST) came into effect on April 1, 1997. This Division contains transitional rules to deal with the implementation of the HST. The four subdivisions of Division X are as follows:

Subdivision a — Interpretation [Sec. 348]

Subdivision b — Application [Sec. 349]

Subdivision c — Transition [Secs. 350–361]

Subdivision d — Special Case [Secs. 362–363.2]

Division XI — Tax Inclusive Pricing [Secs. 364–368]

This Division provides authority for the use of the tax-inclusive pricing which was required under the original HST proposals. However, the rules under tax-inclusive pricing under this Division will not come into effect until the participating provinces that represent at least 51% of Canada's total population have enacted legislation to implement HST.

3. Schedules to the Excise Tax Act

Schedule I   —Rates of Excise Tax

Schedule II   —Tax Rates on Tobacco Products

Schedule II.1   —Specific Tax Rates on Petroleum Products

Schedule III   —Sales Tax Exemptions

Schedule III.1 —Goods Sold by Deemed Manufacturers or Producers

Schedule IV   —Construction Materials and Equipment for Buildings

Schedule V   —Exempt Supplies

Schedule VI   —Zero-Rated Supplies

Schedule VII   —Non-Taxable Importations

Schedule VIII —Participating Provinces and Applicable Tax Rates

Schedule IX   —Supply in a Province

Schedule X   —Non-Taxable Property and Services for Purposes of Division IV.I of Part IX

Schedules V through VII relate to the GST. Schedule V sets out those supplies that are exempt from GST. Schedule VI sets out those supplies that are zero-rated, i.e., subject to tax at the rate of zero per cent. Schedule VII sets out a list of imported goods that are not subject to GST.

B. Overview and Basic Concepts

The GST was implemented on January 1, 1991. The introduction of the GST at the rate of 7% culminated numerous attempts to reform the sales tax regime in Canada. The GST replaced the federal sales tax, which was riddled with inequities and inconsistent administrative practice and often led to distortions in business practices in the Canadian economy. The GST was intended to correct many of these deficiencies and to fulfill certain revenue objectives of the federal government.

The discussion of GST in this book does not attempt to cover all the technical areas that are associated with the GST. The intent, rather, is to give the reader a basic working knowledge of the rules. With this grounding, readers are encouraged to do further research in this important area of taxation that affects virtually every business organization in Canada. Unlike the former federal sales tax system, in which there were few accounting professionals who became actively involved in dealing with sales tax problems, the implementation of GST has resulted in substantial work for tax and other accounting professionals.

The GST is a tax on the consumption of goods and services in Canada. The tax is collected by businesses (referred to as "registrants") who sell goods and provide services (collectively referred to as "supplies") in Canada. GST is collected by registrants throughout the production and distribution chain. Any person who is engaged in a "commercial activity" is required to register and collect GST. This includes persons who carry on business in Canada. "Business" is defined quite broadly in the legislation and does not require a profit motive. For example, charities and non-profit organizations are required to register if they engage in commercial activities, even if these entities are not subject to income tax.

The GST is intended to be a tax on final consumption. Thus, while businesses are charged GST on their purchases, they are entitled to a credit for this tax (referred to as an "input tax credit"). Input tax credits are available to the extent purchases are used in commercial activities. Businesses are required to remit to the government the difference between the amount of GST collected or collectible and the amount of any input tax credit entitlement.

Supplies of goods and services are divided into three categories. "Taxable supplies" are subject to GST at the rate of 7%, and the supplier is entitled to a full input tax credit. "Zero-rated supplies" are subject to tax at the rate of zero per cent, and the supplier may claim a full input tax credit on purchases used to provide these supplies. "Exempt supplies" do not attract GST, and the supplier is not entitled to an input tax credit in respect of purchases used to provide these supplies.

The next two sections will expand on the concepts of "supply" and "input tax credits".

C. Supplies

The concept of "supply" is essential to an understanding of GST. While in many cases the term will be synonymous with sale, it has a much broader scope for GST purposes.

The provision of a supply includes, among other things:

- sales or rentals of goods;
- rendering of services;
- leases, sales or other transfers of real property;
- licensing of copyrights or patents; and
- barter and exchange transactions and gifts.

Once it is determined that there is a supply, a further determination must be made as to the type of supply. As discussed above, there are three types of supplies under the GST: taxable, zero-rated and exempt. A taxable supply is defined as a supply made in the course of a commercial activity, but does not include an exempt supply. Taxable supplies are subject to tax each time they are sold, with no exceptions. Most goods and services are taxable. However, zero-rated and exempt status is extended to a short list of goods and services for which the government has determined that GST should not apply. Only limited relief from the tax is provided in the case of exempt supplies. Goods and services which are zero-rated are completely free of tax.

1. Zero-rated supplies

A short list of goods and services are subject to tax at the rate of 0%. These zero-rated supplies are still considered to be taxable supplies. Although this appears paradoxical, the distinction between taxable and exempt supplies is important. On taxable supplies, including zero-rated ones, the supplier is entitled to recoup the GST paid on its inputs in the form of input tax credits, since input tax credits may be claimed on inputs used in commercial activities. Thus, even though GST is not charged on the supply of zero-rated goods and services, the entitlement to input tax credits ensures that these supplies are effectively tax-free. The following are some examples of goods and services that are zero-rated:

- prescription drugs;

- medical devices;

- basic groceries; and

- exported goods and services.

2. Exempt supplies

Like suppliers of zero-rated supplies, suppliers of exempt goods and services are not required to collect GST on these supplies. However, unlike zero-rated supplies, relief from GST is not available on inputs used in the supply of exempt goods and services. The GST paid by the supplier on purchases attributable to those exempt supplies is buried in the cost of the goods or services. For income tax purposes, however, the GST paid on such inputs represents part of the cost of the inputs, and hence, is deductible.

For example, when a bank purchases inputs to be used in the supply of financial services (which are exempt supplies), the bank is not entitled to recover the GST incurred in respect of those inputs. Consequently, even though the bank does not charge GST on the supply of those exempt financial services, the GST incurred on the bank's purchases is buried in the cost of those financial services. The bank will be able to deduct the GST paid on these purchases for income tax purposes as part of the cost of the purchases.

The following are some examples of exempt goods and services:

- health care and child care services;

- educational services;

- most financial services; and

- sales of used residential housing and rentals of residential premises.

D. Input Tax Credits

An integral part of the GST system is the entitlement to claim refundable input tax credits on business purchases. This relieves business inputs of GST and thus avoids the pyramiding of tax. In order to qualify for an input tax credit (ITC), the goods and services must have been purchased for use in a commercial activity. As the GST is designed to be a tax on consumption to be borne by the end user, there are certain restrictions on the claiming of ITCs. These restrictions generally mirror the restrictions on claiming expenses under the *Income Tax Act*.

Input tax credits claimed by a registrant during a reporting period are subtracted from the tax collected on goods and services during the period to arrive at the net tax payable. Where input tax credits exceed tax payable, the registrant is entitled to a refund. An important concept related to ITCs is that purchases and sales need not be matched in order to claim an ITC. The credit can be claimed when the purchase is paid for or becomes due. Similarly, GST paid on purchases of capital property need not be amortized over the life of the property (see Chapter 5).

Input tax credits are available where goods and services are purchased for use in a commercial activity. Conversely, if an input is not used at all in a commercial activity, no credit is allowed. A full credit is available where an input is used "exclusively" in a commercial activity. "Exclusively" is defined as "all or substantially all" and is interpreted by the CRA to mean 90% or more.

There will be circumstances where a purchase is used in respect of a combination of taxable and exempt activities. In these cases, except for certain capital property, registrants will be required to apportion the ITC between the taxable (including zero-rated) and exempt activities. For example, consider the case of a hospital that purchases an industrial dishwasher for use in its kitchen. The dishwasher will be used to clean dishes from both patients and cafeteria patrons. Because meals provided to patients are exempt and cafeteria sales are taxable, the hospital will be required to apportion the ITC between the taxable and exempt activities.

The legislation does not prescribe allocation methods for use in apportioning ITCs. As long as the allocation is reasonable and is used consistently throughout the year, it will likely not be challenged.

Registrants will be required to maintain certain documentation to support ITCs. These requirements are discussed in Chapter 14.

E. Reform of the GST and Provincial Harmonization

Pursuant to an election promise made in 1993 to replace the GST, the federal government has reviewed a number of alternatives and has had ongoing discussions with the provinces. On April 23, 1996, the federal government announced it had signed Memoranda of Understanding with the governments of Nova Scotia, New Brunswick, and Newfoundland and Labrador (referred to as the "participating provinces") to harmonize the federal goods and services tax (GST) with their respective provincial sales tax systems. Legislation to implement the new Harmonized Sales Tax (HST) received Royal Assent on March 20, 1997. The HST became effective April 1, 1997 and has an impact on businesses resident in these three Atlantic provinces, as well as businesses that make supplies to recipients in those provinces or that acquire goods and services from vendors in those provinces. It is the place where goods and services are supplied or deemed to be supplied that dictates whether GST applies at the rate of 7% or the HST at the rate of 15%. Supplies made or deemed to be made in the HST participating provinces are subject to the 15% rate. The HST applies to the same base of goods and services as the GST. The province of Quebec has already substantially harmonized its provincial sales tax with the GST through the Harmonized Provincial Sales Tax (Quebec Sales Tax or QST).

With the April 1, 1997 implementation of the HST by the three Atlantic provinces, the GST appears here to stay, although with additional technical amendments. Various other provinces, however, have indicated that they are not interested in harmonization. The Ontario government, for example, has repeatedly stated that it is not prepared to harmonize, citing a shift in the tax burden from businesses to consumers of $2 billion to $3 billion a year as the main reason against harmonization. Under a harmonized GST–PST system, businesses would be entitled to input tax credits on purchases used in commercial activities; currently, businesses pay provincial sales tax on many business inputs. Although a number of provinces appear to be opposed to harmonization, the federal government is continuing its efforts to attempt to convince the remaining provinces to harmonize.

EXERCISES

Exercise 1

For each of the following items, identify the appropriate provision of the Act which deals with the item listed. Be as specific as possible in citing the reference to the Act, i.e., Part, Division, Subdivision, Section, Subsection, etc. Use of the Sectional List at the beginning of CCH edition of CANADIAN INCOME TAX ACT and/or the Topical Index at the end of the book may be helpful. However, using the CD included with this text may provide faster search results. Refer to Chapter 19 for instructions on how to search.

(A) Definition of "taxable capital gain".

(B) Deduction for certain annual professional membership dues paid by an employee.

(C) Taxability of payments received as income from property acquired as personal injury award.

(D) Deductibility of an expense based on its magnitude.

(E) Definition of a "parent" under the Act.

(F) Definition of an *"inter vivos"* trust.

(G) Deadline for filing of a tax return for a deceased person.

(H) Taxability of a benefit received from a corporation by a shareholder.

(I) Transaction price in a non-arm's length disposition of property.

(J) Deductibility of fees for investment advice.

Exercise 2

[ITA: Divisions B and C]

Mr. Malcolm Multisource has provided you with a list of various sources of income, deductions and credits for the purpose of determining his basic federal tax.

Inclusions:

His share of tax profit from a partnership business	$10,000
Canadian bank interest	3,000
Retiring allowance from a former employer	20,000
Gross salary from new employer	60,000
Director's fee	5,000
Taxable capital gains	20,000
Imputed interest on a home relocation loan provided by employer	3,000
Rental income from a triplex	25,000

Deductions, Losses or Tax Credits:

Mortgage interest on triplex	$23,000
Canada Pension Plan contributions tax credit	298
Property taxes and insurance on triplex	4,500
Non-capital losses from a previous year	3,000
Allowable capital loss for this year	2,000
Education tax credit transfer from son	80
Net capital losses from a previous year	5,000
Home relocation interest deduction	1,000
Maintenance costs for triplex	1,500
Contribution to employer's registered pension plan	4,000
Basic personal and spousal tax credits	2,411
Fees to a professional engineering society	300
Employment Insurance premiums tax credit	122
Tuition tax credit for night course on computer applications	68
Charitable gifts tax credit	550

— *REQUIRED*

(A) Determine the income, taxable income and basic federal tax based on the above correct information using the ordering rules in sections 3, 111.1 and 118.92 for 2004. Assume that federal tax before credits is $21,459 in 2005.

(B) Cross-reference each amount to the appropriate section of the Act.

ASSIGNMENT PROBLEMS

Problem 1

Identify the provision of the Act which deals with each of the following items. Be as specific as possible in citing the reference to the Act (Part, Division, Subdivision, Section, Subsection, etc.). Use of the sectional list at the beginning of the CCH edition of the Act and/or the topical index at the end of the book may be helpful. However, using the CD included with this text may provide faster search results. Refer to Chapter 19 for instructions on how to search.

(A) Definition of a "person".

(B) Tax credit for donation made by a Canadian resident individual to a Canadian university.

(C) Definition of "balance-due day".

(D) Taxability of group term life insurance premiums paid by an employer on behalf of an employee.

(E) Definition of "capital dividend".

(F) Computation of income tax instalments for individuals.

(G) Definition of a "qualified small business corporation share".

(H) Prescribed requirement to file an information return for a corporation paying a dividend.

(I) Definition of a "testamentary trust".

(J) The calculation of a benefit associated with an interest-free loan from an employer to an employee.

(K) Definition of a "disposition" of non-depreciable capital property.

(L) Limitation on deduction of RRSP administration fees.

(M) General limitation on the amount of deductible expenses.

(N) Deduction from taxable income for taxable dividends that were received by a Canadian corporation.

(O) Tax payable on excess contributions to an RRSP.

Problem 2

[ITA: Divisions B and C]

Ms Ichbin Verblonget had a tumultuous year in 2005. She broke her engagement early in the year and quit her job. She moved to a resort area to take a waitress job and to start up a fitness instruction business. She has had the following items correctly calculated and classified as either inclusions, deductions or tax credits for the purposes of determining her taxable income and federal tax.

Inclusions:

Benefit received from Employment Insurance program	$ 600
Board and lodging provided by employer during busy season of resort	8,000
Bonus from resort employer	500
Business revenue from fitness instruction fees	2,000
Gratuities as a waitress	12,100
Interest on Canada Savings Bonds	775
Rental revenue	6,000
Salary received as a waitress	12,000
Taxable capital gain	3,750
Retiring allowance from previous employer	800

Deductions, Losses or Tax Credits:

Allowable capital loss	4,500
Capital cost allowance on fitness business equipment	1,300
Capital cost allowance on rental building	1,200
Charitable gifts tax credit	26
Child care expenses	1,800
Canada Pension Plan contributions tax credits on employment earnings	230
Medical expenses tax credit	9
Business expenses of earning fitness instruction fees	900
Expenses of objection to a tax assessment	65
Interest on funds borrowed to pay expenses of earning fitness instruction fees	75
Maintenance on rental property	1,100
Mortgage interest on rental property	2,500
Moving expenses	1,700
Non-capital losses from previous year	600
Personal tax credits	1,304
Property tax on rental property	1,000
Employment Insurance premiums tax credit	101
Union dues	100

— REQUIRED

(A) Determine the income, taxable income and basic federal tax based on the above correct information using the ordering rules in sections 3, 111.1 and 118.92 for 2005. Assume federal tax before credits is $4,868 in 2005.

(B) Cross-reference each amount to the appropriate section of the Act.

Problem 3

[ITA: 2]

Many words and terms used in the Act have very specific interpretations. Awareness of these interpretations is fundamental to understanding the scheme and application of the Act. These interpretations come from various sources. The primary source is statutory definition; that is, the term is explicitly defined in the Act. Common law principles also determine interpretations for terms. Many court cases have centred on the interpretation of specific words or phrases which were not explicitly defined in the statute. Once such terms are interpreted by the Courts, that interpretation becomes standard for that term. If a term is neither defined in the statute, nor the subject of a common law definition, the word or term must be assigned the meaning provided by everyday language. The definition is often that which can be found in a common dictionary.

Division A of Part I of the Act outlines who is liable for tax. This Division is a fundamental building block for the Act as it defines to whom the Act will apply. Therefore, it is essential that the terms used in this Division are clearly understood.

— REQUIRED

Identify and define those words and terms found in section 2 of the Act, in the order of their use, which you believe require definition. Indicate the references in the Act to the source of the definition for those words or terms which you have so identified. If you use the CD included with this text the words that are defined elsewhere in the Act are highlighted in red. Refer to Chapter 19 for instructions on how to use the CD.

[For more problems and solutions thereto, see the CD accompanying this book.]

Chapter 2

Liability for Tax

TOPICS DISCUSSED

	Page
LIABILITY OF INDIVIDUALS FOR INCOME TAX	41
Liability of Individual Residents	41
Full-time Residence	42
Part-time Residence	44
Liability of Non-residents	45
International Tax Treaties and Individuals	46
Summary of the Residence Issue for an Individual	48
Comprehensive Consideration of the Residence of an Individual	50
Non-tax Factors affecting Planning for the Residence of an Individual	53
LIABILITY OF CORPORATIONS FOR INCOME TAX	53
Charging Provision	53

	Page
Residence of Corporations	54
Liability of Non-resident Corporations	55
International Tax Treaties and Corporations	55
Comprehensive Consideration of the Residence of a Corporation	56
REGISTRATION REQUIREMENTS AND LIABILITY FOR THE GOODS AND SERVICES TAX	57
Liability for GST	57
Registration Requirements for Residents	59
Registration and Collection Requirements for Non-residents	61
Imports	62

This chapter deals with liability for Canadian income tax and the Goods and Services Tax (GST). The chapter addresses the question of who is liable to pay the tax. Whether it is to the taxpayer's advantage or disadvantage to be a resident/non-resident will depend upon the tax laws of each jurisdiction in which the taxpayer's income is earned, the interaction of these laws and any relevant tax treaty. Many non-tax factors may also impact the choice.

The following chart provides an overview of the provisions of the *Income Tax Act* covered by this chapter.

STRUCTURE OF THE *INCOME TAX ACT*

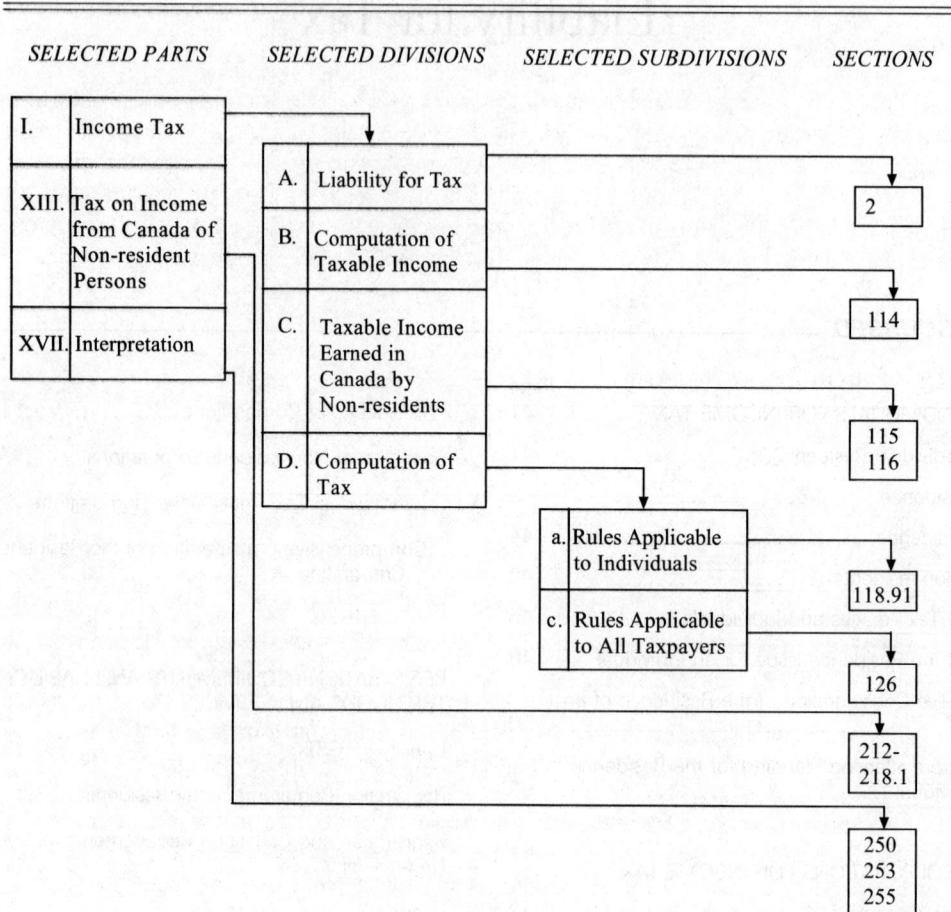

I. LIABILITY OF INDIVIDUALS FOR INCOME TAX

The major issue in this area is the residence of an individual. Residency has become more and more important in recent years as taxpayers with increased mobility attempt to establish residence or non-residence to reduce their income tax liability in a variety of situations.

There are several criteria that can be used to establish income tax liability in a country including citizenship, domicile and residence. In Canada, the major criterion used is residence. Part I, Division A of the Act imposes an income tax on the income of individuals who are resident in Canada. The Act also imposes an income tax on individuals who are not resident in Canada, but only if they are employed in Canada, carry on business in Canada, or dispose of taxable Canadian property.

A. Liability of Individual Residents

[ITA: 2; 249(1); 255]

Subsection 2(1) contains what is known as the charging provision for residents of Canada in respect of income under Part I. The provision charges taxpayers with responsibility for paying the tax by the use of the words "an income tax shall be paid".

Read the following provision carefully and consider some of the key terms used in that subsection:

> An income tax shall be paid as required by this Act on the *taxable income* for each *taxation year* of every *person resident* in *Canada* at any time in the year.

As indicated previously, the word "income" is not defined in the Act. The phrase "taxable income" is a technical phrase with a limited and special meaning [ssec. 2(2)] and the phrase "taxation year" is defined [ssec. 249(1)]. Note that the word "person" is defined to include both an individual and a corporation [ssec. 248(1)]. Also considered to be a person under the definition is a trust which will be discussed in Chapter 18. The word "resident" is not fully defined in the Act and, as a result, is the subject of discussion in much of this chapter. However, a definition of "Canada" is provided for the purposes of the Act [sec. 255]. The existence of a definition for a term or phrase used in a provision like section 2 can be found by checking the "Related Sections" footnotes to the section in the CCH edition of the Act, where defined words or phrases are listed in quotation marks.

The scope of income taxation on a resident of Canada is worldwide. Thus, taxable income of a resident of Canada is subject to Canadian income tax regardless of the country in which the income is earned or generated. To avoid potential double taxation, Canada has negotiated a number of international reciprocal tax agreements which will be discussed in more detail later in this chapter. A key principle followed by these agreements is that the country in which the income is earned has priority in taxing that income and the country of which the taxpayer is a resident allows all or some part of the foreign tax paid as a credit against the domestic tax.

B. Full-time Residence

[ITA: 2; 250(1); IT-221R3]

1. Deemed full-time residence

A full-time resident is taxed on his or her worldwide income for a full year. While the Act does not define resident or residence, it does deem an individual to be a full-time resident if one of the conditions in subsection 250(1) is met. It is important to note the use of the word "deemed" in provisions of the Act. The effect is to establish a set of conditions and treat a taxpayer or an action in a manner or with the consequences desired by the legislation, in this case, like a full-time resident taxed on worldwide income. Were it not for this deeming provision in subsection 250(1), the individual may not be considered to be a resident and, in fact, might be a non-resident. This provision states, among other conditions, that a person is deemed to be resident in Canada throughout the taxation year if he or she "sojourned" in Canada in the year for an aggregate of 183 days or more. The Canada Revenue Agency's (CRA's) practice is to count any part of a day as a "day" for this purpose. The word "sojourn" has the connotation of a temporary visit rather than a permanent stay. It should be noted, however, that spending less than 183 days in Canada does not necessarily make an individual non-resident, if he or she is not merely visiting, but has more substantial residential ties, as discussed below.

2. Common law concept of full-time residence

It is possible for a person to be considered a full-time resident by virtue of principles of the common law or case law which have evolved over the years. Residence is determined by the application of these general principles to the facts of each case.

Consider the following fact situation presented to a British court (*Reid v. C.I.R.*, [1926] 10 T.C. 673). The taxpayer had lived in England throughout her lifetime. For the year in question she stored her furniture, travelled on the Continent with no permanent abode in any one place, stayed in England only a short time, maintained a bank account in England and held no salaried position anywhere. The court held that she was resident in England. The court considered the relationship between a person's life and the place in which the taxpayer spent, at least, part of his or her time. A person's ties to a country need not be manifested in a permanent home.

In another British case (*Levene v. C.I.R.*, [1928] A.C. 217) the following facts were presented. A British subject gave up a leased house in England. He lived on the Continent in an apartment. He made visits of four or five months to London to obtain medical advice, to visit relatives or the graves of his parents, and to take part in certain religious observances. Again, the court held that he was resident in England. An important fact in this case was that he returned to the proximity of relatives and friends. It should be noted that the courts have determined that an individual can be resident in more than one country and that an individual must be resident in at least one country at any moment in time.

A key statement describing the residence of an individual under common law principles was made in a 1921 British decision (*Weymys v. Weymys*, [1921] Sess. Cas. 30, at p. 40) which described residence as "a continuing state of relationship between a person and a place which arises from the durable concurrence of a number of circumstances". Thus, facts must be found to establish the continuing state of relationship, that is, ties to the country. The landmark Canadian case in this area is *Thomson v. M.N.R.*, (S.C.C.) 2 DTC 812 and another often cited case is that of *Meldrum v. M.N.R.*, (T.A.B.) 50 DTC 232. Both cases involved individuals who stayed in Canada for short periods of time on a regular basis. The courts considered facts relevant to establishing the "continuing state of relationship".

3. Departmental practice

IT-221R3 categorizes the type of facts that can be used for an individual to establish residential ties for a "continuing state of relationship". Many of these facts would appear to have held some importance in previous court decisions. However, it must be remembered that statements on administrative practice in an Interpretation Bulletin represent the opinion of the CRA and not the law.

- Maintaining a dwelling, whether owned or leased, suitable for year-round occupancy and available for occupation, would establish an important residential tie. However, the dwelling need not be vacant at all times. If it is rented to a non-arm's length person or to an arm's length person on terms and conditions that are not arm's length, then it may be considered to be available for the taxpayer's use.

- A spouse or common-law partner and other members of the immediate family remaining in Canada when an individual leaves would be regarded by the CRA as an important residential tie. A separation due to the breakdown of a relationship would, of course, reduce the significance of this factor if the individual, in leaving, severs other residential ties.

- Maintaining personal property and social ties in Canada would indicate a "continuing state of relationship" through secondary residential ties. Personal property remaining in Canada might include furniture, clothing, cars, and recreational vehicles. Maintaining provincial or territorial hospitalization and medical insurance coverage and a seasonal residence might also be an indication of residential ties. Social ties such as recreational and religious organization memberships in Canada could be used in a similar way depending on the reasons for maintaining such ties. Economic ties such as employment with a Canadian employer, active investment in a Canadian business and Canadian bank accounts, retirement savings plans, credit cards and securities accounts, are also regarded as secondary residential ties. Other such ties include: Canadian landed immigrant status or appropriate work permits, a Canadian passport, a Canadian driver's license, Canadian vehicle registration and membership in Canadian unions or professional organizations. It should be emphasized that none of the ties in this third category taken singly would be enough to determine full-time residence. However, one or more of these ties in combination with others, particularly in the first two bulleted categories above, would make a strong package of ties indicating such full-time residence. In making a determination of residence, it becomes important to give each fact an appropriate weighting according to its importance in the situation.

In order to establish that an individual is not a full-time resident, the severance of residential ties with Canada and the establishment of residential ties elsewhere is important, although an individual can be a resident of more than one country. An argument for continuing residential ties can be made, in particular, when the return could have been foreseen because of the existence of, perhaps, a contract of employment on return. No particular length of absence results in an individual becoming a non-resident. Occasional, but not regular, return visits for personal or business reasons would not likely jeopardize the severance of full-time residence.

C. Part-time Residence

[ITA: 114; 118.91]

The absence of residential ties, as discussed above, at a point in time would suggest that an individual is not a resident of Canada. Thus, at any particular point in time, an individual is either a resident of Canada, with the income tax consequences discussed above, or a non-resident, with possible income tax consequences to be discussed.

Part-time residence is a transitional position between residence and non-residence. Part-time residence can occur when an individual, having had full residential ties, leaves Canada during a year. Similarly, when an individual who did not have such ties for a prior period, comes to Canada during a year and establishes full residential ties, he or she would be considered to be a part-time resident for that year. The year of exit or entry is the year of part-time residence status.

A part-time resident is taxed in Canada on his or her worldwide income earned during the part of the year in which he or she was resident in Canada. Deductions in the computation of taxable income are allocated, if applicable, to the period of part-time residence [sec. 114]. A similar allocation of amounts deductible as non-refundable tax credits may be made [sec. 118.91]. Note the precise wording of sections 114 and 118.91 which require that during some other part of the year the taxpayer was not resident in Canada. This means that an individual will be taxed in Canada on his or her worldwide income for the period in a year during which he or she was a resident. This period constitutes the taxpayer's taxation year for the computation of income taxable in Canada during the year. Were it not for these rules, an individual might be regarded as a resident for the full year taxable on worldwide income for the whole year. Thus, the part-time residence rules provide an exception to the more general full-time residence rules.

To establish part-time residence, facts must be found to show that the person made either a "clean break" from Canada during the year or a "fresh start" in Canada during the year. An example of a "clean break" might involve a person who has resided in Canada in previous years and leaves Canada with his or her family and all of their belongings in, say, August of the year, severing all ties and indicating an intention not to return. If such a "clean break" or severing of ties can be established by the facts, then the individual becomes a non-resident after the "clean break" and the period of part-time residence. The CRA will consider a "clean break" to have been made on the latest of the date on which:

(a) the individual leaves Canada,

(b) the individual's spouse or common-law partner and/or dependants leave Canada, or

(c) the individual becomes a resident of the country to which he or she is immigrating.

If the ties that have existed are not considered by the facts to have been severed, then the individual remains a full-time resident. An example of a "fresh start" might involve a person who has not previously or not recently resided in Canada and moves to Canada to take up residence in, say, April of the year. In both cases, the person would be in Canada for more than 183 days, but his or her stay in the country for the period in question would not be temporary, as required by the rule in paragraph 250(1)(*a*) to deem an individual to be a full-time resident.[a]

---

[a] The cases of *Schujahn v. M.N.R.*, (Ex. Ct.) 62 DTC 1225 and *Truchon v. M.N.R.*, (T.A.B.) 70 DTC 1277 may illustrate the differences between deemed full-time and part-time residence.

D. Liability of Non-residents

[ITA: 2; 115; 253]

1. General determination of liability

Subject to the provisions of an international tax agreement, a non-resident individual who for a taxation year was employed in Canada, carried on business in Canada or disposed of taxable Canadian property at any time in the year or a previous year, is liable to pay income tax [ssec. 2(3)]. The base for this tax is his or her taxable income earned only in Canada computed under the provisions of section 115. The addition of the phrase "or a previous year" means that income earned in Canada by a non-resident but not received until a later year will be taxed in that later year when the non-resident might not be employed or carrying on business in Canada. Thus, tax cannot be avoided by deferring salaries or business income until a year when no income is earned in Canada. Due to the wording of sections 114 and 118.91 discussed previously, it should be emphasized that a person who is a non-resident for the entire year cannot be a part-time resident. To be a part-time resident, there must be a period in which the person was resident, in the sense of a full-time resident, and a period in which the person was a non-resident.

2. The meaning of carrying on business in Canada

The phrase "carrying on business" is not specifically defined in the *Income Tax Act*. The courts have tended to interpret the phrase as implying a continuous business activity.[b] A "business", on the other hand, is not required to involve a continuous business activity by virtue of its definition in subsection 248(1) which includes an "adventure or concern in the nature of trade". An adventure in the nature of trade can be simply described as a scheme to make a profit in the same manner as a person who is in that line of business.[c] The definition in section 253, "extended meaning of carrying on business", describes activities which, if engaged in by a non-resident person, will result in the non-resident being deemed to have been carrying on business.

Generally speaking, merely soliciting orders makes a non-resident person liable to be deemed to be carrying on business. Normally, the main determinant of carrying on business in a place is the location in which the contract in a transaction is made, not the location of the offering of an item for sale as envisaged by section 253. It should be noted that the courts have also looked beyond the place where the contract was concluded to the place where the operations occur from which the profits arise in substance. This is indicated by where payment is made or where the work is done or delivery of the goods is made. These factors indicate the place of performance of the contract. Recognize, however, that the specific activities listed in section 253 override the common law principle of place of performance.

A non-resident offering something for sale in Canada through an employee who is a salesperson is carrying on business in Canada. On the other hand, a non-resident selling to an independent contractor like a Canadian-based retailer or wholesaler who resells the item in Canada is not carrying on business in Canada. Hence, the distinction between an employee and an independent contractor is important and will be explained more fully in Chapter 3. The distinction must be made on the facts of each case. These facts must establish the degree of responsibility enjoyed by the person who

---

[b] See *Tara Explorations & Development Co. Ltd. v M.N.R.*, (S.C.C.) 72 DTC 6288, affirming (Ex. Ct.) 70 DTC 6370.

[c] See *M.N.R. v. Taylor*, (Ex. Ct.) 56 DTC 1125, and IT-459.

is soliciting orders or offering goods for sale. The courts have considered the following factors in this distinction:

(a) whether the parties describe or refer to their relationship as one of an independent contractor and a supplier;

(b) whether the alleged independent contractor carries on business in the name of the supplier or in his or her own name; and

(c) whether the independent contractor acts for other suppliers.

The greater the independence from the supplier and the greater the degree of responsibility, the greater is the likelihood that the situation involves a non-resident supplier selling to an independent contractor such that the supplier is not carrying on business in Canada and, is, therefore, not taxable in Canada on business income earned in Canada.

Note that the use of words like "carried on" in paragraph 2(3)(*b*) or "carrying on", "solicited" and "offered" in section 253 implies a continuity of activity over a period of time. The courts have indicated that an isolated transaction, even one that is described in section 253, does not fit the concept of continuity over time. Hence, continuity of activity may, depending on the facts, be necessary to establish a "carrying on" of business, unless the isolated transaction in Canada is part of the normal international business activities of the non-resident. On the other hand, the CRA has expressed the view, in a memorandum obtained under Access to Information legislation, that the activity could be carried on in Canada for only a short duration and still be considered to be carrying on business.

E. International Tax Treaties and Individuals

[ITA: 250(5)]

Canada has negotiated many reciprocal tax treaties with other countries with the objective of preventing the incidence of double taxation or tax avoidance. These situations may result from the overlapping of tax provisions applicable to persons subject to tax in the two jurisdictions which are parties in the treaty. The treaty of greatest significance is probably the Canada–U.S. Tax Convention because of the considerable interrelationship of the two countries. Late in 1980 after almost 40 years under the original convention, a new convention was proposed. The new convention was fully ratified through the exchange of instruments of ratification on August 16, 1984 and, as a result, provisions dealing with taxes other than withholding at source came into force for taxation years beginning after 1984. The major provisions are described very briefly below.

The provision in Article XV, regarding employees, in the Canada–U.S. Tax Convention is typical of many treaties that Canada has negotiated with other countries. The provision deals with the taxation of dependent personal services and exempts a resident of Canada from U.S. taxation on salaries, wages and other similar remuneration derived from an employment in the United States under certain conditions. The conditions are:

(a) that the remuneration does not exceed U.S. $10,000, or

(b) that the employee is present in the U.S. for a period not exceeding an aggregate of 183 days in the year and the remuneration is not borne by an employer who is a resident of the U.S. or by a "permanent establishment" or a "fixed base" which the employer has in the U.S.

Note, however, that as a resident of Canada, the individual would be taxable in Canada on worldwide income, including that earned in the U.S. and exempt from taxation in the U.S.

Article XIV deals with income from independent personal services, i.e., from self-employment. For example, an individual who is resident in Canada would only be taxed in the U.S. if the individual has or had a "fixed base", regularly available to him or her in the U.S. The tax in the U.S. would be limited to that on income attributable to the fixed base in the U.S. The provision is reciprocal in relation to residents of the United States performing personal services in Canada under the same conditions.

For the purposes of the Convention, the term "resident" is defined in Article IV, paragraph 1 to mean:

> any person who, under the laws of [one country], is liable to tax therein by reason of his domicile, residence, place of management, place of incorporation or any other criterion of a similar nature. . . .

Paragraph 2 provides "tie-breaker" rules where an individual can be considered by paragraph 1 to be a resident of both countries. In this case, the individual's residence is determined as follows:

(a) he or she is deemed to be a resident of the country in which he or she has a permanent home available; if he or she has a permanent home available in both countries or in neither country, he or she is deemed to be a resident of the country with which his or her personal and economic relations are closer (i.e., centre of vital interests);

(b) if the country in which the individual has his or her centre of vital interests cannot be determined, the individual is deemed to be a resident of the country in which he or she has an habitual abode;

(c) if the individual has an habitual abode in both countries or in neither country, he or she is deemed to be a resident of the country of which he or she is a citizen; and

(d) if the individual is a citizen of both countries, or neither country, the "competent authorities" of the countries will settle the question by mutual agreement.

When these "tie-breaker rules" contained in a treaty apply and it is determined that an individual is a resident of another country, then subsection 250(5) deems the individual to be a non-resident of Canada.

The term "competent authority" is defined in Article III, paragraph 1(g) to mean the Minister of National Revenue in Canada and the Secretary of the Treasury in the United States, or their designates.

While the term "fixed base" is not defined in the Convention, the term "permanent establishment" is defined in Article V to mean "a fixed place of business through which the business of a resident of a [country] is wholly or partly carried on". The term specifically includes a place of management, a branch, an office and a factory, among others. A person, other than an independent contractor, who has and habitually exercises an authority to conclude contracts in, say, Canada in the name of the resident of the U.S., is deemed to constitute a permanent establishment in Canada of the U.S. resident.

However, under paragraph 6 of Article V, the term "permanent establishment" does *not* include a fixed place of business in one country used solely in one or more of the following activities of the resident of the other country:

(a) the use of facilities for the purpose of storage, display or delivery of goods or merchandise belonging to the resident of the other country;

(b) the maintenance of a stock of goods or merchandise belonging to the resident of the other country for the purpose of storage, display or delivery;

(c) the maintenance of a stock of goods or merchandise belonging to the resident of the other country for the purpose of processing by another person;

(d) the purchase of goods or merchandise, or the collection of information, for the resident of the other country; and

(e) advertising, the supply of information, scientific research or similar activities which have a preparatory or auxiliary character for the resident of the other country.

F. Summary of the Residence Issue for an Individual

From the foregoing discussion, it can be concluded, generally, that an individual will be either a full-time resident of Canada or a non-resident. A full-time resident of Canada is taxable in Canada on worldwide income. A non-resident is taxable in Canada, generally, only on Canadian-source income, if any. If, in a particular year, an individual leaves Canada and severs ties to Canada, after having been a full-time resident, or enters Canada and establishes ties to Canada, after having been a non-resident, the individual will be a part-time resident for the part of that year while fully resident in Canada and a non-resident for the other part of the year. Hence, part-time residence is a transitional status. A part-time resident is taxable in Canada on worldwide income only for the part of the year while fully resident. An individual who is a non-resident of Canada can be deemed to be a full-time resident of Canada if one of the conditions in subsection 250(1) is met.

Exhibit 2-1 may provide a helpful checklist of facts to evaluate a case in which there has been a change in the residence status of an individual. In essence, it elaborates on the common law principle of "a continuing state of relationship" by establishing the existence of either continuing ties to Canada or ties elsewhere. In a transitional year, when an individual leaves Canada, having been a full-time resident, the ties to Canada may be severed (i.e., a "clean break" was made). Alternatively, when an individual moves into Canada, having been a non-resident, the ties to Canada may be established (i.e., a "fresh start" was made) and ties elsewhere may be severed. Note that full-time resident status and non-resident status are mutually exclusive. An individual cannot be a full-time resident of Canada and a non-resident at the same time. Therefore, the facts that support one status can usually be used to refute the other, although it is possible for an individual to be a resident of more than one country at the same time.

EXHIBIT 2-1
Checklist of Facts to Consider When Determining Residence
status of an Individual
(Based on IT-221R3)

Factor	Resident	Non-resident
Significant residential ties		
(a) dwelling place		
(b) spouse or common-law partner		
(c) dependants		
Secondary residential ties		
(a) personal property in Canada		
(b) social ties with Canada		
(c) economic ties with Canada		
(d) landed immigrant status or appropriate work permits		
(e) hospitalization and medical insurance coverage from Canada		
(f) driver's license from Canada		
(g) vehicle registration in Canada		
(h) seasonal dwelling place in Canada		
(i) Canadian passport		
(j) memberships in Canadian union or professional organization		
Other residential ties of limited importance		
(a) retention of Canadian mailing address]		
(b) Canadian post office box		
(c) Canadian safety deposit box		
(d) personal stationery or business cards showing Canadian address		
(e) telephone listing in Canada		
(f) Canadian newspaper and magazine subscriptions		
Nature of absence from Canada		
(a) evidence of intention to permanently sever ties with Canada		
(b) regularity and length of visits to Canada		
(c) residence ties outside of Canada		

G. Comprehensive Consideration of the Residence of an Individual

In any of the areas of taxation that are not resolved by a provision of the Act, there are several stages at which the tax adviser may become involved. At one stage, the facts of the case represent completed transactions which have been reported for income tax purposes and have been reassessed by the CRA. At this stage, the question is whether there is a sufficient basis to pursue the issue with the CRA further or to accept the reassessment as issued. At another stage, the facts represent completed transactions, but the client has not yet filed the return which will report the transactions. Here, the issue is how to comply with the law in filing the return. At yet another stage, the facts of the situation are in the planning phase and have not been completed. The issue at this stage is how the fact situation will be regarded for taxation purposes.

At all stages, the type of analysis of the facts that should be done is essentially the same. If a framework of a test or a series of tests is available, as is the case in a residence situation, it should be applied to the facts to systematically evaluate the situation and enable the adviser to arrive at a logical conclusion. No matter how strongly the adviser may feel about a particular conclusion, it is important to consider both sides of the issue. A case for one particular side can be strengthened by considering the arguments for the opposing side and developing arguments against that opposing position. If this can be anticipated before actual discussions with the other side, fewer surprises will result.

While the method of analysis may be essentially the same at all stages of a tax situation, the form of the advice offered may differ, depending on the stage. At the reassessment stage, advice on whether there is a reasonably strong basis to pursue the client's position should be presented. At the initial compliance stage of filing the return, an indication of the alternatives and their tax consequences are needed to help the client decide on a filing position. The planning stage provides the greatest opportunity to help the client structure the situation to achieve the best tax result. At this stage, it is possible to modify the situation and its facts to achieve the desired outcome, because the originally planned facts have not been undertaken at this stage. However, even this stage requires a thorough evaluation of the situation and its potential tax consequences.

The facts described in the following case situation could arise at any of the above three stages. The solution presented outlines a suggested method of systematic analysis based on the framework discussed and summarized in Exhibit 2-2.

Example Problem

· Eighteen years ago, Mr. Har DeHatt, a U.S. citizen, moved to Vancouver with his parents. He went to high school in Vancouver and upon completion of his program he was employed in construction work in the Vancouver area. In time he became a construction supervisor. He married a Canadian five years ago. The couple subsequently purchased a home in Vancouver in which they lived and raised two children. He never became a Canadian citizen.

During the year in question, the state of the construction industry in Vancouver was such that he could not be employed on a regular basis although he did work on several jobs during the year. Effective August 1 of that year, he accepted an offer of employment with a construction company operating in the State of Washington and during the remainder of the year and the entire following year he worked on construction jobs in the State of Washington and in Alaska. He rented an apartment in Seattle, Washington, but maintained his home in Vancouver where his wife and children made their regular home. The household telephone listing in the Vancouver telephone directory was in his name.

He visited his family on such occasions as he was able to take time to go to Vancouver. The Vancouver address was the one to which he always returned when his duties permitted.

During the year in question, he worked a total of 800 hours on the new job, earning substantially more than U.S. $10,000.

— *REQUIRED*

Prepare a memo for the tax person in your firm who will advise Mr. DeHatt on his income tax liability for the year in question. Evaluate in detail the alternatives in the residence issue as they relate to this fact situation for the year in question. Discuss each possible degree of residence and its tax consequences. State your conclusion on the case after considering the relevant international tax agreement and after appropriately weighing the significance of the facts in the case. You may wish to use the framework presented in Exhibit 2-2, as it applies to individuals.

EXHIBIT 2-2
Residency Tests
Framework for Analysis of Residence Fact Situation

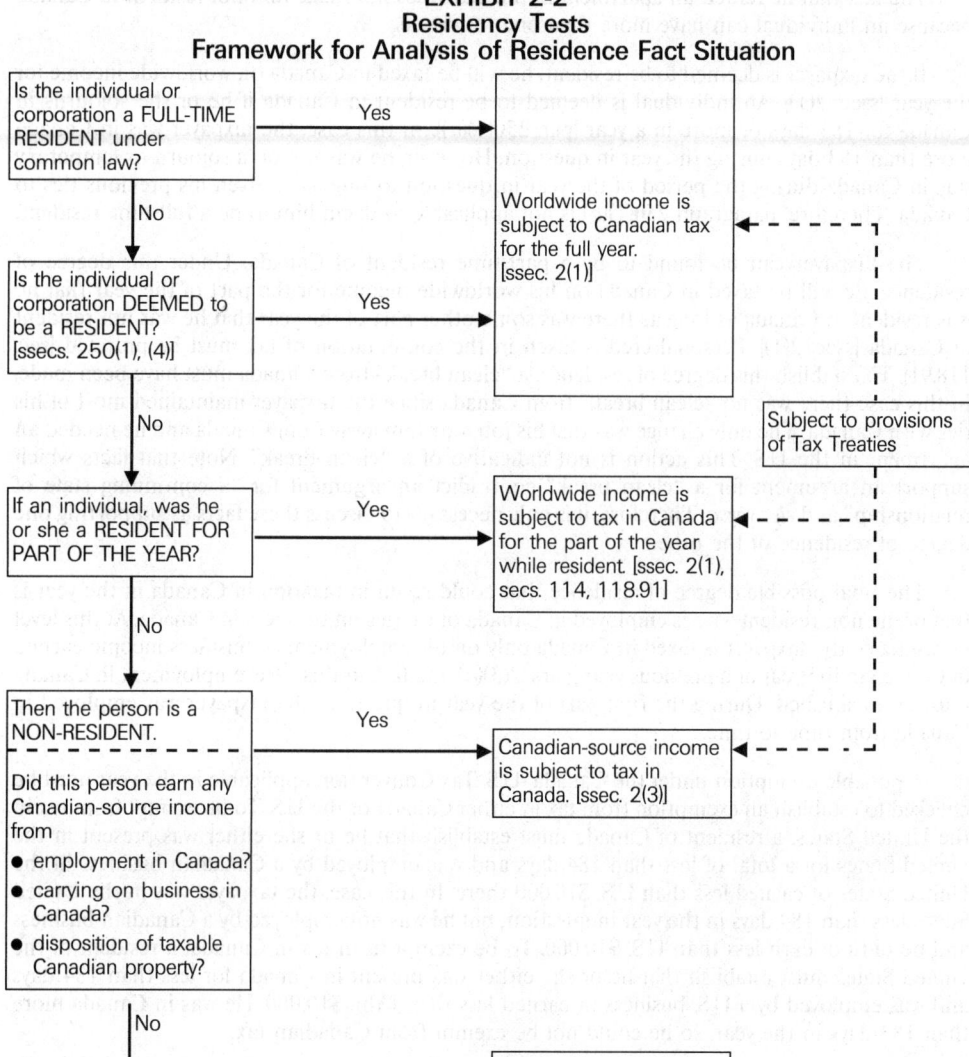

—*SOLUTION* [See *Lawrence C. Gillis v. M.N.R.*, (T.A.B.) 69 DTC 488]

If the taxpayer is found to be a full-time resident of Canada under the common law, he will be taxed in Canada on his worldwide income for the year [ssec. 2(1)]. For this degree of residence to be found, "a continuing state of relationship between the person and a place" must be established. Citizenship is irrelevant to the question of residence. The facts of this case that could be used to establish the continuing relationship between the taxpayer and Canada include the following:

    (a) he lived in Canada on a full-time basis for 18 years in which time he was educated in Canada, employed in Canada and married in Canada;

(b) he owned a house in Canada and the household telephone was listed in his name;

(c) his wife and children lived in Canada; and

(d) he visited his family whenever possible.

The fact that he rented an apartment in the U.S. does not make him not resident in Canada because an individual can have more than one residence.

If the taxpayer is deemed to be resident, he will be taxed in Canada on worldwide income for the year [ssec. 2(1)]. An individual is deemed to be resident in Canada if he or she sojourns in Canada for 183 days or more in a year [par. 250(1)(*a*)]. In this case, the taxpayer was in Canada more than 183 days during the year in question. However, he was not on a sojourn or temporary stay in Canada during the period of the year in question to August 1, given his previous ties to Canada. Therefore, paragraph 250(1)(*a*) is not applicable to deem him to be a full-time resident.

The taxpayer can be found to be a part-time resident of Canada. Under this degree of residence, he will be taxed in Canada on his worldwide income for the part of the year that he was resident in Canada as long as there was some other part of the year that he was not resident in Canada [ssec. 2(1)]. Personal credits taken in the computation of tax must be prorated [sec. 118.91]. To establish this degree of residence, a "clean break" from Canada must have been made. In this case there was no "clean break" from Canada since the taxpayer maintained most of his ties with Canada. The only change was that his job took him away from Canada and he needed an apartment in the U.S. This action is not indicative of a "clean break". Note that facts which support an argument for a "clean break" contradict an argument for "a continuing state of relationship" and *vice versa*. Therefore, it is only necessary to discuss these facts as supporting one degree of residence or the other.

The final possible degree of residence that could result in taxation in Canada in the year is that of the non-resident who is employed in Canada or carries on business in Canada. At this level of residence the taxpayer is taxed in Canada only on his employment or business income earned in Canada in the year or a previous year [pars. 2(3)(*a*) and (*b*)]. In this case, employment in Canada must be established. During the first part of the year in question, the taxpayer was employed in Canada from time to time.

A possible exemption under the Canada–U.S. Tax Convention applicable in the year must be checked to establish an exemption from tax in either Canada or the U.S. To be exempt from tax in the United States, a resident of Canada must establish that he or she either was present in the United States for a total of less than 184 days and was employed by a Canadian business in the United States or earned less than U.S. $10,000 there. In this case, the taxpayer was in the United States less than 184 days in the year in question, but he was not employed by a Canadian business and he did not earn less than U.S. $10,000. To be exempt from tax in Canada, a resident of the United States must establish that he or she either was present in Canada for less than 184 days and was employed by a U.S. business or earned less than Cdn. $10,000. He was in Canada more than 183 days in the year, so he could not be exempt from Canadian tax.

It should be noted that under the Canada–U.S. Tax Convention, income from independent personal services, i.e., non-employment related services, earned by an individual who is resident in one country may be taxed in the other country if the individual has or had a "fixed base" regularly available to him or her in the other country. However, the income is subject to tax in the other country only to the extent that it is attributable to the fixed base in that country. The term "fixed base" is not defined.

The facts of this case indicate that the taxpayer is most likely a full-time resident of Canada. Deemed residence is not a possibility in this case, based on an evaluation of the facts. The evidence of a "clean break" is not very strong in the facts of this case. If a "clean break" is not established in the year the non-resident category is not possible in that year.

H. Non-tax Factors affecting Planning for the Residence of an Individual

Establishing that an individual is taxable as a full-time resident or a non-resident, or not taxable in Canada at all, is not the same as determining the best form of residency in a particular case. For example, being a full-time resident of Canada, taxed on worldwide income, is not always worse than being a non-resident who is not taxable in Canada at all and, hence, taxed completely elsewhere. The best form of residency for an individual in a particular situation depends on many factors, some of which involve tax liability and some of which do not.

Newspaper and other articles frequently appear, presenting comparisons of the net tax burden of a particular individual taxed in Canada and in another jurisdiction. As a result of different income tax rates and allowable deductions in different jurisdictions, the net income tax differences can be considerable. The implication is often that the full-time resident of Canada is better off or worse off on an after-tax basis in the other jurisdiction. These comparisons can be misleading, if they do not consider a number of non-tax factors that might have an impact on the situation. For example, differences in the cost of health care and how it is financed by an individual can offset differences in net tax. A Canadian Minister of Finance, commenting on relatively higher levels of taxation in Canada, was reported to have stated: "if taxes were the only reason [to leave Canada], the Cayman Islands would be the most populated area in the world".

While employment opportunities at the forefront of a particular field of interest or training and higher remuneration levels may be an attraction in a particular jurisdiction, quality-of-life factors should also be considered. For example, if there are differences in the cost of health care, they may result from differences in quality and in availability. On the other hand, differences in climatic conditions may solve certain health problems such as asthma or allergies. Differences in both the standard of living and the cost of living should be assessed. Cultural differences may require adjustments which may be made more difficult by geographic separation from family and social ties. Some countries may be less socially or politically stable, resulting in less personal safety and more crime. Economic differences, such as less availability of credit, may exist. Also, financial exchange risks may be encountered and exchange controls may make it difficult to remove capital from some jurisdictions.

II. LIABILITY OF CORPORATIONS FOR INCOME TAX

The liability of a corporation for income tax in Canada depends on whether it is a resident or a non-resident. The existence of a deeming rule to establish corporate residence, based on incorporation in Canada, means that contentious issues pertaining to corporate residence in Canada are limited. In recent years, there has been little litigation on the residence of corporations.

A. Charging Provision
[ITA: 2; 249]

Since section 2 applies to persons and the word "person" includes a corporation, the charging provision for corporations is the same as that for individuals. The taxation year of a corporation need not be the calendar year, like the taxation year of an individual [sec. 249]. Since the taxation year of a corporation need not coincide with the calendar year and, in fact, need not be a full twelve months, there is no need for a concept of part-time residence pertaining to a corporation. When, at any time, a corporation is incorporated in Canada and commences operations, a taxation year begins. When a corporation terminates its incorporation in Canada, a taxation year ends. The appropriate rules pertaining to resident corporations are applied for those taxation years.

B. Residence of Corporations

[ITA: 250(4)]

1. Deemed residence

Since a corporation is an artificial legal entity, it does not "reside" anywhere in the sense that an individual does. Paragraph 250(4)(*a*) provides that a corporation incorporated in Canada after April 26, 1965, the date of the federal budget that introduced this deeming rule, is deemed to be resident in Canada throughout a taxation year. This deeming rule clearly settles the issue of corporate residence for corporations incorporated *in Canada* in recent years. A corporation incorporated in Canada before April 27, 1965 is deemed to be resident in Canada if it was resident by the common law principle discussed below or it carried on business in Canada during any taxation year ending after April 26, 1965 [par. 250(4)(*c*)].[d] A corporation which does not fall within subsection 250(4), that is, a corporation that is not incorporated in Canada, may still be a Canadian resident under the common law principle that its central management and control are in Canada.

2. Common law concept of corporate residence

A 1906 British case, (*DeBeers Consolidated Mines Ltd. v. Howe*, [1906] A.C. 455), which established the "central management and control rule", was based on the following facts. The company was incorporated in South Africa and had its head office there. The board of directors regularly met in London and the real control was exercised in London, although no business was carried on in the United Kingdom. The corporation was held to be resident in the United Kingdom because "a corporation resides where the real business is being carried on and the real business is carried on where the central management and control actually abide". Usually central management and control exists where the board of directors meets to make decisions on company policy.

In another British case, (*Unit Construction Co. Ltd. v. Bullock*, [1959] 3 W.W.R. 1022), the following facts were presented. The appellant company was a wholly-owned subsidiary of an English company and so were three companies registered in Kenya. The appellant had made some payments to these companies which would be tax deductible only if the companies were resident in the United Kingdom for the year in question. In addition to being registered in Kenya, the companies carried on business entirely outside the United Kingdom and their articles of association expressly provided that their directors' meetings be held anywhere except in the United Kingdom. At a certain point in time, the situation of the companies had become so serious that it was unwise to allow them to be managed in Africa any longer and it was decided that management be taken over by the parent. From that time, any decision of importance that concerned the running of the companies was made in London by the directors of the parent.

The House of Lords of the United Kingdom held the following in this case:

> . . . on these facts the seat of the "central management and control" of the subsidiaries passed from Africa to the United Kingdom. This is a straightforward case of *de facto* control being actively exercised in the United Kingdom while the local directors stood aside from their directorial duties . . .

This case has been used as an authority for the principle that central management and control and, therefore, residence of a company is not necessarily in the country where the board of directors meets even if they have *de jure* or legal control.

---

[d] For the purposes of this chapter, paragraph 250(4)(*b*) can be ignored.

The case of *The King v. British Columbia Electric Railway Company Ltd.*, (S.C.C.) 2 DTC 824 established the principle that the place of incorporation of a company is not relevant by itself. Of course, deemed residence of a corporation requires incorporation in Canada. *Bedford Overseas Freighters Ltd. v. M.N.R.*, (Ex. Ct.) 70 DTC 6072 illustrates the application of the "central management and control" rule to a Canadian fact situation. It should be noted that if a corporation is considered to be a resident in Canada at any time in the year, it is taxed on its worldwide income for the year as if it had been resident throughout the year. Thus, there is no concept of part-time residence for corporations.

C. Liability of Non-resident Corporations

[ITA: 2(3); 253]

To be considered a non-resident, a corporation cannot be incorporated in Canada after April 26, 1965, subject to certain specific exceptions [ssec. 250(4)]. A non-resident corporation may be taxable in Canada on its Canadian-source income [ssec. 2(3)]. Since a corporation cannot be "employed", paragraph 2(3)(*a*) cannot apply to a corporation. It is possible, however, for a corporation that is not incorporated in Canada to carry on business in Canada and, hence, be taxable on its Canadian-source business income. The consideration of what constitutes a carrying on of business by a corporation in Canada is generally the same as that for an individual, as discussed previously. However, one perspective on carrying on business involving a corporation may not exist in the case of an individual. A corporation may be formed for a single business purpose which, if implemented in a single transaction, would involve no continuity of activity in the carrying on of business. In the case of *Placrefid Ltd. v. M.N.R.*, (F.C.T.D.) 92 DTC 6480, the court held that a single transaction in this type of corporate situation constituted a carrying on of business. The provisions of a tax treaty may eliminate the liability for tax in Canada of a non-resident corporation carrying on business in Canada.

D. International Tax Treaties and Corporations

Most of the major treaties carry a provision similar to that in Article VII of the Canada–U.S. Income Tax Convention in which a U.S. enterprise is not subject to taxation by Canada on its "business profits" unless the enterprise carries on business in Canada through a "permanent establishment" located in Canada. If it has such a permanent establishment, it is subject to tax in Canada only on the income attributable to the permanent establishment. As indicated above, the key determinants of a permanent establishment defined in Article V are a fixed place of business or a person who habitually exercises authority to contract for his or her principal. Note that an independent agent is not considered such a person. A list of activities from Article V that do not constitute a fixed place of business is provided in the discussion of international tax treaties and individuals, above.[e] The logic used by the Exchequer Court in the *Tara Explorations* case (cited in footnote (e)) is particularly noteworthy in its comprehensiveness. A similar method of analysis of a residence question is used in the following example problems. It is also illustrated in Exhibit 2-2 which sets out a framework for the analysis of a fact situation on the residence issue in terms of levels or "degrees" of residence.

The definition of the term "resident" quoted above from Article IV applies to a corporation as well as to an individual. Where that definition would determine that a corporation is a resident of both countries, then paragraph 3 of Article IV would deem the corporation to be resident in the country of its incorporation.

---

[e] The cases of *American Wheelabrator & Equipment Corporation v. M.N.R.*, (T.A.B.) 51 DTC 285 and *Tara Explorations and Development Company Limited v. M.N.R.*, (Ex. Ct.) 70 DTC 6370 consider the concept of a permanent establishment.

E. Comprehensive Consideration of the Residence of a Corporation

Example Problem

Thumbusters Corporation was incorporated in the State of New York on March 1, 1981. The head office of the corporation was established in Buffalo, New York, along with production and warehouse facilities. The directors of the company, the president, and the general manager were all U.S. citizens resident in Buffalo. Meetings necessary to maintain the corporate charter as well as major business meetings to discuss corporate strategy were held in Buffalo. The main corporation books and records were maintained at the company's head office.

One of the main reasons for locating the company facilities in Buffalo was to exploit the Canadian market for thumbusters, the company's product. As a result, immediately upon incorporation a sales office was set up in rented premises in Toronto from which orders for thumbusters could be solicited from Canadian customers. A head salesman was hired to manage the sales effort conducted through the Toronto office by himself and two subordinate salesmen. In addition, an office secretary reporting to the head salesman was hired. All of these personnel were Canadian citizens resident in Canada.

The Toronto office was identified by the company name on the door. The office telephone was listed in the company's name. The salesmen solicited orders in the Canadian market, but they had to be approved in Buffalo by the head office there. Once authorized by head office, the merchandise was shipped from the warehouses there. However, the Toronto office invoiced its Canadian customers and payments were made to the Toronto office and deposited to a bank account in the company's name in Toronto. Expenses of operating the Toronto office including the salaries of all Toronto personnel and the commissions of the salesmen were paid from the Toronto bank account by cheques signed by the head salesman in Toronto. Records of these receipts and disbursements were kept in a set of books at the Toronto office. At the end of each month, the Toronto office would remit to head office all but a nominal amount of the balance remaining in the bank account.

By the end of the last year, the Canadian market for thumbusters was such that the expense of maintaining an office in downtown Toronto was not warranted. Effective January 1 of the current year, the head salesman was instructed to carry out all of his duties from a room built to accommodate the work in the basement of his home. The two subordinate salesmen reported to him there. The home telephone with a listing in the head salesman's name was used for the business. All salesmen carried business cards printed with the company name and the number of this residence phone. It was felt that the services of the secretary were unnecessary at this location since the head salesman's wife could be paid to do the secretarial work on a part-time basis. A telephone answering service was hired to take messages when neither the head salesman nor his wife was home.

—REQUIRED

Prepare a memo for the tax person in your firm who will advise Thumbusters Corporation on the income tax consequences of these facts for the current year. Evaluate in detail the alternatives in the residence issue as they relate to this fact situation for the current year. Discuss each possible degree of residence and its tax consequences. State your conclusions on the case after considering the relevant international tax agreement and after appropriately weighing the significance of the facts in the case. You may wish to use the framework in Exhibit 2-1 for your analysis, as it applies to corporations.

—SOLUTION [See *American Wheelabrator & Equipment Corporation v. M.N.R.*, (T.A.B.) 51 DTC 285 and *Tara Explorations and Development Company Ltd. v. M.N.R.*, (Ex. Ct.) 70 DTC 6370]

Since the meaning of residence is not fully defined in the Act it is necessary to make a determination based on the specific facts of each case. A corporation can be found to be a full-time resident by common law principle. If this is the case, the corporation will be taxed in Canada on its worldwide income [ssec. 2(1)]. The common law principle that must be in evidence by the facts is that "central management and control" are in Canada. In this case, the directors, president and general manager managed from head office in the United States. Corporate business and strategy meetings were held in the United States. Corporate books and records, with the exception of the Toronto records, were kept in the United States. The Toronto records are probably not sufficient to establish central management and control since they are subsidiary documents. Also, the management function undertaken by the head salesman would probably not be major enough to indicate central management and control of the company.

A corporation can be deemed resident by meeting the conditions of subsection 250(4) and, as a result, it would be taxed in Canada on its worldwide income [ssec. 2(1)]. To be deemed resident, the corporation must be incorporated in Canada. In this case, since the company was not incorporated in Canada, the date of incorporation is irrelevant and the questions raised in subsection 250(4) of residence (by common law principle) or of carrying on business in Canada need not be addressed.

Under the third degree of residence, the corporation can be considered a non-resident carrying on business in Canada. It can then be taxed in Canada on profits from its business in Canada [par. 2(3)(b)]. Carrying on business in Canada must be established by the facts of the case. Soliciting orders in Canada is enough to establish carrying on business in Canada [sec. 253]. This raises the question as to whether the salesman was an employee of the corporation or an independent contractor. If he is an employee, then the corporation could be considered to be carrying on a business in Canada. The following facts indicate that he is an employee rather than an independent contractor operating his own business in Canada:

(a) he carried on business in the name of the company;

(b) he acted only for the company and no one else;

(c) he had no stock of merchandise of his own; and

(d) the books and records kept in Canada were not those of an independent business, but were only enough to maintain an office in Canada.

The Canada–U.S. Tax Convention must be consulted to determine if the corporation can be exempted from tax in Canada on its profits from carrying on business in Canada. In order to be exempt, the corporation must establish that it is not operating from a "permanent establishment" in Canada. During the current year, the corporation did not have a fixed place of business in Canada. Other facts that can be used to show no permanent establishment in Canada include:

(a) the salesman did not have authority to contract, because acceptance was given only in New York;

(b) there was no stock of merchandise in Canada (note that under Article V paragraph 6(b) of the Canada–U.S. Tax Convention, a fixed place of business used to maintain a stock of merchandise for the purpose of storage, display or delivery will not constitute a permanent establishment);

(c) the only office used was in the house which had no company identification; and

(d) the bank account and records were not sufficient to establish a permanent establishment in Canada.

In conclusion, the corporation would not likely be taxable in Canada. The tax treaty would exempt the company from tax as a non-resident on its profits since they were not earned from a permanent establishment in Canada. Also, the facts do not warrant finding either full-time residence or deemed residence.

III. REGISTRATION REQUIREMENTS AND LIABILITY FOR THE GOODS AND SERVICES TAX

A. Liability for GST

[ETA: 123(1); 142(1); 143; 165(1), (2); 166]

This part of the chapter deals with liability for GST and the requirements to register and charge GST under the *Excise Tax Act* (ETA). While the legal liability for payment of GST rests with the purchaser, the responsibility for collecting and remitting the tax generally lies with the supplier. These rules will also be examined in the context of the residency of the supplier, since the rules are somewhat different for resident and non-resident suppliers.

Subsection 165(1) of the ETA is the charging provision which requires every recipient of a taxable supply made in Canada to pay to Her Majesty in right of Canada a tax of 7% (0% for zero-rated supplies [ETA ssec. 165(2)]) of the value of the consideration of the supply. The *recipient* of a supply is generally the person who enters into the agreement to acquire the property or service and is liable under that agreement to pay consideration for the supply. (Special rules apply where there is no agreement or no consideration is payable [ssec. 123(1)]. A *taxable supply* is defined as a supply made in the course of a commercial activity. The term includes both supplies taxed at the general rate of 7% and those that are zero-rated. (A *zero-rated supply* is defined in ETA subsection 123(1) as a supply included in Schedule VI). Therefore, for a person to be subject to GST, the supply must be (i) made in Canada, and (ii) made by another person who is engaged in a commercial activity. The definition of a commercial activity does not include activities engaged in by a business that involve the making of an exempt supply (which in turn is defined as a supply included in Schedule V [ssec. 123(1)]. Rules have been introduced to determine when a supply is made in Canada and, hence, within the scope of GST.

Section 166 is a relieving provision which provides that if, at the time consideration is paid or becomes due for a supply, the supplier is a small supplier (who is not registered or required to be registered), no GST is payable. However, this relieving provision does not apply to the sale of real property. Small suppliers are discussed in greater detail below.

1. Supplies in Canada

Supplies are subject to GST only if they are made in Canada. (It should be noted that imported goods and services are also subject to GST in certain circumstances.) A sale of goods is deemed to be made in Canada if the goods are delivered or made available to the recipient in Canada [ETA ssec. 142(1)]. In the case of leased goods, the supply is deemed to be made in Canada if possession or use of the goods is given or made available to the recipient in Canada. In the case of a supply of real property or a service in relation to real property, the supply is deemed to be made in Canada if the real property is situated in Canada. In the case of a supply of any other service, if the service is to be performed in whole or in part in Canada, the supply of the service is deemed to be made in Canada.

For supplies of intangible personal property, the determination of whether a supply is made in Canada can be more difficult. Intangible personal property is not defined in the ETA. However, the term "property" is defined to include "any property, whether real or personal, movable or immovable, tangible or intangible . . ." [ETA ssec. 123(1)]. The main categories of property under the ETA are real property, tangible personal property (generally referred to as goods) and intangible personal property (movable and immovable property are terms used under civil law in the province of Quebec). Intangible personal property includes a property that has no intrinsic or marketable value, but is merely evidence of value, and which is enforceable by law, such as contractual rights, stock certificates, intellectual property, etc. Intellectual property includes patents, trademarks, industrial designs, etc. The supply of intangible personal property is deemed to be made in Canada if the property may be used in whole or in part in Canada and the recipient is either a registrant for GST purposes or a resident of Canada [ETA spar. 142(1)(c)(i)]. If the intangible personal property is in respect of real property situated in Canada, or of goods ordinarily situated in Canada, or of a service to be performed in Canada, the supply is also deemed to be made in Canada [ETA spar. 142(1)(c)(ii)].

2. Supplies by non-residents

As a general rule, a supply of goods or services made in Canada by a non-resident is deemed [ETA ssec. 143(1)] to be made in Canada if:

- the supply is made in the course of a business carried on in Canada;
- the non-resident is registered for GST purposes at the time the supply is made; or
- the supply is in respect of a place of amusement, a seminar, an activity or an event, and the non-resident supplies admissions directly to consumers.

Unless any of the above situations apply, supplies by a non-resident are outside the scope of GST.

Now that the rules for determining whether a particular supply is deemed to be made in Canada have been reviewed, the issue of whether GST must be charged by the supplier will be examined. As a general rule, a supply made in Canada will only be subject to GST if it is made by a registrant.

B. Registration Requirements for Residents

[ETA: 123(1); 148; 240(1)]

1. Test for registration

A person who is engaged in a commercial activity in Canada (discussed below) is required to register for GST purposes [ETA ssec. 240(1)]. Persons registered or required to be registered under the legislation are referred to as *registrants* [ETA ssec. 123(1)]. The rights and obligations of registrants under the ETA are discussed in Chapter 14. It should be noted that as agents of the Crown, registrants are required to collect GST as required under the ETA.

The definition of person for the purposes of GST is broadly based to include an individual, partnership, corporation, trust or estate, or a body that is a society, union, club, association, commission, or other organization of any kind [ETA ssec. 123(1)]. Therefore, virtually any kind of organized unit or individual can be considered to be a person and, therefore, can be required to register.

Unlike the *Income Tax Act*, the ETA treats partnerships as persons for purposes of the GST. Therefore, the partnership is considered to be a person for registration purposes and is liable for GST collected on taxable supplies, rather than the individual partners. Similarly, the partnership is eligible for an input tax credit for its purchases attributable to commercial activities.

2. Definition of commercial activity

Central to the determination of whether a person is required to register is the issue of whether the person is engaged in commercial activities. This topic will be discussed in greater detail in Chapter 4. However, for the purposes of the discussion of the registration requirements, it should be noted that a commercial activity is defined [ETA ssec. 123(1)] as:

- a business that is carried on;
- an adventure or concern in the nature of trade; and
- the supply of real property.

Business is defined broadly to include a profession, calling, trade, manufacture, or undertaking of any kind whatever, regardless of whether the activity engaged in is for profit. This test is broader than the business test under the *Income Tax Act* in that there need not be a profit motive present for an activity to be considered a business for GST purposes. The point to remember is that the GST is a tax on consumption or value added, and not on income. Thus, many activities engaged in by non-profit organizations, charities and governments may constitute a business for GST purposes. These entities engage in activities that add value to the economy in competition with profit-motivated businesses. For example, a non-profit organization will be considered to be engaged in a commercial activity for GST purposes if it supplies taxable goods or services for consideration. Therefore, any entity that engages in an activity of a commercial nature, regardless of whether the activity is engaged in primarily for profit, will be considered to be engaged in a commercial activity. Consequently, the entity will be required to register for GST purposes.

An adventure or concern in the nature of trade, which is not defined but has the common law meaning discussed previously, also constitutes a commercial activity. This concept is discussed in Chapter 4. The supply of real property also constitutes a commercial activity unless the supply is exempt. Thus, most sales and leases of non-residential property constitute a commercial activity. Reference should be made to Chapter 7 for a discussion on supplies of real property.

3. Exclusions from commercial activity

The definition of commercial activity contains certain exclusions of which readers should be aware. First, activities that involve the making of exempt supplies do not constitute commercial activities. For example, the supply of medical services by a physician is exempt and, therefore, not a commercial activity. Consequently, physicians providing exempt medical services, only, are not able to register for GST purposes and cannot claim input tax credits in respect of GST paid on inputs. However, the GST component of these expenses can be deducted for income tax purposes.

Second, commercial activity does not include any activity engaged in by an individual (or a partnership comprised of individuals) without a reasonable expectation of profit. Thus, hobbies and recreational pastimes of individuals would not be considered to be commercial activities and, hence, registration would not be required nor permitted. The phrase "reasonable expectation of profit" is discussed in Chapter 4.

4. Exceptions from the registration requirements

The registration requirements contain an exception for *small suppliers* [ETA ssec. 240(1)]. The rules for determining whether a person qualifies as a small supplier are set out in section 148 of the ETA. Basically, this includes persons whose revenues from taxable supplies do not exceed $30,000 in the four preceding calendar quarters. This calculation is based on the supplier's total worldwide sales including any supply made outside Canada by its "associates". Small suppliers, who are not registered, are not required to collect GST on taxable supplies. Persons who qualify as small suppliers and who are engaged in a commercial activity, however, may register on a voluntary basis. Registration would permit these persons to claim input tax credits and may be advantageous if taxable supplies are made to registrants. Since registrants are able to claim input tax credits on their purchases, they will likely prefer to deal with other registrants. Purchases from non-registrants may contain indirect GST because non-registrants are unable to recover GST paid on purchases through the input tax credit mechanism.

In addition to the small supplier exception, a person whose only commercial activity is making supplies of real property by way of sale other than in the course of a business is not required to register. As noted above, supplies of real property are discussed in Chapter 7.

C. Registration and Collection Requirements for Non-residents

[ETA: 123(1); 132; 240]

The place of supply rules discussed earlier in this section must be read in conjunction with the registration requirements to determine when non-residents are required to register and collect GST.

1. Meaning of non-resident

For purposes of the GST, non-residents are defined as "not resident in Canada". In the absence of a definition of "resident", reference should be made to the dictionary meaning of the term and to the interpretation of the term under the *Income Tax Act*, as discussed earlier in this chapter. The ETA does, however, contain deeming provisions in section 132 which provide that a corporation is deemed to be resident in Canada if it is incorporated in Canada, similar to the rules under the *Income Tax Act*. In addition, a corporation originally incorporated in a foreign jurisdiction that is continued (a special form of incorporation) in Canada and not elsewhere is deemed to be resident in Canada.

In the case of a partnership or unincorporated society, club, association, or organization, or a branch thereof, the entity is deemed to be resident in Canada if a majority of its members, having management and control, are resident in Canada at that time. A labour union is deemed to be resident in Canada if it carries on its activities in Canada and has a local union or branch in Canada at that time.

Where a non-resident person has a permanent establishment in Canada, the person is deemed to be resident in Canada in respect of the activities carried on through that particular establishment. For GST purposes, a *permanent establishment* is defined as a fixed place of business, including a place of management, branch, office, factory, workshop, mine, oil or gas well, quarry, timberland, or other place of extraction of mineral resources through which supplies are made. It also includes a fixed place of business of another person (other than a broker, general commission agent, or other independent agent) making supplies on behalf of the person in the ordinary course of business. Because the definition of permanent establishment under the ETA is different from that generally found in Canada's income tax treaties, there may be situations where the existence of a permanent establishment is different for income tax and GST purposes.

2. Mandatory registration

Returning to subsection 240(1), which sets out the registration requirements, non-resident persons, who do not *carry on any business in Canada*, are not required to register. Thus, while the test for residents is based on engaging in a commercial activity, the test for non-residents is based on the narrower concept of carrying on business. In basic terms, the difference for a non-resident is that registration is not required if the activities undertaken in Canada are not of a regular and continuous nature. Again, reference should be made to Chapter 4 for a discussion of the distinction between commercial activity and business.

A non-resident who directly supplies admissions to a place of amusement, a seminar, an activity or an event, must register before making any such supplies in Canada [ETA ssec. 240(2)].

The small supplier exemption, for suppliers with less than $30,000 in sales per year, is also available to non-residents, other than those who supply admissions as described above.

For individuals, an individual is deemed to be resident in Canada, if he or she is deemed, under any of the paragraphs 250(1)(*a*) to (*f*) of the *Income Tax Act*, to be a resident of Canada at that time. Thus, a deemed resident (other than a sojourner) for income tax purposes is also a resident for GST purposes.

3. Voluntary registration

Voluntary registration is available to non-residents, provided certain requirements are met [ETA ssec. 240(3)]. The non-resident person must, in the ordinary course of carrying on business outside Canada,

(a) regularly solicit orders for the supply of goods for delivery in Canada; or

(b) have entered into an agreement for the supply of:

- services to be performed in Canada, or

- intangibles to be used in Canada or that relate to real property in Canada, goods ordinarily situated in Canada or services performed in Canada.

D. Imports

[ETA: 212; 213; 215(1); 217; 218]

As the GST is a tax on consumption in Canada, it also applies to imports. Section 212 of the ETA imposes GST on the value of imported goods. The GST is payable by the person who is liable under the *Customs Act* to pay duty on the imported goods. The value of the goods is based on the value for customs purposes plus duties and excise taxes (excluding GST) [ETA ssec. 215(1)]. No tax is payable on zero-rated goods, such as basic groceries and medical devices [ETA sec. 213].

GST is imposed on the recipient of imported taxable supplies [ETA sec. 218]. Imported taxable supplies are defined [ETA sec. 217] to include intangible personal property (e.g., intellectual property) and services that are supplied outside Canada to a Canadian resident for use in Canada. However, GST is not imposed where the imported taxable supply is for use in Canada exclusively (90% or more) in a commercial activity.

REVIEW QUESTIONS

(1) Canadian citizens pay tax in Canada on their world income. Comment.

(2) If a non-resident vacations in Canada for 180 days during the year, then he or she will be considered a Canadian resident for the full year. Comment.

(3) If an individual sells his or her house and then leaves the country, the person will be considered to be a non-resident. Comment.

(4) Assume that an individual resided in Buffalo and carried on a proprietorship business in St. Catharines. How would he or she pay tax on the business income earned in Canada?

(5) An individual who moves to Canada on March 31 of the year, will be considered resident in Canada throughout the year since he or she was resident here for more than 183 days. Comment.

(6) Since a corporation is an artificial legal entity, it does not "reside" anywhere in the sense that an individual does. Comment on how the residency of a corporation is determined.

(7) A company was incorporated in Canada on November 30, 1965, but has been carrying on business in Bermuda since that date and all of the officers and directors have always been resident there. Comment on the company's tax liability in Canada.

(8) A company was incorporated in Canada on November 30, 1964, but has been carrying on business in Bermuda since that date and all of the officers and directors have always been resident there. In the years from incorporation to 1971 the company actively solicited orders in Canada by telephone. It stopped this activity in Canada at the end of 1971. Comment on the company's tax liability to Canada.

(9) A Canadian executive is transferred to the U.S. with his company on a five-year contract. He and his family sell all their Canadian assets and move to the U.S. in December of the year. Due to the lower personal income tax rates in the U.S., he has the Canadian company defer the

payment of the bonus of $100,000 that he earned in Canada in the year until the next year when he is resident in the U.S. Comment on whether the executive will be taxed in Canada on this bonus.

(10) If a non-resident individual were to buy and quickly resell some land in Canada and earn income of $100,000, would the non-resident be considered to be carrying on business in Canada for purposes of subsection 2(3)?

(11) If a U.S. corporation has an employee located in Canada who is selling goods on behalf of the employer, then would the U.S. company be taxable in Canada?

(12) If a U.S. corporation has an agent located in Canada who is selling goods on behalf of the U.S. company, then would the U.S. company be taxable in Canada?

(13) If a person is resident in Canada, can that same person also be resident in the U.S.?

(14) If a Canadian corporation is carrying on business in the U.S. through a permanent establishment in the U.S., will the Canadian company be considered resident in the U.S. and be subject to tax in the U.S. on the total corporate income?

(15) Mr. Smooth is an independent consultant who provides his services wherever he can get the work. He has been asked by a U.S. company to go to the U.S. to consult with them. He thinks that he will have to spend 25 days travelling to their many locations in the U.S. over the next year and that he will earn $50,000 for his efforts. His lawyer has told him that he will be taxed in the U.S. on this business income. What do you think?

MULTIPLE CHOICE QUESTIONS

Question 1

X Ltd. is a corporation which has always been managed by the *same* Board of Directors. The Board of Directors has always met where the directors reside. Based on these facts, X Ltd. will NOT be resident in Canada for income tax purposes if X Ltd. was:

(A) incorporated in Canada in 1968 and its directors are all U.S. residents;

(B) incorporated in the U.S. in 1970 and its directors are all U.S. residents;

(C) incorporated in the U.S. in 1968 and its directors are all Canadian residents;

(D) incorporated in Canada in 1964 and its directors are all Canadian residents.

Question 2

Joe is legally separated from his wife and has two adult children who live with his wife and are not dependent on him for support. Joe is leaving Canada to take a job in Germany on June 30 of this year. He plans to stay in Germany indefinitely and has purchased a home there. Which one of the following things is the most important for Joe to do to help ensure that he is not a resident of Canada for Canadian income tax purposes after he leaves?

(A) Take his wife and children with him to Germany.

(B) Give up his Canadian citizenship.

(C) Sell his Canadian home or rent it under a long-term lease.

(D) Put all his household furniture and personal effects into storage in Canada.

Question 3

Mr. N is *not* a resident of Canada. In the year, he had worldwide income of $200,000, including $50,000 of employment income earned in Canada (from director's fees) and $10,000 of interest on Government of Canada bonds.

What amount of taxable income must Mr. N report on his Canadian personal income tax return for the year?

(A) $10,000

(B) $50,000

(C) $60,000

(D) $200,000

Question 4

Jerry Dykopf ceased to be a resident of Canada on April 30 of the year and moved to Israel on that date. During the first four months of the year, he earned $25,000 of employment income in Canada and $1,000 of interest income from his bank accounts in Canada. While living in Israel during the remainder of the year, he earned $30,000 (Cdn. $) of employment income in Israel and received $2,000 of interest income from his Canadian bank accounts.

What amount of taxable income must Mr. Dykopf report on his Canadian personal income tax return for the year?

(A) $58,000

(B) $56,000

(C) $26,000

(D) Nil

Question 5

In which of the following situations is the person considered a non-resident of Canada for Canadian income tax purposes in the year in question?

(A) James Hill, a 25-year-old engineer living in Ottawa, accepted a six-month transfer to an office in London, England for the period July 1 to December 31, of the year in question. He returned to Canada in the following year. James is not married and has always lived at his parents' house in Ottawa.

(B) Judy Gordon, a financial analyst, lives in a house she owns in London, England. She had lived in Toronto all her life, until she started a minimum three-year contract with CS Services Inc., which started in July of the year in question. Judy is single and terminated the lease on her apartment in Toronto before moving her belongings to England when her position started in July.

(C) ERT Limited was incorporated in Canada in 1987 and, until recently, its manufacturing plant was located in Ontario. In June of the year in question, it moved all of its operations, including the manufacturing plant, to Mexico.

(D) Doug Stewart, a member of the Canadian Armed Forces, has been stationed in Germany for the last 5 years, including the year in question. Doug was born in Canada and lived in Canada prior to moving to Germany.

Question 6

CART Ltd. is registered for GST purposes. The following is a summary of the transactions for CART Ltd. for the month of December:

Account	Amount (Net of GST & PST)
Sales (Taxable at 7%)	$250,000
Exports	100,000
Purchase of supplies from a registrant	(30,000)
Salaries	(70,000)
Interest Expense.................................	(20,000)
	$230,000

The GST that has to be remitted in respect of the above transaction is:

(A) $10,500

(B) $14,000

(C) $15,400

(D) $21,000

EXERCISES

Exercise 1

[ITA: 2; 114; 115; 250(1)]

Determine the form of residence, if any, for each of the following individuals.

(A) Alpha had lived all of his life in Vancouver until this year when he left with his family on August 27 to live in Los Angeles.

(B) Beta is a Canadian citizen who has lived in the United States with his family for the past nine years.

(C) Gamma lives in Niagara Falls, New York, but works Monday to Friday from 9:00 a.m. to 5:00 p.m. in an office in Niagara Falls, Ontario.

(D) Delta had lived all of his life in Dallas, Texas. He moved with his family to Calgary, Alberta, early this year to take a job with Dome Petroleum. He moved back to Dallas in the summer of this year. While in Canada he invested in the shares of a private corporation operating in Calgary. These shares were later sold during the year after he left Calgary.

(E) Epsilon was born in Philadelphia. He is now ten years old and has never been to Canada but his mother has been consul in the Canadian Consulate there for the past 12 years.

(F) Mu is a German citizen who is married to a member of the Canadian forces stationed in Germany. She has been to Canada only for brief visits when her husband was on leave.

Exercise 2

[ITA: 2; 114; 250; IT-221R3]

This appeal concerns the appellant's place of residence in the taxation year 1964.

At the hearing on August 8, 1967 at Saint John, N.B., both counsel agreed on the following statement of facts:

(A) The appellant was about 58 years old in 1963.

(B) The appellant is and was at all material times an American citizen.

(C) The appellant is a sea captain and sails tankers around the world. His employer is the Cities Services Corporation of New York and the ships bear United States registry. He is paid in United States currency from New York and since 1956 he has been Master of the "S.S. Cities Services, Norfolk.".

(D) Prior to 1962, the appellant and his wife had always lived in the United States. Until June 1962, they owned a house in Massachusetts.

(E) In September 1962, the appellant's wife and two of their children moved to Fredericton. At that time the two children were enrolled at Rothesay Collegiate School. In September 1963, a house was purchased at 146 Cambridge Crescent in Fredericton and was registered in joint tenancy in the names of the appellant and his wife.

(F) Prior to the purchase of the house in September 1963 the appellant's wife rented premises in Fredericton.

(G) The appellant filed a T1 Income Tax Return for his 1963 taxation year on which he stated, "the above taxpayer and his family are American citizens and are merely residents of Canada. He is a U.S. ship captain and is employed full-time by a U.S. company".

(H) The appellant paid $134.24 Canadian income tax for the 1963 taxation year after using his foreign tax credit.

(I) The routine into which the appellant and his wife have settled over the past years is as follows: The appellant receives his orders to sail from New York. He may be gone months at a time. He may dock at U.S. ports such as Galveston, Texas, or San Francisco.

(J) After the appellant's wife moved to Fredericton in 1963, the appellant retained two rooms in his sister's house at 48 Elm Street, Stoneham, Mass., U.S.A. The appellant gave his sister's number as his telephone number in the United States.

(K) At all material times, the appellant:

- worked for a U.S. company;
- was paid in U.S. currency;
- was a member of the First Baptist Church at Wakefield, Mass.;
- had two children living in the United States;
- had a bank account or accounts in the United States;
- had investments, including stocks and bonds, in the United States;
- had a pension plan with a U.S. company;
- intended and still intends to retire in Florida;
- banked his pay at the First National Bank in Malden, Mass. and enough to maintain his wife and children was sent to her. The rest stayed in the United States where he still retains a chequing account in Malden.

(L) The appellant, during 1964:

- had a joint bank account in Fredericton with his wife;
- had a family phone number in his wife's name;
- neither applied for nor received family allowance for his children;
- neither was employed nor carried on business in Canada;
- never belonged to a church or club in Fredericton;
- was never a member of a Canadian union;
- had no Canadian investments;
- owned a car jointly with his wife with a New Brunswick registry.

(M) The appellant's sole connections with Canada during 1964 were:

- his wife lived in Fredericton with one son;
- he visited Fredericton for a total of 166 days at the following times in the year:

January 3 to February 22	51 days
June 1 to August 7	68 days
November 14 to December 31	47 days
	166 days

(N) In June 1966 the house in Fredericton was sold and the appellant's wife moved back to the United States.

According to the appellant's wife's testimony, she moved in 1962 with their furniture from Massachusetts to the city of Fredericton, N.B., where she rented a house in her name to live nearer their two youngest sons, who were attending the Rothesay private boarding college in Saint John, N.B. Their two oldest children were married and another was attending the Springfield (Mass.) College. Upon moving, they sold their nine-room house in the United States.

On the advice of an American lawyer, the appellant and his wife tried to purchase a house in Canada within the year in order to avoid the American capital gains tax; unfortunately, they jointly bought one two months too late and had to pay the tax. As already mentioned, during the year 1964, her husband lived 166 days in Fredericton and spent the rest of the time at sea. While away, his pay cheques were sent directly from the New York office to the First National Bank in Malden, Mass., and his wife received monthly cheques of $600 for living expenditures in Canada. During his vacation, his pay cheques were deposited in a joint bank account in Fredericton. His trips usually lasted three to four months, and six months when bound for foreign ports. When he was unable to come home, his wife would visit him in New York or at his sister's home in Massachusetts. The appellant contended that, in 1964, he resided with his sister and could be reached there at any time, but did not enjoy the exclusive right to the use of rooms and furniture; during that period, his wife stayed there with him for three or four weeks.

— REQUIRED

Prepare an analysis of the residence issue. Evaluate in detail the alternatives in the residence issue as they relate to this fact situation for the year 1964. Discuss each possible degree of residence and its tax consequences. Weigh the relevance of the facts you consider and come to a conclusion on the case.

Exercise 3

[ITA: 2; 250(4)]

Determine the form of residence, if any, for each of the following corporations.

(A) Inch Incorporated was incorporated in 1982 in North Dakota. However, its directors are all residents of Saskatchewan where all meetings of the board of directors have been held since incorporation.

(B) Foot Limited was incorporated in Manitoba in 1972. However, it is managed in Japan where all directors' and shareholders' meetings have been held since incorporation.

(C) Yard Incorporated was incorporated in Ohio in 1967, but until five years ago all of the directors' meetings were held in Ontario and the president of the company was a resident of Ontario. However, five years ago the president moved to Ohio and from then on all directors' meetings have been held there.

(D) Mile Limited was incorporated in Nova Scotia in 1964 where all directors' meetings were held until 1971 when the directors moved to Boston where they met regularly.

ASSIGNMENT PROBLEMS

Problem 1

[ITA: 2; 114; 250; IT-221R3]

The client was born and raised in Canada. After obtaining his MBA in 1968, he began working as a consultant. In July 1976, the corporation of which he was a major shareholder entered into a contract with a Canadian Crown corporation to furnish consulting advice in Nigeria. Services were to commence July 15, 1976 and end January 14, 1978. A daily rate of fees was set, but total billings were not to exceed a specified maximum. The contract also provided for moving, travel and living expenses for the client and his dependants up to a specified maximum.

All fees and expenses were paid to the client's corporation in Toronto. He continued to be a shareholder, director and officer of the corporation and he remained very interested in its activities. The corporation paid the client and was instructed to deposit these payments in the client's Canadian bank account which he continued to maintain for this purpose and for the operation of the rental property that he owned. He felt that the Canadian bank account was necessary because of foreign exchange difficulties that he might otherwise encounter. He instructed the corporation not to withhold any income taxes on these payments because he intended to give up his Canadian residence status to establish an international consulting business abroad upon termination of the Nigerian contract.

Since the client had little time before leaving for Nigeria, he quickly rented the unit that he had been occupying in a duplex that he owned, on a month-to-month basis. He intended to sell the property when the market would provide him with a reasonable profit. He arranged to have his corporation manage the renting of this property for a fee which he paid to the corporation.

He stored his major furnishings and winter clothing in Canada. His smaller household and personal effects were shipped to Nigeria. He sold his car, cancelled his auto insurance and a gasoline company credit card and obtained an international driver's licence. He retained credit cards such as American Express, Visa and MasterCard, as well as his RRSP accounts. Under the contract he was also required to maintain his provincial health insurance coverage.

When he left Canada for Nigeria, he was accompanied by his friend, Martha, who had been a part of his life for over a year before their departure. She had obtained leave from her university program of studies for the fall 1976 term. The couple took up residence in a hotel suite that was converted into an apartment at the Holiday Inn in Lagos, Nigeria. No conventional living quarters were available, because of the housing market. During his stay in Nigeria, the client obtained a Nigerian driver's licence and maintained two bank accounts and two cars. He joined sports, dining and social clubs in Lagos. He was provided with an office by the Nigerian government and he carried business cards which identified him as a consultant with that government. He promoted the consulting business of his Toronto corporation actively in Nigeria in the hope of establishing the business abroad, but he did not generate sufficient business to stay in Nigeria beyond the period of the existing contract. He did not seek to extend his visa or pay any form of tax on his income in Nigeria.

Martha returned to Canada for the winter 1977 term, and then returned to Nigeria for the summer of 1977, but returned again to Canada in September 1977 to begin a new program.

By December 1977 the client had billed the limit under the contract. He vacated his apartment, sold his cars, packed up his possessions, including some artwork, textiles and other souvenirs that he had acquired, and returned to Canada.

— REQUIRED

Prepare a memo for the tax person in your firm who will advise the client on the income tax consequences of these facts. Evaluate in detail the alternatives in the residence issue as they relate to this fact situation. Discuss each possible degree of residence and its tax consequences. State your conclusions on the case after weighing the significance of the facts considered.

Problem 2

[ITA: 2; 114; 250; IT-221R3]

The client is an electronic engineer. He was born in Erith, England, on the 7th day of July 1946. During the relevant times the client held a valid passport for the United Kingdom of Great Britain and Northern Ireland. The passport declares him a British subject with a residence in the United Kingdom with the right of abode therein. The passport was issued on September 26, 1978 for a 10-year period.

Prior to the client's second marriage in 1981, his parents maintained a bedroom for him in Kent, England.

In 1981, the client married Cathy, a Canadian citizen residing in Canada who had no income of her own and was wholly dependent on the client. She has always resided continuously in Canada.

In June of 1981, a house near Apsley, Ontario, was purchased by Cathy with money supplied by the client. In September of 1982, Cathy borrowed money by way of a mortgage. The client guaranteed the mortgage which has an affidavit attached dated September 13, 1982 where he swore that he was not then a non-resident of Canada. For a purchase of property in Ontario, he would otherwise have had to pay a 20% non-resident land transfer tax.

During the three-year period at issue in this case, 1981 to 1983, the client regularly returned to Canada when he was not working. Each time the client entered Canada, his passport was stamped by Immigration Canada with the majority of the entries setting out a date upon which he must leave Canada. The authorized period of stay varied from five days to 45 days. On some of the stamps the word "visitor" was written in by an immigration official. Throughout the three-year period, the client was employed full-time by a non-resident corporation and all work was performed outside Canada on an oil rig at sea. All income was deposited directly into a Canadian bank.

The client indicated that he was charged in Provincial Court for failure to file an income tax return for 1981 and was acquitted (likely on the basis that he was not required to file in Canada for that year).

During the three-year period, the client indicated or claimed that he:

(a) never filed a tax return or paid income tax anywhere;

(b) was not allowed to work in Canada;

(c) was given a fixed date to leave Canada on entry (i.e., not allowed to stay in Canada);

(d) could not join OHIP, pay EI, maintain an RRSP or join a pension plan;

(e) was out of the country more than 183 days per year;

(f) had no desire to work in Canada;

(g) had a residence in Britain in the home of his mother and father;

(h) held a mortgage in Britain on his first wife's house;

(i) could not live a normal life in Canada as he had to leave every 27 days; and

(j) had a bank account with the Royal Bank of Canada both in Canada and the Caribbean.

In 1984, the client purchased a car in Canada. In 1985, the client:

(a) obtained a Canadian driver's licence;

(b) obtained a Canadian visa; and

(c) became a landed immigrant in Canada.

— REQUIRED

Prepare a memo for the tax person in your firm who will advise the client on the income tax consequences of these facts. Evaluate in detail the alternatives in the residence issue as they relate to this fact situation for the period in question. Discuss each degree of residence and its tax consequences as it applies to this fact situation. Note that in this case full-time residence under the common law principle could only result from a "fresh start" at a point in time in the period in question. Therefore, part-time residence would depend on there being a period of non-residence prior to a "fresh start", if any.

State your conclusion on this case after appropriately weighing the significance of the facts considered. Your conclusion should indicate whether the client became a full-time resident at any point in the period or remained a non-resident throughout the period. If you conclude that he became a full-time resident, indicate the point in time when the "fresh start" was made.

Problem 3

[ITA: 2, 114, 250; IT-221R3]

The client is a mechanical engineer, born and educated in England. The client was married in England in 1962 and he and his wife, Dawning, had three sons born in 1964, 1966 and 1969. In 1967, the client and his wife and family moved to Canada where he immediately commenced employment with Imperial Oil in Sarnia, Ontario. With Imperial Oil and/or its parent corporation, Exxon Corporation, the client and his family moved to various locations throughout Canada until 1988. In 1988, while residing and working in Edmonton, Alberta, the client was offered the position as deputy manager of the Exxon refinery at Port Dickson in Malaysia. He accepted the position because it presented the opportunity to likely become manager of this same refinery within a three-year period.

At the time of his acceptance of the above position, the client and his wife were experiencing marriage difficulties. As a result of these difficulties, it was mutually agreed that the client would go to Malaysia on his own. His wife and youngest son remained in the family home in Edmonton. His older sons were living on their own by this time.

The client and his employer undertook the following steps in preparation for his move from Canada:

- his employer obtained a work permit for him in Malaysia;
- he sold his car;
- he cancelled his provincial health plan;
- his employer obtained private health insurance for him;
- he closed all of his existing bank accounts at Royal Bank;
- he opened a savings account at the Bank of Nova Scotia because this bank had a branch in Kuala Lumpur, the capital of Malaysia;
- he allowed his membership in the Edmonton Petroleum Club to lapse; and
- he allowed his participation in the Model Guided Plane Association to lapse.

The client moved to Malaysia in the last few days of September 1988. He stayed in a hotel in Malaysia for the first few weeks and then moved into a company-provided home. His employer charged him with a monthly rent of $1,000 for his use of this house. He took the following items with him from Canada to Malaysia:

- all of his clothes and personal effects; and
- an airplane kit for model guided planes and a radio control transmitter for his hobby of model guided planes.

Once in Malaysia, the client undertook to establish Port Dickson as his home. To this end, he:

- purchased a car;
- obtained a Malaysian driver's licence;
- joined the Port Dickson yacht club which was, in fact, a social/recreational club;
- joined the petroleum club at Kuala Lumpur;
- opened a chequing account at the Bank of Nova Scotia in Kuala Lumpur;
- opened a chequing account at the Standard Chartered Bank at Port Dickson;
- acquired two Malaysian credit cards;
- became a patient at a Port Dickson medical clinic and, as well, made regular visits to a dentist in Port Dickson; and
- joined the Port Dickson Golf Club in 1991.

In accordance with Exxon corporate policy, the client remained on the payroll and in the pension plan of the Canadian subsidiary. His monthly pay was deposited into his Edmonton bank account. There was no income tax withheld at source on the client's salary because the Canadian subsidiary knew that he was working full-time outside of Canada. The total cost of his salary and related benefits (including pension) were charged by the Canadian subsidiary to Exxon Corporation International.

The client made only two visits to Canada during the period from 1989 through 1994. He visited for 14 days in 1990 and 14 days again in 1992. On each of these visits, he stayed in the family home in Edmonton. During the same period, the client's spouse made eight visits to him in Malaysia. She made no visits after January 1992, but prior to that time, the length of her visits ranged from 19 days to 32 days. On each of these visits, she stayed with the client in his Malaysian home. The client and his wife remained married throughout the relevant period.

The client maintained the following Canadian investments while he was residing in Malaysia:

- his 50% interest in the family home in Edmonton;
- a 50% investment in a rental property which his wife purchased after his move to Malaysia, because she thought it would be a good investment;
- his RRSP;
- his company savings plan; and
- a few personal shares in Canadian public companies.

He did maintain his memberships in the Canadian Society of Mechanical Engineers and the Association of Professional Engineers and Geologists of Alberta.

The client became manager of the Port Dickson plant in 1991 and eventually retired from Exxon in the summer of 1995 under the terms of an early retirement package. Upon retirement from Exxon, the client returned to Edmonton to the family home. In late 1995 the client started seeking employment in Malaysia and in January 1996 he and his wife went to Malaysia hoping that he would find employment and they would both live there. His wife returned to Canada in February 1996 and he moved on to Thailand where he stayed through July 1997 (working for the 12-month period from August 1996 through July 1997). When the Thailand employment ended, the client returned to Canada. He and his wife then worked out a plan of separation.

—REQUIRED

Prepare a memo for the tax person in your firm who will advise the client on the income tax consequences of these facts. Evaluate in detail the alternatives in the residence issue as they relate to this fact situation for the period October 1, 1988 through the summer of 1995. Discuss each possible degree of residence and its tax consequences. State your conclusions on this case after weighing the relevance of the facts you have considered.

Problem 4

[ITA: 2; 250; 253]

Far Eastern Airlines is a company incorporated in Korea in 1974. Its general manager and other active officers of the company are resident in Korea and have their offices there. The directors and corporate officers of the company live in Korea as well.

During the year in question, its sole business was operating an international airline which had no landing rights in Canada. However, in that year it had raised capital on the Canadian market for its international operations by selling an issue of its stock through an investment dealer in Vancouver. The vice-president–finance of the company, who believed the stock issue would sell better in Canada, travelled from the head office in Korea to Vancouver to instruct the investment dealer.

The stock issue was highly successful and the proceeds of the issue were accumulated in a bank account in Vancouver. During the several months in the year in question when these funds were being accumulated, the company became aware of an opportunity to purchase a vast quantity of aviation fuel at a very low price. A purchasing agent was dispatched from the head office in Korea to Canada to complete the purchase using some of the funds accumulated from the stock issue. The fuel was stored in Canada temporarily in rented facilities pending shipment to San Francisco, where it could be used by aircraft landing there. Subsequently, the company was unable to make suitable arrangements for shipment. The fuel was sold to a Canadian buyer at a considerable profit. All contracts involved in the purchase and sale transactions were drawn up by a Canadian lawyer under the direction of the purchasing agent who operated from a hotel room in Vancouver during the period of the transactions.

— REQUIRED

Prepare a memo for the tax person in your firm who will advise Far Eastern Airlines on the income tax consequences of these facts. Evaluate in detail the alternatives in the residence issue as they relate to this fact situation. Discuss each possible degree of residence and its tax consequences. State your conclusions on the case after considering the relevant international tax agreement and after appropriately weighing the significance of the facts considered.

Problem 5

[ITA: 2; 250; 253]

Wong Computer Games Inc. (WCG) was incorporated in the state of Illinois in the last decade. The founding shareholder, Mr. Andrew Wong, is an inventor of computer simulation models. His products include a wide variety of computer games as well as some programs which have industrial applications.

Mr. Wong is the controlling shareholder of WCG. His brother owns a minority interest, as does Walter Bends, a long-time associate of Mr. Wong, who often collaborates in the development of new products. All three shareholders are resident in Chicago. In addition to Mr. Wong, the WCG Board of Directors includes George Wolf, who represents the Chicago law firm, which advises WCG, and Tony Aster who represents First National Bank of Chicago, which provides most of the financing for WCG's operations. The Board meets approximately every six months to review financial results, discuss product development and decide on strategic initiatives. The meetings are usually held in the boardroom of George Wolf's law firm.

Two years ago, Mr. Wong achieved an industry breakthrough when he developed his latest game, SuperPilot. SuperPilot is a computer game in which the operator attempts to safely land a disabled airliner. SuperPilot provided special effects which were far beyond those available in any other commercially available product. Although other WCG products were only available in the U.S. market, Wong was convinced that SuperPilot would be a global success. To ensure the competitive advantage would be maintained, Wong Computer Games Inc. took the required legal steps to ensure copyright and patent protection of the program in a variety of countries, including Canada.

By last year, SuperPilot was doing very well in the U.S. market and WCG began to launch the product in other markets. Walter Bends was assigned responsibility for the Canadian market and took a short-term lease on a Toronto apartment in March of last year. WCG established a bank account with a Toronto branch of a Canadian bank. This account was to be used by Bends for promotional expenses and other incidentals. All other expenses, including Bends' salary, continued to be paid from Chicago.

Bends attended a number of Canadian trade shows, exhibiting the SuperPilot program. Prospective purchasers were provided with SuperPilot game cartridges as a promotional item. Bends was given the authority to sign supply contracts which would permit the purchaser a one-month supply of cartridges. At the end of the one month, if the distributor was still interested, a longer-term supply contract would be required. Bends was not permitted, however, to sign any of these long-term agreements without receiving prior approval from the WCG Board. All game cartridges, including promotional cartridges, were supplied from Chicago. If the product began to sell well in Canada, the WCG Board had discussed establishing a Canadian warehouse.

By January of this year, it became obvious that SuperPilot was not going to be a Canadian success. No distributors had requested a long-term supply contract and only one, Pete's Gaming Emporium, had agreed to stock the product for one month. At the end of the month, sales had been so slow that Pete's was not interested in continuing the relationship. Bends returned to Chicago, the bank account was closed, and WCG refocussed its marketing efforts on the U.S. market.

— REQUIRED

Prepare a memo for the tax person in your firm who will advise WCG on the income tax consequences of these facts. Evaluate in detail the alternatives in the residence issue as they relate to this fact situation during last year and this year. Discuss each possible degree of residence and its tax consequences. State your conclusions on the case after appropriately weighing the significance of the facts considered.

Problem 6

[ITA: 2, 250, 253]

Capitol Life Insurance Company ("Capitol") was incorporated in the U.S.A. in the state of Colorado at the turn of the century. Its head office had always been in Denver, Colorado. Capitol was a subsidiary of Providence Capitol Corporation which in turn was a subsidiary of Gulf & Western Industries Inc. ("Gulf"). Gulf owned approximately 600 subsidiaries, 240 of which were in turn owned by Associates Corporation of North America ("Associates"). Six of these latter corporations were Canadian companies.

Capitol was in the business of writing individual and group life and health insurance policies. Capitol also wrote creditor's group life and health insurance policies for the 240 finance companies which were part of the Gulf group of companies. Under a creditor's group insurance policy, Capitol would pay to the finance company, upon the death or disability of the borrower, the outstanding amount of the loan in the case of death or the required instalment payments in the case of disability. The costs of the insurance were effectively passed on to the borrower, either as a separate charge or as a higher interest rate.

In the late 1960s, Capitol planned to expand into Canada and obtained licences in nearly every province and obtained federal registration under the *Foreign Insurance Companies Act* ("FICA"). The FICA registration required that Capitol name a chief agent in Canada and that he be given a power of attorney. Capitol was also required to make deposits with the insurance superintendent and maintain assets in Canada. Two bank accounts were opened in Canada. The planned expansion into Canada was cancelled. However, the licences and registration were maintained. This required that Canadian representatives and agents be retained as locations for the licensing authorities to serve legal notices. All reports to the licensing authorities and all inquiries of the licensing authorities were to be passed through the Canadian chief agent. The reports to the licensing authorities were prepared in Denver and all inquiries were passed on to Denver by the chief agent. The chief agent was required to maintain copies of records required by the superintendent of insurance. None of Capitol's representatives or agents ever solicited insurance or were expected or authorized to do any business.

The chief agent countersigned the cheques on Capitol's general bank account on the requirement of the insurance superintendent. He had no means to verify the legitimacy of the cheques; as all books and records were maintained in Denver where the cheques were prepared. The agent later deposited the premiums received in an effort to streamline the former procedure of having the premiums sent to Denver and then sent back to Canada through the bank for deposit into the Canadian general account to meet licensing requirements. All investments were administered and managed in Denver.

Capitol did not have anyone in Canada who solicited insurance business, collected premiums, processed or paid claims, administered investments or countersigned any claim cheques. Capitol had five group insurance contracts under which the lives of Canadian residents were insured. These policies were all issued to affiliated companies without solicitation in Canada. Two of these policies were creditor's group insurance policies with Associates. They were each drafted in accordance with Denver law and signed in Denver by the president of Associates, who was a resident of Indiana. Associates was shown as the insured company and paid all premiums. On the insistence of the Canadian insurance authorities, the wording of the agreements was amended to reflect "a premium collection fee". The original agreement provided for a retroactive adjustment of premiums based upon past claim experience. Capitol and Associates continued to administer, interpret and apply the agreement in the same manner as the original agreement. Blank insurance certificates were also required to be issued so that they could be provided to borrowers whose loans were insured as a way of informing them of the terms of the coverage. The coverage took place independently of the issuance of a certificate to an individual. These certificates listed the Canadian head office of Capitol as being in Don Mills, Ontario, as required by the federal insurance superintendent. This office was never used as a head office. The federal insurance superintendent also required the issuance of a brochure for the information of the Canadian borrowers whose lives and health were insured.

The income that Capitol received from the Canadian insurance and investments represented a very small proportion of its total revenue. Canadian operations were not kept separately from U.S. operations, no Denver personnel were charged with Canadian operations, and there were no special Canadian claim forms or procedures. The only separation of Canadian business from U.S. operations to be found in the accounts of Capitol was to comply with the Canadian insurance authorities. All corporate meetings as well as all levels of management took place in the U.S.A.

— REQUIRED

Prepare a memo for the tax person in your firm who will advise Capitol on the income tax consequences of these facts. Evaluate in detail the alternatives in the residence issue as they relate to this fact situation. Discuss each possible degree of residence and its tax consequences. State your conclusions on this case after weighing the relevance of the facts you have considered.

[For more problems and solutions thereto, see the CD accompanying this book.]

Chapter 3

Employment Income

TOPICS DISCUSSED

	Page
BASIC RULES	77
Employed vs. Self-employed or Independent Contractor	77
Salary, Wages and Other Remuneration including Gratuities	80
Amounts Received	81
SPECIFIC INCLUSIONS	81
Value of Board and Lodging	81
Other Fringe Benefits	82
Allowances	89
Director's or Other Fees	91
Standby Charge and Operating Cost Benefit for Automobile provided by Employer	91
Employee-owned Automobile Operating Expense Benefit	95
Benefit from Employer-paid GST	96
Employment Insurance Benefits	96
Payments by Employer to Employee	97
Restrictive Covenants	99

	Page
Stock Options	99
DEDUCTIONS FROM EMPLOYMENT INCOME	104
Sales/Negotiating Person's Expenses	104
Travelling Expenses other than Motor Vehicle Expenses	105
Other Expenses	108
Registered Pension Plans	109
CAR ALLOWANCES AND EXPENSES	111
Motor Vehicle Allowances Received from Employers	112
Expenses	113
Application of Rules	119
GST REBATE ON EMPLOYEE DEDUCTIONS	122
APPLICATION OF RULES UNDER SUBDIVISION "a"	125
SUPPLEMENTAL NOTES	147
Salary Deferral Arrangements	147
Registered Pension Plans	147

Subdivision a of Division B defines employment income under the Act. This computation, although very basic, is important because it will be used in subsequent sections to describe the limitations on the deductibility of certain items such as registered retirement savings plan contributions and child care expense deductions. The following list indicates the sections and basic content of this subdivision:

Sec. 5 — Salary, wages and gratuities received.

Sec. 6 — Other income inclusions arising from employment.

Sec. 7 — Stock option benefits.

Sec. 8 — Deductions allowed against employment income.

75

It is worth noting that the only expenses that can be deducted against employment income are those specifically set out in sec. 8 [ssec. 8(2)].

The following chart will help locate the major provisions discussed in this chapter.

PART I — DIVISION B

SUBDIVISION a

EMPLOYMENT INCOME

DIVISION		SUBDIVISION		SECTION	
A	Liability for tax				
B	Computation of income		Basic rules		
C	Computation of taxable income	a	Office or employment	5	Basic rules
		b	Business or property	6-7	Inclusions
D	Taxable income earned in Canada by non-residents	c	Capital gains and losses	8	Deductions
E	Computation of tax	d	Other income		
E.1	Minimum tax	e	Other deductions		
F	Special rules	f	Rules relating to computation of income		
G	Deferred and other special income arrangements	g	Amounts not included in income		
H	Exemptions	h	Cdn corporations and shareholders		
I	Returns, Assessments, payments, appeals	i	Shareholders of non-resident corporations		
J	Appeals to the courts	j	Partnerships		
		k	Trusts		

Examine carefully the contents of these sections, especially sections 6 and 8, which contain many specific inclusions and deductions. Note that the T1 income tax return (an individual's tax return) does not actually calculate net employment income as a single number, since the return separates employment inclusions from employment deductions. While the net result is, of necessity, the same as that achieved by the Act, the T1 return approach does not compute a net income from employment figure that is very important for subsequent calculations.

This chapter will consider, first, whether a person is an employee or self-employed. The major inclusions of employment income and the major deductions from employment income are considered next. Since the system of provisions that allows for deductions pertaining to the employment use of cars is extensive, these rules are considered in a separate part of this chapter. The deduction by an employee of expenditures which include GST may provide the employee with a GST rebate. The income tax implications of this rebate will be considered after the deductions for income tax purposes have been discussed.

I. BASIC RULES

A. Employed vs. Self-employed or Independent Contractor

[IT-504R2; IT-525R]

The issue of whether a person is an employee or self-employed (i.e., an independent contractor) often arises in connection with the deductibility of expenses. The issue is important because independent contractors are allowed to deduct all reasonable expenses incurred for the purpose of gaining or producing income from business [par. 18(1)(*a*), s. 67], except capital outlays [par. 18(1)(*b*)]. Employees, on the other hand, are strictly limited to those deductions specifically listed in section 8 [ssec. 8(2)]. In addition, the employee versus independent contractor issue is important in determining whether the employer is required to withhold income tax, Canada Pension Plan contributions or Employment Insurance premiums from amounts paid to the individual. For labour law purposes, individuals usually prefer to be employees to gain protection for their severance, pension and injury compensation rights. While many individuals would prefer to be an employee for labour law purposes and self-employed for tax purposes this option is not realistic.

There is no single test that is decisive in determining whether an individual is an employee or an independent contractor. The following interrelated tests have evolved in the courts:

(a) economic reality or entrepreneur test;

(b) integration or organization test; and

(c) specific result test.

Each of the tests, which determine the nature of the relationship rather than the nature of the services, must be understood. It is important to know how the tests work to distinguish between an individual who is considered to be employed and an individual who can be considered to be self-employed.

The *economic reality or entrepreneur test* examines several economic factors and draws from them an inference as to the nature of the relationship. In particular, four dimensions have been advanced involving (1) control, (2) ownership of the tools, (3) chance of profit and (4) risk of loss. In the civil law case of *671122 Ontario Ltd. v. Sagaz Industries Canada Inc.*, [2001] 2 SCR 983, the Supreme Court of Canada added another factor to consider: the degree of responsibility for investment and management held by the worker.

The control subtest, listed as part of the economic reality or entrepreneur test above, determines whether the individual is directed by someone who is in a position to order or require not only what is to be done but how it is to be done. Where such control is exercised over the individual, an employer–employee relationship is implied. Hence, control is evidenced by the situation of an individual who is subject to a person who has the right to give orders and instructions to the individual regarding the manner in which to carry out the work.[a] In the view of the CRA, control "exists if the person for whom services are performed has the right to control the amount, the nature, and the management of the work to be done and the manner of doing it".[b]

At the turn of the twentieth century the control test was regarded as a conclusive test. However, in our increasingly complex business environment, control is no longer appropriate as a conclusive test, but is just one of the four tests which must be examined

---

[a] This test was applied in the cases of *Di Francesco v. M.N.R.*, (T.A.B.) 64 DTC 106 and *Compton v. M.N.R.*, (T.A.B.) 65 DTC 578.

[b] IT-525R, "Performing Artists", August 17, 1995, par. 3.

together as part of the economic reality or entrepreneur test. The shortcomings of the control test reveal themselves in circumstances where it is difficult, because of the nature of the work, to exercise any control over the manner in which the work is performed. In particular, the courts have found the test to be too inflexible in determining the issue in respect of professionals and highly skilled tradespeople who are hired for their knowledge and expertise; that is, they do not need to be told how to do a job.

In cases where the taxpayer doing the work supplies neither funds nor equipment needed to do the work, takes no financial risks and has no liability, the courts have applied the economic reality test and held that the taxpayer is an employee.[c] On the other hand, the major tool necessary for some work is the knowledge, expertise or skill of the person doing the work, as in the case of a professional consultant. In that case, the "ownership of the tools" subtest may not be conclusive.[d]

Where the taxpayer doing the work has a chance of making a profit, risks incurring a loss from bad debts, damages to assets or delivery delays, and must cover operating costs, there is evidence of an independent contractor or self-employed status.

The *integration or organization test* examines whether the individual doing the work is economically dependent on the organization. The more dependent the individual is on the organization, the more he or she will appear to be an employee. In the case of *Wiebe Door Services Ltd. v. M.N.R.*, (F.C.A.) 87 DTC 5025, the court held that the correct perspective was that of the individual in terms of how dependent the individual is on the organization. Consideration can be given, for example, to the proportion of the individual's income derived from the organization and the availability to the individual of benefits available to employees of the organization. In applying this test, it is important to determine whether services are performed as an individual in business on his or her own account.

The *specific result test* has been used to distinguish an employee from an independent contractor. An employer–employee relationship usually contemplates the employee putting his or her personal services at the disposal of his or her employer during a given period of time without reference to a specified result and, generally, envisages the accomplishment of work on an ongoing basis. On the other hand, where a party agrees that certain specified work will be done, possibly, with the use of assistants provided by the party, for the other, it may be inferred that an independent contractor relationship exists. In the CRA's view, this test is satisfied where the facts suggest that "a person is engaged to achieve a defined objective and is given all the freedom to obtain the desired result".[e] The facts used in the application of the *integration or organization test* may, also, be useful in the specific result test since the tests appear to be closely related.[f]

All of these tests were reviewed and applied by the Tax Court of Canada in the case of *Lafleur and Polis v. M.N.R.*, (T.C.C.) 84 DTC 1478. In *Wiebe Door Services Ltd. v. M.N.R.*, 87 DTC 5025 (a case dealing with Canada Pension Plan and Employment Insurance issues), the Federal Court of Appeal, a more senior court, re-emphasized the necessity of examining the interaction of all the facts and the above tests.

The CRA does not have a specific Interpretation Bulletin dealing with the differences between employees and self-employed individuals. However, there is a brief

---

[c] The cases of *Latimer v. M.N.R.*, (T.R.B.) 77 DTC 84 and *Hauser v. M.N.R.*, (T.R.B.) 78 DTC 1532 illustrate the application of this test.

[d] On that point, see the case of *Brandes v. M.N.R.*, (T.R.B.) 83 DTC 158.

[e] IT-525R, par. 3.

[f] The specific result test was adopted in the case of *Alexander v. M.N.R.*, (Ex. Ct.) 70 DTC 6006.

description of the general principles involved in IT-504R2, Visual artists and writers, paragraph 2. A more detailed application of the tests or factors used in the case of performing artists is provided in IT-525R, paragraphs 3 to 8.

Example Problem

The taxpayer, a professional pathologist, was appointed Director of the Clinical Chemistry Laboratory of a hospital for a period of five years. He reported to the hospital's Director of Laboratories who advised the taxpayer what his work involved and decided the amount to be paid to the taxpayer. The hospital supplied all the necessary laboratory facilities and equipment. The laboratory conducted tests exclusively for the patients of the hospital, although some tests were referred out by the hospital to private laboratories.

The taxpayer's main responsibility was to ensure that the output and quality of the work done in the laboratory by 15 technologists who were employees of the hospital was acceptable. He did not have the authority to hire or fire any of the technologists who worked under him, but could, if necessary, request additional help from the hospital's administration. The taxpayer did not have to arrange for or pay his replacement if he was absent from the laboratory for vacations or other lengthy periods of time. Substitute pathologists were paid directly by the hospital.

The normal deductions from employees' salaries were made by the hospital in respect of the taxpayer's remuneration. The taxpayer also participated in the group insurance plan toward which the hospital made substantial contributions.

—REQUIRED

Is the taxpayer in this case an employee or an independent contractor? In presenting your answer, discuss the tests that are applied by the courts in this type of situation and consider how the facts relate to these tests. What are the general tax consequences of your findings?

—SOLUTION

The following has been excerpted from the decision of the Chairman of the Tax Review Board in the case of *Hauser v. M.N.R.*, (T.R.B.) 78 DTC 1532.

1. *The Economic Reality or Entrepreneur Test:* The control aspect of this test, which in certain circumstances is still applicable, has been found by the courts to be too inflexible in determining the issue, particularly in respect of professionals and highly trained, skilled tradespeople. In this instance, it is clear that the Director of Laboratories could not or would not interfere in the taxpayer's exercise of his professional skills. However, even though the usual strict controls of an employer over the employee's work are not found in this instance, it does not automatically rule out the possibility that an employer–employee relationship does in fact exist. The taxpayer as a staff member, therefore was under the hospital's control for the general assignment and reporting of his work and for the amount of remuneration that would be allocated to him. Although these factors would not be present if the appellant were in fact a private practitioner, the application of the control test is not, in the circumstances of this appeal, a wholly satisfactory or conclusive one.

The other aspects of the economic reality or entrepreneur test, however, are particularly revealing if we compare the economics of the taxpayer's professional activities in the hospital's chemistry laboratory with that of a private practitioner operating his own private laboratory. In the latter case, the private practitioner runs the risk of financing the equipment, supplying the help necessary to operate and administer his laboratory and he then has to ensure that he has sufficient clients to render his laboratory operation economically viable. The taxpayer, on the other hand, uses the equipment and supplies which are all furnished by the hospital. He neither hires nor fires any of the technologists who work under him but can, if necessary, request additional help from the hospital's administration and all the technologists and clerks working in the hospital's biochemistry laboratory are hired and paid directly by the hospital. The taxpayer does not seek out clients; the tests are made for patients of the hospital. The evidence is that in his absence from the laboratory the taxpayer is not obligated to arrange for or pay his replacement. Substitute pathologists are paid directly by the hospital. Note how, in this case, the "ownership of the tools" subtest pertaining to the knowledge, skills and expertise of the professional is not conclusive. These "tools" are provided by the professional, whether he acts in the capacity of an employee or of an independent contractor, in this type of situation.

On applying the Economic Reality Test to the facts, there is no valid evidence which might support the proposition that the taxpayer was under a contract for services of a self-employed individual. All the evidence tends to establish that, from an economic reality point of view, the taxpayer was under a contract of service and, therefore, an employee of the hospital.

2. *The Integration or Organization Test:* The taxpayer was appointed for a period of five years by the hospital under a contract of service. By this agreement, his knowledge and skills in pathology or in any other related field, in which the taxpayer may have been qualified, was employed in the hospital's general organization in the treatment of patients. The facts suggest an economic dependence on the organization. In such circumstances the courts have held that the taxpayer was an employee.

3. *The Specific Result Test:* This test distinguishes a contract for services of a self-employed individual from a contract of service of an employee. The taxpayer was appointed as Director of the Clinical Chemistry Laboratory of the hospital for a five-year period on a full-time basis. His income from the hospital, though paid periodically, was calculated on a yearly basis. It was the taxpayer's personal professional services which were at the disposition of the hospital and the taxpayer's work was done on a continuous day-to-day basis without there being any limited or specified amount of work that the taxpayer had, by contract, to accomplish. The taxpayer had to do the work personally and did not employ or pay substitute part-time pathologists to do his work in his absence. According to the Specific Result Test one can reasonably conclude that the taxpayer was an employee of the hospital. Note how closely related the conditions of this test are to those used in the Integration or Organization Test. In fact, the Specific Result Test might be regarded as a later stage in the evolution of the Integration or Organization Test.

As a result of applying all three tests to the facts of this case, there is nothing that supports the contention that the taxpayer was under a contract for services or was an independent contractor. All the evidence clearly indicates that the taxpayer was under a contract of service and was an employee.

The consequence of this finding is that the taxpayer's income would be taxed as employment income with the resultant restricted deductions. In this particular case, the taxpayer was allowed a deduction for professional dues in the amount of $366 in 1975, but denied deductions for property taxes, business fees, liability insurance, books and journals, telephone, accounting fees, and travels and conventions in the amount of $2,190. In addition, the payer would be required to withhold from each payment the appropriate taxes at source.

B. Salary, Wages and Other Remuneration including Gratuities

[ITA: 5]

"Salary" and "wages" are terms in common use, but "remuneration" has a somewhat more general meaning. Remuneration includes such items as bonuses, tips, honoraria, and commissions paid to employees subject to the *ejusdem generis* rule discussed in Chapter 1. Numerous court cases have considered remuneration from employment as opposed to some other type of payment.[g] Two cases illustrate how payment by an employer for an expense incurred by the employee can be considered other remuneration or a benefit. In the case of *Pavel Bure v. The Queen* (TCC), 2000 DTC 1507, the payment of the hockey player's agent by the hockey club was included in the player's income. In the case of *Gernhart v. The Queen* (FCA), 98 DTC 6026, a tax equalization payment made by an employer to compensate for higher Canadian taxes was considered to be part of the employee's compensation.

[g] Court cases include: *Bell v. M.N.R.*, (Ex. Ct.) 62 DTC 1115, *Grant v. M.N.R.*, (T.A.B.) 67 DTC 249 and *Curran v. M.N.R.*, (S.C.C.) 59 DTC 1247 which will be considered again under subsection 6(3).

Notice that gratuities are specifically listed in section 5. All amounts, received by an individual in his or her capacity as an employee both from his or her employer and from others by reason of his or her employment, must be included in income. Thus, in addition to any bonus or honorarium received from an employer, an individual must include any tips received from his or her employer's customers. However, if a payment is made to such an individual without reference to his or her employment and primarily as a personal gift, it is not income. This becomes a question of fact and degree with the regularity of payments also being a factor.[h]

C. Amounts Received

The use of the word "received" in section 5 means that the employee must report employment income on the cash basis. Thus, advancing or deferring a payment such as a bonus will affect the level of income of an individual for a given year. However, the voluntary deferment of an unconditional right to receive remuneration has not been accepted and, as a result, has not been held to be taxable in the year of receipt, as illustrated by the case of *Blenkarn v. M.N.R.*, (T.A.B.) 63 DTC 581. For example, an employee who decides not to cash his or her November pay cheque, which was delivered to the employee in December, would be deemed to have received the cheque in December under the principle of constructive receipt. In the case of *Markman v. M.N.R.*, (T.C.C.) 89 DTC 253, the court held that a retroactive pay increase over a number of taxation years is included in income in the year of receipt.

II. SPECIFIC INCLUSIONS

Most benefits that must be included in income from employment are specified in section 6, with section 7 limited to the benefit from employer stock options. The major list of benefits in section 6 is contained in subsection 6(1), with its eleven paragraphs of different taxable benefits. Subsections 6(1.1) to (23) provide mostly amplification, exceptions, formulae or limits for benefits listed in subsection 6(1). Thus, when attempting to determine if a particular benefit is taxable, scanning the list of paragraph headings in subsection 6(1) should be the first step.

Note that before the rules of the paragraphs in subsection 6(1) are presented, there is a preamble which provides that amounts established to be taxable in the following paragraphs are to be "included in computing the income of a taxpayer for a taxation year as income from an office or employment". Also, each paragraph of subsection 6(1) is a continuation of the sentence commenced in the preamble. In essence, the single sentence which is subsection 6(1) covers several pages of the Act! This is a function of the particular drafting style chosen for the Act in which each subsection consists of only one sentence.

A. Value of Board and Lodging

[ITA: 6(1)(a); 6(6); IT-91R4; IT-470R]

Beyond establishing that the value of board and lodging is a taxable benefit, as was the situation in the case of *Cockerill v. M.N.R.*, (T.A.B.) 65 DTC 525, the inclusion of the value of board and lodging presents a valuation problem. IT-470R, pars. 4 and 28 indicate that board and lodging must be valued for tax purposes at the fair market value less any amount charged to the employee. However, if a "reasonable amount" is recovered from the employee, then board and subsidized meals are not subject to this rule. The CRA indicates that a "reasonable amount" is one which covers costs, including

---

[h] For a case on this issue see *McLuhan v. M.N.R.*, (T.A.B.) 63 DTC 211.

food preparation and service costs. Where a lesser amount is recovered, the difference between that amount and the above total costs will be a taxable benefit.

As an exception to the rule in paragraph 6(1)(a) that requires the inclusion of the value of board and lodging, subsection 6(6) excludes from the income of an employee, in carefully defined circumstances of employment at a special work site or remote location, the benefits he or she might otherwise be said to derive from board and lodging and transportation. The conditions that must be met for the exception to apply may be summarized as follows:

(a) the special work site must be a distance away from the employee's ordinary residence such that he or she cannot reasonably be expected to travel daily, and the temporary nature of the duties or the remoteness of the work site must be such that it is not reasonable to establish and maintain a self-contained domestic establishment; and

(b) the board and lodging is necessary for not less than 36 hours and, if an allowance in respect of the board and lodging is paid by the employer, the allowance is not in excess of a reasonable amount.

Note that an employee's ordinary residence, referred to in part (a) above, is one in which he or she maintains a "self-contained domestic establishment" [ssec. 248(1)] as his or her principal place of residence.

This topic is covered in more detail in IT-91R4, *Employment at special work sites or remote locations.*

As an administrative exception to including the value of lodging as a taxable benefit, the CRA has indicated that "the payment or reimbursement of monthly rental costs of an employee's personal residence in a new work location may not result in a taxable benefit to the extent that the payment or reimbursement is on account of reasonable, temporary living expenses while the employee is waiting to occupy new, permanent accommodations".[i]

B. Other Fringe Benefits

[ITA: 6(1)(a), (1.1), (4), (7), (9), (19)–(23); 80.4; 80.5; IT-470R; IT-529]

1. General rules

Paragraph 6(1)(a) itself begins with a preamble which states the general rule for including benefits that arise in the course of or by virtue of an office or employment. The preamble to paragraph 6(1)(a) is very broadly worded, as emphasized by the Supreme Court of Canada in the case of *The Queen v. Savage*, 83 DTC 5409, 5414, so that it would seem to catch any possible benefit which arises from employment. The Court went on to quote from its decision in *Nowegijick v. The Queen*, 83 DTC 5041, where it stated, at 5041, that:

> The words "in respect of" are . . . words of the widest possible scope. They impart such meaning as "in relation to", "with reference to" or "in connection with". The phrases "in respect of" is probably the widest of any expression intended to convey some connection between two related subject matters.

Paragraph 6(1)(a) includes benefits "enjoyed", as well as those benefits received, through an office or employment. Of course, a benefit which is included in employment income because it is enjoyed by the employee-taxpayer raises the whole question of valuation of the benefit.

---

[i] Letter, dated November 5, 1998, from the Director, Business and Publications Division, Income Tax Rulings and Interpretations Directorate, Policy and Legislation Branch, Canada Customs and Revenue Agency, Document 9821655 reproduced in *Tax Windows Files, CCH Canadian TaxWorks.*

The general statement of the rule in paragraph 6(1)(*a*) is followed by specific statutory exceptions to the rule, outlined as follows:

(a) employer's contributions to:

    (i) a registered pension plan (approved by the CRA),

    (ii) a group sickness or accident insurance plan which includes all types of income protection plans,

    (iii) private health services plan premiums and provincial health tax levies, but not provincial health plan premiums,

    (iv) a supplementary unemployment benefit plan, including both public and private plans,

    (v) a deferred profit sharing plan (which is similar to a registered pension plan except that only the employer contributes and the contribution is based on profits), or

    (vi) a group term life insurance policy (refer to subsection 6(4) for the income inclusion);

(b) benefits under a retirement compensation arrangement, an employee benefit plan or an employee trust, already included in income under other provisions;[(j)]

(c) benefits in respect of the use of an automobile (separate benefits for the availability of an employer-provided automobile, a standby charge and an automobile operating expense benefit are discussed later in the chapter);

(d) benefits from counselling services in respect of mental or physical health and re-employment or retirement of the employee; and

(e) benefits under a salary deferral arrangement already included in income by reason of subsection 6(11), which is discussed in supplemental notes later in the chapter.

Provincial health tax levies in part (a)(iii) above are not taxable benefits (e.g., Ontario's Employer Health Tax and similar plans in Manitoba, Northwest Territories, Nunavut, Quebec and Newfoundland and Labrador), since the basis of this tax is the total payroll amount and the liability for this tax belongs to the employer and not the employee. However, premiums paid by employers for provincial health care services plans, where the employee is liable for the premium, are taxable because, as *public* health services plans, they do not fit the specific wording of the exception for *private* plans.

Part (c) above excludes the benefit in respect of the use of an automobile since there is a specific inclusion under paragraph 6(1)(*e*) (discussed later in the chapter) of a standby charge for automobiles and under paragraphs 6(1)(*k*) and (*l*) for all operating

---

[(j)] Part (b) above became an exclusion from paragraph 6(1)(*a*) with the introduction of the following specific income inclusion provisions which prevent employees from deferring the receipt of income to subsequent years:

- retirement compensation arrangements [pars. 56(1)(*x*) and (*z*)];

- employee benefit plans [par. 6(1)(*g*)]; and

- employee trusts [par. 6(1)(*h*)].

Employee benefit plan rules were introduced to prevent a timing difference between the employer's deduction and the employee's income inclusion for non-registered income deferral plans (i.e., non-government-approved pension plans). With the introduction of even further restrictions on deferred salary arrangements in 1986, these employee benefit plan rules have limited applicability. For example, they apply to "offside" retirement compensation arrangement (RCAs) which are discussed more fully in the Supplemental Notes to Chapter 4.

costs paid by the employer for personal use of the automobile, such as gas, oil, maintenance, insurance, etc.

Subsection 6(1.1) clarifies that any benefit related to parking for personal purposes is not considered to be a benefit in respect of the *use* of an automobile. As a result, any benefit related to personal parking will be included in employment income under paragraph 6(1)(*a*). In the case of *Chow and Topchechka v. The Queen* (TCC – Informal Procedure), 2001 DTC 164, the court determined that free parking spaces were not a taxable benefit since the parking spaces were provided for the employer's advantage rather than the employee's advantage. This case rebuts the assumption that free parking spaces are automatically a taxable benefit.

For selected court decisions on fringe benefits that were included in income in respect of:

- holiday trips and prizes[k], see *Philp et al. v. M.N.R.*, (Ex. Ct.) 70 DTC 6237 and *Arsens v. M.N.R.*, (T.A.B.) 69 DTC 81;

- travelling expenses paid for an employee's spouse[l] , see *Hale v. M.N.R.*, (Ex. Ct.) 68 DTC 5326; and

- an economic benefit from a payment made by an employer, see *The Queen v. Huffman*, (F.C.A.) 90 DTC 6405.

An innovation in providing employee fringe benefits is a cafeteria program or flexible benefit program. These programs enable employees to select from a menu of available benefits some of which are taxable and some of which are not. In addition, some of these programs permit employees to select the quantum of the benefit within a certain defined range, e.g., group insurance plans. There is no specific provision within the Act that governs flexible benefit programs; instead each component of the flexible benefit program is governed by its own unique set of rules. However, in designing the program care must be taken to satisfy certain general conditions to ensure that there is no adverse tax consequences for all the benefits provided under the program. IT-529, "Flexible employee benefit programs", discusses in great detail the various types of flexible benefit programs, overriding conditions, specific benefit provisions, and certain administrative interpretations.

2. Fringe benefits and administrative practice

As previously mentioned, Interpretation Bulletins reflect the CRA's position in interpreting a particular section of the Act. Often, the CRA uses an administratively practical interpretation of the law and, in certain cases, does not enforce the law strictly because it is simply not practical to do so.

IT-470R clarifies the Agency's position on several important issues, some of which are summarized below.

- The exclusion from employment income of fees, paid by an employer, for an employee's membership in a social club applies to those situations "where the membership was principally for the employer's advantage rather than the employee's" [IT-470R, par. 34].

---

[k] In the case of *Romeril v. The Queen* (TCC), 99 DTC 221, where an employee attended a convention, it was held that the trip was not taken for pleasure, but was genuinely related to employment. Hence no benefit could be assessed.

[l] In the case of *Lowe v. The Queen* (FCA), 96 DTC 6226, an account executive for an insurance company was requested to accompany a group of prize-winning brokers on a trip to New Orleans. The company paid the costs of the executive and his spouse. It was established that the executive and his spouse had little personal time on the trip and no benefit could be assessed.

- Personal-use benefits from frequent-flyer programs accumulated through employer-paid business trips are specifically included in employment income [IT-470R, par. 14].

- Financial counselling and tax return preparation provided directly or indirectly by an employer except for financial counselling in respect of re-employment or retirement are specifically included in employment income [IT-470R, par. 26, as amended by a special release dated December 11, 1989].

- One-half of the reimbursed actual loss, in excess of $15,000 on the sale of a home, caused by an employer-instigated move to another work location as discussed in more detail in the next section, is included in employment income.

- The CRA's position in respect of business trips for spouses of employees indicates that there is no employment benefit to the employee if the spouse was, in fact, engaged *primarily* in the business activities on behalf of the employer [IT-470R, par. 15] as opposed to engaged primarily in personal activities.

IT-470R is an important reference for employment benefit planning. It contains a list of items which, if received or enjoyed by an employee, must be included in employment income and a second list of items which need not be included, despite the general wording of the preamble in paragraph 6(1)(*a*), if the CRA's conditions outlined in the Bulletin are met. Clearly, it may be worthwhile on an after-tax basis for an employee to trade taxable salary or fringe benefits for an equivalent amount of non-taxable benefits that are desired by the employee.

Effective for the 2001 and subsequent tax years, the CRA has introduced a change in how gifts and awards are taxed for both employers and employees. Previously, IT-470R provided that gifts of up to $100 could be received by an employee without a taxable benefit being assessed. However, the employer could not deduct these non-taxable gifts as an expense. Gifts in excess of $100 were taxable to the employee and deductible to the employer.

In a change in assessing policy that is not yet reflected in IT-470R but was announced at a Canadian Tax Foundation Conference held in September 2001, the CRA will be assessing the taxable benefit under paragraph 6(1)(a) based on the following guidelines:

1. To mark special occasions, such as Christmas, Hanukkah, birthdays, or a marriage, employers can give their employees two non-cash gifts per year on a tax-free basis. In addition, to honour employment achievements, such as years of service or meeting safety standards, employers can give their employees two non-cash awards per year on a tax-free basis.

2. The total cost to the employer, including taxes, of the two gifts or the two awards cannot be over $500 per year.

3. Employers can deduct the total cost of the gifts or awards.

4. Employees do not have to declare the cost of the gifts or awards as part of their taxable income.

5. If the cost of each gift or award is over the $500 limit, the employer must include the full fair-market value of the gift(s) or award(s) in the employee's income.

6. If an employer gives two or more gifts – or two or more awards – in a single year and their total cost is over the $500 limit, the employer may have to include the fair market value of one or more of the gifts or awards in the employee's income.

7. This inclusion is determined by the cost of each gift or award and, also, by the number of gifts or awards given in a single year.

8. The new policy does not apply to cash or near–cash gifts and awards such as gift certificates, gold nuggets, or other items that can easily be converted into cash. The value of a cash or near–cash gift or award is considered a taxable employment benefit.

The CRA also announced an extension of the policy reflected in the guidelines of Income Tax Technical News No. 13 (1999) to home computers supplied by an employer. According to the guidelines, there is no taxable benefit, where providing the computer is primarily to the benefit of the employer.

3. Housing loss and housing cost benefits

Subsections 6(19) to (23) address the income tax consequences of employer-provided compensation in respect of losses on a disposition of the employee's residence and other housing-related payments such as financing subsidies. These provisions apply to 1998 and subsequent taxation years.

Subsection 6(19) includes in income under paragraph 6(1)(*a*) any amount paid in respect of a housing loss. However, this general rule is modified so that only one-half the amount in excess of $15,000 of an employer-paid amount is included in employment income for an *eligible housing loss* [ssec. 6(22)].

- An eligible housing loss is the taxpayer's *housing loss* (see below) that is designated by the taxpayer as such and is in respect of an *eligible relocation* (see below) of the taxpayer or non-arm's length person [ssec. 6(22)].

- In general terms, a housing loss is the cost of the residence to the taxpayer or a non-arm's length person minus the proceeds of disposition or fair market value depending on certain circumstances [ssec. 6(21)].

- An eligible relocation is defined in subsection 248(1) for purposes of these provisions [ssecs. 6(19) and (23)] and deductible moving expenses [sec. 62]. This definition imposes a 40-kilometre minimum on the relative distance between new and old residences and new and old work locations. This kilometre restriction and other limitations are discussed in detail in Chapter 9 under the topic, Moving Expenses.

Finally, the Act contains a catch-all provision, "for greater certainty", that includes in the income of the employee all other employer-provided payments or any other type of assistance by anyone in respect of housing [ssec. 6(23)].

4. Employee loans

Subsection 6(9) brings into employment income a deemed interest benefit on an interest-free or low-interest loan made by an employer and received by an employee in his or her capacity as an employee. Subsection 80.4(1) defines the benefit as being the difference between the interest calculated at the prescribed interest rate, which may change for each quarter in the year during which the loan was outstanding, [Regs. 4300 and 4301], and the actual interest calculated in respect of the calendar year and paid by the employee up to January 30 of the following year. Interest paid or *payable* on behalf of the employee by the employer or related party is also included in the benefit calculation. Only the interest actually *paid* by the employee is deductible. Hence, interest not paid within the above time-frame does not reduce the benefit.

Subsection 80.5 states that this deemed interest benefit is in turn deemed to be interest paid. The effect of this deeming rule is to meet a condition in paragraph 8(1)(*j*) which allows for a deduction of interest *paid* on funds borrowed to purchase a car for use in employment. By deeming the imputed interest benefit, which is included in employment income, to be interest *paid*, one of the conditions of the interest deduction provision is met. A similar effect is provided where funds are borrowed from an employer, for example, to purchase shares of a corporate employer. In this situation, one of the conditions in paragraph 20(1)(c), which provides for a deduction of interest paid on funds borrowed under specified conditions, would be met by the deeming rule in section 80.5. However, it must be emphasized that the interest is deductible only if the amount qualifies under all of the specific provisions of these paragraphs.

Home purchase loans, as defined in subsection 80.4(7), and home relocation loans, as defined in subsection 248(1), use a rate set by the combined application of subsections 80.4(1) and (4) for each quarter the loan is outstanding as the lesser of:

(a) the prescribed rate for the quarter while the loan was outstanding; and

(b) the prescribed rate in effect at the time the loan was made.

The quarter-by-quarter method described above is used by the CRA and may result in a smaller income inclusion than an annual calculation in (a) above involving the prescribed rates for all four quarters that the loan was outstanding.

Part (b) of this calculation is modified every fifth year for home purchase loans, by virtue of subsection 80.4(6), to use the prescribed rate on every fifth anniversary date.

Note that where the Act uses the term "prescribed" as in prescribed rate, the "prescription" will usually appear in an Income Tax Regulation. Refer to the footnotes of the provision in which the term is used under the "Regulation" heading to locate the Regulation that is applicable. Where a form is prescribed, the number of the form will usually be listed in the footnotes.

The Act contains a partial exemption for the imputed interest income inclusion, as described above, for basically the first $25,000 of a "home relocation loan" [ssec. 248(1)]. This type of loan results from any move of at least 40 kilometres by the taxpayer or his or her spouse to a new employment location in Canada. However, this exemption is deducted under Division C (deductions to arrive at taxable income) and is generally deductible during the first five years of the loan to the extent of the imputed interest net of qualified interest payments. This topic will be discussed in further detail in Chapter 10.

Note that the CRA computes interest on a daily basis. Following normal commercial practice, the CRA calculates interest commencing with the first day that a debt is incurred and excluding the day on which the debt is repaid, unless a provision of the Act specifies another method of calculation.

Example Problem

On May 1 of this year, Mr. Roberts borrowed from his employer, Stanley Inc., $35,000 evidenced by a 3% promissory note with principal repayable in five equal instalments on the anniversary date and interest payable monthly. Mr. Roberts spent the $35,000 on the following acquisitions:

(a) $20,000 as a down-payment on a new condominium which he moved into immediately;

(b) $10,000 for a second-hand car which he needs to carry out his duties of employment (approximately 60% of the time); and

(c) $5,000 for acquiring dividend-paying common shares in his brother's corporation.

Assume that the prescribed interest rates for this year are the following:

1st quarter	7%	3rd quarter	8%
2nd quarter	6%	4th quarter	7%

— *REQUIRED*

Discuss the tax consequences of the above transactions, supporting them with all necessary computations.

— SOLUTION

Income:

Mr. Roberts will have an imputed employment income inclusion for the accrued interest from May 1 to December 31[1] of this year under subsection 6(9) by virtue of subsection 80.4(1).

Car and shares portion of loan

2nd quarter: May 1 to June 30 (inclusive)

$$\frac{61}{365} \times 6\% \times \$15,000 = \dots\dots\dots\dots\dots\dots\dots\dots\dots \quad \$\ 150$$

3rd quarter: July 1 to September 30 (inclusive)

$$\frac{92}{365} \times 8\% \times \$15,000 = \dots\dots\dots\dots\dots\dots\dots\dots\dots \quad 302$$

4th quarter: October 1 to December 31 (inclusive)

$$\frac{92}{365} \times 7\% \times \$15,000 = \dots\dots\dots\dots\dots\dots\dots\dots\dots \quad 265 \quad \$717$$

Condominium portion of loan[2]:

May 1 to December 31 (inclusive)

$$\frac{245}{365} \times 6\% \times \$20,000 = \dots\dots\dots\dots\dots\dots\dots\dots\dots \quad \$\ 805$$

Total $1,522

Less: interest for the year paid on all loans

$$\frac{245}{365} \times 3\% \times (\$15,000 + \$20,000) = \dots\dots\dots\dots\dots\dots \quad 705$$

Imputed interest benefit inclusion . . . . $\ 817

Deductions:

Although deductions are really presented in subsequent chapters and the latter part of this chapter, a conceptual discussion of the deduction alternatives may be helpful in understanding the whole issue.

(A) Portion of loan used to acquire condominium ($20,000)

There is no deduction available in connection with a home purchase loan except in Division C where the employee has moved, under certain defined conditions as described in Chapter 10.

(B) Portion of loan used to acquire the car and shares ($15,000)

Under section 80.5, the imputed interest income in respect of both the shares and the car, in this case, is deemed to be paid and, hence, may be eligible for a deduction. However, both of these amounts must meet further tests in paragraphs 8(1)(*j*) and 20(1)(*c*), in order to qualify for a deduction.

— NOTES TO SOLUTION

(1) The days of interest were determined by counting the first day of the contractual arrangement.

(2) The condominium portion of the loan should qualify as a home purchase loan [ssec. 80.4(7)]. Therefore, the imputed interest calculation would be based on the "lesser of" rule demonstrated above [ssec. 80.4(4) in combination with ssec. 80.4(1)]. Since the prescribed rate at the time the loan was made (6%) is less than the subsequent quarterly prescribed rates (8% and 7%), the 6% rate applies to all three quarters. The CRA's administrative practice is to apply these rules on a quarter-by-quarter basis, not on an annual basis.

5. Forgiveness of employee loans

Subsection 6(15) determines, for the purposes of paragraph 6(1)(*a*), the value of an employment benefit arising on the forgiveness of an employee loan. The effect of this provision is to include in employment income the amount of the employer loan or other indebtedness net of any payments made by the employee, i.e., the forgiven amount. This treatment is logical since the principal amount of the loan is not taxed when received. If a repayment with after-tax funds is not required because the loan was forgiven, the employee receives an economic benefit.

C. Allowances

[ITA: 6(1)(*b*), (16); IT-522R]

1. Overview

First, the differences between an allowance and a reimbursement must be identified. Typically, a reimbursement involves the payment by an employee of an expense of his or her employer and the recovery from the employer of the amount paid as substantiated by vouchers or receipts. Generally, a reimbursement is not a taxable benefit to the employee. On the other hand, an allowance is a fixed amount which is paid to an employee in excess of his or her salary without the requirement that the employee substantiate the amounts expended. IT-522R, at paragraphs 40 and 50, adopts these meanings for the terms "allowance" and "reimbursement", respectively.

Two precedent-setting judicial decisions on this issue are presented in *Ransom v. M.N.R.*, (Ex. Ct.) 67 DTC 5235 and *Splane v. The Queen*, (F.C.A.) 92 DTC 6021. Both cases established a two-stage test for determining if a payment to an employee is employment income. First, a determination must be made as to whether the payment is an allowance or a reimbursement. If the payment is an allowance, then the rules in paragraph 6(1)(*b*) apply. If the payment is a reimbursement, then a further determination must be made as to whether the employee has received an "economic benefit". Normally, there is no benefit if the employee is in the same economic position as he or she was in prior to the employer-driven transaction which gave rise to payment.

Again, paragraph 6(1)(*b*) contains a preamble which establishes the general rule for the inclusion of allowances. The general rule in paragraph 6(1)(*b*) is that all such allowances received must be included in the employee's income. However, there are many exceptions to this rule listed in the paragraph, some of which are discussed below. Any allowance received, that is not excepted, is regarded as an allowance in respect of a personal or living expense. Since such an expense is not deductible, an amount received as an allowance for such an expense must be included in income.[m]

Subsection 6(16) modifies subsection 6(1) so as to exclude from employment income certain allowances, reimbursements and other payments in respect of disabled persons for transportation to and from the workplace and for the services of an attendant to assist the employee to perform his or her employment duties. In order for these exemptions to apply the disabled person must be eligible for a disability tax credit [sec. 118.3] which is discussed in some detail in Chapter 10.

2. Exception of allowance for travelling expenses of sales/negotiating persons

A common exception to the taxation of allowances is found in subparagraph 6(1)(*b*)(v) dealing with employees who sell property or negotiate contracts. Note the conditions that must be met for the allowance to be excluded:

(a) the allowance must be reasonable;

---

[m] For a case on the topic of personal or living expenses, see *Henry v. M.N.R.*, (S.C.C.) 72 DTC 6005.

(b) the allowance must be only for travelling expenses, including by implication motor vehicle expenses (this topic is covered separately, later in this chapter); and

(c) the recipient (hereinafter referred to as a "sales/negotiating person") must be involved in the selling of property or the negotiating of contracts for his or her employer.

The word "reasonable" is not defined in the Act and, therefore, must be applied to the particular facts of the situation. For example, in subparagraph 6(1)(b)(v), a reasonable daily allowance for the travelling expense of the president of a large public corporation (a person who negotiates contracts) would be entirely different than a reasonable daily allowance for a salesperson for the same organization.

In the case of *Hudema v. The Queen*, (F.C.T.D.) 94 DTC 6287, the taxpayer claimed that a car allowance was not reasonable because the allowance did not cover all of his expenses of operating the car. This was not sufficient evidence to prove that the allowance was not reasonable because the court was not convinced that the taxpayer was making a reasonable use of his vehicle. Since the taxpayer made very little personal use of the car, averaging about 15% per year over five years, he attributed most of the costs of operating his car to his work. The court indicated that the taxpayer did not establish that it was sensible to make such little personal use of the car that he used for work. The court further indicated that the employer's allowance should only be expected to pay for such reasonable use of his car as his work required. To be reasonable, the allowance should cover virtually all the costs of his car, both capital and operating. The court suggested that the taxpayer should have provided evidence of the number of hours per week for which he had to use the car for work.

In the case of *Lemire v. The Queen*, (T.C.C.) 94 DTC 1772, the judge suggested the type of evidence necessary to determine whether an allowance, to cover reasonable expenses of owning and maintaining a car, was inadequate. The judge indicated, at 1773, that:

> ... I not only must have evidence as to how the allowance was calculated by the employer, but the intent of the employer when setting the allowance. I must also have the complete history of the vehicle such as the expenses over the years an allowance was received. Just looking at the one year, in light of the evidence before me, is not sufficient. An allowance cannot be reasonable for three years and unreasonable the fourth year. Obviously an Appellant has to demonstrate that his vehicle's expenses are reasonable for an employee in his employment.
>
> An employee earning an annual wage of $40,000 with an investment income of several hundred thousand dollars a year may choose to own and drive a $100,000 car. Obviously a normal reasonable mileage allowance would never cover the depreciation of an automobile this expensive. Even though the expense and depreciation for that car would be reasonable, it would not be reasonable for the employer or the taxpayers of Canada to subsidize this hypothetical employee.

Where a sales/negotiating person receives an allowance for the use of a motor vehicle, there are further conditions that must be satisfied in order to exclude such an allowance [spar. 6(1)(b)(x) or (xi)]. These conditions and their effects will be considered separately, later in this chapter.

3. Exception of allowance for travelling expenses of other employees

Another common income exception is set out in subparagraph 6(1)(b)(vii). This concerns other employees and has the following conditions:

(a) the employee (hereinafter referred to as "ordinary employee") does not sell property or negotiate contracts;

(b) the allowance must be reasonable in the circumstances;

(c) the allowance must be for travelling expenses, but not for the use of a motor vehicle (which is discussed under subparagraph 6(1)(*b*)(vii.1) separately, later in the chapter); and

(d) the recipient must travel away from the municipality and metropolitan area of the employer's establishment at which the employee ordinarily worked.

Note the difference between the conditions in subparagraph 6(1)(*b*)(v) (sales/negotiating person) and subparagraph 6(1)(*b*)(vii) (ordinary employee). First, the travelling expenses include motor vehicle expenses for sales/negotiating persons but exclude them for ordinary employees, since these are covered under subparagraph 6(1)(*b*) (vii.i). Second, the ordinary employee has a geographical limitation placed on the travelling expenses. As will be seen in the discussion of subparagraph 6(1)(*b*)(vii.1) later in the chapter, there is no geographical limitation placed on an allowance for the use of a motor vehicle for sales/negotiating employees. This geographical distinction appears to be the reason for separating out such an allowance from subparagraph 6(1)(*b*)(vii).

D.   Director's or Other Fees

[ITA: 6(1)(*c*)]

A corporate director holds an "office", as defined in subsection 248(1). As a result, fees received by a director are received by virtue of an office and, hence, must be included in income under Subdivision a. The effect of including such fees in this Subdivision is to limit the deductions which may be made against that source of income to those listed in section 8, as discussed subsequently.

E.   Standby Charge and Operating Cost Benefit for Automobile provided by Employer

[ITA: 6(1)(*e*), (*k*), (2), (7); IT-63R5]

1.   Calculation of the benefit from the use of the car itself

A standby charge represents a benefit conferred upon an employee through the availability of a company-owned or leased car for any use, whether for employment or personal. Since the employee, who has a company car made available for his or her use, does not have to spend tax-paid dollars on either purchasing or leasing a car, the government reasoned that this benefit should be taxed somehow, on the principle of equity.[n] The concept is not unreasonable. Since availability rather than actual use of the company car is the basis for this calculation, some unsuspecting employee could have an income inclusion of the rather high minimum standby charge.

Subsection 6(2) which, in turn, modifies paragraph 6(1)(*e*) by providing a computational formula, establishes a reasonable standby charge as:

$$\frac{A}{B} \times [2\% \text{ of } (C \times D) + \tfrac{2}{3}\,(E - F)]$$

where A*   is the lesser of:

(a) total personal-use kilometres driven during the available time period, and

(b) the value determined for B (as defined below) during the days the automobile is available;

---

[n] The term "made available" was at issue in *The Queen v. Adams*, (FCA) 98 DTC 6266.

$$B** \quad \text{is } 1{,}667*** \text{ km} \times \left(\frac{\text{total available days}}{30} \right);$$

C **** is the full original cost of an employer-owned vehicle, including both PST and GST;

$$D** \text{ is } \frac{\text{the total available days when the employer owned the automobile}}{30}$$

E   is the lease payments, including both PST and GST, made by the employer;

F   is the portion of the lease payments which pertains to insurance for loss or damages and any liability in using the automobile.

---

* Note that amount A above is deemed to be equal to amount B unless:

(i) the taxpayer is required by the employer to use the automobile in respect of his or her duties of employment, and

(ii) the automobile is used primarily (more than 50%) in his or her duties of employment.

** Rounded according to the rule in the definition (i.e., to the nearest whole number, unless the fractional part is .5, in which case round the fraction down).

*** The monthly limit was increased from 1,000 km to 1,667 km effective 2003.

**** The capital cost limitations in paragraph 13(7)(g) and Regulation 7307, as subsequently described, do not apply.

A separate A/B ratio must be applied to each automobile available for use by an employee in a year. Thus, if an employee had both an employer-owned automobile and an employer-leased automobile available in a year, the formula in subsection 6(2) would be applied with two different A/B ratios as:

$$\frac{A}{B} \times [2\% \text{ of } (C \times D)] + \frac{A}{B} \times [\tfrac{2}{3} (E - F)].$$

2. Alternatives to calculating the operating cost benefit

As previously mentioned, subparagraph 6(1)(a)(iii) specifically excludes a benefit in relation to the use of an employer-provided automobile. However, operating expenses for personal use, which are paid by an employer and not reimbursed by the employee, do give rise to a taxable benefit to the employee [par. 6(1)(k)]. Automobile operating expenses include gasoline, insurance and maintenance costs, but not parking costs. As indicated previously, any benefit related to personal parking is included in income separately [par. 6(1)(a)].

(a) *Election Where Use is Primarily Employment*

If an employee notifies his or her employer in writing before the end of the particular taxation year, he or she may compute his or her operating-cost employment income inclusion [spar. 6(1)(k)(iv)] as 50% of the standby charge minus any reimbursement to the employer made by the employee within 45 days after the end of the year. However, this option is only available in situations where the vehicle is used *primarily* (more than 50%[o]) in the performance of employment duties. The resultant income inclusion is considered to include a GST component and no additional income inclusion is required.

(b) *Kilometre Method*

Subparagraph 6(1)(k)(v) provides an alternative method (henceforth called the "kilometre method") for computing the operating cost benefit to an employee whose

---

[o] As indicated in paragraph 6(d) of IT-63R5.

employer pays for operating costs including those for the personal use of an employer-provided automobile. The kilometre method is available to employees who do not qualify for the calculation based on 50% of the standby charge (because their use is not primarily for employment) or to employees who choose not to elect the 50% calculation method, where the use is primarily for employment.

The kilometre method alternative computes the amount of the operating cost benefit by reference to the number of kilometres driven for personal purposes at 20 cents per personal-use kilometre in 2005.[p] The 20-cent amount is reviewed periodically. Again, the amount computed by this method is reduced by any reimbursement paid within 45 days after the end of the year by the employee to the employer in respect of these operating costs. Again, the inclusion based on 20 cents per kilometre is considered to include a GST component and no further income inclusion is required.

3. Application of the rules

The following examples will demonstrate how the rules in paragraph 6(1)(e), subsection 6(2) and paragraph 6(1)(k) should be applied.

Example Problem 1

Automobile owned by employer

Original cost of automobile, including PST and GST.............	$26,000
Operating costs for the year paid by employer, including PST and GST	$3,000*
Employment-use kilometres	10,000
Total kilometres for year	30,000
Number of months available.................................	12
Reimbursement to employer for personal use (to cover operating costs and standby charge) at 10¢ per kilometre	$ 2,000

* Includes insurance of $600, but excludes parking.

— REQUIRED

Compute the car benefit under paragraphs 6(1)(e) and 6(1)(k).

— SOLUTION

Car benefit

Par. 6(1)(e) and ssec. 6(2) — Standby

$$\frac{20,004 \text{ km}^1}{20,004 \text{ km}} \times [2\% \times (\$26,000 \times 12)] = \dots\dots\dots\dots \$6,240$$

Spar. 6(1)(k)(v)² → operating costs (20,000 km × $0.20) .... <u>4,000</u> $10,240

Less: amount reimbursed....................................... <u>2,000</u>

Total car benefits $8,240

— NOTES TO SOLUTION

(1) The employee does not qualify for the standby charge reduction, since the car is not used more than 50% in the performance of employment duties. Therefore, in this situation, the value of A in the formula (i.e., 20,004 km) is deemed to be equal to the value of B in the formula (i.e., 1,667 × 12 rounded).

(2) The subparagraph 6(1)(k)(iv) election method is also not available, since the car is not used more than 50% in the performance of employment duties. Since this is an employer-provided automobile, the alternative in subparagraph 6(1)(k)(v) must be used.

---

[p] Department of Finance News Release (2004-081) issued on December 17, 2004.

Example Problem 2 —————————————————————————————————————

Automobile owned by employer — The facts are the same as Example Problem 1, except that the employment-use kilometres are 24,000.

— REQUIRED

Compute the car benefit under paragraphs 6(1)(*e*) and 6(1)(*k*).

— SOLUTION

Car benefit

Par. 6(1)(*e*) and ssec. 6(2)

$$\frac{6,000 \text{ km}^1}{20,004 \text{ km}} \times [2\% \times (\$26,000 \times 12)] = \dots\dots\dots\dots\dots\dots\dots 1,872$$

Spar. 6(1)(*k*)(v)^2 → operating costs 936 $2,808

Less: amount reimbursed (6,000 km × 10¢)   600

Total car benefit $2,208

— NOTES TO SOLUTION

(1) Lesser of (a) 6,000 km and (b) 1,667 km × 12 months. In this situation the employee qualifies for the standby charge reduction since the car is used primarily (i.e., more than 50%) in the performance of employment duties.

(2) The subparagraph 6(1)(*k*)(iv) election method is available to the employee, since the car is used more than 50%. This method would result in a lower income inclusion ($936 (i.e., 50% of $1,872) vs. $1,200 (i.e., 6,000km × $0.20)).

Example Problem 3 —————————————————————————————————————

Automobile leased by employer

Lease cost including $500 of insurance, PST and GST .... $ 5,000

Operating costs for the year paid directly by the employer
(includes PST and GST, but excludes parking) .... $ 3,000

Employment-use kilometres 4,000

Total kilometres for the year 16,000

Number of months available 12

Reimbursement to employer for personal use (to cover operating
costs and standby charge) at 5¢ per kilometre .... $ 600

— REQUIRED

Compute the car benefit under paragraphs 6(1)(*e*) and 6(1)(*k*).

— SOLUTION

Car benefit

Par. 6(1)(*e*) and ssec. 6(2)

$$\frac{20,004 \text{ km}^1}{20,004 \text{ km}} \times {}^2\!/_3 (\$5,000 - \$500) \dots\dots\dots\dots\dots \$3,000$$

Spar. 6(1)(*k*)(v) → 12,000 km × $0.20 .... 2,400 $5,400

Less: amount reimbursed 600

Total car benefits $4,800

— NOTE TO SOLUTION

(1) In this situation, the employee does not qualify for the standby charge reduction or the subparagraph 6(1)(*k*)(iv) alternative, because he or she did not use the car more than 50% in the performance of the employment duties.

Example Problem 4

Automobile leased by employer — The facts are the same as Example Problem 3 except that the employment-use kilometres are 12,000.

— REQUIRED

Compute the car benefit under paragraphs 6(1)(e) and 6(1)(k).

— SOLUTION

Car benefit

Par. 6(1)(e) and ssec. 6(2)

$$\frac{4{,}000 \text{ km}^1}{20{,}004 \text{ km}} \times {}^{2}/_{3} \ (\$5{,}000 - \$500) \ \ldots\ldots\ldots\ldots\ldots\ldots \ \$ \ 600$$

Spar. 6(1)(k)(v)[2]	300	$ 900
Less: amount reimbursed (4,000 km × 5¢)		200
Total car benefits		$ 700

— NOTES TO SOLUTION

(1) The employee qualifies for the standby charge reduction, since he or she used the car more than 50% (i.e., 75%) in the performance of his or her duties.

(2) The employee does qualify for the subparagraph 6(1)(k)(iv) alternative method of computing the operating cost benefits, since the car was used more than 50% in the performance of his or her duties. In this situation, the subparagraph 6(1)(k)(iv) election would give a lower gross income inclusion of $300 (i.e., 50% of $600) vs. $800 (4,000 km × $0.20).

F. Employee-owned Automobile Operating Expense Benefit

[ITA: 6(1)(l)]

Paragraph 6(1)(k), discussed in the preceding part of the chapter, pertains to the automobile operating expense benefit arising when an employer provides the automobile and pays for some or all of the operating costs, including costs related to the personal use of the automobile. Paragraph 6(1)(l) applies in cases where the automobile is provided by the employee and where an employer pays for automobile operating costs, including costs for personal use of the automobile. For example, an employee may use his or her own automobile for employment purposes, but the employer pays, through a business credit card, for all operating costs of the automobile, including costs of driving to and from work which are personal costs.

Paragraph 6(1)(l) includes in income the value of any benefit received by an employee for automobile operating expenses attributable to personal use. To arrive at the value of this benefit, the total costs paid by the employer should be prorated by the ratio of personal-use kilometres to total kilometres driven by the employee. Amounts paid by the employee to the employer can be deducted from the benefit. Of course, this method requires record-keeping of employment and personal kilometres in a log, but there is no simpler, alternative method allowed for an employee-provided automobile. Note that the value of this benefit is determined using GST-included operating expenses.

Note the heading for paragraph 6(1)(l) is the single word "*idem*", which is a Latin word meaning "the same". Therefore, the heading for paragraph 6(1)(l) is considered to be the same as that for paragraph 6(1)(k) which is "automobile operating expense benefit".

G. Benefit from Employer-paid GST

[ITA: 6(1)(a), (e), (k), (l), (7)]

Where an employee receives a taxable benefit from his or her employer, the employer is liable for and must remit the relevant GST. The employee in turn is deemed to receive a taxable benefit which generally includes the employer-paid GST. This employment income inclusion of GST places the employee in the same economic position as if he or she acquired the goods or services on the open market. In essence, the Act includes an employer-paid GST in employment income [pars. 6(1)(a) and (e)].

Note that the inclusion of the full GST paid by the employer in providing the benefit ignores any reimbursement by the employee for the taxable benefit/taxable supply. This is logical if the objective is to place the employee in the same position as if he or she acquired the supply on the open market and, therefore, would pay GST on the full amount rather than a partial net payment.

The general rule is that any benefit included in income under either paragraph 6(1)(a) or (e) is subject to the GST. However, two significant exceptions are:

(a) zero-rated supplies found in Schedule VI of the ETA (e.g., gift food baskets); and

(b) exempt supplies found in Schedule V of the ETA (e.g., day-care services, low-rent and rent-free housing, low-interest and interest-free loans, premiums for government health services and tuition fees for exempt education services).

The practical application of including GST paid by the employer in income is fairly limited. The most common applications would be:

(a) personal use of an employer's automobile by way of the standby charge [par. 6(1)(e) and ssec. 6(2)]; and

(b) other payments by the employer which would be considered taxable benefits [par. 6(1)(a)] such as parking costs for personal purposes, travelling expenses relating to vacations, spouse's non-business-related travelling costs, and gifts valued in excess of $500 on which the employer would have paid GST in providing the item to the employee.

H. Employment Insurance Benefits

[ITA: 6(1)(f); IT-428; IT-470R]

Paragraph 6(1)(a) excepts the inclusion in employment income of premiums paid by an employer on behalf of an employee to a group sickness or accident insurance plan. Paragraph 6(1)(f) takes into employment income amounts received as a result of a disability claim by an employee in respect of a sickness or accident, disability or income maintenance plan, if the employer has made any contribution. Hence, such plans become tainted if the employer pays all or any portion of the premium.

In terms of employee benefit planning, there is a basic trade-off in the tax treatment of these plans. On the one hand, all employees can receive a relatively small tax-free benefit by having the employer pay the premium. However, those relatively few employees who become disabled and receive insurance payments will be taxed on those payments. On the other hand, all employees can incur a relatively small cost by paying the premium. In this case, the relatively few employees who become disabled and receive insurance payments will receive those payments tax free.

Where an employee has paid any amount of the premiums, these amounts are deductible from the disability benefits received in arriving at the paragraph 6(1)(f) benefit.

Non-group plans are treated in exactly the opposite manner. The premiums paid by the employer are treated as employment income. However, payments received in respect of these plans are not considered as income. This opinion is confirmed in IT-428 paragraph 20. This bulletin is quite detailed and should be consulted carefully in determining whether the employer has contributed to one of these types of plan.

Example Problem

Mr. Beta is insured under a group plan which pays $3,000 per month while disabled. The premium is $25 per month, of which the employer pays one-half and has been so paying on Mr. Beta's behalf starting January 1, 1982. The employee's share of the premium is waived during the period of the disability. Mr. Beta was struck by a truck and was off work from January 1, 2004 to June 30, 2005.

— REQUIRED

How much must be included in Mr. Beta's income in respect of the disability payments received for the years in question?

— SOLUTION

2004

Total cumulative benefits received in 2004 (i.e., before end of 2004 and after 2003) (12 × $3,000)	$36,000
Less: total contributions made by employee before end of 2004 ($\frac{1}{2}$ × $25 × 12 × 22[1])	3,300
Amount to be included in income	$32,700

2005

Total benefits received in 2005 (i.e., before end of 2005 and after 2004)(6 × $3,000)	$18,000
Less: total contributions made by employee in 2005 (i.e., before end of 2005 and after 2004) ($\frac{1}{2}$ × $25 × 6[2])	75
Amount to be included in income	$17,925

— NOTES TO SOLUTION

(1) 1982 to 2003, inclusive (2004 not counted because employee's share of the premium not paid during disability).

(2) While no premium was paid by the employee during the six months of his disability, the premium was paid during the remaining six months in the year.

I. Payments by Employer to Employee

ITA: 6(3); IT-196R2]

Section 5 is a general statement describing employment income. Other items are specifically listed in section 6 as income from employment, with subsection 6(1) listing several types of such income and subsections 6(1.1) to 6(23) providing further rules in the specification of these items. A few payments received may be regarded as a capital receipt, not subject to tax. However, most payments, such as a signing bonus, might be considered as "other remuneration" under section 5 or as part of "other benefits of any kind whatever" under paragraph 6(1)(a). The payment could also be considered consideration for entering into a contract of employment under subsection 6(3). This provision basically expands employment income to include payments which are received either immediately before or after the actual employment period and which arise from the employment contract. Each of these provisions must be read very carefully to determine the conditions, if any, necessary for the provision to apply.[q] The following example problem illustrates the need for a careful interpretation of these provisions.

Example Problem

The appellant, a geologist highly regarded in his field, had been employed by General Oil Limited for many years. Had he continued until retirement, he would have been entitled to a substantial pension which would be lost if he left General Oil voluntarily.

Mr. Green was a substantial shareholder and chief executive of Prairie Oil Limited which held a large number of shares of Clean Oil Limited. Under an agreement made in the year, Mr. Green paid the appellant $250,000 in consideration of the loss of pension rights, chances for advancement, and opportunities for re-employment in the oil industry. On the same day, the appellant entered into another agreement with Prairie Oil to act as its general manager at a salary of $25,000 per year, subject to the condition that he would serve as manager of another company if the director so decided.

Pursuant to this consideration, the appellant became the president and manager of Clean Oil at a salary of $25,000 per year with no superannuation benefits.

—REQUIRED

Resolve the foregoing fact situation with reference to paragraph 3(*a*), section 5 and subsection 6(3) of the current *Income Tax Act*.

—SOLUTION [see *Robert B. Curran v. M.N.R.*, (S.C.C.) 59 DTC 1247]

The payment of $250,000 can be considered either as a capital receipt or as income from employment. It can be argued that the payment was compensation for substantial benefits forgone including the loss or relinquishment of a source of income which can be regarded as a capital asset. At least that part of the payment for the loss of pension rights, if such a part can be determined, could be regarded as a capital receipt. It has been held that a lump sum paid to commute a pension is a capital payment which is substituted for a series of periodic sums in the nature of income. However, the payment did not come from General Oil to commute the pension.

On the other hand, the payment of $250,000 could be regarded as being made for personal services to be rendered by the appellant to the new employer. The mere fact that the agreement characterizes the $250,000 as a capital payment in consideration of the loss of pension rights, chances for advancement and opportunities for re-employment in the oil industry cannot change the true character of the payment as employment income. Mr. Green was seeking to acquire the skilled services of the appellant as a manager. The consideration was paid so that these services would be made available; therefore, it is income of the appellant within the meaning of paragraph 3(*a*).

Since the payment was not made by the appellant's employer as required by paragraph 6(3)(*b*), it is not *deemed*, for the purpose of section 5, to be remuneration for the appellant's services rendered during the period of employment. Although the payment is not deemed to be employment income, the more general paragraph 3(*a*) can be applied in determining income from employment from a source inside or outside Canada.

The Supreme Court of Canada held that this payment was income from employment under paragraph 3(*a*).

(q) The case of *No. 261 v. M.N.R.*, (T.A.B.) 55 DTC 285 was heard to decide the meaning of the phrase "immediately after" used in paragraph 6(3)(*b*). Cases that resulted in payments which were considered taxable include *Butters v. M.N.R.*, (T.A.B.) 52 DTC 37, *Moss v. M.N.R.*, (Ex. Ct.) 63 DTC 1359 and *The Queen v. Blanchard* (FCA), 95 DTC 5479. Cases that resulted in payments which were considered not taxable include *Wilson v. M.N.R.*, (T.A.B.) 60 DTC 115 and *Segall v. M.N.R.*, (F.C.T.D.) 86 DTC 6486. Cases in which receipts were considered not to be taxable by subsection 6(3) include: *Ballard v. MNR* (TCC), 87 DTC 157, and *The Queen v. Albino* (FCTD), 94 DTC 6071.

J. Restrictive Covenants

Proposed subsection 6(3.1) [Technical Amendments to the *Income Tax Act* dated February 27, 2004] provides that an employee may be required to include in employment income an amount that is receivable at the end of the year in respect of a covenant as to what the employee is, or is not, to do. Normally, only amounts received are included in employment income. This provision deems an amount that is receivable to be received. This provision is part of a comprehensive package of amendments related to payments received for covenants provided by individuals. For a full discussion on the treatment of payments received for restrictive covenants please refer to Chapter 9.

K. Stock Options

[ITA: 7(1), (1.1), (1.3), (5); 110(1)(*d*), (*d*.1); IT-113R4; IC 89-3]

Exercising a stock option will result in employment income if the price paid under the option is less than the fair market value of the shares at the time of their purchase. However, the timing of the inclusion and the ultimate effect on taxable income will depend upon a number of factors:

- the type of corporation issuing the option;
- whether the parties involved are dealing at arm's length;
- the relationship of option price to fair market value of the shares when the option is granted; and
- the value of the shares purchased under the option.

The stock option benefit included in employment income must be received as a result of employment [ssec. 7(5)] from a "qualifying person" that is a corporation or a mutual fund trust [ssec. 7(7)]. Hence, rights or warrants provided by virtue of shareholdings alone would be excluded from this provision.

An employment income inclusion is deemed, for employees of *all* corporations on the exercising of a stock option, equal to the difference between the fair market value at the date the option is exercised and the option price [ssec. 7(1)]. However, there is a partial offsetting deduction, in Division C, equal to one-half of the subsection 7(1) inclusion, if the option price is equal to or greater than the fair market value of the share at the time the option was granted [par. 110(1)(*d*)]. In addition, there are certain limitations on the type of shares to be issued and the relationship of the parties before and after the transaction, all of which are discussed in Chapter 10.

An exception to the general rules described above is provided [ssec. 7(1.1)] for stock options granted by Canadian-controlled private corporations (CCPC) [ssec. 125(7)]. There is still an employment income inclusion, equal to the excess of the fair market value at the date the option is exercised and the option price. However, the inclusion of that benefit occurs at the time that the shares are disposed of, thereby deferring the inclusion of the benefit.

Furthermore, there will be a Division C deduction, equal to one-half of the inclusion, if the shares have not been sold or exchanged before the second anniversary date of the day of acquisition [par. 110(1)(*d*.1)]. For the purpose of determining the length of the holding period of the shares, shares are deemed to have been disposed of in the order in which they were acquired (i.e., first in, first out) [ssec. 7(1.3)]. The excess of the actual selling price over the fair market value at the date the option is exercised will result in a capital gain at the appropriate inclusion rate, as discussed in Chapter 7. Note that stock options issued by CCPCs can qualify for a deduction under paragraph

110(1)(*d*) (referred to above) or under paragraph 110(1)(*d*.1), but not both, even if both sets of conditions are met.

There is another exception to the general rule that the stock option benefit must be included in income in the year of exercise. For public-company securities, issued after February 27, 2000, the inclusion of the benefit can be deferred to the earlier of the year in which the shares acquired under the option are disposed of and the year in which the individual dies or becomes a non-resident. To obtain this deferral, the following conditions must be met [ssec. 7(8) to (16)]:

- The securities are acquired after February 27, 2000 by Canadian residents.

- If the employee option security is a share, the deferral is available only if the share is of a class of shares listed on a Canadian or foreign prescribed stock exchange.

- The deferral does not apply to options granted by Canadian-controlled private corporations, since a deferral is already available on such options under subsection 7(1.1).

- The deferral is available only if the employee is entitled to a deduction under paragraph 110(1)(*d*). Generally, an employee is entitled to a deduction under that paragraph when the following conditions are satisfied:
  - the amount paid by the employee to acquire the security was equal to or greater than the fair market value of the security when the option was granted;
  - the employee was dealing at arm's length, immediately after the option was granted, with the employer; and
  - if the security is a share, it is an ordinary common share.

- If the employee option security is a share, the deferral is not available if the employee was, immediately after the option was granted, a specified shareholder (generally, owning 10% or more of any class of shares) of the employer.

- The deferral is subject to an annual limit of $100,000. The limit is based on the year in which the options vest (i.e., first become exercisable), and on the fair market value of the underlying securities when the options were granted. Thus, for options vesting in a given year, an employee will be able to defer taxation on the acquisition of securities having a total fair market value (determined at the time the options were granted) not exceeding $100,000.

- The deferral is not automatic. It requires that the employee file an election with the employer. The elective nature of the deferral allows an employee who has options in excess of the $100,000 limit vesting in a particular year to choose those options for which the deferral will be claimed.

- The deferral amount is to be reported as a special item on the employee's T4 slip in the year in which the security is acquired. The employee is required to include the deferred amount in computing income from employment when completing the tax return for the year in which the deferral ceases.

For a discussion of the implications on the disposition of shares acquired under a stock option, please refer to Chapter 7.

The following diagram summarizes these rules for inclusions under Division B.

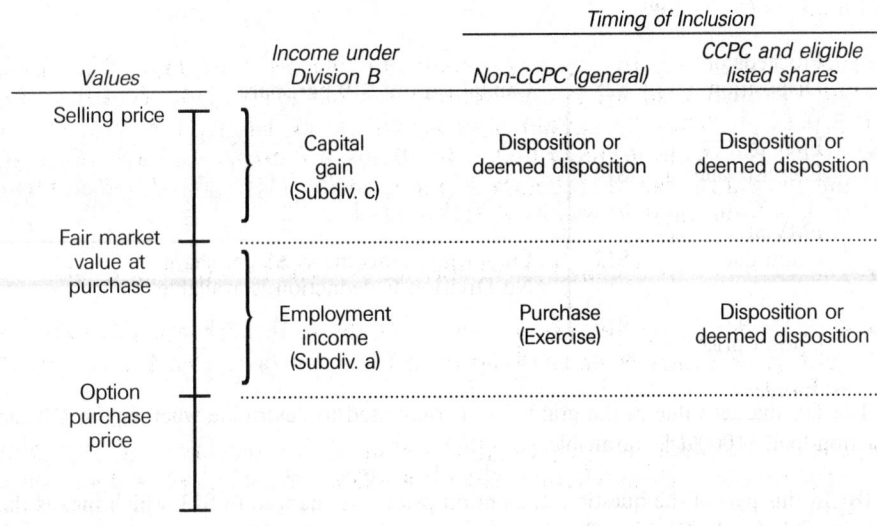

	Values	Income under Division B	Timing of Inclusion	
			Non-CCPC (general)	CCPC and eligible listed shares
Selling price		Capital gain (Subdiv. c)	Disposition or deemed disposition	Disposition or deemed disposition
Fair market value at purchase		Employment income (Subdiv. a)	Purchase (Exercise)	Disposition or deemed disposition
Option purchase price				

Example Problem

Mr. Doubletax, who is employed by Public Co. Ltd., was granted an option in year one to purchase up to 5,000 common shares at $10 after completion of his fifth year of employment. The fair market value of the common shares at the time of granting the right was $12. He does not have any other shares.

During Mr. Doubletax's seventh year of employment he decided to exercise part of his right and purchased 1,000 shares with a fair market value of $15 as at that date.

Three years later, Mr. Doubletax sold the shares at $25 per share.

—REQUIRED

(A) Discuss the tax implications of each of the above transactions.

(B) How would your answer differ if the option price was $13?

(C) How would your answer differ if Mr. Doubletax was employed by a Canadian-controlled private corporation?

—SOLUTION

(A) *Year one, when option is granted:* There is no tax effect when Mr. Doubletax is granted the right to purchase shares through the stock option plan.

Seventh year when option is exercised — Subsection 7(1): Mr. Doubletax must take into employment income the difference between the fair market value and the option price:

1,000 shares × ($15 – $10) = $5,000.

There will be no deduction of one-half, since the option price ($10) is less than the fair market value ($12) at the date the option was granted [par. 110(1)(*d*)]. As a result, one of the conditions necessary to defer the inclusion of the benefit to the year of disposition or deemed disposition is not met.

Note that there has been no disposition at this point; he will have to find the funds to pay the tax from other sources.

Tenth year, when shares are sold: Mr. Doubletax will have a capital gain in the year of disposal calculated on the difference between the proceeds of disposition ($25) and the fair market value as at the date the option was exercised ($15) which is his cost base.[1]

1,000 shares × ($25 – $15) = $10,000.

The taxable capital gain is ½ of $10,000 and is included in Subdivision c of Division B.

The results can be demonstrated as follows:

Proceeds of Disposition	$25	Capital gain of $10 per share
FMV at Exercise date	$15	
FMV at Grant date	$12	Employment income of $5 per share No Division C deduction is available
Option price	$10	

The fair market value at the grant date is only used to determine whether the Division C deduction [par. 110(1)(*d*)] is available.

(B) In this part of the question, the option price was changed to $13, which means that he will be eligible for the Division C deduction [par. 110(1)(*d*)]. In addition, the fair market value of the 5,000 shares at the time the option was granted was $12 per share or $60,000 in total, which is less than $100,000. Therefore, he meets all the conditions for electing to defer reporting the stock option benefit from the year of exercise until the year of sale.

Year one, when option is granted: There is no tax effect in the year the option is granted.

Seventh year, when option is exercised: As mentioned above, he can elect to defer the recognition of the benefit until he sells the shares. In this case he will not report any stock option benefit in his income and he will not be able to take the one-half deduction in the seventh year.

If he does not make this election, he will have to take the stock option benefit into income. This will be calculated as follows:

$$1{,}000 \text{ shares} \times (\$15 - \$13) = \$2{,}000$$

He will also be entitled to the one-half deduction [par. 110(1)(d)], since the exercise price was greater than the fair market value at the date the option was granted. It is calculated as follows:

$$\tfrac{1}{2} \times \$2{,}000 = (\$1{,}000)$$

This one-half deduction, effectively, reduces the income inclusion for eligible stock options to the inclusion rate for capital gains.

Tenth year, when the shares are sold: Assuming that he made the election to defer the stock option benefit then in the year of disposal, since nothing was reported in the seventh year, he will report the following:

$$\text{Stock option benefit: } 1{,}000 \text{ shares} \times (\$15 - \$13) = \$2{,}000$$

$$\text{Division C deduction: } \tfrac{1}{2} \times \$2{,}000 = (\$1{,}000)$$

$$\text{Capital gain: } 1{,}000 \text{ shares} \times (\$25 - \$15) = \$10{,}000$$

The results can be demonstrated as follows:

Proceeds of Disposition	$25	Capital gain of $10 per share
FMV at Exercise date	$15	
Option price	$13	Employment income of $2 per share
		Division C deduction of $1 per share
FMV at Grant date	$12	

The fair market value at the grant date is only used to determine whether the Division C deduction [par. 110(1)(*d*)] is available.

(C) *Subsection 7(1.1)* — If Mr. Doubletax had been employed by a Canadian-controlled private corporation (CCPC), with which he dealt at arm's length, then he would not have to include any amount in employment income upon exercising his right in the seventh year. Upon disposing of the shares in the tenth year, however, he would have employment income equal to the difference between the fair market value at the time he acquired the shares ($15) and his cost ($10):

$$1,000 \text{ shares} \times (\$15 - \$10) = \$5,000.$$

At the same time, he will also have a capital gain of $10,000:

$$1,000 \text{ shares} \times (\$25 - \$15^1) = \$10,000.$$

He would be eligible for a deduction [par. 110(1)(*d*.1)] of one-half of the employment income inclusion of $5,000, since he had retained the shares for more than two years.

Summary	Part A	Part B	Part C
Year 1: (Option granted)	No tax effects in the year the option is granted.	No tax effects in the year the option is granted.	No tax effects in the year the option is granted.
Year 7: (Option exercised)	Recognize employment income benefit and Division C deduction.	No tax effects if election made to defer the recognition of the stock option benefit.	No tax effects until the shares are sold.
Year 10: (Shares sold)	Recognize capital gain only.	Recognize employment income benefit, Division C deduction and capital gain.	Recognize employment income benefit, Division C deduction and capital gain.

Both subsections 7(1) and (1.1) required an employment inclusion of $5,000; the difference was the timing of the inclusion. Where the stock option was offered by a Canadian-controlled private corporation, then the employment inclusion is at the time of disposition of the shares. For stock options from all other corporate employers, the employment inclusion is at the date the option is exercised or when shares are acquired, subject to the proposed $100,000 deferral.

The Division C deductions [par. 110(1)(*d*) or (*d*.1)] were designed to give the same net effect as a capital gain, at the appropriate net inclusion rate, without permitting these amounts to qualify for the capital gains deduction. Both of these deductions will be discussed in further detail in Chapter 10.

— NOTE TO SOLUTION

(1) His cost is determined as the exercise price ($10) plus an addition to his cost base of the amount per share ($5) included in employment income under section 7. Both of these amounts represent tax-paid dollars which, by their inclusion in the cost base, will not be taxed further on disposition.

Valuation of Shares

There is usually little difficulty in establishing the value of shares which are traded regularly as would be the case with shares in a public company. However, establishing the value of shares where there is no listing or open market is more difficult. In recent years, comprehensive methods of determining the value of such shares have been used. For the CRA's approach to valuations of this nature refer to Information Circular 89-3.

III. DEDUCTIONS FROM EMPLOYMENT INCOME

Subsection 8(1) lists all of the deductions that may be claimed in computing income from an office or employment. Subsection 8(2) specifically limits deductions from employment income to those specified in section 8. To qualify for these deductions, the provisions must be strictly adhered to. Note that the preamble to subsection 8(1) restricts these deductions to expenses which relate in some manner to the earning of employment income.

At this point, it should also be noted that section 67 imposes a general limitation on the deductibility of expenses in computing income under Division B from any source. To be deductible by this provision, the amount of the expenditure must be "reasonable in the circumstances". What is reasonable in the circumstances depends on the particular facts of a situation and may be determined by reference to a standard, such as an industry average or a previously accepted historical average, among others. Another general limitation that applies, notwithstanding the deductibility of an expense under a specific provision, is found in subsection 67.5(1), which denies the deduction of an expense incurred to commit an offence under specified sections of the *Criminal Code*.

A. Sales/Negotiating Person's Expenses

[ITA: 8(1)(*f*); IT-522R]

Paragraph 8(1)(*f*) allows the deduction of expenses incurred for the purpose of earning income from employment for employees who sell property or negotiate contracts. The nature or type of the expenses is not restricted, unlike for other employees, except for expenses of a capital nature [spar. 8(1)(*f*)(v)][(r)]. Of course, these expenditures are subject to the general restrictions, just discussed, and a number of specific restrictions and/or exceptions. For example, paragraph 18(1)(*l*), which is one of those

---

[(r)] In the case of *Gifford v. The Queen* (SCC, 2004 DTC 6120), the issues were:

(i) whether the payment made by an employee to a former employee for a client list was a deductible current expense under paragraph 8(1)(*f*) or a non-deductible capital outlay under subparagraph 8(1)(*f*)(v) and

(ii) whether interest on funds borrowed to buy the list was also deductible under paragraph 8(1)(*f*) or non-deductible under subparagraph 8(1)(*f*)(v).

Both payments were held to be "on account of capital" and, hence, were prevented by subparagraph 8(1)(f)(v) from being deducted.

restrictions specified in subparagraph 8(1)(*f*)(vi), prohibits expenditures in respect of the use of a yacht, camp, lodge, golf course, and membership fees in private clubs.

Also excepted by subparagraph 8(1)(*f*)(vii) are payments to reimburse the employer for the personal use of an employer provided automobile, since these payments reduce the previously-included benefit [par. 6(1)(*e*)]. The expenses claimed must be substantiated by vouchers or other records. However, the amount of expenses that can be deducted is limited to the amount of the employee's commission income or other amounts, that are fixed by reference to the volume of sales or contracts negotiated.

Note the conditions in the provision that must be met for the expenses to be deductible.

- Subparagraph 8(1)(*f*)(i) requires that the employee be required to pay his or her own expenses as stipulated in the contract of employment.[s]

- Subparagraph 8(1)(*f*)(ii) requires that the employee be ordinarily required to travel away from the employer's place of business.[t]

- Subparagraph 8(1)(*f*)(iii) requires that the remuneration be dependent on volume of sales or contracts.[u]

- Subparagraph 8(1)(*f*)(iv) requires that a non-taxable allowance cannot be received, if a deduction under paragraph 8(1)(*f*) is to apply.

If the allowance [spar. 6(1)(*b*)(v)] is not reasonable, then the sales/negotiating person must include the allowance in income. An unreasonable allowance is one that is less than a reasonable amount, greater than a reasonable amount, or deemed not to be reasonable. He or she may then deduct the expenses [par. 8(1)(*f*)], since the employee would not be in receipt of an *excluded* allowance in such circumstances.

The relationship between car allowances and car expenses for sales/negotiating persons and other employees is discussed later in the chapter. Other expenses for sales/negotiating persons will be discussed in more detail in Chapter 4, where comparisons with self-employed salespersons are made.

B. Travelling Expenses other than Motor Vehicle Expenses

[ITA: 8(1)(*h*), 8(4), (10); 81(3.1); IT-518R; IT-522R]

1. Overview

The travelling expenses of employees who are not involved in the selling of property or negotiating of contracts are deductible under one of two provisions in subsection 8(1). Paragraph 8(1)(*h*) allows the deduction of travelling expenses other than motor vehicle expenses. Paragraph 8(1)(*h*.1), which will be discussed later in this chapter, pertains to motor vehicle expenses. Two separate provisions are used for reasons which will become apparent after the conditions for these deductions are explored.

Deductible travelling expenses are not restricted as to type of employee or employer under paragraph 8(1)(*h*). However, three specific conditions must be met to obtain the deduction for an expenditure. Many case situations, discussed below, involve an attempt to deduct expenses for travel between an employee's home and his or her place of work. These are not deductible travelling expenses, but personal or living

---

[s] See two Federal Court of Appeal cases: *The Queen v. Moore*, (F.C.A.) 90 DTC 6200 and *The Queen v. Betz*, (F.C.A.) 90 DTC 6201. In these decisions, the Court expanded the concept of a contractual obligation to include unwritten conditions which would result in an unfavourable performance assessment.

[t] *Healy v. The Queen*, (F.C.A.) 78 DTC 6239.

[u] *Neville v. M.N.R.*, (T.C.C.) 88 DTC 1546. A payment that was made as a percent of an employer's gross profit was held not to be an amount based on volume of sales in *Griesbach v. MNR* (TCC), 91 DTC 142.

expenses, unless the travel expenses are incurred between home and worksites away from the employee's usual place of work.[v] The reasonableness of the expenditures and the need for adequate record-keeping to substantiate the deduction were at issue in other court decisions.[w]

2. Conditions

The first condition imposed in subparagraph 8(1)(h)(i) is that the employee must ordinarily be required to carry out his or her duties away from his or her employer's place of business. The CRA's interpretation of the word "ordinarily", in this paragraph only, is habitually or customarily. However, there should be some degree of regularity in the required travelling [IT-522R, par. 32].[x]

The second condition, in subparagraph 8(1)(h)(ii), requires that the payment of the travelling expenses by the employee must be part of his or her contract. The contract can be either in a written or oral form, but the latter may be harder to prove in a court of law. There have been several court cases involving this issue.[y]

The condition in subparagraph 8(1)(h)(iii) is that the employee cannot be in receipt of a tax-exempt allowance for travelling expenses under subparagraph 6(1)(b)(v), (vi) or (vii) which exclude the allowance if it is reasonable. Therefore, employees who have received an allowance that is greater or less than a reasonable amount can include the allowance in income and can deduct the related expenses, because they would not be in receipt of an excluded (reasonable) allowance in such circumstances. Whether an allowance is reasonable depends upon *all* the facts in a particular circumstance.

Note that the receipt of an excluded allowance for employment use of a motor vehicle under subparagraph 6(1)(b)(vii.1) precludes the deduction under paragraph 8(1)(h.1) of motor vehicle expenses, but does not preclude the deduction under paragraph 8(1)(h) of more general travelling expenses. This is likely the reason for the existence of the two separate deduction provisions in paragraphs 8(1)(h) and (h.1). The receipt of an excluded (reasonable) allowance for one type of travelling expense does not preclude the deduction of the other type of travelling expense.

Subsection 8(10) requires that employees who make deductions under paragraph 8(1)(f), (h) or (h.1) and subparagraph 8(1)(i)(ii) or (iii) (office rent and supplies which are discussed in the next section) must file a prescribed form (T2200) signed by their employers certifying that the conditions set out in these provisions were met in the year. However, it appears that the CRA has simplified the administration of the application of some of the conditions in these provisions. For example, IT-522R paragraph 33 indicates that, as long as the form T2200 is completed properly by the employer, then the requirement that there must be a contractual arrangement stipulating that the employee must pay for the travelling expenses will be met. Also this Interpretation Bulletin indicates in paragraph 58 that form T2200 should be kept with the taxpayer's records for examination on request. Thus, the form is not required to be filed with the tax return.

---

[v] The following cases resulted in a decision for personal or living expenses: *Martyn v. M.N.R.*, (T.A.B.) 62 DTC 341; *Luks v. M.N.R.*, (Ex. Ct.) 58 DTC 1194; *Wilkinson v. M.N.R.*, (T.A.B.) 66 DTC 344; and *Carson v. M.N.R.*, (T.A.B.) 66 DTC 424. On the other hand, in *The Queen v. Merten* (FCTD), 90 DTC 6600, the taxpayer was allowed to deduct expenses to travel to worksites away from his usual place of work.

[w] *No. 589 v. M.N.R.*, (T.A.B.) 59 DTC 41, *Niessen v. M.N.R.*, (T.A.B.) 60 DTC 489 and *Winter v. MNR* (TCC) 88 DTC 1143.

[x] The interpretation of the word "ordinarily" was at issue in the cases of *Krieger v. M.N.R.*, (T.R.B.) 79 DTC 269, *The Queen v. Patterson*, (F.C.T.D.) 82 DTC 6326 and *Imray v. The Queen*, (FCTD) 98 DTC 6580.

[y] *The Queen v. Cival*, (F.C.A.) 83 DTC 5168; *Rozen v. The Queen*, (F.C.T.D.) 85 DTC 5611; and *Hoedel v. The Queen*, (F.C.A.) 86 DTC 6535.

3. Limitations

Subsection 8(4) restricts the deduction under paragraphs 8(1)(*f*) and (*h*) of the cost of meals consumed while travelling for an employer. These costs are deductible only where the meal is consumed when the taxpayer is away, for twelve hours or more, from the municipality or metropolitan area where he or she usually reports for work.[(z)]

Section 67.1, located in Subdivision f "Rules Relating to Computation of Income", limits the deduction for the cost of meals consumed and entertainment to 50% of the lesser of the amount paid or payable and a reasonable amount. There are a number of exceptions to these restrictions for meal expenses, as described in some detail in IT-518R:

- moving expenses [sec. 62] (see Chapter 9);

- child-care expenses [sec. 63] (see Chapter 9);

- medical expenses which qualify for non-refundable credit [sec. 118.2] (see Chapter 10);

- the specific products and services of taxpayers who are in the business of providing meals and entertainment;

- meals provided where the primary purpose is for fund-raising for a registered charity;

- reasonable reimbursements to the employer;

- exempted amounts under subparagraph 6(6)(*a*)(ii);

- the cost of meals and entertainment at special and remote work sites [spar. 6(6)(*a*)(i)], subject to some additional restrictions [par.67.1(2)(*e*)]; and

- meals and entertainment, at up to six special events generally available to all employees at the particular place of business.

4. Receipts by part-time employees for travelling expenses

Personal travelling expenses of part-time employees are not deductible under the normal rules in section 8. However, where an individual receives an allowance for or a reimbursement of travelling expenses, the receipts are treated as income which is exempt from tax under subsection 81(3.1) found in Subdivision g — "Amounts Not Included in Income". There are several tests which must be met in order to have these travelling expenses qualify for this provision:

(a) the part-time employee must have other employment or business income;

(b) the amount received cannot exceed a reasonable amount and the travelling expenses must be in respect of travelling only to and from the part-time employment, not travelling expenses incurred *during* the part-time employment; and

(c) the part-time employment location must be at least 80 kilometres away from both the employee's ordinary place of residence and his or her principal place of business or employment.

Condition (a), above, is waived [spar. 81(3.1)(*a*)(ii)] for individuals who are employed part-time as professors or teachers by designated educational institutions [ssec. 118.6(1)]. The purpose of this exception is to facilitate the recruiting of part-time instructors by universities and other educational institutions outside major metropolitan areas.

[(z)] See the case of *Krieger v. M.N.R.*, (T.R.B.) 79 DTC 269.

C. Other Expenses

[ITA: 8(1)(*b*), (*i*), (*l*.1), (5), (10), (13); IT-103R; IT-158R2; IT-352R2; IT-514]

1. Legal expenses

Paragraph 8(1)(*b*) permits the deduction of certain legal expenses incurred by employees. The expenses are limited to those incurred to collect or establish a right to remuneration owed to the employee by an employer or former employer. [The February 27, 2004 Draft Legislation proposed to extend this deduction to amounts not owed to the employee directly by the employer, if the amounts, when received, would be taxable as employment income. For example, legal fees incurred by an employee to collect insurance benefits under a sickness or accident insurance policy provided through an employer would be deductible.]

2. Dues and other expenses[(aa)]

Deductible under paragraph 8(1)(*i*) are:

- annual professional membership dues paid to maintain standing in a profession recognized by statute;
- office rent paid or salary paid to an assistant;
- the cost of supplies paid; and
- annual union membership dues paid.

One of the requirements that must be met in order for an amount to be deductible is that it must be paid by the employee. However, an amount also qualifies for a deduction if the employer paid the amount and added it to the employee's income as a taxable benefit. [Proposed amendment in the February 27, 2004 Draft Legislation.]

There are a number of restrictions that are placed on these expenses [par. 8(1)(*i*)]:

(a) First, a limitation is placed on dues which prohibits the deduction of amounts that are not directly attributable to the ordinary operating expenses of the organization which is levying the dues [ssec. 8(5)].

(b) Second, there are the employment contract requirements placed on the amounts deductible for office rent or salary to an assistant [spar. 8(1)(*i*)(ii)] and for the cost of supplies [spar. 8(1)(*i*)(iii)].

(c) Finally, remember that the preamble to section 8 restricts deductions to those that are wholly applicable to that source. Hence, a professional accountant who teaches English literature in the secondary school system cannot deduct his or her accounting association dues [spar. 8(1)(*i*)(i)], but can deduct his or her teaching association dues [spar. 8(1)(*i*)(iv)].

As long as form T2200 is completed properly by the employer, it appears that the contractual requirement [spar. 8(1)(*i*)(ii) (rent and salary paid to an assistant) and spar. 8(1)(*i*)(iii) (supplies)] will be met through this certification procedure [par. 13 of IT-352R2]. The employer is required to certify by signing form T2200 that the employee was required to maintain an office away from the employer's place of business. Furthermore, IT-352R2 requires that the deductibility of these expenses, except union dues and professional fees, requires a contract of employment (written or "tacitly understood"), certified by the employer signing form T2200, to permit the deduction of office rent, supplies or salaries paid by the employee to an assistant or substitute.

[(aa)] The cases of *Daley v. M.N.R.*, (Ex. Ct.) 50 DTC 877 and *Montgomery, et. al. v. MNR* (FCA), 99 DTC 5186, deal with professional membership dues; the case of *The Queen v. Thompson*, (F.C.T.D.) 89 DTC 5439, deals with the controversial topic of imputed office rent expense; the case of *Felton v. M.N.R.*, (T.C.C.) 89 DTC 233, deals with deductibility of home office expenses generally; and the cases of *Luks v. M.N.R.*, (Ex. Ct.) 58 DTC 1194 and *Thibault v. MNR* (TCC), 86 DTC 1538, deal with the meaning of "supplies".

3. Work space in home

Subsection 8(13) provides restrictions on the deductibility of expenses related to work space in the home for employees. This provision parallels the rules for self-employed individuals [ssec. 18(12)] as discussed in IT-514. The provision only applies to individuals who are entitled to deductions under paragraph 8(1)(*f*) for sales expenses or under paragraph 8(1)(*i*)] for rent or supplies related to a work space in a home. The effect of the provision is twofold. A deduction is then only permitted if the work space is:

    (a) the place where the individual *principally* (more than 50% of the time [par. 2 of IT-352R2]) performs the employment duties; or

    (b) (i) used *exclusively* for the purpose of earning employment income during the period, and

        (ii) used on a regular and continuous basis for meeting customers or other persons in the ordinary course of performing the employment duties.

As long as more than 50% of the employment duties are performed in the home work space, then test (a) above has been met and test (b) above can be ignored. Where test (a) is not met, then the exclusive condition in test (b)(i) above must be met. The word "exclusively" is not defined in the Act. *Webster's English Dictionary* defines "exclusively" as "to the exclusion of all others" which is a much more onerous test.

Once one of the conditions in (a) or (b) above has been met in the year of the expenditure, then the work space deduction is restricted to employment-source income. However, there is an indefinite carry-forward provision as long as the employee can meet either test (a) or (b) above in the future year of deduction [par. 3 of IT-352R2].

Supplies related to a work space in the home [par. 5 of IT-352R2] include expenses paid for the maintenance of the home such as the cost of fuel, electricity, light bulbs, cleaning materials and minor repairs. For an eligible individual, property taxes and insurance paid on a home owned by the individual are deductible [par. 8(1)(*f*)]. All of these expenses must be allocated between the work space and the personal space of the home on a reasonable basis such as floor space.

4. CPP and EI premiums payable in respect of an assistant

Subparagraph 8(1)(*i*)(ii) permits the deduction of a salary paid by an employee to an assistant or substitute, if required by the contract of employment of the payer. Such payments may also require the payment of Canada Pension Plan or Employment Insurance premiums that are the responsibility of an employer. Amounts payable by an employee as premiums for CPP and EI in respect of an assistant are deductible [par. 8(1)(*l*.1)].

D. Registered Pension Plans

[ITA: 8(1)(*m*); 147.2(4); IT-167R6]

1. Overview

There are two different types of registered pension plans (RPPs): defined benefit and money purchase (defined contribution). Defined benefit plans guarantee a predetermined amount of retirement income based on a flat amount per year of service or a percentage of the employee's earnings over a defined period. The defined benefit RPPs are funded by actuarially-determined contributions by the employee and/or employer. Money-purchase RPPs provide whatever pension income that the contributed funds in the plan can purchase through the acquisition of an annuity. No predetermined amount of pension income is guaranteed under a money-purchase plan. Benefits will depend upon the actual contributions, the investment return of the plan and annuity rates at the date of purchase.

The major objective of pension reform, which became effective for years after 1990, was to eliminate the discrepancies among the various tax-assisted retirement plans by imposing a comprehensive single limit of 18% of employee earnings for all employee and/or employer contributions to registered pension plans (defined benefit and defined contribution), registered retirement savings plans (RRSPs) and deferred profit sharing plans (DPSPs).

Total annual comprehensive dollar limits for money-purchase RPPs for employer and/or employee contributions are set at the following amounts:

2004	2005	2006	2007	2008	2009	2010
$16,500	$18,000	$19,000	$20,000	$21,000	$22,000	indexed

The dollar limits for 2006 to 2009 will be increased to the greater of the dollar limits shown above and $18,000 indexed after 2006. After 2009, the maximum amount of $22,000 will be indexed with the increase in the average wage. Contribution limits for RRSPs, which are discussed in detail in Chapter 9, will reflect benefits accruing under defined benefit RPPs and contributions to money-purchase RPPs and DPSPs.

Defined benefit plans also have contribution limits for employees and employers; however, the limits that are imposed are set in terms of the maximum pension which can be received on retirement. Contributions to fund the pension are then actuarially determined. Generally speaking, the maximum defined benefit is calculated as 2% of the employee's income, usually an average of the highest income level for 3 to 7 years, times the number of years of service to a maximum of 70%.

However, under the definition of "defined benefit limit" in regulation 8500(1), there is an additional cap to the maximum pension per year of service equal to the greater of $1,722.22 ($15,500/9) and $1/9$ of the money purchase limit for the year. This cap also translates into an upper pension income limit of the equivalent of 35 years of service of $60,278 ($1,722.22 x 35 years). The employment income needed to contribute $15,500 is $86,111 ($15,500/18%). The following table shows these changes.

Year	Money Purchase Limit	Maximum Pension Per year of Service	Maximum Pension (35 yrs)	Employment Income Needed
2004........	$16,500	$1,833	$64,155	$ 91,667
2005........	$18,000	·$2,000	$70,000	$100,000
2006........	$19,000	$2,111	$73,885	$105,550
2007........	$20,000	$2,222	$77,770	$111,100
2008........	$21,000	$2,333	$81,655	$116,650
2009........	$22,000	$2,444	$85,540	$122,200
2010........	indexed	indexed	indexed	indexed

Limits for a combination of defined benefit plans and money-purchase plans are also provided in the law. However, these rules are extremely complex and require the services of a specialist in the area.

Paragraph 8(1)(*m*) provides the statutory authority for an employment deduction in respect of registered pension plans, but only as determined by subsection 147.2(4), which is found under Division G, "Deferred and Other Special Income Arrangements".

A defined benefit RPP must meet the conditions described above and others in order to be "registered". Meeting the conditions implies that the contributions made by an employee, in whatever amount acceptable under the registration conditions, are deductible by the employee [par. 8(1)(*m*)]. On the other hand, deductible contributions to a money-purchase RPP are restricted annually by the comprehensive dollar limit discussed above.

2. Deductions for post-1989 service contributions

Paragraph 147.2(4)(*a*) allows an individual, when computing his or her income for *a taxation year ending after 1990*, to deduct a contribution *made in the year* to a registered pension plan *in respect of years of service after 1989*, to the extent that the contribution was made in accordance with the terms of the plan as registered with the CRA. Therefore, for years of service after 1989, catch-up contributions can be made in subsequent years for a particular year of service where the individual has not contributed the maximum amount permitted by the terms of the plan. There are a number of supporting provisions and regulations which prescribe these registration requirements; however, they are far beyond the scope of an introductory coverage.

IV. CAR ALLOWANCES AND EXPENSES

The focus of this part of the chapter is on cars that are either owned or leased by employees and used for employment purposes. Provisions pertaining to employer-provided cars were discussed previously in this chapter. Provisions pertaining to capital cost allowance restrictions will be discussed in Chapter 5.

Several definitions in respect of cars can be found in subsection 248(1) and are briefly *summarized* below:

(a) Motor vehicle — an automotive vehicle (undefined) designed to be used on highways and streets but not trolley buses or vehicles on rails.

(b) Automobile — a motor vehicle designed to carry up to nine individuals plus baggage, including vans, certain pick-up trucks and station wagons but excluding ambulances, taxis, hearses, vehicle inventory and clearly marked fire department, police [or Emergency Medical Services (EMS)] vehicles.

(c) Passenger vehicle — an automobile acquired or leased after June 17, 1987.

It is important to determine which of the above definitions is being referred to. For example, paragraph 6(1)(*b*) refers to a motor vehicle; subsection 6(2) refers to an automobile; and section 67.2 (discussed below) refers to a passenger vehicle.

A. Motor Vehicle Allowances Received from Employers

[ITA: 6(1)(*b*)(v), (vii), (vii.1), (x), (xi); ITR: 7306; IT-522R]

1. Overview

As previously discussed, all allowances received by employees are included in income [par. 6(1)(*b*)] with specified exceptions. Two of these exceptions were explained previously: subparagraph 6(1)(*b*)(v) in respect of *all* allowances pertaining to salespersons and persons who negotiate contracts, and subparagraph 6(1)(*b*)(vii) in respect of allowances, except motor vehicle allowances, for all other employees. Note that the motor vehicle allowance rules are separate in subparagraph 6(1)(*b*)(vii.1) for ordinary employees, but included in subparagraph 6(1)(*b*)(v) for sales/negotiating persons. The reason for the distinction is that subparagraph 6(1)(*b*)(vii) allowances for travelling, other than for motor vehicle expenses, have a territorial restriction and are limited to travel away from the municipality and metropolitan area of the employer's establishment. However, subparagraphs 6(1)(*b*)(v) and 6(1)(*b*)(vii.1), as discussed next, do not have this territorial restriction.

2. Conditions of subparagraph 6(1)(*b*)(vii.1) and interpretation

Subparagraph 6(1)(*b*)(vii.1) sets out the initial conditions for exempting motor vehicle allowances for employees, other than those who are salespersons or who negotiate contracts. The conditions for exemption are:

(a) the allowances must be reasonable in the circumstances (therefore, motor vehicle allowances which are not reasonable, i.e., less than a reasonable amount, greater than a reasonable amount, or deemed not to be reasonable (as discussed below), must be included in income); and

(b) the allowances must be in respect of travelling in the performance of the duties of an office or employment.

IT-522R "Vehicle and other travelling expenses — Employees" makes some important administrative comments on the application of subparagraph 6(1)(*b*)(vii.1). First, in paragraph 44, where an employee receives a set periodic amount (i.e., monthly, weekly, etc.) the amount will be considered to be an excluded advance (prepaid reimbursement) rather than a potentially excludable allowance where:

(a) there is a beginning-of-the-year agreement between the employee and employer that the employee will receive a stated amount per kilometre for business-related travelling;

(b) there is a year-end accounting for any difference between the advances and the actual business-related kilometres; and

(c) the amounts above are reasonable.

Paragraph 43 indicates that the CRA will, as a general rule, consider the kilometre allowances permitted as deductions for *employers* in Regulation 7306 as reasonable allowances. These amounts, generally, are 45¢ (for 2005) on the first 5,000 kilometres and 39¢ (for 2005) on the remaining kilometres.[ab] (See Chapter 4 for further comments on these amounts.) However, at the same time, the Department acknowledges that reasonableness of an allowance is normally decided based on the particular fact situation.

[ab] Department of Finance News Release, (2004-081), December 17, 2004.

3. Allowance deemed not to be reasonable

Two additional subparagraphs and the preamble thereto (which appears after subparagraph 6(1)(*b*)(ix)) modify and restrict the exclusion from income of certain motor vehicle allowances. The preamble to subparagraphs 6(1)(*b*)(x) and (xi) deems the allowance received "not to be a reasonable allowance" where:

- the motor vehicle allowance is not based solely on kilometres in respect of use for the employer's business [spar. 6(1)(*b*)(x)], or

- both an allowance and a reimbursement, in whole or in part for expenses in respect of that use, are received. Excepted is the reimbursement of expenses for supplementary business insurance, toll and ferry charges [spar. 6(1)(*b*)(xi)].

Whether an allowance is excluded from employment income based on the reasonableness test is critical in determining the deductibility of expenses by the employee. As has been discussed previously in this chapter, a reasonable allowance that must be excluded from income precludes the deduction of expenses for which the allowance is received.

Subparagraph 6(1)(*b*)(x) deems an allowance to be unreasonable and, therefore, included in income, if it is received for the use of a motor vehicle and is not based solely on the number of kilometres driven for employment purposes.

The CRA has indicated that, if the employer pays an employee both a flat-rate allowance and a per-kilometre allowance for the same use of the automobile, the whole amount is deemed to be one allowance that is taxable, since it is not based solely on the number of kilometers driven. If an employee received a flat monthly rate for fixed expenses plus a reasonable per-kilometre rate then the CRA considers the two allowances to be for the same use and combines them. They have indicated that the two allowances can be separated, if the employer pays a reasonable per-kilometre rate for travel outside the employment area and a flat monthly rate for travel inside the employment area. In this case, the two amounts are not for the same use and the per-kilometre allowance, in this case, would not be taxable, but the flat-rate allowance would be.

B. Expenses

[ITA: 8(1)(*h*), (*h*.1), (*j*), (9); 13(7)(*g*), (*h*); 67.2; 67.3; 80.4; 80.5; ITR: 7307; IT-522R]

1. Overview

Paragraph 8(1)(*h*.1) carves out motor vehicle expenses from general travelling expenses for ordinary employees under paragraph 8(1)(*h*). Motor vehicle expenses for salespersons and negotiating persons (persons who negotiate contracts and who have commission income or income based on volume of sales) still remain deductible [par. 8(1)(*f*)]. The conditions for and issues arising from this paragraph parallel paragraph 8(1)(*h*). Refer to Exhibit 3-1 which summarizes and compares all employee deductions under paragraphs 8(1)(*f*), (*h*) and (*h*.1).

EXHIBIT 3-1
Comparison of Employee Deduction Provisions

Conditions	*Par. 8(1)(f)* *sales/negotiating person's expenses*	*Par. 8(1)(h)* *travelling expenses*	*Par. 8(1)(h.1)* *motor vehicle travelling expenses*
Nature of employment	the taxpayer was employed in the year in connection with the selling of property or the negotiating of contracts for the employer	no restrictions	no restrictions
General type of expenditure	amounts expended by the taxpayer in the year for the purpose of earning income from the employment	amounts expended by the taxpayer in the year for travelling in the course of the taxpayer's employment	amounts expended by the taxpayer in the year in respect of motor vehicle expenses incurred for travelling in the course of employment
Conditions of employment			
Contract*	under the contract of employment was required to pay the taxpayer's own expenses	under the contract of employment was required to pay the travelling expenses incurred by the taxpayer in the performance of the duties of the office or employment	was required under the contract of employment to pay the motor vehicle expenses incurred in the performance of the duties of the office or employment
Duties	was ordinarily required to carry on the duties of employment away from the employer's place of business	was ordinarily required to carry on the duties of the employment away from the employer's place of business or in different places	was ordinarily required to carry on the duties of the employment away from the employer's place of business or in different places
Limits	was remunerated in whole or part by commission or other similar amounts fixed by reference to the volume of the sales made or the contracts negotiated	did not claim a deduction in the year under par. 8(1)(e), (f), or (g)	did not claim a deduction for the year under par. 8(1)(f)
Allowances	was not in receipt of an allowance for travelling expenses in respect of the taxation year that was, by virtue of spar. 6(1)(b)(v), not included in computing his or her income	did not receive an allowance for travelling expenses that was, by reason of spar. 6(1)(b)(v), (vi) or (vii), not included in computing the taxpayer's income for the year	did not receive an allowance for motor vehicle expenses that was, by reason of par. 6(1)(b), not included in computing the taxpayer's income for the year

Conditions	Par. 8(1)(f) sales/negotiating person's expenses	Par. 8(1)(h) travelling expenses	Par. 8(1)(h.1) motor vehicle travelling expenses
Restrictions on type of expenditure**			
Capital outlay....	not outlays, losses, or replacements of capital or payments on account of capital except interest and capital cost allowances described in par. 8(1)(j)	travelling expenses*** other than motor vehicle expenses and capital expenditures	motor vehicle expenses incurred for travelling other than capital expenditures except interest and capital cost allowances described in par. 8(1)(j)
Club dues	not outlays or expenses that would, by virtue of par. 18(1)(l), not be deductible in computing the income for the year if the employment were a business carried on by the taxpayer		
Standby payments	not amounts the payment of which reduced the amount that would otherwise be included in computing the taxpayer's income for the year by reason of par. 6(1)(e)		
Restrictions on amounts of deductible expenditures	not exceeding the commissions or other amounts fixed by reference to the volume of sales made or the contracts negotiated, amounts in respect of the workspace in the home of the individual that meets the conditions set out in spar. 8(13)(a)(i) or (ii) cannot exceed the individual's income for the year from the office or employment computed without reference to any deduction in respect of the workspace	no restrictions	no restrictions

* Subject to the requirements in subsection 8(10) for the filing of form T2200.
** Subsection 8(4) and section 67.1 restrict deductions for meal expenditures.
*** Includes expenses of employee-owned aircraft as well as interest and capital cost allowance on such aircraft as allowed by paragraph 8(1)(j), subject to the limitation in subsection 8(9).

Source: Reproduced with the permission of the Canadian Tax Foundation from, Robert E. Beam and Stanley N. Laiken, "Employee Deductions", Personal Tax Planning Feature (1991), Vol. 39, No. 2 *Canadian Tax Journal*, pp. 338–71, at pp. 340–42, Table 1.

A series of provisions which modify, limit or depend upon paragraphs 8(1)(f), (h) and (h.1) is presented, followed by examples which apply these rules as they pertain to cars.

2. Motor vehicle and aircraft costs

Paragraph 8(1)(j) is the statutory authority to permit the deduction of certain expenses which are, in essence, capital in nature; namely, interest on loans and the depreciation for tax purposes (i.e., capital cost allowance) in respect of motor vehicles and aircraft. A deduction is only available under paragraph 8(1)(j) where an employee may deduct expenditures under paragraph 8(1)(f), (h) or (h.1). Hence, it is critical to establish that the employee was not in receipt of a tax-exempt allowance that would preclude a deduction of expenses under paragraph 8(1)(f), (h) or (h.1). In the case of a sales/negotiating person claiming a deduction under paragraph 8(1)(f), the paragraph 8(1)(j) deduction is not restricted to the amount of commission income or similar amounts received. These deductions for interest and capital cost allowance are further restricted as explained below.

Capital cost allowance will be discussed in some detail in Chapter 5. However, at this stage, all that has to be understood is that accounting depreciation and capital cost allowance (CCA) are quite similar. The major exception is that in respect of depreciable capital properties that are motor vehicles and aircraft the maximum deduction *must* be based on the declining balance method (30% for motor vehicles and 40% for aircraft) and that in the year of acquisition the rates are one-half of the normal rate.

Note that in the case of an aircraft, the use thereof must be *required* for employment purposes. However, a motor vehicle need only be *used* for employment purposes to qualify for a deduction. In addition, subsection 8(9) limits the deduction in respect of an aircraft to the amount that is reasonable in the circumstances in relation to the availability of other modes of transportation.

3. Imputed interest deemed paid

Subsection 6(9) deals with an employment income inclusion for a benefit obtained through a low-interest loan to an employee. These benefits are computed by virtue of subsections 80.4(1) and (3) to (7), as previously discussed in this chapter. Section 80.5 provides that this interest income inclusion in employment income, in respect of interest on funds borrowed to purchase a motor vehicle or aircraft, is *deemed* to be interest *paid*. Hence, this deemed interest payment is eligible for a deduction under paragraph 8(1)(j). Note that subparagraph 8(1)(j)(i) allows for the deduction of "any interest paid", which would include amounts "deemed to be interest paid" by virtue of section 80.5. This amount, however, must be prorated for employment kilometres driven or hours flown to arrive at the allowable deduction.

4. Interest on money borrowed for passenger vehicle

Section 67.2 limits the amount deductible in respect of interest on funds borrowed or debt incurred on the acquisition of a passenger vehicle to the lesser of:

(a) the actual amount payable (or paid, per IT-522R paragraph 28); and

(b) $300[(ac)] for each 30-day period that the automobile loan or debt was outstanding in the year [Reg. 7307(2)].

Note that there is no rounding of the number of periods to an equivalent number of months as there is in the standby charge rules. The resulting lesser amount is further prorated by the portion of employment use to the total use based on kilometres driven.

5. Capital cost for passenger vehicle

Paragraph 13(7)(g) and Regulation 7307(1) place limits on the capital cost of an automobile. The limits are set out Department of Finance News Release (2004-081) issued by Finance Canada on December 17, 2004 as follows:

Acquisition date	Maximum capital cost	Reference
After 2000	$30,000 plus PST and GST on the $30,000	Par. 13(7)(g)

[(ac)] Department of Finance News Release (2004-081), December 17, 2004.

Where the passenger vehicle is acquired from a person with whom the purchaser does not deal at arm's length (see subsection 251(1) for a definition of this term), the capital cost is deemed [par. 13(7)(*h*)] to be the least of:

(a) the fair market value;

(b) the undepreciated capital cost of the seller; and

(c) the dollar maximum found in the above summary.

6. Limitation re cost of leased passenger vehicle

Section 67.3 and Regulation 7307 limit automobile leasing costs in a manner equivalent to the $30,000 capital cost restriction as described above. The following formula calculates the deductible portion of the leasing cost.

Lesser of:

(a) $$\left[\frac{A \times B}{30} \right] - C - D - E$$

(b) $$\left[\frac{F \times G}{.85H} \right] - D - E$$

where A is a dollar monthly maximum, as prescribed (and announced in the Department of Finance News Release, (2004-081), December 17, 2004) and reflected in the notes below*;

B is the aggregate of the number of days the vehicle was leased for all years to the end of the present year;

C is the aggregate of the lease costs deducted in all preceding years;

D is imputed interest, at the prescribed rate, on refundable amounts (e.g., deposits) over $1,000;

E is total reimbursements receivable in respect of the lease in the year;

F is the total lease charges payable (including PST and GST) for the year;

G is the dollar maximum capital cost prescribed**;

H is the greater of:

(a) a dollar maximum prescribed amount***, and

(b) the manufacturer's list price.

Date of lease contract	Maximum monthly deduction	Reference
After 2000	$800 plus PST and GST on the $800	Sec. 67.3 Reg. 7307(3)

** The rules are similar to the capital cost limitations described above. See Reg. 7307(1)(*b*)(iii).

*** Regulation 7307(4) calculates the appropriate number for years after 1997 by multiplying the capital cost maximum amount (see above) by $^{100}/_{85}$, i.e., $^{100}/_{85} \times$ [$30,000 $\times$ (1 + .08 + .07)] = $40,588, assuming a PST rate of 8%.

Note that there is no rounding of the 30-day periods in part (a) above as in subsection 6(2) pertaining to the standby charge.

Part (a) of the above formula provides a dollar limit, $800 (prescribed for years after 2000) plus PST and GST per month. Recognize, however, that a lease could be devised for almost any car, no matter how expensive, so that the monthly lease payments do not exceed that limit. To discourage this strategy, the further limit in part (b) of the formula was necessary. That part allows a fraction of the total lease charges as a maximum deduction. The fraction is based on the $30,000 maximum capital cost for capital cost allowance purposes for years after 2000, relative to 85% of the manufacturer's list price of the car. The higher the list price in the denominator of the fraction, the lower the value of the fraction and the lower the amount of lease payments that can be deducted.

Leasing a car involves paying for both the capital cost of the car consumed during the leasing period and an interest cost for spreading the payments over time. Therefore, the limit on the deduction of lease payments must provide for a limit equivalent to the limit on capital cost allowance and the limit on interest for a purchased car.

7. Summary of interplay among deduction provisions

The following diagram illustrates how the deduction provisions in paragraphs 8(1)(*f*), (*h*), (*h*.1), (*i*), and (*j*) are applied.

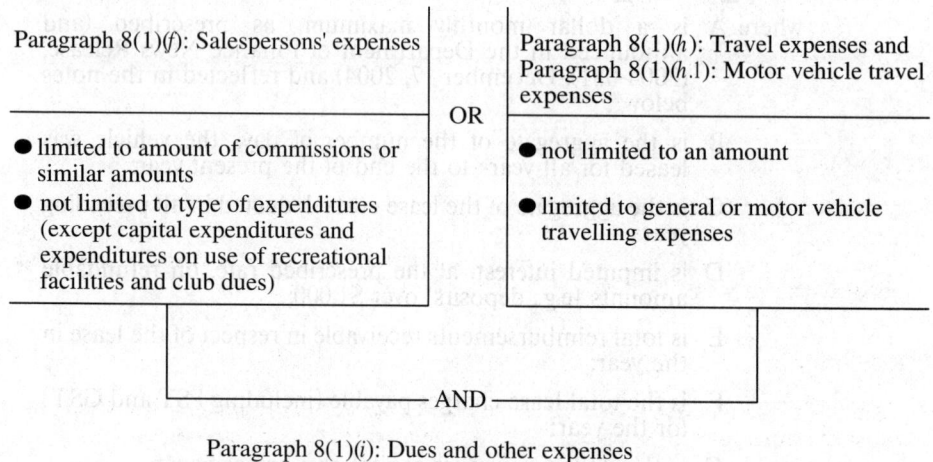

Where travel expenses, alone, exceed the amount of commissions or similar income, it is advantageous to use the deduction under paragraphs 8(1)(*h*) and (*h*.1), instead of paragraph 8(1)(*f*). Where a deduction is possible for an amount either under paragraph 8(1)(*f*) or paragraph 8(1)(*i*), it is better to deduct under paragraph 8(1)(*i*), which is not limited by commissions or similar income, to preserve deduction room under paragraph 8(1)(*f*).

C. Application of Rules

The following examples will demonstrate the rules for car allowances and expenses.

Example Problem 1

Mr. Alex Otto Deduckshun acquired an automobile on July 1, 2005, to be used in connection with his duties of employment. Alex is required by contract to use his own car and to pay directly all the expenses. Alex does not have any commission income. The following information, some of which is estimated, relates to the newly acquired car:

Cost of car (including PST and GST)	$38,000
Total kilometres driven in the ownership period	25,000
Total kilometres in respect of his employer's business	15,000
Capital cost allowance rate ($^1/_2 \times 30\%$)	15%
Interest paid on bank loan in respect of the car	$ 1,950
Gas and oil	1,800
Maintenance	300
Insurance	1,400
Licences	100

Alex lives in a province which has a sales tax of 10% on automobiles; therefore, the effective commodity tax rate would be 17% (10% + 7%).

— REQUIRED

Determine the amount deductible in respect of the car under paragraph 8(1)(*h*.1) in the following situations, on the assumption that the above expenses were reasonable:

(A) no kilometre allowance was received;

(B) a reasonable allowance of 38¢ per kilometre in respect of employment driving was received;

(C) an unreasonable allowance of 5¢ per kilometre in respect of employment driving was received;

(D) a reasonable allowance of 25¢ per kilometre in respect of employment driving plus a yearly allowance of $2,000 was received;

(E) an unreasonable allowance of $1 per kilometre in respect of employment driving was received.

— SOLUTION

Potentially deductible expenses (before prorating for employment use):

Capital cost allowance — par. 13(7)(*g*) limit:

($^1/_2 \times 30\%$) × ($30,000 × 1.17) $5,265

Interest expense — lesser of:

(a) $\underline{\$1,950}$ (actual)

(b) $\$300 \times \dfrac{184}{30} = \underline{\$1,840}$ 1,840

Gas and oil 1,800

Maintenance 300

Insurance 1,400

Licences 100

                                                              $\underline{\underline{\$10,705}}$

Portion relating to employment use:

$$\frac{15,000 \text{ km}}{25,000 \text{ km}} \times \$10,705 = \underline{\underline{\$6,423}}$$

Alternative Fact Situations:

(A) All of the $6,423 automobile expenses would be deductible [pars. 8(1)(*h*.1) and (*j*)], since all the conditions of these provisions have been met. The automobile is used in connection with his employment duties; there is a contractual obligation to use his own car and to pay directly all of the automobile expenses; a reasonable allowance had not been received; and he has not made a deduction under paragraph 8(1)(*f*) in respect of the automobile expenses.

(B) None of the $6,423 would be deductible [spar. 8(1)(*h*.1)(iii)], since subparagraph 6(1)(*b*)(vii.1) exempts reasonable allowances.

(C) Since the 5¢ per kilometre allowance is not a reasonable amount, Mr. Deduckshun must include the allowance in income and would be permitted the $6,423 deduction [pars. 8(1)(*h*.1) and 8(1)(*j*)].

(D) Although the combined package of the two allowances may be reasonable in the circumstances, subparagraph 6(1)(*b*)(x) deems the two allowances not to be a reasonable amount and, hence, taxable under subparagraph (vii.1), since one of the motor vehicle allowances received was not based solely on kilometres. Since these allowances are taxable, the $6,423 would be deductible.

(E) An unreasonable allowance of $1 per kilometre would be taxable [spar. 6(1)(*b*)(vii.1)], since the amount is in excess of a reasonable amount. Hence, the restricted expenses of $6,423 would be deductible.

Example Problem 2

Mr. Jonathan is required by his contract of employment to use his own car in the performance of his employment duties and to pay for all expenses. Mr. Jonathan leased a BMW from Expensive Cars Unlimited. The following facts relate to the leased car:

Lease period .... Jan. 1, 2005 to Dec. 31, 2006

Lease cost per month including GST and PST................. $ 800

Manufacturer's list price, excluding PST and GST.............. $50,000

Mr. Jonathan was not reimbursed for any portion of the lease cost. Mr. Jonathan lives in a province which has a sales tax of 8% and, therefore, would have an effective commodity tax rate of 15% on items subject to both GST and PST.

— *REQUIRED*

Determine the allowable lease cost which qualifies for a deduction under section 67.3 in 2005.

— SOLUTION

Lesser of:

(a) $\dfrac{(1.15 \times \$800) \times 365}{30} = \underline{\underline{\$11,193}}$

(b) $\dfrac{(\$800 \times 12) \times (\$30,000 \times 1.15)}{85\% \text{ of the greater of (i)} \atop \$40,588^1 \text{ and (ii) } \$50,000} = \underline{\underline{\$7,793}}$

Deduction of the lesser amount: $\underline{\underline{\$7,793}}$

— NOTE TO SOLUTION

(1) $\dfrac{100}{85} \times (\$30,000 \times 1.15)$

Example Problem 3 ——————————————————————

Ms. Elana is required by her contract of employment to use her own car in the performance of her employment duties and to pay for all expenses. Ms. Elana leased a Mercedes from Sky's The Limit Leasing. The following facts relate to the leased Mercedes:

Lease period	Oct. 1, 2003 to Sept. 30, 2006
Lease cost per month, including GST and PST	$ 1,600
Manufacturer's list price, excluding PST and GST	$60,000
Total kilometres	30,000
Total employment kilometres	20,000
Gas and oil	$ 1,500
Maintenance	700
Insurance	2,000
Licences	100

— REQUIRED

Determine the amount deductible in respect of the car for the year 2005 on the assumption that a total of $13,000 of leasing costs had been deducted *prior to* 2005. Assume a PST rate of 9% for an effective commodity tax rate of 16%. (Ignore the extra day in 2004 due to the leap year.)

— SOLUTION

Gas and oil	$ 1,500
Maintenance	700
Insurance	2,000
Licences	100

Leasing costs — lesser of:

(a) $\dfrac{(1.16 \times \$800) \times 822 \text{ days}^1}{30} - \$13,000 = \underline{\underline{\$12,427}}$

(b) $\dfrac{(12 \times \$1,600) \times (\$30,000 \times 1.16)}{85\% \text{ of the greater of (i) } \$40,941^2 = \underline{\underline{\$13,101}}}$
   and (ii) $60,000

$\left.\begin{array}{r}\end{array}\right\}$ 12,427

$\underline{\underline{\$16,727}}$

Portion relating to employment use:

$$\frac{20,000 \text{ km}}{30,000 \text{ km}} \times \$16,727 = \underline{\underline{\$11,151}}$$

— *NOTES TO SOLUTION*

(1) 92 days in 2003 + 365 days in 2004 + 365 days in 2005

(2) $(\$30,000 \times 1.16) \times \dfrac{100}{85} = \$40,941$

V. GST REBATE ON EMPLOYEE DEDUCTIONS

[ITA: 6(8); 8(11); 13(7.1); ETA: 123(1); 174; 253(1); Sch. V]

Employees, who are able to deduct GST-paid employment expenses, can obtain a refund of the GST component of these expenses in a similar manner to their employers who are registrants. Although the employee refund mechanism is quite different from the input tax credit system, the effect of this refund is quite similar.

As a general rule, employees do not have GST registration numbers and, hence, are not eligible for input tax credits. However, employees, who have deductible expenses for income tax purposes, may have paid GST on some of those expenses and should be eligible for some sort of refund mechanism. Therefore, in order to refund employees of registrants, other than financial institutions, who have paid GST on non-reimbursed expenses, a GST "rebate" system, as opposed to a GST "input tax credit" system, has been established. The following description is based on subsection 253(1) of the *Excise Tax Act* (ETA).

The GST rebate system is based on amounts which are deductible for income tax purposes under section 8 of the *Income Tax Act*. These deductible amounts will include both the PST and GST components. In the calendar year following the year in which the deduction is made, the employee is eligible to file a rebate application in prescribed form. The employee has four years from the end of the taxation year, in which the expense was claimed for income tax purposes, to apply for the rebate. The amount of GST rebate that is received is then required to be included in income in the year that it is received [par. 6(8)(c)]. This employment inclusion has the effect of offsetting the GST component of the expense deducted in a preceding year. The reason for this effect is that a rebate received in respect of an expense that has been deducted lowers the net cost and, hence, should lower the net deduction.

Subsection 8(11) provides that the goods and services tax rebate is not considered to be a reimbursement received by the taxpayer. As a result, the employee is allowed to deduct, in the year of payment, GST along with the expenses to which it attaches. In view of the required inclusion of the rebate [ssec. 6(8)], the rule in subsection 8(11) is needed to allow the deduction of GST which is ultimately offset by the inclusion.

The employee GST rebate is calculated as $7/107^{(ad)}$ times the amounts deducted for income tax purposes. An employee is not entitled to a GST rebate for expenses in respect of which the employee has received an allowance unless the employer certifies that it did not consider the allowance to be a reasonable allowance for the purposes of subparagraphs 6(1)(b)(v), (vi), (vii), or (vii.1) of the *Income Tax Act*. If the allowance was considered to be a reasonable allowance by the employer, it would have claimed the input tax credit pursuant to section 174 of the ETA. The certification precludes recovery of the GST by both the employer and the employee.

In the year in which the employee actually receives the rebate, there is an offsetting adjustment under the *Income Tax Act* for the GST component, if any, of the deductible expenses. Paragraph 6(8)(c) of the *Income Tax Act* includes in employment income the GST component of the deductible employment expenses of the preceding year, other than capital cost allowance. Paragraph 6(8)(d) deems that the GST component of the capital cost allowance, which is buried in the cost of the asset, is government assistance under subsection 13(7.1) and, thereby, reduces the capital cost of the respective automobile, aircraft or musical instrument.

Example Problem

Ms. G. S. Tax, an employee of Taxable Entity Ltd., which is a registrant for GST purposes, has supplied you with the following information concerning her employment income for 2005.

Ms. Tax uses her own car in the performance of her employment duties away from her employer's place of business and is required by her employment contract to pay for her travel expenses. She is not reimbursed for any of her travel expenses, but she does receive a kilometre allowance. Her employer will certify that it did not consider the allowance to be reasonable at the time it was paid. The example is based on the assumption that her automobile was purchased in early 2005 and was subject to GST.

The following information pertains to Ms. Tax's 2005 employment income as correctly prepared by her accountant. The amount of the expenses indicated reflect all pertinent income tax restrictions (e.g., the limit on capital cost of the automobile, 50% for meals and a proration of employment kilometres to total kilometres). The deductible expenses, where appropriate, include GST and PST, as indicated below.

Employment income

Inclusions:

Salary (see Note (1))	$85,000	
Car allowance (see Note (1))	3,000	
Premiums paid by Taxable Entity Ltd. for non-group disability insurance (see Note (2))	400	
Imputed interest on a car loan (see Note (2))	2,160	$ 90,560

Deductions:

Travel expenses:

Transportation, including PST of $240 and GST of $210	$ 3,550	
Accommodation, including PST of $400 and GST of $280	4,680	
Meals, including PST of $250 and GST of $175	2,925	(11,155)

[ad] 11% for purposes of the HST.

Automobile expenses:

Operating costs, including PST of $120 and GST of $105	$ 1,725	
Interest (see Note (2))	3,120	
Insurance and licence (see Note (2))	800	
Capital cost allowance (see Note (3))	2,000	(7,645)
Professional fees, including GST of $49 (see Note (4))		(749)
Employment income		$ 71,011

Notes

(1) Salary and car allowance are not subject to GST since the definition of property in the ETA under subsection 123(1) excludes money.

(2) Insurance, licence and interest are exempt supplies under Schedule V of the ETA.

(3) Capital cost allowance is not subject to GST or PST. However, there is a GST and PST component in the capital cost allowance claimed.

(4) Membership fees in professional organizations of which an employee must be a member to maintain a professional status recognized by statute, are exempt supplies [Schedule V, Part VI, par. 18 of the ETA]. However, an election is available to these organizations under this provision to deem these fees to be taxable supplies. This election would normally be made where the majority of the members can obtain a refund under either the input tax credit system or rebate system. In addition, the professional organization will also be able to claim an input tax credit on its acquisition of taxable supplies.

— *REQUIRED*

(A) Calculate the amount of GST rebate which Ms. Tax is entitled to receive in 2006.

(B) Indicate the income tax consequences of the GST rebate.

— *SOLUTION*

(A) Ms. Tax can apply for a GST rebate in 2006 based on her deductible expenses in 2005. This would normally be done on the filing of her 2005 income tax return. The amount of the rebate [ETA ssec. 253(1)] would be calculated as:

$7/_{107}$ of the sum of:

(a) Deductible expenses, including GST and PST

Transportation	$ 3,550
Accommodation	4,680
Meals	2,925
Automobile operating expenses	1,725
Professional fees	749
	$13,629

(b) Capital cost allowance......................................	2,000
	$15,629
(c) Less: any expenses for which a reasonable allowance was received...	Nil
	$15,629
$^7/_{107}$ thereof	$ 1,022

(B) On the assumption that Ms. Tax receives the GST rebate in 2006 she would make the following income tax adjustments in 2006:

Par. 6(8)(*c*) employment income inclusion

$$\frac{\$13,629}{\$15,629} \times \$1,022 = \underline{\underline{\$891}}$$

Par. 6(8)(*d*) capital cost reduction

$$\frac{\$2,000}{\$15,629} \times \$1,022 = \underline{\underline{\$131}}$$

VI. APPLICATION OF RULES UNDER SUBDIVISION "A"

The following illustration is a comprehensive example of how "employment income" is determined under Subdivision a of Division B. The solution is cross-referenced to the appropriate section in the Act [secs. 5, 6, 7, and 8]. Read carefully these cross-references and the supporting notes which highlight the key points in each related paragraph. However, note that the assignment problems may contain additional points not covered in this illustration.

Example Problem

Ms. Employee, who lives and works in Ontario, is employed as an internal auditor by Maxi Mumsales Ltd., a public corporation, for the calendar year 2005. She provides you with the following information concerning her receipts, taxable benefits, and expenditures:

Gross salary.....................................		$ 50,000
Income taxes withheld	$16,000	
CPP contributions (max. amount)	1,861	
EI contributions (max. amount)..................	761	
R.P.P. contributions (money purchase)	3,000	
United Way donation	100	
Reimbursement for use of company car and its operating costs.............................	300	(22,022)
Net salary		$ 27,978

Maxi Mumsales Ltd. pays the following amounts on behalf of Ms. Employee:

(A) Premiums for the following medical plans:

    (i) Drug plan — Sun Life .... $ 275

    (ii) Extended health care — Liberty Mutual 350

    (iii) Provincial health insurance plan premiums .... Nil

(B) Maxi Mumsales Ltd. provides Ms. Employee with a car to be used in connection with the duties of her employment. Ms. Employee uses the car 80% for employment and 20% for pleasure based on total kilometres for 2005 of 25,000.

The company paid the following automobile expenses:

    (i) Operating costs (including 8% PST and GST) $3,200

    (ii) Lease costs (including 8% PST of $313 and GST of $274) 4,500

(C) Ms. Employee, who must travel regularly away from her employer's place of business, receives a monthly allowance of $400 to cover her accommodation and meals while travelling. She is, however, required by her contract to pay for these expenses directly. Her actual expenses were $3,000, including PST of $209 and GST of $183, for meals and $4,000, including PST of $278 and GST of $243, for accommodation, all of which were reasonable in the circumstances.

Ms. Employee also supplies you with the following selected expenditures:

    (i) Registered retirement savings plan contributions $1,500

    (ii) Legal fees paid in collecting back pay from a former employer (including GST of $13) 200

    (iii) Professional accounting dues (including GST of $20) 300

— REQUIRED

(A) Calculate Ms. Employee's employment income for tax purposes for 2005 (as determined by Subdivision a of Division B of the Act).

(B) Compute the GST rebate that should be claimed and the income tax consequences of the rebate to be received in 2006.

— SOLUTION

(A) Employment income:

Reference			
Ssec. 5(1)	Salary[1]		$50,000
Par. 6(1)(a)	Provincial health insurance plan[2]		Nil
Par. 6(1)(e)	Standby charge[3]	$ 750	
Par. 6(1)(k)	Operating cost — car[4]	375	$1,125
	Less: payments to company	300	825
Spar. 6(1)(b)(vii)	Travel allowance[5]		4,800
			$55,625

	Less:		
Par. 8(1)(*b*)	Legal fees[6]	$ 200	
Par. 8(1)(*h*)	Travel expenses[7]	5,500	
Par. 8(1)(*i*)	Professional dues[8]	300	
Par. 8(1)(*m*)	R.P.P. contributions[9]	3,000	(9,000)
	Employment income — Subdivision a[10]		$46,625

(B) GST rebate income tax consequences:

(a) Rebate

7/107 of the sum of:

(i) Deductible expenses, including GST and PST:

Legal fees	$ 200
Travel expenses	5,500
Professional dues..	300
	$ 6,000

(ii) Capital cost allowance	Nil
	$ 6,000

(iii) Less any expenses for which a reasonable allowance was received	Nil
	$ 6,000

7/107 thereof	$ 393

(b) Income tax consequences

The GST rebate of $393 must be included in employment income in the year of receipt [par. 6(8)(*c*)]. Since no capital cost allowance was deducted, there will be no capital cost reduction component of the rebate.

—*NOTES TO SOLUTION*

(1) Section 5 refers to remuneration *received* in the calendar year only, but this does not mean that the net salary is the amount included in employment income. Subsection 153(3) deems that taxes withheld have been received at the time remuneration etc. was paid.

(2) Paragraph 6(1)(*a*) includes all benefits received or enjoyed through employment with certain specific exemptions which do not include public medical plan premiums paid by an employer. However, in Ontario, as in several other provinces, provincial medical plan premiums have been replaced by a health services tax based on total payroll; hence, there is no taxable benefit for individual employees.

(3) The standby charge will be computed as:

$$\frac{5,000 \text{ km}}{20,004 \text{ km}} \times (^2/_3 \times \$4,500) = \$750$$

Ms. Employee is entitled to the standby charge reduction, since she uses the car for business more than 50% of the total kilometres.

(4) Ms. Employee qualifies for the election method of determining a benefit derived from employer-paid automobile operating costs [spar. 6(1)(*k*)(iv)], since her employment-use is in excess of 50% of the total use. The operating costs under this election method would result in a reduced

income inclusion of $375 [20% × 25,000 km × $0.20= $1,000 under the kilometre alternative [spar. 6(1)(*k*)(v)] *vs.* (50% × $750) = $375].

(5) Allowances are dealt with in paragraph 6(1)(*b*) which includes all allowances in income with ten specific exceptions. Subparagraph 6(1)(*b*)(vii), which is applicable in this situation, applies to most employees, but not salespersons or persons who negotiate contracts, since there is a special provision for them [spar. 6(1)(*b*)(v)]. There are two specific conditions which must be met in order for the allowance not to be taxable. The first condition is that the allowance must be a reasonable amount. The second condition is that the employee must be travelling outside the metropolitan area where his or her employer is located.

On the assumption that Ms. Employee's travelling expenses were reasonable in the circumstances, the monthly allowance of $400 ($4,800 annually) was not a reasonable amount since the actual expenses were $7,000. Therefore, the allowance is a taxable allowance and she can claim her actual travel expenses [par. 8(1)(*h*)].

(6) Legal fees are deductible only if paid in the year.

(7) Ms. Employee can deduct her travelling expenses because she meets all the conditions of paragraph 8(1)(*h*). First, she must travel regularly away from her employer's place of business. Second, she is required by contract to pay for these expenses. Finally, she is not in receipt of an exempt allowance since the allowance which she receives is less than a reasonable amount and, as a result, has been included in income [spar. 6(1)(*b*)(vii)].

The deductible expenses are composed of:

Accommodation	$4,000
Meals and entertainment expenses (50% × $3,000)	1,500
	$5,500

Note how the determination of the reasonableness of the allowance was based on the full expenditures which were considered reasonable. The result was that the allowance was not reasonable and, hence, it was included in employment income. However, the meals expenditures were only 50% deductible.

(8) Professional dues are deductible only if the dues are for a profession recognized by statute and if the dues relate to the employment income as per the preamble to section 8.

(9) Registered pension plan: an employee is permitted to deduct, for tax purposes, his or her contributions to a money purchase registered pension plan to a maximum of $18,000 in 2005, but this amount is the maximum amount for the combined employee-employer contributions.

(10) Items excluded from computation:

(a) Employers' contributions to a private health plan, such as the drug and extended health care plans and provincial health service tax levies, are not taxable benefits under paragraph 6(1)(*a*).

(b) Registered retirement savings plan contributions are deducted under Subdivision e, not Subdivision a.

(c) Income tax is not deductible — subsection 8(2).

(d) United Way, a charitable donation, is not deductible under Division B.

(e) CPP contributions and EI premiums are eligible for non-refundable tax credits under Division E.

REVIEW QUESTIONS

(1) The best way to calculate employment income is to follow the format used on the personal tax return. Comment on the accuracy of this statement.

(2) It does not matter whether an individual is employed or self-employed since he or she can claim the same expenses under either category as long as the expense was incurred to earn income. Comment on the accuracy of this statement.

(3) If an individual fails any one of the tests which are used to determine employed vs. self-employed status then the individual is employed. Comment.

(4) When determining whether a person is employed or self-employed, one of the subtests used in the economic reality or entrepreneur test is the "control test". What does this test involve?

(5) When determining whether a person is employed or self-employed, one of the tests used is the "integration or organization test". What does this test involve?

(6) When determining whether a person is employed or self-employed, one of the tests used is the "specific result test". What does this test involve?

(7) If a bonus cheque is received by an employee, Ms. Defer, on December 15 of this year and she chooses not to cash her cheque until January 5 of next year, then she will be able to defer the tax on the bonus until the next year since individuals are taxed on the cash basis. Comment.

(8) If a bonus is payable to an employee, Mr. Later, on December 15 of this year and he decides that he wants to be taxed on the income in the following year instead of this year, then he can ask his employer to defer the payment of this bonus until next year and accomplish his goal. Comment.

(9) Employees are taxed on income from their employer to the extent that it is a gross payment before withholding tax or a taxable benefit. The employer can deduct, as an expense, the full amount of the gross payments before withholding tax and taxable benefits that are reported on the employee's T4. Comment.

(10) To maximize the after-tax income from a disability insurance policy to a disabled employee, the employer should not pay *any* of the premium for the coverage. Comment.

(11) On June 2 of this year, Opco loaned $10,000 to an employee and did not charge interest. The employee repaid the loan on June 30 of the same year. How many days are included for purposes of determining the deemed interest benefit under section 80.4?

(12) Explain the differences between a reimbursement and an allowance.

(13) Opco bought a new car for its owner-manager that cost the company $40,000 plus $3,200 for PST and $2,800 for GST. How much is the standby charge for this car for a full year assuming it is driven 40% for business purposes?

(14) What are the five conditions that must be met before a sales/negotiating person can deduct expenses?

(15) What are the four conditions that must be met by an employee, who is not a sales/negotiating person, in order to allow him or her to deduct travelling expenses other than car expenses?

(16) Mr. Tax O. N. Wheels is a part-time lecturer at the University of Waterloo. He lives in a location in Toronto which is 105 km away from the university. The rest of the time he has a tax consulting practice which he operates out of his home. The university pays him $0.37 per km to travel to and from the university. He is issued a T4 at the end of the year for his teaching income on the basis that he is a part-time employee. How is the travel allowance of $0.37 per km treated for tax purposes?

(17) Guidelines for the deductibility of expenses related to work space in the home for employees are included in subsection 8(13). Under paragraph (a) of this provision the expenses are allowed if one of two conditions are met. In these conditions, the words "principally" and "exclusively" are used. What do these words mean for tax purposes?

(18) Ms. Smith has come to you to ask your tax advice. She has just had a large bonus paid to her on December 31 and wants to defer some of it until next year. She is arguing that since the CRA's portion was not sent to the Receiver General until January 15 she should be able to defer that portion until the next year on the basis that it was not received until January 15 when it was sent to the CRA. What do you think?

MULTIPLE CHOICE QUESTIONS

Question 1

In 2005, Bob's employer provided him with an employer-owned automobile costing $34,500 (including GST of $2,100 and PST of $2,400) for 12 months. His kilometres for personal use were 15,000 out of a total of 20,000 kilometres. Operating costs paid by his employer during 2005 were $3,300 (including PST of $100 and GST of $200). Which one of the following statements is TRUE for 2005?

(A) Bob's minimum standby charge is $8,280.

(B) Bob's minimum operating cost benefit is $2,475.

(C) Bob's minimum operating cost benefit is $2,550.

(D) Bob can elect to use ½ of his standby charge as his operating cost benefit.

Question 2

In 2005, Mary earned a $50,000 annual salary as a computer repair person and received a car allowance of $3,500. The car allowance was paid to her monthly and was not based on the number of kilometres that she drove. Her employment-related expenses (all reasonable) were:

Automobile expenses (gas, parking, CCA)	$3,000
Entertainment	2,000

What is Mary's minimum employment income for 2005?

(A) $53,500

(B) $50,500

(C) $49,500

(D) $49,000

Question 3

Susanne Denholm is employed as a provincial payroll tax auditor and is required by contract to maintain an office in her home. Susanne works at home most of the time and has been provided with a laptop computer and a fireproof audit bag for her files. She has not been provided with any reimbursement or allowance in connection with her home office, which occupies 10% of the square footage of her home. She incurred the following costs to maintain her home in 2005:

Telephone (general line)	$ 600*
House insurance	2,000
Property taxes	4,000
Heat, hydro & maintenance	5,000
Mortgage interest	24,000

*Susanne estimates that she used her telephone 50% for employment purposes during the year.

What is the maximum amount that Susanne can claim for the costs she has incurred in respect of her home office?

(A) $500

(B) $1,100

(C) $1,400

(D) $3,800

Question 4

On April 1, 2002, E Ltd. made a loan of $100,000 to Mr. Walker, a new employee of the corporation, to assist him in purchasing a residence when he moved from Quebec to commence employment in British Columbia. The loan bears interest at 2%, which is to be paid monthly. The principal of the loan is to be repaid in full on April 1, 2012. The prescribed interest rate on April 1, 2002 was 4%. Assuming that the prescribed interest rate throughout 2005 was 3% and the interest owing on the loan is paid each month, which one of the following amounts represents the increase in Mr. Walker's employment income in 2005 due to the loan.

(A) $1,000

(B) $2,000

(C) $3,000

(D) $4,000

Question 5

Tanya, an employee of a Canadian public company received an option to purchase 1,000 common shares of her employer at $30 per share in March 2004, when the shares were worth $19 per share. In December 2004, when the fair market value was $40 per share, she exercised her options. In January 2005, she sold all the shares for $38 per share. Tanya wants to know what employee benefit she will have to report on her tax return. She wants to pay the lowest amount of taxes possible and wants to elect under the $100,000 stock option rule if she can.

(A) $5,000 in 2004.

(B) $8,000 in 2004.

(C) $8,000 in 2005.

(D) $10,000 in 2005.

Question 6

Tim began employment as a commissioned salesman in July of this year and received a base salary of $60,000 and $5,000 in commissions based on sales for the year. During the year, Tim worked away from the office negotiating sales contracts. Tim is required to pay his own travelling expenses and his employer has signed a T2200 form certifying that requirement and certifying that no reimbursements are paid for any expenses Tim incurs to earn commissions. Tim incurred the following work-related costs from July through December of this year and all expenses are reasonable:

Meals and entertainment for potential customers...................... $14,000

Automobile costs (90% of the following amounts were for employment
   purposes based on kilometres driven):

Fuel 4,000

Insurance 750

Repairs 2,250

Leasing costs for a car costing $20,000 ($500 per month) 3,000

What is the maximum deduction Tim may claim for employment expenses for the year?

(A) $5,000

(B) $9,000

(C) $14,000

(D) $16,000

EXERCISES

Exercise 1

The appellant is a qualified registered nurse, is entitled to use the traditional letters "R.N." after her name and, in answering the questions contained in her 1966 income tax return, described herself as a "private duty" nurse both in the space provided for employed persons and in the space provided for persons in business or practising a profession. Thus, in trying to answer all the official questions on her return, the appellant indicated, on the one hand, that she was employed "as a private duty nurse" by the Canadian Forces Hospital at Halifax and, on the other hand, that she was in business of practising her profession "as a private duty nurse" in connection with the same hospital. The basic issue to be decided in this appeal is, briefly, what was the taxpayer's correct status vis-à-vis the Canadian Forces Hospital, Halifax in her 1966 taxation year.

The appellant launched the present appeal by Notice of Appeal dated March 7, 1968 in which she alleged (in effect) as follows: that in the relevant 1966 taxation year she was employed by the Canadian Forces Hospital, Halifax, on a day-to-day basis terminable on 24 hours' notice; that the usual so-called fringe benefits made available to and enjoyed by the regular full-time army nursing sisters such as holidays, sick pay, retirement plan, and so on, were not made available to her as a private duty nurse; that the regional surgeon's office in Halifax classified her as a "self-employed R.N."; that in her 1965 return she claimed and was permitted to deduct from her income expenses of a similar type to those disallowed in the 1966 taxation year now under appeal; and that several of her fellow private duty nurses employed at the Canadian Forces Base, Halifax, were employed on the same basis as she was and had claimed expenses of a similar type to those disallowed in this appeal (i.e., the type of expenses one would associate with a private duty nurse). The Minister stated that, in making the assessment now in dispute, he had acted upon the following assumptions of fact — that the appellant is a registered nurse and was employed by the Department of National Defence at the Canadian Forces Hospital and Base, Halifax, during the 1966 taxation year, that in the course of carrying out her engagement as a general duty nurse the appellant was subject to supervision and discipline by the hospital authorities, and that of the expenses allegedly incurred by the appellant only the amount of $25 claimed as "R.N. fees" and the amount of $42.41 being her contribution to the Canada Pension Plan were permitted under the Act.

The appellant testified, in effect, as follows: that she is a registered nurse; that in the relevant 1966 taxation year she was living in Halifax and was employed at the Canadian Forces Hospital (Stadacona Hospital), "not as a staff nurse but more or less as a private duty nurse, though my times were made up ahead of time" (the correct interpretation to be placed on the word "employed" in this appeal appears to be the key to the solution); that private duty nurses are allowed to claim as deductions from income certain expenses such as laundry, uniforms including caps, white shoes and stockings, travelling expenses (in this matter that item amounted to $76.40 made up of 191 days at 40¢ per day) and so on; that the only difference between herself and a private duty nurse is that the hospital deducted her Canada Pension Plan contributions from the per diem amounts payable to her; that she acted as a private duty nurse at Stadacona Hospital in the years 1964, 1965, 1966, 1967 and until April 1968 when she moved from Halifax to Charlottetown and became associated with the Charlottetown Hospital as a relief nurse; that she is presently working under exactly the same conditions under which she carried on at the Canadian Forces Hospital, Halifax, i.e., "If I don't work, I don't get paid, I have no benefits or holidays. I get private duty wages (these amounted to $15 per day in Halifax and now amount to $20 per day). My time is made up. If they get full-time nurses they can let me go"; that she and other private duty nurses were hired by Stadacona Hospital (on a day-to-day basis) to fill in while the hospital "didn't have enough service nurses"; and that in the year 1967 the said hospital "did get a large supply of military nurses in and we were all cut down" (i.e., a number of private duty nurses were simply laid off which was easy to do because they were working on a day-to-day basis). The Hospital supplied all equipment and supplies used by the appellant. The Hospital hired and fired all nursing assistants and other support staff who assisted the appellant in the performance of her duties. The appellant could request the Hospital to hire additional support staff but she personally did not hire them.

During her cross-examination, the appellant also testified, in effect, as follows: that her time sheet in the Canadian Forces Hospital, Halifax, was made out a week in advance; that the said hospital's authority to hire civilian nurses to meet its requirements was only valid while there was a shortage of military nurses; that, as they became available, the civilian nurses were replaced; that the hospital asserted its right to dismiss civilian nurses on 24 hours' notice — "we were told that when we went there to work"; that she, herself, was not replaced by a military nurse in the 1966 taxation year, now under appeal, but later her shifts were cut down and she was eventually replaced in 1968; that she was, of course, obliged to follow hospital regulations with regard to the administration of drugs, medications, and so on, as she would be in any recognized hospital; that, when she was working at the Canadian Forces Hospital, Halifax, she was told which patients to look after; and that she did not sign any form of contract with the above hospital when she started to work there.

— *REQUIRED*

Is the appellant in this case employed or self-employed? In presenting your answer, discuss the tests that are applied by the courts in this type of situation and consider how the facts relate to these tests.

Exercise 2

[ITA: 6(1)(*a*); IT-470R]

William Wage-Slave works for an extremely generous employer, Claude's Fringe-Benefits Ltd. which paid the following amounts on behalf of William:

(a) Registered pension plan contributions (defined benefit) $1,000

(b) Provincial medical plan premiums (not a health service levy) 600

(c) Extended health care premiums — Sun Life 250

(d) Drug plan premiums — Mutual of Omaha 150

(e) Tuition fee for a basket weaving course offered by a local high school 75

(f) Non-cash Christmas gift which the company did expense for tax purposes.. 65

(g) Subsidized lunches at company cafeteria:

　　Fair market value 640

　　Actual cost... 420

　　Amount paid by William...................................... 200

(h) Membership fees in Exclusive Private Club 800

(i) Financial counselling — ABC Investment Counselling Ltd. 1,000

— *REQUIRED*

Comment on whether these amounts are taxable under paragraph 6(1)(*a*) and/or IT-470R.

Exercise 3

[ITA: 6(1)(*a*); IT-470R]

Melanie Manager, a division supervisor for Eli's Ltd., a large department store chain, receives a 35% discount on all merchandise purchased through Eli's Ltd. This discount is available to all executives above assistant department heads. Melanie calculated that the discount saved her $6,000 this year.

— *REQUIRED*

Discuss whether there is a benefit under paragraph 6(1)(*a*) according to IT-470R.

Exercise 4

[ITA: 6(1)(*a*); IT-470R]

John Aggressive, an employee of Isaac's Fast Sell Ltd., lives in Burlington and commutes by Go-Train to Toronto where Isaac's Fast Sell Ltd. is located. John, who is bored by reading, decides to move to Toronto in order to cut down his travelling time. Isaac's Fast Sell Ltd. reimburses him for the following amounts:

Moving van costs...	$ 500
Reimbursement of actual loss suffered in selling the house..............	5,000
	$5,500

— REQUIRED

Discuss whether there is a benefit under paragraph 6(1)(*a*) according to IT-470R.

Exercise 5

[ITA: 6(1)(*a*); 6(1)(*f*)]

Tanya Taxaware, who is chairperson of her union's negotiating team, has approached you concerning the management's offer in connection with fringe benefits. The company proposes to pay one-half of the premiums of the following plans:

(a) provincial medical plan — not a provincial health levy;

(b) extended health care — a private plan;

(c) dental care — a private plan;

(d) an income protection plan — a private group plan covering up to 50% of the wages.

All of these plans have premiums which are approximately the same. The company at present does not contribute to any of these plans.

— REQUIRED

Discuss the tax implications of the company's proposal.

Exercise 6

[ITA: 6(9); 8(1)(*j*); 80.4; 80.5]

Leonard Loans, an employee of Bertha's Generous Employer Ltd., received the following loans on January 1 of this year from his employer:

6% .... $15,000 loan to purchase a car to be used primarily for employment purposes,

4% .... $100,000 loan to purchase a home, and

7% .... $10,000 loan to consolidate his other debts.

Leonard does not receive a mileage allowance and is specifically required by his contract to pay his car expenses. According to Leonard's travel log, he used the car for employment purposes, for 27,000 kilometres out of a total of 45,000 kilometres.

Assume that the prescribed rates for this year were:

1st Quarter — 7%	3rd Quarter — 8%
2nd Quarter — 6%	4th Quarter — 7%

Leonard paid the interest on these loans on January 15th of the following year.

— REQUIRED

Compute the benefit under subsection 6(9) and any deduction under paragraph 8(1)(*j*).

Exercise 7

[ITA: 7; IT-113R4]

Katrina Keyemployee was granted, in year one, an option to purchase 50,000 common shares at $1 per share from her employer, Michael Ltd., a Canadian-controlled private corporation. The shares had an estimated fair market value at this date of $1.50. However, according to the agreement, Katrina could not exercise her option until her fourth employment year. Katrina did exercise her entire option in year five; the fair market value of the shares at that time was $3. Katrina sold all the shares in year six, at $6 per share.

— REQUIRED

Discuss the tax implications of the above transactions.

Exercise 8

[ITA: 6(1)(e), (k), (2)]

Ms. Speedster has full use of an employer-owned Mustang GTS purchased for her use in mid-December of last year. It is now January. The original cost to the employer of this classic is $20,000, including PST of $1,552 and GST of $1,207. Other details of the car for the coming year are as follows:

Capital cost allowance to be claimed by employer	$4,792
Operating costs for the year paid by the employer, including PST, GST, and insurance ($600)	$3,500
Personal-use kilometres	12,000
Number of months available	12
Reimbursement to employer for personal use at 15 cents	$ 400

— REQUIRED

Compute the taxable benefit under paragraphs 6(1)(e) and 6(1)(k), if the business-use kilometres are:

(a) 10,000

(b) 20,000

Exercise 9

[ITA: 8(1)(i), (13); IT-352R2]

Calvin Comptroller, who is employed and lives in Calgary, takes a considerable amount of office work home and, therefore, has built and furnished an office in his fully-paid home. On this year's tax return, he claimed the following expenses under paragraph 8(1)(i) and subsection 8(13) in respect of his office which represents approximately 1/8 of the home.

Estimated rental value for office space	$1,000
Maintenance — 1/8	250
Taxes — 1/8	200
Insurance — 1/8	80
	$1,530

— REQUIRED

Discuss whether Calvin's course of action was correct according to paragraph 8(1)(i), subsection 8(13), and IT-352R2.

Exercise 10

[ITA: 6(1)(b); 13(7)(g); 67.2; IT-522R]

Ms. Internal Auditor, who is employed by Susan's Super Ltd., travels extensively across Canada. According to the terms of her contract, she receives an accommodation allowance of $10,000 per year.

The contract states that she must use her own automobile and pay for all travelling expenses. Ms. Auditor acquired a new car on January 5, 2005 for $32,000 plus GST and PST at 6%. Her kilometres for business purposes were 15,000 out of a total of 21,000 kilometres.

During the year, Ms. Auditor paid the following amounts, all of which are reasonable in the circumstances and which are supported by receipts:

(a) accommodation, including meals of $4,500 (including PST and GST)	$12,000
(b) total car expenses: gas (including PST and GST)	1,500
maintenance (including PST and GST)	500
insurance	1,200
licences	90
interest on bank loan	4,000

Ms. Auditor calculated her capital cost allowance to be:

$$(^1/_2 \times 30\% \times \$32,000) = \$4,800$$

Ms. Auditor also filed the prescribed form (T2200) which her employer had signed. Assume that the employment use of the car is reasonable in the circumstances.

— *REQUIRED*

Discuss the tax consequences of the allowance and related expenses plus the deductibility of the car expenses.

Exercise 11

[ITA: 6(8); ETA: 253(1)]

Based on the facts and solution for Exercise 10 determine the potential GST rebate and income tax consequences upon receipt of this amount.

ASSIGNMENT PROBLEMS

Problem 1

Chow Installation and Repair Ltd. ("Chow") is in the business of installing and repairing overhead doors. Chow maintained a list of qualified installers and repair-persons and would contact them as work became available. Chow informed these workers that they would be considered to be running their own business, so no withholding of income tax, EI or CPP was made. Workers were paid by the job and worked mostly on their own. If the person contacted refused the assignment, Chow would call the next person on the list. The person who agreed to the job would go directly to the job site; he or she was not required to report to Chow's work place, except to pick up a door or parts.

Chow supplied the doors and the parts used in the repair or installation. Each worker maintained his or her own truck and tools. Chow, however, owned specialized racks made for transporting the doors and a special drill which could be used on cement. These items were available to any worker who required them.

Chow guaranteed all work for one year. Under the terms of the agreement between Chow and the workers, if a guarantee had to be honoured, the worker would be responsible to fix any defects. If any parts were required to correct the defect, the worker would have to pay for them.

— REQUIRED

Determine whether the workers should be considered employees of Chow or independent contractors. Evaluate this fact situation in detail before arriving at your conclusion. In presenting your answer, discuss the tests that are applied by the courts in this type of situation and consider how the facts relate to these tests.

Problem 2

[ITA: 5; 6(1)(*a*), (*b*); 80.4; IT-470R]

Miriam, the sole tax adviser of a financial planning firm, is contemplating an offer to become Director of Taxation of Neil Manufacturing Limited (NML) of Dundas, Ontario. The offered compensation package would include the following:

- a salary of $132,000 per year, payable monthly;
- a one-time flat allowance of $25,000, payable on acceptance of the position, to help move her and her family to Dundas;
- a company contribution of 6% of her salary to a defined-benefit registered pension plan;
- company payment of the premiums for extended health coverage and a dental plan provided by Star Insurance;
- company payment, valued at $900, for the preparation of her tax return by the company's accountants;
- company payment, valued at $2,500, for her membership in the Dundas Valley Golf and Curling Club;
- a company loan of $200,000 to help finance the purchase of a new home in Dundas. The loan will bear interest at 3.5% per year payable monthly and will be made on May 1, 2005, the closing date on the purchase of the home.

— REQUIRED

Miriam does not deal with many employment-related tax issues and recognizes the need for a corroborating opinion on the tax consequences of this compensation package. She has asked you for your opinion. Comment on the income tax consequences for employment income of each item in the compensation package. Assume that the prescribed rate of interest for employee loans is 7% in the first quarter of 2005, 6% in the second quarter, 4% in the third quarter and 7% in the fourth quarter.

Problem 3

[ITA: 6(1)(*a*), (*e*), (*e*.1), (*k*), (2), (2.2)]

Your best friend, Mooch, was at a sales conference recently. During one of the breaks, he entered into a conversation with one of the other attendees, Darly, regarding the perks provided by their respective employers. In both cases, the employer provides a car. However, Darly commented on the significant tax advantage available to her since her employer leased the car instead of buying the car. Mooch was able to obtain all of the information from Darly regarding her car.

Mooch has come to you for some "free" tax advice. He has asked you to compare the tax position he is in currently with the employer-owned car to the position that Darly is in with the leased car.

Mooch

Capital cost of the car including PST and GST	$38,772
Capital cost allowance claimed by the employer in 2005	6,375
Operating costs paid by the employer (including PST and GST)	4,250
Kilometres (as calculated from Mooch's log):	
Employment	8,000
Personal	10,000
Amount reimbursed to the company for the personal use at 12 cents per kilometre	$ 1,200

Darly

Lease cost including $1,650 of insurance and PST and GST	$12,450
Operating costs paid by the employer (including PST and GST)	2,975
Kilometres (as calculated from Darly's log):	
Employment	23,000
Personal	9,000
Amount reimbursed to the company for the personal use at 7 cents per kilometre	$ 630

— *REQUIRED*

Calculate the minimum car benefit which would be included in employment income for 2005 for Mooch and Darly.

Problem 4

[ITA: 5; 6; IT-470R]

Anita Lee, Vice-President of Gary Inc., has asked for your assistance concerning the tax implications of certain amounts and benefits she received from her employer during 2005.

Salary, gross		$ 90,000
Payroll deductions:		
Income taxes	$36,000	
Canada Pension Plan premiums	1,861	
Employment Insurance premiums	761	
Group accident disability insurance premiums	110	(38,732)
Net pay		$ 51,268

Additional Information

(1) In November 2005, Anita was in a skiing accident and was unable to work for four weeks. During this period she received disability payments totalling $1,600 from Paris Life Insurance Ltd. Half of the disability insurance premiums were paid by Gary Inc. and half by Anita (see payroll deduction above). Anita has paid a total of $350 in disability insurance premiums since she commenced employment at Gary Inc. in 2002.

(2) In 2005, Gary Inc. paid $428 (including GST of $28) for the preparation of Anita's 2004 income tax return and $535 (including GST of $35) for Anita to see a financial planning consultant regarding retirement planning.

(3) Anita is taking courses towards her M.B.A. degree on a part-time basis during the evening. She is taking the courses on her initiative and for her own benefit. During 2005, Gary Inc. paid for the tuition for these M.B.A. courses which amounted to $1,000. Gary Inc. also paid $400 in tuition for Anita to attend a two-day computer workshop on company time to learn about the new software system that the company had just installed.

(4) Director's fees of $2,000 were received by Anita from Clint's Hi-Tech Ltd., a company owned by Anita's spouse.

(5) Christmas gift of $200 cash was received and was expensed by Gary Inc.

(6) Anita received an employee loan of $8,000 on January 15, 2005, at 3% interest to purchase a notebook computer for personal use. The interest was payable on each anniversary date of the loan, and Anita paid the interest owing on the loan on the due date in 2006. Assume that the prescribed interest rates applicable to employee loans for 2005 are: first quarter, 7%; second quarter, 6%; third quarter, 8%; fourth quarter, 7%.

(7) For 12 months, Gary Inc. paid Anita a monthly gas allowance of $250 regardless of the number of kilometres she drove. In addition, she was provided with a company-owned automobile costing $38,500 (including PST and GST) at the beginning of January. Anita's kilometres for personal use were 16,000 out of a total of 25,000 kilometres. Operating costs paid (excluding gas) by Gary Inc. during 2005 amounted to $2,920, including insurance of $600, PST of $220 and GST of $137.

(8) Anita and her spouse Clint were provided with Gary Inc.'s condo in the Bahamas for a one-week holiday during the winter. Excluding GST considerations, such accommodation during this peak period would have cost them $500 as opposed to the $100 actually paid by Anita.

(9) Anita used her frequent-flyer points accumulated as a result of her business trips (which had been paid by Gary Inc.) for her holiday in the Bahamas. She saved $800, plus $56 of GST, by using the frequent-flyer points.

(10) Anita bought merchandise from Gary Inc. during the year and saved $180 (excluding GST) using its 30% employee discount, which is available to all employees. Gary Inc.'s mark-up is 100%.

— *REQUIRED*

(A) Calculate Anita Lee's employment income inclusions for 2005 in accordance with sections 5 and 6 of the Act and the CRA's administrative position as reflected by IT-470R. Assume a PST rate of 10%.

(B) Explain why you omitted any of the above amounts from your answer in part (A).

(C) If the facts were changed so that Anita had not been provided with a company-owned automobile and instead used her own car for employment purposes, how would this affect the computation of Anita's employment income in accordance with sections 5 and 6 of the Act? Assume that Gary Inc. continues to pay for Anita's car operating costs.

Problem 5

[ITA: 5; 6(3)]

Chrisa had been an employee of David Hardware, a hardware product distributor, for 15 years. Chrisa sold the David hardware products directly to hardware stores. She was a salesperson and she was paid 100% by commission. Chrisa was personally responsible for all of her business expenses. Expenses, for example, for office supplies, stamps, telephone, parking, entertainment, promotion and samples, were supported by receipts and she deducted them.

During the years that Chrisa was employed by David, she sold products and developed the hardware market in her geographic area. One of the ways in which she developed the market was by "renting" floor space in various stores to display the David products. However, no receipts were received from the various stores, because in many ways the money was considered a "tip" by the managers of the hardware stores. Chrisa did not deduct these expenses. Through this process, Chrisa had significantly increased David's sales in her sales region and she had developed a loyal following in the hardware business.

At the time of Chrisa's departure from David, David paid $15,000 to Chrisa. The conditions of the agreement surrounding the $15,000 payment were as follows:

- David was "buying back" Chrisa's sales territory;

- Chrisa agreed not to enter a similar business to that of David's business, in David's distribution area, for a period of three years; and

- David and Chrisa agreed that the $15,000 would constitute a reimbursement of capital invested by Chrisa (i.e., the amounts she had paid to the stores for the rental of floor space for David products).

— REQUIRED

Discuss the income tax implications for Chrisa of the receipt of the $15,000.

Problem 6

[ITA: 5; 6(1); 7; 8(1)]

The following information relates to Leonard, a middle-management accountant, not engaged in negotiating contracts, of a public corporation, Peter Productions Ltd. which is located in Ontario.

(A) Salary — gross		$ 80,000
Payroll deductions:		
Income taxes	$23,500	
Registered pension plan (money purchase; see (B) below)	5,500	
Canada Pension Plan contributions	1,861	
Employment Insurance contributions	761	
Charitable donations	350	
Employee's portion of benefit plans (see (B) below)	800	(32,772)
		$ 47,228

(B) The company paid the following additional matching amounts on behalf of Leonard (an equal amount was withheld from salary as the employee's contribution, as shown in (A) above):

Registered pension plan	$5,500
Dental plan — Sun Life Co.	175
Group income protection — Royal Insurance Co.	225
Extended health care — Liberty Mutual	150
Group term life insurance — General Insurance Co.	250

The group term life coverage for Leonard was $300,000.

(C) Selected additional information concerning Leonard's receipts, disbursements, and other benefits:

(i) Trip to Europe from one of Peter Productions Ltd.'s clients in appreciation of Leonard's services (including PST of $417 and GST of $365) $ 6,000

(ii) Periodic payments received from Royal Insurance under the group income protection plan during a three-month illness. This plan had been in existence since 1993 and Leonard's share of the premium since that date was $2,300   12,000

(iii) Peter Productions Ltd. paid Leonard's annual membership fee in a golf club .... $ 2,100

(iv) Early in 2005, Leonard was granted an option to purchase 1,000 of the company's shares for $2.00 per share. At that time the shares were trading on the market at $3.00 per share. Later in the year, Leonard exercised the option and acquired 1,000 shares when they were trading at $4.50 per share. In December of 2005, he needed cash, so he sold the 1,000 shares for $5.00 each.

(v) Leonard paid the following amounts during the year:

Annual membership fee of a professional accounting body (including GST, no
PST charged) 800

Registered retirement savings plan 3,500

Legal fees in appealing a tax assessment 1,900

— *REQUIRED*

(A) Calculate the employment income of Leonard for 2005 in accordance with Subdivision a of Division B.

(B) Indicate why you omitted any of the above amounts.

(C) Compute the GST rebate that should be claimed and the income tax consequences of the rebate to be received in 2006.

Problem 7

[ITA: 5; 6; 7; 8; 67.1; 67.2; 67.3; IT-352R2]

Robby Beamon has recently been appointed vice-president of sales and marketing for Lori's Unpublished Books Limited, a public company. Robby has come to you for advice regarding the tax implications of his new position. During your meeting you were able to determine the following information:

(A) Remuneration for the year:

Salary — gross		$84,800
Less: Canada Pension Plan contributions	$1,861	
Employment Insurance contributions	761	
Disability insurance premiums	600	3,222
		$81,578
Bonus based on company sales		24,000
Allowances for the year (paid monthly):		
meals, accommodation and air travel		13,000
car		6,300
entertainment..		2,000
Moving allowance		15,000

Robby has also been granted an option to acquire 7,500 previously unissued fully-paid shares of Lori's Unpublished Books Limited at $11.50 per share. The fair market value at the time of the grant was $15. One of the conditions was that he must exercise one-third of the option immediately upon it being granted. He did so and acquired 2,500 shares.

(B) Robby has summarized the following expenses related to his employment:

Gas and oil — automobile....................................	$ 3,900
Painting (office only)	100

Licences — automobile	100
Meals (consumed while travelling away for more than 12 hours)	7,000
House insurance	800
Accommodation (while travelling on company business)	10,000
Interest expense — car loan	3,600
General maintenance (house)	300
Car insurance	1,900
Hydro	700
Air travel	4,200
Car maintenance	1,000
Supplies	700
Fuel (house)	1,200
Property taxes	4,500
Mortgage interest	24,000
Salary (to wife, including payroll taxes and employer contributions)	15,000

(C) Lori's Unpublished Books Limited requires Robby to provide an automobile in order to carry out his duties of employment. Robby is responsible for his travelling expenses. On March 17, 2005, he acquired a new car for $46,000, including PST at 10% and GST, financing part of the acquisition through a bank loan arranged for the same date. The capital cost allowance rate in the first year is effectively 15%. He estimates that he will drive 38,000 kilometres in the course of his employment. He expects his total kilometres to the end of the year to be 45,000. The car and the employment use are reasonable for his position and his work requirements.

(D) Robby's contract also requires that he maintain an office in his home, since no other office is provided. He is responsible for all costs related to the operation of the office. He does not receive an allowance or reimbursement related to any of these costs. Robby has estimated that the office occupies approximately 15% of his home. This estimate is based on square footage. Robby estimates that if he had to rent a comparable amount of space he would have to pay $850 per month plus utilities.

— REQUIRED

(A) Calculate Robby's employment income for 2005, assuming that all expenses are reasonable in the circumstances and will be documented. Ignore consideration of the GST rebate.

(B) If the facts in part (A) were changed as follows, what would be the deductible expenses under subsection 8(1) for 2005?

(i) Lease entered into on March 1, 2005.

(ii) Monthly lease payments are $1,100 including PST at 10% and GST.

(iii) Employment use accounts for 38,000 km out of a total of 45,000 km for 2005.

(iv) Manufacturer's list price is $46,000 excluding PST and GST.

(C) How would your conclusions in parts (A) and (B) change if Robby was an internal auditor and, therefore, did not receive a bonus based on sales?

Problem 8

[ITA: 5; 6; 7; 8; 67.2; 67.3; IT-470R]

Anita Flare is a skilled tool and die worker. She has been working for Car Parts Inc., a large manufacturer of parts for the automobile industry for over 10 years. Car Parts Inc. is a Canadian-controlled private corporation. Anita has become their "Jane on the Spot" as far as diagnosing and quickly retooling machinery that breaks down or needs to be updated to run a short order. Anita is single and she rents a home in north Toronto. Because Anita is required to travel for 75% of the year, Car Parts Inc. actually pays the $1,200 monthly rent on Anita's home in

Toronto. Anita reimburses the company for 25% of this amount ($300 per month) through payroll deduction as set out below.

The head office of Car Parts Inc. is located in north Toronto. The company, however, has plants that are located throughout Ontario and Quebec, wherever there are large automobile manufacturing operations to be supplied with parts. When a plant requires emergency retooling or repair Anita is sent out to that location to supervise and organize the work. As stated above, this involves about 75% of Anita's total employment hours for any given year. She stays at a particular location for a period of days or weeks depending on the nature of the job involved. She is never at a site for less than 36 hours. For the balance of the year, Anita works at the head office in the research department.

Anita's final 2005 pay stub showed the following totals in respect of the 2005 taxation year.

Gross salary		$115,000
Payroll deductions:		
Income tax withheld	$44,224	
Canada Pension Plan contributions	1,861	
Employment Insurance premiums paid	761	
Contributions to company group RRSP	1,750	
RPP contributions on account of current service (matched by company)	5,000	
Union dues to Canadian Union of Automobile Workers (GST exempt)	800	
Group accident income protection insurance premiums (matched by company)	240	
Monthly rent reimbursement (as described above)	3,600	

In discussion with Anita you determined that the company also provides the following fringe benefits.

Payment of board and lodging costs at special work sites as required – at cost to company	$18,000
Bonus based on company profits for the year above budgeted targets	12,500
Provision of safety boots and company uniform consisting of 5 shirts and 5 matching pairs of pants; the shirt is embroidered with her name on the front pocket and has the company name on the back	$ 450
Registered pension plan contributions to defined benefit plan	6,750
Monthly allowance of $150 to cover personal phone calls, laundry costs and other incidentals while travelling. (She estimates that she spends $100 per month.)	1,800
Fitness club membership dues to a club with locations across Ontario (including PST of $56 and GST of $49); Anita feels that it's important to her productivity to remain in top physical shape as her work can be physically demanding	805

Anita was injured on the job early in the year and received total payments of $11,500 out of the company group income protection plan for 2 months while she was recuperating. She had not previously received any payments under this plan and has paid total premiums of $2,880 into the plan since she began employment 12 years ago (this includes all of the year 2005 premiums paid through December 2005).

Due to her extensive travel, Anita's employer requires her to have an automobile for employment purposes. Anita has provided you with the following details of her automobile expenses.

	Owned car[1]	Leased car
Leasing costs[2]	n/a	$3,680
Gasoline and oil (including PST and GST)	$2,880	1,440
Insurance	1,333	667
Maintenance (including PST and GST)	400	240
Licence	90	30
C.C.A.	1,207	n/a

Notes

(1) She owned an automobile until August 31, 2005, at which time she disposed of that vehicle and began leasing a new one. Assume that there are no tax consequences to Anita of the disposition of the automobile other than the fact that she can claim CCA in 2005 on this vehicle, as set out above, since it was a luxury vehicle.

(2) Anita leased the car as of September 1, 2005, at a cost of $920 a month that includes PST of $64 and GST of $56. The lease is for a 3-year period that will expire August 31, 2008. At the time that she leased the car, the manufacturer's list price on the vehicle was $55,000 excluding all taxes.

(3) Anita received an automobile loan to purchase the owned automobile. She received the loan on April 1, 2000, for $40,000 but has been making principal repayments annually on April 1 each year. She made the last principal repayment of $8,000 on April 1, 2005. There was no interest payable on the loan. Assume that the prescribed interest rate for employee loans was 6% for all of 2005.

(4) Anita drove the owned car a total of 40,000 km during 2005 of which 35,000 km was employment related.

(5) Anita drove the leased car a total of 20,000 km during 2005 of which 18,000 km was employment related.

— *REQUIRED*

(A) Determine Anita Flare's income under Subdivision a of Division B of the Act for 2005 and cross-reference your answer to the appropriate section of the Act and/or Interpretation Bulletin. Round your answer to the nearest dollar.

(B) Indicate why you did not include any of the above amounts in your answer with the appropriate cross-reference.

(C) Compute the GST rebate that should be claimed and the income tax consequences of the rebate to be received in 2006.

Problem 9

[ITA: Subdiv. a, Div. B; 67.1; 67.3; IT-470R]

Mr. Ned Negotiator is employed by Snoopy-Snacks Ltd. (a Canadian-controlled private corporation). As of February 15, 2005, Ned was promoted to vice-president sales due to his hard work negotiating puppy snack contracts on behalf of the company. This promotion required Ned to relocate from the Toronto office of Snoopy-Snacks Ltd. to its Victoria, British Columbia office.

Ned has provided you with the following information regarding his 2005 income and expenses. He requests your assistance in determining his 2005 employment income for tax purposes.

Payroll Details:

Gross salary	$125,000
Less:	
Income taxes	$45,000
Canada Pension Plan contributions.........................	1,861

Employment Insurance contributions	761	
Registered pension plan contributions: defined benefit (post-89 service)	6,750	
Group income protection premiums paid	120	
Group term life insurance premiums paid..................	180	54,672
		$ 70,328

Employer-paid Amounts and Fringe Benefits paid by
Snoopy-Snacks Ltd.:

Dental plan premiums — paid to Star Insurance Company	$ 245
Group term life insurance premiums	90
BC provincial health care premiums.......................	640
Group income protection premiums	400
Monthly allowance to cover travel and automobile expenses (based on a flat monthly amount of $400 for travel and $400 for auto).................................	9,600
Travelling expenses for Ned and his wife to Bermuda for a sales conference. Ned's time was spent attending the conference but his wife was on vacation the entire time. No GST or PST was payable on the trip since it was outside of Canada. One-half of the expenses related to Ned and one-half to his wife.	2,800
A birthday gift (a watch) received while in Ontario (including GST of $9 and PST of $10). Snoopy-Snacks Ltd. deducted the cost of this gift as a business expense.	150
Outside financial counseling fees (including GST of $168 and no PST). The counseling firm indicated that 80% of its fees relate to counseling for future retirement while the remaining 20% of its fees relate to tax preparation.	2,568

Other Information:

1. Snoopy-Snacks Ltd. provided Ned with some assistance that relates to his move from Toronto to Victoria. The details of that assistance are set out below.

a) Ned purchased a new home in Victoria just prior to his move. However, he could not take possession of that home until April 30, 2005. Snoopy-Snacks Ltd. paid Ned's rent for a Victoria apartment for the months of February through April 2005. The rent paid was $1,200 per month.

b) Ned and Snoopy-Snacks Ltd. agreed that he would receive reimbursement from Snoopy-Snacks Ltd. for one-half of the loss realized by him on the sale of his Toronto home. Ned received $16,500 as a result of this agreement.

c) Ned received an allowance of $15,000 to cover his moving expenses.

In addition to the above, Ned's employer agreed to reimburse him an amount equal to one-quarter of his annual mortgage interest payment for the first five years of his mortgage on his new Victoria home. This was intended to compensate for higher real estate prices in Victoria. For 2005, Ned received $2,000 under the terms of this agreement.

2. Snoopy-Snacks Ltd. maintains an employee stock purchase plan for certain of its employees. Ned became eligible for this plan after his promotion. During 2005 he was granted an option to purchase 1,000 shares in Snoopy-Snacks Ltd. at an exercise price of $15 per share. At the time this option was granted the fair market value of the shares was $20 per share. On September 15, 2005, Ned exercised the option to purchase 600 of the above shares. The fair market value of the shares was $25 at that time.

3. Ned had unlimited use of the company's private swimming pool. All management level employees are permitted to utilize this pool. The local private swimming pool charges annual fees of $1,800 per year before GST (no PST).

4. Ned had the following expenditures during 2005.

Automobile operating expenditures:

Lease payments for 12 months ($850 a month including
  PST of 8% and GST of 7%).............................. $10,200

(lease commenced July 1, 2004 for a period of three
years; deducted lease costs for 2004 were $4,585)

Gasoline and oil... 1,300

Insurance 1,050

Maintenance... 180

Licence 120

Travelling expenditures:

Meals (consumed while out of metropolitan area for
  greater than 12 hours)..................................... 7,200

Accommodation... 12,000

Ned travelled a total of 36,000 km during 2005 of which 22,500 km were employment-related. The manufacturer's list price on his automobile was $33,000 before GST and PST.

— *REQUIRED*

(A) Determine Ned's employment income for tax purposes for 2005 and cross-reference your answer to the appropriate sections of the Act and/or Interpretation Bulletins.

(B) Indicate why you did not include any of the above amounts in your answer with the appropriate cross-reference.

(C) Compute the potential GST rebate in 2006, and the income tax consequences upon receipt of the GST rebate under subsection 6(8).

[For more problems and solutions thereto, see the CD accompanying this book.]

SUPPLEMENTAL NOTES

(This section can be omitted without losing the continuity of the chapter. None of the review questions, multiple choice questions, exercises, or assignment problems utilize this information.)

A. Salary Deferral Arrangements

[ITA 6(1)(*i*), (11)-(14); ITR: 6801]

Subsections 6(11) to (14) replace and expand the employee benefit plan restrictions, for years after 1985. A salary deferral arrangement (SDA) is broadly defined in subsection 248(1) to include any plan or arrangement under which any person has the right to receive salary or wages in a subsequent period to the period in which services are rendered and one of the main purposes of this right is to postpone taxes payable. A salary deferral arrangement does not include:

(a) rights which have conditions which might give rise to a substantial risk that any condition might not be satisfied and, hence, the deferred payment might not be made;

(b) a number of statutory-approved deferred income plans, such as registered pension funds, deferred profit sharing plans, and employee trusts;

(c) group sickness or accident insurance plans and supplementary benefit plans;

(d) certain employee work-related training plans;

(e) wage deferrals for professional athletes;

(f) bonuses paid within three years of the rendering of the service; or

(g) prescribed plans such as the self-financing sabbatical arrangements described in Regulation 6801 (Part LXVIII).

The amount that is deferred under an SDA is called a "deferred amount" and is also defined in subsection 248(1).

Subsection 6(11) requires that the "deferred amount" must be included in income by virtue of paragraph 6(1)(*a*). Subsection 6(12) brings, into income, accrued interest and similar amounts which relate to the deferred amount. The result of these rules is to require the inclusion and payment of tax on amounts that have not been received, making an SDA generally unattractive. Subsection 6(13) provides an exception to the salary deferral rules in respect of non-resident employees who provide services outside of Canada and, under certain circumstances, former non-residents. Where a plan or arrangement qualifies as both an employee benefit plan and an SDA, subsection 6(14) separates these two components and deems that income from this combined plan comes out of the salary deferral portion first, to the extent of the deferred amount.

Finally, paragraph 6(1)(*i*) includes in income all payments received from an SDA, to the extent that these amounts have not been previously recognized under paragraph 6(1)(*a*) in preceding years. The inclusion is also limited to the amount that qualified as a deduction under paragraph 8(1)(*o*) as a deferred amount which did not meet all the conditions of the arrangement such that the taxpayer's rights under the arrangement have been forfeited.

B. Registered Pension Plans

1. Deductions for pre-1990 service contributions while not a contributor

Paragraph 147.2(4)(*b*) allows an individual, when computing his or her income for *a taxation year ending after 1990*, to deduct a contribution *made in the year or a preceding year* to a registered pension plan for past service contributions, but only *for years of service prior to 1990 while the individual was not a contributor.* This might be the case where an employer had no pension plan during the years in question; where a part-time employee was not permitted to join the plan; or where an employee had the right to opt out of the plan. The deduction is generally restricted to the least of:

(a) the total amount of contributions made by the individual in the year or a previous year under this provision, minus any deductions previously claimed in respect of these contributions;

(b) $3,500; and

(c) $3,500 for each pre-1990 year of service in which the employee was not a contributor to any RPP, minus any deductions previously claimed in respect of these contributions.

Since these rules allow for a contribution made in a preceding year to be deducted in the current year, there is an indefinite carryforward of the deductibility of these contributions.

2. Deductions for pre-1990 service while a contributor

Paragraph 147.2(4)(c) allows an individual, when computing his or her income for *a taxation year ending after 1990*, to deduct a contribution *made in the year or a preceding year* to a registered pension plan *for years of service prior to 1990 while the individual was a contributor.* A deduction for pre-1990 services while a contributor might be made for a period in which an individual was a member of the plan but contributed less than the statutory limit for those years (i.e., $3,500) and the pension plan's specified contribution limits (e.g., 6% of gross salary which did not reach the dollar limit for an individual). The deduction is restricted to the lesser of:

(i) the total amount of eligible contributions made by the individual in the year or a preceding year in respect of years of service prior to 1990 (other than those made in respect of past service while not a contributor), minus any deductions previously claimed under this provision in respect of the year; and

(ii) $3,500 minus all deductions made *in the year* by the individual for post-1989 service contributions and pre-1990 service contributions while the individual was not a contributor.

The limit in (b) above is very restrictive, making it more difficult for an employee to obtain a deduction for such contributions. However, since the rules allow for a contribution made in a preceding year to be deducted in the current year, subject to the above restrictions, there is, again, an indefinite carryforward of the deductibility of these contributions.

Chapter 4

Income from Business:
General Concepts and Rules

TOPICS DISCUSSED

	Page
BASIC RULES	151
The Concept of Business Income	151
Inventory Valuation	160
Sole Proprietorship	163
INCLUSIONS	164
Amounts Received and Receivable	164
Inducement Payments or Reimbursements	164
Restricted Covenants	165
DEDUCTIONS	165
Deductibility of Expenditures	165
Sales/Negotiating Person's Expenses Revisited	185
Ceasing to Carry on Business	190

	Page
Professional Business	191
Scientific Research and Experimental Development	191
THE GST IMPACT ON BUSINESS ACTIVITY	194
Commercial Activity	194
Input Tax Credits	196
Adjustments to Net Tax	198
Application of the Rules	199
SUPPLEMENTAL NOTES	216
Adjustment for Depreciation Allocation in Inventory: An Illustration of the Effect	216
Unregistered Employee Compensation Plans	217

The focus of this chapter is on Subdivision b of Division B, Part I of the Act. In particular, the provisions dealing with income from business (both inclusions and deductions) will be covered. The final section of the chapter presents the impact of GST legislation on the business activity discussed in the earlier sections of the chapter. The following chart will help to locate in the Act the key provisions discussed in this Chapter.

Part I — Division B
Subdivision b
Business or Property

DIVISION		SUBDIVISION		SECTION	
A	Liability for tax				
B	Computation of income		Basic rules		
		a	Office or employment		
C	Computation of taxable income	b	**Business or property**	9-11	Basic rules
				12-17	Inclusions
D	Taxable income earned in Canada by non-residents	c	Capital gains and losses	18-21	Deductions
		d	Other income	22-25	Ceasing to carry on business
E	Computation of tax	e	Other deductions	26-37	Special cases
E.1	Minimum tax	f	Rules relating to computation of income		
F	Special rules				
G	Deferred and other special income arrangements	g	Amounts not included in income		
H	Exemptions	h	Cdn corporations and shareholders		
I	Returns, Assessments, payments, appeals	i	Shareholders of non-resident corporations		
J	Appeals to the courts	j	Partnerships		
		k	Trusts		

Subdivision b of Division B of Part I of the Act contains the primary rules for the computation of income from business. Most of what will be covered will be found in sections 9 through 21. Some of the more important provisions are as follows:

Sec. 9 — A taxpayer's income (loss) for a taxation year from a business is their profit (loss) from that business for the year.

Sec. 10 — Rules related to inventory

Sec. 12 — Income inclusions

Sec. 13 — Rules related to capital cost allowance

Sec. 14 — Rules related to eligible capital property

Sec. 15 — Rules for shareholder benefits

Sec. 18 — Limitations on the deductibility of expenses

Sec. 19 — Limitation on advertising expenses

Sec. 20 — Deductions permitted

The interaction between section 18 and section 20 is interesting. For example, paragraph 18(1)(*b*) does not allow any deduction that is on account of capital, including depreciation. However, paragraph 20(1)(*a*) allows a deduction for capital cost allowance and paragraph 20(1)(*l*) allows a deduction for doubtful debts. Both of these items are capital in nature.

I. BASIC RULES

A. The Concept of Business Income

[ITA: 9; 67.5; 80; IT-218R; IT-256R; IT-273R2; IT-459; IT-479R]

1. Income from a business

The word "business" is very broadly defined in subsection 248(1), although the definition specifically excludes an office or employment. Income from a business for a taxation year is the "profit" therefrom for the year [ssec. 9(1)]. While the word "profit" is not defined in the Act, Subdivision b contains numerous specific rules regarding amounts to be included in income and amounts which may or may not be deducted for income tax purposes. Furthermore, it must be understood that the word "income" when used in the Act means income after the deduction of expenses currently incurred to produce it.

Profit is the portrayal of income, according to common law, on "sound commercial principles", which may include generally accepted accounting principles (GAAP), unless a particular provision of the Act or principle of common law requires otherwise. This issue was recently explored by the Supreme Court of Canada in the case of *Canderel Ltd. v. The Queen*, (S.C.C.) 98 DTC 6100 and the court provided the following framework for analysis.

(1) The determination of profit is a question of law.

(2) The profit of a business for a taxation year is to be determined by setting against the revenues from the business for that year the expenses incurred in earning said income.[a]

(3) In seeking to ascertain profit, the goal is to obtain an accurate picture of the taxpayer's profit for the given year.

(4) In ascertaining profit, the taxpayer is free to use any method which is not inconsistent with:

(a) the provisions of the *Income Tax Act*;

(b) established case law principles or "rules of law"; and

(c) well-accepted business principles.

(5) Well-accepted business principles, which include but are not limited to the formal codification found in GAAP, are not rules of law but interpretive aids. To the extent that they may influence the calculation of income, they will do so only on a case-by-case basis, depending upon the facts of the taxpayer's financial situation.

(6) On reassessment, once the taxpayer has shown that he has provided an accurate picture of income for the year, which is consistent with the Act, the case law, and well-accepted business principles, the onus shifts to the Minister to show either that the figure provided does *not* represent an accurate picture, or that another method of computation would provide a *more* accurate picture.

---

[a] *M.N.R. v. Irwin*, (S.C.C.) 64 DTC 5227; *Associated Investors of Canada Ltd. v. M.N.R.*, [No. 2] (Ex. Ct.) 67 DTC 5096.

Specific provisions of the Act can create considerable differences between income for tax purposes and income for accounting purposes. One of the major causes of such differences results from the write-off of capital expenditures over a period of years. However, in recent years, tax treatment in certain areas of the Act, including the valuation of inventory and the deductibility of prepaid expenses, has moved closer to generally accepted accounting principles.

GAAP are often considered to reflect ordinary commercial principles, the legal concept, held by the courts to be a key determinant of profits. Nevertheless, it should be noted that the word "profit" is not required by the legislation to be interpreted in conformity with GAAP, even where the Act is silent on the treatment of a particular transaction.

While the Canada Revenue Agency (CRA) has often taken the position that profit computed under GAAP most accurately reflects income in these situations, the courts have, on occasion, rejected conformity between income for accounting and tax purposes, particularly in cases where GAAP were at variance with the court's legal concept of ordinary commercial trading and business principles and practices or with a legal concept of income.[b] The case of *The Queen v. Metropolitan Properties Co. Ltd.*, (F.C.T.D.) 85 DTC 5128, on the measurement of business profit, clearly indicates "the desirability of applying generally accepted commercial and business practice as reflected in the generally accepted accounting principles". Thus, according to the reasoning of the court in the *Metropolitan* case, in the absence of a specific provision, a legal principle, or recognized commercial practice to deal with the tax treatment of a particular transaction, GAAP are applied to meet the objectives of the income tax system.

On the other hand, in the case of *Symes v. The Queen*, 94 DTC 6001, the Supreme Court of Canada expressed the view that to rely on GAAP for a determination of profit would suggest a degree of control by professional accountants that was inconsistent with a legal test for profit. The Supreme Court suggested the use of "well accepted principles of business (or accounting) practice" or "well accepted principles of commercial trading", but did not suggest how to determine these principles or how to differentiate them from GAAP. As a result, in the absence of a specific provision of the Act or a clearly stated legal principle, reliance on GAAP may provide a reasonable guideline.

Where GAAP envisage more than one method of determining income, the courts have adopted the "truer picture" approach, choosing the method that provides the truer picture of income as in the case of *West Kootenay Power and Light Co. Ltd. v. The Queen*, (F.C.A.) 92 DTC 6023. In this case, considerable emphasis was placed on the matching of expenses to the income that was generated by the expenditure.[c]

---

[b] There have been many cases in this area, including *M.N.R. v. Publishers Guild of Canada Limited*, (Ex. Ct.) 57 DTC 1017.

[c] For further discussion of the role of GAAP in interpreting profit for tax purposes, see Joanne E. Magee, "The Profit GAAP", *CA Magazine*, April 1995, pp. 32–35.

2. Business income vs. capital receipt[d]

This is a particularly grey area in Canadian income taxation which has given rise to thousands of court cases which attempt to distinguish between a receipt of income and a receipt of capital. The courts have at times applied the analogy of a fruit-bearing tree to cases in which the determination of a capital or income transaction was at issue, in order to focus on how an asset has been used. An investment or capital asset is likened to the tree which produces or can be expected to produce income in the form of fruit. Just as the sale of the tree would be regarded as a capital transaction, the sale of an investment that can produce a form of income from business or property can be regarded as a capital transaction. However, the analogy breaks down under the facts of certain cases.

At the time of a court hearing, the courts can view in perspective the taxpayer's whole course of conduct for the period before, during and after the transaction in question. To help make the distinction between an income and a capital transaction, the courts attempt to assess the intention of the taxpayer in the transaction. The courts attempt to answer the question: did the taxpayer deliberately seek a profit of an income rather than a capital gain nature? An attempt is made to substantiate this by facts which establish the taxpayer's general course of conduct.

Secondary intention is a development of more recent years which is established by looking at whether the taxpayer has built into a transaction, at the time of purchase, a profitable alternative in the event that the primary intention is frustrated. For example, if land is acquired for development, but appropriate zoning changes are not approved or other extraneous circumstances frustrate the original intention and subsequently the land is sold at a profit, that profit may be considered to be the result of the alternative business intention and may be regarded as business income.[e]

The concept of secondary intention was clarified in the case of *Racine et al. v. M.N.R.*, (Ex. Ct.) 65 DTC 5098 as follows:

> To give a transaction which involves the acquisition of capital the double character of also being at the same time an adventure in the nature of trade, the purchaser must have in his mind, at *the moment of the purchase*, the possibility of reselling *as an operating motivation* for the acquisition; that is to say that he must have had in mind that upon a certain type of circumstances arising he had hopes of being able to resell it at a profit instead of using the thing purchased for purposes of capital. (Italics added.)

In the case of *Armstrong v. The Queen*, (F.C.T.D.) 85 DTC 5396, the court stated further "that circumstances which force the sale of property or make such a sale attractive do not have the effect of *retroactively converting* a property held to produce income and as a capital property into something of a trading nature". (Italics added.)

While the courts have indicated that taxpayer intention is the objective in a determination of whether a transaction results in a receipt of business income or capital, it should be recognized that intention is a state of mind. Intention must be inferred from an observation of a taxpayer's behaviour or a taxpayer's whole course of conduct. The observable behaviour of a taxpayer may be classified by a set of behavioural factors which may point to the existence of "an adventure or concern in the nature of trade" from which an intention to enter a profit-making scheme can be inferred. The courts have developed a set of indicators, often referred to as "badges of trade" to determine whether an adventure or concern in the nature of trade was present in a transaction and, hence, whether business income resulted.

---

[d] For a more detailed discussion of this topic, see Robert E. Beam and Stanley N. Laiken, "Adventure or Concern in the Nature of Trade: the Key to Taxpayer Intention", (1996) vol. 44, no. 3 *Canadian Tax Journal*, pp. 888–913.

[e] Two good examples of this situation are given by the cases of *Regal Heights Ltd. v. M.N.R.*, (S.C.C.) 60 DTC 1270 and *Fraser v. M.N.R.*, (S.C.C.) 64 DTC 5224.

To determine whether a gain on the disposition of property is business income from an adventure or concern in the nature of trade or a capital gain, it is useful to apply an analytical framework to a fact situation. The objective of applying such a framework is to systematically evaluate the facts to determine whether a transaction or series of transactions bear the "badges of trade". A list of behavioural factors or badges of trade that can be used as a reference might be comprised of the following.

(1) Relation of the transaction to the taxpayer's business: A transaction may be regarded as an income transaction if it is very similar to one in which the taxpayer would be involved in his or her normal business or profession. If a taxpayer undertakes a transaction in association with others, then the relationship of the transaction to the normal business or profession of these associates can be considered. This factor is helpful in determining whether a taxpayer had a secondary intention to make a profit on the sale of an asset. If a taxpayer has special knowledge or expertise or had direct access to these, it might be inferred that in a particular transaction a profitable "escape hatch" was known at the time of the purchase.

(2) Activity or organization normally associated with trade: The nature of the activity surrounding a transaction or the level of organization of the transaction may be such that the transaction can be considered "an adventure in the nature of trade" or a transaction which is very similar to one which would be undertaken by a business-person normally engaged in such transactions. Two classic cases of this involved British taxpayers one of whom purchased a carload of toilet paper and resold it at a profit (*Rutledge v. C.I.R.*, [1929] 14 T.C. 490) and the other of whom purchased a carload of whisky and sold it at a profit (*C.I.R. v. Fraser*, [1942] 24 T.C. 498). Transacting in such commodities by the carload is an indication of an intention to trade which would result in the gains being assessed as business income. To apply this factor, it is necessary to determine how the transaction in question was organized. If a transaction was handled in the same way as a normal business transaction was handled, in terms of quantities of a commodity purchased, method of promotion and sale, etc., there may be evidence of an adventure in the nature of trade. IT-459 deals with the concept of "an adventure or concern in the nature of trade" in more detail, in particular, under the heading "Taxpayer's Conduct" in paragraphs 5 to 8.

(3) Nature of the assets involved: The courts distinguish between fixed assets, which if sold result in a capital transaction, and "circulating" or working capital assets, which if sold result in an income transaction. Hence, the particular use of an asset by a given taxpayer may determine its nature for that taxpayer. Some assets, by their nature, can only be regarded as inventory. For example, whisky or toilet paper cannot produce income in such forms as interest, dividends, rents, etc. Income from these commodities can only be earned when they are sold, as inventory, for a price higher than their cost. IT-459 deals with this factor under the heading "Nature of the Property" in paragraphs 9 to 11.

(4) Number and frequency of transactions by the same taxpayer in a given period of time: A relatively large number of transactions in a given period of time may indicate that the taxpayer is involved in a business activity which will result in income transactions. Hence, extensive involvement in a particular type of transaction may be indicative of business activity. It should be emphasized, however, that an isolated transaction may still be considered an "adventure in the nature of trade", that is, of a business nature.

(5) Length of the period of ownership of the asset: The length of the holding period for an asset may be used to determine whether the asset is being treated as inventory or as a capital asset. The shorter the period of ownership, the more likely is the gain to be regarded as business income from an adventure in the nature of trade.

(6) Supplemental work on or in connection with the property disposed of in the transaction: Work done on a property to enhance its value or to make it more marketable may indicate an adventure in the nature of trade resulting in business income on

the disposition. Intensive advertising and promotion of the property for sale would be a similar indicator.

(7) Circumstances that caused the disposition: An unsolicited offer that results in the sale or a sale motivated by an unforeseen need for funds may argue against the existence of an adventure in the nature of trade, because of the evidence of the lack of a plan to turn a profit on a sale.

(8) Corporate objects or partnership agreement: Articles of incorporation may suggest that the corporation was engaged in a business which it had been created to carry on. Some judicial decisions, in the past, have held that a transaction, although unrelated to the taxpayer's usual business, fell within the objects of a corporation as represented by its charter and, as a result, was a transaction of a business nature. This can occur when the objects of a corporation are set out in a very broad manner in its charter to provide for future flexibility. On the other hand, in the case of *Sutton Lumber & Trading Company Ltd. v. M.N.R.*, 53 DTC 1158, the Supreme Court of Canada ignored a corporation's objects on the basis that what is relevant is not what a corporation can do under its objects, but what, in fact, it did do. Furthermore, it should be noted that, although some provincial corporation legislation provides for corporations having objects, the *Canada Business Corporations Act* and the *Ontario Business Corporations Act* do not provide for stated corporate objects. Thus, the relevance of this factor may be diminished. It should be noted that the stated objectives of a partnership organization, as outlined in a partnership agreement or other document, might be regarded in the same way.

This is not an exhaustive list of behavioural factors that can be observed. The factors used to determine whether a receipt is one of income or capital may depend on the type of property involved. For example, on the sale of real estate, the CRA has developed a list of about 12 factors which the courts have considered and lists them in IT-218R at paragraph 3.

Factors or badges of trade pertaining specifically to real estate transactions not already indicated in the foregoing list include:

(a) feasibility of the taxpayer's stated intention;

(b) geographical location and zoned use of the real estate;

(c) extent to which stated intention was carried out by the taxpayer;

(d) evidence of a change in stated intention after the purchase;

(e) the extent to which borrowed money was used to finance the acquisition and the terms of the financing; and

(f) factors which motivated the sale.

IT-479R lists some of the factors or badges of trade that are used in distinguishing between a receipt of income and a receipt of capital on the disposition of securities. Some of the factors listed in paragraph 11 and not listed among the factors already discussed include:

(a) knowledge of or experience in securities markets;

(b) time spent studying the securities markets and investigating potential purchases;

(c) financing primarily by margin or other forms of debt; and

(d) advertising or otherwise making it known that the taxpayer is willing to purchase securities.

Exhibit 4-1 diagrams the analytical framework developed. Note how an assessment of the existence of badges of trade from the facts is used to infer intention of the taxpayer at the time of the purchase of the property in question. Evidence of the existence of significant badges of trade suggests an intention to engage in a profit-making scheme or an adventure in the nature of trade. The lack of that evidence may suggest an investment intention.

EXHIBIT 4-1
Analytical Framework for Capital vs. Income Issue

Evidence of Adventure Based on Behavioural Factors or "Badges of Trade"

- relationship of transaction to taxpayer's business;
- activity or organization associated with trade;
- nature of asset;
- number and frequency of transactions in a given period of time;
- length of period of ownership of asset;
- supplemental work on or in connection with property;
- circumstances that caused disposition;
- if transaction completed by organization, stated objectives of organization as outlined in articles of association or partnership agreement;
- other factors.

inference

Intention of the Taxpayer

Primary:

   Did the taxpayer intend to use the asset like an item of inventory or like a capital asset?

Secondary:

   If the primary intention to use the asset like a capital asset was frustrated, did the taxpayer have, *at the time of the purchase*, a motivating intention to sell the property at a profit?

determination

Issue for Determination

   Is the gain (or loss) from the disposition of property a capital gain (or loss) or business income (or loss)?

Source: Reproduced with the permission of the Canadian Tax Foundation from Robert E. Beam and Stanley N. Laiken, "Adventure or Concern in the Nature of Trade: Badges of Trade as the Key Indicator of Taxpayer Intention", (1996) vol. 44, no. 3 *Canadian Tax Journal*, pp. 888–913.

Example Problem

The taxpayer was the president and general manager of a Canadian company involved in the fabrication of various products of non-ferrous metals, including lead. The company purchased all its lead requirements from a Canadian supplier which was the only producer of lead in Canada. However, the Canadian supplier held the company to a quota and, as a result, the company lost considerable business.

In these circumstances, the Canadian company requested the permission of its U.S. parent to import foreign lead. This meant buying it for future delivery in about three months. The risk of importing lead for future delivery was contrary to the business policy set for the Canadian company by the U.S. parent. However, the taxpayer was granted permission to purchase the lead himself and sell it to the Canadian company, assuming personally whatever risk was involved in the transaction.

The taxpayer made arrangements for the purchase of 1,500 tons of the foreign lead and for its sale to the Canadian company, on its arrival, at the market price of lead on the date of its arrival. He did not, himself, have to put up any money for the purchase of the lead. On the transaction, the taxpayer made a substantial profit.

— REQUIRED

Determine whether the profit made by the taxpayer was a capital gain or income from business or property.

— SOLUTION [See *M.N.R. v. James A. Taylor*, (Ex. Ct.) 56 DTC 1125]

The taxpayer purchased the lead with the intention of selling it to the Canadian company. His purpose was to alleviate the short supply of lead to which the Canadian company had been held by its Canadian supplier and, hence, to enable the Canadian company to meet the demand for its products. Since the taxpayer, as president and general manager of the Canadian company, was an employee, he was not carrying on a business of his own. Hence, the transaction in question was not related to a business that he was carrying on personally, as might be the case of a commodity dealer.

If the transaction can be considered "an adventure in the nature of trade", then the profit resulting from the transaction would be income from business. An 1896 British case (*Grainger and Son v. Gough*, (1896) 3 R.T.C. 462) provided the following definition of "trade":

> . . . Trade in its largest sense is the business of selling, with a view to profit, goods which the trader has either manufactured or himself purchased.

A 1904 British case (*Californian Copper Syndicate Ltd. v. Harris*, [1904] 5 T.C. 159) set out a test for determining whether the gain from a transaction was capital or income as follows:

> . . . Is the sum of gain that has been made a mere enhancement of value by realising a security, or is it a gain made in an operation of business in carrying out a scheme for profit-making?

The element of speculation may determine that a transaction is characteristic of what a trader would do. It can be said that the transaction has the "badges of trade". Thus, if the transaction is of the same kind and is carried on in the same way as a transaction of an ordinary trader or dealer in the same kind of property, it may be called an adventure in the nature of trade.

The nature and quantity of the subject matter of the transaction may be such as to exclude the possibility that its sale was the realization of an investment of a capital nature. This would lead to the conclusion that the taxpayer's purchase and sale of 1,500 tons of lead was an adventure in the nature of trade. He could not do anything with the lead except sell it. In fact, he dealt with the lead in the same manner as any dealer in imported lead would have done.

The fact that this was an isolated transaction cannot preclude it from being an adventure in the nature of trade. The word "adventure" implies a single or isolated transaction. Furthermore, it is not essential to a transaction being an adventure in the nature of trade that an organization be set up to carry it into effect. Finally, the fact that a transaction is totally different in nature from any of the other activities of the taxpayer and that he has never entered into a transaction of the kind before or since does not, by itself, preclude it from being an adventure in the nature of trade.

The Exchequer Court of Canada, the predecessor of the Federal Court of Canada, concluded in this case that the taxpayer's transaction was an adventure in the nature of trade and, hence, the profit was taxable as income from business.

3. Damages as a receipt of income or capital

(a) *Non-performance of Business Contracts*

Damages received for non-performance of business contracts are usually intended to place the recipient in the same position as he or she would have been had the contract been performed. Since the performance of a business contract usually results in income, damages for non-performance are generally regarded as income.[f]

(b) *Cancellation of Agency Agreements*

While the cancellation of an agency agreement has been held to be income, if such an agreement is of sufficient importance to constitute part of the company's total business structure, the compensation paid on the termination of such a contract may be capital. This was the situation in *Van den Berghs, Ltd. v. Clark*, [1935] A.C. 431, a United Kingdom decision. In that case an English company entered into an agreement with a competing Dutch company to co-operate in the manufacture and sale of margarine and to share in the resulting profits and losses. The agreement was to last for about 30 years, but it had to be terminated earlier and the Dutch company paid the English company a large sum of money to terminate the agreement. The British House of Lords held that the rights of the English company under the agreement constituted a capital asset and the sum paid for its cancellation was a capital receipt. For a Canadian case in this area see *Parsons-Steiner Limited v. M.N.R.*, (Ex. Ct.) 62 DTC 1148, which dealt with the cancellation of an agency agreement of 22 years standing accounting for 80% of the appellant's business. In *Pepsi-Cola Canada Ltd. v. The Queen*, (F.C.A.) 79 DTC 5388, a payment made on the termination of a bottling and distributorship agreement was held to be for goodwill and, hence, a capital receipt. On the other hand, compensation for cancelling a contract entered into in the course of the appellant's regular business was held to be taxable as income in *The Great Lakes Paper Company, Limited v. M.N.R.*, (T.A.B.) 61 DTC 564.

(c) *Loss of Property*

Damages for loss of property may be regarded as a receipt of capital if the property involved was fixed capital and a receipt of income if the property was working capital such as inventory.[g]

4. Other receipts or benefits

(a) *Profits from an Illegal Business*

A taxpayer may be carrying on a business of an illegal nature and yet be taxable on the profits. This principle was established in a 1932 United Kingdom case (*Mann v. Nash*, [1932] 1 K.B. 752) in which the following statement was made:

> ... The revenue [authorities], representing the state, are merely looking at an accomplished fact. It is not condoning it, or taking part in it. It merely finds profit made from what appears to be a trade, and the revenue laws say that profits made from a trade are to be taxed.

This was re-established in the Canadian case of *No. 275 v. M.N.R.*, (T.A.B.) 55 DTC 439. Having established this principle, the question of deductions arises in terms of

---

[f] The cases of *Sutherland v. M.N.R.*, (T.A.B.) 60 DTC 13 on compensation for losses in construction delays and *Hill v. M.N.R.*, (T.A.B.) 60 DTC 362 on compensation for lease cancellation illustrate this result.

[g] The cases of *Gagnon v. M.N.R.*, (T.A.B.) 53 DTC 273 and *Federal Farms Limited v. M.N.R.*, (Ex. Ct.) 59 DTC 1050 deal with such damages. Whether property was lost or profits were foregone was at issue in *Donald Hart Limited v. M.N.R.*, (Ex. Ct.) 59 DTC 1134, and whether a capital source of income or the income itself was lost was at issue in *Dr. Georges Garneau v. M.N.R.*, (T.A.B.) 68 DTC 132.

substantiating expenses incurred to produce the profits from an illegal business. This was the situation in *M.N.R. v. Eldridge*, (Ex. Ct.) 64 DTC 5338 involving the operator of a call-girl organization who attempted to claim certain cash expenditures. Substantiated, non-capital expenditures incurred to produce income from an illegal business are normally deductible, under conditions discussed later in this chapter. However, section 67.5 prohibits the deduction of specified illegal payments. Hence, illegal payments under specified sections of the *Criminal Code* made to government officials in Canada, officials engaged in the administration of justice in Canada, persons under a duty as agents or employees and persons responsible for collecting fares or admission fees are not deductible where the payments are made to induce, or attempt to induce, the recipient to breach his or her duty and the payment is made for doing anything that is an offence under the specified sections of the *Criminal Code*. Refer to IT-256R for the CRA's position in this area.

(b) *Profits from Betting, Gambling and Windfalls*

The proceeds of private betting or gambling for mere pleasure have generally been regarded as not taxable as long as the activity is not organized and of a business nature. This will be the case even if the bets, perhaps even made with borrowed funds, are high and the gains substantial. However, someone like a bookmaker will be taxable on his or her profits because he or she will be regarded as carrying on a business. The existence of a system for the minimization or management of risk may indicate a professional gambler. In this case, the winnings would be taxable and, conceivably, the losses would be deductible.[h]

A non-taxable windfall can be distinguished from income if the recipient has no expectation of receiving the payment.[i] Perhaps a more widely recognized form of windfall is a lottery winning, which is not taxable.

(c) *Subsidies*

The question of whether a government or any other subsidy is capital or income will depend on the purpose of the subsidy. An income receipt may result from a subsidy to:

- supplement the taxpayer's income or enable him or her to operate at a profit, or
- ensure a reasonable return to the taxpayer on capital invested.

On the other hand, a capital receipt may result from a subsidy to:

- reimburse or assist the taxpayer in respect of a capital outlay, or
- encourage an activity in the public interest such as the prevention of unemployment.

The case of *Saint John Drydock & Shipbuilding Co. Ltd. v. M.N.R.*, (Ex. Ct.) 2 DTC 663 is a leading Canadian decision on the question of whether a subsidy should be regarded as a receipt of income or capital. The general principles followed by the CRA in making this distinction are set out in IT-273R2.

(d) *Forgiveness of Debt Rules*

When a taxpayer incurs a debt obligation, the principal amount that is borrowed is not considered to be income. Hence, there is no deduction on the repayment of this debt. Therefore, repayments of principal are made with after-tax funds. As well, when a debt is settled or forgiven by the creditor for less than its principal amount, there should be no tax consequences. However, where interest was paid or payable on the debt amount and was or could be deducted from a source of income, then the debtor

---

[h] See the case of *Belawski v. M.N.R.*, (T.A.B.) 54 DTC 457 in this area.

[i] As an example of such an amount see *J.E. Cranswick v. The Queen*, (F.C.T.D.) 80 DTC 6057.

has received a tax benefit from the interest expense write-offs. The debt forgiveness rules apply to commercial obligations which are debt obligations incurred for the purpose of earning income from a business or property. Personal debt would normally be excluded from these rules.

Section 80 contains complex rules that reduce certain tax-loss carryovers or tax accounts by the amount of debt forgiven, generally where interest charged on the debt was deductible to the debtor. The forgiven amount of the debt is applied to reduce tax values including non-capital loss and net capital loss carryforwards and the capital costs of assets owned by the debtor [ssec. 80(3) to (12)]. The potential effect of these reductions is to increase income through lower tax-free recovery of costs in the future. The balance of debt forgiven that is not otherwise applied to reduce specified tax-loss carryovers or other tax accounts must be included in computing the income of the debtor at an inclusion rate of 50% (or 100% for a partnership) [ssec. 80(13)]. Where the debt was incurred in a business activity, the income inclusion is considered to be income from the business. The effect of this provision is to fully offset the benefit of not having to repay all or part of a debt with after-tax funds. The specific rules of section 80 are beyond the scope of this text.

B. Inventory Valuation

[ITA: 10; ITR: 1801; IT-473R]

1. Basis of valuation

Subsection 10(1) permits the valuation of each item in an inventory at the lower of cost or market. A degree of variation is permitted by section 1801 of the Income Tax Regulations which allows all of the items in the inventory to be valued at fair market value. Regulation 1801 might be used, where the fair market value of all items is lower than the valuation provided by subsection 10(1), to maximize cost of goods sold, and, thereby, minimize tax. However, there could be situations where the higher value would be desirable, for example, to reduce a loss that might expire. Again, the choice permitted between subsection 10(1) and Regulation 1801 could be used to provide the higher valuation as necessary, but the effect may be minimal, given the choices permitted. Furthermore, as will be seen from a subsequent discussion, the choice may be permanent, such that the long-term effects of the alternate choice should be considered [ssec. 10(2.1)].

Where the cost of items in an inventory can be identified, it is the actual laid down cost that must be used. This would include invoice cost plus duties, freight and insurance. In the case of goods in process and finished goods in the inventory of a manufacturing concern, cost will also include the cost of direct labour and in some cases the applicable share of overhead expenses. According to IT-473R the cost of manufactured goods must include overhead allocated on a direct costing or absorption costing basis. Subsection 10(1.1) requires the inclusion in cost any non-deductible interest and property taxes on vacant land held as inventory of a business.

Where individual items cannot be identified for costing, a convention or assumption, usually "first-in first-out" (FIFO), must be applied for the purpose of determining cost of inventory on hand. The use of "last-in first-out" (LIFO) as an assumption about cost has long been fought by the CRA as illustrated by the case of *M.N.R. v. Anaconda American Brass Ltd.*, (Privy Council) 55 DTC 1220. In that case it was held by the Judicial Committee of the Privy Council of the House of Lords of the United Kingdom (to which decisions of the Supreme Court of Canada could be appealed until the mid-1950s), first, that an assumption of any kind in determining inventory value could only be made to the extent that the facts about actual cost were not ascertainable. Furthermore, in the particular case of Anaconda, the LIFO assumption disregarded the actual flow of inventory through the business. This disregard of facts in relation to the flow of goods also made the use of the LIFO assumption objectionable in the case of *Wickett and Craig Ltd. v. M.N.R.*, (T.R.B.) 78 DTC 1382. While the use of LIFO conforms to generally accepted accounting principles and increases, relatively, the cost of goods sold to reflect the effects of inflation in periods of rising inventory costs, the Act does not recognize such effects.

For the meaning of the word "market" in the valuation of inventory, refer to the C.I.C.A. (Canadian Institute of Chartered Accountants) *Handbook*. Market price may be interpreted to mean:

(a) the current purchase price prevailing for the quantities of goods normally purchased by the taxpayer (useful for raw materials);

(b) realization value, i.e., the selling price which the goods on hand will realize, after deducting the direct cost of making the sale (useful for finished goods); or

(c) replacement value, i.e., the cost of reproducing the article into its present state of completion (useful for semi-finished goods where it is usually not possible to obtain a purchase price and it is not possible to sell the article).

The meaning of the terms "cost" and "market" are further considered in IT-473R.

It is interesting to note that paragraph 10(4)(*b*) specifies that replacement cost must be used for the fair market value of certain property that is advertising or packaging material, parts, supplies or other property of this nature which is considered to be inventory. Note, also, that work in progress of a business that is a profession is considered to be inventory with a fair market value equal to the amount that can reasonably be expected to become receivable after the end of the year [par. 10(4)(*a*)]. Subsection 10(5) establishes, for greater certainty, that these types of property are considered to be inventory and, hence, subject to the valuation rules for inventory in subsection 10(1).

Subsection 10(2) requires that the value attributed to the opening inventory be the same as that attributed to the closing inventory of the year before. This ensures that no profits escape tax by a break in the continuity of the inventory figures between the end of one year and the beginning of the next.

Subsection 10(2.1) requires that a taxpayer value inventory at the end of a year using the same method as that used at the end of the preceding year. The subsection permits a taxpayer to change the valuation method used for inventory of a business where permission is obtained from the CRA. The result is to restrict the flexibility in the choice of inventory valuation method from one year to another. However, there may be some flexibility within a particular inventory valuation method. For example, a business that is required to value its inventory at the lower of cost or market at the end of a year because that method was used at the end of the preceding year, may still have a choice in determining cost for the purposes of this valuation method. Subsection 10(2.1) appears to codify accounting principles requiring that the opening and closing inventories of a given year be valued on the same basis.

Subsection 10(3) allows the CRA to correct the value of opening inventory where it has not been valued as required by subsection 10(1). As a result, corrected opening inventory may differ from closing inventory of the preceding year, thereby forcing the effects of the change on the income of the year of the correction only.

Example Problem

Sam DaBuilder builds houses in various parts of the city. At the end of his fiscal year he has four homes left in his inventory. Sam's records show the following information on each house:

		Actual total cost	Cost to rebuild house	Market list price
1.	Happy Valley Road	$40,000	$50,000	$75,000
2.	Thruway Drive	25,000	20,000	18,000
3.	Low Profit Place	40,000	45,000	42,000
4.	Broken Balloon Lane	25,000	22,000	24,000

From past experience Sam knows that he can sell each house for its market list price less 10% for commissions and bargaining.

— REQUIRED

Using the valuation alternatives available to him, determine the value of Sam's closing inventory. Indicate the basis for each valuation and select the one more advantageous to him, assuming he wants to minimize income for tax purposes. (Ignore the potential application of subsection 10(2.1) in this case.)

— SOLUTION

In this case, since the houses are finished, net realizable value would be the appropriate indicator of market value. This would be calculated from the information given by reducing market list price by the 10% direct cost of making the sale. The following would form the basis of the decision:

House	Cost	Market		Lower on each unit
1	$40,000	$ 67,500	(90% of $75,000)	$ 40,000
2	25,000	16,200	(90% of $18,000)	16,200
3	40,000	37,800	(90% of $42,000)	37,800
4	25,000	21,600	(90% of $24,000)	21,600
		$143,100		$115,600

Using subsection 10(1), the inventory could be valued at $115,600 which is the lower of cost or market for each item. Regulation 1801 would permit the use of the market value of all items ($143,100). In this case, if the business is profitable, the more advantageous valuation would be based on the lower of cost or market for each item because it would provide the lower valuation, thereby increasing cost of goods sold and decreasing income subject to tax. On the other hand, if the business is in a loss position for the year, some of the losses can be absorbed by choosing the Regulation 1801 alternative of market value to decrease cost of goods sold, thereby increasing the gross margin available to offset losses for the year. The choice is limited by the provision in subsection 10(2.1), which requires that the method chosen for ending inventory in the current year must be the same as the method used for closing inventory at the end of the previous year unless ministerial permission for a change is granted.

2. Adjustment for depreciation allocation to inventory: an overview of the issue

To the extent that the cost of closing inventory for financial accounting purposes *includes an allocation* by the use of absorption costing of depreciation, obsolescence or depletion write-offs, such an allocation must be added to income for the year [par. 12(1)(r)]. This rule requires the full add-back of depreciation in the reconciliation of income for tax purposes with income for financial accounting purposes. The add-back is required despite the fact that any depreciation included in the cost of closing inventory is not charged as an expense in the year, because the value of closing inventory reduces the cost of goods sold. Since the same allocation for accounting purposes will be included in the cost of opening inventory of the next year, a deduction of the amount of the allocation added in the current year for tax purposes is made in the subsequent year [par. 20(1)(*ii*)]. These adjustments are unnecessary if the taxpayer has used the direct costing method and, as a result, has not included in the cost of inventory for financial accounting purposes an allowance in respect of depreciation, obsolescence or depletion.

C. Sole Proprietorship

[ITA: 11; 34.1; 34.2; 249.1]

For fiscal periods that begin after 1994, individuals who report business income, including professional income, generally must report that income on a calendar year basis, according to the definition of "fiscal period" [ssec. 249.1(1)]. This requirement applies to a sole proprietorship and a professional corporation, which is any corporation that carries on the professional practice of an accountant, dentist, lawyer, medical doctor, veterinarian, or chiropractor [ssec. 248(1)]. The requirement, also, applies to partnerships in which at least one member is an individual, a professional corporation or another affected partnership.

However, subsection 249.1(4) provides for an alternative fiscal period for a business carried on by an individual. A change in the end of a fiscal period can only be made with ministerial concurrence [ssec. 249.1(7)]. An off-calendar fiscal year-end for an unincorporated business is possible, if an individual files an election in prescribed form by the date on which the individual must file a tax return for the year. The election can be revoked in a future period, in which case the calendar-year fiscal period must be used [ssec. 249.1(6)].

To prevent a deferral in the reporting of income on an off-calendar fiscal period [ssec. 249.1(4)], additional rules for the reporting of business income must be followed. Section 34.1 contains a formula that effectively computes income from an unincorporated business with an off-calendar year-end on a calendar year basis by the use of an estimating procedure.

The system applies to, for example, a January 31 business year-end as follows. First, the taxpayer includes income from the unincorporated business for the fiscal period ended, say, January 31, 2005. To this amount, the taxpayer must add an estimate of business income for the "stub period" from February 1, 2005 to December 31, 2005. The estimate is based on a proration of $^{11}/_{12}$ or 11 months of income in the fiscal period ended January 31, 2005. From the sum, the taxpayer can subtract the stub period addition made in the 2004 tax return. However, the alternative method recognizes that there are valid non-tax business reasons for using an off-calendar year-end and allows such a year-end to be maintained.

When an off-calendar year-end reflects less than 12 months of business operations, due to the commencement of business, the stub-period income addition is adjusted so that an appropriate amount not exceeding 12 months of income is reported in a calendar-year period [ssecs. 34.1(1) and (2)].

Section 34.2 provides a transitional reserve for off-calendar fiscal periods that were changed to a calendar year-end in 1995. This transitional relief is accomplished through a reserve system that brings the 1995 adjustment into income over ten years.

II. INCLUSIONS

A. Amounts Received and Receivable

[ITA: 12(1)(a), (b), (2)]

Amounts received for services to be rendered or goods to be delivered are included in income [par. 12(1)(a)]. This represents a divergence from accounting principles which would defer such amounts of income until the year in which they are earned. However, a reasonable reserve for unearned amounts included in income can be taken [par. 20(1)(m)]. The Act's system for reserves will be discussed later in this chapter. Paragraph 12(1)(a) would include amounts received such as prepaid rent, payments for the warranty of merchandise and container deposits. A deduction for refunds of amounts previously included in income under this paragraph is provided to offset the fact that a reserve would not be available for a refunded amount [par. 20(1)(m.2)].

Amounts receivable in respect of services rendered or property sold during the year in the course of business are brought into income [par. 12(1)(b)]. A complementary reserve (limited to three years by subsection 20(8)) is available at least for property sold [par. 20(1)(n)] to recognize the uncertainty of collecting these amounts. An amount will be deemed to have become receivable on the earlier of the day when the account was rendered and the day on which it would have been rendered had there been no undue delay.

Amounts included under paragraph 12(1)(b) must be legally receivable as a result of the taxpayer's having completed the performance of the service contracted for.[j] Hold-backs, common in the construction industry, are not legally receivable until the year in which the architect's or engineer's final certificate accepting and approving work done is issued. Subsection 12(2) provides that these paragraphs are enacted "for greater certainty" and should not be interpreted to imply that any amount not referred to, such as amounts received and earned in the year, are not to be included in income from business.

B. Inducement Payments or Reimbursements

[ITA: 12(1)(x); IT-359R2]

Paragraph 12(1)(x) requires that all receipts in the nature of reimbursements or inducements in respect of the acquisition of an asset or the incurring of a deductible expense be included in income from business or property unless this amount already has reduced the cost of the property or the amount of the expense. The types of receipts contemplated by this provision include inducements, grants, subsidies, reimbursements, etc., and amounts received indirectly from these sources, perhaps, through a not-for-profit entity. An example of such inducements would be receipts by a commercial tenant who was reimbursed by a landlord for part or all of the cost of making leasehold improvements. As an alternative, the recipient may elect to reduce the capital cost [ssec. 13(7.4)] or the cost [ssec. 53(2.1)] of the related property or the amount of the related expense. The provision brings the tax treatment of such receipts in line with generally accepted commercial principles. This area has been a source of contentious issues which were not fully resolved by the CRA's IT-359R2. Note that this Interpretation Bulletin also deals with the position of the payer which is not specifically dealt with in the legislation.

---

[j] The question of when expropriation proceeds are receivable was addressed in the case of *M.N.R. v. Lechter*, (S.C.C.) 66 DTC 5300.

C. Restricted Covenants

[ITA: 12(1)(x)(v.1) Proposed in the Technical Amendments to the *Income Tax Act*, February 27, 2004]

Starting on October 8, 2003, payments received for a restrictive covenant must be included in income. To the extent that a taxpayer receives an amount for a restrictive covenant, the amount must be included in income except to the extent that a related person is required to take it into income under subsection 56.4(2). For a full discussion on the treatment of payments received for restrictive covenants please refer to Chapter 9.

III. DEDUCTIONS

A. Deductibility of Expenditures

[ITA: 9; 12(1); 18–20; 67; 67.1; 67.2; 67.3; 67.5; 67.6 [Proposed]; 78; 147(5.1); 147.1; 147.2; 248(16); ITR: 4100; IT-109R2; IT-185R; IT-419R2; IT-442R; IT-514; IT-533]

The first test of deductibility is actually contained in the words of subsection 9(1) which state that:

> subject to this Part, a taxpayer's *income* for a taxation year from a business or property is his *profit* therefrom for the year. (italics added)

As previously indicated, the courts have often relied on ordinary commercial practices (which may also embody generally accepted accounting principles (GAAP)) to provide the basis of profit, unless the Act specifically requires an alternate treatment. Hence, the deductibility of an expenditure under GAAP, subject to ordinary commercial practices, should be considered where the Act is silent on the treatment of the expenditure. The specific provisions of the Act that may require an alternate treatment are contained, generally, in sections 18, 19, 20 and 67.[k]

Sections 18 and 19, in essence, prohibit the deduction of specified expenditures through the use of the words "no deduction shall be made". However, the rules in sections 18 and 19 actually establish general principles or tests of deductibility under the Act. If an expenditure is not prohibited by a rule in section 18 or 19, that is, if an expenditure passes the set of sequential tests in these provisions, the expenditure is deductible. If an expenditure fails one of the tests in section 18 or 19, then subsection 20(1) should be consulted for the existence of a specific exception which would allow the deduction of the expenditure. Some of the more common tests of deductibility pertaining to income from business are discussed here.

1. General test

To pass the test of deductibility in paragraph 18(1)(*a*) an expense or outlay must:

(a) be made or incurred by the taxpayer for the purpose of gaining, producing or maintaining income; and

(b) be expected to generate income related to the taxpayer's business or property.

The meaning of "for the purpose of gaining or producing income" has been at issue in many cases. While the club dues at issue in *The Royal Trust Company v. M.N.R.*, (Ex. Ct.) 57 DTC 1055 are now specifically not deductible by virtue of paragraph 18(1)(*l*), added to the Act in 1972, the case is important in demonstrating the relative remoteness between the expenditure and its purpose to produce income. That is, while the items listed in paragraph 18(1)(*l*), including club dues, are not deductible,

---

[k] This system of testing the deductibility of an expenditure was discussed in the case of *The Queen v. MerBan Capital Corporation Limited*, (F.C.A.) 89 DTC 5404.

the principle established in the *Royal Trust* case may still hold for items not specifically prohibited by that paragraph or others.[1]

Generally, all that need be demonstrated is that the expenditure was expected to generate income, although no income may have been generated. This was the issue in *Booth v. M.N.R.*, (T.R.B.) 79 DTC 595 involving a poet and painter who claimed certain expenses as deductions. Also, *The Queen v. Lalande and Watelle*, (F.C.T.D.) 84 DTC 6159 (affirmed by Federal Court of Appeal, 89 DTC 5178) dealt with the deduction by doctors of legal fees and payments under loan guarantees in situations which could increase their clientele. In the case of *Speck v. M.N.R.*, 88 DTC 1518, the Tax Court of Canada held that a full-time teacher, who incurred losses for three years followed by small profits for two years when he started a part-time business involving the restoration of automobiles, had reasonable expectations of turning a profit and these expectations had been met within the expected five years.

2. Expenditure of a capital nature

An expenditure may pass the test of having been made for the purpose of gaining, producing, or maintaining income, but paragraph 18(1)(*b*) prohibits the deduction of an outlay of a capital nature. A capital expenditure has been described in the United Kingdom case of *British Insulated and Helsby Cables Ltd. v. Atherton* [1926], A.C. 205 by the following statement:

> ... when an expenditure is made, not only once and for all, but with a view to bringing into existence an asset or advantage for the enduring benefit of a trade, ... there is very good reason (in the absence of special circumstances leading to an opposite conclusion) for treating such an expenditure as properly attributable not to revenue but to capital.

3. Other prohibited deductions

(a) *Reserves*

Paragraph 18(1)(*e*) prohibits the deduction of a reserve, a contingent liability or a sinking fund except as permitted by the Act. Allowable reserves under subsection 20(1) will be discussed later in this chapter.

(b) *Payments on Discounted Bonds*

When bonds are issued at a discount, usually because the contractual interest rate is lower than the market interest rate, the cost of the discount is incurred on the repayment of the debt at its face value. Paragraph 18(1)(*f*) does not permit a deduction for the amount paid or payable in respect of the discount except as computed under paragraph 20(1)(*f*) which will be discussed subsequently with deductions that are specifically permitted. This prohibition exists to discourage the issue of debt at a relatively large discount which might provide the holder of the debt with more advantageous capital gains treatment.

(c) *Use of Recreational Facilities and Club Dues*

Note the prohibition in paragraph 18(1)(*l*) on the deduction of club and other recreational facilities dues, no matter how important they may be to the revenue-producing process. In addition, this provision denies the deduction of expenses incurred for the *use or maintenance* of a yacht, a camp, a lodge or a golf course, unless these facilities are provided to the general public as in the course of the taxpayer's

---

[1] Other cases include: *Premium Iron Ores v. M.N.R.*, (S.C.C.) 66 DTC 5280 on legal fees to prepare a U.S. tax appeal; *M.N.R. v. Algoma Central Railways*, (S.C.C.) 68 DTC 5096 on the cost of a geological survey; *Canada Starch Co. Ltd. v. M.N.R.*, (Ex. Ct.) 68 DTC 5320 on the cost of protecting a trademark; and *Bowater Power Co. Ltd. v. M.N.R.*, (F.C.T.D.) 71 DTC 5469 on engineering studies.

business.[m] Note, also, that the prohibition applies only to expenditures incurred in respect of a yacht, camp, lodge or golf course. Similar expenditures incurred in respect of a restaurant or hotel would not be prohibited by paragraph 18(1)(*l*). In its decision, the Supreme Court upheld the intention of Parliament to discriminate in this way, based on the very specific words used in the provision. However, in a document dated February 17, 1998, the CRA indicated that it had reconsidered its interpretation of the word "facility" in relation to a golf course in subparagraph 18(1)(*l*)(*i*) of the Act. The Agency will now consider that "facility" as used in that subparagraph should be interpreted in connection with the words "golf course" as to only include recreational amenities provided by a golf club. Accordingly, a "facility" will not include the dining room, banquet halls, conference rooms, beverage rooms or lounges of a golf club and thus the deduction of the cost of meals and beverages incurred at a golf club will not be denied. As a result, the tax treatment of meals and beverages at a golf club will parallel that of meals and beverages consumed at a restaurant.[n]

(d) *Political Contributions*

Paragraph 18(1)(*n*) specifically prohibits the deduction of political contributions. A limited tax credit is provided in subsection 127(3).

(e) *Automobile Expenses*

Paragraph 18(1)(*r*) limits the deduction of an allowance paid or payable to an employee for the employment use of an automobile. However, there is no deduction limit if the amount of the allowance must be included in the employee's income. Regulation 7306 prescribes the deductible limit. According to Department of Finance News Release No. 2004-081 dated December 17, 2004, the present rates are, effective for 2005, 45 cents per kilometre for the first 5,000 kilometres driven and 39 cents per kilometre thereafter, with a four-cent per kilometre premium for driving in the Yukon Territory, Northwest Territories or Nunavut.

(f) *Payments under Act*

Paragraph 18(1)(*t*) denies a deduction in respect of any amount paid or payable under the Act. This provision would prohibit, for greater certainty, the deduction of federal income taxes, interest and penalties, all of which are imposed under the Act. However, paragraph 20(1)(*ll*) allows a deduction for interest paid on a tax refund that a taxpayer is required to repay because the refund was excessive.

(g) *Prepaid Expenses*

In a move to bring the treatment of certain prepaid expenses for tax purposes in line with the treatment for accounting purposes, subsection 18(9) prohibits the deduction of such expenses in the year of outlay. These expenses are deductible only in the taxation year to which the expenses relate. Expenditures treated in this manner are the following: payments for services to be rendered after the end of the year; payments of interest, taxes, rent or royalties in respect of a period after the end of the year and payments for insurance in respect of a period after the end of the year.

(h) *Expenses of Investing in Sheltered Plans*

While interest and certain financing expenses are usually deductible under several provisions in section 20, subsection 18(11) prohibits the deduction of these expenses in respect of indebtedness incurred for the purposes listed therein. Note that the items listed pertain to deductible investments in sheltered retirement plans in which income

---

[m] In the case of *Sie-Mac Pipeline Contractors Ltd. v. The Queen*, (S.C.C.) 93 DTC 5158, the Supreme Court of Canada held that to use a lodge does not require that it be owned or rented or exclusively controlled.

[n] "Entertainment at golf clubs", TAX WINDOWS FILES, Document number 9803677, February 17, 1998.

is not taxed as long as it remains in the plan. Also, the deduction of administration fees and investment counselling fees pertaining to certain plans, as discussed in Chapter 9, are prohibited [par. 18(1)(u)].

(i) Work Space in Home

Subsection 18(12) prohibits the deduction of the costs of maintaining a work space in an individual's home (i.e., "a self-contained domestic establishment in which the individual resides"), unless the office meets one of the following two tests:

(a) the work space is the individual's principal place of business; or

(b) it is used on a regular and continuous basis for meeting clients, customers or patients of the individual in earning income from business.

In the case of these exceptions, the costs are deductible only to the extent of income from the business. Thus, these home office expenses cannot be used to create a loss from the business, although a carryforward is available for excess expenses. This carryforward may be indefinite, according to IT-514, paragraph 5, as long as one of the two tests stated above is met. For the CRA's interpretation of the term "principal place of business" and "regular and continuous basis," see IT-514. The case of *Jenkins et. al. v. The Queen* (TCC — Informal Procedure), 2005 DTC 384, addressed the meaning of "principle place of business" for a fisher. The court concluded that the principal place of business is where the "business elements" of the business are engaged in, such as "telephoning customers and suppliers, filling in invoices, doing payroll, maintaining books and records, contacting authorities for licences, preparing tax returns, chasing down receivables, handling complaints, creating business plans, preparing financial statements, talking to accountants and lawyers, etc." The courts stated that "the actual harvesting of fish is the core of a fishing business, but it is not where the business side of fishing occurs."

(j) Deductibility of Provincial Capital and Payroll Taxes

The Federal Budget of February 26, 1991, proposed to limit the deduction of provincial capital and payroll taxes. However, the implementation of the proposal has been delayed (as a result of a Department of Finance announcement made late in 2004: Department of Finance News Release No. 2004-080, December 16, 2004). Payroll taxes would include any provincial tax imposed on a taxpayer and set by reference to the salary, wages or other remuneration paid by the taxpayer, except pension and worker's compensation contributions. Provincial health levies are an example of a provincial payroll tax. Capital taxes would include any tax imposed by a province and set by reference to a taxpayer's equity, liabilities or assets, but would exclude real property taxes.

Until a solution to the problems of the deductibility of these taxes is implemented, they are fully deductible. However, the government announced interim measures in March 1993 which would deny the deductibility of any increases in provincial payroll and capital taxes, whether by way of rate increases, base changes or the introduction of new taxes. This interim measure has been extended annually, most recently to 2005.

(k) Limitation on Accrued Expenses

In normal circumstances a deductible expenditure incurred by one taxpayer is matched, within a reasonable period of time, by the income receipt in the hands of the creditor. However, section 78 is designed to thwart contrived situations between persons not dealing at arm's length or between employers and employees where the debtor uses the accrual method of accounting and the creditor is on the cash method and where actual payment is unduly deferred.

Subsection 251(1) deems that related persons do not deal at arm's length. Chapter 6 deals with related individuals and Chapter 12 deals with related corporations and individuals. For the time being, assume that the normal interpretation of "related" applies. In addition, the provision indicates that it is question of fact whether persons not related to each other were, at a particular time, dealing with each other at arm's length. IT-419R2 pars. 23–26 list the following criteria that could be used in determining whether a transaction has occurred at arm's length:

- a common mind directs the bargaining for both parties to the transaction;

- the parties to the transaction were acting in concert without separate interests; and

- one party in fact controls the other party.

In order for an expense (e.g., accrued wages) that remains unpaid at the end of the taxation year to be deductible for tax purposes, it must constitute a genuine liability of the taxpayer. For a genuine liability to exist there must be an enforceable claim by the creditor (e.g., the employee) with a reasonable expectation that the debt in fact will be paid [IT-109R2 par. 15(e)]. Where there is not a genuine liability, the amount will be treated as contingent liability or reserve and will be denied [par. 18(1)(e)].[o]

(i) Unpaid Amounts

Unpaid amounts, in non-arm's length circumstances, are subject to the rules in subsection 78(1). Such an unpaid amount must be paid within two years of the end of the taxation year in which it was declared payable or accrued. If an amount remains unpaid after that two-year period, it must be brought back into income on the first day of the third taxation year following that in which the payable was declared. Thus, an unpaid amount declared payable in 2002 must be paid by the end of the 2004 taxation year or be included in income at the beginning of the 2005 taxation year.

Under paragraph 78(1)(b), the two parties can file an election by the date on which the corporation is required to file its tax return for the 2005 taxation year (i.e., by June 30, 2006) that the amount be deemed to have been paid on the first day of the 2005 taxation year and to have been loaned, net of appropriate withholding tax, back to the corporation. Then, the corporation would be liable to remit the amount deemed to have been withheld, by departmental practice, on or before July 15, 2006 in this case, and a repayment of the loan would have no further tax consequences. IT-109R2 provides further explanation of this provision and a more complete discussion of the interplay of these provisions is contained in Chapter 13.

(ii) Unpaid Remuneration and Other Amounts

In the case of items of remuneration, subsection 78(4) requires that salaries, wages or other remuneration (other than specified exceptions) must be paid within 179 days of the end of the taxation year in which the expense was incurred. If an amount is unpaid after that day, it will be deemed not to have been incurred as an expense and, therefore, will not be deductible until the year in which it is actually paid. However, by administrative practice, the CRA indicates in IT-109R2 par. 10 that a payment made on the 180th day is considered to have been made within the time limit and subsection 78(4) will not apply. Other remuneration includes unfunded obligations in respect of pension benefits and retiring allowances. The election for deemed repayment available in subsection 78(1), as described above, is not available for unpaid remuneration. An amount of accrued remuneration must be legally paid.

---

[o] The question of whether an amount was deductible at all as a real liability or not deductible as a contingent liability was at issue in *The Queen v. V & R Enterprises Limited*, (F.C.T.D.) 79 DTC 5399 and *Toronto Heel Limited v. M.N.R.*, (T.R.B.) 80 DTC 1250.

4. Reasonable Expectation of Profit (REOP)

Paragraph 18(1)(*h*) prohibits the deduction of personal or living expenses as defined, in part, as expenses not in connection with a business carried on for profit or with a reasonable expectation of profit [ssec. 248(1)]. Travel between home and work is one of the expenditures prohibited by this provision. In this regard, note the difference in treatment between the case of *Mildred Cohen v. M.N.R.*, (T.A.B.) 52 DTC 356 involving a physically challenged employee who, as a person deriving income from employment, cannot deduct the expenses of travel between home and work, no matter what the hardship may be, and, by contrast, *Cumming v. M.N.R.*, (Ex. Ct.) 67 DTC 5312 involving a self-employed doctor with an office in his home. Since his base of operations was his home, expenses of travel from that base to the hospital where he rendered services were deductible. The provision would also apply to the deductibility of interest on funds borrowed to purchase personal items such as cars and houses.

To be deductible, an expenditure must not only be made or incurred by the taxpayer for the purpose of gaining or producing income, but, as a result of the test in paragraph 18(1)(*h*), it must be made with "a reasonable expectation of profit" as defined in subsection 248(1). What constitutes a reasonable expectation of profit is dependent on the facts of each particular case. For a long period of time, the CRA, sometimes supported by the Canadian courts, attempted to expand the application of this reasonable expectation of profit or REOP test to deny the deduction of losses from business or property sources. Where there was a personal expenditure element to the fact situation, as in the case of a hobby or a partially rented personal residential property, the case for a reasonable expectation of profit was more difficult to make. On the other hand, where the expenditure involved no personal benefit element, that is, it was of a purely commercial nature, the Federal Court of Appeal had suggested in the case of *Tonn et al. v. The Queen*, 96 DTC 6001, and confirmed in the case of *Attorney General of Canada v. Mastri, et al.*, 97 DTC 5420, that the case against a reasonable expectation of profit test is more difficult to make. In the case of *Stewart v. Canada*, 2002 DTC 6969, the Supreme Court of Canada clarified and limited the application of the REOP test. The Court indicated that the REOP test has no application where there is no personal benefit element to a transaction. Where there is a personal benefit element, the test is only one of a number of factors that can be used to assess the commercial nature of an activity, thereby, undertaken in the pursuit of profit.[p]

Exhibit 4-2 provides a checklist for planning purposes to provide evidence of a reasonable expectation of profit, where there is a personal benefit in an activity. The checklist may help to assess the commercial nature of an activity and the businesslike behaviour of the taxpayer in that activity. The factors were derived largely from two U.S. studies of jurisprudence on a similar issue in U.S. tax law. Since the factors are based on U.S. jurisprudence, they have no direct precedent value in Canada. However, they are of more general applicability and may provide a basis or a framework for developing arguments for the existence, or lack thereof, of a predominant intention to make a profit from an activity in a Canadian fact situation.

---

[p] For a more complete discussion of the *Stewart* case and the jurisprudence that led to that decision, see Rayna F. Laiken and Stanley N. Laiken, "Working with the Source Test, the Supreme Court's Replacement for the Reasonable Expectation of Profit Test", (2002) vol. 50, no. 3, *Canadian Tax Journal*, pp.1147-1177.

EXHIBIT 4-2
Checklist of General Factors Used to Determine the Existence of a Reasonable Expectation of Profit or of Operating in a Businesslike Manner

(1) Manner in which activity is operated:
   (a) activity held out to community as a business
   (b) activity operated in a businesslike manner
   (c) activity operated in manner similar to comparable profitable businesses
   (d) unsuccessful methods discontinued and new ones adopted
   (e) formal books and records maintained
   (f) separate bank account maintained
   (g) record-keeping system provides for the determination of segment profits and relevant costs
   (h) detailed non-financial records maintained
   (i) operating methods changed to improve profitability
   (j) level of advertising or promotion undertaken
   (k) development plan formulated, followed and adjusted
   (l) scale of operations sufficient to be profitable.

(2) Elements of personal pleasure or recreation:
   (a) taxpayer obtains personal pleasure from the activity
   (b) facilities are utilitarian
   (c) conduct of activity involves social or recreational functions (apart from the activity itself)
   (d) long-time interest in activity as a hobby
   (e) operating methods constrained by personal motives
   (f) personal use separately accounted for.

(3) Expertise of the taxpayer or his or her advisers:
   (a) prior experience in the activity
   (b) profit potential determined prior to entry
   (c) pre-entry advice (or prior preparation) sought and followed
   (d) post-entry advice sought and followed
   (e) taxpayer belongs to business-related associations.
   (f) new or superior techniques developed

(4) History of income and loss:
   (a) average ratio of receipts to disbursements
   (b) percentage of years where receipts less than 5% of disbursements
   (c) average magnitude of losses
   (d) trend of losses declining
   (e) number of years activity was operated
   (f) losses due to circumstances beyond taxpayer's control
   (g) percentage of years with profits.
   (h) reasonable start-up period
   (i) trend of gross revenues

(5) Time and effort expended:
   (a) competent and well-informed manager employed
   (b) competent labour employed
   (c) average time spent on activity by taxpayer
   (d) taxpayer withdrew from another business to devote most of his/her time to the activity
   (e) taxpayer did physical labour.

(6) Financial status of taxpayer:
  (a) taxpayer's average income before activity loss
  (b) extent of tax savings from net losses
  (c) average ratio of activity losses to other income
  (d) taxpayer maintains an extravagant standard of living
  (e) majority of taxpayer's other income is from investments
  (f) extent of other net assets of taxpayer.
  (g) amount of capital invested in the operation

(7) Amount of occasional profits:
  (a) ratio of average profit to average loss
  (b) amount of largest profit earned
  (c) ratio of net losses to net assets.

(8) Sale or discontinuance of activity:
  (a) activity sold or discontinued because no chance for profit
  (b) activity sold or discontinued for any reason.

(9) Success of taxpayer in other activities:
  (a) extent of experience in similar successful business
  (b) history of losses in a similar activity.

(10) Expected appreciation of asset value:
  (a) taxpayer expected property to appreciate in value as the major source of investment return.

Sources: Jane O. Burns and S. Michael Groomer, "An Analysis of Tax Court Decisions That Assess the Profit Motive of Farming-Oriented Operations," *The Journal of the American Taxation Association*, Fall 1983, pp. 23-39.

Jack Robison, "Tax Court Classification of Activities Not Engaged in for Profit: Some Empirical Evidence," *The Journal of the American Taxation Association*, Fall 1983, pp. 7-22.

Proposed Amendments Related to REOP

[Draft Proposals on Interest Deductibility dated October 31, 2003]

On October 31, 2003, the Department of Finance released draft proposals on interest deductibility which also included legislation related to reasonable expectation of profit.

Proposed subsection 3.1(1) provides that a taxpayer can deduct a loss from a source that is a business or property only if, in that year, it is reasonable to expect that the taxpayer will realize a cumulative profit from the business or property. Then, new subsection 3.1(2) makes it clear that profit, in this context, does not include capital gains or capital losses.

While these changes seem straightforward, consider what would happen if a new business began to have financial difficulty and realized losses in excess of previous income. If they determined that they were going to have to close the business, then this proposed rule would deny any losses from that time forward. These future losses from expenditures such as wages, lease payments, severance and other recurring expenses, were previously deductible.

Since their release, there has been significant discussion between tax professionals and the Department on the implications of their proposals. The report of the Joint Committee on Taxation of the Canadian Bar Association and the Canadian Institute of Chartered Accountants states that:

> . . . we are of the view that the Draft Proposals would introduce a fundamental change to the *Income Tax Act* which goes well beyond the case law and administrative practice prior to recent court decisions. We are concerned that the proposals could be used to disallow losses resulting from wholly-legitimate business expenses the deductibility of which would not have been an issue under prior case law or administrative practice.

They would create significant issues with respect to the treatment of investments in securities.

In the March 23, 2004 federal budget the following statement was made:

> Assurances were given by the Minister of Finance, Finance officials and the CRA that these releases were not intended to adversely affect the past assessing practices regarding the deductibility of interest on equity investments. The Budget materials acknowledge that significant issues have been raised with them that warrant further consideration.

The Budget Plan 2005, published by the Department of Finance to accompany the February 23, 2005 federal budget, contained the following statement at page 410:

> Many commentators expressed concerns with the proposals' structure, in partic- ular, that the proposals' codification of the "reasonable expectation of profit" test might inadvertently limit the deductibility of a wide variety of ordinary commercial expenses. The Department of Finance has sought to respond by developing a more modest legislative initiative that would respond to those concerns while still achieving the Government's objectives. The Department will, at an early opportu- nity, release that alternative proposal for comment. This will be combined with a Canada Revenue Agency publication that addresses, in the context of the alterna- tive proposal, certain administrative questions relating to deductibility.

5. Limitations on amount of deductions for deductible expenditures

Items listed in subsection 18(1) are prohibited from being deducted because of the nature of the expenditure. Section 67 places a limitation on the amount of an outlay or expense that may be deducted. To be deductible, the amount must be "reasonable in the circumstances." This would suggest a comparison of the amount of an expenditure with the amount of similar expenditures made in similar situations by other taxpayers. The question of a reasonable salary paid to the wife of an owner-manager of a corpora- tion for full-time work as the secretary-treasurer was at issue in *Mulder Bros. Sand & Gravel Ltd. v. M.N.R.*, (T.A.B.) 67 DTC 475. The payment of large bonuses to the wife of the major shareholder of a corporation was at issue in *Doug Burns Excavation Con- tracting Limited v. M.N.R.*, (T.C.C.) 83 DTC 528. In the case of *Robinson v. M.N.R.*, 85 DTC 84, the Tax Court of Canada indicated that the costs of operating a luxury vehicle for business purposes should be limited in their deduction to a reasonable charge.

Other expenditures that are deductible under the general principles of deduct- ibility are limited by:

- section 67.1 in respect of food, beverages and entertainment;
- section 67.2 in respect of interest on funds borrowed to purchase a passenger vehicle; and
- section 67.3 in respect of costs of leasing a passenger vehicle.

Each of these provisions has been discussed in Chapter 3 and is equally applicable to the computation of deductions from business income, except that GST is not deduct- ible to a registrant where the GST provides an input tax credit [ssec. 248(16)]. The input tax credit, in effect, eliminates the GST as a cost and, hence, GST should not be deductible in these cases.

Two other limitations are noteworthy:

- section 67.5 in respect of illegal payments and
- section 67.6 in respect of fines and penalties.

Subsection 67.5(1) prohibits a deduction in respect of an expenditure incurred for the purpose of doing anything that is an offence under section 3 of the *Corruption of*

Foreign Public Officials Act involving bribery of a foreign public official to obtain a business advantage or any of the following sections of the Criminal Code:

- section 119 — bribery of judicial officers, etc.
- section 120 — bribery of officers
- section 121 — frauds on the government
- section 123 — municipal corruption
- section 124 — selling or purchasing office
- section 125 — influencing or negotiating appointments or dealing in offices
- section 393 — fraud in relation to fares, etc.
- section 426 — secret commissions

Deductions are, also, prohibited where the payment is made in a conspiracy to commit an offence under one of the above sections or a conspiracy in Canada to commit a similar offence under the law of another country.

Recent court cases have allowed the deductibility of fines and penalties incurred in the ordinary course of earning income unless the underlying action was so offensive that the fine or penalty could not reasonably be considered to have had an income-earning purpose. To bring certainty to this area of tax law, fines or penalties incurred after March 22, 2005 are not deductible if they are imposed by law — whether by a government, government agency, regulator, court or other tribunal, or any other person with statutory authority to levy fines or penalties [sec. 67.6]. This would include fines and penalties imposed under the laws of a foreign country. This would not include penalties or damages paid under private contracts. Part of this provision includes authority to exempt prescribed fines and penalties from its application, although there are no exemptions at this time.

6. Deductions specifically permitted

Usually, the general principles and rules (e.g., sections 18, 67, etc.) determining the deductibility of an outlay or expenditure are to be applied first. If a particular outlay or expenditure does not pass the tests of deductibility set out in section 18 or 19, then the lists in section 20 of exceptions to the general principles and rules should be consulted. The wording of subsection 20(1) recognizes that some of the deductions listed in the subsection may be prohibited by a general rule in subsection 18(1), and negates that effect by inserting the words "notwithstanding paragraphs 18(1)(a), (b) and (h), . . . there may be deducted . . ." The following are some of the more common deductions provided in section 20.

(a) *Write-offs of Capital Expenditures*

While paragraph 18(1)(b) prohibits the deduction of a capital nature, paragraphs 20(1)(a) and (b) override this prohibition and permit the deduction of the capital cost of depreciable capital property and the cost of eligible capital property, respectively, through a system of annual write-offs to be discussed in Chapter 5.

(b) *Interest*

Interest paid or payable on funds borrowed to finance the capital expenditures of a business would be considered as payment on account of capital and, therefore, would be prohibited from deduction [par. 18(1)(b)]. However, paragraph 20(1)(c) specifically provides for the deduction of interest on funds borrowed to earn income, i.e., on the purchase of assets or on indebtedness arising from the acquisition of capital assets. Compound interest is deductible under paragraph 20(1)(d) if the base interest is deductible [par. 20(1)(c)].

On October 31, 2003 the Department of Finance released its Draft Proposals on Interest Deductibility. Along with proposed amendments related to REOP (discussed above) was a new Interpretation Bulletin, IT-533 — Interest Deductibility and Related Issues. This new bulletin is now a prime source for the CRA's administrative position on interest deductibility in that it replaces and cancels five other bulletins and provides commentary on all the key issues and some of the tax planning techniques used to ensure the deductibility of interest. *The Budget Plan 2005*, published by the Department of Finance to accompany the February 23, 2005 federal budget, indicated that an alternative proposal will be released for comment "at an early opportunity".

(c) *Expenses of Issuing Shares or Borrowing Money*

The type of expenses contemplated by paragraph 20(1)(*e*) includes printing and advertising costs, filing fees, legal and accounting fees, registration and transfer fees and commissions or bonuses on the issue or sale of shares. Also, deductible by this provision are similar expenses incurred in the course of becoming indebted on the purchase of capital property acquired to earn income. Similarly, refinancing costs such as rescheduling, restructuring or assumption of debt used for the purpose of earning business income are also deductible under this provision.

Not included in the deduction would be amounts paid or payable on account of the principal amount of the indebtedness. Since the deductible expenditures are still considered to be of a capital nature, paragraph 20(1)(*e*) requires that the deduction be amortized equally over five years (prorated on a daily basis for short taxation years) to achieve a better matching of expenses and revenues. Any undeducted balance of borrowing costs are deductible for the year in which the debt is fully repaid (otherwise than as a part of a refinancing).[q]

Annual fees payable as a standby charge, guarantee fee, registrar fee, transfer agent fee, filing fee or any similar fee in respect of borrowing money, incurring indebtedness or rescheduling or restructuring a debt obligation are deductible under paragraph 20(1)(e.1).

(d) *Premiums on Life Insurance used as Collateral*

Paragraph 20(1)(*e*.2) permits a limited deduction for life insurance premiums where the policy has been assigned as collateral for a loan. The lender must require the assignment of the policy as collateral for the loan. The principal business of the lender must be the lending of money or the purchase of debt obligations. The interest payable on the funds borrowed must be deductible [par. 20(1)(*c*)]. The deduction is limited to the portion of the premium that represents the net cost of pure insurance.

(e) *Discount on Debt Obligations*

Subsection 18(1) contains several provisions that would deny the deduction of all or any part of a discount from the face value of a debt obligation like a bond, debenture, note, mortgage, etc. Since the discount would be considered to be of a capital nature, its deduction is prohibited by paragraph 18(1)(*b*). The amortization of the discount, for financial accounting purposes, over the life of the debt instrument would not be deductible for tax purposes, because the annual amortization would be considered to be in the nature of a reserve prohibited by paragraph 18(1)(*e*). In addition, paragraph 18(1)(*f*) specifically denies the deduction of the *actual cash outlay* on redemption or open market purchase, except to the extent permitted by paragraph 20(1)(*f*). The latter provision permits a full deduction of the discount (an actual cash outlay on redemption or maturity) at the earlier of redemption or maturity if:

---

[q] Two cases heard under this provision are: *Enterprise Foundry Co. Ltd. v. M.N.R.*, (T.A.B.) 59 DTC 318 on a capital reorganization and *Dominion Electrohome Industries Ltd. v. M.N.R.*, (T.A.B.) 68 DTC 256 on a call premium.

(i) the debt security is issued at not less than 97% of face value; *and*

(ii) the yield to maturity is not more than $^4/_3$ of the nominal or coupon interest rate.

If one, or both, of these conditions is not met, then only $^1/_2$ of the discount is deductible, again at the earlier of redemption or maturity. The $^1/_2$ fraction is intended to reflect the allowable or deductible portion of a capital loss.

This rule discourages the issue of debt securities at a large discount by agreeing to pay a low rate of interest relative to the market. The concern is that only the lower than normal interest rate would be taxable to the debtholder at full rates and the gain from the discounted issue price to the par value would be a fractionally taxed capital gain to the debtholder. On the other hand, an acceptable discount of 3% is sufficient to account for normal market fluctuations in interest rates between the time of setting the rate and the time of issue of the debt.

(f) *The System for Reserves under the Act*

Paragraph 18(1)(*e*) prohibits the deduction of a reserve except those that are specifically permitted in Part I of the Act. A number of cases have been heard in this area on the question of distinguishing between a reserve that would be prohibited and an amount that represents a real and subsisting liability resulting in a deductible expense.[r]

Next, subsection 20(1) lists the reserves that may be deducted including:

- reserve for doubtful debts [par. 20(1)(*l*)];

- reserve for goods not delivered and services not rendered or deposits on returnable containers (other than bottles), limited by subsection 20(6) [par. 20(1)(*m*)];

- manufacturer's warranty reserve for amounts paid or payable to an insurer to insure liability under warranty agreement [par. 20(1)(*m*.1)];

- reserve for an amount not due until a later year under an instalment sales contract limited by subsection 20(8) [par. 20(1)(*n*)]; and

Any reserve taken in a given year under one of these provisions must be brought back into income in the following year under one of the following provisions in subsection 12(1):

- reserve for doubtful debts [par. 12(1)(*d*)];

- reserve in respect of certain goods and services, deposits or manufacturer's warranty reserve [par. 12(1)(*e*)]; and

In that following year, a new reserve can be taken based on the taxpayer's circumstances at that time. The inclusion of last year's reserve in income and the deduction of a new reserve this year forces the taxpayer to re-evaluate the circumstances and to establish a new reserve which can be substantiated by these circumstances.

IT-442R paragraph 24 describes the method suggested by the CRA for determining an appropriate reserve for doubtful debts.

Where a debt has been established by the taxpayer to have become a bad debt, rather than merely a debt of doubtful collectibility, the amount of the bad debt can be written off as an expense [par. 20(1)(*p*)]. A bad debt written off in this way need not be included in income in the following year. However, if and when a bad debt is recovered, then the amount of recovery is added to income in the year of receipt [par. 12(1)(*i*)]. It is

---

[r] These cases include: *No. 297 v. M.N.R.*, (T.A.B.) 55 DTC 611 on employee bonuses; *Canada Packers Ltd. v. M.N.R.*, (T.A.B.) 68 DTC 682 on an income normalization reserve; *Time Motors Limited v. M.N.R.*, (S.C.C.) 69 DTC 5149 on credit notes; and *Acadia Overseas Freighters Halifax Ltd. v. M.N.R.*, (T.A.B.) 62 DTC 84 on contributions to a mutual insurance fund.

a question of fact whether a debt has become a bad debt and, hence, uncollectible, rather than simply of doubtful collectibility.

Example Problem 1 ————————————————————————————————

The Greyduck Bus Lines Limited issues books of junior student tickets containing 20 transportation passes for $20 per book. The following information relates to books sold and tickets used:

	Year 1	Year 2	Year 3
Number of books sold	2,000	2,500	4,000
Number of tickets used:			
from Year 1 sales	25,000	11,000	expired
from Year 2 sales		31,250	13,750
from Year 3 sales			50,000

— REQUIRED

Compute the effect of these transactions on the net income from business of this company, assuming 10% of the tickets sold in a year are expected to expire at the beginning of the second year from the end of the year of sale.

— SOLUTION

		Applicable provisions
Year 1		
Include amount received in income ($20 × 2,000)	$40,000	par. 12(1)(*a*)
Less: reserve for services not provided[1]	11,000	par. 20(1)(*m*)
Income	$29,000	
Year 2		
Include amount received in income ($20 × 2,500)	$50,000	par. 12(1)(*a*)
Add: reserve from previous year	11,000	par. 12(1)(*e*)
	$61,000	
Less: reserve for services not provided[2]	13,750	par. 20(1)(*m*)
Income	$47,250	
Year 3		
Include amount received in income ($20 × 4,000)	$80,000	par. 12(1)(*a*)
Add: reserve from previous year	13,750	par. 12(1)(*e*)
	$93,750	
Less: reserve for services not provided[3]	22,000	par. 20(1)(*m*)
Income	$71,750	

— NOTES TO SOLUTION

(1) The reserve is limited to a reasonable amount based on services that it is reasonably expected will have to be provided. In this case, no service will have to be provided for 10% of all tickets sold in the year. Of the 40,000 tickets (20 tickets × 2,000 books) sold in Year 1, 25,000 have been used and 4,000 will expire (10% of 40,000) leaving 11,000 for which service will have to be provided. At $1.00 per ticket ($20.00 ÷ 20) a reasonable reserve would be $11,000 ($1.00 × 11,000). Note that subsection 20(6) limits this reserve to the amount included in income for transportation not provided before the end of the year. In this case transportation has not been provided on 15,000 tickets (40,000 − 25,000) providing a limit at $1 per ticket of $15,000.

(2) Using the above process, service will have to be provided for 13,750 tickets since 5,000 (10% of 50,000) will expire and 31,250 have been used. Thus, a reasonable reserve at $1.00 per

ticket is $13,750. The subsection 20(6) limit on this reserve would be on 18,750 tickets (50,000 – 31,250) at $1.00 per ticket or $18,750.

(3) Service will have to be provided for 22,000 tickets since 8,000 (10% of 80,000) will expire and 50,000 have been used. The reserve at $1.00 per ticket would be $22,000 and the subsection 20(6) limit on that reserve would be on 30,000 tickets (80,000 – 50,000) at $1 per ticket or $30,000.

Example Problem 2

On July 1, 2002, Delta Company sold some inventory with a value of $100,000 and a cost of $40,000. A cash downpayment of $10,000 was made and the balance was payable in four annual instalments of $20,000 and a final payment of $10,000. The purchaser is at arm's length.

— *REQUIRED*

• How much of a reserve under paragraph 20(1)(*n*) can the company take in each year covered by the instalment sale? Use a December 31 year-end.

— *SOLUTION*

Paragraph 20(8)(*b*) limits the reserve available under paragraph 20(1)(*n*) to a three-year period. A reserve is not deductible for a year-end that is more than 36 months after the sale.

Calculation of reserve:

		Accounts receivable	*Profit content*
July 1, 2002	— sale price of article	$100,000	$60,000
	— cash downpayment	10,000	6,000
Dec. 31, 2002	— balance receivable	$ 90,000	
	— reserve allowable[1]		$54,000
2003	— instalment due	20,000	12,000
Dec. 31, 2003	— balance receivable	$ 70,000	
	— reserve allowable[1]		$42,000
2004	— instalment due	20,000	12,000
Dec. 31, 2004	— balance receivable	$ 50,000	
	— reserve allowable[1]		$30,000
2005	— instalment due	20,000	12,000
Dec. 31, 2005	— balance receivable	$ 30,000	$18,000
	— reserve allowable (more than 36 months after sale)...		Nil

Income effect:

			Net reported income
2002	— Profit on sale [par. 12(1)(*b*)]	$ 60,000	
	— Reserve [par. 20(1)(*n*)]	(54,000)	$ 6,000
2003	— Previous year reserve [par. 12(1)(*e*)]	$ 54,000	
	— Reserve [par. 20(1)(*n*)]	(42,000)	12,000
2004	— Previous year reserve [par. 12(1)(*e*)]	$ 42,000	
	— Reserve [par. 20(1)(*n*)]	(30,000)	12,000
2005	— Previous year reserve [par. 12(1)(*e*)]	$ 30,000	
	— Reserve [par. 20(1)(*n*) and ssec. 20(8)]	—	30,000
	Total income reported over four years		$60,000

— *NOTE TO SOLUTION*

(1) Reserve $= \dfrac{\text{gross profit}}{\text{gross selling price}} \times$ amount receivable

(g) *Employer's Contribution to Registered Pension Plan*

Paragraph 20(1)(*q*) permits the deduction of employer contributions to a registered pension plan (RPP) as is permitted by section 147.2. Deductible contributions may be made by the employer either in the year to which the deduction is to apply or within 120 days after the end of that taxation year. Contributions made in the 120-day period which are in excess of the deduction limit for the preceding year may be deductible in the year in which they are made if the deduction limit for the year is not exceeded.

Two types of RPP are envisaged.

- A defined benefit plan promises a defined retirement benefit which is specified by a formula. In the case of a defined benefit RPP, all contributions are deductible if they are determined by an actuary to be necessary to fund the benefits for which the RPP was registered to provide.

- A money purchase or defined contribution plan specifies a contribution requirement with the retirement benefit dependent on the funds accumulated in the plan at the time of retirement.

In the case of a money purchase RPP, the total of employer and employee contributions are limited [ssec. 147.1(8)] to:

the lesser of:

(i) 18% of the employee's compensation defined [ssec. 147.1(1)] to be employment income inclusions under sections 5 and 6 for the particular year; and

(ii) a specified dollar limit, defined [ssec. 147.1(1)] as the money purchase limit.

The limits for money purchase RPPs are as follows:

(i) for 2004	$16,500	(iv) for 2007	$20,000
(ii) for 2005	$18,000	(v) for 2008	$21,000
(iii) for 2006	$19,000	(vi) for 2009	$22,000
		(vii) for 2010	indexed

A violation of the limits set for either type of plan can lead to the revocation of the RPP registration status. If this occurs, all amounts in the plan become taxable, having lost their sheltered status.

(h) *Employer's Contribution under a Deferred Profit Sharing Plan*

Paragraph 20(1)(*y*) provides for the deduction by an employer of contributions to a deferred profit sharing plan (DPSP) as permitted by subsection 147(8). An employer may deduct an amount which is paid in the year or within 120 days after the end of the year to a trustee to the extent that the amount was paid in accordance with the terms of the plan and was not deducted by the employer in a previous year. However, subsection 147(8) is subject to subsection 147(9) which states that if the requirements of subsection 147(5.1) are not met, the employer is not entitled to a deduction under subsection 147(8) except to the extent expressly permitted in writing by the Minister. This rule prevents the deduction of employer DPSP contributions where the terms of the plan are not adequate to ensure that the limits under subsection 147(5.1) are met.

Subsection 147(5.1) provides a formula for the amount of an employer's contribution to a DPSP that is deductible. Generally, where there is no RPP, the employer's contribution limit under paragraph 147(5.1)(*a*) in respect of an employee for a year is the lesser of:

(a) one-half of the money-purchase dollar limit for the year, as discussed above; and

(b) 18% of the employee's compensation (as defined in subsection 147.1(1)) for the year.

Therefore, to be deductible in a year, contributions should not exceed the lesser amount computed.

Where an employer participates in both a DPSP and an RPP for the benefit of an employee, the employer's total contribution to both plans is limited [par. 147(5.1)(*c*)]. It is rare for an employer to provide both a DPSP and an RPP together.

(i) *Cancellation of Lease*

Where the owner of a property is required to pay an amount to a lessee for the cancellation of the lease, paragraph 20(1)(*z*) treats the costs of cancelling the lease as a type of prepaid expense, as long as the property continues to be owned by the lessor or by a non-arm's length person. As a result, the costs may be deducted over what would have been the remaining term of the lease, including renewal periods, to a maximum of 40 years. Paragraph 20(1)(*z*.1) provides for a deduction of the unamortized balance of these costs ($\frac{1}{2}$ of the unamortized balance, in the case of capital property) if the property is sold. An amount that does not meet the conditions of these two paragraphs is not deductible [par. 18(1)(*q*)].

(j) *Landscaping of Grounds*

Paragraph 20(1)(*aa*) allows a deduction of an amount paid in the year for landscaping of grounds around a building that is used to produce income from business. Were it not for this provision the expenditure would be considered to be of a capital nature.

(k) *Expenses of Representation*

The expenses of representation for the purpose of obtaining a licence, permit, franchise or trademark related to the business of a taxpayer are deductible [par. 20(1)(*cc*)]. Given the capital nature of the assets acquired, these expenditures would otherwise be prohibited [par. 18(1)(*b*)]. Note that the representations must be made to a government body or agency to be deductible.

Instead of deducting the full amount allowed by paragraph 20(1)(*cc*), a taxpayer may elect under subsection 20(9) to deduct one-tenth of the full amount in the year of expenditure and the nine immediately following taxation years. Regulation 4100 sets out the documents that must be filed to implement the election.

(l) *Investigation of Site*

Paragraph 20(1)(*dd*) permits the deduction of an amount paid in the year for investigating the suitability of a site for a building or other structure planned for use in the taxpayer's *existing* business.

(m) *Utilities Service Connection*

An amount paid in the year to an arm's length person to make connections for the supply of electricity, gas, telephone service, water or sewers, is deductible [par. 20(1)(*ee*)]. Without this provision no deduction would be permitted, since the expenditure is of a capital nature. Furthermore, no capital cost allowance would be permitted, because the taxpayer normally does not own the service connections.

(n) *Disability-Related Modifications and Equipment*

Paragraph 20(1)(*qq*) allows a deduction in the payment year of the full cost of prescribed renovations or alterations to a building used primarily in a business. The expenditures must be made to enable individuals who have a mobility impairment to gain access to the building or be mobile within it. The building need not be owned by the taxpayer making the expenditure.

Paragraph 20(1)(*rr*) allows the deduction in the payment year of the cost of any prescribed disability-specific device or equipment which assists individuals with a sight, hearing or mobility impairment. The type of expenditure envisaged includes installation of elevator car position indicators, visible fire alarm indicators, telephone devices, listening devices for group meetings and disability-specific computer software and hardware.

If it were not for these provisions, the expenditures could be considered of a capital nature and could not be expensed. Clearly, the rules provide an incentive to implement social policy.

(o) *Convention Expenses*

Attendance at a convention may be considered to give rise to expenditures of a capital nature, perhaps, in the form of increased knowledge. However, subsection 20(10) permits the deduction from a taxpayer's business income of amounts paid in attending up to two conventions per year. Attendance at the convention must be in connection with the business. The location of the convention must be within the territorial scope of the organization holding the convention. Note that an internal business meeting, such as a sales conference within a business, is not considered to be a convention

6. Application of the rules for deduction

To determine the deductibility of an outlay or expenditure after considering the general principles and rules in section 18, the list of deductions under section 20 should be scanned. This can be done quickly by reference to the table of contents for the Act. In addition, commentary under these sections contained in the "Canadian Tax Library" of CCH TAXWORKS lists court case decisions for a wide variety of expenditures. This list is based on court decisions made on the question of the deductibility of many types of expenditure for tax purposes. However, it should be noted that because the commentary list is based largely on case law, the deductibility of any particular type of expenditure is heavily dependent on the specific facts of the case and the specific law in force at the time of the case. Care should be taken to determine the facts that resulted in a particular decision and the wording of the Act at the time of the case, since some court decisions may be at variance with current law.

Example Problem

You are the auditor for Corporate Welfare Bum Limited and you have been given an income statement prepared for financial accounting purposes showing a loss for its fiscal year ended December 31, 2005 of $112,000. Your audit uncovers the following:

(a) appraisal expense contains cost of determining asset values for insurance purposes . . . . $ 4,000

(b) wages expense contains amounts (matched by employees) relating to money-purchase (defined-contribution) registered pension plan contributions, made during the first 120 days of 2006 but allocated by the accountant to 2005, in respect of current services on behalf of the following executives (employment compensation for the year shown in brackets):

President (Mr. C.S. Bum, 100% owner; $150,000)	$ 10,150	
Vice-President ($95,000)	6,000	
Accountant ($80,000)	5,000	
Plant Supervisor ($65,000)	4,000	
Shop Foreman ($48,000)	3,400	
Timekeeper ($27,000)	2,400	30,950

(c) cost of landscaping written off 10,000

(d) legal expenses for

    (i) defence of a suit, brought by a customer, for failure to deliver
       merchandise on time .... $ 2,500

    (ii) articles of amendment to revise company's articles of incorpora-
       tion.. 3,500

    (iii) cost of disputing income tax............................. 4,000   10,000

(e) revenues included a dividend received from a Canadian subsidiary......... 80,000

(f) interest expense included amortization of bond discount on bonds maturing
    in 2006 12,000

(g) opening inventories were valued on the FIFO basis at $184,750 while closing
    inventories were valued on the LIFO basis rather than the FIFO basis which
    would have exceeded the LIFO valuation by............................. 36,950

(h) miscellaneous expense contained donations for the year to

    (i) duly registered charities.................................... $ 4,000

    (ii) the NDP political party 7,000   11,000

(i) insurance expense contained whole life insurance premium paid on the life of
    Mr. C.S. Bum (proceeds payable to the company; not group life) 10,000

(j) salaries expense contained a dividend payable to Mr. Bum 8,000

(k) bad debts expense including $4,000 in respect of a loan to a shareholder of a
    supplier totalled 10,000

(l) extraordinary maintenance arising from conversion of premises including
    replacement of heating and air-conditioning systems, plumbing, electrical wir-
    ing and concrete foundations in respect of a building was written off to repairs
    and maintenance in the amount of 150,000

(m) salaries expense included a bonus paid to Mr. Bum..................... 15,000

(n) interest expense included interest in respect of the acquisition of 90% of the
    shares of another Canadian corporation................................. 115,000

(o) convention expenses over three days of Mr. Bum and his family ($2,000
    thereof represents costs relating to Mrs. Bum and the two little Bums, who
    attended for social purposes only; $500 of the remaining amount relates to the
    cost of meals consumed by Mr. Bum) 5,000

(p) administration expense contains an embezzlement loss caused by a minor
    employee of the company... 10,000

(q) (i) management bonuses included in wages expense but not paid in 2005 ... 50,000

    (ii) bonuses accrued at the end of 2005 which were not, and will not be, paid in
       2006 35,000

(r) property taxes paid in 2005 include an amount paid for the company's fishing
    lodge 1,000

(s) the company as a lessor agreed to pay and expensed $15,000 on June 30, 2005
    to cancel a lease that could have been in force until December 31, 2011 with
    renewal periods, but in 2005 actually paid only 10,000

(t) the company paid damages for failing to deliver goods on time under an action
    for breach of contract brought by one of its suppliers and the amount was
    expensed in the financial accounts 12,000

(u) cost of constructing a cement ramp to facilitate wheelchair access to the
    company's premises, capitalized by the accountant 6,000

— *REQUIRED*

    Compute the company's income or loss from business or property for tax purposes, but do not compute tax deductions in respect of depreciable capital or eligible capital property. Indicate the applicable sections of the Act or brief reasons to substantiate your answer. Indicate in a separate list the applicable section of the Act or brief reasons for not considering an item in your computations. Make sure all items are accounted for.

—SOLUTION

		Applicable sections
Loss for financial accounting purposes......................	$(112,000)	sec. 9
Add items not deductible for tax purposes:		
Excess allocations to 2005 of RPP contributions[1]............................	$ 2,300	par. 20(1)(*q*)
Legal expenses for articles revision[2]	3,500	par. 18(1)(*b*)
Amortization of bond discount[3]..................	12,000	par. 18(1)(*b*)
Excess of FIFO over LIFO[4]....................	36,950	ssec. 10(1)
Donations[5]	11,000	par. 18(1)(*a*)
Life insurance premium[6]	10,000	par. 18(1)(*a*)
Dividend payable[7]	8,000	
Bad debt re: loan to shareholder of supplier[8]	4,000	par. 20(1)(*p*)
Extraordinary maintenance[9]	150,000	par. 18(1)(*b*)
Convention expenses[10]	2,250	par. 18(1)(*h*)
Bonuses accrued and not paid[11].................	35,000	ssec. 78(4)
Property tax on fishing lodge[12].................	1,000	par. 18(1)(*l*)
Non-deductible prepaid lease cancellation amount[13]............................	13,838 $ 289,838	par. 20(1)(*z*)
	$ 177,838	
Deduct items deductible for tax purposes:		
Wheelchair access ramp......................	$ 6,000	par. 20(1)(*qq*)
Income from business or property for tax purposes[14]	$ 171,838	

—NOTES TO SOLUTION

(1) In this case, involving a money-purchase RPP, assuming the employee contributions are matched by the employer corporation and that the employee's contributions are fully deductible, the corporation will have a non-deductible contribution in respect of 2005 computed as follows:

	Pres.	*V.-P.*	*Acct.*	*Super.*	*Fore.*	*Time.*
Least of:						
(a) Employer plus employee RPP contributions	$20,300	$12,000	$10,000	$ 8,000	$ 6,800	$ 4,800
(b) Money-purchase dollar limit for 2005	$18,000	$18,000	$18,000	$18,000	$18,000	$18,000
(c) 18% of compensation......................	$27,000	$17,100	$14,400	$11,700	$ 8,640	$ 4,860
Least amount....................................	$18,000	$12,000	$10,000	$ 8,000	$ 6,800	$ 4,800
Less: employer & employee contributions	20,300	12,000	10,000	8,000	6,800	4,800
Employer's non-deductible contributions for 2005	$ 2,300	$ Nil	Nil	Nil	Nil	Nil

Total amount to be added back: $2,300

Since the $2,300 non-deductible amount was contributed in the first 120 days of 2006, it can be a part of the deductible contribution for 2006 without danger of a revocation of the registration status of the RPP, as long as contributions in 2006 do not exceed deduction limits for 2006.

(2) Expenditures on articles of incorporation or articles of amendment are regarded as eligible capital property and are written off over time for tax purposes. This topic will be covered in Chapter 5.

(3) Paragraph 18(1)(*b*) specifically prohibits the amortization of an amount that is capital in nature. Paragraph 18(1)(*e*) prohibits all reserves, except as expressly provided for in the Act. Paragraph 18(1)(*f*) specifically denies the deduction of an actual cash outlay on redemption or open market purchases except to the extent permitted under paragraph 20(1)(*f*).

(4) Departmental practice has disallowed the use of LIFO as an assumption in the costing of inventory when actual cost cannot be identified. This practice is based on the decision in *M.N.R. v. Anaconda American Brass Ltd.*, (J.C.P.C.) 55 DTC 1220 which established the principle that the facts of inventory flow cannot be disregarded in using an assumption about inventory cost. The same disregard of the facts and substitution of assumptions in relation to the flow of goods made the use of the LIFO method of valuation objectionable in *Wickett and Craig Ltd. v. M.N.R.*, (T.R.B.) 78 DTC 1382.

(5) Donations are not deductible in the computation of income if they were not incurred to earn income. However, charitable donations of a corporation are deductible under section 110.1 in Division C dealing with the computation of taxable income, and political contributions are eligible for a tax credit under subsection 127(3) in Division E dealing with the computation of tax.

(6) Life insurance premiums paid on the lives of officers, employees or shareholders where the policies are payable to the company do not produce income. Hence, the premiums are not deductible unless the policy is required to obtain financing, such as a bank loan. Paragraph 20(1)(*e*.2) limits the amount of a deductible premium to the net cost of pure insurance, determined by reference to standard mortality assumptions.

(7) Dividends are not paid to produce income; they are a distribution of income after it has been earned.

(8) Paragraph 20(1)(*p*) requires that an amount be previously included in income if it is to be written off as a bad debt. On this loan, which was not a trade account receivable, no amount would have been included in sales and, hence, in income. However, a further adjustment may be allowed under section 50 which will be discussed in a subsequent chapter.

(9) An expenditure which prolongs the life of an asset is regarded as capital in nature under paragraph 18(1)(*b*), but an expenditure which restores an asset to its original condition is regarded as an expenditure of an income nature. In this case, the expenditure, as described, appears to be of a capital nature.

(10) Personal or living expenses are specifically prohibited as a deduction in paragraph 18(1)(*h*), except, for example, an item such as convention expenses specifically allowed by subsection 20(10). Subsection 67.1(1) provides that the deductible cost of meals while attending a convention is 50% of the actual cost, on the assumption that the cost is reasonable. Where the fees for a convention do not specify the cost of meals or entertainment included in those fees, subsection 67.1(3) will deem the cost to be $50 per day and that amount will be subject to the 50% limitation. In this case, since the cost is specified, 50% of $500, or $250, is not deductible and must be added in the reconciliation.

(11) The bonuses accrued at the end of 2005 are not deductible in 2005, since they were not paid within the time limit [ssec. 78(4)]. The $35,000 would, therefore, have been added back to 2005 income. These bonuses can only be deducted when they are actually paid.

(12) Paragraph 18(1)(*l*) arbitrarily disallows certain listed expenditures including one made for the maintenance of a lodge.

(13) The costs of cancelling a lease are treated as a prepaid expense under paragraph 20(1)(*z*) as long as the property continues to be owned by the lessor or a person with whom he or she does not deal at arm's length. As such it may be deducted over the remaining term of the cancelled lease, including renewal periods, subject to a maximum limit of 40 years. In this case, the number of days in the remainder of the lease is 184 in 2005 and 6 years of 365 days per year and 1 day for a leap year for a total of 2,375 days. Thus, the deduction for 2004 is given by $184/2,375 \times \$15,000$ or $1,162. Therefore, the non-deductible amount of the $15,000 payment is $13,838 (i.e., $15,000 − $1,162). See paragraph 20(1)(*z*.1) for a deduction of the unamortized balance if the property is sold.

(14) Other items:

(a) The cost of an appraisal made for the purpose of maintaining adequate insurance coverage is regarded as a normal business expense and is deductible.

(b) Paragraph 20(1)(*q*) allows a deduction for an employer contribution to a registered pension plan of the amount calculated in subsection 147.2(1). The amounts calculated in respect of all employees shown other than the President and Vice-President are deductible, as shown in Note (1).

(c) Paragraph 20(1)(*aa*) allows the deduction of landscaping costs even though they might otherwise be considered of a capital nature.

(d) (i) The cost of defending a suit brought by a customer is regarded as a business expense if it pertains to trading transactions.

(ii) The cost of disputing an income tax case has been held in the case of *Premium Iron Ores Ltd. v. M.N.R.*, (S.C.C.) 66 DTC 5280 to be a business expense. The legal expenses of $4,000 could also be deducted under paragraph 60(*o*) in which case they should be added back in the computation of income from business.

(e) A dividend received is to be included in income from property [par. 12(1)(*j*)].

(f) Bad debt expenses are deductible [par. 20(1)(*p*)] as long as the account has previously resulted in an inclusion in income. In the normal course of setting up an account receivable a credit would be made to sales, thereby including the amount in income. The treatment of a bad debt expense for tax purposes is identical to the treatment of the expense for financial accounting purposes. In fact, the tax treatment of both the reserve and the expense parallels the accounting treatment. The previous year's reserve is reversed by including it in current income [par. 12(1)(*d*)] and a new reserve is set up for the current year by taking a deduction [par. 20(1)(*l*)]. A debt established to be bad is written off [par. 20(1)(*p*)] and a recovery of such a debt previously written off is included in income [par. 12(1)(*i*)].

(g) A bonus expense is a deductible business expense [par. 18(1)(*a*)] to the extent that it meets the test in section 67 of being "reasonable in the circumstances." The $50,000 bonus expensed in 2005 is deductible in 2005 as long as it is paid on or before June 28, 2006.

(h) Paragraph 20(1)(*c*) permits the deduction of interest on funds borrowed to buy shares since dividend income will be earned.

(i) Subsection 20(10) permits the deduction of convention expenses (except for part of the cost of meals which is limited by sections 67.1 and 67.3) of Mr. Bum as long as the conditions of that provision are met.

(j) Losses in cash or misappropriation of merchandise sustained by the criminal action of employees or officers will be allowed as deductions from income as being incidental to carrying on of business. However, such a loss attributable to a partner or senior officer is not usually regarded as a normal business risk and is not deductible [IT-185R]. In the case of *Cassidy's Limited v. M.N.R.*, 89 DTC 686, the Tax Court of Canada disagreed specifically with the statement in paragraph 2 (b) of IT-185R in which the CRA stated that, because a theft was committed by a senior employee, the losses resulting from the theft are not deductible by the employer. The Court held that "the amounts lost due to the defalcation were non-capital losses, the deductions of which are deductible in computing profit in accordance with ordinary commercial principles and are not prohibited by the Act" and, hence, allowed the deduction.

(k) Damages for failure to deliver goods are regarded as normal business expenses.

B. Sales/Negotiating Person's Expenses Revisited

[ITA: 8(1)(*f*), (*h*), (*h*.1), (*i*), (*j*), (12); 13(7)(*g*), (*h*); 18–20; 67; 67.1; 67.2; 67.3; ITR: 7306; 7307; IT-352R2; IT-514; IT-518R; IT-521R; IT-522R]

One of the topics dealt with in the preceding chapter on employment income was the deductibility of the expenses of sales/negotiating persons (i.e., individuals employed in connection with the selling of property or negotiating of contracts) under paragraph 8(1)(*f*) and paragraph 8(1)(*j*). Unlike other employees, sales/negotiating persons can deduct expenses incurred to produce employment income. However, these allowable expenses [par. 8(1)(*f*)] are limited to the amount of commission income or other similar amounts, fixed by reference to the volume of sales made or the contracts negotiated, received in the year. It is interesting to compare the limited deductions for expenses available to a sales/negotiating person who is an employee subject to the provisions of Subdivision a of Division B with the broader deductions available to a person performing similar functions as an independent businessperson subject to the provisions of Subdivision b of Division B.

Provisions introduced in Chapter 3 limit certain deductions allowed to taxpayers, whether they are employed or self-employed or whether they are incorporated or unincorporated. Section 67.2 and paragraphs 13(7)(*g*) and (*h*) pertain to passenger vehicles, as defined [ssec. 248(1)], and apply to all taxpayers. Where a passenger vehicle, including a station wagon, a passenger van, or a similar motor vehicle, is acquired, the capital cost used as the basis for capital cost allowance is limited. Regulation 7307(*b*) sets the limit on which capital cost allowance may be claimed at $30,000 after 2000 plus federal and provincial sales taxes (i.e., GST and PST). If GST is paid by a registrant who is eligible for an immediate input tax credit, the GST is not included in capital cost. Any excess of capital cost will not qualify for capital cost allowance. The amount deductible in respect of interest on money borrowed to acquire a passenger vehicle is limited by section 67.2 to $300 for funds borrowed after 2000 per 30-day period (as computed by formula) in the year that the interest is paid or payable. Where a passenger vehicle is leased, the amount deductible under section 67.3 in respect of amounts paid or payable is restricted as discussed in Chapter 3.

As discussed previously in this chapter, paragraph 18(1)(*r*) and Regulation 7306 limit the deduction by an employer of allowances paid to employees for the use of an automobile in the course of employment or business to a prescribed amount per kilometre, except where the allowance is required to be included in the employee's income under paragraph 6(1)(*b*).

Also, as previously discussed, subsection 18(12) restricts the deductibility of the costs relating to a place of business in the residence of a self-employed individual. A prorated portion of these "home office" expenses, such as rent, capital cost allowance, property taxes, and mortgage interest or operating costs, including heating, electricity, insurance or maintenance may be deducted only if the space is either:

- the individual's principal place of business; or
- used exclusively by the individual on a regular and continuous basis for meeting clients, customers or patients.

The deduction for home office expenses is further restricted to the income for the year from the business for which the office is used. However, any excess of deduction disallowed in a year may be treated as home office expenses incurred in a following year, according to IT-514, paragraph 5. Subsection 8(13) contains a parallel provision to restrict the deduction of home office expenses by an employee, as presented in Chapter 3.

Section 67.1 restricts the amount of a deduction by all taxpayers for food, beverage and entertainment to the lesser of 50% of the amount paid or payable or a reasonable amount. This limitation applies to all business meals, including food and beverage, as well as to the cost of meals while travelling or attending a seminar, conference, convention or similar function. The restriction also applies to tickets to an entertainment or sporting event, gratuities and cover charges, room rentals to provide entertainment and the cost of private boxes at sports facilities. The limitation applies to the taxpayer incurring the costs in the case where a reimbursement is made. The following are exclusions from the 50% limitation:

(a) the cost to a restaurant, airline or hotel of providing meals to customers in the ordinary course of business,

(b) meals or entertainment expenses relating to an event intended primarily to benefit a registered charity,

(c) the cost of meals or entertainment that is included as a taxable benefit to the employee or where the employer is reimbursed for the cost, and

(d) the cost of meals and recreation provided by an employer for the general benefit of all employees at a particular place of business in respect of occasional events not exceeding six events per year.

IT-518R presents the CRA's interpretation of this provision.

Example Problem

Ms. Jo Schmaltz is a salesperson who earned a total of $25,000 in 2005, including $4,000 in commissions. She was required to travel in her job and she was required to pay her own expenses, all of which were reasonable in the circumstances and consisted of the following:

(a) entertainment of clients including golf club membership dues of $500 (incurred in equal monthly amounts)		$3,700
(b) home office expenses (allocated by floor space of office portion of home):		
mortgage interest	$ 450	
municipal taxes	400	
capital cost allowance	300	
utilities	1,000	
maintenance and repairs	850	3,000
This is the only office space available for her work.		
(c) capital cost allowance on car used 75% for business		3,570
(d) car operating expenses		3,100
(e) convention dues (excluding meals and entertainment)		1,000
(f) travellers' association (a trade union) dues		300
(g) meals while travelling		900

— REQUIRED

(A) Compute Jo's minimum employment income for 2005.

(B) Compute Jo's minimum business income, assuming she is an independent business-person with $25,000 in sales rather than an employee.

— SOLUTION

			Applicable provisions
(A) Employment income			
Salary and commissions		$25,000	sec. 5
Deductions:			
Entertainment[1] (50% of $3,200)	$ 1,600		par. 8(1)(*f*) par. 18(1)(*l*) ssec. 67.1(1)
Home office[2]: municipal taxes	400		par. 8(1)(*f*)
Car operating expenses (75% of $3,100)	2,325		par. 8(1)(*f*)
Meal expenses (50% of $900)	450		ssec. 67.1(1)
Total	$ 4,775		
Deductions not in excess of commission[3]		$ (4,000)	par. 8(1)(*f*)
		$21,000	
Less: association dues[4]	$ 300		par. 8(1)(*i*)
C.C.A. on car (75% of $3,570)	2,678		par. 8(1)(*j*)
Utilities	1,000		par. 8(1)(*i*)
Maintenance and repairs	850	(4,828)	par. 8(1)(*i*)
Employment income[5, 6]		$16,172	

(B) Business income

Sales	$25,000	sec. 9
Deductions:		
Entertainment[7] (50% of $3,200)	$ 1,600	par. 18(1)(a)
C.C.A. on car (75% of $3,570)	2,678	par. 20(1)(a)
Car operating expenses (75% of $3,100)	2,325	par. 18(1)(a)
Convention expenses	1,000	ssec. 20(10)
Meals (50% of $900)	450	par. 18(1)(a)
Association dues	300 (8,353)	par. 18(1)(a)
Income from business[8] (before home office expense)	$16,647	par. 18(1)(a)
Less: home office expense[9]	(3,000)	par. 20(1)(a)
		par. 20(1)(c)
Income from business	$13,647	

Note that the difference between employment income of $16,172 and business income of $13,647 is $2,525. This amount consists of the following expenses that are not deductible from employment income but are deductible from business income:

Interest and C.C.A. on home office ($450 + $300)	$ 750
Non-deductible excess of employment expenses over commissions	775
Convention expenses	1,000
Total	$2,525

—NOTES TO SOLUTION

(1) To be deductible under paragraph 8(1)(f) an expenditure must be made to earn employment income. However, subparagraph 8(1)(f)(vi) specifically denies deductions which fall under paragraph 18(1)(l), which lists an outlay for the use of a golf course.

(2) Outlays on account of capital are not deductible [spar. 8(1)(f)(v)] except for interest and capital cost allowance on a car used in the course of employment [par. 8(1)(j)]. The interest is on account of the home mortgage and the capital cost allowance is not for a car. Municipal taxes and home insurance are deductible. (See IT-352R2, paragraph 6 which was confirmed by the decision of the Tax Court of Canada in *Felton v. M.N.R.*, 89 DTC 233. In that case, the taxpayer sought to deduct mortgage interest, property taxes, insurance premiums and the cost of utilities for his home as rent under subparagraph 8(1)(i)(ii). The court held that rent involves only a payment arising out of a landlord and tenant relationship, such that the expenses incurred for an owner-occupied home could not be considered as rent. However, the court did recognize the Agency's assessing practices described in IT-352R2 in respect of maintenance costs and utilities. The Federal Court–Trial Division concurred with the *Felton* decision in *The Queen v. Thompson*, 89 DTC 5439.)

Subsection 8(13) sets out two tests, one of which must be met, if any amount of home office expense is to be deductible. Subparagraph 8(13)(a)(i) requires that the work space be the place where the individual principally performs the duties of the office or employment. The alternative test in subparagraph 8(13)(a)(ii) requires that both of the following conditions be met:

(a) the work space is used exclusively for employment during the period in respect of which the deduction relates, and

(b) the work space is used on a regular and continuous basis for meeting customers or other persons in the ordinary course of employment.

If one of the two tests in subparagraphs 8(13)(a)(i) and (ii) is met, the deductible expenses are limited to the employee's employment income for the year. Therefore, work space deduction cannot create a loss from employment. However, the provision allows for what amounts to an indefinite carryforward under paragraph 8(13)(c). In this case, where all expenses are limited to the amount of commission income, by virtue of paragraph 8(1)(f), the limitation in paragraph 8(13)(b) will have no effect.

(3) Note that paragraph 8(1)(f) requires that expenses, to be deductible, cannot exceed the commission.

(4) Paragraph 8(1)(*f*) does not restrict the deductions under paragraph 8(1)(*i*) or 8(1)(*j*) (i.e., interest and capital cost allowance on car, utilities and maintenance) to commission income.

(5) Convention expenses may not be deducted from employment income since they are not listed in subsection 8(1) [ssec. 8(2)].

(6) Due to the limitation placed on deductible expenses in paragraph 8(1)(*f*), i.e., expenses cannot exceed commission income, an alternative set of provisions may be preferable. In this case, the employee could make use of paragraph 8(1)(*h*) covering travelling expenses other than motor vehicle expenses and paragraph 8(1)(*h*.1) covering motor vehicle expenses, rather than paragraph 8(1)(*f*). Although paragraph 8(1)(*h*) does not provide for the deduction of entertainment expenses, there is no commission income limitation on the amount of meals expenses deductible under paragraph 8(1)(*h*) (except for the 50% limitation on the cost of meals) or on car operating expenses deductible under paragraph 8(1)(*h*.1). Thus, the meals expenses and car operating expenses of $2,775 (i.e., $2,325 + $450) would be deductible under paragraphs 8(1)(*h*) and (*h*.1), respectively; office maintenance and utilities expenses of $1,850 would be deductible under subparagraph 8(1)(*i*)(iii) as interpreted by IT-352R2, paragraph 6; the traveller's association dues would be deductible under subparagraph 8(1)(*i*)(iv) and capital cost allowance on the car would be deductible under subparagraph 8(1)(*j*)(ii). This would result in employment income of $17,397 computed as follows:

Salary and commissions		$ 25,000	sec. 5
Deductions:			
Car operating expenses (75% of $3,100)	$2,325		par. 8(1)(*h*.1)
Meal expenses (50% of $900)	450		par. 8(1)(*h*)
Association dues	300		par. 8(1)(*i*)
C.C.A. on car (75% of $3,570)	2,678	(5,753)	par. 8(1)(*j*)
Employment income (before home office expense)		$ 19,247	
Less: home office expense		(1,850)	par. 8(1)(*i*), ssec. 8(13)
Employment income		$ 17,397	

Therefore, in this particular case, using the paragraphs 8(1)(*h*) and (*h*.1) alternative is not better.

(7) Golf club membership dues are not deductible because of the prohibition in paragraph 18(1)(*l*).

(8) The issue of employment versus self-employment was considered in the previous chapter.

The courts have applied the following three tests as discussed in the previous chapter:

(a) the economic reality or entrepreneur test, i.e., control, ownership of the tools, chance of profit and risk of loss;

(b) integration or organization test, i.e., whether the worker is economically dependent on the organization; and

(c) the specific result test, i.e., a contract envisaging the accomplishment of a specific job or task.

(9) All of the home office expenses, including the interest and capital cost allowance, are deductible to the extent incurred to earn income, if the conditions in subsection 18(12) are met. However, she may not want to claim the capital cost allowance because of the principal residence rules which will be discussed in the chapters on capital gains taxation. Subsection 18(12) will allow the deduction of expenses pertaining to work space in a home where it is either the individual's principal place of business or used exclusively on a regular and continuous basis for meeting clients, customers or patients of the individual. Deductible expenses cannot exceed the individual's income from business before the deduction of these expenses. However, excess expenses of this nature may be carried forward. As a result of the restriction in subsection 18(12), home office expenses should be separated from other deductible expenses and deducted last, as shown. Also, see IT-514 for the CRA's interpretation of subsection 18(12).

C. Ceasing to Carry on Business

[ITA: 22; 23; 25]

1. Sale of accounts receivable

In order to deduct a reserve for doubtful debts [par. 20(1)(*l*)] or to write off a bad debt [par. 20(1)(*p*)], an amount in respect of the debt must have been included previously in income. This would not be the case, if accounts judged to be doubtful or bad were purchased from someone else. To alleviate the problems that this may cause where:

- a person has sold all or substantially all of the property used in a business,
- to a purchaser who will continue the business,

section 22 provides for a joint election by the vendor and purchaser which permits the purchaser to take the reserve or write-off in respect of accounts receivable.

To illustrate the operation of section 22, assume that accounts receivable having a face value of $14,000 with an existing reserve of $3,000 are sold for their assessed fair market value of $10,000. The following represents the procedure that must be followed jointly by the buyer and seller to allow the buyer future reserves and write-offs on the accounts purchased:

SELLER

Accounts receivable		Reserve	
$14,000			$3,000
	$10,000(1)		
	4,000(3)	(2) $3,000	
NIL		NIL	

(1) Cash $10,000
　　Accounts receiv-
　　　able $10,000

(2) Reserve 3,000
　　Income 3,000

(3) Business loss 4,000
　　Accounts receiv-
　　　able 4,000

BUYER

Accounts receivable		Reserve	
(1) $14,000			NIL

(1) Accounts receivable $14,000
　　Cash $10,000
　　Income........... 4,000

NOTE: Buyer could then set up an appropriate reserve for doubtful debts and could write off any of these debts should they prove bad.

Note that the loss to the seller under the section 22 election is a business loss. If the election were not made, the loss of $4,000 would be a capital loss, only ½ allowable as a deduction and only deductible against taxable capital gains of $2,000.

2. Sale of inventory

Where a taxpayer disposes of a business or part of a business, any inventory sold is deemed to have been sold in the course of carrying on the business [sec. 23]. Thus, the proceeds of the sale result in income for the seller and become the cost of the inventory to the buyer. The purpose of this provision is to ensure that a lump-sum sale of inventory on the sale of a business is treated in exactly the same way as the usual sale of inventory in the normal course of carrying on business.

D. Professional Business

[ITA: 34; IT-457R]

Amounts receivable in respect of services that have been billed are required to be included in income from the business of a professional. Work in progress at the end of a year, representing unbilled services of a business that is a profession, is considered to be inventory [par. 10(5)(*a*)].

An election is available to a taxpayer whose business is the professional practice of an accountant, dentist, lawyer, medical doctor, veterinarian or chiropractor. The election allows the taxpayer to exclude from business income any amount in respect of work in progress at the end of the year [par. 34(*a*)]. Where the election is made, it must be used in all subsequent taxation years unless the election is revoked with the permission of the CRA [par. 34(*b*)]. The CRA's interpretation of these rules is contained in IT-457R.

E. Scientific Research and Experimental Development

[ITA: 12(1)(*v*); 37; ITR: 2900–2902; IT-151R5; IC 86-4R4 (Draft)]

1. Meaning of scientific research and experimental development [SR&ED]

Subsection 248(1) defines "scientific research and experimental development" to mean the "systematic investigation or search carried out in a field of science or technology by means of experiment or analysis . . . ," including basic research, applied research and experimental development. Activities which result in deductible expenditures in support of the three types of research include engineering or design, operations research, mathematical analysis or computer programming, data collection, testing and psychological research. However, activities which do not result in a deductible expenditure include market research or sales promotion, quality control or routine testing, social sciences or humanities research, natural resource exploration, commercial development of material, products or processes, style changes or routine data collection. The CRA's interpretation of the term "scientific research" is contained in IC 86-4R4 (Draft) which offers some guidelines in the area.[s]

The term "scientific research and experimental development" recognizes that the bulk of industrial scientific research is concentrated on the experimental development of new products or processes rather than pure or applied research. The inclusion of the words "experimental development" confirms that research does not include projects involving only routine engineering or routine development.

2. General deduction of expenditures

Generally, research and development expenditures, including most capital expenditures, made in a year are fully deductible. However, any allowable expenditures that are not deducted in a year are placed in a pool and may be deducted in any future year in which the taxpayer carries on business in Canada.

Subsection 37(1) determines the deduction that can be made from income of a business carried on in Canada of certain scientific research and experimental development expenditures made in the year. Paragraph 37(1)(*a*) contains a list of expenditures of a current nature including payments:

(a) for scientific research and experimental development related to the business and directly undertaken by or on behalf of the taxpayer;

(b) to an approved association that undertakes scientific research and experimental development related to the class of business of the taxpayer;

---

[s] The Tax Court of Canada had occasion to consider the definition of the term in the case of *Sass Manufacturing Limited v. M.N.R.*, 88 DTC 1363.

(c) to an approved university, college, research institute or other similar institution to be used for scientific research and experimental development related to the class of business of the taxpayer;

(d) for scientific research and experimental development in Canada to non-profit corporations resident in Canada;

(e) to a corporation resident in Canada for scientific research and experimental development in Canada related to the business of the taxpayer; or

(f) to an approved organization that makes payments to an association, institution or corporation described in (b) to (d) above, for use in scientific research and experimental development related to the class of business of the taxpayer, and where the taxpayer may exploit the results of such research and development.

Paragraph 37(1)(*b*) describes expenditures on scientific research and experimental development of a capital nature made in Canada by acquiring property (other than land or other non-depreciable property) relating to the business and directly undertaken by or on behalf of the taxpayer.

Proposed subsection 37(1.3) extends the zone in which deductible SR&ED expenditures can be incurred to the area that is up to 200 nautical miles from the low-water line along the costs of Canada, as recognized in the *Oceans Act*. This is known as the exclusive economic zone (EEZ) and includes the airspace above and the subsoil or seabed below that zone.

Paragraphs 37(1)(*a*) and (*b*) require that expenditures be related to a business carried on by the person making the expenditure. As indicated, SR&ED expenditures are added to a pool of such costs. They are eligible for a 100% deduction in the year incurred or may be carried forward indefinitely.

As a further incentive to invest in SR&ED activity, the Act provides for an investment tax credit (ITC, discussed in subsequent chapters) which is a direct reduction of the taxpayer's tax bill. The investment tax credit is calculated as a specified percentage of the SR&ED expenditures made. An investment tax credit in respect of SR&ED, in essence, lowers the cost of the research and development activity. Therefore, the amount of the investment tax credit reduces the amount of the pool available for deduction in the year following the year of the investment tax credit claim [par. 37(1)(*e*)]. In addition, any super-allowance benefit amount, as defined in subsection 127(9), will reduce the pool. If there is no balance in the pool in that year, because all amounts were previously deducted and no new expenditures were made in the current year, then the investment tax credit is included in income [par. 12(1)(*v*)]. A reduction of the balance in the pool reduces the future deduction and has the same effect as the income inclusion. The effect of this adjustment for the investment tax credit is to permit a deduction of the net cost of the expenditure after the partial recovery of cost through the investment tax credit. This effect can be illustrated with the following two options:

	Fully deducted	*Pooled*
Expenditure in year 1	$1,000	$1,000
Deducted in year 1	(1,000)	Nil
Available for future deduction	Nil	$1,000

	Fully deducted	*Pooled*
ITC @ 35% of $1,000 claimed in year 1:		
Income inclusion in year 2	$ 350	
Reduction of pool in year 2		(350)
Available for future deduction		$ 650
Net deduction:		
Deduction in year 1 net of inclusion in year 2 (i.e., net deduction over 2 years)	$ 650	
Available for future deduction		$ 650
Net cost:		
Initial expenditure	$1,000	$1,000
ITC claimed in year 1	(350)	(350)
Tax saving at, say 20%:		
year 1 — $1,000 × .20	(200)	
later years — $1,000 × .20		(200)
Tax cost: year 2 ($350 × .20)	70	70
Net cost	$ 520	$ 520

Subsection 37(2) permits the deduction of certain expenditures only of a current nature made for scientific research and experimental development carried on outside Canada. Deductible SR&ED expenditures incurred outside Canada must be deducted in the year that they are incurred. They are not pooled.

Paragraph 37(8)(*d*) excludes expenditures on buildings from the 100% write-off. This includes the capital cost of a building or rent and lease expense incurred in respect of a building. However, expenditures on structures such as a wind tunnel or an experimental wind or hydro energy prototype are not affected and, hence, are eligible for the 100% write-off.

Paragraph 37(8)(*a*) requires that expenditures eligible for the scientific research and experimental development deduction be all or substantially all attributable to the prosecution or to the provision of premises, facilities or equipment for the prosecution of such research and development. Regulations 2900(2) and (3) amplify the definition of expenditures that are directly attributable to the prosecution of and to the provision of premises, facilities and equipment for the prosecution of SR&ED in Canada.

Current expenditures that are "directly attributable" to scientific research also qualify. This allows for the prorating of the direct costs of personnel who, while not solely involved with research, do directly perform scientific research part of the time, support scientific research personnel or directly supervise researchers. In the case of capital expenditures, minor or incidental use of equipment for non-research purposes is possible under the "all or substantially all" requirement.

3. Election method to determine deduction

Clause 37(8)(*a*)(ii)(B) provides an election as an alternative method for determining which expenditures incurred in Canada will qualify as SR&ED, to be included in the pool. This alternative method, which must be elected in prescribed form each year, is generally simpler for the taxpayer. The taxpayer has a choice of using either the method described in clause 37(8)(*a*)(ii)(A) or the alternative elected method in clause 37(8)(*a*)(ii)(B). If the election is used, clause 37(8)(*a*)(ii)(B) specifically lists six types of expenditures which will be considered to be for SR&ED carried on in Canada and, therefore, will be included in the taxpayer's SR&ED pool under subsection 37(1). The alternative method is described in more detail in Chapters 11 and 12.

This elective method for determining SR&ED expenditures does not account for general overhead expenditures, even if they are directly attributable to the prosecution or the provision of premises for the prosecution of SR&ED in Canada. Such overhead expenditures are treated, under the elective method, as ordinary expenses which are, generally, deductible in the year incurred or eligible for capital cost allowance. However, general overhead expenses are recognized in the method of calculating the investment tax credit discussed in Chapter 12.

IV. THE GST IMPACT ON BUSINESS ACTIVITY

A. Commercial Activity

[ETA: 123(1); 152; 161; 168; 173(1); Sch. V; Sch. VI]

As noted in Chapter 2, the issue of whether the person is engaged in a commercial activity is central to the determination of whether a person is required to register and collect GST. Commercial activity means any business that is carried on, an adventure or concern in the nature of trade, or the making of a supply of real property [ETA: ssec. 123(1)]. The meaning of the first two phrases is discussed below, while supplies of real property will be reviewed, in part, in Chapters 5 and 6.

1. Carrying on business

To some extent, the concept of carrying on business under the *Income Tax Act* has been adopted for GST purposes. Generally, if an entity is carrying on business for income tax purposes, it is also considered to be carrying on business for GST purposes. However, some entities not considered to be carrying on business for income tax purposes may still be considered to be carrying on business for GST purposes, as the comparable provisions under the ETA are generally broader in scope than those under the *Income Tax Act*.

The term "business" is defined to include a profession, calling, trade, manufacture or undertaking of any kind whatever [ETA: ssec. 123(1)]. However, unlike the definition of carrying on business in the *Income Tax Act*, it is not necessary to establish that the business has a reasonable expectation of profit. Therefore, an entity engaged in activities with continuous, repetitive effort is generally considered to be a business for GST purposes, whether the activity or undertaking is engaged in for profit. The definition specifically excludes an office or employment.

Because of the absence of the profit test, a number of organizations established on a not-for-profit basis are considered to be carrying on business for GST purposes and, thus, to be engaged in commercial activities. For example, where a hospital operates a parking lot, this is considered to be a commercial activity and the hospital is required to collect GST on that supply. Therefore, even if an activity is considered ancillary to achieving a not-for-profit purpose for income tax purposes, and, therefore, outside the definition of carrying on business for purposes of the *Income Tax Act*, it is still considered to be a business for purposes of the GST.

Another distinction from the *Income Tax Act* is the inclusion of leasing activities in the definition of business [ETA: ssec. 123(1)]. Any activity that is engaged in on a regular and continuous basis that involves the supply of property by way of lease, licence or similar arrangement, is considered to be a business. Thus, rents received from the rental of an automobile, for example, are regarded as being earned from a business for GST purposes, regardless of the effort required by the owner of the automobile to earn the rental income. This can be contrasted with the treatment under the *Income Tax Act*, where the activity may not be considered to be a business, but rather, may be regarded as income from property. This distinction for income tax purposes will be discussed in Chapter 6.

2. Adventure or concern in the nature of trade

As noted earlier in this chapter, the definition of business for income tax purposes includes an adventure or concern in the nature of trade. In contrast, this latter phrase is referred to separately in the definition of commercial activity under the ETA. In any event, as the phrase is not defined in the ETA, its meaning under the *Income Tax Act* should offer some insight into its meaning for GST purposes. In this regard, the *Taylor* case referred to earlier in this chapter should be reviewed.

3. Exclusions from the definition of commercial activity

There are two key activities which are specifically excluded from the definition of commercial activity [ETA: ssec. 123(1)]. As a result, supplies made in the course of these activities will not be considered to be taxable supplies. The supplier of these goods and services is not required to collect GST on these supplies and, in turn, is not entitled to claim input tax credits. They include:

- that part of a business or adventure or concern in the nature of trade that involves the making of an exempt supply; or
- a business engaged in by an individual, a personal trust or a partnership consisting solely of individuals without a reasonable expectation of profit.

Exempt supplies are set out in Schedule V of the ETA, and include, for example, health care services, educational services, and legal aid services. While the making of exempt supplies is excluded from the definition of a commercial activity, the making of zero-rated supplies is not excluded. Thus, any person who sells zero-rated groceries or exports goods in the course of a business or an adventure or concern in the nature of trade, is considered to be engaged in a commercial activity and is entitled to claim input tax credits in respect of GST paid on purchases. Zero-rated supplies are set out in Schedule VI of the ETA. If a supply is not considered to be made in the course of a commercial activity because it falls within one of these exclusions, or if the supply is not made in the course of a business or an adventure or concern in the nature of trade or is not a supply of real property, the supply will not be a taxable supply and no GST will apply. Although no input tax credit may be claimed for GST paid in respect of these supplies, this GST is deductible for income tax purposes.

4. Value for tax

GST is imposed on the value of consideration for a supply [ETA: ssec. 165(1)]. Consideration is the price paid for property or services and is, generally, expressed in monetary terms.

Goods or services are often sold on terms that allow for a discount for prompt payment, or for a penalty in the case of a late payment. Under section 161 of the ETA, the value on which GST is imposed is not affected by the discount or penalty. In either case, GST applies to the amount of consideration shown on the invoice (i.e., the full sale price). If, however, the invoice is for an amount that is net of a cash discount, GST applies on the net amount.

5. When GST is payable

GST is generally payable by a recipient of a taxable supply at the time the consideration for the supply is paid to the supplier or the time the consideration becomes due, whichever is earlier [ETA: ssec. 168(1)]. Where partial payments are made in respect of a supply, GST must be paid on each payment [ETA: ssec. 168(2)]. GST generally becomes due when it is invoiced [ETA: ssec. 152(1)]. Specifically, the consideration becomes due on the earliest of:

(a) the day on which the invoice for the amount is issued;

(b) the date on the invoice;

(c) the day on which the invoice would have been issued, if not for an undue delay; and

(d) the day on which the amount becomes due under an agreement in writing.

Where property is supplied by way of lease, licence or similar agreement, the consideration is deemed to become due on the day the recipient is required to pay the consideration under the agreement [ETA: ssec. 152(2)].

Notwithstanding the general rule set out in subsection 168(1) of the ETA, a number of special cases are dealt with in other subsections. For example, where the supply involves goods, liability occurs on the earlier of the date determined under the general rule and the end of the month following the month in which ownership or possession of the goods is transferred to the purchaser [ETA: ssec. 168(3)]. In the case of a deposit, GST is not payable on the deposit until the time the supplier applies the deposit against the consideration for the supply [ETA: ssec. 168(9)].

6. Automobile operating cost benefits paid by employer

Recall from Chapter 3 that an employer provides a taxable benefit when the employee's operating costs for an employer-provided automobile are paid by the employer. The value of the benefit is determined by one of two methods [par. 6(1)(k)]. The employee may use a per-kilometre method or elect to value the benefit as 50% of the standby charge in respect of the employer-provided car. Likewise, where the employee uses his or her own car but the operating costs are paid by the employer, an operating cost benefit is required to be determined under the *Income Tax Act* [par. 6(1)(l)]. In either case, the registrant employer is required to remit GST equal to a prescribed percentage of 5%[t] of the benefit, however computed [ETA: l. 173(1)(d)(vi)(A)]. The prescribed percentage is less than 7% to recognize that the benefit includes exempt supplies such as insurance and licence fees.

B. Input Tax Credits

[ETA: 123(1); 169; 170]

1. General rules

Input tax credits are available to registrants for GST paid on goods and services that are purchased for use in a commercial activity [ETA: ssec. 169(1)]. If the use of the input is exclusively in a commercial activity, which is defined in subsection 123(1) of the ETA to mean "all or substantially all" (and which is interpreted to mean 90% or more), a full credit may be claimed. Conversely, if a business input will not be used at all in respect of a commercial activity, no credit will be allowed. Under this latter rule, if the extent of use in a commercial activity is less than 10%, no credit may be claimed. For example, if an input is to be used 90% or more in the course of making an exempt supply, no credit may be claimed. It is important to note that the test for eligibility is the intended use of the input at the time of purchase. Apart from the change-of-use rules for capital real property discussed in Chapter 8, a registrant is not required to adjust the input tax credit for subsequent changes of use. Registrants are entitled to claim the credit in the reporting period in which the GST is paid or, if earlier, when it becomes payable.

---

[t] 11% for purposes of the HST. The prescribed percentages are set out in the Automobile Operating Expense Benefit (GST/HST) Regulations.

There are circumstances where a purchase will be used in respect of a combination of taxable and exempt supplies. In these cases, except for certain capital goods which are discussed in Chapter 5, registrants are required to apportion the input tax credit between the taxable and exempt activity [ETA: ssec. 169(1)]. For example, if use in a commercial activity represents 70% of the total use, a credit equal to 70% of the GST paid or payable may be claimed.

The legislation does not prescribe allocation methods to be used in apportioning input tax credits. Provided the allocation basis is reasonable and is used on a consistent basis throughout the fiscal year, the allocation will likely not be challenged by the CRA. The documentation requirements that are necessary to support input tax credit claims are discussed in Chapter 14.

2. Restrictions

Certain purchases made by a registrant have a personal consumption element or are for goods and services that are available to employees. As a result, there are certain circumstances where input tax credits are not allowed, in full or in part. In many circumstances, the GST restrictions parallel the restrictions contained in the *Income Tax Act* in respect of business deductions. The more significant restrictions include:

(a) *Club Memberships*

Input tax credits are not allowed in respect of membership fees or dues in any club whose main purpose is to provide dining, recreational or sporting facilities [ETA: par. 170(1)(a)]. Common examples of these clubs include business persons' clubs, golf clubs and fitness clubs. However, if meal and entertainment expenses are incurred at the club in respect of a commercial activity, input tax credits are allowed, subject to the recapture rule discussed below.

(b) *Home Office Expenses*

Input tax credits are not allowed in respect of expenses incurred by an individual in respect of a home office where the office is neither the individual's principal place of business nor a place that is both used exclusively for the purpose of earning income from a business and used on a regular and continuous basis for meeting clients, customers or patients [ETA: par. 170(1)(a.1)]. This provision is consistent with the *Income Tax Act*, which denies a deduction in such circumstances [ssec. 18(12)].

(c) *Personal or Living Expenses*

No input tax credit is allowed where a property or service is purchased exclusively for the personal consumption, use or enjoyment of an officer, employee or related individual [ETA: pars. 170(1)(b) and (c)]. This restriction was referred to in Chapter 3, in the context of employee benefits. An exception to this rule is provided where a registrant acquires property or service exclusively for an employee's personal use; but the input tax credit will be disallowed, unless the property is re-supplied for fair market value consideration to the employee in the reporting period. In these circumstances, as GST will be collected on the resale, an input tax credit is allowed. An additional exception where an input tax credit is allowed is where the property or service would not be a taxable benefit for purposes of the *Income Tax Act*.

For leases in respect of property rented to individuals, no input tax credit is allowed where the property is primarily for personal consumption, use or enjoyment. However, similar to the rule discussed above, an input tax credit is allowed where the property is supplied to the individual and GST is collected on the fair rental value.

(d)   *Reasonableness*

Another concept is borrowed from the *Income Tax Act*, namely, that of reasonableness [ETA: ssec. 170(2)]. In claiming an input tax credit, the nature or cost of the property or services purchased by the registrant must be reasonable in the circumstances, having regard to the nature of the commercial activities of the registrant. In addition, the amount of the input tax credit must be calculated on consideration that is reasonable in the circumstances.

(e)   *Automobile Allowances*

Where an employer has paid an automobile allowance to an employee for travel in respect of the employer's business and the employee is not required to include the allowance in income because the allowance is a reasonable one, the employer is permitted to claim an ITC on that amount [ETA: sec. 174].

C.   Adjustments to Net Tax
[ETA: 231; 232(1), (3); 235; 236]

The legislation sets out a series of adjustments in computing the net tax to be remitted by a registrant for a particular period. The most common of these adjustments are discussed below.

1.   Excess charges

Where a supplier has charged an amount of GST in excess of what is collectible under the legislation, the supplier may adjust the amount of GST charged if it has not already been collected [ETA: ssec. 232(1)]. If the excess has already been collected, it may be refunded or credited to the customer, provided a credit note is issued to the customer (or a debit note is issued by the recipient of the supply) [ETA: ssec. 232(3)]. The supplier is permitted to deduct the excess amount refunded or credited in determining his or her net tax for the reporting period in which the credit or debit note is issued. Conversely, the recipient, if a registrant, is required to add that amount to his or her net tax for that period, or a preceding period, to the extent it was deducted in determining his or her net tax. The refund or credit must be made within four years after the day the GST was charged or collected.

2.   Price reductions

Where a registrant reduces the price in respect of a supply for which GST has been charged but not collected, the registrant may adjust the amount of GST charged [ETA: ssec. 232(2)]. If the GST has already been collected, a refund or credit may be given to the customer, provided a credit note (or debit note) is issued, as described above [ETA: ssec. 232(3)]. The refund or credit must be made within four years of the time the price was reduced.

This rule does not apply where section 161 applies [ETA: ssec. 232(4)]. (Section 161, which is discussed earlier in this chapter, contains the rules in respect of cash discounts for prompt payment.) The adjustments outlined above may not be made for cash discounts. Registrants are required to collect GST on the full invoice price, regardless of whether a cash discount is subsequently granted for prompt payment. Similarly, registrants who purchase goods that are subject to a cash discount for prompt payment are entitled to claim an input tax credit based on the full invoice price.

3.   Bad debts

Relief is provided for bad debts [ETA: ssec. 231(1)]. Where GST is remitted but not collected on a debt that is subsequently written off, a registrant is permitted to deduct an amount equal to the tax payable in respect of the supply multiplied by the ratio of the total amount equal to $^7/_{107}$th ($^{15}/_{115}$th for HST) of the bad debt written off to the total amount payable for the supply. To be eligible for this relief, the bad debt must be in respect of a supply made to an arm's length party, and the relief must be claimed in the reporting period in which the debt is written off or within four years after the due date of the return for that period. If a bad debt is subsequently recovered after the deduction is made, the ETA requires that the registrant add back to net tax an amount equal to the amount of the bad debt recovered multiplied by the ratio of the tax payable in respect of the supply to the total amount paid or payable on the supply (including GST and applicable provincial taxes) [ETA: ssec. 231(3)].

4. Lease of passenger vehicles

Where a registrant leases a passenger vehicle, to the extent the lease costs exceed the maximum amount deductible under section 67.3 of the *Income Tax Act*, a portion of the input tax credit will be recaptured [ETA: ssec. 235(1)]. This restriction parallels the restriction that limits the maximum input tax credit that can be claimed in respect of the purchase of a passenger vehicle, which is discussed in Chapter 5. The recapture is provided by way of an adjustment to the net tax determination for the appropriate reporting period [ETA: ssec. 235(2)]. For annual filers, the appropriate reporting period is the taxation year. For quarterly and monthly filers, it is the reporting period that begins immediately after the taxation year.

5. Food, beverages and entertainment expenses

Section 236 of the ETA contains the rules for food, beverages and entertainment expenses that are subject to section 67.1 of the *Income Tax Act*. Input tax credits for GST paid expenses are allowed in full in the reporting period in which they are incurred. However, at the end of the registrant's fiscal year, there will be a recapture of 50% of the total input tax credits in respect of these expenses. The amount recaptured will be included in the registrant's GST return for the first reporting period in the next fiscal year [ETA: ssec. 236(1.1)].

D. Application of the Rules

Example Problem

Reconsider the facts of the Example Problem involving Corporate Welfare Bum Limited beginning on page 181.

— REQUIRED

Outline the proper GST treatment by the corporation of the items presented.

— SOLUTION

(1) General

Since the corporation is carrying on business, it is engaged in a commercial activity [ETA: ssec. 123(1)]. Therefore, the corporation is required to register and collect GST on its supplies, i.e., sales of goods or services, which are "taxable supplies." As a registrant, the corporation is entitled to a full input tax credit (ITC) in respect of GST paid or payable on goods and services that it purchases exclusively for use in its commercial activity [ETA: ssec. 169(1)]. If GST collected or collectible on its sales exceeds its ITCs, the corporation must remit the difference. On the other hand, if ITCs exceed GST collected or collectible, a refund of the excess is available.

(2) Items Listed

 (a) The appraisal expenses incurred for insurance appraisal purposes are for the provision of an exempt supply of a financial service which does not give rise to an ITC since no GST was payable [ETA: Schedule V, Part VII].

 (b) Employer contributions to a registered pension plan involve a payment for an exempt supply on which GST is not charged [ETA: ssec. 123(1)]. As a result, no ITC is available.

(c) Landscaping costs involve a payment for taxable supplies of goods or services resulting in the availability of an ITC.

(d) Payments for legal services give rise to an ITC since the services are taxable supplies.

(e) Dividends received involve an exempt supply of a financial service on which no GST is collected [ETA: Schedule V, Part VII].

(f) The payment of interest is a financial service which is an exempt supply.

(g) The purchase of inventory involves a taxable supply on which GST is paid. Hence, an ITC is available.

(h) No GST is charged on a donation which involves a transfer of money. As a result, no ITC is available [ETA: ssec. 123(1), sec. 164].

(i) Insurance premiums are for an exempt supply of a financial service and no ITC is available since no GST was paid.

(j) The payment of a dividend is an exempt supply of a financial service. No ITC is available.

(k) A loan is a financial instrument which is an exempt supply, on which no GST is charged. Hence, the write-off of this bad debt has no GST effect.

(l) Improvements that are not normal repairs or maintenance are considered to be capital outlays. However, as will be discussed in Chapter 5, there is no amortization of the GST paid on capital outlays. The GST paid provides an ITC at the time of payment.

(m) Amounts paid to employees as remuneration are not supplies, since these amounts are excluded from the definition of services in subsection 123(1) of the ETA. As a result, remuneration is not subject to GST.

(n) Interest paid involves an exempt supply of a financial service.

(o) Initially, an ITC is available on the full amount of GST paid in respect of meals and entertainment. However, 50% of the ITC in respect of such expenditures is recaptured in the first reporting period of the next fiscal year [ETA: sec. 236].

(p) Embezzlement losses involve a transfer of money for which there are no GST implications.

(q) Bonuses are employment remuneration excluded from the definition of service and, hence, are not subject to GST.

(r) Property tax involves an exempt supply on which no GST is charged.

(s) A lease cancellation fee paid by a lessor is subject to GST. The payer is deemed to have paid GST equal to $^7/_{107}$ths of the payment and, hence, an ITC is available.

(t) The payer of damages is deemed to have paid or the recipient deemed to have received GST equal to $^7/_{107}$ths of the damages. As a result, the corporation is entitled to an ITC [ETA: sec. 182].

(u) Construction and repair costs involve a payment for taxable supplies for goods or services resulting in the availability of an ITC.

REVIEW QUESTIONS

(1) Mr. Flip is a commissioned real estate client of yours. He has just bought and sold a piece of land in a "quick flip" transaction. What kind of income might this be to him: employment, business, property or capital gain?

(2) Does the Act require that the "profit" from a business be calculated in accordance with generally accepted accounting principles?

(3) Opco Ltd. is in the business of manufacturing equipment under contract for other manufacturers. One of its customers failed to live up to its contract and would not take delivery of or pay for its order. Opco took the customer to court and was awarded the amount of $100,000 as damages. Can this amount be treated as a non-taxable capital receipt by Opco?

(4) Aco Ltd. and Xco Ltd. entered into an agreement to manufacture a new product for the next 20 years. This represented 80% of Aco's business. After 5 years it was decided that the two

parties could not work together so Xco paid Aco $500,000 to terminate the agreement. Is the receipt of this amount by Aco considered to be business income?

(5) Donald Corleone owns an illegal gambling house. He has made significant "profits" on this activity, but has not reported the income since he believes it is not taxable. Is he correct?

(6) Opco Ltd. took advantage of a program offered by the government and hired two employees whose wages were partially offset by a government subsidy. The owner felt that since he was really just getting some of his tax dollars back through this subsidy, the amount received would not be taxable. What do you think?

(7) As long as an expenditure was made for the purpose of earning income from a business or property then it is deductible under section 18. Is this statement true? Comment.

(8) One of your clients is having some short-term cash flow problems and cannot pay his year-end tax liability. He decides that he will defer his payment to the Receiver General instead of trying to get another short-term bank loan. He reasons that in either case the interest will be deductible. Comment.

(9) Subsection 18(1) lists those items that are prohibited from being deducted because of the nature of the expenditure. If an expense passes those tests, will it be deductible?

(10) A client had to replace the roof on its factory at a cost of $100,000. The client deducted the cost of the roof on the basis that it was simply replacing the previous roof with a new one of the same quality. Is the cost deductible?

(11) Is the portion of the airline ticket that represents the meal subject to the 50% limitation on meal expenses?

(12) Will a company that offers a warranty with its product be able to deduct a reserve under paragraph 20(1)(*m.1*)?

(13) Under certain circumstances, can capital expenditures be written off in the year?

MULTIPLE CHOICE QUESTIONS

Question 1

Which one of the following items is NOT deductible in computing the income of a corporation under Division B of the Act?

(A) Amounts paid for landscaping business premises.

(B) Interest on money borrowed to finance the purchase of a factory for use in its business.

(C) The premium on a $100,000 term life insurance policy on an employee if the beneficiary of the policy is the employee's family.

(D) Interest and penalties on late income tax payments.

Question 2

Which one of the following amounts is DEDUCTIBLE in computing the income of a corporation under Division B of the Act?

(A) $11,000 of accrued legal fees for a pending law suit. The accrual is an estimate because no work has been done to date by the lawyers.

(B) $4,000 of donations to registered charities made for no business reason.

(C) $15,000 spent on three social events in the taxation year for all employees at a particular location.

(D) $1,500 for golf club membership dues for employees.

Question 3

Which one of the following amounts is DEDUCTIBLE in computing income of a corporation under Division B of the Act?

(A) $5,000 of donations to federal political parties.

(B) $44,000 in accrued bonuses paid 7 months after year-end. The amounts were legal liabilities at year-end.

(C) A $10,000 increase in the financial accounting reserve for warranty expenses.

(D) The $2,000 cost of tickets for meals and entertainment at a gala fund-raising event for a registered charity.

Question 4

XYZ Ltd.'s current financial statement shows a deduction for $20,000 of legal and accounting expenses. This amount consists of the following items:

- $5,000 of legal expenses related to the purchase of an investment in shares;
- $5,000 of legal expenses incurred to dispute a tax assessment;
- $5,000 of legal expenses related to the issuance of debt; and
- $5,000 of accounting fees related to the preparation of a prospectus regarding the issuance of shares.

What amount must be added back to XYZ's financial statement income in the computation of its net income under Division B of the Act?

(A) $13,000

(B) $12,000

(C) $9,000

(D) $5,000

Question 5

Ten years ago, Sam, a real estate agent, purchased a piece of land for $50,000. His intention at that time was to build a rental building on the land and use it to earn rental income, which he did four years ago. In the current year, he sold the land and building for $100,000 and $80,000 respectively after receiving an unsolicited offer.

Based on the facts, which one of the following statements is true?

(A) The CRA may argue that the gain on the sale of the land is a capital gain, because Sam is a real estate agent.

(B) The CRA may argue that the gain on the sale of the land is business income, because of the ten-year holding period of the land.

(C) The CRA may argue that the gain on the sale of the land is business income because of the unsolicited offer for sale.

(D) The gain on the sale of the land will likely be treated as a capital gain for income tax purposes.

Question 6

Which of the following amounts is DEDUCTIBLE in computing the income of a corporation under Division B of the Act?

(A) $13,000 of legal fees to defend a lawsuit brought by a customer.

(B) Accounting losses on the sale of a capital property.

(C) The principal amount of a mortgage on a company's warehouse.

(D) The personal and living expenses of the shareholder who works very hard in the business and is not paid a salary.

EXERCISES

Exercise 1

[ITA: 9; IT-218R]

The taxpayer corporation, Singh Enterprises Ltd., purchased a property consisting of some eight separate residential apartment buildings. When purchased, the property was ready for profit-producing operation and immediate arrangements were made for such operations.

The principal shareholder of the corporation, Sam Singh, was an individual with a long history of trading in real estate in many different countries. He fully expected that the property would increase in value in the future.

About eleven months after the purchase of the property, circumstances dictated a change in the investments of the corporation and the property was sold for a substantial profit.

— *REQUIRED*

Determine whether the profit realized by the sale of the property was income from a business or a capital gain.

Exercise 2

[ITA: 9]

Unloadem Limited had a franchise for the distribution in Saskatchewan of Belchfire automobiles made in Argentina. The business had grown rapidly in its ten years of existence. However, soon after the expansion of its facilities, Belchfire Motor Industries terminated the distribution agreement and voluntarily agreed to pay Unloadem Limited $225,000.

— *REQUIRED*

What are the tax implications to Unloadem Limited?

Exercise 3

[ITA: 10]

Holey Mufflers Limited operates a fast-service repair shop. At the end of its fiscal year its inventory records showed the following:

Item	Number	Actual cost	FIFO cost	Replacement cost	Net realization value
Mufflers	64	$17.50	$16.25	$18.40	$15.50
Tailpipes	157	4.75	4.25	5.00	4.50
Exhaust systems	39	16.25	16.30	17.00	15.50
Shock absorbers	256	19.45	18.85	20.50	19.75
Brackets	932	1.40	1.35	1.50	1.30
Clamps	1,746	.65	.70	.75	.80

— *REQUIRED*

What values could be used for the total inventory for tax purposes? (Ignore the potential application of subsection 10(2.1) in this case.)

Exercise 4

[ITA: 18(1)(*l*)]

Foistit Limited, a consulting firm in Calgary, owns a small lodge in the Banff area. The lodge is used throughout the year for the purposes of entertaining clients.

— *REQUIRED*

(A) Comment on the deductibility of maintenance costs in respect of the lodge.

(B) Reconsider the deductibility of these costs if the property is rented during the week to the public and used to entertain clients only on the weekends.

Exercise 5

[ITA: 17; 20(1)]

Mr. M. Bezzle is the controller with responsibility for tax compliance of International Widget Manufacturing Limited based in Calgary. He has called to ask your advice, as the company's accountant, on various matters pertaining to the company's 2005 tax return. He has asked you the following questions.

(A) On March 1, 2006, the company paid $234,000 for the benefit of 30 employees to a defined benefit registered pension plan. Of the $234,000 paid, $129,000 represents an adjustment required as a result of an actuarial valuation; the remainder was based on a current service contribution equal to 6% of each employee's wages for 2005. What is the total amount that can be deducted for tax purposes in 2005?

(B) The company paid $15,000 representation costs to obtain a special licence from the State of Montana to sell its widgets in the state. This amount was written off in the financial accounts but added back and amortized over a 20-year period in calculating income for tax purposes. How should this item be treated?

(C) The amount of $1,500 spent to connect gas lines on conversion from oil to gas in the Toronto plant was added to the cost of the building for financial accounting purposes and depreciated with the building. How should the amount be treated for tax purposes?

(D) The president's wife is employed full-time as his secretary and paid $7,000 per month. Is this amount deductible and if not, how much is deductible?

— *REQUIRED*

Provide brief answers to the questions posed by the controller.

Exercise 6

[ITA: 20(1)(f)]

In August 1999, Steel M. Blind Manufacturing Co. Ltd., a venetian blind manufacturer, issued a series of bonds at $891.90 per $1,000 par value. The issue matured in August 2005 and was redeemed at that time at par value. It bears a coupon rate of 9% to yield 12% to maturity.

— *REQUIRED*

How much of the bond discount can be deducted and in what year can it be deducted?

Exercise 7

[ITA: 9–12; 18–20]

The following information concerning the financial statements of Incredible Incubators Incorporated for its fiscal year ended September 30, 2005 has been presented to you in order to prepare tax returns.

(a)	Net income after tax per financial statements	$150,000
(b)	Provision for income taxes — current	25,000
	— future	130,000
(c)	Depreciation expense	40,000
(d)	Inventory — on LIFO* basis: opening	125,000
	closing	145,000
	— on FIFO basis: opening	140,000
	closing	155,000
(e)	Interest on income taxes paid after due date	2,500
(f)	Bond interest expense (including annual discount amortization of $7,500 re bonds issued this year)	39,500
(g)	Landscaping costs re factory premises — debited to land account	12,000

* LIFO is used by the company for financial statement purposes.

— *REQUIRED*

Using the foregoing information, compute income for tax purposes for Incredible Incubators for their fiscal year ended September 30, 2005. [Ignore tax deductions in respect of depreciable capital property.]

Exercise 8

[ITA: 9; 12(1)(*e*)(ii); 20(1)(*n*)(ii), (8)(*b*)]

Quickturn Land Limited bought for cash 25 acres of land at a cost of $107,500 during the year. About two months later the land was sold to a developer for $250,000 consisting of a $110,000 down payment in cash and a note without interest due in one year for the balance. A real estate commission of $12,500 was paid. The company often engages in this type of transaction.

— REQUIRED

Compute the minimum net income for the company in the year of sale and the next year in respect of this transaction.

Exercise 9

[ITA: 22]

Mr. Flogger has arranged to sell substantially all of the assets of his proprietorship business, including accounts receivable valued at $36,000, to Mr. Sucker who will continue the proprietorship business. At the end of last year, Mr. Flogger had deducted a reserve for doubtful debts of $6,500. The face value of the accounts being sold is $45,000.

— REQUIRED

What are the tax implications to both Mr. Flogger and Mr. Sucker of using section 22 on the sale of accounts receivable?

Exercise 10

[ETA: 123(1); 169(1); Schedule V, Part VII]

Reconsider the facts of Exercise 7.

— REQUIRED

Outline the proper GST treatment by the corporation of the items presented.

ASSIGNMENT PROBLEMS

Problem 1

[ITA: 9; IT-218R]

A piece of land was purchased by Yacumflastor Corporation Ltd. for the purpose of constructing a high-rise residential building. Plans were made for the development of the property, surveys were made and the land was stripped and excavated in preparation for construction. Subsequent to this work on the land, it was determined that the location was not suitable for the intended purpose, due to heavy truck traffic in the area. As a result, the property was listed for sale with the realtor who acted in the original purchase. The sale at a substantial profit took place approximately six months from the purchase.

The corporation had been newly formed when the above land was purchased. At about the same time, another piece of land was purchased and was developed into a commercial/industrial plaza which the corporation continues to own as a rental property. The principal shareholder of the corporation, Jake Yacumflastor, owns and operates an electrical contracting business.

The Articles of Incorporation of the corporation contain the following statement of objects:

... to purchase, lease, acquire, hold, manage, develop, operate, pledge and mortgage, either absolutely as owner or by way of collateral security or otherwise, alone or jointly with others and either as principal or agent, property, real or personal, and assets generally of any and every kind of description.

No mention is made of the purchase and sale of land as a business activity.

— *REQUIRED*

Write a memo for the Yacumflastor Corporation Ltd.'s file evaluating the issue of whether the sale of the land should be treated as a receipt of income or capital gain for tax purposes. Arrive at a conclusion consistent with your analysis of the facts, but indicate the basis for any areas of potential opposition to your conclusion.

Problem 2

[ITA: 18(1)(a), (h); 248(1)]

The taxpayer, in 1959, purchased 200 acres of property in the Calabogie area of Lanark, as a holiday property for himself and his family. In 1961 it became their principal residence. He worked in Ottawa, both at that time and in the subsequent years; initially he commuted between the Lanark property and his Ottawa job on a daily basis. In the early 1970s he began living in Ottawa during the week and commuting home to the property only on weekends. When the property was first purchased, there was an old brick house on it which was not suitable as a residence for the family. A new house (referred to in the evidence as the D.V.A. house) was built; the family moved into it. It is clear that the family's lifestyle was such as to enjoy the rural location.

In 1974 the taxpayer decided to turn part of the property into a campground; 8 serviced campsites and approximately 12 unserviced sites were created for this purpose. There was as well room for at least 10 other unserviced campsites more or less immediately available and potential for expansion to a much larger number (e.g., 100). Outhouses were built; a trout pond constructed; and the requisite service roads installed. The tax treatment of the expenses incurred with respect to this construction is not part of the dispute in this case.

After these initiatives had been taken, sometime towards the end of 1975 or the beginning of 1976, the taxpayer sought the advice of a consultant with the Ontario Ministry of Tourism, a Mr. Bingham. The advice sought was with respect to the possibility of developing the campground and obtaining a business loan for this purpose. The taxpayer had applied in early 1975 for a loan and was turned down in September of that year.

The taxpayer's consultations with Mr. Bingham in the later half of 1975 and beginning of 1976 led to suggestions for the development of the campsite through the construction of additional facilities: additional serviced sites; proper toilets; laundry facilities; a store on the property; a swimming pool; an activities building which might be used by the campers in bad weather. The taxpayer's accountant, Mr. McCoy, in early 1976 prepared projections as to the proposed profitability of the venture if the proposed development took place. These projections showed losses in the first year (1976–77) but a profit thereafter. The projections were based on information given to Mr. McCoy by the taxpayer and they envisaged the obtaining of a $280,000 loan. The taxpayer applied to the Eastern Ontario Development Corporation, in 1979, for a loan ($45,000, not $280,000). Mr. Bingham was asked to evaluate the loan application from the Department of Tourism's point of view. He was asked to consider: whether the taxpayer had the management capability to effect and operate the proposed development; whether there would be any negative effects on competitors in the area if the development took place; whether the taxpayer's marketing plans looked reasonable. Mr. Bingham's evaluation did not involve any financial analysis of the application. Mr. Bingham recommended that the loan application go forward for the next step, evaluation by the Eastern Ontario Development Corporation. The taxpayer was unable to obtain the loan, because the Eastern Ontario Development Corporation's funds are new money for new projects.

The taxpayer purchased a "pre-fab" house for $40,000 which was constructed across the road from the D.V.A. house. The family moved into that house in January of 1980. The taxpayer contends that he had decided to proceed with the plans for the development of the campsite by turning the D.V.A. house into the general activities building envisaged in the projected development. He states that he planned to add laundry facilities, toilets, etc., thereto. During 1980, the taxpayer rented the D.V.A. house to his daughter for $100 per month. This was not sufficient to cover the mortgage costs of the property. In May of 1980 the taxpayer had a massive heart attack. He was incapacitated until at least September of that year. The taxpayer continued to charge the mortgage expenses of the property as a business expense.

The profit and loss record of the taxpayer's business never showed a profit from the first year of its operation, in 1975 to 1985. The taxpayer has consistently reported losses for the years 1977 to 1983 as follows:

1977	$ 7,985.54
1978	$ 8,676.84
1979	$ 8,383.37
1980	$14,491.57
1981	$24,414.44
1982	$14,350.77
1983	$14,508.35

The gross income for the campground itself for the years 1977 to 1980 was:

1977	$ 86
1978	$134
1979	$258
1980	$520

After 1980, the campground income was reported in a combined fashion with that received from the cottage and farmhouse property; therefore, it cannot be separately identified. The evidence is sketchy with respect to the renting of the cottage, the farmhouse and the D.V.A. house. That which exists does not show a vigorous and concerted effort to run a business. The D.V.A. house, as well as being rented to the taxpayer's daughter for $100 per month in 1980, was rented during a few of the winter months in 1981–82 to some loggers and for approximately six months in 1984 to some miners who were prospecting in the area.

Camp Coupland was listed in a Government of Ontario camping brochure published for the 1981 season and the taxpayer had had some calling cards made with Camp Coupland, the address, a map and rates listed thereon. No expenses for advertising of the Camp were included in his 1975–1985 tax returns.

— REQUIRED

Determine whether expenses incurred by the taxpayer during the 1980 and 1981 taxation years are business expenses that are deductible for tax purposes.

Problem 3

[ITA: 12(1); 18(1); 20(1); IT-442R]

TalkTech Inc. is a manufacturer and wholesaler of cellular communication products. TalkTech Inc's customers are retailers who promote TalkTech Inc.'s products to the general public. TalkTech Inc. has an October 31 year-end. You are conducting a review of TalkTech Inc's year-end accounting records for its 2005 fiscal year and have been provided with the following information.

TalkTech Inc. has the following recorded reserves:

Account	Opening	Additions	Subtractions	Closing
Warranty reserve	$35,000	$10,000	$17,500	$27,500
Allowance for doubtful accounts	32,000	7,500	5,000	34,500

TalkTech Inc. provides a 1-year warranty on most of its products. The warranty is for defects in workmanship or component parts. This warranty is provided as part of the purchase price of TalkTech Inc.'s products. TalkTech Inc. honours its own warranties. The 2005 addition of $10,000 represents a standard percentage of sales made in the 2005 fiscal period. The 2005 subtraction of $17,500 represents an amount actually paid to honour warranties.

The addition of $7,500 to the allowance for doubtful accounts is a result of the application of TalkTech Inc.'s annual year-end aging analysis. In conversation with the controller of TalkTech Inc. you determine that this $7,500 increase in the allowance for doubtful accounts was computed by applying the company's historical collection percentages to the aged accounts receivable balances. Also, during its 2005 fiscal period, TalkTech Inc. wrote off $5,000 (the subtraction noted above) of amounts previously expensed and included in the opening allowance for doubtful accounts. TalkTech Inc. also ended up collecting $1,500 of previously written-off bad debts.

In an attempt to attract a particular retail customer, TalkTech Inc. provided this new customer with an incentive to make a large initial purchase of its products. On April 1, 2005 TalkTech Inc. sold $300,000 worth of cellular phones to CellBlock Limited. TalkTech agreed to the following payment terms in an attempt to entice CellBlock Limited to make the purchase:

- $100,000 due and payable May 1, 2005; and

- $50,000 due and payable January 1 each year starting January 1, 2006 through January 1, 2009.

The cost of the good sold under this contract was $180,000. The delivery date for the cellular phones sold under this contract was May 1, 2005.

One of TalkTech's customers was experiencing financial trouble. As a result, TalkTech Inc. had agreed to make shipments only if payments were received well in advance of the anticipated shipping dates. Under the terms of this agreement, TalkTech Inc. received $40,000 from Phones'N'Things on September 30, 2005. This payment was an advance payment for a shipment of new technology cellular phones which TalkTech Inc. expected to be shipping to customers commencing February 1, 2006. In the event that TalkTech Inc. was unable to honour its contract with Phones'N'Things, a full refund of the $40,000 was payable.

— *REQUIRED*

(A) Prepare a schedule showing the effect of the above information on income for tax purposes of TalkTech Inc. for the year ended October 31, 2005. From this comparison, determine any adjustments that would be necessary to reconcile accounting income and income for tax purposes for the year.

(B) What would be the tax consequences if the $5,000 subtraction in the allowance for doubtful accounts in 2005 included an account receivable of $800 which was written off only because it has been outstanding for more than 180 days. In fact, it has been outstanding for one year and is part of the opening allowance of $32,000. This $800 could still be collected and there has been no serious attempt to collect it. In fact, the remainder of that customer's account is current and further sales have been made to that customer.

Problem 4

[ITA: 18; 19; 20(1); 147.2(1)]

You have been assigned to the audit team for B.B. JAMS Ltd., one of your significant clients. Below is the income statement prepared by the company's accountant for the December 31, 2005 year-end.

B.B. JAMS LIMITED
INCOME STATEMENT

FOR THE YEAR ENDED DECEMBER 31, 2005

Sales	$147,840,000
Cost of sales (Note (1))	(119,859,000)
Gross profit	$ 27,981,000
General and administrative expenses (Notes (2)–(7))	(12,374,000)
Selling expenses (Note (8))	(9,311,000)
Income from operations	$ 6,296,000
Other income (Notes (9)–(10))	16,000
Net income before income taxes	$ 6,312,000
Provision for income taxes	(2,528,000)
Net income	$ 3,784,000

Through various discussions with the accountant, you have been able to determine that the following information has been recorded in the financial statements:

(1) JAMS had a number of items of inventory that did not sell well in the current year. For accounting purposes, the accountant has recorded a reserve for inventory obsolescence. The reserve was calculated based on the carrying value of any inventory item that had not had a sale in the last 180 days. The reserve at year-end was $1,285,000.

(2) JAMS provides insurance for employees and paid the following amounts to Nat Insurance Company during the year:

$2,000,000 insurance policy on the life of the president included in insurance expense ($300 per month)	$ 3,600
$1,000,000 insurance policy on the life of the vice-president — marketing included in insurance expense	2,000
Group term life insurance for employees included in salaries and benefits ($37,000 × 12 months)	444,000
Total	$449,600

JAMS is the beneficiary of the policies on the president and vice-president. On June 1, 2005, JAMS renegotiated its bank debt, and due to the ever increasing responsibilities of the president, the bank required the insurance policy on the life of the president as part of the collateral for the loan. The premiums on the policy are equal to the net cost of pure insurance for the policy.

(3) An analysis of the professional fees for 2005 revealed the following expenses:

Legal and accounting fees related to the issuance of shares	$29,300
Legal fees related to amending the articles of incorporation	2,300
Costs incurred regarding the renegotiating of the bank loans	46,100
Costs incurred to defend the company against a wrongful dismissal charge	59,600
Costs related to the structuring of an agreement for the purchase of equipment from a foreign company	38,700
Appraisal costs to determine value of the equipment for the bank	5,100

(4) During the year, there were substantial repairs completed to the outside of the building. After the repairs some of the landscaping had to be redone. The total costs were $139,000. Of this, $23,500 relates to the landscaping costs. The entire $139,000 was included in general and administrative expenses

(5) A review of the other expense accounts included in general and administrative expenses showed the following:

Depreciation and amortization	$4,560,000
Interest on late payment of municipal taxes	900
Severance payments to four managers*	245,000
Loss from theft by accounting clerk	4,500
Donations to various registered charities	57,000

* All of the amounts were paid in the year.

(6) The salaries and benefits account shows contributions for certain employees to the company's registered pension plan. The contributions were not actually made until March 31, 2006. The pension plan is a defined contribution (money purchase) plan. The company matches the employees' contributions on a dollar for dollar basis.

	Registered pension plan	Employment compensation
President	$11,500	$250,000
Vice-president	8,500	150,000
Accountant	5,400	70,000

(7) In early November 2005, JAMS announced an early retirement package that was made available to employees over the age of 60. In order to provide employees with the time required to assess the offer, the deadline for accepting the package has been set at February 15, 2006. While no formal replies were received as of December 31, 2005, the personnel manager anticipates a high acceptance rate. She expects that the costs associated with the packages will be $672,000. This cost has been accrued in the 2005 financial statements.

(8) The following information was taken from the various selling expense accounts:

Cost of sponsoring presentations at a local theatre company	$15,000
Hockey game tickets given to customers	8,000
Meals and entertainment costs of salespeople	109,500
Staff Christmas party and summer barbecue	43,800
Cost of sponsoring local little league teams	5,000
Memberships for salespeople at local golf courses	12,700

(9) The other income includes a loss on the sale of various fixed assets of $35,900.

(10) During the year, the company had cash on hand for a short period of time due to the timing of certain contract payments. The funds earned interest income of $10,400 while they were held.

Other Information:

(11) The accountant has calculated that JAMS is entitled to claim capital cost allowance and CECA of $5,835,000 in 2005. You have confirmed that this calculation is correct.

(12) In reviewing the income tax assessments, you noted that JAMS had been charged interest of $4,900 on the late payment of instalments. You discussed this with the accountant and determined that the interest was recorded in the income tax expense account.

— REQUIRED

Based on the information that you have obtained, calculate the business income for JAMS for December 31, 2005. Show all calculations whether or not they seem relevant to the final answer. Comment on all items omitted from the calculation.

Problem 5

[ITA: Subdivisions a and b]

Coco Hardy is an apprentice with Sepp, a design house in Toronto. In her spare time, during some evenings and on weekends, she operates a sewing service for clothing manufacturers. She has set aside a spare room in her apartment where she keeps her equipment and materials and performs her services. This room occupies approximately 20% of her apartment. She sews for many of the same companies that deal with her employer, Sepp. The demands of her employment with Sepp will continue to prohibit her from expanding her sewing services. Consequently, she has not advertised for additional sewing work. Her sewing billings average approximately $600 per month.

She and the manufacturers mutually agree upon what type of sewing is to be done in order to meet the manufacturers' production deadlines. Her hourly rates are determined by the type of sewing required for a particular manufacturer. At the end of each month, she will issue a bill to the manufacturers bearing her name, home address, and home telephone number. Her clients pay her the gross amount on the invoice which does not include GST.

Ms. Hardy has incurred some direct sewing expenses and has allocated some of her other costs to her sewing services in respect of the past year as follows:

Direct expenses:

Sewing supplies		$ 2,890
Meals and entertainment for manufacturers		500
Sewing machine repairs		425
Long distance telephone calls to manufacturers		710
Delivery of finished product		1,500
Total direct expenses		$ 6,025

Allocated costs:

Rent ($1,000 per month)	$12,000	
Utilities	2,100	
Insurance	400	
	$14,500	
Allocation to sewing room	× 20%	$ 2,900
Capital cost allowance:		
Sewing room furniture	$ 450	
Sewing machine	325	
Automobile for deliveries	1,200	$ 1,975
Total allocated costs		$ 4,875
Total		$10,900

— REQUIRED

(A) Discuss the issues involved in determining whether Ms. Hardy is earning employment income or business income from her sewing service and then reach a conclusion based on the facts.

(B) Compute both income from employment and business, and comment on whether the listed expenses and allocated costs are deductible for income tax purposes under each alternative.

Problem 6

[ITA: 8(1)(*f*), (*h*), (*h*.1), (*i*), (*j*), (3); 18–20]

Mr. Peter Rajagopal, who is a salesman in Regina, Saskatchewan, has incurred the following expenses in connection with his employment in 2005. He was not reimbursed and did not receive an allowance in respect of any of these expenses. Peter has a form T2200, signed by his employer, attesting to all of these expenses.

(1) Peter uses one room in his home exclusively as a home office. He uses his home office most days and evenings to do paperwork and make phone calls and his home office computer is connected to his employer's computer system by modem. He visits his office at his employer's premises approximately once a week and spends the remainder of the time on the road, making sales calls throughout Western Canada.

(2) The following expenses relate to Peter's home office which occupies 10% of the square footage of his house:

Utilities	$ 3,100
Mortgage interest	12,000
House insurance	1,150
Municipal taxes	3,050
Maintenance and repairs	2,700
Total	$22,000
10% thereof	$2,200
Capital cost allowance on computer equipment ($6,900 × 15%)	1,035
Rental of photocopier	1,200
Rental of fax machine	200
Office supplies	750
Monthly charge for telephone extension (12 × $30)	360
Long distance calls	1,000

(3) Peter also has the following promotional expenses:

Meals (with clients in Regina, excluding the cost of his own meals)	$2,100
Theatre tickets	1,200
Promotional gifts	1,300
Country club membership	3,200

(4) Peter paid the following automobile expenses:

Gas & oil	$2,000
Insurance	1,100
Licence	90
Repairs	800
Cellular phone airtime charges (used for employment-related calls only)	700
Parking (employment related)	320

Peter purchased the car that he uses for employment purposes on May 1, 2004 for $50,000 plus $3,500 GST and $5,000 provincial sales tax. Peter did not claim CCA on the car in 2004; therefore, the capital cost allowance rate for the car is 30% in 2005. The car was driven a total of 40,000km in 2005; 32,000 of the kilometres driven related to Peter's employment use.

(5) Peter also incurred the following travel expenses (while away at least 12 hours):

Airfare	$ 4,520
Meals and accommodation (including $2,000 for meals)	4,560
Attendance at convention in Vancouver to increase product knowledge (including $400 for meals)	1,200
Out-of-town entertainment	3,200

(6) Interest on bank loan:

— to buy the computer equipment for the home office in (1) above	$ 320
— to buy the car in (4) above	800

(7) Peter's remuneration from employment is as follows:

Salary	$40,000
Bonus based on company sales	17,000

— *REQUIRED*

Compute the total deductible amount of expense under each of the following sets of assumptions:

(A) Peter chooses to use the following deductions as an employee:

(i) paragraphs 8(1)(*h*), (*h*.1), (*i*), and (*j*), or

(ii) paragraphs 8(1)(*f*), (*i*) and (*j*).

(B) Peter's situation is changed to that of an independent sole proprietor.

Assume that all the amounts given are accurate, supported by receipts and reasonable in the circumstances. Present your answer in tabular form for ease of comparison of alternatives.

Problem 7

[ITA: 37; ITR: 2900(2)(3); 2903]

Joe's Widget Manufacturers Inc. (JWMI) is an established manufacturing company with a growing research and development (R&D) department. JWMI is a Canadian-controlled private corporation with no associated companies. The research part of the business is new and the company's accountant has no experience dealing with the tax implications of the expenditures in this area. He has correctly computed the company's net income for tax purposes before R&D related adjustments as $615,000 and would like your input on the impact of the transactions described below.

For the year ended December 31, 2005 the following R&D related expenditures were made.

Description	Amount
Purchase of lab machinery and lab equipment	$450,000
Purchase of building to house laboratory	120,000
Salaries of lab staff	100,000
Operating costs directly related to the lab	40,000

The lab machinery, equipment and building are used 100% for R&D activities. The lab machinery and equipment have been capitalized for accounting purposes and are being amortized over an eight-year period (net of available investment tax credits as set out below). Thus, amortization expense of $36,562 was recorded for accounting purposes on the lab machinery and equipment. Depreciation expense of $4,800 was recorded on the building.

The company is eligible for investment tax credits at a rate of 35% and has correctly determined that they are eligible for investment tax credits at this rate on all of the above expenditures with the exception of the building. No investment tax credit is allowable on the purchase price of the building. For accounting purposes, the company's accountant has netted the investment tax credits against the related expenditures as follows.

Expenditure	Gross amount	ITC	Amount recorded for accounting purposes
Lab machinery and equipment	$450,000	$157,500	$292,500
Building	120,000	0	120,000
Salaries of lab staff	100,000	35,000	65,000
Operating costs of lab	40,000	14,000	26,000

— REQUIRED

Based on the above information, explain to JWMI's accountant the adjustments necessary in computing income for tax purposes for the years ended December 31, 2005 and 2006.

Problem 8

[ITA: 9–12; 18–20; 37; 67.1; 78; 147]

The *unaudited* income statement for Lomas & Sons Limited for its year ended December 31, 2005 shows the following:

Sales		$ 795,000
Cost of sales	$350,000	
General and administrative expenses	225,000	
Research and development expenditures	76,700	(651,700)
Operating income		$ 143,300
Other income		20,000

Net income before taxes		$ 163,300
Provision for income taxes:		
— current	$ 27,000	
— future	25,000	(52,000)
Net income after income taxes		$ 111,300

The information in the following notes has already been reflected in the above income statement.

(1) Payment made by company on April 1, 2006, to a defined contribution (money-purchase) registered pension plan for the president of the company in respect of current employment service, allocated to 2005 expenses by the company's accountant; in addition, the president had $7,500 withheld from his compensation of $74,000 for the RPP . . . . $ 7,000

(2) Increase in warranty reserve on company's product (net of expense incurred; based on self-insurance warranty program) 16,000

(3) Depreciation expense recorded in the financial statements 30,000

(4) Landscaping costs re: factory premises 2,500

(5) Interest on bank loan obtained for the purpose of purchasing common shares in Advanco Ltd., a dividend-paying Canadian corporation 6,300

(6) Legal costs of arranging an agreement among shareholders 8,500

(7) Legal and accounting fees related to issue of shares 12,700

(8) Interest on municipal real estate taxes paid late in error. 1,000

(9) Golf club membership fees 2,200

(10) Donation to United Way 3,000

(11) Meals and entertainment for clients 4,000

(12) Appraisal fees to determine selling price of fixed assets 6,200

(13) Premium on term insurance on life of president with the corporation as beneficiary; policy was not required to be assigned as collateral for corporate borrowing from the bank 2,800

(14) Management bonuses ($20,000 of the bonuses expensed in 2005, and shown as "Bonus Payable" on the Balance Sheet as at December 31, 2005 has not been paid at the time of filing the corporate tax return on June 30, 2006) 40,000

(15) Amortization of bond discount on bonds issued in 1999 3,400

(16) The company has capitalized and will amortize over five years $90,000 of costs incurred in 2004 related to the purchase of machinery to be used for qualifying research and development. The resultant amortization of the net cost after the investment tax credit was $11,700 and is included in the income statement deduction for research and development expenditures. As well, the company incurred current research and development expenditures of $100,000. These current expenditures will qualify the company for an investment tax credit of $35,000. The $35,000 has been deducted from the expenditure on SR&ED, as shown in the income statement. In the previous year, the company made $95,000 in qualifying SR&ED current expenditures. The company claimed an investment tax credit of $33,250 in respect of these current expenditures.

(17) Interest and penalties on income tax assessments, expensed for accounting purposes 1,250

(18) Items included in the financial accounting statements in arriving at the net profit:

Amount paid by an insurance company on its business interruption insurance to compensate for loss of profits when company was closed down for a month during the year because of a fire 26,800

Dividends received 1,700
Volume rebates and purchase discount 16,000

— REQUIRED

Based on the foregoing information, compute the income from business or property for tax purposes, ignoring tax deductions in respect of depreciable capital or eligible capital property for Lomas and Sons Limited in respect of its 2005 fiscal year. In addition, comment on all items not included in your derivation of income from business or property.

Problem 9

[ETA: 123(1); 161; 164; 169(1); 170(1)(*a*); 232; 236; Sched. V, Part VII]

Reconsider the facts of Problem 8.

— REQUIRED

Outline the proper GST treatment by the corporation of the items presented.

[For more problems and solutions thereto, see the CD accompanying this book.]

SUPPLEMENTAL NOTES

(This section can be omitted without losing the continuity of the chapter. None of the review questions, multiple choice questions, exercises, or assignment problems utilizes this information.)

A. Adjustment for Depreciation Allocation in Inventory: An Illustration of the Effect

To illustrate how the legislation deals with the problem of depreciation in inventory, the following example, which expands a similar example used in the Appendix to IT-473R, is presented.

Assumed facts:	Year 1	Year 2
Inventory at beginning of year	Nil	$ 20,000
Cost of goods sold (COGS)	$100,000	200,000
Inventory at end of year	20,000	25,000
Depreciation for year	35,000	80,000
Depreciation included in closing inventory	7,000	10,000
Net income for year per financial statements	50,000	90,000
Amount of depreciation allocated under absorption costing:		
Opening inventory	Nil	$ 7,000
Cost of goods manufactured	$ 35,000	80,000
	$ 35,000	$ 87,000
Closing inventory	(7,000)	(10,000)
Cost of goods sold	$ 28,000	$ 77,000

	Absorption costing — Depreciation allocated to cost of goods sold		Direct costing — Depreciation not allocated to cost of goods sold	
	Year 1	Year 2	Year 1	Year 2
Cost of goods sold:				
Opening inventory	Nil	$ 20,000	Nil	$ 13,000
Cost of goods manufactured	$120,000	205,000	$ 85,000	125,000
	$120,000	$225,000	$ 85,000	$138,000
Closing inventory	(20,000)	(25,000)	(13,000)	(15,000)
Cost of goods sold	$100,000	$200,000	$ 72,000	$123,000
Income for accounting purposes:				
Revenue	$150,000	$290,000	$150,000	$290,000
Cost of goods sold	(100,000)	(200,000)	(72,000)	(123,000)
Unallocated depreciation	Nil	Nil	(35,000)	(80,000)
Net income (accounting)	$ 50,000	$ 90,000	$ 43,000	$ 87,000
Reconciliation to income for tax purposes:				
Net income (accounting)	$ 50,000	$ 90,000	$ 43,000	$ 87,000
Add: depreciation deducted	28,000	77,000	35,000	80,000
Net income before par. 12(1)(r) and par. 20(1)(ii) adjustments	$ 78,000	$167,000	$ 78,000	$167,000
Add: par. 12(1)(r) adjustment	7,000	10,000	Nil	Nil
	$ 85,000	$177,000	$ 78,000	$167,000
Less: par. 20(1)(ii) adjustment	Nil	7,000	Nil	Nil
Net income (tax) before capital cost allowance	$ 85,000	$170,000	$ 78,000	$167,000

Note that the income for tax purposes before capital cost allowance is higher under absorption costing. The application of paragraph 12(1)(r) results in the add-back of what is, in total, the full depreciation allocated to the cost of goods manufactured, notwithstanding the fact that the depreciation content in closing inventory was not expensed in the year through the cost of goods sold calculation. While the excess add-back required by paragraph 12(1)(*r*) is corrected in the following year by the deduction permitted in paragraph 20(1)(*ii*), it is not clear why those adjustments are necessary. Note that if no adjustments had been made for absorption costing under paragraphs 12(1)(*r*) and 20(1)(*ii*), the net income for tax purposes before capital cost allowance in both years would have been the same as that under direct costing. (See the third line under "Reconciliation to income for tax purposes", above.)

The amendments introducing paragraphs 12(1)(*r*) and 20(1)(*ii*) followed the case of *Quebec North Shore Paper Co. v. The Queen*, 78 DTC 6426, in which the Federal Court — Trial Division held that absorption costing which allocates both variable and fixed overheads including depreciation without the adjustments introduced subsequently was the correct method of reconciling net income. It would now appear that direct costing which allocates variable overheads (excluding depreciation) to inventory and which is acceptable to the CRA according to IT-473R paragraph 8 is preferable because it provides the lower income for tax purposes as illustrated above.

B. Unregistered Employee Compensation Plans

[ITA: 6(1)(*g*), (*h*), (11)–(14); 18(1)(*o*), (*o*.1); 20(1)(*r*); 32.1; 56(1)(*x*), (*y*), (*z*); 207.5–207.7; IT-502]

The type of plan envisaged by the legislation in this area is a benefit arrangement involving an employer contribution to a plan that is not registered under the Act, unlike a registered pension plan or a deferred profit sharing plan. Typical of these unregistered plans is a benefit that is received by the employee at some time after the contribution is made by the employer. The effect of the legislation is to prevent a time lag between the time the employer obtains a deduction for the contribution and the time the employee must include in income an amount received from such a plan.

One type of unregistered plan is termed an "employee benefit plan" which is defined in subsection 248(1). It is an arrangement under which an employer makes contributions to a "custodian" and under which payments are made for the benefit of employees and certain other persons. Paragraph 18(1)(*o*) denies a deduction of the contributions by the employer at the time they are made. However, section 32.1 permits the deduction by the employer of amounts *paid* under the plan to employees in excess of the income of the plan for the year. At this time, the employee must include in income all amounts received from such a plan [par. 6(1)(*g*)] unless these amounts are specifically exempted by that paragraph. Tax on income from investments in the plan must be paid each year by the plan itself, by the employer or by the employee if the earnings are distributed.

Employee benefit plans became particularly popular in situations where the employer was not taxable either because the employer was in a loss position or because the employer was a non-taxable entity. In these cases, the employer's deduction on contributions was of no consequence. In fact, earnings of the plan could be paid out to such employers and contributed back to the plan with no tax consequences. The result was an indefinite deferral of income for the employee. By including the concept of an employee benefit plan in the definition of a "salary deferral arrangement" in subsection 248(1), the legislation now prevents this deferral of salary without eliminating employee benefit plans involving deferrals that relate to services rendered before July 1986. As discussed in Chapter 3, remuneration deferred by an employee through a "salary deferral arrangement" is taxed on an accrual rather than a cash basis. The deferred remuneration is deductible immediately to the employer. A salary deferral arrangement is defined in subsection 248(1) as one that has a main purpose to defer the receipt of remuneration that would otherwise have been paid for services rendered in the year or a preceding year. It excludes a registered pension plan, a profit sharing plan and other statutory plans. It also excludes such arrangements as those governing sabbaticals for teachers and compensation for services as a professional athlete.

Until amendments were made in 1987, the employee benefit plan legislation permitted the deferral of tax on certain pension and retirement arrangements that were not registered plans like RPPs, RRSPs, or DPSPs. To remove the tax benefits from the use of these unregistered plans, rules for retirement compensation arrangements (RCAs) were added to the Act. A "retirement compensation arrangement" is defined at length, with exclusions, in subsection 248(1) to mean, in part, a plan or arrangement between an employer and an employee under which contributions are made by the employer to a custodian. The custodian would be required to make payments to the employee on, after or in contemplation of the employee's retirement or loss of an office or employment.

Contributions made by an employer to an RCA are subject to the withholding of a special refundable tax of 50% under section 207.5 in Part XI.3 of the Act. The employer receives a deduction for the contribution [par. 20(1)(r)]. Income of the plan, including dividends (without the gross-up) and capital gains, is also subject to the 50% refundable tax. When retirement benefits are paid by the custodian to the employee, the tax is refunded at the rate of $1 of refund for each $2 paid to the employee. Payments received by an employee as benefits from an RCA are included in computing the employee's income [par. 56(1)(x)]. The payment of a 50% refundable tax on contributions to the plan and on income earned in the plan removes any deductibility or deferral advantage between the time the employer receives a deduction for contributions and the time the employee receives an amount to be included in income.

Another type of unregistered plan is termed an "employee trust" which is defined in subsection 248(1) where certain qualifying conditions are set out for such a plan. Under this type of plan, which is similar to an employees' profit sharing plan, employer contributions and income of the plan are allocated to employees when made or earned respectively. Employer contributions are deductible when made and, at the same time, the employee must include in income [par. 6(1)(h)] all amounts allocated. As a result, the benefits from such a trust are not taxed when received by the employee. The effect is the same as a salary deferral arrangement described above.

Chapter 5

Depreciable Property and Eligible Capital Property

TOPICS DISCUSSED

	Page
THE CAPITAL COST ALLOWANCE SYSTEM	221
Basic Rules	221
Exceptions to the Declining Balance Method	230
Proceeds of Disposition	231
Involuntary and Voluntary Dispositions	232
Change in Use and Part Disposition Rules	235
Franchises and Similar Property	239
ELIGIBLE CAPITAL PROPERTY	240
Basic Rules	240
Similarities with Capital Cost Allowance System	241

	Page
Election re: Capital Gain	243
CAPITAL PERSONAL PROPERTY AND THE INPUT TAX CREDIT SYSTEM UNDER GST	245
Basic Rules	245
Passenger Vehicles and Aircraft	246
SUPPLEMENTAL NOTES	258
Lease-option Arrangements	258
Leasing Property	260
Capital Personal Property for GST Purposes	261

The system in the Act for amortizing the capital cost of depreciable property and intangibles is fairly straightforward in its concept. Depreciable property write-offs are not encumbered by many of the complicated rules and computations necessary for the financial accounting. However, economic policy incentives to invest in depreciable property are reflected in the rates and methods of write-off of cost.

Although the rules pertaining to depreciable property and eligible capital property (intangibles) have many similarities, the differences require separate discussion in the two major sections of this chapter. The third major section of the chapter discusses the input tax credit system under the GST pertaining to capital property.

The following chart shows that the above rules related to deductions for depreciable and eligible capital property are found in Subdivision b (income or loss from a business or property) of Division B of the Act and in the Regulations.

PART I — DIVISION B
SUBDIVISION b
BUSINESS OR PROPERTY

DIVISION		SUBDIVISION		SECTION	
A	Liability for tax				
B	Computation of income		Basic rules		
		a	Office or employment		
C	Computation of taxable income	b	Business or property	9-11	Basic rules
D	Taxable income earned in Canada by non-residents	c	Capital gains and losses	12-17	Inclusions
				18-21 20(1)	Deductions (incl. CCA/CECA)
E	Computation of tax	d	Other income	22-25	Ceasing to carry on business
E.1	Minimum tax	e	Other deductions	26-37	Special cases
F	Special rules	f	Rules relating to computation of income		
G	Deferred and other special income arrangements	g	Amounts not included in income		
H	Exemptions	h	Cdn corporations and shareholders		
I	Returns, Assessments, payments, appeals	i	Shareholders of non-resident corporations		
J	Appeals to the courts	j	Partnerships		
		k	Trusts		

The major rules related to these deductions are found in the following parts of the Act:

Depreciable capital property

Ssec. 13(1)	Recaptured CCA
Ssec. 13(2)	Luxury automobiles
Ssec. 13(4)	Replacement property
Ssec. 13(7)	Special rules
Ssec. 13(21)	Definitions
Ssec. 13(21.1)	Loss on certain transfers within affiliated groups
Ssec. 13(26)	Available for use
Par. 18(1)(b)	No deduction for depreciation
Par. 20(1)(a)	Deduction for capital cost allowance
Ssec. 20(16)	Terminal loss
Reg. 1100	CCA rules
Reg. 7307(1)	CCA limits on automobiles
Reg. Sch. II–VI	Classes of property

Eligible capital property

Ssec. 14(1)	Recaptured CECA
Ssec. 14(3)	Acquisition of eligible capital property
Ssec. 14(5)	Definitions
Ssec. 14(6)	Replacement property
Ssec. 14(12)	Loss on certain transfers within affiliated groups
Par. 18(1)(*b*)	No deduction for depreciation
Par. 20(1)(*b*)	Deduction for cumulative eligible capital amount

I. THE CAPITAL COST ALLOWANCE SYSTEM

A. Basic Rules

[ITA: 13(1)–(3), (7)(*g*), (7)(*h*), (26)–(32); 20(1)(*a*), (16), (16.1); 37(2.1); 67.2; 248(16); ITR: 1100(1), (2.5), (3); 1101(1af); 7307(1); Sched. II; IT-128R; IT-460; IT-522R; IC 84-1]

1. Classes of assets for tangible capital property

(a) *Common Classes*

An important feature of the capital cost allowance system is the grouping of depreciable property, defined in subsection 13(21), into prescribed classes which are established by the Regulations (Part XI and Schedule II, primarily). When a taxpayer has a number of properties within a particular class, the properties of that class are treated as one unit for the purposes of capital cost allowances. Classes for some of the more common assets are contained in the following list:

Class 1 (4%)	— most buildings or other structures, including component parts such as electrical wiring and fixtures, plumbing, heating and central air conditioning, acquired after 1987;
Class 3 (5%)	— buildings or other structures, including component parts acquired before 1988 and limited costs of an addition or alteration made after 1988;
Class 8 (20%)	— miscellaneous tangible capital property, such as furniture, fixtures and outdoor advertising signs (bought after 1987), and machinery or equipment, such as photocopiers, refrigeration equipment, telephones and tools costing $200 or more, not included in another class (i.e., general default class for tangible capital property);
Class 9 (25%)	— aircraft, including furniture or equipment attached to the aircraft, and spare parts;
Class 10 (30%)	— automotive equipment, such as automobiles (except taxis and those used in a daily rental business), vans, trucks, tractors, wagons and trailers, and general-purpose electronic data processing equipment with its systems software acquired before March 23, 2004;
Class 10.1 (30%)	— a passenger vehicle with a cost in excess of the limit prescribed for paragraph 13(7)(*g*) (i.e., $30,000 if acquired after 2000);
Class 12 (100%)	— tools, instruments and kitchen utensils costing less than $200; linen, uniforms, dies, jigs or moulds; rental video cassettes; computer software;

Class 13   — leasehold interest;

Class 14   — patent,[a] franchise, concession or licence for a limited
                     period;

Class 17 (8%)   — roads, parking lots, sidewalks, airplane runways, storage
                     areas, or similar surface construction;

Class 39 (25%)   — property used in manufacturing or processing acquired
                     after 1987 and before February 26, 1992;

Class 43 (30%)   — manufacturing and processing machinery and equipment
                     acquired after February 25, 1992;

Class 44 (25%)[a] — patents and rights to use patented information acquired
                     after April 26, 1993, for a limited or unlimited period;

Class 45 (45%)   — general-purpose electronic data processing and ancillary
                     equipment acquired after March 22, 2004 and systems
                     software.

A convenient alphabetical list of many depreciable assets can be found in the
Topical Index to the CCH edition of the INCOME TAX ACT, under the heading "capital
cost allowance". However, the latter listing contains only property specifically itemized
in the class descriptions. Hence, property referred to in more general terms in the class
description may not appear in the list.

(b) *Basic Rules of the System*

The basic rules of the capital cost allowance system are illustrated in Exhibit 5-1
and can be stated for many classes quite simply as follows:

(a) whenever an asset of a particular class is purchased, the full purchase cost
    (capital cost) is added to the balance known as undepreciated capital cost
    (U.C.C.) of the class of assets defined in subsection 13(21);

(b) whenever an asset of a particular class is sold under conditions set out in the
    definition of "disposition of property" in subsection 13(21), the full proceeds of
    disposition as defined in subsection 13(21), not in excess of original cost (i.e., the
    lesser of proceeds and capital cost), is subtracted from the balance in the class of
    assets (proceeds in excess of capital cost may give rise to a capital gain); and

(c) at the end of the taxation year,

   (i) if the balance in the class of assets (i.e., U.C.C.) is positive and there are still
       assets in that class,

      (A) subtract from the balance in the account $^{1}/_{2}$ of the excess, if any, of
          purchases minus disposals made in the year (i.e., $^{1}/_{2} \times (a - b)$ above),

      (B) deduct up to the maximum capital cost allowance (C.C.A.) [par. 20(1)(*a*)] at
          the prescribed rate for the class on the positive balance and subtract the
          amount of the capital cost allowance taken from the balance to be carried
          forward to the next year, and

      (C) add back the $^{1}/_{2}$ of the net amount subtracted in (A) above;

   (ii) if the balance in the class of assets is negative, take the negative balance into
        income as recaptured capital cost allowance as outlined in subsection 13(1)
        and set the balance in the class at zero; and

---

[a] Regulation 1103(2h) provides that taxpayers may elect not to use Class 44 for such patents, in which
case the property will be classified in Class 14.

(iii) if the balance in the class of assets is positive, but all of the assets in the class have been disposed of such that there are no more assets physically in the class, take the positive balance, known as a terminal loss as defined in subsection 20(16), as a deduction from income and set the balance in the class at zero.

EXHIBIT 5-1
Basic Rules of the Capital Cost Allowance System
Applied to a Prescribed Class of Assets

Undepreciated capital cost of the class at the beginning of the year..................		$ xxx
Add: purchases during the year		xxx
		$ xxx
Deduct: dispositions during the year at the lesser of (LOCP):		
(a) capital cost	$ xxx	
(b) proceeds of disposition...	$ xxx	(xxx)
Undepreciated capital cost before adjustment		$ xxx
Deduct: 1/2 net amount*		(xxx)
Undepreciated capital cost before C.C.A.		$ xxx
Deduct: capital cost allowance in the class for the year...........................		(xxx)
Add: 1/2 net amount*...		xxx
Undepreciated capital cost of the class at the beginning of the following year		$ xxx

* Purchases during the year..................................	$ xxx	
Deduct: lesser of capital cost and proceeds of disposition above ...	(xxx)	
Net amount (positive amounts only)........................	$ xxx	

Note that the central definition for the above computation is that of undepreciated capital cost which is defined in subsection 13(21). The capital letters in brackets shown after each item below coincide with the letters in the algebraic formula in the definition. Some of the less mainstream items have been omitted. The definition can be paraphrased, in part, as:

the sum of:

(a) the capital cost of depreciable property (A),

(b) all amounts previously included in income as recapture (B), and

(c) all amounts of grants and other assistance deemed [ssec. 13(7.1)] to be capital cost that were repaid (C)

less the sum of:

(a) total depreciation previously allowed [par. 20(1)(a) and ssec. 20(16)] (E),

(b) for dispositions the lesser of (i) proceeds of disposition net of expenses of disposition and (ii) capital cost (F),

(c) all amounts of investment tax credit claimed [ssec. 127(5) or (6)] (I), and

(d) grants and other assistance received or receivable [par. 13(7.1)(f)] (J).

(c) *The Half-year Rule*

The half-net-amount rule, referred to in practice as the half-year rule, illustrated above and set out in subsection 1100(2) of the Regulations under the heading "Property Acquired in the Year" applies to all classes *except* the following:

(a) property described in paragraph 1100(1)(v) of the Regulations pertaining to certified vessels;

(b) Class 12 paragraphs (a) to (c), (e) to (i), (k), (l), and (p) to (s) in Schedule II; and

(c) Classes 13, 14, 15, 23, 24, 27, 29 and 34 in Schedule II.

However, despite these exceptions, an adjustment similar in effect to the half-net-amount rule is provided for some classes as follows:

(a) subparagraph 1100(1)(v)(iv) adjusts property described in paragraph 1100(1)(v) (certified vessels) of the Regulations;

(b) paragraph 1100(1)(b) adjusts property of Class 13 in Schedule II (leasehold improvements); and

(c) paragraphs 1100(1)(t) and (ta) adjust property of Classes 24, 27, 29 and 34 (some accelerated write-off classes) in Schedule II.

Thus, it would appear that the only property for which some form of adjustment to reflect the half-year rule is *not* made is the following:

(a) property in Class 12 paragraphs (a) to (c), (e) to (i), (k), (l), (p) to (s); and

(b) property in Classes 14, 15 and 23.

Exhibit 5-2 lists some common capital property not affected in some manner by the half-year rule [Reg. 1100(2)] . Some of these classes will be discussed further in this chapter.

EXHIBIT 5-2
Common Property not Affected by Half-Year Rule

Class	Paragraph	Property
12	(a) ...	a book that is a part of a lending library
	(b) ...	chinaware, cutlery or other tableware
	(c) ...	a kitchen utensil costing less than $200
	(e) ...	a medical or dental instrument costing less than $200
	(g) ...	linen
	(h) ...	a tool costing less than $200
	(i) ...	a uniform
	(k) ...	rental apparel or costume, including accessories
14		a patent, franchise, concession or licence for a limited period

The half-net-amount adjustment was implemented to correct the fact that assets purchased at the end of a taxation year would, otherwise, provide a balance in a class that would be eligible for the maximum capital cost allowance in the year. By effectively reducing the capital cost allowance on purchases (in excess of dispositions) during the year, whenever they are made, the advantage of a late purchase is reduced. Hence, the Act uses a simple, arbitrary adjustment as an alternative to adjusting for the period of ownership during the year of acquisition or disposition.

Notice that no adjustments other than the half-net-amount adjustment are made for the length of time in the year that an asset is owned. An asset purchased near the end of the year will normally increase the balance in the asset class resulting in a one-half capital cost allowance claim for the year for that asset net of dispositions. On the other hand, an asset sold near the end of the year will normally reduce the balance in the asset class resulting in a decrease in the amount subject to the capital cost allowance for the year.

(d) *Available-for-Use Rule*

Subsections 13(26) to (32) outline an "available-for-use" rule. A similar rule pertaining to capital expenditures in respect of scientific research and experimental development is found in subsection 37(1.2). The rule in subsection 13(26) provides that taxpayers may not start claiming capital cost allowance until the property has become "available for use" by the taxpayer. The rules determining the time at which property becomes "available for use" are provided in subsections 13(27) to (32). Subsections 13(27) and (29) to (32) establish the time at which property, other than a building, is considered to have become available for use. Subsection 13(29) provides a limited exception for long-term projects. Very generally, the property is available for use when it is delivered and capable of performing the function for which it was acquired. Subsection 13(28) establishes the time at which a building is considered to be available for use. Again, very generally, a building is available for use at the earlier of: (a) when all or substantially all of the building is first used for its intended purpose and, (b) the second taxation year after the year of acquisition. These rules are complex and must be consulted for their application to a specific asset under the particular conditions of the asset's purchase.

Since an asset is eligible for a capital cost allowance claim in the year in which it becomes available for use, the half-year rule applies to the asset in that year [Reg. 1100(2)].

(e) *CCA as a Permissive Deduction*

The rate of capital cost allowance applied to each class is specified as a maximum rate. The taxpayer may, therefore, claim any amount of capital cost allowance up to a maximum of the amount given by the capital cost allowance rate multiplied by the balance in the class at the end of the taxation year. Under certain conditions, it may be advantageous for the taxpayer to take less than the maximum amount of capital cost allowance allowed. Only the amount actually taken is deducted from the balance in the class of assets. The remaining balance is carried forward and is available for future capital cost allowance claims. In IC 84-1, the Canada Revenue Agency (CRA) indicates some conditions under which it will accept a request from a taxpayer to reassess a return for a previous year to adjust a permissive deduction such as capital cost allowance.

2. Taxation year less than 12 months

The statement has been made previously that there is no need to prorate capital cost allowance (other than the half-net-amount adjustment) for the period in a taxation year that an asset was owned by the taxpayer. This applies to full 12-month taxation years. However, in the first or last years of the operation of a business or in a year in which there has been a change in fiscal year, it is possible to have a taxation year of less than a full 12 months. In this case, capital cost allowance for classes of assets listed in Regulation 1100 must be prorated by the proportion that the number of days in the taxation year is of 365 [Reg. 1100(3)]. Hence, the proration pertains only to a short taxation year. It is completely independent of the half-net-amount adjustment which must be made, where applicable, irrespective of the length of the taxation year.

A common exception to this short-year proration rule, listed in Regulation 1100(3), is Class 14 which includes limited-life patents, franchises, licences, etc. However, as will be seen later in this chapter, there is a proration of capital cost allowance for assets in Class 14 based on the number of days the asset is owned in a taxation year. Therefore, the effect is quite similar to the short-year proration rule.

Note that an employee does not have to prorate the capital cost allowance on his or her automobile in the first year of use of an existing car for employment purposes, although the half-net-amount rule applies to the purchase of a new automobile [IT-522R par. 24]. Also, where depreciable capital property is used by an individual to produce income from a source that is property (e.g., rental income), rather than business, the full calendar year is considered to be the taxation year of the individual and, therefore, no prorating is necessary.

3. Ownership of property

Generally, in order to be eligible for capital cost allowance on depreciable property, the taxpayer must have either title to the asset or all the incidents of title such as possession, use and risk. An exception is Class 13 leasehold improvements that are made by the tenant but the owner of the building has title to the improvements.

In some circumstances, a taxpayer does not always have ownership or a leasehold interest (Class 13) in a capital asset for which he or she has incurred a cost. In this situation the cost incurred does not give rise to a claim for capital cost allowance. As indicated in paragraph 3 of IT-128R, capital cost allowance may not be claimed for such an expenditure. This was the situation in *Saskatoon Community Broadcasting Co. Ltd. v. M.N.R.*, (T.A.B.) 58 DTC 491 in which the appellant constructed at its cost a new broadcasting gondola in an arena and was given the sole right to use the new gondola, but the facility was the property of the arena company. In this case, the construction costs were held to be a non-deductible capital outlay and the broadcasting company could not take capital cost allowance because it did not own the property and it did not have a leasehold interest in the facility. Under the tax legislation in force since 1972, this type of expenditure would be considered an eligible capital expenditure [IT-143R2]. This concept will be discussed later in this chapter.

4. Disposition of property

A disposition of property is defined [ssec. 248(1)] to *include* "any transaction or event entitling a taxpayer to proceeds of disposition (defined in subsection 13(21)) of property". The use of the word "include" in the definition does not necessarily limit the meaning of disposition of property to a situation where there are proceeds of disposition. Thus, in IT-460, par. 3, the CRA gives examples of events that it considers to be dispositions without any actual proceeds, including cases of property that is stolen, destroyed, confiscated or expropriated without any compensation or property that is lost or abandoned without expectation of recovery. Furthermore, in the case of *The Queen v. Compagnie Immobilière BCN Limitée*, 79 DTC 5068, the Supreme Court of Canada indicated that a claim for capital cost allowance could not be made in lieu of a terminal loss deduction when a building no longer existed. Thus, capital cost allowance can only be claimed when property in a class continues to exist. This follows from the operation of the system in which no claim can be made for capital cost allowance on an asset in the year of its disposition.

5. Automobiles used in employment or business

(a) *Class 10.1 Automobiles*

Recall that employees who use their own automobiles to earn employment income and who are entitled to a deduction:

- for sales/negotiating person's expenses [par. 8(1)(f)],
- for travel expenses (other than motor vehicle expenses) [par. 8(1)(h)], or
- for motor vehicle expenses [par. 8(1)(h.1)]

are entitled to deduct capital cost allowance on the automobiles [par. 8(1)(j)].

Where an automobile is used to earn income from business, capital cost allowance is also deductible. In either case, the capital cost used as the basis for capital cost allowance is limited [Reg. 7307(1)(*b*)] to $30,000 plus federal sales tax (i.e., GST) and provincial sales tax (PST) (for acquisitions after 2000) for all taxpayers, whether employed or self-employed and whether incorporated or unincorporated [pars. 13(7)(*g*) and (*h*)]. In the case of a registrant, since the input tax credit resulting from a purchase is used immediately to offset the GST paid, there is no effective GST cost to add to capital cost and, therefore, GST is excluded [ssec. 248(16)].

Furthermore, the rules relating to recapture of capital cost allowance and terminal losses do not apply to automobiles having a cost in excess of the prescribed limit [ssecs. 13(2) and 20(16.1)]. For this reason, each automobile, having a cost in excess of $30,000 plus PST and GST, must be placed in a separate Class 10.1 [Reg. 1101(1af)] and not pooled.

Since the terminal loss rules do not apply to automobiles in Class 10.1, a special capital cost allowance calculation applies in the year of disposition [Reg. 1100(2.5)]. In the year of disposition of the automobile, one-half of the capital cost allowance that would have been allowed in respect of the automobile, had it not been disposed of, may be deducted. To qualify for this special "half-year rule", the taxpayer must have disposed of an automobile that was included in Class 10.1 and was owned by him or her at the end of the preceding year.

(b) *Class 10 Automobiles*

For automobiles that are not included in Class 10.1, but are in Class 10 because they cost less than the prescribed limit, the amount of capital cost allowance claimed is subject to recapture under subsection 13(1) [ssec. 13(11)], if the automobile was owned by an employee. A terminal loss on the disposition of the automobile is not allowed as a deduction from employment income. The only deduction in respect of the capital cost of an automobile allowed as an employment income deduction is provided in subparagraph 8(1)(*j*)(ii) which allows such part of the capital cost "as is allowed by regulation". A terminal loss is not allowed by regulation. Since a terminal loss is not specifically allowed in section 8, subsection 8(2) would prohibit its deduction.

When an automobile costs less than the prescribed limit and is owned by a taxpayer other than an employee, the usual rules for deducting capital cost allowance, subject to the half-net-amount rule, including recapture, or deducting a terminal loss apply. Hence, these usual rules would apply to an automobile used in a business by and owned by, for example, a proprietor, a partner or a corporation.

6. Comparison of capital cost allowance and depreciation

(a) *Main Differences*

Although capital cost allowance for tangible capital assets is the tax equivalent of depreciation there are a number of important differences which give rise to the need for future income tax accounting. While financial accounting uses useful life as the basis of the write-off of a capital expenditure, the tax system might be based on useful life, legal life (as in the case of leasehold improvements or patents) or fiscal policy. While accounting depreciation must adhere to the principles of consistency, the tax system allows for a deduction of any amount up to the maximum permitted for each class. For accounting purposes, differences between book value and proceeds of disposition are considered gains or losses on the sale of an asset. However, the tax system provides for the write-off of the actual decline in value of assets during their holding period. The system requires the inclusion in income of recapture of capital cost allowance where the capital cost allowance deductions have resulted in an undepreciated capital cost that is less than the proceeds of disposition, and the recognition of a terminal loss where capital cost allowance deductions did not fully reflect the decreased value of the asset pool. Under appropriate circumstances, the sale of an asset may also result in a capital gain. However, there can never, under any circumstances, be a capital loss on depreciable capital property. All declines in value are handled through the capital cost allowance deduction and the final adjustment through either recapture or a terminal loss.

(b) *Recapture and Terminal Loss*

The role of the recapture and terminal loss concepts in the capital cost allowance system is to provide for a deduction for tax purposes of the full decline in value of assets over the period of their use. Thus, capital cost allowance will be recaptured when proceeds of disposition exceed undepreciated capital cost, i.e., when assets in a class have been over-depreciated relative to their disposal value as in the following case where there has been no decline in value of the assets:

```
Proceeds..................... $10,000 ┐
                                      ├→ Capital gain
Capital cost..................   8,000 ┤  Recapture of C.C.A. claimed
                                      ├→ reflecting disposition
Undepreciated capital cost......  7,000 ┘  value in excess of U.C.C.
```

Similarly, a terminal loss provides for a deduction when proceeds of disposition are less than undepreciated capital cost and there are no assets remaining in the class, i.e., when assets in a class have been under-depreciated relative to their disposal value as in the following case where the decline in value of the assets exceeds the amount of capital cost allowance previously taken:

```
Capital cost ............. $ 8,000
Undepreciated capital cost   7,000 ┐ Terminal loss reflecting additional decline
Proceeds ................   5,000 ┘→ in value over CCA previously claimed
```

7. Separate class rule for electronic office equipment

Taxpayers may elect to place one or more specified properties that would ordinarily be classified in Class 8 or Class 10 in a separate class [Reg. 1101(5p)]. The specified properties are:

(a) general purpose electronic data processing equipment and systems software, normally included in paragraph (*f*) of Class 10;

(b) computer software, presumably systems software for electronic process control or monitor equipment and electronic communications control equipment, normally classified in Class 8 (i.e., not classified in Class 10 or Class 12);

(c) a photocopier, normally included in Class 8; and

(d) electronic communications equipment, such as a facsimile transmission device or telephone equipment, normally included in Class 8.

Property placed in separate classes in this manner must have a capital cost of at least $1,000.

The election allows one or more such properties to be placed in a separate Class 8 or Class 10. The advantage of the separate class would be the availability of a terminal loss deduction when all of the assets in such a class are sold for less than the U.C.C. of that class. If assets of this nature decline in value more rapidly than the C.C.A. rates of 20% for Class 8 and 30% for Class 10 imply, perhaps due to technological obsolescence, then a terminal loss on disposition is likely if these assets are separated from other Class 8 or Class 10 assets.

Regulation 1103(2g) provides a special transfer rule to transfer Class 8 and Class 10 assets of a separate class back to their main Class 8 or Class 10 after four taxation years. Hence, if the assets in a separate class have not been disposed of after the four-year period from the end of the taxation year of their acquisition, the potential terminal loss deduction in the separate class will not be available.

The separate class election is extended to manufacturing and processing property included in Class 43 costing more than $1,000 and acquired after February 27, 2000 [Reg. 1101(55)]. The election must be filed with the income tax return for the taxation year in which the property is acquired [Reg. 1101(59)]. After five years, any remaining UCC in each separate class must be transferred into the general Class 43 UCC pool [Reg. 1103(29)].

8. Computer Equipment Acquired After March 22, 2004

In recognition of the short useful life for computers, the CCA rate for general-purpose electronic data processing equipment and related systems software, acquired after March 22, 2004, will increase to 45% (class 45) from 30% (class 10).

Currently, computer equipment is eligible for a separate class election. With the higher rate for compute equipment, the separate class election is no longer available to computer equipment eligible for the higher rate. As a transition provision, taxpayers may elect that computer equipment acquired before 2005 be included in Class 10 and, therefore, be eligible for the separate class election.

Example Problem ————————————————————————————

Portable Tools Rental Unlimited Limited incorporated and commenced business on April 1, 2000 and has a December 31 year-end. The company rents portable tools for short terms and the following are its transactions:

		Computers *Class 10: 30%*
2000	100 tools purchased at various times during the year for $950 each	$ 95,000
2001	20 tools purchased in June for $1,000 each	20,000
2003	30 2000 tools (well maintained) sold in November for $1,000 each	30,000
2005	50 2000 tools sold in February for $700 each	35,000

— *REQUIRED*

Prepare a schedule showing the effects of these transactions on Class 10 and on the income of the company for the period of years indicated. (Ignore the leap year effects.)

— *SOLUTION*

			Portable Tools *Class 10: 30%*
2000	Additions: 100 tools purchased for $950 each		$ 95,000
	U.C.C. at the end of 2000 before adjustment		$ 95,000
	Less: ¹/₂ of net amount during the year		(47,500)
	U.C.C. before C.C.A.		$ 47,500
	C.C.A. claimed @ 30%; prorated, because of short first year, for 275 days ($47,500 × .3 × 275/365)		(10,736)
	Add: ¹/₂ of net amount during the year...............		47,500
	U.C.C. at the beginning of 2001		$ 84,264
2001	Additions: 20 tools purchased for $1,000 each..........		20,000
	U.C.C. at the end of 2001 before adjustment		$104,264
	Less: ¹/₂ of net amount during the year		(10,000)
	U.C.C. before C.C.A		$ 94,264
	C.C.A. claimed @ 30% ($94,264 × .3)		(28,279)
	Add: ¹/₂ of net amount during the year...............		10,000
	U.C.C. at the beginning of 2002		$ 75,985
2002	No additions or dispositions		
	C.C.A. claimed @ 30% ($75,985 × .3)		(22,796)
	U.C.C. at the beginning of 2003		$ 53,189
2003	Disposals: 30 tools sold for $1,000 each (cost: $950 each; $1,500 total capital gain)..................		(28,500)
	U.C.C. before C.C.A.		$ 24,689
	C.C.A. claimed @ 30% ($24,689 × .3)		(7,407)
	U.C.C. at the beginning of 2004		$ 17,282
2004	No additions or dispositions		
	C.C.A. claimed @ 30% ($17,282 × .3)		(5,185)
	U.C.C. at the beginning of 2005		$ 12,097
2005	Disposals: 50 tools sold for $700 each (cost: $950 each; no capital loss on depreciable property)...........		(35,000)
	U.C.C. at the end of 2005		$ (22,903)
	Recapture of C.C.A. taken into income		22,903
	U.C.C. at the beginning of 2006		Nil

— *NOTE TO SOLUTION*

Had all ninety of the remaining tools in the class been sold for less than $12,097 in 2005 there would have been a positive balance in the class at the end of the taxation year. This would have been written off as a terminal loss under subsection 20(16) against income and the balance in the account would have been set at nil to carry forward.

B. Exceptions to the Declining Balance Method

[ITR: 1100; Sched. III; IT-477]

1. Leasehold improvements

Not all classes of assets are treated in the foregoing manner using a declining balance method of computing capital cost allowance. Special treatment is accorded to a leasehold interest [Reg. 1100(1)(b) and Schedule III]. The capital cost allowance that may be claimed for a leasehold interest (Class 13) after the first year of ownership is the lesser of:

(a) ¹/₅ of the capital cost of the leasehold interest; and

(b) the capital cost of the leasehold interest divided by the number of 12-month periods from the beginning of the taxation year in which the cost was incurred to the end of the term of the lease plus the first renewal term (i.e., the number of months in the remainder of the lease term plus one renewal option divided by 12). The divisor is not to exceed a total of 40 such 12-month periods.

The first year write-off would be $1/2$ of the above amount.

For example, if a $16,000 leasehold improvement is made on a rented building on which the taxpayer has a lease for five years with two successive options to renew of three years and two years, the capital cost allowance for a year other than the first year would be calculated as follows:

Lesser of: (a) $1/5$ of the capital cost ($1/5 \times$ $16,000)................... $3,200

(b) capital cost divided by the number of 12-month periods from the beginning of the taxation year in which the cost was incurred to the end of the term of the lease plus first renewal term not to exceed 40 years

$$\frac{\$16,000}{5 + 3}$$ $2,000

Thus, $1,000 capital cost allowance would be taken in the first year, $2,000 in each of the next seven years and the remaining $1,000 in the ninth year.

2. Class 14 limited-life intangibles

Straight-line capital cost allowance is also used for items in Class 14 which generally includes limited-life intangibles such as patents, franchises, concessions or licences. For this class, the capital cost of each property in the class is divided by the remaining legal life, as at the acquisition date, of the property to obtain the amount of capital cost allowance for the year. (Note that the legal life of a patent registered after 1989 is 20 years. If the patent was registered before 1990, its legal life is 17 years.) Paragraph 4 of IT-477 indicates the CRA's view that the capital cost should be prorated over the number of days in the remaining life of the Class 14 asset. Note that this is one of the classes not affected by the half-net-amount rule.

A taxpayer must classify property acquired after April 26, 1993, that is a patent or a right to use patented information for a limited or unlimited period in Class 44 with a 25% declining-balance rate. However, Regulation 1103(2h) allows a taxpayer to elect that such property not be included in Class 44. Under this election, patents for a limited period would be classified in Class 14. This election might be used when the patent is purchased late in its legal life, such that the straight-line capital cost allowance of Class 14 would exceed the 25% declining-balance capital cost allowance of Class 44.

C. Proceeds of Disposition

[ITA: 12(1)(f); 13(21)]

Insurance proceeds expended on damaged depreciable property

The provision in paragraph 12(1)(f) requires the inclusion in income of any part of insurance proceeds payable for damaged depreciable property that has been expended on repairing the damage within the year or within a reasonable time after the damage. The amount included will be offset by the amount that will be deducted as an expense of repairing the property so that there will be no net effect on the taxpayer's income. If any part of the insurance proceeds is not expended in this manner, the unused portion will be treated as proceeds of disposition of depreciable property by paragraph (f) in the definition of "proceeds of disposition" in subsection 13(21) and will, thus, be treated according to the basic rules for proceeds.

D. Involuntary and Voluntary Dispositions

[ITA: 13(4); IT-259R4]

1. Involuntary dispositions

(Consideration of this segment of the chapter can be deferred, without a loss of continuity, until the material under the heading "Exchanges of Property" [sec. 44] is considered in Chapter 8 where the capital gain component of the problem is discussed.)

Ordinarily any insurance recovery for stolen, lost or destroyed (but not merely damaged) depreciable property or any expropriation proceeds would be considered as proceeds of disposition by paragraphs (*b*), (*c*) and (*d*) of the definition in subsection 13(21). A potential recapture might be offset under subsection 13(1) against the cost of property of the same class acquired later in the year. However, a replacement outlay might not be made in the same year for major assets which take some time to replace even if the taxpayer immediately begins to plan the reconstruction or replacement.[b]

The taxpayer may elect [ssec. 13(4)] in the year of replacement of property stolen, lost, destroyed or expropriated to offset any recapture caused by proceeds for the loss as long as replacement is made by the later of either 24 months after the initial taxation year or by the end of the second taxation year following the year in which proceeds are considered receivable. Proceeds are deemed to have become receivable at the earliest of:

(a) the day the taxpayer has agreed to the full amount of the compensation;

(b) the day the compensation is finally determined by a court or tribunal;

(c) the day that is two years from the day of loss, destruction or taking where a claim or suit has not been taken before the courts;

(d) the day the taxpayer dies or ceases to be a resident of Canada; and

(e) the day immediately before the winding-up of a corporation (other than a Canadian subsidiary owned 90% or more) where the taxpayer is a corporation.

Basically, replacement property is depreciable property acquired for the same or a similar use as the original property and used for gaining or producing income from the same or similar business by the taxpayer or related persons [ssec. 44(5)]. Note that replacement property need not be of the same class of depreciable property as the original property. Paragraphs 16 and 17 of IT-259R4 present the CRA's interpretation of the term "same or similar use", applicable in paragraph 44(5)(*a*.1), which is to be interpreted separately from the term "same or similar business", applicable in paragraph 44(5)(*b*). Paragraphs 18 to 21 of IT-259R4 present the CRA's position in respect of a "same or similar business". The CRA indicates that the term is to be "interpreted in a reasonably broad manner", setting out 10 categories of similar businesses.

---

[b] For an example, see the case of *Korenowsky v. M.N.R.*, (T.A.B.) 64 DTC 235.

2. Voluntary dispositions

(Consideration of this segment of the chapter can be deferred, without a loss of continuity, until the material under the heading "Exchanges of Property" [sec. 44] is considered in Chapter 8 where the capital gain component of the problem is discussed.)

The same rules permitting an offset of recapture caused by proceeds of disposition apply on certain voluntary dispositions of depreciable "former business property". However, in this case, replacement must be made by the later of either 12 months after the initial taxation year or by the end of the first taxation year following the year of disposition. The term "former business property" is defined [ssec. 248(1)] to mean real property (i.e., land and buildings) or an interest therein (i.e., a leasehold interest) that is capital property used primarily for the purpose of earning business income. These rules pertaining to a former business property might be used in a business relocation to avoid recapture on the disposition of buildings.

Normally, a building is the only depreciable property eligible for the replacement property rules for voluntary dispositions. However, a limited-period franchise, concession or license will also be eligible if the disposition takes place after December 20, 2002 [Proposed in the Technical Amendments to the *Income Tax Act* — February 27, 2004]. Subsections 13(4.2) and (4.3) extend the replacement property rules where the transferor and transferee jointly elect to have these rules apply.

Example Problem

Dump's is a department store operating in the area. Its operations are carried on in a building which is owned by the company. The capital cost of the building to Dump's in September 2001 was $400,000. The company has been taking capital cost allowance on the structure on the basis that it is a Class 1 asset with a capital cost allowance rate of 4%. In May 2003 a fire virtually destroyed the building. The only asset which was recovered was an F.A.D. Computer and it was substantially damaged. The computer had been purchased by Dump's in December 2002 at a cost of $75,000 and as a Class 10 asset it had been depreciated at a rate of 30% since 2002.

In August 2003, under an insurance policy with the Risk-Averters Insurance Company, Dump's received $385,000 for the destruction of the building and $25,000 for the damage to the computer. Dump's had the computer repaired to its original condition in 2003 at a cost of $23,000. In 2005 a new building was constructed for $465,000.

— REQUIRED

Trace the effects of these events on the balance of the undepreciated capital cost accounts for each asset from 2001 through to the beginning balance for 2006 in the building account and for 2005 in the computer account. As you trace the effects, indicate all deductions from and inclusions in income from the business for the years indicated. Assume that the appropriate election under subsection 13(4) is made.

— SOLUTION

(A) Building

		Building *Class 1: 4%*
2001	Additions: purchase of building	$400,000
	U.C.C. at the end of 2001	$400,000
	C.C.A. claimed @ 4% (($400,000 — ½ × $400,000) × .04)	(8,000)
	U.C.C. at the beginning of 2002	$392,000
2002	No additions or disposals	
	C.C.A. claimed @ 4% ($392,000 × .04)	(15,680)
	U.C.C. at the beginning of 2003	$376,320

		Building *Class 1: 4%*
2003	Disposals: insurance proceeds [ssec. 13(21), par. (*c*) of def. "proceeds of disposition"]	(385,000)
	U.C.C. at the end of 2003	$ (8,680)
	Recaptured C.C.A. taken into income	8,680
	U.C.C. at the beginning of 2004	Nil
2004	No additions or disposals	
	U.C.C. at the beginning of 2005	Nil

2005 File an amended return for 2003 by virtue of ssec. 13(4) as follows:

U.C.C. at beginning of 2003		$376,320

Reduction of U.C.C.
[par. 13(4)(*c*)][1]:
— normal deduction is lesser of:

(i) proceeds	$ 385,000 →	$385,000	
(ii) capital cost	$ 400,000		

— reduced [par. 13(4)(*c*)] by lesser of:

(i) excess, if any, of $385,000 (as determined above) over U.C.C. of $376,320 at the beginning of 2003 (i.e., recapture)	$ 8,680 →	(8,680)	
(ii) cost of replacement property	$ 465,000		(376,320)

U.C.C. at the end of 2003	Nil
Recaptured C.C.A.	Nil
U.C.C. at the beginning of 2004	Nil

2005 Additions: purchase of new building[2]	$465,000
Deemed proceeds of disposition [par. 13(4)(*d*)] (equal to reduction [par. 13(4)(*c*)] calculated above)	(8,680)
U.C.C. at the end of 2005	$456,320
C.C.A. @ 4% (($456,320 − ½ × $456,320) × .04)	(9,126)
U.C.C. at beginning of 2006	$447,194

(B) Computer

	Computer Class 10: 30%
2002 Additions: computer.....................................	$ 75,000
U.C.C. at the end of 2002..............................	$ 75,000
C.C.A. claimed @ 30% (($75,000 — ½ × $75,000) × .3)....	(11,250)
U.C.C. at the beginning of 2003	$ 63,750
2003[3] Disposals: proceeds of disposition in the amount of unexpended insurance proceeds	(2,000)
U.C.C. at the end of 2003..............................	$ 61,750
C.C.A. claimed @ 30% ($61,750 × .3)	(18,525)
U.C.C. at the beginning of 2004	$ 43,225
2004 No additions or disposals C.C.A. claimed @ 30% ($43,225 × .3)	(12,968)
U.C.C. at the beginning of 2005	$ 30,257

—NOTES TO SOLUTION

(1) To generalize the rule set out in paragraph 13(4)(*c*), it would appear that as long as the cost of the replacement property exceeds the recapture that would otherwise result on the disposition (i.e., the $8,680 above), there will be no actual recaptured capital cost allowance on the disposition. In effect, part of the proceeds of disposition of the former property is transferred from the year in which the disposition occurred to the year in which the replacement property is acquired. This avoids recapture in the year of disposition and reduces the undepreciated capital cost of whichever class of property the replacement property falls into.

(2) The rules allow for a replacement with an asset of another class [ssec. 13(4)]. Had the old building been in Class 3, the new building in Class 1 would still qualify as replacement property for the rollover.

(3) In 2003, income would be increased by expended proceeds of insurance of $25,000 [par. 12(1)(*f*)], but this amount would be offset by the deduction of repair expense of $23,000. Thus, the net effect on income is nil which is as it should be. The other $2,000 received is a capital receipt which reduces undepreciated capital cost.

E. Change in Use and Part Disposition Rules

[ITA: 13(7), (7.1); ITR: 1100(2.2); IT-418]

Rules are set out in subsection 13(7) for the determination of capital cost and proceeds of disposition in five situations as follows.

1. Change from income-producing to other purpose

In this case, property is acquired for producing income, but its use is changed to another purpose. Consider the situation where a taxpayer had a house which he or she rented and later lived in himself or herself. At the time of the change in use, the taxpayer is deemed to have disposed of a depreciable asset at its fair market value [par. 13(7)(*a*)]. This deemed disposition may result in either recapture or a terminal loss. The deemed reacquisition at fair market value establishes the cost of the asset for personal use. The problem of determining fair market value without a transaction gives rise to cases such as that of *Tripp v. M.N.R.*, (T.A.B.) 63 DTC 313 in which the value of a house relative to the value of the land on which it was situated was at issue.

2. Change from non-income-producing to income-producing purpose

In this situation, property is acquired for a non-income producing purpose, but its use is changed to producing income. Consider the case if the first situation were reversed. At the time of the change in use, the taxpayer is deemed to acquire a depreciable asset at its fair market value where that value is less than its cost, representing a decline in value [par. 13(7)(*b*)]. But where the fair market value of the asset is greater than its cost, representing an increase in value, the capital cost of the asset will, generally,[c] be limited to the lesser of:

(i) the fair market value of the property at the time of the change in use   xxx

(ii) the total of
   (A) cost at the time of the change in use   xxx
   (B) the fair market value of the property at the time of the
      change in use   xxx
      less: cost at the time of change in use   xxx

      excess, if any   xxx

   ¹/₂ of excess   xxx   xxx

As a result of this latter rule, the capital cost of the asset for the purposes of computing capital cost allowance is limited to the sum of two components. That sum consists of the actual cost of the asset before the change in use plus the amount, if any, of taxable capital gain resulting from the deemed disposition on the change in use. Therefore, there can be no step-up in the capital cost to fair market value, because the step-up in capital cost is limited to ¹/₂ of the gain from actual cost up to fair market value.[d]

The capital cost of the asset after the change in use and the application of the limited step-up will reflect an amount that has been fully tax paid by the owner. Since the taxpayer will pay tax on only ¹/₂ of the capital gain, only ¹/₂ of the gain may be added to the original cost. The rationale for this limitation is that the stepped-up capital cost will provide the base for future C.C.A. which is fully deductible from business or property income. A taxpayer should only expect to fully deduct a cost that was fully tax paid.

The half-net-amount rule to reduce first-year capital cost allowance would appear to apply because the conditions in Regulation 1100(2.2) which provides exceptions to this rule for property of a class in Schedule II are not met. In particular, the condition in Regulation 1100(2.2)(*f*) is not met, because the property subject to the change in use to income-producing purposes would not have been *depreciable* property at the time of the change in use if its previous use was non-income-producing. It makes some sense to impose the half-net-amount rule at the change in use to income-producing purposes, because the half-net-amount rule would usually not have been applied on acquisition for the previous non-income-producing purpose. Note that a change in use from income-producing purpose to non-income-producing purpose should not be affected by the half-net-amount rule, because the property would not be depreciable property if its purpose is not income-producing.

---

[c] The actual formula in paragraph 13(7)(*b*) provides for an adjustment in respect of the capital gains deduction. Such a deduction is only available for qualified farm property which might be subject to a change in use. As a result, the adjustment will not be common.

[d] For a more detailed discussion of paragraphs 13(7)(*b*), (*d*) and (*e*), see Robert E. Beam and Stanley N. Laiken, "Changes in Use and Non-Arm's Length Transfer of Depreciable Property", *Canadian Tax Journal*, Vol. 35, No. 2, March-April 1987, pp. 453.

3. Property acquired for multiple purposes

In this case, property is acquired both for producing income and for another purpose. For example, consider the situation where a taxpayer buys a duplex and lives in one half, renting the other half. At the time of the purchase, $1/2$ of the cost of the building is allocated [par. 13(7)(*c*)] to depreciable assets of the taxpayer. On the sale of the property, $1/2$ of the proceeds is regarded as proceeds of the depreciable asset by the same paragraph.

4. Change in proportion of use for producing income and other purposes

Here, a change occurs in the relation between the use of property for producing income and its use for another purpose. This might be the case where one room out of eight in a house is used for business and at a particular time a second room is converted to business use. Any such increase in the use of the property for income-producing purposes is deemed to be an acquisition of property [par. 13(7)(*d*)]. The capital cost would be deemed to be equal to the proportion (in this case $1/8$) of the fair market value where that value is less than the proportion of its cost of the total property, at the time, representing the increase in use. Where the fair market value of the property is greater than its cost, the capital cost of the additional part of the property used for income-producing purposes is limited in a manner similar to that discussed in paragraph 13(7)(*b*) above.

The calculation of the capital cost of the part of the property converted to income-producing purposes can be computed, generally,[e] as follows:

The aggregate of:

    (A) the fraction of the property converted to income-producing purposes times the lesser of:

       (I) the fair market value of the full property at the time of the increase in income-producing use xxx

       (II) the cost of the full property at the time of the increase in income-producing use.................................... xxx

    fraction above times the lesser amount of (I) and (II)   xxx

    (B)(I) the fraction (used above) of the fair market value of the full property at the time of the increase in income-producing use   xxx

    less:

       (II) the fraction (used above) of the cost of the full property at the time of the increase in income-producing use xxx

    excess, if any xxx

    $1/2$ of excess..   xxx

    Capital cost: (A) + (B)   xxx

The effect of this calculation is similar to that discussed in paragraph 13(7)(*b*) above.

Any decrease in the proportion of income-producing use is treated as a disposition at the proportion of the fair market value of the total property, at the time of the decrease in use. Technically, when an automobile is being used by an employee or in business partially to earn income and the proportion of income-producing use changes from one year to another, there has been a change in the relative use of the asset to which paragraph 13(7)(*d*) would apply. This would result in the need to make a fair market valuation each year and to apply the rules accordingly in the computation of capital cost allowance. In practice, capital cost allowance can be computed first on the

---

[e] The adjustment for the effects of the capital gains deduction, which would only apply to qualified farm property, has been omitted from the formula.

full undepreciated capital cost of the automobile and then reduced by an adjustment for the proportion of personal use of the automobile based on personal mileage to total mileage for the year. The net result is the amount of capital cost allowance that can be considered attributable to the income-producing use.

Example Problem

Mr. Greenjeans purchased a brick building suitable for the relocation of his retail store including storage and office space on March 1, 2003, at a cost of $60,000 (exclusive of land). On September 15, 2004, when the fair market value of the building was $80,000, he converted one-quarter of the building to residential facilities and began to use that area as his personal residence. He continued to use the remainder of the building for his retail operation. On October 31, 2005, when the fair market value of the building was $96,000, he moved out of the residential facilities and converted them back to business use.

— REQUIRED

Assuming that Mr. Greenjeans claims maximum capital cost allowance, prepare a schedule showing the effects of these events for 2003, 2004 and 2005.

— SOLUTION

		Building Class 1: 4%
2003	Addition: purchase building..............................	$60,000
	U.C.C., December 31, 2003	$60,000
	C.C.A. claimed @ 4% (($60,000 — $\frac{1}{2}$ × $60,000) × .04)	(1,200)
	U.C.C., January 1, 2004.....................................	$58,800
2004	Disposal: conversion of $\frac{1}{4}$ of building to personal use resulting in deemed disposition [par. 13(7)(d)] ($\frac{1}{4}$ × $60,000)	(15,000)[1]
	U.C.C., December 31, 2004	$43,800
	C.C.A. claimed @ 4% ($43,800 × .04)...................	(1,752)
	U.C.C., January 1, 2005....................................	$42,048
2005	Addition: conversion of $\frac{1}{4}$ of building to business use resulting in deemed acquisition	22,000[2]
	U.C.C., December 31, 2005	$64,048
	C.C.A. claimed @ 4% (($64,048 — $\frac{1}{2}$ × $22,000) × .04)......	(2,122)[3]
	U.C.C., January 1, 2006....................................	$61,926

— NOTES TO SOLUTION

(1) $\frac{1}{4}$ of the building originally cost $15,000 ($\frac{1}{4}$ × $60,000) and now has a fair market value of $20,000 ($\frac{1}{4}$ × $80,000). The balance in the class is never reduced by more than the equivalent of original cost on a disposition or deemed disposition, that is, the balance in the class is reduced by $\frac{1}{4}$ of the lesser of capital cost ($60,000) and proceeds of disposition ($80,000) [spar. 13(7)(d)(ii)]. The remaining excess of actual or deemed proceeds over original cost may result in a capital gain. For further examples involving partial disposition of depreciable property, one should read IT-418.

(2) The cost of $\frac{1}{4}$ of the building used for residential facilities is equal to its fair market value at the time of the change in use (i.e., $\frac{1}{4}$ × $80,000 = $20,000). Since the fair market value of $\frac{1}{4}$ of the building ($\frac{1}{4}$ × $96,000 = $24,000) is greater than $\frac{1}{4}$ of its cost ($\frac{1}{4}$ × $80,000 = $20,000), the capital cost of $\frac{1}{4}$ of the building will be limited [spar. 13(7)(d)(i)] (applicable to a fractional change in use) to the aggregate of:

(a) 25% of the lesser of:
  (i) fair market value at the time of the increase in income-producing use $96,000

  (ii) cost at the time of the increase in income-producing use $80,000

  25% of $80,000 .... $20,000
(b) proceeds of disposition deemed to result (25% of $96,000) $24,000
  less: cost at the time of the increase in income-producing use (25% of $80,000) .... (20,000)

  excess, if any.. $ 4,000

  ½ of excess .... $ 2,000

  capital cost addition on change in use................. $22,000

(3) Note that the half-net-amount rule would appear to apply on this change in use, because the condition in Regulation 1100(2.2)(*f*) would not be met. Since the previous use of the property was not income-producing, it would not have been depreciable capital property. As a result, the half-net-amount rule would not have been applied to this property in its previous use.

Note, also, that capital cost allowance is not prorated for a short year, in these cases, because the business existed in a year before the year of the change in use or the original acquisition for business use.

---

5. Non-arm's length transfer of depreciable property

Paragraph 13(7)(*e*), discussed in more detail in a subsequent chapter, provides rules that apply where depreciable property is transferred between persons not dealing at arm's length, as defined in section 251 and also discussed in a subsequent chapter. These rules prevent the realization of benefits from a transfer motivated by the fact that the increase in value over cost is taxable to the transferor as a capital gain (i.e., ½ taxable), but would be fully depreciable from fair market value at the time of the transfer to the transferee if it were not for paragraph 13(7)(*e*). The adjustment to the capital cost of property transferred to the non-arm's length transferee is similar to part (ii)(B) of the calculation presented for paragraph 13(7)(*b*) above, with proceeds of disposition substituted for fair market value, as used in that formula.

6. Capital cost reduction for cost assistance

Subsection 13(7.1) applies when a grant, subsidy, forgivable loan, deduction from tax, investment allowance or other assistance is received on the acquisition of property. The amount of such assistance received reduces the capital cost of depreciable property, so that C.C.A. is claimed only on the net cost of the asset.

F. Franchises and Similar Property

[ITA: 13(12); 20(1)(*cc*), (9); ITR: Sched. II; IT-99R5; IT-477]

It should be noted that Class 14 of Schedule II of the Income Tax Regulations includes certain property that is a patent, franchise concession or licence for a limited period. The cost of such property is expensed under the capital cost allowance system by taking straight-line capital cost allowance over the remaining legal life of the property as indicated earlier. Note in particular that this property must have a limited life. The amounts that can be considered as the capital cost of a patent were at issue in *Weinberger v. M.N.R.*, (Ex. Ct.) 64 DTC 5060. The court held that not only the amount paid to have the invention patented but also the costs to produce and perfect the invention to the point where the patent can be obtained are considered to be the capital cost of the patent.

If the cost of a patent is added to Class 14, because the taxpayer has elected [Reg. 1103(2h)] that the property not be included in Class 44, it will be eligible for capital cost allowance on a straight-line basis over its remaining legal life (17 years if registered before 1990 and 20 years if registered after 1989), as discussed previously. However, IT-99R5 paragraph 11 suggests that expenditures incurred in making any representation for the purpose of obtaining a franchise or a patent (among others) to a government or public body relating to a business of the taxpayer would be deductible immediately [par. 20(1)(*cc*)]. In lieu of the paragraph 20(1)(*cc*) deduction, the taxpayer may elect in prescribed manner to deduct one-tenth of the amount otherwise eligible for deduction in each of the 10 consecutive years beginning with the year in which the expenditure is made [ssec. 20(9)]. Thus, three possibilities for dealing with expenses of representation, in this situation, may be available:

(a) an immediate deduction of the cost [par. 20(1)(*cc*)];

(b) a deduction of the cost over a 10-year period [ssec. 20(9))]; and

(c) capitalization of the cost in the appropriate C.C.A. class (14 or 44) or in the eligible capital property pool (see below).

Any amount deducted under paragraph 20(1)(*cc*) or subsection 20(9) is subject to recapture [ssec. 13(12)].

Certain property, such as franchises, may have an indefinite life in contrast to a limited life (Class 14). If this is the case, the property is likely an eligible capital property subject to amortization through the cumulative eligible capital account which will be discussed in the next section of this chapter. It will be seen that eligible capital property excludes intangible property that is depreciable property. A franchise of any kind may be considered as intangible property, but because a franchise for a limited period is listed in Class 14 it is depreciable property and, therefore, cannot be eligible capital property.

II. ELIGIBLE CAPITAL PROPERTY

A. Basic Rules

[ITA: 14; 20(1)(*b*); 24; IT-123R6; IT-143R2; IT-206R]

Under the pre-1972 Act, certain items of intangible property were known as "nothings" because they were capital in nature, and, hence, not deductible as a business expense, but not tangible assets and, hence, not depreciable. Such "nothings" included the cost of purchased goodwill,[f] the cost of a franchise for an indefinite life and incorporation costs among others. When these assets were sold, proceeds were treated by the vendor as a capital receipt with no tax consequences and by the purchaser as a non-deductible, non-depreciable expenditure.

Under the present Act, most of these items and others discussed in IT-143R2 are called "eligible capital expenditures" as defined in subsection 14(5). This definition includes capital outlays that are not otherwise specifically allowed or disallowed as deductions under the Act and made after 1971 for the purpose of earning income (other than exempt income) from business. (See IT-206R for an indication of the concept of a "business".) Note that the definition of the term specifically excludes certain expenditures. Also, note that expenditures made prior to 1972 are not now deductible.

---

[f] The meaning of "goodwill" was considered in *Losey v. M.N.R.*, (Ex. Ct.) 57 DTC 1098.

In general, a fraction of each eligible capital expenditure made after 1971 is added to the "cumulative eligible capital" (CEC) account [ssec. 14(5)]. The fraction changed from $\frac{1}{2}$ to $\frac{3}{4}$ at the "adjustment time" defined [ssec. 14(5)] as:

(a) in the case of a corporation, the beginning of the first taxation year that began after June 30, 1988, and

(b) in the case of an individual, the beginning of the first fiscal period of a business that began after 1987.

The material in this text will only consider implications related to "post adjustment time" eligible capital expenditures.

The change to a $\frac{1}{2}$ capital gains inclusion rate for dispositions after October 17, 2000 does not affect the $\frac{3}{4}$ fraction used to calculate additions to the CEC account or disposals of eligible capital property. Instead, a special "$\frac{2}{3}$" adjustment is applied when calculating the income inclusion for a negative balance in the CEC pool for taxation years ended after October 17, 2000. The $\frac{2}{3}$ adjustment converts a $\frac{3}{4}$ amount in the CEC pool to a $\frac{1}{2}$ amount (i.e., $\frac{2}{3} \times \frac{3}{4} = \frac{1}{2}$).

The February 23, 2004 Technical Amendments propose to make an adjustment to the amount added to the cumulative eligible capital account on a non-arm's length purchase. The adjustment is similar in effect to the adjustment in paragraph 13(7)(*e*) on the purchase of depreciable property. The usual addition of $\frac{3}{4}$ of the purchase purchaser's cost must be reduced by $\frac{1}{2}$ of the non-arm's length seller's business income inclusion under paragraph 14(1)(*b*) from the gain on the sale of eligible capital property [ssec. 14(1.02)].

The balance in the CEC account is amortized under paragraph 20(1)(*b*) on a declining balance basis using a maximum rate of 7% (for fiscal periods commencing after the change dates defined as "adjustment time", indicated above, and 10% for fiscal periods commencing before the change dates above). The amount of annual amortization is referred to as the "cumulative eligible capital amount" (CECA). IT-123R6 discusses the effects of transactions involving eligible capital property on the balance in the CEC account and provides an extended numerical example in Schedule B.

B. Similarities with Capital Cost Allowance System

The system for taking deductions on eligible capital expenditures is very similar to that for depreciable capital property. The major differences, based on the rules in effect after the adjustment time, are:

(a) there is only one account or pool that is used to record purchases and dispositions of eligible capital expenditures (ECE) for a particular business [IT-206R]. This account is called the "cumulative eligible capital" (CEC) account, as indicated above, and is amortized on a declining balance basis [par. 20(1)(*b*)] to a maximum of 7% of the balance in the account. (The definition of the cumulative eligible capital account in subsection 14(5) appears somewhat more complex because it accumulates all adjustments to the account since 1971. Note that the ECE definition in subsection 14(5) parallels directly the definition of undepreciated capital cost in subsection 13(21));

(b) expenditures made prior to 1972 are completely ignored (but dispositions of property whenever purchased are considered);

(c) only ¾ of eligible capital expenditures (ECE) (which is equivalent to capital cost in the capital cost allowance system) and ¾ of proceeds called an "eligible capital amount" (ECA) affect the account;[g] and

(d) there is no half-net-amount rule.

Similar to the capital cost allowance system, it is the balance of cumulative eligible capital (CEC) which is equivalent to undepreciated capital cost at the end of the taxation year or on termination of the business that is important. At that time:

(a) if the balance of CEC is positive and the business is to continue, take amortization as a deduction at a maximum of 7% (after the adjustment time) of the balance of CEC and subtract that amount from the balance to be carried forward to the next year;

(b) if the balance of CEC is negative, for any taxation year ending after October 17, 2000, take into business income:

(i) the lesser of:

(A) the negative balance, and

(B) all cumulative eligible capital amounts claimed in prior years

less

deductions previously recaptured in prior year business income inclusions

PLUS

(ii) ⅔ of the negative CEC balance less (a) above.

The business income is effectively a recapture of previous deductions plus ½ of the absolute gain on the disposal. The ⅔ adjustment factor effectively converts from a ¾ rate to a ½ [⅔ x ¾ = ½].

(c) if the balance of cumulative eligible capital is positive, but the business has been terminated, take the positive balance as a deduction which is the equivalent of a terminal loss from income under section 24;

(d) the provision in subsection 14(3) operates in much the same way as paragraph 13(7)(e) for capital cost allowance purposes. Subsection 14(3) restricts the eligible capital expenditure of a non-arm's length purchaser of eligible capital property where the vendor has claimed a capital gains deduction under section 110.6[h] in respect of the disposition of the eligible capital property; and

(e) subsections 14(6) and (7) operate to defer recognition of recaptured cumulative eligible capital amounts on the disposition of eligible capital property where the property is replaced within one year of the end of the year of disposition, in the same manner as subsection 13(4) does for the CCA system.

---

[g] The eligible capital amount (ECA) is determined in item E of the definition of "cumulative eligible capital" in subsection 14(5) and referred to in subsection 14(1).

[h] Available to an individual who has disposed of qualified farm property, such as a farm marketing quota.

The more common aspects of these rules are illustrated in Exhibit 5-3.

EXHIBIT 5-3
Cumulative Eligible Capital Account
[Sec. 14]

Facts [applicable to a post-October 17, 2000 period]

Assume a corporation commencing business purchases a store in year one and pays $5,000 for goodwill. In year one and in year two the full 7% deduction is claimed. In year three the store is sold and $6,500 is received for goodwill.

In year three, assume that the corporation purchases another store and pays $4,450 for goodwill. In year three the full 7% deduction is claimed. In year four, the corporation ceases to carry on the business and sells the business to a person other than a corporation controlled by it. No part of the proceeds can be attributed to goodwill.

Application of Rules and Definitions

Year	Ssec. 14(5) Cumulative eligible capital item A	Ssec. 14(5) Cumulative eligible capital item E	Par. 20(1)(b) Cumulative eligible capital amount 7% deduction	Ssec. 14(5) Cumulative eligible capital
1 Purchase	$3/4 \times \$5,000$ = $3,750			$3,750
1 CECA			$263 (7% × $3,750)	$3,487
2 CECA			$244 (7% × $3,487)	$3,243
3 Disposal		($3/4 \times \$6,500$ = $4,875)		($1,632)*
3 Purchase	$3/4 \times \$4,450$ = $3,338			$1,706
3 CECA			$119 (7% × $1,706)	$1,587
4 Business Closed			$1,587 (sec. 24)	Nil

* $263 + $244 + 3/4 ($6,500 − $5,000) = $1,632 (equal to the negative balance for post-adjustment time purchases). If the goodwill of $4,450 is not purchased in Year 3, then there would be a business income inclusion as follows:

a) the lesser of:
   i) $1,632
      and
   ii) $263 + $244 = $507
      lesser amount...................................... $507
PLUS
b) 2/3 × ($1,632 − $507) 750
   $1,257

The $1,257 can also be calculated by adding the recaptured CECA of $507 to 1/2 of the gain ($6,500 − $5,000).

C. Election re: Capital Gain

[ITA: 14(1.01)]

Although the capital gains inclusion rate of 1/2 is reflected in the subsection 14(1) income amount, the additions and reductions to the cumulative eligible capital pool are still done at a rate of 3/4. There may be instances where a taxpayer would prefer to recognize an economic gain on eligible capital property as a capital gain rather than as a reduction to the available cumulative eligible capital pool. An example of such an instance would be if the taxpayer has available capital losses, either currently or carried over from another taxation year.

An election is available in subsection 14(1.01) that allows a taxpayer to treat a gain on the disposition of eligible capital property as a capital gain. The following conditions are necessary to take advantage of this provision.

(i) The property disposed must be eligible capital property of a business, but not goodwill.

(ii) The cost of the property to the taxpayer must be determinable.

(iii) The proceeds of disposition of the property must exceed the cost.

(iv) The taxpayer's exempt gains balance in respect of the business must be NIL.

(v) The taxpayer must elect under subsection 14(1.01) in the taxpayer's return of income for the year.

If the above conditions are met, then the proceeds of disposition of the property are deemed to be equal to the cost of that property. Then, the taxpayer is deemed to dispose of a capital property with proceeds equal to the actual proceeds and an adjusted cost base equal to the cost of the eligible capital property. If the property disposed is an eligible capital property that is a qualified farm property (as determined in subsection 110.6(1)), then the capital property deemed to be disposed is deemed to be a qualified farm property.

Example Problem

Ms. Chalupshka has operated an accounting practice with a December 31 year-end since 2002. She paid $16,000 for a client list when she started the practice in 2002. On August 27, 2005, she sold the practice, including her client list which was allocated $28,000 of the proceeds. The balance in the CEC account on January 1, 2005 was $8,976.

— REQUIRED

Compute Ms. Chalupshka's business income from the sale of the client list in 2005.

— SOLUTION

	CEC a/c
Cumulative eligible capital, January 1, 2005	$ 8,976
2005 Disposal: deemed proceeds = cost of client list ($^{3}/_{4}$ × $16,000)	(12,000)
Cumulative eligible capital, December 31, 2005	$ (3,024)
Inclusion in business income	3,024[1]
Cumulative eligible capital on cessation of business	Nil
Deemed disposal of capital property [ssec. 14(1.01)]	
Deemed proceeds...	$ 28,000
Deemed ACB	(16,000)
Capital gain	$ 12,000
Taxable capital gain ($^{1}/_{2}$).....................................	$ 6,000
Income inclusion	
Business income	$ 3,024
Taxable capital gain	6,000
Total	$ 9,024

— *NOTE TO SOLUTION*

(1) The inclusion is computed as follows:

(a) lesser of:

(i) Negative balance...............................$ 3,024

(ii) Total CECA claimed [($^3/_4$ × $16,000) − $8,976] $ 3,024

lesser amount $3,024

(b) $^2/_3$ ($3,024 − $3,024)..................................... nil

Inclusion in business income $3,024

III. CAPITAL PERSONAL PROPERTY AND THE INPUT TAX CREDIT SYSTEM UNDER GST

A. Basic Rules

[ETA: 123; 169]

An integral part of the GST system is the ability to claim input tax credits (ITCs) on business inputs and thus avoid the cascading or compounding of tax through the production and distribution chain. In order to qualify for an ITC, the property or service must have been purchased for use in a *commercial activity*. In determining the net remittance for a reporting period, the total ITC for the period is deducted from the tax collected or collectible for that period. Where the total ITC for the period exceeds the tax collected or collectible, the registrant will be entitled to a refund.

An important feature of the ITC mechanism is that purchases and sales need not be matched in order to claim an ITC. The credit can be claimed for the period in which the tax is paid or becomes payable. Similarly, for purchases of capital property, there is no requirement for amortization. Under the general input tax credit rules, a registrant may claim an ITC for the tax paid on the purchase of property or a service which was acquired for use in commercial activities. However, special rules have been developed for capital property, due to the fact that the useful life of capital property generally often extends for several years and the use of the property may change over that period. Under the *Excise Tax Act* (ETA), capital property is divided into two main groups — capital personal property and capital real property, and different rules apply to each group.

For GST purposes, capital property is defined [ETA: ssec. 123(1)] to include any property that is capital property for income tax purposes, other than property included in Class 12 (for example, small tools or utensils costing less than $200, video tape, computer software, etc.) or Class 14 (for example, patents, franchises, concessions or licences for a limited period, etc.) of the capital cost allowance classes. This definition for GST purposes applies regardless of whether the registrant is a taxpayer under the *Income Tax Act*.

Separate rules apply to passenger vehicles and aircraft that are acquired by an individual or a partnership, and certain input tax credit restrictions apply to all passenger vehicles. These topics are discussed below.

The rules for capital real property are discussed in Chapter 8.

B. Passenger Vehicles and Aircraft

[ETA: 201; 202(1)–(4); 203(1)–(3)]

Restrictions on claiming ITCs apply to passenger vehicles owned by all registrants, with special additional rules applying to passenger vehicles owned by registrants that are individuals or partnerships. Many of these rules are based on the rules for passenger vehicles under the *Income Tax Act*. For example, the definition of passenger vehicle under the ETA has the meaning assigned under subsection 248(1) of the *Income Tax Act*.

1. Passenger vehicles owned by registrants other than individuals and partnerships

Following the rules for deductibility under the *Income Tax Act*, section 201 of the ETA refers to paragraph 13(7)(*g*) or (*h*) of the *Income Tax Act*. As a result, no input tax credit may be claimed on the portion of the cost of a vehicle that exceeds $30,000 for years after 2000 excluding GST and provincial sales tax. Similarly, an input tax credit may not be claimed in respect of an improvement to the extent the accumulated cost of the vehicle, including the improvement, exceeds $30,000 [ETA: ssec. 202(1)].

As with other capital personal property (i.e., capital property other than capital real property), a full input tax credit may be claimed for the first $30,000 of the cost of passenger vehicles where the primary-use test is met. If the use in a commercial activity is 50% or less, no input tax credit may be claimed.

On the actual disposition of a passenger vehicle, the sale is subject to GST only where the vehicle was used primarily in a commercial activity prior to that time. In addition, a registrant may be entitled to claim an input tax credit on all or a portion of the cost of the vehicle that exceeded the prescribed threshold, e.g., $30,000 for years after 2000, which was previously denied [ETA: ssec. 203(1)].

2. Passenger vehicles and aircraft owned by registrants who are individuals or partnerships

Registrants who are individuals (e.g., sole proprietorships) or partnerships are entitled to claim a full input tax credit in respect of the acquisition of a passenger vehicle only if the vehicle is used exclusively (i.e., 90% or more) in a commercial activity [ETA: ssec. 202(2)]. Similarly, a full input tax credit may be claimed in respect of any improvement only if the vehicle was used exclusively in a commercial activity since its acquisition and will continue to be so used immediately after the improvement [ETA: ssec. 202(3)]. As with other registrants, no input tax credit may be claimed on the portion of the cost of a vehicle (or improvements thereto) that exceeds $30,000, exclusive of provincial sales tax and GST.

If the vehicle or aircraft is used less than exclusively in a commercial activity, a full input tax credit may not be claimed in respect of the acquisition or improvement. However, the individual or partnership is entitled to claim an input tax credit equal to $7/107$ths of the capital cost allowance claimed for income tax purposes, to the extent the vehicle or aircraft is used in a commercial activity [ETA: ssec. 202(4)]. For example, if an individual purchases a car for $16,000 (including GST) for use 60% in a commercial activity, the individual would be able to claim an input tax credit equal to $94 (i.e., $1/2 \times$ 30% of $16,000 \times 60% \times 7/107$ths) in the first year. An input tax credit may also be claimed in subsequent years based on capital cost allowance claims.

On the actual disposition of a passenger vehicle or aircraft, GST applies only if the vehicle or aircraft was used exclusively in a commercial activity since its acquisition [ETA: ssec. 203(3)].

Where an individual or partnership sells a passenger vehicle that immediately before that time was used exclusively in a commercial activity the following applies [ETA: ssec. 203(1)]. The individual or partnership is entitled to claim an input tax credit in the same manner as other registrants (as discussed above) on all or a portion of the cost on acquisition and any improvements, that exceeded $30,000 and that was previously denied.

REVIEW QUESTIONS

(1) In the year of acquisition only one-half of the capital cost of an asset is added to the CCA class. Comment.

(2) If an asset is sold for less than the UCC balance in the class then there will be a terminal loss. Comment.

(3) The "cost amount" of depreciable property is the original cost of the asset. Comment.

(4) The "capital cost" of depreciable property is the original cost of the asset before any CCA is claimed. Comment.

(5) The half-net-amount rule applies to all property acquired in all CCA classes. Comment.

(6) The half-net-amount rule is designed to take into account the period of ownership during the year and the fact that not all assets are purchased at the beginning of the year. Comment.

(7) CCA can be claimed in the year that title and the incidence of ownership are acquired by the taxpayer. Comment.

(8) Once a CCA claim has been made a taxpayer cannot go back and change the amount of the prior year's claim. Comment.

(9) When the fiscal period of a business is less than 365 days then the CCA must be prorated for the number of days in the fiscal year. Comment.

(10) Once an asset has been disposed of, then no CCA can be claimed on that asset. Comment.

(11) A client just bought a new piece of equipment that cost her $50,000. Because of the nature of the asset she has received a government grant of $15,000 to help pay for it. She thinks she can only depreciate $35,000. Comment.

(12) It has just cost a client $20,000 in legal fees to obtain a patent on some new equipment. Given his profitability, he is unhappy that he can only depreciate these costs as a Class 14 asset over the 20-year life of the patent but his controller says that he does not have any choice. Comment.

(13) Mrs. Smith has just incorporated her company to carry on a retail business. As part of the start-up costs she has paid $800 to have the company incorporated and $10,000 to obtain the indefinite-life franchise that she wanted. Each of these expenditures are eligible capital expenditures and since they are different they each go into their own CEC pool. Comment.

(14) Mr. Finis has just come to tell you that he has decided to wind up his business and retire. He is in the process of selling all of his assets but he cannot find one buyer who will continue the business and pay him something for goodwill. He is disappointed since he has a balance of $15,000 in his CEC account that cannot be used. Comment.

MULTIPLE CHOICE QUESTIONS

Question 1

X Ltd. purchased a $50,000 passenger vehicle in 2005. What is the maximum amount that X Ltd. may claim as capital cost allowance for the vehicle in 2005, ignoring provincial sales taxes and the goods and services tax?

(A) $7,500

(B) $9,000

(C) $4,500

(D) $4,050

Question 2

R Ltd. owns a restaurant business which it carries on in rented premises. R Ltd. redecorated and renovated and made $80,000 of leasehold improvements. The lease expires on December 31, 2010 (5 years) and has two successive renewal options of 3 years each. Assuming that R Ltd. has a December 31 year-end, what is the maximum CCA that R Ltd. can claim in 2005 in respect of these improvements?

(A) $5,000

(B) $8,000

(C) $10,000

(D) $16,000

Question 3

In the year, ABC Ltd. purchased goodwill relating to a business for $100,000. Assuming ABC Limited has no other depreciable or eligible capital property, what is the maximum writeoff that ABC Ltd. can claim for this goodwill in the year?

(A) $2,500

(B) $3,500

(C) $7,000

(D) $5,250

Question 4

On January 1, 2003, ABC Ltd. signed a 5-year lease for retail space for a store. The lease expires on December 31, 2007, and has two successive renewal options for three years each, In 2005, ABC Ltd. made $60,000 of leasehold improvements to this space. Assuming that ABC Ltd. has a December 31 year-end, what is the maximum capital cost allowance claim that ABC Ltd. can make in 2005 in respect of these improvements?

(A) $3,750

(B) $5,000

(C) $6,000

(D) $7,500

Question 5

During the year, Swiss Restaurants purchased the following assets for its restaurant and catering business:

Moulds for fancy chocolate items ($300 each)	$ 1,200
An accounting program (computer software)	600
Linens for tables in the restaurants	400
Cutlery, dishes and kitchen utensils costing less than $200 each	15,000

What is the maximum CCA claim for these assets?

(A) $8,600

(B) $16,300

(C) $16,900

(D) $17,200

Question 6

The new controller of a pharmaceutical company has asked you how the legal costs to obtain a patent on a new drug are treated for tax purposes. She is not sure whether the costs can be:

I   included in Class 14,

II included in Class 44,

III deducted in the year incurred, or

IV treated as an eligible capital expenditure.

Which of the above is correct?

(A) I, II and III

(B) II, III, and IV

(C) I, III and IV

(D) I, II, III and IV

EXERCISES

Exercise 1

[ITA: 14(5); 20(1)(a); ITR: 1100]

Businesses in two plazas operating on either side of a very busy city street decided to pool their promotional efforts. They also decided to build an overpass so that customers could avoid crossing the street when shopping at the plazas. The overpass was constructed at a cost of $150,000 after appropriate arrangements were made with the city because the footings to the overpass had to be placed on city property. These arrangements did not include a leasehold interest in the city property.

— *REQUIRED*

In what class of assets can the overpass be placed for capital cost allowance?

Exercise 2

[ITA: 20(16.1); 21(1); ITR: 1100(2.5), (6)]

Slick Sales is a commission salesman who has been claiming capital cost allowance on his automobile under paragraph 8(1)(j). The automobile was purchased for $38,000 (including PST of 8% and GST of 7%) in October 2003. The undepreciated capital cost of his automobile at January 1, 2005, was $18,475. In 2005 he sold the automobile for $12,000. Slick does 75% of his driving for employment purposes out of 16,000 kilometres of total driving.

— *REQUIRED*

(A) What are the tax consequences in 2005 to Slick on the sale of the old car?

(B) What are the tax consequences in 2005 if Slick buys a new car in 2005 for $36,000 including PST of $2,504, GST of $2,191? His net commission income after deducting cash expenses for 2005 is $3,000.

Exercise 3

[ITA: 20(1)(*a*); ITR: 1100; Sched. II, III]

The following balances were found in the various classes of depreciable assets on the books of Wasting Assets Ltd., as at January 1, 2005:

Class 1 (see (1) below)	$120,000
Class 8	75,000
Class 10 (truck for transportation of goods)	40,000
Class 13 (see (2) below)	42,000
Class 14 (see (3) below)	54,400

Additional information and transactions during 2005:

(1) The Class 1 undepreciated capital cost represents two buildings costing $100,000 each. One building was sold for $150,000 during 2005.

(2) The Class 13 balance relates to a long-term lease on a warehouse for 30 years with an option to renew for a further 20 years. The original cost of the leasehold improvements in 1989 was $50,000.

(3) Class 14 consists of a patent for 20 years costing $68,000 on January 1, 2001. (Ignore the effects of the leap years in the period).

(4) Purchases during the year:

Manufacturing equipment	$50,000
Office equipment	10,000

— *REQUIRED*

Prepare a schedule showing the maximum capital cost allowance deductions for tax purposes in 2005.

Exercise 4

(If consideration of the topics of involuntary and voluntary dispositions has been deferred to Chapter 8, this exercise should also be deferred.)

[ITA: 13(4)]

Windswept Storage Ltd. had a brick warehouse that was completely destroyed by a tornado early in its 2004 fiscal year ended December 31. The building had cost $300,000 and its Class 3 undepreciated capital cost at the time of its destruction was $221,000. Agreement was reached on the insurance claim later in 2004 when the company received only $295,000. A new brick building was fully constructed by August 2005 for $400,000.

— *REQUIRED*

Trace the effects of these events on the balance of the undepreciated capital cost from 2004 through to the beginning balance for 2006, assuming that the proper election under subsection 13(4) is made.

Exercise 5

[ITA: 13(7)(*d*)]

Smiley Service purchased a car in 2003 for $14,600. His business use of the car during 250 days each year based on mileage of 16,000 kilometres in total and the fair market values of the car in each of the years to the present were as follows:

	Business use	Fair market value
2003	85%	$14,600
2004	80%	12,200
2005	90%	9,800

— *REQUIRED*

Compute the maximum capital cost allowance that can be claimed.

Exercise 6

[ITA: 14(1); 20(1)(*b*)]

Ms Glutton sold her unincorporated grocery business in 2005 and received $45,000 for goodwill. The business had a December 31 year-end.

— REQUIRED

If the grocery store had been purchased on January 2, 1993 with a payment of $10,800 for goodwill at that time, compute the effect of the 2005 sale on Ms Glutton's income. Assume that maximum deductions have been made under paragraph 20(1)(*b*) in previous years, except in the years 1995 to 2003 inclusive when no amount was claimed since the business only had losses.

Exercise 7

[ITA: 14(1); 20(1)(*b*)]

Buylo Ltd., which has been in the same business, except as noted below, since 1997, made the following purchases and sales throughout the period 1997 to 2005.

Jan. 1, 1997	Purchased goodwill at $40,000.
June 1, 1999	Purchased a government licence with an indefinite life for $50,000.
Mar. 1, 2001	Purchased a trademark for $20,000.
Nov. 1, 2002	Purchased goodwill for $50,000.
Sept. 7, 2003	Sold 1997 goodwill for $100,000.
Aug. 3, 2005	Sold all of the remaining assets of the business to a competitor for $500,000 of which $150,000 could be attributed to the licence and $200,000 to the trademark.

— REQUIRED

Calculate the income under subsection 14(1) for the 2003 and 2005 taxation years, assuming the company always took the maximum tax deductions under paragraph 20(1)(*b*) each year for its fiscal years ending December 31. Calculate the amount of cumulative eligible capital as at January 1, 2006.

ASSIGNMENT PROBLEMS

Problem 1

[ITA: 13(1), (2); 20(1)(a), (16.1); ITR: 1100(1), (2.5); 1101(5p); 1103(2h); 7307(1)(b); Sched. II, III]

On March 1, 2004, Jennifer Lobo began operating as a sole proprietorship and purchased the licence to manufacture the computer software version of the latest trivia game, "Tax is a Microcosm of Life on CD". During the remainder of 2004, she acquired the following assets:

Manufacturing equipment	$20,000
Tools (each costing under $200)	16,000
Dies and moulds	8,000
Computer equipment and systems software	12,000
Photocopier	6,000
Office furnishings	15,000
Customer lists (expected to be used indefinitely)	4,000
Delivery van	30,000
T.V. commercial video tape	22,000
Chairs and tables (for the employee eating area)	2,500
Cutlery and dishes (for the employee eating area)	2,000
Table linens (for the employee eating area)	1,200
Automobile (for use by sales personnel visiting clients)	38,000
Licence to manufacture, based on patented information, "Tax is a Microcosm of Life on CD" for 3 years ending February 28, 2007	30,000
Made improvements on the building that she leased on March 1, 2004; the lease was for 3 years with two successive options to renew of 3 years and 4 years	9,000

During 2005, she made the following additional purchases and disposals:

Bought a brick building and land in order to accommodate the expansion of her building; an appraisal indicated that the building represented 45% of the total cost of the property	$200,000
Sold the photocopier	(4,000)
Sold the automobile	(23,000)
Sold the T.V. commercial video tape	(18,000)
Sold some of the tools (costing less than $200 each)	(5,000)

— REQUIRED

Prepare a schedule to show the maximum capital cost allowance for the fiscal years ended December 31, 2004 and December 31, 2005, ignoring GST and PST considerations. Where choices are available, state the reasons for your decision. Ignore the effects, if any, of the leap year.

Problem 2

(If consideration of the topics of involuntary and voluntary dispositions has been deferred to Chapter 8, this problem should also be deferred.)

[ITA: 13(4)]

Elaine Barblaik owns an apartment building which she holds for rental income. In November 2004, Elaine settled with municipal authorities on expropriation proceeds for the property including the building. The agreed expropriation proceeds for the building and the separate sale proceeds for the appliances and fixtures are indicated in the following data:

	Expropriated building Cl.3	Sold appliances & fixtures
Cost	$406,000	$26,000
U.C.C. January 1, 2004	188,500	7,250
Proceeds	362,500	2,600

Since negotiations had been prolonged, Elaine was able to anticipate the approximate date of settlement and, as a result, she was able to replace in 2005 the assets expropriated.

Replacement cost for the building and the cost of new appliances and fixtures were as follows:

Building $1,276,000
Appliances and fixtures 46,400

— REQUIRED

Trace the effects of these events on the undepreciated capital cost for both assets through to the opening balance on January 1, 2006 assuming no further additions are made to either class of assets.

Problem 3

[ITA: 13(7)]

On January 20, 2004, a personal residence which originally cost $280,000 was converted into a rental property. At this time the property had a fair market value of $320,000. On June 1, 2006, the property was converted back to a personal residence. At that time the property had a fair market value of $305,000.

— REQUIRED

If the building is the only asset in Class 1, which has a 4% capital cost allowance rate, how much capital cost allowance may be deducted for the years 2004 through 2006, inclusive?

Problem 4

[ITA: 14; 20(1)(b)]

Sharp is a musician who paid $500 in 1995 for an indefinite-life licence to perform in the subway walkway areas. In 2000, Sharp decided to try a different approach to developing a following. He purchased the name of a popular local band that stopped performing earlier that year. The cost of the name was $16,128 and the appropriate amount was included in the January 1, 2001 balance below. In 2001, he purchased an indefinite-life licence from the city for $5,000 which allowed him to perform on a street-corner on Saturday afternoons. In 2002, Sharp found that he wanted to spend more time in the studio, so he sold the street-corner licence for $6,000. In 2005, Sharp decided to break up his band and pursue a career as an accountant. He sold the band name for $20,000.

Sharp has not yet filed his tax return for 2005. The year-end of the business is December 31. The following information is available with respect to the cumulative eligible capital account:

(a) the balance in the cumulative eligible capital account on January 1, 2001, was $11,492, and

(b) the total cumulative eligible capital amount claimed prior to 2001 was $979.

— REQUIRED

Prepare a schedule calculating the balance of the cumulative eligible capital account on January 1, 2006, and calculating the impact on income for 2005.

Problem 5

[ITA: 14; 20(1)(b), (cc); IT-206R]

Con-Glo Corporation has been involved in various food services businesses since its incorporation in 1991. Con-Glo has a December 31 year-end. You have been asked by the controller to examine the transactions involving various intangible assets due to an impending sale of the business. The controller wants to ensure that he understands the implications on the sale. You have been provided with the following information.

Shortly after the business was incorporated, Con-Glo purchased its first family restaurant. The purchase price included $43,000 for goodwill. After operating this business for a number of years and ensuring that it was profitable, another restaurant was purchased in 1998. The purchase again included goodwill in the amount of $68,000. The second restaurant had more of a roadhouse atmosphere. The business had obtained a liquor licence. The value of the licence at the time of the purchase was $21,133, and this amount was allocated to the licence in the purchase agreement.

Con-Glo operated the two restaurants until 2000 when it purchased a fast food franchise. The franchise was for an undefined number of years and cost $103,000.

The fast food restaurant, while successful, was too much of a drain on the time of the owners of Con-Glo and was sold in 2002. The value of the franchise agreement was determined to be $110,000.

In 2003, it was determined that the original family restaurant would be more successful if it obtained a liquor licence. In order to obtain the licence a presentation had to be made to the liquor licensing board. Con-Glo paid $29,000 in legal fees related to the presentation to the board.

In 2004, the second restaurant was sold. Con-Glo received $80,000 for the goodwill and $60,000 for the liquor licence.

Due to health problems of the owner's wife, Con-Glo is also considering a sale of the balance of their restaurants in 2005. The selling price will include $250,000 for goodwill.

—REQUIRED

Prepare a schedule calculating the balance of the cumulative eligible capital account as of January 1, 2006, and determine the impact of the above transactions on income for 1998 through 2005. Assume that the opening balance on January 1, 1998, was $20,865, the 1992 to 1997 CECA deductions were a total of $11,385, and that the company took the maximum tax write-offs that it was entitled to in each of the years 1998 to 2003. (Hint: consider paragraph 20(1)(*cc*).) Assume also that Con-Glo was deemed to be in the same business in respect of its restaurant and catering business as per IT-206R.

Problem 6

[ITA: 13; 14; 20(1)(*a*), (*b*); ITR: 1100; Sched. II, III]

Jon's Auto Parts Ltd., which manufactures small equipment, was incorporated in 1978 and had the following balances in its records concerning its capital assets as at January 1, 2005.

| Type of asset | Depreciation | | C.C.A. | |
	Straight-line	Book value	Class	U.C.C.
Land	Nil	$102,000		Nil
Building	40 years	272,000	3	$153,000
Equipment	5 years	163,000	8	39,000
Rolling stock — trucks etc. (for transportation of goods)	3 years	306,000	10	170,000
Leasehold improvements (see note (1) below)	life of lease	113,000	13	165,000
Licences	5 years	70,000	14	87,393

Additional Information

(1) The Class 13 assets consist of:

— Improvements to a leased warehouse costing $100,000 in 2004. The remaining length of the lease in 2004 was 6 years with two successive options of 4 years.

— Improvements to a leased office space for head office downtown, costing $81,600 in 2003. The remaining length of the lease was five years with an option to renew for an additional one year.

(2) The licences were purchased to start on April 22, 2003, at a cost of $110,500 and had a life of five years.

(3) During 2005, the company had the following capital transactions:
Additions:
— Purchased a new concrete building costing $1,625,000, including $325,000 for land.
— Additional expenditures re the building:

Paved parking lot for employees	$ 97,000
Erected a steel fence around an outside storage area	65,000
— Further renovations to leased office space, costing	51,000

— Purchased equipment:

Office equipment	$ 47,000
Manufacturing equipment	255,000
Radio communication equipment	60,000

— Purchased a distributing licence on March 1, 2005, for 5 years from a foreign manufacturing company of a related product line, cost: $240,000.
— Paid $34,500 in legal fees in reorganizing the capital structure.

Disposals:

	Cost	Book value	Proceeds
Equipment — office	$ 16,250	$ 4,225	$ 1,950
Brick building in Cl. 3 (excluding land)	390,000	272,000	568,000

— REQUIRED

Prepare a schedule for tax purposes to reflect the above transactions and calculate the maximum write-off for tax purposes. (Ignore the effects of the replacement property rules in subsection 13(4) and the effects of leap years.)

Problem 7

[ITA: 13; 14; 18–20; ITR: 1100; Sched. II, III]

The controller of Choleva Products Limited has provided you with the following draft income statement as well as some notes that she made during the preparation of this statement.

Choleva Products Limited

STATEMENT OF INCOME
For the year ended December 31, 2005

Sales		$8,300,000
Cost of goods sold (Note (1))		(6,800,000)
Gross profit		$1,500,000
Commission income		70,000
		$1,570,000
Administrative and marketing expenses (Note (2))	$500,000	
Depreciation and amortization (Note (3))	80,000	
Interest on long-term debt (Note (4))	70,000	
Interest on bank indebtedness	120,000	(770,000)
		$ 800,000
Gain on disposal of property, plant and equipment (Note (3))		40,000
Net income before income taxes		$ 840,000
Provision for income taxes		(400,000)
Net income after income taxes		$ 440,000

Notes Prepared by Controller:

(1) The cost of goods sold expense includes the following amounts:

(a) A $9,000 loss from a theft by a warehouse employee;

(b) A $15,000 reserve for future decline in the value of inventory because of new products expected to be introduced by the competitor. There was no such reserve in 2004.

(2) Administration and marketing expenses include:

(a) An $11,000 increase in the reserve for warranty expenses;

(b) $4,000 of donations to registered charities;

(c) $1,500 for golf club membership dues for the Vice-President of Sales and $2,000 for meals and entertainment expenses at the golf club. The Vice-President of Sales uses the club to generate sales;

(d) $85,000 in accrued bonuses, including $62,000 paid to employees on May 31, 2006, and $23,000 paid to employees on June 30, 2006;

(e) A $15,000 year-end party for all employees;

(f) $8,000 of financing fees incurred in connection with the mortgage of the corporation's new plant, including legal fees of $6,000 and an appraisal fee of $2,000;

(g) $5,000 of legal fees in connection with the purchase of shares of another company; and

(h) $300 for an upgrade of word-processing software.

(3) The fixed asset section of the controller's working papers indicate the following:

(a) The undepreciated capital cost balances at December 31, 2004 were as follows:

Class 3	$200,000
Class 8	60,000
Class 10	80,000
Class 13	37,500
CEC	5,000

(b) Gain on disposal of property of plant and equipment consists of the profit on the sale of the corporation's only Class 3 asset (proceeds: $180,000; original cost in 1990: $300,000). The land on which the building was situated was also sold for its fair market value which was equal to its cost in 1990.

(c) During 2005 the corporation made the following purchases:

- A new building was purchased for $700,000. The cost of the related land was $400,000. It cost $20,000 to pave part of the land for use as a parking lot and $30,000 to erect fencing;

- New office furniture was purchased for $25,000. This purchase replaced office furniture which was sold for its $4,000 net book value (original cost: $10,000);

- An unlimited life franchise was purchased for $100,000;

- A 10-year licence to use patented information (expiring June 30, 2015) was purchased on July 1 for $20,000; and

- Improvements on its leased head office premises which were rented in 2003 for 4 years with two successive options to renew for 5 years and 5 years. Improvements had originally been made in 2003 in the amount of $45,000. Additional improvements were made in 2005 at a cost of $28,000.

(d) During the year, the corporation sold some small tools (each costing less than $200) for their net book value of $500.

(4) Interest on long-term debt includes:

(a) Bond discount amortization in the amount of $2,000;

(b) $18,000 of interest on bonds issued to buy shares in another company; and

(c) $50,000 of interest on the mortgage on the new plant.

— REQUIRED

Calculate the corporation's minimum income from business or property for the year ended December 31, 2005, under the provisions of the Act. Assume all expenses are reasonable in the circumstances. Support your treatment of each item listed above with a reason or a section reference. Ignore the effects of leap years.

[For more problems and solutions thereto, see the CD accompanying this book.]

SUPPLEMENTAL NOTES

(This section can be omitted without losing continuity of the chapter. None of the review questions, multiple choice questions, exercises or assignment problems utilizes this information.)

A. Lease-option Arrangements

[ITA: 13(5.2)–(5.3); ITR 1101(5g); IT-233R (cancelled)]

As has been shown, the capital cost allowance system allows for the write-off of the decline in value of a pool of assets over the period of their ownership. When the decline in value has not been as great as the capital cost allowance deducted, as evidenced by proceeds of disposition in excess of the undepreciated capital cost of a class of assets, provision is made to recapture the excess capital cost allowance previously deducted. Recapture is included in income, when it arises, to offset the capital cost allowance previously deducted that exceeded the decline in value of the pool of assets.

A similar problem arises on a lease-option arrangement. An asset may be leased for a period of time and at the end of that period an option to purchase the asset may be exercised. If the lease arrangement is regarded as a true rental agreement and not as a purchase, the lease payments would be deducted in full during the years of the lease arrangement. On the purchase of the asset by the exercise of the option, the capital cost of the asset would ordinarily be established at the purchase price under the option. If the asset is sold for more than that capital cost, a capital gain which is partially taxable would ordinarily result. However, the gain in value from the purchase price under the option should be regarded as a recapture of some of the lease payments previously deducted from income in full.

The rules in subsections 13(5.2) and (5.3) provide for the calculation of that recapture. These rules are invoked when the lease arrangement is not regarded as a financing arrangement for the purchase of an asset (i.e., a "capital" lease), but as a rental arrangement (i.e., an "operating" lease). The CRA discusses the indicators of a financing arrangement as opposed to a rental agreement in IT-233R at paragraph 3.

The Interpretation Bulletin provides four conditions under which a transaction will be considered to be a sale rather than a lease, as follows:

(a) the lessee automatically acquires title to the asset after the payment of a specified amount in rentals;

(b) the lessee is required to buy the asset by the termination of the lease;

(c) the lessee has the right to buy the asset, by the end of the lease, at a price which is substantially less than the estimate, at the beginning of the lease, of the fair market value of the property at the time of acquisition; or

(d) the lessee has the right to buy the asset, by the end of the lease, at a price which, at the beginning of the lease, is such that no reasonable person would not buy the asset.

These conditions parallel the first of three conditions for a capital lease set out in the CICA *Handbook* at section 3065.06. (Refer, also, to the issue raised by the Emerging Issues Committee in EIC-30.)

Subsection 13(5.2) applies where a taxpayer has acquired, on the exercise of a purchase option, depreciable capital property or real property (i.e., land and buildings) from a lessor to whom the taxpayer has paid rent under an operating lease for the use of the property at a capital cost or cost less than the fair market value. This situation would usually be regarded as an operating lease, if the option price represented an estimate, at the time the rental arrangement was made, of the fair market value of the asset. However, as a result of market conditions that arise during the rental period, the actual fair market value at the time of the exercise of the purchase option was higher. The taxpayer is deemed to acquire the property, at the time of the exercise of the option, for an amount equal to the lesser of:

> (a) the fair market value of the property at the time of the exercise of the option, and
>
> (b) (i) the actual cost of the property at the time of the exercise of the option, *plus*
>
>   (ii) all previous payments of rent for the use of the property [ssec. 13(5.2)].

The excess, if any, of the deemed cost, determined above, over the actual cost under the option is considered to be capital cost allowance taken by the taxpayer. As a result, any proceeds of disposition from the ultimate sale of the property up to the deemed cost of the property will reduce the undepreciated capital cost balance of the asset class to which the property belongs, thereby creating either potential or actual recapture. This recapture will offset, to some extent, the benefit derived from the previous deduction of rental payments for the property.

When the property, that is leased and then purchased under an option, is non-depreciable real property (e.g., land), the property is deemed to be depreciable property of a separate class as prescribed by Regulation 1101(5g). Class 36 is prescribed for this purpose and is used only to determine the recapture of previous rental payments on the ultimate sale of the non-depreciable real property acquired under a purchase option. The balance in this class is not eligible for capital cost allowance.

Subsection 13(5.3) applies where a taxpayer disposes of the option to purchase depreciable capital property or real property that has previously been rented, rather than exercising the option. In this case, the excess of the proceeds of disposition for the option over the cost of the option is included in income as recapture [ssec. 13(1)].

Example Problem

Mr. Britelite leased a car for the exclusive use of his business for three years at a cost of $500 per month. The lease agreement with the arm's length lessor provided Mr. Britelite with an option to buy the car at the end of the three years for $6,500 which was estimated, at the time of signing the lease, to be the fair market value of the car at the end of the three years. However, at the time the option was exercised, at the end of the third year, the fair market value of the car was actually $8,000 and the car was sold in the following year for $7,500. The car was the only asset in Class 10 of the business and no capital cost allowance was claimed in the class before the car was sold.

— REQUIRED

What are the tax implications of these transactions?

— SOLUTION

The terms of the lease do not appear to classify it as a capital lease. None of the conditions specified in paragraph 3 of IT-233R appears to apply. Ownership of the car by Mr. Britelite at the end of the lease is not assured, given the terms of the lease, including the option purchase price.

During the three years that the lease was in force, the lease payments of $500 per month were fully deductible if the car was used exclusively for business purposes.

When the car was purchased for $6,500, at the end of the third year, paragraph 13(5.2)(*a*) would deem the capital cost to be the lesser of:

(a) the fair market value of the car at the time of its purchase under the option .... $ 8,000

(b) (i) the actual cost of the car at the time of its purchase under the option .... $ 6,500
     plus
     (ii) all previous lease payments for the use of the car ($500 × 12 × 3)........................... 18,000 $24,500

Mr. Britelite's business will be deemed to have deducted capital cost allowance in respect of the car equal to the excess of the deemed cost of $8,000, as computed above, over the $6,500 actual cost [par. 13(5.2)(b)]. As a result, the net addition to the undepreciated capital cost of Class 10 will be $6,500 and Mr. Britelite will be potentially liable for a recapture on proceeds up to the $8,000 of deemed capital cost.

When the car was sold in the fourth year for $7,500, a recapture of $1,000 (i.e. $7,500 – 6,500) would result. Conceptually, this recapture represents an excess of deduction for the lease payments relative to the actual decline in the value of the car. The lease payments were originally computed based on an estimated decline in value of the car to $6,500 but the actual decline in value was only to $7,500 by the time of its sale. This $1,000 of recapture represents lease payments that were fully deducted in excess of the real decline in value of the car.

The effects of the above example on Class 10 can be traced as follows:

	Car Class 10: 30%
Addition of deemed capital cost [par. 13(5.2)(a)]	$ 8,000
Less: deemed capital cost allowance [par. 13(5.2)(b)]	1,500
U.C.C.	$ 6,500
Less: C.C.A. claimed......................................	Nil
U.C.C.	$ 6,500
Disposition — Lesser of:	
(a) proceeds of disposition $7,500	
(b) capital cost....................... $8,000	
lesser amount	(7,500)
Recapture	$(1,000)

Had C.C.A. been claimed on the $6,500 of U.C.C., the amount of recapture would be higher, reflecting the recovery on the disposition of that C.C.A. claimed, as well as some of the past lease payments deducted.

B. Leasing Property

[ITA: 16.1; ITR: 1100(1.1)–(1.3); 1101(5n), (5o); 4302; 8200]

The provisions of section 16.1 are designed to curtail the advantages of leasing in certain situations. Accelerated capital cost allowance is of little or no advantage to an owner of depreciable capital property, if the owner is in a loss position or is otherwise not taxable. In those cases, it becomes advantageous to lease property from a lessor who can benefit from the accelerated capital cost allowance. In return, the lessee can, perhaps, obtain lease-payment terms that are relatively more favourable, because of the tax advantage to the lessor.

By virtue of the Regulations designed to remove this advantage, a limit is placed on the capital cost allowance that a lessor can claim on certain leasing property. An assumption is made that the lease is, in effect, a loan with interest at a rate prescribed in Regulation 4302. The payments received by the lessor are considered to be blended payments of interest and principal. The amount of capital cost allowance that can be claimed by the lessor is, then, limited to the lesser of the principal component of the blended payment and the capital cost allowance (without the application of the half-net-amount rule) that would otherwise be computed by the lessor on the leased property.

This limitation on a lessor applies only to taxpayers whose principal business is leasing. The limitation applies only to "specified leasing property" which is defined to include depreciable property with a fair market value in excess of $25,000, leased to an arm's length lessee for a term of more than one year [Reg. 1100(1.11)].

Certain property is exempt from the limitation on capital cost allowance. "Exempt property" is defined [Reg. 1100(1.13)(a)] to include:

(i) certain general purpose office furniture or office equipment included in Class 8 or certain general purpose electronic data processing equipment included in Class 10;

(ii) furniture, appliances and other similar properties designed for residential use;

(iii) passenger vehicles, vans or pick-up trucks;

(iv) highway trucks or tractors with a "gross vehicle weight rating" of under 11,778 kilograms;

(v) trailers designed to be hauled by a truck or tractor described in (iv) above; and

(vi) a building, or part of a building, including component parts.

Property that appears to be subject to the restrictions might be characterized very generally as high-cost, heavy equipment. However, the specifics of these definitions must be consulted in a particular case. Exempt property might generally be characterized as property for which capital cost allowance rates fairly closely approximate physical or economic depreciation rates, rather than investment incentive rates.

Lessees are, generally, not affected by the restrictions on capital cost allowance claimed by lessors. As a result, lessees may deduct the full amount of lease payments made. However, a special election is available [ssec. 16.1(1)] for property (other than prescribed property, defined in Regulation 8200) leased from certain arm's length lessors for more than one year. If the election is filed jointly by the lessee and the lessor, the lessee will be treated as if he or she had borrowed an amount equal to the fair market value of the leased property at the rate prescribed in Regulation 4302. The lessee can deduct capital cost allowance and the assumed interest payment in each rental payment. The lessor's tax position is not affected by the election, although the lessor's capital cost allowance deduction may be limited by the rules applicable to lessors [Reg. 1100(1.1)], as discussed above.

C. Capital Personal Property for GST Purposes

[ETA: 123(1); 199(2), (4); 200(3)]

A full input tax credit will be allowed where capital personal property is purchased for use primarily in a commercial activity [ETA: ssec. 199(2)]. If the primary-use test is not satisfied, no part of the tax will be creditable. "Primarily" is interpreted by the CRA to mean greater than 50%.

It should be noted that any subsequent change in the proportion of commercial use over the life of the capital property may trigger adjustments in the GST.

There may be cases where improvements are made to capital personal property. A registrant is allowed to claim an ITC for GST paid or payable on an improvement that has been made to capital personal property [ETA: ssec. 199(4)]. For this rule to apply, the property must be used primarily in a commercial activity at the time the tax is paid or payable on the improvement.

The term "improvement" is defined [ETA: ssec. 123(1)] to include any consideration paid or payable in respect of capital property that would be included in determining the adjusted cost base (capital cost) of the property for the purposes of the *Income Tax Act*.

The sale of capital personal property is subject to GST where the property is being used primarily in commercial activities prior to sale [ETA: ssec. 200(3)]. If the primary-use test is not met, the sale is not subject to GST.

Modified rules apply to capital personal property acquired and used by financial institutions [ETA: sec. 204].

Chapter 6

Income from Property

TOPICS DISCUSSED

	Page
INCLUSIONS	265
Interest Income	265
Payments Based on Production or Use	268
Dividends from Corporations Resident in Canada	269
Shareholder Benefits and Loans	271
Income Attribution	278
DEDUCTIONS	285
Carrying Charges on Land	285
"Soft Costs" relating to Construction of Buildings or Ownership of Land	287
Rental Properties	287
Depreciation-based or Similar Tax Shelters	289

	Page
Interest	290
Personal Loan Planning and Interest Deductibility	293
DIFFERENCES BETWEEN BUSINESS AND PROPERTY INCOME	297
GST AND PROPERTY INCOME	298
Interest and Dividends	298
Shareholder Benefits	298
"Soft Costs"	299
SUPPLEMENTAL NOTES	311
Prescribed Debt Obligations	311
GST and Property Income	313

Income from property is generally regarded as the return on invested capital when little or no time, labour or attention is expended in producing the return. Income from property would normally include dividends, interest, rents and royalties. It should be noted, however, that even such receipts might constitute income from a business if sufficient time and effort are expended in earning them. As was the case for income from a business, income from property is the "profit therefrom for the year" [ssec. 9(1)].

Note that income or loss from property does not include capital gains or capital losses [ssec. 9(3)]. This exclusion is important when considering the deductibility of an expenditure which depends on producing income from property.[a]

---

[a] The case of *The Queen v. Young*, (F.C.A.) 89 DTC 5234, illustrates this issue of deductibility.

The GST implication of several of the topics introduced in the discussion of the Act are presented in the final major section of this chapter.

The following chart provides an overview of the location of most of these provisions.

PART I — DIVISION B
SUBDIVISION b
BUSINESS OR PROPERTY

DIVISION		SUBDIVISION		SECTION	
A	Liability for tax				
B	Computation of income		Basic rules		
C	Computation of taxable income	a	Office or employment		
D	Taxable income earned in Canada by non-residents	b	Business or property	9-11	Basic rules
				12-17	Inclusions
		c	Capital gains and losses	18-21	Deductions
E	Computation of tax	d	Other income	22-25	Ceasing to carry on business
E.1	Minimum tax	e	Other deductions	26-37	Special cases
F	Special rules	f	Rules relating to computation of income	67	General limitation
G	Deferred and other special income arrangements			67.1	Meals and entertainment
		g	Amounts not included in income	67.2-67.4	Automobiles
H	Exemptions	h	Cdn. corporations and shareholders	67.5	Illegal payments
I	Returns, Assessments, payments, appeals			68	Allocation of price
		i	Shareholders of non-resident corporations	69	Inadequate consideration
J	Appeals to the courts			70-72	Death
		j	Partnerships	73-75.1	Attribution
		k	Trusts	76	Security in satisfaction of income debt
				77	Bond conversion
				78	Unpaid amounts
				79-79.1	Foreclosure
				80-80.04	Settlement of debt
				80.1	Expropriation re foreign property
				80.2	Reimbursement re Crown resource propeerty
				80.3	Drought-induced sale of livestock
				80.4-80.5	Deemed interest

Subdivision b of Division B of Part I of the Act contains the primary rules for the computation of income from property. Like the rules for business income discussed in Chapter 4, most of what will be covered will be found in sections 9 through 21.

Some of the more important provisions are as follows:

Sec. 9 Income (loss) for a taxation year from a property is the profit (loss) from that property for the year.

Sec. 12 Income inclusions

Sec. 13 Rules related to capital cost allowance

Sec. 15 Rules for shareholder benefits

Sec. 18 Limitations on the deductibility of expenses

Sec. 20 Deductions permitted

In addition, Subdivision f of Division B also provides some rules that are relevant to the computation of property income. For example, the attribution rules in sections 74.1 to 74.5 determine who is to report the property income received by a particular person. In addition, section 80.4 calculates the amount of the deemed interest benefit to be reported in section 15 by an individual who received a loan by virtue of their shareholding.

I. INCLUSIONS

A. Interest Income

[ITA: 12(1)(c), (3), (4), (11); 16(1); 20(14), (21); 146.1; IT-396R]

1. The meaning of interest

The term "interest" is not defined in the Act. The Supreme Court of Canada has defined interest to be "the return or consideration or compensation for the use or retention by one person of a sum of money, belonging to, in a colloquial sense, or owed to, another." This definition has been adopted by the Canada Revenue Agency (CRA) [IT-396R, par. 12]. It is unclear in many situations whether an amount paid or payable is in the nature of interest or, as in the case of a discount on a bond, is something else. Partly in order to clarify the issue and to forestall taxpayers from converting amounts from interest to capital, provisions have been legislated in the Act and the Regulations deeming amounts to be interest and requiring them to be brought into income at specified intervals.

2. Method of reporting income

In effect, the primary method for computing interest on a "debt obligation" is the annual accrual method. The requirement to use this method is found in subsection 12(3) for corporations, partnerships and certain trusts and in subsection 12(4) for individuals. The term "debt obligation" is not defined in the Act, although the term is used in the definition of an "investment contract" [par. 12(11)(a)]. The CRA indicates that "the term 'debt obligation' is considered to include, for example, bank accounts, term deposits, guaranteed investment certificates, Canada Savings Bonds, mortgages, corporate bonds and loans" [IT-396R, par. 19]. Thus, the annual accrual method would appear to be required for most common sources of interest income. However, when interest is received, it must be included in income to the extent that the interest has not been included previously by the accrual method [par. 12(1)(c)]. As a result, it is not possible to defer the recognition of, for example, compounding interest by using the cash method to report that interest only when it is received. Therefore, there may be a disadvantage to a compounding-interest debt security, because interest must be accrued and reported annually such that tax is levied in a year when no payment of interest is actually made.

3. Accrual rules for individuals

Subsection 12(4) requires that individuals holding an interest in an investment contract[b] include in income, on every anniversary of that contract, any interest accrued to that day, to the extent that it has not previously been included in income. Paragraph 12(11)(*a*) defines an "investment contract" as any debt obligation other than a salary deferral arrangement, various types of income-based debt, certain government-sponsored debt for small businesses and prescribed contracts (of which there are none at the present). "Anniversary day" is defined as the day that is one year after the day before the date of issue and every successive one year interval, unless the contract is disposed of before such a day [par. 12(11)(*b*)].

Example Problem

Ms. N. Vestor purchased a $1,000 face value bond on January 2, 2005, for $1,000. The bond was issued on the same date, January 2, 2005. Interest is payable at 8% compounded semi-annually on uncashed coupons on each of June 30 and December 31 at the investor's option.

— REQUIRED

(A) If Ms. Vestor does not exercise her option to receive interest, when would she first have to include an amount in income?

(B) What would be the result if she exercised her option on December 31 for interest payable on both June 30 and December 31, 2005?

— SOLUTION

(A) The first "anniversary day" would be January 1, 2006, which is the day that is one year after the day before (January 1, 2005) the date of issue (January 2, 2005) [ssec. 12(11)]. As a result, $81.61 would be required to be included in income in 2006 [ssec. 12(4)]. The inclusion was computed as follows:

$$\$1,000.00 \times .04 \times {}^{180}/_{181} = \quad \$39.78$$
$$\$1,039.78 \times .04 \qquad\qquad = \quad \underline{\quad 41.59}$$
$$\$81.37$$
$$\$1,081.37 \times .04 \times {}^{1}/_{181} = \quad \underline{\quad .24}$$

Total accrual to
January 1, 2006 . . . . $81.61

(B) The $81.37, received on December 31, 2005, would be included in income to the extent it had not previously been included in income [par. 12(1)(*c*)]. Thus, only $0.24 (i.e., $81.61 − $81.37) would be included in income in 2006. Interest is included to the extent that it was not otherwise included in computing the taxpayer's income for the taxation year or any previous taxation year [ssec. 12(4)].

---

[b] Acquired or materially altered after 1989.

4. Other interest income provisions

Interest that is accrued to the date of transfer on bonds sold or otherwise transferred is brought into the income of the transferor [par. 20(14)(*a*)]. For example, a bond earning 9% interest per annum paid annually is purchased for face value of $1,000 and sold for $1,045 mid-way through the year. The excess of $45 over cost reflects interest for a half year and must be included in full. It is not a capital gain. Note that paragraph 20(14)(*b*) allows the recipient (transferee) of the bonds to deduct an amount equal to that included in the income of the transferor.

Where a loan is made at a discount, but repayable at par, or is made at par, but repayable at a premium, the question arises as to whether the discount or premium is interest or a capital gain. Here, paragraph 12(1)(*c*) must be read together with subsection 16(1), which states that where a payment can reasonably be regarded as being in part a payment of interest and in part a payment of capital, the part that can reasonably be regarded as interest is to be included in the income of the recipient. In making the distinction, a number of factors must be considered. For example, if no interest is charged, a discount or a premium may be considered in the nature of interest as is the case with Treasury Bills which do not bear interest but are issued at a discount. Also, where the interest rate is low and a substantial bonus payment is made, the bonus may well be considered as additional interest. Excepted from the rule in subsection 16(1) is an annuity payment [ssec. 16(4)]. An annuity contract, by its nature, pays an annual amount which is a blend of capital paid for the annuity and interest on that capital. The taxation of annuities is discussed in a later chapter.

There is not necessarily an interest component in all payments of this nature. A taxpayer need not charge interest in such a transaction. If the property is sold at fair market value, no interest component in the payments will be assumed. On the other hand, the provision in subsection 16(1) will apply to the sale of property if the contractual price, in total, exceeds the fair market value of the property.[(c)]

Interest on a scholarship trust fund is not taxable to a parent or grandparent who establishes the fund under the registered education savings plan (RESP) legislation in section 146.1.[(d)] This provision, which is discussed in more detail in Chapter 9, shelters the accumulated interest such that no tax is paid on it until it is paid out for the benefit of the child. At that time, if it arises, the interest is considered to be the income of the recipient child.

[(c)] This was the situation in the case of *Groulx v. M.N.R.*, (S.C.C.) 67 DTC 5284.

[(d)] Interest on scholarship trust funds has had an interesting history. The CRA, initially, took the position in an Interpretation Bulletin that such interest credited to a taxpayer's account with the trust would be considered annual interest income of the contributing taxpayer. However, in some of these trusts the interest cannot be withdrawn, but is used to provide scholarships for the taxpayer's children if they qualify under the terms of the trust. If the children do not qualify, the interest is used to provide scholarships for other people's children and the original capital contributed is returned. This position was appealed by the taxpayer in the case of *The Queen v. Quinn*, (F.C.T.D.) 73 DTC 5215. The court held that no taxpayer should be required to pay tax on money he had not received beneficially or had not the right to receive and might never, in fact, receive. This situation illustrates the fact that a departmental position, even if it is published as an Interpretation Bulletin, can be successfully challenged by the taxpayer, notwithstanding the weight that might be given to such administrative policy and interpretation by the courts as reiterated by the Federal Court of Appeal in *The Queen v. Royal Trust Corporation of Canada*, 83 DTC 5172 at page 5177.

B. Payments Based on Production or Use

[ITA: 12(1)(g); IT-462]

Concept of the provision

Any amount received that is dependent on the use of or production from property is taxed as income [par. 12(1)(g)]. Despite the clarity of the provision, it has been the subject of many appeals because ordinary instalment payments of principal which are not taxed as income may not be substantially different from payments based on production or use which are taxed.[(e)] Also, the distinction between a receipt of income or a receipt of capital has some bearing in this area. Payments that may be expressed as instalments of the sale price of property, but are actually payments depending on the use of or production from that property are taxed under paragraph 12(1)(g), although they may appear to be capital in nature. In certain circumstances, therefore, payments that would otherwise be considered capital and given capital gains treatment are brought into income and fully taxed. Furthermore, property is broadly defined [ssec. 248(1)] as including not only real and personal property, but also intangible property such as patents, franchises and rights of all kinds.

Example Problem

The appellant, a farmer, entered into an agreement with the Department of Highways of Alberta under which she granted the Department the right to enter upon her land for the purpose of taking clay for use in the construction of a highway. Employees of the Department removed the crop growing on the land designated in the agreement, removed the topsoil from the area, removed the quantity of clay subsoil required for highway construction, replaced the topsoil and levelled off the area. Pursuant to the agreement, the appellant received compensation of $2,271 in full settlement of "general damages, loss of crop, cost of restoring areas and reduction of yields." The Minister, relying on subsection 9(1) and paragraph 12(1)(g), added the $2,271 to the appellant's declared income. The appellant objected.

— REQUIRED

Decide this case on the basis of whether the receipt of $2,271 can be considered business or property income under either or both of the sections cited by the Minister.

— SOLUTION [see *Randle v. M.N.R.*, (T.A.B.) 65 DTC 507]

Consider first whether the receipt was one of business or property income under subsection 9(1). At best the situation involved an adventure in the nature of trade which is part of the definition of the word business [ssec. 248(1)], thereby making the receipt part of business income. The receipt was not like normal income from property in the nature of dividends, interest, rents or royalties and there is little to connect the payment to business activity. There was no intention either of a primary or secondary nature to make a profit from a business operation in this situation. The receipt was more like a reimbursement for a capital item. The relation of the transaction to farming is fairly remote except for the compensation for current crops. The nature of the asset involved is more like fixed capital in land than working capital in inventory except, again, for the current crop. Furthermore, it is unlikely that this was a frequent transaction, indicating a non-business income receipt. Finally, damages for loss of earnings capacity, as this seemed to be, are not income, but are generally regarded as a capital receipt.

[(e)] Cases under this provision can be classified by the type of property sold. Oil and gas rights were an issue in the case of *Ross v. M.N.R.*, (Ex. Ct.) 50 DTC 775. Timber was the subject of the cases of *Mouat v. M.N.R.*, (T.A.B.) 58 DTC 694; *Hoffman v. M.N.R.*, (T.A.B.) 65 DTC 617 and *The Queen v. Mel-Bar Ranches Ltd.*, (F.C.T.D.) 89 DTC 5189. Gravel and rock were sold in the cases of *Pallet v. M.N.R.*, (T.A.B.) 59 DTC 230 and *M.N.R. v. Lamon*, (Ex. Ct.) 63 DTC 1039. The rights to books and manuals were at issue in *Gingras v. M.N.R.*, (Ex. Ct.) 63 DTC 1142 and *LaRue v. M.N.R.*, (T.A.B.) 67 DTC 553, and the sale of equipment was considered in *R. C. Huffman Construction Co. Ltd. v. M.N.R.*, (T.A.B.) 65 DTC 597. A payment for the use of patents was considered in *Porta-Test Systems Ltd. v. The Queen*, (F.C.T.D.) 80 DTC 6046. Finally, the sale of a franchise was the subject of *M.N.R. v. Waintown Gas and Oil Co. Ltd.*, (S.C.C.) 52 DTC 1138.

The exception for sales of agricultural land in paragraph 12(1)(g) does not apply to mineral and oil rights on the land. This was the situation in the case of *Ade v. M.N.R.*, (T.A.B.) 67 DTC 23.

Next, consider whether the payment was dependent on production or use [par. 12(1)(g)]. No relation between the amount received and the amount of clay taken is indicated. There was no continuing activity in the sale of clay which might indicate more clearly a payment dependent on production or use. Finally, the agreement indicated that the appellant did not sell the clay or the land, but received money in compensation for damages sustained.

It might be concluded, therefore, that most of the money was compensation for the loss of a portion of a capital asset and for restoring it to its former state of production. However, the amount paid for the current crop in the designated area as part of the appellant's inventory should be included in income.

C. Dividends from Corporations Resident in Canada

[ITA: 12(1)(j); 82(1); 121]

Gross-up and tax credit procedure

Dividends from corporations resident in Canada are to be included in income [par. 12(1)(j)]. The amount to be included in income is set out in subsection 82(1) which is part of Subdivision h. The provision stipulates that taxable dividends received in the year from Canadian corporations must be included in income and that, where the taxpayer is an individual, a further amount of one-quarter of the taxable dividends must also be added to income. Then, an individual pays tax on $5/4$ of an actual dividend received. This is part of a scheme of integration (to be discussed in detail in Chapter 12) which provides relief from the potential double taxation of dividends for certain corporations, once at the level of the corporation when its income is taxed and once at the level of the shareholder when dividends received are taxed.

The one-quarter gross-up when added to the actual dividend received is designed to place the individual shareholder in approximately the same income position that the corporation was in before it paid corporate tax on its income. That is, the grossed-up dividend of $5/4$ of the actual dividend is an approximation of the earnings the corporation must generate before tax on its income for it to be able to pay the actual dividend from after-tax income. (See Exhibit 12-1.) Thus, the individual shareholder's income [par. 12(1)(j)] would include the grossed-up dividend.

Note that the taxpayer may elect to include the dividends of his or her spouse in his or her own income following the same rules as for his or her own dividends [ssec. 82(3)]. This provision will be discussed fully in Chapter 10.

Chapter 10 will consider the computation of tax on individuals under Division E, Subdivision a. Since the grossed-up dividend is included in the individual's income, it will be subject to tax in full at the individual's tax rate which is dependent on the level of his or her income. However, section 121 provides for a dividend tax credit which effectively reduces the tax on dividends paid to the individual. This federal tax credit (equal to $2/3$ of the dividend gross-up, $13^1/3$% of the grossed-up dividend or $16^2/3$% of the dividend paid, all of which are mathematically equal) together with a provincial dividend tax credit approximates the tax that the corporation has paid on the shareholder's behalf. Thus, the shareholder computes his or her tax on the grossed-up dividend (which approximates the corporation's pre-tax earnings). Then the individual shareholder receives the dividend tax credit to reduce that computed tax on the grossed-up dividend (by an amount which approximates the payment of tax the corporation has already made on that pre-tax profit). The result is the elimination of most or all of the potential double taxation. (See Exhibit 12-1.) Also, the combined federal and provincial dividend tax credit approximates the dividend gross-up. For example, if a $100 dividend is received, the gross-up is $25 (25%). The combined federal and provincial dividend tax credit will be approximately $25 ($\frac{2}{3}$ of gross-up federal and $\frac{1}{3}$ provincial).

Note that the dividend gross-up and tax credit procedure applies to individual shareholders on dividends received from a corporation resident in Canada. The procedure does not apply to corporate shareholders which benefit from other provisions used to mitigate potential double taxation, as discussed in Chapter 11. Also, the procedure does not apply to dividends received by an individual from corporations not resident in Canada. In this case, the individual must include the amount of the dividend with no gross-up in income and no dividend tax credit is available.

As an example of the effect of the dividend treatment for individuals, consider two individuals, one paying federal tax at a marginal rate of 16% and the other paying federal tax at the top marginal rate of 29%. Assume that both individuals live in a province with a tax on income rate of 10% and 17%, respectively. Also assume that the combined federal and provincial dividend tax credit is equal to the gross-up. Each shareholder receives a dividend of $300 from a Canadian security and the following computation would be made:

		26%	46%
Taxpayer's marginal tax rate (federal and provincial)		26%	46%
Dividend	(A)	$300.00	$300.00
Add: gross-up of 25% of dividend		75.00	75.00
Grossed-up dividend subject to tax		$375.00	$375.00
Tax on grossed-up dividend at marginal tax rate		$ 97.50	$172.50
Less: federal and provincial dividend tax credit (equal to the gross-up)		(75.00)	(75.00)
Net tax payable	(B)	$ 22.50	$ 97.50
After-tax dividend [(A) − (B)]		$277.50	$202.50

Example Problem

I.M.A. Plunger faces a 12% provincial tax on income and a federal tax rate of 22% at the margin. On an investment of $5,000 in the shares of a Canadian corporation, he receives $362.50 of taxable dividends for a yield of 7.25%. He is considering the alternative of investing his funds in a bond paying 9%. Assume that the combined federal and provincial dividend tax credit is equal to the gross-up.

— REQUIRED

Compute the after-tax return from the alternative investments to compare their desirability.

— SOLUTION

(A) Dividend

Dividend	$362.50
Add: gross-up of 25% of dividend	90.63
Grossed-up dividend subject to tax	$453.13
Tax on grossed-up dividend @ 34% (ie., 22% + 12%)	$154.06
Less: dividend tax credit (federal and provincial)	(90.63)
Net tax payable	$ 63.43
After-tax dividend ($362.50 − $63.43)	$299.07

(B) Interest

Interest income (9% of $5,000) $450.00

Tax payable @ 34% $153.00

After-tax interest ($450.00 − $153.00) $297.00

— NOTE TO SOLUTION

Although the pre-tax dividend yield of 7.25% is lower than the pre-tax interest yield of 9%, the after-tax return from the dividend of $299.07 or 5.98% of the investment is greater than the after-tax return from the interest of $297.00 or 5.94% of the $5,000 invested. Furthermore, it should be remembered that there may be a greater potential for a return from capital gains on the shares compared to the bond. This would influence the decision when the after-tax dividend yield is lower than the after-tax interest yield.

D.   Shareholder Benefits and Loans

[ITA: 15(1)–(2.1), (9); 20(1)(*j*); 69(4); 80.4; 80.5; IT-119R4; IT-432R2; IT-533]

1.   Benefit conferred on shareholder[(f)]

The provisions in subsection 15(1) are designed to prevent the distribution of part of the accumulated surplus of a corporation (other than by way of taxable dividends) to shareholders while the corporation is a going concern. Paragraphs (*a*) to (*d*) provide exceptions to the broad application of subsection 15(1) because these particular situations are dealt with elsewhere in the Act, notably in the provision dealing with the taxation of dividends and options. In all other cases, subsection 15(1) applies to require an amount to be included in income, but the amount is not deemed to be a dividend and, therefore, is not eligible for the dividend tax credit. This provision was applied in the case of *No. 403 v. M.N.R.*, (T.A.B.) 57 DTC 120 in which a controlling shareholder purchased a house from his company at $38,000 when it had been purchased a year earlier by the company for $45,000. The $7,000 benefit to the shareholder was included in his income from property. In this situation, the corporation will be considered to have received proceeds equal to its fair market value at the time of the sale to the shareholder. If this sale triggers any income, it must be included by the corporation [ssec. 69(4)]. In this particular case, if the corporation's cost was $45,000, there would have been no income with proceeds of $45,000.

Where a loan to a shareholder is forgiven by a corporation, that is, the shareholder is not required to repay all or some part of the principal amount of the loan, subsection 15(1.2) indicates that the amount of the principal forgiven must be included in the shareholder's income under subsection 15(1).

Example Problem

Smartmoney Manufacturing Ltd. built a 21-room house for its principal shareholder-officer on a country property owned by him. The company expensed the costs as promotion expenses on the basis that he would use the property to entertain distributors of the company's products to ensure continuing outlets for the company's products.

[(f)] For a more detailed discussion of subsection 15(1), see Robert E. Beam and Stanley N. Laiken, "Benefits under Subsection 15(1)," Personal Tax Planning Feature (1994), Vol. 42, No. 2, *Canadian Tax Journal*, pp. 479–511.

— REQUIRED

Consider the tax consequences to the individual and the company in this case.

— SOLUTION

Subsection 15(1) would include the value of the house plus the GST, if any, on that value in the income of the shareholder since it represents a benefit conferred on the shareholder. Since the company does not own the property on which the house was built and it has expensed the cost on its books, it appears clear that the shareholder has received a taxable benefit.

The company would ordinarily be allowed to deduct an expenditure made or incurred to produce income. In this case, the house would be a capital asset subject to the capital cost allowance system to the extent that some part of the house was used for business purposes. However, if the house is considered to be a lodge, in any way, subparagraph 18(1)(*l*)(i) would prohibit the corporation from deducting any expense or outlay considered for the use or maintenance of that property.

2. Shareholder loans

(a) *Principal*

Normally, when funds are borrowed, the principal amount of the debt, that is, the amount borrowed, is not considered to be income and the amount of the debt repaid is not deductible. Incurring and repaying the debt is a capital transaction. However, in the case of a shareholder, particularly a significant shareholder who can influence the decisions of the corporation, it would be easy to escape tax on the distribution of corporate surplus, if it were not for the rules in subsection 15(2). In the absence of subsection 15(2), a shareholder could borrow funds from the corporation, instead of receiving taxable salary, interest or dividends from the corporation, and never repay these funds.

The basic rule for the taxation of shareholder loans is contained in subsection 15(2). The exceptions to the basic rule, as discussed below, are found in subsections 15(2.2) to (2.6).

Loans and other forms of indebtedness to shareholders (other than corporate shareholders) or to persons not at arm's length with the shareholder (i.e., connected with a shareholder [ssec. 15(2.1)]) are required to be included in income of the borrower for the year in which the loan was made. In the case of *The Queen v. Silden*, 93 DTC 5362, the Federal Court of Appeal confirmed that subsection 15(2) must be applied where a loan is made to a shareholder. The capacity in which the individual receives the loan, i.e., as a shareholder or as an employee, is not relevant to the application of subsection 15(2), but maybe relevant for certain specific exceptions. Related persons [sec. 251], discussed in the next segment of this chapter, do not deal with each other at arm's length.

(b) *Exceptions*

There are two general exceptions to the application of subsection 15(2). The first, in subsection 15(2.2), excepts indebtedness between non-resident persons. The second, in subsection 15(2.3), excepts debt that arises in the ordinary course of the lender's business, as long as *bona fide* arrangements are made at the time the loan is made for repayment within a reasonable time. This exception protects a borrower who happens to be a shareholder of, for example, a bank at which he or she borrowed.

Subsection 15(2.4) provides specific exceptions for four types of loans, for which the principal amount can be excluded from a shareholder's income if received:

(a) a loan made by the corporation to a shareholder who is, also, an employee, but not a specified employee (defined in subsection 248(1), very generally, as an employee who, together with non-arm's length persons, owns at least 10% of the shares of any class of a corporation or who does not deal at arm's length with the corporation); or

(b) a loan made by the corporation to a shareholder who is, also, an employee to assist him or her to acquire:

(i) a home for his or her own occupation (even if the loan is made to the employee's spouse) [par. 15(2.4)(*b*)],

(ii) previously unissued shares of the corporation purchased directly from the corporation [par. 15(2.4)(*c*)], or

(iii) a motor vehicle (as defined in subsection 248(1)) to be used in the performance of his or her duties of employment [par. 15(2.4)(*d*)].

For the principal amount of the loan to be excluded, there are two additional conditions. The first condition requires that the loan arise because of the employee's employment (often referred to, using the Latin, *qua* employee) and not because of his or her shareholdings (*qua* shareholder) [par. 15(2.4)(*e*)]. The second condition requires that *bona fide* arrangements be made at the time of the loan for repayment within a reasonable period of time [par. 15(2.4)(*f*)]. Paragraph 12 of IT-119R4 suggests that normal commercial practice is used as the basis for *bona fide* arrangements. For example, a 25-year amortization period would be appropriate for a housing loan and the security of a mortgage on the property should be taken for large loans.

Thus, for subsection 15(2) to apply, the recipient of the loan must be a shareholder. Note that all of the exceptions in subsection 15(2.4) require that the recipient also be an employee. Therefore, to exclude the principal amount of the loan under all four of the exceptions in subsection 15(2.4), the recipient must be an employee. Paragraph 15(2.4)(*e*) imposes an employee-capacity condition on these exceptions which results in subsection 15(2) not being applicable if the other conditions of subsection 15(2.4) are met. That is, the loan must be received by the employee in his or her capacity as an employee, in addition to meeting the other conditions, for the loan to be excluded.

Subsection 15(2.6) excludes a loan that is fully repaid within one year of the end of the taxation year of the lender in which it was made if the repayment is not part of a series of loans and repayments.

(c) *Deduction of Repayment*

Where an amount has been included in income for a preceding year [ssec. 15(2)], the taxpayer is permitted to deduct any repayment of the loan from his or her income in the year of repayment provided the repayment was not part of a series of loans and repayments [par. 20(1)(*j*)]. While the CRA states in IT-119R4 paragraph 29 that whether a repayment is part of such a series is a question of fact, it also states that a shareholder's loan account with several loan and repayment transactions will give rise to a series unless there is clear evidence otherwise.

The CRA also states in IT-119R4 that, notwithstanding that there is a series of loans and repayments, they will administratively allow a deduction for a decrease in the loan account, unless the decrease is temporary [par. 20(1)(j)]. Paragraph 36 provides a numerical example of the application of the CRA's policy on how the net decrease should be calculated, based on a FIFO allocation of repayments of the loan balance. However, the calculation of both the inclusion in income under subsection 15(2) and the deduction under paragraph 20(1)(j) are based on administrative practice only. However, since this is a particularly tricky area in practice, the Bulletin should be studied carefully.

(d) *Imputed Interest Benefit*

Where the principal amount of the loan is not included in income because it meets one of the exclusion conditions in subsection 15(2), section 80.4 dealing with imputed interest on loans may apply. The Act requires any person who received a loan or otherwise incurred a debt by virtue of:

- an individual's employment or intended employment (as discussed in Chapter 3),

- shareholdings in a corporation, or

- a shareholding of a person who does not deal at arm's length with a shareholder,

to include in his or her income an amount in respect of interest on low-interest or interest-free loans. It is always a question of fact whether a person will receive a benefit under this section by virtue of his or her employment through subsection 6(9) or by virtue of his or her shareholdings through subsection 15(9).

Subsection 80.4(1) imputes an interest benefit as a consequence of a previous, a current or an intended office or employment. Subsection 80.4(2) imputes an interest benefit by virtue of the taxpayer's shareholdings in the lending corporation or a related corporation. A taxpayer may fall into either category, subsection 80.4(1) or (2), depending on the facts under which the loan was granted. Therefore, a decision will have to be made as to the source of this benefit based on the facts of the situation.[g]

If the loan is a "home purchase loan" [par. 80.4(7)(a)] or a "home relocation loan" [ssec. 248(1)], the definitions of which are applicable only to loans by virtue of employment, the imputed interest benefit is calculated for each quarter[h] as the lesser of [ssec. 80.4(4)]:

(a) the prescribed rate in effect at the time the loan was received; and

(b) the prescribed rate (changed on a quarterly basis) in effect during that quarter.

However, subsection 80.4(6) will deem a new loan to have been received every five years on longer-term home purchase or relocation loans. This deemed disposition will have the effect of changing the rate of imputed interest at least every five years. Finally, the

---

[g] For a more detailed analysis of this and other issues arising in the interpretation of subsection 15(2), see Robert E. Beam and Stanley N. Laiken, "The 'Capacity' Issue in Corporate Transactions with Shareholders," Personal Tax Planning Feature (1992), Vol. 40, No. 2, *Canadian Tax Journal*, pp. 412–439.

[h] The quarter-by-quarter method is used by the CRA for the "lesser of" calculation and may result in a slightly smaller income inclusion than the traditional annual calculation.

interest benefit is the amount of imputed interest in excess of the interest actually paid in the year or within 30 days after the end of the taxation year on the loan.

Note that a home relocation loan is eligible for a deduction under certain specific rules in paragraph 110(1)(*j*) in Division C which will be explained more fully in Chapter 10.

Subsection 80.4(2) imputes an interest benefit to a person who receives a loan by virtue of shareholdings rather than as a consequence of employment. The recipient of the loan may include a shareholder or a person not at arm's length with a shareholder of a corporation who receives a loan from, or incurs a debt to, the corporation or a related corporation. Since the special provisions for a home purchase loan or a home relocation loan [ssec. 80.4(4)] refer only to a loan received by virtue of an office or employment, these provisions cannot apply where the loan is received by virtue of shareholdings. In this case, the individual must include in income the amount by which interest on the loan computed at the prescribed rate [Reg. 4300(7)] tied to the treasury bill rate exceeds the interest actually paid in the year or within 30 days after the end of the taxation year on such a loan.

Subsection 80.4(3) provides two additional exceptions to the application of the imputed interest rules. First, paragraph 80.4(3)(*a*) provides that a benefit will not arise where the rate of interest payable is equal to or greater than the rate of interest that would have been agreed upon in an arm's length transaction at the time the obligation was incurred. Second, paragraph 80.4(3)(*b*) exempts a loan where the principal amount of the loan has already been included in the income of a person from imputed interest [ssecs. 80.4(1) and (2)].

Receiving a loan by virtue of shareholding and receiving a deemed interest benefit under subsection 80.4(2) is not as common as receiving a loan by virtue of employment and receiving a deemed interest benefit under subsection 80.4(1). This is the case since receiving a loan by virtue of shareholding may result in the loan principal being included in income under subsection 15(2). However if an individual receives a loan by virtue of shareholding and repays it within the time period required to avoid including the principal in income, then there will be a deemed interest benefit calculated under subsection 80.4(2) and included in income.

Section 80.5 deems the interest benefit [sec. 80.4] to be interest paid or payable in the year pursuant to a legal obligation for purposes of paragraphs 20(1)(*c*) and 8(1)(*j*) as long as the provisions of these two paragraphs are met. Thus, an offsetting deduction may be available for interest deemed to have been paid, depending on the use of the borrowed funds [sec. 80.5].

(e) *Application of Shareholder Loan Rules*

Exhibit 6-1 provides a flow chart of the shareholder loan rules in sections 15 and 80.4 and the consequences of their application.

EXHIBIT 6-1
Shareholder Loans
Section 15 and Section 80.4

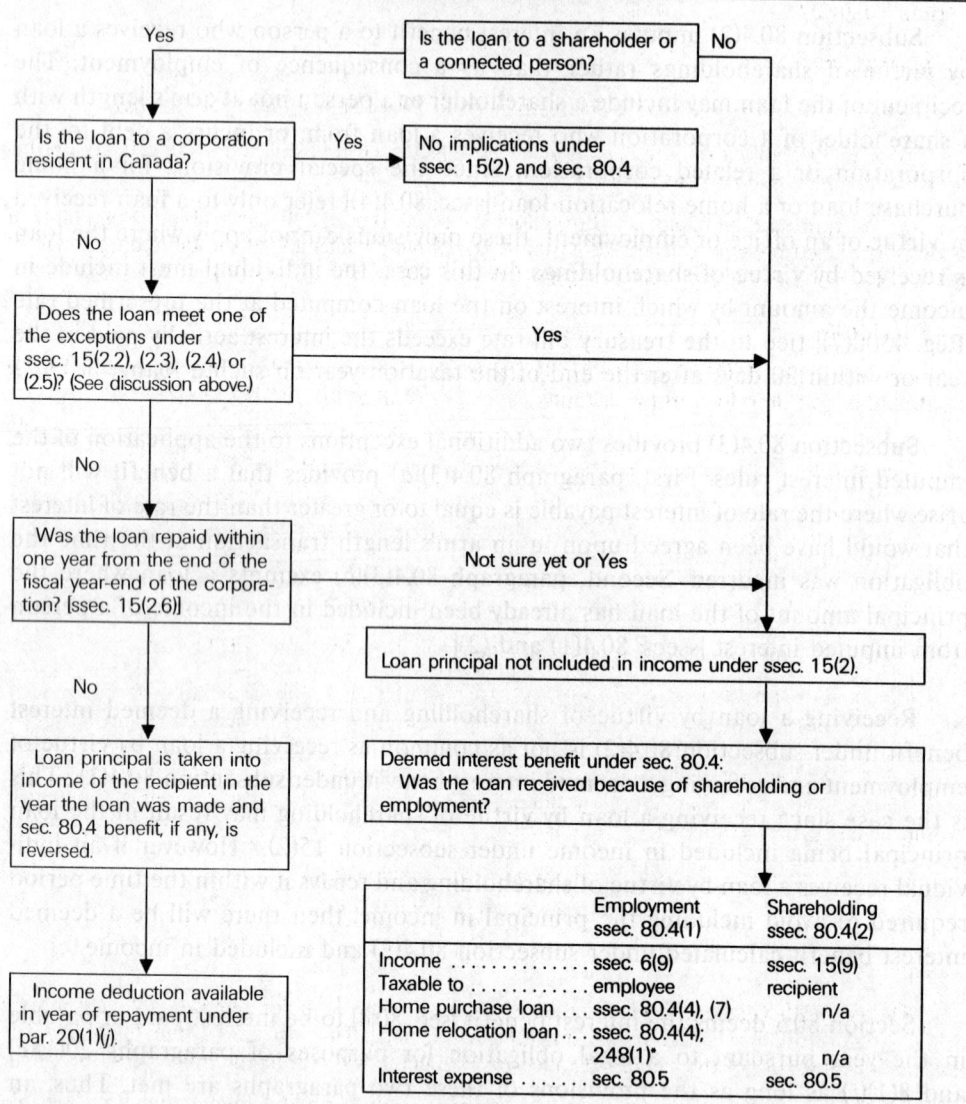

* Eligible for a deduction in Division C [par. 110(1)(*j*)].

Example Problem

Mr. I. M. Portly owns all the outstanding shares of Run for Your Life Limited, a health and fitness club. He is the company president. On July 1, 2005, the company made a loan to Mr. Portly of $19,500 which he used to acquire an automobile at fair market value. All of the other six employees of the corporation are eligible to receive this type of loan on the same terms and four have, in fact, taken advantage of the opportunity. He requires the automobile to carry out his business duties for the company. (He drives behind members of the club in case of an emergency while they are jogging.) The loan is repayable in two equal annual instalments starting July 2006 without interest.

— REQUIRED

(A) Does Mr. Portly receive a taxable benefit in 2005? Substantiate your answer.

(B) Can the company's income position be affected either positively or negatively by this loan? Again, substantiate your answer.

Assume a prescribed rate of 4% throughout the relevant period in this problem. For a table of actual prescribed rates set out in Regulation 4301(1), see Chapter 14, or the table on p. xxviii of the CCH Edition of the CANADIAN INCOME TAX ACT. Ignore the effects of the leap year.

— SOLUTION

(A) Subsection 15(2) applies to Mr. Portly since he is a shareholder, but subsection 15(2.4) permits the loan described to be exempted from inclusion in income because:

(i) the loan was to assist a shareholder/employee to purchase a motor vehicle to be used by him in the performance of the duties of his office [par. 15(2.4)(*d*)];

(ii) the loan was received because of his employment and not because of his shareholdings, since all employees were eligible for this type of loan and four have received one [par. 15(2.4)(*e*)];

(iii) *bona fide* repayment arrangements were made; and

(iv) repayment was scheduled within a reasonable time [par. 15(2.4)(*f*)].

However, the fact that this was an interest-free loan results in the application of section 80.4. Since Mr. Portly is probably acting in his capacity as an employee, he will be deemed to have received a benefit equal to the unpaid interest on the loan calculated at the prescribed rate in effect during the period in the year that the loan was outstanding [ssec. 80.4(1)]. The prescribed rate, for this purpose, is given as 4% for all relevant quarters. Therefore, the amount of the benefit would be calculated as follows:

$$4\% \text{ of } \$19,500 \times {}^{92}\!/_{365} = \$ \ 196.60$$
$$4\% \text{ of } \ \ 19,500 \times {}^{92}\!/_{365} = \ \ \ \underline{\ \ \ 196.60}$$
$$\$ \ 393.20$$

The $393.20 will be considered interest paid on a car loan for purposes of determining Mr. Portly's deduction under paragraph 8(1)(*j*) [sec. 80.5]. This will allow him to deduct the business-use portion of the interest deemed to have been paid within the limits of section 67.2.

(B) From the company's position, the foregone interest on the loan is not an allowable deduction. In fact, if the loan had been for more than the fair market value of the car and the car was bought from the company, interest income could be imputed to the company [ssec. 16(1)]. However, there is no need to charge interest in a *bona fide* loan and no interest will be imputed in a fair market value transaction.

If the company borrowed the funds which it loaned to Mr. Portly, it would be able to deduct the interest it paid provided it was part of reasonable total remuneration to Mr. Portly as an employee. (See IT-533, paragraph 26.)

E. Income Attribution

[ITA: 56(4.1)–(5); 73(1); 74.1; 74.3; 74.4; 74.5; 248(5); 251; 252; IT-419R2; IT-510; IT-511R]

1. The reason for attribution rules

Progressive income tax rates applied to individuals provide an incentive to split income, particularly among family members. The highest rate of federal income tax, applied to taxable income in excess of $115,739 in 2005, is 29%. The lowest rate of federal income tax, applied to taxable income up to $35,595, is only 16%. If income-producing property can be acquired by family members in lower tax brackets, income tax can be saved. For example, if an individual who is taxable in the 29% federal income tax bracket earns an additional $50,000 on investments, the incremental federal tax is $14,500. If the same $50,000 of investment income is earned by another family member who has no other source of income, the $50,000 will attract about $7,560 of federal tax, resulting in a federal tax savings of about $6,940. When provincial tax is computed, the total tax savings will be even greater. Hence, the Act contains rules which attribute income from property (but not income from business) to an individual who may have transferred or loaned the property to split income. This is despite the fact that the property is legally owned by the transferee.

Attribution of capital gains on transfers or loans to a spouse is discussed in a subsequent chapter.

2. Transactions subject to income attribution

Attribution of income or loss from property (and, as will be seen in a subsequent chapter, capital gains and losses) will occur where an individual transfers or loans property to a spouse or common-law partner or to a person who becomes his or her spouse or common-law partner [sec. 74.1(1)].

Subsection 248(1) defines a "common-law partner" as a person who cohabits at that time in a conjugal relationship with the taxpayer and either

(a) has so cohabited with the taxpayer for a continuous period of at least one year, or

(b) would be the parent of a child of whom the taxpayer is a parent.

Where at any time the taxpayer and the person cohabit in a conjugal relationship, they are deemed to be cohabiting in a conjugal relationship unless they were not cohabiting at the particular time for a period of at least 90 days because of a breakdown of their conjugal relationship. This definition covers both common-law spouses and same-sex partners.

Attribution of income or loss from property, but usually not capital gains or losses, will, also, occur on a transfer or loan to a minor (i.e., under the age of 18) who is a non-arm's length person [secs. 251 and 252] (plus a niece or nephew) as interpreted in IT-419R2. Attribution continues until that person attains the age of 18 [ssec. 74.1(2)]. Both subsections pertain to direct or *indirect* transfers or loans to or *for the benefit of* the person. Thus, a transfer or loan to a trust in which the spouse or common-law partner or minor is a beneficiary will result in attribution [ssec. 74.3], as discussed in more detail in Chapter 18. Attribution means that the income or loss earned by the spouse or common-law partner or minor is considered to be the income or loss of the transferor during his or her lifetime as long as he or she is resident in Canada.

3. Related persons

As indicated above, the attribution rules apply to certain non-arm's length individuals. Paragraph 251(1)(*a*) deems related persons not to deal at arm's length with each other. Exhibit 6-2 attempts to present schematically all of the provisions in sections 251 and 252 defining related individuals, as well as the CRA's interpretations in IT-419R2. Related individuals are diagrammed in relation to a taxpayer (i.e., "you"). On the horizontal axis, do not attempt to make the individuals at the extreme outer limits (i.e., the second bullet) related to each other. They are only related to "you" in respect of this chart. Note that where the word "spouse" is used, it is intended to include the concept of a common-law partner, including a same-sex partner.

EXHIBIT 6-2
Schematic Diagram of Related Individuals

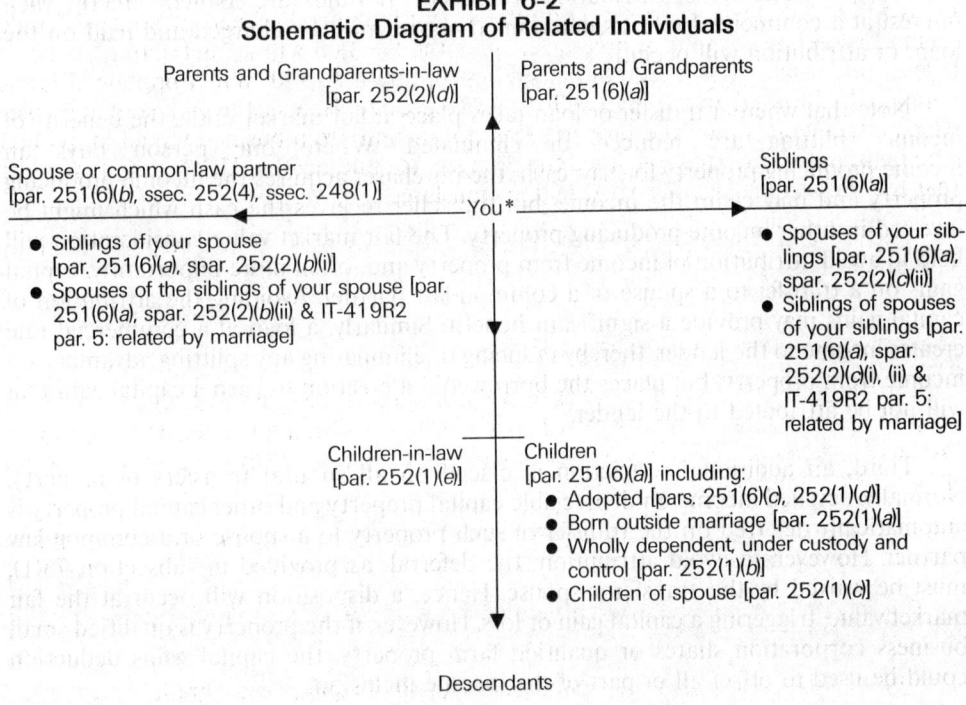

Parents and Grandparents-in-law [par. 252(2)(*d*)]

Parents and Grandparents [par. 251(6)(*a*)]

Spouse or common-law partner [par. 251(6)(*b*), ssec. 252(4), ssec. 248(1)]

You*

Siblings [par. 251(6)(*a*)]

- Siblings of your spouse [par. 251(6)(*a*), spar. 252(2)(*b*)(i)]
- Spouses of the siblings of your spouse [par. 251(6)(*a*), spar. 252(2)(*b*)(ii) & IT-419R2 par. 5: related by marriage]

- Spouses of your siblings [par. 251(6)(*a*), spar. 252(2)(*c*)(ii)]
- Siblings of spouses of your siblings [par. 251(6)(*a*), spar. 252(2)(*c*)(i), (ii) & IT-419R2 par. 5: related by marriage]

Children-in-law [par. 252(1)(*e*)]

Children [par. 251(6)(*a*)] including:
- Adopted [pars. 251(6)(*c*), 252(1)(*d*)]
- Born outside marriage [par. 252(1)(*a*)]
- Wholly dependent, under custody and control [par. 252(1)(*b*)]
- Children of spouse [par. 252(1)(*c*)]

Descendants

* Under the Act, an individual is deemed to be related to herself or himself where she or he owns shares in two or more corporations [par. 251(5)(*c*) and ssec. 256(1.5)]. Note, however, that an individual is more than likely not dealing at "arm's length" with herself or himself by virtue of the definition of this term [par. 251(1)(*b*)] which bases this type of relationship on the facts of the particular situation at a particular moment in time. Therefore, be careful which term is being used — "related" or "arm's length."

It should be noted that the word "transfer" (which is used continually throughout the attribution rules) is considered to include a sale, whether or not at fair market value, and a gift. Since it was held by the courts that a transfer did not include a loan,[i] genuine loans escaped the attribution rules, until the legislation was changed, effective May 23, 1985. Note that loans are now specifically subject to the attribution rules.

[i] See the case of *Oelbaum v. M.N.R.*, (Ex. Ct.) 68 DTC 5176, involving a loan to a spouse, and the case of *Dunkelman v. M.N.R.*, (Ex. Ct.) 59 DTC 1242, involving a loan to a trust for minors.

4. Avoiding income attributions

An exception to the application of these attribution rules is provided in section 74.5. This provision requires a number of very specific conditions to be fulfilled before the taxpayer will be exempted from the attribution rules. First, if the fair market value of the property transferred does not exceed the fair market value of the consideration received in return, that is, if the property is sold for its fair market value, then these attribution rules will not apply. Therefore, all gifts of income-earning property are subject to the attribution rules as are transfers for consideration which is less than the fair market value of the property transferred. Second, if the transferor takes back a debt, then interest that is at least equal to the lesser of the prescribed rate or an arm's length rate (to be referred to here as a "commercial" rate) must be charged. In addition, the interest must be paid within thirty days of the end of each and every year in which the debt was outstanding, or attribution will occur. If funds are loaned directly, then interest at a commercial rate, as determined above, must be charged and paid on the loan, or attribution will occur.

Note that where a transfer or loan takes place at fair market value, the benefits of income splitting are reduced or eliminated. Where one person buys an income-producing property for, say, cash, the purchaser acquires the income-producing property and may claim the income, but the seller receives the cash which might be invested in other income-producing property. The fair market value consideration will help to avoid attribution of income from property and, often more importantly, capital gains on a transfer to a spouse or a common-law partner. Avoiding the attribution of capital gains may provide a significant benefit. Similarly, a loan at a commercial rate creates income to the lender, thereby reducing or eliminating any splitting advantage on income from property, but places the borrower in a position to earn a capital gain that will not be attributed to the lender.

Third, an additional restriction is placed on all spousal transfers of property. Normally, accrued income on depreciable capital property and other capital property is automatically deferred on the transfer of such property to a spouse or a common-law partner. However, to avoid attribution, the deferral, as provided in subsection 73(1), must be waived by the transferor spouse. Hence, a disposition will occur at the fair market value, triggering a capital gain or loss. However, if the property is qualified small business corporation shares or qualified farm property, the capital gains deduction could be used to offset all or part of the income inclusion.

For example, consider the case of Spouse A, whose income is taxed in the top bracket and who owns a property worth $50,000 that produces $5,000 of income. If that property is sold for cash to Spouse B who has no other source of income and Spouse A elects to transfer the property at its fair market value [ssec. 73(1)], Spouse B will have the $5,000 of income from property. However, Spouse A will have the $50,000 in cash proceeds on the sale of the property. If that $50,000 is reinvested in Spouse A's hands, the income will attract tax at the top rate and the benefits of income splitting would be negated, unless the original property generated a large capital gain on its ultimate disposition by Spouse B. At that time, the capital gain would not be subject to attribution because the original transfer of the property took place for fair market value consideration.

Fourth, there is an exception to the attribution rules [ssec. 74.5(3)] which applies where spouses live separate and apart by reason of a breakdown of their marriage. Any income or loss that relates to the period of separation is excepted from attribution.

> **Summary**
> **Avoiding Income Attribution On Transferred Property**
> *Subsection 74.5(1)*
>   1. Fair market value consideration must be received by the vendor.
>   2. If part of the consideration is debt, then interest must be charged at the prescribed rate and always paid by January 30th.
>   3. If it is a transfer to a spouse or common-law partner, then they must elect out of the rollover in subsection 73(1).
> *Subsection 74.5(3)*
>   4. If the spouses or common-law partners are living separate and apart by reason of the breakdown of their relationship. (This exception applies to property income, but not capital gains, unless an election has been made.)

5. Anti-avoidance rules relating to attribution

A number of anti-avoidance rules are contained in these attribution provisions. The rule in subsection 74.1(3) prevents the refinancing of an old loan by the substitution of a commercial rate loan for a loan that would result in attribution under the rules [ssecs. 74.1(1) and (2)]. This rule applies to attribute income from property financed with the original loan or property substituted therefor.

An anti-avoidance rule is provided to prevent circumventing the attribution rules by the use of "back-to-back" loans and transfers [ssec. 74.5(6)]. The rule envisages a situation where property is deposited with a financial institution paying no interest with an agreement that the same amount as that deposited be loaned to the depositor's spouse at a nominal rate of interest, say, 2%. In this case, the use of the intermediary would be disregarded. The attribution rules will apply to include, in the income of the original transferor, the income earned by the property owned by the ultimate transferee. Of course, if such a back-to-back loan is made at a commercial rate or a back-to-back transfer is made for fair market value consideration, then no attribution will take place.

The avoidance of the attribution rules by the use of loan guarantees is prevented [ssec. 74.5(7)]. For example, instead of Spouse A lending income-producing property to Spouse B, Spouse A could guarantee a loan made by another person or a financial institution to Spouse B who would use the proceeds of the loan to buy income-producing property. Unless a commercial rate of interest is charged and paid on the loan to Spouse B, Spouse A will have to include the income from the property.

A general anti-avoidance rule is provided to prevent "artificial transactions" which would benefit from the application of the attribution rules [ssec. 74.5(11)]. In the past, taxpayers have devised transactions or a series of transactions known as "reverse attribution plans" to have income attributed to a low-income taxpayer. Therefore, if one of the main reasons for a loan or transfer is to reduce the amount of tax that would be paid, the attribution rules discussed will not apply in cases where such reverse attribution is attempted. Another example of such artificial attribution is given in paragraph 26 of IT-511R.

Both IT-510, paragraph 18, and IT-511R, paragraph 25, indicate that an individual can remunerate a spouse or a related minor for services provided in a business carried on by the payer as long as the conditions in paragraph 74.5(12)(*b*) are met. That paragraph requires that the amount paid must be deductible in determining the payer's business income (according to the general rules of deductibility discussed in Chapter 4) and included in the recipient's income. Payments under the child tax benefits program are excepted from the income attribution rule applicable on transfers or loans to minors [ssec. 74.1(2)]. As a result, the income attribution rules do not apply to income arising from child tax benefits transferred or loaned to the child.

Finally, section 74.4 generally prevents income splitting through the use of a corporation. This provision is discussed at greater length in Chapter 13.

6. Type of income subject to attribution

Note that the income attribution rules apply only to the transfer of property that results in income or loss from property rather than income or loss from business. This distinction was at issue in the case of *Lackie v. The Queen*, (F.C.A.) 79 DTC 5309 in which the taxpayer transferred a farm to his wife from which she sold gravel at an agreed price per ton. The amounts received were taxable as income [par. 12(1)(g)]. The CRA argued that this income was from property transferred by the taxpayer to his spouse and, therefore, was subject to the attribution rules and taxable as income in the hands of the taxpayer. On the other hand, the taxpayer contended that attribution was improper because the income was from business rather than property. The court held that the income was from property because the taxpayer's wife did not sell gravel as a business but granted a licence to work a gravel pit on her land. It was clear to the court that the amounts received were dependent on the use of property.

The term "property" includes substituted property, as defined in subsection 248(5), but does not include income earned on attributed income, often referred to as "second-generation" income. For example, if a $10,000 bond, bearing interest at 10% annually, is given to a spouse, the $1,000 of interest income received by the recipient of the bond is attributed to the transferor spouse. If the $1,000 is reinvested by the recipient spouse at, say, 10%, the $100 of interest earned on the reinvested interest is not attributed to the transferor spouse. The $100 is income earned on income, i.e., the $1,000, that has been attributed. Hence, the $100 is referred to as second-generation income.

7. Loans to non-arm's length individuals

The attribution rules [secs. 74.1 to 74.5] do not apply to loans or transfers to non-arm's length persons who are 18 years of age or older. However, anti-avoidance rules [ssecs. 56(4.1) to (4.3)] prevent the avoidance of tax on *loans* between non-arm's length individuals. Income from property resulting from a low-interest or a no-interest loan by an individual to another non-arm's length individual will be attributed back to the lender in situations where section 74.1 does not apply. The key condition for the attribution rule in subsection 56(4.1) to apply is that one of the main reasons for the loan is to reduce or avoid tax on income from the property or substituted property. Therefore, loans between non-arm's length individuals, both of whom are taxed at the same rate, would appear not to be caught by these provisions. Similarly, if the loaned funds are spent on non-income-producing property (e.g., personal-use property, living expenses, etc.), then the "one of the main reasons" test would not be met. Note that the attribution rules in subsection 56(4.1) apply only to loans, but not to sales or gifts.

Loans that bear a commercial or arm's length rate of interest are exempt from the attribution rule [ssec. 56(4.1)] by virtue of subsection 56(4.2). The interest must, in fact, be paid within 30 days of the end of the year in respect of which it was charged for the exemption to apply. Refinancing a loan subject to subsection 56(4.1) with another loan will not circumvent the attribution rule [ssec. 56(4.3)].

8. Summary of income attribution rules

Exhibit 6-3 attempts to summarize the major rules pertaining to the attribution of income from property.

EXHIBIT 6-3
Attribution of Income* from Property**
Conceptual Summary

	Transaction		
Recipient	*Transfer by gift*	*Transfer by sale*	*Transaction involving loan*
Spouse or common-law partner*** [ssec. 74.1(1)]	• Income or loss from property attributed to transferor	• If no fair market value consideration received: Income or loss from property attributed to transferor • If fair market value consideration received:**** No attribution	• If no interest at a commercial rate paid: Income or loss from property attributed to transferor • If interest at a commercial rate paid:**** No attribution
Minors who are not at arm's length [secs. 251 and 252] or who are nieces and nephews [ssec. 74.1(2)]	• Income or loss from property attributed to transferor	• Same as for transfer by gift (dependent on whether fair market value consideration received)	• Same as for transfer by gift (dependent on whether fair market value consideration received)
Other non-arm's length individuals not subject to section 74.1 [ssec. 56(4.1)]	• No attribution	• No attribution	• Income only from property attributed to transferor, if one of the main reasons for the loan was to reduce or avoid tax and market rate of interest not paid

* Excluding second-generation income.

** Including substituted property as defined in subsection 248(5). Income from business is not attributed in any of these transactions. Attribution of capital gains or losses is discussed in Chapter 8.

*** Attribution of capital gains and losses on transfers or loans to a spouse is discussed in Chapter 8.

**** To avoid attribution, the taxpayer must elect to waive the deferral of accrued income under subsection 73(1) (discussed in Chapter 8) and must transfer for fair market value consideration. Where a loan is involved, interest at a commercial rate must be paid within 30 days of the end of every year in which the loan is outstanding.

9. Tax on split income

Note that the income attribution rules discussed above do not apply to income from a business, such as a proprietorship or a partnership, transferred to a minor. As will be seen in a subsequent chapter, corporate attribution rules do not attribute dividends from certain private corporation that carry on business in Canada. Therefore, the attribution rules do not prevent income-splitting on business income. To address this exclusion from attribution, there is a special income-splitting tax on certain income of minors [sec. 120.4]. A separate tax on certain sources of, essentially, business income earned by individuals age 17 or under at the end of a calendar year is imposed.

The special income-splitting tax applies to the following types of income that are earned by persons under 18 years of age:

- taxable dividends from shares that are not listed on a prescribed Canadian or foreign stock exchange (i.e., essentially, shares of a private corporation) and that are received directly or indirectly through a trust or partnership;

- shareholder benefits included in the minor's income under section 15;

- partnership or trust income derived from the provision of goods and services to a business that is carried on by

  (i) a person related to the minor,

  (ii) a corporation which has a specified shareholder [ssec. 248(1)] who is related to the minor, or

  (iii) a professional corporation which has a shareholder who is related to the minor.

The specified income is:

- subject to tax at the top marginal rate, including applicable surtax, instead of the graduated rates;

- not eligible for any deductions or credits, except for the dividend tax credit and foreign tax credits;

- eligible for an offsetting deduction from taxable income equal to the specified income, so that this amount would not be taxed again normally under Part I of the Act; and

- not subject to the regular attribution rules. [ssec. 74.5(13), 56(5)]

The special income-splitting tax does not apply to:

- taxable dividends from shares listed on prescribed Canadian or foreign stock exchanges;

- minors who have no parent who is resident in Canada at any time in the year;

- income from property inherited by a minor from a parent;

- income from any inherited property, if the minor is in full-time attendance at a post-secondary institution or is eligible for the disability tax credit; and

- income from employment or personal services business carried on by the minor.

Note how these rules tax the minor, at the top rate, on income that would not otherwise be subject to the attributions rules and, therefore, that would not be taxed in the hands of a transferor, usually at the top tax rate.

II. DEDUCTIONS

A. Carrying Charges on Land

[ITA: 10(1.1); 18(2)–(3); 53(1)(*h*)]

Limitation on deduction

The deduction of carrying charges (i.e., interest and property taxes) in respect of vacant land, which is not used to produce income from holding it, is limited [ssecs. 18(2) and (3)]. There is an exception to this rule where the land can reasonably be considered to be used or held in the carrying on of business (excluding the unincorporated business of selling or developing land) or held primarily for the purpose of gaining or producing income from the land. This treatment does not apply to a building and the land on which it is situated or adjoining land used in connection with the building. Notice, also, that interest and property taxes on land subject to this treatment [ssec. 18(2)] can be deducted only to the extent that gross revenues exceed all other expenses. If the land is regarded as a capital asset, the non-deductible part of interest and property taxes can be added to the cost base of the land [par. 53(1)(*h*)] in the computation of cost for capital gains purposes. On the other hand, if the land is regarded as inventory, the non-deductible costs can be added to the cost of inventory [ssec. 10(1.1)].

The limitation [ssecs. 18(2) and (3)] extends to land held primarily for resale or development and vacant land held by a business but not used in the course of the business. However, corporations whose principal business is the leasing, rental or sale, and the development for lease, rental or sale of real property are permitted to deduct carrying charges on vacant land, in excess of net income before deducting carrying charges [par. 18(2)(*f*)]. The limit of this deduction is the corporation's "base level deduction" [ssec. 18(2.2)]. That limit is interest computed at the prescribed rate (as previously discussed in this chapter in respect of shareholder loans) on a loan of $1,000,000 outstanding throughout the year.

Example Problem

In 2003, Mr. Walkovia acquired a vacant lot in a downtown area of the city, intending to build an office complex. By late 2005 he decided to abandon the project. The property was disposed of just before the end of the year. It was not considered to have been held for speculation because of the unforeseen problems encountered in the development.

While the property was owned by Mr. Walkovia, it had been used as a city parking lot with the following results:

	2003	2004	2005
Net income (loss) before interest and property taxes*	$11,000	$ 6,000	$ (3,000)
Interest and property taxes	9,500	10,000	10,500

*This amount is equal to gross revenue in excess of all other expenses

— *REQUIRED*

(A) Consider the effect of these data on the income of Mr. Walkovia for tax purposes.

(B) If the land had been owned by a corporation whose principal business was the development and sale of land, what would be the effects of these data? Assume a prescribed rate of interest of 8% throughout the period in question.

—SOLUTION

(A) Since the land, held for development in this case, is not excluded from the limitation [ssec. 18(2)], interest and property taxes will be deductible only to the extent of gross revenues in excess of all other expenses, i.e., net income before interest and property taxes. As a result, the following amount would be reported as income for the years indicated:

	2003	2004	2005
Gross revenue less expenses other than interest and property taxes	$11,000	$ 6,000	$ (3,000)
Less: Interest and property taxes	9,500	6,000	Nil
Income (loss) for the year	$ 1,500	Nil	$ (3,000)
Non-deductible interest and property taxes added to adjusted cost base of land	Nil	$ 4,000	$10,500

(B) Paragraph 18(2)(*f*) would permit a loss created by the deduction of interest and property tax. However, the excess of interest and property tax that is deductible is limited to an amount of interest computed at the 8% prescribed rate, assumed in this case, on a notional principal amount of $1,000,000. The $80,000 limit in this case is referred to as the base level deduction. The following losses would be reported by a corporation:

	2003	2004	2005
Gross revenue less expenses other than interest and property taxes	$11,000	$ 6,000	$ (3,000)
Less lesser of:			
(a) interest and property taxes	$ 9,500	$ 10,000	$ 10,500
(b) base level deduction	$ 80,000	$ 80,000	$ 80,000
lesser amount	(9,500)	(10,000)	(10,500)
Income (loss) for the year	$ 1,500	$ (4,000)	$(13,500)

Note that the losses are of value to a corporation if it generates sufficient income from other sources to be shielded by the deduction of the losses. That is, the value of losses is inherent in the ability to shield income from tax.

B. "Soft Costs" relating to Construction of Buildings or Ownership of Land

[ITA: 18(3.1)–(3.7); 20(29); IT-371]

Expenses attributable to the period of construction, renovation or alteration of a building or in respect of the ownership of the related land must be capitalized to the building rather than deducted on a current basis. Subsection 18(3.1) requires this treatment even if the expenses would otherwise be specifically allowed as deductions under the Act. These expenses are known in practice as "soft costs" and, if attributable to the period of construction, renovation or alteration, might include, among other items, interest, legal and accounting fees, insurance and property taxes. Capital cost allowance and landscaping expenses are exempted from this treatment [par. 18(3.1)(*a*)]. Also exempted are disability-related modifications to buildings, deductible under paragraph 20(1)(*qq*) [par. 18(3.1)(*a*)]. The legislation also permits a taxpayer to deduct soft costs incurred in a year to the extent of the taxpayer's income, if any, from the rental of the building for the year [ssec. 20(29)]. Certain interest payments, which otherwise might not be specifically identified with the construction, renovation or alteration of a particular building or the ownership of a particular piece of land, are subject to the capitalization rules [ssec. 18(3.2)]. Thus, for example, where surplus funds are used to pay for the construction work and money is borrowed to finance business operations, a portion of the interest on borrowed funds would have to be capitalized. Subsection 18(3.3) provides for the determination of the date on which the work is completed. Transitional provisions are provided in subsections 18(3.5) to (3.7).

C. Rental Properties

[ITR: 1100(14)–(20); 1101(1ac); Sch. II; IT-195R4; IT-434R]

1. Separate classes

Recall that, in general, capital cost allowances are computed on the balance at the end of the year in a pool or class of similar assets. Dispositions throughout the year reduce the balance in a class and may even cause the balance to be negative. However, such a negative balance, to the extent that it is offset by a purchase of more assets for the class during the year, will not result in recapture. Thus, the ability to offset a negative balance in a class of assets with purchases of similar assets during the year reduces or eliminates the need to pay tax on income from recapture of capital cost allowances.

As an exception to this rule, each rental building purchased after 1971 and costing $50,000 or more must be placed in a separate capital cost allowance class [Reg. 1101(1ac)]. This will result in immediate recapture when such a building is sold for proceeds in excess of the undepreciated capital cost in the class, because no further purchases of rental buildings can be added to the class during the year. Since the recapture cannot be offset it must be taken into income in the year of disposition.

2. Losses from rental property

Again recall that, in general, capital cost allowances may be deducted to a maximum of the amount obtained by applying the prescribed rate for a class to the undepreciated capital cost in the class at the end of the year. If such amounts, when added to the other expenses of a business, exceed revenues from the business a loss is created. This loss, in general, can be offset against other sources of income.

As an exception to this rule, losses created by capital cost allowances on rental property will not be deductible from non-rental income [Regs. 1100(11) to (14)]. However, rental property is narrowly defined to mean the rental building, thereby excluding furniture and fixtures from this treatment. As a result, Regulations 1100(15) to (20), dealing with leasing properties, were added to prohibit the deduction of losses from non-rental income created by capital cost allowance on furniture and fixtures leased in a building except for corporations in the business of leasing property [IT-195R4]. Thus, a taxpayer cannot shelter other sources of income by offsetting a loss created by capital cost allowances on a rental building or leasing properties against those other sources of income, unless the taxpayer is a corporation or a partnership of corporations whose principal business was the property rental or leasing business.

Example Problem

Auntie Inflation owns six rental buildings with the following information pertaining to each:

	Building					
	1	*2*	*3*	*4*	*5*	*6*
Cost	$30,000	$132,000	$71,000	$49,000	$350,000	$47,000
U.C.C., January 1, 2005	22,000	90,000	49,000	40,000	238,000	38,000
Rental revenue in 2005	1,600	17,000	8,000	3,800	45,000	6,000
Cash expenses:						
Interest	Nil	$ 1,200	$1,700	Nil	$ 3,200	$1,400
Property taxes	$400	3,000	1,500	$ 800	8,000	1,200
Other expenses	800	11,000	7,500	1,600	29,000	5,800

Late in 2005, buildings 1 and 2 were sold for proceeds of $40,000 and $91,000 respectively. Building 5 was purchased in 1980. All other buildings were purchased after 1987.

— REQUIRED

Prepare a schedule showing the maximum capital cost allowance which may be claimed for tax purposes assuming she owns no other rental properties. Assume all buildings are of brick construction.

— SOLUTION

	Class 1: 4%			Class 3: 5%
	Under $50,000	Building 2	Building 3	Building 5
U.C.C., January 1, 2005	$100,000	$90,000	$49,000	$238,000
Dispositions during the year	30,000[1]	91,000	—	—
U.C.C., December 31, 2005	$ 70,000	$ (1,000)	$49,000	$238,000
C.C.A. for 2005 (max.: $4,300 below)	2,800[2]	—	1,500[2]	Nil[2]
Recapture	—	1,000	—	—
U.C.C., January 1, 2006	$ 67,200	Nil	$47,500	$238,000

Total rental revenue in 2005	$81,400
Add: recapture [ssecs. 13(1)–(3)]	1,000
Less: total cash expenses	(78,100)
Net before C.C.A.	$ 4,300
C.C.A. — Amount deductible re: limitation[2]	(4,300)
Loss on rental properties	Nil

— NOTES TO SOLUTION

(1) The balance is never reduced by more than the original cost on the disposition of an asset; capital gain of $10,000 (i.e., $40,000 – $30,000).

(2) C.C.A. potentially available in 2005:

Buildings with cost under $50,000 (4% of $70,000)	$ 2,800
Building 3 (4% of $49,000)	1,960
Building 5 (5% of $238,000)	11,900
Total	$16,660

Where deducting the maximum allowable C.C.A. is not possible, as in this case, or not desirable, it is usually advisable to take C.C.A. in lower-rate classes first. This preserves a higher balance in the higher-rate classes for the future when it may be possible to deduct relatively higher amounts of C.C.A. in the higher-rate classes.

D. Depreciation-based or Similar Tax Shelters[j]

[ITA: 96(2.2)]

Depreciation-based or similar tax shelters such as residential buildings, films, yachts, hotels, recreational vehicles and nursing homes have been available in the past. They have been used as a tool of fiscal policy to encourage investment in certain areas by providing a fast write-off. For example, a high CCA rate, or a large absolute dollar write-off of an amount invested will reduce the after-tax cash outflow of the initial investment. As extensive use of these shelters is perceived as abuse of the system by the Department of Finance, the ability to shelter other income with losses created by capital cost allowances has been either eliminated or reduced in effect. This was the case for residential buildings, films, yachts, hotels, nursing homes, recreational vehicles, computer software and other similar properties. On December 1, 1994, the federal government announced further restrictive measures with the stated objective to "improve the fairness of the tax system and prevent abuses through aggressive tax shelter promotion." However, from time to time, other assets become the subject of depreciation-based tax shelters and, therefore, it is important to understand, conceptually, how they are used.

Consider the following typical example of a simple tax shelter, based on a hypothetical Class 10 asset. An investor could purchase a percentage of the asset through a partnership. The investor could be required to pay as little as 5% of the full investment in cash and he or she typically would sign an unconditional note for the balance which is usually payable in two to seven years. As long as the full investment amount is at risk by the investor, he or she could take Class 10 declining balance capital cost allowance of 30%, subject to the half-net-amount rule, of the full amount of the investment in the year in which the investment was made. This principle was supported by the case of *Mandel v. The Queen*, (F.C.A.) 78 DTC 6518 and subsection 96(2.2) codifies these "at risk" rules under specified conditions where a limited partnership is used. In the case of *Signum Communications Inc. v. The Queen*, 88 DTC 6427, based on facts which pre-dated subsection 96(2.2), the Federal Court — Trial Division held that in the absence of a statutory at-risk rule, there was no reason to limit losses to the amount of capital invested in a partnership, despite the decision in the *Mandel* case.

Assets sold as tax shelters have been very high risk investments, with probably only a small chance that the investment would be profitable. The main advantage of an investment in a sheltered asset has been a tax deferral which was most valuable to those in the higher tax brackets. For example, an investor purchasing a $100,000 interest in an asset may have had to pay only $5,000 in the first year, but was entitled to a $15,000 tax deduction of capital cost allowance at the 30% rate for Class 10, subject to the half-net-amount rule. However, the $95,000 balance will have to be paid, and the investor

---

[j] For a discussion of the general tax and investment implications of tax shelters which provide for an immediate or a rapid write-off of costs, see Lawrence I. Gould and Stanley N. Laiken, "Depreciation-Based Tax Shelters: Are They Worth the Risks?" *CA Magazine*, April 1983, pp. 38–41.

may be confronted by cash flow problems if he or she receives no income from the asset. These investments are also usually very illiquid.

It should be realized that *all* investments shelter the cost of the investment from taxation. For example, it will be demonstrated in the next two chapters how the cost of an investment in stock is "written off" against the proceeds of disposition when the stock is sold. It can be shown that the advantage of the faster write-off of a tax shelter cannot provide a profit for an investment that does not return both its cost and its after-tax carrying charges. Thus, an investment decision should be made primarily on its value as an investment without regard to any accelerated tax write-off that may be available and should not be based solely on the advantage of an early or large write-off of the investment. There is little advantage to making a $100,000 investment that turns out to be almost worthless, in order to write off the $100,000 and save about $50,000 in taxes!

E. Interest

[ITA: 18(11); 20(1)(*c*), (*d*), (2.1), [(3.1), (3.2); 20.1; 20.2]; 21; 80.4; 80.5; IT-533]

1. Current legislation

On October 31, 2003, IT-533 — Interest Deductibility and Related Issues was released as part of the Draft Proposals on Interest Deductibility. This Interpretation Bulletin replaced five other bulletins and establishes the CRA's assessing position on interest deductibility. Not all of the material in this bulletin is included in this section. Refer directly to the bulletin for specific details. Throughout this section, reference will be made to this bulletin wherever appropriate.

Reasonable interest paid or payable in the year is deductible [par. 20(1)(*c*)] if the borrowings were used to produce income or to acquire property to produce such income.[k] In addition, the first level of compound interest is allowed [par. 20(1)(*d*)] if the original amount borrowed meets the test for interest deductibility in paragraph 20(1)(*c*).

Remember that section 80.5 provides that where a benefit is included in the income of a taxpayer under section 80.4, the amount of the benefit will be regarded as an interest expense which might be deductible under subparagraph 8(1)(*j*)(i) or paragraph 20(1)(*c*) if the tests of those provisions are met. Thus, where the borrowed funds are used for investing in securities a deduction of interest imputed as income under section 80.4 will be possible under paragraph 20(1)(*c*).

There are some statutory limits on the deduction of interest provided in section 18 of the Act which apply notwithstanding the general provision for a deduction in paragraph 20(1)(*c*). Most of these exceptions have been discussed previously in this chapter or Chapter 4. Paragraph 18(1)(*t*) denies a deduction for interest imposed under the Act. Subsection 18(2), previously discussed, limits the deduction of interest on funds borrowed to purchase land in certain circumstances. Subsection 18(3.1) capitalizes interest as part of "soft costs" pertaining to real property ownership. The thin capitalization rules provided in subsections 18(4) to (8) limit deductible interest paid to certain non-resident shareholders. Subsection 18(9) prohibits the deduction of prepaid interest. Where interest has been prepaid by corporations, partnerships and trusts, rules in subsections 18(9.2) to (9.8) compute interest payable. Finally, subsection 18(11) prohibits the deduction of interest on funds borrowed to make a contribution to sheltered or tax-assisted retirement savings plans, discussed in Chapter 9.

---

[k] The question of this income-producing capability was addressed in the Supreme Court of Canada decision, *The Queen v. Bronfman Trust*, 87 DTC 5059.

2. Loss of the source of income

The general principle of interest deductibility in paragraph 20(1)(*c*) is that the borrowed money must be used for the purpose of earning income from a business or property. Consider the following case. A taxpayer borrows $10,000 to acquire an income-producing property. During the holding period of that property the interest is deductible. When the property declines in value to $6,000, the property is sold and the taxpayer invests the $6,000 of proceeds in another income-producing property. The courts have held that interest on only $6,000 of borrowings is deductible, because the other $4,000 of borrowing cannot be traced to an income-producing source.

However, section 20.1 [IT-533, paragraph 19] would apply in this case, where because of a loss of the source of income, borrowed money ceases to be used for an income-producing purposes. These rules ensure that interest on such borrowed money will, in specified circumstances, continue to be deductible under paragraph 20(1)(*c*). The rules operate to deem the portion of borrowed money that has been lost because of a decline in the value of property to continue to be used for the purpose of earning income from the property.

In the example, above, subsection 20.1(1) applies to deem the $4,000 of borrowed money to continue to be used for the purpose of earning income from the property, as long as the original property was capital property (other than real estate or depreciable property). This allows the interest on the $4,000 to qualify for a deduction [spar. 20(1)(*c*)(i)]. The interest on the $6,000 that was reinvested continues to be deductible, because the borrowed funds are being used to produce income [par. 20(1)(*c*)].

If the taxpayer uses the $6,000 from the proceeds of the original property for personal expenditures, interest on the $6,000 of borrowed funds would no longer be deductible, because those funds are not being used for income-producing purposes. However, interest on the $4,000 would be deductible as discussed above.

In another example, consider the case of an individual who has borrowed $25,000 for use in a business. During the year, the individual ceases to carry on the business, because it is not successful. Several months later, the individual sells the assets of the business to an arm's length purchaser for $10,000 and uses the proceeds for personal purposes.

In this case, paragraph 20.1(2)(*c*) deems the $25,000 to continue to be used for the purpose of earning income from the business from the time of the cessation of operations until the time of the sale of the assets. Therefore, interest on the $25,000 continues to be deductible in that period [spar. 20(1)(*c*)(i)]. The $15,000 of lost capital is deemed to have been borrowed to continue to be used for the purpose of earning income from the business from the time of the sale of the business assets until the time of repayment of the debt [par. 20.1(2)(*c*)]. However, interest on the $10,000 of borrowings used for personal purposes is not deductible after the sale of the assets, since the borrowed funds are no longer used for income-producing purposes [par. 20.1(2)(*a*)].

3. Draft legislation (December 20, 1991)

Draft Legislation on Interest Deductibility was released on December 20, 1991 (Department of Finance Release No. 91-141). At the time of writing (June 2005) it had not been introduced to Parliament. The proposals address the deductibility of interest on borrowed money:

(a) used to make low-interest or no-interest loans to employees and shareholders [spars. 20(1)(*c*)(v) and (vi)];

(b) used to buy shares which are not expected to earn income in excess of interest charges [par. 20(1)(*qq*): note that if this provision is ultimately passed, it will have to be renumbered because paragraph 20(1)(*qq*) has now been used for another provision in the law];

(c) loaned to a corporation or partnership in which the taxpayer seeking the deduction has an ownership interest [ssecs. 20(3.1) and (3.2)]; and

(d) used to make distributions to shareholders or partners [secs. 20.1 and 20.2: note that if the proposed provision for section 20.1 is ultimately enacted, it will have to be renumbered, because section 20.1 has now been used for the provisions pertaining to the loss of a source of income, discussed above.].

Where an employer borrows funds to make a low-interest or no-interest loan described in subsection 80.4(1) to an employee, the interest incurred on the employee's loan is deductible [spar. 20(1)(c)(v)], as long as the other conditions of paragraph 20(1)(c) and section 67 are met. A similar rule is provided for interest on money borrowed by a corporation to make a loan described in subsection 80.4(2) to a shareholder [spar. 20(1)(c)(vi)]. However, on a loan to or for the benefit of a shareholder, interest is deductible only to the extent of the amount included in the borrower's income [ssec. 80.4(2)] for the year from the shareholder loan. Refer to IT-533, paragraph 26.

Taxpayers may borrow money to acquire shares bearing a fixed dividend rate that is lower than the rate of interest on the borrowings. In such a case, no net income from the shares will be generated. Proposed paragraph 20(1)(qq) (or its renumbered equivalent when passed) appears to legislate the Department's current practice and provides an interest deduction which is limited to the amount included in the borrower's income from the shares acquired with the borrowed money. In the case of an individual, the interest deduction would be limited to the amount of grossed-up dividends included in the shareholder's income. Interest not deductible in a particular year, due to this limit, may be added to interest on borrowings for the next year to be deducted in that next year subject to the same limit of taxable dividend income. This limit on the deductibility of interest would not apply to common shares, because the rules of paragraph 20(1)(c) allow for the deduction of interest if there is a reasonable expectation of earning income. On common shares there is always an expectation of a dividend, even if the dividend only occurs on the ultimate liquidation of the corporation.

In some cases, a shareholder or partner may be required to borrow money and incur an interest expense to make low-interest or no-interest loans to his or her business or to acquire shares with little or no dividend entitlement in his or her corporation. Since there is no reasonable expectation of profit from the borrowed funds, the general rules of interest deductibility in paragraph 20(1)(c) may deny the deduction. However, the provisions in subsections 20(3.1) and (3.2) deem the borrowings to have been made for the purpose of earning income from property. As a result, the interest on funds borrowed by the shareholder or partner will be deductible. However, two further conditions must be met. First, the corporation or partnership receiving the funds must use them for the purposes of earning Canadian-source, non-exempt income. Second, the corporation or partnership could not have been in a financial position to borrow the funds on its own on terms comparable to those obtained by the shareholder or partner. Refer to IT-533, paragraph 25.

The provisions in proposed sections 20.1 and 20.2 (or their renumbered equivalents when passed) would facilitate the deduction of interest on funds borrowed by a corporation or a partnership to make a distribution of retained earnings or capital. The rules, effectively, deem the use of the borrowed funds to be for the purpose of earning income from business or property, allowing the interest to be deductible under paragraph 20(1)(c). Interest deductible by these rules is limited to interest on an amount borrowed up to the equity, as specifically defined, of the corporation or partnership making the distribution. These rules address some issues raised in the *Bronfman* case and facilitate a distribution without the need to sell income-earning assets to provide the funds to make the distribution.

4. Capitalization of interest

At the taxpayer's election, section 21 permits certain borrowing costs and interest to be treated as non-deductible expenses and added to the cost of depreciable property in respect of which the expenses were incurred. This election might be made, for example, if the deduction of such costs would create a loss that could not be absorbed in the loss carry-over period which will be discussed in a later chapter. The costs eligible for such deferment are amounts otherwise deductible as interest [pars. 20(1)(c) and (d)] and other expenses of borrowing money [par. 20(1)(e)]. This is particularly advantageous if the interest is in respect of assets in fast write-off classes such as Class 12.

F. Personal Loan Planning and Interest Deductibility

[ITA: 20(1)(c); 67; IT-533]

1. Deductibility of interest expenses

In general, as indicated above, expenditures made or incurred for the purpose of gaining or producing income from property are deductible from that income. The amounts of such expenditures must be reasonable in the circumstances by virtue of the last phrase in paragraph 20(1)(c). Under the current concept of interest deductibility, there need only be a reasonable expectation of earning income. No income need actually be earned in a year, in order to deduct interest paid or payable in that year. In the case of *Fallis v. M.N.R.*, (T.A.B.) 66 DTC 233 the taxpayer was not allowed to deduct interest when he could never hope to receive as much interest as he paid. In the case of preferred shares held by an individual, the CRA will allow an interest expense deduction to the extent of the grossed-up dividend income. On the other hand, if the preferred shares can be freely converted into common shares, interest expense on funds borrowed to buy the preferred shares will be fully deductible irrespective of the dividend rate on those shares. Also, interest at a reasonable rate on funds borrowed to buy common shares will be fully deductible irrespective of the dividend yield, which may even be zero, because of the reasonable expectation of an increase in the dividend rate on common shares. Refer to IT-533, paragraph 31.

The deductibility of interest is determined by the use of the borrowed funds. Thus, interest paid on a mortgage, the proceeds of which are used to invest in certain securities, is deductible because the interest is paid in respect of funds used to produce income. On the other hand, interest on funds borrowed to purchase personal property is not deductible because it is not used to produce income. Also, interest on funds borrowed to invest in commodities as a capital investment was held by the Tax Court of Canada not to be deductible in *Hastings v. M.N.R.*, 88 DTC 1391. The Court agreed with the Crown's position that the ordinary rules relating to expenses being deducted in the income-earning process do not apply to the capital gains sections of the Act.

Loan planning would suggest that the taxpayer borrow funds which will be used to produce income, thereby making the interest tax deductible. This permits the taxpayer to allocate his or her savings to purchases such as assets used for personal purposes including the family home or a car not used for business which do not produce income.

Great care must be taken in maintaining the connection between the interest paid and the use of the funds borrowed. In one case, a taxpayer received a loan from his employer and used the proceeds to finance the purchase of securities. He secured the loan with a mortgage on his house. In this situation, the interest on the loan was deductible. However, when the taxpayer was transferred and he sold his house, he had to pay off the loan from the proceeds of sale. He then purchased another house in his new work location and financed the purchase with a mortgage. He deducted mortgage interest on the new house against his investment income on the same basis as before, but the CRA disallowed that interest deduction. It was argued that the money was not used to produce income, but to acquire the new house. In this case, the taxpayer did not maintain the connection between the loan and the use of the funds. Had he not paid off the employer's loan but secured the loan with a new mortgage on the new home, he would have maintained that connection. Refer to IT-533, paragraphs 9 to 14.

This position, taken by the CRA, was confirmed in the case of *The Queen v. Bronfman Trust*, 87 DTC 5097, when the Supreme Court of Canada held that what was important was the use of the borrowed funds. In this case, the Supreme Court, in its examination, was not able to trace the funds borrowed directly to an income-earning source (eligible use source) and, hence, denied the deduction of the related interest. The December 20, 1991 Draft Legislation on Interest Deductibility does not address the situation of an individual who borrows initially for a non-income-producing purpose and later directs savings to an income-producing purpose. It would appear that in these cases, the decision in the *Bronfman Trust* case would stand. Therefore, in order for interest on borrowed funds to be deductible, the taxpayer must still trace the funds borrowed to an income-producing purpose. Refer to IT-533, paragraph 13.

2. Commentary on Two Supreme Court Decisions on Interest Deductibility — *Singleton* and *Ludco*

The following is an excerpt from a commentary[1] on two major Supreme Court of Canada decisions on the topic of interest deductibility in two very different types of fact situations. The excerpts of the commentary relate to the facts and reasons for judgement of the cases and are provided here to refer the reader to the type of commentary provided by practitioners. While obviously not the law, such commentaries provide interpretations of practitioners, in much the same manner as CRA publications like *Interpretation Bulletins* present the interpretations of the CRA.

On September 28, 2001, the Supreme Court of Canada released its decisions in the *Singleton* and *Ludco* appeals (2001 DTC 5533 and 2001 DTC 5505, respectively). Both cases dealt with the deduction of interest under paragraph 20(1)(c)... The *Singleton* appeal was concerned with the "use" of the borrowed money requirement, while the Ludco appeal focused on the "purpose" of the use requirement. Both appeals were decided in favour of the taxpayers.

The *Singleton* case involved a lawyer who withdrew funds from the capital account at his law firm, used the funds to purchase a house, and on the same day, borrowed from a bank to refinance the capital account. The taxpayer attempted to deduct the interest on the borrowing on the grounds that it was used for the purpose of earning income from the law practice. The Minister denied the deduction. The Minister took the position that the taxpayer's transactions, when viewed as a whole, effectively resulted in the borrowed money being used for the purpose of purchasing the house.

... [T]he Tax Court of Canada had held in favour of the Crown, but on appeal, the Federal Court of Appeal overturned the decision...

By a five-to-two majority, the Supreme Court upheld the Federal Court of Appeal decision and allowed the interest deduction... The majority rejected the Crown's argument that the "economic realities" of the taxpayer's transactions should be considered in determining whether the use requirement of paragraph 20(1)(c) had been met. The Court relied on its previous decision in the *Shell* case (99 DTC 5669) where it held that, absent a sham or specific provision in the Act to the contrary, the economic realities of a transaction cannot be used to recharacterize a taxpayer's *bona fide* legal relationships. The Court concluded that, giving effect to the legal relationships in the case at hand, the taxpayer borrowed money and used that money to refinance the capital account in the law firm. This was a direct and eligible use within the meaning of paragraph

---

[1] Joseph Frankovic, "No Surprises in Supreme Court Decisions on Interest Deductibility", *Tax Topics Report* #1545, CCH Canadian Limited, October 18, 2001.

20(1)(*c*). The characterization of this use was not altered by the fact that the taxpayer had used the money previously withdrawn from the capital account to purchase a house. Nor was it altered by the fact that all of the transactions occurred on the same day.

. . .

The taxpayers in the *Ludco* case were Canadian residents who purchased shares in two offshore companies for $7.5 million. The taxpayers borrowed to purchase the shares and paid $6 million of interest expense on the borrowing over the investment period. During that period, the shares generated dividend income of $600,000 that was subject to tax in Canada, while the bulk of the companies' income was reinvested. The taxpayers' investments were tax-motivated, in that the objective was to have the companies earn significant investment income that was not subject to immediate taxation in Canada and that could be repatriated to Canada in the form of a tax-deferred capital gain. When the shares were ultimately redeemed, the taxpayers realized a capital gain of $9.2 million. The Minister disallowed the deduction of the $6 million interest expense incurred on the borrowing on the grounds that the shares were acquired for the purpose of earning a capital gain and not for the purpose of earning income from property.

The Federal Court of Appeal decided in favour of the Crown (99 DTC 5153), holding that the taxpayers used the borrowed money to acquire the shares for the real purpose of earning a capital gain and not dividend income. In a dissenting judgment, Létourneau, J.A. [Associate Justice] disagreed and held that the borrowed money was also used for the purpose of earning the dividend income. Létourneau, J.A. held that as long as one of the purposes was to earn income from property (the dividend income), the interest deduction should have been allowed. He also held that "income" in paragraph 20(1)(*c*) refers to gross income rather than net income, so that only a reasonable expectation of some income was required.

The Supreme Court of Canada agreed with most of the analysis provided by Létourneau, J.A. and allowed the taxpayers' appeal. The Court held that the text of paragraph 20(1)(*c*) does not indicate that a taxpayer's purpose must be *bona fide*, exclusive, primary or dominant, or that multiple purposes are to be somehow ranked in order of importance to determine a taxpayer's "real" purpose. Therefore, according to the Court, it is perfectly consistent within the language of the provision that a taxpayer who uses borrowed money to make an investment with dual purposes be entitled to deduct the interest on the borrowing, provided that one of the purposes is to earn income. Furthermore, and absent a sham or "window dressing" or other vitiating circumstances, a taxpayer's ancillary purpose is equally capable of fulfilling the requisite purpose for interest deductibility in comparison with a more significant purpose. The Court thus concluded that the proper test to determine the purpose under paragraph 20(1)(*c*) is whether, considering all the circumstances, the taxpayer had a reasonable expectation of income at the time the borrowed money was used to make the investment. In this regard, the Court agreed that paragraph 20(1)(*c*) refers to gross income rather than net income or profit. The Court noted that the plain meaning of the provision supported neither a quantitative determination of income nor a judicial assessment of sufficiency of income. Accordingly, and again in the absence of a sham or window dressing, the Court was not concerned with the sufficiency of income expected or received.

Applying these findings to the facts of the case, the Court held that even though earning income was not the principal factor that motivated their investments, the taxpayers had a reasonable expectation of receiving dividends. There was no sham involved, and the amount of the dividends received on the shares could not be characterized as window dressing. Accordingly, the taxpayers had a reasonable expectation of income when they used the borrowed money, and the requisite purpose test had been met.

. . .

3. Proposed Amendments to Interest Deductibility and REOP

[Draft Proposals on Interest Deductibility dated October 31, 2003]

On October 31, 2003, the Department of Finance released draft proposals on interest deductibility which also included legislation related to reasonable expectation of profit.

Proposed subsection 3.1(1) provides that a taxpayer can deduct a loss from a source that is a business or property only if, in that year, it is reasonable to expect that the taxpayer will realize a cumulative profit from the business or property. Then, new subsection 3.1(2) makes it clear that profit, in this context does not include capital gains or capital losses.

While these changes seem straightforward, consider what would happen if a new business, began to have financial difficulty and realized losses in excess of previous income. If they determined that they were going to have to close the business, then this proposed rule would deny any losses from that time forward. These future losses from expenditures such as wages, lease payments, severance and other recurring expenses, were previously deductible.

Since their release, there has been significant discussion between tax professionals and the Department on the implications of their proposals. The report of the Joint Committee on Taxation of the Canadian Bar Association and the Canadian Institute of Chartered Accountants states that:

> we are of the view that the Draft Proposals would introduce a fundamental change to the *Income Tax Act* which goes well beyond the case law and administrative practice prior to recent court decisions. We are concerned that the proposals could be used to disallow losses resulting from wholly-legitimate business expenses the deductibility of which would not have been an issue under prior case law or administrative practice. They would create significant issues with respect to the treatment of investments in securities.

In the March 23, 2004 federal budget, the following statement was made:

> Assurances were given by the Minister of Finance, Finance officials and the CRA that these releases were not intended to adversely affect the past assessing practices regarding the deductibility of interest on equity investments. The Budget materials acknowledge that significant issues have been raised with them that warrant further consideration.

The Budget Plan 2005, published by the Department of Finance to accompany the February 23, 2005 federal budget, contained the following statement at page 410:

> Many commentators expressed concerns with the proposals' structure, in particular, that the proposals' codification of the "reasonable expectation of profit" test might inadvertently limit the deductibility of a wide variety of ordinary commercial expenses. The Department of Finance has sought to respond by developing a more modest legislative initiative that would respond to those concerns while still achieving the Government's objectives. The Department will, at an early opportunity, release that alternative proposal for comment. This will be combined with a Canada Revenue Agency publication that addresses, in the context of the alternative proposal, certain administrative questions relating to deductibility.

Example Problem

A parent with two children is preparing a will. One child is active in the parent's business and the other is not. The parent is considering the following two options with respect to the business:

(a) leave the business to the child who will be active in the business on the condition that the child give the other child an amount equal to the 50% of the fair market value of the business on the parent's death, and

(b) leave 50% of the business to each of the two children on the condition that the child who will be active in the business buy the 50% left to the other child.

In either case, the active child will have to borrow the funds to pay the other child.

— REQUIRED

Advise the parent on the better alternative for the child who will be active in the business.

— SOLUTION

Based on the use of the borrowed funds, the interest incurred under the second alternative will be deductible, because the funds will be used to buy shares which will produce income. Interest incurred under the first alternative will not be deductible, because the use of the borrowed funds will not produce income.

4. Investing in your mortgage

Since interest paid on mortgage funds used to buy a personal house is, generally, not deductible, this interest must be paid with after-tax dollars. Every dollar of the mortgage that can be paid down will save the rate of interest on the mortgage for every year that it would otherwise be outstanding. If that rate of interest is, say, 5%, the rate of return on paying down the mortgage will be 5% per year after taxes. This rate of return is risk-free. Such a riskless after-tax return is quite rare.

If a mortgage can be prepaid without penalty, this return can be achieved immediately by using current savings to pay down the mortgage. However, if the mortgage is not open for such payments in full or in part, it may be worthwhile setting aside savings for the purpose of paying down the mortgage when it is due for renewal as shown above. In any case, it is necessary to compare the after-tax return possible on available funds invested in other media. Paying down an old, low-interest mortgage may not be the best investment, but certainly paying down a mortgage held at higher current rates will compare very favourably with alternatives.

III. DIFFERENCES BETWEEN BUSINESS AND PROPERTY INCOME

At this point, it would be worthwhile comparing some of the provisions which have been examined so far and which distinguish between business and property income.

(1) Applicable to business income only:

- write-off of eligible capital property [par. 20(1)(b)];

- reserves [pars. 20(1)(m), (m.1), (m.2) and (n)];

- certain specific expenses:

  — expenses of representation [par. 20(1)(cc)];

  — site investigation [par. 20(1)(dd)];

  — utilities services connection [par. 20(1)(ee)];

- convention expenses [ssec. 20(10)];

- short-year proration for capital cost allowance [Reg. 1100(3)].

(2) Applicable to property income only:

- restriction on capital cost allowance for rental properties [Reg. 1100(15)];
- attribution rules [sec. 74.1];
- foreign taxes on property income in excess of 15% deductible [ssec. 20(11)].

IV. GST AND PROPERTY INCOME

A. Interest and Dividends

[ETA: 123(1); Sch. V, Part VII]

Interest and dividends are exempt from GST. A number of provisions and definitions in the *Excise Tax Act* (ETA) must be reviewed to explain the basis for this exemption. First, financial services rendered to residents in Canada are exempt from GST [ETA: Part VII of Schedule V]. A "financial service" is defined [ETA: ssec. 123(1)] to include a broad range of transactions and services. For example, the payment or receipt of interest, dividends, or any other amount in respect of a "financial instrument" is included in the definition of financial service. A "financial instrument" is defined [ETA: ssec. 123(1)] to include a debt security, an equity security, an insurance policy, etc. A "debt security" is defined in the same subsection to mean a right to be paid money and includes a deposit of money. An "equity security" is defined to mean a share of the capital stock of a corporation or any interest in or right to such a share. Consequently, payments of interest and dividends in respect of financial instruments are exempt from GST. It is important to note that the definition of financial service contains several exclusions. For example, paragraph (r) of the definition excludes the provision of a professional service by an accountant, actuary, lawyer or notary in the course of a professional practice. Consequently, these services are subject to GST in the normal manner.

B. Shareholder Benefits

[ETA: 170; 173]

Shareholders may be subject to GST on certain shareholder benefits that they receive from a corporation. The rules applicable to shareholder benefits are the same provisions that deal with employee benefits [ETA: sec. 170 and ssec. 173(1)]. As these provisions were discussed in Chapter 3 in the context of employee benefits, the discussion in this section will only briefly review the relevant rules. Reference may be made to Chapter 3 for further analysis of these provisions.

Where a shareholder receives a benefit from a corporation that is required to be included in income pursuant to subsection 15(1) of the *Income Tax Act*, the corporation is deemed to have made a taxable supply to the shareholder and to have collected the GST in respect of the benefit [ETA: ssec. 173(1)]. In turn, the shareholder is required to include the corporation-paid GST in income as a taxable benefit. This income inclusion places the shareholder in the same economic position as if he or she acquired the property or services on the open market.

However, as noted in Chapter 3, there are a number of significant exceptions to the above general rule. For example, no income inclusion of GST is required if the supply of the benefit is exempt or zero-rated under the ETA, or if the benefit is monetary in nature, such as an allowance.

C. "Soft Costs"

[ETA: 123(1); 192; Sch. V, Part I; Sch. V, Part VI, 21; Sch. V, Part VII]

GST applies to sales and rentals of real property unless the supply is specifically exempt under Part I of Schedule V (such as sales of *used* residential housing and long-term residential rents). The GST affects real estate developers and builders in the same manner that it affects other businesses that make taxable supplies. To the extent property and services are purchased for use in commercial activities, input tax credits in respect of the GST paid on those purchases may be claimed. For example, when a builder incurs GST in respect of legal and accounting fees during the period of construction, renovation or alteration of a building or in respect of the ownership of the related land, the tax may be recovered as an input tax credit.

Certain other soft costs incurred by builders are classified as exempt supplies under the ETA, and hence, not subject to GST. These would include, for example, interest, insurance, and property taxes. As discussed above, interest is exempt as a financial service [ETA: Part VII of Schedule V]. Similarly, insurance premiums are exempt as financial services. Property taxes are exempt [ETA: sec. 21 of Part VI of Schedule V].

Since sales of *used* residential properties are exempt from GST, special rules have been incorporated into the ETA to deal with "substantial renovations" of used residential properties. These rules are intended to ensure that persons in the business of renovating homes for resale are treated in the same manner as builders of new homes. The term "substantial renovation" is defined [ETA: ssec. 123(1)] to mean:

> . . . the renovation or alteration of a building to such extent that all or substantially all of the building that existed immediately before the renovation or alteration was begun, other than the foundation, external walls, interior supporting walls, floors, roof and staircases, has been removed or replaced where, after completion of the renovation or alteration, the building is, or forms part of, a residential complex.

Since the sale of a substantially renovated home is treated as the sale of new residential property, GST is charged on the sale and the builder is able to claim input tax credits on purchases of property and services. Consequently, any GST paid on soft costs would be recoverable.

Where a residential property is renovated and the renovation is not considered to be substantial, the sale of the property is exempt as a sale of used residential property [ETA: Part I of Schedule V]. However, the renovator is required to pay GST on certain costs incurred in renovating the property [ETA: sec. 192]. The GST is calculated by reference to all costs of completing the renovation or alteration that would be included in determining the adjusted cost base of the property for income tax purposes, other than:

- the costs of acquiring the property;

- interest and the cost of other financial services; and

- the cost of other purchases on which the renovator previously paid GST.

REVIEW QUESTIONS

(1) Billy Hilly has come to you to tell you that he has found a great way of generating income of which only one-half is taxable as a capital gain. He buys a bond that pays interest annually and he holds it until just before the payment date and then he sells it, including the accrued interest, at a gain. Comment.

(2) One of your clients does not want to buy the compounding series Canada Savings Bonds any more since the new interest accrual rules cause the interest earned to be taxable annually rather than at maturity. Comment.

(3) Ms. Jones is the President and sole shareholder of a construction company. She has two vice-presidents who are not related to her. As part of their compensation package she has agreed that all employees of the company are entitled to an interest-free loan from the company of up to $25,000. Ms. Jones herself has taken her $25,000 loan and bought a boat. Comment.

(4) Mr. Saleprop owns an unincorporated business. In recognition of his wife's considerable contribution of her time and skills to the business he gives her a one-half share of the business income. Comment.

(5) Mr. Smith has just guaranteed a bank loan that his wife has taken out to buy shares in a corporation carrying on a business that she is starting. He is concerned about the attribution rules. Comment.

(6) Opco Inc. recently borrowed $300,000 to buy 30 acres of industrial land. The corporation has constructed a building, shipping and receiving areas and parking for employees on this property using up 20 acres. The remaining 10 acres is available for future needs. Is all of the interest on the $300,000 loan deductible?

(7) Rent Co. Ltd. is a corporation in the residential rental business. Because of some recent purchases, its financing costs are high and it is operating at a break-even before CCA this year. However, in the prior three years it made a profit. Can the corporation claim CCA to create a loss this year to carry back to the prior years, using the carryover rules in Division C, to offset income in those years?

(8) Ms. Cautious has just bought some gold as a protection against inflation. However, she did not have the cash to make the purchase so she borrowed from the bank to buy the gold. This is the first time that she has done this and she plans to hold the gold for some time. She is repaying the loan over three years. Will she be able to deduct all or some of her interest expense? Explain.

(9) You have been told of a court case where a taxpayer borrowed money initially to purchase a home, because some of the funds that he was to receive from Iran had not arrived when expected. When the funds at last arrived, interest rates had risen above that rate he was paying on his house mortgage. He then chose to invest his money at these higher interest rates instead of paying off the mortgage. He deducted the interest portion of his mortgage payments on his tax return. Comment.

(10) A client is in the process of selling his house and buying a bigger one. However, the real estate market has slowed down and in order to sell his existing house he is going to have to take back a mortgage for $100,000 at 8% for a five-year term. Since he does not have any extra cash, he is going to have to borrow that $100,000 from you in order to buy his new house. Is the interest going to be deductible on his mortgage? If not, how might he restructure the transaction to make it deductible?

(11) You have just interviewed a new client and have discovered that she borrowed to buy shares in a private corporation five years ago. The loan is still outstanding but the corporation has since gone bankrupt. Is the interest she is paying on the loan still deductible?

MULTIPLE CHOICE QUESTIONS

Question 1

Max is planning to invest in preferred shares of taxable Canadian corporations which are paying a $12,000 dividend per year. Assuming that Max is in the top federal tax bracket (29%) and that the provincial tax on income rate in his province is 17%, how much income tax will Max pay on this income? Also assume that the combined federal and provincial dividend tax credit is equal to the dividend gross-up.

(A) $1,350

(B) $3,900

(C) $6,900

(D) $5,520

Question 2

Wendy Jang owns three rental buildings. All of the buildings were purchased after 1987 and are of brick construction:

	Property		
	1	*2*	*3*
Original cost	$120,000	$ 80,000	$150,000
UCC at Jan. 1	100,000	75,000	150,000
Rental revenue for the year	58,000	22,000	20,000
Expenses for the year:			
Interest	20,000	10,000	8,000
Property taxes	13,000	6,000	11,000
Other	17,000	4,000	1,000

What is the maximum CCA that Wendy Jang can claim on the rental properties for the year?

(A) $13,000

(B) $10,000

(C) $7,000

(D) $6,500

Question 3

In 2005, S Ltd., which has a December 31 year-end, made the following loans to shareholders. All of the shareholders are resident in Canada and are not related to S Ltd. This was the first time that these shareholders had received a loan or had become indebted to S. Ltd. Since S Ltd. was not in the business of lending money, it was very careful, in each case, to ensure that *bona fide* arrangements were made at the time the loan was made for repayment of the loan within a reasonable time. Taking all this into consideration, which one of the following loans will be included in the borrower's income in 2005 pursuant to subsection 15(2)?

(A) A loan to Mrs. A, a vice-president and 20% shareholder. The loan was made to assist Mrs. A in the purchase of newly issued shares of S Ltd. The loan was made on April 1, 2005, and repaid on April 1, 2006. No other employees have received similar loans.

(B) A loan made to B Ltd., a corporation which is a 20% shareholder of S Ltd. The loan was used to help B Ltd. repurchase some of its shares for cancellation and pay off a bank loan.

(C) A loan to Mrs. C, a vice-president and 20% shareholder. The loan was made to assist Mrs. C in the purchase of a home. The loan was made on April 1, 2005, and will be repaid on April 1, 2007. No other employees have received similar loans.

(D) A loan to Mr. D, an S Ltd. vice-president and 5% shareholder. Mr. D deals at arm's length with S Ltd. The loan was made to assist Mr. D in the purchase of a home computer for employment use. Five other employees of the company currently work at home and have received similar loans. None of the other employees are shareholders. Mr. D's loan was made on April 1, 2005, and will be repaid on April 1, 2007.

Question 4

In the year, Mr. P made the following loans and gifts to family members to split income with his family members. Which one of the loans and/or gifts will result in income being attributed to Mr. P?

(A) A gift of $100,000 to his son, Peter, age 21. Peter invested the money in a term deposit and earned $3,000 of interest income.

(B) An interest-free loan of $100,000 to his mother-in-law, Mabel, age 81. Mabel invested the money in mutual funds and earned $12,000 of dividend income.

(C) An interest-free loan of $100,000 to his daughter, Daphne, age 28. Daphne bought a cottage and used it for personal use.

(D) A gift of $100,000 to his wife, Debbie. Debbie put the money in her non-interest bearing chequing account and paid all the family's household expenses from the account. She then used $100,000 of her own money to invest in the stock market and earned $10,000 of dividend income.

Question 5

Which of the following items is DEDUCTIBLE by Canadian taxpayers in the computation of income from business or property in Subdivision b of Division B of the Act?

(A) Commissions paid on the purchase of an investment in common shares.

(B) The premium paid on a $100,000 term life insurance policy on the taxpayer's life which is required as collateral for a $100,000 bank loan used to purchase a $100,000 investment in common shares.

(C) Interest expenses on a loan to invest in a registered retirement savings plan.

(D) Commissions paid on the sale of an investment in common shares.

Question 6

During 2005 Mike received two cheques, one in the amount of $20,000 Cdn., the other in the amount of $8,500 Cdn. The $20,000 cheque was a dividend from a taxable Canadian corporation. The $8,500 cheque was a dividend from a foreign corporation, net of the $1,500 of foreign tax withheld by the foreign country from the dividend payment. Which of the following amounts must Mike include in his income for Canadian income tax purposes in respect of these two dividend cheques?

(A) $20,000

(B) $28,500

(C) $30,000

(D) $35,000

Question 7

Ron Bordessa is 18 years of age. He inherited shares of Royal Roads Ltd., a private corporation, on his grandfather's death three years ago. Which of the following statements is true?

(A) Any dividend that Ron receives on these shares will be subject to the tax on split income.

(B) The tax on split income does not apply to any dividends on these shares because they were inherited.

(C) Any capital gains that Ron received on these will be subject to the tax on split income.

(D) The tax on split income does not apply to any dividend on these shares because Ron has reached the age of 18.

EXERCISES

Exercise 1

[ITA: 12(1)(c), (4), (11)]

What would be the *first* year in which the taxpayer would have to include interest in income in each of the following cases and to which years would that interest relate?

(A) A corporation with a June 30 year-end buys a bond that pays interest semi-annually on March 31 and September 30 from its previous owner on January 1, 2005.

(B) An individual buys a compounding GIC on November 1, 2005.

(C) An individual buys a zero coupon bond, issued on January 1, 2005, in 2005.

(D) An individual buys a compound Canada Savings Bond issued November 1, 2005.

(E) On June 1, 2005, an individual buys a $1,000 bond paying $40 interest by cheque each May 31 and November 30. The bond was issued on December 1, 2004.

Exercise 2

[ITA: 15(2); 20(1)(j)]

Mr. Skimit is a shareholder of Wonder-Benefits Ltd. which has a December 31 year-end. Consider the following transactions in his shareholder loan account:

Date	Loan (repayment)	Balance
Dec. 31/Year 1	—	Nil
Jan. 31/Year 2	$ 20,000	$20,000
Apr. 30/Year 2	25,000	45,000
June 30/Year 3	(15,000)	30,000
Sept. 30/Year 3	(17,000)	13,000
Mar. 31/Year 4	(12,000)	1,000
Nov. 30/Year 4	10,000	11,000
May 31/Year 5	(11,000)	Nil
Nov. 30/Year 5	23,000	23,000
July 31/Year 6	(14,000)	9,000
Dec. 31/Year 6	—	9,000

— *REQUIRED*

(A) If it is assumed that these transactions result in the conclusion that there is a series of loans and repayments, compute the amounts that must be included under paragraph 15(2)(b) or that may be deducted under paragraph 20(1)(j) for each of the years indicated according to the guidelines in IT-119R4.

(B) If there has not been a series of loans and repayments, how would the amounts differ from the above? How would you argue there was no series of loans and repayments?

Exercise 3

[ITA: 15(2); 80.4; ITR: 4300]

Cohber Marlach is a major shareholder and senior executive of Burlon Ltd. He was required to use a car about 60% for the duties of his employment. On April 1, under a plan available to the five other senior executives of the corporation, he was granted a loan of $35,000 at a rate of interest of 3% per annum and agreed to annual payments on the anniversary day of $7,000 for principal and monthly payments of interest at the end of each month. During the year he faithfully made the monthly interest payments for seven months, but neglected to make the interest payments for the last two months of the year.

— REQUIRED

What are the income tax consequences to the taxpayer? Assume that the prescribed rates were as follows:

first quarter	.... 5%	third quarter	.... 5%
second quarter	.... 4%	fourth quarter	.... 6%

Ignore the effects of the leap year, if applicable.

Exercise 4

[ITA: 74.1; 74.5]

(A) A husband wants his wife to have a $1,000 Canada Savings Bond that he owns paying interest at 7%. What are the consequences to the couple during the year if:

(i) he gives the bond to her without receiving any financial consideration from her in return?

(ii) he sells the bond to her for $1,000 plus accrued interest to the date of sale in return for cash?

(iii) he sells the bond to her for $1,000 plus accrued interest to the date of sale in return for a demand note which she signs payable to him without interest?

(iv) he cashes the bond lending the proceeds to her in return for a promissory note which she signs payable to him without interest but with a definite repayment period and she uses the funds from the loan to buy a similar bond?

(B) Would any of the above answers change for the current year if he undertook the same transactions with a trust set up in favour of a child aged 15 instead of his wife?

(C) Would any of the above answers change if he undertook the same transactions with a child aged 20?

Exercise 5

[ITA: 18(2)]

A downtown hotel bought a vacant lot adjacent to the hotel building. Comment on the deductibility of property taxes and interest paid on funds borrowed to buy the property if:

(i) the property is used as a parking lot for hotel guests;

(ii) the property was bought for potential gains on future sale but in the meantime it is being used as a public parking lot generating net revenues before the taxes and interest of 75% of the expenditures for taxes and interest;

(iii) the property was bought for future expansion of the hotel and in the meantime is being used under the same condition as in (ii) above.

Exercise 6

[ITR: 1100]

Mr. Provident is a salaried employee who invests in small rental properties. He bought one such property last year and at the beginning of this year the undepreciated capital cost balances for that property were as follows:

Class 1 — brick building	$148,000
Class 8 — furniture and fixtures	25,000

This year he bought another property for $150,000 including land valued at $12,500. The net income before capital cost allowance for each property this year was:

property 1 . . . . $ 9,270
property 2   3,750

— REQUIRED

Compute the maximum capital cost allowance on these rental properties for the current year.

Exercise 7

[ITA: 18(1)(a); 20(1)(c)]

Ms. Prudent has always considered investing her savings to be a high priority. This year she has saved $5,000. However, she has just discovered that she will need to purchase a new car which will cost an additional $5,000 with her trade-in. She can borrow the funds for the car from the dealer at a very favourable rate of 5.9% while funds borrowed from a stockbroker will cost 7%. She is in a 25.5% (combined federal and provincial) tax bracket.

— REQUIRED

Advise Ms. Prudent as to how she can accomplish her goals at a minimum cost in this situation.

Exercise 8

[ITA: 20(1)(a); ITR: 1100; 1101(1ac)]

Ms. Alimeag owns two rental properties. One produced rental revenue of $13,500 and had allowable expenses (excluding capital cost allowance) of $11,250. The other had rental revenue of $22,500 and expenses of $18,750. Data on the two Class 3 buildings are as follows:

	Property A	Property B
Capital cost	$360,000	$600,000
U.C.C., January 1	$330,000	$480,000

During the year, Property A was sold for net proceeds of $336,000.

— REQUIRED

(A) What is the effect of the above information on the income of Ms. Alimeag for the year?

(B) Can an election be made under subsection 13(4) if Property A is replaced by the end of the next year?

Exercise 9

[ETA: 123(1); 173(1); Schedule V, Part VII]

Reconsider the facts of Exercise 4.

— REQUIRED

Discuss the GST implications to the receipt of the loan.

ASSIGNMENT PROBLEMS

Problem 1

[ITA: 12(1)(g); IT-462]

The Country Pie is a highly recognized baker of quality pies in Beamsville, Ontario. The current proprietor, Rudolph Strudel, started the business about 20 years ago with an initial purchase of equipment of $150,000 and built up the name of the company by closely supervising the pie production process. Many have said that it is this attention and his recipes that have made the business a success. Rudolph has decided to sell his business and move to the coast to get away from the pressures of running a business. An offer has been made for the assets of The Country Pie by Big Food Corporation Ltd. ("BFC"). There was a meeting of the minds as to the value of the fixed assets of The Country Pie. However, there was considerable dispute as to the value of The Country Pie name in generating pie sales after a purchase by BFC. Consequently, it is proposed that the full proceeds be determined in part by future sales.

The BFC offer is for $50,000 cash; $60,000 to be paid on the basis of sales over the next three years with any balance of the $60,000 remaining at the end of the third year payable at that time; and 25% of gross sales in the next five years. As part of the agreement, Rudolph would provide consulting services to BFC as needed during the next three years.

— REQUIRED

Discuss the income tax implications to Rudolph of the proposal from BFC.

Problem 2

[ITA: 15(2), (2.3), (2.4), (2.6); 20(1)(j); 80.4; ITR: 4300(7)]

In 2004, Sunshine Publishing Ltd., a book publishing company with a fiscal year-end on December 31, made a loan of $100,000 to Stuart Sunshine, the president and majority shareholder. Both Stuart and Sunshine Publishing Limited are Canadian residents.

This is the first loan that Stuart ever received from the company, and it helped him finance the purchase of a new home which was built just outside Toronto, ten kilometres farther from the corporate headquarters than Stuart's previous home. The loan was made on May 1, 2004, and a mortgage agreement was signed on that date. This agreement requires that the $100,000 owing be repaid over five years in equal instalments of $20,000 on each anniversary date without interest. Early prepayments of principal are allowed.

Assume that the prescribed rates applicable to taxable benefits are: 6% for the first quarter of 2004, 8% for the second quarter, 9% for the third quarter, 7% for the fourth quarter and 6% for all of 2005.

— REQUIRED

(A) It is now December 2004 and Stuart has asked you to advise him on the tax consequences of the loan. It is not a company policy to make housing loans to employees and no other loans have been made to employees on similar conditions. What are the income tax consequences of this loan to Stuart in 2004 and 2005?

(B) If it was a company policy to make such loans to employees and other loans had been made to employees on similar terms and conditions, how would this change your answer to Part (A)?

(C) Assume the following facts: it was a company policy to make such loans to employees; other loans had been made to employees on similar terms and conditions; Stuart was a 9.5% shareholder rather than a majority shareholder; he was not related to any shareholders of the company; and the loan was to buy a rental property rather than a home. How would this change your answer to Part (B)?

Ignore the effects of the leap year.

Problem 3

[ITA: 12(1)(c), (j); 74.1; 74.5; 82(1); IT-510; IT-511R]

Mr. Wiser is contemplating investing in two different mutual funds. His investment options are set out below.

Amount	Mutual Fund	Distribution
$2,000	International Income Fund	Annual interest of 8.0%
$2,000	Canadian Dividend Fund	Annual dividend of 6.0%

Mr. Wiser contemplates holding both mutual funds for the same period of time — from purchase to December 31, 2009 Mr. Wiser is in the top federal income tax bracket (29%). Mr. Wiser's provincial tax on income rate is 17%. Assume that the combined federal and provincial dividend tax credit is equal to the dividend gross-up.

— REQUIRED

(A) Based on the above information, which mutual fund should Mr. Wiser prefer?

(B) Can Mr. Wiser achieve any advantage by purchasing the above mutual fund in the name of his 8 year old daughter who has no other source of income?

(C) Mr. Wiser's spouse is currently attending university on a full-time basis and has no source of income. Can Mr. Wiser achieve any advantage by lending $2,000 to his spouse and having her purchase the above mutual fund? The $2,000 loan would be evidenced by a promissory note repayable in 4 equal annual installments on each of December 31, 2005–2008 and bearing interest at a commercial rate.

Problem 4

[ITA: 18(2)–(3)]

Furniture Focus Limited provides competitive prices to consumers by using a no-frills approach to displaying its product in large stores surrounded by ample parking. Furniture Focus Limited has excess land that is not currently used in its business. This vacant land is rented to the adjacent automobile dealer who stores new cars on it.

For the year ended December 31, 2005, Furniture Focus Limited had the following operating expenses:

Sales	$35,000,000
Cost of goods sold	(20,000,000)
Gross profit	$15,000,000
Selling expenses	(5,000,000)
General and administrative expenses	(2,000,000)
	$ 8,000,000
Other income	50,000
Net income	$ 8,050,000

The general and administrative expenses include $30,000 of interest and $5,000 of property taxes on the vacant land rented to the automobile dealer. There are no other expenses connected with this land. Other income includes $10,000 of rental income paid by the automobile dealer.

— REQUIRED

Determine the income tax consequences of the various payments related to the vacant land.

Problem 5

[ITA: 20(1)(*a*); ITR: 1100 (11); 1101(1ac); Sched. II]

Sara Shimizu is the owner of two rental properties, 509 Brunswick Avenue and 356 Spadina Road. These properties were purchased six years ago for $525,000 and $600,000, respectively. In 2005, 509 Brunswick Avenue was sold for $550,000. A reasonable allocation of this amount is considered to be 75% to the building and 25% to the land. The following income and expenses were incurred in renting out the two properties in 2005:

Rental	$ 60,000
Interest on mortgage	(40,000)
Operating costs	(15,000)
Promotion costs for sale of property	(5,000)
Net income	0

There are no meal or entertainment expenses included in the $5,000 of sales promotion costs. At December 31, 2004, the undepreciated capital cost of 509 Brunswick Avenue was $383,500 and that of 356 Spadina Road was $400,000.

— REQUIRED

Determine the income from property for income tax purposes assuming Sara wishes to report the least amount possible for tax purposes in 2005.

Problem 6

[ITA: 18; 20]

It is early January 2005 and the president of BDC Distributing Limited, a client of your firm, called recently to discuss the tax implications regarding the construction of a new building. BDC has been growing rapidly and needs new warehouse space. They have been unable to locate any suitable space in the existing buildings in town and, therefore, have decided that their only option is to build their own building. They have identified the site and have estimated the costs of the project. These projected costs (and dates of completion) are as follows:

The land that has been identified will be purchased on February 15, 2005, for $405,000. There is no significant site preparation required so construction of the building can commence immediately. The cost of the building is estimated to be $1,348,000 plus the costs noted below. It is anticipated that BDC will be able to occupy the building on October 31, 2005.

BDC currently has an architect finalizing the drawings for the building. The architect fees, which will all be paid in 2005, will amount to $7,200. There will also be fees of $2,100 for an engineer to examine the drawings.

BDC has arranged for the financing required for the project. The project will be financed with a mortgage of $875,000 and $1,000,000 of preferred shares issued on January 15, 2005. Interest on the mortgage is payable semi-annually on July 15 and January 15 at a rate of 8% per annum. The preferred shares pay dividends of 5% per annum, payable semi-annually on July 15 and January 15. There will be a number of costs incurred in order to issue the debt and shares. These costs are legal and accounting fees of $18,450, commissions of $58,300 and registration fees of $1,800 for amending the articles of incorporation to allow the issuance of the preferred shares.

The balance of the costs related to the building are summarized below:

Building insurance from April 15, 2005 @ $450 per month	$ 3,825
Property taxes from February 15, 2005 @ $770 per month	8,085
Soil testing to determine location of footings for building	1,825
Relocation expenses	34,100
Utilities service connections estimated to be completed on May 20, 2005	3,800
Mortgage insurance premium from March 1, 2005 of $325 per month	3,250
Maintenance from October 31, 2005	2,500
Utilities from October 31, 2005	6,300
Landscaping	15,500

— REQUIRED

Advise the corporation of the impact of the proposed transactions on their December 31, 2005 income tax return.

Ignore the effects of the leap year.

Problem 7

[ETA: 123(1); Schedule V, Parts VI and VII]

Reconsider the facts of Problem 6. Assume that GST was paid, where applicable, in addition to the amounts shown.

— REQUIRED

Calculate the GST consequences of the transactions presented.

Problem 8

[ITA: Subdivision b]

John Investor has provided you with the following information related to his various investment holdings as of December 31, 2005.

Interest earned on joint bank account with his spouse (spouse contributes equally)	$ 2,000
Interest earned on his investment account (not joint) with his investment broker	800
Interest earned on 2004 personal income tax assessment	450
Interest on short-term investments:	
$20,000 term deposit taken out November 30, 2005 (interest at maturity in six months)	
Accrued interest from December 1 — December 31, 2005	85
$200,000 GIC purchased November 1, 2004 (interest payable at maturity on October 31, 2007)	
Accrued interest from November 1, 2004 — October 31, 2005	16,000
Accrued interest from January 1, 2005 — December 31, 2005	16,214
Government of Canada Treasury Bills purchased for $9,009 on January 1, 2005	
Amount received on maturity on December 31, 2005	10,000
Cash dividends received from investment in common shares of taxable Canadian corporations	24,000
Cash dividends received from common shares in US corporations (net of $3,000 of foreign withholding taxes; all in $CDN)	17,000

Rental details from operation of two separate rental properties:

	Property 1	Property 2
Gross rental revenue	$ 30,000	$ 46,000
Utilities	5,000	8,000
Property taxes	2,400	3,500
Repairs	1,500	4,800
Mortgage interest	20,000	32,000
Opening UCC	$368,209	$520,225

John has his own small business which is incorporated. He is the sole shareholder of this business. On May 21, 2005, his corporation (which has a December 31 year end) loaned him $40,000 free of interest. He used this money to help his oldest son make a downpayment on his first home. He did sign a note with his corporation agreeing to pay these funds back in equal instalments over the next 4 years. No other employees of the corporation are eligible to receive loans on similar terms. Show the ultimate effect on income assuming the loan is not repaid for three years.

Interest expenses paid during 2005:

Interest on bank line of credit used for investing in shares described above	$50,000
Interest on loan to acquire an automobile for his daughter for her 18th birthday	3,200
Interest on a parcel of vacant land (purchased in 2000, the land does not generate any income)	10,000

— *REQUIRED*

Prepare a calculation of John's property income. Assume that the prescribed rates for 2005 were: 5% for the first quarter, 4% for the second quarter and 6% for the third and fourth quarters. Comment on the income tax implications of items not included in your calculations.

Problem 9

[ITA: 18(1); 20(1)(*c*); [20(1)(*qq*)]; IT-533]

Funds are borrowed by an individual from a financial institution at an 11% per annum interest rate to purchase the following unrelated investments:

(a) gold coins on which gains or losses will be treated as capital gains or losses;

(b) an RRSP portfolio of investments yielding 12.5% in interest;

(c) a five-year GIC paying interest at 8% per annum;

(d) common shares of a taxable Canadian corporation paying no dividends;

(e) preferred shares of a taxable Canadian corporation paying 7% dividends;

(f) preferred shares of a U.S. corporation paying 9% dividends;

(g) $100,000 of assets used in an unincorporated business which generated net income of $9,750 before drawings of $18,000 for the year;

(h) lottery tickets which yielded $75,000 in winnings which were reinvested in short-term securities yielding 13%; and

(i) common shares of a taxable Canadian corporation paying dividends of 6%; later in the year the shares were sold at a small gain to repay a 14% second mortgage on a principal residence.

— *REQUIRED*

Determine the deductibility of the interest expense in each of the unrelated cases.

[For more problems and solutions thereto, see the CD accompanying this book.]

SUPPLEMENTAL NOTES

(This section can be omitted without losing the continuity of the chapter. None of the review questions, multiple choice questions, exercises, or assignment problems utilizes this information.)

A. Prescribed Debt Obligations

[ITA: 12(9); ITR: 7000]

Regulations define specific methods of determining the interest deemed to accrue for debt obligations that have a variety of interest payment terms, including variable and contingent interest obligations. These Regulations apply, by virtue of subsection 12(9), for purposes of determining the accrued interest under subsections 12(3), (4), (11), 20(14) and (21). There are four prescribed debt obligations.

A Type I debt obligation [Reg. 7000(1)(*a*)] is one that does not have an interest payment that is stipulated to be payable in respect of a principal amount; for example, a zero coupon bond. The accrued interest is determined by multiplying the principal amount by the interest rate equal to the yield that equates the cost of the debt obligation with the present value of all future payments [Reg. 7000(2)(*a*)].

A Type II debt obligation [Reg. 7000(1)(*b*)] has disproportional rights to principal and interest such as a stripped bond where the coupons and residue are sold separately. The accrued interest will be determined in the same manner as Type I if there is a single future payment [Reg. 7000(2)(*b*)]. Where there is more than one payment, the method used to calculate the interest income is the same as Type III, which is described below.

A Type III debt obligation [Reg. 7000(1)(*c*)] is one, other than a Type I or Type II debt obligation, that has a stated interest rate (including any bonus [Reg. 7000(3)]) that increases at some point in time — for example, a guaranteed investment certificate (GIC) that has a higher interest rate after the first two years. The accrued interest is prescribed to be the greater of (1) the maximum interest stipulated for the year and (2) the accrued interest based on the yield that equates the principal amount of the debt to the present value of all maximum future payments [Reg. 7000(2)(*c*)].

Paragraph 7000(2)(*c*.1) expands a debt obligation that can be classified as Type III. The interest payable on this type of obligation is fixed at the date of issue and the rate of interest never decreases. An example would be a GIC which pays interest at stipulated rates per year which increase by one percentage point per year from the year of issue through its five-year term. In this case, the accrued interest would be determined on a yield to maturity basis. The actual interest payable would not be relevant in determining accrued interest for this type of obligation.

A Type IV debt obligation [Reg. 7000(1)(*d*)] does not qualify as any of the first three types and has an interest rate that is contingent upon a subsequent event, such as an interest rate that increases if the debt is held maturity. Another example would be a GIC that has a return which is tied to a stock market index. The accrued interest is determined to be the maximum interest rate potentially payable [Reg. 7000(2)(*d*)].

Example Problem 1 ————————————————————————————

A zero coupon bond (one paying no interest) is issued on July 1, 2005, for $659. It matures on June 30, 2009 for $1,000.

— REQUIRED

(A) If Tacks E. Nuff purchased the bond on the issue date and held it to maturity, when and how much interest would he be required to include in income each year?

(B) How would your answer differ if the purchaser was a corporation with a December 31 taxation year-end?

— SOLUTION

(A) A zero coupon bond is a prescribed debt obligation [Reg. 7000(1)(a)]. The amount of interest deemed to accrue [Reg. 7000(2)(a)] is determined as follows:

Step 1

Compute the yield (i) on the bond: $659 = \dfrac{\$1,000}{(1 + i)^4}$

i = approximately 11%

Step 2

Compute the annual accrued interest on the accrued value of the bond:

An individual taxpayer would recognize the following accrued income, beginning in the year of the first anniversary day on June 30, 2006:

Year	Accrued income of an individual for tax purposes	Total accrual on bond
2005	Nil	
2006	$659 × .11 = $ 72	$659 + $72 = $ 731
2007	731 × .11 = 80	731 + 80 = 811
2008	811 × .11 = 89	811 + 89 = 900
2009	900 × .11 = 99	900 + 99 = 999
	$340	

(B) A corporation would include the accrued interest in income on an annual basis (e.g., $36 in 2005, assuming the corporation had a fiscal year ending December 31). Since the "anniversary day" definition applies only to an "investment contract" and the term "investment contract" does not apply to a corporation subject to the accrual rule in subsection 12(3), a normal annual accrual method must be used by a corporate taxpayer.

Year ended December 31	Accrued interest	Amount owing on bond
2005	$659 × 0.054* = $36	$659 + $36 = $ 695
2006	695 × 0.11 = 76	695 + 76 = 771
2007	771 × 0.11 = 85	771 + 85 = 856
2008	856 × 0.11 = 94	856 + 94 = 950
2009	950 × 0.054 = 51	950 + 51 = 1,001
	$342**	

———————————

* Approximate six-month rate resulting in annual 11 per cent effective rate.

** Difference in total from (A), above, due to rounding.

Example Problem 2 ————————————————————————————————————

Mr. Lot Stu Learn acquired a non-transferable $5,000 five-year compound-interest GIC in 2005. The GIC pays 9% annual interest; however, the interest is reduced to 7% per annum if the GIC is cashed early.

— *REQUIRED*

(A) At what rate must interest be included in the taxpayer's income each year?

(B) What are the tax consequences of cashing the GIC early?

— *SOLUTION*

(A) This GIC is a prescribed debt obligation [Reg. 7000(1)(*d*)] because the interest payable depends on a contingency (holding period) existing after the year. The CRA uses this example in paragraph 23 of IT-396R, although it considers the GIC to fall under Regulation 7000(1)(*c*), a debt in which the interest in a year is less than interest in a subsequent year. Regardless, Regulation 7000(2) would deem interest income to accrue at 9% per year.

(B) If the certificate is disposed of before maturity, any overaccrued interest already recognized for tax purposes would be deductible in the year of disposition [ssec. 20(21)]. Note, however, that the taxpayer may have been forced to pre-pay tax on interest that he ultimately does not receive.

B. GST and Property Income

[ETA: 123(1); 142(1), (2); 162; Schedule V, Part 1, 6]

1. Payments based on production or use

The definition of supply [ETA: ssec. 123(1)] provides, among other things, that supply means the provision of property or a service in any manner, including licence, rental or lease. Consequently, most rents, royalties and similar payments that are dependent on the use of or production from property are subject to GST, provided that they do not relate to exempt or zero-rated supplies. For example, where the author of a book receives royalty payments that are based on the number of books sold in Canada, the payments will be subject to GST. Under the place of supply rules [ETA: ssec. 142(1)] (discussed in Chapter 2), a supply of rights to intangible personal property (such as intellectual property) that may be used in whole or in part in Canada will be deemed to be made in Canada. For example, if the worldwide rights to use a patent or copyright are granted, the supply is deemed to be made in Canada, even if the Canadian rights are never exercised. Conversely, a supply is deemed to be made outside Canada if the property cannot be used in Canada [ETA: ssec. 142(2)]. For example, the supply of a copyright that does not include Canadian rights is deemed to be made outside Canada.

The supply of most rights to explore for or exploit natural resources is deemed not to be a supply and, hence, any consideration paid in respect of such a right is not subject to GST [ETA: sec. 162]. This includes any right to an amount computed by reference to the production (including profit) from, or to the value of production from, any mineral deposit or peat bog or deposit of peat, or any forestry, water or fishery resources. However, this provision does not apply to the supply of a natural resource property right to consumers, or to non-registrants who acquire the right in the course of making resales to consumers. As a result, these fees are subject to GST.

2. Rental properties

Long-term leases of residential real property are exempt from GST [ETA: sec. 6 of Part I of Schedule V]. For this exemption to apply, the tenant must occupy the particular residential complex (such as a house) or unit (such as an apartment) for a period of at least one month. This exemption does not apply to hotels, motels, etc., where all or substantially all of the units are rented out for periods of less than sixty days. However, an exemption is available for short-term stays in rooming and boarding houses. While residential landlords need not collect GST on rents, input tax credits may not be claimed in respect of GST paid by these landlords on purchases of property and services. The net GST remitted by the landlord may be added to the adjusted cost base for capital property, and to other deductible expenses for income tax purposes. However, a residential rental property rebate is available for landlords, equal to 36 per cent of the tax imposed (or 2.5 percentage points of tax), for newly-constructed, substantially-renovated or converted residential rental accommodation used for long-term rental accommodation. The rebate also applies to the construction of additions to residential rental property and to the leasing of land that is used for residential purposes. The full rebate is available for units valued up to $350,000. The rebate is phased out for residential units valued between $350,000 and $450,000, and is eliminated for units valued at $450,000 or more.

On leases of commercial property, landlords are required to charge GST and are eligible to claim input tax credits in the normal manner for tax paid on purchases of property and services.

Chapter 7

Capital Gains: An Introduction

TOPICS DISCUSSED

	Page
OVERVIEW OF THE TAXATION OF CAPITAL GAINS	317
History	317
Capital Receipt vs. Income Receipt Revisited	318
Terminology	319
Capital Gains Deduction	320
Election re: Disposition of Canadian Securities	321
Avoidance	321
GENERAL RULES	321
Computation of Capital Gains and Capital Losses	321
Adjustments to the Cost Base	324
SPECIFIC PROVISIONS FOR THE TAXATION OF CAPITAL GAINS	325
Principal Residence Exemption	325
Personal-use Property	328
Listed Personal Property	329

	Page
Pooling of Identical Assets Purchased after 1971	329
Disposition of Shares Acquired under a Stock Option	331
Cost of Certain Properties	335
Adjustments to the Cost Base	336
Superficial Losses	337
COMPUTATIONAL RULES	339
Section 3 Revisited	339
Allowable Business Investment Losses	340
SUPPLEMENTAL NOTES	354
Cost of Assets Owned on December 31, 1971	354
Additional Rules For a Residence Owned On and After December 31, 1981	355
Principal Residence on Farm Land	361
GST Rules For Dispositions of Residential Property and Used Goods	361

Subdivision c of Division B of Part I of the Act contains the primary rules for the computation of taxable capital gains and allowable capital losses.

The following chart will help to locate these provisions in the Act.

Part I — Division B
Subdivision c
Capital Gains & Losses

DIVISION		SUBDIVISION		SECTION	
A	Liability for tax				
B	Computation of income		Basic rules		
C	Computation of taxable income	a	Office or employment		
		b	Business or property		
D	Taxable income earned in Canada by non-residents	c	Capital gains and losses	38	TCG/ACL
		d	Other income	39	CG/CL
E	Computation of tax	e	Other deductions	39.1	Exempt CG balance
E.1	Minimum tax	f	Rules relating to computation of income	40	General rules
F	Special rules			41	LPP
G	Deferred and other special income arrangements			42	Warranty
		g	Amounts not included in income	43	Part disposition
				43.1	Life estates
H	Exemptions	h	Cdn corporations and shareholders	44	Replacement property
I	Returns, Assessments, payments, appeals	i	Shareholders of non-resident corporations	44.1	Small business share rollover
				45	Change in use
J	Appeals to the courts	j	Partnerships	46	Personal-use property
		k	Trusts	47	Identical property
				48.1	SBC goes public
				49	Options granted
				50	Loss on debt/shares
				51	Convertible prop
				52	Cost of certain prop
				53	ACB adjustments
				54	Definitions
				54.1	Exception: principal residence
				54.2	Shares and capital property
				55	Deemed capital gain

Some of the more important provisions are as follows:

Sec. 39 Meaning of capital gain, capital loss and business investment loss

Sec. 40 General rules including principal residence exemption

Sec. 41 Listed personal property

Sec. 44 Replacement property rules

Sec. 45 Change in use

Sec. 46 Personal-use property

Sec. 47 Identical properties

Sec. 52 Cost

Sec. 53 Adjustments to cost base

Sec. 54 Definitions

In addition, subdivision f of Division B also provides some rules that are relevant to the computation of property income. For example, the attribution rules in sections 74.2 and 74.3 determine whether the capital gains or losses received by a particular person should be attributed to someone else.

This chapter introduces the concepts needed and the following chapter discusses them in further detail.

I. OVERVIEW OF THE TAXATION OF CAPITAL GAINS

A. History

Prior to 1972, capital gains were not taxed under the Act. Canada was one of the few western nations which had never levied a tax on the disposition of capital property. With our government's concern for equity among taxpayers, a complete set of rules for the taxation of capital gains was introduced to the legislation. These rules have become an additional source of confusion for tax practitioners, the Canada Revenue Agency (CRA) and taxpayers. Slowly since 1972, the government has been revising the rules in this particular subdivision, although these revisions have introduced more complexity during this time.

One of the most significant changes is to the inclusion rate for capital gains. The inclusion rate is the percentage that is applied to the capital gain with the result being included in income as a taxable capital gain. Since tax on capital gains was introduced in 1972 this inclusion rate has changed four times as shown below:

Time Period	Inclusion Rate
1972 to 1987	50%
1988 and 1989	66 2/3 %
1990 to February 27, 2000	75%
February 28 to October 17, 2000	66 2/3%
After October 17, 2000	50%

B. Capital Receipt vs. Income Receipt Revisited

[ITA: 38; 39(1); IT-218R; IT-459; IT-479R]

The Act does not define a capital gain. The provisions merely set out the technical computations to be made once it has been determined whether a transaction is an income receipt or a capital receipt. Hence, taxpayers and their advisers must turn to the guidelines which have been laid down by the courts through past judicial decisions. Even then, there is no clear-cut set of rules which will apply unequivocally in all situations. The result has been one of the most confusing and controversial areas of taxation giving rise to thousands of court cases since the advent of federal income taxation in Canada.

A set of behavioural factors which were introduced in Chapter 4 were developed by the courts to help in determining whether the transaction may fall into the capital category or the income category. However, each situation must be judged in relation to facts surrounding the particular transaction and in many cases may warrant professional advice. In determining the facts, the taxpayer's whole course of conduct before, during and after the transaction in question should be reviewed.

The objective of most decisions is to determine the intention of the taxpayer. First, there may be an indicator in the taxpayer's behaviour of *primary intention*, that is, did the taxpayer intend to make a business or trading profit on the transaction? If the answer to this question, as determined by observing the facts of the taxpayer's behaviour, is affirmative, then the transaction is likely income.

The courts may, also, examine the evidence of the taxpayer's behaviour to establish whether the taxpayer had any *secondary intention*, especially in respect of, but not limited to, real estate transactions. Secondary intention may be thought of as an alternative or secondary objective in the mind of the taxpayer at the time of the purchase which motivated the purchase and which would come into operation later if the primary objective is thwarted. For example, a developer purchases a piece of property for an apartment complex which he or she plans to operate as an investment property by collecting rent. However, zoning bylaws cannot be altered to accommodate the proposed project and the developer subsequently sells the property at a profit. The courts would likely view this as an income transaction by way of the taxpayer's secondary intention, on the assumption that the taxpayer, as a developer, would know at the time of purchase that he or she could remove himself or herself from the situation at a profit when the primary objective could not be achieved.[a]

The factors, often referred to as "badges of trade", used to establish intention to engage in an adventure or concern in the nature of trade and previously discussed in Chapter 4, include but are not limited to:

(a) the relationship of the transaction to the taxpayer's business;[b]

(b) the nature of the activity or organization associated with trade (recall the British cases of the large quantities of toilet paper and whiskey referred to in Chapter 4 and refer to IT-459 on the concept of an adventure in the nature of trade, also discussed in Chapter 4);

(c) the nature of the assets involved in the transaction;[c]

---

[a] The cases of *Rosenblatt v. M.N.R.*, (Ex. Ct.) 55 DTC 1205, *Stekl v. M.N.R.*, (Ex. Ct.) 59 DTC 1262 and *Regina Shoppers Mall Ltd. v. The Queen*, (F.C.A.) 89 DTC 5482, illustrate the focus on intention by the courts.

[b] This factor is illustrated by the cases of *Atlantic Sugar Refineries v. M.N.R.*, (S.C.C.) 49 DTC 602 and *Gairdner Securities v. M.N.R.*, (S.C.C.) 54 DTC 1015.

[c] This factor is illustrated by the case of *Great West Exploration Ltd. v. M.N.R.*, (T.A.B.) 57 DTC 444.

(d) the number and frequency of transactions within a given period of time;

(e) the length of the period of ownership of the asset;

(f) any supplemental work on or in connection with the property; and

(g) if the transaction was completed by an organization, the stated objectives of the organization, as outlined in articles of association or incorporation or a partnership agreement.[d]

The more complete description of these factors presented in Chapter 4 should be reviewed. Reference should also be made to IT-218R, at paragraph 3, where the CRA lists about 12 factors pertaining to real estate transactions. Where a disposition of securities is at issue, the CRA lists some relevant factors to consider in IT-479R at paragraph 11.

C. Terminology

[ITA: 39; 54]

Before attempting to read the pertinent sections in Subdivision c, it is necessary to become acquainted with the basic terminology and abbreviations illustrated below.

Accounting terminology			*Income tax terminology*	
Selling price..............		$xx	Proceeds of disposition (P of D)	Sec. 54
Cost..........................	$xx	....	Adjusted cost base (A.C.B.)	Sec. 54
Selling costs..............	xx (xx)	....	Expenses of disposition (S.C.)	Ssec. 40(1)
Profit (Loss)..............		$xx	Gain (Loss)	
		(xx)	Exemption or reserve, if any	Sec. 40
		$xx	Capital gain (C.G.) or Capital loss (C.L.)	Sec. 39
		$xx	Taxable capital gain (T.C.G.) or Allowable capital loss (A.C.L.)	Sec. 38

Capital gains treatment requires a disposition. Subsection 248(1) contains the definition of "disposition" of property. Generally, a disposition includes any transaction entitling a taxpayer to proceeds of disposition. This definition, then, specifies situations that are considered to be dispositions. In some cases, transfers of property, which do not give rise to actual proceeds, will be deemed to be dispositions for tax purposes. These will include deemed dispositions:

● on the change in use of property [ssec. 45(1)];

● on the death of a taxpayer [ssec. 70(5)];

● by way of gift during the lifetime of a taxpayer [ssec. 69(1)]; and

● when a taxpayer ceases to be a resident of Canada [ssec. 128.1(1)].

"Proceeds of disposition" defined in section 54 is a much broader term than "selling price" because it includes deemed proceeds.

"Adjusted cost base" defined in section 54 also encompasses more than the traditional accounting "laid-down cost". Section 53 has over forty specific adjustments to the accounting actual cost. Selling costs are not included in the adjusted cost base and, hence, may in themselves give rise to a capital loss.

---

[d] This factor is illustrated by the cases of *Sutton Lumber & Trading Co. Ltd. v. M.N.R.*, (S.C.C.) 53 DTC 1158; *Laverne Asmussen Ltd. v. M.N.R.*, (T.A.B.) 61 DTC 440; and *Western Leaseholds v. M.N.R.*, (S.C.C.) 59 DTC 1316.

"Exemptions" are deducted from the "gain" in order to arrive at the capital gain. There are two major exemptions: one pertains to a principal residence (a permanent exemption from tax) and the other provides a reserve for amounts not due in the year (a tax deferral). These are discussed in detail later in this chapter.

A taxable capital gain (allowable capital loss) is the portion of the capital gain (capital loss) taken into income. The inclusion rate is $^1/_2$ after October 17, 2000.

Business investment losses (B.I.L.s), as defined in paragraph 39(1)(c), are capital losses which occur on the disposition of either shares or debt of a small business corporation. The term "small business corporation" is defined in subsection 248(1) and discussed in more detail in a subsequent chapter. Generally, a small business corporation is a Canadian-controlled private corporation. All or substantially all of its fair market value of its assets are:

(a) used to carry on an active business primarily in Canada;

(b) shares or debt of connected (as discussed in a subsequent chapter) small business corporations; or

(c) a combination of (a) and (b).

While these BILs are still capital losses, only fractionally deductible, they are given special treatment as an incentive for investment. The fractional amount deductible, which uses the same inclusion rate as capital losses (i.e., $^1/_2$ after October 17, 2000), is called an allowable business investment loss (A.B.I.L.). The use of A.B.I.L.s will be discussed later in this chapter.

Another way of looking at the terminology is to compare the description before (100%) and after (50%) the inclusion rate has been applied. For example,

100%	50%
Capital gain	Taxable capital gain
Capital loss	Allowable capital loss
Business investment loss	Allowable business investment loss
Capital gains exemption	Capital gains deduction

D. Capital Gains Deduction

[ITA: 110.6]

From 1985 until February 22, 1994, there was a lifetime exemption for capital gains of $100,000 for individuals, other than trusts. This deduction was eliminated for taxable capital gains realized after February 22, 1994, but individuals were given an opportunity to elect to realize taxable capital gains accrued to February 22, 1994, which could be offset by the deduction in their 1994 tax return. The benefit of the election was to gain an increase in the adjusted cost base of the property on which the election was made or to create a notional account balance of elected gains. The increase in A.C.B. reduces future capital gains exposed to tax. The notional account balance for eligible capital property or mutual funds can be used to reduce future gains on these properties. There continues to be a capital gains exemption of up to $500,000 of capital gains on qualifying shares of a small business corporation and certain farming property. The application of these rules will be discussed in some detail in Chapter 13 which deals with planning for the corporate owner-manager.

E. Election re: Disposition of Canadian Securities

[ITA: 39(4)–(6); IT-346R; IT-479R]

Subsections 39(4) to (6) contain legislation which permits a taxpayer to elect (on form T123) that the disposition of "Canadian securities" *only* will always be a capital receipt, despite the aforementioned common law guidelines. Until the introduction of these rules, the CRA had not consistently assessed taxpayers on trading transactions in which there was an obvious intention to make a quick profit rather than to hold the shares as an income-producing investment. The dilemma is resolved with the inclusion of subsections 39(4) to (6). It should be noted, however, that once this election is made, it will remain in force forever unless the taxpayer, at the time of a disposition, is one of the prescribed taxpayers listed in subsection 39(5) who are not permitted this election. One of the exclusions is a "dealer in securities" and, of course, it will be a matter of fact whether an individual will be considered to be a "dealer" because of his or her past and present trading activities. IT-479R outlines the general rules used by the CRA to determine whether securities transactions will be afforded capital or income treatment.

The CRA's administrative position in respect of commodity transactions, including futures, is quite similar to the statutory provisions in respect of Canadian securities discussed above. IT-346R sets out a number of guidelines which must be adhered to.

F. Avoidance

[ITA: 55; 245; IC 88-2]

Prior to Tax Reform in 1987, there was a very broad anti-avoidance provision in respect of capital gains in Subdivision c. Many tax advisers were of the opinion that the provision was too wide in scope and could not be enforced. The provision was replaced by a general anti-avoidance rule (GAAR) found in subsection 245(2) which will be described in some detail in Chapter 13. However, there are a number of aspects concerning the GAAR to be aware of even at this stage.

(1) According to the CRA, the GAAR is a provision of last resort and all other avenues (i.e., specific statutory anti-avoidance provisions) must be exhausted before the GAAR will be applied.

(2) The CRA has prepared an extensive Information Circular on section 245 [IC 88-2], including numerous examples as to when the GAAR would or would not apply in the opinion of the Department.

(3) The GAAR will not apply to a transaction(s) which is primarily motivated by a non-tax purpose, e.g., estate planning.

Subsection 55(2) provides specific anti-avoidance provisions to prevent a corporation from converting a capital gain into a dividend which would normally avoid income tax when the parties involved are corporations. These rules will be covered in more detail in Chapter 16.

II. GENERAL RULES

A. Computation of Capital Gains and Capital Losses

[ITA: 40(1), (1.1); 52; 53; 54; IT-185R; IT-220R2; IT-236R4 (archived); IT-259R4; IT-460]

A gain on the disposition of property is determined [spar. 40(1)(a)(i)] as:

(a) proceeds of disposition [sec. 54]

minus

(b) the aggregate of:

(i) adjusted cost base [sec. 54], and

(ii) expenses of the disposition.

A loss is generally a negative amount resulting from the application of the above, that is, adjusted cost base and expenses of disposition minus proceeds of disposition. However, there can be no such loss on depreciable capital property, since the total decline in value should have been accounted for through the capital cost allowance system [spar. 39(1)(b)(i)].

1. Proceeds of disposition

In most cases, proceeds of disposition will be the value of the consideration received or receivable. Where a deemed disposition occurs, the proceeds usually will be deemed to be the fair market value of the property at the time of the disposition.

Section 54 provides the definitions for purposes of capital gains and losses. The definition of "proceeds of disposition" found in this section provides some very specific inclusions and exclusions that go beyond our normal idea of proceeds. In addition, the following is a list of Interpretation Bulletins that give further guidance:

IT-185R	Losses from theft, defalcation or embezzlement
IT-220R2	Capital cost allowance — proceeds of disposition of depreciable property
IT-259R4	Exchanges of property
IT-460	Dispositions — absence of consideration

One of the components of the proceeds of disposition of shares, a partnership interest or business assets might be an agreement not to compete with the purchaser. This is known as a restrictive covenant. This topic is covered by a comprehensive package of provisions related to payments received by individuals for covenants. For a full discussion on the treatment of payments received for covenants, please refer to Chapter 9.

2. Adjusted cost base and capital cost

The "adjusted cost base" of most capital property, as defined in section 54, is usually its cost plus or minus the adjustments found in section 53. Cost is not defined for taxation purposes. The usual starting point is *cost* for accounting purposes which comprises laid-down cost, including the invoice cost, relevant provincial sales, excise, and customs taxes, insurance, freight and, perhaps, some start-up costs. Where the person is a GST registrant and is eligible for an input tax credit, the GST should be excluded from adjusted cost base, because the GST is not a cost if it is recovered by an input tax credit.

Cost for accounting purposes is then modified by section 52 which establishes the cost base as amounts in respect of the value of the property which have been included in the taxpayer's income. For example, the cost of property received as a dividend in kind is the fair market value of the property received [ssec. 52(2)]. Similarly, the cost of certain stock dividends is established as a defined amount depending upon the time frame in which the stock dividends were issued [ssec. 52(3)]. Note that a stock option benefit, as determined by section 7, is excluded from the application of the general rule in subsection 52(1) because the amount of the stock option benefit determined on the acquisition of shares is added to the actual cost of the shares purchased as discussed in Chapter 3 [par. 53(1)(*j*)].

There is an important exception to the above general rules in respect of depreciable property. In order to preserve the integrity of the capital cost allowance system, the adjusted cost base of depreciable property cannot be allowed to fluctuate as a result of the previously-mentioned adjustments through sections 52 or 53. Hence, section 54 defines the "adjusted cost base" of depreciable property to be its capital cost, which in turn takes us back to *cost* for accounting purposes without adjustments under sections 52 and 53. The next chapter shows that some of these adjustments are done to proceeds of disposition rather than capital cost.

From the gain, certain exemptions, such as the exempt portion relating to a principal residence and reserves relating to amounts not yet due, could be deducted in order to arrive at the capital gain.

3. Reserves

A capital gains reserve for dispositions, where all or part of the proceeds are payable after the end of the year, is the lesser of a reasonable amount and an amount that brings 20% of the gain into income in the year of disposition and each of the immediately following four years. As a result, the usual maximum period over which the gain can be spread for inclusion in income is five years, including the year of disposition. A reasonable reserve is not defined in the Act. The CRA has taken the position [IT-236R4 (archived and no longer in force), par. 4] that a reasonable reserve is based on prorated uncollected proceeds times the gain. The following examples are based on the CRA's interpretation of a reasonable reserve. The formula for the reserve [spar. 40(1)(*a*)(iii)] is:

$$\text{Lesser of (a)} \frac{\text{proceeds not yet due}}{\text{total proceeds}} \times \text{gain} = \begin{array}{l}\text{reasonable reserve (i.e., the fraction}\\ \text{of the gain represented by the}\\ \text{portion of total proceeds not due at}\\ \text{the end of}\\ \text{the year)}\end{array}$$

(b) ($\frac{1}{5}$ of gain) $\times$ (4 – number of preceding taxation years ending after disposition)

The CRA's interpretation of the applicability of the reserve provision [IT-236R4 (archived and no longer in force), par. 2] has indicated that the reserve is based on amounts that are payable to the taxpayer after the end of the year. Where a demand note is accepted on a disposition, eligibility for a reserve can be perfected by adding a condition that the note be payable, say, 10 days after demand. A demand made at the end of the year does not require payment until 10 days later with this condition.

Subsection 40(1.1) provides for a claim for a similar reserve with a maximum 10-year period (rather than five years) on the transfer of certain farm property, shares in a family farm corporation, an interest in a family farm partnership and shares of a small business corporation to a child.

Consistent with the general scheme of the Act for the deduction of reserves, in the year following the deduction of a reserve, the preceding year's reserve will be taken into income [spar. 40(1)(*a*)(ii)], and a new reserve will be deducted in accordance with the above rules.

Example Problem ————————————————————————————

Ms. Gamma sold a capital property for $200,000 on December 31, 2005. Of that price, $180,000 was not due until December 2006. The adjusted cost base of the property was $130,000 and the selling costs were $20,000.

— REQUIRED

Determine the taxable capital gain for 2005 and 2006 using the reserve provision in paragraph 40(1)(a).

— SOLUTION

		2005
Proceeds of disposition		$200,000
Adjusted cost base	$130,000	
Expenses of disposition	20,000	(150,000)
Gain		$ 50,000

Less reserve — lesser of:

(a) $\frac{\$180,000}{\$200,000} \times \$50,000 =$ .... $ 45,000

(b) $(1/5 \times \$50,000) \times (4 - 0) =$ .... $ 40,000

} (40,000)

Capital gain		$ 10,000
Taxable capital gain (1/2 of capital gain)		$ 5,000

		2006
Inclusion in income of 2005 reserve		$ 40,000

Less 2006 reserve — lesser of:

(a) $\frac{Nil}{\$200,000} \times \$50,000 =$ .... Nil

(b) $(1/5 \times \$50,000) \times (4 - 1) =$ .... $ 30,000

} Nil

Capital gain		$ 40,000
Taxable capital gain (1/2 of capital gain)		$ 20,000

Note that the $50,000 of original capital gain is included in income over the two years in which proceeds were collected. The reserve simply allows the original gain to be spread over a maximum of 5 or 10 years, or the period of collection if that period is shorter.

Since a reserve is a permissive or optional deduction, it may not always be wise to take the reserve. For example, if the gain was triggered in a year in which the taxpayer's income and tax rate were lower than other years, deferral of the gain through a reserve would be pointless. However, a time-value of money advantage may be gained by a deferral to a future year, even if income will be taxed at a higher rate in that year. Similarly where the taxpayer wishes to use up the capital gains exemption for qualified small business corporation shares or qualified farm property immediately, the reserve should not be claimed.

B. Adjustments to the Cost Base

[ITA: 40(3); 53]

As previously noted, the laid-down cost of capital assets may be subjected to certain adjustments which are not recognized for accounting purposes. These adjustments are found in section 53, which describes a variety of specific additions to and deductions from adjusted cost base. These adjustments reflect amounts that would otherwise be treated as capital gains or losses or amounts of ordinary income, but have instead been deferred. The result of the adjustments is to reduce or increase the cost base of the property for purposes of measuring a future capital gain or loss. For example, non-deductible interest and property taxes on unproductive land prohibited under subsection 18(2) can be added to the adjusted cost base of the land [par. 53(1)(*h*)], as discussed in Chapter 6. A benefit under a stock option plan included in income under section 7 can be added to the cost base of the shares acquired [par. 53(1)(*j*)], on the basis that the amount of the benefit represents a tax-paid cost of the shares. On the other hand, grants, subsidies and other types of government assistance of this nature must be deducted from the cost base of the non-depreciable capital property acquired, on the basis that the cost of the asset has been reduced by the amount of assistance [par. 53(2)(*k*)].

A negative adjusted cost base could result at any time if the sum of the amounts deducted is greater than the cost of the property plus the sum of amounts added to it. With the exception of a partnership interest in a general (but not a limited) partnership, such a negative amount is deemed [ssec. 40(3)] to be an immediate capital gain at the time that an adjustment causes the adjusted cost base to become negative. At the same time, the adjusted cost base is brought to zero [par. 53(1)(*a*)] and future adjustments under section 53 are made from that zero base.

III. SPECIFIC PROVISIONS FOR THE TAXATION OF CAPITAL GAINS

A. Principal Residence Exemption

[ITA: 40(2)(*b*), (*c*), (6); 54; IT-120R6]

Since the rules for principal residences are complex, this chapter demonstrates only the basic concepts. The next chapter will expand upon these basic concepts and look at some important exceptions.

Generalizing that there are no capital gains subject to tax on principal residences may be inaccurate. In fact, there may be a gain but it can be exempted, wholly or partially, by designating the home as the taxpayer's principal residence for certain *specific* years. Note that the CRA, in paragraph 5 of IT-120R6, states that a taxpayer may designate any residence as his or her principal residence as long as he or she ordinarily inhabits the home, even for a short period. This may be the case when the residence was disposed of early in the year or acquired late in the year. Also, a seasonal residence can be considered to be ordinarily inhabited.

A "principal residence" defined in section 54 is virtually any housing unit or right to such a unit owned by the taxpayer either by himself or herself or jointly and ordinarily inhabited by the taxpayer, the taxpayer's spouse or former spouse, or the taxpayer's child at any time in the year. To be a principal residence, the property must be designated as such in the year of disposal. The exemption applies not only to the building but also up to one-half hectare of subjacent and adjacent land. If all of the land exceeds one-half hectare, the additional land must be shown to be necessary to the taxpayer's use and enjoyment to be eligible for this exemption. There have been a number of court cases dealing with this issue of necessity to use and enjoyment.[e]

A taxpayer owning more than one residence can designate only one of his or her residences for a given year as the principal residence for years after 1981. This is done at the time when an actual or deemed disposition is reported. Although the regulations require that a designation form (T2091) be filed with the tax return in the year of the disposition, IT-120R6, paragraph 7 states that the CRA does not require this form to be

---

(e) See *The Queen v. Yates*, (F.C.T.D.) 83 DTC 5158, affirmed by (F.C.A.) 86 DTC 6296; *Haber v. The Queen*, (F.C.T.D.) 83 DTC 5004; *Augart v. The Queen*, (F.C.A.) 93 DTC 5205; and *Carlile v. the Queen*, (F.C.A.) 95 DTC 5483.

filed unless there is a taxable capital gain after applying the exempt portion according to the designation rules.

The exempt portion of a gain on the disposition or deemed disposition of a principal residence is calculated [par. 40(2)(b)] by the following *oversimplified* formula:

$$\frac{1 + \text{number of years designated}}{\text{number of years owned}} \times \text{gain}$$

In using this formula the following points should be noted:

(a) only one housing unit can be designated as a principal residence, after December 31, 1981, per family unit which is defined in the definition of "principal residence" in section 54 to include spouses and their unmarried minor children;

(b) the years referred to in the numerator and denominator refer to those years after 1971;

(c) deemed dispositions and the resultant modification to the formula will be discussed in the next chapter;

(d) the taxpayer must be resident in Canada for tax purposes; and

(e) the actual formula contains a factor that reduces the gain by an amount based on an election made in 1994 to utilize the general capital gains deduction of $100,000 which was eliminated on February 22, 1994.

Since a family can only designate one housing unit as a principal residence for any particular year, the 1 + in the numerator of the fraction was intended to protect one housing unit in a situation where a family sells one house and buys another in the same year. In that situation, the family owns two houses in the year, but can only designate one as the principal residence for that year. In the following examples, the 1 + rule will be used in other situations involving the ownership of more than one housing unit by a family in a particular year.

Note that to be in the position to use the 1 + in the numerator, the taxpayer must be willing to designate the housing unit as a principal residence for at least one year. That is, the numerator can never be 1 + 0. The exemption formula containing the 1 + is not applicable at all if the taxpayer does not designate the housing unit as the principal residence for any year. Therefore, the minimum numerator will be 1 + 1.

Example Problem

Mr. Taxobservant is in the process of retiring and moving to another city. He decides to sell his two residences and provides you with the following information as at September 30, 2005, the date of sale.

Residence	Date of purchase	Selling price	Cost
City home	1996	$170,000	$100,000
Cottage	2001	90,000	40,000

— *REQUIRED*

Calculate the minimum total taxable capital gain on the disposition of the two residences.

— *SOLUTION*

In the five taxation years 1996 to 2000, Mr. Taxobservant owned only one residence — the city home. Therefore, there is no option in these years but to designate the city home as his principal residence.

The remaining problem is to find the allocation of the five "option" years 2001–2005 which will minimize the total capital gain on the two residences. To find this allocation, note two facts:

(1) Mr. Taxobservant can designate only one residence as his principal residence in any year.

(2) From the formula for the exempt portion of the capital gain, it can be seen that designating a particular residence as a principal residence for an additional year generally will decrease the capital gain on that residence by its gain per year of ownership.

Therefore, a first guess, as to the best allocation of the option years, is to use all of these years to designate, as a principal residence, the residence with the higher gain per year of ownership.

The city home has been owned during 10 years (1996–2005, inclusive) while the cottage has been owned during 5 years (2001–2005, inclusive). The gains per year are $7,000 for the city home and $10,000 for the cottage:

	City home	Cottage
P of D	$170,000	$90,000
A.C.B.	(100,000)	(40,000)
Gain	$ 70,000	$50,000
Gain per year	$\dfrac{\$70,000}{10 \text{ years}} = \$7,000$	$\dfrac{\$50,000}{5 \text{ years}} = \$10,000$

Thus, a first guess would be to designate the cottage for all of the option years 2001–2005 (and to designate the city home for the no-option years 1996–2000). This produces a total capital gain on the two residences of $28,000, all of which is on the city home:

	City home	Cottage
Gain	$70,000	$50,000
Exemption	$\dfrac{1+5}{10} \times \$70,000 =$ (42,000)	$\dfrac{1+5}{5} \times \$50,000 =$ (50,000)*
Capital gain	$28,000	Nil

_____
* The exemption cannot exceed the gain.

This first guess can be improved upon. Note that because of the "one plus" in the formula for the exempt portion of the capital gain, it is wasteful to designate the cottage for all of its years of ownership. The cottage would still have a zero capital gain if it was designated as a principal residence for 4 years instead of 5 years. This reduces the total capital gain to the minimum possible amount of $21,000:

	City home	Cottage
Gain	$70,000	$50,000
Exemption	$\dfrac{1+6}{10} \times \$70,000 =$ (49,000)	$\dfrac{1+4}{5} \times \$50,000 =$ (50,000)
Capital gain	$21,000	Nil
Taxable capital gain ($\frac{1}{2} \times \$21,000$)	$10,500	Nil

> **Principal Residence Exemption**
> **Steps to Follow**
> 1. Calculate the capital gain per year for each principal residence.
> 2. Determine if any of the years of ownership have been allocated to previous principal residences.
> 3. Allocate the years available to each residence to optimize the exemption. More years are initially allocated to the residence with the highest gain per year. Change that allocation if you can increase the exemption.

B. Personal-use Property

[ITA: 40(2)(g)(iii); 46; 50(2); 54]

While gains on "personal-use property" (P.U.P.), defined in section 54 as property used primarily for personal use or enjoyment, are subject to tax, losses on such property may not be deducted [spar. 40(2)(g)(iii)]. The loss on any particular item is considered to be a personal or living expense. Personal-use property will typically generate losses on disposal because such property often declines in value over time through use.

Subsection 46(1) provides that for the purpose of calculating the capital gain or loss on any disposal of P.U.P., the taxpayer's cost is deemed to be the greater of the adjusted cost base of the property and $1,000. Similarly, the taxpayer's proceeds of disposition are deemed to be the greater of actual proceeds and $1,000.

If a taxpayer disposes of any part of a personal-use property, for the purposes of computing the capital gain or loss on the disposal, subsection 46(2) provides that the $1,000 minimum cost and the $1,000 minimum proceeds must be apportioned on the basis of the proportion of the P.U.P. attributable to the part disposed of. These "part disposition" rules also apply to a disposition of part of a personal-use property that would ordinarily be disposed of as a set [ssec. 46(3)]. Thus, several dispositions of pieces of the set would be considered to be parts of a single P.U.P. disposition. If all of the pieces of a set are acquired by one person or by a group consisting of persons who are not dealing at arm's length, the taxpayer is deemed to have made a single disposition.

Example Problem ───

Consider the sale of the following personal-use properties:

	P.U.P. #1	P.U.P. #2
A.C.B.	$ 800	$1,300
P of D	1,200	700

— *REQUIRED*

Compute the capital gain or capital loss in the two above situations.

— *SOLUTION*

P.U.P. #1		P.U.P. #2	
P of D	$1,200	Deemed P of D	$1,000
Deemed A.C.B.	(1,000)	A.C.B.	(1,300)
C.G.	$ 200	C.L.	Nil

Losses arising from debts, which are personal-use property and are uncollectible, will be recognized to the extent that the gain was previously recognized on the disposition of personal-use property in return for the debt [ssec. 50(2)].

C. Listed Personal Property

[ITA: 40(2)(g)(iii); 41; 54]

"Listed personal property" (L.P.P.), which is specifically defined in section 54, is a special subset of personal-use property. Hence, all of the personal-use property rules previously described also apply to listed personal property, except that capital losses arising on the disposition of L.P.P. can be utilized, but only to the extent of L.P.P. capital gains. In addition, there are carryover provisions so that unused L.P.P. capital losses can be carried back three years and forward seven years but once again to be applied only against L.P.P. gains. Unlike all other loss carryover provisions which are found in Division C, these carryovers are applied in Division B, using the capital loss amount rather than the allowable capital loss amount, i.e., 100% of the loss instead of $1/2$. This result is achieved through a special term "net gain", which is defined in subsection 41(2) as listed personal property capital gains minus:

(a) listed personal property capital losses in the year; and

(b) listed personal property capital losses arising from the seven preceding years or the three years immediately following.

As a result of the specification of the carryover amounts in this way, there need be no concern for differing capital gains inclusion rates in the carryover period for L.P.P.s. Furthermore, these losses can be deducted at the option of the taxpayer, except that the earliest losses must be deducted before any losses of a subsequent year.

Examine carefully the very restrictive list of capital property, which qualifies for the listed personal property rules found in the definition of the term in section 54. The list is limited to a taxpayer's personal-use property that is a:

(a) print, etching, drawing, painting, sculpture, or other similar work of art,

(b) jewellery,

(c) rare folio, rare manuscript, or rare book,

(d) stamp, or

(e) coin.

If an item cannot be found in that list, it is not L.P.P. and, therefore, capital losses cannot be applied against capital gains.

D. Pooling of Identical Assets Purchased after 1971

[ITA: 47; IT-387R2]

There are many and varied methods of arriving at a cost base for identical assets for accounting purposes. However, for tax purposes, there is only one method, namely, the *"floating weighted-average method"*.

For stock transactions, the floating weighted-average cost is calculated by dividing the aggregate of the costs of the identical properties by the number of such identical properties.

For bonds, debentures, notes, etc., the floating weighted-average cost is calculated by dividing the aggregate of the cost of the identical properties by the quotient obtained when the principal amounts of all the identical properties are divided by the principal amount of the property disposed of. For example, assume that an individual purchased three $1,000 bonds of a corporation for $2,880. Later, a $500 bond of the same series of bonds of the corporation was purchased for $490. The weighted-average cost of one of the $1,000 bonds is:

$$\frac{\$2,880 + \$490}{((3 \times \$1,000) + \$500)/\$1,000} = \$963$$

Similarly, the weighted-average cost of the $500 bond is:

$$\frac{\$2,880 + \$490}{((3 \times \$1,000) + \$500)/\$500} = \$481 \text{ (or one-half the cost of a \$1,000 bond)}$$

Many investors purchase shares or units of mutual funds to hold outside of RRSP investments. Mutual funds allocate their income to their investors, such that the income is taxable to the investors and not to the mutual fund. As a result, investors must include in their income for tax purposes the amount of net investment income, such as interest and dividends, and net taxable capital gains paid or payable to them in the year. Often income so allocated to the investor is reinvested in additional units in the fund. Since reinvested income amounts would have been taxed in the hands of the investor, whether or not actually distributed, these amounts can be added to the adjusted cost base of the investor's units in the fund. However, the adjusted amount for capital gains would be the full capital gain rather than the taxable capital gain. For dividends, the adjusted amount would be the actual dividend, not the grossed-up dividend. After the reinvestment, the A.C.B. of each unit owned in the mutual fund must be averaged by dividing the total A.C.B. of all units in the mutual fund owned by the investor by the total number of units owned.

When an investor redeems or disposes of units in a mutual fund, a capital gain (or loss) is realized. The calculation of the capital gain (or loss) follows the normal formula of proceeds of disposition minus the sum of the investor's A.C.B. and selling costs. This capital gain (or loss) is separate and distinct from the taxable capital gains allocated from the income of the fund which are made annually and taxed as paid or declared payable.

Example Problem

Consider the following transactions in the shares of Dachshund Airways Ltd:

Date	Type of transaction	Number of shares	Cost per share (selling price)	Total cost (selling price)
April 1994	Purchase	100	$1	$ 100
March 1996	Purchase	150	2	300
Aug. 1997	Sale	(200)	(3)	(600)
June 2000	Purchase	100	4	400
July 2002	Purchase	300	5	1,500
Oct. 2005	Sale	(250)	(6)	(1,500)

— REQUIRED

Compute the taxable capital gains, if any, on the 1997 and the 2005 sales.

— SOLUTION

August 1997 sale:

P of D (200 shares @ $3)	$ 600
A.C.B. (200 shares @ $1.60[1])	(320)
C.G.	$ 280
T.C.G. (³/₄ × $280)	$ 210

October 2005 sale:

P of D (250 shares @ $6)	$1,500
A.C.B. (250 shares @ $4.40[2])	(1,100)
C.G.	$ 400
T.C.G. (¹/₂ × $400)	$ 200

There are 200 shares with a weighted average cost of $4.40 on hand after the 2005 sale.

— NOTES TO SOLUTION

(1)
100 shares @ $1 =	$100
150 shares @ $2 =	300
250	$400

$400 ÷ 250 = $1.60 per share

(2)
50 shares @ $1.60 =	$ 80
100 shares @ $4.00 =	400
300 shares @ $5.00 =	1,500
450	$1,980

$1,980 ÷ 450 = $4.40 per share

E. Disposition of Shares Acquired under a Stock Option

[ITA: 7(1.3); 7(1.31); 53(1)(j); 47(3)]

1. Disposition of newly-acquired securities

Under the stock option benefit rules there is a special provision [subsection 7(1.31)] which applies when a taxpayer disposes of a security that is identical to other securities owned by the taxpayer. The provision deems a particular security, as designated by the taxpayer, to be the security that is the subject of the disposition. In order for this subsection to apply, certain conditions, as set out in the technical notes to this subsection, must be met.

1. The particular security must have been acquired under an employee stock option agreement, as described in subsection 7(1) of the Act.

2. The disposition must occur no later than 30 days after the taxpayer acquires the particular security.

3. There must be no other acquisitions or dispositions of identical securities in the intervening period; that is, after the acquisition of the particular security and before the disposition in respect of which the designation is being made. It should be noted, however, that this does not preclude the taxpayer from acquiring other identical securities at the same time as the disposition in respect of which the designation is being made.

4. The taxpayer must make the designation in the return of income that is filed for the year in which the disposition occurs. It is expected that the CRA will accept, as the form of designation, the calculation of the capital gain or loss in respect of the disposition on the basis that it is the particular security that is the subject of the disposition.

5. The taxpayer must not have designated the particular security in connection with the disposition of any other security.

Consider the following facts. On May 1, 2004, Joseph acquires 750 shares of his corporate employer on the open market. On May 1, 2005, he acquires another 750 shares on the open market. On May 1, 2006, he acquires an additional 1,000 shares under employee stock options. Immediately thereafter, he sells 1,500 shares. In his return of income for 2006, he designates the 1,000 stock option shares as constituting part of the shares that were sold. Pursuant to subsections 7(1.3) and (1.31), the 1,500 shares being sold by Joseph are deemed to be comprised of the 1,000 stock option shares and 500 of the 750 shares that Joseph acquired on the open market.

It should be noted that the provisions of subsection 7(1.31) accommodate the practice of specific identification that is currently permitted by the CRA. The significance of subsection 7(1.31) for the purpose of new paragraph 110(1)(*d*.01) should also be noted. That paragraph allows a taxpayer to deduct a portion of the employment benefit that the taxpayer is deemed by subsection 7(1) to have received in respect of the taxpayer's acquisition of a qualifying employee option security, if the taxpayer disposes of the security by donating it to a qualifying charity within 30 days after its acquisition.

It should also be noted that subsection 47(3) of the Act provides that securities to which subsection 7(1.31) apply are deemed, for the purpose of the cost-averaging rule in subsection 47(1), not to be identical to any other securities owned by the taxpayer. Consequently, the adjusted cost base (ACB) of each such security and, thus, the capital gain or loss on the disposition of the security, is determined without regard to the ACB of any other securities owned by the taxpayer.

Subsection 7(1.31) applies to securities acquired after February 27, 2000. It also applies to securities acquired, but not disposed of, before February 28, 2000.

2. Adjusted cost base of shares

Paragraph 53(1)(*j*) of the Act provides for an addition to the ACB of a share acquired by a taxpayer under an employee option agreement. The amount that is added to the ACB is the amount of the employment benefit that the taxpayer (or a non-arm's length person) is deemed by subsection 7(1) to have received in connection with the acquisition of the security. The amount is generally equal to the excess of the fair market value of the security at the time it is acquired over the amount paid to acquire the security under the option. The amount is added to the ACB in the year in which the benefit is deemed to have been received, which is generally the year in which the taxpayer acquires the security. However, in the case of an option granted by a Canadian-controlled private corporation (CCPC) to an arm's length person, subsection 7(1.1) applies to defer recognition of the benefit to the year in which the taxpayer disposes of the security.

Paragraph 53(1)(*j*) provides that, for all employee option securities acquired after February 27, 2000, the employment benefit is included in the ACB of the security from the time of acquisition, even if recognition of the employment benefit is deferred, for tax purposes, until the taxpayer disposes of the security. This will be primarily relevant where securities for which a deferral is provided under either subsection 7(1.1), or new subsection 7(8) (which applies to publicly-listed shares and units of a fund trust), are exchanged for new securities in accordance with subsection 7(1.5), but in circumstances in which there is no rollover available, in respect of the disposition of the old securities, for capital gains purposes. The immediate inclusion in the ACB of the old securities ensures that the determination of the capital gain or loss on the disposition of those securities is not distorted by the exclusion of the deferred employment benefit associated with the acquisition of those securities.

3. Identical properties

Subsection 47(1) of the Act requires that the cost of identical properties acquired by a taxpayer be averaged over all such properties. Generally, this results in each of the properties having the same adjusted cost base (ACB), thus, ensuring that the capital gain or loss on the disposition of any one of the properties can be determined without having to identify a particular property as the property that has been disposed of.

Subsection 47(3) exempts certain securities acquired after February 27, 2000, from the cost-averaging rule by deeming such securities not to be identical to any other securities acquired by the taxpayer for the purposes of subsection 47(1). The specific securities to which subsection 47(3) applies are as follows:

- Securities (i.e., shares of a corporation and units of a mutual fund trust) acquired under an employee option agreement for which a deferral is provided under existing subsection 7(1.1) or new subsection 7(8) of the Act, and securities acquired in exchange for such securities under circumstances to which subsection 7(1.5) of the Act applied.

- Securities acquired under an employee option agreement where the securities are designated by the taxpayer and deemed by new subsection 7(1.31) of the Act to be the securities that are the subject of a disposition of identical securities occurring within 30 days after the acquisition.

- Employer shares received by an employee as part of a lump sum payment on withdrawing from a deferred profit sharing plan (DPSP), where the employee filed an election in respect of those shares under subsection 147(10.1) of the Act. Such an election allows the taxpayer to defer taxation on the growth of the shares while they were held by the plan until such time as the employee disposes of the shares.

The effect of a security being exempted from the cost-averaging rule in subsection 47(1) is that the ACB of the security and, thus, the capital gain or loss on its disposition, is determined without regard to the ACB of any other securities owned by the taxpayer. In other words, each security to which subsection 47(3) applies has its own unique ACB.

It should be noted that, under amended subsection 7(1.3) and new subsection 7(1.31) of the Act, it is possible to determine when each security which is exempted from the cost averaging rule by subsection 47(3) is disposed of by the taxpayer. As noted above, subsection 7(1.31) deals with situations in which there is an acquisition of an employee option security and a disposition of an identical security within 30 days. Amended subsection 7(1.3) deals with securities for which a deferral is provided under subsection 7(1.1) or (8) or 147(10.1) of the Act (referred to in these notes as "deferral securities"). In general terms, subsection 7(1.3) deems a taxpayer to dispose of deferral securities only after having disposed of non-deferral securities, and then to dispose of deferral securities in the order in which they were acquired. Since it is possible to determine exactly when a particular security to which subsection 47(3) applies is disposed of, the fact that the security has its own unique ACB is not problematic.

It should also be noted that, where an employee acquires a security after February 27, 2000, under circumstances to which subsection 7(1.1) or (8) apply, the deferred employment benefit is added, pursuant to amended paragraph 53(1)(*j*) of the Act, to the ACB of the security at the time it is acquired even though the benefit is not subject to taxation until the security is disposed of.

The following example problem illustrates the effect of subsection 47(3), in conjunction with the rules in subsections 7(1.3) and 7(1.31) for determining the order of disposition of identical securities and the amended ACB rule for employee option securities in paragraph 53(1)(j) of the Act.

Example Problem

2003	Simon acquired 500 shares of Pubco Inc. (a public company) on the open market at a cost of $20 each.	
2004	Simon exercised an employee stock option and acquired 700 more shares of Pubco Inc. at a cost of $15 each. The fair market value of the shares at exercise was $25 per share and the fair market value of the shares at the time the option was granted was $13 per share.	
	Simon elected to defer the recognition of the employment benefit associated with this option.	
2005	Simon sold 400 shares of Pubco Inc. for $30 per share.	

— REQUIRED

Compute the income effect of the sale of the shares, the remaining deferral of employment benefit and the adjusted cost base of the remaining shares.

— SOLUTION

Because of the election [ssec. 7(8)] to defer the recognition of the employment benefit associated with the stock option the shares acquired under the option are in a separate pool for ACB purposes [ssec. 47(3)]. Therefore the ACBs of the two pools of Publco Inc. shares are:

Open market:	Cost	500 shares × $20	$10,000
Stock option:	Cost	700 shares × $15	$10,500
	Benefit	700 shares × $10	7,000
	Total ACB		$17,500

The ACB of the shares acquired under the option is the actual cost ($15) plus the deferred employment benefit ($25 − $15 = $10) [par. 53(1)(j)].

Employment income deferral:	700 shares × $10	$7,000

The 400 shares that are sold are deemed to have come out of the open market pool first [ssec. 7(1.3)]. As a result, the only income to report is a taxable capital gain, which is calculated as follows:

Proceeds	400 shares × $30	$12,000
ACB	400 shares × $20	(8,000)
Capital gain		$ 4,000
Taxable capital gain		$ 2,000

The employment income deferral of $7,000 continues until the stock option shares are sold.

The ACB of the 100 open market shares remaining is $20 per share.

The ACB of the 700 stock option shares remains at $25 per share.

F. Cost of Certain Properties

[ITA: 52; IT-88R2]

The cost of property is usually incurred by the acquisition of the property with after-tax funds. Thus, when a capital property is acquired for $100, the funds used in the purchase have usually been subjected to income tax. That is why, on the disposition of the property for, say, $150, the $100 of cost is not taxed; only the $50 of gain above cost is taxed. Thus, cost is recovered tax free on a disposition, because it represents an amount on which tax was already paid.

Normally the cost of capital property or the capital cost of depreciable capital property is the laid-down cost for accounting purposes. However, section 52 contains a number of provisions which deem the *cost* to be an amount other than laid-down cost. For purposes of Subdivision c, where a taxpayer has acquired property and an amount in respect of the value of the property is included in the taxpayer's income that amount is added to the cost of the property [ssec. 52(1)]. For example, if a shareholder had a benefit in kind (i.e., in property) which was included in his or her income under subsection 15(1), then the income inclusion would be added to the cost of the property so received. Since the income inclusion in respect of the benefit would be taxed, the amount of the benefit can be considered as a tax-paid cost of the property, according to the concept of cost discussed above. There is one notable exception to the rule in subsection 52(1), namely, an employment income inclusion arising from a stock option benefit under section 7 which is discussed in the next part of the chapter.

The cost of property in respect of dividends in kind (non-cash dividends) and lottery prizes is the fair market value [ssecs. 52(2) and (4)]. Note that the prize itself is not subject to an income inclusion [par. 40(2)(f)].

Subsection 52(3) determines the cost of stock dividends which have had varying tax treatments over the years. Prior to April 1, 1977, a stock dividend was treated in the same manner as any other dividend for purposes of determining income. Its cost base, however, was deemed to be equal to its paid-up capital which is generally the stated capital[(f)] on the accounting balance sheet. This treatment is also applied to all stock dividends after May 22, 1985. For the period after March 31, 1977 to May 22, 1985, stock dividends, for public companies only, were deemed not to be dividends. Hence, there was no income inclusion, and the cost base of the stock received as dividend was deemed to be nil. This treatment resulted in a larger eventual capital gain. Therefore, public companies could offer to their shareholders different classes of shares paying either ordinary dividends subject to the gross-up and tax credit rules or stock dividends which resulted in future capital gains treatment. With the introduction of the capital gains exemption in 1985, this latter option was removed.

TAXATION OF STOCK DIVIDENDS

Time Period	Taxation of Dividend	ACB Adjustment
Prior to April 1/77	Taxed on increase in PUC	ACB increased by PUC increase
April 1/77 to May 22/85	Not taxed (public companies)	No ACB adjustment
After May 22/85	Taxed on increase in PUC	ACB increased by PUC increase

(f) In some provinces, this amount may be the par value.

Example Problem _____

Mr. Adjusted-Shares purchased 1,000 shares of Sure-Fire Limited, a public corporation, at $50 per share in 1983. Mr. Adjusted-Shares received the following dividends subsequent to that time:

1984	A stock dividend of 10% which resulted in an increase in the paid-up capital of $10 for each share issued.
1996	A stock dividend of 10% which resulted in an increase in the paid-up capital of $10 for each share issued.
1998	Cash dividend of $5 per share.
2003	A stock dividend of 10% which resulted in an increase in the paid-up capital of $10 for each share issued.

— REQUIRED

Compute the taxable capital gain or allowable capital loss if Mr. Adjusted Shares sold 100 of the above shares in 2004 for $45 per share plus brokerage of $100.

— SOLUTION

2005	P of D (100 shares @ $45)			$4,500
	A.C.B. (100 shares @ $39.23[1])		$3,923	
	Selling cost		100	(4,023)
	Capital gain			$ 477
	Taxable capital gain ($1/2 \times $477)			$ 239

— NOTE TO SOLUTION

(1)	1983	1,000	shares — purchased @ $50 each		$50,000
	1984	100	shares — stock dividend of 10%		Nil
		1,100			
	1996	110	shares — stock dividend of 10% @ $10 each	1,100	
		1,210			
	2003	121	shares — stock dividend of 10% @ $10 each	1,210	
		1,331			$52,310

$52,310 \div 1,331 = $39.30

G. Adjustments to the Cost Base

[ITA: 40(3.6)(*b*); 53; 54; 82(3); 84(1)]

As previously noted, the term "adjusted cost base" is defined in section 54, the definitions section of Subdivision c. This provision states that the adjusted cost base of depreciable property is its capital cost and for all other capital property the cost of the property adjusted in accordance with section 53. The definition then further restricts this adjusted cost to a positive amount.

Subsection 53(1) (additions) and subsection 53(2) (reductions) set out a number of adjustments some of which we have already examined.

(a) Paragraph 53(1)(*h*) adds to the cost base of land interest and property taxes denied [ssec. 18(2)].

(b) Paragraph 53(1)(*j*) adds the employment income inclusion arising from the acquisition of shares through a stock option [sec. 7].

(c) Paragraph 53(1)(*n*) adds to the cost base reasonable costs of surveying or valuing property in respect of its acquisition or disposition which are denied [par. 18(1)(*b*)].

(d) Paragraph 53(2)(*k*) provides for a reduction for government assistance for capital property as subsection 13(7.1) does for depreciable capital property.

(e) Paragraph 53(2)(*l*) reduces the cost base by the amount of accrued interest paid for on the purchase of a bond and deducted from interest earned during the holding period of the bond [ssec. 20(14)].

There are also a number of adjustments in respect of shares of a corporation, many of which will be described in more detail in later chapters. But a conceptual understanding of these adjustments is necessary in determining the adjusted cost base of a particular class of shares.

(1) Paragraph 53(1)(*b*) adds to the cost base deemed dividends under subsection 84(1) which arise in transactions (with some exceptions) where the paid-up capital of the corporation is increased by more than the increase in the fair market value of the net assets of the corporation. (Paid-up capital of shares is generally (but not always) the stated or par value for accounting purposes and is discussed in more detail in Chapter 15.)

(2) Paragraph 53(1)(*f*.2) adds to the cost base of shares received as consideration for any transfer of property to a corporation the amount of any capital loss denied by reason of paragraph 40(3.6)(*b*).

H. Superficial Losses

[ITA: 40(2)(*g*)(i); 53(1); 54; 251.1(1)]

A "superficial loss", defined in section 54 is usually, but not necessarily, associated with the trading of securities. A taxpayer might own securities with an accrued capital loss at the end of the year. The securities are sold to trigger the loss which is used to offset a capital gain previously realized in the year. Then the taxpayer repurchases the same or identical securities, almost immediately, because of their long-term potential. In this case, the taxpayer has converted a "paper" loss into a realized loss, but after the repurchase continues to own essentially the same securities. This is the essence of a superficial loss in which the taxpayer is denied the loss at the time of the disposition but is permitted to add the superficial loss to the adjusted cost base of the substituted property [paragraph 53(1)(*f*)]. This adjustment has the effect of delaying the triggering of the loss. There are three conditions necessary in order to establish a superficial loss:

(a) the taxpayer or an "affiliated person" [ssec. 251.1(1))], in essence, the taxpayer's spouse or a corporation controlled by either the taxpayer or the taxpayer's spouse, must dispose of the property;

(b) the taxpayer or an affiliated person acquires or re-acquires the same or identical property during the period beginning 30 days before the disposition and ending 30 days after the disposition; and

(c) the taxpayer or an affiliated person, at the end of the period referred to in point (b), still owns at least some of the property.

Example Problem 1

Mr. Sureloss buys 1,000 shares of Nogain Ltd. at $10 per share on October 1, 2004. On December 15, 2004, Mr. Sureloss sells 1,000 shares at $5. On January 3, 2005, he buys 1,000 shares at $6. On November 15, 2005, he sells 1,000 shares at $10.

— *REQUIRED*

Compute the taxable capital gain or allowable capital loss on each of the above transactions.

— *SOLUTION*

Dec. 15,	P of D (1,000 shares @ $5)	$ 5,000
2004	A.C.B. (1,000 shares @ $10)	(10,000)
	Capital loss	Nil

There is a superficial loss of $5,000, since he purchased the shares within the 30-day time limit and still owns the shares at the end of the period which is 30 days after December 15th. In essence, the purchase on January 3, 2005 allows him to maintain his ownership position in the shares after the sale.

Nov. 15,	P of D (1,000 shares @ $10)	$10,000
2005	A.C.B. (1,000 shares[1])	(11,000)
	Capital loss	(1,000)

Since Mr. Sureloss has no shares on hand 30 days after the sale on November 15, 2005, there cannot be a superficial loss.

— *NOTES TO SOLUTION*

(1)	1,000 shares @ $6 =	$ 6,000
	Dec. 15 Sup. loss =	5,000
		$11,000

Example Problem 2

Ms. Taxconfused is considering selling all of her remaining shares of Overrated Mining Ltd., a public corporation. She is uncertain of the adjusted cost base of the shares. The following is the historical data concerning her holdings in Overrated Mining Ltd.

June 1, 1982	Purchased 500 shares @ $2 per share.
Jan. 15, 1984	Received a stock dividend of 10%. The paid-up capital of the corporation was credited with one dollar for each share issued.
July 1, 1991	Purchased additional 1,000 shares @ $5 per share.
April 15, 1999	Received a stock dividend of 10%. The paid-up capital of the corporation was credited with $6 for each additional share.
June 19, 2005	Purchased an additional 1,000 shares @ $9.
Aug. 1, 2005	Sold 500 shares @ $5 plus commission of $150.

— *REQUIRED*

Determine the adjusted cost base of Ms. Taxconfused's shares in Overrated Mining Ltd.

—SOLUTION

Adjusted cost base

June 1, 1982	500	shares @ $2 — purchase	$ 1,000
Jan. 15, 1984	50	shares — 10% stock dividend	Nil
July 1, 1991	1,000	shares @ $5 — purchase	5,000
	1,550		
April 15, 1999	155	shares — 10% stock dividend @ $6	930
June 19, 2005	1,000	shares at $9	9,000
	2,705		$15,930
Aug. 1, 2005	(500)	P. of D. 500 shares @ $5	$2,500

$$\text{A.C.B. (500 shares} \times \frac{\$15,930}{2,705}) \ldots \ldots \ (2,945) \quad (2,945)$$

		$ (445)
S.C.		(150)
Capital loss		$ 595
2,205	shares @ $5.89	$12,985

IV. COMPUTATIONAL RULES

A. Section 3 Revisited

[ITA: 3]

In Chapter 1, a cursory examination was made of section 3 in the process of section identification. Now that several technical components have been examined, the carryover rules contained in section 3 will be highlighted.

Paragraph 3(*a*) includes the aggregate of all income from each non-capital source: property, business, office and employment, plus the other non-capital sources of income found in Subdivision d of Division B which is examined in Chapter 9. The amount determined for each source must be a positive amount (i.e., losses or an excess of deductions over inclusions from a particular source are not considered here).

Paragraph 3(*b*) deals with taxable capital gains and allowable capital losses, and is composed of the excess of:

(1) all taxable capital gains, excluding those from L.P.P.s

plus

(2) listed personal property taxable net gains as computed in subsection 41(2) and discussed previously

minus

(3) allowable capital losses, except for

(i) L.P.P. losses, and

(ii) allowable business investment losses (A.B.I.L.s).

Paragraph 3(*c*) adds together paragraphs 3(*a*) and (*b*) and subtracts Subdivision e deductions such as moving expenses, alimony, RRSPs, etc. All of these topics will be covered in Chapter 9.

Paragraph 3(*d*) subtracts various types of losses from any excess amount calculated in paragraph 3(*c*). The losses deducted are from the following sources:

(i) office, employment, business and property (i.e., losses from non-capital sources), and

(ii) A.B.I.L.s.

Note the special treatment accorded to A.B.I.L.s. Normally, allowable capital losses can only be claimed against taxable capital gains (see paragraph 3(*b*)). However, A.B.I.L.s. have no such restriction and, hence, are deducted under paragraph 3(*d*) along with other losses from non-capital sources (e.g., losses from business and property). Deducting A.B.I.L.s under paragraph 3(*d*), effectively, against all sources of income, rather than only against net taxable capital gains may result in a more rapid deduction of A.B.I.L.s, which is the intent of the A.B.I.L. investment incentive. As a capital loss, however, A.B.I.L.s are still only $^1/_2$ deductible.

B. Allowable Business Investment Losses

[ITA: 39(1)(*c*); 39(9)]

The definition of a business investment loss [par. 39(1)(*c*)] includes capital losses arising from the disposition of shares and debts of a small business corporation (S.B.C.) as defined in subsection 248(1). An S.B.C. is generally defined to be a Canadian-controlled private corporation, where all or substantially all of the fair market value of the assets were, at that time, used principally in an active business carried on primarily in Canada. Assets would include the shares of S.B.C.s which were connected [ssec. 186(4)] to the holding corporation. (The concept of a "connected" corporation is discussed in Chapter 12.) For the purposes of paragraph 39(1)(*c*) only, an S.B.C. which ceases to meet the conditions in the definition of an S.B.C. will still be considered as an S.B.C. if at any time in the 12 months preceding the disposition it met the conditions in the definition of an S.B.C.

Since business investment losses (B.I.L.s) are really only a subset of capital losses, allowable business investment losses (A.B.I.L.s) for a particular year are determined by the same inclusion rates as allowable capital losses as follows:

Time Period	Inclusion Rate
Prior to 1988	50%
1988 and 1989	66 $^2/_3$%
1990 to February 27, 2000	75%
February 28 to October 17, 2000	66 $^2/_3$%
After October 17, 2000	50%

A portion of a B.I.L., equal to an amount of capital gains that has previously benefited from a capital gains deduction, is disallowed [ssec. 39(9)]. The capital gains deduction referred to is either a past claim for the general capital gains deduction that was eliminated or the continuing capital gains deduction for shares of a qualified small business corporation or qualified farm property. This disallowed portion reduces the B.I.L. and resultant A.B.I.L., for purposes of the deduction under paragraph 3(*d*). In effect, an individual cannot obtain a benefit of the capital gains deduction on capital gains that are not offset by capital losses in the form of B.I.L.s, at the same time as he or she obtains a benefit from A.B.I.L.s which offset non-capital sources of income under paragraph 3(*d*). A fraction ($^1/_2$ for years prior to 1988, $^2/_3$ for 1988 and 1989, $^3/_4$ for 1990 to February 27, 2000; $^2/_3$ for February 28 to October 17, 2000; and $^1/_2$ after October 17, 2000) of the disallowed B.I.L. reverts to an allowable capital loss for the year realized. This allowable capital loss will possibly offset taxable capital gains which will not be available for the capital gains deduction, as a result.

Any portion of the A.B.I.L. (i.e., an amount that has not been disallowed), which is not deducted under paragraph 3(*d*), is added to the non-capital losses for the year subject to the non-capital loss carryover rules, discussed in Chapter 10 for individuals and Chapter 11 for corporations. However, if the A.B.I.L., which was treated as a non-capital loss, is not used by the end of the 10th carryforward year, it becomes a net capital loss, in essence, reverting to its original character as an allowable capital loss, restricted by the net capital loss carryover rules.

The portion of a B.I.L. that is disallowed is computed [ssec. 39(9)] as the lesser of:

(a) the B.I.L. for the year (before deducting the disallowed portion) ..... $xxxx

(b) the cumulative capital gains deduction claimed in previous years ×
a factor (the factor is 2 for years prior to 1988, $3/2$ for 1988 and
1989, $4/3$ for 1990 to February 27, 2000, $3/2$ for February 28, 2000 to
October 17, 2000 and 2 after October 17, 2000 to adjust the capital
gains deduction to a full capital gain amount which is parallel with
the full B.I.L. amount) .... $xxxx

    minus: the cumulative disallowed portion of B.I.L.s in preceding
        years .... (xxxx)

        $xxxx

Note that part (a) above uses the full business investment loss (not the fractional allowable business investment loss). However, the capital gains *deduction* is a fractional amount. Therefore, to make parts (a) and (b) comparable, the capital gains deduction must be adjusted to convert the deduction to a full amount of gain that has been exempted. Hence, multiplying a 1999 capital gains deduction, for example, by $4/3$ adjusts the $3/4$ fractional amount to the required full amount (i.e., $4/3 \times 3/4 = 1$).

Exhibit 7-1 attempts to map the treatment of B.I.L.s under the provisions described above.

EXHIBIT 7-1
Treatment of a Business Investment Loss

Example Problem

	2003	2004	2005
Employment income	$10,000	$12,000	$15,000
Business income (loss)	(25,000)	6,000	10,000
Property income (loss)	3,000	(2,000)	1,000
Capital gains (capital losses)			
L.P.P.	2,000	(5,000)	7,000
P.U.P.	(4,000)	8,000	2,000
Other	10,000	(17,000)*	4,000

* Includes a business investment loss of $2,000.

— *REQUIRED*

Determine the income under Division B according to section 3, after filing any necessary amended returns for each of the years indicated above. (For the purposes of this type of problem, dealing with each item, line-by-line, across the years, will help keep track of carryovers more easily than dealing with income one year at a time.)

— *SOLUTION*

	2003	2004	2005
Par. 3(*a*) — Sum of income from non-capital sources (non-negative):			
Employment	$ 10,000	$12,000	$15,000
Business (no losses)........	—	6,000	10,000
Property (no losses)	3,000	—	1,000
	$ 13,000	$18,000	$26,000
Par. 3(*b*) — Sum of net taxable capital gains (non-negative):			
L.P.P.	Nil[1]	Nil	$ 2,000[2]
P.U.P.	Nil[3]	$ 4,000[4]	1,000[5]
Other	$ 5,000[6]	(4,000)[7]	2,000[8]
	$ 5,000	Nil	$ 5,000
Sum of par. 3(*a*) and par. 3(*b*)	$ 18,000	$18,000	$31,000
Par. 3(*d*) — Sum of losses from non-capital sources:			
Business loss	(18,000)[9]	—	—
Property loss	—	(2,000)	—
A.B.I.L.	—	(1,000)[10]	—
Income under Division B	Nil	$15,000	$31,000

— NOTES TO SOLUTION

(1) The $2,000 listed personal property capital gain in 2003 was offset and removed by amending the 2003 return for the 2004 loss, carried back to 2003. Note how L.P.P. losses are carried over in their full amount, not their fractional allowable amount. Therefore, no consideration need be given to changing capital gains inclusion rates, if applicable, in the carryover period for L.P.P.s.

(2) There was still $3,000 of the listed personal property capital loss in 2004 to be applied against the listed personal property gain in 2005, of $7,000 (($7,000 − $3,000) × $\frac{1}{2}$ = $2,000).

(3) No losses are allowed on the personal-use property assets.

(4) $\frac{1}{2}$ × $8,000.

(5) $\frac{1}{2}$ × $2,000.

(6) $\frac{1}{2}$ × $10,000.

(7) Only $4,000 of the allowable capital loss of $7,500 [$\frac{1}{2}$ ($17,000 − $2,000)] was applied to reduce paragraph 3(*b*) amount to nil. The remaining $3,500 will be applied to another year but under Division C, not Division B.

(8) $\frac{1}{2}$ × $4,000.

(9) Only $18,000 of the business loss of $25,000 was applied to bring the income under Division B to nil. The remainder ($7,000) may be carried back three years and forward seven, but these losses are deductible in the carryover year in Division C, not Division B.

(10) The *allowable* business investment loss is $1,000 ($\frac{1}{2}$ × $2,000).

REVIEW QUESTIONS

(1) Tom, Dick and Harry formed a partnership in order to invest in a tract of land just outside a large urban area. Five years later, the partnership sold the property making a large profit. According to the partnership agreement, profits from this venture were to be split equally. Discuss whether this is an income or a capital receipt.

(2) Rachel Real-Estate-Salesperson invests her spare cash in "good land buys" which she occasionally finds. This year Rachel sold one of these properties and realized a large profit. Is this an income or a capital receipt?

(3) Winston Windfall, an accountant, uses his spare time and cash to trade in low-cost mining shares listed on a Canadian stock exchange. Winston made a large profit this year on his stock market transactions. Is this profit income or capital gain?

(4) Diana Developer purchased some land to erect a shopping centre which she intended to sell. However, zoning bylaws could not be changed and Diana sold the property at a large profit. Is this profit income or a capital gain?

(5) Doug Daily-Double spends his Saturday afternoons at the race track. This year Doug was extremely fortunate and his net winnings were $15,000. How will these winnings be taxed?

(6) A client invested in a rental property some years ago and paid $10,000 as a down payment and $150,000 was in the form of a mortgage. Recently, the vacancy rate has climbed and the value of the property has fallen. She thinks that she will just walk away from the property and let the mortgage company take over the property. What will her proceeds of disposition be?

(7) As a result of a reorganization in a company in which Mr. Smith is a shareholder, he has just had a return of some of the corporation's capital. As a result, the adjusted cost base of his shares has become negative. This does not bother him since he has been told that as long as he continues to own the shares he will not have to recognize this built-in capital gain. Comment.

(8) Mr. Confused has come to you with a problem. He owns the family cottage and his wife owns the house in town. Both housing units were purchased after 1981. They are thinking of selling both of these properties and moving to another province. He thought they could each claim the principal residence exemption to avoid any tax but someone has told him that they can only claim one of the residences. In general terms can you explain the rules to him?

(9) Ms. Spill bought a cottage property on a lake that has since become polluted. As a result, the value of the property has declined and she has sold it, since no one wants to go there

anymore. She realized a loss on the sale and wants to claim the loss on her personal return. Can she do it?

(10) What is the "$1,000 rule" as it relates to personal-use property? Does the same rule apply to listed personal property?

(11) Mr. Div has come to you to have his personal tax return done. He sold some shares of a public corporation that he has owned for some years and wants help in minimizing his tax on the transaction. One point that is confusing him is the stock dividend that he received this year. He does not know how to treat the dividend for tax purposes. Please help him.

(12) Under Divisions B and C, what happens when the capital losses exceed the capital gains in any one year?

(13) If you were to win a Mazda Miata in a lottery, what would the cost base be to you given that you might want to sell it to buy a car more fitting (boring) for an accountant?

(14) Ms. Devious has had her company buy her a car and register it in her name. The CRA discovered this and has assessed her with a benefit under subsection 15(1) for $35,000, the value of the car. Ms. Devious is going to have to sell the car to pay the tax liability. What will her cost base be on the car?

MULTIPLE CHOICE QUESTIONS

Question 1

On April 1, 2005, X Ltd., with a December 31 year-end, sold a parcel of land, a capital property with an adjusted cost base of $100,000, for $600,000. The $600,000 proceeds were payable in the form of a mortgage, with principal payments of $90,000 due every six months, starting on October 1, 2005. What is the minimum taxable capital gain that X Ltd. must report in 2005?

(A) $100,000

(B) $50,000

(C) $75,000

(D) $37,500

Question 2

During the year, Mina sold the following personal assets, all of which she had acquired after 1971:

	Cost	Proceeds
Automobile	$20,000	$18,000
Boat	600	1,500
Painting	600	1,300
Jewellery	1,400	200

Her capital gain for the year from these dispositions is:

(A) $900

(B) $800

(C) $500

(D) $400

Question 3

Mike purchased 100 shares of Pubco (a taxable Canadian corporation and public company) in 2002 for $3.11 per share plus $39 in commissions. In 2003, Mike purchased another 100 shares of Pubco for $4 per share plus a brokerage commission of $50. On March 1, 2005, when the shares were worth $6 per share, Mike gifted half the Pubco shares to his eight-year old son and half to his wife (no special elections were filed). What is the amount of the taxable capital gain that Mike must report in 2005?

(A) $100

(B) $122

(C) $200

(D) $400

Question 4

Amanda sold her cottage for $130,000 in May 2005. The cottage cost her $50,000 in 1998 and qualifies as a principal residence. The only other principal residence that Amanda has owned during her lifetime was her Toronto home, which she owned from 1996 to 2004. Even though she sold it for $200,000 more than it cost, she did not report the gain on her 2004 tax return because it was her principal residence. What is the minimum taxable capital gain that Amanda must report on her 2005 tax return in respect of the sale of the cottage?

(A) $80,000

(B) $25,000

(C) $30,000

(D) $50,000

Question 5

A Canadian resident individual received a stock dividend from a public corporation of one share. The dividend is a taxable dividend. The stock dividend resulted in an increase in the paid-up capital of $4 for each share issued but the fair market value of each share is $10. Which of the following statements is correct about the stock dividend received?

(A) The cost of the stock is deemed to be $4 and the individual's net income increases by $4.

(B) The cost of the stock is deemed to be $4 and the individual's net income increases by $5.

(C) The cost of the stock is deemed to be $10 and the individual's net income increases by $10.

(D) The cost of the stock is deemed to be $10 and the individual's net income is deemed to be $12.50.

Question 6

Donna Jailal has provided you with the following information in connection with her income tax return for the year:

Capital Gains:

Shares	$1,600
Personal-use property	700
Listed personal property	500

Capital Losses:

Shares	$ 820
Personal-use property	1,000
Listed personal property	140
Listed personal property losses from the previous year	100

What is the minimum net taxable capital gain that she must report as Division B income for the year?

(A) $370

(B) $740

(C) $870

(D) $920

EXERCISES

Exercise 1

[ITA: 40(2)(b)]

Peter Principal-Residence has only two residences which he wishes to dispose of in 2005. The following facts relate to those residences:

	Date purchased	Cost	Real estate commission	Estimated selling price
City home	1990	$180,000	$12,000	$247,000
Cottage	1995	90,000	6,000	164,000

— REQUIRED

Determine how Peter must designate residences in order to achieve the minimum capital gain.

Exercise 2

[ITA: 41; 54]

Karl Kapitalgains disposed of the following assets in 2005, all of which were bought subsequent to 1972:

	Sale price	Cost	Selling cost
Painting...............................	$2,000	$ 300	$100
Antique clock...........................	1,200	250	20
Outboard motor........................	750	500	15
Gold coin	600	1,000	10

— REQUIRED

Determine Karl's net taxable capital gain for the year.

Exercise 3

[ITA: 53(1)(f); 54]

Ivan Investor purchased the following shares of Solid Investments Ltd.:

March 1, 2004.......................	100 shares @ $30 including brokerage
June 1, 2005	150 shares @ $35 including brokerage
January 10, 2006	200 shares @ $26 including brokerage

On December 15, 2005, Ivan sold 200 shares @ $25 less brokerage of $75.

— REQUIRED

(A) Determine Ivan's taxable capital gain or allowable capital loss on his December 15, 2005 disposition.

(B) Compute the adjusted cost base of the shares on hand on January 10, 2006.

Exercise 4

[ITA: 53(2)]

Miriam Marketwise decided to purchase shares in Strippit Limited, a public company, listed on the Canadian Venture Exchange. Miriam purchased 1,000 shares at $35 per share plus brokerage of $500 on December 10, 1973.

Miriam received the following dividends during the intervening years:

February 1, 1974	A stock dividend of 5% with a paid-up capital of $10 per share.
April 10, 1985	A stock dividend of 10% with a paid-up capital of $10 per share.
August 1, 2000	A stock dividend of 20% with a paid-up capital of $10 per share.

— *REQUIRED*

Determine the adjusted cost base of Miriam's shares as at December 31, 2005.

Exercise 5

[ITA: 53]

Imanin Vestor invested $2,000 on April 1, 2004, in Suckers Mutual Fund sold by a major financial institution. Her investment purchased 72.788 units of the fund. On December 31, 2004, the fund allocated $96.37 of capital gains to her account. As a result, the $96.37 was reinvested in the fund to purchase 3.774 units at the market value of $25.535 per unit.

On June 30, 2005, she sold 25 of her units for a total of $718.

— *REQUIRED*

Compute the effects of these events on income for tax purposes in 2004 and 2005.

Exercise 6

[ITA: 3; 39; 41]

Simple Simon has the following sources of income and losses for tax purposes:

	2004	2005
Employment income	$25,000	$30,000
Property income	10,000	(4,000)
Business income — other	8,000	(9,000)
Capital gains (capital losses):		
— Listed personal property (Note 1)	4,000	(1,500)
— Personal-use property	8,000	(1,000)
— Shares — Canadian-controlled private corporation		
(Note 2)	(6,000)	(2,000)
— Public corporation	(12,000)	9,000

Additional Information

(1) Simon has a capital loss from listed personal property of $1,000 carried forward from 2001.

(2) These losses qualify as business investment losses. No capital gains deduction has ever been claimed.

— *REQUIRED*

Determine Simple Simon's Division B income according to the ordering rules in section 3 for 2004 and 2005. (Deal with each item line-by-line across the years, rather than computing income one year at a time.)

ASSIGNMENT PROBLEMS

Problem 1

Jean-Luc, the taxpayer in this case, was experienced in retail real estate, having originally been employed by a fast-food chain of restaurants. His duties were to locate, acquire and open restaurants on behalf of his employer. He acquired extensive knowledge in packaging sites for retail operations.

Two years ago, Jean-Luc began to work as an employee for Jorge, a successful builder of homes and condominiums, real estate developer for investment of rental apartments and retail plazas, and trust company owner. Jean-Luc was employed on a salary and bonus basis. At the time, Jean-Luc was also a licensed real estate broker and owned a brokerage firm.

Jean-Luc's first project for Jorge involved developing a retail complex in Toronto. He was instrumental in obtaining two anchor tenants as well as two others. This was a successful venture.

His second venture involved a strip plaza in London, Ontario. By the time Jean-Luc and Jorge were prepared to purchase the property, most of the pre-development work had been completed and two nationally recognized restaurant chains had signed letters of intent and/or offers to lease. These two tenants represented 60% of the rentable area of the plaza. With those tenants in place, other tenants were prepared to rent because of the traffic which would be generated by the presence of the two popular fast-food restaurants. As a result, financing the project would not be a problem.

All of the leases which were negotiated were of the "net-net" type — the landlord being responsible only for its financing costs. The tenants were responsible for all other costs and expenses involved with the plaza, in addition to their own businesses.

A partnership of Jorge (74%), Jean-Luc (24%) and Shloimie (2%), the long-time accountant for Jorge, was established to own the plaza. Neither Jean-Luc nor Shloimie paid for his respective interest in the partnership. Jean-Luc considered this to be a long-term project that would provide income for his children's future. Jorge and Shloimie regarded the project as an opportunity to acquire and own an income-producing property with very little investment, since most of the funds were provided by debt financing.

City planning and zoning for the plaza was approved and most of the financing was in place. Last year, about a year after the purchase by the partnership, the building was completed to the point where the tenants took possession. Shortly thereafter, the tenants completed their respective areas and were in operation and paying rent. Temporary financing was in place and permanent financing was being negotiated pending a drop in interest rates at the time.

This year, Jorge began to have financial difficulties and his assets were liquidated by his creditors. Since his creditors did not have security on the plaza project, Jorge was in a position to sell that asset in an orderly manner. Although Jorge controlled the partnership, he received Jean-Luc's consent to sell the property. Jean-Luc's share of the gain on the sale was about $157,000.

Jean-Luc filed his tax return for this year showing the gain as a capital gain.

— *REQUIRED*

A CRA assessor has just called to indicate that she is considering a reassessment of the income in question as income from a business, an adventure in the nature of trade, or from a profit-making undertaking or concern.

As Jean-Luc's tax adviser, evaluate the fact situation and recommend a course of action.

Problem 2

[ITA: 20(1)(*n*), (8); 40; IT-152R3]

Loof Lirpa bought a parcel of land in 1986. It was his intention that he would build a family home on the land some day. However, the city continued to delay issuing permits to landowners in the area and eventually Loof purchased another home. He held onto the land for a number of years but has now decided that he needs the cash and will sell the property. The details related to his purchase of the land are set out below.

Purchase Price: $4,000; Purchase Date: May 21, 1986

Loof has received an offer from an acquaintance to purchase the land. The payment terms are set out below and are considered to represent fair market value.

Purchase Price: $160,000; Purchase Date: October 1, 2005

Payment terms: $40,000 down payment on purchase date; $20,000 payable on January 1 each year for the period January 1, 2006 through January 1, 2011 inclusive. Interest: Interest is payable at 6% annually on the unpaid balance.

Loof is uncertain as to whether the disposition is on account of capital or income.

— REQUIRED

Compare the income tax consequences to Loof of this sale if the sale is on account of capital and, alternatively, if it is on account of income. Do not calculate the interest income. Ignore the consequences and calculation of the interest income.

Problem 3

[ITA: 40(2)(*b*); 54]

Mr. Doug Hart, who lives in Ontario, is contemplating moving to Switzerland. He came to you to discuss the tax consequences of disposing of his residences, as indicated below, in April 2005. He is single and ordinarily inhabits each of the residences for several months each year. He has never used his principal residence exemption since purchasing these properties.

The following information relates to the proposed 2005 dispositions.

Residence	Date of purchase	Cost	Selling price
Toronto home	1998	$160,000	$240,000
Farm in Quebec...................	2000	100,000	148,000
Condominium in Florida............	2003	150,000	186,000

— REQUIRED

Compute the minimum amount of taxable capital gains that Mr. Hart will have to report in 2005.

Problem 4

[ITA: 40(2)(*b*); 54]

Ms. Twoholmes has come to you for advice on the tax consequences of the disposition of the following two residences in 2005:

Residence	Date of purchase	Cost	Selling price
Regina home	1994	$400,000	$517,500
Cottage	1999	250,000	375,000

— REQUIRED

Compute the minimum amount of taxable capital gains.

Problem 5

[ITA: 41; 46]

Mr. Ar Fl sold the following assets in 2005, all of which were purchased in the 1990s:

	Cost	Proceeds
Oil painting	$2,500	$ 500
Canoe	700	500
Rare coin	1,300	500
Bible produced in 1635	800	5,000
Antique car	15,000	10,000
Antique chair	300	1,200
Antique table	1,500	2,000

Mr. Ar Fl has an unclaimed capital loss on listed personal property of $1,200 arising in 2002.

— *REQUIRED*

What is the amount of Mr. Ar Fl's net taxable capital gain for 2005?

Problem 6

[ITA: 47; 53]

Sherman Stockwatcher likes to invest in the stock market for the long term. While some of his investments have been failures, some have been very successful. Generally, he has been very fortunate in buying certain stocks at a relatively low price and selling them at their peak. One such stock is Headed For the Sky Corporation, a public corporation. Sherman has provided the following trade information related to this investment:

Nov. 8, 1981	Purchased 1,000 shares at initial offering price of $5.
Apr. 15, 1982	Purchased 2,000 shares at price of $3.50.
June 6, 1983	Sold 500 shares at $2.75, incurred brokerage commission of $50.
July 2, 1983	Purchased 2,000 shares at $4.
Apr. 30, 1984	Received a stock dividend of 10% of shares held; stock dividend increased corporation's paid-up capital by $.50/share.
June 20, 1992	Two-for-one stock split.
Nov. 8, 1996	Purchased 2,000 shares at $6.
Jan. 12, 1999	Received a stock dividend of 10% of shares held; stock dividend increased corporation's paid-up capital by $1/share.
Nov. 5, 2005	Sold 10,000 shares for $7.50/share, incurred brokerage commission of $650.

— *REQUIRED*

Calculate the taxable capital gain or allowable capital loss on the above transactions.

Problem 7

[ITA: 3; 41]

Dave Stieb reported the following information for tax purposes:

	2003	2004	2005
Business income	$ 60,000	$ 65,000	$70,000
Property income	2,000	3,000	(1,000)
Capital gains:*			
Listed personal property	5,000	(7,000)	3,000
Personal-use property	(2,000)	5,000	4,000
Other	(8,000)**	6,000	(16,000)

    * Brackets indicate capital loss.
    ** Includes a $4,000 business investment loss.

— *REQUIRED*

Compute the income under Division B for each year *after* making the necessary amendments to the returns of other years. (Deal with each item line-by-line across the years, rather than computing income one year at a time.) Assume that no capital gains deduction was ever claimed.

Problem 8

[ITA: Division B, Subdivisions a, b, c]

Mr. Rich, a new client, has invested in rental properties, principal residences and other capital property with inheritance monies and other liquid cash. He provides you with the following information with respect to his 2005 taxation year.

Mr. Rich is employed by Wealth Inc., a Canadian-controlled private corporation, and received the following income and benefits:

(1) Salary (net)		$50,578
Payroll deduction:		
Income taxes	$15,100	
CPP	1,861	
EI	761	
Registered pension plan (defined benefit: current service)	3,700	21,422
		$72,000

(2) Mr. Rich paid professional fees of $500 to the Professional Engineers of Ontario.

(3) Mr. Rich, who is engaged in negotiating contracts for his employer, received for the entire year a monthly allowance for travelling and car expenses of $550 and $650, respectively.

In September of 2005, Mr. Rich sold his car for $12,500 and purchased a new car costing $35,000, including PST of 8% and GST of 7%. Mr. Rich purchased his previous car in January 2002 for $30,000 plus PST and GST. The UCC at January 1, 2005, was $10,000. CCA has been taken each year on a prorated basis to reflect the use for employment purposes. Mr. Rich's kilometres for personal use were 6,250 out of a total kilometres of 25,000.

Mr. Rich's employment contract requires him to use his own car and pay all of his expenses.

Travelling expenses:	
Meals	$ 3,500
Accommodation	4,500
Gas and oil	2,100
Insurance	800
Maintenance	500
Licence	85
	$11,485

(4) Mr. Rich sold two lots of his stock options. He provides you with the following:

1st lot — 450 shares sold on March 15, 2005, for $26.50 per share. These shares were purchased in February 1998 for $8 at which time the shares were valued at $10.50.

2nd lot — 600 shares sold on December 5, 2005, for $25 per share. These shares were purchased on April 12, 2005, for $15 at which time the shares were valued at $21. The fair market value at the date of grant was $17.

(5) Mr. Rich received an interest-free loan of $9,000 on March 12, 2005, to enable him to purchase shares of Wealth Inc. The loan was outstanding until the shares were sold on December 5th, at which time the loan was repaid. Assume that the prescribed rate throughout the year was 7%.

In addition, during 2005, Mr. Rich received the following income from various sources including certain capital dispositions.

(A) Mr. Rich sold the following assets:

	Cost	Proceeds
Antique foot stool	$1,100	$ 900
Painting	950	1,500
Stamp collection	250	850

(B) During 2005, Mr. Rich sold his two residences, in order to purchase a larger home in an expensive suburb. The following facts relate to these two residences:

	Date purchased	Cost	Commission	Proceeds
City home..............	1996	$95,000	$21,000	$350,000
Cottage	1991	15,500	12,000	200,000

(C) In addition to his residences, Mr. Rich owns two rental properties. The following information pertains to these two properties:

	Wealthier St.	Richmount St.
Cost of land	$70,000	$100,000
Cost of building	$55,000	$ 80,000
UCC — January 1, 2005, Class 1	$39,000	$ 65,000
Rental revenue in 2005	$18,000	$ 7,600
Expenses:		
Taxes (property)................	$ 2,100	$ 1,800
Other expenses................	4,300	6,100
Mortgage interest	3,600	Nil
	$10,000	$ 7,900

The Richmount St. rental property was sold in November for $250,000, including $140,000 for the land, before a commission of $9,000. Mr. Rich took back a $100,000 first mortgage on the property for 5 years. Mr. Rich will receive a capital repayment each year, excluding the first year, of $20,000.

Mr. Rich purchased the Wealthier St. rental property by placing a mortgage on his home. His monthly payments are $450 per month, of which $300 per month represents interest.

(D) Mr. Rich gifted his wife $10,000 in June 2005 to allow her to invest in the stock market. Mrs. Rich decided to be a cautious investor for the first while; as a result, she invested the $10,000 in Treasury Bills which earned $600 from June to December of 2005.

(E) In addition, Mr. Rich decided to provide his younger brother, who is 22, with a non-interest bearing loan of $5,000 to allow him to complete his Masters in Marine Biology. Mr. Rich's brother paid his tuition fees with the funds.

(F) Mr. Rich gifted $8,500 to each of his twin children, Dolly and Camp, aged 15. Both children placed their monies in high interest-bearing savings accounts each receiving interest of $1,050 in 2005.

(G) Mr. Rich received dividends from the following investments:

Foreign Co. — a foreign corporation (net of $88 withholding tax) ... $500
Wealth Inc. — a taxable Canadian corporation   800

(H) Mr. Rich owns two mutual funds, Dumark Mutual Fund and Paget Mutual Fund. He received a T3 slip from Dumark Mutual Fund indicating the following income amounts allocated to his account and reinvested in 2005:

Capital gains $1,200
Actual amount of dividends   400
Taxable amount of dividends   500

Mr. Rich had invested $20,000 in the Dumark Fund in 2004. This resulted in the purchase of 1,640.824 units of the fund. In 2004, income of $46.31 was allocated to his account and reinvested. The reinvestment resulted in the purchase of 3.845 units at the market value of $12.044 per unit. The 2005 income allocation resulted, on reinvestment of the $1,600, in the purchase of 119.358 units at the market value of $13.405 per unit. Late in 2005, after the income allocation, Mr. Rich sold 1,000 units for a total of $12,912.

He also received a T5 slip from Paget Mutual Fund indicating that he had received a $280 capital gains dividend during 2005.

(I) Mr. Rich sold a $100,000 Government of Canada bond for $115,327. This bond paid interest semi-annually at an interest rate which was much higher than current interest rates. The proceeds received of $115,327 included accrued interest of $5,327. Mr. Rich had purchased the bonds when they were originally issued for $98,000.

(J) In 2002, Mr. Rich loaned $120,000 to his brother-in-law's company which was a small business corporation. The loan paid interest at commercial rates, but no interest was received in 2005 because the company went into receivership. As an unsecured creditor, Mr. Rich received 10 cents on the dollar ($12,000) in 2005 in full payment of this loan.

(K) Mr. Rich has a listed personal property loss, carried forward from 1999, of $500.

— *REQUIRED*

Determine Mr. Rich's Division B income according to the ordering rules in section 3 for 2005. Assume that Mr. Rich claimed $60,000 of his capital gains exemption in prior years.

Problem 9

[ITA: 52; 53]

Ms. Plummet decided to purchase shares in Schvantz Ltd., a public company. She purchased 800 shares at $25 per share plus brokerage of $690 on May 24, 1981.

The following additional transactions took place:

June 30, 1982	— Purchased 500 shares of Shtupp Metals Ltd., a public company, at $35 plus brokerage of $600.
Aug. 20, 1982	— Purchased 1,100 additional shares of Schvantz Ltd. at $30 plus brokerage of $940.
June 9, 1983	— Received a 10% stock dividend from Shtupp Metals Ltd. of which $25 per share issued was credited to paid-up capital.
Aug. 27, 1984	— Sold 900 shares of Schvantz Ltd. at $24.50 per share plus brokerage fee of $760.
Sept. 20, 1984	— Purchased 600 additional shares of Schvantz Ltd. at $19.50 plus brokerage of $400.
Oct. 31, 1984	— Sold 200 shares of Shtupp Metals Ltd. at $32 per share plus brokerage fee of $220.
May 8, 1985	— Received a 6% stock dividend from Shtupp Metals Ltd. of which $28 per share issued was credited to paid-up capital.
June 9, 1992	— Sold 250 shares of Schvantz Ltd. at $32 per share plus brokerage fee of $275.
May 24, 1996	— Received a 10% stock dividend from Shtupp Metals Ltd. (i.e., 37 shares) of which $20 per share issued was credited to paid-up capital.
June 30, 1999	— Sold 150 shares of Shtupp Metals Ltd. at $31.50 per share plus brokerage fee of $165.
Aug. 20, 2002	— Received 10% stock dividend from Schvantz Ltd. of which $20 per share issued was credited to paid-up capital.
Dec. 28, 2005	— Sold 350 shares of Schvantz Ltd. at $29 per share plus brokerage fee of $355, settlement date January 4, 2006.

— *REQUIRED*

Calculate the taxable capital gain or allowable capital loss for Ms. Plummet from each of the above sales.

[For more problems and solutions thereto, see the CD accompanying this book.]

SUPPLEMENTAL NOTES

(This section can be omitted without losing the continuity of the chapter. None of the review questions, multiple choice questions, exercises or assignment problems utilizes this information.)

A. Cost of Assets Owned on December 31, 1971

[ITAR: 24; 26(3), (7); IT-84]

Since the government did not want to tax capital gains which had accrued up to December 31, 1971, certain special transition rules, called the Income Tax Application Rules, 1971 (ITARs), were developed to eliminate these gains from taxation under this subdivision when property purchased prior to 1972 was disposed of after 1971.

The median rule or tax-free zone method [ITAR 26(3)] applies automatically to all taxpayers. The rule establishes the cost of non-depreciable capital property owned on December 31, 1971 for the beginning of the new system which taxes capital gains, as follows:

A.C.B. = The middle figure of:

(a) Proceeds of disposition
(b) Valuation-day value
(c) Cost

if any two of these are equal they become the initial A.C.B.

The Valuation-day (V-Day) value rule [ITAR 26(7)] is an election which applies only to individuals. As an alternative to the median rule, this V-Day rule establishes the cost of capital property owned on December 31, 1971, for the beginning of the new system, as follows:

A.C.B. = Valuation-day value

Two Valuation days were designated [ITAR 24] to establish cost at the beginning of the new system under this rule. December 22, 1971 was chosen for publicly-traded securities and December 31, 1971 was chosen for all other capital property.

It is presumed by law that a taxpayer will use the median rule unless he or she elects under ITAR 26(7). The CRA has taken the position that when the capital gain is the same under both methods, then the taxpayer has the right to defer making the election until there is a difference between the two methods. Also, IT-139R, paragraphs 3 and 4 outline other situations in which the election may be postponed. From then on the taxpayer must adhere to the method chosen for all property owned prior to 1972.

The following six cases illustrate the application of the median rule (alternatively referred to as the tax-free zone method) and the V-Day rule. Note how the rule used establishes a base against which gains or losses under the new system of taxation of capital gains are measured. The objective is to prevent pre-1972 gains or losses from being taxable or allowable.

| | *Facts* | | | *Capital gain* | | | |
| | | | | *Under median rule* | | *Under V-day rule* | |
Case	*Actual cost*	*V-day value*	*P of D*	*Adjusted cost base*	*Capital gain (loss)*	*Adjusted cost base*	*Capital gain (loss)*
1	$2,000	$3,000	$5,000	$3,000	$2,000	$3,000	$2,000
2	5,000	3,000	2,000	3,000	(1,000)	3,000	(1,000)
3	3,000	2,000	5,000	3,000	2,000	2,000	3,000
4	3,000	5,000	2,000	3,000	(1,000)	5,000	(3,000)
5	2,000	5,000	3,000	3,000	Nil	5,000	(2,000)
6	5,000	2,000	3,000	3,000	Nil	2,000	1,000

Note how the adjusted cost base is established at the same value under both rules in Cases 1 and 2. Note, also, how in Case 1, the $1,000 (i.e., $3,000 − $2,000) gain that accrued before 1972 is not included in the capital gain. Similarly, in Case 2, the $2,000 (i.e., $3,000 − $5,000) of loss that accrued prior to 1972 is not considered part of the capital loss. Note that when the median rule is used and the proceeds of disposition amount is the middle number, there is no gain or loss. That is because proceeds fall in the "tax-free zone" between cost and V-Day.

B. Additional Rules For a Residence Owned On and After December 31, 1981

Amendments made effective for 1982 and subsequent years introduced rules to prevent certain perceived abuses of the principal residence rules. For years prior to 1982, it was possible for both spouses to each designate a residence as his or her principal residence as long as each residence was inhabited by the owner-spouse some-time during the year. For example, one spouse could designate the city home as a principal residence while the other spouse could designate a recreational residence. Hence, both residences could be fully protected from tax on capital gains by the maximum use of the designation rules. The following changes were made to eliminate the above situation.

(1) Paragraph (c) in the definition of "principal residence" in section 54 was modified for taxation years after 1981 such that the principal residence designation is limited to one per family unit, which generally includes the spouses and their single children under 18. A trust of which a spouse is the beneficiary (i.e., a spousal trust) can benefit from the principal residence exemption. Certain personal trusts that are not spousal trusts, i.e., not established for the benefit of a spouse, may also qualify for the principal residence exemption.

(2) For residences owned on December 31, 1981, there is a transitional rule found under subsection 40(6) which modifies the exemption rules to provide for the calculation of a gain equal to the lesser of:

(a) an amount determined under the rules in paragraph 40(2)(b), as discussed above, applied to the gain for the total period of ownership to the date of sale, including the one-plus rule but with the family unit restriction for years after 1981; and

(b) the sum of:

   (i) an amount determined under the rules in paragraph 40(2)(b) (see (a) above) applied to the gain to December 31, 1981 [par. 40(6)(a)], and

   (ii) an amount determined under the rules in paragraph 40(2)(b) applied to the gain from December 31, 1981 to the date of sale, including the family unit restriction but no one plus in the numerator of the exemption fraction [par. 40(6)(b)]

   minus

   (iii) the excess of the fair market value as at December 31, 1981 over the actual proceeds [par. 40(6)(c)].

Part (b) of the above calculation applicable on an eventual disposition after 1981 assumes that there was a disposition on December 31, 1981, at the fair market value at the time and a reacquisition at the same value on January 1, 1982. The purpose of the above rules is to provide for residences owned on December 31, 1981, the same measure of protection, as formerly allowed, before the change in legislation. There is no one plus provided in the numerator of the exemption fraction in part (b)(ii) above, because it is not needed for the intended purpose discussed previously. As a result of the assumed disposition on December 31, 1981, and reacquisition on January 1, 1982, an individual would not be assumed to sell the house and repurchase it in the same year. Hence, there is no need for the intended protection of the one-plus rule in this situation.

The following schematic diagram summarizes the applicability of the appropriate rules outlined above:

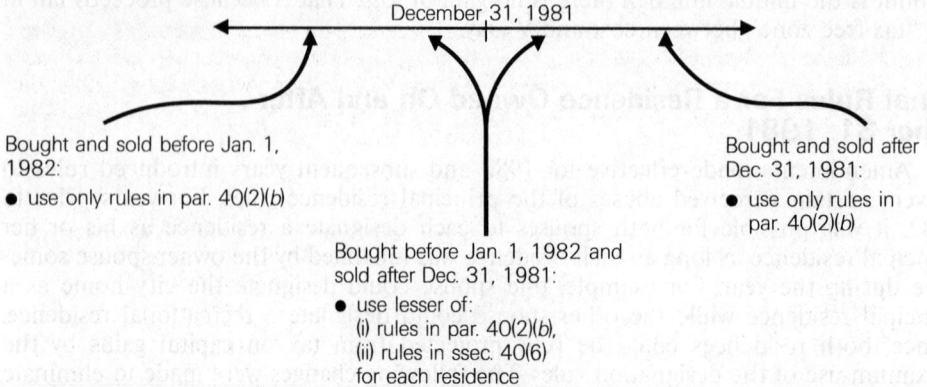

December 31, 1981

Bought and sold before Jan. 1, 1982:
● use only rules in par. 40(2)(b)

Bought before Jan. 1, 1982 and sold after Dec. 31, 1981:
● use lesser of:
  (i) rules in par. 40(2)(b),
  (ii) rules in ssec. 40(6)
  for each residence

Bought and sold after Dec. 31, 1981:
● use only rules in par. 40(2)(b)

Example Problem 1

Ms. Observanttax decides to sell the two residences listed below in 1999. She has not elected under ITAR 26(7) to use V-Day value to establish cost at the beginning of 1972; that is, the median rule must be used.

Residence	Date of purchase	Cost	Dec. 31/71 V-Day value	December 31, 1981 — FMV	Selling price
City home	1968	$60,000	$100,000	$180,000	$322,500
Cottage	1978	40,000	—	100,000	152,500

— *REQUIRED*

Calculate the minimum total capital gain on the disposition of the two residences.

— *SOLUTION*

(Note that the following analysis only applies to homes owned on December 31, 1981.)

Determine options to calculate.

By subsection 40(6), the capital gain on a residence is the lesser of the paragraph 40(2)(b) gain on that residence and the subsection 40(6) gain on that residence. This is true for each residence separately. Therefore, by simple arithmetic, the total capital gain on the two residences must be the least of the following four amounts:

(a) the paragraph 40(2)(b) gain on the city home plus the paragraph 40(2)(b) gain on the cottage;

(b) the subsection 40(6) gain on the city home plus the subsection 40(6) gain on the cottage;

(c) the paragraph 40(2)(b) gain on the city home plus the subsection 40(6) gain on the cottage;

(d) the subsection 40(6) gain on the city home plus the paragraph 40(2)(b) gain on the cottage.

The following schematic diagram outlines the four alternatives described above:

City home
(bought before '82/sold after '81)

Cottage
(bought before '82/sold after '81)

Par. 40(2)(b)   Par. 40(2)(b)

Ssec. 40(6)   Ssec. 40(6)

The four options are joined with arrows and lettered according to the description above.

To obtain the minimum total capital gain, each of the four amounts above must be minimized separately by appropriately choosing, for each year, the residence Ms. Observanttax should designate as her principal residence. Then, the least of the four minimized amounts will be the minimum total capital gain.[g] The principal residence designations filed with her tax return should be chosen accordingly.

The first step is to calculate the gains per year of ownership on the two residences. For gains determined under paragraph 40(2)(b), this should be the gain per year of ownership over the total post-1971 period as computed above. However, for gains determined under subsection 40(6), the gains per year should be computed separately for the period after 1971 and before 1982 (the pre-1982 gain) and the period after 1981 (the post-1981 gain).

Step 1 — Determine gain per year of ownership

	City home	Cottage
Par. 40(2)(b): Total period gain		
P of D	$322,500	$152,500
A.C.B.	(100,000)	(40,000)
Gain	$222,500	$112,500
Gain per year	$\frac{\$222,500}{28 \text{ years}} = \$\ 7,946$	$\frac{\$112,500}{22 \text{ years}} = \$\ 5,114$
Par. 40(6)(a): Pre-82 gain		
P of D — deemed	$180,000	$100,000
A.C.B.	(100,000)	(40,000)
Gain	$ 80,000	$ 60,000
Gain per year	$\frac{\$\ 80,000}{10 \text{ years}} = \$\ 8,000$	$\frac{\$\ 60,000}{4 \text{ years}} = \$15,000$
Par. 40(6)(b): Post-81 gain		
P of D	$322,500	$152,500
A.C.B. — deemed	(180,000)	(100,000)
Gain	$142,500	$ 52,500
Gain per year	$\frac{\$142,500}{18 \text{ years}} = \$7,917$	$\frac{\$\ 52,500}{18 \text{ years}} = \$\ 2,917$

Step 2 — Assignment of no-option years

The years 1972–77 should be used to designate the city home, which was the only residence owned in those years.

The option years 1978–1999 are allocated below in steps 3 to 7.

Step 3 — Gains determined under par. 40(2)(b) for both dwellings

From Step 1, the gains per year of ownership over the total period (28 years) are $7,946 for the city home vs. $5,114 for the cottage. Hence a first guess is to allocate all of the 22 option years 1978–1999 to the city home. However, as before, this results in one year being wasted because of the one-plus rule. This is corrected by designating the cottage as the taxpayer's principal residence for one year and allocating the remaining 21 option years to the city home.

	City home	Cottage
Par. 40(2)(b): Total period gain		
Gain	$222,500	$112,500
Exemption	(222,500)[1]	(10,227)[2]
Capital gain	Nil	$102,273

---

[g] This procedure follows Alan Macnaughton, "Minimizing Tax on Capital Gains on Principal Residences", a paper presented at the 1986 annual meeting of the Canadian Academic Accounting Association.

Step 4 — Gains determined under ssec. 40(6) for both dwellings

From Step 1, the cottage has the higher pre-1982 gain per year ($15,000 vs. $8,000) while the city home has the higher post-1981 gain per year ($7,917 vs. $2,917). Therefore, as a first guess, all pre-1982 option years should be allocated to the cottage while all post-1981 years should be allocated to the city home.

As before, the one-plus rule causes us to move one year in the pre-1982 period to the city home. This leaves the cottage's pre-1982 gain at zero while decreasing the pre-1982 gain of the city home. Thus, the cottage should be designated as a principal residence for all but one of the four pre-1982 option years (1978–81). The city home should be designated for one of the pre-1982 option years as well as the six no-option years (1972–77).

Under subsection 40(6), the one-plus rule is used only in computing the pre-1982 gain and is not used in calculating the post-1981 gain. Therefore, there is no reason to change the allocation of all post-1981 years to the city home.

	City home	Cottage
Sum of:		
(a) Par. 40(6)(a): Pre-82 gain		
Gain	$ 80,000	$60,000
Exemption	(64,000)[3]	(60,000)[4]
Capital gain	$ 16,000	Nil
and		
(b) Par. 40(6)(b): Post-81 gain		
Gain	$142,500	$52,500
Exemption	(142,500)[5]	Nil[6]
Capital gain	Nil	$52,500
Total ssec. 40(6) capital gain	$ 16,000	$52,500

Step 5 — Gains determined under par. 40(2)(b) for city home and ssec. 40(6) for cottage

Since the city home's gain is computed under paragraph 40(2)(b), its gain per year from Step 1 is $7,946. This should be compared to the subsection 40(6) gains per year for the cottage of $15,000 for the pre-1982 period and $2,916 for the post-1981 period. Therefore, our first guess is to assign all pre-1982 option years to the cottage and all post-1981 years to the city home.

Again, because of the one-plus rule, our first guess should be changed by moving one pre-1982 option year to the city home. This leaves the cottage's pre-1982 gain at zero while reducing the paragraph 40(2)(b) gain of the city home. Thus, the city home should be designated for the 1972–77 no-option years, one pre-1982 option year, and all of the years 1982–99. The cottage should be designated for just four years (the remaining pre-1982 option years).

	City home	Cottage
Par. 40(2)(b): Total period gain		
Gain	$222,500	
Exemption	(206,607)[7]	
Capital gain	$ 15,893	
Sum of:		
(a) Par. 40(6)(a): Pre-82 gain		
Gain		$60,000
Exemption		(60,000)[8]
Capital gain		Nil
and		
(b) Par. 40(6)(b): Post-81 gain		
Gain		$52,500
Exemption		Nil[9]
Capital gain		$52,500
Total ssec. 40(6) capital gain		$52,500

Step 6 — Gains determined under ssec. 40(6) for city home and par. 40(2)(b) for cottage

The gain per year of $5,114 over the total period for the cottage should be compared to the gains per year on the city home of $8,000 in the pre-1982 period and $7,917 in the post-1981 period. The first guess is to allocate all option years to the city home. Because of the one-plus rule, this allocation can be improved by moving one pre-1982 option year to the cottage.

	City home	Cottage
Par. 40(2)(b): Total period gain		
Gain		$112,500
Exemption		(10,227)[10]
Capital gain		$102,273

Sum of:

(a) Par. 40(6)(a): Pre-82 gain

Gain	$ 80,000	
Exemption	(80,000)[11]	
Capital gain	Nil	

and

(b) Par. 40(6)(b): Post-81 gain

Gain	$142,500	
Exemption	(142,500)[12]	
Capital gain	Nil	
Total ssec. 40(6) capital gain	Nil	

Step 7 — Comparison of total gains on the two dwellings under Steps 3 to 6

Step 3:	0 +	$102,273 =	$102,273
Step 4:	$16,000 +	52,500 =	68,500
Step 5:	15,893 +	52,500 =	68,393
Step 6:	0 +	102,273 =	102,273

The conclusion is that the minimum capital gain is produced under Step 5 and, therefore, the principal residence designations should be made as recommended in that step. Thus, Ms. Observanttax could designate the cottage as her principal residence for the years 1979 to 1981 and designate the city home as her principal residence for the years 1972 to 1978 and 1982 to 1999. This will produce a total capital gain on the two residences of $68,393 with a taxable capital gain of $51,295 (at the $3/4$ inclusion rate).

— *NOTES TO SOLUTION*

(1) $\frac{1 + 27}{28}$ × $222,500 = $222,500; years designated — 1972–76 and any 21 years from 1978–99

(2) $\frac{1 + 1}{22}$ × $112,500 = $10,227; year designated — any one of 1978–99 not designated in (1) above

(3) $\frac{1 + 7}{10}$ × $80,000 = $64,000; years designated — 1972–77 and any one of 1978–81

(4) $\frac{1 + 3}{4}$ × $60,000 = $60,000; years designated — any three of 1978–81 not designated in (3) above

(5) $\frac{18}{18}$ × $142,500 = $142,500; years designated — 1982–99

(6) $\frac{0}{18}$ × $52,500 = 0; years designated — none

(7) $\frac{1 + 25}{28}$ × $222,500 = $206,607; years designated — 1972–77, 1982–99 and any one of 1978–81

(8) $\frac{1 + 3}{4}$ × $60,000 = $60,000; years designated — any 3 of 1978–81 not designated in (7) above

(9) $\dfrac{0}{18}$ × \$52,500 = 0; years designated — none

(10) $\dfrac{1 + 1}{22}$ × \$112,500 = \$10,227; years designated — any one of 1978–81

(11) $\dfrac{1 + 9}{10}$ × \$80,000 = \$80,000; years designated — 1972–77 and any three of 1978–81 not designated in (10) above

(12) $\dfrac{18}{18}$ × \$142,500 =\$142,500; years designated — 1982–99

Example Problem 2

Mr. Dwellings owns two residences in British Columbia: a cottage and a Vancouver home, both of which were purchased prior to 1982. He anticipates disposing of his Vancouver home in 1999 and would like some advice on how to minimize the taxable capital gain on this disposition and yet provide maximum protection to the cottage (purchased in 1970), which has a smaller capital gain. The following facts relate to the Vancouver home:

Cost — 1965	\$250,000
F.M.V. — 1971	300,000
F.M.V. — 1981	510,000
F.M.V. — 1999	450,000

—REQUIRED

Calculate the minimum capital gain on the anticipated sale of the Vancouver home while saving the maximum number of designations for the cottage.

—SOLUTION

The Vancouver home has actually declined in value from the December 31, 1981 value (\$510,000 to \$450,000). Since paragraph 40(6)(c) permits a reduction of the gain under the sum of the preceding two paragraphs, the optimum solution should take this fact into account.

Step 1 — Determine gain per year of ownership
Par. 40(2)(b): Total period gain

P of D	\$450,000
A.C.B.	(300,000)
Gain	\$150,000

Gain per year of ownership..... $\dfrac{\$150,000}{28 \text{ years}}$ = \$ 5,357

Par. 40(6)(a): Pre-1982 gain

P of D — deemed	\$510,000
A.C.B.	(300,000)
Gain	\$210,000

Gain per year of ownership..... $\dfrac{\$210,000}{10 \text{ years}}$ = \$ 21,000

Therefore, assume that the capital gain will be determined by subsection 40(6) and designate the Vancouver home for enough years to remove all of the gain.

Step 2 — Determine the number of years of designation to remove all the gain

Gain (pre-1982)		\$210,000
less: par. 40(6)(c) reduction		
F.M.V. — December 31, 1981	\$510,000	
less actual P of D	(450,000)	(60,000)
		\$150,000

$\dfrac{\$150,000}{\$21,000}$ = 7.14 years required to remove entire gain

Therefore, designate only six years to the Vancouver home in the pre-1982 period using the one-plus rule for the other year.

Step 3 — Calculate minimum capital gain
Lesser of:
(a) Par. 40(2)(*b*): Total period gains
Gain as per Step 1 . . . . $150,000
Exemption: $\frac{1+6}{28} \times \$150,000$ . . . . (37,500) $112,500
(b) Par. 40(6)(*a*): Pre-1982 gain
Gain as per Step 1 . . . . $210,000
Exemption: $\frac{1+6}{10} \times \$210,000$ . . . . (147,000) $ 63,000
plus: par. 40(6)(*b*): Post-1981 gain . . . . Nil
less: par. 40(6)(*c*) excess
F.M.V. — December 31, 1981 . . . . $510,000
Actual P of D . . . . (450,000) (60,000)
Net gain under ssec. 40(6) . . . . $ 3,000

Therefore, the minimum capital gain is $3,000 and 22 years of designations remain to be assigned to the cottage as follows:
Pre-1982 — 4 years
Post-1981 — 18 years to 1999

C. Principal Residence on Farm Land

The gain on the disposition of land used in a farming business that included a principal residence may be computed in one of two ways. The gain on the housing unit plus up to one-half hectare of land may be reduced by an amount computed by the general formula in paragraph 40(2)(*b*). Alternatively, the farmer may elect under paragraph 40(2)(*c*) to compute an exemption of $1,000 plus $1,000 for every year after the later of 1971 and the last acquisition date that the property was designated as a principal residence and during which he or she was resident in Canada. The CRA's interpretation of these provisions can be found in IT-120R6, paragraphs 20–24.

D. GST Rules For Dispositions of Residential Property and Used Goods

The disposition of capital personal property for GST purposes was discussed in Chapter 5 while the rules relating to dispositions and changes in use of capital real property will be discussed in Chapter 8. The sale of shares, which is discussed in Chapter 15, is an exempt supply under the GST and, hence, there are no GST consequences. This part of the chapter will address the GST rules relating to dispositions of used residential or personal-use property and dispositions of used goods.

1. Sales of used residential or personal-use real property
[ETA: 123(1); 136(2); Sch. V, Part I, 2, 9]

GST applies to all sales of real property unless a specific exemption is provided. For example, sales of new residential housing are subject to GST. Pursuant to section 2 of Part I of Schedule V of the *Excise Tax Act* (ETA), sales of used residential complexes, or interests therein, are exempt from GST. Unlike the principal residence exemption under the *Income Tax Act*, the exemption for GST purposes is not limited to a single property.

The term "residential complex" is defined [ETA: ssec. 123(1)] to include a detached house, semi-detached house, rowhouse unit, multi-unit residential condominium or apartment complex, together with any common areas and land that are reasonably necessary for the use and enjoyment of the residential unit. A residential complex does not include a hotel, a motel, an inn, a boarding or lodging house, or other similar property that provides all, or substantially all, accommodation for periods of less than 60 days. A building generally constitutes a residential complex only in respect of the part that includes residential units. Thus, if an apartment building contains one floor of commercial space and ten floors of residential units, only the latter ten floors will constitute a residential complex.

A residential complex includes a single family dwelling in which a business is carried on, provided the dwelling is used primarily (i.e., more than 50%) as a residence for individuals. If the "primarily test" (i.e., the more than 50% test) is not met, a supply of real property that includes a residential complex and other real property that is not part of the residential complex is deemed to be two separate supplies [ETA: ssec. 136(2)]. Accordingly, the supply of the residential portion will be exempt if it qualifies as a used residential complex, and the other part of the property will be subject to the general rules. This rule will apply, for example, where an accountant uses a house primarily for his or her practice and not primarily as a residence.

Although the sale of the residential complex may be exempt, various fees related to the sale are subject to GST. These include, for example, real estate commissions, legal fees, appraisal fees, survey fees, and home inspection fees. No GST is payable in respect of exempt financial services, such as mortgage brokerage or mortgage insurance fees.

Section 9 of Part I of Schedule V of the ETA exempts sales of real property by an individual or a personal trust, other than:

- real property that is capital property used primarily
  — in a business carried on by the individual or trust with a reasonable expectation of profit, or
  — if the individual or trust is a registrant
    - in making taxable supplies of the real property by way of lease, licence, or similar arrangement, or
    - in any combination of the uses described above;
- real property sold
  — in the course of a business of the individual or trust, or
  — where the individual or trust has filed an election with the Minister in prescribed form and manner and containing prescribed information, in the course of an adventure or concern in the nature of trade of the individual or trust;
- a parcel of land that was subdivided or severed by the individual, trust or settlor of the trust (subject to certain exemptions);
- certain deemed supplies;
- a residential complex or an interest in a residential complex; or
- where an individual or personal trust has bought taxable real property and pursuant to a joint election, subsequently sells it back to the vendor within one year, pursuant to a right or obligation under the original purchase and sale agreement between the parties.

A "personal trust" is defined as a testamentary trust, or an *inter vivos* trust that is a personal trust (within the meaning assigned by subsection 248(1) of the *Income Tax Act*) all the beneficiaries (other than contingent beneficiaries) of which are individuals, and all the contingent beneficiaries of which, if any, are individuals, charities, or public institutions.

Under this provision, most sales of country properties kept for personal use, non-commercial hobby farms and other non-business land are exempt from GST. Sales of residential complexes are excluded from this exemption because they are covered in another provision, as discussed above. Where real property is sold in the course of an adventure or concern in the nature of trade, an election may be made to treat the sale as taxable. Such an election may be made, for example, by an individual or trust who acquires real property for resale purposes and not for personal use. If such an election is made, the individual or trust, if a registrant, would be entitled to recover any GST paid on the acquisition of the property (for example, if it was not purchased from another individual who held the property as personal-use real property) and on any subsequent improvements. As discussed in Chapter 6, sales of substantially renovated used housing in the course of a business are treated as sales of new housing and, therefore, are subject to GST.

The rules relating to exempt sales of real property by public sector bodies will not be discussed in this chapter.

The conversion of a commercial property to a residential complex, and *vice versa*, will be discussed in Chapter 8.

2. Sales of used goods and acceptance of trade-ins

[ETA: 153(4)]

Under the general GST rules, the sale by a registrant of a used good is subject to GST. If a used good sold by a registrant is purchased by another registrant for use in a commercial activity, the normal input tax credit rules apply. The sale of a used good by a non-registrant is not subject to GST.

Where a registrant accepts a used good (or a leasehold interest therein) as full or partial consideration for another good, the supplier has to collect GST only on the net amount if the trade-in is for consumption, use or supply by the supplier in the course of commercial activities and the person trading in the property is not required to collect GST (i.e., is not a registrant) [ETA: ssec. 153(4)]. For example, this rule would apply to an automobile dealer who accepts a trade-in from a consumer. The dealer would charge tax on the difference between the value of the new car and the value of the trade-in.

There are certain exceptions to this rule. For example, it does not apply to any supply of a trade-in that is a zero-rated supply (e.g., a supply of zero-rated farming equipment), or to a supply made outside Canada (e.g., a trade-in delivered outside Canada to the supplier of the new good).

If the used good is traded in by a registrant, the purchase of the new good and the trade-in are treated as two separate transactions, both of which are subject to GST.

Chapter 8

Capital Gains: The Finer Points

TOPICS DISCUSSED

	Page
VARIOUS CAPITAL GAINS PROVISIONS	367
Foreign Exchange Gains and Losses	367
Part Disposition	367
Exchanges of Property	368
Proceeds on Disposition of Building	376
Property with more than One Use	378
Principal Residence Revisited	380
Leaving and Entering Canada	385
Options	386
Debts Established to be Bad Debts	389
Convertible Properties	389
Capital Gains Deferral	390
Certain Shares Deemed to be Capital Property	392

	Page
CONSIDERATION IN NON-ARM'S LENGTH TRANSFERS AND THE ATTRIBUTION RULES REVISITED	392
Consideration in Non-arm's Length Transfers	392
Attribution Rules	394
DEATH OF A TAXPAYER	398
INCOME RECONCILIATION REVISITED	399
SUPPLEMENTAL NOTES	411
Pre-1972 Assets Revisited	411
Exempt Capital Gains Balance and Exempt Gains Balance	413
Warranties	414
Attribution and the CRA Policy Change on Substituted Property	415
GST and Capital Real Property	416

This chapter will re-examine some of the topics introduced in the preceding chapter and enlarge upon some of the technical refinements involved in the application of these rules. Additional areas of the capital gains system will also be explored. Furthermore, the chapter expands upon the GST implications of capital property acquisitions and dispositions.

As mentioned in chapter 7, Subdivision c of Division B of Part I of the Act contains the primary rules for the computation of taxable capital gains and allowable capital losses. Some of the more important provisions were reviewed at the beginning of the last chapter.

In addition, Subdivision f of Division B also provides some rules that are relevant to the computation of property income. For example, in this chapter we will look at the rules in section 70 related to the deemed disposition of capital property on the death of an individual as well as the attribution rules and non-arm's length transfers in sections 73 and 74.2.

In Division F the rules dealing with the treatment of capital property when an individual ceases to be or becomes a resident of Canada will be reviewed.

The following chart will help to locate in the Act, the major provisions dealt with in this chapter.

Part I — Division B
Subdivision c
Capital Gains & Losses

DIVISION		SUBDIVISION		SECTION	
A	Liability for tax				
B	Computation of income		Basic rules		
		a	Office or employment		
C	Computation of taxable income	b	Business or property		
D	Taxable income earned in Canada by non-residents	c	Capital gains and losses	38	TCG/ACL
				39	CG/CL
E	Computation of tax	d	Other income	39.1	Exempt CG balance
E.1	Minimum tax	e	Other deductions	40	General rules
F	Special rules	f	Rules relating to computation of income	41	LPP
				42	Warranty
G	Deferred and other special income arrangements	g	Amounts not included in income	43	Part disposition
				43.1	Life estates
H	Exemptions	h	Cdn corporations and shareholders	44	Replacement property
I	Returns, Assessments, payments, appeals	i	Shareholders of non-resident corporations	44.1	Small business share rollover
				45	Change in use
J	Appeals to the courts	j	Partnerships	46	Personal-use property
		k	Trusts	47	Identical property
				48.1	SBC goes public
				49	Options granted
				50	Loss on debt/shares
				51	Convertible property
				52	Cost of certain property
				53	ACB adjustments
				54	Definitions
				54.1	Exception: principal residence
				54.2	Shares and capital property
				55	Deemed capital gain

I. VARIOUS CAPITAL GAINS PROVISIONS

A. Foreign Exchange Gains and Losses

[ITA: 39(2); IT-95R]

Taxpayers must first determine whether the foreign exchange gain or loss arose from an income or a capital receipt, using the common law rules discussed in Chapters 4 and 7. For income receipts, the full gain or loss will be included in arriving at business or property income under Subdivision b. For capital receipts, the net capital gain or loss is determined in the normal manner. However, for individuals the net capital gain or loss is reduced by a maximum of $200 [ssec. 39(2)].

Example Problem

Mr. Fast-Dollar made the following capital transactions which resulted in currency gains and losses during the following years:

	2003	2004	2005
Total currency gains........................	$800	$180	$250
Total currency losses	300	40	400

— REQUIRED

Compute the capital gains (losses) on foreign currency for each of the years shown.

— SOLUTION

	2003	2004	2005
Net capital gain (loss)	$500	$140	$(150)
Exempt portion of excess	200	140	(150)
Capital gain (loss)	$300	Nil	Nil

It should be noted that a currency gain or loss must be distinct and separate from another transaction that may have given rise to the currency transaction. For example, the sale of an article must be computed in Canadian dollars valued at the time of the sale in order to arrive at a gain or loss on that disposition. A subsequent conversion of foreign funds received would give rise to the currency gain or loss.

B. Part Disposition

[ITA: 43; IT-264R]

If a taxpayer makes a partial disposition of a capital property, section 43 requires that he or she allocate a reasonable portion of the total adjusted cost base of the capital property to the proceeds of partial disposition to determine the capital gain or loss. The portion of this cost allocated to the part sold should be in the ratio of the value of the part sold to the total value of the capital property. A valuation problem is very likely to arise, particularly if the value of the part sold is not, in fact, proportional to total value. This might be the case, for example, where a taxpayer owns land with lake frontage and the half of the property fronting on the lake is sold leaving the other half without such lake access.

C. Exchanges of Property

[ITA: 13(4); 44; IT-259R4; IT-491]

1. The basic deferral

This particular provision permits the deferral of some or all of the capital gain on property which is disposed of and which is subsequently replaced. There are two basic types of disposition which qualify for this deferral (often referred to in practice as a "rollover"):

(a) an involuntary disposition of property which has been lost, stolen, destroyed or taken by order of statutory authority (e.g., expropriation, bankruptcy); and

(b) a voluntary dispositions of real property referred to as "former business property" that usually occur on the relocation of a business.

The deferral for a voluntary disposition is limited to former business property. "Former business property" as used in paragraph 44(1)(*b*) is defined in subsection 248(1) as real property which has a common law definition of "land and buildings" and limited-period franchises, concessions or licences on which an election under subsection 13(4.2) has been made [proposed in the Technical Amendments to the *Income Tax Act* dated February 27, 2004].

This topic has been partly covered in Chapter 5 in connection with the deferral of recapture [ssec. 13(4)] realized on depreciable property. That material should be reviewed as preparation for the following discussion of the deferral of a capital gain in these situations. An election under subsection 13(4) or subsection 44(1) is deemed to be an election under the other subsection [ssec. 44(4)].

In the year of the disposition, a taxpayer may choose to:

(a) recognize the usual capital gain (i.e., P of D minus A.C.B. and selling costs), or

(b) elect to report the capital gain as the lesser of:

   (i) the actual capital gain in (a) above, and

   (ii) the excess, if any, of proceeds for the old property over the cost of replacement,

if he or she has replaced the property,

(a) in the case of a voluntary disposition, by the later of the end of the first taxation year after the year of disposition and 12 months after the end of the year of disposition, or

(b) in the case of an involuntary disposition, by the later of the end of the second taxation year after the year of disposition and 24 months after the end of the year of disposition.

The disposition of the old property is deemed to have occurred only when the proceeds are "receivable". In the case of involuntary dispositions, the rules for determining when proceeds are receivable are found in subsection 44(2) and can be summarized (for situations excluding the death of a taxpayer or the winding-up of a corporation) as the earliest of:

(a) the day the taxpayer has agreed to the full amount of the compensation;

(b) the day the compensation is finally determined by a court or tribunal; and

(c) the day that is two years from the day of loss, destruction or taking where a claim or suit has not been taken before the courts.

The election does not apply immediately where the taxpayer does not purchase the replacement property in the same year the proceeds of disposition become receivable. In the year in which proceeds of disposition become receivable, the disposition is handled in the normal manner by reporting the gain. If the replacement property is acquired within the allowed time, an amended return would be filed for the year in which the proceeds became receivable to implement the rollover.

The adjusted cost base for the replacement property under the election above will be reduced by the deferred capital gain [par. 44(1)(f)]. This is the essence of a rollover or deferral which, in this case, is accomplished by the reduction of the adjusted cost base of the new property. By reducing the adjusted cost base, a future capital gain (or reduced capital loss) in the amount of the deferred gain will arise on the ultimate disposition of the new property.

Replacement property is defined in subsection 44(5) as property acquired for the same or a similar use as the original property and for gaining or producing income from the same or a similar business. See IT-259R4 for the Department's present liberal interpretation of "same or similar use" (paragraphs 16-17) and "same or similar business" (paragraphs 18-21).

Net capital gains reserves may arise from exchanges of property situations. For example, proceeds may become receivable in a year, but they are not due until a subsequent year, such that a capital gains reserve is available. When the reserve is included in income in the year after the reserve is deducted, the included reserve would normally qualify for this election.

Example Problem 1

Quick Growth Stores Ltd. has decided to change the present location of its retail store, now in a suburban mall, to the Yonge Street strip in downtown Toronto. The following facts relate to the disposition of the original property in March 2004.

	Land	Cl.3 Building	Cl.8 Equipment
Cost	$30,000	$50,000	$5,000
U.C.C.	—	30,000	1,500
Proceeds	70,000	100,000	500

Quick Growth Ltd. purchased its Yonge Street property in August 2005 for the following amounts:

Land	$100,000
Building — brick	150,000
Equipment	20,000

The company wishes to elect to defer both the capital gain and the recapture.

— REQUIRED

Indicate the tax consequences if Quick Growth Stores Ltd. elects under section 44 and subsection 13(4), assuming that its fiscal year-end is December 31.

— SOLUTION

This situation involves the voluntary disposition of a former business property in respect of the land and building. As a result, the taxpayer corporation must replace the land and building within the later of one taxation year or 12 months from the end of the December 31, 2004 taxation year (i.e., the taxation year of the disposition), in order to obtain the benefits of the rollover. It is often helpful to use a time line to graph the qualifying period of replacement as follows:

(A) Effect of section 44 election — Filed on an amended return for 2004

Gain to be recognized in year of disposal — 2004 [par. 44(1)(e)]

			Land	Building
(i)	Capital gain, computed as:			
	Lesser of: (I)	P of D	$ 70,000	$100,000
		A.C.B.	(30,000)	(50,000)
		Capital gain	$ 40,000	$ 50,000
	(II)	P of D	$ 70,000	$100,000
		Replacement cost	(100,000)	(150,000)
		Excess, if any	Nil	Nil

Adjusted cost base of replacement land is

$100,000 − $40,000 = $60,000 [par. 44(1)(f)]

Adjusted cost base of replacement building is

$150,000 − $50,000 = $100,000 [par. 44(1)(f)]

(ii) Equipment — Nil

Equipment does not qualify as "former business property". In any case there is a loss which is not allowed as a capital loss [spar. 39(1)(b)(i)].

Comments:

(1) In the above situation, the entire capital gain is deferred through the reduction of the adjusted cost base of the replacement property, since the amount actually spent on the replacement property was greater than the proceeds of disposition for the old property. The intent of the provision is to allow a deferral of all or some part of the actual capital gain and, hence, the tax on that gain, where the proceeds have been spent to acquire a new property. Conceptually, if the proceeds have been spent in this manner, there would be no funds from the disposition of the old property to pay the taxes, so the taxes are deferred. Note how the reduction in the adjusted cost base of the replacement property implements the deferral. Consider the replacement land which was acquired at a cost of $100,000. Its cost base is $60,000 after the adjustment for the deferred gain. If that land were sold immediately for its indicated value of $100,000 (it was just purchased for that amount), a capital gain of $40,000 (i.e., $100,000 − $60,000) would be realized. That capital gain is exactly the gain on the old land that was deferred.

(2) Since the replacement property was acquired after the filing of the 2004 corporate tax returns (June 30, 2005), according to IT-259R4, paragraph 3, the resultant capital gain and any recapture must be reported in the year of disposition. A request for an amended return must be made in the year of acquisition. Acceptable security may be provided in lieu of the payment of outstanding taxes.

(B) Effect of subsection 13(4) election re building — Filed on an amended return for 2004.

2004

		Cl.3: 5%
U.C.C. immediately before disposal		$30,000
Less: deemed disposal reducing U.C.C. [par. 13(4)(*c*)]		
— normal deduction: lesser of:		
(i) cost ($50,000)		
(ii) P of D ($100,000)	$50,000	
— reduced [par. 13(4)(*c*)] by the lesser of:		
(i) amount determined above ($50,000) less U.C.C. above ($30,000)	20,000	
(ii) cost of replacement ($150,000)	30,000	
U.C.C., December 31, 2004		Nil

Comment:

As long as the cost of replacement ($150,000) is greater than the amount of the recapture ($20,000) that would otherwise result on the disposition, there will be full deferral of the recapture.

2005

		Cl.1: 4%
Add: Capital cost of replacement property [par. 13(4)(*d*)]		
Cost of replacement	$150,000	
Less: reduction for deferred gain [par. 44(1)(*f*)]	50,000	
Deemed capital cost	$100,000	
Less: reduction for deferred recapture [par. 13(4)(*d*)]	20,000	$80,000
U.C.C., December 31, 2005		$80,000
C.C.A., 2005 (4% of ¹/₂ × $80,000)		1,600
U.C.C., January 1, 2006		$78,400

Comment:

Normally, when depreciable property of a class is sold and replaced with property of the same class in the year of disposition, all or some part of the potential recapture on the disposition is offset by the purchase before the end of the year. For example, if the new building had been purchased for $100,000 in 2004 and if it could have been added to the *same* class as the old building, the following U.C.C. balance would have resulted:

U.C.C. immediately before disposal		$ 30,000
Less lesser of:		
(i) cost of building disposed of................	$ 50,000	
(ii) proceeds of disposition	$100,000	
lesser amount		(50,000)
Add: capital cost of replacement building		100,000
U.C.C., December 31, 2004		$ 80,000

Note that this is the same amount as the U.C.C. balance at December 31, 2005 after the rollover [ssec. 13(4)] is implemented.

In deferring the recapture, subsection 13(4) provides two additional benefits:

(i) it allows for a replacement to take place in a subsequent year, and

(ii) it allows for a replacement with a property in a different class.

Example Problem 2

Reconsider the facts in Example Problem 1. In this example, Quick Growth Ltd. purchased less expensive land in 2005.

Land...	$ 45,000
Building — brick (same as Example Problem 1)...............	150,000
Equipment (same as Example Problem 1)....................	20,000

— REQUIRED

Indicate the tax consequences for the land only, if Quick Growth Ltd. elects under section 44 (assuming that its fiscal year-end is December 31).

— SOLUTION

The gain on the land to be recognized in year of disposal (2004) is now $25,000, computed as:

Lesser of: (A) P of D......................................	$70,000
A.C.B.	(30,000)
C.G.	$40,000
(B) P of D	$70,000
Replacement cost	(45,000)
Excess, if any	$25,000

Adjusted cost base in 2005 of replacement property is:		
Replacement cost	$ 45,000	
Deferred gain [$40,000 − $25,000]	(15,000)	
A.C.B. of replacement property	$ 30,000	[par. 44(1)(f)]

2. Subsection 44(6) election for additional deferral

This particular election permits the proceeds on the dispositions of former business property (land and buildings) to be reallocated between the two components so that less capital gain or recapture would be triggered. This election appears to recognize the fact that when a property consisting of land and building is sold, it is usually sold for proceeds which represent the fair market value of the total property. In this situation, the land and building are not priced separately. Therefore, the original allocation of proceeds between land and building may have been fairly arbitrary.

Example Problem

Reconsider the facts in Example Problems 1 and 2 above.

— REQUIRED

Indicate tax consequences of electing under subsection 44(6) in respect of the building, based on the facts in Example Problem 1, and the land, based on the facts in Example Problem 2.

— SOLUTION

Re-examining the facts of Example Problem 2 above, it would be possible to elect to transfer $25,000 of the land proceeds to the building proceeds, thereby eliminating the capital gain. Note that the trade-off is a reduced capital cost of the building and, hence, a lower capital cost allowance base. Therefore, the cost of deferring tax on $25,000 of capital gain now is less capital cost allowance over the holding period of the building in the future.

(A) Effect of subsection 44(6) election

Gain to be recognized in year of disposal (2004) [par. 44(1)(e)]

			Land	Building
(i) Capital gain, computed as:			<u>Land</u>	<u>Building</u>
Lesser of: (I)	Actual P of D...............		$ 70,000	$100,000
	Ssec. 44(6) election		(25,000)	25,000
	Deemed P of D		$ 45,000	$125,000
	A.C.B.		(30,000)	(50,000)
	C.G.		$ 15,000	$ 75,000
(II)	Deemed P of D above		$ 45,000	$125,000
	Replacement cost		(45,000)	(150,000)
	Excess, if any		Nil	Nil

Adjusted cost base of replacement land is:

$45,000 – ($15,000 – Nil) = <u>$30,000</u> [par. 44(1)(f)]

Adjusted cost base of replacement building is:

$150,000 – ($75,000 – Nil) = <u>$75,000</u> [par. 44(1)(f)]

Comment:

Note that the key to a reallocation of proceeds that will successfully defer more of the capital gain is a replacement cost of one of the assets (i.e., either land or building) that is sufficiently in excess of original proceeds of disposition to allow for an increase in proceeds on that asset without triggering a gain. In this case, the replacement cost of the building, at $150,000, exceeds the original proceeds of the old building of $100,000. Therefore, up to $50,000 can be added to the proceeds and still leave the excess of proceeds over replacement cost of nil. In this case, only $25,000 needs to be removed from the proceeds of the land to allow all of the gain to be deferred.

(B) Effect of subsection 13(4) election on building — Filed on an amended return for 2004.

2004

		Cl.3:5%
U.C.C. immediately before disposal		$30,000
Less: deemed disposal reducing U.C.C. [par. 13(4)(c)]		
— normal deduction: lesser of:		
(i) cost ($50,000)		
(ii) P of D ($100,000)[1]	$ 50,000	
— reduced [par. 13(4)(c)] by the lesser of:		
(i) amount determined above ($50,000) less U.C.C. above ($30,000)	20,000	
(ii) cost of replacement ($150,000)	30,000	
U.C.C. after disposal		Nil

2005

			Cl.1:4%
Add:	Capital cost of replacement property [par. 13(4)(d)]		
	Cost of replacement	$150,000	
	Less: reduction for deferred gain [par. 44(1)(f)]	75,000	
	Deemed capital cost	$ 75,000	
	Less: reduction for deferred recapture [par. 13(4)(d)]	20,000	$55,000
U.C.C., December 31, 2005			$55,000
C.C.A., 2005 (4% of ½ × $55,000)			1,100
U.C.C., January 1, 2006			$53,900

Comment:

The results of using the subsection 44(6) election can be compared with the original application of the deferral as follows:

	Without ssec. 44(6)	With ssec. 44(6)	Difference
Capital gains recognized:			
land	$ 25,000	Nil	$25,000
building	Nil	Nil	Nil
A.C.B. of replacement property:			
land	30,000	$30,000	Nil
building	100,000	75,000	25,000
U.C.C. (before C.C.A.) of replacement building	80,000	55,000	25,000

The above shows that $25,000 less capital gain on the land has to be recognized as a result of the subsection 44(6) election. This is reflected in the adjusted cost base of the building which is $25,000 lower. This lower A.C.B. will potentially result in a higher capital gain on the ultimate disposition of the building, if it is sold for a capital gain. Also, the U.C.C. of the building is $25,000 lower, resulting in less annual C.C.A. To evaluate the trade-off the following should be compared:

    (i) the tax that would be paid now on a capital gain of $25,000 or a taxable capital gain of $12,500 (i.e., $\frac{1}{2} \times \$25,000$), and

    (ii) the present value of the C.C.A. tax shield[2] from $25,000 of capital cost in Class 1.

— NOTES TO SOLUTION

(1) Note that the deemed proceeds arising from subsection 44(6) are not applicable for the purpose of section 13, since subsection 44(6) is only applicable to Subdivision c which deals with taxable capital gains and allowable capital losses.

(2) The present value of the C.C.A. tax shield, including the effect of the half-net-amount rule, can be computed from the following:

$$PV = \frac{C \times R \times T}{R + I} \times \frac{1 + I/2}{1 + I}$$

where PV = present value of the C.C.A. tax shield,
       C = capital cost of the asset,
       R = rate of C.C.A. for the class,
       I = after-tax discount rate,
       T = tax rate.

Replacement Property
Deferral of Capital Gain
Summary

Key Question: Did you spend at least the proceeds on the replacement property?

If you spend at least the proceeds from the sale of the former property to buy the replacement property, then the full amount of the gain will be deferred. The deferral is built into the reduction of the cost base of the replacement property.

If you sell both land and building then this concept applies to the combined proceeds and the combined replacement cost.

Deferral of Recapture
Summary

Key Question: Did you spend at least the amount of the recapture on the replacement property?

If you spend at least an amount equal to the potential recapture from the sale of the former property to buy the replacement property, then the full amount of the recapture will be deferred. The deferral is built into the reduction of the undepreciated capital cost of the replacement property.

D. Proceeds on Disposition of Building

[ITA: 13(21.1)]

An interesting situation arose in the case of *The Queen v. Malloney's Studio Limited*, (S.C.C.) 78 DTC 6278 in which the taxpayer agreed to sell land clear of buildings and, therefore, had to demolish an existing building before disposing of the land. The Minister allocated part of the proceeds of disposition for the property to the demol-ished building resulting in recapture. The taxpayer argued that all of the price related to the land. The Supreme Court of Canada held that the price related only to the land because the building was not part of the sale. No part of the price was for property "damaged, destroyed, taken or injuriously affected" because the purchase did not cause the damage as envisaged by the definition of "proceeds of disposition" in subsec-tion 13(21). Since none of the proceeds for the property had to be allocated to the building, the taxpayer could deduct a terminal loss on the building and, at the same time, all of the proceeds created a capital gain which was only fractionally taxable.

Perhaps as a reaction to the result of the above case, subsection 13(21.1) was added to the Act to provide rules to allocate proceeds of disposition between land and buildings on their sale. Where a building is sold for proceeds that are less than its proportionate share of the undepreciated capital cost of its class, subsection 13(21.1) will apply. In the situation where the land is sold in the same taxation year as the building, the amount which is treated as proceeds of disposition of the building may be greater than the fair market value of the building, thereby reducing or eliminating the potential terminal loss. At the same time, the capital gain on the sale of the land will be reduced by the amount of the terminal loss eliminated on the building. As a result, the potential terminal loss on the building will be used to offset the gain on the land. The result is to convert what might have been a terminal loss fully deductible into a reduction of a capital gain, in essence, three-quarters deductible.

Where the land is not disposed of in the same year, one-half of the apparent terminal loss on the building will be deductible, resulting in what is, in effect, an allowable capital loss on the sale of the building instead of an ordinary loss. However, the deductible amount of the loss will technically be considered a business loss.

Example Problem

Trash-it Limited owned a real property which it sold during the current taxation year for a total of $200,000. The land had a fair market value of $150,000 and an adjusted cost base of $100,000. The building had a fair market value of $50,000. It was the only building in the class which had an undepreciated capital cost of $75,000 and a capital cost of $90,000.

— REQUIRED

(A) Determine the tax consequences of the sale of the building in this transaction.

(B) If the purchaser wanted to buy only the building for $50,000 and remove it at his or her own expense to another location, what would be the tax consequences of the sale of the building?

— SOLUTION

(A) If proceeds of disposition of the building are considered to be equal to its fair market value of $50,000 which is less than the undepreciated capital cost of the class and the capital cost, the proceeds of disposition of the building will be deemed [par. 13(21.1)(a)] to be the following:

P of D of building = lesser of:

(i)	(I) F.M.V. of land and building		$200,000	
	minus			
	(II) lesser of:			
	— A.C.B. of land	$100,000		
	— F.M.V. of land	$150,000		100,000
				$100,000

(ii) greater of:

    (I) F.M.V. of building $50,000

    (II) lesser of capital cost and U.C.C. of

        building . . . . $75,000 $ 75,000

= $75,000

Since proceeds of disposition are deemed to be equal to the undepreciated capital cost of the class, there is no terminal loss and no recapture. Note that proceeds of disposition of the land will be deemed to be:

    (i) P of D of land and building $200,000

    minus

    (ii) deemed P of D of building (above) 75,000 $125,000

This will result in a capital gain of $25,000 on the land (i.e., $125,000 – $100,000).

If it were not for the rule in paragraph 13(21.1)(*a*), there would have been a capital gain on the land of $50,000 (i.e., $150,000 – $100,000) and a terminal loss on the building of $25,000 (i.e., $50,000 – $75,000). The effect of paragraph 13(21.1)(*a*) can be seen from the following comparison:

Income effect	*Without* *par. 13(21.1)(a)*	*With* *par. 13(21.1)(a)*
Taxable capital gain on land:		
$^1/_2 \times$ $50,000	$ 25,000	
$^1/_2 \times$ $25,000		$12,500
Terminal loss on building	(25,000)	(Nil)
Effect on net income	NIL	$12,500

Paragraph 13(21.1)(*a*) has converted the terminal loss on the building, which is normally fully deductible, into an amount that is, in effect, only $^1/_2$ deductible by reducing the gain on the land (which is only $^1/_2$ taxable).

(B) In this case, proceeds of disposition of the building will be deemed [par. 13(21.1)(*b*)] to be the following:

P of D of building = (i) P of D of building (without ssec. 13(21.1)) $ 50,000

    plus

    (ii) greater of:

        (I) U.C.C. of building

           (Class 3) $75,000

        (II) F.M.V. $75,000

           of building . . . $50,000

        minus P of D of building

           in (i) above $50,000

        excess $\times$ 1/2 . . . . $25,000 $\times$ $^1/_2$ $ 12,500

                                              $ 62,500

U.C.C. of class 75,000

Terminal loss . . . . $(12,500)

Note how the decline in value of $25,000 from undepreciated capital cost to fair market value of the building has been rendered, essentially one-half deductible in this situation. This effect parallels that illustrated in part (A) above.

Disposal of Land and Building
Ssec. 13(21.1)
Summary

Key Question: Was there a capital gain on the land and a terminal loss on the building?

If so, an amount equal to the terminal loss (but not greater than the capital gain) will reduce the proceeds on the land and increase the proceeds on the building. This will reduce the capital gain and the terminal loss will be eliminated.

E. Property with more than One Use

[ITA: 45; IT-218R]

When a taxpayer changes the use of property, he or she is deemed to have sold that property at the fair market value and to have reacquired the same property immediately thereafter at the fair market value which becomes his or her new adjusted cost base [par. 45(1)(a)]. Where property has a dual use, its cost must be apportioned between the uses on a percentage basis and that basis will be used on the disposition of the property [par. 45(1)(b)]. If the percentage for a particular use is changed either up or down, there will be a proportionate deemed disposition and reacquisition at the fair market value at that time [par. 45(1)(c)].[a] Note that these rules are similar in concept to the rules in subsection 13(7) with respect to changes of use and the capital cost allowance system.

In IT-218R, the Canada Revenue Agency (CRA) indicates, at paragraph 11, that a change in use does not include a transfer of property from one income-producing use to another such use by the same taxpayer. As examples, the CRA suggests that the change-in-use rules do not apply when real estate used to produce income from a business or property is converted to inventory, because holding the property as inventory is still an income-producing use. Similarly, the rules do not apply where inventory is converted to capital property which is used to produce income from a business or property. The Interpretation Bulletin provides numerical examples of how to handle these conversions to separate income gains from capital gains by the use of a "notional disposition" described in paragraph 15. It is only on an actual disposition that income gains alone may be realized in these situations.

For personal-use property *only*, a taxpayer may elect to defer the capital gain until such time as he or she:

- decides to dispose of the asset;
- is deemed to dispose of the asset; or
- decides to rescind the election.

This election applies only when the property was used originally for personal use and remains in force until one of the above conditions occurs. For example, a taxpayer may have a yacht which is used for personal use. Later, the taxpayer decides to rent out his or her yacht. He or she may elect to defer the potential gain on the change in use by using subsection 45(2). This election will remain in force even when he or she changes its use back to personal use unless, of course, he or she rescinds the election. However, this election is not available in a situation where the property was first used to produce income and then is changed to personal use.

[a] The case of *Woods v. M.N.R.*, (T.R.B.) 78 DTC 1576 illustrates the application of subsection 45(1) and the consequences of a deemed disposition.

Example Problem

A taxpayer purchased a yacht in 1997 at a cost of $24,000. In 1999, the taxpayer changed the use and rented the yacht for the next two years. The fair market value at the time the property became an income-producing asset was $30,000. During 2001, he converted the yacht back to exclusive personal use. The fair market value at this time was $33,000. In 2005, the taxpayer sold the yacht for $60,000.

— REQUIRED

Compare the taxable capital gain arising with and without the subsection 45(2) election.

— SOLUTION

	No election made by taxpayer	Ssec. 45(2) election made by taxpayer
1999		
Deemed proceeds of disposition	$30,000	
Less: adjusted cost base	24,000	
Capital gain	$ 6,000	
Taxable capital gain ($3/4 \times$ $6,000)	$ 4,500	Nil
2001		
Deemed proceeds of disposition	$33,000	
Less: adjusted cost base	30,000	
Capital gain	$ 3,000	
Taxable capital gain ($1/2 \times$ $3,000)	$ 1,500	Nil
2005		
Proceeds of sale	$60,000	$60,000
Less: adjusted cost base	33,000	24,000
Capital gain	$27,000	$36,000
Taxable capital gain (1/2)	$13,500	$18,000

Notes to Example Problem

Theoretically, there should be no difference in the total taxable capital gain between the two options available, only a timing difference in the payment of the tax. Where the inclusion rate is constant, the subsection 45(2) election would normally be the preferred treatment, since the change in use has not generated any cash. Hence, there are a number of other factors to be considered:

(a) Does the taxpayer have any capital losses which he or she may wish to trigger?

(b) Will the taxpayer move to a higher tax bracket in the future?

(c) Conversely, does the taxpayer anticipate a decrease in income at some time in the future?

If the facts in the example problem had been reversed and the taxpayer had acquired the yacht for rental purposes and subsequently converted the yacht to personal use, this election would not be available. However, if the property was a rental building which was converted to personal use and was designated as a principal residence in a subsequent disposition, subsection 45(3) would provide a rollover as discussed in the next section.

If an election is made under subsection 45(2) not to have a change in use, then subsection 13(7) will not apply to determine the UCC of the yacht, since it is deemed to still be personal-use property. If an election is not made, then subsection 13(7) will apply and these rules as explained in Chapter 5 will result in a UCC in 1999 of $28,500 (cost of $24,000 plus the TCG at 75% of $6,000). On the deemed disposition in 2001, there may be recapture to the extent that any CCA was claimed on the yacht.

F. Principal Residence Revisited

[ITA: 40(2), (4); 45; 54; 54.1; ITR: 1102(1)(*c*); IT-120R6; IT-437R]

1. Application of subsection 45(2) and 45(3) elections

The aforementioned subsection 45(2) election can also be used in connection with a principal residence where the initial change of use is from personal use to income-producing use. Paragraph (*d*) of the definition of a "principal residence" in section 54 permits a taxpayer, who changes the use of his or her home, to choose to designate this home as his or her principal residence for up to four years, as long as he or she has elected under subsection 45(2). One should note that the subsection 45(2) election and the designation as a principal residence are two separate and distinct acts. IT-120R6 normally permits a taxpayer to file a retroactive subsection 45(2) election in connection with a principal residence *only*. A further consequence of the subsection 45(2) election is that the taxpayer cannot claim capital cost allowance against any income from that property [Reg. 1102(1)(*c*)].

For dispositions of principal residences (after 1984), subsection 45(3) and the definition of a "principal residence" in section 54 provide for a similar four-year maximum designation in situations where the property was converted from an initial income-producing purpose to personal use and is designated as a principal residence. This election must be made on the earlier of 90 days after a ministerial demand or the normal filing due date (see Chapter 14) for the year of the disposition of the property. Note that this provision is not applicable in respect of recapture and subsection 45(4) will revoke this election if any capital cost allowance is claimed. The combination of the designations under subsections 45(2) and (3) cannot exceed four years.

The exemption formula [par. 40(2)(*b*)] discussed in the last chapter must now be modified to take into account a possible change in use as follows:

$$\frac{1 + \text{the number of years for which the property is designated after the later of December 31, 1971 and the date on which it was last acquired}}{\text{Number of years during which the property was owned after the later of December 31, 1971 and the date on which it was last acquired}} \times \text{gain realized}$$

"The date on which it was last acquired" can, if applicable, refer to a deemed reacquisition for personal use after a change in use.

Example Problem

Mr. On-the-Move owned a home in Calgary which he purchased in 1994. During 1997, he decided to relocate because of business reasons and moved to Vancouver. He rented an apartment in Vancouver and rented out his Calgary home. In 2003, he returned to Calgary to live in his original home. He anticipates selling the Calgary home in 2005 and retiring. The following data relates to his home:

Calgary home:	Cost	1994	$140,000
	F.M.V.	1997	200,000
	F.M.V.	2003	320,000
	Proceeds	2005 (estimated)	415,000

— *REQUIRED*

(A) Compute the minimum capital gain, based on the above information. Assume Mr. On-the-Move makes the subsection 45(2) election on a late-filed basis when he files his 2003 tax return as per paragraph 28 of IT-120R6.

(B) Re-do Part (A) on the assumption that Mr. On-the-Move does not elect under subsection 45(2).

— SOLUTION

Part (A) — Subsection 45(2) election

When Mr. On-the-Move moves out of the Calgary home and begins to rent it out, there is a deemed disposition on the change in use. However, if he makes an election under subsection 45(2) then the result is that there is no change in use and the property remains a personal-use property. In addition, paragraph (d) of the definition of a "principal residence" in section 54 provides that it is possible for this property to be designated as his principal residence for up to four additional years even though he is not living there. This would allow him to designate the property as his principal residence for the years 1994-1997 and 2003-2005 based on the years he lived there and for the years 1998-2001 based on the four additional years. The only year missing is 2002 and it is protected with the "1+" rule.

	Calgary home
Gain	$ 275,000
Exempt portion	(275,000)[1]
Capital gain	Nil
Taxable capital gain	Nil

Since an election is made under subsection 45(2) to deem there not to be a change in use of the Calgary home, then subsection 13(7) does not apply.

Part (B) — No subsection 45(2) election

In 1997, when Mr. On-the-Move moves out of his Calgary home and begins to rent it to earn income, there is a deemed disposition on the change in use [ssec. 45(1)]. Since he has been living in the house since he bought it in 1994, he can claim the principal residence exemption on the gain that results from the deemed disposition. By designating the years 1994 to 1996 he can eliminate the full gain as shown below.

	Calgary home
1998	
P of D, deemed	$ 200,000
A.C.B.	(140,000)
Gain	$ 60,000
Exempt portion	(60,000)[2]
Capital gain	Nil

Since no election was made under subsection 45(2) on the Calgary home, then subsection 13(7) will apply to deem the UCC in 1997 to become $185,000 (cost of $140,000 plus the TCG at 75% of $60,000). On the deemed disposition of the Calgary home in 2003, there will be recapture to the extent that any CCA was claimed on the home between 1997 and 2003.

In 2003, when he returns to Calgary and moves back into the house, there is another change in use and a resulting deemed disposition. In this case the principal residence exemption can be claimed for the years 1997 and 2003, since the house was his principal residence at some point during each of those years.

	Calgary home
P of D — actual	$ 320,000
A.C.B. — deemed	(200,000)
Gain	$ 120,000
Exempt portion	(51,429)[3]
Capital gain	$ 68,571
Taxable capital gain (½)	$ 34,286

Finally, when the Calgary home is sold in 2005, there would be no capital gain as shown below.

	Calgary home
P of D — estimated	$ 415,000
A.C.B. — deemed	(320,000)
Gain	$ 95,000
Exempt portion	(95,000)[4]
Capital gain	Nil

In summary, by making no elections, he will report a capital gain of $34,286 in 2003 along with any recaptured CCA that also has to be reported.

If he had made the subsection 45(3) election in 2003 when the house was changed from income producing to personal-use property then the capital gain could be deferred and would not have to be reported until the actual disposition in 2005.

— NOTES TO SOLUTION

(1) $\frac{1 + 11}{12} \times \$275,000 = \$275,000$; 94–97 — owner-occupied
98–2001 — paragraph (*d*) of the definition of "principal residence" in sec. 54, maximum 4 years
2003–2005 — owner-occupied.

(2) $\frac{1 + 3}{4} \times \$60,000 = \$60,000$; 94–96.

(3) $\frac{1 + 2}{7} \times \$120,000 = \$51,428$; 97, 2003 — owner-occupied.

(4) $\frac{1 + 2}{3} \times \$95,000 = \$95,000$; 2004–2005.

2. Interpretation Bulletin IT-120R6

The Interpretation Bulletin is an excellent example of how administrative practice differs from the actual law. For example, the term "ordinarily inhabited" has been interpreted by the CRA, for purposes of this section only, to mean "a short period of time in the year" [par. 5]. However the facts of each particular case must be considered. Therefore, a taxpayer who abuses the application of this CRA interpretation could conceivably be reassessed and potentially taken to court on this issue.

One should note the difference between partial changes in use where there are no structural changes [par. 30] and partial changes where there are structural changes [par. 31]. In cases where the change in use is "ancillary" or secondary to the main purpose of the residence, the CRA's view is that no change has taken place for the purpose of this section. Therefore, the taxpayer may still designate the residence as a principal residence as long as he or she does not claim any capital cost allowance. Where the change is more substantial, then this option does not exist and subsection 45(1) will apply. In this case, the residence will have more than one use and each must be treated differently for tax purposes.

3. Section 54.1

This relieving provision was added to aid taxpayers and their spouses who are transferred by their employers to another location. In such an event, paragraph (*b*) of the definition of a "principal residence" in section 54 applies, without the four-year limitation, as long as the taxpayer complies with the specific conditions of this subsection. Since nothing is said to the contrary, the aforementioned interpretation of the word "ordinarily" should stand.

4. Subsection 40(4)

(a) *Single-ownership Situations*

This provision enables the transfer of a wholly-owned principal residence from one spouse to another, where subsection 73(1) or 70(6) is applicable, with complete or partial relief from the taxation of the capital gain depending upon the principal residence designation circumstances. Subsection 40(4) does not apply to the inter-spousal transfer of a home which was previously *jointly-owned* (discussed later in this part of the chapter). The provision does apply where one spouse owns a residence solely and transfers this residence to the other spouse.

Paragraph 40(4)(*a*) determines the period of ownership for the transferee spouse for purposes of the principal-residence exempting formula [par. 40(2)(*b*)]. The result is that the transferee spouse is deemed to have owned the property since the time the transferor spouse originally acquired it. Thus, the recipient spouse will be able to designate the home as a principal residence for the same years that it would have qualified for the transferor spouse.

Paragraph 40(4)(*b*) ensures that the years of designation by the transferee spouse for the period of ownership by the transferor spouse are those years which were actually designated by the transferor spouse, plus those years after the transfer for which the transferee spouse ordinarily resided in the transferred residence. Subsection 73(1) must be applicable (i.e., no election out of subsection 73(1)) [spar. 40(4)(*b*)(ii)], so no gain would be recognized on the transfer.

It is recommended that a designation form be completed by the transferor spouse, even if it is not filed, so that the recipient spouse can determine the appropriate designation on the ultimate disposition of the property. This would fully protect the capital gain on the residence, if it had been the only one owned by the family unit.

If the transfer to the recipient spouse takes place as a result of the death of the transferor spouse, by the application of subsection 70(6), the actual designation requirement by the transferor spouse is removed, but the residence must have been ordinarily inhabited by the transferor spouse for the years before death that the recipient spouse chooses to designate the home [spar. 40(4)(*b*)(i)].

Where two residences are owned by one spouse, the transfer of one of the residences to the other only offers partial relief because of the limitation of one principal residence per family unit for years after 1981. In this situation, the transferee spouse will be deemed to have owned the property since the time the transferor spouse originally acquired the property. However, the years of designation will be limited to those years in which the transferor actually designates the transferred residence as his or her principal residence plus those years in which the transferee spouse "ordinarily inhabited" the transferred residence. (See the CRA technical interpretation document 9502557, February 9, 1995.) Therefore, one of the two properties will be left unsheltered at least, in part, by the designation rules in paragraph (*c*) of the definition of a "principal residence" in section 54. A disposition by, or the death of the spouse who owns the two properties would trigger a taxable capital gain on the less-designated property minus an exemption based on the ever-present extra year of designation (one-plus rule) and the number of years owned.

Example Problem

Spouse A owns two residences:

	Residence 1	Residence 2
F.M.V.	$100,000	$200,000
A.C.B.	50,000	100,000
Year of acquisition	1994	1994

Both spouses have resided in the home since 1994. In 2000, Spouse A transferred Residence 2 to Spouse B as a gift. Spouse B sold the transferred residence in 2005 for $300,000. Spouse A has not designated, at any time, Residence 2 as his principal residence.

— REQUIRED

(A) Compute the effect of the above transaction as if subsection 40(4) did not exist.

(B) Apply subsection 40(4) to the transaction.

(C) Apply subsection 40(4) to the transaction on the assumption that spouse A had previously designated Residence 2 for two years.

— SOLUTION

(A) As if subsection 40(4) did not exist

> 2000 —Transfer of residence to Spouse B (section 73 automatically applies since the facts do not indicate that Spouse A elected not to have section 73 apply; refer to the discussion of the attribution rules later in this chapter for a more detailed explanation of this provision)

P of D (deemed)	$100,000	[sec. 73]
A.C.B.	(100,000)	
Gain	Nil	

> Note that no principal residence designation was required to reduce the gain to nil.

> 2005 —Spouse B sells home

P of D	$300,000
A.C.B. (deemed sec. 73)	(100,000)
Gain	$200,000
Exemption ..... $\dfrac{1 + 5 \text{ years designated by B}}{6 \text{ years owned by B}} \times \$200,000 =$	(200,000)
Capital gain	Nil

Years of designation: any five of 2000 to 2005.

The gain of $200,000 was completely eliminated by Spouse B designating Residence 2 for five years under the principal residence rules, because:

- Spouse B owned the residence for six years (2000 to 2005, inclusive), and

- Spouse B ordinarily inhabited the residence for those years.

Hence, the entire gain is eliminated and Spouse A has saved the designation of years 1994 to 1999, plus one year of 2000 to 2005.

Note that there is no attribution since the capital gain is nil. However, depending upon the use of the $300,000 proceeds by Spouse B, there is potential attribution under the substituted property rule, discussed later in this chapter.

(B) With subsection 40(4)

2005 —Spouse B sells home

P of D	$ 300,000
A.C.B. (deemed by sec. 73)	(100,000)
Gain	$ 200,000
Exemption . . . . $\frac{1 + 10^{1}}{11^{2}} \times \$200,000 =$	(200,000)
Capital gain[3]	NIL

The application of subsection 40(4) results in the same nil capital gain, but has eliminated all the principal residence designation years for Spouse A for Residence 1, except for one year.

(C) The answer would be the same as Part (B). The years designated would be the two years designated by Spouse A, plus eight years by Spouse B for a total of 10 years, thereby, eliminating the entire gain.

—NOTES TO SOLUTION

(1) Spouse B can designate the transferred residence for the actual years or deemed years that he or she owned and ordinarily inhabited the residence (10 years) plus any other years for which Spouse A made a designation (in this case nil).

(2) The number of years owned includes the ownership years of Spouse A [par. 40(4)(*a*)].

(3) The taxable capital gain, if any, will be attributed back to Spouse A, if realized during his or her lifetime.

(4) If this transfer had been as a consequence of Spouse A's death, the years of designation available would be expanded to include the potential designations available to Spouse A (or his or her legal representative). Hence, the entire gain would be exempt, but Residence 1 could not be designated for the years used to designate Residence 2.

(5) This example was designed to demonstrate how subsection 40(4) is applied and no tax planning was taken into account. Some of the factors which should be considered would be:

● the relative size of the future gain on the two homes;

● the tax rates of the respective spouses who own the homes; and

● the potential application of the attribution rules to the ultimate non-exempt capital gains on the homes.

(b) *Joint-ownership Situations*

Where two residences are each jointly owned by spouses, subsection 40(4) does not have any effect, since the definition of a "principal residence" in section 54 governs years of joint ownership. Hence, each spouse enjoys an unrestricted right to designate either residence as his or her principal residence under the exemption formula [par. 40(2)(*b*)]. A transfer of ownership so that one residence is wholly-owned by one spouse and the other residence is wholly-owned by the other spouse will maximize the potential principal residence designation for years owned before 1982. Therefore, there will be no tax consequences, since both spouses have owned, although only partially, the residence for the entire period. The transferee spouse can designate the entire residence as his or her principal residence.

As previously mentioned in Chapter 7, after 1981 the legislation permits only one principal residence exemption per family which would include spouses and single children under 18.

G. Leaving and Entering Canada

[ITA: 128.1; IT-451R]

Section 128.1 sets out the tax rules for taxpayers who become or cease to be resident in Canada. When a taxpayer ceases to be a resident of Canada, subsection 128.1(4) deems that all of that person's capital property has been disposed of at its fair market value. Such capital property would consist of shares, including shares of private corporations, bonds, real estate outside Canada, boats, recreational vehicles and automobiles, among others. Where the taxpayer is an individual, the following properties, generally, those that would be subject to Canadian tax in the hands of a non-resident, are exempted from the deemed disposition:

(a) Property that can be described, conceptually, as:

- Canadian property that is not very movable, such as real property or capital property used in a business carried on through a permanent establishment in Canada, or

- Canadian property that is not very liquid or marketable, such as employment-related stock options.

    The taxpayer will continue to be liable for tax on the disposition of such property, but as a non-resident [ssec. 2(3)]. However, the taxpayer may elect not to have this exemption apply so that capital gains (losses) are triggered to offset other capital losses (gains).

(b) Property of a business carried on by the individual in Canada. Income from such property, including capital property, eligible capital property and property described in the inventory of the business, will be taxable as business income earned by a non-resident [ssec. 2(3)].

(c) The right to receive certain payments such as pension payments and other retirement benefits, including rights under RRSPs, RPPs and DPSPs, or a right under a registered education savings plan on which the taxpayer will be liable for withholding tax.

A taxpayer is prevented from triggering only allowable capital losses while protecting potential taxable capital gains through the available elections previously described. In this situation, losses, except listed personal property losses, are restricted to the taxable capital gains actually triggered by subsection 128.1(4).

Subsection 128.1(4) provides an exception in the case of a short-term resident of Canada. The tax on departure does not apply to capital property which an individual owned on last becoming a resident of Canada, if he or she resided in Canada for 60 months or less during the ten years preceding his or her departure. Under these conditions, he or she will be exempt from the deemed disposition on any property, which he or she brought with him or her and took away again. Also exempt is property acquired by inheritance or bequest after the individual last became resident in Canada. However, the taxpayer will still be subject to the rules of this section on other property he or she acquired while he or she was resident in Canada.

To set the cost of property for a person entering Canada such that the taxpayer is taxed only on gains subsequent to his or her entry, subsection 128.1(1) provides that where a taxpayer becomes a Canadian resident, he or she is deemed to have acquired all of his or her property other than taxable Canadian property and inventory or eligible capital property of a business carried on in Canada at its fair market value at the time.

H. Options
[ITA: 49; IT-96R6; IT-403R; IT-479R]

There are two basic types of option: an option to buy property (known as a call option) and an option to sell property (known as a put option). As a general rule, when an option is granted, there is a disposition of a property with an adjusted cost base of nil by the grantor or issuer [ssec. 49(1)]. The result is a capital gain to the grantor in the amount of the proceeds for the option. The grantee or holder of the option has acquired a capital property with an adjusted cost base equal to the amount paid for the option. If the option expires, the grantor's or issuer's tax position remains unchanged and the grantee has a capital loss in the year of expiration.

There are two exceptions to the general rule noted above.

- When an option in respect of a principal residence is granted, there is no disposition [par. 49(1)(a)]. As a result, if an option on a principal residence expires, there would have been no inclusion for the grantor and, therefore, no tax effect. The grantee would be denied a loss on expiration [spar. 40(2)(g)(iii)], because the option on a principal residence would be regarded as a personal-use property [par. (c) of the definition in sec. 54].

- The other exception is for an option granted by a corporation to another person to buy securities to be issued by the corporation. In this case, the corporation has no disposition at the time the option is granted. However, if the option expires, the corporation is deemed to have disposed of a capital property with an adjusted cost base of nil. The proceeds are deemed to be equal to the amount, if any, received for granting the option [ssec. 49(2)]. As a result, when this type of option expires, a capital gain is realized.

If an option to acquire property (i.e., a call option) is exercised, then the granting of the option and its exercise are deemed not to be a disposition [ssec. 49(3)]. Also, note that when the option is exercised, there is a disposition of the property underlying the option and the grantor or issuer becomes a vendor and the grantee or holder becomes a purchaser. On the exercise of the option, the vendor of the optioned property must include the consideration, received for the option, in proceeds of disposition of the property sold in the year in which the option is exercised. The vendor, who was the grantor of the option, can file an amended return for the year, in which the amount received for the option was included in income, to remove the amount received for the option from income for that year [ssec. 49(4)]. This amended return must be filed by the time the return for the year, in which the option was exercised, must be filed. The purchaser of the property must add the cost of the option held to the cost of the property.

If an option to sell property (i.e., a put option) is exercised, the rules in subsection 49(3.1) are similar to those in subsection 49(3). Note, however, that the grantor of a put option is the purchaser of the property on exercise of the option and will have been paid an amount by the vendor of the underlying property. The granting of the option and its exercise are deemed not to be a disposition of property. The vendor of the optioned property, who paid for the right to "put" or sell the property to the purchaser of the optional property, must deduct the amount paid for the option from proceeds of disposition of the property sold. The purchaser of the optioned property must deduct the amount received for the put option from the cost of the property acquired. The grantor of the option (i.e., the purchaser of the property in this case) can file an amended return for the year in which the amount received for the option was included in income and to exclude the amount received for the option from income in the year of the grant [ssec. 49(4)].

The basic rules for the taxation of options as capital property are summarized in Exhibit 8-1.

EXHIBIT 8-1
Basic Rules for Taxation of Options as Capital Property

	Option to buy property (Call)		Option to sell property (Put)	
Event	**Grantor (Seller)**	**Grantee (Buyer)**	**Grantor (Buyer)**	**Grantee (Seller)**
Option granted	• Amount received for option included as capital gain	• Amount paid for option is ACB of option	• Amount received for option included as capital gain	• Amount paid for option is ACB of option
Option exercised	• Amount received for option added to proceeds of underlying property sold	• Amount paid for option added to ACB of underlying property purchased	• Amount received for option deducted from cost of underlying property purchased	• Amount paid for option deducted from proceeds of underlying property sold
	• File amended return (if necessary) for year option granted to remove capital gain from income		• File amended return (if necessary) for year option granted to remove capital gain from income	
Option expired	• No change in tax position	• Amount paid for option realized as a capital loss	• No change in tax position	• Amount paid for option realized as a capital loss

Example Problem

Ms. Smart owned a capital property that had an adjusted cost base of $100,000. In 2003, she granted Mr. Shnook an option to buy the property from her by the end of 2005 at an option price of $160,000. Mr. Shnook paid $16,000 to Ms. Smart for the option.

— REQUIRED

(A) What are the income tax implications to Ms. Smart and Mr. Shnook in 2003?

(B) What are the income tax implications to Ms. Smart and Mr. Shnook in 2005 if:

(i) the call option expires?

(ii) the call option is exercised?

— SOLUTION

(A) In 2003, Ms. Smart has granted a call option with an adjusted cost base of nil and proceeds of disposition of $16,000. On this disposition, in 2003 she must report a capital gain of $16,000. Mr. Shnook has acquired a capital property in the option with an adjusted cost base of $16,000.

(B)(i) If the option expires at the end of 2005, because Mr. Shnook chooses not to exercise it and acquire the capital property, then there are no further tax implications to Ms. Smart. She has already included the capital gain in 2003 on granting the option and she retains the capital property with an adjusted cost base of $100,000. In 2005, Mr. Shnook has a capital loss of $16,000, since the option held at that cost has become worthless on expiration. Of course, that capital loss can only be applied to a capital gain in the current year, 2005, the three preceding years, 2002, 2003 and 2004, or any year subsequent to 2005.

(ii) If the call option is exercised in 2005 and Mr. Shnook acquires the property for $160,000, then Ms. Smart can file an amended return for 2003 to remove the $16,000 capital gain from her income in that year. However, her proceeds of disposition on the sale in 2004 will amount to the $160,000 received as the agreed price under the option plus the $16,000 received for the option in 2003. Thus, she will report in 2005 a capital gain of $76,000 (i.e., $160,000 + $16,000 − $100,000). Mr. Shnook will have acquired the property which will have an adjusted cost base of $176,000 (i.e., $160,000 + $16,000).

I. Debts Established to be Bad Debts

[ITA: 50; IT-159R3]

Where a debt taken back from the purchaser of a capital property is established to have become a bad debt, the seller can elect to have disposed of the debt and to have reacquired it immediately at a cost equal to nil [ssec. 50(1)]. The deemed disposition results in a capital loss to offset any part of the gain on disposition of the property represented in the debt. The deemed reacquisition at a nil cost may result in a further capital gain if any part of the debt is ultimately collected.

A deemed disposition of the shares of an insolvent corporation occurs [spar. 50(1)(b)(iii)] to realize the capital loss if:

- neither the corporation nor a corporation controlled by it carries on business in the year;
- the fair market value of the shares is nil;
- it is reasonable to expect that the corporation will be dissolved or wound up and will not start to carry on business; and
- the taxpayer elects to have this provision apply.

There will be another deemed disposition [ssec. 50(1.1)] for proceeds of disposition equal to the A.C.B. of the shares before the subsection 50(1) deemed disposition if:

- the taxpayer elects a deemed disposition under the conditions of subparagraph 50(1)(b)(iii); and
- within 24 months of the disposition the corporation or a corporation controlled by it carries on business and the taxpayer or a non-arm's length person owns the shares.

This deemed disposition will result in the realization of a capital gain equal to the capital loss realized by the subparagraph 50(1)(b)(iii) election. The shares are deemed to be reacquired at a cost equal to the proceeds established under subsection 50(1.1).

Note that there is no provision for an "allowance for doubtful debts" in computing capital gains. At best, paragraph 40(1)(a) provides for a reserve for the uncollected gain portion of the proceeds, payable after the end of the year. This, of course, does not help the taxpayer when the amount of the debt is payable in the year but not collectible, because the debt has become bad. Also, the treatment of a bad debt resulting from the disposition of personal-use property is different and is handled by subsection 50(2).

J. Convertible Properties

[ITA: 51]

Where a taxpayer acquires shares from a corporation on the conversion of a convertible security, referred to as a convertible property, the exchange is deemed not to have been a disposition of property. The cost to the taxpayer of the shares received is deemed to be the adjusted cost base to him or her of the convertible property immediately before the exchange. There is a further condition in this rollover provision that the taxpayer must not have received any consideration (such as cash) other than shares in exchange for his or her convertible property.

Consider, as an example, a convertible debenture acquired at face value of $100. The conversion privilege entitles the holder to five common shares. If the privilege is exercised, the taxpayer is deemed to have acquired the new shares at $20 each ($100/5). If the fair market value of the shares is $30 each, the taxpayer has effectively deferred recognition of a $50 per bond or a $10 per share capital gain.

K. Capital Gains Deferral

[ITA: 44.1]

Subsection 44.1(2) permits an individual to defer the recognition of a capital gain in respect of certain small business investments. To obtain the deferral, the proceeds from the sale of the small business investment must be used to acquire other small business investments. The deferred gain on the old investments will reduce the ACB of the new investments, which is similar to the treatment of replacement property discussed earlier.

The following are some of the considerations:

- The individual can establish a permitted deferral less than the maximum amount available by designating a lesser amount of replacement shares.

- The permitted deferral is the amount of a capital gain from the disposition that can be deferred. It reduces the gain of the individual for the disposition.

- A "permitted deferral" of an individual is calculated using the formula

    $(G/H) \times I$ where

    G   is the lesser of the individual's proceeds of disposition from the old small business investment and the cost to the individual of a replacement share;

    H   is the individual's proceeds of disposition from the old small business investment; and

    I   is the individual's capital gain from the old small business investment.

- A qualifying disposition of an individual is a disposition of common shares of the capital stock of a corporation owned by the individual where each such share was:

    (1) an eligible small business corporation share of the individual,

    (2) a common share of the capital stock of an active business corporation throughout the time it was owned by the individual, and

    (3) owned by the individual throughout the 185-day period that ended immediately before the disposition.

- The active business of the corporation has to be carried on primarily in Canada at all times in the period that began when the individual last acquired the share and ended when the disposition occurred (the "ownership period"), if that period is less than 730 days [ssec. 44.1(9)]. In any other case that active business has to be carried on primarily in Canada for at least 730 days during the ownership period.

- The term "eligible small business corporation" is relevant for the purposes of the term "eligible small business corporation share". An eligible small business corporation, at a particular time, means a Canadian-controlled private corporation all or substantially all of the fair market value of the assets of which is, at that time, attributable to assets of the corporation that are

    - assets used principally in an active business carried on primarily in Canada by the corporation or an eligible small business corporation related to it,

    - shares of or debt issued by other eligible small business corporations related to the corporation, or

    - a combination of those two types of assets.

An asset of the corporation that is a share or a debt issued by a related corporation is deemed to have a carrying value of nil.

An eligible small business corporation share of an individual is a common share issued by a corporation to the individual where:

- at the time the share is issued, the corporation was an eligible small business corporation and immediately before, and
- after that time the total carrying value of its assets and the assets of corporations related to it does not exceed $50 million.

Example Problem

Jennifer S. Lee disposes of shares of corporation A with an adjusted cost base of $3,000,000 for proceeds of disposition of $4,500,000. Jennifer immediately purchases replacement shares in corporations B with a cost of $2,200,000 and in corporation C with a cost of $2,300,000. All shares are eligible small business corporation shares.

—REQUIRED

Compute the capital gain, after the deferral, on the disposition of the shares of corporation A and the ACB of the replacement shares in corporations B and C.

—SOLUTION

Jennifer's capital gain without the deferral would be calculated as:

Capital gain otherwise determined:

Proceeds	$4,500,000
ACB	3,000,000
Capital gain	$1,500,000

Permitted deferral:

G/H $\times$ I = $4,500,000/$4,500,000 $\times$ $1,500,000 =	$1,500,000

G = lesser of:

1. Proceeds of disposition =	$4,500,000
2. Cost of replacement shares =	$4,500,000
H = Proceeds of disposition =	$4,500,000
I = Capital gain =	$1,500,000

Jennifer's capital gain that will be reported is calculated as follows:

Capital gain otherwise determined	$1,500,000
Less: Permitted deferral	1,500,000
Capital gain	$ Nil

The ACB reduction is determined by the formula D $\times$ (E/F) found in the definition of that expression in section 44.1(1):

Corporation B: $1,500,000 $\times$ ($2,200,000/$4,500,000) =	$ 733,333
Corporation C: $1,500,000 $\times$ ($2,300,000/$4,500,000) =	$ 766,667

Note that the sum of the ACB reductions is $1,500,000, which is equal to the total capital gain deferred.

The adjusted cost base of the replacement shares is, therefore:

Corporation B: $2,2000,000 – $733,333 =	$1,466,667
Corporation C: $2,300,000 – $766,667 =	$1,533,333

Note that the sum of these ACBs is $3,000,000, which is actual cost net of the permitted deferral.

L Certain Shares Deemed to be Capital Property

[ITA: 54.2]

Where a person disposes of all or substantially all of the assets used in an active business to a corporation, the shares received in consideration are capital property of that person. This provision allows a person to transfer business assets to a corporation in exchange for shares, then sell the shares and have the gain or loss treated as a capital gain or loss. It should be noted that the definition of "business" [ssec. 248(1)] for purposes of this provision does not include an adventure or concern in the nature of trade. As a result, it must be an ongoing business that is transferred, not just a trading asset.

II. CONSIDERATION IN NON-ARM'S LENGTH TRANSFERS AND THE ATTRIBUTION RULES REVISITED

A. Consideration in Non-arm's Length Transfers

[ITA: 13(7)(*e*); 69; 251; IT-209R; IT-419R2]

The rules in subsection 69(1) are designed to prevent tax avoidance in certain transactions between persons not dealing at arm's length. Paragraph 251(1)(*a*), in effect, defines the term arm's length by providing that related persons are deemed not to deal with each other at arm's length. Paragraph 251(1)(*b*) provides that a taxpayer (or anyone not dealing at arm's length with the taxpayer) and an *inter vivos* or testamentary trust cannot deal at arm's length, if the taxpayer is an income or capital beneficiary of the trust.

Finally, paragraph 251(1)(*c*) provides that it is a question of fact whether persons not related to each other are dealing with each other at arm's length. In IT-419R2, the CRA sets out the following criteria which have generally been used by the courts to determine whether a transaction has occurred at "arm's length":

- was there a common mind which directs the bargaining for both parties to a transaction?;
- were the parties to a transaction acting in concert without separate interests?; and
- was there "de facto" control?

Refer to paragraphs 24 and 25 of the bulletin for more details on these points. These conditions may arise in dealings between business partners or close friends.[b]

Summary
Who Does Not Deal at Arm's Length
Subsection 251(1)

1. Related persons.
2. A beneficiary, or anyone not dealing at arm's length with the beneficiary, and the *inter vivos* or testamentary trust.
3. It is a question of fact.

Related persons are further defined [ssec. 251(2)] in terms of individuals and corporations. Related individuals are those connected by blood, marriage or adoption

---

[b] In the case of *Grant et al. v. M.N.R.*, 87 DTC 16, the Tax Court of Canada describes in some detail the factors to be taken into account in determining whether unrelated persons are not dealing at arm's length.

and these connections are further specified in subsection 251(6). A schematic diagram of related individuals under the Act was presented in Chapter 6 as Exhibit 6-2. Non-arm's length relationships between persons and corporations require control, either by one person or a group of related persons [par. 251(2)(*b*) and interpreted in IT-419R2, par. 11]. Control in this situation means control of more than 50% of the voting shares. Subsection 251(5) expands the concept of control in situations involving related groups and in the case of a person holding certain options. The subsection also indicates that a person is deemed to be related to himself or herself in cases where the person owns shares in two or more corporations. Remember that the word "person" is defined in subsection 248(1) to include a corporation such that two corporations can be related. Furthermore, two corporations are related if they meet one of the six conditions set out in paragraph 251(2)(*c*).

Generally, in situations involving the non-arm's length transfer of anything, including both tangible and intangible property, the transferor is deemed to receive proceeds equal to its fair market value at the time of the transfer, if the actual transfer price is less than fair market value. This rule would include gifts for no proceeds. Note, however, that no downward adjustment is made to the actual price received if it is more than fair market value. On the other side, the transferee is deemed to have acquired property at a cost equal to its fair market value at the time of the transfer if he or she paid more than fair market value or if he or she received it as a gift, bequest or inheritance, but not if he or she paid less than fair market value. In the case of a payment of less than fair market value, no adjustment is made to the actual price paid. There are exceptions to these rules on the transfer of such property to a spouse under certain conditions.

As mentioned previously, non-arm's length transfers, for a price either greater than or less than fair market value, can involve a one-sided adjustment to the transfer price. This can be more easily seen in Exhibit 8-2. Where the amount is in excess of fair market value only the purchaser is deemed to have transacted at fair market value with the seller having received proceeds at the higher price. Thus, the seller may have income or a capital gain on the transaction and the purchaser may ultimately have to include a similar amount of income or capital gain on disposition. Where the amount is less than fair market value, but the transfer is not a gift, the seller is deemed to have received proceeds equal to fair market value while there is no adjustment made to the actual price paid by the purchaser. Again, the seller may have income or a capital gain on the transaction and the purchaser may ultimately have to include a similar amount of income or capital gain on disposition. In this case, a gift would be better since both the transferor and the transferee are deemed to have made the transfer at fair market value and no double-counting will result.

These rules have implications for the operation of the capital cost allowance system in these cases. Deeming proceeds of disposition and cost of acquisition to be the fair market value will affect potential recapture of capital cost allowance on disposition and the base on which capital cost allowance is computed on acquisition.

EXHIBIT 8-2
Consideration in Gifts and Non-arm's Length Transfers

Non-arm's length transfer	Seller or transferor	Purchaser or transferee
Proceeds greater than fair market value	no adjustment to actual proceeds received	deemed acquisition at fair market value [par. 69(1)(a)]
Proceeds less than fair market value	deemed proceeds at fair market value [par. 69(1)(b)]	no adjustment to actual amount paid
Gift, bequest or inheritance	deemed proceeds at fair market value [par. 69(1)(b)*]	deemed acquisition at fair market value [par. 69(1)(c)*]

* Note that these fair market value rules apply to gifts even at arm's length.

Where the property being transferred between non-arm's length parties is depreciable property, there are special rules [subsection 13(7)(e)] to determine what the undepreciated capital cost (UCC) of the property is to the acquirer. The results depend on whether an election is made under subsection 73(1) not to have the automatic rollover apply and whether there is an accrued gain on the property at the time of transfer.

If no election is made under subsection 73(1), then the property will automatically roll over at UCC and subsection 13(7)(e) does not apply. If an election is made, then the property will be disposed of at fair market value and subsection 13(7)(e) will deem the UCC of the property to the acquirer will be equal to:

Cost of the property to the transferor immediately before the transfer plus the taxable capital gain realized on the transfer

This restricts the UCC of the property to the transferee to the amount on which the transferor has paid tax.

B. Attribution Rules

[ITA: 73; 74.1; 74.2; 74.5; 75.1; IT-510; IT-511R]

1. Capital gains on spousal transfers or loans

In Chapter 6, the attribution rules, relating to income from property only, were discussed for transfers and loans. Capital gains and losses are also similarly attributed back, but only to the transferor spouse or common-law partner [ssec. 74.2(1)] for all transfers (i.e., gifts and sales) or for loans. Capital gains and losses arising from transfers and loans to related and deemed related minors do not result in attribution to the transferor (except for *inter vivos* transfers of farming property which is tax-deferred by a rollover [sec. 75.1] and beyond the scope of this text). A series of anti-avoidance provisions apply attribution to transactions such as:

(a) back-to-back loans and transfers to third parties [ssec. 74.5(6)],

(b) repayment of loan through additional transfers and loans [ssec. 74.1(3)],

(c) loan guarantees for all or part of the principal and/or interest [ssec. 74.5(7)], or

(d) artificial transactions which use the attribution rules to the taxpayer's advantage [ssec. 74.5(11)].

Subsection 248(1) defines common-law partner as two persons, regardless of sex, who co-habit in a conjugal relationship and have done so for a continuous period of at least 12 months. This change will be effective for the 2000 and subsequent years.

The justification for the attribution of capital gains on property transferred between spouses or common-law partners is found in section 73, which has the effect of deferring any accrued gains on transfers between spouses or common-law partners. The deferral occurs because the transferor is automatically deemed to have transferred the property at proceeds exactly equal to his or her adjusted cost base immediately prior to the transfer. Note here that the transfer is an actual transaction which must be reported, even though the gain is nil. The transferee spouse, or common-law partner, will have an adjusted cost base exactly equal to the deemed proceeds of disposition at the time of transfer (the transferor spouse's, or common-law partner's, adjusted cost base). When the transferee spouse, or common-law partner, disposes of the property, the gain or loss will be attributed back to the transferor spouse, or common-law partner, as long as they are married or in a common-law relationship.

Paragraph 74.5(3)(*b*), which pertains to the attribution of capital gains, applies to spouses, or common-law partners, living apart by reason of a breakdown of their marriage or common-law relationship. In this situation, when both spouses [or common-law partners] have jointly elected, section 74.2 does not apply. The election must be filed with the tax return of the transferor spouse or common-law partner in the year in which the aforementioned separation occurs. Note that this provision is much harsher than the attribution relieving provision for income from property [par. 74.5(3)(*a*)] which does not require that an election be filed.

Alternatively, the transferor spouse or common-law partner can elect not to have subsection 73(1) apply and the normal non-arm's length rules apply under section 69 as previously discussed. Hence, the property will be deemed to have been disposed of at the fair market value at the date of transfer. There would be no capital gains attribution on subsequent dispositions of transferred property, as long as consideration equal to the fair market value of the property transferred was received by the transferor and the taxpayer elected not to use section 73 [pars. 74.5(1)(*a*) and (*c*)]. If the consideration included a loan, then the interest rate must be on a commercial basis (the lesser of the prescribed rate at the time the loan was made and the non-arm's length rate as determined by the marketplace) and the accrued interest must be actually paid no later than 30 days after each and every December 31 that the loan is outstanding [par. 74.5(1)(*b*)].

If the property is sold to a spouse or common-law partner at less than the fair market value and the taxpayer elects not to use section 73, there would be a double penalty.

- First, the attribution rules would apply to both income and capital gains, since the fair market value of the property transferred and the consideration received are not equal [par. 74.5(1)(*a*)].

- Second, the adjusted cost base of transferred property would be the actual price paid by the acquiring spouse and not the deemed proceeds of disposition of the transferor spouse since paragraph 69(1)(*c*) is a one-sided adjustment. Hence, the avoided capital gain would be taxed twice.

If, however, the transfer had been a gift, then both the proceeds and the adjusted cost base would be bumped to the fair market value [spar. 69(1)(b)(ii) and par. 69(1)(c)]. Again, the attribution of future income and capital gain would not have been avoided, however, since no consideration was received.

2. Recapture

In order to prevent the avoidance of recapture on the transfer of depreciable property between spouses, the following additional rules [ssec. 73(2)] apply. When the undepreciated capital cost is less than the capital cost to the transferor, then for purposes of capital cost allowance computations:

(a) the capital cost to the transferee is deemed to be the capital cost to the transferor; and

(b) the difference between the capital cost and the deemed capital cost to the spouse will be treated as a capital cost allowance taken by the transferee.

3. Summary of provisions

Summary
Avoiding Income Attribution
On Transferred Property

Subsection 74.5(1)

1. Fair market value consideration must be received by the vendor.

2. If part of the consideration is debt then interest must be charged at the prescribed rate and always paid by January 30th.

3. If it is a transfer to a spouse or common-law partner, then they must elect out of the rollover in subsection 73(1).

Subsection 74.5(3)

4. The spouses or common-law partners are living separate and apart by reason of the breakdown of their relationship.

Exhibit 8-3 expands the exhibit on property income attribution rules introduced in Chapter 6 to include the application of the capital gains attribution rules discussed in this chapter.

EXHIBIT 8-3
Transfers or Loans of Property to Spouse or Common-law Partner
Conceptual Summary

(A) Proceeds and Cost on Transfer

Transaction	Transferor's proceeds	Transferee's cost
(1) gift ● no election made under ssec. 73(1)*	Transferor's A.C.B./U.C.C.	Transferor's A.C.B./U.C.C.
● elect under ssec. 73(1) not to have rollover	F.M.V. par. 69(1)(*b*)	F.M.V. par. 69(1)(*c*)
(2) sale ● no election made under ssec. 73(1)	Transferor's A.C.B./U.C.C.	Transferor's A.C.B./U.C.C.
● elect under ssec. 73(1) not to have rollover	greater of: ● actual proceeds ● F.M.V. ssec. 69(1)	Lesser of: ● actual cost ● F.M.V. ssec. 69(1)

(B) Attribution of Income and Capital Gains

	Business income	Property income**	Capital gains***
On transferred or loaned property and substituted property****	n/a	Attributed ssec. 74.1(1)	Attributed sec. 74.2

However, neither property income nor capital gains are attributed if the following two conditions of ssec. 74.5(1) are met:

(1) fair market consideration is received*****, and

(2) the ssec. 73(1) election out of the rollover is used.

---

* The provision in subsection 73(1) applies *automatically* on a transfer of property between spouses or common-law partners at the A.C.B. of the property; that is, the transferor spouse or common-law partner is deemed to have received proceeds of disposition equal to A.C.B. and the transferee spouse or common-law partner is deemed to have acquired the property at the same A.C.B. However, the provision contains an election that allows the spouses or common-law partners not to have the rollover apply, in which case the normal non-arm's length rules apply to the transaction which will be considered to have taken place at fair market value.

** Including losses but excluding second-generation income from property.

*** Including capital losses and including second-generation capital gains (losses) after December 31, 1987.

**** Substituted property is defined in subsection 248(5).

***** To avoid attribution, the taxpayer must elect to waive the deferral of accrued income [ssec. 73(1)] and must transfer for fair market value consideration. Where a loan is involved, interest must be paid within 30 days of the end of every year in which the loan is outstanding.

EXHIBIT 8-4
Transfers or Loans of Property to Minors and Other
Non-arm's Length Individuals
Conceptual Summary

(A) Proceeds and Cost on Transfer

	Transferor's proceeds	*Transferee's cost*
(1) gift	F.M.V. par. 69(1)(*b*)	F.M.V. par. 69(1)(*c*)
(2) sale	greater of: ● actual proceeds ● F.M.V. ssec. 69(1)	Lesser of: ● actual cost ● F.M.V. ssec. 69(1)

(B) Attribution of Income and Capital Gains

	Business income	*Property income**	*Capital gains*
Minors[†] who are not at arm's length (secs. 251 and 252) or who are nieces and nephews......	n/a	Attributed ssec. 74.1(2)	n/a
● on transferred** or loaned property and substituted property***			
Other non-arm's length individuals not subject to section 74.1	n/a	Attributed ssec. 56(4.1)	n/a
● only on loaned property if one of the main reasons for the loan was to reduce or avoid tax			

* Including losses but excluding second-generation income from property.

** To avoid attribution the taxpayer must transfer for fair market value consideration. Where a loan is involved, interest must be paid within 30 days of the end of the year in which the loan is outstanding.

*** Substituted property is defined in subsection 248(5).

[†] An income-splitting tax applies at the top marginal tax rate for years after 1999 on dividends or shareholder benefits received by minors from private corporations and certain income from a partnership or trust. (See Chapter 6 for a discussion of this provision.) Income that is subject to the income-splitting tax is not be subject to the attribution rules.

III. DEATH OF A TAXPAYER

[ITA: 70; 73; IT-305R4]

Capital gains may be triggered upon the death of a taxpayer depending on the status of the beneficiaries and the type of assets transferred. Death is the final opportunity to tax unrealized gains that have accrued to the taxpayer. Generally, the taxpayer is deemed to have disposed of all his or her capital assets at their fair market value as at the date of his or her death [par. 70(5)(*a*)].

In respect of non-depreciable capital assets transferred on death to a spouse, the basic rules similar to those under section 73 still apply and are contained in subsection 70(6). The deceased is deemed to have disposed of them at his or her adjusted cost base and the surviving spouse or common-law partner assumes that cost base. Hence, no capital gain or recapture will be triggered unless the estate so elects [ssec. 70(6.2) as discussed in IT-305R4] not to have subsection 70(6) apply, or until the surviving spouse or common-law partner disposes of the assets.

Depreciable property received by a beneficiary, other than a spouse or common-law partner, is also deemed to be disposed of at fair market value at the date of death [par. 70(5)(*a*)]. Any resulting capital gain or recapture would be included on the deceased's final return. The beneficiary's deemed cost would be the fair market value of the property received. However, if the fair market value was less than the original cost, then the beneficiary's cost would be the deceased's cost and the excess of cost over fair market value would be deemed to have been taken as CCA. As a result, the beneficiary's U.C.C. is the fair market value. Where a spouse or common-law partner is the beneficiary of depreciable property and where no subsection 70(6.2) election has been filed, the proceeds of disposition are deemed to be the undepreciated capital cost prorated on a capital cost basis.

Chapter 14 discusses, in some detail, the various filing alternatives available upon death of a taxpayer.

IV. INCOME RECONCILIATION REVISITED

[ITA: 9; 38]

One of the major adjustments to accounting income in its conversion to income for tax purposes is the exclusion of book gains and losses on the disposition of capital property and the inclusion of taxable capital gains and allowable capital losses.

Example Problem

Capital Transactions Ltd. has disposed of the following capital assets during 2005:

	Proceeds of disposition	Cost	Book value	Undepreciated capital cost
Securities	$ 500	$ 5,000	n/a	n/a
Land	52,500	30,000	n/a	n/a
Building*	76,250	20,000	$ 3,000	$4,500
Equipment**	500	10,000	1,000	1,500

* Ignore section 44 considerations.
** Only asset in class.

— *REQUIRED*

Indicate the adjustments to be made in the reconciliation of accounting income to income for tax purposes.

—SOLUTION

Reference	ADDITIONS	
Sec. 3	Securities — book loss: ($500 – $5,000)	$ 4,500
Sec. 38	Land — taxable capital gain: ($52,500 – $30,000) × ½	11,250
Sec. 38	Building — taxable capital gain: ($76,250 – $20,000) × ½	28,125
Sec. 13	Building — recapture: ($4,500 – $20,000)	15,500
Sec. 3	Equipment — book loss: ($500 – $1,000)	500
		$ 59,875

Reference	DEDUCTIONS	
Sec. 38	Securities — allowable capital loss: ($500 – $5,000) × ½	$ 2,250*
Sec. 3	Land — book gain: ($52,500 – $30,000)	22,500
Sec. 3	Building — book gain: ($76,250 – $3,000)	73,250
Par. 39(1)(b)	Equipment — capital loss........................	Nil
Ssec. 20(16)	— terminal loss ($1,500 – $500)	1,000
		$ 99,000

* Can only be deducted to the extent that there are taxable capital gains.

REVIEW QUESTIONS

(1) Mrs. Snowbird has been going south for many years and usually keeps some U.S. currency handy in case she needs it. This year, because of some unusual fluctuations in the Canadian dollar, she realized an exchange loss on her U.S. dollar transactions of $2,500. How will this be taxed?

(2) Mr. Cottage bought six acres of lake-front property 15 years ago for $24,000. This year, he sold the three acres that are not on the lake to a neighbour who wanted the woodlot. His proceeds on the three acres sold are $30,000. Discuss what the cost base of the three acres sold would be.

(3) Mr. Farmer had 20 acres of his farm expropriated by the city for industrial land in 2004. Because he disputed their value, the proceeds were not finally decided until 2005. How soon does he have to replace the land in order to defer the tax on the capital gain realized on the sale of the land?

(4) Opco Ltd. had a large piece of equipment destroyed by fire with the insurance proceeds being paid and the machine replaced in the same year. Can the replacement property rules be applied?

(5) Mrs. Smith owns 100% of Holdco Inc. which in turn owns 100% of Opco Inc. Holdco owns the building which is used by Opco in its active business and rents it to Opco under a 5-year lease. Mrs. Smith wants to sell the building and buy a bigger one for the same purpose, but she has been told that the building is considered to be a rental property and, therefore, does not qualify for the replacement property rules since it is not a "former business property" [ssec. 248(1)]. She has asked for your comments.

(6) Mr. Carr bought and operated a parking lot for the past 10 years. He has now decided that it is time to do something different. However, instead of selling the parking lot he wants to rezone the property and develop and sell condominium apartments. On July 1 of last year, he applied for rezoning and on December 1 of last year, he received the zoning change and a

building permit. By October 31 of this year, he had completed construction and sold the units. What kind of income would he have to report and when?

(7) On July 1 of this year, John Smith died leaving his wife and four children in financial difficulty. In order to earn extra income Mrs. Smith painted the basement, put carpet down, and then rented it to students. Comment on the tax issues.

(8) On July 1 nine years ago, Ms. Mover was transferred with her family to Victoria from Toronto by her employer, a large public company. She was sure that the value of her Toronto house would go up significantly so she kept it and rented a house in Victoria. It was this year that the same employer moved Ms. Mover and her family back to Toronto, at which time they moved back into their house. However, they found that the neighbourhood had changed significantly so they decided to sell the house and buy in another location. Discuss how much of the principal residence exemption she can claim on the sale of the Toronto home.

(9) Last year Ms. Madeit inherited $5 million from her uncle's estate and is now appalled by the amount of tax that she has to pay on her interest income. She has always liked the Cayman Islands and has decided to move there permanently in order to avoid Canadian tax. Her only assets are $5 million of term deposits but she has heard that there is a lot of tax to pay on leaving the country. What do you think?

(10) Mr. State was transferred to Canada by his employer four years ago and is now being transferred back to the U.S. At the time he entered Canada he held shares in his U.S. employer which are listed on the TSX Stock Exchange. He still owns all these shares and is unhappy about all the tax he is going to have to pay on the deemed disposition [ssec. 128.1(4)]. Advise him.

(11) Ms. Green has been told that a good way to create a capital gain is to buy shares on the stock market and then sell someone an option to buy the shares at a price slightly higher than the current market price. Her understanding is that the proceeds on the sale of the option is a capital gain. What advice can you give her?

(12) Mr. Oats is a farmer who is fortunate enough to have farm land close to the city. Because of the prime location he has been approached to sell the land, but he is reluctant to do so since he wants to farm for the next five years. However, he is willing to sell someone an option to buy the land in five years at what he thinks is a generous price. He is to receive $50,000 for granting this option. He thinks he can defer the gain on granting the option until the year of sale by reducing the A.C.B. of his land by $50,000. What do you think?

(13) Last year Ms. Sorry sold some land that was capital property and realized a capital gain of $150,000. As part of the proceeds she took back a note for $100,000 at 12% which unfortunately was unsecured. This year she realized that the note will become a bad debt, but since she has not disposed of the note she does not think that it can be used for tax purposes. What is your advice to her? What would be the result if the land that was sold was personal-use property?

(14) Mr. Roller bought a convertible debenture two years ago for $10,000 and is now in the process of converting it into common shares of the company. The debenture is convertible into 1,000 common shares. At the time of the conversion the common shares are worth $20 each. What are the tax effects of the disposition of the debenture and the acquisition of the shares?

(15) Mrs. Generous owns 20 acres of land that have an appraised value of $100,000. She is considering selling the land to a friend for $50,000 in order to have the friend living closer to her. The two individuals are not related. What tax issues would you discuss with her?

(16) Scott was 25 years old when his father Bill gave him shares in Bell Canada as a gift. Bill had paid $1,000 for them 10 years ago and they were worth $5,000 at the time of the gift. Scott has come to you to find out how much tax he will have to pay. Discuss the tax implications to Scott and Bill of the gift.

MULTIPLE CHOICE QUESTIONS

Question 1

Mega Ltd., which has a May 31 year-end, had its land and building expropriated on June 30, 2005 and received $1 million of compensation from the government for the expropriation. Which one of the following is the deadline for Mega Ltd. to replace the property with another property costing at least $1 million in order to defer the entire recapture and capital gain on the disposition of the expropriated property?

(A) On or before May 31, 2007.

(B) On or before June 30, 2007.

(C) On or before December 31, 2007.

(D) On or before May 31, 2008.

Question 2

On December 31 of this year, Ms. Y gave her six-year old child some common shares of a public corporation with an adjusted cost base of $900,000 and a fair market value of $1,000,000. Which one of the following statements is TRUE?

(A) The attribution rule will apply to attribute to Ms. Y any future dividends received by her child on the shares. This attribution will continue until the year in which the child becomes 18 years old.

(B) The attribution rule will apply to attribute to Ms. Y any future dividends received by her child on the shares as well as any capital gains or losses if her child sells the shares. This attribution will continue until the year in which the child turns 18 years of age.

(C) Ms. Y will report no gain or loss on the transfer of property this year because it is a gift.

(D) Ms. Y will report a $100,000 taxable capital gain on the gift this year.

Question 3

Ms. Y sells a stock (adjusted cost base $900,000) to her husband for $800,000 cash (the fair market value of the stock) and elects out of the rollover in subsection 73(1) of the Act. Which one of the following statements is TRUE?

(A) Ms. Y will report an allowable capital loss of $50,000 which she can only deduct against taxable capital gains.

(B) Ms. Y does not have a capital loss because transfers to a spouse are made for proceeds equal to adjusted cost base.

(C) Ms. Y does not have a capital loss because of the superficial loss rules.

(D) The attribution rule will apply to attribute to Ms. Y any future dividends received by her husband on the shares as well as any capital gains or losses if her husband sells the shares.

Question 4

Mr. T ceased to be a resident of Canada on September 1, 2005. At that date, he owned the following assets:

	Year acquired	Cost	Fair market value Sept. 1, 2005
Rental real estate in Canada...	1990	$50,000	$100,000
Registered retirement savings plan	1998	60,000	80,000
Painting	2001	6,000	10,000
Shares of a public corporation (listed) resident in Canada (owns less than 1%)	2002	10,000	40,000

Which one of the following amounts represents Mr. T's minimum taxable capital gain on the above assets for 2005?

(A) $15,000

(B) $17,000

(C) $27,000

(D) $42,000

Question 5

Mr. Smith died on June 30th of this year and left his entire estate to his son, Mark. His executor has provided you with a list of assets and their fair market value at the date of death.

List of Assets	Cost	Fair Market Value
Toronto home (sole principal residence since 1988).....................................	$100,000	$240,000
Rental property in London, Ontario		
— Land	50,000	100,000
— Building (UCC: $2,000).....................	25,000	35,000
Mutual fund units	12,000	60,000
Shares of a public companies	90,000	100,000

What is the amount that must be included in Mr. Smith's Division B income for the year of death?

(A) $59,000

(B) $70,500

(C) $82,000

(D) $152,000

Question 6

Gary Chin purchased his first and only principal residence in 1988 for $50,000. The residence was in Toronto, and when he was transferred to Windsor because of a promotion to managing partner in 1999, he rented the residence. The residence was worth $150,000 in 1999 and he elected under subsection 45(2) in respect of it. Gary rented an apartment in Windsor with the expectation of moving back into his Toronto residence on retirement. On January 1, 2005,

Gary received an unsolicited offer of $250,000 for the Toronto residence and sold it. Which of the following is a true statement?

(A) There is no taxable capital gain to report in 1999 or 2005 in respect of the principal residence.

(B) There is no capital gain to report in 1999 in respect of the principal residence. The taxable capital gain is $5,556 in 2005 in respect of the principal residence.

(C) The taxable capital gain is $50,000 in 1999 and $50,000 in 2005 in respect of the principal residence.

(D) The taxable capital gain is $100,000 in 2005 in respect of the principal residence.

EXERCISES

Exercise 1

[ITA: 39(2)]

When he was vacationing in Florida this year, Joe Retired sold, for U.S. $10,000, his antique car which he purchased four years ago for Cdn. $4,000. Joe was paid in U.S. dollars. The Canadian currency was valued at 80¢ U.S. at the time of the sale. When Joe returned, he converted the U.S. currency to Canadian dollars and received $12,500 Canadian dollars.

— *REQUIRED*

Compute the taxable capital gain or allowable capital loss, if any, arising on the above transactions.

Exercise 2

[ITA: 13(4); 44]

Tax Processing Ltd.'s computer was completely destroyed in a fire in 2003. The insurance company has been disputing the claim. In the meantime, the company is renting computer time until the claim is settled. The following facts relate to the destroyed computer:

Capital cost	$50,000
U.C.C. immediately before the fire — Class 10	17,150

During 2004, the insurance company paid $60,000 in respect of the claim. The company continued to rent computer time for another 24 months when it then purchased a new-generation computer for $70,000.

— *REQUIRED*

Indicate the tax consequences for Tax Processing Ltd. for the above years.

Exercise 3

[ITA: 40(2)(b); 45; 54; 54.1]

Howard Homeowner, who presently lives in Vancouver, is considering moving to Montreal. Although Howard intends to purchase a home in Montreal, he does not want to sell his fully-paid Vancouver home in case he decides to return some time in the future. Howard would rent his Vancouver home which cost him $50,000 in 1991 and now has a fair market value of $350,000.

— REQUIRED

Discuss the tax implications concerning Howard's Vancouver home if:

(A) Howard is self-employed; or

(B) Howard is employed.

Exercise 4

[ITA: 128.1(4); 115]

Mr. Emigrant, a United States citizen, entered Canada on June 1, 2000, and became resident in Canada for tax purposes. Mr. Emigrant had a capital asset A which he brought with him upon his entry to Canada. The cost of the asset was $2,000 and the fair market value was $5,000 at the time of entry. In 2001 Mr. Emigrant purchased another capital property B for $10,000. Mr. Emigrant is considering returning to the United States on a permanent basis in 2005. He estimates that the two properties will have fair market values of $12,000 for A and $20,000 for B.

— REQUIRED

Discuss the tax consequences of Mr. Emigrant's pending departure from Canada.

Exercise 5

[ITA: 49]

Doctor Quick, a general practitioner, has decided to move into a larger office/residence. On July 1, 2004, he paid $5,000 to Devalued Properties Ltd., a developer, for a one-year option to purchase a residential building which he would use 50% for business and 50% as his principal residence. On February 1, 2005, Dr. Quick assigned his option to another medical practitioner, Dr. Slow, for $2,000. On May 1, 2005, Dr. Slow exercised the option and paid $100,000 for the building.

— REQUIRED

Discuss the tax implications in the above situation for Doctors Quick and Slow and for Devalued Properties Ltd.

Exercise 6

[ITA: 251]

Which of the following individuals are not at arm's length with Ms Gamma:

(A) her brother's wife?

(B) her niece?

(C) her husband from whom she is legally separated?

(D) an unrelated person?

Exercise 7

[ITA: 69]

James Meadows is not at arm's length with his son Hayden. James wants Hayden to have a painting that cost him $1,200 and now has a fair market value of $1,500. What are the consequences under subsection 69(1) to James and Hayden if:

(A) he sells the painting to him for $2,000?

(B) he sells the painting to him for $1,200?

(C) he gives the painting to him without any financial consideration?

Exercise 8

[ITA: 73; 74.1; 74.2; 74.5; IT-511R]

Alice Attribution is considering the following courses of action in transferring assets to her spouse this year:

(A) gifting to her husband shares with a fair market value of $15,000 and an adjusted cost base of $12,000;

(B) selling to her husband shares with a fair market value of $15,000 and an adjusted cost base of $12,000 for cash of $15,000. An election under subsection 73(1) was made;

(C) selling to her husband shares with a fair market value of $15,000 and an adjusted cost base of $12,000 for a $15,000 non-interest bearing promissory note with a definite repayment period;

(D) gifting to her husband $15,000 such that he purchases the shares on the open market; and

(E) lending her husband $15,000 evidenced by a non-interest bearing promissory note with a definite repayment period such that he purchases the shares on the open market.

— *REQUIRED*

Discuss the tax implications arising from the above transactions and any subsequent disposition by the spouse.

Exercise 9

[ITA: 20(1)(*l*), (*p*); 22; 38; 39; 50]

Reconsider Exercise 9 of Chapter 4 and explain the tax implications if Mr. Flogger and Mr. Sucker do not use the section 22 election on the sale of the accounts receivable.

ASSIGNMENT PROBLEMS

Problem 1

[ITA: 13(4); 44]

During its year ended December 31, 2005, Power Boat Corporation Ltd. sold its facilities in downtown Toronto. As the sale occurred in December, business activity was at a low. New facilities were purchased in February 2006 in Parry Sound on the shores of Georgian Bay. The corporation sold its Toronto land and building for $300,000 and $200,000, respectively. This land and building had a cost in 1989 of $50,000 and $100,000, respectively. At the end of 2004, the building had an undepreciated capital cost of $55,000 for income tax purposes. In Parry Sound, the corporation purchased land and building for $75,000 and $350,000, respectively.

— *REQUIRED*

(A) Prepare two calculations of the income tax consequences of the above move, one without an election under subsection 44(6) and one with this election.

(B) If the property disposed of by the corporation in 2005 had been an apartment building held for rental purposes:

   (i) what would the tax consequences of a sale of the property have been after a replacement of the property with another apartment complex in 2006?

   (ii) what would the tax consequences on an expropriation have been after a replacement of the property with another apartment complex in 2006?

Problem 2

[ITA: 13(4); 44]

On March 1, 2005, Raymond Fan, a sole proprietor, sold his garden supply store in downtown Toronto to a competitor because of declining sales caused by competition from large suburban hardware and grocery stores. The following information relates to the sale of the business:

	Proceeds	Cost	U.C.C./ C.E.C. Jan. 1, 2005
Accounts receivable	$ 6,000	$10,000	—
Land	120,000	65,000	—
Building — Class 3	170,000	62,000	$28,000
Equipment — Class 8	3,000	1,200	300
— Class 10	4,000	12,000	800
Inventory	5,200	7,000	—
Goodwill	52,000	—	—

Raymond's business year-end coincided with the calendar year. Raymond has been in the same business since 1987. As of December 31, 2004, there was a balance in the allowance for doubtful accounts for tax purposes of $1,300.

Subsequent to the sale of the business, Raymond worked for his brother, Kevin, who owned a shoe store. However, Raymond became bored and when a garden supply store on a busy highway north of Toronto came on the market in late November 2006, he immediately bought it. The following information relates to his purchase of assets of the new business:

Land	$105,000
Building	220,000
Equipment — Class 8	9,000
— Class 10	11,000
Goodwill	Nil

— *REQUIRED*

(A) Compute the minimum amount Raymond must include on his 2005 tax return in respect of the sale of the business, before any election is made under section 44 or subsection 13(4).

Problem 5

[ITA: 7; 69; 73; 74.1; 74.2; 74.5; 56(4.1); 110(1)(*d*)]

During 2004, Madame Moneybucks exercised a stock option that she held in her employer (a CCPC). It is now November 2005. She is currently contemplating a number of scenarios in terms of the shares she received under the 2004 stock option exercise. She has asked you to explain the tax consequences of her actual and contemplated transactions.

The details of the stock option exercised during 2004 are as follows.

Number of shares purchased	Exercise price	Fair market value of shares at exercise date	Fair market value of shares at grant date
6,000	$20	$35	$20

The current fair market value of a share is $42.

Madame Moneybucks is married and has two children (ages 21 and 15). She is expecting large dividends to be paid on the above shares in December 2005 and each December on an ongoing basis. She also expects that the shares will increase in value quite considerably over the near future. As a result, she is looking for a means of splitting income with her immediate family. She is proposing the following scenarios in terms of distributing these shares amongst her immediate family:

(1) gift the shares to her spouse and children (¹/₃ to her spouse and ¹/₃ to each child);

(2) sell the shares to her spouse and children (¹/₃ to her spouse and ¹/₃ to each child) for cash proceeds of $20 per share; or

(3) sell the shares to her spouse and children (¹/₃ to her spouse and ¹/₃ to each child) in exchange for a note payable of $42 per share.

The note payable described in (3) above will be payable over five years with no interest. Since the note pays no interest and is repayable over future years, the estimated present value of the note is $25 per share.

— REQUIRED

Prepare a memorandum to Madame Moneybucks explaining the income tax consequences of her completed and proposed transactions.

Problem 6

[ITA: Subdivisions b and c; ETA: 123(1); 169(1); 170(1)(*a*); 174; 231; 236]

PITA Co. Ltd. is a nutritional consulting firm that advises manufacturers and distributors on consumers' dietary needs and preferences. For its year ended December 31, 2005, it reported net income before taxes of $900,000 for financial statement purposes. This amount included a gain on the disposition of land held as capital property of $50,000 and of a building (not the only one in the class) of $95,000. The corporation also realized an accounting loss of $20,000 on securities and of $10,000 on a trademark. These assets were acquired for the following amounts:

land .... $120,000 in 1994
building .... 100,000 in 1994 (UCC of the class is $125,000)
securities ...... 50,000 in 2003
trademark ..... 80,000 in 2002

The proceeds of disposition of these assets were as follows:

land $150,000
building 120,000
securities 30,000
trademark 70,000

The corporation has reported accounting depreciation of $80,000 and wishes to claim the maximum available capital cost allowance of $100,000. During 2005, the corporation also made payments in respect of interest on unpaid income taxes ($1,500), charitable donations ($10,000), and an annual employee dinner-dance in December 2005 ($14,000). During 2005, the corporation established that an unsecured $5,000 note receivable in respect of the sale (as capital property) of a parcel of land in the prior year had become a bad debt. This was not reflected in the financial statements.

— REQUIRED

(A) Prepare a reconciliation between net income for financial statement purposes and net income for income tax purposes for the year ended December 31, 2005. Support your reconciliation with references to the *Income Tax Act*.

(B) Discuss in general terms the treatment of these items by the corporation for purposes of the GST.

Problem 7

[ITA: 13(7)(*e*); 70(5)(*a*), (*b*), (*c*); 70(6)(*d*), (*e*); ITR: 1100(2)(*h*); 1102(14)(*d*)]

On July 31, 2005, Mary McArthur passed away after a lengthy illness. Mary was survived by her husband and one adult child, Margaret. Both her husband and daughter are residents of Canada. Information related to Mary's assets as at July 31, 2005, is set out below.

Description	Cost	UCC	Fair market value	Beneficiary
Rental property — Toronto, Ontario				
Land	$40,000	n/a	$ 100,000	Spouse
Building (Class 3)	55,000	$15,000	145,000	Spouse
Rental property — Stratford, Ontario				
Land	25,000	n/a	45,000	Daughter
Building (Class 1)	65,000	42,000	93,000	Daughter
CBS shares (see Note below)	nil	n/a	1,000,000	Spouse
Bell Canada shares (see Note below)	nil	n/a	150,000	Daughter

Note:

Mary inherited these shares from her father upon his death in 2003. Her father had an adjusted cost base of $250,000 in the CBS shares. The fair market value of the CBS shares on the date of his death was $500,000. Her father had an adjusted cost base of $150,000 in the Bell Canada shares. The fair market value of the Bell Canada shares on the date of his death was $180,000.

— REQUIRED

(A) Compute the minimum income and/or taxable capital gains to be reported by Mary McArthur for 2005 in respect of the above noted assets. Ignore any available elections.

(B) Determine the cost amounts of the above assets to the respective beneficiaries.

[For more problems and solutions thereto, see the CD accompanying this book.]

SUPPLEMENTAL NOTES

(This section can be omitted without losing the continuity of the chapter. None of the review questions, multiple choice questions, exercises or assignment problems utilizes this information.)

A. Pre-1972 Assets Revisited

I. Non-depreciable capital property

[ITAR: 26]

In the preceding chapter, several section 53 adjustments to the cost base were demonstrated for assets purchased *subsequent* to December 31, 1971. However, with non-depreciable assets held on this date, the median rule, as described in ITAR 26(3), is one of the two methods used to establish adjusted cost base at the beginning of 1972. The effect of ITAR 26(3)(*c*) is to adjust proceeds of disposition, as used in the median rule, by reversing any section 53 adjustments that are made to adjusted cost base after 1971. Note that despite the length of time elapsed since 1971, long-term fixed assets, such as land, may be still disposed of currently.

There are three distinct steps in arriving at the adjusted cost base of non-depreciable assets owned on December 31, 1971.

Step 1. Calculate the "adjusted proceeds" by taking the actual proceeds and reversing the section 53 adjustments, that is, by adding to proceeds of disposition reductions to the cost base listed in subsection 53(2) and deducting from proceeds of disposition additions to the cost base listed in subsection 53(1).

Step 2. Use the adjusted proceeds in Step 1, in arriving at the median figure or "deemed cost," that is, in comparing the three relevant amounts in the median rule, to establish adjusted cost base at January 1, 1972.

Step 3. Calculate the adjusted cost base at the time of the disposition by adding or subtracting the actual section 53 adjustments, as required, to the "deemed cost".

Step 4. Calculate the capital gain or loss in the normal manner.

Example Problem

The following information relates to the sale of land which is capital property purchased in 1968:

	Situation (a)	Situation (b)	Situation (c)
	(Expressed in thousands (000s))		
Cost (1968)	$ 80	$ 80	$ 80
Valuation-day value	120	120	120
Proceeds of disposition in 1999	150	100	50
Ssec. 18(2) denial of interest and property taxes	10	10	10

— REQUIRED

Determine the taxable capital gain on the 1999 disposition using ITAR 26(3).

412 Introduction to Federal Income Taxation in Canada

— SOLUTION

The denial of the deduction for interest and property taxes [ssec. 18(2)] results in a paragraph 53(1)(h) addition to the cost base.

Situation (a)

Step 1:	Adjusted proceeds ($150 − $10)		$140
Step 2:	Deemed cost = median of:		
	(a) Cost	$ 80	
	(b) Valuation-day value	120	$120
	(c) Adjusted proceeds	140	
Step 3:	A.C.B. ($120 + $10)		$130
Step 4:	P of D (actual)	$150	
	A.C.B.	(130)	
	C.G.	$ 20	
	T.C.G. (³/₄ × $20)		$ 15

Situation (b)

Step 1:	Adjusted proceeds ($100 − $10)		$ 90
Step 2:	Deemed cost = median of:		
	(a) Cost	$ 80	
	(b) Valuation-day value	120	$ 90
	(c) Adjusted proceeds	90	
Step 3:	A.C.B. ($90 + $10)		$100
Step 4:	P of D (actual)	$100	
	A.C.B.	(100)	
	C.G.	Nil	
	T.C.G. (³/₄ × Nil)		Nil

Situation (c)

Step 1:	Adjusted proceeds ($50 − $10)		$ 40
Step 2:	Deemed cost = median of:		
	(a) Cost	$ 80	
	(b) Valuation-day value	120	$ 80
	(c) Adjusted proceeds	40	
Step 3:	A.C.B. ($80 + $10)		$ 90
Step 4:	P of D (actual)	$ 50	
	A.C.B.	(90)	
	C.L.	$ (40)	
	A.C.L. (³/₄ × $40)		$ (30)

2. Depreciable property

[ITAR: 20(1)(a)]

One of the important exceptions to the use of the median rule is "depreciable property". Paragraph (a) of the definition of "adjusted cost base" in section 54 defines the adjusted cost base of depreciable property as being its capital cost. Hence, for depreciable property, the median and fair market value rules [ITAR 26(3) and (7)] which determine the adjusted cost base at the beginning of 1972 for capital assets owned on December 31, 1971, cannot apply. However, in order to avoid taxing the accrued gain until Valuation day, a special rule [ITAR 20(1)(a)] applies, to adjust proceeds of disposition rather than adjusted cost base. The adjustment is necessary only when the capital cost is less than both:

(a) Valuation-day value, and

(b) proceeds of disposition.

Where the capital cost is greater than either of the above amounts, then ITAR 20(1)(a) is not applicable. The capital cost is the adjusted cost base. It should be emphasized that there can be no capital loss on the disposition of depreciable property. Any such decline in value is handled through the capital cost allowance system.

Assume, for example, that proceeds of disposition are $10,000; V-day value is $7,000; and capital cost is $5,000. In this case, the capital gain would be computed in the following manner:

Capital cost		$5,000
Plus the excess, if any		
Proceeds of disposition	$10,000	
Less: V-day value	7,000	3,000
Deemed proceeds....................................		$8,000
Less: capital cost..................................		5,000
Capital gain		$3,000

Note that the effect of ITAR 20(1)(a) is to adjust actual proceeds so that the difference between the adjusted or deemed proceeds and capital cost is equal to the capital gain since V-day. In the example, this amount is $3,000 (i.e., $10,000– $7,000). The definition of adjusted cost base for depreciable property [par. (a) of the definition in sec. 54] is the original capital cost with no adjustment. Therefore, were it not for the ITAR, the capital gain would be computed as proceeds minus capital cost. In the example, this amount is $5,000 (i.e., $10,000 – $5,000), not V-day value of $7,000. Consequently, the effect of ITAR 20(1)(a) is to obtain protection from being taxed on gains accrued up to Valuation day, because capital cost cannot be adjusted according to the definition of adjusted cost base for that property.

B. Exempt Capital Gains Balance and Exempt Gains Balance

[ITA: 14(5); 39.1; 52(1)(p)]

Where an individual made an election on an investment in a flow-through entity held on February 22, 1994, an exempt capital gains balance [defined in ssec. 39.1(1)] was created. A flow-through entity includes a mutual fund and a partnership [ssec. 39.1(1)]. These entities flow their income out to their investors to be taxed in the hands of the investors. The individual investor would have made an election in his or her 1994 tax return to trigger all or some of the accrued capital gains on the investment in order to use up the expiring general capital gains deduction. Instead of increasing the A.C.B. of the investment to the individual, the elected gain was added to this special account, called the exempt capital gains balance, of the individual in respect of the particular entity. An election would have been made separately on each flow-through entity held by the investor to the extent necessary to absorb the capital gains deduction. Hence, the individual would have an exempt capital gains balance for each separate entity for which an election was made.

The exempt capital gains balance can be used to shelter either a capital gain of the entity that is flowed out to the individual or a capital gain realized on the disposal of the interest in the entity itself. However, the balance must be used before January 1, 2005. At that time, any unused balance will expire. However, paragraph 53(1)(*p*) allows an addition of, in essence, the exempt gains balance at the end of the year 2004 to the A.C.B. of the investment in the flow-through entity. The balance for a particular entity will also expire when the individual disposes of all of the interest in the entity and the realized gains have not been large enough to use up the remainder of the exempt capital gains balance.

A similar election was available for a component of the gain on eligible capital property. If a taxpayer owned eligible capital property on February 22, 1994, and had not used all of the general capital gains deduction available, a special election on a component of the accrued gain was possible. The effect of the election was to trigger as much of the accrued taxable capital gain component of eligible capital property as could be offset by available capital gains deduction. Since the elected taxable capital gain was offset by an equal amount of capital gains deduction, no incremental taxable income resulted from the election.

The benefit of the election results from the addition of the elected taxable capital gain on eligible capital property to the "exempt gains balance" defined in subsection 14(5). That balance can be used to reduce a negative balance in the CEC account on a disposition after February 22, 1994. The election had no effect on the balance in the CEC account used for the purposes of the deduction under paragraph 20(1)(*b*). Therefore, the election had no immediate effect on the annual deduction, but only a future effect on a disposition.

C. Warranties

[ITA: 42; IT-330R]

The traditional method of accounting for warranties through a reserve, in respect of items sold as inventory, is not permitted for tax purposes. Such a reserve is denied [par. 18(1)(*e*)], since there is no specific provision for the deduction of this type of reserve. Only the actual expenditures incurred on servicing inventory sold under warranty may be deducted for tax purposes as ordinary business expenses.

In respect of *capital property*, like land used as a fixed asset in a business, proceeds of disposition must include all amounts received or receivable as consideration for warranties. Then, a reduction of proceeds is recognized, if a cost is incurred before the filing-due date for the year of sale or a capital loss is recognized for a cost incurred subsequently, to the extent that the cost incurred was laid out to fulfil the legal obligation under the warranty [sec. 42]. In effect, either adjustment to income at the time the warranty cost is incurred is intended to offset the amount included in proceeds of the disposition which may have resulted in a capital gain at the time of disposition. Recall that capital losses can only be applied to capital gains realized in the year of loss, in the preceding three years or in any subsequent year.

The type of situation in which this adjustment might be used would be, for example, the sale of land held as a capital asset subject to a warranty that it is environmentally clean. Proceeds of disposition would include all amounts received or receivable in respect of the sale, including any amount received or receivable in respect of the warranty. If it is discovered later that the land is polluted in some manner, any expenditure made to clean the land under the warranty obligation will be considered to be a reduction of proceeds or a capital loss, depending on when the cost is incurred.

D. Attribution and the CRA Policy Change on Substituted Property

[ITA: 73(1), 74.1, 74.2; IT-511R]

Prior to May 22, 1985, the CRA took the position in IT-258R2 that there would be no further attribution on capital gains which had been included in the transferor's income even though these subsequent transactions were technically caught by the substituted property rules [ssec. 248(5)]. However, IT-511R, dated February 21, 1994, reverses this policy. An analysis of the example presented in paragraph 27 of this Bulletin appears to indicate that only capital property transferred to a spouse after December 31, 1987, is subject to the new interpretation of including, in income, all capital gains on substituted property. Therefore, pre-1988 capital property acquisitions will only have an income inclusion to the extent the capital gain realized has not been previously attributed. However, proceeds on the sale of pre-1988 capital property acquisitions invested in substituted capital property after 1987 will be subject to full attribution.

Example of Capital Gains Attribution between Spouses (IT-511R, paragraph 27)

1978	*Facts*	One spouse (transferor) gifted property with the following attributes to the other spouse (transferee):
		A.C.B. .... $ 50,000
		F.M.V. $100,000
	Results	Proceeds of disposition are automatically deemed to be the adjusted cost base of the transferred property ($50,000) under subsection 73(1); hence, there is no capital gain in the year of transfer. (Note 1)
		The transferee has an A.C.B. of $50,000.
1982	*Facts*	The transferee sold the transferred property for $120,000 and acquired substituted property for the same amount.
	Results	A capital gain of $70,000 ($120,000 – $50,000) is attributed back to the transferor under section 74.2.
		The transferee's A.C.B. of the substituted property is $120,000.
1988	*Facts*	The transferee sold the substituted property for $200,000 and reinvested all of the proceeds in new substituted property.
	Results	A portion of the capital gain ($66,667) is attributed back to the transferor, since the acquisition of the property occurred in the pre-1988 period.
		A capital gain of $80,000 ($200,000 – $120,000) is realized.
		The attributed portion of the $80,000 capital gain is computed as:

$$\frac{\text{F.M.V. at the date of original transfer}}{\text{Proceeds of disposition of the previous sale (1978)}} \times \frac{\text{Capital gain on}}{\text{present sale}}$$

$$\frac{\$100,000}{\$120,000} \times \$80,000 = \$66,667$$

The transferee's A.C.B. of the second substituted property is $200,000.

| 1999 | *Facts* | The transferee sold the second substituted property acquired in 1988 for $250,000. |
| | *Results* | All of the resultant capital gain of $50,000 ($250,000 − $200,000) is attributed back to the transferor since the acquisition was post-1987. Any future capital gain arising from the investment of the $250,000 will be fully attributable to the transferor. |

Note 1: If the transferor had elected in 1978 not to have section 73 apply, then proceeds of disposition would have been F.M.V. of $100,000, triggering a capital gain of $50,000 in the hands of the transferor. The transferee's A.C.B. would have been $100,000. The overall numerical result would not change because of the election, except that $50,000 of capital gain would be recognized earlier.

Note 2: Any income from property earned on the transferred property and property substituted therefor would also be subject to attribution under section 74.1.

E. GST and Capital Real Property

1. Input tax credits on acquisitions of capital real property
[ETA: 123(1); 206; 208]

This part of the chapter will focus on the input tax credit rules for capital real property. These rules apply to real property that is capital property of a registrant; they do not apply to real property that is held as inventory. As noted in Chapter 5, capital property is defined in subsection 123(1) of the *Excise Tax Act* (ETA) to include any property that is capital property for income tax purposes, other than property included in Class 12 or Class 14 of the capital cost allowance classes. This definition for GST purposes applies regardless of whether the registrant is a taxpayer under the *Income Tax Act*.

The term "real property" is defined in subsection 123(1) of the ETA to include:

(a) in respect of real property in the Province of Quebec, immovable property and every lease thereof,

(b) in respect of property in any other place in Canada, buildings and adjacent land, land and tenements of every nature and description, and every estate or interest in real property, whether legal or equitable, and

(c) a mobile home, a floating home and any leasehold or proprietary interest therein.

Separate sets of rules relating to input tax credits for capital real property are applicable, depending on whether the registrant is an individual (i.e., a sole proprietorship), or any other type of business. The rules for individuals are designed to account for any personal use of capital property. The special rules that apply to public sector bodies and financial institutions will not be discussed in this chapter.

Section 206 of the ETA contains the rules for capital real property owned by a registrant that is not an individual. Unlike acquisitions of capital personal property, acquisitions of capital real property generate proportional input tax credits based on the extent of use in a commercial activity (i.e., the same as the rules for the acquisition of goods and services in general). As an example, if capital real property is acquired for use 30% in a commercial activity, an input tax credit equal to 30% of the GST paid or payable on acquisition may be claimed. This may occur, for example, where a portion of a residential apartment building is rented to retailers. Since residential rents are exempt supplies, only the portion of the building used by the retailers will generate input tax credits. The apportionment may be done on the basis of floor space or rental income.

No input tax credit is available, however, where the extent of commercial use is less than 10% of total use. On the other hand, a full input tax credit may be claimed where use in a commercial activity is exclusive, i.e., 90% or more. (In the case of financial institutions, exclusive use is interpreted as 100%.)

Subsection 206(2) of the ETA applies where a registrant who was previously unable to claim an input tax credit, for example, when the capital real property was used exclusively in non-commercial activities, begins to use the property in a commercial activity. In these circumstances, a proportional input tax credit may be claimed at that time. For example, if a medical practice acquires a building to be used exclusively for the provision of exempt health services, no input tax credit may be claimed. If, at some later date, 40% of the building is rented to other businesses, a proportional input tax credit may be claimed at that time.

Section 208 of the ETA deals with acquisitions of, and improvements to, capital real property by a registrant who is an individual. Pursuant to subsections 208(1) and (4), no input tax credit may be claimed on the acquisition or subsequent improvement of the property, respectively, if the use of the property is primarily (i.e., more than 50%) personal. For example, if an accountant acquires a building to be used 40% for his or her practice and 60% for his or her residence, no input tax credit can be claimed. If the property is used primarily in a commercial activity, an input tax credit in proportion to the commercial use is allowed.

Acquisitions of Capital Real Property

Registrants	Proportion of use	Amount of credit
Entities other than individuals	Commercial use≤10%	No input tax credit
	10%<Commercial use<90%	Input tax credit based on proportion of commercial use
	Commercial use≥90%	Full input tax credit
Individuals	Personal use>50%	No input tax credit
	Personal use≤50%	Input tax credit based on proportion of commercial use

2. Change-of-use rules for capital real property

[ETA: 123(1); 190; 197; 206–208]

Capital real property may undergo several changes in use over its useful life. The change-of-use rules for capital real property require registrants to carefully monitor the use of such property and to keep records of any GST paid in respect of the property. There is also the need to track the cost of subsequent improvements to the property, since these may impact the amount of the input tax credit claimed on a change in use. An improvement in respect of property is defined in subsection 123(1) of the ETA to mean any property or service that is supplied for the purpose of improving the property, to the extent that the cost would be included in determining the adjusted cost base of the property for purposes of the *Income Tax Act*.

A specific rule deals with minor changes in use. Section 197 of the ETA provides that if the change in use is less than 10% of the total use of the property, the use of the property will be deemed not to have changed.

3. Dispositions of capital real property

[ETA: 123(1); 193(1); 257]

Where a registrant other than an individual sells capital real property, the sale is generally subject to GST. The definition of commercial activity in subsection 123(1) includes the making of a supply of real property. However, where the property was used as a residential apartment building, the sale is exempt and no GST need be collected. If, on the other hand, the vendor previously claimed an input tax credit, for example, for the use of the building by retailers, the sale would be taxable, as discussed below.

Where the property was used partially in commercial activities prior to sale, the registrant must account for GST based on the full sale price. However, the registrant is entitled to claim an input tax credit under subsection 193(1) of the ETA equal to the "basic tax content" of the property. This term means, generally, the amount of GST that the person was required to pay on the property at the time of acquisition and on improvements thereto, after deducting any amounts (other than input tax credits) the person was entitled to recover by way of a rebate, remission, or otherwise, and after taking into account any depreciation in the value of the property. Thus, any GST paid on the original acquisition that was not previously claimed as an input tax credit may be recovered, provided the value of the property has not declined.

Where an individual who is a registrant sells real property, the GST status of the sale depends on the use of the property before the sale. Where the property was used primarily for personal purposes, the sale is exempt. Where the property was used in commercial activities and not primarily for personal purposes, the sale is subject to GST and the individual is entitled to an input tax credit under subsection 193(1) of the ETA, as described above.

Special rules are contained in section 257 of the ETA to provide rebates to non-registrants on taxable sales of capital real property. Since non-registrants are not entitled to claim input tax credits, the rebate mechanism was established to prevent double taxation. For example, where a doctor sells a building used exclusively in supplying exempt medical services, GST must be charged but no input tax credit may be claimed. Under section 257 of the ETA, the doctor is able to claim a rebate equal to the basic tax content of the property. The application must be filed within two years after the day the consideration for the sale became due or was paid without becoming due.

Chapter 9

Other Sources of Income and Deductions in Computing Income

TOPICS DISCUSSED

	Page
OTHER SOURCES OF INCOME	421
Benefits in the Nature of Pensions	421
Retiring Allowances and Other Payments on Termination of Employment	421
Support Receipts and Payments	422
Annuity Payments	424
Amounts Received from Deferred Income Plans	424
Education Assistance Payments	426
Other Inclusions	426
Indirect Payments	427
Restrictive Covenants	428
AMOUNTS NOT INCLUDED IN COMPUTING INCOME	429
DEDUCTIONS IN COMPUTING INCOME	430

	Page
Capital Element of Annuity	430
Registered Retirement Savings Plans	430
Transfers of Retirement Income and Sheltered Amounts	447
Overpayments and Other Deductions	449
Moving Expenses	450
Child Care Expenses	452
Attendant Care Expenses [Disability Support Deduction]	455
Expenses of Residents Absent from Canada	456
SUPPLEMENTAL NOTES	470
RRSP's and Net Past Service Pension Adjustments and Pension Adjustment Reversals	470

This chapter will highlight the following:

Division B — Computation of Income

    Subdivision d — Other sources of income

    Subdivision e — Deduction in computing income

    Subdivision g — Amounts not included in income

Division G — Deferred and Other Special Income Arrangements

The sectional list for these subdivisions of the Act, located at the front of the CCH edition of the CANADIAN INCOME TAX ACT, should be used to find quickly specific inclusions and deductions in doing the problem material in this and subsequent chapters.

PART I — DIVISION B
SUBDIVISION d
OTHER INCOME

DIVISION		SUBDIVISION		SECTION	
A	Liability for tax				
B	Computation of income				
C	Computation of taxable income		Basic rules	56	General
				56.1	Support
D	Taxable income earned in Canada by non-residents	a	Office or employment	56.2-56.3	Debt forgiveness
		b	Business or property	56.4	Restrictive Covenants
E	Computation of tax			57	Certain pensions
E.1	Minimum tax	c	Capital gains and losses	58	Gov't annuities
F	Special rules			59-59.1	Resource property
G	Deferred and other special income arrangements	d	Other income		
		e	Other deductions	60	Other deductions
H	Exemptions	f	Rules relating to computation of income	60.1	Support
I	Returns, assessments, payments, appeals			60.2	Refund of AVC's
				61-61.1	IAAC's
J	Appeals to the courts	g	Amounts not included in income	61.2-61.4	Debt forgiveness
		h	Cdn corporations and shareholders	62	Moving expenses
				63	Child care expenses
		i	Shareholders of non-resident corporations	64	Attendant care
				64.1	Individual absent from Canada
		j	Partnerships	65-66.8	Resource
		k	Trusts		
				81	Amounts not included in income

146	RRSP
146.01	Home Buyers' Plan
146.02	Lifelong Learning Plan
146.1	RESP
146.3	RRIF
147	DPSP
147.1-147.4	RPP
148	Life insurance policies
148.1	Eligible funeral arrangements

I. OTHER SOURCES OF INCOME

Section 56 presents a list of miscellaneous types of income from a non-capital source, other than employment in Subdivision a and business or property in Subdivision b. Section 56.1 extends the rules pertaining to marital breakdown situations. Sections 57 to 59.1, which will not be discussed in this text, deal with certain pension plans, government annuities and resource properties in more detail.

A. Benefits in the Nature of Pensions

[ITA: 56(1)(*a*); IT-499R]

This provision includes in income superannuation or pension benefits including those received under the *Old Age Security Act* and the Canada Pension Plan [spar. 56(1)(*a*)(i)]. IT-499R discusses the inclusion of these benefits. "Retiring allowances" [defined in ssec. 248(1)] are included, as discussed further below [spar. 56(1)(*a*)(ii)]. "Death benefits" are also defined very precisely for the purposes of the Act [ssec. 248(1)] and are included [spar. 56(1)(*a*)(iii)]. Note the exemption of a maximum of $10,000 of death benefit contained in the definition of the term. Any benefits received under the *Employment Insurance Act* are taxable [spar. 56(1)(*a*)(iv)].

Spouses or common-law partners, who meet certain conditions [ssec. 248(1): "common-law partner"], can split equally their Canada Pension Plan income. The term "spouse or common-law partner" is defined as two persons, regardless of sex, who co-habit in a conjugal relationship and have done so for a continuous period of at least 12 months. The amount which can be shared is 50% of the combined CPP benefits received but prorated by the length of the time the individuals have been living together in relation to the contributory period. This income sharing arrangement would be most useful where the individuals have different tax rates and amounts of income. Where one individual was a contributor and the other individual was not, then the non-contributor must be at least 60 years of age at the time of this election. Applications are available from the Income Security Programs Department of Human Resources Development Canada.

B. Retiring Allowances and Other Payments on Termination of Employment

[ITA; 6(3)(*b*); 56(1)(*a*)(ii); IT-337R4]

In the absence of any express terms as to termination in a contract of employment, which is covered under subsection 6(3) in Chapter 3, the general principle is that all other payments on the termination of employment are taxable [spar. 56(1)(*a*)(ii)] as a retiring allowance. The provision excepts amounts out of an employee benefit plan, a retirement compensation arrangement, or a salary deferral arrangement. All three of these are plans specifically defined [ssec. 248(1)] and are not particularly common.

The definition of a retiring allowance [ssec. 248(1)] excludes pension income and death benefits, but specifically includes payments in respect of:

(a) retirement from an office or employment in recognition of long service; or

(b) loss of office including court-awarded damages received by the taxpayer, or as a bequest, by a dependant or relation of the taxpayer or his or her legal representative.

In the case of *Schwartz v. The Queen*, 96 DTC 6103, the Supreme Court of Canada had an opportunity to determine that a lump sum payment was not a retiring allowance on the facts of the case. The taxpayer had entered into a written agreement for employment, but before the employment had commenced, the taxpayer was informed that his services were not required. He received the lump sum payment as damages for the termination of the employment contract. The Canada Revenue Agency (CRA) argued that the lump sum was a retiring allowance [spar. 56(1)(*a*)(ii)]. However, the Supreme Court of Canada concluded that the argument was inconsistent with the requirement in the definition of "retiring allowance" [ssec. 248(1)] of retirement from employment.

Since the employment was only intended and not actual, there was no "employment" according to the definition of that term [ssec. 248(1)].

C. Support Receipts and Payments

[ITA: 56(1)(b); 56.1; 60(b); 60.1; IT-99R5]

1. Overview

Paragraph 56(1)(b) for support income inclusions and paragraph 60(b) for support deductions are mirror images of each other. If the amount paid is not deductible [par. 60(b)] then the receipt is usually not income to the recipient [par. 56(1)(b)]. The following discussion is applicable to both the receipts and payments.

In the case of *Thibaudeau v. The Queen*, 94 DTC 6230, the Federal Court of Appeal ruled that a separated custodial parent did not have to include child support payments as part of her income. However, the court did not rule on the deductibility of the husband's payments in this case. The court's decision was based on a finding of instances of discrimination against separated custodial parents in the Act. As an example of such discrimination, the court indicated that a non-separated custodial parent is not required to include support payments from a spouse in income. (Of course, the payer spouse does not get a deduction in that case.) If this situation had been allowed to stand, such support payments, deductible to the payer but not includable by the recipient, would escape tax altogether.

In the decision of the Supreme Court of Canada on the appeal of the *Thibaudeau* case (*The Queen v. Thibaudeau*, 95 DTC 5273), the Court ruled that the custodial parent was required to include the child support payments in her income. The majority opinion concluded that the fact that the tax saving resulting from the inclusion/deduction system does not benefit both parents equally does not infringe the equality rights protected by the Canadian Charter of Rights and Freedoms.

As a result of the *Thibaudeau* case, the inclusion–deduction system related to child support only was changed, as discussed below. These changes are applied to agreements or orders made or changed after April 30, 1997.

2. Spousal support

Support amounts [ssec. 56.1(4)], except amounts that relate to child support, are deductible [par. 60(b)] if the following five tests are met:

(a) the payments are made as allowances on a periodic basis, as discussed below;

(b) the payments are made for the maintenance of the recipient;

(c) the recipient has discretionary use of the amounts;

(d) the payments are made to a spouse or common-law partner or former spouse or common-law partner who is living apart from the payer because of the breakdown of their marriage or common-law partnership, or paid by a natural parent of a child of the recipient; and

(e) the payments are made pursuant to an order of a competent tribunal or a written agreement.

A spouse or common-law partner is described as an individual of either sex who cohabited with the recipient in a conjugal relationship or is the parent of the child of the recipient [ssec. 248(1): "common-law partner"].

The definition of an allowance for purposes of the above paragraphs is embodied in the definition of the term "support amount" [ssec. 56.1(4)]. The provision does not completely define an allowance, but does limit an allowance to an amount over which the recipient has discretion as to how the funds will be spent.

In the case of *Gagnon v. The Queen*, 86 DTC 6179, the Supreme Court of Canada considered the meaning of allowance. Three conditions must be met for an amount to be regarded as an allowance in the Court's view:

(a) the amount must be limited and predetermined;

(b) the amount must be paid to enable the recipient to discharge a certain type of expense; and

(c) the recipient must be able to dispose of the amount completely.

The Court elaborated on the last condition. As long as the recipient benefits from the amount, it is not relevant that he or she has to account for it or that he or she cannot apply it to certain types of expense at his or her complete discretion.

As noted previously, all of these provisions require that the payments be made on a periodic basis. The Federal Court of Appeal decision in *The Queen v. McKimmon*, 90 DTC 6088 listed some of the criteria which should be used in determining whether a payment is made on a periodic basis and whether in fact the payment is a deductible allowance or an instalment of a lump or capital sum which is not deductible.

Section 56.1 deems received and section 60.1 deems paid, respectively, certain receipts/payments to third parties made under an order or agreement or any variation of either. Subsection 56.1(1) deals generally with third-party payments made for the benefit of the recipient. Payments envisaged include medical bills, mortgage payments or tuition fees.

Third-party payments, whether or not they are made on a periodic basis, will be deemed [ssecs. 56.1(2) and 60.1(2)] to be an allowance for the discretionary use of the recipient for the purposes of sections 56.1 and 60.1 if they meet the following criteria:

- the payments are made in the year or preceding year under an order of a competent tribunal or written agreement;

- the expense was incurred for the maintenance of a spouse or common-law partner or former spouse or common-law partner; and

- the court order or written agreement alludes specifically to subsections 56.1(2) and 60.1(2).

Note that the use of this provision requires the agreement of both parties. If they do not agree to include the effects of these provisions in their documentation, the third-party amounts will not be deemed to be an allowance. These payments exclude the acquisition of tangible property, unless it involves an expenditure on medical expenses or educational expenses. The acquisition, improvement or maintenance of a self-contained domestic establishment, as defined [ssec. 248(1)], also qualify as payments that are deemed to be an allowance. Note that interest and principal payments are limited to 20% of the original principal amount of the debt.

Amounts that are received/paid in respect of support before a court order or written agreement is made, are considered to have been received/paid under the order or agreement. However, the subsequent order or agreement must be made before the end of the year following the receipt/payment. In addition, the subsequent order or agreement must provide for the prior support to be deemed to have been received/paid under the order or agreement]ssec. 56.1(3)[.

The CRA is very strict on its interpretation of support receipts [par. 56(1)(b)] and deductions [par. 60(b)]. All aspects of these rules must be adhered to.

3. Child support

Amounts paid in respect of support or maintenance of a child are not deductible by the payer and are not included in the income of the recipient. Any amount not identified in the agreement or order as being solely for the support of the recipient spouse or former spouse will be considered to be an amount payable for child support.

For this purpose, the term "child support amount" is defined [ssec. 56.1(4)]. These rules apply to new written agreements or court orders made or to existing written agreements or court orders changed after April 30, 1997.

4. Legal fees in connection with support payments

Under current common law, it appears that legal fees incurred to enforce pre-existing rights to support payments are deductible.[a] Paragraph 18 of IT-99R5 suggested that legal and accounting fees incurred to enforce pre-existing rights to support are deductible.[b] In *Income Tax Technical News*, No. 24, October 10, 2002, the CRA announced that it had reconsidered its position in paragraph 17 of IT-99R5 which indicates that legal costs incurred to establish rights to support are considered to be non-deductible capital outlays or personal or living expenses. The CRA now considers legal costs incurred to obtain spousal support under the *Divorce Act*, or under the applicable provincial legislation, in a separation agreement to have been incurred to enforce a pre-existing right to support. This position is based on the case of *Gallien v. The Queen* (TCC – Informal Procedure) 2000 DTC 2514. The CRA further indicated that it now accepts that legal costs of seeking to obtain an increase in support or to make child support non-taxable are also deductible.

D. Annuity Payments

[ITA: 56(1)(*d*), (*d*.2)]

An "annuity" is defined in subsection 248(1). The full amount of an annuity payment is included in income unless it is required to be included under another provision of the Act or unless it is subject to income accrual rules [ssec. 12.2(1)]. If the full amount of the annuity payment is included in income [par. 56(1)(*d*)], then the capital portion of the annuity, if any, is deducted [par. 60(*a*)].

The full amount of an annuity payment that resulted from certain registered retirement savings plan contributions that were deductible by the taxpayer is included in income [par. 56(1)(*d*.2)].

E. Amounts Received from Deferred Income Plans

[ITA: 56(1)(*h*), (*h*.1), (*h*.2), (*i*), (*q*), (*t*); 146.1]

1. Inclusion provisions

The following paragraphs take into income amounts received by the taxpayer through the deferred income plans indicated:

Paragraph 56(1)(*h*)	Registered retirement savings plan (RRSP)
Paragraph 56(1)(*h*.1)	Home buyer's plan (HBP)
Paragraph 56(1)(*h*.2)	Lifelong learning plan (LLP)
Paragraph 56(1)(*i*)	Deferred profit sharing plan (DPSP)
Paragraph 56(1)(*q*)	Registered education savings plan (RESP)
Paragraph 56(1)(*t*)	Registered retirement income fund (RRIF)

The detailed rules governing these plans are found in Division G "Deferred and Other Special Income Arrangements". RRSPs and RRIFs will be discussed in more detail later in this chapter.

---

[a] See the *McColl* case, (TCC) 2000 DTC 2148, which cites for support the cases of *Burgess*, (FCTD) 81 DTC 5192, *Evans*, (SCC) 60 DTC 1047, and *Wakeman* (TCC, Informal Procedure) 96 DTC 3220.

[b] Paragraph 18 of IT-99R5 also refers to the *Sembinelli* case (FCA), 94 DTC 6636.

2.   Registered education savings plans (RESPs)

RESPs, as defined in subsection 146.1(1), allow individuals to contribute up to $4,000 per year to a plan to fund post-secondary education of a qualified beneficiary. The lifetime contribution limit in respect of a beneficiary is $42,000 over a maximum of 21 years. The maximum number of years is 25 for a single beneficiary RESP under which the beneficiary is an individual who is entitled to a disability tax credit. Contributions are not deductible when contributed to the plan and, hence, they are not taxable when the plan allows their withdrawal. Neither the trust holding the property of a plan [ssec. 146.1(5)] nor the contributor or subscriber [ssec. 146.1(6)] is taxable on the income earned by that property, so the investment income of the plan is sheltered.

The accumulated investment income is taxable to a beneficiary as he or she receives the funds to pay for education expenses while enrolled as a full-time student in a post-secondary educational institution [par. 56(1)(q)], called "educational assistance payments" [ssec. 146.1(1)]. Educational assistance payments can be made in connection with occupational skills programs at educational institutions certified by the Minister of Human Resources and Skills Development.

A family plan RESP can be established for a number of beneficiaries related by blood or adoption. The income from such an RESP can be paid to any one or more of the beneficiaries who pursue higher education. However, the RESP cannot allow an individual to become a beneficiary after he or she turns 21.

To increase the attractiveness of saving for education through an RESP, beginning in 1998, the government provides a Canada Education Savings Grant (CESG) of 20% of the first $2,000 of annual contributions to an RESP for the benefit of children up to age 18. [Part III.1 of the *Department of Human Resources Development Act.*] This amounts to a maximum grant of $400 per year per child. The CESG is paid directly to the RESP. The maximum CESG that can be *paid* to an RESP in respect of a particular beneficiary is $7,200 (i.e., $400 × 18 years). In the case of a family plan RESP involving more than one beneficiary, the maximum CESG that can be *received* by a particular beneficiary as educational assistance payments is $7,200. CESG contribution room of $2,000 per year is accumulated for each child under 18 years old. Thus, where less than the maximum or no contribution is made in a year, the 20% grant will be paid in a subsequent year when RESP contributions are made. If a child does not pursue higher education to qualify for educational assistance payments, the CESG must be repaid to the government by the RESP.

The CESG matching rate for contributions made to an RESP by low and middle-income families on or after January 1, 2005 is determined as follows. Where a child is the beneficiary of the RESP and under the age of 18 throughout the year, the first $500 contributed in the year will attract:

- a 40% CESG matching rate, if the qualifying net income of the child's family is $35,000 or less and

- a 30% CESG matching rate if the qualifying net income of the child's family is between $35,000 and $70,000.

There is no carry-forward of the enhanced rate to future years and the income thresholds are indexed to inflation for 2005 and subsequent taxation years.

In addition, a Canada Learning Bond (CLB) provides a source of education savings for children of low-income families. Each child born on or after January 1, 2004 is eligible for an initial CLB of $500 and subsequent annual CLB's of $100 in each year up to and including the year the child turns 15, provided that the child's family is entitled to the National Child Benefit (NCB) supplement in the year (Chapter 10). The total amount of the CLB payments cannot exceed $2,000 per child and can be transferred to an RESP at any time before the child reaches 18. While no separate application is required, eligibility is linked to entitlement for the National Child Benefit supplement. The CLB is payable into an RESP of which the child is a beneficiary.

An RESP is permitted to distribute any part of its accumulated income to the subscriber after 1997, under certain conditions, as follows:

- the subscriber is alive;
- each beneficiary of the RESP is either:
  - (i) over 21 years of age and not eligible to receive educational assistance payments, or
  - (ii) has died; and
- the RESP has been in existence for at least 10 years [par. 146.1(2)(d.1)].

These distributions are included in the subscriber's income. The Minister may waive the "over 21 years of age" and the "at least 10 years" restrictions where a beneficiary under an RESP is mentally impaired [ssec. 146.1(2.2)]. The distributions may be rolled over to the subscriber's (or his or her spouse's) RRSP, to the extent that the subscriber has contribution room. The limit on this rollover is $50,000. A 20% tax is imposed on the amount of the RESP distribution received in excess of the limited amount transferred to RRSPs [sec. 204.94].

F. Education Assistance Payments

[ITA: 56(1)(*n*), (*o*); 56(3); ITR: 7700; IT-75R4; IT-340R]

These provisions include in income:

(a) scholarships, fellowships, bursaries or prizes for achievement in a field of endeavour of the taxpayer in excess of the taxpayer's scholarship exemption for a taxation year [par. 56(1)(*n*) and par. 56(3)(*c*)], and project grants, received by artists, net of the related, contractual project expenses [par. 56(1)(*n*)]; and

(b) research grants in excess of expenses which are unreimbursed, non-personal or living expenses, except for *bona fide* travelling expenses, incurred in carrying on the research [par. 56(1)(*o*)].

The scholarship exemption is generally $500 [par. 56(3)(*a*)]. However, the exemption is $3,000 for scholarships, fellowships and bursaries received by a taxpayer in connection with the taxpayer's enrolment in a program in respect of which the taxpayer may claim the education tax credit, that is, a designated educational institution [par. 56(3)(*b*)].

There are certain restrictions on the amounts which qualify as scholarships, bursaries, prizes, etc. Amounts received from a registered education savings plan, amounts received in the course of a business and amounts received in respect of employment are excluded [par. 56(1)(*n*)]. Note that the grant portion of provincial or federal education assistance payments is considered to be income under this paragraph. Certain prescribed prizes are excluded from income completely [Reg. 7700]. Generally, these prizes may be described as recognition by the general public for meritorious achievement in the arts, sciences or public service; thus these amounts do not represent a payment in respect of a contract of service.

G. Other Inclusions

[ITA: 56(1)(*l*), (*l*.1), (*s*), (*u*), (*v*)]

Included in income are amounts received as legal costs awarded by a court on an appeal from an assessment of any tax, interest or penalties, as well as any reimbursement of costs received as a result of decisions under the *Employment Insurance Act* or Canada Pension Plan [par. 56(1)(*l*)]. These receipts are included if the expenses incurred are deducted or deductible [par. 60(*o*)].

A taxpayer must include amounts received as an award or reimbursement of legal expenses paid to collect or establish a right to a retiring allowance or benefits under a pension plan [par. 56(1)(*l*.1)]. Excluded are legal expenses relating to a division or settlement of property arising from a marriage or other conjugal relationship.

Social assistance payments are included in income and, if the recipient is married, the amount received must be included by the spouse with the higher income [par. 56(1)(*u*)]. Finally, Workers' Compensation is included [par. 56(1)(*v*)].

H. Indirect Payments

[ITA: 56(2), (4), (4.1), (4.2), (4.3)]

These anti-avoidance provisions invoke the principle of constructive receipt by imputing to the taxpayer:

(a) income diverted at his or her direction to someone else either for the taxpayer's benefit or to satisfy the desire of the taxpayer to benefit the other person [ssec. 56(2)];[(c)]

(b) any rights to income transferred by the taxpayer, while resident in Canada, to someone with whom he or she was not dealing at arm's length [ssec. 56(4)]; and

(c) income earned on non-arm's length loans which do not yield a commercial rate of interest [ssecs. 56(4.1), (4.2) and (4.3)] (see Chapter 6).

Subsection 56(2) specifies the following four conditions:

- there must be a payment or transfer of property to a person other than the taxpayer;

- the payment or transfer must be made pursuant to the direction or with the concurrence of the taxpayer;

- the payment or transfer must be for the benefit of the taxpayer, or a benefit that the taxpayer desired to confer on the other person; and

- the payment or transfer would have been included in the taxpayer's income if it had been made to the taxpayer.

If all of these conditions are met, the payment or transfer is included in the taxpayer's income to the extent that it would be if the payment or transfer had been made directly to the taxpayer.

The CRA has attacked certain family income splitting schemes by applying these indirect payments provisions. In the case of *Champ v. The Queen*, (F.C.T.D.) 83 DTC 5029, part of the dividends payable on shares owned by the taxpayer's wife was included in the taxpayer's income. It was found that the taxpayer had directed the payment of dividends on his wife's shares without the payment of dividends on his shares which were essentially the same. On the other hand, in the case of *The Queen v. McClurg*, (S.C.C.) 91 DTC 5001, subsection 56(2) was held not to be applicable in facts very similar to *Champ* but where there were contractual restrictions upon the payment of dividends. The case of *The Queen v. Neuman*, (F.C.A.) 96 DTC 6464, involved facts that were slightly different from those in the *McClurg* case. The decision to apply subsection 56(2) in the *Neuman* case was based on the power of the taxpayer to ratify the dividends paid to his wife and the distinction with the *McClurg* case on the wife's lack of contribution to the corporation.

In its decision on the case of *Neuman v. The Queen*, (S.C.C.) 98 DTC 6297, the Supreme Court of Canada held that subsection 56(2) does not apply to the dividend income received by Neuman's wife. This decision established that there is no requirement for the shareholder to make a business contribution to the corporation in order to earn the dividend. Dividends are paid to shareholders simply as a return on their investment in the corporation, not as compensation for work done for the corporation. This conclusion clarifies the uncertainty left by the *McClurg* case on the issue.

[(c)] For a more detailed analysis of this provision, see Robert E. Beam and Stanley N. Laiken, "Recent Developments on Subsection 56(2): Indirect Payments", Personal Tax Planning Feature (1995), Vol. 43, No. 2, *Canadian Tax Journal*, pp. 447–469.

I. Restrictive Covenants

[ITA: 56.4]

Section 56.4 [Proposed in the Technical Amendments to the *Income Tax Act* — February 27, 2004] sets out rules with respect to amounts that are received or receivable after October 7, 2003 in respect of a restrictive covenant.

The term "restrictive covenant" is defined in subsection 56.4(1) to mean an arrangement, an undertaking or a waiver of a right or advantage that affects, in any way, the acquisition or provision of property or services by the taxpayer or someone not dealing at arm's length with the taxpayer.

The starting point under subsection 56.4(2) is to include in income the total of all amounts received or receivable by the taxpayer, or non-arm's length person, in respect of a restrictive covenant.

Then, subsection 56.4(3) sets out the amounts to which the income inclusion in subsection 56.4(2) do not apply. Basically, the exceptions are for those amounts that are included in income somewhere else. The result is that payments for restrictive covenants will be taxable in some manner. The following are the three items that are not taxed under section 56.4 because they are taxed elsewhere:

Employment income: Subsection 56.4(2) will not apply if the amount is included in employment income or will be included when received. This might be the case where an employee leaves and is paid an amount not to work for a competitor. In this case there may not be any shares or assets sold that might cause part of the payments to be allocated in a different way. While employment income is normally taxed on the received basis, if the employee agreed to the covenant more than 36 months before the end of the taxation year, then subsection 6(3.1) may cause the payments for the restrictive covenant to be included in employment income even though it is not actually received.

Eligible capital property: Subsection 56.4(2) will not apply to an amount if the payment received is required by the description E in the definition "cumulative eligible capital" in subsection 14(5) to have $3/4$ of the payment credited to the pool. The purchaser and the taxpayer must jointly elect for this exception to apply. This might apply, for example, where a partnership sells its business and the restrictive covenant proceeds are included in with the proceeds for the goodwill.

Proceeds of disposition: Subsection 56.4(2) will not apply to the extent that the amount is added to the proceeds of disposition of an "eligible interest". An "eligible interest" is capital property that is a partnership interest or a share of a corporation where the partnership or the corporation is carrying on a business. This might occur where the share or the partnership interest is disposed of and the shareholder or partner enters into a restrictive covenant. For this to be the case, the following conditions must be met:

- the amount must directly relate to the taxpayer's disposition of an "eligible interest" [subsection 56.4(1)];

- the disposition of the "eligible interest" must be to the purchaser of the restrictive covenant;

- the amount received or receivable must be consideration for an undertaking not to compete with the purchaser;

- the amount cannot exceed the amount determined by a formula;

- the amount is included in the proceeds of disposition of the "eligible interest"; and

- the taxpayer and the purchaser of the restrictive covenant have elected to apply this exception.

Paragraph 60(*f*) provides a deduction for a bad debt if the amount was previously included in income under section 56.4. Section 68 addresses the allocation of amounts between restrictive covenants and the other property being disposed of.

The following diagram illustrates how section 56.4 fits into the taxation of restrictive covenant payments:

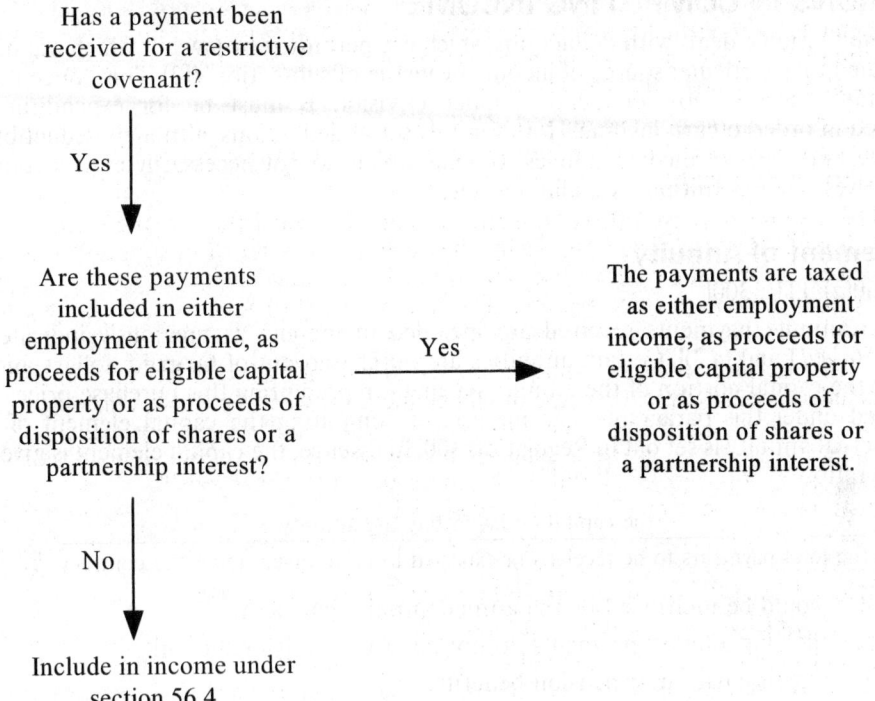

II. AMOUNTS NOT INCLUDED IN COMPUTING INCOME

[ITA: 81]

Section 81 lists a number of specific types of income that would ordinarily have to be included in income subject to tax, but are excluded from the computation of income. Note the very limited scope of these exclusions each of which meets a specific problem area. The more common components of this section are summarized below:

(a) amounts exempted by other federal statutes or foreign tax agreements [par. 81(1)(*a*)];

(b) certain pension or other payments related to war services [par. 81(1)(*d*)];

(c) war service pensions of a country which has reciprocal arrangements with Canada [par. 81(1)(*e*)];

(d) compensation by the Federal Republic of Germany, for war victims [par. 81(1)(*g*)];

(e) income and capital gains from personal injury award property for individuals under 21 years of age [pars. 81(1)(*g*.1) and (*g*.2)];

(f) social assistance payments based on a needs test [par. 81(1)(*h*)];

(g) payments out of a profit sharing plan [par. 81(1)(*k*)];

(h) expense allowances of elected municipal officers and members of provincial legislature [ssecs. 81(2) and (3)]; and

(i) allowance for or reimbursement of part-time employment travel expenses [ssec. 81(3.1)]. (See Chapter 3 for a detailed discussion of this provision.)

III. DEDUCTIONS IN COMPUTING INCOME

Subdivision e deals with deductions which are permitted by law but which are not attributed to a particular source of income by virtue of subsection 4(2). This concept is important because most deductions under Division B must be for expenditures incurred in order to earn income. However, this set of deductions, although deductible from certain types of income, applies to items which do not necessarily earn income themselves, such as tuition fees, alimony, etc.

A. Capital Element of Annuity

[ITA: 60(*a*); ITR: 300]

All annuity payments received are included in income as previously indicated [pars. 56(1)(*d*) and (*d*.2)]. Certain annuities are purchased out of tax-paid dollars and, hence, the capital portion of the annuity payment, representing this purchase price, is removed under this paragraph. The method of computing the capital element of a contractual annuity is set out in Regulation 300. In essence, the capital element is given by the ratio:

$$\frac{\text{the capital outlay to buy the annuity}}{\text{the total payments to be received or expected to be received under the contract}}$$

This ratio would be multiplied by the annual annuity payment.

The following annuity payments do not qualify for this deduction:

(a) a superannuation or pension benefit;

(b) a payment under a registered retirement savings plan or registered retirement income fund; or

(c) a payment resulting from a deferred profit sharing plan.

These types of annuities are excluded because they are paid out of income which has not been subjected to tax; that is, the cost of these annuities has been allowed as a deduction in computing income.

B. Registered Retirement Savings Plans

[ITA: 18(1)(*u*), (11); 40(2)(*g*)(iv); 60(*i*)–(*l*); 74.5(12); 146(1), (5), (5.1), (8)–(8.3), (8.6); 146.01; 146.02; 146.3(5.1), (6.1); 204.1(2.1); 204.2(1.1); ITR: 103(4), (6); 7308]

The rules regarding the tax treatment of registered retirement savings plans (RRSPs) reflect a comprehensive overhaul of the taxation of retirement savings, referred to as pension reform. Pension reform received Royal Assent on June 27, 1990, after six years of government task forces, studies, green papers, press releases and draft legislation. The scope and impact of the pension legislation on Canadians is pervasive and, as a result, it is complex. Many of the Regulations relating to the legislation are very technical in nature and will not be dealt with in this text.

1. Objectives of pension reform

The objectives of pension reform were:

- to provide equal access to tax assistance regardless of the type of plan with which an individual funds his or her retirement;

- to provide flexibility in the pension system; and
- to tighten up the system to close both actual and perceived loopholes.

These objectives have been accomplished through the integration of limits for various types of pension plans with the limits for RRSPs.

In order to provide the same amount of tax assistance to an individual for retirement savings, regardless of whether the retirement is funded through a registered pension plan (RPP), a deferred profit sharing plan (DPSP) or an RRSP, under pension reform a comprehensive annual limit for tax-assisted retirement savings — 18% of earned income up to a maximum dollar limit of $18,000 — is phased in, reaching the maximum in 2006. The fairly generous contribution limits give individuals an incentive to provide for their retirement years.

2. Types of tax-assisted retirement plans

There are several basic types of pension plans, and the pension legislation attempts to equalize the tax assistance provided to an individual whether he or she earns retirement income through a defined-benefit registered pension plan (DBP), a money-purchase registered pension plan (MPP), a DPSP, or an RRSP.

(a) Defined-Benefit Registered Pension Plans

Under a DBP, *the benefit that is to be paid* to each employee *is defined* usually in regard to a certain percentage of an employee's earnings in the last few years of employment, regardless of the cost to the employer or the earnings experience of the plan. The benefit that is tax-assisted is limited to a maximum. The employer contributions are deductible, provided that they are certified by an actuary to be necessary to fund the accruing benefits of the plan as registered with the CRA. The employee contributions are deductible, subject to a maximum.

The maximum tax-assisted benefit that may be provided to an individual under a defined-benefit registered pension plan is 2% per year of the individual's average best 3 years of remuneration times the number of years of pensionable service, with a dollar limit of $60,278 before 2004. This amount had not changed since the early 1970s. The government assumed that this maximum amount was generous in that if an individual had pre-retirement earnings of $86,111, it would provide for a maximum tax-assisted pension of $60,278, or 70% of the individual's pre-retirement earnings. Assuming that the individual has 35 years of pensionable service, $86,111 × 2% = $1,722.22 per year, which buys a pension of $60,278, if expended annually over an effective period of 35 years. The maximum tax-assisted benefit that may be provided under a defined benefit pension plan increases to $1,833.33 in 2004 and $2,000 in 2005. Further increases are scheduled.

The following table summarizes this.

Year	Money Purchase Limit	Maximum Pension Per year of Service	Maximum Pension (35 yrs)	Employment Income Needed
2004	$16,500	$1,833	$64,155	$ 91,667
2005	$18,000	$2,000	$70,000	$100,000
2006	$19,000	$2,111	$73,885	$105,550
2007	$20,000	$2,222	$77,770	$111,100
2008	$21,000	$2,333	$81,665	$116,650
2009	$22,000	$2,444	$85,540	$122,200
2010	indexed	indexed	indexed	indexed

(b)   *Money-Purchase Registered Pension Plans*

Under an MPP, which is sometimes called a defined contribution plan, *the contribution*, that is required by the employer and the employee, *is defined* rather than the benefit. The retirement benefit for the individual is acquired through the purchase of an annuity on the open market with the contributions made to the plan plus the earnings generated from those contributions while they are held in the plan. The tax-assisted contributions of both employees and employers are limited to a maximum each year as indicated in Exhibit 9-1.

(c)   *Deferred Profit Sharing Plans*

Under this type of arrangement, only an employer may contribute a limited amount to a plan for the employee, which is based on the performance or the profits of the business. The funds must vest irrevocably in the employee after two years of employment, and the plan may invest in equity shares of the employer if they qualify.

(d)   *Registered Retirement Savings Plans*

Basically, an RRSP is a tax shelter provided under the Act to give an individual an incentive to save money for his or her retirement years. Within certain limits, the individual can claim tax deductions for contributions to his or her own RRSP, or a spousal RRSP. Since income can accumulate in the plan on a pre-tax basis, RRSPs can play an important part in an individual's overall retirement and tax planning.

If funds are withdrawn from an RRSP prior to maturity, the proceeds are subject to tax when received. If an RRSP is held until maturity, the accumulated RRSP funds may be received as a lump sum, in which case the funds are included in the individual's income and taxed at his or her marginal rate in the year received. Alternatively, the funds may be used to purchase a retirement annuity or may be transferred to a registered retirement income fund (RRIF). Both of these options would defer the receipt of the funds and, consequently, would defer tax on these funds until received in the form of retirement income. Tax savings will be realized if the funds are received and taxed in years when the individual's marginal tax rate is lower than in his or her pre-retirement years. The effect of the deferral of tax on income accumulating within the shelter can even offset the effect of a higher marginal tax rate on retirement income, making the RRSP shelter very attractive to most investors.

Technically, an RRSP is a contract, accepted for registration by the Minister of National Revenue, between an individual (the annuitant) and an entity that is authorized to carry on the business of selling such contracts (the carrier). RRSPs are available from banks, trust companies, life insurance companies, credit unions, caisses populaires, mutual funds and stockbrokerage firms.

3.   Types of RRSPs

In general, the RRSPs available may be categorized into three types, all of which are of a money-purchase nature:

- life insurance company plans;
- other financial institution plans; and
- self-administered plans.

(a)   *Life Insurance Company Plans*

Life insurance companies are currently the only kind of financial institution permitted to offer deferred life annuities. Deferred annuities accumulate funds on behalf of the policy owner until maturity, at which time the annuity is converted into income.

Some deferred annuities have guaranteed rates of interest for specified terms and others are invested in segregated funds or mutual funds which are professionally managed by the insurance company. Some companies also offer RRSPs with a life insurance component, in which case only the RRSP or savings portion of the total premium is tax deductible. In certain provinces and in specified circumstances, insurance company RRSPs are protected against creditors.

(b) *Other Financial Institution Plans*

Other financial institutions, such as banks, trust companies or credit unions, sponsor plans which are invested in savings deposits, term deposits and guaranteed investment certificates (GICs). They also offer plans which are invested in mutual funds or pooled fund trusts. These funds may be invested in mortgages, bonds, equities, money market instruments or a combination thereof. Some specialized funds are invested in high-risk investments providing venture capital. Others are invested in specific segments of the economy. Although one can select the type of fund for one's RRSP, the underlying investments are selected by the fund manager. Typically, investment management charges are levied against the underlying investment funds rather than the RRSP. However, sales or redemption charges may be applied against the RRSP on purchases or sales of units in the fund.

(c) *Self-administered Plans*

A self-administered RRSP can be set up with most financial institutions or a stock broker. A trustee will hold and administer the RRSP investments, but the individual can select investments or, if desired, an investment adviser can do it.

A self-administered RRSP can be invested in a wide variety of qualified investments, including publicly-traded debt and equity securities, as well as publicly-traded warrants or rights to acquire qualified investments. It can also be invested in certain mutual funds, mortgages, Canada Savings Bonds, treasury bills, and strip coupon bonds and certificates.

Often, administration fees are paid by a taxpayer in respect of a self-administered RRSP (or RRIF, as discussed subsequently). Investment counselling fees may, also, be paid in respect of property in these retirement shelters. However, no amount is deductible by a taxpayer in respect of payments made for services pertaining to these sheltered plans [par. 18(1)(*u*)].

4. **Integration of limits**

In order to provide the same amount of tax assistance to an individual for retirement savings, regardless of whether it is funded through an RPP, a DPSP, an RRSP or a combination thereof, a comprehensive annual limit for tax-assisted retirement savings is being phased in.

This comprehensive annual limit is determined using certain key assumptions with respect to retirement savings.

First, the maximum amount of tax-assisted retirement savings that the government is willing to fund through tax assistance for each individual is $70,000 in 2005. That amount was derived as $2\frac{1}{2}$ times the average wage at the time that the $70,000 was determined. Second, it is assumed actuarially that $9 of contributions buys $1 of annual pension income.

Under a DBP, an individual generally must have a combined pension contribution of $2,000 a year over the equivalent of 35 years to pay out the 2005 maximum pension of $70,000, and so at the maximum it will be possible to make combined employer/employee contributions equal to the lesser of 18% of the individual's compensation from the employer for the year, or $18,000 ($2,000 × 9) a year.

Under an MPP, tax-assisted contributions at the maximum may equal the lesser of 18% (9 × 2%) of earnings or $18,000 per year (total contributions made by the employer and employee) and should result in an accumulation of funds in the plan of up to $70,000 of 2005 pension income, generally, after the equivalent of 35 years. The cap of $18,000 for 2005 limits the amount of pensionable earnings that may receive tax assistance to $100,000 (18% of $100,000 is $18,000).

Under a DPSP, the maximum contribution limit is the lesser of 18% of earnings and 50% of $18,000 for 2005, since only the employer may make contributions. This lower limit will leave more contribution room for the individual to make a deductible RRSP contribution.

To integrate the tax assistance provided to individuals who fund their retirement savings with a combination of RRSPs, pension plans and deferred profit-sharing plans, the RRSP contribution limit, when the phase-in period is over, will be 18% of earned income for the *prior* year to a 2005 maximum of $18,000, plus or minus any adjustments for benefits provided to the individual under an RPP or a DPSP in the *prior* year.

5. Contribution limits for RRSPs

Using these assumptions, and starting with a phase-in period ending in 2005, a system has been put in place to determine an individual's RRSP deduction limit and RRSP dollar limit. These limits are defined in subsection 146(1) and are described in Exhibit 9-1.

Employers are to report the Pension Adjustment (PA) (a measure of the pension benefits an employee is entitled to under an RPP and/or a DPSP) on an employee's T4 slip on or before February 28th of the year following the year in which the benefits accrued. From February to August of that year, the CRA will use the PA reported by the employer plus the prior year's earned income as calculated from the individual's personal tax return to create a pension account for each individual. The CRA will then provide an RRSP contribution limit statement with the taxpayer's Notice of Assessment for the tax return filed. For example, the Notice of Assessment for a taxpayer's 2004 tax return filed by April 30, 2005 will contain a calculation of the RRSP contribution limit for 2005.

According to subsection 146(5), an individual may contribute to an RRSP at any time up to and including 60 days after the year-end, or, for example, until March 1, 2006 in order to claim an RRSP deduction on his or her 2005 tax return. The CRA will check the deduction against its pension file to determine if the RRSP contribution is deductible.

An added advantage of the system is that if an individual is not able to contribute the maximum amount to an RRSP, he or she is allowed to "carry forward" any unused deduction limit. There is no time restriction on the carryforward of an individual's unused RRSP deduction room. This feature is discussed in more detail subsequently.

If funds are borrowed to make contributions to an RRSP (or an RPP or DPSP), interest on the borrowed funds is not deductible [ssec. 18(11)]. The reason for this denial of an interest deduction is probably that the income from the investments in the sheltered retirement plans is not taxed as long as it remains in the plan.

The annual deduction limits for 2004 to 2011 are outlined in Exhibit 9-1.

EXHIBIT 9-1
2004–2011 Annual RRSP Deduction and Dollar Limits
[ssec. 146(1)]

If the individual is:	The annual contribution limit for 2004–2011 is:
• a member of an RPP or a DPSP,	(A) the individual's unused RRSP deduction room carried forward from the previous year*
	plus
	(B) the lesser of:
	(i) the RRSP dollar limit
	— for 2004, $15,500,
	— for 2005, $16,500,
	— for 2006, $18,000
	— for 2007, $19,000
	— for 2008, $20,000
	— for 2009, $21,000
	— for 2010, $22,000
	— for 2011, indexed
	and
	(ii) 18% of earned income for the prior year
	minus
	(C) the pension adjustment for the prior year reported to the CRA by the individual's employer and any past service pension adjustment reported by his or her employer during that particular year.
• a self-employed individual or an individual not described above,	(A) the individual's unused RRSP deduction room carried forward from the previous year*
	plus
	(B) the lesser of:
	(i) the RRSP dollar limit
	— for 2004, $15,500,
	— for 2005, $16,500,
	— for 2006, $18,000
	— for 2007, $19,000
	— for 2008, $20,000
	— for 2009, $21,000
	— for 2010, $22,000
	— for 2011, indexed
	and
	(ii) 18% of earned income for the prior year.

*There cannot be unused RRSP deduction room carried forward from a year prior to 1991.

EXHIBIT 9-2
RPP and RRSP Limits

	2004	2005	2006	2007	2008	2009	2010	2011
RRSP								
RRSP Dollar Limit	$15,500	$16,500	$ 18,000	$ 19,000	$ 20,000	$ 21,000	$ 22,000	indexed
Earned income needed	$86,111	$91,667	$100,000	$105,550	$111,100	$116,650	$122,200	indexed
RPP								
Money Purchase Limit	$16,500	$18,000	$ 19,000	$ 20,000	$ 21,000	$ 22,000	indexed	indexed
Defined benefit maximum	$ 1,833	$ 2,000	$ 2,111	$ 2,222	$ 2,333	$ 2,444	indexed	indexed
Maximum pension	$64,167	$70,000	$ 73,885	$ 77,770	$ 81,655	$ 85,540	indexed	indexed

6. Definition of earned income for RRSPs

If an individual was a resident of Canada throughout the year, earned income, as defined [ssec. 146(1)], will include the individual's income for a period in the year throughout which the individual was a resident in Canada from:

- an office or employment, generally including all taxable benefits, less all employment-related deductions, but not including any deduction for RPP contributions, employee contributions to a retirement compensation arrangement (RCA) or a clergyman's residence;

- a business carried on by the individual either alone, or as a partner actively engaged in the business;

- property, when derived from the rental of real property or from royalties in respect of a work or invention of which the individual was the author or inventor;

- support payments included in computing the individual's income;

- an amount included in income from supplementary unemployment benefit plans, net research grants, and support receipts in computing the individual's income; and

- the amount of disability pension received after 1990 by an individual under the Canada or Quebec Pension Plan;

less the total of the individual's loss or deduction for a period in the year throughout which the individual was resident in Canada from:

- a business carried on by the individual either alone, or as a partner actively engaged in the business;

- property, where the loss is sustained from the rental of real property; and

- support payments deductible in computing the individual's income.

For the purposes of determining the earned income of such an individual, the income or loss of the individual for any period in a taxation year is the individual's income or loss computed as though that period were the whole taxation year.

Note that earned income does not include superannuation or pension benefits (including CPP/QPP and OAS benefits), retiring allowances, Employment Insurance benefits, death benefits, amounts received from an RRSP or taxable benefits from a DPSP or a revoked plan. It also does not include investment income, taxable capital gains, or scholarships and bursaries.

Also note that it is the earned income of the preceding year which is relevant for purposes of calculating the maximum deductible RRSP contribution.

7. Calculation of the pension adjustment (PA)

Since an individual's pension adjustment is reported to the individual by his or her employer on a T4 slip, in most cases it will not be necessary for the individual to calculate his or her PA. To do some advance tax planning for an individual, it may be necessary to get a rough idea of what the individual's PA will be for future years. Conceptually, the PA represents the value of tax-assisted or sheltered benefits accruing to the taxpayer in a year. Hence, it reflects the amount of the dollar limit that has been used by employer and employee contributions to an RPP and/or DPSP, leaving the balance of the dollar limit available for a deductible RRSP contribution.

For example, if an individual's earned income is $72,000 and PA is $11,960, that individual's RRSP contribution would be limited to:

18% of earned income (18% of $72,000)	$12,960
Less: PA	11,960
Net limit for RRSP	$ 1,000

The following provides a non-technical indication of how the PA is determined.

(1) *PA for DBP:* The PA for a DBP is based on a formula which reflects the actuarial assumptions made about contributions providing pension income. The objective of the formula is to quantify the contribution room used by contributions to an RPP. The formula is beyond the scope of this text.

(2) *PA for MPP:* The PA for an MPP is equal to the total of the employer's and the employee's contributions in the year.

(3) *PA for DPSP:* The PA for a DPSP is equal to the employer's contributions in the year.

8. RRSP contribution room carried forward

An advantage of the system is that if an individual is not able to contribute the maximum amount, he or she is allowed to "carry forward" the unused deduction limit. There is no time restriction on this carryforward. The "unused RRSP deduction room" is defined in subsection 146(1). For example, if an individual's maximum annual RRSP contribution limit in 1997 is $10,000, but he or she made a contribution of only $7,000, he or she will be permitted to make an additional deductible RRSP contribution of $3,000 at any time in the future. However, even if he or she makes up the contribution in, for example, 2005, remember that he or she will lose the tax-sheltering on the income that would have been earned on the $3,000 from 1997 until 2005, and on any future income earned on this amount for the balance of his or her career. Therefore, it is important to contribute the maximum to an RRSP as soon as possible.

9. Excess contribution

(a) *Penalties for Excess Contributions*

The penalty provisions for RRSP overcontributions are fairly severe. There is a 1% per month penalty until the "excess" for the year is removed from the plan [ssec. 204.1(2.1)].

In determining whether there is an excess, the individual includes all amounts contributed by the individual to the plan (other than specified transfers) and all gifts made to the plan, other than gifts made by the individual's spouse. Overcontributions of premiums in the 60-day grace period after the end of the year usually are not considered to be part of the "excess", since the individual can claim them in the year or in the following year.

In order to avoid the 1% per month penalty, the excess amount may be withdrawn from the plan, but it will be included in the individual's income in the year of receipt [ssec. 146(8)]. This income can be reduced by an offsetting deduction if it is withdrawn in the year in which the excess was contributed or in the following year [ssec. 146(8.2)]. The withdrawal of contributions on a tax-free basis is allowed only where the taxpayer is not deliberately making excess contributions.

If the excess is not withdrawn in those particular years, but is instead left in the plan, then the individual will include in income this excess contribution when it is eventually withdrawn and there will be no offsetting deduction, resulting in double taxation. It is, therefore, not advisable to leave an excess contribution in an RRSP, as benefits of tax-free compounding in the plan are unlikely to offset the combination of the 1% per month penalty and the double taxation on withdrawal.

(b) *Additional Contribution*

There is a threshold amount for an excess contribution, which has been set at a cumulative amount of $2,000 [ssec. 204.2(1.1)]. This means that at any point in time[d] an individual may contribute up to $2,000 in excess of his or her deductible contribution limit without incurring a penalty. The purpose of this excess allowance is to provide a margin of error for inadvertent excess contributions and for the operation of group RRSP arrangements. In a family context, both spouses [or common-law partners] may contribute an additional $2,000, so that in total $4,000 may be sheltered without penalty. Children who did not attain the age of 18 in the previous year may not make this additional contribution [ssec. 204.2(1.1)]. Individuals who contribute to both their own RRSP and a spousal RRSP may not make an additional contribution of more than $2,000 in total.

Even though the individual will not be able to deduct the excess $2,000 contribution for tax purposes as would be the case if it was a regular RRSP contribution, a sum of money could be accumulated using the benefits of tax-free compounding. If, however, the individual makes a maximum deductible contribution every year, when the excess is eventually withdrawn the individual may be subject to double tax, as the funds were not deductible when the contribution was made, but they are taxable when the individual withdraws them. This double tax may be avoided, since the rules provide for an indefinite carryforward of undeducted contributions. If the individual simply reduces the contribution that he or she would otherwise make in a later year (prior to the withdrawal) and claims the additional $2,000 contribution as a deduction under the carryforward provisions, no double tax will result, because all contributions will have been fully deducted.

Even if the individual was not certain that he or she would use the carryforward rules to eliminate double taxation, it may still be advantageous to make additional contribution. Assuming a 10% rate of return and a 50% personal tax rate, if the individual leaves the $2,000 in the RRSP for 15 years or longer, the benefits of tax-free compounding will outweigh the cost of the taxes that must be paid when the funds are withdrawn.

All or part of an individual's additional $2,000 contribution can be made by the individual to a spousal RRSP, but care must be taken so that the spousal attribution rules (see below) and the regular attribution rules [ssec. 74.5(12)] do not apply.

10. Contributions of property

In addition to cash contributions, an individual may be able to contribute certain types of property, such as shares, units of a mutual fund, or Canada Savings Bonds, to an RRSP. The individual will generally need to have a self-administered RRSP if he or she wishes to make a non-cash contribution. If an individual contributes property, he or she is entitled to a deduction equal to the fair market value of the property at the time of the contribution, but keep in mind that the individual is still subject to the

---

[d] After February 26, 1995.

normal contribution limits and that the Act restricts the type of property that may be held in an RRSP.

The individual will be considered to have sold the property at its fair market value at the date of contribution. Although any resulting capital gain is subject to tax in the individual's hands, the individual cannot claim any capital loss that arises [spar. 40(2)(g)(iv)].

Example Problem ───

Mr. Confused reported the following income for tax purposes in 2004:

Employment income — Subdivision a	$81,000
Dividend received from taxable Canadian corporation (grossed up)	1,200
Rental loss...	(2,500)
Total...	$79,700

Included in the employment income computation was a deduction for a current contribution to a registered pension plan of $3,200. His employer reported a Pension Adjustment (PA) on his T4 for 2004 of $10,000. Mr. Confused made $5,000 of tax-deductible support payments to his former spouse in 2004.

—REQUIRED

Calculate the maximum RRSP contribution that Mr. Confused can deduct under paragraph 60(*i*), as determined under the definition of "RRSP deduction limit" in subsection 146(1), in respect of the 2005 taxation year and advise Mr. Confused as to when he can make his contribution. Is there any other advice that you might want to give Mr. Confused in 2005 regarding his contributions?

—SOLUTION

Mr. Confused's earned income for 2004 is calculated as follows:

Employment income — Subdivision a	$81,000
Add back RPP contribution	3,200
Deduct: Support payment made............................	(5,000)
Rental loss.......................................	(2,500)
Total earned income for 2004	$76,700

In respect of 2005, Mr. Confused is able to deduct the following:

Lesser of:

(a) 18% of 2004 earned income of $76,700 = $13,806, and

(b) the dollar limit for 2005 of $16,500

less PA for 2004 of $10,000 reported by his employer in respect of the year.

Mr. Confused is able to contribute $3,806 (i.e., $13,806 – $10,000) to his RRSP in respect of 2005. The contribution may be made at any time in 2005 and within the first 60 days of 2006, which is by March 1, 2006. However, Mr. Confused will probably have to wait until the end of February 2005 to make an early 2005 contribution, since he will not know his PA for 2004 until he receives his T4. If Mr. Confused was really cautious, he might want to wait until he receives his Notice of Assessment for his 2004 tax return in which the CRA will issue him a 2005 RRSP contribution limit statement. However, he will have lost the benefit of tax-free compounding on his contribution from March until he receives his Notice of Assessment and makes his contribution. You should inform him that if he has the information at hand respecting the pension benefits that he accrued in the year, you could assist him by calculating his PA and he could make his contribution on the first day of January in 2005.

You should also advise Mr. Confused that because of the way the penalties for an over-contribution work, he may make a one-time additional contribution of up to $2,000 in 2005 and the funds may be left to accumulate tax-free in his RRSP. Although this contribution is not tax-deductible, a sum of money can be built up over the life of his RRSP. This will be preferable to Mr. Confused investing in debt instruments or stocks outside of his RRSP, since the income will not be taxed. In order to avoid tax when Mr. Confused withdraws the $2,000 from his plan, he may be able to use the carryforward rules to his advantage by making a contribution that is $2,000 less than his allowable contribution in a year just prior to the withdrawal of the $2,000 from the plan. Then, he will have room to deduct the $2,000. Even if Mr. Confused is not able to use the carryforward rules to eliminate the tax when he withdraws the funds from the plan, if Mr. Confused is able to leave the additional $2,000 in the plan for a period of about 15 years, assuming that his rate of return on the funds was 10%, he would still be better off making the additional contribution.

11. Contributions to a spousal (or common-law partner) RRSP

A "spousal (or common-law partner) plan", which is a defined term [ssec. 146(1)], is a plan under which an individual makes contributions to an RRSP but his or her spouse (or common-law partner) is the annuitant. An individual's contributions to both his or her plan and a spousal (or common-law partner) RRSP are restricted in total to the individual's own contribution limit [ssec. 146(5.1)]. Therefore, a contribution made by an individual to a spousal (or common-law partner) RRSP does not affect the spouse's or common-law partner's personal RRSP contribution limit for the year.

A spousal RRSP could be set up for a common-law partner. Two individuals of either sex are considered to be common-law partners of each other when they are cohabiting in a conjugal relationship and either (a) they have so cohabited throughout the preceding 12 months, or (b) they are parents of the same child [ssec. 248(1): "common-law partner"].

A spousal (or common-law partner) RRSP can be used to achieve income splitting on retirement. Tax savings will be realized if the retirement income from the RRSP will be taxed at lower marginal tax rates in the spouse's or partner's hands. For example, assuming an individual intends to retire in 20 years and his or her RRSP earns a 10% annual rate of return, the individual could contribute $5,000 to a spousal (or common-law partner) RRSP for the next three years. At retirement, this would give the individual's spouse or partner a 15-year annuity of about $12,000 per year. If the spouse or partner will pay tax on this income at a marginal tax rate of about 26%, compared to about 46% in the individual's hands, the individual will realize annual tax savings of about $2,400 on this retirement income. To the extent that the contributions to a spousal (or common-law partner) RRSP exceed the individual's deductible limit, the income on withdrawal will be attributed back to the individual and will be subject to tax in his or her hands, because the non-deductible contribution would not meet the exception to the attribution rules [par. 74.5(12)(a)].

Provided an individual has earned income, contributions can be made to a spousal (or common-law partner) RRSP until the end of the year in which the spouse attains 69 years of age. These deductible contributions can be made even if the contributor is over 69.

There are other factors that an individual should consider when deciding whether to contribute to a spousal (or common-law partner) RRSP. The individual should be aware that amounts contributed to a spousal plan become the property of his or her spouse. This should be considered in view of any provincial laws governing the division of assets in the event of a marital breakdown.

12. Attribution on spousal (or common-law partner) RRSPs

An individual may contribute to a spousal (or common-law partner) RRSP to gain some benefit from income-splitting. However, special rules apply to curtail such income-splitting if the RRSP is used for short-term income splitting.

Attribution applies to include in the contributing individual's income all premiums paid to any spousal (or common-law partner) RRSP in a three-year period, even if the premiums are not deducted or deductible in the three years [ssec. 146(8.3)]. As a consequence, attribution will apply on withdrawal of the funds by the spouse if:

- the individual paid a premium to *any* spousal (or common-law partner) plan in the current year or the preceding two years; and
- the premium is required to be included in computing the income of the individual's spouse or common-law partner [ssec. 146(8)].

If such withdrawals are included in the spouse's or partner's income, the amount withdrawn, up to the amount of the premiums paid by the individual in the three-year period, will also be included in the individual's income. In order to eliminate double counting, if the income is attributed to the individual who made the contribution, an offsetting deduction is allowed to the spouse or common-law partner [ssec. 146(8.6)].

Similar rules apply where the individual's spouse or common-law partner receives an amount in excess of the minimum amount from an RRIF and the RRIF received property from an RRSP to which the individual paid a premium in the three-year period. The amount received by the individual's spouse or common-law partner in excess of the minimum amount will be included in the individual's income rather than the spouse's or partner's [ssec. 146.3(5.1)].

13. Withdrawals before retirement

An RRSP may generally be terminated at any time prior to maturity (generally retirement) and the proceeds distributed to the individual. However, the gross amount received must be included in his or her income. Of course, the benefit of a tax-free accumulation of funds will be lost. An individual may make partial withdrawals from an RRSP without terminating the plan.

The trustee of the RRSP must withhold tax from the amount withdrawn by the individual. The tax withheld may be claimed as a credit on the individual's income tax return as income taxes paid in the year. The withholding tax rate is based on the amount withdrawn — 10% of the amount if it is $5,000 or less; 20% of the amount if it is between $5,000 and $15,000; and 30% of the amount if it exceeds $15,000, except in Quebec [Regs. 103(4) and (6)].

Tax withheld at source from RRSP withdrawals may be minimized by making sure that each withdrawal is for $5,000 or less. Any tax liability related to the withdrawal in excess of the amount withheld must be paid when the individual files his or her tax return for the year.

14. Home Buyers' Plan (HBP)

Under the Home Buyers' Plan [sec. 146.01], individuals may withdraw up to an aggregate of $20,000 from any of their RRSPs to buy an owner-occupied home without having to pay tax on the withdrawal. Form T1036 must be used to report the withdrawal and to get the exclusion from income. These withdrawals must be repaid in annual instalments over a maximum period of 15 years. The repayment period begins in the second calendar year following the calendar year in which the withdrawal is made. However, the individual may elect to have a repayment made in the first 60 days of a year treated as having been made in the preceding year. Hence, if $20,000 is withdrawn in 2005, the minimum annual repayment of $1,333 (i.e., $20,000/15) must be made on or before March 1, 2008, being 60 days after 2007 which is the second calendar year after the 2005 year of withdrawal.

A qualifying home must generally be acquired before October 1 of the calendar year following the year of the withdrawal. Under specified conditions, this acquisition deadline can be extended. Only a first-time home buyer may make use of this plan. An individual will be considered to be a first-time home buyer, if neither the individual nor the individual's spouse or common-law partner owned a home and lived in it as the "principal place of residence" in any of the five calendar years beginning before the time of withdrawal. An individual is excepted from this five-year requirement on the termination of the marriage or common-law relationship.

An individual is allowed to participate in an HBP more than once in his or her lifetime. However, the individual must have repaid all amounts previously withdrawn under the HBP before the beginning of the year in which he or she participates in a new HBP.

The first-time home buyer condition need not be met, also, under specific circumstances. The conditions are that:

(a) the individual is entitled to claim the disability tax credit [ssec. 118.3(1), as discussed in Chapter 10]; and

(b) the HBP withdrawal by the disabled individual or a related individual is to enable the disabled individual to acquire and live in a dwelling that is more accessible by the individual or that is better suited for the personal needs and care of the individual.

Ordinary contributions made to an RRSP within 90 days before a withdrawal will not be allowed as a deduction, except to the extent that the RRSP balance after the withdrawal is more than the amount of the contribution. Hence, an amount that is both contributed and withdrawn within the 90-day period will not be deductible as an RRSP contribution.

Any amount scheduled for repayment, but not repaid in the appropriate year will be included in the individual's income for the year. For example, if the minimum annual repayment is $1,333 and the individual only repays $1,000, the $333 will be included in income and subjected to tax. On the other hand, an individual may repay more than the minimum scheduled repayment for a year. In this case, there will be less to repay over the remainder of the 15-year period and the minimum annual repayments can, but need not, be reduced for subsequent years.

15. Tax-free RRSP withdrawals for lifelong learning plan (LLP)

Individuals are allowed to make tax-free withdrawals from their RRSPs for lifelong learning, effective January 1, 1999 [sec. 146.02]. The objective is to give taxpayers greater access to funds for retraining. Similar to the Home Buyers' Plan, individuals must repay the amount they withdraw over a fixed period of time.

A maximum of $10,000 per year can be withdrawn from an RRSP by an individual who is enrolled at a designated educational institution [ssec. 118.6(1)] in full-time training or higher education requiring not less than 10 hours per week on courses or work in the program for at least three consecutive months during the year. Students with disabilities qualify if engaged in part-time studies. Further withdrawals can be made for a period of up to four years, but total withdrawals cannot exceed $20,000. Also, contributions made within 90 days of a withdrawal are not eligible for tax-free withdrawal.

Amounts withdrawn are repayable in 10 equal annual instalments. The first repayment must be made at the earlier of:

(a) the year following the last year that the student was enrolled on a full-time basis, that is, where the student is not entitled to annual full-time education tax credits for at least three months in two consecutive years; or

(b) 60 days following the fifth year after the first withdrawal.

Repayments simply replenish, without interest, amounts withdrawn from the RRSP. Hence, these repayments are not deductible. If an amount is not repaid on time, it is included in the individual's income in that year.

Individuals may participate in this withdrawal program any number of times during their lifetime. However, no new withdrawals are permitted until all repayments from a previously started program have been made. Of course, while the funds are not in the RRSP, they are not earning sheltered income and there is no opportunity to replenish that income.

16. Retirement options

Although an RRSP must mature by the end of the year in which the individual reaches the age of 69, the individual does not have to wait until then to obtain retirement income from the RRSP. An RRSP can be matured at any time before the end of the year in which an individual reaches the age of 69. As an alternative, the individual can make withdrawals from the plan. This allows an individual the flexibility to take an early retirement should he or she so desire.

At maturity, the accumulated funds may be withdrawn from an RRSP. Tax must be paid at the individual's marginal tax rate on these funds. As an alternative, he or she may purchase one or a combination of available maturity options. These options provide an individual with retirement income in varying amounts over different periods of time. Tax is deferred until he or she actually receives retirement income.

Retirement options which are currently available are:

Fixed-term annuities	• provide benefits up to age 90, or if the spouse or common-law spouse is younger than the individual, and he or she so elects, until the spouse or common-law partner reaches age 90.
	• may provide fixed or fluctuating income.
Life annuities.....................	• provide benefits during the individual's life, or during the lives of the individual and his or her spouse or common-law partner.
	• may have a guaranteed pay-out option.
	• may provide fixed or fluctuating income.
Registered retirement income funds	• are essentially a continuation of an RRSP.
	• provide the individual with retirement income from the investment of the funds accumulated in a matured RRSP for the individual's life.

Under federal and provincial pension legislation, the proceeds of locked-in RRSPs that arise on the transfer of a lump-sum payment of vested benefits from an RPP must be used to purchase a life annuity or RRIF at retirement.

(a) *Considerations when Choosing an Option*

A number of factors should be considered when deciding which option or combination of options to choose upon maturity of an RRSP:

- the rate of return;
- current and future income needs;
- the tax that would be payable currently if an annuity or RRIF were not purchased to defer tax;
- the income stream that would result from a particular annuity or RRIF;
- the present age of the individual and that of his or her spouse or common-law partner;
- the extent to which the individual wants to personally manage his or her retirement income; and
- the size of the estate the individual wishes to leave to his or her beneficiaries.

(b) *Fixed-term and Life Annuities*

With a fixed-term annuity, all of the funds accumulated in an RRSP will be paid out over the term of the annuity. The monthly retirement income the individual receives will vary, depending on the interest rate the issuer anticipates earning on the funds. However, with a life annuity, the retirement income will also depend on the sex and age of the individual and the options he or she chooses to attach to the annuity. Retirement income is highest for a straight life annuity (i.e., payments cease upon death, even if this occurs shortly after purchasing the annuity). Retirement income is lower if a guaranteed pay-out or guaranteed term option is added. These options guarantee that a certain amount of funds will be paid out, or that funds will be paid for a specified number of years, regardless of when the individual dies.

When an annuity is purchased, the retirement income will be determined for the term of the annuity. Once the annuity is in place, no further involvement with regard to investment decisions is required on the individual's part. In addition, no adjustments in income occur if interest rates subsequently rise or fall.

17. RRIFs

Generally the following rules [sec. 146.3] apply.

- An RRIF may be established at any time before the end of the year in which the individual reaches the age of 69. Early retirement can therefore be accommodated by an RRIF.
- It is possible to have more than one RRIF at a time. As a result, several different RRIFs can be set up in order to diversify an RRIF portfolio.
- Although a minimum amount must be withdrawn each year, an individual may withdraw any amount in excess of this minimum.

The fact that an individual is able to withdraw any amount in excess of the minimum allows him or her to match cash needs in any given year. The minimum required withdrawal for ages under 79 is calculated as the value of the RRIF at the beginning of each year, divided by the quantity 90 less the age of the individual at the beginning of the year [Reg. 7308(3)]. Thus, in the first year of the RRIF, no amount need be withdrawn unless he or she so desires. In the second year, if the individual was 65 years old when the RRIF was established, he or she must withdraw at least $1/25$ of the value of the fund at the beginning of the year. The amount withdrawn in the year may be received in one lump-sum payment or periodically throughout the year (e.g., monthly), depending upon the terms of the RRIF. For ages after 78, the minimum amount is derived by multiplying the value of the RRIF at the beginning of the year by a prescribed factor for the age of the annuitant or the annuitant's spouse or common-law partner, if elected. The factors are contained in Regulation 7308.

Amounts withdrawn from an RRIF in excess of the minimum amount, however, will be subject to withholding tax at the same rates that are applicable to RRSP lump-sum withdrawals.

If an individual so elects at the commencement of the RRIF and his or her spouse or common-law partner is younger, the individual may have the minimum payment out of the RRIF based on the age of the spouse or common-law partner. This election does not automatically make the spouse or common-law partner the annuitant under the RRIF after the individual's death.

Generally, RRIF funds may be invested in the same types of investments as RRSPs. The RRIF may be self-administered. That is, an individual may personally determine, along with the trustees of the RRIF, what investments are made by it. As with an RRSP, an RRIF is not taxed on its earnings. Thus, income accumulates on a tax-free basis in the RRIF.

When choosing which investments to hold in an RRIF, an individual should consider the same factors that he or she would have considered in choosing investments for an RRSP. Liquidity is a particularly important factor when choosing investments to be held in an RRIF, since a portion of the funds must be withdrawn each year to provide retirement income.

18. Treatment of RRSPs and RRIFs on death

If the individual has an RRIF at the time of death, his or her spouse or common-law partner may continue to receive the income from the RRIF (become the annuitant under the RRIF) or receive a lump sum under the RRIF (become the beneficiary under the RRIF), provided that the individual specified that this was his or her intention, either in the RRIF contract or under the terms of his or her will.

If the spouse or common-law partner becomes the annuitant under the RRIF, payments may continue to be made to the spouse or partner, or to the estate for the benefit of the spouse or partner. If the spouse or partner becomes the beneficiary under the RRIF, the lump sum may be paid directly to him or her, or to an estate for the benefit of the spouse or partner. In the situation where the spouse or partner does not become the annuitant or the beneficiary under the RRIF, the RRIF must be collapsed and the value of the RRIF must be paid to any other named beneficiary or the individual's estate.

Amounts paid to a spouse or common-law partner as a named beneficiary from an RRSP (whether lump-sum or otherwise), or as an annuitant or beneficiary under an RRIF, will be taxable to the spouse or partner when received. Amounts paid from an RRSP to the individual's estate for the benefit of his or her spouse or partner will also be taxable to that spouse or partner, provided that the spouse or partner and the legal representatives of the estate file a joint tax election to this effect. If this election is not filed, the fair market value of all of the property of the RRSP fund at the time of his or her death will be included in the deceased's income for the year of death. If the individual intends to have his or her spouse or partner as beneficiary, it will generally be preferable for the individual to name the spouse or partner as beneficiary under the RRSP, rather than to file the election after death, in order to minimize probate fees. The election is made by filing T2019 (RRSP refunds of premiums designation — Spouse).

In the CRA's view, a similar election may not be available where an amount out of an RRIF is paid to an individual's estate for the benefit of his or her spouse or common-law partner. If the individual intends to have his or her spouse or partner as an annuitant or a beneficiary under the RRIF, the individual should name the spouse or partner as an annuitant or as a beneficiary under the contract or under the terms of the will, so that the RRIF amounts will not be included in the individual's income for the year of death.

Where amounts received out of an unmatured RRSP are taxed in the spouse's or partner's hands, he or she may defer tax on all or any portion of the amount by using the provisions of paragraph 60(*l*) to make either a direct or indirect transfer of the funds to an RRSP (if the spouse or partner is under the age of 69), an RRIF, or by purchasing a fixed-term or life annuity within 60 days after the taxation year of receipt.

Where the spouse or common-law partner is not the beneficiary, or the beneficiary or annuitant in the case of an RRIF, the proceeds from an RRIF, an unmatured RRSP or the commuted value of an RRSP annuity must be included in the individual's income for the year of death. An exception occurs in certain circumstances where the beneficiary is a financially dependent child or grandchild even if the deceased individual had a surviving spouse or partner when he or she died, if the proceeds are considered to be a "refund of premiums" as defined [ssec. 146(1)].

A child or grandchild is not considered financially dependent, if his or her income for the year preceding the year in which the annuitant died exceeded the basic personal credit amount ($8,148 in 2005) for that preceding year. This amount is increased by $6,596 to $14,744 if that child or grandchild is infirm.

In these circumstances, it is possible to have, or to elect [ssec. 146(8.1) or ssec. 146.3(6.1)] to have such proceeds taxed in the hands of the child or grandchild. The tax on such proceeds may be deferred by the deduction under paragraph 60(*l*). In the case where a dependent child or grandchild is mentally or physically infirm, tax may be deferred on such proceeds if either a direct or indirect transfer is made by the child or grandchild, or his or her representative, under paragraph 60(*l*) to an RRSP (if under the age of 69), an RRIF or an annuity within 60 days after the taxation year of receipt.

In the case where the child or grandchild is not physically or mentally infirm, tax may be deferred on such proceeds if they are used to acquire an annuity with a term not exceeding 18 minus the age of the child or grandchild at the time the annuity is acquired. The annuity must be acquired in the year the proceeds are included in the child or grandchild's income. In these cases, it will generally be preferable for the individual to name the child or grandchild as the beneficiary under the terms of the will.

If the individual names a person other than his or her spouse or common-law partner (or, in limited circumstances, a child or grandchild) as a beneficiary under the RRSP or as beneficiary or annuitant under the RRIF, the estate will be faced with paying any tax liability resulting from the individual's death, even though it may not have sufficient funds to do so because the proceeds have been paid to the named beneficiary.

If, at the time of death, the individual has not made an RRSP contribution for the year of death, his or her legal representative may make a spousal or common-law partner RRSP contribution under the normal rules. Such a contribution will be deductible in the year of death, provided the contribution is made within 60 days of the end of the year of death [ssec. 146(5.1)].

C. Transfers of Retirement Income and Sheltered Amounts

[ITA: 60(j.1); 146(16); 147(19), (20); 147.3]

In general, lump-sum amounts of retirement income can be transferred on a tax-free basis, but only where the amounts are transferred directly from one plan to another [sec. 147.3]. When amounts are transferred directly, they generally are not included in income and consequently it is not necessary to claim an offsetting deduction.

The rollover of periodic pension income out of an RPP, DPSP, Old Age Security (OAS) and Canada Pension/Quebec Pension Plan (CPP/QPP) is generally prohibited. Restrictions are also placed on the amounts that may be transferred from defined benefit RPPs to money purchase RPPs and RRSPs. The result is to restrict the opportunity for individuals to obtain further tax deferral on receipts of periodic pension income.

1. Direct transfer

Lump-sum RPP and DPSP amounts are transferable on a tax-free basis, but *only through a direct transfer* for:

- lump-sum amounts out of RPPs (other than lump-sum amounts that relate to an actuarial surplus) to another RPP or to an RRSP under which the individual is an annuitant [sec. 147.3];

- lump-sum amounts of DPSPs to an RPP, an RRSP or to certain DPSPs [ssecs. 147(19) and (20)]; and

- property from an unmatured RRSP to an RPP, to another RRSP or to an RRIF [ssec. 146(16)].

When such direct transfers are made, the amount transferred is not included in income, and does not give rise to a deduction. If, however, the individual receives the funds personally, the amount will be included in his or her income for tax purposes in the year it is received and the individual will not be able to contribute the funds (i.e., transfer them indirectly) to his or her RRSP to avoid the income inclusion.

Unlimited lump-sum transfers may be made directly from one MPP to another, from an MPP to a DBP, from a DBP to another DBP, but transfers from a DBP to an MPP or RRSP are limited to prescribed amounts.

2. Retiring allowances

Retiring allowances may be transferred tax-free, within certain dollar and time limits, to an RRSP or an RPP. A retiring allowance is defined [ssec. 248(1)] to be an amount received (other than a superannuation or pension benefit, an amount received as a consequence of the death of an employee or employment benefits derived from certain specified counselling services) [spar. 6(1)(a)(iv)]:

(a) upon or after retirement of an individual from an office or employment in recognition of his or her long service, or

(b) in respect of a loss of an office or employment of an individual, whether or not received as, on account or in lieu of payment of damages or pursuant to an order or judgment of a competent tribunal

by the individual or, after his or her death, by a dependant or relation of the individual or by the legal representative of the individual.

The rollover of a retiring allowance to an RRSP or an RPP may be made [par. 60(j.1)] within the following limits:

- $2,000 for each year or part thereof during which the individual was employed by the employer or related employer with respect to service before 1996;

plus

- $1,500 for each year or part year of service counted for the $2,000 limit prior to 1989 for which the employer RPP and DPSP contribution did not vest at the time of retirement.

The $1,500 limit is technically computed as the number of pre-1989 years or part years of employment in excess of the equivalent number of pre-1989 years in respect of which employer contributions had vested. The use of the term "equivalent number of years" allows for a fractional number of years to be used, when, to use the example presented in explanatory notes, an employee has worked seven pre-89 years and 60% of the employer's contributions have vested. In that case, the non-vested years would be counted as 2.8 years (i.e., 7 years − 60% of 7 years) and, hence, at $1,500 per non-vested years, $4,200 (i.e., 2.8 × $1,500) could be deducted on a transfer of a retiring allowance.

The amount that may be deducted may not exceed the total of the amounts paid by the individual in the year or in the 60 days after the end of the year as a contribution to an RPP. Excluded from that limit are amounts deductible: (1) under paragraph 8(1)(*m*) (contributions to an RPP), and (2) as a premium to an RRSP under which he or she is the annuitant, other than the portion that has been designated for the purposes of paragraph 60(*l*) (as a transfer of a refund of premiums to a spouse or child as a consequence of death or for certain direct transfers of amounts out of an RRIF or an RRSP).

The following is a *simplified* formula for the deductible amount of a retiring allowance transferred to an RRSP. The deductible transfer cannot exceed the least of:

(a) the sum of:

    (i) $2,000 × the number of pre-'96 years during which the individual was employed (as described above) xxx

    (ii) $1,500 × the equivalent number of non-vested pre-89 years (as described above)... xxx

                                                                                                                                                                                xxx

(b)* total RRSP premium contributions xxx

(c) the amount of the retiring allowance xxx

---

*Item (b), in the actual legislation, consists of total RRSP contributions and non-deductible RPP contributions made by the employee. However, it would be unusual for an employee to have made a non-deductible RPP contribution under the current legislation (unless past service contributions were made) and, as a result, that part of the rule has been omitted for simplicity.

The limit in part (b) above reflects the fact that an individual cannot deduct more than the amount actually transferred or contributed into a sheltered plan.

Example Problem

Consider the following facts:

Retiring allowance received by I. Wasfired in 2005	$30,000
Earned income in 2004	66,000
PA reported by employer in 2004	10,880
Number of pre-'96 years during which he was employed since November of 1984...	12
Percentage of vesting for pre-1989 years of service	60%

— REQUIRED

Determine the amount that I. Wasfired is able to deduct under paragraph 60(*j*.1) if he transfers the maximum he can to his RRSP.

— SOLUTION

I. Wasfired is only able to contribute $27,000 under paragraph 60(*j*.1) to his RRSP without overcontributing to the plan in 2005, determined as:

Sum of $2,000 × 12^1 =..	$24,000
$1,500 × 2^2 =..	3,000
Total..	$27,000

I. Wasfired may deduct a $27,000 transfer in respect of his $30,000 retiring allowance to an RRSP, plus his annual contribution for 2005.

— NOTES TO SOLUTION

(1) Since the legislation only refers to years, not full years, it is reasonable to assume part years would qualify.

(2) In the five pre-1989 years (i.e., 1984 to 1988, inclusive) during which the taxpayer was employed, 60% of the employer's contributions vested. Therefore, the equivalent non-vested years would be counted as two years (i.e., 5 years − 60% of 5 years) and, hence, an additional $1,500 may be deducted in respect of each of those two equivalent non-vested years.

D. Overpayments and Other Deductions

[ITA: 60(*n*), (*o*), (*o*.1), (*q*), (*v*.1), (*w*); 180.2]

The Act permits the deduction of certain overpayments of receipts which have already been included in income, but to which the taxpayer was not entitled, and, hence, must repay (e.g., pension benefits, unemployment insurance and education assistance payments [pars. 60(*n*), (*q*) and (*v*.1)]).

Also, deductible are amounts paid in the year in respect of fees or expenses incurred in an objection or appeal under the Act and other specified legislation [par. 60(*o*)]. The expenditures that are deductible could include accounting fees incurred in the preparation of an objection or appeal as well as legal costs.

Legal expenses paid by the taxpayer to collect or establish a right to a retiring allowance or pension benefits are deductible [par. 60(*o*.1)]. The deduction of legal expenses is limited to the amount of retiring allowance or pension benefits at issue, net of any transfers to an RRSP or RPP under paragraph 60(*j*.1). Excess legal expenses can be carried forward seven years to be deducted against related retiring allowance or pension benefits in those years.

Paragraph 60(*w*) permits a deduction for the amount of Old Age Security (OAS) benefits that a taxpayer must repay under the clawback provision of the Act [sec. 180.2]. Where an individual's income under Division B, before deducting the clawback under paragraph 60(*w*), exceeds $60,806 in 2005, all or some part of the Old Age Security benefits are taxed back. The amount of repayment is computed as:

The lesser of:		
(a) OAS benefits		$xxx
(b) income under Division B without par. 60(*w*) deduction	$ xxx	
Less:	60,806	
Excess, if any.......................................	$ xxx	
15% of excess, if any		$xxx

OAS benefits are currently about $5,700 per year. Therefore, a Division B income of $65,000 (before the paragraph 60(w) deduction) would result in a clawback of $629 (i.e., 15% of ($65,000 − $60,806)). Since $629 of the benefits must be repaid as a Part I.2 tax, the clawback is allowed as a deduction [par. 60(w)]. In essence, the deduction equates net income effects with cash effects as follows:

	Income effect	Cash effect
Receipt [par. 56(1)(a)]	$ 5,700	$ 5,700
Clawback [par. 60(w)]	(629)	(629) (Part I.2 tax)
Net effect	$ 5,071	$ 5,071

E. Moving Expenses

[ITA: 62; IT-178R3]

Taxpayers are permitted to deduct the moving expenses [ssec. 62(3)] in respect of an eligible relocation [ssec. 248(1)] under certain prescribed limitations imposed by the Act.

These deductible expenses include:

(a) reasonable travelling costs in moving the family members to the new residence;

(b) transporting or storing household effects;

(c) the cost of meals and accommodation near the old residence or an acquired new residence for a period not exceeding 15 days;

(d) lease cancellation costs in respect of the old residence;

(e) selling costs of the old residence;

(f) the cost of legal services, transfer taxes or registration taxes, but not goods and services tax, in respect of the new residence but only where the old residence is being sold;

(g) mortgage interest, property taxes, insurance premiums and costs associated with maintaining heat and power, to a maximum of $5,000, payable in respect of a vacant "old residence" for a period during which reasonable efforts are being made to sell the "old residence"; and

(h) the cost of revising legal documents to reflect the taxpayer's new address, replacing driving licences and automobile permits and obtaining utility connections and disconnections.

Note that selling costs of the old residence may be deducted as moving costs or as selling costs for capital gains purposes.

By administrative CRA practice, taxpayers may choose a simplified method to calculate certain travel expenses for moving. Instead of substantiating actual expenses by receipts, the taxpayer may use various pre-established flat rates. Individuals may claim a flat rate of $15 a meal, to a maximum of $45 per day, per person, without receipts. An individual may determine the deduction for vehicle expenses by multiplying the number of kilometres driven by the flat rate in the following list for the province or territory from which travel begins:

Province or Territory	2004 Cents/km*
Alberta	43.5
British Columbia	43.0
Manitoba	40.5
New Brunswick	43.5
Newfoundland and Labrador	47.5
Northwest Territories	49.0

Nova Scotia	44.0
Nunavut	49.0
Ontario	45.5
Prince Edward Island	44.0
Quebec	47.5
Saskatchewan	40.0
Yukon	50.5

*www.cra.gc.ca/travelcosts

Vehicle expenses covered by the flat rate include operating and ownership expenses as follows:

- operating expenses: fuel, oil, tires, licence fees, insurance, maintenance and repairs

- ownership expenses: depreciation, provincial tax and finance charges

There are two distinct categories of taxpayers contained in the definition of "eligible relocation" [ssec. 248(1)]:

(a) taxpayers who move to a new business or employment location in Canada may deduct their moving expenses from their income in that new work location; or

(b) students who move to attend a post-secondary institution on a full-time basis either in or out of Canada [ssec. 62(2)] may deduct their moving expenses from scholarship income.

There are a number of specific limitations imposed upon the above two groups of taxpayers. The following are the most important:

(a) the taxpayer must move 40 kilometres (measured by the shortest normal route available to the travelling public)[e] closer to his or her new work location or post-secondary institution;

(b) moving expenses, which exceed the income from the new work location in the year of move, can be deducted, but only in the following year, against income from that new work location; and

(c) the taxpayer cannot be reimbursed by or be in receipt of an allowance from his or her employer for the moving expenses he or she is claiming, unless the reimbursement or allowance is included in income.

The income limitation on moving expenses [par. 62(1)(c)] may not be clear in its application to the situation of an individual who fits both categories of taxpayer recognized in paragraph (a) of the definition of "eligible relocation" [ssec. 248(1)]. For example, a full-time student who moves to a university over 40 kilometres away may have both scholarship income and part-time employment income in the new location. Paragraph 62(1)(c) limits the *aggregate* of moving expenses,

(a) in the case of an employee or self-employed individual, to income from employment or business in the new location, *and*

(b) in the case of a full-time student, to income from a scholarship or research grant.

The use of the word "and" between cases (a) and (b) above may allow a deduction of moving expenses from the sum of both categories of income in the case of the student, as presented. IT-178R3 does not address the issue directly. The Bulletin deals with the two cases separately in paragraphs 2(*d*) and 10(*c*), but does not comment on a

---

[e] The case of *Giannakopoulos v. The Queen*, (F.C.A.) 95 DTC 5477, appears to have established this method of measurement of the 40 kilometres.

situation involving a combination of the two categories of income for a student. The authorized form T1-M and the accompanying information are not entirely clear either.

Also it appears that the actual move does not have to be accomplished in the same year as the change in the work location.[f]

F. Child Care Expenses

[ITA: 63; IT-495R3]

Child care expenses are permitted to be deducted in the same year that the taxpayer incurs these expenses in the process of earning income. Note that these provisions restrict the deduction to the parent or supporting individual with the lower income, except during a period where that individual is:

- a student in full-time [par. 63(2)(b), clause (i)(A) of factor C] or part-time [par. 63(2)(b), par. (ii) of factor C] attendance at a designated educational institution or a secondary school in Canada;

- infirm and incapable of caring for children for at least two weeks [par. 63(2)(b), clause (i)(B) of factor C];

- confined to prison for at least two weeks [par. 63(2)(b), clause (i)(C) of factor C]; or

- living apart from the higher-income taxpayer throughout a period of at least 90 days commencing in the year due to a marital or common-law relationship breakdown [par. 63(2)(b), clause (i)(D) of factor C].

Income for this purpose is determined to be the income before the child care expense deduction and the deduction in paragraph 60(w) for the clawback of certain social assistance payments [ssec. 63(2)]. Where the incomes of two taxpayers are equal, the individuals must agree to treat the income of one of them as higher [ssec. 63(2.1)].

The case of *Fiset v. M.N.R.*, (T.C.C.) 88 DTC 1226, challenged successfully the above interpretation. In this particular situation, the Tax Court of Canada determined that since one spouse had no income and since nil is not an amount (of income), the provision could not be applied. However, section 3 was amended subsequently so that no income is zero amount, not nil. Therefore, a taxpayer with no income will have a zero "amount".

Another interesting judicial development involving child care expenses is the case of *Symes v. The Queen et al.*, (S.C.C.) 94 DTC 6001. In this case, the self-employed taxpayer claimed the expenses under subsection 9(1) and paragraph 18(1)(a) rather than section 63. The CRA had denied the expenses as personal living expenses [par. 18(1)(h)]. The taxpayer also argued that there was a violation of rights under subsection 15(1) of the *Charter of Rights and Freedoms*. The Supreme Court of Canada held that the language of section 63 specifically encompasses the purpose for which the taxpayer had incurred her nanny expenses. As a result, section 9 and paragraphs 18(1)(a) and (h) could not be interpreted to permit her a child care business expense deduction. Furthermore, the taxpayer failed to show that women disproportionately pay child care expenses, to prove that section 63 violates subsection 15(1) of the Charter. The taxpayer's evidence showed only that women disproportionately bear the responsibility for caring for children in society.

There are several additional restrictions which should be noted:

(a) an eligible child [ssec. 63(3)] includes a child who turned 16 years of age during the year, since he or she was "during the year" under 16 years of age;

---

[f] See *Beyette v. M.N.R.*, (T.C.C.) 89 DTC 701 for a decision on this issue.

(b) the payments cannot be made to certain individuals listed under paragraph *(b)* of the definition of "child care expense" in subsection 63(3), including persons under 18 years of age who are related to the taxpayer by blood, marriage or adoption [ssec. 251(6)] and a person claimed as a dependant [sec. 118];

(c) the maximum amount claimable for a child's attendance at a boarding school or camp is $175 (i.e., $1/40$ of $7,000) per week for each child under the age of seven at the end of the year or for a child who has a severe and prolonged mental or physical impairment and $100 (i.e., $1/40$ of $4,000) per week for any other eligible child. These rules are set out in paragraph *(c)* of the definition of "child care expense" and the definition of "periodic child care expense" in subsection 63(3);

(d) earned income, which is one of the limiting factors in determining the child care deduction, is defined very specifically [ssec. 63(3)] (note the difference between this definition and the "earned income" definition for a registered retirement savings plan in subsection 146(1)). Specifically, the definition of "salary or wages" [ssec. 248(1)] does not apply to section 63. This definition of earned income reflects the original purpose of the child care expense deduction provision which was to encourage individuals who had to care for young children to enter the workforce as employees, to carry on a business, to carry on research under a grant, or attend an educational institution to upgrade work skills and knowledge; and

(e) expenses must be substantiated by receipts bearing the social insurance number of the person performing the service [ssec. 63(1)].

The following formulae reflect the maximum child care deduction.

(a) The lower income spouse is restricted [ssec. 63(1)] to a deduction of the least of:

　(i) generally an amount paid in the year by the taxpayer or supporting person;[g]

　(ii) $4,000 for each eligible child seven years of age or older, $7,000 for each eligible child under age seven at the end of the year and $10,000 for each child who has a severe and prolonged mental or physical impairment [definition of "annual child care expense amount" in ssec. 63(3)]; and

　(iii) $2/3$ of the earned income of the taxpayer [par. 63(2.3)*(e)* as defined in subsection 63(3)

　minus the amount deducted by the higher-income spouse under part (b) below [par. 63(1)*(f)*].

(b) The higher income spouse, where the lower income taxpayer is a person described in clauses (i)(A) to (D) and subparagraph (ii) of the definition of factor C in the formula in paragraph 63(2)*(b)*, is restricted [ssec. 63(2)] to a deduction of the lesser of:

　(i) the least of (i)[h], (ii) and (iii) described in (a) above and computed using the earned income of the higher income supporting person; and

　(ii) the sum of:

　　(A) $250 (i.e., $1/40$ of $10,000) times the number of children who have a severe and prolonged mental or physical impairment,

---

[g] A supporting person is defined in subsection 63(3). However, where the taxpayer is the higher-income spouse, the payments made by a supporting person and deductible by the taxpayer are restricted to those payments made by a person living separate and apart from the taxpayer for a period of at least 90 days due to marital or common-law relationship breakdown [par. 63(1)*(a)* and spar. 63(2)*(b)*(vi)].

[h] Paragraph 63(1)*(c)* excludes, from part (a)(i) above, amounts used in computing a child care deduction of another individual.

        (B) $175 (i.e., $^1/_{40}$ of $7,000) times the number of children under seven years of age at the end of the year, and

        (C) $100 (i.e., $^1/_{40}$ of $4,000) times the number of other eligible children,

        times the number of weeks the lower income spouse was a person described in clauses (i)(A) to (D) and subparagraph (ii) of the definition of factor C in the formula in paragraph 63(2)(*b*).

    Clause (i)(A) of the definition of factor C in the formula in paragraph 63(2)(*b*) describes a full-time student, that is, one who is enrolled in a program of not less than three consecutive weeks duration that requires not less than 10 hours per week on courses or work. The dollar limit on the deduction that may be claimed by the working spouse when the other spouse is a part-time student, described in subparagraph (ii) of the definition of factor C, is, also, $175 (i.e., $^1/_{40}$ of $7,000) per child under age 7 and $100 (i.e., $^1/_{40}$ of $4,000) per child age 7 to 16. However in the case of a part-time student, the limit is computed for each month of studies. Months are counted where the part-time student is enrolled at an educational institution in Canada in an eligible program lasting at least three consecutive weeks and involving a minimum of 12 hours spent on courses each month.

    The legislation provides a child care expense deduction to single parents in full-time or part-time attendance at either a designated educational institution or a secondary school in Canada and to two-parent families when both parents are in full-time attendance in school at the same time [ssecs. 63(2.2) and (2.3)]. Full-time attendance is defined, for that purpose, as enrolment in a program of at least three consecutive weeks duration that requires the individual to spend at least 10 hours per week on courses or work in the program [spar. 63(2.2)(*a*)(i)]. Part-time attendance is defined as enrolment in a program of at least three consecutive weeks duration that requires the individual to spend not less than 12 hours per month on courses in the program [spar. 63(2.2)(*a*)(ii)]. The limits of the deduction are the amounts paid in respect of child care to a maximum of $250 (i.e., $^1/_{40}$ x $10,000) per week of attendance per child who has a severe and prolonged mental or physical infirmity, $175 (i.e., $^1/_{40}$ of $7,000) per week of attendance per child under 7 at the end of the year and $100 (i.e., $^1/_{40}$ of $4,000) per week of attendance per child over age 6 and under age 16 at any time during the year. The income limit for this deduction is based on all amounts included in computing the individual's Division B income for the year, not just earned income [par. 63(2.3)(*b*)].

Example Problem

    Efficacious and Useful Xiao are married. The cost of child care expenses for three eligible children (ages 4, 5 and 9) was $175 per week for 52 weeks.

Efficacious' earned income	$45,000
Useful's earned income	12,000

    Useful was determined to be physically infirm by a qualified medical practitioner and he was confined to bed for a period of 10 weeks.

— REQUIRED

Compute the child care expense deduction under section 63 for 2005.

— SOLUTION

    Since the lower-income spouse (Useful) is infirm and incapable of caring for children for at least two weeks in the year, it is possible for the higher-income spouse (Efficacious) to claim a deduction for part of the child care expenses as demonstrated below.

Efficacious' child care deduction is the lesser of:

(a) the least of:
  (i) an amount paid in the
      year ($175 × 52) ..... $ 9,100
  (ii) $7,000 × 2 children = $14,000
       $4,000 × 1 child =.... 4,000 $18,000 ....$9,100
  (iii) ⅔ × $45,000 =....... $30,000

(b) the sum of:
  (i) $175 × 2 children =...... $350
  (ii) $100 × 1 child =......... 100 $450 × 10 weeks = $4,500

Lesser amount: $4,500

Useful's child care deduction is the least of:
  (i) ($175 × 52 weeks) = ... $ 9,100
  (ii) ($7,000 × 2 children) + ($4,000 × 1 child)
       = ... $18,000 $8,000
  (iii) (⅔ × $12,000) = ... $ 8,000

minus the amount deducted by Spouse A 4,500

$3,500

Therefore, the sum of both spouses' claim ($4,500 + $3,500) is limited, in this case, to the $8,000 amount which is ⅔ of the lower income spouse's earned income. The computational format used above is similar to that found in form T778. The format simplifies the effect on the calculation of paragraph 63(1)(c) which might otherwise require that the amount used in part (a)(i) of Efficacious' deduction calculation be determined as the minimum amount after all other parts of the calculation, so that only the $4,500 amount actually deductible by Efficacious is shown in part (a)(i). This follows from a possible strict interpretation of paragraph 63(1)(c) which would not permit Useful to deduct an amount that is "included in computing the amount deductible" by Efficacious, in this case. Technically, the full $9,100 used in part (a)(i) of Efficacious's calculation was included in computing the amount deductible by Useful. The simplified calculation used in the example problem, above, arrives at the correct distribution between Efficacious and Useful and is apparently acceptable, as evidenced by the computational format used in the authorized form, T778.

G. Attendant Care Expenses [Disability Support Deduction]

[ITA: 64]

For 2004 and subsequent years, the attendant care expenses deduction found in section 64 is replaced by a disability support deduction. Disability support expenses incurred for purposes of employment or education are treated as attendant care expenses and are fully deductible from the disabled person's income. The deduction is subject to the attendant care deduction limit. The following services or equipment used by disabled persons qualify for the new deduction: sign-language interpretation services, real-time captioning services, teletypewriters, optical scanners and electronic speech synthesizers.

In addition, for 2004 and subsequent years the refundable medical expense supplement (RMES) includes 25% of the total of the allowable expenses claimed under the non-refundable medical expense tax credit and the new disability supports deduction. For details on this supplement, please refer to Chapter 10.

An individual, who has a specified impairment, such as speech, hearing, eyesight or learning or who has a severe and prolonged mental or physical impairment and who qualifies for the impairment credit in section 118.3, may deduct expenses paid to an unrelated attendant, who is at least 18 years of age, to enable the individual to work as an employee, carry on a business, carry on research, or attend a designated educational institution or a secondary school at which the individual is enrolled in an educational program. The deduction under section 64 is limited to the lesser of:

(a) the amount paid in the year to the attendant net of any reimbursement; and

(b) the sum of:

    (i) the total of:

        (A) employment income inclusions or the taxable portion of scholarships and bursaries or net research grants, or

        (B) income from business, and

    (ii) where the taxpayer is a student, the least of:

        (A) $15,000,

        (B) $375 times the number of weeks in the year during which the individual attends the institution or school, and

        (C) the amount by which the individual's total income exceeds the individual's earned income, that is items (A), (B) and (C) in (b)(i), above.

H. Expenses of Residents Absent from Canada

[ITA: 64.1]

Section 64.1 extends the deductibility of child care expenses under section 63 and attendant care expenses under section 64 to an individual who is absent from, but still resident in Canada. Such an individual, who is physically absent from Canada throughout all or some part of a taxation year, would otherwise be precluded from these deductions for expenditures made outside of Canada by the wording contained in sections 63 and 64. The addition of section 64.1 is an apparent reaction to the strict interpretation of sections 63 and 64 taken by the courts in cases involving members of the Canadian Armed Forces. The provision appears to be directed to individuals who are physically absent from Canada for most of a year, but are deemed to be resident [ssec. 250(1)]. However, the wording of the provision would also appear to apply to individuals who are considered to be resident by the common law principle of continuing ties to Canada.

REVIEW QUESTIONS

(1) Ms. Tired had been working for the same employer for the past ten years and was tired of her job. She decided to quit and travel to Australia for a year. On leaving, her employer paid her a lump-sum amount of $15,000, since Ms. Tired had been a good employee of theirs and they were hoping she might come back to work for them when she returned to Canada. Ms. Tired had no intention of working for them again but was grateful for the payment. Comment on how this payment should be taxed.

(2) Mr. Early has worked for the provincial government for the past 35 years and was now eligible for early retirement. As part of his retirement package he is entitled to a lump-sum payment for unused sick days in the amount of $20,000 and unused vacation days of $25,000. On retirement, he is going to receive a cheque for $45,000 as payment for the above amounts. How will this amount be taxed?

(3) Charles and Dee Vorce have decided to end their 12-year marriage. As part of their written separation agreement, they agree that Charles will pay Dee $3,000 per month for her personal support and maintenance, including $1,200 per month for the mortgage on the house that Dee will be living in. The original principal amount of the mortgage is $120,000. What limitations, if any, will Charles encounter when deciding the deductibility of the payments related to the mortgage?

(4) Mark and Ann have agreed to a separation agreement that requires Ann to pay $2,000 per month to Mark as an allowance for his maintenance. Initially, this payment will consist of $1,500 paid to Mark directly and $500 paid to the financial institution that holds the mortgage on his condominium. Mark may change this arrangement at any time to have the full $2,000 paid to him directly. Comment on the deductibility of these payments.

(5) Sam Student reached an agreement with his employer to pay for his education and living expenses while he returned to university. The agreement was that, if he returned to work for his employer when he graduated, there would be no repayment of the amounts he received. If he did not return to work for his employer, the payments he received would have to be repaid in full. How would this be treated for tax purposes?

(6) Mrs. Smith, a 75 year-old widow, has applied for and received the Old Age Security Supplement. This payment is based on the fact that her income is below a certain threshold amount. She has asked you to tell her how this is treated for tax purposes.

(7) Mr. Slippery, a consultant, did some work for ACME Corporation with the agreed-upon fee being $15,000. When the time came for the billing to be done, Mr. Slippery sent an invoice to ACME with instructions that the cheque be made payable to his wife. What would your comments be to Mr. Slippery and his wife on this arrangement?

(8) How do you determine how much of the employer's contributions to a defined benefit pension plan are deductible?

(9) What is the maximum tax-assisted benefit that may be provided to an individual under a defined benefit plan?

(10) What is the major difference between a defined benefit pension plan and a money purchase pension plan?

(11) One of the RRSP contribution limits is 18% of the prior year's earned income. How was the "18%" arrived at?

(12) In 2006, one of the RRSP contribution limits will be $18,000. How was this "$18,000" arrived at?

(13) Joe is confused. He is trying to understand the pension rules and he cannot understand why the limit on a money purchase pension plan is based on 18% of this year's income while the limit for an RRSP is based on last year's income. Explain this difference to him.

(14) It has been said that if an individual makes a $2,000 overcontribution (i.e., under the penalty limit) to an RRSP, and as long as the money is left in the RRSP for 15 years or longer at a 10% return and a 46% personal tax rate, then the benefits of compounding will outweigh the cost of the taxes that might be paid when the funds are withdrawn, even if the $2,000 is never deductible. Can you show how this calculation was arrived at? If the rate of return was only 8%, how long would the funds have to be left in the RRSP?

(15) Jennifer wanted to withdraw $20,000 from her RRSP in January in order to buy a new car. She had spent a long time accumulating this amount, but felt that it was more important to buy a car now than accumulate for retirement later. How can she minimize the tax that is withheld on the $20,000 taken out of the plan?

(16) Mr. Mort, a widower, has died and now his executor has come in to administer the will. His only assets on his death were an RRSP worth $150,000 and his house and other personal assets worth $150,000. Both of his children were grown up so he thought that his was a simple estate. He left the RRSPs to his daughter, Kim, and the residue to his son, Jim. Is there likely to be any conflict between the beneficiaries?

(17) Joan had worked for the same employer for 20 pre-'96 years. Two years ago she was fired. She took legal action against her former employer on the basis that it was wrongful dismissal. This year she won her case and was awarded $40,000. She then paid her legal fees of $8,000 and contributed $35,000 to her RRSP as a retiring allowance under paragraph 60(j.1). She is glad the case has been settled since she has not worked since her dismissal. What would you show on her personal tax return for the year based on this information?

MULTIPLE CHOICE QUESTIONS

Question 1

Max retired in 2005 and received a $100,000 retiring allowance. Max worked for his employer from April 1975 to January 2005. He never belonged to a registered pension plan or a deferred profit sharing plan during any of those years. What is the maximum amount of retiring allowance that Max can shelter from tax by transferring it to his RRSP?

(A) $42,000

(B) $59,500

(C) $63,000

(D) $83,000

Question 2

Ms. Assad wants to know the maximum RRSP contribution she can make in 2005 or in the first 60 days of 2006 that will be fully deductible on her 2005 tax return. The following information was taken from Ms. Assad's 2004 tax return:

Income from employment	$44,000
RPP contributions	1,000
Moving expenses	300
Support received	3,600
Pension income	6,000
Real estate rental income	1,400
Interest income	500

The pension adjustment reported by Ms. Assad's employer for 2004 was $4,000. Ms. Assad also has a $1,000 unused RRSP deduction limit room which has carried forward from 2004.

What is the maximum RRSP contribution that Ms. Assad can make in 2005 or in the first 60 days of 2006 and deduct fully on her 2005 tax return?

(A) $4,920

(B) $5,000

(C) $6,000

(D) $12,500

Question 3

Meg and James Rashev were both employed full-time during the year. The Rashevs have 4 children: Joanne (age 17), Susie (age 14), Sarah and Kelly (4 year old twins). The Rashevs employed a nanny to look after their children and paid her $15,000 for the year. In addition, during July, the 14-year old went to overnight camp for two weeks at a cost of $250 per week. The Rashevs' family income is summarized below:

	Meg	James
Salary & taxable benefits	$ 46,000	
Employment expenses [sec. 8]	(2,800)	
Business income:		
Revenues		$ 50,000
Expenses deductible for tax purposes		(32,000)
Interest income	800	1,500

Which one of the following represents the maximum child care deduction that can be claimed by the Rashevs in the year?

(A) James can claim a deduction of $12,000.

(B) Meg can claim a deduction of $13,000.

(C) James can claim a deduction of $18,000.

(D) James can claim a deduction of $15,200.

Question 4

Ms. Chiu moved from Toronto to Vancouver to start a new job. She earned $40,000 from her Toronto job and $50,000 from her Vancouver job in the year of the move. Ms. Chiu incurred the following costs of moving all of which can be substantiated by receipts:

Moving van to transport household effects....................	$ 5,000
Travelling costs — self, spouse and two children	1,800
Legal fees — Vancouver house	900
Legal fees — Toronto house	1,100
Loss on sale of Toronto house	25,000
Hotel costs while waiting for Vancouver house — $100 per day for 30 days	3,000
House hunting trip (prior to Vancouver move).................	800

Which one of the following amounts represents the maximum amount that Ms. Chiu can deduct as moving expenses on her personal income tax return for the year of the move?

(A) $8,300

(B) $10,300

(C) $11,800

(D) $12,600

Question 5

Sahar's income for tax purposes for 2004 and 2005 is as follows:

	2004	2005
Salary	$100,000	$110,000
Taxable benefits under sections 6 and 7	8,000	8,000
Travel expenses under section 8	(3,000)	(2,000)
Registered pension plan contributions under s. 8.........	(4,200)	(4,200)
Business losses	(1,000)	(1,200)
Rental income (net of expenses and CCA)	3,200	3,600
Spousal support paid................................	(12,600)	(12,000)
Net income under Division B........................	$ 90,400	$102,200

Which of the following statements is correct?

(A) The earned income that should be used to calculate her child care expense deduction for 2005 is $110,000.

(B) The earned income that should be used to calculate her RRSP deduction for 2005 is $106,400.

(C) The earned income that should be used to calculate her child care expense deduction for 2005 is $102,200.

(D) The earned income that should be used to calculate her RRSP deduction for 2005 is $94,600.

Question 6

Natalie Doak moved 1,000 km on March 1, 2005 to a new job and earned $40,000 in her new work location. Her employer reimbursed the costs of selling her old residence and purchasing her new residence. She did not receive any allowance or reimbursement in respect of the following expenses, all of which she paid in 2005:

Moving van	$ 2,600
Travelling costs to move Natalie and family	1,200
Cost of cleaning house in new work location	100
Cost of painting and installing new carpets and windows	10,000
Cost of maintaining vacant former residence for 3 months until it was sold (mortgage interest and property taxes of $3,000 per month)	9,000
Cost of changing address on legal documents	100
House hunting trips for new residence	3,000
	$26,000

What amount can Natalie claim for moving expenses in 2005?

(A) $26,000

(B) $15,900

(C) $12,900

(D) $8,900

EXERCISES

Exercise 1

[ITA: 56(1)(*b*); 56.1; 60(*b*); 60.1]

Uriah and Ursalla Unhappy decided to terminate their marriage of ten years. On June 1 Uriah moved out. From the period of June 1 to October 31, Uriah paid Ursalla $900 per month, made up of $200 for the support of herself and $700 for their two children. On November 1, 2005, Uriah and Ursalla signed a written separation agreement which confirmed the $900 a month payment. In addition the agreement provided that Uriah would pay the monthly mortgage payment of $400 on the home which is in Ursalla's name and all medical expenses for the children. During November and December Uriah made the appropriate payments as per the written agreement and paid $100 of dental bills in respect of the children.

— *REQUIRED*

Discuss the tax implications of the above facts for both Uriah and Ursalla.

Exercise 2

[ITA: 60(*i*); 146(1); 146(5)]

Don Deplanner contributed $5,000 to a spousal RRSP on February 15, 2006. Don's income for tax purposes for 2004 is as follows:

Salary	$70,000
Taxable benefits	1,200
	$71,200
Less: Registered pension plan contributions — defined contribution	(2,800)
Employment income — Subdivision a	$68,400
Rental loss	(5,000)
Dividend income from taxable Canadian corporations grossed up	800
Interest income — Canada Savings Bonds	400
Division B income	$64,600

Don's employer reported a PA of $6,084 in respect of 2004.

— *REQUIRED*

Determine the maximum amount Don can deduct on his 2005 tax return in respect of his 2006 contribution to his spouse's RRSP and the amount, if any, that he can deduct in respect of his own RRSP.

Exercise 3

[ITA: 60(*i*), (*j*.1)]

I. M. Retired received the following amounts for 2005, the year of his retirement:

Employment income (see (1) below)	$ 7,000
Pension income:	
Lump-sum RPP payment from a defined benefit plan	100,000
Superannuation payments (eight monthly pension payments of	
$3,000)	24,000
Old Age Security pension	5,700
Canada Pension Plan	12,000
Retiring allowance	50,000
Interest income	8,000
	$206,700

Additional Information

(1) I. M. Retired resigned his position on April 1, 2005. The employment income for tax purposes above includes a $300 contribution to his employer's registered pension plan.

(2) On April 1, 2005, Mr. Retired had his employer transfer directly the lump-sum payment from the RPP to his RRSP. In addition, Mr. Retired transferred all but $10,000 of his retiring allowance directly to his RRSP.

(3) Mr. Retired has been employed by the same employer for 22 pre-'96 years beginning in October 1974 and all of the employer pension contributions have vested.

(4) Mr. Retired was 65 on October 31, 2004.

(5) Mr. Retired's employer reported a PA for him of $700 in respect of 2004. Mr. Retired's earned income for 2004 was $120,000.

— REQUIRED

Determine the tax consequences of the above transactions for 2005, supported by your computations.

Exercise 4

[ITA: 62]

Edwin Employee was transferred from Vancouver to Montreal by his employer on October 1, 2005. The following expenses were incurred by Edwin:

Air fare for family	$ 1,300
Moving cost of furniture	1,000
Cost of disposing of Vancouver home	
— legal fees	500
— real estate commission	10,000
Cost of purchasing Montreal home	
— prepaid realty taxes	500
— legal fees	1,000
— Quebec transfer tax	300

Edwin's employment income for tax purposes earned in Montreal during 2005 was $7,000. Edwin's employer reimbursed Edwin for $5,000 of the moving expenses.

— REQUIRED

Calculate the amount that Edwin can deduct under section 62.

Exercise 5

[ITA: 63]

Charles Childcare was a university student in full-time attendance for 30 weeks and worked as a salesman for the balance of the year. His wife, Cathy, was also employed. The Childcares have four children: Sharon 17, Shawn 14, Sally 6 and Stephen 4. Child care expenses for the year amounted to $200 per week for 52 weeks. Charles' and Cathy's receipts and withholdings are summarized below:

	Charles	*Cathy*
Gross salary	$23,000	$47,000
Taxable fringe benefits	850	4,000
Interest income	200	—
Scholarship	3,600	—
Student loan	2,500	—

Deductions from Charles' and Cathy's employment income were:

	Charles	*Cathy*
Income taxes withheld	$ 3,800	$13,700
RPP contributions	2,000	3,700

— *REQUIRED*

Calculate the child care expenses deduction allowed to Charles and Cathy Childcare for 2005.

ASSIGNMENT PROBLEMS

Problem 1

[ITA: 60(*i*), (*j*.1); 146(5), (5.1), (8.2), (8.3); 147.3(4), (9)]

Mr. Rui retired from his job with Wise and Foresighted Consulting Ltd. on January 31, 2005. He had been employed continuously by the same employer since December 1980. Mr. Rui expects that his 2005 income for tax purposes will be as follows:

Employment income	$ 7,000
Pension income:	
Monthly superannuation (11 months of $3,000)	33,000
Old Age Security	5,700
Canadian Pension Plan	12,000
Retiring allowance	55,000
Farming income	20,000
Income from rental of apartment	10,800
Royalty income from books written by Mr. Rui	14,200
Interest income	12,000
Total income	$169,700

Additional Information

(1) Mr. Rui's 2005 employment income is net of an RPP contribution of $300. His PA for 2005 is expected to be $600.

(2) Mr. Rui has been a member of his employer's pension plan since he commenced working there in 1980. The employer's contributions have vested in Mr. Rui for each year he has been a member of the plan.

(3) Mr. Rui will be 69 in February 2006. His wife is now 65.

(4) In 2005 Mrs. Rui withdrew $6,000 from her RRSP. Mr. Rui had made the following contributions to Mrs. Rui's RRSP: January 2005 — $2,000; April 2004 — $1,000; February 2003 — $1,000; December 2002 — $3,000. Mr. Rui did not deduct the January 2005 contribution in 2004.

(5) Mr. Rui's employer reported a PA for him of $7,000 in 2004. His earned income in 2004 was $66,000.

(6) Mr. Rui's employer paid the retiring allowance to Mr. Rui in 2005 and Mr. Rui contributed his entire $55,000 retiring allowance to his RRSP in January 2006.

(7) Mr. Rui has unused RRSP deduction room from prior years of $5,000.

— REQUIRED

(A) Determine the tax implications of Mrs. Rui's $6,000 RRSP withdrawal.

(B) Determine Mr. Rui's maximum tax deductible RRSP contribution for 2005. What additional RRSP contribution should Mr. Rui make for 2005?

(C) It is now February 2006. What are the tax implications to Mr. Rui of the $55,000 transfer of his retiring allowance to his RRSP?

(D) What additional planning steps would you advise Mr Rui to take in connection with his RRSP in 2006?

Problem 2

[ITA: 5; 6; 8; 12; 20; 39; 40(2); 56; 60; 75; 146]

Ms. Sui is an executive of a large public retail corporation, Clothes to You Ltd., situated in Dundas, Ontario. Ms. Sui is not married. However, she has two adopted children, ages 8 and 10, who reside with her.

Ms. Sui has provided you with the following information for 2005:

Clothes to You Ltd.:

Gross salary	$150,000
Commission income	30,000
Canada Pension Plan contributions	(1,861)
Employment Insurance premiums	(761)
Registered pension plan contributions (money purchase)	(6,000)
Income taxes deducted	(55,000)

(1) Clothes to You Ltd. provides Ms. Sui with an automobile. The annual lease cost of the car, including PST of $1,280 (at 8%) and GST of $1,120, is $18,400. Ms. Sui is reimbursed for her operating expenses when using the car for business. Clothes to You Ltd. also pays for any insurance, licence fees and repairs and maintenance related to the operation of the automobile. The operating expenses for the year totalled $6,200, including PST of $431 and GST of $378. She used the car 10,000 km for pleasure and 30,000 km for business. She is charged $200/month for the use of the car and operating costs.

(2) Ms. Sui received stock options in the year. She has the option to purchase 20,000 shares at $3.50/share. The value of the shares at the date of the issue of the option was $3.50/share. Ms. Sui has not yet exercised any of her options.

(3) Ms. Sui received a piece of artwork worth $750, including PST of $52 and GST of $46, from the company at Christmas time.

(4) Clothes to You Ltd. paid $1,300, including GST of $85, for her membership in a fitness club. The corporation also paid Private Health Insurance premiums of $350.

Investment Receipts:

Interest income	$1,100
Dividends received from taxable Canadian corporations	7,500
Dividends from U.S. corporation — net of 15% withholding tax (in Cdn. $)	680

Other Items:

(1) Annuity payments under contract from Profound Life Assurance Co. The capital portion of the annuity was $650 .... $2,000

(2) Net proceeds on the sale of her house on March 15, 2005 — net of real estate commission of $12,000 .... $188,000

The house cost $90,000 in 1992. She had previously sold her pre-1971 cottage in 1994, giving the cottage the maximum designation as a principal residence in order to have a nil taxable capital gain.

(3) At Christmas 2004, Ms. Sui gave each of her children a 6%, $2,000 five-year bond.

(4) Ms. Sui received a termination payment of $28,000 from her previous employer. She contributed all of this amount to her RRSP. Ms. Sui worked for her previous employer from February 15, 1986 to January 10, 2005. In that period, 80% of that employer's contribution had vested.

Expenditures/Losses:

(1) Investment counsellor's fees	$ 1,100
(2) Interest on bank loan to purchase shares	850
(3) Registered retirement savings plan contribution	4,000

Ms. Sui's earned income in 2004 was $170,000. The PA on her 2004 T4 was $6,000.

(4) Ms. Sui incurred meals and entertainment expenses	$ 8,300
(5) Rental loss (before CCA)	3,500

(6) Ms. Sui invested in a limited partnership tax shelter in 2005. The loss per form T5013 is $3,200. She invested $5,000 in the partnership units in early 2005.

— REQUIRED

Calculate Ms. Sui's income under Division B for 2005, using the ordering rules in section 3.

Problem 3

[ITA: 62; IT-178R3]

Sue and George Shaker lived in Halifax, Nova Scotia, while George completed his combined law and MBA degree at Dalhousie University. The Shakers purchased a home in Halifax when they first moved to Nova Scotia. Due to contracting mononucleosis in his second year of the program, George completed his degree in December of 2005 rather than in the spring of 2005.

George excelled in the program and had numerous job offers. He finally accepted a job with NorthAm Co. in Toronto. In order to convince George to accept the job, NorthAm Co. offered to pay the Shakers an amount equal to any loss that they incurred on the sale of their Halifax home and provide them with a $10,000 moving allowance.

Sue has been working for an insurance company in Halifax while George has been attending school. Sue intends to find work in Toronto, but will be unable to continue working for the same insurance company.

George accepted the job with NorthAm Co. in September 2005. During October 2005, George and Sue flew to Toronto to look for a home. They spent a week in Toronto and on the fifth day managed to find and purchase a home with the purchase contract closing on December 15, 2005. The remaining two days were spent arranging for painting and cleaning of the new home. Their expenditures on that trip were:

Two Air Canada tickets (return Halifax to Toronto)	$500
Motel room, 7 days @ $75 per day	525
Meals, 7 days @ $50 per day	350
Car rental	350

George and Sue managed to sell their Halifax home. That sale closed on December 15, 2005. The statement of account from the lawyer (dated January 15, 2006) revealed the following expenses:

Real estate commission	$7,000
Legal fees, old home	2,000
Legal fees, new home	2,500
Land transfer tax, new home	1,000

The house in Halifax was sold for $140,000. The Shakers had originally paid $160,000 for the house. NorthAm Co. provided a cheque for $27,000 in February 2006 to reimburse them for the loss and the real estate commission. (NorthAm Co. did not include the legal costs when calculating the loss eligible for reimbursement.)

Subsequent to finalizing the sale of their Halifax home and George's completion of his exams, Sue and George packed up their car and drove to Toronto. The trip took 7 days due to a leisurely pace and some bad weather delays, and since their home was not ready when they arrived, they stayed in a nearby motel for 11 days.

The cost of trip and stay in motel was as follows:

Meals, 18 days @ $100 (substantiated by receipts)	$1,800
Motel room, 18 days @ $80	1,440
Gasoline (2000 kilometres driven)	250

In late December, the Shakers paid a moving bill consisting of $5,000 for the actual move and $250 for storage. George received the $10,000 allowance for moving expenses in December 2005. He commenced work for NorthAm Co. in January 2006 at a salary of $80,000 per year. Sue commenced work for Toronto Insurance Co. in September 2006 at a salary of $50,000 per year.

— *REQUIRED*

Calculate the allowable moving expenses for the Shakers for both 2005 and 2006. Discuss the tax treatment of the loss reimbursement. Assume that all expenditures made were reasonable and can be substantiated by receipts.

Problem 4

[ITA: 63]

Nina Diamond and Len Dirkfeld are married and have five children: Lindsay age 18, Trevor age 15, James age 7, Ben age 5, and Rebecca age 3. During 2005, they paid a nanny $250 per week for 50 weeks to look after their children while they worked. During July, they paid $3,000 ($1,500 each) for Trevor and James to go to an overnight summer camp for four weeks. In addition, they paid their child Lindsay $300 to babysit the other children at various times when they worked late.

Len is a doctor and has his own practice. Nina worked full-time as a computer consultant during the first eight months of the year. In September, she went back to university on a full-time basis for 13 weeks. On December 11, her courses were finished and she went back to work.

Nina and Len's incomes are summarized below:

	Nina	Len
Salary...	$50,000	
Taxable benefits	3,000	
Employment expenses	(800)	
Employment income	$52,200	
Business income		$120,000
Interest income	2,000	3,000
Rental income		6,000
RRSP contribution	(5,000)	(10,000)
Net income under Division B	$49,200	$119,000

— *REQUIRED*

(A) Compute the maximum 2005 child care deductions for Nina Diamond and Dr. Len Dirkfeld. Show all calculations.

(B) How would your answer to (A) change if Nina went back to university for 13 weeks on a part-time basis rather than a full-time basis. Assume Nina took a minimum of 12 hours of courses each month, but do not redo all the calculations.

Problem 5

[ITA: 56(1)(*a*); 60(*b*), (*i*), (*j*.1), (*o*); 60.1; 62; 63; 146(1), (5), (8.2); 147.3]

In early July 2005, Dr. Elaine Matthews separated from her husband of some years. She maintained full custody of the couple's only child, a six-year-old girl. Since May 1, 1985, Dr. Matthews had been working as a public health consultant for the Oshawa region. Just prior to her separation she had chosen to take advantage of a severance package from the Oshawa region. She accepted a staff position at Joseph Brant Memorial Hospital in Burlington, Ontario and moved directly from Oshawa to Burlington on September 1, 2005. She sold the former family home in Oshawa on September 15, 2005. Her husband had rented an apartment in Oshawa in late July 2005.

Dr. Matthews has some experience preparing her own tax returns but she has been particularly busy in recent months. She started her 2005 return but quickly decided she simply did not have time to finish it. She requested your assistance in completing her return.

You met with Dr. Matthews to go over her tax information related to 2005 and determined that she had correctly calculated her income under Subdivisions a, b and c of Division B to total $158,488. Included in this correct computation were the following items:

Salary (from former employer)	$ 96,000
Salary (from Joseph Brant Memorial Hospital)	60,000
Taxable benefits under section 6 of the *Income Tax Act*	1,743
Registered pension plan contributions (defined benefit plan)	(6,750)
Consulting income (reported as business income)	8,000
Interest income from investments	540
Taxable dividends from investments	1,250
Share of rental loss from childhood home inherited from her parents	(1,495)
Net taxable capital gains	4,800
Interest paid on investment loans	(2,400)
Loss from limited partnership investment (rental property)	(3,200)
	$158,488

She provided you with the following *additional details* relating to 2005:

Miscellaneous income

Severance from former employer	$ 41,538

Transfer of RPP accrued from former employer

Her former employer made a direct transfer of her accumulated RPP benefits (within prescribed limits) to her RRSP; her former employer had made vested contributions for the years 1987 through 2005	$210,000

Spousal support

Under the terms of her separation agreement signed in September 2005, Dr. Matthews paid the following amounts for support of her husband:

Support ($500 a month for September — December)	$ 2,000
Rent on his new Oshawa apartment ($750 a month for September — December)	3,000

Moving Expenses from Oshawa to Burlington

Gas for house-hunting trips (4 trips made during late August 2005)	$ 40

Selling costs of former Oshawa home (owned 100% by her; sold September 15, 2005):

Real estate commissions	$ 12,000
Legal fees	1,050

Costs of purchasing new Burlington home:

Legal fees	$ 850
Land transfer tax	3,250

Costs of moving herself and her household effects:

Moving van to transport belongings	$ 600
Gas to drive herself and her daughter (120 kms. driven)	15
Hotel (2 nights while new home was being painted and cleaned; 2 × $100)	200
Meals (same two days as above 2 × $55)	110

You have determined that the distance from her new home to Joseph Brant Hospital is 3.5 km. The distance from Joseph Brant Hospital to her former home was 115 km.

Care of her daughter

Part-time nanny employed January 1–August 31	$ 8,976
YMCA summer camp for two weeks in July while nanny was on vacation ($200 a week)	400
Fall term (September–December) tuition fees for private school (excluding before and after school daycare)	4,000
Before and after school daycare for September–December (provided on premises of private school)	720
Fall term (September–December) transportation to private school	1,200

Registered retirement savings plan contributions

Transfer of severance pay from former employer	$ 30,000
Personal contributions through employment (March–December 2005)	7,000
Personal contributions through employment (January–February 2006)	1,000

Her 2004 earned income for RRSP purposes was $120,000; her employer had reported a pension adjustment on her 2004 T4 of $7,000; she had no unused RRSP contribution room at the start of 2005 and no undeducted balance of RRSP contributions

Legal fees paid

Legal representation during separation proceedings to establish requirements to make support payments	$ 1,600
Appeal of her 2003 income tax assessment (which she won)	1,200

—REQUIRED

Complete the calculation of income under Division B. Show all calculations whether or not they are necessary to the final answer. Explain briefly any items not used in your calculations.

Problem 6

[ITA: Division B]

Ms. King had a busy year in 2005. During the year, she formally separated from her husband and retained custody of her five year-old daughter, Kelly. She also decided that she needed a fresh start in another city, so she quit her job in Belleville, Ontario, and got a new job in Windsor. Ms. King and her daughter moved to Windsor, Ontario, in November 2005. She has asked you to help her estimate her 2005 personal income tax liability. In order to help you, she has prepared the following list of all the transactions which she thinks might be of interest to you.

(1) Her employment income from her employer in Belleville for the first 11 months of 2005 was $55,000. Her deductions at source included CPP/EI of $2,622 and income tax of $20,000.

Her Belleville employer paid her a retiring allowance of $15,000 to compensate her for the fact that she was not a member of a pension plan and to reward her for years of service to the company (from 1980 to 2005).

Before she left the Belleville employer, a public company, she exercised a stock option that she had for 800 shares. When this option had originally been granted, the share price was $15. The exercise price of the option was $17. At the time she exercised the option, the market price was $25. She immediately sold these shares on the open market for $25.

(2) Her new employer in Windsor agreed to pay some of her moving expenses, but in order to simplify things, they were going to give her an allowance of $8,000. She was responsible, then, for her own expenses.

Her moving costs were as follows:

Moving company charges	$5,500
Gas for trip to Windsor at the time of the move (600 kms. driven)	50
Motel in Belleville for one night on the day of the move	75
Meals during the day of the move and during the trip to Windsor	100
Lease cancellation charge in Belleville	200
	$5,925

She had made a trip to Windsor to look for an apartment for her and Kelly and she had incurred the following expenses:

Gas for trip to Windsor	$ 50
Motel costs in Windsor	150
Meals	75
	$275

(3) Her income from her new employer in Windsor during the month of December was $5,000.

(4) During the year she incurred the following expenses for the care of Kelly:

Food and clothing	$6,000
Babysitter costs while she was at work	3,000

(5) Ms. King incurred legal fees of $3,200 to establish her right to support payments in connection with the finalization of the separation agreement. She feels that this was well spent, since her lawyer was successful in getting her husband to pay child support to her for Kelly in the amount of $800 per month, starting in February 2005. So far, her husband has been making these payments on time.

She also had trouble with her 2003 tax return and had to pay her previous accountant $400 to deal with the CRA. It turns out that the CRA has correctly assessed her return.

(6) She is totally confused by the RRSP rules, so she wants you to tell her what the maximum amount is that she can contribute to her RRSP for 2005. She wants you to assume that she will make these payments within the time deadlines when you calculate her tax liability.

(7) Five years ago, Ms. King inherited some shares in a Canadian public company, Facai Ltd., from her mother. She believed that the shares were capable of making money for her. She sold the shares in 2005, in order to put money into a mutual fund that a friend recommended. Her mother had paid $5,000 for these shares in 1980 and at the time of her mother's death, the shares were worth $60,000. Ms. King sold them for $180,000.

Ms. King received cash dividends from these shares during the year in the amount of $10,000.

(8) One of her good friends had been a battered wife, so Ms. King had donated $2,000 to the local registered charity which protects battered women.

(9) Ms. King gave you a copy of her 2004 tax return and it showed employment income of $55,000, child care expenses of $2,000 and taxable dividends of $10,000. She made the maximum RRSP contribution for 2004.

— REQUIRED

Calculate Ms. King's income under Division B for 2005. Explain why you omitted any amounts from your calculations. Show all calculations.

[For more problems and solutions thereto, see the CD accompanying this book.]

SUPPLEMENTAL NOTES

(This section can be omitted without losing the continuity of the chapter. None of the review questions, multiple choice questions, exercises or assignment problems utilize this information.)

A. RRSP's and Net Past Service Pension Adjustments and Pension Adjustment Reversals

Pension benefits can be increased on a retroactive basis through the provision of credits for additional periods of service, or the retroactive upgrading of plan benefits. An employer wishing to upgrade an existing plan by providing additional benefits in respect of past service or wishing to provide credits for additional periods of service will have to calculate a net past service pension adjustment (NPSPA). This amount is defined in subsection 146(1) and represents the value of the additional benefits to an individual. The NPSPA must be reported to the Canada Revenue Agency. In addition, a procedure for the processing of past service amendments to pension plans is in force. The upgrade will be permitted if it is within the overall rules for tax assistance, but it will reduce an individual's RRSP contribution room accordingly.

The legislation contains a measure designed to provide greater equity to individuals where participation in an RPP or DPSP is terminated prior to retirement. A pension adjustment reversal (PAR) is intended to restore lost RRSP contribution room in situations where a pre-retirement termination benefit or pension entitlement is less than the individual's foregone RRSP contribution room for past years. The PAR allows an individual to make additional RRSP contributions which make up for the lost room. The PAR provides additional room for the individual to roll over large severance payments to an RRSP on a tax-deferred basis.

Chapter 10

Computation of Taxable Income
and Taxes Payable for Individuals

TOPICS DISCUSSED

	Page
COMPUTATION OF TAXABLE INCOME FOR AN INDIVIDUAL	473
Miscellaneous Division C Deductions and Additions	473
Loss Carryovers	478
Capital Gains Deduction — Historical Overview	481
Ordering of Division C Deductions	482
Taxable Income of Non-Residents	486
COMPUTATION OF TAX FOR INDIVIDUALS	487
Basic Computation of Tax	487
Section 118 Tax Credits	489
Charitable Gifts Credit	496
Medical Expense Credit	498
Credit for Mental or Physical Impairment (Disability Tax Credit)	504
Tuition and Education Credits	505
Credit for Employment Insurance Premiums and CPP Contributions	508

	Page
Transfer of Unused Credits to Spouse or Common-law Partner	508
[Adoption Expense Tax Credit]	510
Dividend Tax Credit and Subsection 82(3) Election	511
Credits for Part-Time and Non-Residents	513
Ordering of Credits	514
Income Not Earned in a Province	515
Credit for Employment outside Canada	515
Refundable Goods and Services Tax Credit (GSTC)	515
Refundable Medical Expense Tax Credit Supplement	517
Refundable Canada Child Tax Benefit	517
Foreign Tax Credits	519
Federal Political Contribution Tax Credit	520
Tax on Old Age Security Benefits	520
Tax Reduction on Retroactive Lump-sum Payments	521
Application of Rules for Computation of Tax and Credits	522
Minimum Tax	524

This chapter is divided into two major parts. The first major segment deals with a discussion of the provisions used to compute taxable income. Subsection 2(2) simply defines taxable income as income plus or minus amounts permitted under Division C. This chapter will cover a list of miscellaneous items in Division C which specifically pertain to individuals. The enhanced capital gains deduction contained in section 110.6 will be introduced briefly in this chapter and discussed more fully in Chapter 13. This chapter will deal with the carryover of losses incurred in another year from the perspective of an individual taxpayer.

The second major segment of this chapter discusses the computation of tax for individuals, including coverage of tax rates, tax credits and minimum tax. This discussion follows a long list of tax credits for such things as marital status, dependants, age, pension income, charitable donations, medical expenses and disability, among others, and for transfers of certain of these credits to another taxpayer. Many of the tax credits in Division E are dependent in some way on Division B income. Therefore, it is necessary first to calculate Division B income and, then, to determine if a Division E tax credit is deductible to the limit of tax on Division C taxable income. If the Division C deductions result in a negative taxable income, taxable income becomes zero.

The following chart will help locate the major provisions of the Act considered in this chapter.

PART I — DIVISIONS C, E & E.1
COMPUTATION OF TAXABLE INCOME
COMPUTATION OF TAX

DIVISION		SUBDIVISION		SECTION	
				110	Deductions
				110.2	Lump-sum payments
				110.6	CG exemption
				110.7	Prescribed zone
				111	Losses
				111.1	Ordering
				114-114.2	Part-year resident
				117-117.1	Tax rates
				118-118.95	Personal credits
				120	Income from o/s prov
				120.2	Min tax c/over
				120.4	Tax on split income
A	Liability for tax			121	Dividend tax credit
B	Computation of income			122	Tax on trust
C	Computation of taxable income			122.3	Empl o/s Canada
D	Taxable income earned in Canada by non-residents			122.5	GST credit
		a	Individuals	122.51	Refundable medical expense supplement
		a.1	Child tax benefit		
E	Computation of tax	b	Corporations	122.6-122.64	Child tax benefit
E.1	Minimum tax	c	All taxpayers	126	Foreign tax credit
				126.1-127.41	Other tax credits
F	Special rules			127.5	Obligation
G	Deferred and other income arrangements			127.51	Minimum amount
H	Exemptions			127.52	Adjusted Taxable Inc
I	Returns, assessments, payments, appeals			127.53	Basic exemption
				127.531	Basic credit
J	Appeals to the courts			127.54	Definitions
				127.55	Application of 127.5

I. COMPUTATION OF TAXABLE INCOME FOR AN INDIVIDUAL

A. Miscellaneous Division C Deductions and Additions

[ITA: 7(1), (1.1); (8) to (16); 53(1)(*j*); 80.4; 110(1)(*d*), (*d*.1), (*f*), (*j*), (1.4); IT-113R4]

1. Employee stock options

Employees, who acquire shares from a corporation other than a Canadian-controlled private corporation under a stock option agreement, are required to include in their employment income a benefit [ssec. 7(1)]. The benefit is computed as the amount by which the fair market value of the shares at the time the shares were acquired exceeds the price actually paid (i.e., the exercise price). The employment benefit is then added to the adjusted cost base of the shares [par. 53(1)(*j*)], so that any resultant capital gain reflects the increase in value since the acquisition date. Also, the adjusted cost base reflects the sum of amounts that have been previously taxed, that is, amounts that have been tax-paid.

There is a deduction of $1/2$ of the employment benefit referred to as a "stock option deduction" available in Division C in the computation of taxable income. The stock option deduction can be claimed if the exercise price was not less than the value of the share at the time the option was granted [par. 110(1)(*d*)]. In addition, there are certain limitations on the type of shares issued (i.e., prescribed shares which are described as, in essence, common shares [Reg. 6204]). Also, an arm's length relationship of the parties must exist before and after the exercising of the option. Note there are no tax consequences upon the granting of an option.

In some instances where employees have been granted stock options the value of the shares has subsequently declined to the point where the fair market value is less than the exercise price. As a result of this decline, employers may want to reduce the exercise price to the current fair market value. This, however, will disqualify the option for the Division C deduction under paragraph 110(1)(*d*) since the exercise price may be less than the fair market value at the time the option was granted. [In recognition of this, a proposed amendment [subsections 110(1.7) and (1.8)] in the draft legislation of December 20, 2002 allows employers to reduce the exercise price without jeopardizing the employee's paragraph 110(1)(*d*) deduction, as long as the following conditions are met:

1. the exercise price is reduced at a time when the fair market value of the securities is less than the old exercise price,

2. the old exercise price was not less than the fair market value of the securities when the option was granted, and

3. the new exercise price was not less than the fair market value of the securities at the time of the price reduction.

For example, assume that the original option was granted when the fair market value of the shares was $20 and the option had an exercise price of $22. This option would have qualified for the paragraph 110(1)(*d*) deduction. If the share value drops to $10 and the company reduces the option price to $12 then these proposed amendments allow this security to continue to qualify for the deduction.]

One exception to the requirement to include the benefit in the year of exercise of the option is provided for stock options on publicly-listed shares where certain conditions are met. These conditions were listed in Chapter 3. Where the employment income benefit is deferred on the first $100,000 worth of shares acquired under option, the stock option deduction is also deferred to the year of disposition of the shares.

Another exception to the requirement to include the benefit in the year of exercise of the option is provided for stock options granted by a Canadian-controlled private corporation (CCPC) [ssec. 7(1.1)]. There is an employment inclusion of the same amount, but the income is deferred until the year the shares are disposed of. Furthermore, the stock option deduction can be claimed if the shares have not been sold or exchanged before the second anniversary date of the day of acquisition [par. 110(1)(*d*.1)].

Note that for stock options granted by a CCPC, there are two possibilities for a stock option deduction. Either the shares acquired under the option are held for the two-year period and, thus, qualify under paragraph 110(1)(*d*.1), or the exercise price is not less than the value of the shares at the date the option was granted and, thus, qualify under paragraph 110(1)(*d*). However, only one of the two possibilities can apply.

Where the stock option deduction is claimed, effectively, only ½ of the difference between the exercise price and the value at the date of exercise is taxable, similar to a capital gain. While the net numerical result is a ½ inclusion, the net amount is not a taxable capital gain and, therefore, not eligible for the capital gains deduction on qualified small business corporation shares (Q.S.B.C.S.).

The schematic diagram on stock options introduced in Chapter 3 can be expanded now to include the effects of the stock option deduction.

Values	Income under Division B	Division C deduction = 50% of benefit		Timing of inclusion and deduction	
		Non-CCPC	CCPC	Non-CCPC (general)	CCPC and eligible listed shares*
Selling price	Capital gain ½ taxable (Subdiv. c)			Disposition or deemed disposition	Disposition or deemed disposition
Fair market value at purchase	Employment income (Subdiv. b)	if: FMV at date option granted ≤ exercise price	if: FMV at date option granted ≤ exercise price	Purchase	Disposition or deemed disposition
			or		
			shares held ≥ 2 years from date of purchase (except for deemed disposition at death)		
Option exercise price					

*The inclusion of the stock benefit and, hence, the deduction in Division C is deferred in the case of publicly-listed shares on the first $100,000 of optioned shares, valued at the grant date, in any one year. Other conditions for the deferral are outlined in Chapter 3.

Note that the fair market value of the shares at the date that the option is granted is relevant only for the condition that allows the ½ stock option deduction.

Example Problem

Malenkov Mfg. Ltd. granted Ms. Yampolsky, its Vice-president, an option to purchase 10,000 shares for $5 per share. On March 10, 2005, she acquired the 10,000 shares under the option. The following pertains to the shares:

	Date	F.M.V.
Option granted	March 10, 1999	$10
Option exercised	March 10, 2005	20
Shares sold	March 10, 2008	30

— REQUIRED

(A) Determine the tax consequences on the above dates if Malenkov Mfg. Ltd. was:

    (i) a public company, or

    (ii) a Canadian-controlled private corporation.

(B) Redo Part (A) assuming the exercise price had been set at $10 per share.

— SOLUTION

(A) (i) March 10, 1999 — No tax consequences

    March 10, 2005 — Employment income of $150,000 (10,000 shares × ($20 – $5)) [ssec. 7(1)]

    — No stock option deduction and no $100,000 deferral since the exercise price ($5) was less than the value on the grant date ($10) [par. 110(1)(*d*); par. 7(9)(*b*)]

    — Adjusted cost base of each share increased by $15 per share to $20, so that the $15 per share benefit is not taxed again on disposition [par. 53(1)(*j*)]

    March 10, 2008 — Taxable capital gain of $50,000 ($\frac{1}{2}$ ($30 – $20) × 10,000 shares)

    (ii) March 10, 1999 — No tax consequences

    March 10, 2005 — No tax consequences

    March 10, 2008 — Employment inclusion of $150,000 (10,000 shares × ($20 – $5)) [ssec. 7(1.1)]

    — Adjusted cost base of each share increased by $15 per-share to $20 [par. 53(1)(*j*)]

    — Stock option deduction of $75,000 ($\frac{1}{2}$ × $150,000), since the shares were held over two years [par. 110(1)(*d*.1)]

    — Taxable capital gain of $50,000 ($\frac{1}{2}$ ($30 – $20) × 10,000 shares); may qualify for the qualified small business corporation share capital gains deduction

(B) If the exercise price had been $10, equal to the fair market value of the shares at the date of grant, the two results would have been as follows:

	(B)(i)	(B)(ii)
Employment income (10,000 shares × ($20 – $10)) ...	$100,000	$100,000
Pars. 110(1)(*d*), (*d*.1) ($\frac{1}{2}$ × $100,000)	(50,000)	(50,000)
	$ 50,000	$ 50,000
Taxable capital gain	50,000	50,000
	$100,000	$100,000

In addition, the public company shares would have qualified for the $100,000 deferral [ssec.7(8)], by being eligible for the par. 110(1)(d) deduction.

The primary difference between (A) and (B) is that the stock option deduction [par. 110(1)(*d*)] is available to the non-CCPC, since the exercise price is not less than the fair market value at the time the option was granted. Also, for the CCPC option, the benefit does not have to be reported until the year of disposal.

The effect of these provisions is to give a treatment equivalent to capital gains for stock option benefits accruing up to the date of acquisition and included in employment income, without providing eligibility for the Q.S.B.C. share capital gains deduction where applicable.

2. Deduction for certain receipts

A number of refundable and non-refundable tax credits provided to an individual taxpayer are reduced by the individual's Division B income. Certain social assistance payments received by individuals are included in their Division B income and may affect these tax credits. However, there is no intention to tax these payments in the hands of the recipient. As a result, a deduction is provided in Division C [par. 110(1)(*f*)], in the computation of taxable income, to offset the inclusion of the payments in Division B. The sources of income which qualify for this treatment are:

- the Guaranteed Income Supplement,
- social assistance payments,
- workers' compensation, and
- amounts that are exempt income by virtue of a tax treaty.

3. Home relocation loan

A special deduction is available to partially offset an interest income inclusion under section 80.4 in situations where an employee has obtained a "home relocation loan" as a result of an employment relocation [par. 110(1)(*j*)]. A home relocation loan is defined [ssec. 248(1)] as, in essence, a loan used to acquire a home which is at least 40 kilometres closer to an employee's new work location than his or her old residence. The intention of this special deduction is that an employee could receive the equivalent of a $25,000 interest-free loan without including a deemed interest benefit in taxable income. The maximum deduction is the section 80.4 benefit and the duration of the deduction is the lesser of five years or the life of the home relocation loan. A loan received by a taxpayer that is used to repay a home relocation loan is deemed to be the same loan as the home relocation loan and to have been made on the same day [ssec. 110(1.4)]. In addition, the same "lesser of" benefit is provided [ssec. 80.4(4)] for a home relocation loan as is provided for a home purchase loan (refer to Chapter 6). Hence, the low-interest benefit [sec. 80.4] can be computed on the principal amount of the loan outstanding in the year at a rate which is the lesser of (a) the prescribed rate at the time the loan was made and (b) the changing prescribed rates during the year the loan was outstanding.

The deduction is computed as the least of three amounts [par. 110(1)(*j*)]:

(a) interest on the whole home relocation loan as computed under paragraph 80.4(1)(*a*) using the "lesser of" rule in subsection 80.4(4) *minus* interest paid during that year and 30 days thereafter (i.e., the net imputed interest benefit on the home relocation loan itself);

(b) interest on a $25,000 home relocation loan under paragraph 80.4(1)(*a*) using the "lesser of" rule in subsection 80.4(4) but restricted to a maximum of five years (i.e., interest at the appropriate prescribed rate computed on a principal amount of $25,000); and

(c) total benefits from all low-interest or no-interest loans computed under section 80.4.

Exhibit 6-1 can be expanded now by adding a box containing the above "least of" calculation at the bottom of the right-hand side of the exhibit.

Example Problem

Ms. Kishke joined May Kostcha Ltd. on February 1, 2005 as chief corporate tax officer. On that date she received an interest-free loan of $100,000 to assist her in the financing of a new home, since she was moving from Kingston in eastern Ontario, to Dundas in southern Ontario, to take the position. In addition, she was given a loan of $20,000 bearing interest at 3% payable on December 31 of each year that the loan is outstanding. This loan was to assist her with other costs associated with her move. The interest was paid when due.

— REQUIRED

Determine the effects of these loans on Ms. Kishke's taxable income in 2005. Assume prescribed rates for 2005 as follows: 4% for the first quarter, 5% for the second quarter, 4% for the third and fourth quarters.

— SOLUTION

The imputed interest benefit would be computed on these loans under subsection 80.4(1) with the "lesser of" rule provided in subsection 80.4(4) for a home relocation loan as follows.

Par. 80.4(1)(*a*) and ssec. 80.4(4): loan to purchase house:

The "lesser of rule" can be applied in each quarter of the year during the year that the loan is outstanding. Since the 4% rate applicable in the first quarter of the loan is less than or equal to the prescribed rate in each of the other three quarters, the 4% rate will be applicable for all of the year, computed as follows:

4% of $100,000 × $^{334}/_{365}$ =		$3,660
Par. 80.4(1)(*a*) loan for general purposes:		
4% of $20,000 × $^{59}/_{365}$ =	$ 129	
5% of $20,000 × $^{91}/_{365}$ =	249	
4% of $20,000 × $^{92}/_{365}$ =	202	
4% of $20,000 × $^{92}/_{365}$ =	202	782
		$4,442
Par. 80.4(1)(*c*): interest paid (3% of $20,000 × $^{334}/_{365}$)		(549)
Sec. 80.4 benefit		$3,893

Since the $100,000 loan is a home relocation loan, the following deduction may be taken in the calculation of taxable income [par. 110(1)(*j*)]:

Least of:

Spar. 110(1)(*j*)(i): benefit computed [sec. 80.4] on $100,000 home relocation loan net of reduction for interest paid (interest-free loan)	$3,660
Spar. 110(1)(*j*)(ii): interest computed [par. 80.4(1)(*a*)] on a $25,000 loan 4% of $25,000 × $^{334}/_{365}$)	$ 915
Spar. 110(1)(*j*)(iii): total sec. 80.4 benefit net of interest paid for year	$3,893

Therefore, the paragraph 110(1)(*j*) deduction would be $915 in 2005.

It may be rare to see a case where the deduction [par. 110(1)(*j*)] is equal to the total section 80.4 benefit for the year.

B. Loss Carryovers

[ITA: 111; IT-232R3]

Commentary in previous chapters has alluded to the fact that losses which cannot be applied in the year in which they occur because of a restriction in Division B may be deducted in Division C by carrying the losses back three years through amended returns and/or applying the balance of the losses to future years, subject to any further restrictions as indicated below.

1. Non-capital loss carryovers deductible by par. 111(1)(a)

A "non-capital loss" (non-C.L.) available for carryover is defined in subsection 111(8). For individuals, the definition can be summarized in computational form as follows:

Aggregate of:		
Amounts computed in par. 3(d):		
Loss from an office or employment		$xxx
Loss from business.......................................		xxx
Loss from property		xxx
Allowable business investment loss.......................		xxx
Amount deducted under section 110.6 (capital gains deduction)		xxx
Amount deducted under par. 111(1)(b) (net capital losses)		xxx
Amount deductible under:		
Pars. 110(1)(d), (d.1), (d.2), (d.3) — Stock options	$xxx	
Par. 110(1)(f) — Social assistance and other payments	xxx	
Par. 110(1)(j) — Home relocation loan	xxx	xxx
		$xxx
Less: aggregate of the amount determined under par. 3(c):		
Income from office or employment	$xxx	
Income from business	xxx	
Income from property	xxx	
Income from other sources [secs. 56–59]	xxx	
Taxable capital gains (other than from listed personal property)	$xxx	
Taxable net capital gain from listed personal property	xxx	
	$xxx	
Less: allowable capital losses (other than from listed personal property and allowable business investment losses)	xxx	xxx*
		$xxx
Less: other deductions [secs. 60–66]	xxx	xxx*
		$xxx*
Less: farm loss (included in loss from business above)..................		xxx
Non-capital loss carryover		$xxx*

---

* Cannot be negative [sec. 257].

Note that in order to become a carryover non-capital loss, a current year's loss from non-capital sources must, in essence, exceed income from all other sources in the current year. Any non-capital loss may be carried back three years or forward ten (for taxation years that end after March 22, 2004) years with the earliest losses being applied first. Note the portion of an allowable business investment loss, which is discussed in some detail in Chapters 7 and 13, not used in the year of loss, becomes a non-capital loss and is available for carryover in the manner just described.

2. Net capital loss carryovers deductible by par. 111(1)(*b*)

A "net capital loss" (net C.L.) for a particular taxation year available for carryover to another year is defined to be the excess of allowable capital losses over taxable capital gains for that particular year plus allowable business investment losses not absorbed in the seven-year carryforward period as a non-capital loss, as discussed above [ssec. 111(8)]. Net capital losses may be carried back three years and forward indefinitely. It is important to note that net capital losses for a particular year are calculated using the inclusion rate of that year. The following are the historical inclusion rates.

Capital Gains Inclusion Rate:

Years	Inclusion Rate
1972–1987	$1/2$
1988, 1989	$2/3$
1990–February 27, 2000	$3/4$
February 28, 2000 – October 17, 2000	$2/3$
After October 17, 2000	$1/2$

Since net capital losses may arise in years with different capital gains inclusion rates to be deducted against other net taxable capital gains computed by other inclusion rates, it is necessary to convert net capital losses to the capital gains inclusion rate appropriate to the carryover year in which the net capital loss is deducted. Net capital losses realized in a year with a lower inclusion rate must be increased when carried forward to a year with a higher inclusion rate. Net capital losses realized in a year with a higher inclusion rate must be decreased when carried back to a year with a lower inclusion rate.

Subsection 111(1.1) calculates the amount of the net capital loss to be deducted in the year taking into account any differences in the rates of inclusion by the following formula:

the lesser of:

(a) net taxable capital gains computed under par. 3(*b*) for the year; and

(b) the total of each amount for different years of net capital losses determined by the formula

$$A \times \frac{B}{C}$$

where A is the amount of the net capital loss arising from a particular "loss year" and claimed under par. 111(1)(*b*);

B is the inclusion rate for the year in which the net capital loss is to be deducted; and

C is the inclusion rate for the year in which the loss was realized.

For example, a net capital loss of $9,000 realized in 1999 with its $3/4$ inclusion rate would be converted to $6,000 in 2004 with its $1/2$ inclusion rate (i.e., $9,000 × $1/2/3/4 = $6,000). Conceptually, the $9,000 net capital loss in 1999 resulted from a $12,000 capital loss (i.e., $9,000 × $4/3$). The same $12,000 capital loss in 2004 would result in a net capital loss of $6,000 (i.e., $12,000 × $1/2$).

Note that subsection 111(1.1) uses both the words "deducted" and "claimed" in reference to net capital losses. The word "claimed", as used in clauses 111(1.1)(*b*)(iii)(A) and (B), appears to refer to net capital losses in their original, unadjusted amount as computed in the "loss year" at the inclusion rate for that year. The word "deducted" appears to refer to the net capital losses after they have been adjusted by the formula to the inclusion rate appropriate for the year in which they will offset taxable capital gains.

Example Problem

Larry Loser had net capital losses of $10,000 in the taxation year ending December 31, 1987 and $2,000 in each of the taxation years ending December 31, 1988 and 1990. He had capital gains of $5,000 in 1998, $4,000 in 1999 and $3,000 in 2005. He has had no other capital gains or losses.

— REQUIRED

Determine the maximum amount to be deducted in the taxation years 1998, 1999 and 2005 under paragraph 111(1)(b) as modified by subsection 111(1.1).

— SOLUTION

	1998	1999	2005
Par. 3(b) inclusion:			
Capital gains realized	$ 5,000	$ 4,000	$ 3,000
Taxable capital gain...	$ 3,750	$ 3,000	$ 1,500
Par. 111(1.1)(a) deduction —			
Lesser of:			
(i) T.C.G. under par. 3(b) above	$ 3,750	$ 3,000	$ 1,500
(ii) total of adjusted net capital losses of loss years (see below)	$19,250	$15,500	$ 8,333
Lesser amount	$3,750	$3,000	$1,500

Net capital loss carryovers:

Year loss incurred	1987	1988	1990	Total
Unadjusted net C.L.	$10,000	$2,000	$2,000	
Adjusted to 1998 inclusion rate	$15,000[1]	$2,250[1]	$2,000	$19,250
Utilized in 1998 (see above)	(3,750)	Nil	Nil	(3,750)
Available in 1999	$11,250	$2,250	$2,000	$15,500
Utilized in 1999 (see above)	(3,000)	Nil	Nil	(3,000)
Available in 2005	$ 8,250	$2,250	$2,000	$12,500
Adjusted to 2005 inclusion rate	$ 5,500[2]	$1,500[2]	$1,333[2]	$ 8,333
Utilized in 2005	(1,500)	Nil	Nil	(1,500)
Available in 2006	$ 4,000	$1,500	$1,333	$ 6,833

— NOTE TO SOLUTION

(1) The $10,000 of 1987 net capital loss is a fractional amount computed at a $1/2$ inclusion rate. This amount is adjusted to the 1998 inclusion rate of $3/4$ as follows:

$$\$10,000 \times {}^{3}/_{4}/{}^{1}/_{2} = \$15,000$$

The $2,000 of 1988 net capital loss is a fractional amount computed at a $2/3$ inclusion rate. This amount is adjusted to the 1998 inclusion rate of $3/4$ as follows:

$$\$2,000 \times {}^{3}/_{4}/{}^{2}/_{3} = \$2,250$$

The $2,000 of 1990 net capital loss is a fractional amount computed at a $3/4$ inclusion rate. Therefore, it need not be adjusted for use before February 28, 2000.

(2) The losses are adjusted from the $3/4$ inclusion rate (as adjusted above) to the $1/2$ inclusion rate as follows:

1987: $$\$8,250 \times {}^{1}/_{2}/{}^{3}/_{4} = \$5,500$$

1988: $2,250 × ¹/₂/³/₄ = $1,500

1989: $2,000 × ¹/₂/³/₄ = $1,333

These adjustment factors do nothing more than convert the fractional loss of a particular year into a full loss by dividing by ¹/₂, ²/₃ or ³/₄ in the denominator (i.e., item C in the formula) and then computing the net capital loss at the inclusion rate for the year of the deduction by multiplying by ³/₄, ²/₃, or ¹/₂ in the numerator (i.e., item B in the formula). Hence, $10,000 divided by ¹/₂ is $20,000 which was the full capital loss in 1987 before the ¹/₂ inclusion rate was applied. Then $20,000 multiplied by ³/₄ produces $15,000 which is the net capital loss stated in terms of a ³/₄ inclusion rate used before February 28, 2000.

Note that the losses carried forward from the "loss year" are those from the earliest loss year [ssec. 111(3)]. This is illustrated in the net capital loss carryover calculation presented above. Note, also, how net capital losses deducted in a particular year under paragraph 111(1)(*b*), as modified by the adjustments in paragraph 111(1.1)(*a*), are limited to net taxable capital gains of that year.

3. Restricted farm loss carryovers deductible by par. 111(1)(*c*)

Restricted farm losses (R.F.L.) available for carryover (i.e., losses not deductible in the current year under section 31 because they exceed the limit of losses up to $2,500 plus one-half of losses in excess of $2,500 to a maximum of another $6,250) may be carried back three years and forward ten years. They may be deducted only to the extent of income from a farming business.

4. Farm loss carryovers deductible by par. 111(1)(*d*)

Farm losses are business losses but are given an extended carryforward of 10 years, as compared to seven years for other business losses. A farm loss is defined in subsection 111(8) and is separated from other business losses in the definition of non-capital loss carryovers, to accommodate the longer carryforward period. The three-year carryback is also available.

C. Capital Gains Deduction — Historical Overview

[ITA: 39(1)(*c*), (9); 110.6]

Individuals can shelter up to $500,000 of capital gains on qualified small business corporation shares and qualified farm property by claiming a capital gains deduction in the computation of taxable income.

The capital gains deduction originated in 1985. The 1985 federal Budget introduced a lifetime cumulative deduction for net taxable capital gains (net T.C.G.s) for individuals (other than trusts) resident in Canada. The announced purpose of this deduction was to provide an incentive for investment. Until the February 25, 1992 federal Budget, the deduction was virtually unrestricted as to type of capital gains on a disposition. The February 25, 1992 federal Budget imposed a restriction on the capital gains deduction resulting from the disposition, after February 1992, of most real property (i.e., land and buildings), described as non-qualifying real property. Since the whole thrust of the present Act is to tax a fraction of capital gains, the introduction of this provision created considerable complexity in the legislation, to accommodate this exception.

The February 22, 1994 federal Budget eliminated the $100,000 lifetime general capital gains deduction for gains realized on dispositions of property occurring after the budget date. However, the budget did not eliminate the $500,000 lifetime capital gains exemption for shares of a qualified small business corporation or for qualified farm property. This exemption uses the same rules and calculations as the exemption that was eliminated, so much of the complexity remains.

The budget which eliminated the $100,000 lifetime general capital gains exemption contained a provision which would allow an individual to recognize all or any part of the gains on the taxpayer's capital property accrued to February 22, 1994. Generally, the individual had to file an election with his or her 1994 tax return to recognize an amount of accrued gain that could be offset by the available capital gains exemption. The gain that was recognized by this election will reduce future capital gains by either increasing the cost of the property elected on or creating a special account which can be drawn down by future capital gains on those assets. These special accounts are called "exempt gains balance" for eligible capital property and "exempt capital gains balance" for mutual funds.

For example, consider the case of an individual who owns capital property, such as shares of a public corporation, which cost $10,000 and had a fair market value of $40,000 on February 22, 1994. The individual had $15,000 of the lifetime general capital gains exemption left in 1994. On filing the 1994 tax return, the individual could elect to have received proceeds of disposition on the shares of $25,000, resulting in a capital gain of $15,000 which would be offset by the exemption. The adjusted cost base of the shares could then be increased to the elected proceeds of $25,000.

Since the general capital gains exemption has been eliminated, it will not be discussed further. The capital gains deduction available on qualified small business corporation shares will be discussed in Chapter 13.

D. Ordering of Division C Deductions

[ITA: 111; 111.1]

1. General ordering rules for Division C

Section 111.1 provides the following order of relevant deductions under Division C:

Sec. 110	Other deductions
Sec. 110.2	Lump-sum payments
Sec. 111	Loss carryovers
Sec. 110.6	Capital gains deduction
Sec. 110.7	Residing in prescribed zone.

2. Ordering of section 111 loss carryovers

Loss carryovers can be applied in any order within section 111, subject to the general ordering rules for Division C [sec. 111.1], except that the oldest losses are always applied first [par. 111(3)(*b*)]. Therefore, careful consideration should be given as to which type of losses are used first. Generally speaking, the most restricted types of loss carryovers should be applied first. For example, since net capital losses can only be applied against net taxable capital gains, then net capital losses should be applied in years in which net taxable capital gains arise, unless it is expected that these gains will arise regularly in the future. Losses which have a carryback provision should be used immediately, if possible, so that taxes are refunded as soon as possible.

Example Problem 1

The following information has been provided by your client, Karl Konfused:

	2003	2004	2005
Capital gains (C.G.)	—	$84,000	$44,000
Capital losses (C.L.) (excluding B.I.L.)	$ 6,000	—	—
Business investment loss (B.I.L.) before ssec. 39(9) adjustment	18,000	—	30,000

Additional Information

(1) Karl had a $10,000 net capital loss which arose in 1998, and has not been deducted previously.

(2) Karl had no capital gains prior to 2003 and he did not claim any net capital losses in any preceding years.

(3) In 2005, Karl had a rental property loss of $1,000 and had no property income in 2003 or 2004.

— REQUIRED

(A) Determine Karl's income from the sources indicated for 2003 to 2005 according to the ordering rules in section 3.

(B) Determine Karl's taxable income from the sources indicated for 2003 to 2005 according to the ordering rules in Division C after amending the returns.

— SOLUTION

(A)	2003	2004	2005
Par. 3(*a*): income from non-capital sources (≥0)	Nil	Nil	Nil
Par. 3(*b*): net taxable capital gains (≥0):			
taxable capital gains	Nil	$ 42,000	$ 22,000
allowable capital losses	$ (3,000)	—	—
	Nil	$ 42,000	$ 22,000
Par. 3(*c*): par. 3(*a*) + par. 3(*b*)	Nil	$ 42,000	$ 22,000
Par. 3(*d*): losses from non-capital sources and A.B.I.L.s:			
rental property loss	—	—	(1,000)
A.B.I.L.	$ (9,000)	—	(15,000)
Division B income	0	$ 42,000	$ 6,000

(B)	2003	2004	2005
Division B income from (A)	0	$ 42,000	$ 6,000
Less: net capital losses [par. 111(1)(*b*)]	Nil	(9,667)[1]	Nil
non-capital losses [par. 111(1)(*a*)] (2002 A.B.I.L. carried forward to 2003)	Nil	(9,000)	Nil
Taxable income	Nil	$ 23,333	$ 6,000

The foregoing solution illustrates how the various components fit into the full calculation of Division B income and taxable income.

— NOTE TO SOLUTION

(1) Loss continuity schedule	1998	2003	Total
Unadjusted net C.L.	$ 10,000	$ 3,000	
Adjusted to 2004 inclusion rate ($10,000 × ½ / ¾)	$ 6,667	$ 3,000	$ 9,667
Utilized in 2004	(6,667)	(3,000)	(9,667)
Available in 2005	Nil	Nil	Nil

Example Problem 2

Larry Loss-Carryover provides you with the following income (losses) for tax purposes for the years 2003 to 2005:

	2003	2004	2005
Employment income	$25,000	$ 32,000	$40,000
Business income:	20,000	(36,000)	40,000
Property income from Canadian interest	3,000	4,000	5,000
Capital gains (capital losses):			
Listed personal property	6,000	(10,000)	12,000
Other	15,000	(14,000)	2,250

Larry also provides the following additional information:

(1) Loss carryovers:

Listed personal property loss arising in 1997	$ 2,000
Non-capital loss arising in 1998 from a business	35,000
Net capital loss arising in 1999	18,000

(2) Larry did not claim a capital gains deduction or net capital losses in the years 1985 to 2002.

— REQUIRED

Dealing with each item line-by-line across the years, rather than one year at a time:

(A) determine Larry's income for 2003 to 2005 according to the ordering rules in section 3, and

(B) determine Larry's taxable income for 2003 to 2005 according to the ordering rules in Division C after amending the returns.

— SOLUTION

(A)

Par. 3(*a*): income from non-capital sources (≥0):

	2003	2004	2005
Employment	$25,000	$ 32,000	$ 40,000
Business income	20,000	Nil	40,000
Property from Canadian interest	3,000	4,000	5,000
	$48,000	$ 36,000	$ 85,000

Par. 3(*b*): net taxable capital gains (≥0):

Listed personal property[1]	Nil	Nil	$ 3,000
Other	$ 7,500	(7,000)	1,125
	$ 7,500	Nil	$ 4,125

Par. 3(c): sum of pars. 3(a), 3(b)...............	$55,500	$ 36,000	$ 89,125
Par. 3(d) Losses from non-capital sources		(36,000)	
Income — Division B	$55,500	Nil	$ 89,125

(B)

Income — Division B	$55,500		$ 89,125
Net capital loss[2] [par. 111(1)(b)]	(7,500)		(4,125)
Non-capital loss[3] [par. 111(1)(a)].............	(35,000)		Nil
Taxable income	$13,000		$ 85,000

— NOTES TO SOLUTION

   (1) The listed personal property loss from 1997 is applied against the 2003 listed personal property gain of $6,000 leaving $4,000 which will be offset by the listed personal property capital loss of 2004 carried back. The remaining 2004 listed personal property capital loss of $6,000 will be carried forward and applied against the 2005 listed personal property capital gain of $12,000 leaving a net capital gain of $6,000 of which $1/2$ will be taken into income. Note that listed personal property losses are carried over in their full capital loss amounts.

   (2) (A) Net capital losses [pars. 111(1)(b), 111(1.1)(a) and 111(8)]

	2003	2004	2005
Lesser of:			
(i) net T.C.G.s for the year	$ 7,500	N/A	$ 4,125
(ii) total of adjusted net capital losses of loss years	$12,000	N/A	$11,500
Lesser amount.....	$ 7,500		$ 4,125

   (B) Net capital loss continuity schedule

	1999	2004	Total
Unadjusted net C.L.	$18,000	$7,000	
Adjusted to 2003 inclusion rate	$12,000	N/A	$12,000
Utilized in 2003	(7,500)	N/A	(7,500)
Available in 2004..........................	$ 4,500	—	$ 4,500
Realized in 2004	—	$7,000	7,000
Utilized in 2004	Nil	Nil	Nil
Available in 2005..........................	$ 4,500	$7,000	$11,500
Utilized in 2005	(4,125)	Nil	(4,125)
Available in 2006..........................	$ 375	$7,000	$ 7,375

(3) Non-capital loss continuity schedule

Non-capital loss — 1998		$35,000
2003 application		(35,000)
Balance of 1998 non-capital loss		Nil
Non-capital loss — 2004		
Business loss	$36,000	
less: par. 3(*c*)	(36,000)	Nil
Balance		Nil

Since individuals are eligible for non-refundable tax credits, it is advantageous to have at least $7,756 of taxable income in 2003. This amount increases to $8,012 in 2004 and $8,148 in 2005, as discussed later in this chapter.

E. Taxable Income of Non-Residents

[ITA: 2(3); 114; 115(1); IT-420R3]

In the discussion of residence in Chapter 2, it was established that a part-time resident of Canada is taxed on worldwide income for the part of the year that the individual is resident in Canada. The taxable income for the period of part-time residence of an individual is calculated under section 114. A non-resident individual is subject to Part I tax on income from employment in Canada, from carrying on business in Canada and from the disposition of taxable Canadian property [sec. 115]. In addition, a non-resident is subject to Canadian withholding tax on Canadian-source income such as interest, dividends, alimony and pension receipts [sec. 212].

Consider the case of an individual who is an international business consultant who decided to move the base of operations of the business to another country and to continue to provide service to Canadian clients from that base. Assume the individual ceases to be a resident on May 15 of the year, but continues to carry on the unincorporated business of providing consulting services in Canada periodically after that date. This individual would be taxed in Canada on worldwide income for the period to May 15 [par. 114(*a*)] and only on Canadian-source business income after that date for the rest of the year [par. 114(*b*)]. If the individual remains a non-resident in the following year, then only Canadian-source business income would be taxed in that year.

Income for the period of part-time residence is computed in the normal manner, including the deduction of most amounts allowed in Division B. The Division C deductions reasonably applicable to the period of part-time residence are also deductible. The taxable income of a non-resident with Canadian-source income is computed under Division D. Certain Division C deductions may be claimed in respect of that income earned in Canada.

Non-residents are required to pay tax on their "taxable income earned in Canada" for the year [ssec. 2(3)]. "Taxable income earned in Canada" is the income that would be determined under section 3 with some adjustments to confine the calculation to Canadian-sources of the non-resident. In particular, the term "taxable Canadian property" necessary under paragraph 2(3)(*c*) for the determination of income from its disposition is defined [par. 115(1)(*b*)]. Then, Division C deductions as appropriate to the Canadian-source income may be claimed [pars. 115(1)(*d*) to (*f*)]. These deductions include those in respect of stock options exercised [pars. 110(1)(*d*) and (*d*.1)], charitable donations [ssec. 110.1(1)], and loss carryovers reasonably applicable to Canadian-source income [sec. 111]. The Canada Revenue Agency's (CRA) interpretation of these provisions is contained in IT-420R3.

II. COMPUTATION OF TAX FOR INDIVIDUALS

A. Basic Computation of Tax
[ITA: 117(1); 117.1; IT-519R2]

1. Tax rates

Subsection 117(2) sets out the rates of tax applicable to individuals. These amounts, which have been indexed for 2005, are presented in Exhibit 10-1.

EXHIBIT 10-1
2005 Federal Income Tax Brackets

Taxable income	Tax
$35,595 or less	16%
In excess of $35,595	$5,695* + 22% on next $35,595
In excess of $71,190	$13,526** + 26% on next $44,549
In excess of $115,739	$25,109*** + 29% on remainder

* Computed as 16% of $35,595 = $5,695 (rounded)

** Computed as $5,695 + 22% of $35,595 = $13,526 (rounded)

*** Computed as $13,526 + 26% of $44,549 = $25,109 (rounded)

2. Annual indexing adjustment

Section 117.1 provides for the annual indexing of certain dollar amounts used in the calculation of tax or tax credits.

The indexing formula is based on the annual increase in the Consumer Price Index for the 12-month period ending September 30 of the year before the year in which the indexing is to apply.

3. Overview of tax credit and tax calculation system

Exhibit 10-2 summarizes the key items in the calculation of tax credits and income tax payable. The first line in Exhibit 10-2 results from applying the tax table in Exhibit 10-1 to the taxpayer's taxable income for the year. Total federal income tax is reduced by two basic types of credits, non-refundable and refundable, which are deducted at one of three different stages of the calculation.

EXHIBIT 10-2
Summary of Income Tax Calculation

Total federal income tax on taxable income [ssec. 117(2) and sec. 117.1]		$xxx
Subtract: Total non-refundable tax credits (see Exhibit 10-3)	$xxx	
Federal dividend tax credit [sec. 121]	xxx	xxx
Basic Federal Tax		$xxx
Subtract: Federal foreign tax credits [sec. 126]		xxx
Federal tax		$xxx
Subtract: Federal political contributions tax credit [ssec. 127(3)]	$xxx	
Other federal tax credits	xxx	xxx
Net federal tax		$xxx
Add: Tax on Old Age Security benefits [sec. 180.2]		xxx
Total federal tax		$xxx
Add: Provincial tax	$xxx	
Provincial surtax	xxx	xxx
Total payable		$xxx
Subtract: Total income tax deducted at source	$xxx	

Federal refundable tax credits (e.g., employee and partner GST rebate)	xxx	
Tax paid by instalments	xxx	
Provincial refundable tax credits	xxx	xxx
Balance payable or refundable		$xxx

Non-refundable tax credits like the marital status tax credit or the dividend tax credit are subtracted from federal tax. To the extent that these credits exceed federal tax, the excess is not refundable and, therefore, is of no value to the taxpayer. Some non-refundable tax credits are referred to as "above-the-line tax credits", because they are subtracted from federal tax to arrive at Basic Federal Tax. Exhibit 10-3 lists these non-refundable tax credits. Some non-refundable tax credits like federal foreign tax credits and federal political contributions tax credits can be termed "below-the-line tax credits", because they are subtracted after the calculation of Basic Federal Tax. These "below-the-line tax credits" are not magnified by the territorial or non-resident tax effects, discussed below.

EXHIBIT 10-3
Types of Non-refundable Tax Credits

- Basic personal amount
- Spousal amount
- Equivalent-to-spouse amount
- Amounts for dependent children (if ≥18 years and infirm)
- Additional personal amounts
- Caregiver amount
- Age amount
- Canada or Quebec Pension Plan contributions
- Employment Insurance premiums
- Pension income amount
- Disability amount
- Disability amount transferred from a dependant other than spouse
- Tuition and education amounts
- Tuition and education amounts transferred from a child
- Amounts transferred from spouse
- Medical expenses
- Donations and gifts
- Interest paid on student loans
- Dividend tax credit

Some tax credits are refundable and, hence, are subtracted last. To the extent that these tax credits, such as the federal credit for employment outside Canada or certain provincial tax credits, exceed total tax payable, the excess is refunded, along with excess tax withholdings from payroll or excess tax instalments on income not subject to withholdings. Other tax credits like the GST credit and the child tax benefit involve a calculation of an amount that is deemed to be tax-paid and, hence, result in a "refund" of the deemed tax.

It is important to understand the difference between a tax credit and a tax deduction. A tax deduction reduces a taxpayer's income subject to tax at a particular marginal tax rate. Therefore, a deduction from income or taxable income saves the taxpayer an amount that increases with the taxpayer's level of income and, hence, tax rate. For some taxpayers, it may take $4 of deduction to save $1 in tax (i.e., at a 25% tax rate), while for other taxpayers, only $2 of deduction will save the $1 in tax (i.e., at a 50% tax rate). A tax credit is a direct reduction of the taxpayer's tax bill at a specified rate. A "below-the-line" credit of $1 results in a tax reduction of $1. An "above-the-line" credit of $1 results in a tax reduction of $1 plus the savings in non-resident tax, discussed below. The objective of the tax credit system is to provide all taxpayers with the same level of tax reduction regardless of their marginal tax rate.

4. Provincial and Territorial Tax

The significance of Basic Federal Tax is that it is the base for additional tax on non-residents [sec. 120]. Therefore, any tax credit subtracted before Basic Federal Tax reduces this non-resident tax which is based on a "tax on tax" structure. As a result, a 16% federal tax credit for, say, marital status, has a magnified effect in reducing total tax by 23.7% where the non-resident tax rate is 48% of Basic Federal Tax (i.e., $.16 \times (1 + .48) = .237$). These tax credits are non-refundable tax credits.

All of the provinces and territories use a "tax on income" (TONI) structure for computing provincial tax. In such a structure, provinces may adopt the federal calculation of taxable income or make adjustments to it. Provinces may use the federal brackets or change them. Provincial rates are specified for income in these brackets. Provinces specify their own non-refundable credit amounts. For provincial tax rates, tax brackets and tax credit amounts, see the preface material in a current edition of the CCH CANADIAN INCOME TAX ACT. For the purposes of this book, where provincial tax is calculated for individuals, the following table, using the federal brackets, will be used. In addition, the provincial rate for the non-refundable credits will be assumed to be 10% of the federal base. For example, the provincial basic personal amount will be 10% of $8,148 or $815.

Taxable income	Tax
$35,595 or less	10%
In excess of $35,595	$3,560* + 12% on next $35,595
In excess of $71,190	$7,831** + 15% on next $44,549
In excess of $115,739	$14,513*** + 17% on remainder

* Computed as 10% of $35,595 = $3,560 (rounded)

** Computed as $3,560 + 12% of $35,595 = $7,831 (rounded)

*** Computed as $7,831 + 15 % of $44,549 = $14,513 (rounded)

B. Section 118 Tax Credits

[ITA: 118; IT-513R; IT-513R]

Subsection 118(1) begins by presenting the following general formula for computing non-refundable personal tax credits:

$$A \times B$$

where A is the appropriate percentage for the year, defined to mean the lowest percentage referred to in subsection 117(2) (i.e., 16% for 2005) [ssec. 248(1)],

B is the aggregate of the following tax credit bases:
(a) married status,
(b) wholly dependent person (i.e., equivalent-to-married status),
(c) single status,
(c.1) in-home care of relative,
(d) dependants, and
(e) additional amount.

Therefore, the personal tax credits are computed as 16% of a dollar amount indexed for 2005. The personal tax credit for individuals, other than the taxpayer, are limited by the Division B income of the dependant. However, dependants are allowed to earn a certain amount of Division B income before the tax credit is reduced.

For the purposes of this chapter, the amount of Division B income of a dependant before the tax credit is reduced will be called the "threshold income".

1. Married status credit allowed by par. 118(1)(*a*)

The tax credit base for married status is computed as the sum of the following two amounts [par. 118(1)(*a*)]:

Basic personal tax credit base in 2005		$8,148
Spouse's tax credit base in 2005		$6,919 7344
Less: greater of spouse's Division B income or $692 in 2005	$ xxx	
minus: threshold income in 2005	(692)	
Net amount (non-negative [sec. 257])	xxx	xxx
Total tax credit base		$ xxx
Tax credit (16% of total)		$ xxx

The total tax credit is a maximum of $2,411 (i.e., 16% of $8,148 + 16% of $6,919 max.). This tax credit is available if an individual supports his or her spouse. Note, however, that the spouse's tax credit base is reduced by the Division B income of the dependent spouse for the whole year, even if the marriage occurred in the year.

On the other hand, if the individual was living apart from his or her spouse at the end of the year because of a marriage breakdown, only the spouse's income for the year, while married and not separated, is considered.

The base for an individual's basic personal tax credit to $10,000 in 2009. The increase will be phased-in beginning in 2006 [ssec. 118 (3.1)]. Similarly, proposed new subsection 118(3.2) will increase the base for the credit in respect of a spouse or common-law partner and for a wholly dependent relative to $8,500 for 2009 with the phase-in increases starting in 2006. The net income threshold for these latter credits will be increased to $850 for 2009, with the phase-in increases starting in 2006 [ssec. 118 (3.1)].

The CRA's position has been that in the year of marriage both spouses cannot claim each other even if the quantum limitations have been adhered to since they both cannot have supported each other.[a]

A common-law partner is treated like a spouse. The term "common-law partner" [ssec. 248(1)] is defined as two persons, regardless of sex, who co-habit in a conjugal relationship and have done so for a continuous period of at least one year or who is the parent of a child of whom the taxpayer is also a parent.

Hence, the married status tax credit is allowed in a common-law relationship if the conditions in the extended meaning are met and the conditions in paragraph 118(1)(*a*) are met.

2. Equivalent-to-married status for wholly dependent person credit allowed by par. 118(1)(*b*)

A tax credit base equal to the tax credit base for married status is provided in respect of a wholly dependent person where the taxpayer is not entitled to a married credit (i.e., an individual who is not married or living in a common-law relationship) [par. 118(1)(*b*)]. This provision might apply to an individual who, at any time in the year, was single, divorced, separated, widowed and who supported a relative. The calculation

---

[a] This position has been confirmed by a decision by the Federal Court–Trial Division in *The Queen v. Robichaud*, 83 DTC 5265.

of the credit is the same as that shown for paragraph 118(1)(*a*), with the Division B income of the wholly dependent person in excess of the threshold reducing the credit.

A number of additional conditions must apply for the tax credit to be available.

(1) The dependent person must live, at some time in the year, in the same self-contained domestic establishment [ssec. 248(1)] as the taxpayer claiming the tax credit. The dependant must be wholly dependent for support on that taxpayer and/or other persons. (See IT-513R, pars. 11–22, for the CRA's comments on the phrase "wholly dependent" and other aspects of the equivalent-to-married tax credit.) The taxpayer need not own the residence. A rental unit qualifies.

(2) The dependant must be related to the taxpayer by blood, marriage or adoption [ssec. 251(6)]. As a result, nieces, nephews, aunts, uncles and cousins would not qualify as a marital equivalent under this provision (unless they fit the definition of child which is very broad and should be examined carefully [ssec. 252(1)]).

(3) Unless the dependant is a child of the taxpayer, the dependant must be resident in Canada.[b]

(4) Unless the dependant is the parent or grandparent of the taxpayer or is dependent by reason of physical or mental infirmity, the dependant must be under 18 years of age at any time in the year. In the case of *The Queen v. Mercier*, (F.C.T.D.) 97 DTC 5081, the taxpayer argued that the age requirement for children discriminates against single parents with children 18 years of age or older who, in the opinion of the taxpayer, should qualify for the credit and, hence, violates the Charter of Rights and Freedoms. The Court held that the provision does not violate the equality guarantee of the Charter.

(5) Only one paragraph 118(1)(*b*) tax credit is available to a taxpayer [par. 118(4)(*a*)].

(6) The dependant cannot be claimed under this tax credit if the dependant has been claimed under the married status credit by another taxpayer [par. 118(4)(*a*.1)].

(7) Where two taxpayers are eligible for a paragraph 118(1)(*b*) tax credit in respect of the same person or the same domestic establishment, only one person is permitted the tax credit and only one equivalent-to-married tax credit can be claimed for a given domestic establishment. If the taxpayers cannot agree as to who should have the tax credit, then neither can have the tax credit [par. 118(4)(*b*)]. For example, Tom and Donna, who are both single, support their mother in the same domestic establishment. Either Tom or Donna can have the paragraph 118(1)(*b*) tax credit, but not both. If they cannot agree, then neither can have the tax credit.

(8) Where a taxpayer has claimed a dependant under this paragraph, neither the taxpayer nor any other taxpayer can claim that dependant for the 18 years of age or older and infirm credit or the caregiver credit [par. 118(4)(*c*)]. For example, if a married couple with one infirm child, 20 years of age, separates during the year and the spouse who supports the child claims the child under paragraph 118(1)(*b*), then that spouse cannot make an additional claim under paragraph 118(1)(*d*) (dependent children 18 years of age or older and infirm). The other spouse also cannot make a claim under paragraph 118(1)(*d*) for that child even if he or she did, in fact, wholly support the child during part of the year.

(9) Where an individual is required under the terms of a written agreement or court order to make payments in the year in respect of the support of a child, the individual is not entitled to claim any tax credit under section 118 in respect of the child [sec. 118(5)].

---

[b] Refer to *Ruzicka v. The Queen*, (T.C.C.) 95 DTC 365, for a discussion of the rules related to non-residents.

It might be noted that the interpretation of the phrase "at any time in the year is an unmarried person" appears to have the effect of enabling a person who presently qualifies for a tax credit under paragraph 118(1)(*b*) and marries during the year to still qualify for this tax credit in the year of marriage but not subsequently. This position appears to be supported by IT-513R, paragraphs 11 and 17. Of course, the person claiming a dependant under paragraph 118(1)(*b*) would not be allowed a claim for marital status under paragraph 118(1)(*a*).

3. Single status — Basic personal tax credit allowed by par. 118(1)(*c*)

The base of the basic personal tax credit [par. 118(1)(*c*)] is set at $8,148 in 2005 and, when multiplied by 16%, provides a tax credit of $1,304 (rounded) for 2005.

4. Caregiver credit for in-home care of relative allowed by par. 118(1)(*c*.1)

Individuals are entitled to a credit of up to $616 (i.e., 16% of $3,848) for residing with and providing in-home care for an adult relative. For this purpose, the relatives include the individual's child or grandchild or the individual's or spouse's common-law partner's parent, grandparent, brother, sister, aunt, uncle, nephew or niece. A parent or grandparent must either have attained the age of 65 years or be dependent because of physical or mental infirmity. All other dependent relatives must have attained the age of 18 and be dependent because of mental or physical infirmity.

The base amount of $3,848 is reduced by the dependant's income in excess of $13,141. The credit is not available if the dependant's income exceeds $16,989.

Where an individual is entitled to a caregiver credit for a dependent, no one can claim the credit for equivalent-to-married [par. 118(4)(*c*)] or for infirm dependants age 18 or older [par. 118(4)(*d*)] in respect of that dependant.

5. Dependants credit allowed by par. 118(1)(*d*)

A dependant is defined to include for the purposes of paragraph 118(1)(*d*) a child, grandchild, parent, grandparent, brother, sister, uncle, aunt, niece or nephew of the taxpayer or the taxpayer's spouse or common-law partner [ssec. 118(6)]. However, the dependants must have attained the age of 18 before the end of the year in order to qualify for the tax credit [spar. 118(1)(*d*)(i)]. Also, the individual must be dependent on the taxpayer because of mental or physical infirmity [spar. 118(1)(*d*)(ii)].

The tax credit is computed for 2005 as [par. 118(1)(*d*)]:

Dependant's tax credit base		$3,848
Less: dependant's Division B income	$ xxx	
threshold amount	5,460	
Net amount (non-negative)		xxx
Net tax credit base (non-negative)		$ xxx
Dependant's tax credit (16% of net) (maximum of $616 — rounded)		$ xxx

Appendix A of IT-513R indicates that mental or physical infirmity in respect of paragraph 118(1)(*d*) should require the infirm person to be dependent during a considerable period of time and not just temporarily.[c]

Note that the maximum amount of the dependant credit is the same as that of the caregiver credit, but the income threshold is much lower for the dependant credit. Thus, the dependant credit can be eliminated more quickly, making the caregiver credit more attractive, numerically. However, the caregiver credit has the more restrictive

[c] A court case dealing with this issue is *The Queen v. Diaz*, (F.C.T.D.) 81 DTC 5112.

condition that the dependant must ordinarily reside in the same self-contained domestic establishment as the taxpayer claiming the credit.

The tax credit available under paragraph 118(1)(*d*) must be shared by all individuals who are entitled to a tax credit in respect of the same dependant [par. 118(4)(*e*)]. Where these supporting individuals cannot agree on an allocation of the tax credit, the Minister may make the allocation. Furthermore, a taxpayer who is entitled to a deduction for support payments for a spouse under paragraph 60(*b*) is not entitled to claim a tax credit for the spouse [ssec. 118(5)]. However, the CRA does permit a tax credit claim in the year of separation or divorce according to IT-513R, paragraph 27. Where an individual is required under the terms of a written agreement or court order to make payments in the year in respect of the support of a child, the individual is not entitled to claim any tax credit under section 118 in respect of the child [ssec. 118(5)]. This provision is necessary to parallel the non-deductibility of child support payments as discussed in Chapter 9. The subsection ensures that, since the child support payments are not deductible, the supporting parent would not be able to claim this deduction.

6. Additional amount allowed as a credit by par. 118(1)(*e*)

Where a taxpayer is entitled to claim a dependant for the equivalent-to-married (ETM) credit, the dependant cannot be claimed under the caregiver credit or the credit for infirm dependants age 18 or older [par. 118(4)(*d*)].

Where the caregiver credit or the credit for an infirm dependant age 18 or older would have been larger than the ETM credit, the difference can be claimed under this provision as an additional credit. The effect is to allow the equivalent of the caregiver credit for a person in respect of whom the ETM credit is claimed.

7. Age credit allowed by sec. 118(2)

The non-refundable age tax credit is computed on a base of $3,979 for 2005 [ssec. 118(2)]. Since the appropriate percentage for the year is 16%, the tax credit for 2005 is $637 (rounded). It is available to an individual who has attained the age of 65 years before the end of the year.

However, this age tax credit is reduced by 15% of the excess of the individual's Division B income over $29,619 and is, thus, completely eliminated when the net income exceeds $56,146.

For example, if an individual's Division B income is $45,000, the age tax credit would be computed as:

Age tax credit base		$3,979
Less: base reduction of lesser of:		
(a) Credit base		$3,979
(b) Division B income	$45,000	
Less: threshold	29,619	
Excess, if any	$15,381 × .15 = $2,307	
Lesser amount		2,307
Net base		$1,672
Age tax credit: 16% of $1,672		$ 268

8.   Pension credit allowed by sec. 118(3)

This non-refundable pension tax credit is determined as follows:

Age 65 and Older

The pension credit is equal to 16% of the lesser of:

1. $1,000 and

2.   the "pension income"

Pension income includes, but is not limited to [ssec. 118(7)]:

(a)   a payment in respect of a life annuity arising from a superannuation pension fund or plan;

(b)   an annuity payment under a registered retirement savings plan or a payment under a registered retirement income fund;

(c)   an annuity payment under a deferred profit sharing plan; and

(d)   the income portion of other annuity payments.

Under Age 65

The pension credit is equal to 16% of the lesser of:

1. $1,000 and

2.   the "qualified pension income"

The only difference is to change the definition of pension income to qualified pension income [ssec. 118(7)]. Qualified pension income includes:

(a)   a payment in respect of a life annuity arising from a superannuation pension fund or plan; or

(b)   certain annuities or payments received by the individual as a consequence of the death of the individual's spouse.

Certain amounts are not included in pension income or qualified pension income [ssec. 118(8)]. These excluded amounts are:

(a)   the Old Age Pension or Supplement;

(b)   the Canada Pension Plan (or provincial plan) pension;

(c)   a death benefit [ssec. 248(1)];

(d)   the amount of any payment which is included in income and then deducted under another provision such as lump-sum payments from withdrawing from a pension fund, an RRSP or a DPSP, retiring allowances, or pension benefits or DPSP benefits transferred into a spousal RRSP; and

(e)   a payment out of or under a salary deferral arrangement, a retirement compensation arrangement, an employee benefit plan, an employee trust or a prescribed provincial pension plan.

9.   Summary of personal tax credits

Exhibit 10-4 provides a summary of the numerical components of the section 118 tax credits discussed.

EXHIBIT 10-4
Section 118 Tax Credits (rounded)

	Maximum tax credit	Tax credit base	Division B income threshold
Par. 118(1)(a) or (b):			
Basic personal	$1,304	$8,148	N/A
Spouse or equivalent	1,107	6,919	$ 692
Par. 118(1)(c): Single person	1,304	8,148	N/A
Sec. 118(1)(c.1) Caregiver	616	3,848	13,141
Par. 118(1)(d): Dependants, age 18 and infirm	616	3,848	5,460
Ssec. 118(2): Age.............................	637	3,979	29,619
Ssec. 118(3): Pension	160	1,000	N/A
Sec. 118.3: Impairment........................	1,055	6,596	N/A

For the purposes of this book, where provincial tax credits are calculated for individuals, a rate of 10% (equal to the lowest provincial rate used in this book) will be applied to the above federal tax credit base, net of any applicable reduction for income in excess of the federal Division B income threshold.

Example Problem

George, age 50, has the following dependants, each of whom has Division B income as indicated for 2005:

Dependant	Age at year-end	Division B income
Spouse	45	$3,500
Son	14	2,725
Son	16	2,800
Daughter (physically infirm)	18	4,000
Mother (age 65)	70	6,000

— REQUIRED

Determine the personal tax credits available under section 118 for each of George's dependants for 2005. All of the dependants live with George.

— SOLUTION

	Wife [par. 118(1)(a)]	Daughter (18 and infirm) [par. 118(1)(d)]	Mother (age 65) [par. 118(1)(c.1)]
Division B income	$3,500	$4,000	$ 6,000
Threshold income	(692)	(5,460)	(13,141)
Excess income	$2,808	$ 0	$ 0
Tax credit base	$6,919	$3,848	$ 3,848
Excess income	(2,808)	0	0
Net tax credit base	$4,111	$3,848	$ 3,848
Tax credit @ 16% (rounded)....................	$ 658	$ 616	$ 616

Note that neither of the sons provides a dependant tax credit under paragraph 118(1)(d). They are covered under the Child Tax Benefit system, discussed later in this chapter.

C. Charitable Gifts Credit

[ITA: 118.1; IT-297R2]

1. Basic rules

The non-refundable charitable donation tax credit is calculated by the following formula [ssec. 118.1(3)]:

$$(A \times B) + C (D - B)$$

where A is 16% (i.e., the appropriate percentage for the year);

B is the first $200 of total gifts [ssec. 118.1(1)];

C is 29% (i.e., the highest federal marginal tax rate for the year); and

D is the individual's total gifts (if over $200) for the year.

In essence, the tax credit amounts to 16% of total gifts up to $200 and 29% for total gifts in excess of $200. For the purposes of this book, where provincial tax credits are calculated for individuals, a rate of 10% will be applied to total gifts up to $200 and 17% (equal to the highest provincial tax rate used in this book) for total gifts in excess of $200.

The definition of total gifts indicates the following four components:

(a) total charitable gifts, including gifts to:

- Canadian registered charities (including Canadian universities),
- registered Canadian amateur athletic associations,
- prescribed universities outside Canada,
- certain tax-free housing organizations in Canada,
- Canadian municipalities,
- the United Nations or its agencies, and
- charities outside Canada to which the Government of Canada has made a donation in the year or the preceding year;

(b) total Crown gifts;

(c) total cultural gifts; and

(d) total ecological gifts.

2. Income limit and carryforward

If the eligible donations in a year exceed the maximum of 75% of Division B income, the excess amount should be carried forward and claimed first, before the current year gifts, in the next five years. Donations may only be carried forward five years subject to the 75% limitation in that year. The income limitation is found in the definition of "total gifts" [ssec. 118.1(1)]. This carryforward is permitted to the extent that the donations are not claimed in the current year, even though they may not exceed 75% of Division B income in the current year. The annual Division B income limitation of 75% of the donor's net income for the year is increased by 25% of:

- recapture of CCA arising on a gift of depreciable capital property; and
- taxable capital gains arising on the donation of a capital property.

A limit of 100% of Division B net income applies for gifts:

- made in the year of death [ssec. 118.1(4)]; or
- of ecologically sensitive land [ssec. 118.1(1)].

The 75% of Division B income limit should not be expected to apply in most cases. However, the limit would become an effective limit, if gifts are made in an unusual year of relatively low income or a loss year.

3. Total charitable gifts

Gifts made to certain types of organizations listed under the definition of "total charitable gifts" [ssec. 118.1(1)] may be eligible for the tax credit to a maximum tax credit base of 75% of Division B income. Only the gifts to these specified organizations are eligible and they must be supported by proper receipts [ssec. 118.1(2)].

Where gifts of capital property and works of art, which are inventory to the donor, have a fair market value greater than adjusted cost base or cost amount, and the gift is not cultural property [ssec. 118.1(1)], the taxpayer may make a designation of a transfer price. The taxpayer can designate a transfer price between fair market value[d] and adjusted cost base [ssec. 118.1(6)] or cost amount as proceeds of disposition and the value of the gift [ssec. 118.1(7)]. Capital gains or income could, thus, be avoided by selecting the adjusted cost base or cost amount; but the value of the gift and the resultant tax credit under these paragraphs would be lower.

If personal-use property is acquired as part of an arrangement under which the property is gifted to a charity, then the $1,000 rule [sec. 46] will not apply. This rule is designed to prevent abuses connected with the donation of art and other personal-use property.

4. Gifts of publicly traded securities

The income inclusion rate for capital gains from gifts of publicly traded securities (unless donated to private charitable foundations) is reduced by $\frac{1}{2}$. For this purpose, the inclusion rate is 25% instead of the usual 50% [par. 38(a.1)]. Securities eligible for this treatment include shares listed on a prescribed stock exchange [Regs. 3200 and 3201].

5. Total cultural gifts

Where an artist makes a cultural gift that is a work of art created by the individual and that is property in the artist's inventory, the artist is deemed to have received proceeds of disposition equal to the cost to the artist of the work of art [ssec. 118.1(7.1)]. A cultural gift is included in the definition of "total cultural gifts" [ssec. 118.1(1)] and means objects that the Cultural Property Export Review Board has determined meets certain conditions. The result of this provision is that the artist is entitled to a credit based on the full fair market value of the art donated, but has no income to report as a result of the donation and its consequent disposition of the art from inventory. There is no net income limitation and there is a five-year carryforward.

Where a charitable organization issues receipts for the price of tickets to fund-raising events involving an element of entertainment or other benefit for the donor, only the excess of the amount paid over the fair market value of the benefit received is allowed to be considered part of the charitable gift.

6. Total Crown gifts

Gifts made to the Government of Canada or to the government of a province are considered to be gifts made to Her Majesty and are defined as Crown gifts [ssec. 118.1(1)]. There is a 75% of net income limitation to equal the limitation on other charitable gifts. Again, there is a five-year carryforward on these gifts.

---

[d] An interesting court case on the issue of fair market valuation in this context is *Friedberg v. The Queen*, (F.C.T.D.) 89 DTC 5115, affirmed by the Federal Court of Appeal (92 DTC 6031).

7. Total ecological gifts

A net income limitation of 100% applies to donations of certain ecologically sensitive land. This provision is meant to encourage the conservation and protection of Canada's environmental heritage and applies to qualified donations of land including qualified donations of covenants, servitudes and easements. As a further incentive, for ecological gifts made after February 27, 2000, any capital gain realized on the donation (other than gifts to a private foundation) will be subject to one-half the regular capital gains inclusion rate [par. 38(a.2)].

D. Medical Expense Credit

[ITA: 118.2, ITR: 5700; IT-519R2]

1. Calculation of the credit

Not all medical and health care costs are fully covered by a provincial health insurance plan or by a private health services plan. Expenses that must be borne by the taxpayer may qualify for the non-refundable medical expense credit. For example, certain cosmetic or elective procedures and a fraction of dental services may not be covered.

For the 2004 and subsequent tax years, the medical expense tax credit [ssec. 118.2(1)] is calculated as:

$$A [(B - C) + D]$$

where

A   is 16% (i.e., the appropriate percentage for the year)

B   is medical expenses listed in subsections 118.2(2) and (3) for the individual, spouse or common-law partner and children not reaching 18 before the end of the year

C   is the lesser of:
- $1,844 (indexed for 2005), and
- 3% of the individual's net income

D   is the lesser of:
- $10,000 and
- E – F where

E   is the total of all medical expenses incurred by the taxpayer on behalf of any other dependant [ssec. 118(6)] and

F   is the lesser of:
- $1,844 (indexed for 2005)
- 3% of the other dependant's net income

In essence, the federal tax credit is 16% (10% used for provincial tax credit) of medical expenses in excess of the $1,844 for 2005 or 3% of the Division B income threshold. The medical expenses must be proven by filing receipts and must be paid within any 12-month period ending in the year unless the individual dies in the year. Where the individual dies in the year, the medical expenses must be paid by the claimant for the deceased person within any period of 24 months that includes the date of death.

2. Medical expenses

Subsection 118.2(2) includes over 30 detailed paragraphs outlining the very technical rules and conditions defining medical expenses. A brief description of these paragraphs is provided below; however, a careful examination of these provisions and IT-519R2 must be made in order to determine the eligibility of each item[d]

(*a*) — This paragraph includes in the tax credit base general medical expenses (illness, hospitalization, etc.) paid to dentists, nurses and medical practitioners (a wider term than medical doctors [ssec. 118.4(2) and IT-519R2, par. 3] for the taxpayer, his or her spouse and dependants of the individual. Hence, either spouse may qualify for a tax credit for the expenses of each other. For other dependants, the definition includes most individuals related to the taxpayer and dependent on the taxpayer for support [ssec. 118(6)].

(*b*), (*b*.1), (*b*.2), (*c*) and (*d*) — These five provisions deal with full-time or part-time attendants or attendants for the care of an individual eligible for the impairment credit [sec. 118.3] and/or full-time care in a nursing home, group home or otherwise. Each provision has its own unique conditions. The amount eligible for the credit in respect of attendant care for an individual eligible for the impairment credit is limited to $10,000 ($20,000 in the year of death). More than $10,000 can be claimed in respect of an individual, but no impairment credit or attendant care deduction can be claimed in respect of that individual.

(*e*) — This category of expense, for care and training for the mentally or physically handicapped, is not completely medical in nature.

(*f*), (*g*) and (*h*) — These provisions deal with the transportation of taxpayers to medical centres. Note that for travel expenses envisaged in paragraph (*h*), individuals may choose a detailed or simplified method to calculate certain travel expenses. The detailed method would use actual costs, substantiated by receipts. The simplified method applies to meals and vehicle expenses which can be based on flat rates. The flat rate for meals is $15 per meal to a maximum of $45 per day, per person. The flat rate for vehicle expenses is based on the province or territory in which the individual travels and varies by province or territory. (See Chapter 9, under moving expenses, for a detailed list of rates for vehicle expenses.)

(*i*), (*i*.1) — These provisions deal with certain specific medical equipment or products.

(*j*) — These paragraph allows for the expenses of eyeglasses, etc. for the taxpayer, his or her spouse or a dependant.

(*k*) — The cost of specialized equipment dealing with oxygen and of insulin and of other specified substances is allowable by virtue of this paragraph.

(*l*) — This paragraph permits certain specific expenses related to the care of a trained dog who assists the blind or deaf and the cost of an animal trained to assist an individual who has a severe and prolonged physical impairment.

(*l*.1) — This paragraph allows a reasonable cost for arranging a bone marrow transplant or organ transplant.

---

[d] For cases dealing with a variety of medical expense claims, see: *Demont v. The Queen* (TCC–Informal Procedure), 2002 DTC 3924, dealing with health care services and transportation expenses; *Weeks v. The Queen* (FCA), 2001 DTC 5035, dealing with the cost of devices, equipment or other chattels purchased for in-home care of a disabled person; *Pagnotto v. The Queen* (TCC–Informal Procedure), 2001 DTC 3797, dealing with medical services and drugs; *Donahue v. The Queen* (TCC–Informal Procedure), dealing with medical services and devices; *Klywak v. The Queen* (TCC–Informal Procedure) 2004 DTC 3143, dealing with medical devices; *Motkowski v. The Queen* (TCC–Informal Procedure), 2003 DTC 3968, dealing with home alterations and *Seely v. The Queen*, 2002 DTC 4009, dealing with home alterations.

(*l*.2), (*l*.21) — These paragraphs allow expenses for modifying a home if an individual is confined to a wheelchair for a long period of time, lacks normal physical development, or has a severe and prolonged mobility impairment.

(*l*.3) — This paragraph allows expenses for rehabilitative therapy to adjust for speech or hearing loss, including training in lip reading and sign language.

(*l*.4) — Amount paid on behalf of an individual with a speech or hearing impairment for sign language interpretation or real-time captioning services if the payment is made to a person who is in the business of providing such services.

(*l*.41) — Amount paid on behalf of an individual with a mental or physical impairment for note-taking services if the payment is made to a person who is in the business of providing such services and the individual has been certified as requiring those services.

(*l*.42) — The cost of voice recognition software used by an individual with a physical impairment if the individual has been certified as requiring that software.

(*l*.5) — This paragraph allows a maximum of $2,000 incurred to move an individual to housing that is more accessible or in which the individual is more mobile or functional.

(*l*.6) — This paragraph allows reasonable expenses relating to alterations to a home driveway to facilitate access to a bus by an individual with a severe and prolonged mobility impairment.

(*l*.7) — This paragraph allows the lesser of $5,000 and 20% of the cost of a van adapted within six months of its purchase for use by an individual using a wheelchair.

(*l*.8) — This paragraph allows reasonable expenses incurred to train an individual to care for a relative having a mental or physical infirmity. The relative must be either a member of the taxpayer's household or dependent on the taxpayer for support.

(*l*.9) — This paragraph allows expenses for remuneration for therapy provided to the patient because of the patient's severe and prolonged impairment.

(*l*.91) — This paragraph allows expenses for remuneration for tutoring services that are rendered to, and are supplementary to the primary education of, the patient who has a learning disability or mental impairment.

(*m*) — This paragraph provides the statutory authority for Regulation 5700 which supplements the equipment listed in paragraphs (*i*) and (*k*) noted above and may stipulate a dollar limit for claims in respect of a particular device or equipment.

(*n*) — Drugs and prescriptions, etc., as prescribed by a medical practitioner and administered by a pharmacist, are allowed by virtue of this paragraph.

(*o*) — This provision allows certain diagnostic services such as x-rays, laboratory tests, etc.

(*p*) — The cost of dentures made in a province by an authorized person is allowed by this provision.

(*q*) — This paragraph allows a premium for a private health services plan. To the extent that the premium has been deducted in computing the individuals business income, it is not deductible as a medical expense.

(*r*) — The incremental cost, to an individual who suffers from celiac disease,of acquiring gluten-free products if the individual has been certified as requiring a gluten-free diet.

[The February 23, 2005 federal budget proposed to add another eight types of expenses eligible for the medical expense tax credit, although the proposal was not included in Bill C-43 which implemented the 2005 federal budget. The proposed additions were as follows:

- to purchase, operate and maintain phototherapy equipment for the treatment of psoriasis or other skin disorders;

- to operate and maintain an oxygen concentrator;

- for deaf-blind intervening services used by an individual who is both blind and profoundly deaf (if paid to persons engaged in the business of providing such services);

- for reading services used by an individual who is blind or who has a severe learning disability, if the need for the service is certified in writing by a medical practitioner and paid to persons engaged in the business of providing such services;

- for drugs or medical devices obtained under Health Canada's Special Access Programme;

- for the purchase of medical marihuana or marihuana seeds, from Health Canada, for use by a patient who is authorized to possess marihuana for medical purposes under the Marihuana Medical Access Regulations (MMAR) or who holds an Exemption for possession under Section 56 of the *Controlled Drugs and Substances Act* (CDSA); and

- for the purchase of medical marihuana, for use by a patient who is authorized to possess marihuana for medical purposes under the MMAR or who holds an Exemption for possession under Section 56 of the CDSA, from an individual who possesses a Designated-person Production Licence under the MMAR to cultivate or produce marihuana for medical purposes on behalf of that patient or who holds a designated person Exemption for cultivation or production under Section 56 of the CDSA to cultivate or produce marihuana for medical purposes on behalf of that patient.]

Example Problem

Mr. Taxpayer has income under Division B of $25,000 and $30,000 for 2004 and 2005, respectively. His wife and children have no income in these years. He incurs the following receipted medical expenses on behalf of himself, his wife, and three dependent children.

2004 — None prior to August

August	Dental bills for children	$ 325
September	Hospital bill and drugs	200*
November	Prescription drugs	65
December	Prescription drugs	125
	Total medical expenses	$ 715 (B)

Less the lesser of:

(a) $1,813

(b) 3% of Division B income (3% of $25,000) . . . .   750 (C)

Net base for tax credit (B − C) . . . .   Nil

2005 — January	Eyeglasses for himself and wife	$ 225
February	Eyeglasses for 3 children	340
March	Orthodontic work for children	1,500
July	Chiropractor for Mr. Taxpayer	400*
	Total medical expenses	$2,465

* Excess over amount paid by a provincial medicare program.

— REQUIRED

Determine the maximum amount Mr. Taxpayer can claim as a medical expense tax credit under subsection 118.2(1) in 2005.

— SOLUTION

Since the only restriction on the twelve-month period is that it must end in the particular taxation year, Mr. Taxpayer should choose the twelve months ending in July 2005.

The medical expense tax credit is computed by the following formula:

$$A\,((B - C) + D)$$

where A = .16

B = total medical expenses (as computed below)

C = lesser of:
(a) $1,844
(b) 3% of Division B income (as computed below)

D = nil in this case

2004 — August to December: total medical expenses	$ 715
2005 — January to July: total medical expenses	2,465
Total	$3,180 (B)
Less the lesser of:	
(a) $1,844	
(b) 3% of Division B income (3% of $30,000)	900 (C)
Net base for medical expense tax credit (B – C)	$2,280
Medical expense tax credit: A (B – C) = .16 × $2,280 = ...	$ 365

Note that had Mr. Taxpayer's wife had some income that would attract tax in excess of her other tax credits, but less than her husband's, there may be a greater benefit to the family if she claimed the medical expense tax credit because the 3% threshold would be lower.

3. Notch provision for dependants

As discussed above, a taxpayer may claim a medical expense tax credit for the medical expenses of the taxpayer, the taxpayer's spouse or any dependent individual [ssec. 118(6)]. Where a person, other than the taxpayer's spouse, qualifies as a dependant, despite a level of income above the $8,148 base for the basic personal tax credit, the taxpayer may include the medical expenses of that person when computing the medical expense tax credit [ssec. 118.2(1)]. However, the taxpayer must reduce the total medical expense tax credit for the year by 68% of the excess, if any, of the other person's net income under Division B over $8,148 for 2005. This reduction is embedded in item D of the medical expense tax credit formula above.

[For the 2004 and subsequent tax years, caregivers can claim more of the medical and disability-related expenses that they incur on behalf of dependent relatives [ssec. 118(6)]. Specifically, medical expense claims made on behalf of minor children are pooled with those of the taxpayer and his or her spouse or common-law partner, subject to the taxpayer's minimum expense threshold (the lesser of 3% of net income and $1,844) without regard to the income of the minor child. For medical expenses, to a maximum of $10,000 for 2005, paid on behalf of other dependent relatives (e.g., parent, grandparent, niece, nephew, etc.) taxpayers can claim qualifying medical expenses paid on behalf of such a dependant that exceed the lesser of 3% of the dependant's net income and $1,844.

Example Problem

Mr. Taxpayer's father is a dependant [ssec. 118(6)]. His father's Division B income is only $8,500 for 2005. During the year, Mr. Taxpayer paid medical expenses of $1,000 on behalf of his father and $2,500 for himself. Mr. Taxpayer's Division B income is $100,000 for 2005.

— REQUIRED

Determine the maximum amount that Mr. Taxpayer can claim as a medical expense tax credit under subsection 118.2(1) in 2005.

— SOLUTION

The medical expense tax credit is computed by the following formula

$$A \, [(B - C) + D]$$

If Mr. Taxpayer claims his father's medical expenses:

A = 16%

B = total medical expenses, i.e., $2,500 for taxpayer

C = lesser of $1,844 and 3% of $100,000, i.e., taxpayer's Division B income
   = $1,844

D   is the lesser of:
   ● $10,000 and
   ● E − F

where

E = the total of all medical expenses incurred by the taxpayer on behalf of the father, i.e., $1,000 and

F = lesser of:
   ● $1,844 and
   ● 3% of the father's net income, i.e., 3% of $8,500 = $255

$$16\% \times [\, (\$2,500 - \$1,844) + (\$1,000 - \$255)] = \$224$$

E. Credit for Mental or Physical Impairment (Disability Tax Credit)
[ITA: 118.3; 118.4; IT-519R2]

1. Amount of and conditions for impairment credit

Subsection 118.3(1) provides the formula for calculating the non-refundable tax credit for an individual with a mental or physical impairment and the conditions for entitlement to the credit. The tax credit for 2005 is $1,055 (i.e., 16% of $6,596). This tax credit is available to taxpayers who have a "severe and prolonged impairment in physical or mental function" that has been certified by a medical doctor. A health professional, other than a medical doctor, may be eligible to certify the impairment. An optometrist may certify the existence of an impairment of sight. An audiologist may certify an impairment of hearing. An occupational therapist may certify the existence of an impairment with respect to an individual's ability to walk or to feed or to dress himself or herself. A psychologist may certify to the existence of an impairment with respect to an individual's ability to perceive, think and remember. A speech-language pathologist may certify a severe and prolonged speech impairment. A physical therapist may certify a marked restriction in walking. Cumulative effects of multiple restrictions must usually be certified by a medical doctor.

The impairment, or the cumulative effect of multiple restrictions, must have caused the individual to be markedly restricted all or almost all of the time in his or her basic activities of daily living. The impairment must have lasted or be expected to last for a continuous period of at least 12 months [ssec. 118.4(1)]. Such impairment would include blindness, deafness and other listed impairments. It would also occur where, even with the use of appropriate devices, medication or therapy, the individual is generally unable (or requires an inordinate amount of time) to feed or to dress himself or herself or perform specified fundamental functions[e]

No claim can be made under this subsection if a claim has been made under subsection 118.2(1) for a full-time attendant or care in a nursing home. However, a claim under paragraph 118.2(2)(b.1) for expenses of an attendant costing less than $10,000 in computing the medical expense tax credit will not deny this impairment tax credit.

A supplement amount of $3,848 for 2005 is available for each disabled child under the age of 18 years at the end of the year. The supplement amount is reduced by the excess of the total of child care and attendant care expenses paid in the year and deducted in respect of the child, over $2,254 (for 2005).

2. Transfer of impairment credit

A transfer of this credit is available to a taxpayer who has claimed dependants under paragraph 118(1)(b) (marital equivalent), paragraph 118(1)(d) (children and grandchildren only), or paragraph 118(1)(c.1) (caregiver tax credit), if the dependants themselves cannot use all or some part of this credit [ssec. 118.3(2)]. The impaired dependant must use as much of the credit as necessary to reduce his or her federal income tax to zero, before the remainder can be transferred. The transfer of the unused part of the impairment credit is available to a taxpayer if:

- the taxpayer claimed an equivalent-to-married credit for the dependant;
- the dependant was the taxpayer's child, grandchild, parent, grandparent (including in-laws), brother, sister, aunt, uncle, nephew or niece, and the taxpayer

---

[e]) For cases on various impairments, see *The Queen v. Hamilton* (FCA), 2002 DTC 6836, dealing with celiac disease; *Johnston v. The Queen* (FCA), 98 DTC 6169, dealing with arthritis; *Overdyk v. MNR* (TRB), 83 DTC 307, dealing with partial paralysis; *Tanguay v. The Queen* (TCC), 97 DTC 3309, dealing with an individual who could not dress himself due to a hip problem; and *Radage v. The Queen* (TCC–Informal Procedure), 96 DTC 1615, dealing with intellectual limitations or perceiving, thinking and remembering.

could have claimed an equivalent-to-married credit for that dependant if the taxpayer did not have a spouse or common-law partner and if the dependant did not have any income;

- the dependant was the taxpayer's child or grandchild and the taxpayer claimed the dependant under paragraph 118(1)(*d*) or (*c*.1);

- the dependant was the taxpayer's child or grandchild and the taxpayer could have claimed the dependant under paragraph 118(1)(*d*) or (*c*.1) if the dependant had no income; or

- the dependant was the taxpayer's parent or grandparent (including in-laws) and the taxpayer could have claimed the dependant under paragraph 118(1)(*d*) or (*c*.1) if the dependant had no income.

The net result of these rules is that if a parent supports two or more disabled children, the parent is entitled to the transfer of the unused portion of the impairment tax credit of those children, even though only one child may be claimed as an equivalent-to-married tax credit.[f] The spousal transfer of this credit occurs in section 118.8 which is discussed later.

Subsection 118.3(3) deals with the allocation of the impairment tax credit where more than one individual is entitled to the credit for the same dependant. A definition of impairment is contained in section 118.4 and applies not only to section 118.3, but also to section 118.2 dealing with medical expenses. A definition of the term used to describe a medical practitioner is contained in subsection 118.4(2) and appears to codify the description in IT-519R2, paragraph 3.

F. Tuition and Education Credits

[ITA: 118.5; 118.6; 118.61; 118.8; 118.81; 118.9; IT-515R2; IT-516R2]

1. Tuition fees

The federal tuition fee tax credit is equal to 16% (10% used for provincial tax credit) of eligible tuition fees paid in respect of that year [sec. 118.5]. Paragraph 118.5(1)(*a*) provides for a tax credit in respect of tuition fees paid to an educational institution in Canada. The fees must be paid to a university, college or other educational institution in respect of courses at a post-secondary school level, or an institution certified by the Minister of Human Resources Development providing courses that furnish a person, who is at least 16 years of age at the end of the year, with skills for an occupation. The total of fees paid to a qualified institution in a year must exceed $100.[g]

Tuition fees for full-time and part-time students include items such as library and laboratory charges. Also, eligible for the credit are mandatory ancillary fees, other than student association fees, required to be paid by all full-time and part-time students for courses at the post-secondary school level. Eligible fees include those charged for health services and athletics. In addition to student association fees, the following are excluded: charges for property to be acquired by students, services not ordinarily provided at post-secondary educational institutions in Canada and tax exempt financial assistance to students. Also, mandatory charges paid for the construction, renovation or maintenance of a building or facility, generally, do not qualify for the credit. A fee that would be eligible, but for the fact that it is not required from all students, may be claimed to a limit of $250.

---

[f] See *Blais v. M.N.R.*, (T.C.C.) 85 DTC 61.

[g] See *Dumas v. M.N.R.*, (T.R.B.) 79 DTC 726, which was decided when the threshold was $25.

The tax credit for tuition paid in the year to a university outside Canada is more restricted [par. 118.5(1)(*b*)]. The student must be in full-time attendance at a university in a course leading to a degree. The course must be of at least 13 consecutive weeks' duration. Paragraph 118.5(1)(*c*) provides a tax credit for fees paid by a Canadian resident who commuted to an educational institution providing courses at the post-secondary level in the United States. Again, the amount of the fees paid in the year to a particular institution must exceed $100.

2. Education credit

This federal credit is calculated by a formula which multiplies 16% (10% used for provincial tax credit) of $400 by the number of months in the year during which the individual was enrolled in a qualifying educational program as a full-time student at a designated educational institution [ssec. 118.6(2)]. Part-time students at a qualifying post-secondary educational institution who are eligible for the disability tax credit or who, by reason of their certified mental or physical impairment, cannot be enrolled on a full-time basis are treated like full-time students [ssec. 118.6(3)]. The enrolment must be proven by filing a certificate issued by the educational institution. Where the student is enrolled at an institution certified by the Minister of Human Resources Development, the purpose of the enrolment must be to obtain or improve skills for an occupation. The terms "designated educational institution" and "qualifying educational program" are defined [ssec. 118.6(1)].

Part-time students (other than students eligible for the impairment tax credit) may claim a federal credit of 16% (10% used for provincial tax credit) of $120 per month during which he or she was enrolled at a designated educational institution and specified educational program. The program must require the student to spend not less than 12 hours in the month on courses in the program.

Post-secondary students enrolled in distance education programs or correspondence courses may meet the full-time or part-time requirements if the courses meet the required standards.

IT-515R2 and IT-516R2 discuss the detailed rules governing the education tax credit and tuition fee tax credit, respectively. These bulletins provide some very important interpretation of the technical terms relating to these credits and should be examined carefully. In particular, note the difference between the interpretation of "full-time attendance" in IT-516R2, paragraphs 9 to 12 and that in IT-515R2, paragraphs 9 to 11.

3. Carryforward

The unused portion of a student's tuition fee and education tax credits can be claimed by the student in a subsequent taxation year [sec. 118.61]. This allows an indefinite carryforward of these credits by the student to the extent that they are not transferred in the year earned to a spouse or supporting individual. Students are permitted to transfer part of the unused credits and carry forward the remainder.

4. Transfer of tuition and education credits to spouse and parent and grandparent

The tuition fee and education credits may be transferred to a spouse [sec. 118.8] or to a parent or grandparent of the student [sec. 118.9]. To qualify, the student must designate, in writing, an amount transferred to a spouse or to a parent or grandparent. The formula for calculating the amount that may be claimed as a tax credit by the spouse or by the parent or grandparent is [sec. 118.81] the lesser of:

(a) the amount determined by the formula A − B

where A is the lesser of:

(a) $800 (i.e., 16% of $5,000), and

(b) the student's tuition credit and education credit for the year (excluding unused amounts carried forward).

B is the amount of the student's Part I tax payable after deducting credits in section 118 (personal, age and pension credits), section 118.3 (mental or physical impairment credit), section 118.7 (EI and CPP credits), and section 118.61 (unused tuition and education tax credits), and

(b) the amount designated by the student in writing for the transfer to a spouse or to a parent or grandparent.)

In effect, this formula allows the transfer of the excess of up to $800 of a student's tuition and education credits over those credits required by the student to reduce federal tax to nil.

Example Problem

Debbie, who is not dependent upon any person, was enrolled as a full-time student at the University of Toronto for ten months during 2005. Debbie provides you with the following information for 2005:

Scholarship income	$12,000
Interest income — Canadian	1,000
Qualified tuition fees paid in 2005 (10 months)	3,600

— *REQUIRED*

(A) Determine the amount of Debbie's federal tuition and education credits which can be deducted by her parent.

(B) Determine the amount of Debbie's unused federal tuition and education tax credits at the end of 2005.

— *SOLUTION*

(A) Scholarship income ($12,000 − $3,000)	$ 9,000
Interest	1,000
Division B and taxable income	$10,000
Federal tax @ 16%	$ 1,600
Basic personal tax credit ($8,148 × 16%)	(1,304)
Federal tax payable	$ 296

Tuition fee and education tax credit:

Tuition fee tax credit (16% of $3,600)	$ 576
Education tax credit (16% of $400 × 10)	640
Total tax credit	$ 1,216

Tuition fee and education tax credit transfer to parent:

Lesser of:

(a) $800	
(b) Student's tuition fee and education tax credit: $1,216	$ 800
Less: amount of student's Part I tax net of secs. 118, 118.3, 118.61 and 118.7	
deductions	296
Net amount available for transfer	$ 504

(B) Unused tuition and education tax credits at Dec. 31, 2004................		Nil
Plus: 2005 tuition and education credits	$1,216	
Less: Debbie's tax payable before deducting the current year's tuition and education credits	(296)	$ 920
Minus: Unused tuition and education credits deducted in 2005 ...		(Nil)
Tuition and education credit transferred..........		(504)
Unused tuition and education tax credits at Dec. 31, 2005		$ 416

5. Credit for interest on student loans

A student may deduct a federal tax credit of 16% (10% used for provincial tax credit) of interest on a federal or provincial student loan payable in respect of the year or in any of the five preceding taxation years ending after 1997 [sec. 118.62]. Qualifying loans are those made under the *Canada Student Loans Act* or a similar provincial statute.

G. Credit for Employment Insurance Premiums and CPP Contributions

[ITA: 118.7]

Section 118.7 provides for a federal tax credit equal to 16% (10% used for provincial tax credit) of:

(a) all amounts payable by the individual in respect of an employee's premiums for Employment Insurance;

(b) all amounts payable by the individual as an employee's contributions under the Canada (or Quebec) Pension Plan; and

(c) all amounts payable by the individual as a contribution for self-employed earnings under the Canada (or Quebec) Pension Plan.

For 2005, the Employment Insurance premium rate for the employee is 1.95% of earnings to a maximum annual earnings amount of $39,000. At this level of earnings the maximum level of premium of $760.50 is reached. (Employers must pay a premium of 2.73% (i.e., 1.4 times the employee payment), for a maximum of $1,064.70.)

The rate of contribution to the Canada Pension Plan for 2005 is 4.95% of pensionable earnings. The maximum pensionable earnings is $41,100 with a basic exemption of $3,500. Thus, the maximum contribution is calculated as follows:

$$4.95\% \text{ of } (\$41,100 - \$3,500) = \$1,861.20$$

For a self-employed individual, the maximum is twice the above amount or $3,722.40.

H. Transfer of Unused Credits to Spouse or Common-law Partner

[ITA: 118.8; 118.81]

Certain unused tax credits may be transferred to a spouse or common-law partner [sec. 118.8]. These tax credits are:

(a) the tuition credit [sec. 118.5] and the education credit [sec. 118.6] (to a maximum of $800);

(b) the age credit [ssec. 118(2)];

(c) the pension credit [ssec. 118(3)]; and

(d) the mental or physical impairment credit [ssec. 118.3(1)].

The amount that may be transferred is calculated by the following formula:

$$A + B - C$$

where   A is the lesser of:
- $800, and
- the spouse's tuition fee and education tax credits;

B is the sum of the following tax credits available to the spouse:
- the age credit,
- the pension credit, and
- the mental or physical impairment credit; and

C is the amount, if any, by which

(a) the spouse's Part I tax payable after deducting:
- the basic personal credit in paragraph 118(1)(*c*),
- unused tuition and education credits in section 118.61 and
- the EI and CPP credit in section 118.7

exceeds

(b) the lesser of:

(i) the tuition and education credit deductible by the spouse; and

(ii) the spouse's Part I tax payable after deducting:
- the basic personal credit,
- the impairment credit,
- the unused tuition and education credits, and
- the EI and CPP credit.

Example Problem

Mrs. Aged, age 75, received the following income in 2005:

Registered pension plan payments	$ 700
Old Age Security pension	5,500
Canada Pension Plan payments	500
Interest from Canadian corporations	700
Division B income	$7,400

Mrs. Aged has been confined to a wheelchair for several years but is quite active and is registered as a full-time student at a post-secondary institution for eight months, paying tuition of $2,000 at the senior citizens' rate.

— REQUIRED

Calculate the amount of federal tax credit transfer available to her husband under section 118.8 for 2005.

— SOLUTION

Transfer of credits to Mr. Aged in accordance with the formula:

$$A + B - C$$

(A)   Tuition and education credits transferred [sec. 118.81]

Lesser of: (a) dollar limit		$ 800
	(b) tuition and education tax credits [16% of ($2,000 + $400 × 8)]	$ 832
	lesser amount	$ 800

(B)	Age credit	$ 637	
	Pension credit[1]	112	
	Impairment credit	1,055	1,804
			$2,604

(C) Mrs. Aged's Part I tax ($1,184 = 16% of $7,400) net of
     the basic personal tax credit ($1,304), unused tuition
     and education credits (nil), and CPP and EI credits
     (nil)... $ nil

Minus lesser of:
(i) tuition and education tax credits deductible
    by Mrs. Aged... nil
(ii) Mrs. Aged's Part I tax ($1,184) net of the
    basic personal tax credit ($1,304), the impair-
    ment credit ($1,055), the unused tuition and
    education credits (nil), and CPP and EI cred-
    its (nil) .... nil

| lesser amount .... | nil | (nil) |
| | | $2,604 |

—NOTE TO SOLUTION
(1) The Old Age Security pension and CPP payments do not qualify for the pension tax credit [ssec. 118(8)]. The tax credit is calculated as 16% of the lesser of:

(a) $1,000; and

(b) pension income of $700.

I. [Adoption Expense Tax Credit]

A proposed (not included in Bill C-43 which implemented the 2005 budget) non-refundable tax credit in the year in which an adoption is completed for 2005 and subsequent taxation years for up to $10,000 (indexed after 2005) of expenses paid for eligible adoption expenses incurred during the adoption period. Details of the credit, as announced in the 2005 federal budget, are as follows:

● eligible adoption expenses include:

(i) fees paid to an adoption agency licensed by a provincial or territorial government,

(ii) court costs, legal and administrative expenses,

(iii) reasonable travel and living expenses of the child and the adoptive parents,

(iv) document translation fees,

(v) mandatory fees paid to a foreign institution, and

(vi) any other reasonable expenses required by a provincial or territorial government or an adoption agency licensed by a provincial or territorial government,

● the adoption period is the period that:

(a) begins at the earlier of the time that the child's adoption file is opened with a provincial or territorial ministry responsible for adoption (or with an adoption agency licensed by a provincial or territorial government) and the time, if any, that an application related to the adoption is made to a Canadian court, and

(b) ends at the time of the adoption.

J. Dividend Tax Credit and Subsection 82(3) Election

[ITA: 82(3); 121; IT-295R4]

The dividend tax credit available to an individual is a non-refundable tax credit [sec. 121] and is equal to $^2/_3$ of the gross-up [par. 82(1)(*b*)]. Since the gross-up is $^1/_4$ of the dividend, the dividend tax credit can be calculated in three different ways depending on the information available:

(a) $^2/_3 \times$ the gross-up;

(b) $16^2/_3\% \times$ the dividend paid (i.e., $^2/_3 \times {}^1/_4 \times$ dividend paid); or

(c) $13^1/_3\% \times$ the grossed-up dividend (i.e., $^2/_3 \times {}^1/_4 \times {}^4/_5 \times$ grossed-up dividend).

For the purposes of this book, unless otherwise stated, where provincial tax credits are calculated for individuals, a dividend tax credit rate of 6 $^2/_3\%$ of the grossed-up dividend will be applied. (Theoretically, the combined federal and provincial dividend tax credit should equal the gross-up of 25% of the dividend or 20% of the gross-up dividend. This will be explored in Chapter 12. This would imply a provincial dividend tax credit rate of 6 $^2/_3\%$, i.e., 13 $^1/_3\%$ federal + 6 $^2/_3\%$ provincial for a total of 20% of the grossed-up dividend. However, provinces using the TONI structure may specify their own rate of dividend tax credit.)

An election is available to deem taxable dividends from taxable Canadian corporations received by one spouse or common-law partner, who cannot use the dividend tax credit because of low income, to be received by the other spouse or common-law partner [ssec. 82(3)]. However, this election can only be used if the married personal tax credit claimed by the higher income spouse for the dependent spouse or common-law partner is increased or created by transferring the dividend income in this way. If the election can be made, the taxpayer must include the grossed-up dividends transferred from the spouse or common-law partner, but may deduct the dividend tax credit available on the dividends.

Consider the following situations where the low-income spouse has $300 of grossed-up dividends from Canadian corporations plus some other source of income.

Calculation of taxpayer's married tax credit	*Case 1*	*Case 2*	*Case 3*	*Case 4*
Spouse's Division B income before election	$7,700	$5,950	$1,500	$ 450
Married credit:				
Spouse base	$6,919	$6,919	$6,919	$6,919
Spouse's Division B income in excess of $692	(7,008)	(5,258)	(808)	Nil
Net credit base	Nil	1,661	$6,111	$6,919
Credit @ 16% of net credit base	Nil	266	$ 978	$1,107
Spouse's Division B income after election	$7,400	$5,650	$1,200	$ 150
Married credit:				
Spouse tax credit base	$6,919	$6,919	$6,919	$6,919
Spouse's Division B income in excess of $692	(6,708)	(4,958)	(508)	Nil
Net credit base	$211	$1,961	$6,411	$6,919
Credit @ 16% of net credit base (rounded)	$34	$ 314	$1,026	$1,107

In Case 1, an election is available, since after the election, a credit for the spouse has been created. In Case 2, the spousal credit has increased from $266 to $314 by the transfer of the dividends and, hence, the election is available. In Case 3, the election is available, since the spousal credit has increased from $978 to $1,026. However, in Case 4, the election is not available since the spousal credit has not increased but remains the same after the election.

Example Problem ───

Mr. and Mrs. Senior Citizen, ages 68 and 65, respectively, received the following income for 2005:

	Mr.	Mrs.
Registered pension plan payments......................	$21,510	$1,300
Old Age Security pension (Mrs. Citizen not eligible)........	5,700	—
Canada Pension Plan	12,000	—
Interest from Canadian sources	940	—
Dividends from taxable Canadian corporations............	—	600
	$40,150	$1,900

— REQUIRED

Compute Mr. Senior Citizen's federal tax, assuming that he elects under subsection 82(3). Ignore provisions which apply after section 121.

— SOLUTION

	With ssec. 82(3)	Without ssec. 82(3)
Income received	$40,150	$40,150
Spouse's grossed-up dividends deemed received under subsection 82(3)	750	—
Division B and taxable income...............	$40,900	$40,150
Tax @ 16% on $35,595	$ 5,695	$ 5,695
Plus 22% (Taxable income — $35,595)....	1,167	1,002
	6,862	6,697

Less tax credits:				
Basic personal....................	$1,304		$1,304	
Spouse[1].........................	1,010		890	
Age[2].............................	366		384	
Pension..........................	160		160	
Spouse transfer[3]	797		797	
Dividend tax credit (13$^1/_3$% of $^5/_4$ × $600)...........................	100	$ 3,737	—	$ 3,535
Net federal tax payable up to section 121[4]......		$ 3,125		$ 3,162

In this example, it makes sense to elect to transfer the dividends since Mr. Senior Citizen's tax liability has been reduced without any increase in his wife's tax liability.

— NOTES TO SOLUTION
(1) Spouse tax credit:

	With ssec. 82(3)	Without ssec. 82(3)
Income received plus dividend gross-up	$2,050	$2,050
Less: dividends transferred [ssec. 82(3)]........	(750)	—
Division B and taxable income after election ...	$1,300	$2,050

Married credit:

Spouse base............................		$6,919		$6,919
Spouse's Division B income........	$1,300		$2,050	
Less: threshold	(692)	(608)	(692)	(1,358)
Net credit base		$6,311		$5,561
Credit @ 16% of net credit base		$1,010		$ 890

Mr. Senior Citizen is eligible for a subsection 82(3) election, since his married credit will increase by $120 (i.e., 16% of $^5/_4 \times$ $600). Without the election, his married credit would have been $890.

(2) Age credit:

	With ssec. 82(3)		Without ssec. 82(3)	
Age amount................................	$ 3,979		$ 3,979	
Net income $40,900		$40,150		
Threshold..................... (29,619)		(29,619)		
Less 15% of excess............. $11,281	(1,692)	$10,531	(1,580)	
	$ 2,287		$ 2,399	
Credit @ 16%	$ 366		$ 384	

(3) Transfer of spouse's credits:

	With ssec. 82(3)		Without ssec. 82(3)	
Age (16% × $3,979)	$ 637		$ 637	
Pension (16% × $1,000)......................	160		160	
	$ 797		$ 797	
Less: Part I tax @ 16%.............. $ 208		$ 328		
minus personal tax credit ...... (1,304)	Nil	(1,304)	Nil	
	$ 797		$ 797	

(4) Tax savings from subsection 82(3) election:

Increase in tax @ 22% on grossed-up dividend of $750		$ (165)
Increase in married tax credit ($1,010 – $890)	$ 120	
Increase in dividend tax credit (13$^1/_3$% × $750)...........	100	
Reduction in age credit ($366 – $384)....................	(18)	202
Net tax savings		$ 37

Note that there may be cases where the lower-income spouse's or common-law partner's income with the dividends is high enough to require the use of a transferable credit if the subsection 82(3) election is not made by the higher-income spouse or common-law partner. In these cases, making the election may result, for the higher-income spouse, not only in an increase in the married credit and dividend tax credit, but also an increase in the other credits transferred from the lower-income spouse. Of course, the increase in these credits to the higher-income spouse will be offset, at least to some extent, by the increase in tax on the dividend income deemed received by the higher-income taxpayer under the subsection 82(3) election.

K. Credits for Part-Time and Non-Residents

[ITA: 118.91; 118.94]

Generally, for the period of residence in Canada of a part-time resident, the individual can deduct specified tax credits prorated by the number of days that the individual is resident in the year divided by the number of days in the calendar year [sec. 118.91]:

- basic personal amount, married amount, equivalent-to-married amount, dependant amount and caregiver amount [ssec. 118(1)];
- age amount [ssec. 118(2)];
- impairment amount either for the taxpayer or transferred from a dependant [sec. 118.3];
- unused credits transferred from a spouse [sec. 118.8]; and
- unused tuition and education amounts transferred from a child or grandchild [sec. 118.9].

All other personal amounts may fully be claimed if they relate to the period of residence. These include:

- the pension credit [ssec. 118(3)];
- charitable gifts [sec. 118.1];
- medical expenses [sec. 118.2];
- tuition and education credits [secs. 118.5 and 118.6]; and
- credit for interest on student loan [sec. 118.62]; and
- EI and CPP credits [sec. 118.7].

A non-resident individual (i.e., an individual who at no time in the year is resident in Canada) may deduct tax credits for the following amounts:

- charitable donations, including Crown gifts and cultural gifts [sec. 118.1];
- impairment amount for the taxpayer, but not for a dependant [ssec. 118.3(1)];
- tuition credit [sec. 118.5]; and
- EI, CPP (or QPP) credits [sec. 118.7].

Credits for all other personal amounts may be deducted if all or substantially all of the individual's worldwide income for the calendar year is included on the return [sec.118.94].

L. Ordering of Credits

[ITA: 118.92]

Section 118.92 provides an ordering rule for computing basic federal tax payable by an individual under Part I of the Act. The tax credits discussed, all of which are above-the-line non-refundable tax credits, must be applied in the following order:

Ssec. 118(1)	— married, equivalent-to-married, single, dependant, and caregiver tax credits;
Ssec. 118(2)	— age credit;
Sec. 118.7	— Employment Insurance and Canada (or Quebec) Pension Plan credits;
Ssec. 118(3)	— pension credit;
Sec. 118.3	— mental or physical impairment credit (including dependant's unused credit);
Sec. 118.61	— unused tuition and education tax credit carryforward;
Sec. 118.5	— tuition fee credit;
Sec. 118.6	— education credit;
Sec. 118.9	— transfer of tuition fee and education credits;
Sec. 118.8	— transfer of unused spouse's credits;
Sec. 118.2	— medical expense credit;
Sec. 118.1	— charitable gifts credit;

Sec. 118.62 — credit for interest on student loan;

Sec. 121 — dividend tax credit.

M. Income Not Earned in a Province

[ITA: 120(1), (4); ITR: 2600]

This provision imposes a surtax of 48% on federal tax of an individual applicable proportionally to income for the year not earned in a province [ssec. 120(1)]. A definition of the term "income earned in the year in a province" is provided [ssec. 120(4) and Reg. 2600].

The purpose of this provision is to achieve a tax rate on income earned outside of Canada and taxable in Canada which approximates the total federal and provincial income tax on income earned in Canada.

N. Credit for Employment outside Canada

[ITA: 122.3; IT-497R4]

Some relief is provided for an employee who is employed outside Canada on a temporary basis. Since, in most cases, the employee will not have made a clean break from Canada, he or she will still be resident in Canada for tax purposes. In order to provide a standard of living equivalent to that in Canada, employers have had to offer increased salaries or living allowances which resulted in a higher tax burden with no increase in disposable income to the employee. This section was enacted to help the competitive position of Canadian corporations in bidding for export contracts.

This section applies to employees of specified employers who perform specified duties outside of Canada for more than six consecutive months. The tax credit is based on the proportion of tax otherwise payable. The fraction is the lesser of:

(a) $80,000, prorated on a daily basis; and

(b) 80% of the employment income which can reasonably be attributed to those specified duties, to his or her total income;

reduced by:

(c) certain deductions provided in Division C.

This credit is not available where employment is by an employer that is, in essence, an "incorporated employee" (as discussed in Chapter 12).

O. Refundable Goods and Services Tax Credit (GSTC)

[ITA: 122.5]

The amount of the refundable goods and services tax credit (GSTC) is provided in subsection 122.5(3). This credit is designed to offset all or part of the GST for families and individuals with lower incomes. Application for the credit is made with the taxpayer's income tax return, but the credit is received separately in quarterly instalments. The payments based on the taxpayer's 2005 income tax return are made in July and October 2006 and in January and April 2007. Section 122.5 provides that eligibility for the credit and the amount paid in each quarter reflects changes in family circumstances that occurred before the end of the preceding quarter. Thus, for example, the birth of a child during the year can increase the GSTC in the next quarter, rather than only in the next year. For 2005, the amount is the sum of:

(a) $227 for an eligible individual, other than a trust, who is, at the end of the year resident in Canada and married, a parent or over 18 years of age [ssecs. 122.5(1) and (2)];

(b) $227 for a qualified relation (as discussed below) or for a qualified dependant (as discussed below) in respect of whom the individual is entitled to deduct an amount under paragraph 118(1)(b) (equivalent to married status);

(c) $120 for each other qualified dependant of the individual; and

(d) where the individual has no qualified relation for the year:

(i) $120 if the individual has one or more qualified dependants for the year,

(ii) if the individual has no qualified dependants for the year, the lesser of:

(A) $120 and

(B) 2% of the excess, if any, of the individual's Division B income for the year over the base (i.e., $7,377 in 2005).

A qualified relation [ssecs. 122.5(1) and (2)] is a cohabiting spouse or common-law partner [sec. 122.6]. However, the credit cannot be double counted (i.e., the individual or the spouse or common-law partner may make the claim but not both). A qualified dependant is also defined as, in essence, a person who is claimed as a dependant under section 118 or a child of the individual who resides with the individual at the end of the year [ssecs. 122.5(1) and (2)]. Two credits cannot be claimed in respect of the same person as an eligible individual [ssecs. 122.5(1) and (2)] and as a qualified dependant.

The credit is reduced by 5% of combined incomes, as set out in subsection 122.5(1) in the definition of adjusted income over a $29,618 threshold for 2005. The refundability feature arises from the wording in subsection 122.5(3) which deems the amount of the credit to have been paid as tax like the refundable child tax credit.

Example Problem

Woody Carver is divorced and has custody of his two children, ages 8 and 13. Woody had net income of $30,000 for 2005.

— REQUIRED

Compute the refundable goods and services tax credit, beginning in July 2006, assuming no changes in his family situation.

— SOLUTION

Credit ($227 + $227 + $120 × 1)		$574
Add the GSTC supplement for single parents		120
		$694
Deduct: Income	$ 30,000	
Threshold	(29,618)	
Excess	$ 382	
5% of the excess		$ (19)
GST credit..		$ 675

This credit will be paid in four instalments of $168.75 in July and October 2006 and January and April 2007.

P. Refundable Medical Expense Tax Credit Supplement

[ITA: 122.51]

A refundable medical expense tax credit (METC) supplement is provided for eligible individuals [sec. 122.51]. An eligible individual is an individual who is resident in Canada throughout the year and 18 years of age or older at the end of the year. The individual's total business and employment income (excluding disability benefits) for the year must be at least $2,857 for 2005 [ssec. 122.51(1)]. The individual's adjusted income for a taxation year is defined as being the total of the income of the individual and of the individual's cohabiting spouse [ssec. 122.51(1)].

The supplement is calculated as follows:

lesser of:
  (a) $750 (for 2005), and
  (b) the total of
    (i) $25/16$ of the medical expense tax credit claimed by the eligible individual for the year, and
    (ii) 25% of the amount deductible under section 64 from disability support
less: 5% of the amount, if any, by which
  (a) the individual's adjusted income
  exceeds
  (b) $21,663.

Since this is a refundable federal tax credit, it does not affect provincial tax. However, an adjustment for the effect of provincial tax is contained in the $25/16$ fraction used in the above calculation.

This supplement is completely eroded by the 5% reduction, when adjusted income is $36,663 (i.e., ($750/.05) + $21,663).

The supplement is deemed to be tax paid as part of the individual's tax liability for the year, like income tax withheld [ssec. 122.51(1)]. Thus, it is available for refund if total tax paid or deemed paid exceeds tax payable for the year.

For 2004 and subsequent taxation years the refundable medical expense supplement to add to the amount subject to 25% of the disability supports deduction is increased as shown above. This ensures that disabled persons do not see their refundable medical expense credit reduced if they claim their cost of disability support as a deduction instead of a credit.

Q. Refundable Canada Child Tax Benefit

[ITA: 122.6–122.64]

The Canada Child Tax Benefit (CCTB) is the main federal instrument for the provision of financial assistance to families with children. The CCTB has two components: the base benefit, which is targeted to low and middle-income families, and the National Child Benefit (NCB) supplement, which provides additional assistance to low-income families. In recognition of the special needs of low and modest-income families with a disabled child, there is a $2,000 (for payments after June 2005 and indexed for payments after June 2006) Child Disability Benefit (CDB). The CDB is a supplement to the CCTB and is paid for children who meet the eligibility criteria for the disability tax credit.

The Canada Child Tax Benefit (CCTB) is paid monthly. The amount of the payments is based on family income and child care expenses of the base taxation year, as defined [sec. 122.6]. The payments are not taxable and not subject to clawback.

An eligible individual [sec. 122.6] is entitled to a CCTB calculated in subsection 122.61(1) in respect of qualified dependants who are generally children who have not attained the age of 18 years [sec. 122.6].

The following is a table of the maximum benefits available under the CCTB.

	July 2004	July 2005
Base Benefit		
Basic amount per child	$ 1,208	$ 1,228
Additional benefit for 3rd and subsequent children	84	86
Additional benefit for children under 7 years	239	243
NCB Supplement		
First child	1,511	1,722
Second child	1,295	1,502
Third and subsequent child	1,215	1,420
Total CCTB Benefit — 7 and older		
First child	2,719	2,950
Second child	2,503	2,730
Third and subsequent child	2,507	2,734
Total CCTB Benefit — under 7		
First child	2,958	3,193
Second child	2,742	2,973
Third and subsequent child	2,746	2,977
Child Disability Benefit		
Each child	1,653	2,000
Phase-Out Thresholds		
Base benefit phase-out starts at	35,000	35,595
Supplement phase-out ends at	35,000	35,595
Disability benefit phase-out starts at	35,000	35,595

To target the increase in the NCB supplement to lower-income families, the income threshold at which the NCB supplement begins to be phased out will be adjusted.

Since tax preparation software manages the complex calculations the point to remember is who qualifies for this benefit.

The child must be a "qualified dependent" which means a person, who:

1. has not attained the age of 18 years,

2. is not a person who has been claimed for the equivalent to married credit, and

3. is not a person in respect of whom a special allowance under the *Children's Special Allowances Act* is payable.

The person receiving the benefit must be an "eligible individual" which means a person, who:

1. resides with the child,

2. is the parent of the child who primarily fulfils the responsibility for care and upbringing,

3. is resident in Canada,

4. is not an employee of a country other than Canada, and

5. is, or whose cohabiting spouse or common-law partner is, a Canadian citizen or a person who is a permanent resident, a temporary resident or a protected person. Each of these terms is defined under federal legislation.

R. Foreign Tax Credits

[ITA: 126]

Since a resident of Canada is subject to tax on worldwide income, any income earned from a foreign source must be included in total income being taxed in Canada. However, the foreign income may also have been taxed in the country in which it was earned. In the absence of a tax treaty which removes the income from the tax base of either Canada or the other country, the income would be taxed twice. Section 126 provides tax credits deductible from tax payable in Canada for income tax paid in another country. Residents of Canada may claim a tax credit for non-business income tax paid (such as tax on investment income) in another country [ssec. 126(1)] and a tax credit for business income tax paid in another country [ssec. 126(2)]. Both credits are limited to a proportion of tax payable in Canada that can be considered to be attributed to the income from the foreign source. This limit is computed by formula.

For individuals, the foreign non-business tax credit is computed as the lesser of [ssec. 126(1)]:

(a) non-business income tax paid to a foreign country, and

(b) $\dfrac{\text{net non-business foreign income included under Division B}}{\text{total income included under Division B net of certain adjustments}} \times$ tax for the year otherwise payable under Part I

Note that part (b) attempts to estimate the Canadian tax paid on the foreign income. As a result, the credit against Canadian tax cannot exceed the estimated Canadian tax paid on the foreign income.

The definition of "non-business income tax" [ssec. 126(7)] excludes an amount that was deductible under subsection 20(11) in respect of foreign taxes in excess of 15% on income from property and an amount that was deducted under subsection 20(12) in respect of foreign non-business income tax paid.

The denominator of the fraction, which uses total income under Division B as the base, is reduced by amounts that are attributable to specific types of income which are offset by Division C deductions and, hence, do not generate tax. These amounts include:

(a) amounts deducted as net capital losses [par. 111(1)(b)]; or

(b) amounts deductible in respect of:

(i) shares [pars. 110(1)(d), (d.1), (d.2) or (d.3)],

(ii) a deduction for workers' compensation or social assistance [par. 110(1)(f)], or

(iii) a home relocation loan [par. 110(1)(j)].

The term "tax for the year otherwise payable under this Part" is defined in paragraph (a) of the definition in subsection 126(7) for the purposes of the foreign non-business income tax credit. As it applies generally to individuals, it is the tax payable under Part I of the Act before specified deductions from tax, including the deduction of the dividend tax credit and the credit for employment outside Canada.

The foreign business income tax credit, also, applies to individual taxpayers and is similar in its calculation. The major difference is that any business income tax paid but not deducted is available as an "unused foreign tax credit" [ssec. 126(7)] to be carried back three years and forward 10 years. This foreign tax credit will be dealt with in more detail, as it applies to corporations, in the next chapter.

Where either non-business or business income taxes paid are not deductible as a credit [sec. 126], all or part of the excess may be eligible for a deduction from an individual's liability for surtax [ssec. 180.1(1.1)]. Furthermore, a non-deductible excess of non-business income tax paid may be eligible for a provincial foreign tax credit.

S. Federal Political Contribution Tax Credit

[ITA: 127(3)]

A tax credit is available for contributions to a registered federal political party or a candidate for election to the House of Commons [ssec. 127(3)]. Receipts signed by the registered agent of the party or the official agent of the candidate are required to substantiate the credit claimed. The maximum credit is $650 which is reached with a contribution of $1,275 or more on the following sliding scale:

Contribution	Credit
$400 or less	75% of the contribution
More than $400, but not more than $750.............................	$300 + 50% of the contribution over $400
More than $750, but not more than $1,275	$475 + 33$\frac{1}{3}$% of the contribution over $750
More than $1,275	$650

T. Tax on Old Age Security Benefits

[ITA: 60(w); 180.2]

The Part I.2 tax [sec. 180.2] results in the repayment of federal Old Age Security benefits included in computing the taxpayer's income, to the extent that the taxpayer's income is in excess of an indexed threshold ($60,806 for 2005). The repayment is computed as:

the lesser of:

(a) Old Age Security benefits .... $xxx

(b) income under Division B without par. 60(w) deduction $ xxx

     less 60,806

     excess, if any .... $ xxx

     15% of excess, if any.. $xxx

Note that the amount of this tax is deductible under paragraph 60(w); however, offsetting the Part I.2 tax in part (b) above through the paragraph 60(w) deduction removes the potential double tax on this amount, as discussed in Chapter 9.

Example Problem

Jimena Buck, a widow, received the Old Age Security benefit of $5,700 in 2005. Her Division B income, excluding the deduction under paragraph 60(w) for the Part I.2 tax, is $62,000.

— REQUIRED

Outline all of the tax implications of receiving the Old Age Security benefit in this case.

— SOLUTION

(a) The amount of the Old Age Security benefit received must be included in Jimena's income [par. 56(1)(a)].

(b) The following repayment of the Old Age Security payment is required [sec. 180.2]:

the lesser of:		
(i) Old Age Security benefit		$ 5,700
(ii) Division B income (excluding par. 60(w) deduction)..	$62,000	
less	60,806	
excess, if any	$ 1,194	
15% of excess		$ 179

(c) The $179 repayment is deductible [par. 60(w)].

(d) The net effect is as follows:

(i) inclusion of Old Age Security benefit	$5,700	
(ii) deduction of repayment.......................	(179)	$ 5,521
(iii) cash received	$5,700	
(iv) repayment of Old Age Security benefit (paid special Part I.2 tax)	(179)	$ 5,521

U. Tax Reduction on Retroactive Lump-sum Payments

[ITA: 110.2, 120.31]

When an individual receives a lump-sum payment in a year that relates to prior years, the graduated tax rate schedule, when applied to the lump sum, may result in more income tax payable in the year of receipt than in the prior years had the lump sum been spread over those previous years. The legislation provides for a reduction of tax on the following lump sums received after 1994:

- income from an office or employment or income received because of the termination of an office or employment, received under the terms of a court judgement, arbitration award or in settlement of a lawsuit;

- superannuation or pension benefits, other than non-periodic benefits;

- spouse or child support payments; and

- employment insurance and other benefits that may be prescribed by regulations.

The right to receive the lump sum must have existed in a prior year. For the tax reduction to apply, the lump sum received in the year must be at least $3,000.

The amount of income that is eligible for this special treatment is deducted in arriving at taxable income [sec. 110.2] and then subject to notional tax [sec. 120.31]. The notional tax is calculated as if the lump-sum payment had actually been received in the year to which it related.

This calculation will not affect any income-base benefits or deductions in those prior years.

V. Application of Rules for Computation of Tax and Credits

[ITA: 117; 118; 118.1; 118.7; 118.8; 121; 126; 127(3); 180.1(2)]

Example Problem

The following 2005 correct computation of taxable income for John Q. Citizen has been prepared for your analysis:

Income — Division B		
Employment income for tax purposes...............		$41,550
Business and property income, composed of:		
Dividends from taxable Canadian corporations		
(grossed-up)	$ 4,500	
Dividends — Foreign ($150 of tax withheld)......	1,000	5,500
Pension income (including OAS benefit of $5,700)		15,000
Taxable capital gain.....................		1,000
		$63,050
Less: Subdivision e deductions:		
RRSP contributions	$ 1,000	
Old Age Security benefit clawback	29	
Moving expenses.................................	1,050	(2,079)
Division B income		$60,971
Less: net capital losses.................................		(1,000)
Taxable income...		$59,971

Additional Information

(1) John, age 67, and his wife Jill, age 64, are both resident in your province. Jill has no income and is blind.

(2) John has made the following selected payments in 2005:

Donations:	
Federal political party (registered)	$ 500
Provincial political party (registered)	400
United Appeal (registered)....................................	500

(3) John's employer correctly withheld the following amounts:

Employment Insurance.......................................	$ 761
Canada Pension Plan	1,861

(4) John filed his return on April 30, 2006.

—REQUIRED

Compute the total amount of federal taxes payable for the year.

—SOLUTION

Sec. 117	Federal tax on first	$35,595	....	$ 5,695
	Tax on balance	24,376	@ 22%.................	5,363
		$59,971		
	Total.....................................			$11,058
	Less: federal non-refundable tax credits:			
Ssec. 118(1)	Basic personal credit base		$ 8,148	
	Married credit base........................		6,919	
Ssec. 118(2)	Age credit base[1]		—	
Sec. 118.7	Employment Insurance credit base		761	
	Canada Pension Plan credit base		1,861	
Ssec. 118(3)	Pension credit base		1,000	
Sec. 118.8	Transfer of spouse's impairment credit base		6,596	
			$25,285	

	16% thereof...............................			(4,046)
				$ 7,012
Sec. 118.1	Charitable donations tax credit			
	First $200 @ 16%......................	$	32	
	Excess $300 @ 29%......................		87	(119)
	$500			
Sec. 121	Federal dividend tax credit (13⅓% × $4,500)			(600)
	Basic federal tax			$ 6,293
	Less: other federal tax credits:			
Sec. 126	Federal foreign tax credit[2]			
	Lesser of:			
	(a) $150			
	(b) $\dfrac{\$1,000}{\$60,971 - \$1,000} \times (\$6,293 + \$600) = \underline{\$115}$			$ (115)
	Federal tax			$ 6,178
Ssec. 127(3)	Federal political donations[3]			(350)
	Net federal Part I tax payable.................			$ 5,828
Sec. 180.2	Old Age Security benefit clawback[4]...........			29
	Net federal tax payable......................			$ 5,857

— NOTES TO SOLUTION

(1) The age credit is not available since Division B income is too high.

Age tax credit base		$3,979
Less: base reduction of lesser of:		
(a) Amount of credit base	$3,979	
(b) Division B income..................	$60,971	
Less: threshold	29,619	
	$31,352 × .15 =	$4,702
Lesser amount		3,979
Net base		Nil

(2) In this case, the foreign non-business tax credit is computed as the lesser of:

(a) the foreign non-business tax paid, and

(b) $\dfrac{\text{the foreign non-business income included under Division B}}{\text{Division B income less net capital losses claimed}} \times$ basic federal tax plus dividend tax credit

(3) Subsection 127(3) permits the deduction of a contribution to a federal registered party or person nominated as a candidate to serve in the House of Commons. The formula is:

75% of first $400	$300
50% of next $350 ($500 – $400 in this situation)	50
33⅓% on next $525 (none in this situation).......................	Nil
	$350

The maximum credit is $650 on $1,275 of contributions.

(4) Lesser of:

    (a) Old Age Security benefit .... $\underline{\$5,700}$

    (b) income under Division B (excluding par. 60(w)

        deduction) $61,000

        less 60,806

        excess, if any.............................. $\ \ \ \ 194$

        15% of excess.. $\underline{\$\ \ \ \ 29}$

W. Minimum Tax

[ITA: 120.2; 127.5]

The minimum tax addresses a government concern about the ability of some high-income individuals to take advantage of tax incentives and shelter virtually all of their income. Thus, a signal that minimum tax might apply in a particular case would be large deductions of CCA on tax shelters or large resource property deductions.

1. Minimum amount

An individual's minimum tax is calculated by the following formula [sec. 127.51]:

$$A (B - C) - D$$

where A is 16%. (i.e., the appropriate percentage for the year),

      B is adjusted taxable income [sec. 127.52],

      C is the basic exemption [sec. 127.53], and

      D is the basic minimum tax credit [sec. 127.531].

This "minimum amount" minus a special foreign tax credit provided in subsection 127.54(2) is then compared to regular Part I tax, net of all non-refundable tax credits (generally, before adding the 48% surtax for income not earned in a province). The greater amount becomes the basis of federal Part I tax for the year. The special foreign tax credit, which is basically equal to the greater of the foreign tax credit determined under normal rules or 16% of foreign income is the only credit available to a taxpayer subject to minimum tax.

All other tax credits, such as dividend tax credits and political donation credits will not be deductible from the minimum amount. In addition, even where the minimum amount is less than Part I tax, the restricted tax credits will be available only to the extent that Part I tax payable for the year does not go below the minimum amount.

2. Adjusted taxable income

Section 127.52 sets out the rules for computing adjusted taxable income, being a recalculation of taxable income using certain assumptions set out in the section. The CRA's form T691, for simplicity, starts with regular taxable income and adds back or subtracts amounts to arrive at adjusted taxable income. The amounts added back include:

    (a) the portion of the loss (including a share of a partnership loss) from certified film or videotape properties that relates to CCA or carrying charges such as interest and financing charges;

    (b) losses on resource properties as a result of certain incentive deductions such as Canadian exploration expense, Canadian development expense, depletion allowance, or Canadian oil and gas property expense;

    (c) 30% of the excess of capital gains over capital losses for the year;

(d) ³/₅ of the employee stock option deductions [pars. 110(1)(*d*) and (*d*.1)] and the other share deductions [pars. 110(1)(*d*.2) and (*d*.3)];

(e) the home relocation loan deduction [par. 110(1)(*j*)]; and

(f) losses of investments required to be identified under the tax shelter identification rules.

Deducted in computing adjusted taxable income are:

(a) the gross-up of Canadian dividends; and

(b) the non-deductible fraction of allowable business investment losses claimed in the year.

3. Basic exemption

An individual's basic exemption is set out in subsection 127.53(1). In the case of an individual, other than a trust, it is $40,000. Therefore, it is only adjusted taxable income in excess of $40,000 that is subject to minimum tax.

4. Basic minimum tax credit

An individual's basic minimum tax credit is the sum of the following tax credits that may be deducted in computing tax payable under Part I of the Act [sec. 127.531]:

Ssec. 118(1)	— Personal credits for married status, equivalent-to-married status, single, dependants, and caregiver;
Ssec. 118(2)	— Age credit;
Sec. 118.1	— Charitable gifts credit;
Sec. 118.2	— Medical expense credit;
Ssec. 118.3(1)	— Mental or physical impairment credit;
Sec. 118.5	— Tuition credit;
Sec. 118.6	— Education credit;
Sec. 118.61	— Unused tuition and education tax credits;
Sec. 118.62	— Credit for interest on student loan; and
Sec. 118.7	— Credit for Employment Insurance premium and CPP contribution.

5. Minimum tax carryforward

To recognize that a taxpayer who is not normally subject to minimum tax may, through unusual circumstances, be subject to minimum tax in a given year, section 120.2 of the Act contains a carryforward provision. A taxpayer may carry forward for seven years the excess of the minimum tax over regular Part I tax for a particular year. The amount of the carryforward deductible in a subsequent year is restricted to the excess of regular Part I tax over the minimum tax in that subsequent year. As a result, in a carryforward year in which Part I tax exceeds the minimum tax, all or some part of the minimum tax paid in the previous year is recoverable as, in essence, a tax credit against Part I tax payable.

6. Impact of the minimum tax

The minimum tax directly affects only a small minority of Canadian taxpayers. The $40,000 basic exemption generally protects most non-top bracket taxpayers from minimum tax. Most top bracket taxpayers who do not invest in tax shelters are also unlikely to be affected by the minimum tax. However, it is necessary for taxpayers who could potentially be affected to do minimum tax calculations as a part of their tax planning each year. Thus, the tax adds a significant additional degree of complexity to the tax system.

Example Problem 1

Determine the federal tax payable in 2005 by Scoop, an unmarried taxpayer, with the following sources of income and deductions and a $400 federal political donation tax credit.

Employment income for tax purposes	$ 90,000
Interest income	15,000
Cash dividend	12,800
Gross-up on dividend	3,200
Taxable capital gain ($\frac{1}{2} \times$ $112,500)	56,250
RRSP contribution	(7,500)
Support of former spouse	(20,000)
Tax shelter loss due to film CCA	(25,000)
Net income for tax purposes	$124,750
Q.S.B.C. share capital gains deduction	(50,000)
Taxable income	$ 74,750

Maximum Employment Insurance of $761 and CPP of $1,861 were withheld from salary.

—SOLUTION

Regular Part I tax			
on first	$71,190		$ 13,526
on balance of	3,560	@ 26%	926
	$74,750		$ 14,452

Less tax credits:		
Basic personal	$1,304	
Employment Insurance (16% of $761)	122	
CPP (16% of $1,861)	298	
Dividend tax credit (13$\frac{1}{3}$% of $16,000)	2,133	$ (3,857)
Basic federal tax under regular rules		$ 10,595(A)
Less: political donation tax credit (75% of $400)		(300)
Federal tax under regular rules		$ 10,295(B)

Adjusted taxable income:		
Taxable income		$ 74,750
Add back: 30% of capital gain		33,750
CCA loss		25,000
Less: dividend gross-up		(3,200)
Adjusted taxable income		$130,300
Less: basic exemption		(40,000)
Net		$ 90,300

Minimum tax before minimum tax credit (16% of $90,300)		$ 14,448
Less basic minimum tax credit:		
Basic personal	$1,304	
Employment Insurance premium	122	
CPP	298	(1,724)
Minimum amount		$ 12,724(C)
Federal tax — greater of (B) and (C)		$ 12,724

Therefore, minimum tax is incurred in this situation.

REVIEW QUESTIONS

(1) Ms. Gnu, a new client of yours, has brought in her tax information and is confused. In prior years, she has had some financial difficulties and has lost money in a number of her business ventures. As a result, she has some net capital and some non-capital losses. This year, she earned some income, but she does not know how to decide which losses to apply against this income. What advice do you have for her?

(2) Mr. Izzy Dumorwhat earns over $130,000 of employment income and has come to you to talk about his investment income. He earns $10,000 of dividend income from a taxable Canadian corporation in the year. He wants you to tell him what his marginal tax rate is on this dividend income.

(3) Mr. Phil D. Ayer earns over $130,000 of employment income and has come to you to talk about his investment income. He earns $10,000 of interest income in the year. He wants you to tell him what his marginal tax rate is on this interest income.

(4) Ms. Borscht earns over $130,000 of employment income and has come to you to talk about her investment income. She realized a $10,000 capital gain in the year and wants you to tell her what her marginal tax rate is on this capital gain.

(5) Ms. Aarts is a painter who specializes in watercolours. In the artistic tradition, she does not make a great deal of money. In fact, she has never made over $20,000 of taxable income in any year. This year is no exception. She expects to have taxable income of $20,000 but she is also planning to donate one of her watercolours to a local charity to be used in one of their fundraising events. The value of the painting is $8,000 and her cost of the painting is $200. She has heard that there are special rules for artists making charitable donations of their work but she does not know if these rules will help her. She does not make any other donations. What is your advice?

(6) During the year Ms. Hurry had full-time employment income from employer A of $45,000 and from employer B of $40,000. In addition, she had income from an unincorporated business of $30,000. Both employer A and employer B each deducted $1,861 from her salary for CPP. What impact will the CPP contributions for her employment and business income have on her personal tax return?

(7) ABC Contracting Inc., a taxable Canadian corporation, has a construction contract in Kuwait. Mr. Jones has been asked to move from Canada to Kuwait to help with the supervision. He will be there for a period of 15 months, after which time he will move back to Canada to take up his duties with the company. Due to the short-term nature of the work he will not move his family with him. He will move to Kuwait on January 1, 2005, and will not come back to Canada until April 1, 2006. His income for 2005 while in Kuwait will be $120,000. Comment on the tax issues in 2005.

MULTIPLE CHOICE QUESTIONS

Question 1

Banbury Ltd. (BL) is a Canadian-controlled private corporation. Brad King is one of BL's employees and deals at arm's length with BL. On April 30, 2002, Brad was granted an option to purchase 1,000 BL shares at $2 per share. Brad exercised the stock option on June 30, 2003, when the market price was $5 per share. In December 2005, Brad sold the shares for $7 each. The fair market value of the shares on April 30, 2002, was $2.50.

Which one of the following amounts represents the increase in Brad's taxable income resulting from the above transactions?

(A) $3,000 in 2003 and $1,000 in 2005

(B) $2,250 in 2003 and $1,000 in 2005

(C) $2,500 in 2005

(D) $4,000 in 2005

Question 2

Bob, a widower who is 65 years old, has correctly calculated his taxable income for 2005 as follows:

Employment income under Subdivision a	$10,000
Pension income (registered pension plan)	20,000
Old Age Security and Canada Pension Plans	10,000
Dividends from taxable Canadian corporations (grossed up)	2,500
Interest income	5,000
	$47,500

What is the maximum amount (rounded to the nearest dollar) of federal income tax credits that Bob can claim on his 2005 tax return?

(A) $1,671

(B) $1,844

(C) $2,004

(D) $2,433

Question 3

In 2005, Shabir Hassam attended McGill University on a full-time basis for eight months, paying tuition fees of $3,900 for that period. In April 2005, Shabir moved back to Toronto to stay with his family and worked as a waiter. Shabir earned $7,500 in wages and $500 in tips during the summer. His moving costs were $200 to Toronto in April 2005 and $500 to Montreal in September 2005. Shabir also received a $1,100 scholarship from McGill in September 2005.

What is the maximum amount of federal personal income tax credits that Shabir can transfer to a parent in respect of his university education in 2005?

(A) $624

(B) $760

(C) $800

(D) $1,136

Question 4

Kyle, who is employed by a Canadian-controlled private corporation, had the following sources of income for the year:

Salary	$ 60,000
Canadian source dividends (amount received)	20,000
Employee stock option benefit	200,000
Capital gain	200,000

The stock option benefit relates to 50,000 shares that Kyle acquired under an employee stock option plan in January 2005 when the fair market value of the shares was $10 per share. Kyle paid $6 per share for the stock, which was the fair market value of each share at the time that the employee stock options were granted to him. He sold the stock when it was worth $14 per share.

Kyle is married and his wife works full-time. Their three children attend university. Each child has transferred the $5,000 maximum amount of education and tuition credits to Kyle.

Based on this information, what is Kyle's federal Part I tax for the year under the regular rules, ignoring the minimum tax rules?

(A) $67,158

(B) $69,041

(C) $70,491

(D) $96,158

Question 5

Based on the information in Question 4, above, what is Kyle's minimum amount of federal tax for the year under section 127.53, after deducting minimum tax credits?

(A) $56,296

(B) $53,896

(C) $46,696

(D) $37,096

EXERCISES

Exercise 1

[ITA: 3; 111]

The following information has been provided by your client, Ms. C.G. Investor.

	2003	2004	2005
Capital gains (C.G.)	$37,500	$50,000	$11,250
Capital losses (C.L.) (excluding B.I.L.)	15,000	—	22,500
Business investment loss (B.I.L.)	—	30,000	—

Additional Information

(1) The above capital gains do not include capital gains from qualified farm property or qualified small business corporation shares.

(2) Ms. Investor had a $7,500 net capital loss which was realized in 2001.

(3) Ms. Investor has never had a taxable capital gain prior to 2003 and did not claim any net capital losses in 1985 to 2002.

(4) Ms. Investor had a property loss of $7,000 in 2004 and property income of $1,000 and $2,000 for 2003 and 2005, respectively.

— *REQUIRED*

(A) Determine Ms. Investor's income from the sources indicated for 2003 to 2005 according to the ordering rules in section 3.

(B) Determine Ms. Investor's taxable income from the sources indicated for 2003 to 2005 according to the ordering rules in Division C after amending the returns.

Exercise 2

[ITA: 118; 122.6; 122.61; IT-513R]

Dan Dependant, age 50, supported the following persons during 2005:

	Net income for tax purposes
Wife, Dolly, age 45	$3,000
Son, Don, age 24	3,800
Son, Dave, age 18, infirm	3,200
Daughter, Doris, age 17	2,800
Son, Dan Jr., age 14	Nil
Mother, infirm, age 83	6,000

Don is attending university; Dave has been unemployed most of the year; and Doris and Dan Jr. attend high school. Ages are given as of the end of 2005.

— *REQUIRED*

Determine Dan's total federal personal tax credits under section 118 for 2005.

Exercise 3

[ITA: 118; IT-513R]

Jack and Jill were married on December 1, 2005. Jill and her two children of a previous marriage moved into Jack's home. Jill's children are 14 and 16 years of age and have no income.

Jack and Jill have the following income for tax purposes for 2005:

	Prior to the marriage	Subsequent to the marriage
Jack	$33,000	$3,000
Jill	8,800	800

— *REQUIRED*

(A) Determine the optimum personal tax credits under section 118 for both Jack and Jill for 2005.

(B) How would your answer change in 2005 if the income levels remain the same?

Exercise 4

[ITA: 8(1)(*m*); 56(1)(*a*); 118(3)]

Sluggo Transient was employed for a little under two years at the Banff Springs Hotel as a bellboy. When Sluggo resigned his position, he withdrew his total contributions of $800 from his employer's pension plan. Sluggo's contribution to this plan for his last year was $300.

— *REQUIRED*

Determine the tax consequences of the above situation.

Exercise 5

[ITA: 118.6; 118.8; 118.9]

Sammy Student, who was a resident of Canada and who attended the University of Alberta on a full-time basis for eight months during 2005, has employment income for tax purposes of $5,000. He paid tuition fees of $1,800 in 2005. Withheld from his income were $100 in Employment Insurance premiums and $75 in CPP contributions.

— *REQUIRED*

(A) Determine the amount Sammy can transfer under section 118.8 or 118.9 to another qualified person.

(B) List the potential persons to whom Sammy can transfer his tuition and education tax credits.

Exercise 6

[ITA: 118.8]

Tina Transfer, age 72, has income for tax purposes from the following sources in 2005:

Pension income:		
Old Age Security pension	$5,700	
Canada Pension Plan	2,755	
Registered pension plan	450	$ 8,905
Investment income:		
Canadian bank interest		100
Total Division B income		$ 9,005

— *REQUIRED*

Determine the amount Tina can transfer to her husband Tom in 2005.

Exercise 7

[ITA: 82(3)]

Mr. Eighty-Two-Three, a resident of your province, cannot decide whether it would be advisable to elect under subsection 82(3) in respect of his wife's dividends of $900 received from taxable Canadian corporations. This is her only income for 2005.

— *REQUIRED*

Determine whether Mr. Eighty-Two-Three should elect under subsection 82(3) for 2005 assuming his federal tax rate is 29%.

Exercise 8

[ITA: 126(1)]

The following selected information has been taken from the 2005 tax return of Adam Amazing, who is a bachelor:

Income — Division B	$156,800
Taxable income	150,800
Basic federal tax	34,000

Included in the Division B income was foreign interest of $1,500. Withholding tax of $225 had been deducted by the foreign government. This income is not subject to an international tax agreement.

Also included in the computation of Division B income were $300 of dividends received from taxable Canadian corporations. Included in the computation of taxable income were deductions for net capital losses of $6,000 under paragraph 111(1)(b).

— REQUIRED

Determine the amount of the federal foreign tax credit that can be claimed.

Exercise 9

[ITA: Divisions E and E.1]

Compute the federal tax at the top bracket, under minimum tax and regular Part I tax for 2005 on $100 of:

(A) interest;

(B) Canadian-source cash dividends;

(C) capital gains.

Exercise 10

[ITA: Divisions E and E.1]

The following is a correct calculation (ignoring surtaxes) of Betty Bucks' Division E tax payable for 2005:

Employment income		$160,000
Canadian dividends		30,000
Gross-up		7,500
Loss created by resource property shelter		(97,500)
Net income for tax purposes and taxable income		$100,000

Tax on first	$ 71,190		$ 13,526
on next	28,810 @ 26%		7,491
	$100,000		$ 21,017

Less tax credits:

Basic personal (16% × $8,148)	$1,304	
Employment Insurance premiums (max.) (16% × $761)	122	
CPP contributions (max.) (16% × $1,861)	298	
Dividend tax credit (13⅓% of $37,500)	5,000	(6,724)
Division E tax		$ 14,293

— REQUIRED

Determine if Betty Bucks is subject to minimum tax in 2005.

ASSIGNMENT PROBLEMS

Problem 1

[ITA: Divisions B and C]

The following tax information is extracted from Mrs. Hawkins' books and records:

Employment income per T4s (excluding effects of items below)	$72,000
Interest income	5,000
Capital gains (on securities)	9,900
Deductible carrying charges	1,000

The following balances are losses carried forward from December 31, 2004:

Non-capital loss arising — 1999	$24,000
— 2000	26,000
— 2003	28,000
Total non-capital losses	$78,000
Net capital loss arising in 2004	$12,000

During the latter part of 2005, Mrs. Hawkins moved from Montreal to Toronto to commence working for Leaves Co. Ltd. She received a $100,000 housing loan from Leaves Co. Ltd., which she used to help purchase a house in Toronto. Mrs. Hawkins received the interest-free loan on October 1, 2005.

Mrs. Hawkins previously worked for Les Habitants Co. Ltée (a public company). Prior to leaving Les Habitants Co. Ltée, Mrs. Hawkins exercised the stock option that she held in Les Habitants Co. Ltée. Mrs. Hawkins was able to purchase 2,000 listed common shares of Les Habitants Co. Ltée for $4 per share (the fair market value of the shares at the time the option was granted). The shares were trading at $10 per share at the time she exercised her option to purchase the shares.

Assume that the prescribed interest rate for the last quarter of 2005 is 7%.

— REQUIRED

Calculate Mrs. Hawkins' income and taxable income in 2005, in accordance with the ordering rules of Divisions B and C.

Problem 2

[ITA: 3; 111]

The following information has been provided by your client, Mr. Stanley Norman:

	2003	2004	2005
Employment income	$75,000	$80,000	$ 90,000
Property income (loss)	(4,000)	3,000	(6,000)
Capital gains (C.G.)	144,000	—	160,000
Capital losses (C.L.) (excluding B.I.L.)	18,000	22,500	80,000
Business investment loss (B.I.L.)	36,000	54,000	—

Additional Information

(1) The above capital gains do not include capital gains from qualified farm property or qualified small business corporation shares. The capital and business investment losses in 2003 were realized in December.

(2) Mr. Norman had a $21,000 net capital loss which was realized in 2001.

(3) Mr. Norman has not had a capital gain prior to 2003 and did not claim a net capital loss in the period 1985 to 2002.

— REQUIRED

Dealing with each item line-by-line across the years, rather than one year at a time:

(A) determine Mr. Norman's income from the sources indicated for 2003 to 2005 according to the ordering rules in section 3, and

(B) determine Mr. Norman's taxable income from the sources indicated from 2003 to 2005 according to the ordering rules in Division C after amending the returns.

Problem 3

[ITA: 3; 111; 111.1]

The following selected tax information has been taken from the books and records of your client, Mr. Taxloss.

	2004	2005
Employment income	$ 30,000	$ 38,000
Other business income (loss)	(14,000)	(23,000)
Property income:		
Canadian interest	7,000	14,000
Rental income from real property (loss)	3,000	(5,000)
Other income — pension	7,000	7,000
Capital gains (capital losses)*:		
Listed personal property	6,000	20,250
Other personal-use property	2,000	(4,000)
Other capital property	6,000	(45,000)
Other deductions:		
RRSP	1,000	3,000
Support of former spouse	7,000	7,000

* The 2005 other capital property loss includes a business investment loss of $24,000.

The following balances are losses carried forward from December 31, 2003:

Non-capital loss arising in 2001	$33,000
Net capital loss arising in 2002	25,000
Listed personal property loss arising in 2001	5,000

Mr. Taxloss was not a member of a registered pension plan and, hence, his pension adjustment for the relevant years was nil. His earned income for 2003 was $33,250.

— REQUIRED

Prepare a schedule for the calculation of income and taxable income for 2004 and 2005, in accordance with the ordering rules under Divisions B and C, after applying any loss carryforward and loss carryback provisions through an amended return. (Deal with each item line-by-line across the years, rather than computing income one year at a time.)

Problem 4

[ITA: 56(1)(u), (v); 74.1(1); 110(1)(f); 118; 118.3; 118.6; 118.9; 122.6; 122.61]

Mrs. Plant, age 47, is married and has three children: Amanda, age 24, Joan, age 17, and Courtney, age 16. Her own income for tax purposes of $60,000 includes employment income of $52,000.

Amanda has been certified as impaired by a medical doctor. Her only income is $6,000 from social assistance payments relating to her disability. She took a university course on a part-time basis for four months. Mrs. Plant paid her tuition fees of $300.

Joan attended a university on a full-time basis in another city for eight months, had employment income for tax purposes of $4,200 from a summer job while living at home and received a $2,500 scholarship. Mrs. Plant paid Joan's tuition fees of $3,000 and Joan paid her own moving costs to and from the university which were $150 each way.

Courtney, who is attending high school, had employment income for tax purposes of $2,800 from summer employment and a part-time job.

Mr. Plant, age 50, has the following sources of income:

Worker's Compensation payment	$5,000
Cash dividends from shares of taxable Canadian corporations purchased with Mrs. Plant's savings	4,000
Bank account interest earned from reinvestment of dividend income	100

— REQUIRED

(A) Calculate the non-refundable tax credits available to Mrs. Plant for 2005. Compute Joan's taxable income to determine if any of her tuition and education tax credit will be available to Mrs. Plant. Prepare detailed calculations supporting your claim. All ages are given as of the end of 2005.

(B) Determine whether Mrs. Plant is entitled to claim the Canada Child Tax Benefit.

Problem 5

[ITA: 118; 118.2–118.9; IT-513R]

Mrs. Hopeful, age 66, separated from her husband on October 17, 2005. She started receiving support payments from Mr. Hopeful of $2,500 per month in November 2005. All of the support payments made commencing in November 2005 are considered to be pursuant to the divorce settlement. Of the $2,500 monthly payment, $1,000 is for the support of their daughter, Rachel. (In 2005, Mr. Hopeful earned a salary of $100,000 per year and also earned other investment income.) Mrs. Hopeful has income of $26,200.

Their eldest daughter Rachel is 40 and infirm and lives with Mrs. Hopeful since she is severely mentally handicapped. She has been certified as impaired by a medical doctor. A part-time attendant helps care for Rachel at a cost of $12,000 per year. Rachel has no income.

— REQUIRED

Discuss the tax credits related to her daughter Rachel that are available to Mrs. Hopeful.

Problem 6

[ITA: 118.2]

Mr. Unfortunate provides you with the following medical expenses and additional information for himself and members of his family who live with him, when he asks you to prepare his 2005 tax return.

Assume that you have correctly computed the incomes under Division B for 2005 as follows:

Mr. Unfortunate	$55,000
Mrs. Unfortunate	Nil
Son, age 16	8,000
Son, age 15	2,000
Daughter, age 14	1,800

Medical expenses for 2005:

February	Prescription drugs for daughter	$ 20
May	Doctor's bill paid for son, 16	15*
June	Chiropractor's bill for the past year	1150*
July	Glasses for Mr. and Mrs. Unfortunate	300
		$1,485

Medical expenses to March 31, 2006:

February	Orthodontist fee for daughter		$2,550
March	Expenses relating to older son's car accident:		
	Hospital	$1,500	
	Surgery	1,000	
	Drugs	200	2,700*

Additional expenses anticipated by May 31, 2006:

(a)	Additional medical bills from son's accident	$ 500*
(b)	Eyeglasses for his mother and daughter ($100 each)	200
(c)	Dental bills (²/₃ for Mr. & Mrs. Unfortunate)	125
(d)	Chiropractor's bill for the past year	800
(e)	Prepayment of chiropractor's bill for next 12 months	1,000

* Excess over provincial plan payments.

— *REQUIRED*

Discuss the tax implications of Mr. Unfortunate claiming the above medical expenses for each of 2005 and 2006. Assume that all income amounts for 2006 will be the same as those for 2005.

Problem 7

[ITA: 82; 118; 118.8]

Mr. and Mrs. Realestate, ages 55 and 50, received the following income during 2005:

Mr. Realestate:

Employment income (commission)	$15,000
Employment expenses	(13,000)
Investment income:	
Canadian interest	2,000
Dividends received (in Cdn $):	
Canadian corporations	950
U.S. corporations (net of 15% withholding tax)	680

Mrs. Realestate:

Employment income	54,000
Investment income:	
Canadian interest	1,000
Canadian dividends	2,000

— *REQUIRED*

Calculate Mrs. Realestate's federal tax (ignoring the foreign tax credit) under the following situations:

(A) No subsection 82(3) election.

(B) With a subsection 82(3) election.

Problem 8

[ITA: 118.5; IT-516R2]

Stuart Student presents to you the following information concerning tuition fees paid for 2003, 2004 and 2005.

2003	Harvard University, Masters in Business Administration, fall term	$15,000
2004	Harvard University, Masters in Business Administration, winter and fall terms	30,000
2005	Harvard University, Masters in Business Administration, winter term	15,000
	Re-read fee for failed course	300
	Make-up course at Harvard for failed course, July–August	3,000
	Income tax course at University of Toronto, fall term; the tuition fee of $500 was waived, since Stuart's father was a member of the faculty	Nil
	Fitness course taken at a local secondary school in Ontario	35

— *REQUIRED*

Discuss the tax implications of the above tuition fee payments.

Problem 9

[ITA: 117; 118; 121; 122.2; 122.5; 122.6–122.64; 180.1]

Patty Parent, a single parent of two children (ages 4 and 2) works part-time as a clerk in a law office. She has provided you with the following information for 2005:

Income:

Workers' Compensation payments	$ 9,000
Employment income (Subdivision a)	20,000
Cash dividend from taxable Canadian corporations	480
University scholarship received	600

Expenses:

Canada Pension Plan contributions	817
Employment Insurance contributions	390
Cost of subsidized day care for the children (3 days a week)	2,400
University tuition paid for a 3-month evening course	600

Patty receives the Workers' Compensation payment because of the accidental death of her husband two years ago. Her two children have no income.

Patty had $700 of tax withheld from her employment income and has paid no income tax instalments.

— *REQUIRED*

(A) Based on the information above, compute Patty's total federal and provincial tax for 2005 and her tax refund or balance due.

(B) Determine if Patty is eligible for the refundable goods and service tax credit and Canada Child Tax Benefit. Explain.

Problem 10

[ITA: Divisions B, C, and E]

Hymie and Alan, both age 70, married, and retired successful businessmen, love to argue. The one fact that they agree upon is that they pay too much income tax. They both receive $5,700 of Old Age Security payments each year. Hymie has $51,000 of income from a registered pension plan. Alan receives $51,000 in dividends from his incorporated business which is now managed by his son. The spouses of both Hymie and Alan have no income for tax purposes and are under 65 years of age.

— *REQUIRED*

Determine which one of the two pays the most federal income tax for 2005. Ignore ssec. 82(3).

Problem 11

[ITA: Divisions E and E.1]

Mrs. Entrepreneur, a client of yours, generally has employment income from her company and some investment income. In early 2005, you arranged Mrs. Entrepreneur's affairs such that she would crystallize her $500,000 capital gains exemption on qualified small business corporation shares. For 2005, her income is estimated as follows:

Employment income (CPP $1,861)	$ 42,500
Interest	12,000
Dividends	20,000
Gross-up	5,000
Taxable capital gains	250,000
Interest expense	(10,000)
RRSP contribution	(14,500)
Capital gains deduction	(250,000)
Taxable income	$ 55,000

— *REQUIRED*

Calculate what effect, if any, minimum tax will have on Mrs. Entrepreneur's 2005 federal tax payable.

[For more problems and solutions thereto, see the CD accompanying this book.]

Chapter 11

Computation of Taxable Income and Tax after General Reductions for Corporations

TOPICS DISCUSSED

	Page			Page
COMPUTATION OF TAXABLE INCOME FOR A CORPORATION	539		Abatement from Federal Tax for Income earned in a Province	575
Overview	539		Tax on Large Corporations	580
Deduction of Taxable Dividends	539		MANUFACTURING AND PROCESSING PROFITS DEDUCTION	583
Charitable Donations	542		Introduction	583
Loss Carryovers	543		Eligibility	583
Acquisition of Control of a Corporation and Its Effect on Losses	553		Elements of the Formula for Determining Manufacturing and Processing Profits	585
Taxable Income of a Corporation in General	571		Application of the Rules	586
			CREDITS AVAILABLE TO ALL TAXPAYERS	588
BASIC COMPUTATION OF TAX FOR ALL CORPORATIONS	573		Foreign Tax Deduction	588
			Investment Tax Credit	595
Objectives of Provisions Affecting Taxation of Corporations	573		SUPPLEMENTAL NOTES	616
General Rates for Corporations	574		Branch Tax	616

In the computation of the taxable income of a corporation, several deductions may be taken from the income determined in Division B of Part I of the Act. Three of these, namely, charitable donations, loss carryovers and intercompany dividends, are covered in the example problem material of this chapter. The computation of tax for a corporation is made under the provisions of Part I, Division E, Subdivisions b (which applies only to corporations) and c (which applies to all taxpayers). This chapter introduces the basic computation of tax for corporations. Next to be introduced is the manufacturing and processing profits deduction which is available only for qualifying corporations. Then two tax credits that are available to all taxpayers, including corporations and individuals, are presented with a focus on their applicability to corporations: the foreign tax deduction and the investment tax credit.

The following chart will help to position in the Act some of the major provisions dealt with in this Chapter.

PART I — DIVISIONS C
TAXABLE INCOME — CORPORATE

DIVISION		SUBDIVISION		SECTION	
A	Liability for tax				
B	Computation of income				
C	**Computation of taxable income**			110.1	Donations
				110.5	Foreign tax addition
D	Taxable income earned in Canada by non-residents			111	Loss carryovers
				112	Dividends–Canadian
				113	Dividends–foreign
E	**Computation of tax**	a	Individuals		
		a.1	Child tax benefit		
E.1	Minimum tax	b	Corporations		
F	Special rules	c	All taxpayers	123-123.3	Tax rates and surtax
				123.4	Tax reductions
G	Deferred and other special income arrangements			124	Prov abatement
				125	Small Business ded'n
				125.1	Mfg and Proc credit
H	Exemptions			125.2	Ded'n of Part VI tax
I	Returns, Assessments, payments, appeals			125.3	Ded'n of Part I.3 tax
				125.4 - 125.5	Cdn film/video credit
J	Appeals to the courts			126	Foreign tax credit
				126.1-127.41	Other tax credits

I. COMPUTATION OF TAXABLE INCOME FOR A CORPORATION

A. Overview

[ITA: 110.1; 111; 112]

Recall that taxable income results from the deduction of certain amounts listed in Division C of Part I from income computed under Division B of Part I. Exhibit 11-1 lists the common Division C deductions and indicates which of these are available to corporations.

EXHIBIT 11-1
Selected Division C Deductions

Provisions	Deduction	Individuals	Corporations
Par. 110(1)(d), (d.1)	Employee stock options	X	
Par. 110(1)(f)	Deductions for certain social assistance payments	X	
Par. 110(1)(j)	Home relocation loan	X	
Par. 110.1(1)(a)	Charitable gifts*		X
Par. 110.1(1)(b)	Gifts to Her Majesty*		X
Par. 110.1(1)(c)	Gifts of cultural property to institutions*		X
Par. 110.1(1)(d)	Ecological gifts*		X
Sec. 110.6	Capital gains deduction	X	
Par. 111(1)(a)	Carryover of non-capital losses	X	X
Par. 111(1)(b)	Carryover of net capital losses	X	X
Par. 111(1)(c)	Carryover of restricted farm losses	X	X
Par. 111(1)(d)	Carryover of farm losses	X	X
Par. 111(1)(e)	Carryover of limited partnership losses	X	X
Sec. 112	Dividends from Canadian corporations		X
Sec. 113	Dividends from foreign affiliates		X

* Non-refundable tax credits available in subsection 118.1(3) for an individual.

B. Deduction of Taxable Dividends

[ITA: 112]

Certain dividends received by a corporation are deductible in the calculation of the taxable income of the recipient corporation [ssec. 112(1)]. This deduction offsets the inclusion of the dividend under Subdivision b of Division B, so that qualifying dividends have no effect on the taxable income of the corporation. The dividends that qualify for the deduction are from:

(a) taxable Canadian corporations [par. 112(1)(a)];

(b) taxable subsidiary corporations resident in Canada [par. 112(1)(b)];

(c) non-resident corporations carrying on business in Canada and, hence, taxable in Canada [ssec. 112(2)]; and

(d) foreign affiliates which have been appropriately taxed in a foreign jurisdiction which has a treaty with Canada [sec. 113].

1. Purpose

The purpose of the deduction is to prevent the double taxation of corporate income. When dividends are paid, the source of the dividends is usually after-tax retained earnings of the payer corporation. If a recipient corporation were to pay tax on the dividends it receives, the income that gave rise to the dividends would effectively be taxed twice. Subsection 112(1) prevents that second imposition of tax at the level of the recipient corporation. In fact, retained earnings can, in many cases, be flowed through any number of shareholder corporations in the form of taxable dividends without attracting tax under Part I. When the retained earnings are ultimately paid as dividends to an individual shareholder, the dividend gross-up and tax-credit mechanism will operate to reduce, at the individual taxpayer level, the potential double taxation of income generated by a corporation.

The dividend deduction is the second building block of the theory of integration. The first building block, the dividend gross-up and tax credit for individual shareholders, was previously discussed in Chapters 6 and 10. The function of the dividend deduction for a corporation is to remove some of the potential multiple taxation of dividend income as the income moves through a series or chain of corporations.

Simply stated, the integration concept requires that a tax system should be designed so that a taxpayer is indifferent (i.e., pays the same amount of tax), no matter what type of entity or person earns the income. In the context of corporations and their shareholders under a perfectly integrated tax system, the total tax burden should be identical whether the individual receives the income directly or indirectly, as a shareholder, from dividends through the corporate structure.

The Canadian income tax system is not perfectly integrated. Near perfect integration occurs numerically only where the combined corporate rate of tax (federal and provincial plus surtaxes) is equal to 20%. However, even at the 20% rate there are flaws in the system. For example, the dividend tax credit should represent the underlying tax paid by the corporation. However, under our present income tax system, even when the corporation has not paid any tax due to losses, for example, shareholders still receive a dividend tax credit. The source of these dividends are usually paid from positive retained earnings that have been taxed. Similarly, low-rate taxpayers should receive a tax refund where the tax credit is greater than their tax liability, but the dividend tax credit is non-refundable.

To illustrate the corporate dividend deduction aspect of integration, consider the following example. Assume that there is a chain of three taxable Canadian corporations: A Ltd. owns 100% of B Ltd. which in turn owns 100% of C Ltd. Also, assume that each of the corporations and the individual shareholders of A Ltd are all taxed at a combined rate of 40% and that all of the after-tax income is passed up to the next level in the form of dividends. In the absence of a corporate deduction for dividends received from another corporation the following would result.

Person	Income	Tax	Dividend
C Ltd.	$1,000	$400	$600
B Ltd.	600	240	360
A Ltd.	360	144	216
Shareholders of A Ltd.	270*	54**	162***
		$838	

* $216 × ⁵⁄₄ (i.e., the grossed-up dividend)
** ($270 × .40) − ((.1333 + .0667) × $270) = $54 where .0667 reflects the provincial dividend tax credit.
*** Cash received (i.e., $216 − $54).

The result of this example is that on the $1,000 of income initially earned by C Ltd., the ultimate tax burden is $838. The dividend deduction, as discussed above, partially offsets this multiple taxation effect. Both B Ltd. and C Ltd. would be eligible for a deduction for the dividends received and no income tax would be levied on these amounts. The tax burden remaining would be composed of the $400 on the income earned initially by C Ltd. and the tax of $150 on the $750 grossed-up dividend received by the individual shareholders calculated as follows:

Dividend received by shareholders of A Ltd.	$ 600
Gross-up ($1/4 \times$ $600)	150
Grossed-up dividend	$ 750
Tax @40%	$ 300
Dividend tax credit @($13^1/3$% federal + 6 $^2/3$% provincial) of $750	(150)
Net tax on shareholders of A Ltd.	$ 150

The total income tax is now $550 compared to $838. However, as can be seen, there is still a high degree of double taxation even with the dividend tax credit when the corporate tax rate is at this level (i.e., $550 v. $400 under perfect integration).

From the above example, one can conclude that where dividend income flows through a series of corporations there will be only two incidences of income tax. Initially, the corporation that earns the business or property income will pay income tax and eventually the individual shareholder who receives the income in the form of a dividend will also pay some income tax. In the next chapter, the topic of integration will be expanded even further with different corporate rates and other factors.

2. Dividends paid from untaxed income

Over the years, the intercorporate dividend deduction has created problems which the government has attempted to rectify. For example, a corporation may pay a dividend from income that was not taxed in the payer corporation. This might occur when income for accounting purposes is higher than income for tax purposes, due to a more rapid write-off of assets for tax purposes. The utilization of carried-over losses may also offset income, so that some amounts that are distributed as dividends may not be taxed fully in the corporation that pays the dividend, usually due to timing differences between the payment of the dividend and the offset of losses. In these cases, there is a breakdown of the assumption that underlies the intercorporate dividend deduction, namely, that the dividend deduction prevents double taxation because the income that gave rise to the dividends *was* taxed in the payer corporation. This problem is compounded when individual shareholders gross up the dividends and deduct a dividend tax credit, on the assumption that the payer corporation or a predecessor corporation paid tax on the income it distributed as dividends. The purpose and effect of the dividend gross-up and tax-credit mechanism will be discussed more fully in the next chapter. A subsequent chapter will discuss provisions designed to deal with this type of problem which arises from the intercorporate dividend deduction.

3. "After-tax financing"

Another problem that is linked with the intercorporate dividend deduction occurs when what has become known as "after-tax financing" is undertaken. A corporation that has generated losses in the past may not find debt financing attractive. This is because the deduction for interest expense provides no immediate tax relief where the corporation does not have to pay tax currently. Instead, the interest expense deduction merely increases the corporation's non-capital losses which may be deductible in the future or may expire. Alternatively, a corporation with unused losses could issue preferred shares to another corporation, such as a financial institution, to obtain the necessary financing. The result is that the corporation that issues the preferred shares will, obviously, not receive a deduction for dividends paid on the preferred shares. However, the financing corporation, because of the intercorporate dividend deduction, will not ordinarily pay tax on the dividends it receives. Consequently, because interest income is taxable and dividends are ordinarily not, the financing corporation may be prepared to lend funds at a rate lower than the market rate of interest. Subsections 112(2.1) to (2.9) contain rules which are designed to eliminate the benefits of after-tax financing on "term preferred shares", "short-term preferred shares" [ssec. 248(1)] and collateralized preferred shares.

4. Dividends paid on shares subsequently sold for a loss

The intercorporate dividend deduction is also linked to a potential problem when dividends are received on shares held by a corporation for a short period and subsequently sold at a loss. Such dividends would ordinarily be deductible in computing taxable income, or in the case of certain dividends (e.g., capital dividends), would be tax exempt. On the other hand, the loss on the disposition of the shares would be deductible as an allowable capital loss (if held as a capital property), or as a business loss (if held as inventory). It may be argued that, to some extent, the loss on disposition may have been caused by the payment of the dividend; for example, witness the normal decline in the value of shares after the ex-dividend date.

Consequently, subsections 112(3) and (4) contain rules which, when certain conditions are present, will reduce the corporation's capital loss or inventory loss by an amount equal to the aggregate of certain types of dividends received on such shares prior to the disposition. The loss reductions will occur if one of the following conditions [ssec. 112(3.01)] is present:

(a) the corporation owned the shares for less than 365 continuous days immediately prior to the disposition date, or

(b) the corporation owned more than 5% of the issued shares of any class of the capital stock on which the dividends were received.

The type of dividends that will reduce such capital losses are essentially taxable dividends (deductible in computing the corporation's taxable income), and tax-exempt capital dividends received on the shares during the period of ownership [ssec. 112(3)]. Similarly, inventory losses are reduced by deductible taxable dividends received by any taxpayer-shareholder plus non-taxable dividends received [ssec. 112(4)].

C. Charitable Donations

[ITA: 110.1]

While individuals are provided with a non-refundable tax credit for various donations, as discussed in Chapter 10, corporations are permitted a deduction in Division C [ssec. 110.1(1)]. The types of donation that provide a corporation with this deduction are the same as the types of donation that provide an individual with a tax credit. Also, a corporation's deduction for both charitable gifts and Crown gifts is limited to 75% of the corporation's income under Division B. The base is the same for an individual's tax credit. An additional limit of 25% of the amount of a taxable capital gain in respect of gifts of capital property is provided. Therefore, the limit on the taxable capital gain component of a gift of appreciated capital property would be 100% of the taxable capital gain. For a similar purpose, an additional limit of 25% of any CCA recapture arising on the gift of depreciable capital property is allowed.

Any unused donations for a given year can be carried forward five years to be deducted in a carryforward year. The total claim for donations carried forward to a year and current donations made in that year cannot exceed the Division B income limit. The maximum donation need not be deducted in a given year, such that undeducted amounts are available within the carryforward period. To be deducted, a donation must be proven, if necessary, by a receipt that contains prescribed information [ssec. 110.1(2)].

D. Loss Carryovers

[ITA: 111; IT-206R; IT-232R3; IC 84-1]

1. Non-capital loss

A non-capital loss for a particular year, as it affects a corporation (for the purposes of this text), is generally defined [ssec. 111(8)] to include:

Aggregate of:		
losses from business..............................		$ xxx
losses from property		xxx
allowable business investment losses		xxx
net capital losses deducted in the year		xxx
dividends deductible under sec. 112 (and certain other dividends)		xxx
		$ xxx (E)
Less aggregate of the amounts determined under par. 3(*c*):		
income from business	$ xxx	
income from property (including dividends deductible under sec. 112)	xxx	
income from other sources [secs. 56–59]......	xxx	
taxable capital gains (other than from listed personal property)	$ xxx	
taxable net gains from listed personal property	xxx	
	$ xxx	
less: allowable capital losses (other than from listed personal property) in excess of allowable business investment losses that are included in allowable capital losses	(xxx)*	xxx *
		$ xxx
less: other deductions [secs. 60–66]..........	(xxx)	$(xxx)*(F)
		$ xxx *
Less: farm loss (included in losses from business above)		(xxx)(D)
Non-capital loss...		$ xxx *

* Cannot be negative.

This definition is designed to offset the current year's losses from various sources against the current year's income from other sources. Then the balance or the unabsorbed excess loss can be carried over and deducted in another year. Non-capital losses may be carried back three taxation years and forward 10 (for taxation years ending after March 22, 2004). To carry losses back to a taxation year for which a return has been filed, the corporation need only file one form (Schedule 4) and not a full, amended tax return. Farming and fishing losses, defined as "farm loss" [ssec. 111(8)], can be carried back three years and forward 10 years, to be deducted [par. 111(1)(*d*)].

Since it is possible for carried-over losses to expire, planning should be undertaken to ensure that the losses are utilized within the carryover period. Income can be increased to absorb non-capital losses by omitting optional or permissive deductions such as capital cost allowances, cumulative eligible capital amounts, scientific research and experimental development expenditures or reserves. The deduction of these amounts can be deferred to future years when there is offsetting income. The Canada Revenue Agency (CRA) usually permits the revision of a permissive deduction for a prior year. IC 84-1, paragraph 11, indicates that a letter, to the director of the district taxation office of the taxpayer, which outlines the requested revisions will be sufficient if other conditions set out in paragraphs 9 and 10 are met. In addition, the corporation should consider the sale of unnecessary or redundant assets to generate income which could be used to absorb losses. The CRA may also allow the substitution of one type of loss for another, as long as the year in which the substitution is made is still open to assessment (as discussed in Chapter 14). For example, a non-capital loss may have been carried back to a year in which there was a net taxable capital gain. Subsequently, an allowable capital loss may arise. The resultant net capital loss may be carried back and substituted for the non-capital loss, leaving the freed non-capital loss available for carryforward.

Example Problem

The operations of Bigloss Ltd. generated the following data for its December 31, 2005 taxation year:

Business losses	$(60,000)
Dividends received and deducted under sec. 112	10,000
Bond interest	5,000
Allowable business investment loss	(3,000)
Taxable capital gains	15,000
Allowable capital losses	(7,000)
	$(40,000)

In its 2004 taxation year, its first profitable year in several, Bigloss Ltd. had taxable income under Division C of $40,000.

— REQUIRED

Compute the non-capital loss for Bigloss Ltd. in 2005 and determine the amount of that loss that can be carried back to 2004.

— SOLUTION

Before calculating the non-capital loss for 2005, a review of the construction of section 3 income would be useful in understanding the basic concept. The following calculation reorganizes the above information using the ordering and application rules in section 3.

Par. 3(a)	Income — business	Nil	
	— property: dividends	$10,000	
	interest	5,000	$15,000
Par. 3(b)	Net taxable capital gains:		
	Taxable capital gains	$15,000	
	Allowable capital losses	(7,000)	8,000
Par. 3(c)	(No Subdivision e deductions taken)		$23,000
Par. 3(d)	Business loss	$60,000	
	Allowable business investment loss	3,000	(63,000)
Net income from Division B			Nil

Non-capital loss arising in 2005:	
Business loss	$ 60,000
Allowable business investment loss	3,000
Dividends	10,000
	$ 73,000

Less: Par. 3(*c*) income (as shown above):

Income from property [par. 3(*a*)]

Bond interest	$ 5,000	
Dividends (see commentary below)	10,000	$15,000

Net taxable capital gains [par. 3(*b*)]

Taxable capital gains	$15,000		
Allowable capital loss	(7,000)	8,000	(23,000)

Non-capital loss for 2005 . . . . $ 50,000

Carryback of non-capital loss to 2004:

Lesser of:

(a) Non-capital loss (as calculated above) . . . . $ 50,000

(b) Taxable income for 2004 . . . . $ 40,000

Thus, $40,000 of the 2005 non-capital loss could be carried back to 2004 leaving $10,000 to carry forward to 2006 through 2015.

Dividend income deductible under section 112 (i.e., $10,000), when added to the business loss and the allowable business investment loss, has the effect of offsetting the dividend income included in the paragraph 3(*c*) income under paragraph 3(*a*). As a result, this dividend income has no effect on the amount of losses available for carryover. As previously discussed, dividends are deductible [sec. 112] to offset the dividend income inclusion [par. 12(1)(*j*)] and, therefore, have no effect on the taxable income of a corporation. Therefore, a similar adjustment is necessary to the non-capital loss calculation to remove the effect of the inclusion of these dividends in property income, as shown above. If the addition of taxable dividends to the business loss had not been made, the 2004 non-capital loss available for carryover would have been only $40,000 (i.e., $60,000 + $3,000 − $23,000), not $50,000 as shown above.

---

2. Treatment of allowable business investment loss

A business investment loss [par. 39(1)(*c*)] is a capital loss that arises from the disposition of shares or debt of a small business corporation [ssec. 248(1)]. The concept of a small business corporation is discussed in some detail in Chapter 13. A business investment loss (B.I.L.) must arise from either an arm's length disposition of the shares and/or debt, establishing a debt to be bad, or a bankruptcy action as described in subsection 50(1).

An allowable business investment loss (A.B.I.L.) is defined [par. 38(*c*)] as ¹/₂ of a business investment loss. Unlike an allowable capital loss, an allowable business investment loss may, in the year in which it is realized, be deducted against any source of income [par. 3(*d*)]. Hence, the deductibility of an allowable business investment loss is less restricted than an allowable capital loss. To the extent that it cannot be absorbed against these other sources of income in the year in which it is incurred, it becomes part of the aggregate of non-capital losses to be carried over in the manner discussed above. Furthermore, any amount of allowable business investment loss that cannot be utilized within the carryover period of a non-capital loss can be added to net capital losses which can be carried forward indefinitely as discussed next. See Exhibit 7-1 for a flow-chart summary of these rules.

Example Problem

The operations of Biggerloss Limited generated the following data for the year ended December 31, 2005:

Business investment loss on sale of shares	$116,000
Capital gains	4,000
Other capital losses	10,000
Other Division B income	30,000

— REQUIRED

Compute the taxable income of the corporation for 2005 and indicate the loss carryovers available for other years.

— SOLUTION

Par. 3(*a*)	Other Division B income		$30,000
Par. 3(*b*)	Taxable capital gains ($1/2 \times \$4,000$)	$ 2,000	
	Allowable capital losses ($1/2 \times \$10,000$)	(5,000)	Nil
Par. 3(*c*)	Income		$30,000
Par. 3(*d*)	Allowable business investment loss deductible (max: $1/2 \times \$116,000 = \$58,000$)		(30,000)
	Income and taxable income		Nil
	Net capital loss available for carryover		$ 3,000[1]
	Non-capital loss available for carryover		$28,000[2]

— NOTES TO SOLUTION

(1) ($1/2 \times \$10,000$ capital loss incurred in the year) *less* ($2,000 claimed in the year as an allowable capital loss) = $3,000.

(2) ($1/2 \times \$116,000$ business investment loss incurred in the year) *less* ($30,000 claimed in the year as an A.B.I.L.) = $28,000.

3. Net capital losses

A net capital loss (C.L.) for a year is defined in subsection 111(8). For corporations a net C.L. is, essentially, the excess of allowable capital losses, excluding losses on listed personal property and allowable business investment losses, over taxable capital gains, including taxable net gains from listed personal property.

This is given by the following computational format:

Allowable capital losses excluding losses on listed personal property and allowable business investment losses	(A)	$xxx
Less: taxable capital gains including taxable net gains from listed personal property	(B)	(xxx)
	(A – B)	$xxx
Add: allowable business investment loss unutilized in the tenth year of its carryforward as a non-capital loss (see comment in previous section)		xxx
Net capital loss		$xxx

The exclusion of allowable capital losses on listed personal property results from the fact that listed personal property losses are carried forward and back under Division B, not Division C, as are all other allowable capital losses. (See Chapter 7 for a more complete discussion.) The term "net gain" from listed personal property refers to the amount of taxable capital gain net of the application of any listed personal property current losses and loss carryovers.

Net capital losses can be carried back three taxation years and forward indefinitely. However, they can only be deducted to the extent of the excess, if any, of taxable capital gains over allowable capital losses in the carryover years. Rules which determine the amount that a person may deduct in respect of net capital losses are the result of the differing inclusion rates for capital gains and capital losses discussed in Chapter 10 [ssec. 111(1.1)].

The historical inclusion rates are as follows:

Prior to 1988	$1/2$
1988 and 1989	$2/3$
1990 to February 27, 2000	$3/4$
February 28 to October 17, 2000	$2/3$
After October 17, 2000	$1/2$

The purpose of the rules is to ensure that the amount of net capital losses, carried forward or carried back from a taxation year with a particular inclusion rate, is converted to the inclusion rate of the taxation year in which the net capital losses are deducted. This is done by means of a formula as illustrated below.

Assume the following facts for a corporation which has $45,000 of net capital losses (representing $3/4$ of a $60,000 capital loss) realized in 1997 and available for carryforward:

	2000	2001
Capital gains realized	$60,000	$10,000
Capital losses realized...........................	(10,000)	(4,000)
Net capital gains	$50,000	$ 6,000
Inclusion rate for the year	$2/3$*	$1/2$

* After February 27, 2000 and before October 18, 2000.

The following net capital losses could be deducted under par. 111(1)(*b*):

Net taxable capital gain for the year	$33,333	$ 3,000
Net capital loss deduction under par. 111(1)(*b*) per ssec. 111(1.1) as computed below..............	(33,333)	(3,000)
Effect on taxable income	Nil	Nil

The limit on the net capital loss deduction is given by [ssec. 111(1.1)]:

Lesser of:
(a) Net taxable capital gain for the year [par. 3(*b*)] $33,333 $ 3,000

(b) $A \times \dfrac{B}{C}$

Where A = net capital loss from a loss year available for deduction in the particular year (see below)	$45,000	$ 7,500
B = inclusion rate in particular year of deduction	$2/3$	$1/2$
C = inclusion rate in loss year	$3/4$	$3/4$
$45,000 \times 2/3 / 3/4$	$40,000	
$7,500 \times 1/2 / 3/4$		$ 5,000
Net capital loss deduction (lesser amount)	$33,333	$ 3,000

To deal with the carryover of these losses conceptually, it may be easier to carry full amounts of capital losses realized either back or forward against full gains in the carryover year. Then the appropriate inclusion rate could be applied to the net full gains in the carryover year. Unfortunately, as discussed below, the definition of net capital loss (i.e., the amount available for carryover) is given in terms of the fractional allowable capital losses.

The amount of net capital loss realized in 1997 and deducted in 2000 and 2001 and, hence, the amount of net capital loss available for carryforward after 2001 can be reconciled as follows:

	Capital loss (gross amount)	Net capital loss at 1997 inclusion rate of ¾	Adjustment factor B/C	Adjusted net capital loss deducted
Loss realized in 1997	$60,000	$45,000		
Loss deducted in 2000 limited to net gains realized in the year	(50,000)	(37,500)	⅔ / ¾	$33,333
Loss available in 2001	$10,000	$ 7,500		
Loss deducted in 2001 limited to net gains realized in the year	(6,000)	(4,500)	½ / ¾	$ 3,000
Loss available after 2001	$ 4,000	$ 3,000	½ / ¾	$ 2,000

4. Restrictions and ordering of deductions

A taxpayer can choose how much of any of its previously unclaimed carried-over losses to deduct in a particular year and in which order to deduct such losses and other Division C deductions. However, the taxpayer must deduct a loss of a particular type (that is, non-capital loss, net capital loss, restricted farm loss or farm loss) in the chronological order in which the loss was incurred [ssec. 111(3)]. Logic would suggest that those deductions in Division C, which are more restricted in their deductibility, be claimed as soon as possible and before those deductions which are less restricted.

There are two basic types of restriction on losses available for carryover. The first is a restriction on the type of income against which the loss carryover can be deducted. This type of restriction is often referred to as "streaming". The other is a restriction on the number of years a loss can be carried over. For example, a net capital loss can only be applied against net taxable capital gains, but is unrestricted as to carryforward time. A non-capital loss can be applied against any source of income, but is time-restricted. A restricted farm loss is restricted both as to the type of income against which it can be applied and to time. Therefore, restricted farm losses should usually be deducted first. Between net capital losses and non-capital losses, the decision depends on whether taxable capital gains are anticipated. If there are current taxable capital gains and an examination of the corporation's balance sheet indicates no accrued capital gains, then net capital losses should probably be deducted before non-capital losses.

EXHIBIT 11-2
Summary for Carryover Rules for Division C Deductions

		Carryover	
Type of deduction	*Type of income applied against*	*Back*	*Forward*
Dividends......................	Any type	*	*
Donations	Any type	0	5
Net capital losses	Net taxable capital gains	3	Indefinitely
Non-capital losses................	Any type	3	7/10**
Restricted farm losses.............	Farm income	3	10
Farm losses	Any type	3	10

Application of Division C deductions
Consider: (1) Type of income the deduction can be applied against.
       (2) Number of years available in the carryover period.
       (3) The likelihood that the type of income needed will arise in the carryover period.
Generally apply most restrictive first.

    * Technically, no carryover rule applies specifically to dividends, although they have an impact on the non-capital loss carryover balance.
    ** 10 for taxation years ending after March 22, 2004.

5. Choice to deduct net capital losses to preserve non-capital losses

Item E in the definition of non-capital loss [ssec. 111(8)] enables taxpayers, at their option, to deduct net capital losses to preserve non-capital losses. The purpose of this choice is to correct a long-standing anomaly in the legislation which inadvertently penalized taxpayers in certain specific situations, as shown in the example below. Whether a taxpayer decides to utilize this option depends upon whether the corporation is expected to generate, in the near future, adequate business income or taxable capital gains.

The non-capital loss can be increased by the amount of any net capital loss actually deducted for that year. For example, assume that a corporation (or an individual) has in 2005 a business loss of $100,000, a net taxable capital gain of $40,000 and an adjusted net capital loss of $60,000 carry forward. The tax consequences are as follows:

Par. 3(*a*):	Income from business	Nil
Par. 3(*b*):	Net taxable capital gain........................	$ 40,000
		$ 40,000
	Less: Subdivision e deductions..................	Nil
Par. 3(*c*):	....	$ 40,000
Par. 3(*d*):	Business loss	(100,000)
Par. 3(*f*):	Division B income	0

If the definition of non-capital loss did not contain the addition for net capital losses deducted, a corporation could deduct $40,000 of the net capital loss of $60,000 (equal to the net taxable capital gain [par. 3(*b*)]) but would not do so because such a deduction would have no impact upon the taxable income which would still be zero. In addition, if the $40,000 was deducted, the taxpayer would no longer have a potential use of the $40,000 net capital loss in the future when the taxpayer is in a taxable position.

The non-capital loss for the 2005 taxation year without the addition would be:

Par. 3(*d*):	Business loss	$ 100,000
Par. 3(*c*):	— see above calculation	(40,000)
Non-capital loss	....	$ 60,000

The result is that the net taxable capital gain has been used to offset the business loss resulting in a lower non-capital loss (i.e., $60,000 vs. $100,000). The taxpayer may or may not be happy with this result depending upon the taxpayer's expected future income sources. Since net capital losses can only be applied to net taxable capital gains (i.e., $40,000) a potential net capital loss deduction has been blocked by the current business loss of $100,000.

The addition of deducted net capital losses to the non-capital loss balance provides a positive tax consequence to claiming a net capital loss deduction, even though the deduction has no impact upon the taxable income as shown below.

Division B income — see previous sec. 3 computation	0
Division C — net capital loss deduction [par. 111(1)(*b*)] limited to par. 3(*b*) amount	$ (40,000)
Taxable income	Nil

However, as a result of the deduction of net capital losses, the non-capital loss is increased by a net capital loss deducted:

Par. 3(*d*): Business loss.............................	$100,000
Add: Net capital loss deducted in the year	40,000
	$140,000
Less: Par. 3(*c*) balance — see above	40,000
	$100,000

The result is that $40,000 of the net capital loss carryover has been deducted under Division C to offset the $40,000 of net taxable capital gain under paragraph 3(*b*). This preserves the full $100,000 of business loss to be carried over as a non-capital loss, which can be deducted from any source of income in a carryover year.

Example Problem

The following data summarize the operations of Parliamentary Fertilizers Limited, a Canadian-controlled private corporation, for the years 2002 to 2005 ended December 31.

	2002	2003	2004	2005
Income (loss): fertilizer business	$ 62,500	$(187,500)	$75,000	$100,000
Dividend income — taxable Cdn. corporation.............................	37,500	62,500	12,500	—
Capital gains (losses)	25,000	(50,000)	7,500	12,000
Charitable donations made	(18,750)	(10,000)	(12,500)	(6,000)
Income (loss): other business............	7,500	(20,000)	2,500	5,000
Income (loss) per financial accounting statements	$113,750	$(205,000)	$85,000	$111,000

The corporation has a net capital loss balance of $18,000 which arose in 1997.

—REQUIRED

Calculate the taxable income of the company for each of the years indicated, on the assumption that future other business income and taxable capital gains are uncertain, and tabulate the losses available for carryover at the end of 2005. (For the purposes of this type of problem, dealing with each item, line-by-line, across the years, will help keep track of carryovers more easily than dealing with income one year at a time.)

—SOLUTION

		2002	2003	2004	2005
Par. 3(*a*)	Income from business				
	— fertilizer	$ 62,500	—[1]	$75,000	$100,000
	— other	7,500	—[1]	2,500	5,000
	Income from property	37,500	$ 62,500	12,500	—
		$107,500	$ 62,500	$90,000	$105,000
Par. 3(*b*)	Taxable capital gain	12,500	—	3,750	6,000
	Allowable capital loss	—	—[2]	—	—
Par. 3(*c*)	Total	$120,000	$ 62,500	$93,750	$111,000
Par. 3(*d*)	Loss from business				
	— fertilizer	—	(187,500)[3]	—	—
	— other	—	(20,000)	—	—
	Income for the year[4] ...	$120,000	Nil[3]	$93,750	$111,000
Sec. 112	Dividends from taxable Canadian corporations	(37,500)[5]	—[6]	(12,500)[5]	—
		$ 82,500	Nil	$81,250	$111,000
Sec. 110.1	Donations made				
	— carryover	—	—	(10,000)	—
	— current	(18,750)	—	(12,500)[7]	(6,000)
		$ 63,750	Nil	$58,750	$105,000
Par. 111(1)(*b*)	Net capital losses	(12,000)[8]	—	(3,750)[8]	(6,000)[8]
		$ 51,750	Nil	$55,000	$ 99,000
Par. 111(1)(*a*)	Non-capital losses	(51,750)[9]	—	(55,000)[9]	(99,000)[9]
	Taxable income	Nil	Nil	Nil	Nil

—NOTES TO SOLUTION

(1) Items aggregated from the various non-capital sources under paragraph 3(*a*) cannot be negative. Losses from these sources are deducted under paragraph 3(*d*).

(2) Allowable capital losses are only deductible to the extent of taxable capital gains under paragraph 3(*b*). The remainder is available for carryover to another year.

(3) Losses from the various non-capital sources and from allowable business investment losses are only deductible under paragraph 3(*d*). However, the net income amounts after the deductions in paragraph 3(*d*) cannot be negative. Note that the excess of the deductions in paragraph 3(*d*) over the aggregate income in paragraph 3(*c*) is only one component of the addition to the non-capital loss carryover balance computed below.

(4) Income for the year cannot be negative. There is no statutory order in which Division C deductions must be taken. However, the time and source restrictions of loss carryovers, as previously discussed, should be taken into account. In addition, where the income under Division B is not large enough to cover all potential Division C deductions, then the dividend deduction under section 112 should always be taken first. Dividends from taxable Canadian corporations are the only Division C deduction for corporations which do not have a carryover clause.

(5) Dividends from taxable Canadian corporations should be deducted first in case there is not enough income for any further Division C deductions. Undeducted dividends cannot be carried over.

(6) A deduction in the computation of taxable income should not be taken if it reduces the balance to a negative number, since normally negative taxable income has no meaning. The one exception to this rule is in respect of net capital losses which can be added to the non-capital loss balance if they are deducted in a particular year.

(7) The deduction of charitable donations is limited to 75% of Division B income for the year. Donations not deducted in the year they are made, can be carried forward to the next five taxation years. However, the Division B income limitation applies to the sum of donations

carried forward and current donations. Since the unused donations of a particular taxation year have a time restriction of 5 years, it would be advisable to claim them prior to claiming current year donations.

(8) Deductions for net capital loss carryovers are restricted to the extent of the net taxable capital gains for the carryover year [par. 3(*b*)].

Subsection 111(1.1) adjusts the 2002 net capital loss deduction by a formula which corrects for the fact that in the loss year (1997) the inclusion rate for capital gains was three-quarters, while in the year that the loss is being claimed (i.e., 2002) the inclusion rate is one-half.

Lesser of (a) amount under par. 3(*b*) in 2002..............	$12,500

$$(b)\ A \times \frac{B}{C} = \$18,000 \times \frac{1}{2} / \frac{3}{4} = \dots\dots\dots\dots\quad \$12,000$$

where: A is the amount of the net capital loss available (i.e., $18,000) from 1997 (the loss year),
 B is the $\frac{1}{2}$ inclusion rate for the deduction year (i.e., 2002), and
 C is the $\frac{3}{4}$ inclusion rate for the loss year (i.e., 1997).

Since the inclusion rate is the same for 2003 and 2004, no ssec. 111(1.1) adjustment is necessary for the 2003 capital loss:

Net capital loss for 2003 ($\frac{1}{2} \times \$50,000$)...................	$25,000
Loss deductible to the extent of net capital gains under par. 3(*b*):	
2004 — limited to T.C.G.............................	(3,750)
	$21,250
2005 — limited to T.C.G.............................	(6,000)
Remaining carryforward	$15,250

(9) "Non-capital loss" is computed for carryforward in [ssec. 111(8)]:

	2002	2003	2004	2005
Sum of:				
(a) loss from business or property...........	Nil	$207,500	Nil	Nil
(b) A.B.I.L..............	Nil	Nil	Nil	Nil
(c) dividends deductible under sec. 112	$ 37,500	62,500	$ 12,500	Nil
(d) net capital loss deducted	12,000	Nil	3,750	$ 6,000
	$ 49,500	$270,000	$ 16,250	$ 6,000
Less:				
(e) par. 3(*c*) total	(120,000)	(62,500)	(93,750)	(111,000)
Non-capital loss for the year	Nil	$207,500	Nil	Nil
Non-capital loss carryforward balance:				
Non-capital loss carryforward to the year..............	Nil	Nil	$155,750	$100,750
Added in the year	Nil	$207,500	Nil	Nil
Applied................	Nil	(51,750)*	(55,000)	(99,000)
Non-capital loss carryforward balance	Nil	$155,750	$100,750	$ 1,750

* Carried back to 2002.

E. Acquisition of Control of a Corporation and Its Effect on Losses

[ITA: 10(1); 12(1)(*i*); 20(1)(*a*), (*b*), (*l*), (*p*); 111(4)–(5.5); 249(4); ITR: 1801; IT-206R; IT-259R4; IT-302R3; IT-442R]

When control of the corporation is acquired by another person or another group of persons, a corporation's ability to carry forward or carry back non-capital losses or farm losses is severely restricted. In addition, net capital losses, losses from property and allowable business investment losses (A.B.I.L.s) that are unutilized at the time of the acquisition of control may not be carried forward — they simply expire. The rules which impose the restrictions are found mainly in subsections 111(4), (5), (5.1), (5.2) and (5.3), while the rules in subsections 249(4), 10(1) and Regulation 1801 have an indirect effect. The rules are discussed below.

Corporations are often unable to generate appropriate or sufficient income to utilize losses and, hence, are unable to recover taxes previously paid or reduce taxes payable. Consequently, such loss corporations become attractive targets for acquisition by profitable corporations which, through a variety of strategies, could shelter their income from tax by utilizing the losses of the acquired corporation. Because such strategies ultimately result in reduced tax revenues, the government, understandably, does not view such transactions with favour. As a result, over the years the government has introduced increasingly restrictive legislation to curb such transactions which are sometimes referred to as "tax-loss trading".

Two of the more common loss utilization strategies are outlined as follows: In the first, after control of the loss corporation is acquired, the operations of the income-earning acquirer corporation and the loss corporation are restructured so that income is generated in the latter corporation. For example, the assets of a profitable business or division in the income-generating corporation are transferred to the loss corporation. Usually the transfer will be accomplished by means of a tax-free rollover [ssec. 85(1)] by moving profit-generating assets to the loss corporation (discussed in Chapter 16). The income that is so generated is used to absorb the losses of the loss corporation. The second strategy involves implementing intercompany transactions which produce expense deductions to the income-generating corporation while generating income for the loss corporation. Interest on loans, rental contracts and commission contracts are examples of such intercompany transactions.

As mentioned previously, the loss utilization restrictions become operative when control of a corporation is acquired by another person or another group of persons. The acquisition of control is considered to occur when control over the voting rights (i.e., *de jure* control that exists where more than 50% of the votes necessary to elect the Board of Directors is held) of the corporation is acquired by a person or group of persons. While it is clear that control refers to voting control, some uncertainty exists as to how the CRA will interpret the phrase "group of persons" for the purposes of these rules. The CRA has indicated that it will look for evidence of a group's intention to "act in concert" to control a corporation [IT-302R3, pars. 3–6].

The legislative restrictions which are aimed at curtailing the utilization of tax losses, are based on certain transactions and events which are deemed to occur when there has been an acquisition of control. These transactions and events, as well as other rules that comprise the restrictions, are discussed below.

1. Deemed year-end

The corporation is deemed to have a taxation year-end immediately before the time of the acquisition of control of the corporation (referred to hereinafter as the "deemed taxation year-end") [ssec. 249(4)]. The result is that various adjustments that are normally made at a year-end, are required to be made before the acquisition of control. For example, the requirement that inventory be valued at the lower of cost or market at a taxation year-end [sec. 10 or Reg. 1801] will cause any accrued losses in inventory to be realized. This adjustment will increase the corporation's pre-acquisition non-capital losses or farm losses. As will be explained later, such pre-acquisition losses are available for carryforward, but only after certain restrictive conditions are satisfied. The advent of the deemed year-end causes other adjustments (discussed below) to increase the corporation's pre-acquisition of control non-capital losses and farm losses.

As a result of the deemed year-end, the corporation is required to satisfy the normal compliance requirements of filing tax returns, reviewing unpaid amounts [ssecs. 78(1), (4)], determining the status of charitable donations and loss carryovers and their carryforward period, etc.

[However, a short taxation year that may result from an acquisition of control will not advance the replacement period required to benefit from the rollovers under subsections 13(4) and 44(1) on an involuntary or voluntary disposition. The February 27, 2004 Revised Draft Legislation proposes to allow a full 24 months and 12 months after an involuntary and voluntary disposition, respectively, from the end of the short taxation year in which such a disposition occurs.]

As well, unless the deemed year-end coincides with the corporation's normal year-end, the corporation may have two taxation years lasting less than 24 months in total. To illustrate this, assume that a corporation whose normal taxation year-end is December 31, experiences an acquisition of control on April 1, 2005. The corporation will have a deemed year-end of March 31, 2005 [ssec. 249(4)]. If the corporation chooses to return to its original taxation year-end of December 31, the corporation will have two taxation years ending in the 12-month period ending December 31, 2005. The first taxation year will be 3 months long, the second 9 months long. If the corporation chose a date for its subsequent taxation years to be, say, March 31, as permitted [par. 249(4)(*d*)], it would then have two taxation years lasting a total of only 15 months — namely, the deemed taxation year ending on March 31, 2005 will be 3 months long and the taxation year ending March 31, 2006 will be 12 months long. The foregoing example can be illustrated with the following diagram:

The upshot of this is that the normal 156-month (3 years back plus 10 years forward) carryover period for non-capital losses is reduced. This, in itself, represents a constraint in that the corporation has a shorter period over which to generate income to utilize the losses. A short taxation year will also cause any capital cost allowance or small business deduction (discussed in Chapter 12) to be proportionately reduced.

2. Accrued or unrealized losses on inventory

A taxpayer is required to value its inventory at the end of each taxation year. The rule in subsection 10(1) requires that each item of inventory be valued at the lower of cost and market (LCM), while regulation 1801 permits valuation at the fair market value of the entire inventory. Either way, the result is that any accrued or unrealized inventory losses are realized in the deemed taxation year, thus, decreasing the taxpayer's income or increasing its non-capital losses or farm losses in the pre-acquisition period.

3. Accrued or unrealized losses on accounts receivable

The restrictions and their consequences that apply to accrued inventory losses are paralleled in the provisions that relate to accrued losses on accounts receivable. The largest amount that a corporation could deduct as a reserve for doubtful accounts [par. 20(1)(*l*)] for each separate trade receivable, must be claimed as an actual bad debt [par. 20(1)(*p*)] in the deemed taxation year [ssec. 111(5.3)]. That is, where there has been an acquisition of control, the normal method of computing a reserve by aging the accounts and applying a fixed percentage to each age category [IT-442R par. 24] is not permitted. Instead, each debt must be considered individually as to its collectibility and, if collection is doubtful, the debt must be written off as a bad debt. The amount deducted [ssec. 111(5.3)] is deemed to be a separate debt and any amount or amounts subsequently received in respect of the separate debt must be included in income [par. 12(1)(*i*)].

As is the case in accrued inventory losses, accrued losses on accounts receivable become part of time-limited non-capital or farm losses, which are deductible only if certain restrictive conditions are satisfied.

4. Accrued or unrealized losses on depreciable capital property

Accrued or unrealized losses on depreciable capital property are measured as the amount by which:

(a) the undepreciated capital cost (UCC), at the deemed year-end, in a prescribed class

exceeds the aggregate of:

(b) the fair market value of all the property in the class at the deemed year-end, plus

(c) any capital cost allowance (CCA) and any terminal losses deducted in that class in the deemed taxation year [ssec. 111(5.1)].

The excess is deemed to be claimed as a capital cost allowance deduction from income [par. 20(1)(*a*)] for the deemed taxation year [ssec. 111(5.1)]. Thus, the corporation's income/loss for the deemed taxation year is increased or decreased accordingly. Where there is a loss, the ultimate effect is to increase the corporation's pre-acquisition non-capital losses or farm losses. At the same time, the balance of the undepreciated capital cost is reduced by the amount of the excess.

The restrictive aspects of the rule are, therefore, as follows:

- first, an accrued loss (i.e., unclaimed capital cost allowance) that would otherwise not be subject to any time limitation, as far as its deductibility is concerned, becomes part of a time-limited non-capital loss or farm loss;

- second, the corporation commences the first post-acquisition of control taxation year with a reduced undepreciated capital cost balance in the particular class.

5. Accrued or unrealized losses on eligible capital property

The rules in subsection 111(5.2) apply to eligible capital property in much the same way as subsection 111(5.1) applies to depreciable capital property. The accrued or unrealized losses on eligible capital property are measured as the amount by which:

(a) the cumulative eligible capital (CEC) balance of a particular business at the deemed year-end

exceeds the aggregate of:

(b) three-quarters[a] of the fair market value, at the deemed year-end, of the eligible capital property of the business, plus

(c) any amount deducted, in respect of that business [par. 20(1)(*b*)] (cumulative eligible capital amount) in the deemed taxation year.

The consequences of the rules in subsection 111(5.2) apply to eligible capital property in a like manner with respect to the time restrictions that affect non-capital losses and farm losses, as well as the impact that the adjustment has on the cumulative eligible capital balance of the corporation in the first taxation year after the acquisition of control.

6. Accrued or unrealized losses on non-depreciable capital property

Accrued or unrealized capital losses on non-depreciable capital property are deemed to have been realized at the deemed taxation year-end [pars. 111(4)(*c*) and (*d*)]. The accrued losses are measured as the excess of:

(a) the adjusted cost base (ACB)
over
(b) the fair market value,

at the deemed year-end, of each non-depreciable capital property (e.g., marketable securities, land used in the business) of the corporation. These rules result in the following:

- first, the capital losses that are so triggered, offset any capital gains produced in the deemed taxation year or increase any existing net capital losses of the corporation;
- second, the adjusted cost base of each affected capital property is reduced by the amount of the applicable excess.

Therefore, any deemed realized allowable capital losses that cannot be utilized against taxable capital gains realized in the deemed taxation year become part of the corporation's net capital losses immediately before the acquisition of control. If nothing further is done, these allowable capital losses, now embedded in the net capital loss balance, will expire. However, there are two possible remedies to this situation. First, the net capital losses can be deducted in arriving at taxable income for the deemed taxation year to the extent of net taxable capital gains in that year. As previously discussed, these deducted net capital losses will increase the non-capital loss balance.

---

[a] The three-quarters fraction is used in order to place components (a) and (b) of the formula on a common basis.

However, a further set of restrictions (discussed later in the chapter) is imposed on the utilization of non-capital losses on an acquisition of control. The second alternative is to create elective taxable capital gains to offset the deemed allowable capital losses as described in the next section.

7. Elective capital gains and recapture

A corporation is permitted to elect to have a deemed disposition for any depreciable or non-depreciable capital property on which capital gains or recapture have accrued [par. 111(4)(e)]. The objective of the elective provision is to permit the corporation to trigger capital gains or recapture, which is income from business, to reduce the amount of net capital losses or non-capital losses that would otherwise expire on account of the acquisition of control. Upon making the election, the corporation must also choose (i.e., designate) an amount to represent the deemed proceeds of disposition. The designated amount or deemed proceeds must be equal to the lesser of:

(a) the fair market value of the property; and

(b) the greater of:

(i) the adjusted cost base of the property, and

(ii) an amount designated (or chosen) by the corporation.

The effect of the above rule is that the corporation can choose proceeds of disposition (amount designated) at any point between fair market value and the adjusted cost base of the particular capital property. This rule also prevents the designated amount from being greater than the fair market value of the property. In addition, the designated amount (proceeds of disposition) cannot be less than the adjusted cost base (capital cost in respect of depreciable property). Note that the election is not available where an accrued terminal loss exists since subsection 111(5.1) applies in the situation where fair market value is less than undepreciated capital cost. However, the above formula does allow a corporation to elect proceeds of disposition which would trigger recapture on depreciable capital property.

In determining the optimal or minimum amount which should be designated [par. 111(4)(e)] where there are losses about to expire, the following formula should be used to trigger a taxable capital gain. This taxable capital gain should be sufficient to offset expiring losses. The elected proceeds will be:

the sum of:

(a) 2 (based on a $\frac{1}{2}$ inclusion rate) times the sum of:

(i) any allowable capital loss arising in the deemed taxation year about to expire,

(ii) the net capital losses about to expire, and

(iii) the sum of the property losses and A.B.I.L.s about to expire; and

(b) the adjusted cost bases of the properties chosen to be elected upon.

The taxable capital gain, using the above deemed proceeds of disposition, should result in the utilization of all of the losses about to expire upon the acquisition of control.

This procedure of creating only enough taxable capital gains to offset the property losses and capital losses about to expire also optimizes the step-up in the cost base of an asset elected upon as discussed below. In addition, this minimum elected amount preserves the business losses which can be utilized after the acquisition of control.

In summary, the deemed proceeds on the asset(s) chosen to be elected upon can be determined as follows:

$$\text{Deemed proceeds of disposition} = \frac{2 \times ((\text{i}) + (\text{ii}) + (\text{iii}))}{(\text{as described above})} + \text{the A.C.B.(s) of properties chosen to be elected upon}$$

The properties and amounts elected upon must be designated in the corporation's tax return for the deemed taxation year. While a corporation will focus mainly on the capital gain implications of an election [par. 111(4)(*e*)], an election made in respect of a depreciable capital property may, also, give rise to recaptured capital cost allowance which may affect the non-capital losses of the corporation. Consequently, both the capital gain and recaptured capital cost allowance implications must be carefully considered when an election [par. 111(4)(*e*)] is contemplated.

The rules also provide for a deemed reacquisition of the depreciable or non-depreciable capital properties that are elected upon [par. 111(4)(*e*)]. A non-depreciable capital property is deemed to be reacquired at a cost equal to the amount of the deemed proceeds of disposition. For the purpose of computing future capital gains or losses, a depreciable capital property is deemed to be reacquired at a cost equal to the amount of the deemed proceeds of disposition. On the other hand, for the purpose of determining future capital cost allowance and recapture amounts, a depreciable capital property is deemed to be reacquired at a cost equal to the amount that is the capital cost plus the realized taxable capital gain (i.e., $\frac{1}{2}$ of the capital gain elected) [par. 13(7)(*f*)]. The effect of paragraph 13(7)(*f*) is to limit the increase in the base for capital cost allowance to the amount of the gain that has been included in income, i.e., the taxable capital gain plus recapture.

Where the deemed proceeds give rise to recapture, but no capital gain is triggered at the same time, the capital cost is deemed to be that amount immediately before the disposition (original capital cost) [spars. 111(4)(*e*)(iii) and (iv)]. Capital cost allowance is deemed to have been taken equal to the excess of the original capital cost over the deemed proceeds calculated according to the formula described above. The result of this provision is to retain the original capital cost for purposes of future recapture calculations and to prevent double counting of the recapture recognized on the exercise of the paragraph 111(4)(*e*) election.

For example, Multi-losses Inc. needs to trigger enough income to offset the expiry of $10,000 of property losses just prior to an acquisition of control. Multi-losses Inc. has already elected and designated an amount equal to the accrued capital gain on all the other capital and depreciable assets. The only asset remaining is a depreciable one that has a capital cost of $70,000, an undepreciated capital cost of $35,000 and fair market value of $60,000.

Obviously, there is no accrued capital gain on the depreciable asset. In fact, there is a capital loss, but capital losses are denied on depreciable assets [spar. 39(1)(*b*)(i)]. There is, however, potential recapture to a current maximum amount of $25,000 (i.e., $35,000 – $60,000), depending upon the designated amount or proceeds of disposition. Therefore, Multi-losses Inc. may attempt to designate, in this fact situation, an amount of $45,000 as the proceeds of disposition so that a desired $10,000 of recapture will be triggered.

In this case, however, the elected amount or deemed proceeds must be equal to the lesser of:

(a) the fair market value of the asset . . . . $60,000 ⎫
                                                                            ⎬ $60,000

(b) the greater of:

    (i) the A.C.B. of the asset . . . . . . $70,000 ⎫
                                               ⎬ $70,000
    (ii) the amount designated . . . . . $45,000 ⎭

As a result of the formula [par. 111(4)(e)], the full $25,000 of recapture must be included in income, calculated as:

U.C.C. $35,000
Less: the lower of:
    (a) capital cost $70,000
    (b) proceeds 60,000   60,000
Recapture $25,000

Therefore, in some cases, it may not be worthwhile to elect, because all of the unrealized recapture will be triggered.

From the perspective of the Multi-losses Inc., the capital cost is deemed to be the original capital cost of the acquired corporation, i.e., $70,000. In addition, Multi-losses Inc. is deemed to have taken capital cost allowance equal to the difference between the capital cost of $70,000 and the proceeds of $60,000. The effect of these two deeming provisions is to make Multi-losses Inc. assume responsibility for the remaining potential recapture of $10,000. The undepreciated capital cost, on which future capital cost allowance may be computed, is now set at $60,000.

8. Allowable business investment losses and losses from property

As a general rule, non-capital losses include allowable business investment losses (ABILs) and losses from property. However, when there has been an acquisition of control of a corporation, the rules in subsection 111(5) restrict the carryover of non-capital losses or farm losses to those losses which can reasonably be attributed to the carrying on of a business. As a result, unutilized allowable business investment losses and losses from property expire after the deemed taxation year and must be removed from the non-capital loss balance. Even ABILs and property losses created in years prior to the acquisition of control are removed from the non-capital loss balance.

9. Unused charitable contributions

A corporation's unused charitable contributions cease to be deductible after the deemed year-end resulting from an acquisition of control [ssec. 110.1 (1.2)]. Furthermore, the deduction of a gift of property made after an acquisition of control is denied if the property was owned at the time of the acquisition of control and it was expected that a gift of the property would be made after the acquisition of control. The purpose of these provisions is to discourage charitable deduction trading transactions.

10. Non-capital losses and the requirement that the loss business be carried on with a reasonable expectation of profit

Non-capital losses and farm losses carried forward to taxation years beyond the deemed taxation year are deductible only if the following conditions are satisfied [spar. 111(5)(a)(i)]:

(a) the business that generated the losses must be carried on throughout the year in which the corporation seeks to make a deduction for non-capital losses [par. 111(1)(*a*)] or farm losses [par. 111(1)(*d*)]; and

(b) the particular business must be carried on for profit or with a reasonable expectation of profit.

An important feature of this rule is that the legislation identifies the non-capital losses and farm losses with a particular business. Note that the word "business" is not synonymous with the word "corporation"; that is, a corporation can carry on more than one business.

With regard to the condition (b) above, there are no guidelines in the Act dealing with the "expectation of profit" test in this context. Accordingly, there is some uncertainty as to how the CRA will apply this test. One court case on the issue is *Garage Montplaisir Ltée v. M.N.R.*, (T.C.C.) 92 DTC 2317 where the court discovered that the acquisition of the loss corporation was for the purpose of eliminating a competitor, not for the purpose of earning income from the loss business. On appeal to the Federal Court – Trial Division (96 DTC 6557), it was found that there was no evidence that the taxpayer had continued to carry on any significant part of the loss business "for profit or with a reasonable expectation of profit". The latter decision was affirmed by the Federal Court of Appeal (2001 DTC 5366).

11. Requirement that non-capital losses must be applied only against income from the same or similar products or services

The principle of identifying non-capital losses and farm losses with a particular business is only the first step in determining the deductibility of these losses. As a second step in the determination, non-capital losses and farm losses that are carried forward beyond the deemed taxation year are deductible only against income generated by the particular business [spar. 111(5)(*a*)(ii) and IT-302R3, par. 13] and by any other business substantially all of whose income is derived from the sale, leasing, rental or development of similar properties or the rendering of similar services. This other business is often referred to, generally, as a "similar" business, but the wording of the Act may be more restrictive in specifying "similar properties" or "similar services". The CRA's opinion of the meaning of the word "similar" in this context is given in IT-302R3, paragraph 14, where the word "similar" is interpreted as "of the same general nature or character". The CRA addresses the concept of a similar business (but not similar properties or services) in IT-206R and IT-259R4. Note that, in addition to the more obvious horizontally integrated business, a vertically integrated business is also considered a similar business. It is not clear whether products or services from various stages of a vertically integrated business are considered to be similar for the purposes of this provision. The case of *Manac Inc. Corp. v. The Queen*, (FCA) 98 DTC 6605, presents facts to address this issue. Although the decision in this case was based on the "substantially all" condition in the provision, the court made the following comments on the vertical integration and the "similar properties" issue: "we do not see how property which loses its identity when incorporated into an end product can be described as property similar to the end product".

In any case, only income from a business can be offset by losses that are carried over. The wording of the Act, therefore, precludes income from property, for example, from being offset by these carryover losses.

The principle of matching the losses of a particular business against income from that business or the income of similar products and services is sometimes referred to as "streaming". Because the stream of income against which the losses can be applied is limited, there is an increased possibility that losses will not be deductible in the appropriate carryover period. Hence the principle of streaming is inherently restrictive as far as the utilization of losses is concerned.

12. Loss carryback rules

The preceding commentary focuses on the carryforward of non-capital losses and farm losses. In general, the restrictions that were described above apply with equal effect in situations where post-acquisition of control losses are carried back to a taxation year preceding the acquisition of control [par. 111(5)(*b*)]. Again, only income from a business can be offset by these carryover non-capital losses.

13. Summary

The effects of the restrictive legislation on loss utilization, following an acquisition of control, may be summarized as follows:

(a) net capital losses, allowable business investment losses, property losses and unused charitable contributions expire and are not carried forward beyond the deemed taxation year;

(b) accrued losses of various kinds are deemed to be realized and, thus, increase the amount of non-capital losses and farm losses of a corporation; as non-capital losses or farm losses they are subject to time restrictions as to their deductibility; and

(c) the principle of streaming which matches losses from a particular business against income from the particular business and a similar business, increases the likelihood that non-capital losses and farm losses will not be deductible within their carryforward periods.

Example Problem 1

Wonder Inc.'s tax return for its year ended December 31, 2005, showed the following balances in its loss accounts:

Type of Loss	Balance	Year Incurred
Net capital loss	$ 8,000	2003
Non-capital loss	$10,000	2004

During the period January to December 2006, Wonder Inc. earned business income of $1,000 per month, computed in accordance with the *Income Tax Act*. On April 1, 2006, an unrelated person acquired 51% of the voting shares of Wonder Inc.

— REQUIRED

Discuss the tax implications of the above information.

— SOLUTION

Legal control (greater than 50% of the voting shares) of Wonder Inc. has been acquired by an unrelated person [par.256(7)(*a*)]. This has the following tax implications for Wonder Inc.:

(1) The taxation year of Wonder Inc. is deemed to have ended on March 31, 2006, being immediately before the acquisition of control [par. 249(4)(*a*)].

(2) A new taxation year is deemed to begin April 1, 2006 [par. 249(4)(*b*)].

(3) Wonder Inc. can choose any date up to 53 weeks in the future as its new taxation year end [par. 249(4)(*d*)].

(4) The net capital loss expires on March 31, 2006, and can never be deducted by Wonder Inc. after that date [par. 111(4)(*a*)].

(5) The non-capital loss, to the extent that it is a loss from carrying on business (not a loss from a property source), can be deducted in future taxation years, provided the following tests are met:

   (i) the business in which the loss was incurred is carried on at a profit or with a reasonable expectation of profit throughout the taxation year the loss is claimed [spar.111(5)(a)(i)], and

   (ii) the non-capital loss is deducted against income from the business that generated the non-capital loss and/or income from a business selling similar products or providing similar services [spar.111(5)(a)(ii)].

Thus, Wonder Inc. will claim $3,000 of its non-capital loss to offset its taxable income for the deemed year ended March 31, 2006. As to whether the remaining $7,000 will ever be deducted depends on point (5) above.

The net capital loss cannot be deducted in the deemed year ended March 31, 2006, as there are no capital gains to deduct it against. Since it expires on March 31, 2006, it will never be used.

Example Problem 2

On May 1, 2005, an unrelated person acquired 60% of the voting shares of Novell Inc. The values of the assets owned by Novell Inc. at May 1, 2005, were as follows:

Assets	Cost	UCC/CEC	FMV
Inventory	$10,000	N/A	$ 8,000
Accounts receivable	20,000	N/A	15,000
Equipment	30,000	$28,000	12,000
Marketable securities	40,000	N/A	10,000
Eligible capital property	50,000	36,000	42,000

In determining the value of the receivables, the collectibility of each debt was considered individually.

— REQUIRED

Which of the accrued (unrealized) losses in the above assets must be recognized by Novell Inc. in determining its income for tax purposes for the deemed year ended April 30, 2005?

— SOLUTION

The accrued loss in the inventory must be recognized. Inventory is valued at the lower of cost or market [sec.10(1) and Reg. 1801]	$ 2,000
The largest amount that Novell Inc. could deduct as a reserve for doubtful accounts [par. 20(1)(*l*)] for each trade receivable, must be claimed as a bad debt [par. 20(1)(*p*) and ssec.111(5.3)]	5,000
The UCC of the equipment is reduced to $12,000 [ssec.111(5.1)]. The reduction is deducted as CCA in the deemed year-end	16,000
The ACB of the marketable securities is reduced to $10,000 [par. 111(4)(*c*)]. The reduction is deemed to be a capital loss in the deemed year-end [par. 111(4)(*d*)]. The allowable capital loss is $30,000 × ½ = $15,000 and is deductible only to the extent there are taxable capital gains in the deemed year ended April 30, 2005, or in any of the three preceding years. No such gains are evident in this case.	
The CEC for the eligible capital property is reduced to $31,500, being ¾ × FMV ($42,000) [ssec.111(5.2)]. The reduction is deducted as CECA in the deemed year-end	4,500
Total reduction to the business income of Novell Inc. for its deemed year ended April 30, 2005	$27,500

Example Problem 3

Universal Ltd.'s tax return for its year ended December 31, 2004, showed the following balances in its loss accounts:

Type of Loss	Balance	Year Incurred
Net capital loss	$12,000*	1999
Non-capital loss	$10,000	2004

*In 1999 the capital gain inclusion rate was 75% so the adjusted net capital loss is $12,000 \times {}^1/_2 / {}^3/_4 =$ $8,000.

On June 1, 2005, an unrelated person acquired 75% of the voting shares of Universal Ltd. The accountant has calculated the business loss for the deemed year ended May 31, 2005, to be $25,000, including the accrued losses required to be recognized on the acquisition of control. The capital assets owned by Universal Ltd. at June 1, 2005, had the following values:

Capital Assets	Cost	UCC/CEC	FMV
Land	$ 40,000	N/A	$ 70,000
Building	60,000	$45,000	90,000
	$100,000		$160,000

The accountant is projecting income of $100,000 for Universal Ltd. over the next twelve months. The projected income is from the business that incurred the losses.

—REQUIRED

Universal Ltd. is considering making an election under paragraph 111(4)(e) of the *Income Tax Act*. Recommend the asset(s) that should be designated and the amount(s) which should be designated in the election.

—SOLUTION

Universal Ltd. should elect to recognize a taxable capital gain of $8,000 in order to utilize the $8,000 adjusted net capital loss expiring May 31, 2005. The election should be made on the land and not on the building as recapture would be incurred on the building. Such recapture would reduce the current year's business loss and, thus, would be disadvantageous, because there would be $15,000 (i.e., $60,000 − $45,000 = $15,000 recapture) less in non-capital losses to carry forward.

To trigger a $8,000 taxable capital gain on the land, proceed of $56,000 should be designated. (Current ACB of the land ($40,000) + desired taxable capital gain grossed up to the full capital gain ($8,000 × 2) = $56,000). The resulting income under section 3 and taxable income for the year would be calculated as follows:

par.3(a) income from business, property		$ Nil
par.3(b) taxable capital gains ($56,000 − $40,000) × ¹/₂	$ 8,000	
allowable capital loss	0	8,000
par.3(c)		$ 8,000
par.3(d) loss from business	$(25,000)	
loss from property	0	(25,000)
Division B net income (technically cannot be negative)		$(17,000)
Division C deductions:		
Net capital losses		(8,000)
Non-capital losses		0
Non-capital loss for the deemed year ended May 31, 2005		$(25,000)

Universal has non-capital losses of $10,000 + $25,000 = $35,000 at May 31, 2005. This is the same with or without the election under paragraph 111(4)(e). The advantage of the election is that the ACB of the land is bumped up to $56,000.

Example Problem 4

Chandra Inc. is a ladies' shoe retailer with a December 31 year-end. During its first fiscal year in 2004, the corporation incurred non-capital losses of $37,500 and capital losses of $4,000. On December 1, 2005, the voting shares of Chandra Inc. were sold to Maysha Ltd., a retailer of ladies' handbags, belts and costume jewellery. Maysha Ltd. is a well-established business that operates a number of profitable retail outlets.

Accounting and income tax data relating to Chandra Inc.'s operations from January 1 to November 30, 2005, were assembled for the purpose of the share-sale transaction. The data contained the following information:

(1) Loss from retail operations $12,500

(2) Long-term debt from Farrford Inc. written off (Farrford Inc., a small business corporation and manufacturer of ladies' shoes, was declared bankrupt on March 1, 2005.) 12,000

(3) Values of various assets at November 30, 2005:

Assets	Cost	UCC	FMV
Inventory	$24,000	—	$22,000
Store fixtures and equipment	36,000	$35,000	30,000
Marketable securities	9,000	—	5,000
Land	86,000	—	126,000
Building	110,000	104,000	118,000

During the short year ended December 31, 2005, Chandra Inc. produced net income for tax purposes of $3,500. No other income or losses were incurred. Chandra Inc. chose to return to its December 31 year-end for business reasons.

During its 2006 taxation year, the financing and marketing operations of Chandra Inc. were revamped and integrated with those of Maysha Ltd. As well, Chandra Inc.'s inventory was expanded to include merchandise carried in the Maysha Ltd. stores.

Chandra Inc.'s operations during the year ended December 31, 2006, produced the following income (losses):

Retailing operations — ladies' shoes	$ (5,000)
— handbags, belts, jewellery	12,000
Taxable capital gain on marketable securities	8,000

— REQUIRED

(A) Discuss the income tax implications of the acquisition of control of Chandra Inc. on December 1, 2005, ignoring all possible elections/options.

(B) Determine the income tax consequences of the acquisition of control of Chandra Inc. under the assumption that:

(i) the maximum amount of elections/options is utilized, and

(ii) the partial amount of all elections/options is utilized so that only enough income is generated to offset the losses which would otherwise expire in the acquisition of control.

For each of the above alternatives, determine the appropriate cost, undepreciated capital cost or adjusted cost base value for each of inventory, shop fixtures, marketable securities and paintings at December 1, 2005.

— SOLUTION

First, it is necessary to determine the losses and potential elections available at the deemed year-end as follows:

Non-capital losses carried forward from 2004	$37,500
Current-year losses from non-capital sources and ABIL:	
Retail operations	$12,500
ABIL (Farrford Inc. loan: ¹/₂ × $12,000)	6,000
Inventory loss ($22,000 − $24,000) [ssec. 10(1) and Reg. 1801]	2,000
Deemed CCA on store fixtures ($30,000 − $35,000) [ssec. 111(5.1)]	5,000
	$25,500
Potential election of recapture on building ($110,000 − $104,000) [par. 111(4)(*e*)]	$ 6,000
Net capital losses carried forward from 2004 $4,000 × ¹/₂	$ 2,000
Current-year allowable capital losses:	
Securities (¹/₂ × ($5,000 − $9,000)) [ssec. 111(5.1)]	$ 2,000
Potential election of taxable capital gain [par. 111(4)(*e*)]:	
Land (¹/₂ × ($126,000 − $86,000))	$20,000
Building (¹/₂ × ($118,000 − $110,000))	$ 4,000

The preceding data can be summarized as follows:

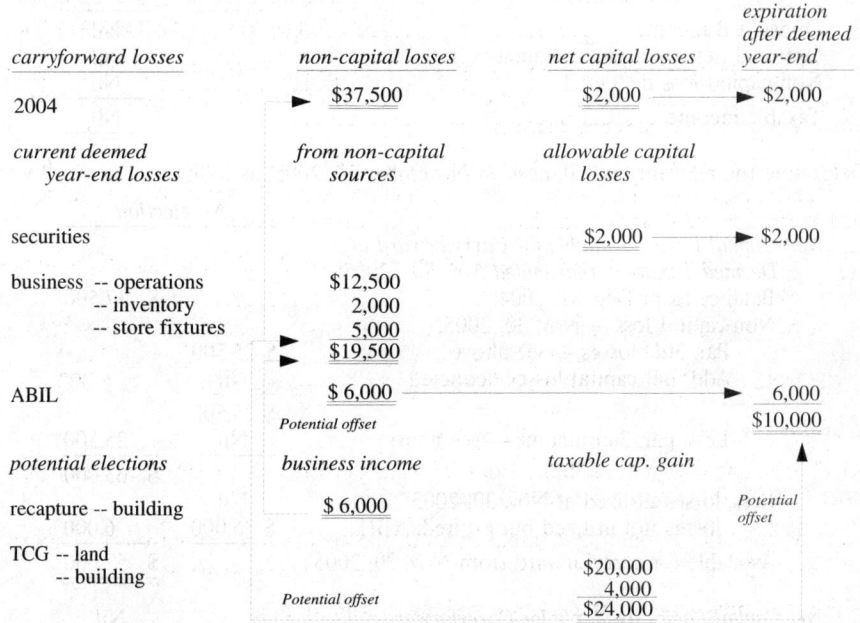

Note that if no election is made, there is no income to offset the current business loss of $19,500 or the non-capital loss carryforward of $37,500. Therefore the non-capital loss available to carry forward from November 30, 2005, is $57,000 (i.e., $19,500 + $37,500).

If the maximum election is made, the $6,000 of recapture offsets the business loss, leaving $13,500 (i.e., $19,500 − $6,000) of net business loss. The $24,000 of taxable capital gain offsets the $10,000 of expiring losses, leaving $14,000 (i.e., $24,000 − $10,000) to offset the remaining $13,500 of business loss. There is still $500 (i.e., $14,000 − $13,500) of taxable capital gain which offsets some of the $37,500 non-capital loss carryforward. As a result, the non-capital loss available for carry forward from November 30, 2005, is $37,000.

If only a partial election is made to offset the $10,000 of expiring losses, the current business loss of $19,500 is not offset and, hence, is available to carry forward, along with the $37,500 of non-capital losses, from November 30, 2005, for a total of $57,000.

(A) Compute the Division B income of Chandra Inc. for its taxation year deemed by subsection 249(4) to end on November 30, 2005 as a result of the acquisition of control on December 1, 2005. Division B income is calculated, using the ordering rules in section 3, as follows:

		No election
Par. 3(*a*): Income from non-capital sources (≧ 0)............		Nil
Par. 3(*b*): Net taxable capital gains (≧ 0):		
Deemed taxable capital gain (elective):		
land............................	Nil	
building	Nil	
Accrued allowable capital loss (automatic):		
securities	$ (2,000)	Nil
Par. 3(*c*): par. 3(*a*) + par. 3(*b*)		Nil
Par. 3(*d*): Losses from non-capital sources and		
ABILs:		
Loss from retail operation..............	$(12,500)	
Deemed recapture (elective) on building	Nil	
ABIL — Farrford Inc. loan	(6,000)	
Accrued losses — Inventory (automatic) ...	(2,000)	
Deemed CCA — Store fixtures		
(automatic)	(5,000)	$(25,500)
Division B income		Nil
Optional net capital loss deducted		Nil
Non-capital loss deducted		Nil
Taxable income		Nil

Determine the relevant tax balances, at November 30, 2005, as follows:

		No election
Non-Capital Losses available for Carryforward at		
Deemed Taxation Year ended Nov. 30, 2005:		
Balance from Dec. 31, 2004		$ 37,500
Non-capital loss — Nov. 30, 2005:		
Par. 3(*d*) losses — see above.............	$ 25,500	
Add: net capital losses deducted	Nil	
	$ 25,500	
Less: par. 3(*c*) income — see above	Nil	25,500
		$ 63,000
Less: losses utilized at Nov. 30, 2005	Nil	
losses not utilized but expired: ABIL	$ 6,000	6,000
Available for carryforward from Nov. 30, 2005		$ 57,000
Net Capital Losses available for Carryforward		Nil
Other Tax Balances:		
Inventory[1]		$ 22,000
Store fixtures[2] — UCC.............................		$ 30,000
Marketable securities[3] — ACB		$ 5,000
Land[4] — ACB......................................		$ 86,000
Building[5] — UCC		$ 104,000
ACB		$ 110,000

In the one-month taxation year ended December 31, 2005, Division B income is $3,500. This would allow a deduction of $3,500 from the non-capital loss balance carried forward from November 30, 2005, leaving a non-capital loss balance to carry forward from December 31, 2005, of $53,500 (i.e., $57,000 – $3,500). The $3,500 is deductible [par. 111(1)(a)] because the ladies' shoe retail business ("the particular business") was carried on throughout the year ending December 31, 2005, for profit; as well, the non-capital loss is applied against income from the particular business.

Division B income for the full year ended December 31, 2006, is calculated, using the ordering rules in section 3, as follows:

Par. 3(a):	Income from handbags, etc. retailing.................	$12,000
Par. 3(b):	Taxable capital gains — securities....................	8,000
Par. 3(c):	par. 3(a) + par. 3(b).............................	$20,000
Par. 3(d):	Loss from shoes retailing	(5,000)
Division B income	....	$15,000

Non-capital losses available for carryforward from December 31, 2006, are computed under two possible assumptions as follows:

Assumption 1: The retailing of handbags, belts, jewellery is the sale of "similar" products.

Balance from Dec. 31, 2005 (see above)..................	$ 53,500
Less: Non-capital losses claimed against "streamed"	
income included in net income in the year..........	12,000[6]
Balance at Dec. 31, 2006	$ 41,500[7]

Assumption 2: The retailing of handbags, belts, jewellery is not the sale of "similar" products.

Balance from Dec. 31, 2005	$ 53,500
Less: Non-capital losses claimed against "streamed"	
income included in net income in the year..........	Nil[8]
Balance at Dec. 31, 2006	$ 53,500[9]

(B)(i) The analysis, in (A) above, of Division B income, non-capital losses available for carryforward from November 30, 2005, and the other tax balances is repeated under the assumption that all possible elections/options are utilized. The "no election" results, as determined above, are presented for comparative purposes.

		No election		Maximum election	
Par. 3(a):	Income from non-capital sources (≧ 0)		Nil		Nil
Par. 3(b):	Net taxable capital gains (≧ 0):				
	Deemed taxable capital gains (elective):				
	land	Nil		$ 20,000	
	building	Nil		4,000	
	Accrued allowable capital loss (auto-				
	matic): securities	$ (2,000)	Nil	(2,000)	$ 22,000
Par. 3(c):	Par. 3(a) + par. 3(b)		Nil		$ 22,000
Par. 3(d):	Losses from non-capital sources and				
	ABILs:				
	Loss from retail operations	$(12,500)		$(12,500)	
	Deemed recapture (elective): building	Nil		6,000	
	ABIL — Farrford Inc. loan	(6,000)		(6,000)	
	Accrued losses (automatic): inventory	(2,000)		(2,000)	
	Deemed CCA (automatic): store fix-				
	tures........................	(5,000)	$(25,500)	(5,000)	(19,500)
Division B income......................			Nil		$ 2,500
Optional net capital loss deducted..........................			Nil		(2,000)[10]
Non-capital loss deducted...........................			Nil		(500)
Taxable income			Nil		Nil

Determine the relevant tax balances, at November 30, 2005, as follows:

Non-Capital Losses available for Carryforward at Deemed Taxation Year ended Nov. 30, 2005:

		No election		Maximum election	
Balance from Dec. 31, 2004		$ 37,500		$ 37,500	
Non-capital loss — Nov. 30, 2005:					
Par. 3(*d*) losses — see above	$ 25,500		$ 19,500		
Add: net capital losses deducted	Nil		2,000		
	$ 25,500		$ 21,500		
Less: par. 3(*c*) income — see above	Nil	25,500	22,000	Nil	
		$ 63,000		$ 37,500	
Less: losses utilized at Nov. 30, 2005	Nil		$ 500		
losses not utilized but expired: ABIL.....	$ 6,000	6,000	Nil	500	
Available for carryforward from Nov. 30, 2005		$ 57,000		$ 37,000	
Net Capital Losses available for Carryforward		Nil		Nil	
Other Tax Balances:					
Inventory..		$ 22,000		$ 22,000	
Store fixtures — UCC		$ 30,000		$ 30,000	
Marketable securities — ACB		$ 5,000		$ 5,000	
Land — ACB.......................................		$ 86,000		$126,000[11]	
Building — UCC....................................		$104,000		$114,000[12]	
— ACB		$110,000		$118,000[12]	

Note how under the "no election" alternative, the non-capital loss balance is larger than in the "maximum election" alternative. However, under the latter alternative, the ACBs of the land and building and the UCC of the building are larger. Non-capital losses must be recovered by offsetting them against income in what remains of their seven-year carryforward. The ACBs of the land and building will be recovered on their sale. The UCC will be recovered through CCA at the Class 1 rate of 4% declining balance. The better alternative depends on how optimistic the new owners are about generating enough income within the next seven years to offset the non-capital losses. If they are optimistic, then the "no election" alternative is better, because the non-capital losses will shield income from tax more quickly than the CCA tax shield and the ACB. shield of capital gains on a disposition.

(B)(ii) The amount of the partial election should be sufficient to offset the ABIL of $6,000, the allowable capital loss of $2,000 and the net capital loss of $2,000 that will expire if not used in the deemed taxation year. This requires income, therefore, of $10,000. Since creating recapture only serves to reduce the loss in paragraph 3(*d*) and a taxable capital gain is needed to offset the expiring allowable capital loss and net capital losses, a taxable capital gain of $10,000 should be created. This will require a capital gain of $20,000 (i.e., 2 × $10,000). If an election is made on the land to be deemed to have disposed of it at $106,000 (i.e., $86,000 + $20,000), a deemed taxable capital gain of $10,000 will result. None of the capital gain on the building should be elected, because if the election is made, recapture will result, in addition to the capital gain, when an election is made for deemed proceeds above capital cost.

Under the assumption that a partial election of a capital gain of $20,000 is made on the land, the analysis, in (B)(i) above, of Division B income, non-capital losses available for carryforward from November 30, 2004 and the other tax balances is repeated. The "no election" and the "maximum election" results, as determined above, are presented for comparative purposes.

	No election		Maximum election		Partial election	
Par. 3(a): Income from non-capital sources (≥ 0)	Nil		Nil		Nil	
Par. 3(b): Net taxable capital gains (≥ 0):						
Deemed taxable capital gains (elective):						
land	Nil		$ 20,000		$ 10,000	
building	Nil		4,000		Nil	
Accrued allowable capital loss (automatic):						
securities	$ (2,000)	Nil	(2,000)	$22,000	(2,000)	$ 8,000
Par. 3(c): Par. 3(a) + par. 3(b)		Nil		$22,000		$ 8,000
Par. 3(d): Losses from non-capital sources and ABILs:						
Loss from retail operations	$(12,500)		$(12,500)		$(12,500)	
Deemed recapture (elective): building	Nil		6,000		Nil	
ABIL — Farrford Inc. loan	(6,000)		(6,000)		(6,000)	
Accrued losses (automatic): inventory	(2,000)		(2,000)		(2,000)	
Deemed CCA (automatic): store fixtures..............	(5,000)	$(25,500)	(5,000)	(19,500)	(5,000)	(25,500)
Division B income...........................		Nil		$ 2,500		Nil
Optional net capital loss deducted		Nil		(2,000)[10]		$ (2,000)[10]
Non-capital loss deducted		Nil		(500)		Nil
Taxable income		Nil		Nil		Nil

Determine the relevant tax balances, at November 30, 2005, as follows:

Non-Capital Losses available for Carryforward at Deemed Taxation Year ended Nov. 30, 2005:

	No election		Maximum election		Partial election	
Balance from Dec. 31, 2004................	$ 37,500		$ 37,500		$ 37,500	
Non-capital loss — Nov. 30, 2005:						
Par. 3(d) losses — see above ...	$25,500		$19,500		$25,500	
Add: net capital losses deducted	Nil		2,000		2,000	
	$25,500		$21,500		$27,500	
Less: par. 3(c) income — see above	Nil	25,500	22,000	Nil	8,000	19,500[13]
		$ 63,000		$ 37,500		$ 57,000
Less: losses utilized at Nov. 30, 2005	Nil		$ 500		Nil	
losses not utilized but expired: ABIL	$ 6,000	6,000	Nil	500	Nil	Nil
Available for carryforward from Nov. 30, 2005		$ 57,000		$ 37,000		$ 57,000
Net Capital Losses available for Carryforward ...		Nil		Nil		Nil
Other Tax Balances:						
Inventory.........................		$ 22,000		$ 22,000		$ 22,000
Store fixtures — UCC.................		$ 30,000		$ 30,000		$ 30,000
Marketable securities — ACB		$ 5,000		$ 5,000		$ 5,000
Land — ACB.......................		$ 86,000		$126,000		$106,000
Building — UCC.....................		$104,000		$114,000		$104,000
ACB		$110,000		$118,000		$110,000

Note that the amount of non-capital losses available for carryforward of $57,000 under the "partial election" alternative is the same as the amount under the "no election" alternative. In the list of other tax balances, the only difference between the "partial election" and the "no election" alternatives is the ACB of the land which is higher for the "partial election" alternative. Therefore, the "partial election" alternative is better than the "no election" alternative.

Comparing the "maximum election" alternative with the "partial election" alternative, the amount of the non-capital losses available for carryforward under the "partial election" alternative is higher than the amount under the "maximum election" alternative, because some of the business losses of the deemed year-end were offset by income elected. However, the tax balances for the land and building are higher for the "maximum election" alternative. Only the increased UCC balance under the "maximum election" alternative shields income from tax immediately after the deemed year-end through increased CCA. The maximum present value of the CCA shield from the increased UCC of \$10,000 (i.e., \$114,000 - \$104,000) can be calculated by formula to be about \$714, assuming a 20% corporate tax rate and a 10% rate of return (i.e., C(d/(d + r))t = \$10,000 × (.04/(.04 + .10)) × .20 = \$571). However, the increased non-capital loss balance is available to shield income from tax in the next seven years. The better alternative depends on how optimistic the new owners of the corporation are in generating at least the additional \$20,000 (i.e., \$57,000 − \$37,000) of income against which the additional non-capital losses available for carryforward can be offset in the next ten years.

— *NOTES TO SOLUTION*

(1) The tax cost at December 1, 2005 is \$22,000, being either the value based on LCM or FMV.

(2) The undepreciated capital cost balance at December 1, 2005 is \$30,000, being the previous \$35,000 undepreciated capital cost balance less the \$5,000 excess that was deemed to be a deduction of capital cost allowance claimed [par. 20(1)(*a*)] in the year ending November 30, 2005 [ssec. 111(5.1)]. Capital cost allowance claimed for the short taxation years ended November 30, 2005, and December 31, 2005, must be prorated for the number of days in each of those taxation years.

(3) The adjusted cost base balance at December 1, 2005, is \$5,000, being the previous \$9,000 adjusted cost base less the \$4,000 excess which was deemed to be a capital loss in the year ending November 30, 2005.

(4) The adjusted cost base balance at December 1, 2005, remains at \$86,000, since no election was made [par. 111(4)(*e*)].

(5) The adjusted cost base at December 1, 2005, remains at \$110,000 and the UCC remains at \$104,000, since no election was made [par. 111(4)(*e*)].

(6) The corporation's income for tax purposes for the year ending December 31, 2006, is \$15,000 as computed by section 3. The corporation may apply the losses of the ladies' shoe retail business against the total of the corporation's *income* from that business and from the sale of similar products [spar. 111(5)(*a*)(ii)]. The result of the aggregation is, therefore, \$12,000, being nil from the ladies' shoe retail business plus \$12,000 from the sale of similar products with the \$8,000 taxable capital gain being excluded. Thus, the maximum deduction is \$12,000.

(7) This amount is available for carryforward as follows:

2004 Dec. 31 non-capital loss balance:			
2004 non-capital loss		\$37,500	
Less: Dec. 31, 2005 deduction	\$ 3,500		
Dec. 31, 2006 deduction	12,000	15,500	\$22,000
2005 Nov. 30 non-capital loss:			
Loss from retail operation		\$12,500	
Deemed CCA — store fixtures		5,000	
Inventory loss...........................		2,000	19,500
			\$41,500

The 2004 loss expires on December 31, 2013, i.e., in 10 taxation years, including the deemed taxation year at November 30, 2005, and the one-month taxation year at December 31, 2005. The November 2005 loss expires on December 31, 2014.

(8) The corporation's income for tax purposes for the year ending December 31, 2006, is \$15,000. However, the corporation may make a deduction to the extent of nil under this assumption because the ladies' shoe retail business generated no income in the year and there was no income from the sale of similar products or services by the assumption made in this alternative [spar. 111(5)(*a*)(ii)].

(9) This amount is available for carryforward as follows, assuming a December 31 taxation year-end is chosen:

— $34,000   (being the 2004 loss of $37,500 – $9,500 claimed in the December 31, 2005 year) expires on December 31, 2013;

— $19,500   (see note (7)) expires on December 31, 2014.

(10) On the assumption that the optional net capital loss deduction is taken in order to increase the non-capital losses for the deemed taxation year.

(11) The adjusted cost base balance at December 1, 2005 is $126,000, being the deemed proceeds of disposition in the deemed disposition elected upon [par. 111(4)(e)].

(12) The adjusted cost base balance (i.e., capital cost, in the case of depreciable property) at December 1, 2005, for future capital gains purposes, is $118,000, being deemed proceeds of disposition in the deemed disposition elected upon [par. 111(4)(e)]. The UCC $114,000 at the same date is increased by all of the recapture of $6,000, but only ½ of the capital gain of $8,000 elected as deemed proceeds on the deemed disposition [par. 13(7)(f)], (i.e., $104,000 + $6,000 + ½ × $8,000).

(13) The addition of $19,500 to the non-capital loss balance is logical, since the $19,500 represents the loss from business sources for the deemed year-end.

F. Taxable Income of a Corporation in General

[ITA: 110–112]

Recall that the starting point for the calculation of a corporation's taxable income is its income computed under Division B. Where financial statements have been prepared using generally accepted accounting principles, it may be necessary to adjust income for financial accounting purposes to income for tax purposes as determined by Division B. This usually involves a reconciliation process, introduced in previous chapters. Generally, expenditures deducted for financial accounting purposes but not deductible for tax purposes, must be added to financial accounting income, and expenditures not deducted for financial accounting purposes but deductible for tax purposes may be deducted in the reconciliation. To perform this reconciliation in the preparation of a corporate tax return, Schedule 1 is completed.

Example Problem

Frenzied Taxpayers Limited reported a net loss for financial accounting purposes of $53,000 for 2004 and a net income of $126,000 for 2005. It showed a provision for income taxes of $113,000 for 2005 only. Expenses deducted for financial accounting purposes in both years included: charitable donations of $15,000 per year, depreciation of $105,000 per year and bond discount amortization of $5,000 per year. The corporation included in financial accounting income, in both years, dividends from taxable Canadian corporations of $23,000 and dividends of $15,300 net of a 15% withholding tax from foreign corporations which were not foreign affiliates. The corporation had no capital gains in either year.

In 2004, capital cost allowance of $14,800 (i.e., less than the maximum of $14,844) had been taken on a brick building (Class 1) leaving an undepreciated capital cost balance of $356,250 on January 1, 2005, the beginning of the 2005 taxation year. In addition, $44,800 in capital cost allowance had been taken on equipment leaving an undepreciated capital cost balance of $179,200 on January 1, 2005. In 2005, no additions or disposals were made to these classes of assets.

The corporation had non-capital losses of $18,000 available for carryover until 2007 and a 1999 net capital loss of $5,000 available for carryover.

— REQUIRED

Calculate the taxable income of the corporation for the years indicated.

—SOLUTION

	2004		2005	
Net income (loss) per financial statements		$ (53,000)		$126,000
Add items not deductible for tax purposes:				
Provision for income taxes[1]		—		$113,000
Withholding tax on foreign dividends[2]	$ 2,700		2,700	
Charitable donations[3]	15,000		15,000	
Depreciation	105,000		105,000	
Amortized bond discount[4]	5,000	127,700	5,000	240,700
Deduct items tax deductible:				
Capital cost allowances[5]		(59,600)		(50,090)
Income for tax purposes		$ 15,100		$316,610
Deductions in computation of taxable income:				
Inter-company dividends [sec. 112] ...	$ 23,000[6]		$ 23,000	
Charitable donations [par. 110(1)(a)]				
— carried over	—		15,000[7]	
— current	Nil[7]		15,000[7]	
Non-capital loss carryover [par. 111(1)(a)][8]	—		18,000	
Net capital loss carryover [par. 111(1)(b)][9]	—	(23,000)	—	(71,000)
Taxable income		Nil		$245,610

—NOTES TO SOLUTION

(1) Income tax is not an expenditure made to produce income. It is an appropriation of profits after they have been earned.

(2) This is not an expenditure made to produce income for tax purposes, but an appropriation of profits after they have been earned. However, a foreign tax credit may be available in the computation of tax.

(3) Donations, normally, are not deductible in the computation of income, but are deductible in the computation of taxable income of a corporation.

(4) Bond discount amortizations are prohibited [par.h 18(1)(f)], but payments reflecting bond discounts are deductible at the earlier of redemption or maturity [par. 20(1)(f)].

(5) Capital cost allowances for 2005 were computed as follows:

	Building Class 1: 4%	Equipment Class 8: 20%
2005: U.C.C., January 1, 2005	$356,250	$179,200
C.C.A. for 2005 (expense $50,090)	(14,250)	(35,840)
2006: U.C.C., January 1, 2006	$342,000	$143,360

(6) Even though $23,000 was deducted, only $15,100 of the dividends deducted have any effect since there is no loss carryover for dividends not deducted. Even where there is a loss from business and property, the addition to the non-capital losses of dividends deducted under section 112 is offset by the paragraph 3(c) income which in fact includes the dividends in question. The dividend deduction only neutralizes the paragraph 3(c) inclusion, as can be seen by a substitution of these numbers in the definition of non-capital loss [ssec. 111(8)].

(7) The amount of charitable donations that may be deducted in a year is limited to 75% of income as computed in Division B of Part I [par. 110.1(1)(a)]. However, charitable donations not deducted in the current year can be carried forward five years.

(8) Non-capital losses would not be deducted in 2004, because after the dividends have been deducted, there is no income against which to absorb them in that year.

(9) Net capital loss carryovers cannot be deducted in 2004 and 2005 because there were no taxable capital gains against which to absorb them in these years. However, if there are net taxable capital gains available under paragraph 3(*b*) in the future or in the 3 years before 2004 (to the extent the taxable capital gains have not been offset by allowable capital losses), there is a potential increase in the non-capital losses at the taxpayer's discretion. The decision to utilize this option will depend upon which source of income will be generated first, business income or net taxable capital gains.

II. BASIC COMPUTATION OF TAX FOR ALL CORPORATIONS

A. Objectives of Provisions Affecting Taxation of Corporations

Although a corporation is regarded as a separate entity, in an economic sense the separation of a corporation and its shareholders may be artificial. However, the flexibility provided by corporations, often involving tax planning, has resulted in considerable complexity of the legislation pertaining to the taxation of corporations. This legislation appears to have three main objectives.

The first objective is the alleviation of the multiple taxation of corporate income by taxing income at the level of the corporation and, then, at the level of the shareholder on dividends received from after-tax corporate earnings. The Act attempts to integrate these two taxes primarily by way of the dividend gross-up and tax credit mechanism. If the system of integration were perfect, it would completely eliminate the double taxation of corporate income, as previously discussed at the beginning of this chapter and demonstrated in Chapter 12. The Canadian system of integration is not perfect in this sense, but it does remove much of the effect of double taxation on investment income and some types of business income. The examination of this aspect will be continued in detail in the next chapter.

The second objective of these provisions is to prevent the avoidance of tax through the use of a corporation. In prior years, there was a considerable incentive to convert amounts that would normally be distributed to *individual* shareholders as dividends into amounts that resulted in capital gains. This was known as "dividend stripping" and many provisions were put in place to stop this practice. The incentive to convert dividends into capital gains was renewed with the introduction of the capital gains deduction which continues for shares of qualified small business corporations. Major anti-avoidance provisions are found in sections 110.6, 245 and 246. However, in making distributions to *corporate* shareholders, there has been an incentive to convert what might be taxed as a capital gain into a non-taxable intercorporate dividend. Hence, provisions to prevent such "capital gains stripping" have been implemented [ssec. 55(2)].

The third objective of these provisions is to provide tax incentives to certain types of corporations. The small business deduction, which will be discussed in the next chapter, is probably the most important of these. The small business deduction will be shown to substantially reduce tax for a Canadian-controlled private corporation. Also discussed will be the manufacturing and processing profits deduction and investment tax credits including the credit for scientific research expenditures.

B.   General Rates for Corporations

[ITA: 89(1); 123; 123.2; 123.4; 125(6)(*a*); ITR: 3200; 4800]

The general federal rate of tax to be paid on the taxable income of all corporations under Part I of the Act is set out in section 123. However, the basic federal rate of 38% is subject to modification, depending on the type of corporation, by provisions such as those in sections 123.2 through 127. Section 123.2 levies a surtax, the rates for which have fluctuated over the years, on a defined base of federal tax payable. Section 123.4 provides for a tax rate reduction for corporations. Section 124 reduces the federal tax payable, in recognition of provincial income taxes, by an amount equal to 10% of the corporation's taxable income earned in a province or territory of Canada. Sections 125 and 125.1 reduce federal tax payable, for certain corporations, by means of the small business deduction and manufacturing and processing profits deduction, respectively. Section 126 sets out the rules for determining foreign tax credits which reduce federal tax payable. Section 127 contains the rules of a number of tax credits, including the political contribution tax credit and the investment tax credit, which reduce the amount of federal tax payable.

Federal corporate surtax is computed, generally, as follows:

Base amount of Part I tax	38.00%
Deduct: 10% of taxable income	10.00
Net amount	28.00%
Corporate surtax @4% of net amount	1.12%

The base amount of Part I tax is 38% of taxable income. The surtax, generally, is 1.12% (i.e., 4% of (38% − 10%)) of taxable income.

The 2005 federal budget, proposed the elimination of the 4% federal surtax effective January 1, 2008. However, this proposal was excluded from the main budget bill in June 2005.

In addition to the federal taxes imposed, each province levies an additional income tax on a corporation's taxable income. Furthermore, the taxable income calculation may vary from province to province because of provincial taxing statutes. The provincial rate varies from province to province, but on the whole lies between 8.9% and 17%.

As mentioned previously, the type and status of the corporation has a bearing on how its income is taxed. There are three major classifications of corporations to be concerned with. These are described as follows:

(1) a public corporation [ssec. 89(1)] is one which is resident in Canada and has a class of shares listed on a prescribed [Reg. 3200] Canadian stock exchange or meets certain conditions prescribed in Part XLVIII of the Regulations and either elects to be a public corporation or is so designated by the Minister;

(2) a private corporation [ssec. 89(1)] is a Canadian resident company which is not a public corporation and is not controlled by one or more public corporations or prescribed federal Crown corporations; and

(3) a Canadian-controlled private corporation [ssec. 125(7)] is a private corporation not controlled directly or indirectly by non-residents, public corporations or any combination of the two.

As a result of the combined federal and provincial rate and several of the modifications to that rate, the rates of tax applicable to Canadian corporations will vary from a low of about 15.6% to a high of about 39.1%, depending on the classification of the corporation and the type of income earned.

Subsection 123.4(2) provides a corporation with a deduction from tax, computed by multiplying the corporation's "general rate reduction percentage" [ssec.123.4(1)] by its "full-rate taxable income" [ssec. 123.4(1)]. The "general rate reduction percentage" is 7% in 2004 and subsequent years. The "full-rate taxable income" of a corporation, generally, is a corporation's taxable income that has not benefited from special rate reductions, such as the manufacturing and processing profits deduction (discussed later in this chapter) and the small business deduction (discussed in Chapter 12), among others. The amount of the rate reduction is dependent on the nature of the corporation. Paragraph (a) of the definition of "full-rate taxable income" in subsection 123.4(1) applies to corporations other than Canadian-controlled private corporations (CCPCs). For the purposes of this chapter, full-rate taxable income is the amount of the corporation's taxable income minus income, if any, eligible for the manufacturing and processing profits deduction. Examples of this calculation are presented later in this Chapter.

The 2005 federal budget, proposed to increase the general rate reduction by one-half a percentage point for 2008, one percentage point for 2009 and two percentage points for the 2010 and later calendar years. This would mean that by 2010 the general rate reduction would be 9%. However, this proposal was excluded from the main budget bill in June 2005.

C. Abatement from Federal Tax for Income earned in a Province

[ITA: 124; ITR: 400; 402; IT-177R2]

1. Purpose of the provision

A federal abatement of 10% of a corporation's taxable income is deducted from income tax otherwise calculated [ssec. 124(1)]. This abatement is based on taxable income earned in a Canadian province or territory; that is, the reduction allows for the imposition of such a provincial tax. All of the provinces and the territories impose an income tax on corporations at basic rates which vary from 8.9% to 17%. In all but Alberta, Ontario and Quebec, this tax is collected by the federal government together with the federal tax. Alberta, Ontario and Quebec have their own rules for the taxation of corporations. All of these tax rates are set out in the "Current Tax Rates and Credits" section at the beginning of the CCH edition of the CANADIAN INCOME TAX ACT.

Exhibit 11-3 shows a hypothetical calculation, applicable to most corporations, of effective total tax on taxable income eligible for the abatement. Note that the provincial tax is calculated separately on a tax base which may or may not equal taxable income under the federal Act depending on the particular province levying the tax. For illustrative purposes only, Exhibit 11-3 *assumes* that the tax base for income earned in a hypothetical province is equal to taxable income for federal corporate income tax. However, as a result of particular provincial legislation, there may be differences in these bases. The exhibit also assumes that the provincial corporate rate of tax is 13% of the taxable income earned in that province. In fact, the provincial tax rates vary from province to province. The basic provincial rate for the majority of the provinces hovers around 8.9% to 17%. The real effective total tax rates will vary because of different provincial rates of tax.

EXHIBIT 11-3
Hypothetical Tax Rates applicable to
Taxable Income eligible for Abatement

Basic federal tax rate [ssec. 123(1)]	38.00%
Federal abatement for provincial tax [ssec. 124(1)]	(10.00)
Net federal tax	28.00%
Federal surtax @ 4% of net federal tax of 28.00% [sec. 123.2]	1.12
Total	29.12%
Federal tax reduction for 2005	(7.00)
Net federal tax	24.12%
Provincial tax (assumed)	13.00
Effective total tax	35.12%

2. Applicable income tax regulations

Part IV of the Regulations provides the prescribed method to determine the taxable income earned in a province by a corporation. The term "taxable income earned in the year in a province" by a corporation is defined as being the aggregate of the taxable incomes of the corporation earned in the year in each of the provinces [Reg. 400(1)]. The Regulations also set out the method of calculating the taxable income earned in a particular province during the year. The taxable income earned in a particular province is that taxable income which is attributable to a *permanent establishment* that the corporation has in the province [Reg. 402]. If a company has no permanent establishment in a province, it will not have earned any taxable income in that province for the purposes of the abatement.

The term "permanent establishment" is defined as a fixed place of business of the corporation, including an office, a branch, a mine or oil well, a farm, a timber land, a factory, a workshop or a warehouse [Reg. 400(2)]. Where the corporation does not have a fixed place of business, its permanent establishment is the principal place in which the corporation's business is carried out. A corporation is deemed [Reg. 400(2)(*b*)] to have a permanent establishment in a place, if the corporation carries on business through an employee or agent, established in a particular place:

(a) who has general authority to contract for his or her employer or principal; or

(b) who has a stock of merchandise owned by his or her employer or principal from which he or she regularly fills orders which he or she receives.

However, the fact that a corporation has business dealings through a commission agent, broker or other independent agent, or maintains an office solely for the purchase of merchandise, does not of itself mean that the corporation has a permanent establishment [Reg. 400(2)(*f*)]. The use of substantial machinery or equipment in a particular place at any time in a taxation year constitutes a permanent establishment in that place [Reg. 400(2)(*e*)] as does the ownership of land in a province by a corporation that, otherwise, has a permanent establishment in Canada [Reg. 400(2)(*d*)]. IT-177R2 indicates that the application of the criteria for a permanent establishment set out in Regulation 400(2) will often involve questions of fact which must be answered by the circumstances of each case.

3. Cases on the meaning of permanent establishment

The case of *M.N.R. v. Panther Oil and Grease Manufacturing Co. of Canada Ltd.*, (Ex. Ct.) 61 DTC 1222 presents a specific fact situation. Here the taxpayer had a factory in Ontario, but maintained a sizable sales force throughout Canada under the direction of district sales managers. These sales managers were under the direction of division managers, one of whom lived in Quebec. He had an office, not listed as the company's, in his home. The division and district managers kept a small quantity of the company's goods on hand for small orders when quick delivery was requested. However, most orders were filled from Ontario.

It was held that the extensive sales organization in Quebec, itself, constituted a branch in that province and district managers constituted "agencies" of the company. It was also found that the stock of merchandise from which small orders were filled qualified as a permanent establishment.

In the case of *Enterprise Foundry (N.B.) Ltd. v. M.N.R.*, (T.A.B.) 64 DTC 660 the appellant was incorporated in New Brunswick, but all of its sales were made to customers in Quebec. About 40% of its orders were filled from a stock of merchandise maintained in a public warehouse in Montreal. The taxpayer's key employee had the authority to deliver goods from the stock of merchandise and also had general authority to contract for his employer. It was held that there was a permanent establishment in Quebec.

Example Problem

The taxpayer corporation, whose head office was in Ontario, manufactured electrical appliances which it sold exclusively to wholesalers throughout the country. The company employed a sales representative and junior salesmen in the Province of Quebec. Orders received by the sales representative, who had no authority to accept them, were forwarded to head office and, if accepted there, the goods were shipped directly to the purchaser. During the years in question, the Quebec representative maintained an office in his home at his own expense. There was no agreement with the company to set up the office, but he found it convenient to do so. The company supplied him with company stationery and literature, price sheets, catalogues, sales promotional material and inter-office memoranda. He was also supplied with substantial quantities of samples of the company's products the value of which varied from $4,700 to $11,000 to be used in demonstrations and in promoting sales. The telephone directory did not list the representative's residence as the company's place of business and there was no business sign of any type on the premises. The office was used for taking orders and for training junior salesmen.

During six months of one year, the company maintained a stock of appliances valued at about $120,000 in rented warehouse space in Montreal and filled Quebec orders from this stock. The company had no employees at that warehouse; the handling of goods there was carried out by the warehouse personnel. The company had no control over any part of the warehouse and the public had no knowledge of the company's goods being stored there.

— REQUIRED

Determine whether or not the company has a "permanent establishment" in the Province of Quebec by reference to Regulation 400(2).

— SOLUTION

[Reference: *M.N.R. v. Sunbeam Corporation (Canada) Ltd.*, (Ex. Ct.) 61 DTC 1063]

The definition of "permanent establishment" [Reg. 400(2)] begins with a general statement and then lists seven situations which describe specific permanent establishments. Consider the potentially applicable specific provisions first.

(1) A corporation must carry on business through an employee or agent who has general authority to contract or who has a stock of merchandise owned by the employer from which he regularly fills orders [Reg. 400(2)(*b*)]. In this case, the sales representative had no authority to accept orders. Furthermore, orders were filled from head office in Ontario. Therefore, the conditions for a permanent establishment [Reg. 400(2)(*b*)] are not met.

(2) Did the company meet the condition of Regulation 400(2)(*e*)? The use of the company's sample appliances for demonstration purposes was not "the use of substantial machinery or

equipment" in Quebec. The provision was probably intended to refer to the use of heavy or large machinery or equipment by such persons as contractors or builders who may move such equipment from one province to another in carrying out their normal operations.

If none of the specific conditions in Regulation 400(2) are met, the analysis should turn to the more general definition of "permanent establishment". The following questions can be posed.

(1) Did the company have a fixed place of business including an office, a branch or a factory? The office of the Quebec sales representative was not an office of the company. This office was maintained by the sales representative in his home for his own convenience and at his own expense. There was no business sign of any sort on the premises and the telephone directory did not list the residence as the company's place of business.

(2) Did the company have a warehouse in the Province of Quebec? The company merely used the facilities of another company's warehouse for the storing of goods. The company had no control over the warehouse. As a result, the warehouse cannot be considered a fixed place of business of the company.

On the basis of this analysis, it was held that the company did not have a permanent establishment in Quebec.

---

4.   Taxable income earned in a province or territory

Once it is determined that a corporation has a permanent establishment in a province or territory, a portion of the company's taxable income is attributed to that jurisdiction. To determine the attribution, a formula must be used [Reg. 402]. The formula is based on the proportion of gross revenues earned through a permanent establishment in a province or territory and the proportion of salaries and wages expense paid through the same permanent establishment in that jurisdiction, relative to total gross revenues and salaries and wages expense, respectively, of the corporation. The total taxable income allocated to all provinces and territories provides the basis for the 10% abatement. The allocations to individual jurisdictions, other than Alberta, Ontario and Quebec, provide the basis for provincial or territorial corporate income tax.

A taxpayer must first determine the gross revenue for the year which is reasonably attributable to each permanent establishment [Reg. 402(3)(a)]. Rules are provided for determining the permanent establishment to which gross revenue is attributable where merchandise is shipped by a corporation to its customers outside of Canada [Reg. 402(4)].

Where the gross revenue reasonably attributable to a permanent establishment in a province has been determined, this amount will be divided by the corporation's total gross revenue for the year and the resulting fraction will be multiplied by its taxable income for the year [Reg. 401]. Certain types of investment income including interest on securities, dividends and rentals or royalties from properties not used in the main business of the corporation are excluded from gross revenue [Reg. 402(5)].

It will also be necessary to determine the aggregate of the salaries and wages paid in the year by the corporation to employees of a permanent establishment in each particular jurisdiction [Reg. 402(3)(b)]. This will then be divided by the aggregate of all salaries and wages paid in the year by the corporation and the resulting fraction will be multiplied by its taxable income for the year [Reg. 401].

Example Problem

Barry and the Wild Bunch Limited, with its head office in Ottawa, Ontario and other permanent establishments in the provinces of New Brunswick and Quebec, and in the United States, has taxable income of $325,000.

Assume that the corporation's gross revenue and salaries and wages are attributable [Reg. 402] to its permanent establishments as follows:

	Gross revenue	Salaries and wages
Ontario	$ 780,000	$ 130,000
New Brunswick	2,340,000	520,000
Quebec	2,600,000	585,000
U.S.	390,000	65,000
Total	$6,110,000	$1,300,000
Dividends not attributable [Reg. 402(5)]	130,000	—
	$6,240,000	$1,300,000

— REQUIRED

Compute the amount of the company's taxable income attributable to each province and determine the amount of the company's abatement [ssec. 124(1)].

— SOLUTION

The proportion of taxable income attributable to each province would be computed as follows [Reg. 402]:

	Gross revenue		Salaries & wages		
	Amount	%	Amount	%	Average %
Ontario	$ 780,000	12.8%	$ 130,000	10.0%	½ (12.8% + 10.0%) = 11.4%
New Brunswick	2,340,000	38.3	520,000	40.0	½ (38.3% + 40.0%) = 39.2%
Quebec	2,600,000	42.6	585,000	45.0	½ (42.6% + 45.0%) = 43.8%
Subtotal	$5,720,000	93.7%	$1,235,000	95.0%	½ (93.7% + 95.0%) = 94.4%
U.S.	390,000	6.3	65,000	5.0	
Total	$6,110,000	100.0%	$1,300,000	100.0%	

Allocation of taxable income to each province:

Ontario	11.4% of $325,000 = $ 37,050
New Brunswick	39.2% of $325,000 = 127,400
Quebec	43.8% of $325,000 = 142,350
Total taxable income earned in a province or territory	$306,800

The amount deductible from the corporation tax otherwise payable would be computed as follows [ssec. 124(1)]:

10% of $306,800 .... $30,680

Note, however, that, in this case, the surtax is applied to federal tax otherwise payable after a deduction of 10% of the full taxable income of $325,000 [sec. 123.2].

D. Tax on Large Corporations

[ITA: 125.3; 181–181.9; ITR: 8600]

This tax is being phased out over the period January 1, 2004 to December 31, 2007.

Part I.3 of the Act provides for a Tax on Large Corporations (LCT) which is in effect a corporate minimum tax. It is levied at a rate of 0.200% (for 2004) of capital in excess of $50 million employed in Canada [ssec. 181.1(1)]. To phase out the tax, the rates are reduced to the following for calendar years 2004 to 2008: 2004 - 0.200%, 2005 - 0.175%, 2006 - 0.125%, 2007 - 0.0625%, and 2008 - nil [ssec. 181.1(1.1)].] Taxable capital employed in Canada is computed (on Schedule 33) for non-financial corporations, generally, as follows [ssecs. 181.2(2) to (5)]:

Share capital			$xxx
Add: contributed surplus	$xxx		
retained earnings and other surpluses	xxx		
reserve funds (except amounts deducted under Part I)	xxx		
loans and advances	xxx		
indebtedness represented by bonds, debentures, notes, mortgages, etc.	xxx		
other indebtedness outstanding for more than 365 days before the year-end	xxx		
dividends payable	xxx	xxx	
Capital [ssec. 181.2(3)]			$xxx
Less: allowance for investments in other corporations [ssec. 181.2(4)]			xxx
Taxable capital			$xxx
Percentage of capital employed in Canada			× x%
Taxable capital employed in Canada			$xxx

The investment allowance is calculated, generally, as follows [ssec. 181.2(4)]:

Add the carrying values at the end of the year of the following assets:	
shares of another corporation	$xxx
loans or advances to another corporation	xxx
dividends receivable	xxx
investment allowance	$xxx

The amounts added to the investment allowance of a particular corporation represent amounts that would be in the Large Corporations Tax base of another corporation and, hence, will be taxed in that other corporation.

Taxable capital is calculated using the unconsolidated balance sheet accounts of a corporation determined in accordance with generally accepted accounting principles for the current taxation year [ssec. 181(3)]. While current accounts payable, including current income taxes payable, are excluded from this base, deferred income tax reserves and other non-tax-deductible reserves are included in the tax base. Taxable capital employed in Canada is then determined by applying the federal abatement percentage of taxable income earned in a province as discussed in the preceding part of this chapter.

The Large Corporation Tax is then calculated as follows:

Taxable capital employed in Canada	$xxx
Less: capital deduction (up to $50,000,000) [sec. 181.5]	xxx
	$xxx
Part I.3 tax at 0.200% thereof	$xxx(A)

The changes to the LCT, before its full phase-out in calendar year 2008 can be summarized as follows for the indicated calendar years:

Calendar year	2004	2005	2006	2007
Rate	.200%	.175%	.125%	.0625%
Threshold (millions)	$ 50	$ 50	$ 50	$50

The $50 million basic capital deduction must be allocated within a group of related corporations [sec. 181.5]. However, for Canadian-controlled private corporations the allocation is based on the associated corporation rules rather than related person rules [ssec. 181.5(7)]. The rate of tax is 0.175% in calendar year 2005 and is payable in instalments following the same pattern as corporate instalments of income tax, as discussed in Chapter 14 [ssec. 181.7(1)]. The Part I.3 tax is then reduced by the amount of the Canadian surtax, which is the federal surtax that can be attributed to a permanent establishment in Canada [par. 181.1(4)(a)].

Federal surtax [sec. 123.2]	$xxx
Canadian surtax (federal abatement percentage times the total federal surtax)	$xxx(B)
Part I.3 tax less Canadian surtax (i.e., (A − B))	$xxx(C)

The corporation's LCT liability for the current year may be reduced further by the excess of the corporation's surtax over its LCT liability in a carryover year, i.e., its unused surtax credits [par.181.1(4)(b)]. For years after 2003, neither the Part I.3 tax rate of 0.200% nor the capital deduction of $50 million will be changed for the purposes of computing the unused surtax credits [ssec. 181.1(1.2) and ssec. 181.1(4.1)]. This will maintain consistency in the carryover amounts over the years. A carryover year is any of the seven preceding years or three subsequent years. The result is that an excess of surtax over LCT can be carried back three years and forward seven years to be deducted from net LCT in the year to which the excess is carried.

The element of a corporation's total federal surtax attributable to its Canadian income (Canadian surtax) is determined as the ratio of its taxable capital employed in Canada to its total taxable capital (i.e., the ratio determined by Part IV of the Regulations for purposes of the federal abatement [Reg. 8601]).

Example Problem

Mammoth Corporation, a public corporation in the retailing business, had the following balance sheet as at December 31, 2005:

	($ 000's)
Current assets	20,000
Investment in Little Corp.	10,000
Loan receivable from Cash Poor Limited	15,000
Fixed assets, net of $260,000,000 of accumulated depreciation	300,000
Goodwill, net of $30,000,000 of amortization	55,000
Total assets	400,000

	($ 000's)
Accounts payable	25,000
Income taxes payable	5,000
Dividends payable	10,000
Mortgages payable	160,000
Future income taxes	40,000
Contingent liability (re: lawsuit)	10,000
Common shares	100,000
Retained earnings	50,000
Total liabilities and equity	400,000

The investment in Little Corp. represents 100% of its common shares and is accounted for at cost.

Mammoth's taxable income for its taxation year ending December 31, 2005, was $40,000,000 and 88% of its taxable income was earned in a province.

— *REQUIRED*

Determine Mammoth's Part I.3 tax liability for the year. Assume that Mammoth is allocated all of the capital deduction for its related group of corporations, and that Mammoth has no unused surtax credits from preceding years.

— *SOLUTION*

Capital	
Capital stock [par. 181.2(3)(*a*)]	$100,000,000
Retained earnings [par. 181.2(3)(*a*)]	50,000,000
Mortgages payable [par. 181.2(3)(*d*)]	160,000,000
Dividends payable [par. 181.2(3)(*e*)]	10,000,000
Future income taxes [par. 181.2(3)(*b*)]	40,000,000
Contingency [par. 181.2(3)(*b*)]	10,000,000
Total capital	$370,000,000
Investment allowance [ssec. 181.2(4)]	
Investment in Little Corp.	$ 10,000,000
Loan receivable from Cash Poor Limited	15,000,000
Total investment allowance	$ 25,000,000
Taxable capital ($370,000,000 – $25,000,000)	$345,000,000
Taxable capital employed in Canada (88% of $345,000,000)	$303,600,000
Capital deduction [ssec. 181.5(1)]	50,000,000
Amount subject to Part I.3 tax	$253,600,000
Part I.3 tax at 0.175%	$ 443,800(A)
Surtax for the year (4% of 28% of $40,000,000)	$ 448,000
Canadian surtax payable (88% of $448,000)	$ 394,240(B)
Part I.3 tax liability after credit for Canadian surtax — (A) minus (B) ($443,800 – $394,240)	$ 49,560[1]

— *NOTE TO SOLUTION*

(1) This amount can be offset by unused surtax credits in the following three years. There are no unused surtax credits from the preceding seven years to offset this amount currently.

III. MANUFACTURING AND PROCESSING PROFITS DEDUCTION

A. Introduction

[ITA: 125.1]

This deduction from tax (i.e., a tax credit) is a tax incentive to all incorporated Canadian manufacturing and processing businesses taxable in Canada. The provision operates to reduce the net rate of federal tax, after the federal abatement, on manufacturing and processing income to 21%. In general, the reduced rate of tax applies to the lesser of the corporation's Canadian manufacturing and processing profits (a specifically defined term) and the portion of the corporation's taxable income considered to be derived from eligible manufacturing and processing activities [par. 125.1(1)(a)]. The base for this deduction excludes manufacturing and processing profits eligible for the small business deduction, discussed in the next chapter. Exhibit 11-4 summarizes the provision in subsection 125.1(1) as they would apply to a corporation that is not a Canadian-controlled private corporation.

EXHIBIT 11-4
Manufacturing and Processing Profits Deduction
for Public Corporations

7% of lesser of:

(a) manufacturing and processing profits, and

(b) taxable income, less 3* times the foreign tax deduction (computed without reference to the section 123.4 rate reduction) in respect of business income [ssec. 126(2)].

* [Proposed in the February 27, 2004 Revised Draft Legislation.]

Exhibit 11-5 illustrates how the manufacturing and processing profit deduction affects the calculation of effective total corporate tax introduced in Exhibit 11-3.

EXHIBIT 11-5
Hypothetical Tax Rates applicable to Taxable Income
eligible for Manufacturing and Processing Profits Deduction

Federal tax rate [ssec. 123(1)]	38.00%
Abatement for provincial tax [ssec. 124(1)]	(10.00)
Net federal tax after abatement	28.00%
Federal surtax @ 4% of above net federal tax of 28% [sec. 123.2]	1.12
M & P deduction [par. 125.1(1)(a)]	(7.00)
Net federal tax	22.12%
Provincial tax (assumed)*	11.00
Effective total tax	33.12%

* Some provinces have a reduced tax rate for M&P profits.

B. Eligibility

[ITA: 125.1(3)(b); IT-145R]

Corporations with income from a manufacturing or processing business qualify if gross revenues from Canadian manufacturing and processing exceed 10% of gross revenue from all Canadian active businesses [par. (l) in the definition of "manufacturing or processing" in ssec. 125.1(3)]. The term "manufacturing and processing" is not defined in the Act. Thus, the general meaning of the term as modified by case law applies. The term "manufacture" has been interpreted to mean the application of physical labour or mechanical power. The CRA indicates that the manufacture of goods normally involves "the creation of something or the shaping, stamping or forming of an object from something" [IT-145R].

"Processing" implies the use of some raw material to begin with. The ordinary meaning of the word (from a dictionary) would appear to include most food service establishments in terms of food preparation (but not serving) and packaging. The CRA views packaging and wrapping activities as "processing" provided that they are carried on in conjunction with other manufacturing and processing activities [IT-145R]. Breaking bulk and repackaging are generally considered processing. Thus, processing appears to include all of those operations which render a product more usable, that is, more marketable.

The following are some examples of cases in which the meaning of the term "manufacturing or processing" has been addressed. In *Nova Scotia Sand and Gravel Ltd. v. M.N.R.*, (F.C.A.) 80 DTC 6298, the Federal Court of Appeal held that excavating and extracting gravel for sale constituted manufacturing and processing. Intercepting and distributing a television signal was held not to be processing of goods in *London Cable TV v. M.N.R.*, (T.R.B.) 76 DTC 1328. However, packaging of potatoes and carrots after various preparatory steps was held to be processing in *Federal Farms Ltd. v. M.N.R.*, (Ex. Ct.) 66 DTC 5068; and slitting, levelling and shearing of steel was held to be processing in *Admiral Steel Products Ltd. v. M.N.R.*, (T.R.B.) 66 DTC 174. In *Mother's Pizza Parlour et al. v. The Queen*, (F.C.A.) 88 DTC 6397, the Federal Court of Appeal held that a restaurant building was not used primarily for the preparation of food and, hence, was not used in a processing activity.

The Act specifically lists in the definition of "manufacturing or processing" twelve activities that are not considered to be "manufacturing or processing" [ssec. 125.1(3)]. Note how an exception to the negative definition of manufacturing or processing can be used such that, for example, processing of iron ore beyond the pellet stage is considered to be manufacturing or processing [par. (g) of the definition of "manufacturing or processing" in ssec. 125.1(3)]. Furthermore, IT-145R provides the CRA's view on the excluded activities of construction, farming and fishing.

Once manufacturing or processing activities have been identified, it is necessary to determine Canadian-source manufacturing and processing profits. Part LII of the Regulations prescribes the rules referred to in the definition of "Canadian manufacturing or processing profits" [ssec. 125.1(3)] for determining manufacturing or processing profits. Regulation 5200 sets out a formula presented in Exhibit 11-6 for the computation of that portion of a corporation's profits that can be attributed to manufacturing and processing profits. Certain activities are considered to result in manufacturing and processing profits while other activities do not. "Qualified activities" are listed in Regulation 5202 along with a list of activities that are not included in the term "qualified activities". It is essential to become thoroughly familiar with the specific wording of all of the definitions in Regulation 5202.

EXHIBIT 11-6
Manufacturing and Processing Profits Formula for Most Corporations

$$MP = \frac{ML + MC}{L + C} \times ADJUBI$$

MP — Canadian manufacturing and processing profits eligible for the reduced rate of income tax.

ML — Cost of manufacturing and processing labour, i.e., $^{100}/_{75}$ths of direct manufacturing and processing labour, to a maximum of L, below.

L — Cost of labour, i.e., total labour related to income earned in Canada.

MC — Cost of manufacturing and processing capital, i.e., $^{100}/_{85}$ths of direct manufacturing and processing fixed annual capital cost (i.e., 10% of gross cost), to a maximum of C, below.

C — Cost of capital, i.e., total fixed annual capital cost (i.e., 10% of gross cost) related to active business income earned in Canada.

ADJUBI — Adjusted business income, i.e., net active business income earned in Canada (other than resource profits).

C. Elements of the Formula for Determining Manufacturing and Processing Profits

[ITR: 5202]

1. Adjusted business income

This is the base of income from which a portion is segregated for special treatment as manufacturing and processing profits by applying the low rate of tax. That base is essentially all active business income from Canadian sources [Reg. 5202] including the activities listed in the definition of "manufacturing or processing" [ssec. 125.1(3)]. Net resource income which reduces adjusted business income is, in general terms, income on which a depletion allowance is permitted [sec. 65] plus any income that arises from the sale of resource properties [Reg. 5203(1)]. For the purposes of this Regulation, the definition of "active business" [ssec. 248(1)] should be used. In the case of *Canadian Marconi Company v. The Queen*, (S.C.C.) 86 DTC 6526, the Supreme Court of Canada held that income from short-term investments was income from an active business and that it could be included in "adjusted business income". Perhaps, that is why subparagraph 125.1(1)(b)(iii) removes only Canadian and foreign investment income of Canadian-controlled private corporations, from taxable income in determining the base for the manufacturing and processing profit deduction. For such a corporation, investment income is treated separately for purposes that will be discussed fully in Chapter 12.

2. Cost of capital and cost of manufacturing and processing capital

The definitions of these terms are contained in Regulation 5202. "Cost of capital" includes virtually all depreciable property of the corporation other than such assets used in foreign business operations and those used to earn income other than active business income. The "gross cost" of an asset means its capital cost with some adjustments such as [Reg. 5202]:

(a) add back grants, subsidies, investment tax credits, etc. that were subtracted from capital cost [ssec. 13(7.1)];

(b) eliminate capitalized interest added [sec. 21]; and

(c) add back amounts deducted due to debt forgiveness [sec. 80].

Note that the definition uses only 10% of the gross cost of property to, in a sense, annualize the cost of capital property and put such property on a parallel basis with the cost of labour which is an annual cost.

"Rental cost" means the rents incurred under a lease, whether a "net" lease or a "gross" lease, for the use of a property [Reg. 5202].

To determine the "cost of manufacturing and processing capital", it is necessary to identify depreciable assets which are used directly in "qualified activities" and to determine the extent of such use. For certain assets such as buildings, material handling equipment, etc., it is necessary to make an allocation of cost on some reasonable basis. The definition of "qualified activities" begins with a list of nine specific activities [Reg. 5202]. The definition, then, adds all other activities that are performed in Canada directly in connection with manufacturing or processing and scientific research and experimental development as defined in Regulation 2900. Then, it concludes with a list of six activities that are not to be considered qualified activities. Note how receiving and storing of raw materials are considered to be qualified activities but purchasing of raw materials is not and storing of finished goods is not. The 100/85 gross-up applied to the cost so determined is to allow for costs which, while not directly related to manufacturing and processing, are ancillary to that activity. Note that the grossed-up cost cannot exceed the "cost of capital".

3. Cost of labour and cost of manufacturing and processing labour

The definitions of these terms are included in Regulation 5202. "Salaries and wages" is defined to mean salaries, wages and commissions, but does not include remuneration in the form of pension benefits, living allowances, stock option benefits, automobile standby charges, etc. [Reg. 5202]. Fringe benefits need not be excluded if insignificant. Also, included in the cost of labour are fees paid or payable to non-employees for functions relating to management or administration, scientific research [Reg. 2900] and services normally performed by an employee.

To determine the "cost of manufacturing and processing labour", it is necessary to calculate that portion of the cost of labour that reflects the extent to which salaries and wages and fees were paid or payable in connection with qualified activities as discussed above. Similarly, a 100/75 gross-up allows for ancillary costs. However, the grossed-up cost of manufacturing and processing labour cannot exceed the "cost of labour".

D. Application of the Rules

[ITA: 125.1; ITR: 5200]

Example Problem

The following data pertain to Effluent Processing Company Limited, a public corporation, for its taxation year ended December 31, 2005:

Processing revenues in Canada		$2,500,000
Processing expenses:		
direct labour	$1,427,500	
allocated portion of administration, material and plant overhead expenses	947,500	$2,375,000
Wholesale sales of fertilizer in Canada		$1,350,000
Wholesale expenses:		
direct labour	$ 322,500	
allocated portion of administration, material and plant overhead expenses	865,000	$1,187,500

The company's processing and wholesaling capacity is provided by owned fixed assets having a capital cost of $3,125,000 and leased fixed assets having an annual lease cost of $62,500. Seventy per cent of the owned fixed assets and 85% of the leased assets are used in processing.

In addition to the revenues noted above, the company received dividends in the amount of $25,000 from a Canadian subsidiary and interest income (i.e., investment income) of $40,000 from long-term government bonds which will be held to maturity in 2010. Administration and overhead expenses include $125,000 paid in salaries and wages to people not engaged in qualified manufacturing and processing activities.

— *REQUIRED*

(A) Calculate Canadian manufacturing and processing profits for the company in 2005.

(B) Calculate the manufacturing and processing profits deduction [par. 125.1(1)(*a*)] for 2005 assuming that the company is not eligible for a small business deduction.

(C) Calculate Part I taxes payable for 2005, assuming that all taxable income is earned in a province which uses federal taxable income as its base for a 11% provincial tax rate. Ignore any effects of LCT.

— *SOLUTION*

(A) (i) Calculation of "adjusted business income":

Processing sales	$2,500,000	
Less: processing expenses	2,375,000	$ 125,000
Wholesaling sales	$1,350,000	
Less: wholesaling expenses	1,187,500	162,500
Total (ADJUBI)		$ 287,500

Note that dividend and interest income is not income from an active business and, therefore, it is not included in adjusted business income.

(ii) Calculation of "cost of capital":

10% of gross capital cost of owned assets (10% of $3,125,000)	$ 312,500
Rental cost of assets	62,500
Cost of capital (C)	$ 375,000(I)

(iii) Calculation of "cost of manufacturing and processing capital":

Portion of cost of capital used in qualified M&P activities	
70% of $312,500	$ 218,750
85% of $62,500	53,125
Total	$ 271,875
100/85 of total (100/85 × $271,875) (MC)	$ 319,853(II)
Lesser of (I) and (II)	$ 319,853

(iv) Calculation of "cost of labour":

Salaries and wages (direct labour)	
Processing	$1,427,500
Wholesaling	322,500
Administration and overhead	125,000
Total (L)	$1,875,000(III)

(v) Calculation of "cost of manufacturing and processing labour":

Portion of cost of labour used in qualified M&P activities	
Direct processing labour	$1,427,500
100/75 of labour (100/75 × $1,427,500)	$1,903,333(IV)
Lesser of (III) and (IV)	$1,875,000

(vi) Calculation of "manufacturing and processing profits":

$$MP = \frac{MC + ML}{C + L} \times ADJUBI$$

$$= \frac{\$319,853 + \$1,875,000}{\$375,000 + \$1,875,000} \times \$287,500$$

$$= \underline{\$280,453}$$

(B) Calculation of manufacturing and processing profits deduction from tax:

7% of the lesser of:

(i) Canadian manufacturing and processing profits $280,453

(ii) Taxable income:
Income from all sources

Business income (see (A)(i) above)	$287,500	
Dividend income	25,000	
Interest income	40,000	$352,500
Less: inter-company dividends	25,000	$327,500

7% of $280,453 = (19,632)

(C) Calculation of Part I taxes payable:

Taxable income	$327,500
Basic federal tax (.38 × $327,500)	$124,450
Deduct: federal tax abatement (10% of $327,500)	32,750
Net amount	$ 91,700
Add: corporate surtax [sec. 123.2] (4% of ($124,450 – 10% of $327,500))	3,668
	$ 95,368
Deduct: manufacturing and processing profits deduction	(19,632)

tax reduction [ssec.123.4(2)]

taxable income	$327,500
less: 100/7 × M&P profits deduction (100/7 × $19,632) (should be equal to M&P profits)	280,453
net	$ 47,047

7% of $47,047	(3,293)
Part I tax payable (federal)	$ 72,443
Provincial tax (11% of $327,500)	36,025
Total tax payable	$108,648

IV.   CREDITS AVAILABLE TO ALL TAXPAYERS

A.   Foreign Tax Deduction

[ITA: 126]

1.   Purpose and approach

Residents of Canada, including corporations, are taxable on their world income even though part of this income may have been subject to tax in a foreign country. Section 126 is designed to mitigate the effects on a Canadian individual or corporate taxpayer of double taxation on income arising from a source outside Canada. Relief is granted by means of a deduction, from the Canadian tax otherwise payable, of all or part of the foreign tax.

The theory underlying this arrangement for a tax deduction is that the country where the income is earned has the first right to tax the income. If the country of the taxpayer's residence levies a higher rate of tax on the income, the taxpayer will pay tax at the higher rate, but part of that tax is paid to the country where the income was earned while the remainder will be paid to the country of the taxpayer's residence.

Since the foreign tax deduction is meant to reduce Canadian tax on foreign income that has been taxed elsewhere, there is no foreign tax deduction available on foreign income that is not taxed in Canada. If a source of income is exempt from tax in Canada, there is no Canadian tax to reduce with a foreign tax deduction. For example, certain dividends received by corporations resident in Canada from corporations, such as foreign subsidiaries, resident in another country are not taxable in Canada. Such dividends are, effectively, not taxable in Canada because, although they are included in Division B income, they are deductible under section 113. This provision is similar to section 112, which provides a deduction for dividends received from taxable Canadian corporations. These dividends, from foreign affiliates, that are deductible under section 113 are not eligible for the foreign tax credit, since any tax "that may reasonably be regarded as having been paid by the taxpayer in respect of income from a share of the capital stock of a foreign affiliate of the taxpayer" is excluded from foreign tax which is eligible for the credit [par. 126(1)(a)]. A foreign affiliate is defined, basically, as a corporation in which the taxpayer has at least 10% equity ownership [ssec. 95(1)].

On the other hand, types of foreign income that are included in Canadian income and, hence, are eligible for a foreign tax deduction include: income from an unincorporated foreign branch, dividend income that is not eligible for deduction under section 113 (e.g., dividends from a country with which Canada does not have a tax treaty, such as the Cayman Islands), or dividends income from a corporation which is not a foreign affiliate.

The Act takes three separate approaches to the foreign tax deduction. The first two, on which this chapter will focus, apply to residents of Canada. One refers to "non-business-income tax" [ssec. 126(1)]. The other refers to "business-income tax" [ssecs. 126(2)–(2.1)]. The third applies to non-residents of Canada referring to tax on certain capital gains on "taxable Canadian property" [ssec. 126(2.2)]. Where the taxpayer is eligible for a foreign tax deduction for "non-business-income tax" or on "business-income tax" paid to more than one foreign country, the taxpayer is required to compute separate deductions for each country [ssec. 126(6)]. It should be emphasized that with few exceptions, the same rules apply to both individuals and corporations. However, the following discussion will focus on the foreign tax deduction rules as they apply to corporations.

2. Non-business income tax deduction

Where a taxpayer has non-business income (e.g., interest income) from another country and has paid foreign income or profits taxes to the government of that country or to the government of a state, province or other political subdivision of that country [ssec. 126(7)], the taxpayer may take a deduction from Canadian tax equal to the lesser of [ssec. 126(1)]:

(a) the foreign non-business-income tax paid in respect of that foreign income; and

(b) foreign non-business income

$$\frac{\text{(Div. B)}}{\substack{\text{Income (Div. B) for the year} \\ \text{(from all sources) plus or} \\ \text{minus certain amounts}}} \times \text{tax otherwise payable [ssec. 126(7)]}$$

Note that part (b) attempts to estimate the Canadian tax paid on the foreign income. As a result, the credit against Canadian tax cannot exceed the estimated Canadian tax paid on the foreign income.

Both the numerator and denominator of the fraction in part (b) above are limited to the amounts of income (excluding income from a foreign affiliate) attributable to the period in the year during which the taxpayer was resident in Canada.

The amounts to be subtracted from the Division B income of a corporation in the denominator of the fraction are:

(a) the claims for net capital losses carried over [par. 111(1)(b)] because they directly offset taxable capital gains, with the result that they are not taxed; and

(b) the amount of taxable dividends received and deductible [sec. 112] and the amount of dividends received from a foreign affiliate and deductible [sec. 113], because they are not taxed under Part I.

The term "tax otherwise payable" is defined [ssec. 126(7)]. For purposes of the non-business income tax deduction, "tax otherwise payable" is defined in paragraph (a) of the definition of the term [ssec. 126(7)]. For corporations, it is the tax for the year after deducting the 10% abatement, but before deducting the tax rate reduction of a Canadian-controlled private corporation [sec. 123.4], the small business deduction [sec. 125], the manufacturing and processing profits deduction [sec. 125.1], the foreign tax deduction [sec. 126] and the deductions in section 127 and sections 127.2 to 127.4. The surtax [sec. 123.2] is included in tax otherwise payable. The net result is to determine an amount of tax that would include the Canadian tax on foreign non-business income. That amount would be net of the abatement and the general reduction for a corporation, other than a Canadian-controlled private corporation. Note that if a Canadian resident corporation's only source of income is from a foreign non-business asset,[b] all of its taxable income would be considered to be earned in a province and the corporation would receive a tax abatement of 10% of its full taxable income. Therefore, the Canadian tax otherwise payable on that income would be after the 10% reduction.

The following should be noted about the term "non-business income tax paid" used in subsection 126(1) as it applies to a corporation and defined in subsection 126(7):

(a) the foreign tax must be paid, not merely payable and the conversion of the foreign tax into its Canadian-dollar equivalent must be made at the rate of exchange prevailing at the time payment is made;

(b) the foreign tax must generally be in the nature of an income or profits tax;

(c) the term includes such income tax paid to the government of another country or to the government of a state, province or other political subdivision of that country;

(d) the term excludes "business income tax" paid in the other country; and

---

[b] This statement is not correct where the non-business income-producing asset is real property located in a foreign jurisdiction. In this situation, the presence of real property would normally result in a permanent establishment in that country and, hence, the corporation would not be eligible for the federal abatement.

(e) foreign non-business income tax deducted under subsection 20(12) must be excluded. Unlike a foreign "business" income deduction, described below, an unused foreign non-business income deduction cannot be carried forward. Therefore, consideration should be given to using the deduction under subsection 20(12) for these amounts. Since a deduction from tax (i.e., a tax credit) is preferable to a deduction from income, eligibility for a foreign tax credit should be determined first, with any unused balance of foreign taxes paid being taken as a deduction. This may result in a circular calculation because of the credit's dependence on net income after the deduction. An algebraic approach may be necessary to solve this problem.

3. Business income tax deduction

Where a resident of Canada carries on business in a foreign country, the foreign tax deduction rules allow for a three-year carryback and a seven-year [10-year proposed for taxation years ending after March 22, 2004 in the March 23, 2004 federal budget] carryforward of unabsorbed foreign business income tax paid in a taxation year. Thus, foreign business income tax paid in a taxation year but not deducted may be carried over and treated as if it were paid in a carryover taxation year.

In the case of a corporation resident in Canada, it would be considered to carry on business in a foreign country if the corporation had an *unincorporated* branch in that foreign country. If the Canadian resident corporation established a subsidiary in the foreign country, the business income of the subsidiary would be taxed by the foreign country as a separate entity and no business foreign tax credit would be available to the parent. Where the corporation operates in foreign countries through unincorporated branches, a business foreign tax credit will arise.

The deduction, as it applies to a corporation, is computed as the least of [ssec. 126(2)]:

(a) the total of the business-income tax paid [ssec. 126(7)] for the year in respect of all businesses carried on through an unincorporated branch by the taxpayer in a particular country, plus any "unused foreign tax credit" [ssec. 126(7)] from other years in respect of the same country as the taxpayer may wish to claim;

(b) $\dfrac{\text{foreign business income}}{\substack{\text{income (Div. B) for the year}\\ \text{(from all sources) plus or}\\ \text{minus certain amounts}^1}} \times$ tax otherwise payable[2]

(c) the tax otherwise payable[3] for the year after deducting any non-business income tax deduction under subsection 126(1).

NOTES: (1) The amounts to be added to and subtracted from Division B income are the same as those that were identified for the non-business income tax deduction.

(2) The tax otherwise payable, in this case, is defined in paragraph (c) of the definition of the term in subsection 126(7). It is the tax before any deduction for the tax rate reduction for a Canadian-controlled private corporation [sec. 123.4(3)] the federal tax abatement [sec. 124] and the deductions in sections 125 to 127 and 127.2 to 127.41 inclusive, but after the addition of the surtax in section 123.2 and the deduction for the large corporations tax liability in section 125.3. Note that, if foreign business income were a Canadian resident corporation's only source of income, none of its taxable income would likely be considered to be earned in a province and the corporation would receive no tax abatement. Therefore, the Canadian tax otherwise payable on that income would be before the 10% abatement.

(3) The tax otherwise payable, in this case, is defined in paragraph (b) of the definition of the term in subsection 126(7). It is the same amount as that computed pursuant to paragraph (c) of the definition of the term in subsection 126(7) in Note (2) above.

Example Problem 1 ——————————————————————————————————

You have audited the books of International Moneygrubbers Limited, a public corporation, and have determined that the income for tax purposes of $472,000 for the year ended December 31, 2005, has been calculated correctly. The following additional data are available:

Interest received from:

a U.S. company (net of $3,000 tax withheld).....................	$17,000
a British company (net of $1,500 tax withheld)	8,500
Business income (net of $9,800 tax paid) earned from an unincorporated branch in Turkey......................................	18,200
Donations	20,000
Dividend received from a taxable Canadian corporation.............	52,000
Taxable income earned in a province (computed by Reg.).............	375,000

— REQUIRED

Compute the maximum foreign tax credit available to the corporation for 2005 on the assumption that there is no Part I.3 tax liability.

— SOLUTION

(a) Calculation of taxable income:

Income for tax purposes.............................		$472,000
Less: donations [par. 110(1)(a)]	$20,000	
dividends [sec. 112]	52,000	72,000
Taxable income		$400,000

(b) Calculation of tax otherwise payable:

(i) For foreign non-business income tax credit:

Tax otherwise payable (38% of $400,000) ....(A)		$152,000
Less: 10% of $375,000		37,500
Net		$114,500
Surtax (4% of ($152,000 − 10% of $400,000))		4,480
Tax rate reduction @ 7% of $400,000		(28,000)
Tax otherwise payable ....(B)		$ 90,980

(ii) For foreign business income tax credit:[1]

Tax otherwise payable, per (A) above.........................	$152,000
Add: surtax	4,480
Less: tax rate reduction	(28,000)
Tax otherwise payable ....(C)	$128,480

(c) Calculation of foreign tax deduction:[2]

(i) Foreign non-business income:

Interest from U.S. company
lesser of:

(I) tax paid	$3,000	→ $3,000

$$(II) \quad \frac{\text{income from U.S.}}{\text{income less dividends}} \times \begin{array}{l}\text{tax otherwise} \\ \text{payable (B)}\end{array}$$

$$= \frac{\$20,000}{\$472,000 - 52,000} \times \$90,980 \quad .... \quad \underline{\$4,332}$$

Interest from British company
    lesser of:
        (I) tax paid . . . . $1,500 → $1,500

        (II) $\dfrac{\text{income from Britain}}{\text{income less dividends}} \times \begin{array}{l}\text{tax otherwise}\\ \text{payable (B)}\end{array}$

        $= \dfrac{\$10,000}{\$472,000 - 52,000} \times \$90,980$ $2,166

(ii) Foreign business income:
    least of:
        (I) tax paid . . . . $ 9,800

        (II) $\dfrac{\text{income from Turkey}}{\text{income less dividends}} \times \begin{array}{l}\text{tax otherwise}\\ \text{payable (C)}\end{array}$

        $= \dfrac{\$28,000}{\$472,000 - 52,000} \times \$128,480$ . . . . $ 8,565 → $8,565

        (III) tax otherwise payable (C) less
           non-business income tax deduction
           ($128,480 − ($3,000 + 1,500)) $123,980

(d) Total foreign tax deduction:
    Foreign non-business income
        U.S. source . . . . $ 3,000
        British source . . . . 1,500 $ 4,500

    Foreign business income 8,565

    Total deduction from tax $13,065

— NOTES TO SOLUTION

(1) If the Canadian income tax effects on foreign investment income could be isolated, as in the case where the corporation's only source of income was foreign non-business income, such as interest income, it would be considered to be earned in the province of which the taxpayer is a resident and, therefore, would be eligible for the federal tax abatement. As a result, it is the tax otherwise payable (B) after the abatement on which the non-business income tax deduction is based. On the other hand, foreign business income is assumed to be earned in a permanent establishment in the foreign country and, therefore, is not eligible for the federal tax abatement. Thus, the tax otherwise payable (C) before the abatement is the relevant base for the business income tax deduction.

(2) Note how these credits against Canadian tax do not exceed foreign tax paid on the foreign income. These reductions of Canadian tax are also restricted to the estimated amount of Canadian tax paid on the foreign income.

Example Problem 2

Reconsider the facts in Example Problem 1 with the additional information that income for tax purposes of $472,000 includes manufacturing and processing profits (MP, as determined by Regulation 5200) of $360,000.

— REQUIRED

Calculate total tax payable under Part I using a 11% provincial rate of tax applied to federal taxable income earned in a province.

—SOLUTION

Taxable income (as computed in Example Problem 1)		$400,000
Part I tax on taxable income:		
Tax @ 38% on $400,000		$152,000
Deduct: Federal tax abatement (10% of $375,000)		37,500
Net amount		$114,500
Add: Corporate surtax[1]		4,480
		$118,980
Deduct: M & P deduction[2]	$25,200	
Tax rate reduction[3]	2,800	
Non-business foreign tax credit[4]	4,500	
Business foreign tax credit[4]	8,565	41,065
Total federal tax		$ 77,915
Provincial tax @ 11% of $375,000		41,250
Total taxes payable		$119,165

—NOTES TO SOLUTION

(1) Corporate surtax

Tax @ 38% of $400,000	$152,000
Deduct: 10% of taxable income	40,000
	$112,000
4% of $112,000 (or 1.12% of $400,000 taxable income)	$ 4,480

(2) M & P deductions:
7% of lesser of:

(a) manufacturing and processing profits	$360,000
(b) taxable income	$400,000
deduct: foreign business tax credit × 3 ($9,800 × 3]) — see Note (3) below	29,400
	$370,600
7% of lesser amount (7% of $360,000)	$ 25,200

(3) Tax rate reduction

Taxable income:	$400,000
Less: 100/7 × M & P profits deduction (100/7 × $25,200)	360,000
Net	$ 40,000
7% of $40,000	$ 2,800

(4) Foreign non-business tax deduction and business deduction — See part (c) of Example Problem 1.

B. Investment Tax Credit

[ITA: 12(1)(*t*); 13(7), (7.1); 127(5)–(11); 127.1; ITR: 2900; 4600–4602; IC 78-4R3; IC 86-4R3]

1. Purpose

The investment tax credit (ITC) was introduced in 1975 as a temporary extra incentive to stimulate new investment in Canada in certain specific business sectors and regional locations. Since that time, the credit has been pared back to apply regionally only to the Gaspé and the Atlantic provinces for certain specific capital expenditures and to all of Canada for scientific research and experimental development expenditures (SR&ED).

Conceptually, the available investment tax credit is simply calculated by applying a "specified percentage" for one of the two categories described above to the capital cost of the asset acquired or the expenditure incurred. The actual amount of the ITC claimed by the taxpayer is deducted in the following taxation year from the capital cost of the asset acquired or the SR&ED pool. In addition, there is a carryover mechanism for available investment tax credits not claimed in a particular year.

Unfortunately, this simple concept is mired in a large number of complex provisions and regulations all of which often change. Rate changes alone require a constant monitoring of the taxation year in which ITCs are earned. In most situations, the assistance of a tax person, who specializes in this area, will be necessary. Therefore, the purpose of this section is to introduce, conceptually, the ramifications of this extremely important tax credit and to provide some simple examples of its application.

2. Computation of investment tax credit

Subsection 127(9) defines the basis for the computation of the available investment tax credit: the category of the asset or expenditure that is eligible for a credit, the "specified percentage" applicable to that category and the carryover rules. All of these variables have changed at least once and in some cases many times. The key to this maze of information is the year of the asset acquisition or the year of the expenditure since both the specified percentage and the carryover rules are governed by this date.

The cost of the capital asset to which the "specified percentage" is applied must be reduced by all government assistance (e.g., grants, subsidies, loans, etc.) and non-arm's length third-party assistance including certain specified contract payments for goods and services [ssecs. 127(11.6) to (11.8) and (16) to (21)].

The amount of the *available* investment tax credit which can be applied in a year is limited only by the Part I tax remaining after the deduction of any of the other corporate tax credits. Those available ITCs that are not applied in the year of acquisition or expenditure can be carried back three taxation years and forward ten taxation years. Because of the generous carryforward time-frame, it is reasonable that ITCs should be deducted last.

Exhibit 11-7 lists the investment tax credit rates which apply to the most common types of properties and expenditures, incurred by taxpayers other than Canadian-controlled private corporations (which are discussed in Chapter 12), which give rise to such credits. The specified percentages listed in the Exhibit vary, depending on the geographic location and nature of the property or expenditure.

All of the terms describing property will be discussed in more detail following the Exhibit.

EXHIBIT 11-7
Rates of Investment Tax Credits
(Non-Canadian-controlled private corporations only)
[ssec. 127(9)]

	Atlantic provinces and Gaspé	Balance of Canada
Qualified property	10%	0%
Qualified SR&ED*	20	20

* SR&ED refers to scientific research and experimental development as discussed in Chapter 4.

3. Qualified property

(a) *Time of Acquisition*

"Qualified property" is property that is a prescribed [Reg. 4600)] building, grain elevator or machinery and equipment [ssec. 127(9)]. Generally, a taxpayer is considered to have acquired depreciable property when title passes or when the taxpayer obtains all the incidents of title including possession, use and risk. Property is deemed not to have been acquired and, hence, not eligible for ITC until the property is "available for use", as discussed in Chapter 5 [ssec. 127(11.2)].

(b) *Type of Property*

To be "qualified property" the property must be new property which has not been used for any purpose prior to its acquisition. It must also meet certain other conditions prescribed by Part XLVI of the Regulations which lists prescribed buildings and prescribed machinery and equipment.

(c) *Use of the Property*

To qualify for the credit, the prescribed building or machinery and equipment must be used primarily in one of a broad range of activities. There is no minimum use period and no provision for recapture of the credit in the event of a change to a non-qualifying use or the sale of the asset. Uses of qualified property are listed in paragraphs (c) and (d) of the definition of "qualified property" in subsection 127(9). In the case of *Mother's Pizza Parlour (London) Limited et al. v. The Queen*, 85 DTC 5271, the Federal Court–Trial Division (affirmed by the Federal Court of Appeal, 88 DTC 6397) held that buildings from which dining room, take-out and delivery service was provided were not used for processing goods for sale, but for selling finished goods, since all ingredients for the pizza, including the dough, were purchased from independent suppliers. Hence, the building was not "qualified property" eligible for an investment tax credit at the time. In the case of a building, which is used primarily for eligible activities and partly for functions such as administration or warehousing, the entire cost would be recognized, providing the principal use of the building is an eligible activity.

(d) *Capital Cost Reduction*

In the taxation year following the year in which the investment tax credit is claimed, the capital cost of the depreciable asset is reduced by the amount of the credit claimed [par. 13(7.1)(e)]. In situations where the asset no longer exists (i.e., the property has been disposed of), there would be an income inclusion [par. 12(1)(t)] as a substitute for the capital cost reduction of the capital asset.

4. Qualified scientific research expenditure

Scientific research and experimental development expenditures are very generously treated by Canadian tax legislation. Not only is there a potential 100% write-off of qualifying expenditures and equipment [sec. 37], but there is also a 20% investment tax credit available. In addition, many of the provincial governments provide additional incentives for SR&ED expenditures. In the next chapter it will be shown that certain qualifying Canadian-controlled private corporations benefit from an even greater "specified percentage" and a potential refund for unclaimed ITCs.

"Qualified expenditure" is defined [ssec. 127(9)] to include scientific research and experimental development expenditures on new property and described in paragraph 37(1)(*a*) (current expenditures) and subparagraph 37(1)(*b*)(i) (capital expenditures). Excluded are prescribed expenditures listed in Regulation 2902. Note that paragraph 37(8)(*d*) excludes any capital expenditure made in respect of a building, including a leasehold interest (other than a prescribed special purpose building [Reg. 2903]). The definition also excludes any rental expense incurred for a building (other than a prescribed special purpose building). The provision further excludes payments made to others to enable the recipient to acquire a building or a leasehold interest in a building.

In the taxation year following the year in which an ITC deduction is made, the amount of the ITC claimed is deducted from the pool of unclaimed SR&ED expenditures. Remember that both current and capital expenditures that are eligible SR&ED expenditures are either written off in the year of the expenditure or placed in a pool of unclaimed expenditures. Therefore, for capital expenditures that are eligible SR&ED expenditures there is no capital cost from which the ITC could be deducted; hence, the deduction reduces the unclaimed SR&ED expenditure pool. Where this pool is nil, then there would be an income inclusion [par. 12(1)(*t*)].

Example Problem

In 2005, Investit Limited has acquired $100,000 of Class 8 (20%) assets eligible as "qualified property" for the 10% investment tax credit in the Gaspé area. The corporation's federal income tax rate after the abatement and the general rate reduction is 22.12%. Its taxable income before capital cost allowance on the eligible property is $30,000.

The corporation is not eligible for any other tax credits and paid no tax in the preceding three years.

— REQUIRED

(A) What is the maximum investment tax credit available?

(B) Compute the net federal Part I tax payable after the investment tax credit.

(C) What is the amount of the investment tax credit available for carryover?

(D) Compute the U.C.C. balance in Class 8 at the end of the following year, assuming the new assets are the only assets in the class.

— SOLUTION

(A) The maximum investment tax credit available will be $10,000 (i.e., 10% of $100,000).

(B) Taxable income before capital cost allowance on qualified
     property $30,000
    Less: capital cost allowance on qualified property:
     $1/2 \times 20\%$ of $100,000 .... (10,000)

    Taxable income $20,000

    Net federal tax @ 22.12% .... $ 4,424
    Less: investment tax credit .... (4,424)

    Net federal tax payable under Part I .... Nil

(C) The remaining investment tax credit of $5,576 (i.e., $10,000 − $4,424) may be carried back three and forward ten years.

(D) U.C.C. in Class 8 before C.C.A. in first year $100,000
    Less: C.C.A. claimed in first year .... (10,000)

    U.C.C. at beginning of second year .... $ 90,000
    Less: ITC claimed in first year .... (4,424)

    U.C.C. before C.C.A. in second year .... $ 85,576
    Less: C.C.A. claimed in second year .... (17,115)

    U.C.C. balance after C.C.A. .... $ 68,461

Note that any investment tax credit for depreciable property carried over to another year and used to reduce tax in that year will reduce the undepreciated capital cost balance in the year following the year of use or the year following the purchase, whichever is later. This will occur until the remaining investment tax credit is fully utilized or expires. The undepreciated capital cost balance will not be reduced by expired investment tax credits. Under certain conditions, it may be worthwhile to deduct no capital cost allowance in order to be able to claim more investment tax credit that would otherwise expire. However, the facts of each case must be analyzed carefully.

Example Problem

In 2005, Developit Limited incurred $100,000 of qualified scientific research and experimental development expenditures eligible for the 20% investment tax credit. The corporation's federal income tax rate after the abatement and the general rate reduction is 22.12%. Its taxable income before the deduction of the SR&ED expenditures under section 37 is $150,000.

The corporation is not eligible for any other tax credits and paid no tax in the preceding three years.

— REQUIRED

(A) What is the maximum investment tax credit available?

(B) Compute the net federal Part I tax payable after the investment tax credit.

(C) What is the amount, if any, of the investment tax credit carryover?

(D) Compute the corporation's deduction or income included in the following year if no further SR&ED expenditures are made.

—SOLUTION

(A) The maximum investment tax credit is:
20% of $100,000 = $20,000

(B) Taxable income before sec. 37 deduction................. $150,000

Sec. 37 deduction.. (100,000)

Taxable income .... $ 50,000

Net tax @ 22.12%....................................... $ 11,060

Investment tax credit (maximum)........................ (11,060)

Net federal tax payable under Part I   Nil

(C) The remaining investment tax credit of $8,940 (i.e., $20,000 −$11,060) may be carried back three years and forward 10 years. In this particular case, the corporation paid no tax in the preceding three years, so it must carry the balance of ITC forward.

(D) Sec. 37 SR&ED expenditures in 2005 .... $100,000

Sec. 37 SR&ED deduction in 2005 .... (100,000)

Balance at the beginning of 2006 .... Nil

ITC claimed in 2005 .... (11,060)

Recapture in 2006 [par 12(1)(t)] 11,060

Balance of ITC claimed in 2005........................ Nil

As the remaining ITC of $8,940 is claimed in a carryforward year, the amount claimed must be brought into income, as recapture, in the year following the year of claim.

Had there been a balance of the $100,000 that was not deducted under section 37, the balance would form a pool of SR&ED expenditures which could be deducted in a future year. Where a balance in the SR&ED pool exists, the amount claimed as ITC in a year is deducted from the balance in the SR&ED pool in the following year.

5. Prescribed Proxy Amount

Where business overhead expenses can be allocated to scientific research and experimental development costs, such overhead expenses will be included in the base on which the 20% investment tax credit for SR&ED expenditures is calculated. In a situation where a business is unable to allocate overhead expenses to SR&ED, the investment tax credit base would be relatively lower, resulting in a lower investment tax credit. As an alternative to allocating overhead expenses, for the purposes of computing the investment tax credit, use of a prescribed proxy amount (PPA) is permitted [ssec 127(9) in paragraph (b) of the definition of "qualified expenditure"]. The PPA is computed by formula which is based on salaries paid to employees directly engaged in SR&ED in Canada [Reg. 2900(4) and (5)]. Use of the PPA method to account for overhead expenses in the calculation of the SR&ED investment tax credit must be elected annually. A more elaborate discussion of the PPA method and an example in which the calculation is demonstrated is presented in Chapter 12, where the application of the SR&ED investment tax credit to Canadian-controlled private corporations is discussed. However, it should be recognized that the PPA election is available to all taxpayers eligible for a SR&ED investment tax credit [ssec. 127(5)].

REVIEW QUESTIONS

(1) Mr. Confused has been trying to prepare the corporate tax returns for his company and cannot seem to get the treatment of charitable donations sorted out. He cannot find the place to put the tax credit for the donations and he is not sure what the limits are. Can you help him?

(2) If a company finds that it has non-capital loss carryovers that are going to expire in the next few years, what tax planning steps can be taken to use up some of these losses without selling the company or buying another company?

(3) Mr. Jones has just bought all of the shares of a company that has some net capital losses being carried forward as well as accrued capital losses on some of its assets. What happens to them? Is there any relief?

(4) There are two basic types of restrictions on losses available for carryover. What are these restrictions and how do they affect the application of losses?

(5) Mr. Magoo bought all the shares of Profitco Ltd. on July 1 of this year, and is expecting to combine the profitable operations of Profitco with the loss operations of his current corporation. However, for Profitco's deemed year-end of June 30, he hopes to offset the six months of profitable operations with a full year of CCA in order to minimize the tax liability. Profitco's normal year-end was December 31. Comment on his plan.

(6) What are the three main objectives of tax provisions affecting the taxation of corporations?

(7) MultiCo Inc. has permanent establishments in Ontario and Alberta. The Alberta operation normally accounted for 20% of the allocation of taxable income. However, in the current year, a salesman in Ontario sold a large order to a customer in Alberta and the goods were shipped directly from Ontario. How does this special sale impact the allocation to Alberta?

(8) Export Inc. is a company located in Windsor that manufactures fire-fighting equipment for the City of Detroit. It does not have any domestic sales; everything is exported to the U.S. Will the company qualify for the M & P profits deduction?

(9) Since residents of Canada are taxable on their world income, why does Canada give a foreign tax credit for taxes paid to another country?

(10) In the calculation of non-business foreign tax credit the "tax otherwise payable" calculation is reduced by the 10% federal abatement. Why?

(11) LossCo Inc. has a loss from operations for the year while at the same time earning interest of $5,000 from the U.S. on which $750 of tax was withheld. How can LossCo. treat the $750 of foreign tax paid on its tax return?

MULTIPLE CHOICE QUESTIONS

Question 1

Helen acquired all of the voting shares of Loss Co. from a non-related individual on February 1, 2005. Loss Co. has always had a December 31 year-end since its incorporation. Which one of the following statements is TRUE?

(A) Loss Co. had a deemed year-end February 1, 2005.

(B) Loss Co. may select any date, within the 53-week period commencing February 1, 2005, as its new year-end.

(C) Loss Co. must continue to have a December 31 year-end unless the CRA grants permission for a change.

(D) Loss Co. had a deemed year-end on January 31, 2005 and is required to keep January 31 as its year-end for the future.

Question 2

Jim acquired control of Smart Ltd. from an unrelated person on May 15, 2005. The following information relates to the inventory and capital assets owned by Smart Ltd. at that time.

	Cost	FMV
Inventory	$120,000	$100,000
Land	200,000	140,000
Building	100,000	75,000
Marketable securities	20,000	30,000

For its taxation year ended on May 14, 2005, Smart Ltd. is required to recognize a capital loss of:

(A) $85,000

(B) $80,000

(C) $60,000

(D) $50,000

Question 3

On April 1, 2005, Calm Corp purchased 72% of the voting shares of X Ltd. from an unrelated person. The tax position of the fixed assets of X Ltd. at that time is summarized below.

	Cost	UCC	FMV
Automobiles (Class 10)	$100,000	$ 42,000	$45,000
Computer equipment (Class 10)	64,000	38,000	33,000
Computer software (Class 12)	30,000	Nil	5,000
Office furniture & equipment (Class 8)	80,000	58,000	48,000

The business loss of X Ltd. for the year ended March 31, 2005, will be increased by deemed CCA of:

(A) $7,000

(B) $10,800

(C) $15,000

(D) $23,000

Question 4

For its year ended December 31, 2004, its first year-end since its incorporation, Loss Co reported the following income (losses) for tax purposes.

Business loss (retailer of widgets)	$ (20,000)
Capital loss	(6,000)

On January 1, 2005, Profit Co acquired control of Loss Co from an unrelated person and transferred its profitable gadget retailing business to Loss Co. For its year ending December 31, 2005, Loss Co is expected to have the following income/losses.

Business loss (widgets)	$ (3,000)
Business income (gadgets)	15,000
Taxable capital gain on sale of capital asset in March 2005 (capital asset was owned since March 2004)	6,000

Assuming widgets and gadgets are similar products, which one of the following statements is TRUE?

(A) For its year ending December 31, 2005, Loss Co will be able to deduct net capital losses of $3,000, provided the widget retailing business is carried on throughout the taxation year ended December 31, 2005 with a reasonable expectation of profit.

(B) For its year ending December 31, 2005, Loss Co will be able to deduct non-capital losses of $18,000 (maximum), provided the widget retailing business is carried on throughout the taxation year ended December 31, 2005, with a reasonable expectation of profit.

(C) For its year ending December 31, 2005, Loss Co will be able to deduct non-capital losses of $12,000 (maximum), provided the widget retailing business is carried on throughout the taxation year ended December 31, 2005, with a reasonable expectation of profit.

(D) For its year ending December 31, 2005, Loss Co will be able to deduct non-capital losses of $15,000 (maximum), provided the widget retailing business is carried on throughout the taxation year ended December 31, 2005, with a reasonable expectation of profit.

Question 5

During 2005, Curran Ltd, a public corporation, has net income for tax purposes of $600,000, including $100,000 of dividends from taxable Canadian corporations and $250,000 of manufacturing and processing profits eligible for the M & P deduction. It made $200,000 of charitable donations during the year. Income earned in a province was 90%.

What is Curran Ltd's taxable income for the year?

(A) $600,000

(B) $500,000

(C) $400,000

(D) $300,000

Question 6

Refer to the facts given in Question 5 above. What is Curran Ltd's federal tax payable for the year?

(A) $51,860

(B) $68,520

(C) $69,360

(D) $72,860

EXERCISES

Exercise 1

[ITA: 110.1; 111]

Generous Limited has income (loss) under Division B of $(7,350) in 2003, $22,050 in 2004 and $14,700 in 2005. During this period it made donations to registered charities of $2,625 in 2003, $4,700 in 2004 and $12,000 in 2005. It also made a donation of ecologically sensitive land valued at $19,700 to the Government of Canada in 2004. The company began operations in 2003.

— REQUIRED

Compute the corporation's taxable income for the years indicated.

Exercise 2

[ITA: 110.1; 111]

Determined Limited predicts, with reasonable accuracy, its income under Division B before capital cost allowances will be: $100,000 in 2003, $115,000 in 2004 and $132,250 in 2005. Capital cost allowances available are expected to be $200,000 in 2003, $170,000 in 2004 and $150,000 in 2005. It made charitable donations of $10,000 in 1999 and $11,500 in 2000 which it could not absorb before 2003.

— REQUIRED

How can the company maximize its charitable donation deduction while minimizing the taxes it pays in the period shown? (Hint: Take advantage of the loss carryover rules.)

Exercise 3

[ITA: 111(8)]

Losses Unlimited Limited has computed the following income (loss) for the year ended December 31, 2005:

Loss from business..	$(129,000)
Income from property including dividends of $10,750 received from taxable Canadian corporations......................	32,250
Capital gains	46,400
Capital losses	(12,000)
Business investment loss...	(16,000)

The corporation has a net capital loss of $27,000 arising from 1999.

— REQUIRED

Compute the corporation's non-capital loss for the year.

Exercise 4

[ITA: 111(8)]

Capital Losses Limited had a large allowable capital loss of $51,750 on one transaction during its taxation year ended December 31, 2005. In addition, the following information pertains to its situation for the year:

Income from business	$155,250
Income from property	17,000
Taxable capital gain	4,700
Allowable business investment loss (not included in above allowable capital loss)	(8,300)

— REQUIRED

Compute the corporation's net capital loss for the year.

Exercise 5

[ITA: 111(1), (1.1)]

Given income from business of $55,500 and a taxable capital gain of $37,000 in 2005, how much of the following losses will be available for carryforward after this year:

Non-capital losses (expiring beyond 2006)	$82,500?
Net capital losses (1999)..	$60,000?

Exercise 6

[ITA: 111(4), (5), (5.1), (5.2)]

All of the voting shares of Loser Limited, a manufacturer of widgets, have been acquired by Holdco Ltd., an investment holding company. At the time of the acquisition on March 10, 2005, Loser Limited had non-capital business losses of $600,000 generated in 2004. Loser Limited also had $30,000 of net capital losses carried forward from 1999. As well, at the time of the acquisition, it was discovered that the balance of undepreciated capital cost in its Class 8 was $70,000 while the fair market value of the assets in that class was only $40,000. The balance in its cumulative eligible capital account (being from the acquisition on August 31, 2004, of an exclusive customer list) was $50,000 while the fair market value of the customer list was $68,000. The corporation's inventory had a cost of $630,000, while its market value was $680,000. The book value of the corporation's receivables was $240,000, while its realizable value was estimated at $225,000. The corporation's only non-depreciable capital property, land, had accrued gains of $56,000 over its cost of $200,000. Loser Limited has a December 31 year-end.

The corporation had business losses of $3,000 from January 1 to March 9, 2005.

The holding company will inject added capital and augment the management of Loser Limited in an attempt to turn Loser's widget manufacturing business around.

—REQUIRED

(A) What are the tax implications of the acquisition of the shares of Loser Limited by Holdco Ltd., assuming the maximum election under paragraph 111(4)(e) is made?

(B) Determine the minimum amount of elected proceeds under paragraph 111(4)(e) to offset expiring losses, if the accrued gains on the land were $100,000 instead of the $56,000 and Loser Limited had an additional loss arising from property of $10,000.

Exercise 7

[ITA: 3; 110.1–112]

Reconsider the example problem of Frenzied Taxpayers Limited in this chapter at page 571. If $7,900 less capital cost allowance had been taken in 2004, all $23,000 of the inter-company dividends could have been deducted, pursuant to section 112, in 2004.

—REQUIRED

Re-calculate the taxable income of the corporation for the years indicated after taking $7,900 less in capital cost allowance for Class 8 in 2004. Comment on whether the corporation is in a better tax position at the end of 2005 with respect to capital cost allowance and taxable income under this alternative.

Exercise 8

[ITA: 110.1; 111; 112]

Puttingitall Together Limited, a Canadian corporation, had its net income under Division B computed as follows for the year ending December 31:

Par. 3(a)	Income from non-capital sources:	
	Income from business operations...........	$ 66,625
	Income from foreign property	7,175
	Dividends from taxable Canadian corporations	12,300
Par. 3(b)	Net taxable capital gains	30,750
	Income under Division B	$116,850

During the year the corporation made charitable donations of $80,000. Its carryforward position from the previous year was as follows:

Charitable donations	$10,250
Non-capital losses	61,500
Net capital losses (realized in 1999)	41,000

—REQUIRED

Compute the corporation's taxable income for the current year.

Exercise 9

[ITA: Part I.3]

Takem-Over Unlimited Ltd., a widely-held public company operating mainly in the investment business, had the following balance sheet as at its year-end, December 31, 2005:

	($000's)
Cash	5,000
Accounts receivable, net of $1,000,000 allowance	45,000
Inventory	50,000
Investments	600,000
Fixed assets	100,000
Total assets	800,000
Accounts payable	175,000
Deferred revenue	15,000
Bonds payable	350,000
Common shares	360,000
Deficit	(100,000)
Total liabilities and equity	800,000

The investments consist of $100,000,000 in 3-year term deposits at a Canadian chartered bank, $250,000,000 in shares of Canadian public companies, $175,000,000 in shares of U.S. public companies and a $75,000,000 demand loan to a private company.

The accounts payable include a trade debt of $5,000,000 to a related company that has been left outstanding for 18 months while Takem-Over works out its cash flow problems.

The deferred revenue consists of $5,000,000 of prepaid rent and $10,000,000 of loan guarantee payments that are being amortized over the 24-month life of the guarantee.

Takem-Over's taxable income for this taxation year ended December 31, 2005, was $20,000,000. The federal abatement amounted to $1,840,000.

— REQUIRED

Determine Takem-Over's Part I.3 tax liability for the year, assuming no unused surtax credits are available. Assume also that Takem-Over is allocated all of the capital deduction in its related group of corporations.

Exercise 10

[ITA: 125.1]

Processor Limited is a wholly-owned subsidiary of a foreign corporation. Processor Limited is incorporated in Canada and is engaged in processing activity in Canada. In its current taxation year ended December 31, the corporation's income under Division B for tax purposes was $500,000. Its available non-capital loss carryforward was $250,000.

The corporation's adjusted business income was computed at $375,000. Its direct processing labour was determined to be $2,855,000 out of a total cost of labour of $3,750,000. Its direct processing cost of capital was $543,750 out of a total cost of capital of $750,000.

Processor Limited was eligible for a foreign business tax credit of $15,000. It also had interest income from the investment of short-term cash surpluses in Canadian marketable securities. This amounted to $19,000 and had been included in income under Division B as determined above.

— REQUIRED

Calculate the manufacturing and processing profits deduction for the current year.

Exercise 11

[ITA: 126]

Exporter Limited is a Canadian public company carrying on a part of its business through an unincorporated branch in Japan. Its income from that business in Japan for the current taxation year ended December 31 was 61,318,408 yen. The corporation paid income tax instalments on that income during the year of 24,527,363 yen. During the year the exchange rate was 1 yen = .01206 Canadian dollars.

During its current taxation year ended December 31, Exporter's income under Division B was $2,500,000 excluding the income from Japan. During the year, the corporation received dividends of $100,000 from taxable Canadian corporations. This amount was included in the computation of Division B income. The corporation was also able to deduct $25,000 of its net capital losses carried forward. There was no foreign investment income during the year.

— *REQUIRED*

Compute the corporation's foreign business tax credit for the year.

Exercise 12

[ITA: 110–112; 123; 124; 125.1; 126; 127]

Maxprof Limited is a Canadian public company with the following income under Division B for its taxation year ended December 31, 2005:

Manufacturing profits (computed by Reg. 5200)	$1,495,000
Foreign business profits (before $36,800 in taxes paid)	115,000
Dividends from taxable Canadian corporations	517,500
Dividends from foreign investments (before $25,875 in taxes withheld)	172,500
Canadian interest income (investment income)	345,000
Income under Division B	$2,645,000

During the year the company made donations of $69,000 to registered charities and $5,750 to federal political parties. It was carrying forward non-capital losses of $127,600. It is considered to earn 86% of its taxable income in Canada, as computed by the Regulation.

— *REQUIRED*

Compute the federal Part I tax payable for the year. (For the calculation of the manufacturing and processing profits deduction, assume that the foreign tax credit is equal to the foreign tax paid. However, show the full calculation of the foreign tax credits, including the effect of the general tax reduction.)

Exercise 13

[ITA: 127]

Consider the following data:

Cost of qualified property eligible for investment tax credit in Nova Scotia	$900,000
Capital cost allowance class (rate)	Class 1 (4%)
Taxable income before capital cost allowance on above	$300,000
Federal tax rate after abatement, surtax and reduction	22.12%
Federal political contributions tax credit	$500

— *REQUIRED*

Compute the amount of the investment tax credit that will be deductible for the year and the net federal Part I tax payable after the investment tax credit.

Exercise 14

[ITA: 110–112; 123; 125.1; 126; 127; 127.1]

Reconsider the data in Exercise 11. Assume that "qualified property" for Class 43 has been purchased in the Atlantic provinces for $3,500,000 in the year. Also, assume that manufacturing profits given as $1,495,000 in Exercise 11 will be reduced by capital cost allowance on this new property to equal the amount computed by Regulation 5200.

— REQUIRED

Compute the maximum investment tax credit deduction for the year. (For the calculation of the manufacturing and processing profits deduction, assume that the foreign tax credit is equal to the foreign tax paid. However, show the full calculation of the foreign tax credits, including the effect of the general tax reduction.)

ASSIGNMENT PROBLEMS

Problem 1

[ITA: 3; 110.1–112]

The following data summarize the operations of Red Pocket Limited for the years of 2002 to 2005 ended September 30.

	2002	2003	2004	2005
Income (loss) from business...........	$54,000	$32,000	$(75,000)	$62,500
Dividend income — Taxable Canadian corporations	42,500	22,500	18,000	10,500
Taxable capital gains	11,000	2,500	5,000	9,000
Allowable capital losses..............	2,000	4,500	3,500	—
Allowable business investment loss.....	3,750	—	—	—
Charitable donations	23,000	9,000	3,000	13,000

The corporation has a net capital loss balance of $13,500 which arose in 1998.

— REQUIRED

Compute the taxable income for Red Pocket Limited for the years indicated and show the amounts that are available for carryforward to 2006. (Deal with each item line-by-line across the years, rather than computing income one year at a time.)

Problem 2

[ITA: 111(4), (5), (5.1); 249(4)]

On November 1, 2005, Chris purchased all the issued shares of Transtek Inc. from an acquaintance, Tom. Transtek carries on a transmission repair business and has done so since its incorporation on January 1, 2004. In addition to the transmission repair business, Transtek rents out a small building it owns. Neither the transmission repair business nor the rental endeavour has been successful.

When Chris purchased Transtek, his financial projections indicated that Transtek would have significant income within two years. Chris credited Transtek's failure to Tom's brash personality and laziness. Chris, on the other hand, has a strong work ethic and has many contacts in the automotive industry to refer work to him.

The values of the capital assets owned by Transtek at the time of purchase by Chris are as follows:

	Repair shop		Rental property	
	Land	Building	Land	Building
F.M.V.....................	$140,000	$230,000	$70,000	$120,000
Cost/A.C.B.	80,000	150,000	90,000	120,000
U.C.C...................	—	147,000	—	120,000

Chris selected June 30, 2006, as the first fiscal year-end for Transtek after his purchase. The following is a schedule of Transtek's income (and losses) from its inception, January 1, 2004, through June 30, 2007.

Period	Transmission repair business	Rental income (loss)	Capital Loss
Jan. 1/2004–Dec. 31/2004	$(40,000)	$(2,000)	$(10,000)
Jan. 1/2005–Oct. 31/2005	(60,000)	(5,000)	—
Nov. 1/2005–June 30/2006	(25,000)	6,000	—
July 1/2006–June 30/2007	54,000	11,000	—

— REQUIRED

(A) Discuss the tax implications of the acquisition of Transtek Inc. on November 1, 2005, ignoring all possible elections/options.

(B) Determine the tax consequences of the acquisition of Transtek Inc. under the assumption that:

(i) the maximum amount of all elections/options is utilized; and

(ii) the partial amount of all elections/options is utilized so that only enough income is generated to offset most or all of the losses which would otherwise expire on the acquisition of control.

Problem 3

[ITA: 111(4), (5), (5.1); 249(4)]

In 2002, a chain of bakeries, called Buscat Ltd., commenced operation. The industry is highly competitive and because of Mr. Buscat's lack of marketing skills, the corporation incurred losses in the first three taxation years of operations as follows:

Taxation year-end	Non-capital losses	Capital losses
Dec. 31, 2002	$60,000	$12,000
Dec. 31, 2003	45,000	8,000
Dec. 31, 2004	25,000	4,000

On July 1, 2005, Mr. Buscat decided to sell 75% of his common shares to Mr. Bran, owner of Buns Plus Ltd. Mr. Bran has been in the business of supplying bread dough, pastry dough and bun bags for ten years and has been very successful. Buns Plus Ltd. has two divisions: a bakery and a coffee shop, which it intends to transfer to Buscat Ltd.

The following income tax data relates to Buscat Limited's operations from January 1, 2005 to June 30, 2005:

(a) Business loss (before inventory valuation)	$10,000			
(b) Allowable capital loss	2,000			
(c) Property loss	5,500			
(d) Assets at June 30, 2005:				

	Cost/A.C.B.	U.C.C.	F.M.V.
Inventory	$ 85,000	—	$ 65,000
Land	155,000	—	195,000
Building	65,000	$45,000	75,000
Bakery equipment..................	100,000	86,000	70,000

During the later part of the 2005 calendar year, the bakery/coffee shop of Buns Plus Ltd. was transferred to Buscat Ltd. For the six-month period ending on December 31, 2005, Buscat Limited had net income of $90,000 from all its businesses.

The net income earned was as follows:

Buscat bakery......................................	$(55,000)
Buns Plus bakery...................................	130,000
Coffee shop	15,000
	$ 90,000

In the 2006 taxation year, Buscat Ltd. expects to earn $250,000, of which $65,000 will be from the original Buscat bakery business and $20,000 from the coffee shop business.

— REQUIRED

Prepare an analysis of the income tax implications of the acquisition of shares. In your analysis, consider the two election options from which an election choice is most likely to be made.

Problem 4

[ITA: 9–20; 38–55; 110.1–112]

The controller of Video Madness Inc. has prepared the accounting income statement for the year ended April 30, 2005:

VIDEO MADNESS INC.

INCOME STATEMENT

FOR THE YEAR ENDED APRIL 30, 2005

Sales		$995,000
Cost of sales	$523,000	
Administrative expenses	185,000	708,000
Operating income		$287,000
Other income and expenses		55,000
		$342,000
Provision for income taxes		102,000
Net income		$240,000

Other Information

(1) Included in the calculation of "Administrative expenses":

(a) Interest on late income tax payments	$ 435
(b) Depreciation and amortization (maximum capital cost allowance of $149,500)	104,900
(c) Club dues for the local Country Club	1,750
(d) Federal political contributions	2,500
(e) Donations to registered charities	22,500
(f) Property tax with respect to vacant land not being used in the course of the business	3,000
(g) Life insurance premium with respect to the president (the company is the beneficiary; not required for financing)	1,950

(2) Included in the calculation of "Other income and expenses":

(a) Landscaping of ground around new premise	4,800
(b) Fees paid with respect to the investigation of a suitable site for the company's manufacturing plant	5,500
(c) Dividends received from taxable Canadian corporation of $42,800 and foreign corporation dividends received (not from a foreign affiliate) of $5,500 (Cdn.)	48,300
(d) Gain from the sale of another piece of land, used in the business, sold for $200,000 in March (purchased for $73,800)	126,200
(e) Loss on sale of investments held as capital property purchased for $85,000 and sold for $75,000	10,000

(3) Loss carryforwards from 2004 are:

(a) Non-capital losses	73,800
(b) Net capital losses (realized in 1999)	75,000

—*REQUIRED*

Prepare a schedule reconciling the accounting net income to income for tax purposes and taxable income. Indicate the appropriate statutory reference for your inclusions or exclusions.

Problem 5

[ITA: 124; ITR: 400]

The taxpayer, whose head office was in Manitoba, manufactured and sold various fans. Local sales agencies were maintained in Ontario and in Quebec. At the Ontario agency, two qualified representatives handled business under the company name. They were authorized to sign quotations. Contracts could be made, terms of payment arranged and credit given without reference to the head office in Winnipeg. The company name was displayed for public visibility, was used on calling cards, and was listed in the telephone directory. The Ontario agency, occupying one-half of a building with warehouse facilities, maintained an inventory worth about $6,000. Orders for standard-sized fans were filled from stock-in-trade. Orders for large fans were filled from the head office in Winnipeg. The Quebec agency was substantially similar to that in Ontario.

— REQUIRED

Determine whether or not the company has a "permanent establishment" in the provinces of Ontario and Quebec. In reaching a conclusion, compare this situation with the case of *M.N.R. v. Sunbeam* discussed in this chapter.

Problem 6

[ITA: Part I.3]

Larger Than Life Inc., a public corporation in the service industry, had the following balance sheet as at December 31, 2005:

	($ 000's)
Cash	40,000
Accounts receivable (net)	50,000
Inventory	60,000
Investment in Canadian subsidiary	120,000
Unsecured demand loan to Mr. Filth E. Rich	60,000
Future income taxes (debit)	20,000
Total assets	350,000
Accounts payable	55,000
Bank indebtedness (due on demand)	75,000
Mortgage due to Mrs. Low N. Shark	35,000
Common shares	65,000
Retained earnings	120,000
Total liabilities and equity	350,000

The investment has been accounted for using the equity basis with the carrying value being computed as follows:

Original cost of shares	$110,000
Accumulated share of subsidiary's earnings	20,000
Accumulated dividends received	(10,000)
Carrying value	$120,000

Larger Than Life's taxable income for its taxation year ended December 31, 2005, was $9,000,000 with 82% of its income being earned in a province. Larger Than Life grew significantly during 2005 In 2004, the corporation was not even subject to Part I.3 tax and its taxable income was only $800,000 (all earned in the province of Ontario). The corporation had no taxable income in the prior six years.

— REQUIRED

Determine Larger Than Life's Part I.3 tax liability for its 2005 tax year. Assume that Larger Than Life is allocated $40,000,000 of the capital deduction in its related group of corporations.

Problem 7

[ITA: 125.1]

One of your manufacturing clients, Mano-Pac Limited, a public company, provides you with the following information in order to calculate their manufacturing and processing profit deduction:

(a) Salary expenses are represented by:	
Accounting staff	$ 200,000
Quality control staff	150,000
Plant staff	800,000

Plant supervisors and maintenance	90,000
Distribution staff (responsible for distribution of finished products)	65,000
Receiving department staff (responsible for receiving and storing raw materials).....................................	45,000
Clerk responsible for purchasing raw materials	35,000
	$1,385,000

(b) Fixed assets of Mano-Pac Ltd.:

Data processing equipment	$ 50,000
Manufacturing equipment	900,000
Office equipment	100,000
Vending machines etc. in employee cafeteria	10,000
	$1,060,000

(c) Taxable income is comprised of:

Manufacturing income	$ 375,000
Investment income.......................................	65,000
Division B income..	$ 440,000
Less: charitable donations	15,000
Taxable income..	$ 425,000

— *REQUIRED*

Calculate the manufacturing and processing profit deduction Mano-Pac Ltd. can claim.

Problem 8

[ITA: 123; 124; 126]

Barltrop Limited is a Canadian public company involved in the software consulting business. Its controller provided you with the following information related to its 2005 taxation year ended December 31:

Income under Division B from consulting business including $100,000 earned in U.S. operations (before deducting $16,000 U.S. tax paid)	$264,000
Canadian investment royalty income	10,000
U.K. non-foreign affiliate income (before $3,000 tax withheld)	20,000
Taxable dividend received from non-connected Canadian corporations	5,000
Taxable capital gains...	6,000
Charitable donations	100,000
Unused foreign tax credit in respect of U.S.	3,000
Net capital losses carried forward arising in 1999	12,000

Barltrop Limited has permanent establishments in the U.S., B.C. and Alberta. Its gross revenues and salaries and wages data have been allocated as follows:

	British Columbia	Alberta	U.S.
Gross revenues	$3,000,000	$3,000,000	$4,000,000
Salaries and wages............	500,000	300,000	200,000

Assume that the British Columbia corporation tax rate is 13.5% and the Alberta rate is 11.5%. Also, assume that taxable income for Alberta is computed on the same basis as federal taxable income.

Gross revenues exclude income from property not used in connection with the principal business operation of the corporation.

— *REQUIRED*

Compute the total tax payable by the company for the 2005 taxation year, including provincial tax. Show all calculations.

Problem 9

[ITA: 12(1)(*t*); 37; 127(5)–(11); ITR:2900]

Infotech is a public company in its first year of business in the information technology industry. It operates out of a plant in Ottawa, Ontario. In 2005, it incurred $2,200,000 of scientific research and experimental development expenditures (SR&ED) which qualify for deduction under subsection 37(1) of the Act. The breakdown of these expenses is as follows:

Current SR&ED expenditures [par. 37(1)(*a*)]		$1,700,000
Capital SR&ED expenditures [spar. 37(1)(*b*)(i)]		
• new equipment	$300,000	
• used equipment	200,000	500,000
Total SR&ED expenditures		$2,200,000

Infotech's federal income tax rate after abatement is 22.12%. Its taxable income before deducting the $2,200,000 claim under section 37 is $3,200,000.

— *REQUIRED*

(A) Compute the maximum investment tax credit available to Infotech in 2005.

(B) Compute the company's net federal Part I tax payable after the investment tax credit, assuming a maximum section 37 deduction is claimed.

(C) What is the amount, if any, of the investment tax credit carryover?

(D) Compute the company's deduction or income inclusion in the following year if no further SR&ED expenditures are made.

Problem 10

[ITA: 123; 124; 125.1; 126; 127(5)]

Up, Up and Away Limited is a public corporation that manufactures hot air balloons in the province of New Brunswick. For the year ended September 30, 2005, its accounting income statement was as follows:

Sales	$1,225,000
Cost of sales and other expenses including C.C.A.	(725,000)
Operating profit	$ 500,000
Other net income	198,500
Net income before taxes	$ 698,500
Provision for taxes	(200,725)
Net income	$ 497,775

Selected Additional Information

(1) Other income includes:

Dividends from taxable Canadian corporation	$ 85,000
Canadian interest income	52,500
Foreign interest income, net of withholding taxes of $10,000	61,000

(2) Up, Up and Away Limited has a non-capital loss carryforward of $255,545.

(3) Up, Up and Away Limited purchased qualified equipment costing $250,000 which is eligible for the investment tax credit.

(4) The M&P profits calculation under Regulation 5200 yielded $435,000.

(5) Donations to registered charities were $9,755 (deducted from accounting income).

— *REQUIRED*

Calculate the total taxes payable for 2005 using a 13% provincial rate of tax. (For the calculation of the foreign tax credit, assume that there is no general tax reduction. Then, calculate the general tax reduction to show that this assumption is accurate.)

Problem 11

[ITA: 123; 124; 125.1; 126; 127(5)]

Tecniquip Limited is a public corporation whose head office is located in Toronto, Ontario. The activities of the corporation are carried on through permanent establishments in the provinces of Ontario and Alberta, and in the United States.

The following is an allocation of selected items for the fiscal year ended December 31, 2005.

	Ontario	Alberta	U.S.	Total
	($ 000)	($ 000)	($ 000)	($ 000)
Sales	$ 6,000	$ 400	$ 4,600	$11,000
Salaries:				
Production employees	$ 900	$ 300	$ 1,000	$ 2,200
Payroll benefits for production employees	10	0	0	10
Office employees	320	170	410	900
Purchasing agents	120	90	180	390
Raw material receiving & storing employees	200	220	280	700
Finished goods warehouse employees	500	0	0	500
Plant maintenance staff	80	20	60	160
Finished product inspectors	110	60	130	300
Sales staff	300	100	300	700
	$ 2,540	$ 960	$ 2,360	$ 5,860
Assets owned (capital cost):				
Office buildings	$ 300	$ 0	$ 250	$ 550
Office equipment	90	0	70	160
Equipment used in SR&ED	250	0	0	250
Manufacturing plants	1,750	40	900	2,690
Warehouses for finished goods	800	40	1,220	2,060
Land	1,000	10	600	1,610
	$ 4,190	$ 90	$ 3,040	$ 7,320
Assets leased (annual rental cost):				
Production machinery	$ 540	$ 10	$ 80	$ 630
Automobiles for sales staff	2	0	2	4
	$ 542	$ 10	$ 82	$ 634

For the year ended December 31, 2005, Tecniquip Limited obtained the following results:

Income from manufacturing operations in Ontario	$1,000,000
Income from manufacturing operations in Alberta	240,000
Income from manufacturing operations in the United States (before $200,000 Cdn. of US taxes paid)	800,000
	$2,040,000
Canadian-source interest income (investment)	12,000
Foreign-source investment income (before $3,000 in foreign tax withheld)	20,000
Taxable capital gain	10,000
Taxable dividends from taxable Canadian corporations	15,000
Net income under Division B	$2,097,000

In computing income from manufacturing, the corporation claimed a deduction of $150,000 under subsection 37(1) of the Act for scientific research and experimental development (SR&ED). $100,000 of the deduction related to expenditures of a current nature and $50,000 was the cost of equipment purchased during the year for use by it in scientific research and experimental development carried on in Canada.

During the year, the corporation made charitable donations totalling $50,000 and claimed non-capital losses of $60,000 and the net capital losses carried forward from 1999 of $9,000.

— REQUIRED

Compute the federal Part I tax payable and provincial tax at 12% for Ontario and 11.5% for Alberta, assuming that taxable income allocated to those provinces is the appropriate provincial tax base. Show all calculations, whether or not necessary to your final answer. (For the calculation of the manufacturing and processing profits deduction, assume that the foreign tax credit is equal to the foreign tax paid. However, show the full calculation of the foreign tax credits, including the effect of the general tax reduction.)

[For more problems and solutions thereto, see the CD accompanying this book.]

SUPPLEMENTAL NOTES

(This section of the text can be omitted without losing the continuity of the chapter. None of review questions, multiple choice questions, exercises, or assignment problems utilizes this information.)

Branch Tax

[ITA: 219; IT-137R3]

Section 219 imposes a branch tax on non-Canadian corporations carrying on business in Canada through a branch that is not a separate entity incorporated in Canada. A Canadian corporation is defined as a corporation which is presently resident in Canada and was incorporated in Canada or has been resident in Canada continuously since 1971 [ssec. 89(1)]. This tax is charged in addition to any Part I tax and is computed as 25% (unless reduced by a tax treaty) of after-tax Canadian-source income, after a number of technical adjustments such as an allowance for investment in property in Canada which is defined [Reg. 808]. The branch tax is intended to put the branch in the same position as a Canadian subsidiary which must withhold tax on dividends paid to the foreign parent. The branch tax, in essence, is paid on Canadian-source income of the branch that is not retained and reinvested in Canada, just as a withholding tax is levied on dividends which represent income that is not retained and reinvested in Canada.

Section 219 applies only to non-resident corporations. The base of the tax is taxable income earned in Canada, with adjustments to that base outlined in subsection 219(1). IT-137R3 details the calculation.

This tax is subject to any overriding provisions within any of the income tax treaties. For example, the rate under the Canada–U.S. Tax Treaty is 5%. IT-137R3 discusses the effect of the tax treaties on branch tax. The comprehensive treaties exempt corporations resident in the other country from Canadian tax unless there is a permanent establishment in Canada.

Example Problem

International Links Inc. is a telecommunications company incorporated in the U.S. with a December 31 year-end. It began operating one small pilot project office in Toronto in fiscal 2004 in addition to its 52 U.S. offices. The corporation is not resident in Canada; however, the Canadian office is considered a permanent establishment. The corporation's taxable income from Canadian operations was $280,000 in 2005. It received $60,000 in dividends from investments in other Canadian-controlled private corporations and realized a $20,000 capital gain on land used in the Canadian business. The corporation has $50,000 of qualified investment property in Canada. At the end of fiscal 2004, it had $20,000 of qualified investment property.

— REQUIRED

Compute the corporation's branch tax liability under Part XIV of the Act on the assumption that the Ontario provincial corporate tax rate is 14%. (Ignore surtaxes.)

— SOLUTION

5%[1] of:

Taxable income earned in Canada	$280,000	[par. 219(1)(*a*)]
Add: Amounts deducted under par. 115(1)(*d*.1)....	60,000	[par. 219(1)(*b*)]
Non-taxable portion of capital gain on a taxable Canadian property (land) used in Canadian business	10,000	[par. 219(1)(*d*)]
Amount claimed in previous year as investment allowance........................	20,000	[par. 219(1)(*g*)]

Deduct: Tax payable under Part I less tax attributable to net taxable capital gain on non-business property	(78,400)[2]	[par. 219(1)(*h*), (1.1)]
Tax payable to a province less tax attributable to net taxable capital gain on non-business property	(39,200)[3]	[par. 219(1)(*h*), (1.1)]
Allowance in respect of qualified investment property in Canada	(50,000)[4]	[par. 219(1)(*j*)]
	$202,400	
Branch tax (5% × $202,400)	$ 10,120	

— *NOTES TO SOLUTION*

(1) The Protocol to the Canada–U.S. Tax Treaty now limits the rate of branch tax to 5%.

(2) $280,000 × (38% − 10%). This tax rate is the basic federal rate net of the federal abatement. Note that the taxable capital gain realized was on business property. Hence the tax on the gain is not removed from federal Part I tax.

(3) $280,000 × 14%. This tax rate reflects a provincial rate of tax on Canadian business income. Note that the taxable capital gain realized was on business property. Hence the tax on the gain is not removed from provincial tax.

(4) Regulation 808(2) lists the specific components of qualified investment property in Canada. Although the regulation is quite detailed with numerous exceptions, it is clearly written. Reference to this regulation will be necessary when determining qualified investment property.

Chapter 12

Integration for Business and Investment Income of the Private Corporation

TOPICS DISCUSSED

Page

THE CONCEPT OF INTEGRATION 621

Problems Addressed by Integration 621

Objectives of Integration 621

The Major Tool for Integration in the Income Tax Act 621

SMALL BUSINESS DEDUCTION ON INCOME FROM
AN ACTIVE BUSINESS 624

Introduction 624

Mechanics of Calculation of Small Business
Deduction 625

Definition of "Active Business" 627

Associated Companies......................... 629

Corporate Partnerships......................... 638

Manufacturing and Processing Profits Revisited...... 638

Investment Tax Credit Revisited 640

Page

Incorporated Business Income and Integration 644

INCOME FROM INVESTMENTS 649

Overview of Integration for Income from Investments 649

Special Refundable Taxes in Respect of Income from
Investments 653

Actual Application of the Scheme 662

Imperfections in the Integration System for Income
from Investments 665

COMPREHENSIVE SUMMARY OF TYPES OF
CORPORATE INCOME AND FEDERAL CORPORATE
INCOME TAX RATES 672

SUPPLEMENTAL NOTES 695

Common Law Background to Current Legislation on
Definition of "Active Business" 695

This chapter deals with the provisions of the Act which attempt to integrate the taxation of private corporations with the taxation of the shareholders of those corporations. Following an introduction to the concept of integration, this chapter will consider both the integration of business income and investment income. While the word "integration" is not used in the Act, a series of provisions attempts to implement a system of integration which is designed to achieve certain objectives.

One of the most important reductions of tax available to corporations is the small business deduction which applies to Canadian-controlled private corporations as defined in subsection 125(7). This chapter will discuss the rules for computing the small business deduction. It will also deal with the rules which reduce the base in the calculation of the manufacturing and processing profits deduction and rules for computing the investment tax credit where a corporation is eligible for the small business deduction. Then the chapter considers the integration of investment income, including the refundable tax system. This chapter presents the remaining rules that must be followed to make a complete calculation of the tax payable by a corporation. The format of the T2 corporate tax return is discussed, but the actual forms are not presented in this chapter.

The following chart will help to position in the Act some of the major provisions dealt with in this Chapter.

PART I — DIVISIONS E AND F

DIVISION		SUBDIVISION		SECTION	
A	Liability for tax				
B	Computation of income				
C	Computation of taxable income	a	Individuals		
		a.1	Child tax benefit		
D	Taxable income earned in Canada by non-residents	b	Corporations	123-123.3	Tax rates and surtax
		c	All taxpayers	123.4	Tax reductions
				124	Prov abatement
E	Computation of tax			125	Small Business ded'n
E.1	Minimum tax			125.1	Mfg and Proc credit
F	Special rules			125.2	Ded'n of Part VI tax
				125.3	Ded'n of Part I.3 tax
G	Deferred and other special income arrangements			125.4 - 125.5	Cdn film/video credit
H	Exemptions			126	Foreign tax credit
I	Returns, Assessments, payments, appeals			126.1-127.41	Other tax credits
J	Appeals to the courts			128	Bankruptcy
				128.1	Change in residence
				129	Dividend refund

I. THE CONCEPT OF INTEGRATION

A. Problems Addressed by Integration

From a legal perspective, a corporation is an entity separate from its shareholders. In economics, however, there is no more separation between a corporation and its shareholders than between a proprietorship and its proprietor, a partnership and its partners or an investment portfolio and its owner.

As a taxpayer, a corporation is a person which is taxed separately from the natural persons (individuals) who are its shareholders. Hence, this could give rise to double taxation, with the same income being taxed, first, at the corporate level and then, again, at the individual shareholder level. Conceptually, a corporation should really be treated as a non-taxable conduit through which income flows to the individual shareholders, in the same way that a proprietorship business or a partnership business is a conduit through which income flows to the individual proprietor or partners. However, as subsequent comments in this chapter will illustrate, if only individuals and not corporations are subject to tax, problems of an economic or political nature may arise.

B. Objectives of Integration

Ideally, integration should cause the total tax paid by a corporation and its shareholders to be equal to the total tax paid by an individual who carries on the same economic activity directly and not through the corporation. By integrating the corporate and personal tax systems, the double taxation of corporate income can be avoided. This would make the tax system neutral with respect to the form of organization, used to carry on an economic activity, because there would be no tax advantage or disadvantage to one form of organization over another. Integration would also make the system equitable by ensuring that the tax imposed on income passed through a corporation to an individual is equal in amount to the tax that is imposed on the same amount and type of income earned directly by an individual. Stated differently, the total tax levied on the corporation and the individual in the former situation should be equal in amount to the tax imposed on the individual in the latter situation.

Perfect integration depends on the existence of two assumptions in the tax system. First, where the corporation itself pays tax, the shareholder should include in income and pay taxes on the full pre-tax income earned by the corporation and then receive a full credit for all of the income tax paid by the corporation. To the extent that the shareholder's tax on this income is less than the corporation's tax paid on behalf of the shareholder, the shareholder should get a refund of the difference. This approximates the approach that is taken for employment income. Salaries or wages are subject to withholding, but the employee gets full credit for all taxes withheld. If taxes withheld exceed taxes payable for the year, a refund is due. The second assumption is that all after-tax income of the corporation should be either paid out as dividends in the year earned or taxed at the shareholder level in that year to avoid the indefinite deferral of tax. This potential deferral would occur if corporate tax rates were lower than individual tax rates. This assumption equates the position of the shareholder with the position of the proprietor, partner or owner of investments who must pay tax on income from his or her economic activity whether or not it is distributed.

C. The Major Tool for Integration in the Income Tax Act

The mainstay of the integration system as it applies to individual shareholders of all taxable Canadian corporations is the gross-up and tax credit procedure which is illustrated in Exhibit 12-1. The gross-up is intended to add to the dividend received by the individual shareholder an amount equal to the total income tax (including provincial tax) paid by the corporation on the income that gave rise to the dividend. Thus, the grossed-up dividend is intended to represent the corporation's pre-tax income. The shareholder will pay tax on the grossed-up dividend at his or her personal rate. The combined federal and provincial tax credit is intended to give the shareholder credit for the total tax paid by the corporation on the shareholder's behalf. This procedure is intended to equalize the tax paid on the income that is flowed through the corporation to its shareholders, with the tax paid on the same income that is earned directly. The potential double taxation of corporate income is thereby avoided, but only where the combined federal and provincial corporate rate is approximately 20% under current legislation. Were it not for the gross-up and tax credit mechanism, the shareholder in the example in Exhibit 12-1 would have to pay tax on an $800 dividend at an assumed rate of 34%, for tax of $272, after the corporation had already paid tax of $200. This $472 in total tax would exceed the tax of $340 on the income earned directly by an individual paying tax at 34%.

EXHIBIT 12-1
Theoretical Taxation of Dividends to Individuals
That Demonstrates Perfect Integration

Corporation	
Corporate income	$1,000
Corporate tax, including provincial tax (*theoretical* rate, i.e., 20%)	(200)
After-tax earnings available for dividends	$ 800
Individual Shareholder	
Dividend	$ 800
Gross-up (*theoretically* equal to corporate tax or ¼ of the dividend)	200
Taxable income (*theoretically* equal to pre-tax corporation income)	$1,000
Personal tax, including provincial tax (assumed rate of 34%)	$ 340
Dividend tax credit, including effect of provincial tax (*theoretically* equal to corporate tax/gross-up)	(200)
Net tax	$ 140
Total Taxes Paid	
Corporation	$ 200
Shareholder	140
Total	$ 340
Earned Directly by Individual (tax @ 34%)	$ 340

Where the combined federal and provincial corporate rate of tax is 20%, integration is potentially perfect no matter what the federal personal tax rate is. This is because the one-quarter gross-up applied to the after-tax corporate distribution of dividends brings the shareholder's taxable dividend up to the exact amount of corporate pre-tax income. Furthermore, the total effect of the dividend tax credit is about 20% which is about equal to the corporate tax paid, in essence, on behalf of the shareholder. Assuming the theoretical rate of provincial tax on individuals is 50%, the total dividend tax credit in Exhibit 12-1 can be derived as:

Federal dividend tax credit
13⅓% of grossed-up dividends of, say, $1,000 .... $133
Provincial dividend tax credit
6⅔% of grossed-up dividend of $1,000 67
Total dividend tax credit $200

However, if the provincial dividend tax credit exceeds 6⅔% of the grossed-up dividend, as is the case in some provinces, then the combined dividend tax credit will exceed the underlying corporate tax. The above example can be modified to show this using a provincial dividend tax credit rate of 8%.

Federal dividend tax credit on $1,000 grossed up dividend $133

Plus provincial tax credit of 8% of $1,000 80

Total dividend tax credit $213

As a result, as the provincial dividend tax credit rate exceeds 6 $^2/_3$%, there may be a greater advantage to paying dividends if the personal tax reduction through the dividend tax credit exceeds the underlying corporate tax.

The federal dividend tax credit is determined pursuant to the rules in section 121 which provide for the credit to be equal to two-thirds of the gross-up [par. 82(1)(*b*)] on dividends received. The 13$^1/_3$ percentage, that is used in the above computation and on the T1 General form, is determined as follows:

Cash amount of dividend received $100.00

Gross-up [par. 82(1)(*b*)]: 25% 25.00

Grossed-up taxable amount of dividend $125.00

Federal dividend tax credit [sec. 121]: $^2/_3$ of $25 gross-up . . . . $ 16.67

Federal dividend tax credit as a percentage of grossed-up taxable amount of dividend: $16.67/$125 $\times$100 = ... 13$^1/_3$%

Under perfect integration, the corporate tax is like a withholding tax on the shareholder's income which the corporation earns on behalf of the shareholder. In a sense, it is similar to the withholding of tax on the salary or wages of an employee. Thus, the corporate tax prevents the tax on income earned by a corporation from being deferred until a dividend is paid and is then taxed in the hands of the shareholder. When the shareholder receives a dividend, the full pre-tax income earned by the corporation is reported by the shareholder, through the gross-up mechanism, just as an employee reports gross salary or wages. Then, tax is computed at the shareholder's personal rate. In the same way that taxes withheld from salary or wages are used to reduce the employee's final tax payable, so the dividend tax credit (representing the tax paid by the corporation) reduces the shareholder's tax payable on the dividend income.

Where the combined federal and provincial corporate rate of tax is anything other than 20%, the system of integration breaks down. The imperfections in the integration system will be considered in more detail in this chapter. The chapter will also consider some tools of integration that help to bring the corporate rate of tax close to the perfect 20% on the first $300,000 of active business income and on all of the investment income earned by a Canadian-controlled private corporation.

II. SMALL BUSINESS DEDUCTION ON INCOME FROM AN ACTIVE BUSINESS

A. Introduction

[ITA: 89(1); 125; 127(9); IT-458R2]

The small business deduction represents a credit against the tax otherwise payable on income "from an active business carried on in Canada" and is designed for only small "Canadian-controlled private corporations" in order to assist them to retain capital to expand their businesses. Note, however, that the corporation does not have to be "small" in order to qualify for the credit.

The benefits of the small business deduction are phased out for very large Canadian-controlled private corporations. The rules that implement this phase-out are presented in the next segment of this topic.

Exhibit 12-2 illustrates how the small business deduction affects the calculation of effective total corporate tax introduced in Exhibit 11-3.

EXHIBIT 12-2
Tax Rates Applicable to Taxable Income Eligible for Small Business Deduction

Federal tax rate [ssec. 123(1)]	38.00%
Federal abatement for provincial tax [ssec. 124(1)]	(10.00)
Net federal tax after federal abatement	28.00%
Federal surtax @ 4% of above net federal tax	1.12
Small business deduction [ssec. 125(1)]	(16.00)
Total federal tax	13.12%
Provincial tax (hypothetical) on income qualifying for small business deduction	5.00
Effective total tax	18.12%

Note that the effective total tax rate is close to the 20% total corporate tax rate that results in perfect integration.

The hypothetical provincial tax rate of 5% used in Exhibit 12-2 above reflects an average provincial equivalent of the federal small business deduction. Remember that in Chapter 11, Exhibit 11-3 used an assumed provincial rate of 13% because most provincial basic tax rates lie between 8.9% and 17%. Most provinces also give an equivalent small business tax credit, giving an effective provincial rate of approximately 5% on the first $300,000 (for calendar year 2005 and later years) of active business income.

The prime qualification that a corporation must meet to get the benefit of the small business deduction is that it be, throughout the taxation year, a "Canadian controlled private corporation" (CCPC) [ssec. 125(7)]. This term is discussed by Canada Revenue Agency (CRA) in IT-458R2. A Canadian-controlled private corporation is distinguished, on the basis of control, from a "private corporation" [ssec. 89(1)]. A "private corporation" is further distinguished from a "public corporation" [ssec. 89(1)], primarily on the basis of whether any of the corporation's shares are listed on a prescribed Canadian or foreign stock exchange.

B. Mechanics of Calculation of Small Business Deduction

[ITA: 123.4(3); 125]

1. The basic limits

A Canadian-controlled private corporation calculates its tax liability by first applying the standard corporate rate to its total taxable income. After this basic tax amount is determined, the corporation makes various additions (e.g., surtax) and deductions (e.g., M&P profits deduction, investment tax credit, etc.) to determine the final taxes payable. One such deduction is the small business deduction.

A corporation must be a Canadian-controlled private corporation *throughout* the year to qualify for the small business deduction which is a credit deducted from the tax otherwise payable. For such a corporation, the deduction is calculated by the following formula [ssec. 125(1)]:

Small business deduction = 16% of the least of:

(a) net Canadian active business income (i.e., income minus losses);

(b) taxable income earned in Canada achieved by removing from the total taxable income, foreign-source income estimated as the sum of:

(i) foreign-source investment income, estimated as $10/3^{(a)}$ times the foreign tax credit on foreign non-business income [ssec. 126(1)], determined without reference to the additional refundable tax on investment income,

(ii) foreign-source business income, estimated as $3^{(a)}$ times the foreign tax credit on foreign business income [ssec. 126(2)], and

(iii) taxable income exempt from Part I tax by reason of an enactment of Parliament; and

(c) the business limit, i.e., $300,000 [ssec. 125(2)] *less* any portion allocated [ssec. 125(3)] to associated corporations (to be discussed later in this chapter).

Items (b)(i) and (ii) ensure that foreign income not taxed in Canada, because of a foreign tax credit, is removed from the base amount on which the small business deduction is calculated. This is necessary since Canada should not allow the small business deduction on income on which the corporation does not pay tax as a result of a foreign tax credit or base a tax credit on income that is not Canadian-source active business income. Conceptually, the first adjustment removes from taxable income an estimate of foreign investment income by multiplying by $10/3$ the tax credit which is assumed to be 30% of the foreign investment income. The 30% rate is based on an assumed corporate rate of 40% reduced by the 10% federal abatement for income earned in a province or territory. Investment income is subject to that abatement, because it is thought to be earned in a province or territory where the corporation is established, as explained in the previous chapter in the discussion of the foreign tax credit calculation. Conceptually, the second adjustment removes from taxable income an estimate of foreign business income by multiplying by 3 the tax credit which is assumed to be $33^{1}/_{3}$% of the foreign business income. The $33^{1}/_{3}$% rate is intended to approximate corporate income tax rates on this type of income (i.e., 38% + 1.12% − 7% (general rate reduction) = 32.12%, say, 33.33%).

Similarly, item (b)(iii) removes from the base for the small business deduction an amount that is not subject to tax. This removal follows from the concept that an amount that is not taxed in Canada should not be in the base for a tax credit which reduces taxes payable in Canada.

(a) [The February 27, 2004 Revised Draft Legislation proposes to change the factor applied to the business foreign tax credit from 10/4 for the 2003 and subsequent taxation years. While the December 20, 2002 Draft Legislation proposed to change the factor applied to the non-business foreign tax credit to 4, the February 27, 2004 Revised Draft Legislation no longer proposes this change.]

2. CCPC Rate Reduction

[ITA: 123.4; 181.1(1.2)]

The CCPC rate reduction has been repealed starting in 2005. However, for taxation years that begin in 2004 and end in 2005 this rate reduction is still in effect.

3. Elimination of small business deduction for large CCPCs

Large Canadian-controlled private corporations are not fully eligible for the small business deduction. The amount of the small business deduction is phased out [ssec. 125(5.1)] with a formula based on the amount of taxable capital employed in Canada for purposes of the large corporations tax [Part I.3] for the preceding taxation year. The phase-out range is taxable capital employed in Canada between $10 and $15 million. The business limit of $300,000 (for calendar year 2005 and later years) for purposes of the small business deduction is reduced by $1 for every $16.67 (i.e., ($15,000,000 – $10,000,000) ÷ $300,000) of taxable capital employed in Canada in excess of $10 million. To offset the effect of short taxation years on this reduction of a CCPC's business limit, the large corporations tax base is grossed up to reflect a full taxation year. Reductions in the business limit for short taxation years are based on a daily proration.

The above limitation also applies to a group of associated corporations. Therefore, the associated corporations' total taxable capital employed in Canada in excess of $10 million serves as the basis for the corporate group's business limit reduction.

This reduction in the small business deduction is implemented through the formula [ssec. 125(5.1)]:

$$A \times \frac{B}{\$11,250}$$

where,

A   is the corporation's business limit for the year, and

B   is the corporation's Part I.3 tax (large corporations tax) payable for its pre-ceding taxation year before the reduction for surtax and the adjustment for short fiscal years.

While the reduction is theoretically based on taxable capital employed in Canada, the formula uses the large corporations tax. The $11,250 in the formula represents the former Part I.3 tax rate of 0.225% on $15 million of taxable capital employed in Canada (0.225% × ($15 million – $10 million) = $11,250).

Subsection 181.1(1.2) ensures that the LCT rate reductions under subsection 181.1(1) does not apply to subsection 125(5.1). As a result, a corporation will continue to apply subsection 125(5.1) as if the LCT rate were 0.225%.

Example Problem

Little-Big Inc., a Canadian-controlled private corporation, has a fiscal year-end of December 31. Little-Big Inc. is not associated with any other corporation and all of its income is earned in Canada. The following selected tax information has been provided for 2005:

Active business income	$ 350,000
Taxable income	500,000
Taxable capital employed in Canada in 2004	13,000,000

— *REQUIRED*

Determine Little-Big Inc.'s small business deduction for the 2005 taxation year.

— SOLUTION

Business limit:

Before reduction .... $ 300,000

Reduction:

$$\$300,000 \times \frac{\$3 \text{ million} \times .00225}{\$11,250} =$$ (180,000)

Business limit... $ 120,000

Small business deduction for 2005:

16% of least of:

(a) active business income $350,000

(b) taxable income $500,000

(c) business limit........................ $120,000

Least amount .... $ 120,000

16% of $120,000 .... $ 19,200

C. Definition of "Active Business"

[ITA: 125(7); IT-73R6]

As will be discussed in more detail later in this chapter, one of the major problems with the implementation of the small business deduction in 1972 was the lack of a statutory definition of "active business". An Interpretation Bulletin outlined the CRA's opinion of the meaning of the term, but it was often successfully challenged in the courts. A definition of "active business" was subsequently added to the legislation.

The current definition of the term [ssec. 125(7)] reads as follows:

"active business carried on by a corporation" means any business carried on by the corporation other than a specified investment business or a personal services business and includes an adventure or concern in the nature of trade.[b]

A "specified investment business" (S.I.B.), which is excluded from that definition of "active business", is defined [ssec. 125(7)] to mean: a business (other than the business of a credit union or of leasing property other than real property) the principal purpose of which is to derive income from property (including interest, dividends, rents and royalties), *unless* the corporation employs in the business throughout the year *more than* five full-time employees. In the unusual case of *The Queen v. Hughes & Co. Holdings Ltd.*, (F.C.T.D.) 94 DTC 6511, the court first considered, in detail, the meaning of full-time employee. The court then held (at 6518) that the condition of "more than five full-time employees" means "more full-time employees than five (full-time employees)", that is, at least six full-time employees. Therefore, the taxpayer could not combine five full-time employees with several part-time employees to meet this condition. The CRA adopts the court's interpretation on this point and interprets this condition to mean six or more full-time employees [IT-73R6, par. 15]. In paragraph (b) of the definition "specified investment business" [ssec. 125(7)], the Act goes on to allow an exception where a corporation would have employed more than five full-time employees but does not because another corporation associated with it provides the services that would otherwise have been performed by its own employees.

A specified investment business is restricted to a business which generates property income, including dividends, interest, rent (leasing) and royalties. Note that by virtue of the exception contained in the brackets in the definition, the business of leasing movable property (i.e., not real property) is an active business. The taxation of

---

[b] Note that this definition is used only for the purpose of section 125. A definition of "active business" can be found in subsection 248(1) which is to be used whenever the term is used elsewhere in the Act. The phrase, "an adventure or concern in the nature of trade", is not included in the definition of "active business" in subsection 248(1). However, the phrase is part of the definition of "business" in subsection 248(1).

investment income, including income from a specified investment business, will be discussed later in the chapter.

A "personal services business" (P.S.B.) is also excluded from the definition of the term "active business". A "personal services business" is defined [ssec. 125(7)] to mean:

- a business of providing services where

    (i) an individual who performs services on behalf of the corporation ("incorporated employee"), or

    (ii) any person related to the incorporated employee

    is a specified shareholder defined [ssec. 248(1)] to mean, in part, an owner, directly or indirectly, of 10% or more of the shares of the corporation;

- the incorporated employee would reasonably be regarded as an officer or employee of the entity to which services are provided;

- *unless*

    (iii) the corporation employs throughout the year more than five full-time employees, or

    (iv) services are provided to an associated corporation (to be discussed subsequently).

To determine whether "the incorporated employee would reasonably be regarded as an officer or employee of the entity to which services are provided", it may be necessary to perform an employee versus self-employed analysis, as presented in Chapter 3. The package of common law tests should be applied to the facts pertaining to the relationship between the incorporated employee and the entity to which services are provided. This was done in the case of *Criterion Capital Corporation v. The Queen* (TCC), 2001 DTC 921. Criterion was held not to be carrying on a P.S.B. and, hence, was eligible for the small business deduction, in part, on the application of the "control" and "ownership of tools" tests.

A corporation carrying on such a personal services business is not eligible for a small business deduction in respect of its P.S.B. income. Furthermore, such a corporation is denied any deductions from the income of the personal services business of the corporation, other than salary, wages and other benefits provided to the individual who performed the services in respect of the personal services business. In addition, the corporation may deduct amounts, in respect of the P.S.B., that would have been deductible by an employee as costs incurred in selling property or negotiating contracts or legal expenses incurred in collecting amounts owing for services. This limitation on the deductions of a personal services business is found in paragraph 18(1)(*p*). As indicated in Chapter 11, the credit for employment outside Canada [sec. 122.3] is not available to a corporation carrying on a P.S.B.

"Income of the corporation for the year from an active business" [ssec. 125(7)] includes any income for the year from an "active business", including any income for the year pertaining to or incident to that business; income from a property held for investment in Canada is specifically excluded.

Ancillary income incidental to the carrying on of an active business will, therefore, be considered as income from an active business in addition to income directly from an active business. Examples of such ancillary income include interest from short-term investment of surplus cash, recaptured capital cost allowance on assets used in the active business, interest on accounts receivable and bad debt recoveries, among others. IT-73R6, paragraph 5 indicates the CRA's interpretation of the concept of ancillary income.

It is important to note that a corporation may have income from more than one source. Therefore, it is necessary to analyze the corporate income (Division B) and break it down into its components.

D. Associated Companies

[ITA: 251; 256; IT-64R4; IT-419R2]

1. Overview

When two or more Canadian-controlled private corporations are associated for tax purposes, the business limit of $300,000, or the reduced amount, must be allocated annually, in any manner, among the associated companies for the purpose of determining the small business deduction in each company [ssec. 125(3)]. A number of other provisions of the Act, also, rely on the concept of association. These include the definitions of the terms "specified investment business" [ssec. 125(7)] and "personal services business" [ssec. 125(7)] which were introduced previously in this chapter. The concept of association is, also, used to determine certain limits and rates for the investment tax credit [ssec. 127(10.1) and sec. 127.1], as discussed later in this chapter.

The deeming rule [ssec. 129(6)], which will be discussed subsequently in this chapter, pertaining to certain intercorporate payments, depends on association between corporations.

2. Related persons

The term "associated corporations" [sec. 256] may depend on the definition of "related persons" contained in section 251. Related persons include relationships between individuals, between individuals and corporations and between corporations. The key to the definition of relationships is found in relationships between individuals who are connected by blood relationship, marriage or adoption. Exhibit 12-4 (which was introduced in Chapter 6 as Exhibit 6-2) attempts to diagram these relationships (i.e., individuals who are related to a taxpayer (i.e., "you")) schematically. On the horizontal axis, do not attempt to relate individuals at the extreme outer limits (i.e., the second bullet) to each other. They are related to "you".

EXHIBIT 12-4
Schematic Diagram of Related Individuals

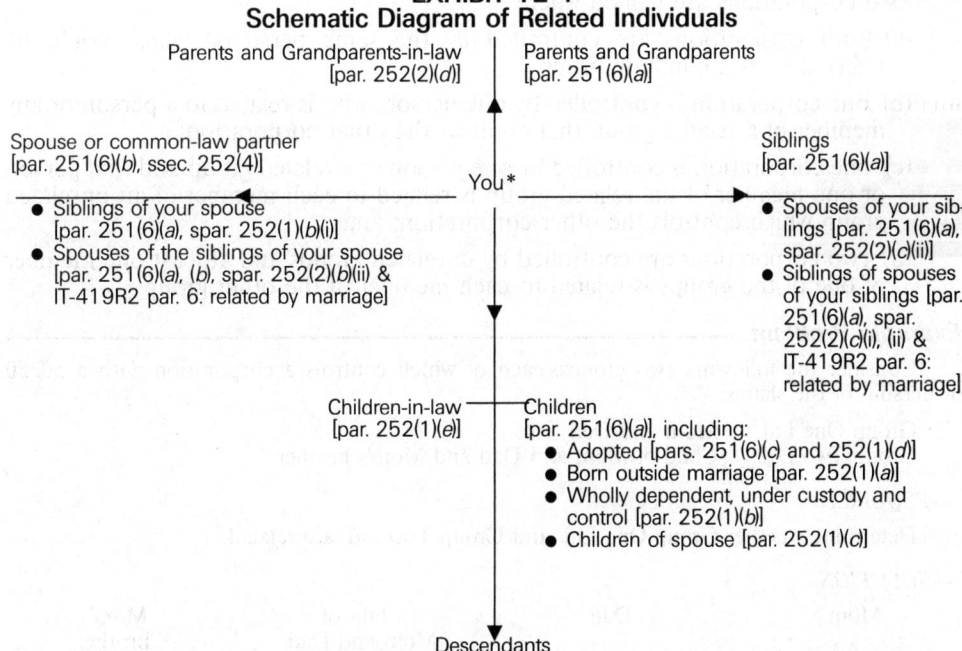

---

* Under the *Income Tax Act*, an individual is deemed to be related to herself or himself where she or he owns shares in two or more corporations [par. 251(5)(c) and ssec. 256(1.5)]. Note, however, that an individual is more than likely not dealing at "arm's length" with herself or himself by virtue of the definition of this term under paragraph 251(1)(b) which bases this type of relationship on the facts of the particular situation at a particular moment in time. Therefore, be careful which term is being used — "related" or "arm's length".

Certain individuals who would normally be regarded as related to other individuals are not considered to be related for tax purposes. These individuals, who do not appear in Exhibit 12-4, include: aunts, uncles, nieces, nephews and cousins.

Note that where the word "spouse" is used, the provision extends to a "common-law partner". This term is defined [ssec. 248(1)] as two persons, regardless of sex, who co-habit in a conjugal relationship and have done so for a continuous period of at least 12 months.

Corporations can be related to individuals and other corporations. The key to understanding corporate relationships is the concept of control. In this context, control refers to legal (*de jure*) control which is generally understood to mean the right of control that rests in the ownership of such number of shares of the corporation as to give a majority of the voting power in the corporation. Control can either be direct or indirect. The latter, for example, could be accomplished through an intermediary corporation.

An example of indirect control would be where A, an individual, owns 80% of the voting shares of A Ltd. which in turn owns 60% of the voting shares of B Ltd. A has more than 50% of the votes of A Ltd. and in turn controls 60% of the votes of B Ltd. through his or her control of A Ltd.

The rules that govern corporate relationships are found in paragraphs 251(2)(*b*) and (*c*). Conceptually, a person (an individual or corporation) is related to a corporation if that person controls the corporation [spar. 251(2)(*b*)(i)]. Similarly, if a person is a member of a related group that controls the corporation, then the person and the corporation are related. A related group is a group of persons each of whom is related to each member of the group. In addition, persons, who are themselves related to the controlling person(s), are deemed to be related to the controlled corporation.

Paragraph 251(2)(*c*) expands these concepts to include control by related and unrelated groups, as defined in subsection 251(4) and is summarized below.

Two corporations are related where:

(a) both corporations are controlled by the same person(s) which could be referred to as a common group;

(b) one corporation is controlled by one person, who is related to a person or any member of a related group that controls the other corporation;

(c) one corporation is controlled by one person or a related group and that person or one member of the related group is related to each member of an unrelated group which controls the other corporation; and

(d) two corporations are controlled by unrelated groups and at least one member of one of the groups is related to each member of the other group.

Example Problem

Consider the following two groups, each of which controls a corporation with a 50/50 ownership of the shares:

Group One Ltd.   Mom and Dad
Group Two Ltd.   Child of Mom and Dad and Mom's brother

— *REQUIRED*

Determine whether Group One Ltd. and Group Two Ltd. are related.

— *SOLUTION*

Mom	Dad	Child of Mom and Dad	Mom's Brother
50%	50%	50%	50%
Group One Ltd.		Group Two Ltd.	

Group Two Ltd. is controlled by an unrelated group since it is composed of an uncle and a niece/nephew. Group One Ltd. is controlled by a related group, because Mom and Dad are related through marriage. In this situation, each member of the related group that controls Group One Ltd. is related to each member of the unrelated group that controls Group Two Ltd.

Therefore, the corporations are related [spar.252(2)(c)(v)].

3. Basic association rules

Conceptually, two companies are associated for tax purposes, when one company controls the other [par. 256(1)(a)], or both companies are controlled by the same person or group of persons [par. 256(1)(b)]. However, the definition of associated corporations goes on to list other conditions for association [sec. 256]. Therefore, the definition must be consulted to properly evaluate a particular set of facts. The rules in paragraphs 256(1)(a) and (b) each require that only one straightforward condition be met in order to apply.

The rules in paragraphs 256(1)(c), (d) and (e) each contain three conditions, all joined by the word "and", which means that all three conditions must be satisfied for the rule to apply.

(a) *Paragraph 256(1)(c)*

The three conditions that must be met for this paragraph to apply are:

(i) each of the corporations must be controlled, directly or indirectly in any manner whatever, by a person (which includes an individual or another corporation) (hereinafter referred to as the "control test");

(ii) the person who controls one of the corporations must be related to the person who controls the other corporation (hereinafter referred to as the "related test"); and

(iii) either of the two persons owns not less than 25% of the issued shares of any class, other than a specified class (as defined below), of the capital stock of each corporation (hereinafter referred to as the "cross-ownership test").

Shares of a "specified class" are excluded from the cross-ownership conditions in subsection 256(1). The term "specified class" is defined [ssec. 256(1.1)] to mean a class of shares where:

(a) the shares are neither convertible nor exchangeable;

(b) the shares are non-voting;

(c) dividends payable on the shares are fixed in amount or rate;

(d) the annual rate of dividend on the shares, expressed as a percentage of the fair market value of the consideration for which the shares were issued, does not exceed the prescribed rate of interest at the time the shares were issued; and

(e) the amount that a holder of the shares is entitled to receive on their redemption, cancellation or acquisition by the corporation (or by a person not at arm's length with the corporation) cannot exceed the fair market value of the consideration for which the shares were issued (usually, their paid-up capital) plus any unpaid dividends.

The exclusion of a specified class of shares and the 25% cross-ownership test allow a person to invest funds in a corporation controlled by a related person without subjecting his or her own corporation to the consequences of association.

Example Problem

Dad and Son (age 25) both own 100% of the common shares of their respective corporations: Dadco Ltd. and Sonco Ltd. Dad owns 100% of the preferred shares of Sonco Ltd. The preferred shares are voting, bear a dividend rate of 8%, and are redeemable at $100,000. At the time the preferred shares were issued, the prescribed rate was 10% and the fair market value was $100,000.

— REQUIRED

Determine whether Dadco Ltd. and Sonco Ltd. are associated under subsection 256(1). Substantiate your conclusions by reference to the related provisions of the Act and the conditions contained therein.

— SOLUTION

Dadco Ltd. and Sonco Ltd. are associated [par. 256(1)(c)] because:

(a) the corporations are controlled directly by either Dad or Son;

(b) Dad and Son are related by blood (i.e., parent–child) [par. 251(1)(a) and ssec. 251(6)];

(c) one of the persons (Dad) owns not less than 25% of issued shares of any class of both corporations, other than specified shares (i.e., 100% of the common shares of Dadco Ltd. and 100% of the preferred shares of Sonco Ltd.); and

(d) the preferred and common shares are not specified shares [ssec. 256(1.1)] since both classes have voting rights.

(b) *Paragraph 256(1)(d)*

Whereas paragraph 256(1)(c) applies to two corporations each controlled by a single person, paragraph 256(1)(d) applies to a situation in which one corporation is controlled by a single person and the other corporation is controlled by a group of persons. The three conditions (involving a control test, a related test and a cross-ownership test) that must be met are:

(i) one of the corporations must be controlled, directly or indirectly in any manner whatever, by one person;

(ii) that person must be related to each member of a group of persons (not necessarily a related group) that controls the other corporation; and

(iii) that person must own not less than 25% of the issued shares of any class, other than specified shares, of the capital stock of the other corporation.

Example Problem ————————————————————————————————

Mom owns 100% of the common shares of Momco Ltd. Her adult daughters, No. 1 and No. 2, each own 35% of the common shares of Sibco Ltd. Mom owns the remaining 30% of the outstanding common shares of Sibco Ltd.

— REQUIRED

Determine whether Momco Ltd. and Sibco Ltd. are associated under subsection 256(1). Substantiate your conclusions by reference to the related provisions of the Act and the conditions contained therein.

— SOLUTION

Momco Ltd. and Sibco Ltd. are associated [par. 256(1)(*d*)] because:

(a) one person (Mom) controls one corporation (Momco Ltd.);

(b) that person (Mom) was related to each person (daughters No. 1 and No. 2) in the group that controls the other corporation (Sibco Ltd.) because of the parent–child relationship [pars. 251(1)(*a*) and 251(6)(*a*)]. Note that the condition would also be met if the controlling group was either Mom and Daughter No. 1 or Mom and Daughter No. 2, since Mom is deemed to be related to herself as a shareholder of both corporations [par. 251(5)(*c*)];

(c) that person (Mom) owns not less than 25% of non-specified shares in the other corporation (30% of the common shares of Sibco Ltd.); and

(d) the common shares of Sibco Ltd. are not specified shares since these shares have voting rights and no restriction on the amount of dividends.

(c) *Paragraph 256(1)(e)*

Finally, this paragraph applies to two group-controlled corporations if the following three conditions (involving a control test, a related test and a cross-ownership test) are met:

(i) each of the corporations must be controlled, directly or indirectly in any manner whatever, by a related group;

(ii) each member of one of the related groups must be related to all of the members of the other related group; and

(iii) one or more members of both related groups must own, either alone or together, not less than 25% of the issued shares of any class, other than a specified class, of shares of the capital stock of the other corporation.

Example Problem

Alpha and Beta, who are married, each own 50% of the common shares of AB Ltd. Their son, Alpha Jr., age 30, and his wife own 40% and 30%, respectively, of the common shares of Junior Ltd. Beta owns the other 30% of the common shares of Junior Ltd.

— REQUIRED

Determine whether AB Ltd. and Junior Ltd. are associated under subsection 256(1). Substantiate your conclusions by the related provisions of the Act and the conditions contained therein.

— *SOLUTION*

AB Ltd. and Junior Ltd. are associated [par. 256(1)(e)] because:

(a) each corporation (AB Ltd. and Junior Ltd.) is controlled by a related group:

- AB Ltd. is controlled by Alpha (50%) and Beta (50%) who are related by marriage [pars. 251(1)(a) and 251(6)(b)],
- Junior Ltd. is controlled by any of:

  (i) Alpha Jr. (40%) and his wife (30%) who are related by marriage [pars. 251(1)(a) and 251(6)(b)],

  (ii) Beta (30%) and Alpha Jr. (40%) who are related by blood [pars. 251(1)(a) and 251(6)(a)],

  (iii) Beta (30%) and Alpha Jr.'s wife (30%) who are related through the extended definition of child [par. 252(1)(e)],

  (iv) Alpha Jr. (40%), Alpha Jr.'s wife (30%) and Beta (30%), all of whom are related;

(b) each member of one related group (Alpha and Beta) is related to all members of the other related group. Note that in cases (ii), (iii) and (iv) above, Beta is related to herself as a shareholder of both corporations [par. 251(5)(c)];

(c) one (or more) member of *both* related groups (Beta) must own not less than 25% (Beta owns 30% in Junior Ltd.) of the issued shares of any class other than specified shares of the other corporation; and

(d) common shares are not specified shares [ssec. 256(1.1)].

The following is a list of the key words used in each of the paragraphs of subsection 256(1).

Par. (a)	controlled
Par. (b)	controlled, person, group of persons
Par. (c)	controlled, person, related, owned not less than 25%, specified class
Par. (d)	controlled, person, group of persons, related, owned not less than 25%, specified class
Par. (e)	controlled, related group, owned not less than 25%, specified class

4. Concept of control

As a first approximation to the interpretation of the concept of control, the common law definition of legal or *de jure* control can be applied. Legal control means ownership of more than 50% of the voting shares or, more precisely, "ownership of such a number of shares as carries with it the right to a majority of the votes in the election of the Board of Directors".[c] Indirect control applies to the situation where there are

---

[c] Stated in the case of *Buckerfield's Limited et al. v M.N.R.*, (Ex. Ct.) 64 DTC 5301.

multi-tiered corporations but is still based on legal control of more than 50% of the voting shares. For example, assume there is a chain of corporations whereby each parent corporation has 60% of all the voting shares of its subsidiary:

| A Ltd. | —60%→ | B Ltd. | —60%→ | C Ltd. | —60%→ | D Ltd. |

In each situation, the parent corporation controls its subsidiary. A Ltd. directly controls B Ltd. and indirectly controls C Ltd. and D Ltd. B Ltd. directly controls C Ltd. and indirectly controls D Ltd. Note that control is not multiplicative. Since A Ltd. controls B Ltd., A Ltd. can cause B Ltd. to vote all of B Ltd.'s shares in C Ltd. according to A Ltd.'s wishes. Therefore, A Ltd. controls, indirectly, C Ltd.[d] Furthermore, IT-64R4 should be consulted for the CRA's view of these rules.[e]

A broadening of the concept of legal control may occur in fact situations to which the concept of "control in fact" applies. Using factual control to determine association further restricts the multiplication of the small business deduction by extending the circumstances under which corporations are considered to be associated. As indicated, the concept of control has been interpreted to mean legal or *de jure* control that vests in the ownership of more than 50% of the voting shares, as set out in the *Buckerfield's* case.[f] Subsection 256(5.1), which is applicable to the expression "controlled, directly or indirectly in any manner whatever" when used throughout the Act, extends the concept of control to actual or *de facto* control which might exist by virtue of a person having any direct or indirect influence. The Technical Notes which accompanied the introduction of the legislation provided the following example of actual control: "where a person held 49% of the voting control of a corporation and the balance was widely dispersed among many employees of the corporation or held by persons who could reasonably be considered to act in respect of the corporation in accordance with his wishes". The Note stated further that "whether a person can be said to be in actual control of a corporation, notwithstanding that he does not legally control more than 50% of its voting shares, will depend in each case on all of the circumstances".

5. Extended meaning of control

The concept of control is further broadened in subsection 256(1.2). In determining whether a corporation was controlled by a group of persons, a group means any two or more persons each of whom owned shares of the same corporation [par. 256(1.2)(a)]. A rule similar to that in paragraph 251(5)(a) is provided such that a corporation can be considered to be controlled at the same time by several persons or groups of persons [par. 256(1.2)(b)]. This concept is shown in the preceding example problem dealing with paragraph 256(1)(e). Note how four different groups control Junior Ltd.

A person or group of persons will be deemed to control a corporation [par. 256(1.2)(c)] when the person or group owns:

(i) shares representing more than 50% of the fair market value of all issued and outstanding shares of the corporation, or

(ii) common shares representing more than 50% of the fair market value of all issued and outstanding common shares of the corporation.

---

[d] For a case on indirect holdings resulting in control see *Vineland Quarries and Crushed Stone Ltd. v. M.N.R.*, (Ex. Ct.) 66 DTC 5092.

[e] As examples of the application of subsection 256(1) to a fact situation see the cases of *Radio CFUN Limited* and *Wellport Broadcasting Limited v. M.N.R.*, (T.A.B.) 69 DTC 420; *Southside Car Market Ltd. et al. v. The Queen*, (F.C.T.D.) 82 DTC 6179; *Wynndel Logging Co. Ltd. v. M.N.R.*, (T.R.B.) 80 DTC 1125; *Roclar Leasing Ltd. et al. v. M.N.R.*, (T.R.B.) 81 DTC 544; and *B.B. Fast & Sons Distributors Ltd. v. The Queen*, (F.C.T.D.) 84 DTC 6554, affirmed by the Federal Court of Appeal (86 DTC 6106).

[f] See also the case of *The Queen v. Imperial General Properties*, (S.C.C.) 85 DTC 5500.

Note how this rule ignores the voting rights of the shares and looks at the underlying value of the shares in question. For example, assume that a corporation is capitalized with $1,000,000 of non-voting retractable shares owned by Individual A and $1,000 of common shares owned by Individual B. Both A and B control the corporation — Individual B through his or her voting rights and Individual A through the preferred shares which represent more than 50% of the total fair market value of the share capital of $1,001,000.

Since the value of a share can be affected by voting rights and certain other special features, these features are to be disregarded for the purposes of determining the fair market value of a share under section 256 [par. 256(1.2)(g)]. Likewise, "term preferred shares" [ssec. 248(1)] and shares included in a "specified class" [ssec. 256(1.1)] should be disregarded for purposes of making the fair market valuation in subsection 256(1.2) [ssec. 256(1.6)].

6. Ownership of shares

The rules in subsection 256(1) use the words "controlled" and "owned". As previously demonstrated, indirect control of a corporation can flow through a chain of corporations through *de jure* control. However, the courts have held that ownership, including indirect ownership, cannot be traced through a chain of corporations. Therefore, paragraphs 256(1.2)(*d*), (*e*) and (*f*) were enacted to provide a series of indirect ownership rules which are referred to as the "look-through" rules which apply where shares of a corporation are held by another corporation, a partnership or a trust. A shareholder of a corporation, a member of a partnership or a beneficiary of a trust that holds shares in a corporation would be deemed to own a number of the shares of the corporation as is proportionate to his or her economic interest in the corporation, partnership or trust that actually owns the shares.

Consider the facts in the following diagram:

With its 60% ownership of the common shares of Controlled One Ltd., Controller Ltd. controls Controlled One Ltd. Since Controller Ltd. controls Controlled One Ltd., it can cause Controlled One Ltd. to vote the latter's 55% controlling interest in Controlled Two Ltd. in the interest of Controller Ltd. Therefore, Controller Ltd. controls Controlled Two Ltd. through Controlled One Ltd. Controller Ltd. does not own any shares directly in Controlled Two Ltd. through its ownership of shares in Controlled One Ltd. However, paragraph 256(1.2)(*d*) deems Controller Ltd. to *own* 33% (i.e., 60% of 55%) of Controlled Two Ltd.

Another such rule deems that shares of a corporation owned by a minor child are owned by each parent of the child [ssec. 256(1.3)]. Even if the shares are deemed to be owned by the minor child by another provision of section 256, the shares will be deemed to be owned by each parent. However, an exception is provided if it may reasonably be considered that the child manages the business and affairs of the corporation and does so without a significant degree of influence by the parent. This exception is intended to accommodate young entrepreneurs.

Subsections 256(1.4) and (1.5) enact, for the purposes of section 256, the provisions in paragraphs 251(5)(*b*) and (*c*), respectively. Subsection 256(1.4) pertains to rights to acquire shares (e.g., options) or rights to cause a corporation to redeem shares of other shareholders. The holder of such rights is deemed to be in the same position as if the rights were exercised. Subsection 256(1.5) deems a person to be related to himself or herself in his or her capacity as shareholder of two or more corporations.

7. Association with third corporation

Where two corporations, that would not otherwise be associated, are both associated with a third corporation, subsection 256(2) normally deems the two corporations to be associated with each other. However, relief from this deeming rule is available, for the purposes of the small business deduction only [section 125], if the third corporation is not a Canadian-controlled private corporation or if the third corporation elects not to be associated with either of the other two corporations. For this election to apply, the two corporations associated by subsection 256(2) cannot be associated by any other rule. Note that the election is an annual one. The result of the election is that the business limit of the third corporation is deemed to be nil.

Example Problem

H and W, a married couple, have incorporated their separate businesses, H Ltd. and W Ltd., both of which are CCPCs. In order to avoid duplication of administrative costs, H and W incorporated a management corporation, M Ltd., to provide support services for H Ltd. and W Ltd. H and W each own 50% of the common shares of M Ltd.

— *REQUIRED*

Determine whether H Ltd., W Ltd. and M Ltd. are associated.

— *SOLUTION*

H Ltd., W Ltd. and M Ltd. are all associated with each other.

H Ltd. and M Ltd. are associated [par. 256(1)(*d*)]:

- H controls (100% of common shares) H Ltd.;

- H and W control M Ltd. (50% of common shares each);

- H is related to:

    (a) W through marriage [pars. 252(1)(*a*) and 252(6)(*b*)]; and

    (b) H through the deemed related rule for a shareholder [ssec. 256(1.5)]; and

- H owns not less than 25% of non-specified shares of the other corporation (100% of H Ltd. and 50% of M Ltd.).

W Ltd. and M Ltd. are associated also [par. 256(1)(*d*)], using the same logic.

Therefore, H Ltd. and W Ltd. are associated through a common third corporation, M Ltd. [ssec. 256(2)]. Note that without M Ltd., H Ltd. and W Ltd. would not be associated.

However, if M Ltd. elects, in prescribed form and on a year-by-year basis, not to be associated with either of the other two corporations, then H Ltd. and W Ltd. are deemed not to be associated for that particular year for purposes of the small business deduction. The business limit of M Ltd. is deemed to be nil for the taxation year, so that M Ltd. cannot, itself, benefit from the small business deduction. No election is needed if M Ltd. is not a Canadian-controlled private corporation.

8. Deemed association

Subsection 256(2.1) provides a deemed association rule where one of the main reasons for the separate existence of two corporations is tax considerations. The provision also contains a reasonableness test.[g] The decisions in the *Jutan Importers* and *Leggat Leasing* cases suggested that if the taxpayer can show a valid, non-tax reason for the separate existence of a corporation, the presence of a tax reason should not result in the application of the deemed association rule.

E. Corporate Partnerships
[ITA: 125(1)(a); 125(6)]

The associated corporations rules were designed to prevent the splitting of a business into numerous corporations each of which could qualify for the maximum small business deduction. Thus, corporations within an associated group must share that maximum small business deduction. To prevent the splitting of a business into numerous non-associated corporations operating as partners and each qualifying for the maximum small business deduction, further rules were designed to require that the maximum annual small business deduction limit of $250,000 for calendar year 2004 be shared by corporate partners or groups of corporate partners. These rules are necessary because partnerships are not taxed as separate entities as will be discussed in Chapter 18.

F. Manufacturing and Processing Profits Revisited
[ITA; 125.1]

In the previous chapter, the manufacturing and processing profits deduction was discussed without reference to the effect of the small business deduction on the manufacturing and processing profits deduction [ssec. 125.1(1)]. Essentially, there is no manufacturing and processing profits deduction on that portion of Canadian manufacturing and processing profits eligible for the small business deduction. The amount of manufacturing and processing profits deduction for a CCPC is computed as the excess of manufacturing and processing profits over the amount of income eligible for the small business deduction [par. 125.1(1)(a)]. However, the manufacturing and processing deduction is further limited by taxable income in excess of certain types of income that have already been taxed at preferential rates. Income eligible for the small business deduction is one of those types of income [par. 125.1(1)(b)]. Hence, the amount eligible for the small business deduction must be computed before the manufacturing and

---

[g] For examples of fact situations in which the predecessor to subsection 256(2.1) (i.e., subsection 247(2)) was at issue, see the cases of *Doris Trucking Company Limited v. M.N.R.*, (Ex. Ct.) 68 DTC 5204; *Jordans Rugs Ltd. et al. v. M.N.R.*, (Ex. Ct.) 69 DTC 5290; *Griffin Head Farms Limited v. M.N.R.*, (T.R.B.) 72 DTC 1225; *C.P. Loewen Enterprises Ltd. v. M.N.R.*, (F.C.T.D.) 72 DTC 6298; *Jutan Importers Ltd. v. M.N.R.*, (T.R.B.) 76 DTC 1289; *Leggat Leasing (Halton) Limited v. M.N.R.*, (T.R.B.) 78 DTC 1035; *Lenco Fibre Canada Corp. v. The Queen*, (F.C.T.D.) 79 DTC 5292; *Covertite Limited v. M.N.R.*, (T.R.B.) 79 DTC 136 and *Alpha Forming Corp. Ltd. et al. v. The Queen*, (F.C.T.D.) 83 DTC 5021. A more recent Tax Court of Canada case on this issue, where the decision was in favor of the taxpayer, is *LJP Sales Agency Inc. v. Her Majesty the Queen* (TCC), 2004 DTC 2007.

processing profits deduction can be calculated. Exhibit 12-5 summarizes the full provision in subsection 125.1(1).

EXHIBIT 12-5
Manufacturing and Processing Profits Deduction

7% of lesser of:

(a) manufacturing and processing profits in excess of the amount eligible for the small business deduction [ssec. 125(1)];

(b) taxable income, less sum of:

(i) amount eligible for the small business deduction [ssec. 125(1)],

(ii) 3* times the foreign tax deduction in respect of business income [ssec. 126(2)], and

(iii) where the corporation was a Canadian-controlled private corporation throughout the year, its aggregate investment income for the year (discussed subsequently) [ssec. 129(4)].

* [Proposed in the February 27, 2004 Revised Draft Legislation.]

Exhibit 12-2 and Exhibit 12-3 are equally applicable in determining the effective total corporate tax rate for income from manufacturing and processing activity that is eligible for the small business deduction.

Example Problem

During its first taxation year (of 365 days) which ended December 31, 2005, Touchee-Feelee Ltd., a Canadian-controlled private corporation, reported the following incomes:

Manufacturing and processing profits	$ 80,000
Total active business income earned in Canada (including M&P)	105,000
Foreign active business income (foreign tax paid $1,125)	5,000
Taxable income	75,000
Division B income	110,000
Taxable dividends paid in the year	40,000

The corporation carries on business in Canada and is not associated with any other Canadian-controlled private corporation. All foreign tax paid is recovered as a foreign tax credit under subsection 126(2). According to the formula in Regulation 402, 96% of the corporation's taxable income is earned in a province in Canada.

— REQUIRED

Compute the tax payable for 2005 by the corporation under Part I of the Act, assuming a 5% provincial rate of tax.

— SOLUTION

Taxable income		$ 75,000
Basic federal tax (38% of $75,000)		$ 28,500
Federal abatement (10% of 96% of $75,000)		(7,200)
Federal surtax (4% of 28% of $75,000)		840
Foreign business tax credit		(1,125)
Small business deduction:		
16% of least of:		
(a) Income from active business carried on in Canada	$105,000	
(b) Taxable income	$75,000	
Less: 3 × foreign business income tax credit (see above: 3 × $1,125)	(3,375) $ 71,625	
(c) Business limit	$300,000	
16% of $71,625		(11,460)

Manufacturing and processing profits deduction:
7% of lesser of:
  (a) M&P profits minus amount eligible for SBD
      ($80,000 – $71,625) .... $ 8,375

  (b) Taxable income .... $ 75,000
     Less:
     (i) Amount eligible for SBD $71,625
     (ii) Foreign business income (3 ×
     $1,125) 3,375
     (iii) Aggregate investment income ..... Nil   75,000
                                                 Nil

7% of Nil .... Nil
Federal Part I tax payable .... $ 9,555
Provincial tax @ 5% of 96% of $75,000................... 3,600
Total tax payable...................................... $ 13,155

G. Investment Tax Credit Revisited

[ITA: 13(7.1), 127(5), (9), (10.1), (10.2); 127.1; ITR: 2900; 4600–4602]

1. Overview

The investment tax credit (ITC), as described in Chapter 11, is also available for Canadian-controlled private corporations. However, additional incentives are provided for CCPCs. These incentives are obtained by adhering to a strict set of limitations many of which are similar to the restrictions for the small business deduction. This section will describe the advantages and limitations imposed by the legislation.

2. The ITC rate for CCPCs

Investment tax credits are presently restricted to qualifying scientific research and experimental development (SR&ED) expenditures for all jurisdictions within Canada. The one very limited exception is the credit for qualifying property expenditures for the Atlantic provinces and the Gaspé at a rate of 10% as described in Chapter 11. The basic SR&ED rate is 20% for all taxpayers including individuals, trusts and corporations [ssec. 127(9)]. This basic ITC rate of 20% has no dollar limit, except that all of the qualifying expenditures must meet the rules set out in section 37, as described in Chapter 4.

An additional ITC incentive of 15% is provided where the taxpayer is a CCPC throughout the taxation year in which the expenditure is made [ssec. 127(10.1)]. This additional rate results in a combined tax credit rate of 35%. However, the 15% additional credit bears additional restrictions as described below.

The additional 15% credit is restricted in total to $2,000,000 of qualifying expenditures, referred to as the SR&ED expenditure limit, but only where the preceding year's taxable income of the corporation and all associated corporations does not exceed the small business deduction limit for the year (i.e., $300,000 for the calendar year 2005 and later taxation years)[ssec. 127(10.2)]. Where the preceding year's taxable income of the corporation and all associated corporations exceeds $300,000, the SR&ED expenditure limit of $2,000,000 is reduced by $10 for every dollar of excess. Once the corporate group's taxable income reaches $500,000 the SR&ED expenditure is reduced to zero. The actual calculation of the expenditure limit in the provision is $5,000,000 minus ten times the greater of $300,000 and the taxable income of the associated group for the immediately preceding taxation year, where the taxation year is co-incident with the calendar year.

Note that ITCs are phased out for large CCPCs in a similar manner to the reduction of the small business deduction for corporations with taxable capital in excess of 10 million dollars.

3. Refundable investment tax credit

Since many small Canadian businesses may not be in a position to pay taxes because of a weak profit position or losses incurred, the investment tax credit is not a strong incentive to invest. Therefore, cash refunds are available to certain taxpayers, in respect of available investment tax credits which cannot be used to offset taxes payable in a particular year [sec. 127.1]. The extent to which a refund is available is a function of the status of the taxpayer, the nature of the expenditure that gave rise to the credit and when the expenditure was made. Investment tax credits that are available for deduction in a taxation year and which cannot be offset against taxes payable or converted into a cash refund, are available for carryover back three taxation years and forward ten taxation years. However, any ITC that is deducted or refunded in the year must be included in income for the following year in respect of current SR&ED expenditures [par. 12(1)(*t*)] or deducted from the capital cost of qualifying depreciable capital property acquisitions [ssec. 13(7.1)].

The refundable investment tax credit rates available to a qualifying CCPC are:

(a) 100% cash refund of the available 35% ITC based on qualifying SR&ED current expenditures not in excess of the expenditure limit for the year;

(b) 40% cash refund of the available 35% ITC based on qualifying SR&ED capital expenditures; and

(c) 40% cash refund of the available 20% ITC on qualifying SR&ED current expenditures in excess of the expenditure limit.

Note that the available ITC refers to the ITC as determined by the rules described in the previous section of this chapter.

Example Problem

Small Limited, a CCPC with a December 31 year-end, spent $2,000,000 in current SR&ED expenditures in 2005. Small Limited is not associated with any other corporation and may be eligible for an ITC of 35%.

— REQUIRED

Determine the amount of ITCs and refundable ITCs for 2005 on the assumption that its taxable income for the preceding year was:

(a) $300,000,

(b) $400,000, and

(c) $500,000.

— SOLUTION

Taxable income of preceding year	Expenditure limit	Refundable ITC	Non-refundable ITC
(a) $300,000	$2,000,000	$700,000[1]	Nil
(b) 400,000	1,000,000[2]	430,000[3]	$120,000[4]
(c) 500,000	Nil[5]	160,000[6]	240,000[7]

— NOTES TO SOLUTION

(1) 35% × $2,000,000

(2) $5,000,000 – ($400,000 × $10)

(3) ($1,000,000 × 35%) + ($1,000,000 × 20%) × 40%

(4) ($2,000,000 – $1,000,000) × 20% × 60%

(5) $5,000,000 – ($500,000 × $10)

(6) $2,000,000 × 20% × 40%

(7) $2,000,000 × 20% × 60%

4. Prescribed proxy amount

As indicated in Chapter 11, an elective alternative for the treatment of SR&ED overhead expenditures eligible for the investment tax credit was introduced to reduce the amount of record-keeping required. Under this annual election, referred to as a prescribed proxy amount (PPA), a prescribed amount rather than the actual overhead expenditure is eligible for ITC. Under the PPA election, the actual overhead expenditures are deductible from business income as ordinary expenditures rather than as SR&ED expenditures, which are credited to the SR&ED expenditure pool and written off as required [sec. 37]. For a more detailed explanation of the treatment of SR&ED expenditures, see Chapter 4. The major difference in the write-off treatment of the two methods is the limited period of carryforward for ordinary business expenses (i.e., 7 years for non-capital losses) as compared to the indefinite carryover for the SR&ED expenditure pool under section 37.

The PPA is only used in respect of the determination of ITCs related to SR&ED expenditures, not the deduction of overhead expenditures. The statutory reference to a PPA is found in the definition of the ITC base, a qualified expenditure [ssec. 127(9)]. The PPA itself is defined in and computed by Regulations 2900(4) and (5).

The PPA is basically a substitute for an item-by-item accounting for and allocating of overhead expenditures *directly* attributable to SR&ED in Canada. Regulation 2900(4) determines the PPA (i.e., the amount eligible for the ITC) as 65% of the salary base which is the portion of the salaries of employees directly engaged in SR&ED in Canada. The "portion", referred to above, is determined on a reasonable time allocation basis for each employee engaged in SR&ED, including direct technical management activities. For employees who spend all or substantially all (i.e., 90%) of their time on qualifying SR&ED activities, the whole amount of their salaries is included in the salary base.

A modification to this rule relates to "specified employees" [ssec. 248(1)]. A specified employee is one who is a specified shareholder of the corporate employer or who does not deal at arm's length with the employer-entity. A specified shareholder is defined [ssec. 248(1)] as a person who owns, together with the shares of related persons, 10% or more of any class of shares of the corporation. The salary base for specified employees is limited to the lesser of three-quarters of their full salary and 2.5 times the year's maximum pensionable earnings for CPP purposes (i.e., $41,100 for 2005) [Reg. 2900(7)].

Where a PPA election is used, eligible expenditures for SR&ED [sec. 37] and the related ITC are restricted to the following non-overhead expenditures:

(a) wages and benefits of employees *directly* engaged in SR&ED activities;

(b) leasing expenses of equipment, other than general-purpose office equipment or furniture, used *all or substantially all* in SR&ED activities;

(c) qualifying third-party payments for subcontracted SR&ED activities;

(d) costs of materials used directly in SR&ED activities;

(e) qualified SR&ED capital expenditures used *all or substantially all* (i.e., at least 90%) in SR&ED activities but excluding general purpose office equipment or furniture — see the next topic below; and

(f) capital cost allowance on 50% of the cost of leased equipment, other than general-purpose office equipment or furniture used *primarily* (i.e., more than 50%, but less than 90% (see (b) above)), for SR&ED activities. (See the next topic heading for an expansion of this topic.)

Regulation 2900(6) contains a restriction which prevents the PPA from being greater than the total amount, with some adjustments, that would otherwise be deductible as business expenses.

As a consequence of this election, the definition of a qualified expenditure has been expanded to include PPAs. Therefore, ITCs in respect of a PPA are treated in the same manner as all ITCs in respect of SR&ED and reduce the SR&ED expenditure pool. ITCs in respect of PPAs are also eligible for refundable investment tax credit treatment as previously discussed.

5. Capital expenditures

Under the normal SR&ED rules [sec. 37], a qualifying capital expenditure must be intended to be used *all or substantially all* (i.e., 90%) in SR&ED activities. This rule is a particularly harsh one since equipment, which is used less than 90% for SR&ED purposes and, therefore, is *shared* with other business activities, does not qualify for an ITC unless it can meet the 90% test.

Therefore, ITC rules have been introduced for equipment which is *shared* between SR&ED activities and other business activities, referred to as *shared-use-equipment*. The ITC rate on shared-use-equipment is one-half the normal rate and is earned on a usage basis over two time-periods (one-quarter for each time-period). These shared-use-equipment capital expenditures are not deductible as SR&ED under paragraph 37(1)(*b*) but must be deducted under the normal CCA rules.

The first time-period starts with the initial usage of the shared-use-equipment until the end of the next taxation year which must be at least 12 months after the initial use. The second time-period again begins with the initial use but ends at the second following taxation year that is at least 24 months after the initial usage. Furthermore, the equipment can only qualify for the second time-period ITC if it qualified initially for the first time-period ITC.

Example Problem

Mr. A owns all the common shares of ABC Limited, a Canadian-controlled private corporation. ABC Limited incurred certain costs in the development of a new process that qualifies for SR&ED expenditures treatment.

Direct material	$250,000
Direct labour	200,000
Indirect material and labour costs	150,000

Of the indirect costs, Mr. A believes that approximately 20% is applicable to the development of the new process, but the corporation's accounting system is not sophisticated enough to identify the direct overhead costs.

Included in the direct labour costs is a salary of $50,000 paid to Mr. A's daughter, a professional engineer who spent 90% of her time on SR&ED activities.

ABC Limited has not had any SR&ED expenditures in the past and had taxable income for the preceding year of $135,000. ABC Limited is not associated with any other corporation. The corporation does not anticipate that it will have any taxable income for this taxation year.

— REQUIRED

Describe the tax treatment of the direct and indirect development costs of the new process on the assumption that the new process meets the requirements as SR&ED expenditures for the taxation year ending December 31, 2005.

— SOLUTION

All of the direct material and direct labour costs, for a total of $450,000, are deductible as current SR&ED expenditures since they are directly attributable to the development of the new process [sec. 37]. Any amount of these expenses that are not deductible this year will qualify for the SR&ED expenditure pool and can be deducted in any future year. Any ITC claimed or small business deduction business refunded in this year or in future years is deducted from the expenditure pool.

In addition, all of the direct material and direct labour costs qualify for an ITC of 35% since ABC Limited's taxable income in the preceding year was under the small business deduction limit (i.e., $300,000 for the calendar year 2005 and later years) and the total of these direct costs was less than the expenditure limit of $2,000,000. The ITC would be $157,500, i.e., 35% of $450,000.

Since the indirect material and labour costs cannot be traced directly to the development of the new process, they are not deductible under section 37 but are expensed in the normal manner under section 9. An ITC can also be claimed on the indirect material and labour costs of $100,000 by electing the proxy amount method for the current taxation year. The amount of the ITC is calculated below:

Direct labour costs	$200,000
Less: Daughter's salary (a specified employee)	50,000
	$150,000
Plus: Eligible portion of the daughter's salary — Lesser[1] of:	
(a) 75% of $50,000 = $ 37,500	
(b) 2.5 × $41,100 = $102,750	$ 37,500
	$187,500
Amount eligible for the proxy amount (65% of $187,500)	$121,875
ITC 35% thereof	$ 42,656

Note that these labour costs are used as the basis of the proxy amount for overhead. The deduction of labour expenses and other overhead expenses as business expenses is not affected by this proxy amount calculation.

Mr. A's daughter is considered to be a specified shareholder [ssec. 248(1)] since she is *deemed* to own all of her father's shares [par. (*a*) of definition of "specified shareholder" in ssec. 248(1)] and, therefore, owns not less than 10% of the issued shares (i.e., 100% in this situation).

Since ABC Limited does not expect to have any taxable income this year it can apply for a 100% cash refund of the total ITCs of $200,156 ($157,500 + $42,656). Alternatively, ABC Limited can apply these ITCs against taxes payable in the three preceding years or against future taxes in the next 10 years.

In the following taxation year, ABC Limited will have to include in income the amount of the ITC deducted or refunded of $200,156 [par. 12(1)(*t*)].

— NOTE TO SOLUTION

(1) Limited by Regulation 2900(7) for a specified employee, but cannot exceed the portion of actual salary allocated to SR&ED (i.e., 90% of $50,000 or $45,000, in this case).

H. Incorporated Business Income and Integration

Now that the complete system for the taxation of business income has been presented, an analysis can be done to determine whether there is a tax advantage to incorporating business income. The answer to the question is affected largely by the corporate tax rate applicable to the business income. Generally, business income not eligible for the small business deduction at the corporate level will attract higher tax costs when earned through a corporation than when earned directly by an individual. This is the case regardless of whether the business income is eligible for the manufacturing and processing profits deduction at the corporate level. Exhibits 12-6 and 12-7 illustrate this point, using the corporate tax rates developed in Exhibits 11-3 and 11-5.

However, there may be the possibility of a tax deferral to the extent that dividends from the business income earned are not paid out immediately. This deferral possibility exists when the personal taxes which must be paid immediately on directly-earned business income exceed the corporate taxes, on the same business income. For example, in Exhibit 12-7, for the top tax bracket, the combined federal and provincial personal tax rate is 46%. Hence, item (C) is $460 and (C) – (A) in the last line of the exhibit reflects a deferral of $109. If the time value of money is considered, this deferral advantage may outweigh the added tax cost of incorporating this business income in a province with relatively high personal tax rates. Of course, there are other, non-tax reasons for incorporating such business income.

On active business income eligible for the small business deduction, a small tax saving results from the incorporation of such income compared to receiving it directly if the total corporate tax rate is lower than the theoretical 20% where integration is perfect. There is, however, the possibility of deferring tax on dividends ultimately distributed to the shareholders by delaying that distribution. Exhibit 12-8 illustrates these effects which result in a small tax saving using the theoretical corporate tax rates developed in Exhibit 12-2. Remember that although most provincial corporate rates lie between 8.9% and 17%, the equivalent of the federal small business deduction is also given by most provinces to give an approximate effective rate of 5%.

It will take a provincial rate of tax below 6.88% to provide tax savings from the incorporation of income eligible for the small business deduction. For all higher provincial income tax rates, the total corporate tax rate will be above the 20% rate necessary for perfect integration and, as a result, there will be a tax cost to incorporation.

EXHIBIT 12-6
Taxation of Active Business Income Not Eligible for Small Business Deduction or Manufacturing and Processing Profits Deduction

Corporation			
Income		$1,000	
Corporate tax — 37.12%			
(38% – 10% + 1.12% – 7% + 15%) .... (A)		(371)	
Available for dividend		$ 629	
Individual			
Dividend		$ 629	
Add: gross-up..		157	
Income subject to tax		$ 786	
Combined federal and provincial tax rate		*26%*	*46%*
Tax on dividend before credit		$ 204	$ 362
Total dividend tax credit ((13¹/₃% + 6 ²/₃%) of $786)...........		(157)	(157)
Net tax		$ 47	$ 205
Add: tax paid by corporation .... (A)		371	371
Total tax .... (B)		$ 418	$ 576
Tax on income if unincorporated .... (C)		$ 260	$ 460
Tax cost of incorporating on $1,000 of income .... (B)–(C)		$ 158	$ 116
Deferral (prepayment) of tax through a corporation ...... (C)–(A)		$ (111)	$ 89

The concept of a "tax cost" is based on the excess of the total tax liability when the income is flowed through a corporation as compared to income earned through an unincorporated business. Under the tax cost concept it is assumed that all of the after-tax cash of the corporation will be paid out in dividends. In Exhibit 12-6, the tax cost at an individual's lowest rate of tax (26%) is $158 whereas the tax cost at the highest tax rate (46%) is only $116. The difference between the two is $42 which is due largely to the difference in the tax rates of 20% (46% – 26%) times the $214 difference between the individual's unincorporated business income of $1,000 and the grossed-up dividend income of $786. Therefore, as an individual's tax increases, the tax cost of using a corporation decreases.

A tax prepayment or deferral is based on a similar concept except for the assumption that none of the corporate after-tax cash is paid out immediately but is retained in the corporation. The ultimate benefits of a deferral are twofold: the present value of the deferred tax payment and after-tax financing costs avoided by the use of its retained earnings. In Exhibit 12-6, at the lowest rate of an individual's tax (26%) there was a prepayment of taxes of $111 because of the difference between the individual's low rate (26%) and the corporate rate of 37.12% or 11.12% on the business income of $1,000. At the highest rate of individual tax (46%), there was a small tax deferral of $89 (rounded) (i.e., 46% – 37.12% = 8.88%; 8.88% × $1,000 = $88.80 of business income) because of the lower corporate tax rate. The higher the individual tax rate relative to the corporate tax rate, the greater the potential deferral.

EXHIBIT 12-7
Taxation of Active Business Income Not Eligible for Small Business Deduction But Eligible for Manufacturing and Processing Profits Deduction

Corporation		
Income	$1,000	
Corporate tax — 35.12%		
(38% – 10% + 1.12% – 7% + 13%) .... (A)	(351)	
Available for dividend	$ 649	
Individual		
Dividend	$ 649	
Add: gross-up	162	
Income subject to tax	$ 811	
Combined federal and provincial tax rate	*26%*	*46%*
Tax on dividend before credit	$ 211	$ 373
Total dividend tax credit ((13⅓% + 6⅔%) of $811)	(162)	(162)
Net tax	$ 49	$ 211
Add: tax paid by corporation .... (A)	351	351
Total tax .... (B)	$ 400	$ 562
Tax on income if unincorporated .... (C)	$ 260	$ 460
Tax cost of incorporating on $1,000 of income .... (B)–(C)	$ 140	$ 102
Deferral (prepayment) of tax through a corporation ...... (C)–(A)	$ (91)	$ 109

EXHIBIT 12-8
Taxation of Active Business Income Eligible for Small Business Deduction

Corporation			
Income		$1,000	
Corporate tax — 18.12%			
(38% – 10% + 1.12% – 16% + 5%).........................	(A)	(181)	
Available for dividend		$ 819	
Individual			
Dividend		$ 819	
Add: gross-up...		205	
Income subject to tax		$1,024	
Combined federal and provincial tax rate		*26%*	*46%*
Tax on dividend before credit		$ 266	$ 471
Total dividend tax credit ((13 1/3% + 6 2/3%) of $1,024)		(205)	(205)
Net tax		$ 61	$ 266
Add: tax paid by corporation	(A)	181	181
Total tax	(B)	$ 242	$ 447
Tax on income if unincorporated	(C)	$ 260	$ 460
Tax cost (saving) of incorporation on $1,000 of income (B)–(C)		$ (18)	$ (13)
Deferral of tax equivalent through a corporation......... (C)–(A)		$ 79	$ 279

The foregoing calculations can be summarized by Exhibit 12-9 which averages the tax cost and deferral or prepayment between the two personal tax rates.

EXHIBIT 12-9
Summary of Tax Cost and Deferral from Incorporating Business Income

Type of business income	Average tax cost (saving)*	Average tax deferral (prepayment)*
Not eligible for small business deduction or manufacturing and processing profits deduction (Exhibit 12-6).................	13.7%	(1.1)%
Not eligible for small business deduction but eligible for manufacturing and processing profits deduction (Exhibit 12-7)...........	12.1	(0.9)
Eligible for small business deduction but not manufacturing and processing profits deduction (Exhibit 12-8).................	(1.5)	17.9

* Average of highest and lowest tax rates.

Note from Exhibits 12-6 to 12-8 that tax costs decrease as personal tax rates increase and the deferral advantage increases as personal tax rates increase. The above averages show that tax cost decreases as corporate tax rates decrease and the deferral advantage increases as corporate tax rates decrease.

From the foregoing analysis, it should be possible to draw some conclusions of both a tax and non-tax nature regarding the incorporating of business operations. The advantages of incorporation appear to include the following:

(a) limited liability, although it should be recognized that to the extent creditors of an incorporated business demand personal guarantees from shareholders, limited liability is negated;

(b) tax savings if the combined corporate tax rate is under 20%;

(c) tax deferral at higher personal income levels on business income not eligible for the small business deduction or the manufacturing and processing profits deduction and at all personal income levels on business income eligible for the small business deduction;

(d) income splitting potential in carefully planned and very restrictive situations (as discussed previously with respect to the attribution rules and tax on split income) with family members as employees or shareholders;

(e) estate planning advantages on the transfer of future growth in the corporation's shares to children (as discussed in a subsequent chapter);

(f) availability of registered pension plans, including defined-benefit plans, to the owner as an employee of a corporation is not possible in the unincorporated form;

(g) separation of business and personal activities;

(h) stabilization of income of the individual through salary payments or greater flexibility in the timing of the receipt of income subject to personal tax;

(i) continuity of the separate legal entity;

(j) deferral of accrued capital gains on transfer of shares to a spouse (as discussed in a subsequent chapter);

(k) potentially easier access to financing;

(l) availability of the capital gains exemption for qualified small business corporation shares; and

(m) availability of the deferral of capital gains on the sale of eligible small business corporation shares [ssec. 44.1(1)], if replacement shares are acquired.

The disadvantages of incorporating business operations appear to include:

(a) a tax cost if the combined corporate tax rate is over 20%;

(b) a prepayment of tax at lower levels of personal income on business income not eligible for the small business deduction;

(c) the additional costs of maintaining a corporation including payment of provincial capital and payroll taxes; and

(d) a loss of the availability of business and capital losses to offset personal income. While this disadvantage may be offset, to some extent, by the availability of allowable business investment loss treatment for shares of a small business corporation, the loss is only one-half deductible and it is deductible only on sale of the shares or bankruptcy of the corporation.

Often the tax saving, if any, or deferral will, in many cases, outweigh the disadvantages of incorporating such income, at least for rates of corporate tax in existence at less than 20%. This is particularly so where business income eligible for the small business deduction is earned through a corporation.

III. INCOME FROM INVESTMENTS

A. Overview of Integration for Income from Investments

1. Purpose

(a) *Investment Income*

The tax system provides special rules for private corporations which are meant to eliminate some of the tax biases between income earned by an individual and income earned by a corporation. One bias arises from the potential double taxation of investment income. For the moment, think of investment income as property income (i.e., interest, rents, etc., but not dividends). Later on, a more precise definition will be given. Without special rules, investment income would be taxed once in the corporation and again at the shareholder level when dividends are paid. To eliminate this bias, the concept of a refundable tax was developed, whereby a portion of the initial corporate tax on such income is refunded when dividends are paid. The tax on investment income was intended to be reduced to an approximate rate of tax of 20%. The dividend tax credit then would allow the shareholder credit for that 20% tax paid by the company and complete integration of corporate and personal taxes would be achieved. Thus, a Canadian who transfers his or her investments to a private corporation and flows the income through the corporation, would, theoretically, retain the same amount of after-tax investment income as he or she would if the investments were held personally and had received the income from the investments directly.

When investment income is flowed through a corporation, an indefinite deferral of tax is possible if the initial corporate tax rate is relatively low and if the investment income is left in the corporation and not distributed by way of dividends to the shareholders. In contrast, an individual Canadian who holds his or her investments personally, is required to pay tax on the income as it is received or accrued. The tax system attempts to eliminate this bias by ensuring that investment income earned in a corporation is taxed initially at a high corporate rate. Then the corporate tax is partially refunded when the investment income is distributed, by way of taxable dividends, to the corporation's shareholders who then pay tax on the income at their personal rate.

The system of integration was intended to bring the effective corporate rate of tax on investment income down to 20%. This rate is the same rate that was intended to apply on up to $300,000 of active business income for calendar year 2005 and later years. As mentioned previously, at a corporate rate of 20% the objective of theoretically perfect integration is achieved. However, the specific rules applied to each type of income achieve the objective in opposite ways. On the one hand, the rules applied to active business income provide for a low initial rate of corporate tax, after the small business deduction, to allow for greater retention of income for reinvestment in the business. On the other hand, the rules applied to investment income provide for a high initial rate of corporate tax to prevent the use of a corporation as a means of deferring tax on investment income. When retained earnings are distributed as dividends, the dividend refund was intended to bring the total effective corporate tax rate on that investment income down to 20%.

Exhibit 12-10 shows the tax rates on which the refundable system for investment income was based theoretically to achieve perfect integration.

EXHIBIT 12-10
Theoretical Corporate Tax Rates for Perfect Integration on Investment Income
Eligible for a Dividend Refund and the First $300,000 of Active Business Income
of a Canadian-Controlled Private Corporation

	Investment income	Active business income
Federal tax rate (theoretical)	40%	40%
Abatement for provincial tax	(10)	(10)
Net federal tax	30%	30%
Small business deduction	—	(16)
Refund of tax paid on investment income on the payment of dividends......................	(20)	—
Net federal tax after dividend refund and small business deduction	10%	14%
Provincial tax (theoretical)	10%	6%
Effective total tax................................	20%	20%

However, the theoretical model in Exhibit 12-10, in reality, does not operate perfectly for a number of reasons. First, the basic federal tax rate is 38%, not 40%. Second, the theoretical model ignores surtaxes, which are supposed to be only temporary taxes, but in reality have become a permanent part of the system. Finally, provincial taxes are generally greater than the theoretical model, e.g., 11.5% to 17% for investment income and up to 8.9% for the first $300,000 of active business income for calendar year 2005 and later years.

Even with these imperfections, it would be possible to defer tax on investment income through the use of a corporation, because the total tax at the corporate level would be less than the top personal tax rate in most provinces. In order to remove the deferral of tax on investment income, an additional refundable tax of $6^2/3$% is levied [sec. 123.3].

Exhibit 12-11 shows the effective tax rate on investment income, including the additional refundable tax of $6^2/3$%.

EXHIBIT 12-11
Effective Tax Rate on Investment Income*

Federal tax rate..	38.00%
Abatement for provincial tax	(10.00)
Net federal tax	28.00%
Federal surtax: 4%	1.12
Additional refundable tax....................................	6.67
Refund on the payment of dividends............................	(26.67)
Net federal tax after dividend refund	9.12%
Provincial tax** (theoretical)	14.50
Effective total rate	23.62%

* Investment income includes all types of property income such as interest, royalties and rent, but does not include dividends from taxable Canadian corporations.

** A provincial corporate tax rate of 10.88% on investment income would result in an effective total tax rate of 20% which would result in perfect integration. However, provincial taxes vary between 11.5% and 17%.

Exhibit 12-12 shows a calculation of effective total tax applicable to taxable investment income of a Canadian-controlled private corporation eligible for a refund on the payment of dividends, referred to as a dividend refund, using an average provincial rate and including the $6^{2}/_{3}\%$ additional refundable tax on investment income.

EXHIBIT 12-12
Comparison of Theoretical Tax Rates Applicable to Investment Income Eligible for a Dividend Refund and on the First $300,000 Active Business Income of a Canadian-controlled Private Corporation

	Investment income[1]	Active business income[2]
Federal tax rate [par. 123(1)(*a*)]	38.00%	38.00%
Abatement for provincial tax [ssec. 124(1)]	(10.00)	(10.00)
Net federal tax	28.00%	28.00%
Federal surtax @ 4% of above net	1.12	1.12
Additional refundable tax on investment income	6.67	Nil
Small business deduction	—	(16.00)
Refund on payment of dividends from investment income [ssec. 129(1)]	(26.67)	—
Net federal tax after dividend refund	9.12%	13.12%
Provincial tax (theoretical)	14.50[3]	5.00[4]
Effective total tax.	23.62%	18.12%

(1) Investment income includes all types of property income except dividends from taxable Canadian corporations.

(2) This column of the table reflects the tax on the first $300,000 of active business income for calendar year 2005 and later years. Over $300,000, there is no small business deduction; therefore, the effective tax rate would be 43.62%, assuming a full theoretical provincial tax rate of 14.5%.

(3) A provincial corporate tax rate of 10.88% on investment income would result in an effective total tax of 20% (excluding surtaxes) which would allow for perfect integration. However, provincial tax rates tend to be around 13%.

(4) Several provinces also give a small business deduction on the first $300,000 of active business income for calendar year 2005 and later years. In this example, a 5% provincial small business deduction was assumed.

Exhibit 12-12 clearly demonstrates that effective tax rates for investment income and active business income, at or below $300,000 for the calendar year 2005 and later years, are approximately the same and close to perfect integration. However, where the $300,000 active business income has been exceeded, there is a significant difference in the effective tax rates on these two types of income (i.e., 43.62% for business income v. 23.62% for investment income.) This difference may encourage some taxpayers to attempt to re-characterize some of their active business income (over $300,000) as investment income so as to attract the investment income net rate (23.62%) which has no cap (like the $300,000 business limit). Remember, however, that one important downside of investment income is that the initial corporate tax rate is at the high 43.62% rate plus a $6^{2}/_{3}\%$ additional refundable tax and that dividends must be paid in order to trigger the refund of Part I tax of $26^{2}/_{3}\%$. While the corporate rate after the refund is low at 23.62% (i.e., 43.62% + 6.67% − 26.67%), the shareholders receive a dividend which is taxable to complete the integration process.

(b) *Portfolio Dividends*

Another bias arises because intercorporate dividends are deductible in order to arrive at taxable income and, therefore, not subject to tax under Part I of the Act. By placing dividend-yielding investments in a corporation, an individual, particularly one in a high tax bracket, could defer tax on dividend income indefinitely. A $33^1/_3\%$ Part IV refundable tax that certain corporations pay on such dividends is intended to eliminate this bias. The Part IV tax rules are provided in section 186.

If it were not for the Part IV tax on what are referred to as "portfolio dividends", it would be extremely attractive for an individual to make portfolio investments in dividend-producing shares through an investment holding corporation. No tax would be paid under Part I on the dividends received by the holding corporation. By contrast, an individual who owned the portfolio investments directly, would pay tax under Part I at his or her personal rate on any dividends received. Thus, the Part IV tax of $33^1/_3\%$ levied on the recipient corporation is an initial tax roughly equivalent to the tax that would be paid by the individual in the top federal tax bracket receiving a dividend from a taxable Canadian corporation. See Exhibit 12-13 which uses an approximate tax rate of 34% for an individual. The Part IV tax is fully refundable when the recipient corporation itself pays a dividend to its shareholders. Thus, after the refund, the corporation is effectively not taxed on the dividend that it received from another corporation and passed on to its shareholders. This preserves the integration system by preventing double taxation of the income that gave rise to the original dividend from the originating corporation to the holding corporation.

2. Conceptual illustration of integration

Exhibit 12-13 illustrates conceptually how investment income, such as interest income, capital gains and portfolio dividends are integrated through a private corporation that qualifies for refundable tax treatment. Recall, one of the objectives of the integration system is to ensure that income from investments, which flows through a qualifying private corporation to its shareholders, bears the same total tax burden (at the combined corporate and individual level) that would be borne on that income if it were earned directly by an individual. For simplicity of illustration, and to demonstrate total integration, the corporate tax is assumed to be 40% plus the additional refundable tax of $6^2/_3\%$ and the dividend tax credit, including the provincial tax effect, is assumed to be equal to the $^1/_4$ gross-up. The combined federal and provincial tax rates for individuals is assumed to be 34% for this illustration, although *any individual's combined federal and provincial marginal tax rate* could have been used to show perfect integration. Under these assumptions, this objective of integration is met perfectly.

EXHIBIT 12-13
Conceptual Illustration of Integration

	$100 Interest income	*$200* Capital gain		*$100* Portfolio dividend
		Taxable	Non-taxable	
Company				
Income	$100	$100	$100*	$100
Tax: @ 40% on investment income [Part I]	(40)(A)	(40)(A)		—
@ 33¹/₃% on portfolio dividend [Part IV]				(33)(A)
Additional refundable tax @ 6²/₃%	(7)(B)	(7)(B)		—
	$ 53	$ 53		$ 67
Refund on payment of dividend (see amounts below)				
26²/₃% of investment income	27(C)	27(C)		—
33¹/₃% of portfolio dividends	—	—		$ 33(C)
Available for payment of dividend	$ 80	$ 80		$100
Shareholder (34% hypothetical *combined* marginal tax rate)				
Dividend received	$ 80	$ 80		$100
¼ gross-up	20	20		25
Income for taxes	$100	$100		$125
Tax @ 34% (assumed)	$ 34	$ 34		$ 43
Less: dividend tax credit, including provincial (approx.)	(20)	(20)		(25)
Net tax paid	$ 14	$ 14		$ 18(D)
Summary of tax paid				
Corporation (net of refund) (A) + (B) – (C) ...	$ 20	$ 20		NIL
Shareholder	14	14		$ 18
Total	$ 34	$ 34		$ 18
Tax paid on equivalent amount of income if received directly by investor	$ 34	$ 34		$ 18**

*This amount can be paid as a capital dividend which is received by the shareholder tax free (as discussed in a subsequent chapter).

** The calculation would be identical to that resulting in amount (D).

B. Special Refundable Taxes in Respect of Income from Investments

[ITA: 82; 83(2); 89(1); 111(1)(*b*); 123.3; 129; 186; 187]

1. Investment income

Aggregate investment income is broadly defined [ssec. 129(4)] to include income from property, plus net taxable capital gains, less certain adjustments. Property income, for the purposes of this definition, includes net income from all property, other than (a) exempt income and (b) dividends which are deductible in computing taxable income. The meaning of the term "income from property" is amplified by the definition "income" or "loss" [ssec. 129(4)] which includes income from a specified investment business *carried on in Canada*, but excludes income from the following sources:

(a) from any property that is incident to or pertains to an active business carried on by a corporation, or

(b) from any property used or held primarily for the purpose of earning income from an active business carried on by the corporation.

Net losses from property are deducted from the foregoing amounts of property income.

Foreign investment income [ssec. 129(4)] is calculated as aggregate investment income from foreign sources. Hence, aggregate investment income includes that income from both Canadian and foreign sources.

As part of the system of integration, one-half of the capital gains and capital losses that is not included in income, is included in the corporation's capital dividend account (discussed in a subsequent chapter) [ssec. 89(1)]. The Act permits the corporation to pay a dividend out of the capital dividend account [ssec. 83(2)]. The capital dividend is received free of tax by the shareholder. This completes the full integration of capital gains through a private corporation or Canadian-controlled private corporation and, with respect to the tax-free portion of the capital gains, places the shareholder in the same position as if he or she received the gain directly.

2. Additional refundable tax (ART)

(a) *Basic Rules*

For Canadian-controlled private corporations, a refundable tax [sec. 123.3] is imposed on "aggregate investment income". This tax can be summarized as follows:

$6^2/_3\%$ × the lesser of:

    (a) aggregate investment income [ssec. 129(4)], and

    (b) taxable income minus the amount on which the small business deduction is based.

Aggregate investment income (AII) [ssec. 129(4)] can be summarized as follows:

- Net taxable capital gains for the year,
- Less: net capital losses deducted under Division C,
- Plus: income from property (Canadian and foreign)*,
- Less: dividends deducted under Division C,
- Less: losses from property (Canadian and foreign).

* Includes interest, royalties, rents and dividends.

(b) *Avoiding the Potential Circular Calculation with ART*

The calculation of the ART has been complicated by the fact that a number of the components of the corporate tax calculation are interrelated. For example:

    (a) the small business deduction must be calculated in order to complete the ART;

    (b) the foreign tax credit (FTC) calculations are needed to calculate the small business deduction; and

    (c) the "tax for the year otherwise payable under this Part" [ssec. 126(7)], which normally would include the ART, is needed to calculate the FTCs.

As a result, there could have been a circular calculation if the following provisions were not introduced:

    (a) the "tax for the year otherwise payable under this Part" for the business FTC excludes ART [ssec.126(7)]; and

    (b) the small business deduction calculation that grosses up the non-business FTC ($^{10}/_3$ × non-business FTC) must be calculated on the assumption that the non-business FTC calculation does not include the ART [spar. 125(1)(*b*)(i)].

To minimize confusion, Exhibit 12-14 sets out the steps that should be taken when calculating the ART when foreign tax credits are involved.

EXHIBIT 12-14
Steps to be taken to Calculate ART when FTCs are Involved

(1) Calculate the non-business FTC excluding ART from the "tax for the year otherwise payable under this Part" [ssec.126(1), spar. 125(1)(*b*)(i)].

(2) Calculate the business FTC (by definition, this excludes ART from "tax for the year otherwise payable under this Part" [ssec.126(2)].

(3) Calculate the small business deduction using the above numbers.

(4) Calculate the ART.

(5) Recalculate the final non-business FTC and include ART in the "tax for the year otherwise payable under this Part".

(6) Recalculate the business FTC with the final non-business FTC (normally, no change will result).

3. "Refundable dividend tax on hand" (RDTOH)

"Refundable dividend tax on hand" (RDTOH) may be viewed as an account which accumulates all of the tax paid by a private company on its portfolio dividend income (i.e., Part IV tax at $33^1/_3\%$) and a portion of the Part I tax paid by a Canadian-controlled private corporation on other investment income. The principal components of the account are as follows:

- the refundable portion of Part I tax (including the ART) that is paid on investment income [par. 129(3)(*a*)];

- the amount of Part IV tax [sec. 186] that is paid on taxable dividends (the Part IV tax is discussed in more detail below) [par. 129(3)(*b*)]; and

- the RDTOH balance at the end of the previous year [par. 129(3)(*c*)], less "dividend refunds" (explained below) of the previous year that arise when the corporation pays taxable dividends [par. 129(3)(*d*)].

The taxes that are accumulated in the RDTOH account are refundable to the company at the rate of $1 of refund for every $3 of taxable dividends paid [spar. 129(1)(*a*)(i)]. These refunds are commonly referred to as "dividend refunds", which reduce the balance in the refundable dividend tax on hand account [par. 129(3)(*d*)].

The following diagram of a "gravity bin" or "water tank" illustrates these rules conceptually:

- Refundable portion of 6 2/3 %
  Part I tax (includes ART)

- All of Part IV tax 33.33 %

current-year additions

- RDTOH balance at previous
  year-end

- Minus: dividend refund of
  previous year

previous year balance

taxable dividends paid: $3

Dividend refund: $1

"Refundable dividend tax on hand" (RDTOH) [ssec. 129(3)] is illustrated, in part, in Exhibit 12-15. The basic purpose of the calculation is to aggregate the two types of refundable taxes (i.e., refundable portion of Part I tax for investment income (shown in the Exhibit) and Part IV tax for portfolio dividends), net of the amount of refundable taxes actually received.

EXHIBIT 12-15
Refundable Portion of Part I Tax [par. 129(3)(a)]

The amount added to RDTOH in a taxation year in respect of Part I tax is the total of:
   (a) where the corporation was a CCPC throughout the year, the least of:
      (i) $26^2/_3\%$ × aggregate investment income
         less the net of: non-business foreign tax credit
               minus: $9^1/_3{}^*$ × foreign investment income
      (ii) $26^2/_3\%$ × the quantity of:
        (taxable income
        less the total of: the amount eligible for the small business deduction
               $25/_9{}^{**}$ × non-business foreign tax credit
               3^{***} × business foreign tax credit)
      (iii) Part I tax minus surtax.

---

* The December 20, 2002 Draft Legislation had proposed to replace this factor with $^1/_{30}$, but the February 27, 2004 Revised Draft Legislation does not. The notional federal tax rate for non-business income is 36% (i.e., 38% − 10% + 1.12% + 6.67% = 35.7%). $9^1/_3\%$ is the notional 36% rate less $26^2/_3\%$.

** The December 20, 2002 Draft Legislation had proposed to replace this factor with $^{10}/_3$, but the February 27, 2004 Revised Draft Legislation does not. $^{25}/_9$ is the equivalent of $^{100}/_{36}$, based on the notional 36% rate.

*** $33^1/_3\%$ is the notional federal tax rate for foreign business income (38% + 1.12% − 7% (general reduction) = 32.12%, say, 33.33%)). [Proposed in the February 27, 2004 Revised Draft Legislation.]

The refundable portion of the Part I tax is designed to produce a refundable tax equal to $26^{2}/_{3}\%$ of investment income (excluding most dividends). The provisions establish aggregate investment income, net of expenses, from which net capital losses deducted in the year [par. 111(1)(*b*)] and losses for the year from property sources are subtracted [ssec. 129(4)]. The justification for deducting the net capital losses is that since investment income is computed at the net income level, it is possible that taxable capital gains included in income could be offset by net capital losses which are deducted at the taxable income level after the computation of income for tax purposes. Since no Part I tax would be payable on such taxable capital gains, no refund of unpaid tax should apply to such gains. Hence, net capital losses claimed [par. 111(1)(*b*)] are deducted from aggregate investment income eligible for refundable treatment.

The calculations ensure that no refundable tax is calculated on foreign investment income which gives rise to a foreign tax credit in the year. Such foreign income will, therefore, not result in a refund of Canadian taxes that have not been paid as a result of the foreign tax credit.

The adjustments to taxable income are made to restrict the amount of the refund where other items (i.e., the small business deduction and foreign-source income) have reduced the taxable income below the investment income subject to tax.

Finally, the refundable portion of Part I tax is limited by the amount of tax payable under Part I, because there should not be a potential refund of a portion of Part I tax that has not been paid. Such non-payment of Part I tax may be due to the carryover of losses, deductions such as the small business deduction and the M&P deduction, or credits such as foreign tax credits, investment tax credits and political donations credits.

4. "Deeming rules"

Subsection 129(6) provides what are known in practice as "deeming rules". This provision is an anti-avoidance provision that converts what would be property income (e.g., rent and interest) into active business income. However, this deeming provision only applies in situations where the income was derived from an associated corporation that had deducted the same amount in determining its active business income.

Were it not for these deeming rules, it would be possible for a corporation that was approaching the $300,000 business limit for its small business deduction to transfer certain of its assets to a new associated corporation which would rent the assets back to the original corporation. The rental expense incurred by the original corporation would be deductible, thereby reducing its active business income and preventing income in excess of $300,000 from being taxed at full corporate rates. The rental income to the new corporation would be considered income from property or income from a specified investment business and would, therefore, be eligible for refundable treatment. However, as a result of subsection 129(6), the amounts received are deemed to be active business income of the recipient.

As a result, the combined active business income of the original corporation and of the new corporation, which receives rent deemed to be active business income is the same as it would have been if the new corporation had not been set up; that is, the fact that the two corporations must share the $300,000 business limit has no effect on the total active business income of the group. Thus, any active business income in excess of $300,000 within the associated group will be taxed at full corporate rates as it would have been without the new corporation. These deeming rules are summarized in Exhibit 12-16.

EXHIBIT 12-16
"Deeming Rules" [ssec. 129(6)]

Conditions	(1) Amount that would be income of the recipient corporation from property.	(2) Amount deductible in computing income from an active business of an *associated* payer corporation.	
Effect	(1) Amount not included in income from property.	(2) Amount deemed to be income of the recipient from an active business [spar. 129(6)(*b*)(*i*)].	
Application of small business deduction	Eligible for the small business deduction to the extent that the associated group of corporations has not exceeded the $300,000 business limit [ssec. 125(1)].		

5. Part IV tax on portfolio and other dividends

Normally, when a private corporation (or a "subject corporation", which is discussed below) receives a taxable dividend from another Canadian company (or an exempt dividend from a foreign affiliate), the dividend is deductible, under section 112 (or 113), in computing taxable income. However, a 33⅓% tax must be paid on some of these dividends [par. 186(1)(*a*)]. A calculation of the Part IV tax is made in the T2 corporate tax return to meet the filing requirements for this tax [ssec. 187(1)]. Late-filed payments of this tax are subject to interest at the prescribed rate [ssec. 187(2)]. This special Part IV tax is fully refundable to the corporation when the dividend income is passed on to its shareholders as previously discussed [par. 129(3)(*b*)].

Part IV tax is a temporary tax of 33⅓% levied on "assessable dividends" received by a "private corporation" or a "subject corporation" with an exception for dividends received from "connected corporations".

(a) *Assessable Dividends*

Dividends subject to Part IV tax have often been referred to as "portfolio dividends" even though the Act does not use this term. The term "assessable dividend" is defined to include dividends that are deductible under Division C [ssec. 186(3)].

(b) *Private Corporation*

A private corporation is a corporation that is resident in Canada and that is neither a public corporation nor controlled by a public corporation [ssec. 89(1)].

(c) *Subject Corporation*

A "subject corporation" a corporation resident in Canada (other than a private corporation) [ssec. 186(3)]. A subject corporation is controlled (in the common law sense of ownership of shares with more than 50% of the votes), whether because of a beneficial interest in one or more trusts or otherwise, by or for the benefit of an individual or related group of individuals. An example is a Canadian public corporation that is controlled in the manner described above. This part of the Part IV tax provision was directed to investment holding corporations which were, essentially, private corporations, but which could otherwise avoid Part IV tax by listing a class of their shares on a prescribed exchange to meet the definition of a public corporation. The result of being a "subject corporation" is to be treated as a private corporation with respect to Part IV tax and its refund only (i.e., the refundable Part I tax provisions do not apply). The rules which provide for a subject corporation to keep track of its RDTOH are found in subsection 186(5).

(d) *Connected Corporation*

A corporation is connected with another corporation [ssec. 186(4)] where:

(a) the corporation is controlled by the other corporation (where control represents ownership of more than 50% of the voting shares by any combination of the other corporation and persons with whom it does not deal at arm's length); or

(b) the corporation's shares are held by the other corporation and these shares represent more than 10% of the voting shares and more than 10% of the fair market value of all the issued shares in the corporation.

Subsection 186(2) expands the definition of control for purposes of subsection 186(4). The provision requires that in determining "control", shares owned by non-arm's length persons must be included in that determination. For example, this provision allows avoidance of the Part IV tax where the share ownership is split in lots of 10% among family members.

This concept of a "connected corporation" is illustrated in Exhibit 12-17.

EXHIBIT 12-17
Concept of Connected Corporations

Assumptions
(1) A, B and C are private corporations resident in Canada;
(2) A, B and C are not related; and
(3) The percentage of ownership reflects both votes and value.

C is connected to both A and B — A because of the control rule or the votes and value rule, and B because of the votes and value rule.

C is connected to A and B because of the votes and value rule.

C is connected with A because of the control rule.
A is not subject to Part IV tax on dividends from C.
C is not connected to B because the votes and value are not greater than 10%.
B is subject to Part IV tax on dividends from C.

Note the "connected" concept flows from C to A and B. Therefore, C may be connected to A and B, but A and B are not connected to C.

Example Problem

Mr. and Mrs. Control hold common shares in two private corporations resident in Canada, as shown in the chart below. These corporations in turn hold common shares in another private corporation, Opco Ltd. The balance of the common shares are held by unrelated individuals. Assume that the share-ownership percentage also reflects their underlying value.

—REQUIRED

Determine whether Opco Ltd. is connected to Holdco Ltd. and Control Ltd.

—SOLUTION

Opco Ltd. is not connected to Holdco Ltd. through the votes and value rule [par. 186(4)(*b*)] since Holdco Ltd. holds less than 10% of the common shares (i.e., 5%). However, Opco Ltd. is connected to Holdco Ltd. by virtue of the control rule [par. 186(4)(*a*)] as modified by the extended meaning of control [ssec. 186(2)]. This latter provision extends the meaning of control by including shares belonging to non-arm's length persons, including other corporations and persons who do not deal at arm's length with the other corporations. In this situation, Control Ltd. and Holdco Ltd. are not dealing at arm's length since both corporations are related [spar. 251(2)(*c*)(ii)] because Mr. and Mrs. Control are related through marriage [pars. 251(2)(*a*) and 256(2)(*b*)]. Therefore, for purposes of determining control, Holdco Ltd. is deemed to own the shares held by Control Ltd. (i.e., 46%) plus the shares owned directly (i.e., 5%) giving Holdco Ltd. effective voting control of Opco Ltd.

Opco Ltd. is connected to Control Ltd. through both the votes and value rule [par. 186(4)(*b*)] and the extended meaning of control rule [par. 186(4)(*a*) and ssec. 186(2)] as described above.

---

6. Dividend refund

The private corporation will obtain a dividend refund each year equal to the lesser of [par. 129(1)(*a*)]:

(a) $\frac{1}{3}$ of all taxable dividends paid in the year, and

(b) the corporation's RDTOH at the end of the year.

A dividend refund is only available to a private corporation if it has that status at the time that it pays the taxable dividend. Thus, where plans exist for control of a private corporation to be acquired by a public corporation, consideration should be given to paying taxable dividends to shareholders prior to the time when control changes in order to maximize the dividend refund to the corporation.

7. Anti-avoidance rule

The Part IV tax is generally not payable on dividends received from companies with which the private corporation (or a "subject corporation") is "connected", i.e., where the recipient corporation has more than merely a portfolio interest in the shares of the payer corporation. However, where a connected private corporation has been entitled to a refund of tax in the year, the receiving corporation will pay a refundable Part IV tax [par. 186(1)(*b*)]. The amount of the tax represents its share of any tax refunded to the payer corporation as a result of the dividend. This prevents corporations in a connected group from escaping the Part IV tax by the payment of dividends from a corporation in the group, receiving portfolio dividends, to another corporation in the group.

For example, assume A Ltd. owns 100% of B Ltd. and B Ltd. received a $100 portfolio dividend from some other corporation. B Ltd. would pay the $33\frac{1}{3}\%$ Part IV tax of $33 on the dividend it received. If B Ltd. then paid A Ltd. a dividend of $100, B Ltd. would receive its dividend refund of $33. The $100 dividend would not be a portfolio dividend to A Ltd. because A Ltd. controls B Ltd. and, therefore, is "connected" (as discussed above and illustrated in Exhibit 12-18) with B Ltd. If it were not for paragraph 186(1)(*b*), A Ltd. would thus not be taxable on the dividend from B Ltd. This would defeat the purpose of the Part IV tax which is to avoid indefinite deferrals of tax on dividends of this nature. Thus, paragraph 186(1)(*b*) prevents such an escape from the Part IV tax by taxing A Ltd. under Part IV on the $33 dividend refund received by B Ltd. on the payment of the $100 dividend. Had A Ltd. owned only 51% of B Ltd., A Ltd. would have paid the Part IV tax only on its share of the dividend refund to B Ltd., i.e., on 51% of $33 for a tax of $16.83. Thus, A Ltd. pays Part IV tax on its proportionate share of the B Ltd. dividend refund triggered by the dividend paid by B Ltd.

8. Summary of conditions for Part IV tax

Exhibit 12-18 summarizes the conditions under which the Part IV tax is paid on dividends received based on the percentage ownership of a recipient corporation in a payer corporation.

EXHIBIT 12-18
Liability for Part IV Tax

9. Application of non-capital losses

The recipient private corporation may *choose* to reduce the amount subject to the Part IV tax by applying otherwise available non-capital losses of the year or of a carryover year [pars. 186(1)(c) and (d)]. These losses *cannot* be deducted subsequently from other income under Division C. Either the non-capital losses can be deducted, in effect, from dividend income subject to Part IV tax or they can be deducted in the calculation of taxable income subject to Part I tax. The same non-capital losses *cannot* be deducted under both provisions. It is, therefore, usually preferable to use the losses against income taxed at normal corporate rates, under Part I if that is possible, since the tax savings are usually greater and the Part IV tax otherwise payable is potentially refundable to the corporation.

C. Actual Application of the Scheme

[ITA: 125; 129; 186]

The following two examples demonstrate the interaction of Part I tax and the refundable taxes. The first example problem deals with Canadian investment income and active business income. The second example adds the element of portfolio dividends subject to Part IV tax and then demonstrates the interaction of the two refundable taxes on Refundable Dividend Tax on Hand and the Dividend Refund.

Example Problem 1

Microtax Corporation Limited, a Canadian-controlled private corporation with a December 31, 2005 year-end, has made the following calculation of its taxable income.

Canadian investment income	$1,000
U.S. investment income ($150 withheld at source)	1,000
Canadian active business income	1,000
	$3,000
Donations	500
Taxable income	$2,500

— REQUIRED

Compute the refundable portion of the corporation's Part I tax for 2005. Assume a 10% provincial tax rate and that the foreign tax credit is equal to the amount of foreign tax withheld.

— SOLUTION

Part I tax on taxable income:		
Tax @ 38% on $2,500		$ 950
Deduct: Federal tax abatement (10% of $2,500)		250
Net amount		$ 700
Add: Corporate surtax @ 4% of ($950 − 10% of $2,500)		28
Additional refundable tax (6²/₃% × $1,500[1])		100
		$ 828
Deduct: Non-business foreign tax credit (assumed equal to tax paid)	$ 150	
Small business deduction (16% of $1,000)	160	
Tax reduction[2]	nil	310
Total federal tax under Part I		$ 518
Provincial tax @ 10% of $2,500		250
Total tax		$ 768

Refundable portion of Part I tax:
Least of:
(a) $26^2/_3\% \times$ aggregate investment income (AII)
    $(26^2/_3\% \times \$2,000)$ .... $\$533$
       Less: non-business foreign tax credit .... $\$\ \ 150$
          minus: $9^1/_3\% \times$ foreign investment income
             $(9^1/_3\% \times \$1,000)$ .... (93)   (57) $\underline{\underline{\$476}}$

(b) Taxable income .... $\$\ 2,500$
       Less: Amount eligible for the SBD .... (1,000)
          $^{25}/_9 \times$ non-business FTC .... (417)
          $3 \times$ business FTC .... —
                              $26^2/_3\% \times$ $\underline{\$\ 1,083}$ = $\underline{\underline{\$289}}$

(c) Part I tax – surtax ($518 – $28) .... $\underline{\underline{\$490}}$

Least amount... $\underline{\underline{\$289}}$

—NOTES TO SOLUTION
(1) $6^2/_3\% \times$ lesser of:

       Aggregate investment income (AII)........................... $\underline{\underline{\$2,000}}$

       Taxable income (TI) – income eligible for SBD ($2,500 – $1,000) $\underline{\underline{\$1,500}}$

(2) There is no tax reduction in this case since all active business income is eligible for the small business deduction and any other income of this CCPC is aggregate investment income.

Example Problem 2

Lifetax Limited is a Canadian-controlled private corporation with its first fiscal year ended December 31, 2005. The following data resulted in the indicated computation of taxable income and Part I tax payable:

Taxable dividends paid during the year .... $\underline{\underline{\$\ 30,000}}$

Active business income (assume equal to income eligible for the small
    business deduction)... $148,560
Investment income:
    Taxable capital gains less allowable capital losses .... $\ \ 3,000
    Net income from property:
        Canadian-source rental income 2,000
        Foreign-source (before foreign tax of $375) interest
        income 2,500

    Total Canadian and foreign investment income.................. 7,500
Dividends (eligible for deduction under sec. 112 from non-connected
    corporations) 13,000

Total net income $169,060
Deduct: dividends [sec. 112] 13,000
       net capital losses....................................... 700

Taxable income .... $\underline{\underline{\$155,360}}$

Part I tax on taxable income:
    Tax @ 38% on $155,360... $\ 59,037
    Deduct: Federal tax abatement (10% of $155,360) 15,536

    Net amount.. $\ 43,501
    Add: Corporate surtax @ 4% of ($59,037 – 10% of $155,360)......... 1,740
        Additional refundable tax ($6^2/_3\% \times \$6,800^*$).................. 453
                                      $\underline{\underline{\$\ 45,694}}$

Deduct: Non-business foreign tax credit (assumed equal to

	tax paid)	$ 375	
	Small business deduction (16% of $148,560)	23,770	
	Tax reduction**	nil	24,145
Total federal tax under Part I			$ 21,549
Provincial tax (assumed) @ 10% of $155,360			15,536
Total tax			$ 37,085

---

*$6^{2}/_{3}$% × lesser of:

    (a) AII ($3,000 + $2,000 + $2,500 − $700) = $6,800

    (b) TI − SBD amount ($155,360 − $148,560) = $6,800

**There is no tax reduction in this case, since all active business income is eligible for the small business deduction and any other income of this CCPC is aggregate investment income.

—REQUIRED

Compute the refundable dividend tax on hand at the end of the 2005 taxation year and the dividend refund for the 2005 taxation year.

—SOLUTION

Part IV tax on taxable dividends received:

Taxable dividends subject to Part IV tax			$13,000
Part IV tax payable: $33^{1}/_{3}$% of $13,000			$ 4,333[1]

Refundable dividend tax on hand:

Refundable portion of Part I tax:

Least of:

(a) $26^{2}/_{3}$% × aggregate investment income			
(AII) ($26^{2}/_{3}$% × $6,800)		$ 1,813	
Less: non-business foreign tax credit ...	$ 375		
minus: $9^{1}/_{3}$% × foreign investment			
income ($9^{1}/_{3}$% × $2,500)	(233)	(142)	$ 1,671
(b) Taxable income	$ 155,360		
Less: Amount eligible for SBD	(148,560)		
$^{25}/_9$ × non-business FTC ($375)	(1,042)		
3 × business FTC..............	—		
$26^{2}/_{3}$% ×	$ 5,758	= $ 1,535	
(c) Part I tax − surtax ($21,549 − $1,740)			$19,809
Refundable portion of Part I tax..............................			$ 1,535
Part IV tax payable...			4,333
Refundable dividend tax on hand			$ 5,868

Dividend refund:

Taxable dividends paid: $30,000 × $^{1}/_3$	$ 10,000(F)	
Refundable dividend tax on hand at year end	$ 5,868(G)	
Dividend refund: lesser of (F) and (G)		$ 5,868

Summary of taxes payable:

Part I tax (including assumed provincial tax)	$37,085
Part IV tax	4,333
	$41,418
Less: dividend refund	5,868
Net taxes payable	$35,550

—NOTE TO SOLUTION

(1) Had any of the dividends deductible under section 112 been received from a connected corporation, such dividends would not have been subject to the Part IV tax, unless those dividends gave rise to a dividend refund to the connected corporation.

D. Imperfections in the Integration System for Income from Investments

1. Tax deferral at higher tax rates on personal income

When investment income or portfolio dividends are received by a corporation and ultimately distributed to shareholders as a dividend, the corporation pays tax when the income is earned and the shareholder pays tax when the dividend is received. There may be a time lag between the time the income is earned by the corporation and the time the corporation pays a dividend from that income. However, when such income is earned directly by an individual, tax must be paid on the income when received. If a taxpayer pays taxes at personal rates higher than the effective corporation rate on such income, there may be a tax deferral benefit of incorporating the income if the corporation does not pay dividends in the same year as it earns the income. Exhibits 12-19 through 12-22 illustrate the flow-through of portfolio dividends subject to the Part IV tax, dividends not subject to the Part IV tax, capital gains and interest, respectively. The effects of different rates of personal tax on the shareholder receiving dividends from the after-tax earnings of the corporation are being illustrated in these exhibits. Note that in all but one of these cases, there is a tax deferral when the shareholder is taxed at personal rates in excess of the $46^{2}/_{3}$% theoretical corporate tax rate (combined provincial and federal rates) which is possible in the top tax bracket in provinces that have a personal tax rate in excess of $17^{2}/_{3}$%. In the case of the flow-through of dividends not subject to Part IV tax (Exhibit 12-20) there is a tax deferral at all personal rates for shareholders.

EXHIBIT 12-19
Theoretical Flow-through of Portfolio Dividends
Subject to Part IV Tax

Corporation		
Taxable dividend included in net income		$1,000
Deduction for taxable dividend [sec. 112]		(1,000)
Taxable income		Nil
Part IV tax paid currently at $33^{1}/_{3}$%	(A)	$ 333
Income remaining after tax		$ 667
Potentially refundable tax [ssec. 129(3)]	(B)	333
Total available for dividends		$1,000

[*Exhibit 12-19 — continued*]

Shareholder (combined federal plus provincial tax rate)	*26%*	*46%*
Taxable dividend received	$1,000	$1,000
Gross-up	250	250
Taxable income	$1,250	$1,250
Total combined tax	$ 325	$ 575
Dividend tax credit (theoretically equal to gross-up)	(250)	(250)
Net tax (C)	$ 75	$ 325
Total tax paid: (A) – (B) + (C)	$ 75	$ 325
Tax payable by shareholder if $1,000 dividend earned directly	$ 75	$ 325

NOTE: Some tax on this income can be deferred by shareholders whose total personal rates of tax exceed 46²/₃% (i.e., (46²/₃ of $1,250) – $250 = $333) if the corporation does not immediately distribute dividends from income received.

EXHIBIT 12-20
Theoretical Flow-through of Dividends Not Subject to Part IV Tax

Corporation		
Taxable dividend included in net income		$1,000
Deduction for taxable dividend [sec. 112]		(1,000)
Taxable income (A)		Nil
Total available for dividends		$1,000

Shareholder (theoretical federal plus provincial tax rate)	*26%*	*46%*
Taxable dividend received	$1,000	$1,000
Gross-up	250	250
Taxable income	$1,250	$1,250
Total combined tax	$ 325	$ 575
Dividend tax credit (theoretically equal to gross-up)	(250)	(250)
Net tax (B)	$ 75	$ 325
Total tax paid: (A) + (B)	$ 75	$ 325
Tax payable by shareholder if $1,000 dividend earned directly	$ 75	$ 325

NOTE: All tax on this income can be deferred by all shareholders regardless of their personal rates of tax if the corporation does not immediately distribute dividends from income received.

EXHIBIT 12-21
Theoretical Flow-through of Capital Gains Eligible for Refundable Tax

Corporation	
Actual capital gain	$1,000
Taxable capital gain (¹/₂* $1,000)	$ 500*
Part I	
Tax on taxable capital gain (theoretical — 40%)	$ 200
Additional refundable tax at 6²/₃% of $500	33
(A)	$ 233
Income remaining after tax ($500 – ($200 + $33))	$ 267
Potentially refundable tax (26²/₃% of $500) (B)	133
Total available for dividend on taxable capital gain	$ 400

[*Exhibit 12-21 — continued*]

Shareholder (theoretical federal plus provincial tax rate)	26%	46%
Taxable dividend received	$ 400	$ 400
Gross-up	100	100
Taxable income	$ 500	$ 500
Total combined tax	$ 130	$ 230
Dividend tax credit (theoretically equal to gross-up)	(100)	(100)
Net tax (C)	$ 30	$ 130
Total tax paid: (A) – (B) + (C)	$ 130	$ 230
Tax payable by shareholder if $500 taxable capital gain in excess of capital gains deduction earned directly	$ 130	$ 230

* The other $500 can be distributed tax free as a capital dividend.

NOTES: (1) Some tax on this income can be deferred by shareholders whose total personal rate of tax exceeds 46²/₃% if the corporation does not immediately distribute dividends from income received.

(2) If the capital gains had not been generated by a Canadian-controlled private corporation and, therefore, had not been eligible for refundable tax, the total tax paid through the corporation would have been higher than that paid by an individual generating the capital gain directly.

EXHIBIT 12-22
Theoretical Flow-through of Interest Eligible for Refundable Tax

Corporation		
Interest income	$1,000	
Part I		
Tax in corporation (theoretical — 40%)	$ 400	
Additional refundable tax at 6²/₃%	67	
(A)	$ 467	
Income remaining after tax ($1,000 – $400 – $67)	$ 533	
Potentially refundable tax (26²/₃% of $1,000) (B)	267	
Total available for dividends	$ 800	

Shareholder (theoretical federal plus provincial tax rate)	26%	44%
Taxable dividend received	$ 800	$ 800
Gross-up	200	200
Taxable income	$1,000	$1,000
Total combined tax	$ 260	$ 460
Dividend tax credit (theoretically equal to gross-up)	(200)	(200)
Net tax (C)	$ 60	$ 260
Total tax paid: (A) – (B) + (C)	$ 260	$ 460
Tax payable by shareholder if $1,000 interest income earned directly	$ 260	$ 460

NOTES: (1) Some tax on this income can be deferred by shareholders whose total personal rate of tax exceeds 46²/₃% if the corporation does not immediately distribute dividends from income received.

(2) If the interest had not been earned by a Canadian-controlled private corporation and, therefore, had not been eligible for refundable tax, the total tax paid through the corporation would have been higher than that paid by an individual earning the interest directly.

2. Permanent tax savings or costs

(a) *Dividend Tax Credit*

Recall the following about the dividend gross-up and tax credit procedure:

(i) the gross-up is intended to place the shareholder in an income position equivalent to that of the corporation before it paid corporate taxes; and

(ii) the tax credit is intended to give the shareholder credit against his or her taxes for the taxes paid by the corporation on the income from which the dividend was paid.

Theoretically, the tax credit (including the effect on provincial tax) for the shareholder should equal the gross-up because the gross-up represents taxes paid by the corporation for which the shareholder gets a tax credit. In practice, however, the tax credit may be greater than the gross-up.

The following calculations illustrate the situation of a shareholder in a province with a provincial dividend tax credit rate of 8%:

Gross-up 25.0%

Tax credit:
Federal ($^2/_3$ × 25% = 13$^1/_3$% of 125%) 16.7%
Provincial tax credit (8% of 125%) 10.0
Total tax credit 26.7%

The total or combined tax credit, which includes the provincial dividend tax credit, is often used in illustrations where a combined federal and provincial tax rate is also used. Exhibit 12-23 illustrates this effect for all provinces.

EXHIBIT 12-23
Tax Saving Resulting from Operation of Dividend Tax Credit Generated by Incorporating Investment Income other than Dividends

Province	Dividend tax credit Federal (13$^1/_3$% × 125%)	Provincial*	Total	Net tax saving (cost)**
Alberta	16.7%	8.0 %	247 %	(0.3)
British Columbia	16.7	6.4	231	(1.9)
Manitoba	16.7	6.3	230	(2.0)
New Brunswick	16.7	4.6	21.3	(3.7)
Newfoundland and Labrador	16.7	6.3	230	(2.0)
Nova Scotia	16.7	9.6	263	(1.3)
Nunavut	16.7	5.0	21.7	(2.3)
Ontario	16.7	6.4	231	(1.9)
P.E.I.	16.7	9.6	263	(1.3)
Quebec	16.7	13.5	302	5.2
Saskatchewan	16.7	10.0	267	(1.7)
Western Territory	16.7	7.5	242	(0.8)
Yukon Territory	16.7	7.3	240	(1.0)

* on actual dividend, excluding surtax effect

** compared to theoretical dividend tax credit of 25%

(b) *Others*

Either a tax saving or a tax cost will result from changes in the federal corporate tax rate. Exhibit 12-24 shows the effects of a range of such federal rates, including the additional refundable tax of 6$^2/_3$%, between 40% and 50% while other factors are held constant. The Exhibit shows that, below the 46²/₃% corporate rate, there is an advantage to incorporating investment income. Hence, the 38% federal rate, introduced in Exhibit 12-12, will provide for such an advantage. Where the corporate rate is above 46²/₃%, there is a tax cost to incorporating investment income. Exhibit 12-25 shows a reduction in the tax advantage of incorporating investment income with all other factors held constant, when provincial corporate rates are in excess of 12%.

All factors, including the effects of the federal tax rate, the provincial personal rate and the provincial corporate rate, can be combined using data for a given province. This is done for Ontario in Exhibit 12-26 and for Nova Scotia in Exhibit 12-27. Exhibit 12-26 shows that there is a tax cost to incorporating investment income in Ontario, at least, in the lower brackets. By comparison, the cost resulting from incorporating investment income in Nova Scotia is a little lower in the low bracket and higher in the high bracket. This type of analysis is important and should be understood in order to react to future rate changes.

EXHIBIT 12-24
Tax Saving or Cost Resulting from Changes in the Federal Corporate Tax Rate Generated by Incorporating Investment Income other than Dividends

Federal corporate rate before provincial abatement (theoretical)	40%	50%
Income (assume interest eligible for refundable tax)	$300	$300
Corporate tax including additional refundable tax @ 6²/₃%	(120)	(150)
Net before tax refund potentially available	$180	$150
Add: refundable tax (26²/₃% of $300)	80	80
Available for dividend	$260	$230
Add: gross-up	65	58
Taxable income of shareholder	$325	$288
Tax on shareholder @ 40% overall (assumed)	$130	$115
Less: dividend tax credit (assumed equal to gross-up)	(65)	(58)
Net tax on shareholder	$ 65	$ 57
Add: tax paid by corporation (net of refund)	40	70
Total tax paid	$105	$127
Tax if income earned directly and taxed @ 40%	$120	$120
Tax saving (cost)	$ 15	$ (7)

EXHIBIT 12-25
Tax Cost Resulting from Provincial Corporate Rate greater than 10% Generated by Incorporating Investment Income other than Dividends (assuming a 38% federal rate and a 10% federal abatement)

Provincial rate (corporate)	12%	17%
Combined federal and provincial rate (corporate)	47%	52%
Income (assume interest eligible for refundable tax)	$300	$300
Corporate tax (38% + 6²/₃% – 10% + provincial rate)	(141)	(156)
Net before tax refund potentially available	$159	$144
Add: refundable tax (26²/₃% of $300)	80	80
Available for dividend	$239	$224
Add: gross-up	60	56
Taxable income of shareholder	$299	$280

[*Exhibit 12-24 — continued*]

	12%	17%
Provincial rate (corporate)		
Combined federal and provincial rate (corporate)	47%	52%
Tax on shareholder @ 40%	$120	$112
Less: dividend tax credit (assumed equal to gross-up)	60	56
Net tax on shareholder	$ 60	$ 56
Add: tax paid by corporation (net of refund)	61	76
Total tax paid	$121	$132
Tax if income earned directly and taxed @ 40%	$120	$120
Tax cost	$ 1	$ 12

EXHIBIT 12-26
Incorporating Investment Income Eligible for Refundable Tax other than Dividends in Ontario for 2005

Corporation		
Interest income		$ 300
Corporate tax (38% – 10% + 1.12% + 14%)		(129)
Additional refundable tax at 6²/₃%		(20)
Net before tax refund potentially available		$ 151
Add: refundable tax (26²/₃% of $300)*		80
		$ 231

Individual		
Dividend		$ 231
Add: gross-up		58
Income subject to tax		$ 289

	22.0%	46.4%
Combined federal and provincial rate		
Tax before credit	$ 64	$ 134
Total dividend tax credit ((13¹/₃% + 5.1% × $289))	(53)	(53)
Net tax	$ 11	$ 81
Add: tax paid by corporation (net of refund)	69	69
Total tax	$ 80	$ 150
Tax if income earned directly	$ 66	$ 139
Cost on $300 of income	$ 14	11
Cost as percentage of income	4.7%	3.7%

* If the investment income had not been earned by a Canadian-controlled private corporation and, therefore, had not been eligible for refundable tax, there would have been a greater tax cost in using a corporation rather than receiving the income directly.

EXHIBIT 12-27
Incorporating Investment Income Eligible for Refundable Tax other than Dividends in Nova Scotia for 2005

Corporation

Interest income	$ 300	
Corporate tax (38% – 10% + 1.12% + 16%)	(135)	
Additional refundable tax at 6²/₃%	(20)	
Net before tax refund potentially available	$ 145	
Add: refundable tax (26²/₃% of $300)*	80	
Available for dividend	$ 225	

Individual

Dividend	$ 225	
Add: gross-up	56	
Income subject to tax	$ 281	

Combined federal and provincial rate	25.8%	47.3%
Tax before credit	$ 72	$ 133
Total dividend tax credit ((13¹/₃% + 7.7%) of $281)	(59)	(59)
Net tax	$ 13	$ 74
Add: tax paid by corporation after refund	75	75
Total tax	$ 88	$ 149
Tax if income earned directly	$ 77	$ 142
Cost on $300 of income	$ 11	$ 7
Cost as percentage of income	3.7%	2.3%

* If the investment income had not been earned by a Canadian-controlled private corporation and, therefore, had not been eligible for refundable tax, there would have been a greater tax cost in using a corporation rather than receiving the income directly.

3. Summary of advantages and disadvantages of incorporating investment income eligible for refundable tax

The advantages of incorporating investment income eligible for refundable tax would appear to include the following:

(a) a tax deferral if the shareholder's combined marginal tax rate is greater than the theoretical combined corporate rate of 46²/₃%;

(b) a negligible absolute tax saving as a result of the operation of the dividend tax credit in some provinces and a small tax saving where the combined federal and provincial corporate tax rate is less than the theoretical 46²/₃%;

(c) greater flexibility in the timing of the receipt of income subject to personal tax;

(d) estate planning advantages on the transfer of property and the transfer of future growth to children (as discussed in a subsequent chapter);

(e) possible family income splitting in carefully planned and very restrictive situations (to be discussed subsequently with respect to the corporate attribution rules) through family members as shareholders and, perhaps, employees; and

(f) possible avoidance of foreign estate taxes by placing foreign property in a Canadian corporation.

On the other hand the disadvantages of incorporating investment income would appear to include the following:

(a) a prepayment (as opposed to a deferral) of tax if the shareholder's combined marginal tax rate is less than the corporate tax rate plus the additional refundable tax;

(b) an additional tax cost if the combined federal and provincial corporate tax rate is ever raised to a rate in excess of the theoretical $46^2/_3\%$;

(c) an additional cost of maintaining a corporation in the form of administrative, accounting and legal costs as well as provincial capital taxes; and

(d) a loss of the availability to the individual of investment and capital losses.

Given the relatively small tax savings resulting from the incorporation of investment income in many cases, these disadvantages may outweigh the advantages. However, the beneficial effects of estate planning and income splitting must be analyzed.

IV. COMPREHENSIVE SUMMARY OF TYPES OF CORPORATE INCOME AND FEDERAL CORPORATE INCOME TAX RATES

Exhibit 12-28 presents a comprehensive summary of types of corporate income that can be earned by a Canadian corporation and the federal marginal income tax rates applicable to each type of income.

EXHIBIT 12-28
Summary of Corporate Income Types and Federal Marginal Tax Rates

	ABI			Investment		Cdn. dividends	
	Cdn.	For'n.	PSB	Cdn.	For'n.	Conn.	Port.
Business & property:							
Business	X						
Interest, rent				X	X		
Foreign branch		X					
Dividends						X	X
Employment			X				
Taxable capital gains				X	X		
Net Income for Tax							
	%	%	%	%	%	%	%
Federal Part I tax rates:							
Basic	38.00	38.00	38.00	38.00	38.00		
Abatement	(10.00)		(10.00)	(10.00)	(10.00)		
	28.00	38.00	28.00	28.00	28.00		
Surtax (4% × 28%)	1.12	1.12	1.12	1.12	1.12		
	29.12	39.12	29.12	29.12	29.12		
Eligible for:							
SBD	16.00						
M&P > SBD	7.00						
RDTOH				26.67	26.67	33.33	33.33
FTC		Yes			Yes		
General rate reduction	7.00	7.00	7.00				
Additional refundable tax				6.67	6.67		
Part IV tax:							
3 × dividend refund						33.33	
Portfolio dividend							33.33

Example Problem

James Fish Processors Inc. (JFPI) is a Canadian-controlled private corporation located in Burnaby, British Columbia. The company's income for tax purposes for its December 31, 2005 taxation year-end was calculated correctly as follows:

Processing income[1]	$ 145,000
Wholesaling income	195,000
Maintenance service contract loss	(65,000)
Patent income[2]	45,000
Rental income[3]	35,000
Taxable capital gains net of losses[4]	55,000
Recapture of CCA[4]	15,000
Interest income on outstanding account receivable on wholesaling income	10,000
Interest income from loan to wholly-owned subsidiary[5]	20,000
Interest income from a sinking fund trust for replacement of a building	50,000
Foreign business income (gross amount — $Cdn.)[6]	40,000
Foreign non-business income (gross amount — $Cdn.)[7]	25,000
Dividends from taxable Canadian corporations (non-connected)	12,500
Dividends from the wholly-owned subsidiary which received a $1,500 dividend refund as a result of paying this dividend	17,500
Profit on sale of excess land[8]	90,000
Net income for tax purposes — Division B	$ 690,000

(1) Processing income was correctly computed according to the provisions of Regulation 5200.

(2) The patent income has been determined to be property income.

(3) The rental income was derived from leasing the entire space on a 5-year lease in an unused warehouse in a small town in the northern part of the province.

(4) The net taxable capital gain and the recapture concerned the disposition of certain specialized maintenance service equipment.

(5) The funds were used to buy equipment for its active business.

(6) Foreign income tax in the amount of $10,000 ($Cdn.) was paid on the foreign business income.

(7) Withholding tax on the non-business income was $4,000 ($Cdn.).

(8) The land had been held for approximately 5 years. It was purchased with the intent of realizing a profit on sale.

Additional Information:

(1) JFPI made the following selected payments during the year:

Political donations	$ 7,500
Charitable donations	22,500
Dividends paid on July 15, 2005	37,500

(1) The balances in the tax accounts on January 1, 2005 were:

Charitable donation carryforward	$ 2,500
Unused business foreign tax credit	3,500
Non-capital losses	42,500
Net capital losses (arising in 1999)	13,500
RDTOH balance	nil

(3) Taxable income earned in British Columbia, which is the only Canadian jurisdiction in which JFPI operates, is approximately 85% of the total.

(4) The business limit is all allocated to JFPI.

—REQUIRED

(A) Calculate the federal tax and provincial tax at a 13.5% rate on federal taxable income payable by the company for 2005.

(B) Compute the refundable dividend tax on hand balance as at December 31, 2005, and compute the dividend refund for 2005.

—SOLUTION

Analysis of Division B Income

| | ABI | | | Investment | | Dividend | | |
Source	Cdn.	For'n.	PSB	Cdn.	For'n.	Conn.	Port.	Total
Processing.............	$145,000							$145,000
Wholesaling	195,000							195,000
Maintenance service	(65,000)							(65,000)
Patent				$ 45,000				45,000
Rental				35,000				35,000
Net taxable capital gains				55,000				55,000
Recapture	15,000							15,000
Interest — A/R..........	10,000							10,000
loan	20,000[1]							20,000
sinking fund....				50,000				50,000
Foreign		$40,000			$25,000			65,000
Dividend						$17,500	$12,500	30,000
Profit................	90,000							90,000
Division B income	$410,000	$40,000	Nil	$185,000	$25,000	$17,500	$12,500	$690,000

(A) Tax Payable

Division B income..................................		$ 690,000
Division C deductions:		
Charitable donations ($22,500 + $2,500) — max. 75% of $690,000...........................	$25,000	
Dividends from taxable Canadian corporations ($17,500 + $12,500)........................	30,000	
Non-capital losses	42,500	
Net capital losses ($13,500 × ½ / ¾)	9,000	(106,500)
Taxable income....................................		$ 583,500
Tax @38% of $583,500		$ 221,730
Deduct: Federal abatement (10% of 85% of $583,500) ...		49,598
Net amount		$ 172,132
Add: Corporate surtax (4% of 28% of $583,500).........		6,535
Additional refundable tax (Schedule 1)............		13,400
		$ 192,067
Deduct: Non-business foreign tax credit (Schedule 2)....	$ 4,000	
Business foreign tax credit (Schedule 3)	13,500	
Small business deduction (Schedule 4)	48,000	
M&P profits deduction (Schedule 5)...........	nil	
Tax reduction (Schedule 6)	5,775	
Federal political contributions tax credit — max. ...	650	(71,925)
Part I tax payable		$ 120,142
Provincial tax @ 13.5% of 85% of $583,500		66,957
Part IV tax payable ((33⅓% of $12,500) + $1,500)		5,667
Total tax..		$ 192,766

Schedule 1: Additional refundable tax

    $6^2/_3$% of lesser of:

        (a) AII ($185,000 + $25,000 + $17,500 + $12,500 − $9,000

              − $30,000)...................................... $ 201,000

        (b) Taxable income − SBD amount[2] ($583,500 − $300,000) $ 283,500

      $6^2/_3$% of $201,000 = $13,400

Schedule 2: Non-business foreign tax credit

    Lesser of:

        (a) Amount paid..................................... $ 4,000

        (b) $\dfrac{\text{Foreign non-business income}}{\text{Div. B − (sec. 112 + par. 111(1)(}b\text{))}}$ × tax after abatement + surtax + ART

           $\dfrac{\$25,000}{\$690,000 − (\$30,000 + \$9,000)}$ × $192,067 .... $ 7,376

      Lesser amount = $4,000

Schedule 3: Business foreign tax credit

    Least of:

        (a) Amount paid + unused amount ($10,000 + $3,500) ...... $ 13,500

        (b) $\dfrac{\text{Foreign business income}}{\text{Div. B − (sec. 112 + par. 111(1)(}b\text{))}}$ × tax before abatement + surtax − general tax reduction

           $\dfrac{\$40,000}{\$690,000 − (\$30,000 + \$9,000)}$ × ($221,730 + $6,535 − $5,775) .... $ 13,670

        (c) Tax otherwise payable − non-business FTC:

           ($221,730 + $6,535 − $5,775) − $4,000 =..................$218,490

      Least amount = $13,500

Schedule 4: Small business deduction

    16% of least of:

        (a) Active business income (Canadian-source)............... $410,000

        (b) Taxable income $583,500

           Less: $^{10}/_3$ × NBFTC ($^{10}/_3$ × $4,000) $13,333

                  3 × BFTC (3 × $13,500)   40,500   53,833 $529,667

        (c) Business limit (all allocated to JFPI).................... $300,000

      16% of $300,000 = $48,000

Schedule 5: M&P profits deduction

    7% of lesser of:

        (a) M&P profits (given) − SBD amount ($145,000 − $300,000)   nil

        (b) Taxable income $583,500

           Less: Income eligible for SBD $300,000

               Aggregate investment income   201,000

               3 × BFTC (3 × $13,500) ...   40,500   541,500 $ 42,000

      7% of nil = nil

Schedule 6: General tax reductions

taxable income			$583,500
less: $100/7$ of the M&P profits deduction	$	Nil	
$100/16$ of the small business deduction		300,000	
AII		201,000	(501,000)
net			$ 82,500
7% of $82,500			$ 5,775

(B) *Refundable Portion of Part I Tax*

Least of:

(a)	$26^{2}/_{3}$% of AII ($26^{2}/_{3}$% of $201,000)			$ 53,600
	Less: non-business foreign tax credit . . .	$ 4,000		
	minus: $9^{1}/_{3}$% of foreign investment income ($9^{1}/_{3}$% of $25,000).	2,333	1,667	$ 51,933
(b)	Taxable income		$583,500	
	Less: Amount eligible for SBD	$300,000		
	$25/_{9}$ × NBFTC ($25/_{9}$ × $4,000). . . .	11,111		
	3 × BFTC (3 × $13,500)	40,500	351,611	
	$26^{2}/_{3}$% of.		$231,889	$ 61,837
(c)	Part I tax – surtax ($120,142 – $6,535)			$113,607

Least amount = $51,933

RDTOH

Balance, January 1, 2005		nil
Add: Refundable portion of Part I tax		$ 51,933
Part IV tax		5,667
Balance, December 31, 2005		$ 57,600

Dividend refund

Lesser of:

(a)	Taxable dividends paid × $1/_{3}$ ($37,500/3)	$ 12,500
(b)	RDTOH balance, December 31, 2005	$ 57,600

Lesser amount = $12,500

—NOTE TO SOLUTION

(1) The interest on the loan to the subsidiary is deemed to be active business income [ssec. 129(6)]. JFPI and the subsidiary are associated. The interest is ordinarily income from property, but is deducted from the ABI of the associated payer.

(2) Initially, the SBD amount is assumed to be $300,000, since Canadian-source ABI is $410,000. This assumption, which is verified later in Schedule 4, allows for a calculation of ART.

REVIEW QUESTIONS

(1) Explain the purpose behind the concept of integration.

(2) It has been said that "ideal integration depends on the existence of two factors in the tax system". Briefly explain what they are.

(3) The dividend gross-up and tax credit has been described as the major tool of integration in the Act. Give a brief explanation of how it works in theory.

(4) What is the purpose of the small business deduction?

(5) On July 15th of this year, Mr. Smith bought all the shares of a company which was the Canadian subsidiary of a U.S. parent. There are no losses or ITCs being carried forward by the company. What advice would you have for Mr. Smith with regard to his choice of year-end for the acquired corporation?

(6) Give an example of when paragraph 125(1)(*b*) will give a lower limit for the small business deduction than paragraph 125(1)(*a*).

(7) What is the purpose of subparagraphs 125(1)(*b*)(i) and (ii)? Explain the overall concept and why they use the fractions they do in each of them.

(8) List some tax and non-tax advantages of incorporation.

(9) List some tax and non-tax disadvantages of incorporation.

(10) Mr. Mould has just started up a manufacturing operation to supply parts to the auto industry. Given his need for start-up capital, he is happy that his tax rate is reduced by both the small business deduction of 16% and the M & P profits deduction of 6%. Comment.

(11) Are there any tax rules that prevent an individual from deferring tax on portfolio dividends by flowing them through a corporation?

(12) What are five tools that are used in the tax laws to integrate the taxation of investment income earned through a corporation?

(13) Theoretically, what does the 25% gross-up on dividends from taxable Canadian corporations represent?

(14) Theoretically, what does the dividend tax credit represent?

(15) Explain how integration theoretically works if a $1,000 capital gain is realized in a CCPC.

(16) Mr. Owner owns all the shares of Holdco which in turn owns all of the shares of Opco, a CCPC carrying on an active business in Canada. In recent years, Opco has done very well and its income is well in excess of the business limit. Last year Mr. Owner paid a dividend of $150,000 from Opco to Holdco. However, since he needed the cash in Opco to expand, he loaned the money back to Opco and charged 10% interest. The interest charged to Opco amounted to $15,000 in the year. How will this interest income be taxed in Holdco?

(17) A number of years ago a reorganization was undertaken so that now A Ltd. owns voting preferred shares in B Ltd. These preferred shares have only 7% of the votes and are now only worth 7% of the value. The other shares of B Ltd. are owned by the son of the only shareholder of A Ltd. Are A Ltd. and B Ltd. connected?

(18) Under paragraphs 186(1)(*c*) and (*d*), the recipient private corporation may choose to reduce the amount subject to the Part IV tax by applying otherwise available non-capital losses of the year or of a carryover year. Either the non-capital losses can be deducted from dividend income subject to Part IV tax or they can be deducted in the calculation of taxable income subject to Part I tax. What factors should be considered in deciding which option to choose?

MULTIPLE CHOICE QUESTIONS

Question 1

Concept Corp, a CCPC, correctly calculated its taxable income for its year ended December 31, 2005 as follows:

Income from retailing business carried on in Canada................	$ 120,000
Loss from retailing business carried on in United States	(20,000)
Interest income from long-term bonds	30,000
Taxable capital gain from sale of a capital asset	5,000
Net income	$ 135,000
Non-capital losses	(3,000)
Taxable income	$ 132,000

Concept Corp and X Ltd. are associated corporations. X Ltd. claimed a 16% small business deduction on $185,000 for 2005. The taxable capital of Concept Corp and X Ltd. is significantly less than $10,000,000. Which one of the following amounts is the maximum 16% small business deduction for Concept Corp for 2005?

(A) $16,000

(B) $18,400

(C) $19,200

(D) $21,120

Question 2

M Ltd. provides management advisory services to ACC Ltd. and is not involved in any other business. Mr. Mud is the sole shareholder and only employee of M Ltd. Mr. Mud and his son each own 50% of the issued shares of ACC Ltd. Which one of the following statements is TRUE?

(A) If Mr. Mud would reasonably be regarded as an employee of ACC Ltd., but for the existence of M Ltd., then M Ltd. is carrying on a "personal services business".

(B) M Ltd. is carrying on a "personal services business", unless it employs in the business more than five full-time employees throughout the year, which it does not.

(C) M Ltd. is carrying on a "specified investment business".

(D) M Ltd. is carrying on an "active business".

Question 3

B Ltd. is a Canadian-controlled private corporation which manufactures plastic bottles. The following information relates to its year ended June 30, 2005.

Active business income earned in Canada.........................	$305,000
Canadian manufacturing and processing profits.....................	310,000
Net income, Division B	320,000
Taxable income	320,000

B Ltd. is not associated with any other corporation. B Ltd. did not earn any foreign business income nor any investment income. B Ltd.'s taxable capital is well below $10,000,000. Which of the following amounts is the maximum manufacturing and processing profits deduction for the June 30, 2005 year:

(A) $700

(B) $1,400

(C) $18,340

(D) $21,700

Question 4

A Ltd., a private corporation, received dividends from B Ltd. and C Ltd. during its year ended December 31, 2005.

	B Ltd.	C Ltd.
Amount of dividend received by A Ltd.	$120,000	$120,000
Percentage of shares owned by A Ltd. (votes and value)	70%	8%
Dividend refund received by the payer of the dividend	$ 40,000	$400,000

A Ltd. and C Ltd. are not related. All three are taxable Canadian corporations. Which one of the following amounts is the Part IV tax payable by A Ltd.?

(A) $60,000

(B) $64,000

(C) $68,000

(D) $80,000

Question 5

Joanne owns 55% of the common shares of J Co. and Doug (her spouse) owns 55% of the common shares of D Co. Which of the following would make J Co. and D Co. associated?

(A) If Joanne owned 25% of the common shares of D Co.

(B) If Doug owned 25% of the common shares of J Co.

(C) If a trust for their twin two year-old daughters controls T Co. and no special elections were made.

(D) All of the above.

Question 6

In which of the following situations are X Ltd. and Y Ltd. NOT associated?

(A) Rod owns 10% of voting shares of X Ltd. and 50% of the voting shares Y Ltd. and Patrick owns 60% of the voting shares of X Ltd. and 10% of the voting shares of Y Ltd. Rod and Patrick are not related.

(B) The adult son of the controlling shareholder of X Ltd. controls Y Ltd. and owns 25% of the voting shares of X Ltd.

(C) A mother controls Company X. Her two adult daughters each own 30% of the voting shares of Y Ltd. Her adult son owns 25% of the voting shares of Y Ltd.

(D) Both (A) and (C)

EXERCISES

Exercise 1

[ITA: 125(7)]

The taxpayer company carried on the business on a comparatively small scale of lending money on mortgages. The company was operated by two individuals who also owned and managed a number of other companies. All the companies operated out of the same office premises and used more or less the same office staff and equipment. The taxpayer company had no full-time employees. It was listed in the telephone directory but did no direct advertising. No attempt was made to keep track of the amount of time spent by the office staff on the work of each company and no specific charge was made for office space, use of telephones and equipment or staff.

The company made loans to potential borrowers referred to it by independent agents. Its clientele came mainly from those who found it difficult to obtain loans through the normal commercial channels. The agents had a general idea of the sort of loans which might be acceptable, but because those were relatively high-risk loans, the company had to examine them very carefully. Occasionally, an outside appraisal was made, but normally someone from the company would visit the property to examine it. Often considerable negotiations as to terms were involved. Post-dated cheques for five years would be obtained from borrowers and turned over to the bank as collateral for the company's line of credit.

For the year in question, the company held three mortgages involving $11,084. The sale of a small property, interest and other income resulted in total income of $4,609. Net income before taxes was shown as $3,479. The mortgages outstanding and net income of the company increased continuously from the year in question to the present time. During the year in question, the company's line of credit at the bank was estimated at $7,500 to $15,000, but it is now $25,000.

— *REQUIRED*

From the facts provided in the case, determine the type of business that is carried on by the company under the current legislation.

Exercise 2

[ITA: 251]

(A) Which of the following individuals or groups of individuals are not at arm's length with Alpha Corporation Limited:

(i) Mr. Beta who owns 25% of the shares of Alpha and is not related to any other shareholders?

(ii) Mr. Beta and his brother who together own 55% of the shares of Alpha and they are not related to any other shareholder?

(iii) Mr. Delta, who has an option to purchase all of the shares held by Mr. Beta and his brother, anytime during the next three years?

(iv) Mr. Epsilon, who has an option to purchase all of the shares held by Mr. Beta and his brother, from their estates within five years of their death?

(B) Under which of the following conditions do Tau Corporation Limited and Lambda Corporation Limited not deal with each other at arm's length:

(i) Tau is controlled by two brothers, A and B, and Lambda is controlled by A?

(ii) three unrelated individuals together control Tau and one of these individuals controls Lambda?

(iii) Tau is related to Sigma Corporation Limited and Sigma is related to Lambda?

Exercise 3

[ITA: 251; 256]

Consider each of the following unrelated cases:

(A) Janna owns 55% of the shares of Jay-one Ltd. and 70% of the shares of Jay-two Ltd. Jay-one Ltd. owns 60% of the shares of Jay-three Ltd. The remaining shares in all three corporations are owned by persons unrelated to Janna.

(B) Rayna owns 30% of the common shares of Famco Ltd. and all of the shares of Rayco Ltd. The other 70% of the common shares of Famco Ltd. are owned by Rayna's cousin. However, Rayna's mother owns all of the voting preferred shares of Famco Ltd. and has sufficient votes to elect more than 50% of the Board of Directors of Famco Ltd.

(C) Adam owns 100% of the shares of Adamco Ltd. and 25% of the shares of Kidco Ltd. His daughter and son-in-law each own 20% of the shares of Kidco Ltd. and the remainder of the shares are owned by persons unrelated to all three.

(D) Sister One and Sister Two each own 50% of Sisco Ltd. and 25% of Cousco Ltd. Each sister has a daughter over the age of 18 who owns 25% of Cousco Ltd.

— *REQUIRED*

In each unrelated case, determine whether the corporations named are associated. Substantiate your answer by reference to specific provisions of subsection 256(1).

Exercise 4

[ITA: 125(1); 256(1), (2.1)]

Alpha and Beta are two sisters living in Halifax. While Alpha controls Taxit Ltd., Beta owns 25% of the shares of the corporation. Beta also owns 100% of the shares of Sibling Ltd. The active business income for Taxit during the current taxation year was $465,000 and for Sibling was $560,000. The taxation years for both corporations end December 31.

— *REQUIRED*

How much should each company claim as a small business deduction on their active business income for the taxation year?

Exercise 5

[ITA: 251; 252; 256]

The common shares of Chutzpah Enterprises Limited were owned by the three Chutzpah brothers as follows:

Aleph Chutzpah	40%
Bett Chutzpah	40%
Gimmel Chutzpah	20%

The common shares of Shlock Sales Limited were owned by the following:

Bett Chutzpah	45%
Dalled Chutzpah	45%
Unrelated person	10%

Aleph Chutzpah is married to Dalled Chutzpah.

— *REQUIRED*

Determine whether the two corporations are associated. Substantiate your answer by reference to specific provisions of subsection 256(1).

Exercise 6

[ITA: 123–126]

The following data pertains to Moosonee Company Limited, a Canadian-controlled private corporation for its fiscal year ended December 31, 2005:

Canadian-source business income including $84,000 of manufacturing and processing profits	$110,000
Foreign investment income ($1,050 in tax withheld)	7,000
Income under Division B	117,000
Taxable income all of which is earned in Canada	79,700

— REQUIRED

Compute the federal Part I tax payable plus provincial tax at a 12% rate for 2005 if all of the business income is considered to be active. Assume that the foreign non-business tax credit is equal to the foreign tax paid through withholding.

Exercise 7

[ITA: 186]

Ex Ltd., a Canadian-controlled private corporation, received a taxable dividend of $90,000 from its Canadian subsidiary Little Ex Ltd. The subsidiary had paid a total dividend of $120,000 and had received a dividend refund of $18,000.

— REQUIRED

Compute the Part IV tax payable by Ex Ltd.

Exercise 8

[ITA: 123–127; 129; 186]

Why Limited is a Canadian-controlled private corporation operating solely in Newfoundland and Labrador. For its taxation year ended December 31, 2005, the company reported the following income under Division B:

Active business income	$ 85,000
Taxable capital gain	37,500
Canadian-source interest income	45,000
Taxable portfolio dividends from Canadian corporations	18,750
Income under Division B	$186,250

The corporation is carrying forward the following amounts:	
Non-capital losses	$ 37,500
Net capital losses (arising in 1999)	68,750

The balance in the refundable dividend tax on hand account at December 31, 2004 was nil. On November 30, 2005, the company paid $112,500 in taxable dividends to its shareholders all of whom are individuals. The taxable portfolio dividends of $18,750 were received on November 1, 2005.

— REQUIRED

(A) Compute the federal Part I tax and provincial tax at a 12% rate payable by the company for 2005.

(B) Compute the refundable dividend tax on hand balance as at December 31, 2005 and compute the dividend refund for 2005.

Exercise 9

[ITA: 123–127; 129; 186]

Ay Ltd. is a Canadian-controlled private corporation with a December 31, 2005 fiscal year-end. The company operates primarily in Alberta, but has a very small business operation in the U.S. where 5% of its total taxable income as calculated by Regulation 402(3) is generated. Taxable income for the year is calculated as follows:

Canadian-source business income		$ 90,000
Dividends from taxable Canadian corporations:		
Non-connected corporations		30,000
Wholly-owned corporation which received a dividend refund of $4,000		
as a result of paying the dividend		20,000
Canadian-source investment income		50,000
Foreign-source non-business income (foreign tax credit will be $4,000)		30,000
Foreign-source business income (foreign tax credit will be $1,000)		20,000
Canadian-source taxable capital gains		20,000
Income under Division B		$ 260,000
Less: donations	$ 40,000	
taxable dividends from Canadian corporations	50,000	
non-capital losses	20,000	
net capital losses	20,000	130,000
Taxable income		$ 130,000

The refundable dividend tax on hand account had a nil balance at the end of the previous year. No dividends were paid in the preceding year. Dividends of $70,000 had been paid during the year to the only shareholder, an associated corporation which has only income from investments.

— REQUIRED

(A) Compute the federal Part I tax and provincial tax at a 9% rate (using federal taxable income as the tax base) payable by the company for the 2005 taxation year.

(B) Compute the refundable dividend tax on hand balance at the end of the year and the dividend refund for the taxation year.

Exercise 10

[ITA: 125; 129; 186; 256(1)]

Splitinc Limited is owned 50% by Husband Ltd. and 50% by Wife Ltd. The two holding companies are 100% owned by Mr. Split and Mrs. Split, respectively. Splitinc Limited derives all of its income from active business carried on in Canada. It rents facilities from Husband Ltd. to which it pays $120,000 in annual rent, deducting this amount as a business expense. Splitinc also pays dividends to the two holding companies which is the only other income of those corporations.

— REQUIRED

(A) What is the nature of the rental income to Husband Ltd.?

(B) Is there a Part IV tax liability for the two holding companies on the dividends received from Splitinc Limited?

Exercise 11

[ITA: 125; 129; 256]

Janna Management Limited owns a building most of which it rents to Rayna Consulting Services Limited which carries on an active business. Janna and Rayna each own 50% of both corporations. Janna Management Limited also provides managerial, administrative and maintenance services to the unincorporated professional practice of Dr. Adam. The result of these transactions is that Janna Management Limited receives 60% of its income from rent and 40% from providing services and has available an excess business limit for the purposes of the small business deduction.

— REQUIRED

Determine the nature of its income and the deductions from tax available to Janna Management Limited.

Exercise 12

[ITA: Parts I and IV]

Dane Tee lives in a province with a 15.5% corporate tax rate and owns an investment portfolio that generated the following Canadian-source income during the year:

Interest	$ 7,000
Portfolio dividends	15,000
Capital gains	6,000

Her cash needs require that $15,000 of the corporation's after-tax profits be distributed as a dividend. The corporation will retain and reinvest the remainder. She already has taxable income of $20,000 from other sources. She has federal personal tax credits of $1,300 and provincial tax credits of $813.

— REQUIRED

Compare the total tax on the income from the portfolio with the total tax if a corporation owned the securities.

ASSIGNMENT PROBLEMS

Problem 1

[ITA: 125(7)]

The taxpayer company, a private corporation, owned and operated a small shopping centre from which it received rental income. There were seven separate tenants, only one of them being what is sometimes referred to as a "Triple A" tenant, namely, a Canadian bank. The corporation, through its principal officer, negotiated all the leases, took care of all the complaints from the tenants and arranged for the maintenance of the shopping centre. It required some activity by the company almost daily. The rental income of the company was mainly for use of the property, but also, to a much lesser extent, for services and other things supplied by the company such as heat, repairs, etc.

— *REQUIRED*

From the facts provided in the case, determine the type of income that the corporation derives from the business that it carries on under the current legislation.

Problem 2

[ITA: 256]

Consider each of the following unrelated cases, involving the ownership of the common shares of Canadian-controlled private corporations, for taxation years of all corporations ending on December 31:

(A) Leah Ltd. owns 55% of the shares of Elaine Ltd.

(B) Ms. Miriam owns 51% of the shares of Miri Ltd. and 60% of the shares of Ethan Jay Ltd.

(C) Ms. Irene and Mr. Mordechai each own 50% of the shares of IL Ltd. In addition, they each own 50% of the shares of Frim Ltd. Ms. Irene and Mr. Mordechai are not related.

(D) Mrs. Lyn owns 60% of the shares of LBD Ltd. and Mrs. Sarah owns the other 40%. Mrs. Lyn and Mrs. Sarah each own 50% of the shares of Alex Ltd. Mrs. Lyn and Mrs. Sarah are not related.

(E) Janna Ltd., Rayna Ltd. and Adam Ltd. each own $^1/_3$ of the shares of Stan Ltd. Janna Ltd. and Rayna Ltd. each own 50% of the shares of Jonathan Ltd.

(F) Ms. Ruth owns all of the shares of Rick Ltd. Ms. Ruth owns 25% of the shares of Daniel Ltd. and Ms. Ruth's daughter, Elana, who is over 18 years old owns the other 75%.

(G) Mr. Joshua owns 100% of the shares of Gord Ltd. and Ms. Dahlia owns 100% of the shares of Rosalyn Ltd. Mr. Joshua and Ms. Dahlia each own 30% of the shares of Rebecca Ltd. The other 40% of the shares of Rebecca Ltd. are owned by strangers. Mr. Joshua is the brother of Ms. Dahlia's husband.

(H) Mrs. Yael owns 60% of the shares of Birdco Ltd. and 30% of the shares of Livi Ltd. Another 25% of the shares of Livi Ltd. are owned by Birdco Ltd. and the remaining 45% of the shares of Livi Ltd. are owned by strangers.

(I) Ms. Daniella owns 60% of the shares of Veggie Ltd. and 25% of the shares of Beef Ltd. Mr. Adam, who is not related to Ms. Daniella, owns the other 75% of the shares of Beef Ltd. Ms. Daniella holds an option to buy all of the shares owned by Mr. Adam at any time in the next 10 years.

(J) Mr. and Mrs. Jonathan each own 50% of Ethan Ltd. Mr. Jonathan and his three brothers and sisters each own 25% of Maya Ltd.

— *REQUIRED*

In each of the above *unrelated* cases determine whether the corporations are associated. Substantiate your answer by reference to the specific conditions in the provisions of section 256, and consider all possible alternatives.

Problem 3

[ITA: 256]

Consider each of the following unrelated cases, involving the ownership of shares of Canadian-controlled private corporations. Assume all of the issued shares are common shares unless specifically stated otherwise.

(A) Rachel and Monica, friends, each own 50% of the issued shares of A Ltd. In addition, Rachel owns 80% and Monica owns 20% of the issued shares of B Ltd.

(B) Charlie and Claudia are siblings. Charlie owns 80% of A Ltd. which in turn owns 40% of B Ltd. Claudia owns 60% of B Ltd.

(C) Bob, Bill and Bert are three brothers who share equally the income of a professional partnership. The partnership owns 100% of the shares of A Ltd. Bert owns 100% of the shares of B Ltd.

(D) Anne and Barbara are sisters. They each own 100% of their respective corporations, A Ltd. and B Ltd. A Ltd. and B Ltd. each own 40% of the shares of C Ltd.

(E) Valerie, Brandon, and Claire are strangers. They each own $\frac{1}{3}$ of the shares of A Ltd. Brandon owns 40% of the shares of B Ltd. The remaining 60% are owned by Claire. Claire also owns 100% of the shares of C Ltd.

(F) Valerie and her two nieces each own 25% of the shares of A Ltd. Valerie's husband, Dilon, and his nephew each own 50% of the shares of B Ltd. Dilon also owns the remaining 25% of the shares of A Ltd.

(G) Father owns 100% of the shares of F Ltd. His son, Sean, age 17, owns 100% of the common shares of S Ltd. F Ltd. owns 30% of the issued preferred shares of S Ltd. The preferred shares have the following characteristics:

- non-voting,
- dividend rate fixed at 6%,
- redeemable at $1,000 per share, and
- issue price $1,000 per share.

The prescribed rate of interest was 8% at the time the preferred shares were issued.

— *REQUIRED*

Determine which of the corporations are associated and substantiate your answer by reference to specific provisions of the Act.

Problem 4

[ITA: 256]

Both corporations in this case were incorporated for the purpose of buying and selling anti-freeze products. Warren Packaging Limited sold its product ("Dual Duty") to wholesalers who serviced and supplied garages and service stations ultimately for the consumers. Its sole shareholder and president was Mr. Warren. Bradford-Penn Oil Inc. sold its product ("Viceroy") to retailers who sold it on a cash and carry basis to its clients. Mr. Warren's wife was the sole shareholder and president of the latter company.

In essence, both companies were directed by the same person in the same premises. They both had the same year-end. The product came in bulk from the same supplier and was packed in smaller quantities with the different brand names.

Management of the companies felt that it was too risky to have the same company distribute the anti-freeze product to both the wholesalers and the retailers. There was only one supplier of bulk anti-freeze available to the two corporations and that supplier marketed its own brand and, as a result, was also in competition with Warren Packaging and Bradford-Penn Oil. Maintaining the source of supply at a competitive price made the business risky.

Management also felt that it was necessary to have two companies with two different brand names to cover the wholesale market and the retail market. Experience had shown that if the same brand were supplied to both the wholesalers and the retailers, one or the other of the markets would be lost. Even if the same company name appeared on the package of the two different brands, it would be difficult to maintain both markets because of price differentials from the different outlets to the ultimate consumers.

In his testimony, Mr. Warren testified that he did not remember his counselor discussing taxation with him when he decided to separately incorporate the two companies. He also testified that he had given a personal guarantee to the bank to obtain a loan for Warren Packaging Limited and he felt it was necessary to have a limited liability in that corporation. He believed that limited liability was accomplished by his wife's sole ownership of the shares of Bradford-Penn Oil Inc.

— *REQUIRED*

(A) Would subsection 256(5.1) apply in this case and, if so, what would be the effect of that application?

(B) Assuming that subsection 256(5.1) does not apply, determine whether Warren Packaging Limited and Bradford-Penn Oil Inc. are associated. Provide reasons for your determination by reference to the legislation and to the facts of the case.

Problem 5

[ITA: 125, 125.1]

The accountant, Ryan Mailling, of Double-D Manufacturing Ltd. (DML), a Canadian-controlled private corporation, has requested your assistance with respect to the calculation of the company's small business deduction and manufacturing and processing profits deduction.

Ryan has provided you with the following information.

(1) DML is not associated with any other corporation.

(2) For DML's December 31 taxation year-end, the corporation reported:

Active business income	$289,000
Taxable income	250,000
Investment income (all Canadian source)	5,000
Net capital loss deducted	2,000

(3) The accounting records show the cost of equipment and salaries as follows:

	Warehouse: finished products	Processing plant	Admin. bldg.	Warehouse: raw materials	Total
Land	$ 15,000	$ 40,000	$ 10,000	$ 20,000	$ 85,000
Building	156,300	416,400	104,100	208,200	885,000
Machinery	3,000	450,000	15,000	9,000	477,000
Salaries	75,000	900,000	200,000	85,000	1,260,000

— *REQUIRED*

Calculate the 16% small business deduction and manufacturing and processing profits deduction for the taxation year ended December 31, 2005. Show all calculations whether or not relevant to the final answer.

Problem 6

[ITA: 37; 127(5)–(11); 127.1]

Natalia, a resident of Canada, owns 100% of the shares of New Age Limited (NAL). NAL carries on scientific research and experimental development (SR&ED) activities with respect to finding the ingredients for a cream which will reduce fat and tone muscles when massaged into the skin.

During its fiscal year ended December 31, 2005, NAL incurred the following costs related to its SR&ED activities:

Salaries for research technicians and assistants	$600,000
Materials consumed	200,000
Supplies consumed	40,000
Small equipment purchased for the laboratory	80,000
A special machine purchased to mix the ingredients in a temperature controlled environment	100,000

The machine and the lab equipment will have no value when the research project is completed.

Additional overhead costs were incurred in 2005 because of the SR&ED project. The accounting system was not sophisticated enough to properly allocate these expenses. Overhead expenses for the year totalled $500,000.

NAL paid Natalia a bonus of $40,000 in 2005 in addition to her salary of $80,000. Natalia spent 25% of her time on the SR&ED project in 2005.

NAL does not expect to have any taxable income for 2005. It had taxable income of $100,000 in 2004. Its taxable capital does not exceed $10,000,000. It is not associated with any other corporation.

— REQUIRED

(A) Which of the above costs incurred by NAL in 2005 qualify for deduction under subsection 37(1) as qualifying SR&ED expenditures?

(B) Determine the amount of ITCs and refundable ITCs for 2005.

Problem 7

[ITA: 110.1–112; 123–126; 127(3)]

Neville Ltd. is a Canadian-controlled private corporation which was incorporated in 1985 with a December 31 year-end. In 2005, Neville Ltd. earned net income of $250,000 before taxes for accounting purposes. Included in the calculation of that amount were the following items:

Canadian active business income:	
— manufacturing profits (as defined in ssec. 125.1(3))	$ 74,000
— other Canadian active business income	85,000
Dividends from taxable Canadian subsidiary corporations	8,000
Other Canadian investment income:	
— rental income	$ 4,000
— interest income	15,000
— royalty income	1,000
— taxable capital gain	9,000
U.S. interest income ($2,000 withheld)	15,000
U.S. business income ($20,000 tax paid)	96,000
Income under Division B	$307,000
Donations to registered charities	$ 60,000
The company also has the following balances at January 1, 2005:	
1997 Non-capital loss	$ 20,000
1999 Net capital loss	15,000
Charitable donations carried forward from 2004	10,000

The company is a retailer and sells its products in Canada and the U.S. Its total proportion of taxable income earned in Canada, as per Regulation 402, is 75%. Assume that the provincial tax rates on taxable income are 12% and that Neville Ltd.'s foreign tax credits are equal to the U.S. tax withheld on the income.

Neville Ltd.'s 100% owned subsidiary has used $250,000 of the business limit for the small business deduction in 2005. Together, Neville Ltd. and its subsidiary have $8 million of taxable capital in Canada.

— *REQUIRED*

Compute the federal Part I tax and provincial tax payable by Neville Ltd. for 2005. Show *all* calculations.

Problem 8

[ITA: 123–127; 129; 186]

The following selected information has been taken from the records of Sharp Ltd., a Canadian-controlled private corporation, for its fiscal year ended December 31, 2005.

(1) Income for tax purposes:

Active business income (retailing)	$100,000
Foreign business income (retailing)	60,000
Canadian bond interest	20,000
Foreign bond interest	10,000
Taxable dividends received from taxable Canadian corporations	40,000
Taxable capital gains	30,000
Net income under Division B	$260,000

(2) Division C deductions claimed:

Donations	(2,000)
Net capital losses	(5,000)
Non-capital losses	(13,000)
Taxable dividends received from taxable Canadian corporations	(40,000)

(3) Taxable income ... $200,000

(4) Part I tax payable is $23,657 including surtax of $2,240 and additional refundable tax of $3,667. In computing Part I tax, the following deductions were made:

Small business deduction	$16,000
Foreign non-business tax deduction	1,500
Foreign business tax deduction	18,000

(5) Summary of taxable dividends received from taxable Canadian corporations:

Date received	Payer	% of voting shares owned	Amount of dividend received	Dividend refund received by payer corp.
Aug. 1, 2005	A Ltd.	6%	$20,000	$30,000
Oct. 1, 2005	B Ltd.	80%	20,000	5,000
			$40,000	

(6) Summary of dividends paid by Sharp Ltd.:

Type of dividend	Amount	Date declared	Date paid
Taxable dividend	$60,000	July 15, 2005	Aug. 15, 2005
Tax-free ssec. 83(2) dividend	20,000	Oct. 15, 2005	Nov. 15, 2005
Taxable dividend	24,000	Dec. 15, 2005	Jan. 15, 2006

(7) The refundable dividend tax on hand balance at December 31, 2004 was $12,000. The dividend refund for 2004 was $4,000.

— REQUIRED

(A) Compute the dividend refund for 2005.

(B) What would change if Sharp Ltd. was a private corporation, and not a CCPC? Explain.

Problem 9

[ITA: 123–127; 129; 186]

Multi Enterprises Ltd. is a Canadian-controlled private corporation whose fiscal period coincides with the calendar year. For the year 2005, the company's taxable income was calculated as follows:

Income from manufacturing net of C.C.A.		$191,000
Dividends from taxable corporations:		
(a) connected corporation, dividend payment triggering a dividend refund of $2,750 to the wholly-owned subsidiary		11,000
(b) non-connected corporation (portfolio dividends)		20,000
Taxable capital gain	$29,000	
Allowable capital losses	12,000	17,000
Royalties		9,000
Recapture of C.C.A. on disposal of sales equipment		4,000
Income from rental of an apartment building (no full-time employees and tenants provide virtually all of their own services)		14,000
Foreign non-business income (i.e., interest income) (foreign tax credit of $3,450 equal to foreign tax withheld)		23,000
Foreign business income (foreign tax credit of $1,800 equal to foreign tax paid)		6,000
Interest charged on accounts receivable		5,000
Net income for tax purposes		$300,000
Less: net capital losses carried over	$ 7,000	
non-capital losses carried over	10,000	
donations	26,000	
dividends from taxable Canadian corporations	31,000	74,000
Taxable income		$226,000

At December 31, 2004 there was a nil balance in the refundable dividend tax on hand account. The company paid $72,000 in dividends during 2005 to individual shareholders.

It has been agreed that $150,000 of the business limit for small business deduction will be claimed by the parent, Multi Enterprises Ltd., leaving the remainder for the subsidiary.

The gross capital cost of the company's depreciable assets for capital cost allowance purposes is as follows:

Rental property	$144,000
Manufacturing building	290,000
Manufacturing equipment	97,500
Other non-manufacturing assets	32,500
Total	$564,000

The manufacturing building is also used 10% for finished goods inventory, 10% by the shipping department and 5% by the accounting and sales departments. Rental expenses totalled $30,000 for the manufacturing operations.

Salaries and wages for the year were allocated as follows:	
Rental operation (in Canada)	$ 14,000
Manufacturing operation (including sales)	240,000
Total	$254,000

The manufacturing division salaries include $155,000 with respect to time engaged in manufacturing activities.

The company has a permanent establishment in New Brunswick and in the United States. Its gross revenue, net of dividends and net of rentals, and its salaries and wages are attributed to its permanent establishments as follows:

	Gross revenue	Salaries & wages
New Brunswick	$1,776,000	$238,000
United States	220,000	16,000
Totals	$1,996,000	$254,000

In the United States a salesman worked out of his home in which he kept a small stock of merchandise from which he filled orders.

During the year the company purchased machinery and equipment (Class 43) in the amount of $32,000 for use in its southern New Brunswick manufacturing facilities. Capital cost allowance for the year has been adjusted for this purchase.

— REQUIRED

(A) Compute the federal Part I tax and provincial tax at a 11.5% rate on federal taxable income payable by the company for 2005. Show in detail the calculation of all deductions in the computation, using a separate schedule for each special deduction. In calculating the small business deduction list all ineligible items of income, if any, and indicate the amount of the business limit available for the subsidiary.

(B) Compute the refundable dividend tax on hand balance as at December 31, 2005, showing, in detail, your calculations and compute the dividend refund for 2005.

Problem 10

[ITA: 110.1–112; 123–127]

The controller of Tek Enterprises Ltd. provided the Accountant with the following information.

Tek Enterprises Ltd.
Income
For the fiscal year ended December 31, 2005

Canadian manufacturing and processing profits (Reg.5200)		$251,500
Canadian retail business income		50,000
Foreign retail business income (before foreign tax paid of $15,000)		40,000
Taxable capital gains		4,500
Interest income:		
Canadian long-term bonds	$20,000	
Interest on accounts receivable outstanding for more than 30 days in the Canadian retail business	5,000	25,000
Dividend income:		
From taxable Canadian corporations	$ 9,000	
From foreign corporations (before foreign tax of $1,800) (Tek Enterprises Ltd. owns less than 5% of the shares)	12,000	21,000
Net income		$392,000

Notes:

(1) Tek Enterprises Limited is a CCPC. It is not associated with any corporations. It paid federal Part I tax of $35,000 and Part I.3 tax, large corporations tax, of $400 (before deducting surtax credits) in 2004.

(2) The following items were deducted in the computation of income above:

SR&ED expenditures (current in nature)	$50,000
Charitable donations	75,000
Federal political contributions	1,000

(3) The taxable capital gain was calculated as follows:

	Marketable securities	Equipment	Total
Proceeds	$15,000	$ 200	$15,200
Cost	3,000	3,200	6,200
Gain (Loss)	$12,000	$ (3,000)	$ 9,000
			× ½
			$ 4,500

(4) The corporation has net capital losses (incurred in 1999) of $13,000. It has unused foreign business tax credits (from 2004) of $100.

The Accountant assigned a junior staff member to calculate the federal Part I tax payable for Tek Enterprises Ltd. The following is his calculation.

Net income	$392,000
Dividends	(21,000)
Donations	(75,000)
Net capital losses	(13,000)
Taxable income	$283,000
Basic federal tax (40% × $283,000)	$113,200

Abatement: Taxable income $283,000
Foreign business income .... (40,000)

$243,000 × 10% = 24,300

$137,500

Surtax (4% × $137,500) 5,500

$143,000

Foreign tax credit:
Lesser of: (a) Foreign tax paid ($15,000 + $1,800) = $16,800

(b) $\dfrac{\text{Foreign income } \$52,000}{\$283,000 + \$21,000 + \$13,000} \times \$143,000 = \$23,457$ (16,800)

Small business deduction:
16% × the least of: (a) Active business income:

M&P	$251,500
Cdn. retail business	50,000
Foreign retail business	40,000
	$341,500

(b) $283,000 – 4 × $16,800   = $215,800

(c) Business limit: $300,000   (34,528)

M&P deduction: 7% × the lesser of:
(a) Cdn M&P profits $251,500

(b) Taxable income $283,000
Small business deduction .... (34,528)
$16,800 × 3 .... (50,400)

$198,072   (13,865)

Political contribution tax credit ....   (650)

Federal Part I tax payable .... $ 77,157

— *REQUIRED*

Write a memo in point-form explaining to the junior staff member the errors in his calculation. Do not redo the calculations. Only describe his incorrect procedures in arriving at Part I tax so that the calculation may be redone correctly.

Problem 11

[ITA: 123–127; 129; 186]

Rob's Shameless Self-Promotion Sales (RSS-PS) Inc. is a Canadian-controlled private corporation located in London, Ontario. For its fiscal year ended December 31, 2005, the corporation had correctly calculated its income for tax purposes under Division B as follows:

Canadian source:

Consulting income	$160,000
Advertising agency loss	(30,000)
Rental income from warehouse fully rented on a 5-year lease	20,000
Retailing income	75,000
Interest on outstanding accounts receivable in retailing business	25,000
Recapture of CCA from sale of fixtures used in retailing business	25,000
Interest income from 5-year bonds	75,000
Taxable capital gain	70,000
Dividends from non-connected taxable Canadian corporations	12,000

Foreign sources:

Interest earned on Bermuda bank account (no withholding tax)	20,000
U.S. business income (foreign tax credit of $7,581 equal to foreign tax paid)	23,000
Division B net income for tax purposes	$475,000

Additional information:

RSS-PS Inc. made the following selected payments during the year:

Scientific research and experimental development (current expenses and new equipment)	$100,000
Charitable donations	14,000
Taxable dividends	120,000

The balance in the tax accounts on December 31, 2004 were:

Charitable donations from 2002	$ 1,000
Non-capital losses from 2001	56,000
Net capital losses from 1999	18,000
Refundable dividend tax on hand	20,000
Dividend refund for 2004	9,000

Taxable income earned in Canada is considered to be 90% of the total earned by RSS-PS Inc. RSS-PS Inc. allocated $170,000 of its $300,000 business limit to other associated corporations. Taxable capital of the associated group for large corporations tax purposes was $8,380,000. The only scientific research and experimental development expenditures of the associated group were made by RSS-PS Inc.

— *REQUIRED*

(A) Compute the federal Part I tax and provincial tax at a 13% rate on federal taxable income for the 2005 taxation year.

(B) Compute the dividend refund for 2005 and the amount of any Refundable Dividend Tax on Hand to be carried forward.

Problem 12

[ITA: 125; 129; 186; 256]

Carl owns 100% of the issued shares of Compunet. He incorporated Compunet earlier this year to provide computer consulting services to Vitamins Inc., a retailer of energy-producing vitamins. Prior to the incorporation of Compunet, Carl headed the computer service division of Vitamins Inc. One hundred per cent of the issued shares of Vitamins Inc. are owned by Carl's cousin, Vince.

Carl's daughter, Sulee, received a degree in computer science from the University of Toronto in April and has been employed by Compunet as a computer consultant since then. Sulee and Carl work well together. They are the only employees of Compunet.

Compunet owns a warehouse. One-half of the warehouse is rented to Vitamins Inc. and the remainder is rented to Mindblasters, a wholly-owned subsidiary of Compunet. Mindblasters is a successful retailer of computer games.

During the current year, Compunet received taxable dividends from Mindblasters and paid taxable dividends to Carl.

— *REQUIRED*

Determine the type(s) of income being earned by Compunet, the rate of tax for each type and any refunds available.

Problem 13

[ITA: 125; 129; 256]

Lemon Ltd. provides management services for Toys-4-U Limited (Toys), a manufacturer of educational toys, and for certain other corporations described below. Les Lemon is the sole shareholder and only employee of Lemon Ltd. Prior to this year, Les had been employed by Toys as vice-president of financial and administrative services.

Les owns all of the common shares of Slum Landlord Ltd. (Slum), which is in the business of renting commercial properties. Slum has no employees, except for Les, and subcontracts all maintenance and administrative services. Slum's income for tax purposes can be broken down as follows:

Lemon Ltd.	10%
Cheap Leasing Ltd. (see below)	25%
Arm's length parties	65%
	100%

Les is also involved with Cheap Leasing Limited (Cheap), which is in the business of leasing educational equipment. The ownership of the common shares of Cheap is as follow:

Les Lemon	25 shares
Lucy Lemon, Les' wife	20 shares
Lemon Ltd.	30 shares
Larry Lemon, Les' uncle	10 shares
Arm's length parties	15 shares

Cheap derives approximately 80% of its income from the educational equipment leasing business. The balance of its income is interest from a loan to Toys. Cheap has four employees in addition to Les.

All of the above corporations are Canadian-controlled private corporations and have December 31 year-ends.

— *REQUIRED*

Identify the various sources of income for the above corporations indicating the reasoning behind your conclusions. Also indicate the *federal* tax rate and any refundable taxes applicable to each income source.

Problem 14

[ITA: Parts I and IV]

Mr. Horseshoes, a resident of a province with a 41% effective corporate tax rate (before the additional refundable tax), has just won a lottery prize of $750,000. He is considering the following investment of these funds: $200,000 of bonds yielding 8% and $550,000 of common shares of Growth Unlimited Limited which pay a dividend to yield 5%. Having taken a course in security analysis, Mr. Horseshoes can predict with great confidence that he will realize a 10.5% capital gain on the shares within the year. Mr. Horseshoes currently has taxable income of $30,000. He has federal personal tax credits of $2,000.

— *REQUIRED*

(A) Advise Mr. Horseshoes on whether he should use an investment corporation with a permanent establishment in the province of which he is a resident to hold the securities he proposes to purchase. Include in your analysis the realization of the predicted capital gain. Use 2005 personal tax rates. Also, consider any non-quantitative factors that may be relevant to the decision.

(B) Do the above analysis again, using a 40% effective corporate tax rate before the additional refundable tax.

[For more problems and solutions thereto, see the CD accompanying this book.]

SUPPLEMENTAL NOTES

(This section of the text can be omitted without losing the continuity of the chapter. None of review questions, multiple choice questions, exercises, or assignment problems utilizes this information.)

Common Law Background to Current Legislation on Definition of "Active Business"

As long as Canadian tax legislation has provided for a low rate of tax on relatively low amounts of corporate income, there has been an incentive for taxpayers to incorporate their operations. Certainly, non-tax advantages, as discussed later in the chapter, are present in the incorporated form. However, the small business deduction overshadowed the other benefits of incorporation and many businesses were incorporated to qualify for that deduction.

To provide some perspective on the rules that currently exist in this area, some common law history is important. Many of the rules that are in force resulted from court decisions that are presented in this discussion.

Over the years, the CRA has looked very carefully at corporations which appeared to have been formed solely for the reduction of taxes. It has used a number of types of arguments against such corporations. In a relatively early case, *Kindree v. M.N.R.*, (Ex. Ct.) 64 DTC 5248, the incorporated practice of a medical doctor was challenged on the grounds that a corporation cannot practise medicine under the particular provincial law governing such practice. This precedent-setting decision still stands today where provincial corporate legislation does not allow for the incorporation of "personal corporations" as are allowed, for example, in Alberta.

Another approach taken by the CRA was to argue that a corporation was a sham creating an appearance that was not justified in substance. A corporation found to be such a sham could be disregarded for tax purposes. This type of argument was not successful[h] and this line of argument has not been used by the CRA for a number of years.

As a refinement of the sham arguments, the CRA used the approach that for a corporation to avoid being considered a sham it had to have a valid business purpose other than the purpose of reducing taxes. The arrangements in the case of *M.N.R. v. Leon et al.*, (F.C.A.) 76 DTC 6299, were judged not to have such a legitimate business purpose and, further, to be for the sole purpose of reducing taxes. However, the majority of subsequent cases did not support this extended definition of a sham (i.e., no business purpose).[i] In the case of *The Queen v. Daly*, (F.C.A.) 81 DTC 5197, the court indicated that the "business purpose" test was unnecessary and, in fact, that the saving of tax is a good reason for entering a transaction. This conclusion was confirmed by the Supreme Court of Canada in *Stubart Investments Limited v. The Queen*, (S.C.C.) 84 DTC 6305 which indicated that the conclusion in the *Leon* case could be disregarded in many situations. The decision in *The Queen v. Vivian*, (F.C.A.) 84 DTC 6452, on the issue of a management services corporation being a sham, followed the *Stubart* reasoning.

---

[h] *Sazio v. M.N.R.*, (Ex. Ct.) 69 DTC 5001 and *M.N.R. v. Cameron*, (S.C.C.) 72 DTC 6325.

[i] Other cases heard on the question of the business purpose included: *The Queen v. Burns*, (F.C.T.D.) 73 DTC 5219; *Petritz v. M.N.R.*, (F.C.T.D.) 73 DTC 5243; *Holmes et al. v. the Queen*, (F.C.T.D.) 74 DTC 6143; *Connor v. M.N.R.*, (T.R.B.) 75 DTC 85; *Fotheringham v. M.N.R.*, (T.R.B.) 77 DTC 275; *Handa v. M.N.R.*, (T.R.B.) 78 DTC 1191; and *Mendels v. M.N.R.*, (F.C.T.D.) 78 DTC 6267.

If a corporation could not be challenged by the foregoing arguments, then the question arose as to whether or not it could qualify for the very favourable small business deduction. The small business deduction, which was introduced in 1972, was computed on the corporation's Canadian-source active business income. However, as previously indicated, there was no statutory definition of the term "active business". (In general terms, "active business", as a defined term for use in computing the small business deduction, was applicable to taxation years commencing after 1979.) While the applicability of the term to many situations was obvious, it was not necessarily clear in a large number of situations which gave rise to a number of key appeals.

The appeals that were heard in this area can be categorized by the type of corporation that argued that its income should be considered to be derived from an active business. One such type of corporation was the small investment corporation which was formed to hold income-producing property such as real estate, shares, bonds or mortgages. In such cases, the issue was whether the income of the corporation came from property or from business.[j] A case involving the rental of buildings became a leading case in this area. In that case, *The Queen v. Cadboro Bay Holdings*, (F.C.T.D.) 77 DTC 5115, a very liberal interpretation of "active business" was used. It would appear that the issues addressed in this category of cases have now been resolved by the statutory definition of a "specified investment business" [ssec. 125(7)]. If a corporation carries on such a business, the income from that business is treated as investment income and, therefore, is not eligible for the small business deduction. However, if the corporation's business does not fit that definition, the income might be considered active.

A second category of corporation can be termed the personal service corporation and is sometimes referred to as an incorporated employee. The *Sazio* and *Cameron* cases provide good examples of such corporations while the *Leon* case shows an unsuccessful attempt to establish such a corporation. These situations often involve a contract of employment being replaced by a contract between the former employer and a corporation owned by the former employee whereby the corporation would provide the services of the former employee. The new corporation hires the former employee to perform those services. Typically, the corporation would have one major client (i.e., the former employer) and few, if any, employees other than the owner of the new corporation. This type of business activity became a particularly troublesome area. As a result, to limit the potential benefits of incorporation where corporations provided personal services, such as that in the *Daly* case, further rules were introduced which excluded a "personal services business" [ssec. 125(7))] from the definition of "active business". The first reported case on the definition of a "personal services business" was *Hushi v. M.N.R.*, (T.C.C.) 89 DTC 30, in which the court applied the tests for determining whether an individual was employed or self-employed (as discussed in Chapter 3).[k]

A third category of corporation can be called a management corporation. This type of corporation was formed to provide management services to an unincorporated professional practice that could not itself be incorporated because of the laws governing the particular profession. The unincorporated professional practice would hire the corporation at a fee usually equal to cost plus 15% to provide administrative, management and other services as well as facilities and equipment. The professional or that person's spouse would own the corporation.[l] Such arrangements now seem to be included in the definition of "active business" unless they fall into the definition of a "personal services business". Even if the operations of the management corporation are considered an "active business", the CRA will attempt to minimize the advantage of the small business deduction by challenging the 15% mark-up on certain services and items provided to the professional practice. Since it is the 15% mark-up that is taxed at a potentially low rate in the corporation, the advantage of the corporation can be reduced by this assessment practice.[m]

---

[j] Cases heard to determine whether the lending of money on mortgages could be considered to result in income from an active business included *MRT Investments Ltd. et al. v. The Queen*, (F.C.T.D.) 75 DTC 5224 and *The Queen v. Rockmore Investments*, (F.C.A.) 76 DTC 6156.

[k] For another case on this topic, see *Toushan v. M.N.R.*, (T.C.C.) 89 DTC 568.

[l] The case of *DBSK Management Ltd. v. M.N.R.*, (T.R.B.) 75 DTC 219 involves a good example of such a corporation.

[m] See the court decision in *R.L. Smith v. M.N.R.*, (T.C.C.) 87 DTC 132 for a case in this area.

Chapter 13

Planning the Use of a Corporation and Shareholder-manager Remuneration

TOPICS DISCUSSED

	Page
EMPLOYMENT REMUNERATION	698
Considerations in Choosing Elements of Shareholder-manager Remuneration	698
Salaries, Bonuses and Other Payments to the Shareholder-manager	701
Shareholder Benefits and Loans	704
Other Planning Considerations for Shareholder-manager Remuneration	708
SALARY vs. DIVIDENDS	710
The Basic Trade-off	710
Amounts of Taxable Dividends that can be Distributed Tax-free	711
Distribution out of Income Taxed at Small Business Rate	711
Distributions out of Income not Eligible for the Small Business Deduction	716

	Page
Summary of the Salary vs. Dividends Issue	717
OTHER PLANNING ASPECTS OF USING CORPORATIONS	718
Use of Holding Companies	718
Qualified Small Business Corporation Shares (QSBCS)	720
Capital Gains Deduction	727
Attribution through a Corporation	731
Income-splitting Tax ["Kiddie Tax"]	733
GENERAL ANTI-AVOIDANCE RULE UNDER THE INCOME TAX ACT	734
SUPPLEMENTAL NOTES	750
Other Salary/Dividend Considerations	750
General Anti-avoidance Rule Under the Excise Tax Act	753

The previous chapter demonstrated that the integration system, when applied to business income earned by a corporation, can result in tax savings in certain cases where the combined federal and provincial rate of tax on corporations is less than 20%. Further tax savings and flexibility through the use of a corporation for business income are possible, if proper planning is undertaken. This chapter discusses planning considerations by beginning with the planning of employment remuneration for the shareholder-manager. It then examines the question of whether to pay salaries and similar income or to pay dividends. While much of the discussion is set out in terms pertaining to an individual owner of a business, the principles can be applied, with appropriate modification, to a group of owners controlling the business. Some other planning aspects of using corporations pertaining to holding companies, the qualified small business corporation share (QSBCS) capital gains exemption [sec. 110.6] and attribution [sec. 74.4] are discussed next. The final section of the chapter discuss the general anti-avoidance rule (GAAR) of the *Income Tax Act* [sec. 245], which may limit more aggressive planning and, hence, must be considered.

For the purposes of computing the total income tax of an individual, the following table will be used in this chapter. Provincial rates of tax are hypothetical. Actual provincial rates vary. In addition, provincial tax brackets may vary, due to the use of a provincial Consumer Price Index and the impact of provincial surtaxes. Provinces may also establish a different number of tax brackets.

Combined Federal and Provincial Tax Rates

		Federal		Provincial		Total	
Taxable Income		*Tax on lower limit*	*Tax rate on excess*	*Tax on lower limit*	*Tax rate on excess*	*Tax on lower limit*	*Tax rate on excess*
—	$ 35,595	—	16%	—	10%	—	26%
$ 35,596	71,190	$ 5,695	22%	$ 3,560	12%	$ 9,235	34%
71,191	115,739	13,526	26%	7,831	15%	21,357	41%
115,740	and over	25,109	29%	14,513	17%	39,622	46%

I. EMPLOYMENT REMUNERATION

A. Considerations in Choosing Elements of Shareholder-manager Remuneration

The prime consideration in deciding on remuneration for the shareholder-manager is his or her cash requirements, both immediately and in the future on retirement. The objective of the decision is to find the optimum method of providing the share-holder-manager with the necessary cash while at the same time leaving the corporation with maximum cash for reinvestment. This process might involve paying out more than necessary in salaries and bonuses, as long as this is reasonable. The purpose of such payments would be to be taxable at the corporate level only on income eligible for the small business deduction or to qualify for Canada Pension Plan, registered retirement savings plan, deferred profit sharing plan or registered pension plan contributions. Any after-tax salary paid to the shareholder-manager in excess of his or her cash requirements can be loaned back to the corporation for reinvestment.

Also important to the remuneration decision are the other sources of income that the shareholder-manager may have. If he or she is already in a high tax bracket, it might be wise to freeze salaries and bonuses to take advantage of a tax deferral on the income left in the corporation, even though the ultimate total tax may be higher. The time value of money may make the saving now greater than the added cost at some time in the future.

For example, consider the case of a corporation taxable at a net 36% rate, including provincial tax. This corporation faces the choice of whether to pay a bonus of $100 now or a dividend of $100 at some time in the future. Exhibit 13-1 shows the comparative calculation that might be made assuming that the individual tax rate (federal plus provincial) is approximately 46%.

EXHIBIT 13-1
Comparison of $100 Paid as a Bonus Now or as a Dividend in the Future

	Bonus now	Dividend later
Corporation		
Corporate income..	$100	$100
Bonus...	100	—
Corporate taxable income	Nil	$100
Corporate tax @ 36% (rounded)	—	(36)
Funds available for dividend	Nil	$ 64
Shareholder		
Income...	$100	$ 64
Dividend gross-up	—	16
Taxable income	$100	$ 80
Combined federal and provincial tax @ 46% (rounded)	$ 46	$ 37
Dividend tax credit @ 25% of actual dividend (combined federal and provincial effect)	—	(16)
Net tax...	$ 46	$ 21
Cash available...	$ 54	$ 43
Tax deferral ($46 – $36)	$10	
Tax cost ($46 – ($36 + $21))	$11	

Note, there is a tax deferral of $10 (i.e., $46 – $36) because the initial tax on the corporation for the dividend alternative is $36 while the tax on the individual for the bonus alternative is $46, but when the dividend is paid, personal tax of $21 must be paid on the dividend. Thus, paying a dividend in the future will result in a lower tax now by $10 and a higher tax later by $11.

The number of years that the dividend must be deferred for the tax deferral advantage to exceed the tax cost can be determined using the following analysis involving the time value of money. Assume that the pre-tax time value of money is 10% for both the owner-manager and the corporation. This is reasonable if the owner-manager can reinvest a bonus in the corporation by lending the after-tax bonus amount to the corporation at a pre-tax 10% interest rate. A $100 bonus will attract tax at an assumed 46% rate in the hands of the owner-manager who can reinvest the $54 (i.e., $100 (1 – .46)) at a pre-tax 10% rate or an after-tax rate of 5.4% (i.e., 10% (1 – .46)) for n years. Income earned by the corporation on the reinvested bonus will be offset by the tax deductible interest paid by the corporation on the loan from the owner-manager.

On the other hand, if the corporation does not pay the bonus, it will pay tax at the assumed 36% total rate, leaving it with $64 (i.e., $100 (1 – .36) after tax. That $64 can be reinvested by the corporation at a pre-tax 10% or an after-tax 6.4% (i.e., 10% (1 – .36)) for n years. However, in n years, the accumulated amount will be paid as a dividend and taxed at a net combined federal and provincial rate, after the dividend gross-up and tax credit in the top bracket, of about 33%.

In this case, the number of years, n, for the accumulated after-tax bonus to equal the accumulated after-tax dividend in the hands of the owner-manager is about 22 years.[a] After about 24 years, the deferral advantage from the dividend alternative is higher than the tax cost of not paying the bonus immediately. The lower the discount

---

[a] This result was achieved by solving the following equation for n:

(continued on next page)

rate used, the higher is the breakeven number of years, n. Also, the higher the corporate tax rate used, the higher is the breakeven number of years. This analysis assumes a constant time value of money and constant personal and corporate tax rates over the period.

A tax deferral of this nature will be possible wherever the initial corporate rate of tax is less than the individual's personal rate of tax. In cases of lower corporate tax rates, it can be shown with an analysis similar to the above that a tax deferral is possible with negligible additional tax on the ultimate dividend. Therefore, the deferral advantage can be much greater than that shown, particularly for a corporation eligible for the small business deduction.

As shown in the previous chapter, the availability of the small business deduction is essential to certain tax deferrals and possible savings on business income. Thus, the remuneration policy should be designed to maintain corporate income below the business limit of $300,000 (for the calendar year 2005 and later years) to prevent Canadian business income from being taxed at full corporate rates and, hence, to be double-taxed when integration is not perfect. Yet, such a policy must recognize that added salary or bonuses necessary to its implementation, taxed at a high personal rate of a shareholder-manager, may have adverse tax consequences not considered in the above breakeven analysis. Salary may increase a payroll tax such as the health levy, used in several provinces to finance health care. The interim measure limiting the deductibility of payroll taxes to November 1994 levels (i.e., any increases by way of rate increases or new taxes will not be deductible) will have further planning implications for the payment of salary.

The payment of interest or dividends is favoured, if it is desirable to reduce the cumulative net investment loss (C.N.I.L.) account, as will be discussed later in this chapter, to preserve access to the QSBCS capital gains deduction. Note that interest paid on shareholder debt has the same effect as salary in reducing corporate income to the business limit of $300,000 (for calendar year 2005 and later years) and attracts the same tax as salary in the hands of the individual. However, interest income reduces the cumulative net investment loss and salary does not.

Other considerations would include the company's need for funds to be used in the business, as indicated above. They would also include the effects of the remuneration decision on the value of the company's shares which may be important if a sale of the business is contemplated. Finally, changes in tax rates and tax law in general must be monitored constantly in terms of their effect on the remuneration decision.

(continued from previous page)
$$\$100 \, (1 - .46)(1 + .10 \, (1 - .46))^n = \$100 \, (1 - .36)(1 + .10 \, (1 - .36))^n(1 - .33)$$

$$n \approx 22 \text{ years.}$$

The formula can be generalized as follows:

$$\$100 \, (1 - t_p)(1 + r \, (1 - t_p))^n = \$100 \, (1 - t_c)(1 + r \, (1 - t_c))^n(1 - t_{pd}).$$

The number of years, n, can be solved using logarithms.

B. Salaries, Bonuses and Other Payments to the Shareholder-manager

[ITA: 5; 9; 18; 67; 78; 80; IT-109R2]

1. General guidelines

A primary guideline to follow is to ensure that various basic deductions and personal tax credits available to employees and individuals, in general, are fully utilized by the payment of salaries and bonuses or other similar amounts of employment income. These basic deductions and credits would include items listed in section 8 of the Act and Division C and personal tax credits listed in Division E.

As already indicated, another guideline would involve the payment of salaries and bonuses, perhaps to reduce active business income to as low a level approaching the business limit of $300,000 business limit (for the calendar year 2005 and later years), as would be considered reasonable to avoid double taxation on income taxed at a corporate rate in excess of 20%. This can also be accomplished by having a shareholder, who cannot be paid a salary, hold some of his or her investment in the corporation in the form of debt such that the corporation can make interest payments which will reduce corporate income. Again, payments of this nature, which are not needed immediately by the shareholder, can be loaned back to the corporation. When needed, the funds can then be withdrawn as a repayment of debt with no further tax consequences.

2. Salaries and bonuses

In order to be deductible by the corporation, salaries and bonuses paid, must be reasonable in the circumstances [sec. 67]. There are no concrete guidelines as to what is meant by the word "reasonable". Where the employee is at arm's length with the corporation, generally any salary and/or bonus would qualify as "reasonable". However, this is not the case in the situation of a controlling shareholder-manager. In such a case, the value of his or her services may be assessed. The Canada Revenue Agency (CRA) could look at what executives in other corporations are being paid. The gross revenue and profitability of the corporation are probably the major factors to consider when justifying a large salary or bonus to a key person.[b]

On the other hand, there may be no incentive for the CRA to use section 67 to challenge the amount of salary paid to a controlling shareholder-manager. While the salary may be deductible to the corporation, it is included in the income of the recipient shareholder-manager. At high salary levels, the tax on the income in the hands of the shareholder-manager will generally be higher than the tax saving from the deduction of salary by the corporation.

In the case of *Totem Disposal Co. Ltd. v. M.N.R.*, (T.R.B.) 81 DTC 493, the court held that the company's policy of limiting its net income to below the small business deduction limit by the accrual of management salary was for the purpose of tax reduction and not for the purpose of gaining or producing income. Therefore, the accrued salary expense was not allowed. This decision would not necessarily preclude the actual payment, as opposed to accrual, of a reasonable salary or bonus to achieve the same objective. In contrast to the *Totem Disposal* case, the Tax Court of Canada, in rejecting the argument that accruals were not made to produce income, set out the following criteria[c] for deductibility:

(a) reasonableness of the bonus in relation to profit and services rendered;

(b) payment for real and identifiable service;

---

[b] For a case on the issue of the reasonableness of bonuses, see *La Compagnie Ideal Body Inc. v. The Queen*, (F.C.T.D.) 89 DTC 5450. See also "Shareholder/Manager Remuneration" in *Income Tax Technical News No. 22*, Canada Customs and Revenue Agency, January 11, 2002.

[c] These criteria were quoted in the case of *Earlscourt Sheet Metal Mechanical Limited v. M.N.R.*, (T.C.C.) 88 DTC 1029.

(c) some justification for expecting a bonus over regular salary (e.g., a company policy);

(d) reasonableness of the time between determining profit and establishing the bonus; and

(e) a legal obligation to pay the accrued bonus.

Where a director's resolution authorizing payment of management bonuses contained uncertainties regarding the actual payment, the Tax Court of Canada, in *Samuel F. Investments Limited v. M.N.R.*, 88 DTC 1106, held that the liability was contingent in nature and, therefore, not deductible.

The CRA's position on the issue of reasonableness of salaries or bonuses is that the reasonableness of salaries or bonuses paid to employee-shareholders is to be determined based on the facts of the case. However, they will generally not challenge the reasonableness of salaries or bonuses to shareholder-managers if profits are usually distributed by way of bonuses to the shareholder-managers or the company has a policy of paying bonuses to compensate them for their special knowledge or skills.[d]

3. Accrued bonuses and other amounts

Where an amount in respect of employee remuneration (including salaries, wages, pension benefits, and retiring allowances) is unpaid 180 days after the end of the employer's fiscal period, the amount is deductible only in the employer's fiscal period in which the amount is actually paid [ssec. 78(4)]. (By administrative practice, the CRA allows payment on the 180th day [IT-109R2, par. 10], despite the clarity of the legislation on this point.) Thus, the accrual method is denied to the employer on amounts unpaid after the 179-day period. Note that a shareholder-manager has far greater flexibility when the corporation's fiscal year ends during the last 179 days of the calendar year. Since a bonus can be paid at any time during the following 179 days from the year-end of the accrual, income can be triggered in the current calendar year by a payment to the owner-manager. Alternatively, income can be deferred to the following year by an accrual in the fiscal period and a payment in the following year, if this is more beneficial. Of course, the benefit from deferring the payment of the bonus to the employee is reduced considerably by the requirement by the employer to withhold tax at the time of paying the bonus. With a fiscal year-end in the first half of the calendar year, the accrued bonus must be paid in the same calendar year, as it is accrued, thereby reducing the deferral flexibility.

Where an amount, other than remuneration, is deductible by a taxpayer, like a corporation, and owed to a non-arm's length person, like a majority shareholder, the provisions in subsection 78(1) apply to the unpaid amount. As an example of the application of these rules, consider a situation where *property* owned by a majority shareholder personally is transferred to a corporation in return for certain income payments, such as, a royalty payment. The royalties can be accrued by the corporation as an expense in one year and paid up to two years after the taxation year of the corporation in which the amount was accrued. This gives the company an immediate expense deduction, but the shareholder, if using the cash basis, has no income until the amount is paid. The amount must be paid prior to the end of the second taxation year after the year in which it is expensed where the shareholder is not at arm's length with the corporation [ssec. 78(1)]. If it is not paid by the end of the second taxation year following the year of accrual, the amount must be added back to the income of the corporation in the third taxation year of the corporation following the year of accrual [par. 78(1)(a)]. This could result in double taxation, unless the shareholder forgives the amount payable, because on ultimate payment the corporation would not get a deduction, while the shareholder would have to report the income. On the forgiveness of a

---

[d] Question 42 of the "CRA Round Table" in the *1981 Conference Report* of the Canadian Tax Foundation.

debt of this nature, the rules in section 80 would ordinarily be invoked. However, if section 78 applies, the amount payable is considered "an excluded obligation" [ssec. 80(1)] and the debt forgiveness rules in section 80 will not apply.

To avoid this problem, the corporation and the shareholder-manager must file an agreement on or before the date on which the corporation must file its tax return for the third taxation year following the year of accrual [par. 78(1)(b)]. This agreement deems the amount to have been paid by the corporation and received by the shareholder-manager on the first day of the third taxation year following the year of accrual. In addition, the amount deducted is deemed to have been lent back to the corporation by the shareholder-manager.

For example, assume a corporation's year-end is June 30. Royalties accrued on June 30, 2003 must be paid by June 30, 2005 or added back to the corporation's income for the year ended June 30, 2006 unless a paragraph 78(1)(b) election is filed on or before December 31, 2006. In that case, the royalties are deemed to have been received by the non-arm's length shareholder-manager and loaned back to the corporation on July 1, 2005. The effect of the election is to put the shareholder in the same position as he or she would have been had the royalties actually been paid. When the corporation ultimately repays the loan resulting from the unpaid royalties, there are no further tax consequences because the royalties were already taxed on their deemed receipt under the election.

The election under paragraph 78(1)(b) can be filed late, that is, after the filing deadline. However, if the election is filed late, 25% of the unpaid amount is added back in the third year under paragraph 78(1)(a) to the corporation's income [ssec. 78(3)]. This will not affect the treatment of the full unpaid amount under paragraph 78(1)(b). Thus, in the above example, 25% of the unpaid amount would be added back to the corporation's income in the 2006 taxation year, but under the election the entire amount of unpaid royalties would be deemed to have been paid by the corporation and received by the shareholder-manager and to have been loaned back on July 1, 2005. When the corporation ultimately pays back the loan, there will be no further tax consequences. The corporation will have deducted the entire amount of royalties in its 2003 taxation year, but will have added back 25% in its 2006 taxation year. Thus, the 25% amount will, in effect, not have been deducted, thereby creating a penalty for a late-filed election.

See IT-109R2 for the CRA's interpretation of these provisions. Note, in particular, paragraph 12(e) of the Interpretation Bulletin which suggests that if an unpaid amount does not constitute a genuine liability, no deduction will be allowed [par. 18(1)(e)]. The Interpretation Bulletin states that "for genuine liability to exist, there must be an enforceable claim by the creditor with a reasonable expectation that the debt will in fact be paid by the debtor."

There are other potential problems with the accrual of amounts. In order to be deductible in the year accrued, there must be a legal obligation to pay the amount. If the legal obligation is not established, then a deduction would be allowed only in the year of payment and not in the year of accrual. Thus, the liability should be established by recording the amount in the minutes of the directors' meeting prior to the year-end and by attempting to establish, in the case of a bonus, some formula for computing the bonus representing objective standards. The payment should not be made contingent on some event which might take place after the year-end. Having established a real liability in this manner, if the amount is not paid on time and if the election is not filed, the shareholder may decide to forgive the amount so that the corporation need not pay it, subject to the double taxation previously mentioned.

The foregoing rules in subsections 78(1) and (3) and their effects, which apply if the accrual is not actually paid within two years, can be diagrammed as follows, assuming a $10,000 royalty accrual:

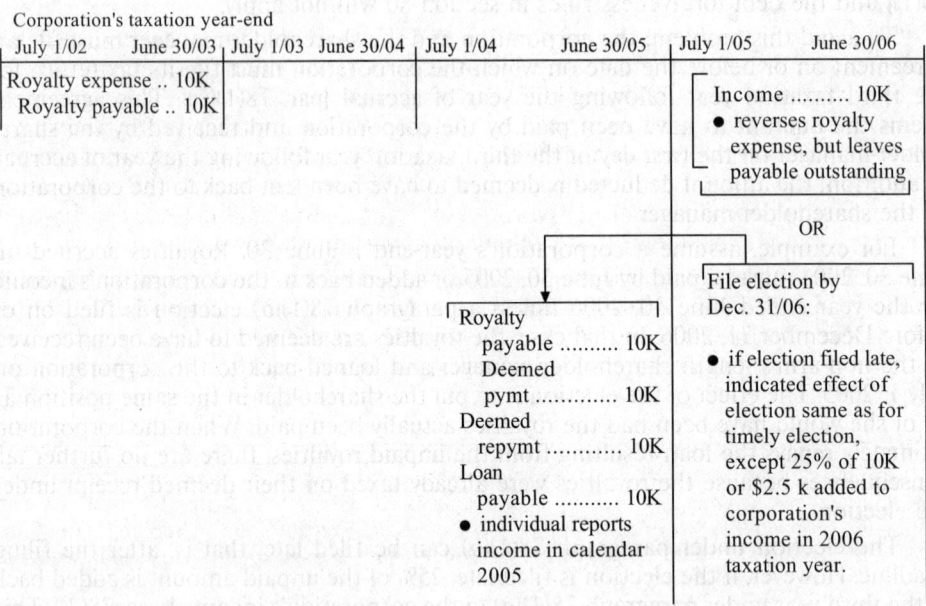

Corporation's taxation year-end

| July 1/02 | June 30/03 | July 1/03 | June 30/04 | July 1/04 | June 30/05 | July 1/05 | June 30/06 |

Royalty expense .. 10K
Royalty payable .. 10K

Income 10K
• reverses royalty expense, but leaves payable outstanding

OR

Royalty
payable 10K
Deemed
pymt 10K
Deemed
repymt 10K
Loan
payable 10K
• individual reports income in calendar 2005

File election by Dec. 31/06:

• if election filed late, indicated effect of election same as for timely election, except 25% of 10K or $2.5 k added to corporation's income in 2006 taxation year.

C. Shareholder Benefits and Loans

[ITA: 15; 20(1)(*j*); 80.4; 80.5; 110(1)(*j*), (1.4); ITR: 4301; IT-119R4; IT-421R2; IT-432R2; IT-533]

1. Shareholder benefits

Subsection 15(1) includes in income benefits conferred on shareholders just as paragraph 6(1)(*a*) includes in income benefits conferred on employees. Many of the related subsections in section 15 provide a treatment similar to section 6, as shown in Exhibit 13-2.

EXHIBIT 13-2
Selected Shareholder and Employee Benefits

	Shareholder subsection 15(1) and	Employee paragraph 6(1)(a) and/or
Automobile.................	Subsection 15(5)*	Paragraphs 6(1)(e), (k) and subsection 6(2)
Interest on loans	Subsections 15(9) and 80.4(2)	Subsections 6(9) and 80.4(1)
Forgiveness of loans	Subsection 15(1.2)	Subsection 6(15)

* Refers to subparagraph 6(1)(*e*)(i) and subsections 6(1.1) and (2).

The question often arises, when dealing with a shareholder-manager, as to which provision is applicable — section 6 dealing with employees or section 15 dealing with shareholders. The capacity (often referred to by the Latin word *qua*) in which the person is operating and which, in turn, depends upon the specifics of the particular relationship, will determine which provision will apply. A good rule of thumb is that a person operates in his or her capacity as shareholder (that is, *qua* shareholder) if he or she receives a benefit which he or she would not have received if he or she was an ordinary employee.[e]

The word "benefit" is another of those key words that is undefined and yet sprinkled liberally throughout the Act. The standard test to determine whether a benefit has been conferred on a shareholder is the "*bona fide* transaction" test as set out in *M.N.R. v. Pillsbury Holdings Ltd.*, (Ex. Ct.) 64 DTC 5184. The court made the distinction between a *bona fide* transaction and transactions that are devices and arrangements for conferring benefits or advantages on a shareholder. A *bona fide* transaction might occur where a shareholder deals with the corporation in the same manner or capacity as a customer (i.e., *qua* customer) or as a supplier (i.e., *qua* supplier).

Once it has been established that a benefit has been conferred, then the next step is to determine its value, if any. In *Youngman v. The Queen*, (F.C.A.) 90 DTC 6322, the court determined that the value of a benefit of a house provided to its shareholders was not based on the equivalent rental fair market value, but instead was based on the value of the house itself.

Example Problem

Mr. Edwards owns all of the outstanding shares of Edwards Inc., a large property management company, which manages over 20 large apartment buildings. One spring Mr. Edwards had the repair crew spend five days at his cottage making extensive repairs to the building. The value of these repairs was $8,500 (excluding GST). Because of his busy schedule, Mr. Edwards apparently forgot to tell his controller to send him a bill for the work done.

— REQUIRED

If the CRA were to discover this transaction during their audit, how would they reassess?

— SOLUTION

The CRA would begin by assessing Mr. Edwards a shareholder benefit in the amount of $8,500 plus GST of $595 (i.e., 7% of $8,500), since funds of the corporation were directed to the benefit of a shareholder [ssec. 15(1)]. This amount would be treated as income from property in the calendar year that the repairs were made.

The company, Edwards Inc., would probably also be reassessed to deny the deduction for the cost to the company of the repairs on the basis that the expenses were not incurred to earn income since no billing was ever sent [par. 18(1)(*a*)], or on the basis that the expense was a personal or living expense [par. 18(1)(*h*)].

As a result, there is double taxation. Mr. Edwards includes an amount in income for which the company does not receive a deduction.

2. Shareholder loans and other indebtedness

This topic was covered in some detail in Chapter 6 and should be reviewed before reading this section. In particular, review carefully the example problem. This part of the text will not review all of the technical rules previously covered, but will attempt to summarize and categorize some of the concepts and results of these provisions.

The capacity issue, in particular, *qua* shareholder, is not relevant for determining the application of subsection 15(2) as indicated in *The Queen v. Silden*, (F.C.A.) 93 DTC 5362. The only requirement for the application of subsection 15(2) is that the person was, in fact, a shareholder in the taxation year in question. The capacity issue is, however, relevant to the exceptions to subsection 15(2) found in subsection 15(2.4) and to the companion provision, section 80.4, dealing with imputed interest, as discussed below.

---

[e] For a more detailed discussion of this topic see Robert E. Beam and Stanley N. Laiken, "The 'Capacity' Issue in Corporate Transactions with Shareholders", Personal Tax Planning Feature (1992), Vol. 40, No. 2, *Canadian Tax Journal*, pp. 412–439.

The basic rule for the taxation of shareholder loans is contained in subsection 15(2). The exceptions to the basic rule, as discussed below, are placed in subsections 15(2.2) to (2.6). As stated above, for subsection 15(2) to apply, the loan or indebtedness must be due from anyone who is a shareholder. In addition, loans or indebtedness due from a person who is connected with a shareholder are also subject to these rules. A connected person is defined [ssec. 15(2.1)] as someone who does not deal at arm's length with the shareholder. Related persons do not deal at arm's length and it is a question of fact whether unrelated persons deal at arm's length [sec. 251]. The definition of related persons is found in section 252.

Subsection 15(2.2) excepts indebtedness between non-residents persons from the application of subsection 15(2). Subsection 15(2.3) excepts loans made in the ordinary course of the lender's business. Therefore, a loan made to an individual by a large public bank would be excepted if the individual happened to be a shareholder of the bank.

Paragraphs 15(2.4)(a) to (d) overrride subsection 15(2) for persons who are shareholders or connected persons, but are also employees. Paragraph 15(2.4)(a) excepts a loan made to an employee who is *not* a specified employee. A specified employee is defined in subsection 248(1), very generally, as an employee who, together with non-arm's length persons, owns at least 10% of the shares of any class of a corporation. The last three exceptions in subsection 15(2.4) are transaction-specific and deal with the acquisition of a dwelling for the employee's habitation, acquisition of previously unissued, fully paid shares of the employer, or a car to be used in the performance of employment duties. However, each of these exceptions in subsection 15(2.4), also, carries the conditions that the loan or debt was made in the shareholder's capacity as an employee [par. 15(2.4)(e)] and that *bona fide* arrangements were made, at the time the loan or debt was incurred, for repayment within a reasonable time frame [par. 15(2.4)(f)].

If none of the above exceptions is applicable, the taxpayer can only escape by repaying the loan or debt. Subsection 15(2.6) permits an avoidance of the income inclusion by repaying the loan within one year from the end of the taxation year of the corporate lender. However, this repayment cannot be made as part of a series of loans and repayments (i.e., repay a loan on December 31, and obtain a new loan on January 1). Repayments of all or part of a loan that has been included in income will be eligible for a deduction in the payment year [par. 20(1)(j)].

Consider the following facts. Sally owns all the outstanding shares of Sally Inc. On July 15, 2005, Sally Inc. loans Bob, Sally's brother, $10,000 to buy a sailboat. Sally Inc. has a December 31 year-end. On January 1, 2007, the loan is still outstanding. In this case, Bob received a loan from Sally Inc. and Bob is connected to his sister Sally, the shareholder, because they are related. Since the loan was not repaid before January 1, 2007, Bob will have to take the principal amount of the loan, $10,000, into income in the year the loan was received which was 2005.

The exceptions found in subsection 15(2.6) and the deduction for repayments in paragraph 20(1)(j) both contain an important restriction, as noted above. The payment cannot be part of a "series of loans or other transactions and repayments". IT-119R4, paragraphs 28 to 36 describe the Agency's interpretation and application of this phrase. The CRA's practice is to consider that dividends, salaries or bonuses paid or credited to the shareholder loan account (i.e., amounts owing to the shareholder by the corporation) to repay the balance at the end of the previous year are not part of a "series of loans or other transactions and repayments" for purposes of these two provisions. Income Tax Technical News, No. 3, dated January 30, 1995 and IT-119R4, paragraph 29, indicate that the Agency has based its position on two Tax Court of Canada cases.[f]

---

[f] *Joel Attis v. M.N.R.*, 92 DTC 1128, and *Uphill Holdings Ltd. et al. v. M.N.R.*, 93 DTC 148.

Note that not all charges to a shareholder loan account are necessarily *bona fide* loans. Some charges might be construed as salary, dividends or an appropriation. Therefore, it is necessary to properly document loans. If the corporation incurs interest charges, it should in turn charge interest to the shareholder or some of the interest it pays may be disallowed as not for the purpose of earning income. This applies even if the loan falls under the exception rules applicable in respect of subsection 15(2). [Draft legislation on interest deductibility, released on December 20, 1991, but not introduced into Parliament, addressed the issue of deducting interest paid to a third party to provide funds for employee and shareholder loans. Proposed subparagraph 20(1)(*c*)(v) would permit the deduction of reasonable interest paid by an employer on funds borrowed to make a loan to an employee or a prospective employee. Similarly, proposed subparagraph 20(1)(*c*)(vi) would allow the deduction of interest paid by a corporation on funds borrowed to make a loan to a shareholder. However, the deduction in this case is limited to the amount of the shareholder's imputed interest benefit under subsection 80.4(2).] IT-533 comments on the deductibility of interest on borrowed money used to make interest-free loans to employees and shareholders in paragraph 26. The CRA's position is similar to that proposed in the 1991 Draft Legislation for loans to employees. However, the CRA makes the statement that "interest on money borrowed to make interest-free loans to individuals in their capacity as shareholders would not generally qualify."

3. Imputed interest under section 80.4

The first point to note is that section 80.4 is not applicable if there has been an income inclusion under subsection 15(2) [par. 80.4(3)(*b*)]. As a result, a loan made to a shareholder in his or her capacity as a shareholder will not pass the test for exclusion in paragraph 15(2)(e) and, hence, will not be affected by section 80.4. The second point to note is that the *qua* or capacity issue is also very relevant for purposes of section 80.4. There are separate charging provisions for employees and shareholders (i.e., subsections 80.4(1) and (2), respectively). Each provision refers to the capacity issue by using the phrase "by virtue of", or a similar phrase, in reference to an office or employment or to shareholdings. It would appear, however, that subsection 80.4(2) would apply to a shareholder loan in limited circumstances, such as the case of a loan to a shareholder that is excluded by virtue of subsection 15(2.6) by being repaid within the established time limit.

Depending upon the resolution of the capacity issue, the imputed interest calculated under section 80.4 is included in the income of that capacity. Subsection 6(9) brings the imputed interest into employment income and subsection 15(9) brings the imputed interest into property income. Similarly, section 80.5, by deeming imputed interest to be paid, provides the opportunity for an offsetting interest deduction, subject of course to the conditions of subparagraph 8(1)(*j*)(i) (interest in respect of automobiles used in employment) and paragraph 20(1)(*c*) (interest in respect of business and property).

Finally, the actual calculation of the interest may also depend upon the capacity of the individual. For example, a "home purchase loan" and a "home relocation loan" are only available to individuals receiving the loan in their capacity as employees. Therefore, the "lesser of" rule, as described in Chapter 6, is only available on loans made *qua* employee. Similarly, the interest benefit reduction on the first $25,000 of a home relocation loan is also restricted to loans made *qua* employees [par. 110(1)(*j*)].

D. Other Planning Considerations for Shareholder-manager Remuneration

[ITA: 6(1); 60(j.1); 146; 147; 147.1; IT-470R]

1. Income splitting

It is possible to pay a spouse or other family members a tax-deductible salary. Of course, the salary must be reasonable in the circumstances and based on the value of the actual services performed for the business, as discussed previously. Such payments will split the income of a business so that it is subject to tax at lower personal tax rates. The trade-off for this benefit is the possible loss of a marital status tax credit for the spouse.

Unlike the case of remunerating a controlling shareholder-manager with salary, there may be an incentive for the CRA to use section 67 to challenge the amount of salary paid to relatives, because they may be in a lower tax bracket than the corporation after the payment of salary. The case of *Gabco Limited v. M.N.R.*, (Ex. Ct.) 68 DTC 5210 presents an interesting situation of this nature. Late in 1962, Jules, the president of a construction company, hired Robert, his brother aged 19, with the intention of making him the number two man. Robert immediately became an energetic and innovative driving force in the company and, according to his brother Jules, gave better service than anyone in the company, including the superintendent who was Robert's immediate superior. The company deducted the following sums from its income as expenses for Robert's remuneration: $20,371 for three months in 1962 consisting of $851 in salary and $19,520 in bonus and $35,673 in 1963 consisting of $5,280 in salary and $30,393 in bonus. These bonuses were paid in accordance with the company's practice of paying its permanent employees mainly by way of a yearly bonus proportionate to each employee's shareholdings which were based on service.

The CRA took the position that only $1,800 in 1962 and $7,200 in 1963 was a reasonable deduction for remuneration in the circumstances. This position was based on Robert's youth, his record of academic failures and the fact that his earnings for the three months in 1962 were greater than the superintendent's salary for that year. An expert appearing for the company testified that Robert was, in fact, the number two man in the company and that, as such, he would normally receive 70% of the most senior man's salary. Jules' salary was $48,000 in 1962 and $57,000 in 1963.

The company's position was upheld on the basis that Robert's remuneration was reasonable in the circumstances. The question to be answered was: would a reasonable businessperson have paid the remuneration in the circumstances? It was found that the bonus arrangement was a legitimate way of remunerating the company employees. Having regard to Robert's contemplated status in the company, which was subsequently fulfilled, and to the legitimate consideration of future benefits to be derived from his employment, the court found that his remuneration for the three-month period in 1962 was not unreasonable but in proportion to the value of his services to the company. The court also found, on the basis of the evidence that 70% of the most senior person's salary was a normal salary for his second in command, that Robert's remuneration for 1963 was reasonable.

2. Fringe benefits

The remuneration package for a shareholder-manager may include a number of fringe benefits such as private health insurance and group sickness or accident insurance, among others discussed in IT-470R. It might include retirement benefits from an employer's contribution to a registered pension plan. Since only employees are eligible, the owner of an unincorporated business, who is not considered to be an employee, cannot participate in such a pension plan. However, a personal contribution to a registered retirement savings plan could still be made. Section 147.1 should be consulted for the criteria which must be met by a registered pension plan for a shareholder-manager.

Sometimes the life and disability insurance coverage provided in the group insurance package is not adequate to meet the needs of the shareholder-manager. If the company were to pay for additional life insurance premiums on an individual policy owned by the shareholder-manager (in his or her capacity as a shareholder), then the full premium would be a shareholder benefit [ssec. 15(1)]. Similarly, if the company were to pay the premiums on a disability insurance policy owned by the shareholder-manager, and if the benefit was received in his or her capacity as shareholder, then the full amount of the premium would be a shareholder benefit.

A retiring allowance could also be paid by the company which would receive a tax deduction. The tax on that income could be deferred by the shareholder-manager by rolling the allowance into a registered retirement savings plan or a registered pension plan. Note, however, that paragraph 60(j.1) will restrict the amount that can be rolled in this manner. A limit, for years of service prior to 1989, of $3,500 will apply for each year that the taxpayer was not a member of a registered pension plan, or was a member of a plan whose benefits for those years did not vest, and $2,000 for each year that the taxpayer was a member of such a plan whose benefits did vest. For years of service after 1988 and before 1996, there is a single limit of $2,000 for each year of service. Therefore, no amount in respect of years of service after 1995 can be rolled into an RRSP.

Finally, a company car can be provided as a fringe benefit. Exhibit 13-3 presents an example which shows the possible advantage of the company providing a car subject to the standby charge in comparison with the individual providing himself or herself with the same car. The decision in this comparison will depend on the specific facts of each case. However, the calculation at the bottom of Exhibit 13-3 would suggest a benefit to a company car when the actual cost of the personal use of the company car exceeds the amount of the benefit that must be added to the shareholder-manager's income under subsection 6(1) for the particular car in question. It should be noted that if the car is used primarily for personal purposes as a perquisite there may be a difference in favour of the company providing the car as illustrated in the example. Note that the example neutralizes the company's position by assuming that lease costs and operating costs would be added to the salary of the shareholder-manager where he or she assumed these expenses. Exhibit 13-3 is a relatively simple example. The analysis can be much more complex (e.g., luxury cars with a cost or lease payments over $30,000 or $800, respectively).

EXHIBIT 13-3
Company Car as a Fringe Benefit

Assumptions:

Annual car lease cost (added to salary if leased by shareholder-manager), including PST (8%) and GST (7%)	$ 6,000
Annual operating costs of car (added to salary if leased by shareholder-manager)	2,880
Shareholder-manager has taxable income before car benefit of:	
if car leased by company	54,000
if car leased personally ($54,000 + $6,000 + $2,880)	62,880
Business use of car (4,800/24,000 km)	20%
Personal tax credits (federal and provincial)	$ 2,118

Shareholder-Manager Pays Tax on Benefit			*Shareholder-Manager Leases Car Personally*	
Taxable income		$54,000	Taxable income	$62,880
Benefit from use of car:			Less: deduction for business use of car	
— value of operating costs of personal use [par. 6(1)(k)] (20¢ × 19,200 km)	3,840		(20% of ($2,880 + $6,000))	(1,776)
				$61,104
— standby charge* [par. (1)(e)] (²/₃ × $6,000)	4,000		GST rebate (⁷/₁₀₇ × $1,776)	$ 116
		$61,840		
Tax net of $2,118 of personal tax credits on $61,840 of taxable income (incl. prov.)		$16,060	Tax net of $2,118 of personal tax credits on $61,104 of taxable income (incl. prov.)	$15,810
			Tax on GST rebate ($116 × .34)	$ 39
Retained after tax ($54,000 − $16,060)		$37,940	Retained after tax ($62,880 − $15,810 − $6,000− $2,880 + $116 − $39)	$38,267

Difference: $327

Conclusion: If considering only net cash in shareholder-manager's hands he or she would choose to lease the car personally.

Reason: Cost of personal use of car ($8,880 — $1,776)+GST rebate included in the year of receipt ($116)	$7,220
Less: benefit added to income under ssec. 6(1) ($3,840 + $4,000)...	7,840
Net income difference	$ 620
Federal tax on net saving @ 22%	$ 136
Provincial tax @ 12%	75
GST rebate received	116
Total cash difference	$ 327

Note that present value considerations on the rebate which is received and taxed in the following year have been ignored, although the tax on the rebate inclusion is considered by the inclusion of the rebate in income. Also, ignored is the effect of the input tax credit (ITC) received by the corporation if it incurs the annual lease and operating costs. If the corporation pays additional salary equal to its net costs for these items after ITC and, hence, if the shareholder-manager must pay the GST from other sources, it can be shown that the shareholder-manager's after-tax retention is reduced by the after-tax equivalent of the GST costs.

---

* Since business travel does not comprise the primary (usually more than 50%) purpose of the distance travelled, the reduction factor in subsection 6(2) does not apply (i.e., A/B=1 in the formula). Lease costs in this calculation include PST @ 8% and GST @ 7%.

II. SALARY VS. DIVIDENDS

A. The Basic Trade-off

On the one hand, salaries which are deductible by the corporation are subjected to personal tax. On the other hand, dividends which are not deductible by the corporation must be generated from income that is subjected to corporate tax; in turn, such dividends are subjected to personal tax which is reduced by the dividend tax credit.

Exhibit 12-1 demonstrated that integration of personal and corporate income tax works perfectly if the combined corporate tax rate is 20%. Since the federal tax rate on income eligible for the small business deduction is 13.12%, a provincial corporate tax rate of 6.88% (20.00% − 13.12%) on this type of income would provide perfect integration. If the provincial tax rate is less than 6.88% then there is an advantage from incorporating income eligible for the small business deduction and receiving dividends, since the dividend tax credit claimed on the personal tax return will be greater than the underlying corporate tax. If the provincial corporate tax rate is higher than 6.88%, then there will be a disadvantage from incorporating this type of income since the dividend tax credit will be less than the underlying corporate tax. In this case, salary, and not dividends, will generally be preferred.

Further, salaries can reduce income to maintain corporate income at or below the $300,000 business limit for the small business deduction in the calendar year 2005 and later years, whereas dividends will not. On the other hand, dividends reduce the cumulative net investment loss balance, to help preserve access to the capital gains deduction and may generate a dividend refund, but salaries do not.

B. Amounts of Taxable Dividends that can be Distributed Tax-free

[ITA: 82; 121]

Exhibit 13-4 demonstrates that it is possible to distribute a considerable amount of dividends which will be received tax-free by the shareholder, if he or she has no other sources of income. This fact might be advantageous in family income splitting where various members of a family hold different classes of shares. However, in the case of *Champ v. The Queen*, (F.C.T.D.) 83 DTC 5029, the court rejected such an arrangement where the two classes of common shares were identical, but dividends were only paid on one class. The court treated the two share classes as one and assigned a proportional share of the dividends to each class. The basis for this decision was the corporate common law rule that dividends must be shared *pro rata*.

The case of *The Queen v. McClurg*, (S.C.C.) 91 DTC 5001 presents a different set of facts resolved in favour of the taxpayer because the Articles of Incorporation allowed the "sprinkling" of dividends among various classes of shares at the discretion of the directors. However, it must be remembered that in order for the company to pay the dividends indicated it must generate income which will be subjected to corporate taxes.

EXHIBIT 13-4
Amounts of Taxable Dividends that can be distributed almost Tax-Free in 2005

	Single	Married
Taxable dividend[1,2]	$31,754	$41,973
¼ gross-up	7,939	10,493
Taxable income	$39,693	$52,466
Federal tax	$ 6,596	$ 9,407
Less: personal tax credits[3]	(1,304)	(2,411)
dividend tax credit	(5,292)	(6,996)
Basic federal tax[4]	Nil	Nil
Provincial tax	4,052	5,585
Less: provincial tax credits	(815)	(1,507)
dividend tax credit	(2,646)	(3,498)
Total tax	$ 591	$ 580
Net cash retained	$31,163	$41,392

NOTES: (1) Amounts will change with indexing of tax brackets. The increase in dividends will be approximately equal to the increase in the indexing factor for the year.

(2) None of these amounts will be affected by the minimum tax.

(3) Uses the basic personal tax credit on base amount of $8,148 and the married tax credit on base amount of $6,919. Assumes that the spouse or common-law partner has no Division B income.

(4) Federal tax cannot be negative, since the tax credits are non-refundable. Therefore, the dividend was calculated to arrive at a basic federal tax of nil. As a result, some provincial tax must be paid, but the provincial tax rate is lower than the federal tax rate.

C. Distribution out of Income Taxed at Small Business Rate

[ITA: 82(1); 117; 121; 123–125.1]

Exhibit 13-5 shows the tax saving resulting from the payment of a dividend rather than salary from income eligible for the small business deduction in a province with a 5% corporate tax rate. Generally, dividends are preferred to salary at all personal rates when total corporate rates are less than 20%. This is because the dividend tax credit is larger than the tax paid by the corporation, resulting in what is known as "over-integration" which produces a tax savings from the use of a corporation. Corporate rates will be less than 20% where a corporation is eligible for the federal small business deduction and where the provincial corporate tax rate is about 7% or less.

However, there is a range which will vary annually with indexing within which a combination of salaries and dividends will provide the lowest tax cost. Below the lower limit of the range, which is approximately equal to the level of the individual's total personal credit base (i.e., the level of income at which tax is offset by personal tax credits), salaries alone result in the lowest tax cost because they are deductible by the corporation and in the hands of the individual are offset by personal credits and, therefore, not taxable. Above the upper limit of the range, dividends alone result in the lowest tax cost. The latter case is demonstrated in Exhibit 13-6 using a $120,000 level of pre-tax corporate income. In that case, the payment of the salary is not fully integrated, because it is deductible by the corporation at a relatively low tax rate, assumed to be 18.12%, and taxable to the individual at a relatively high rate, including provincial tax, at a 46% rate. On the other hand, the dividend benefits from "over-integration" because the total corporate rate of tax is less than 20%.

An appropriate range can be computed for situations where the corporate income accrues to a single owner-manager or for more than one owner-manager. When corporate tax rates total 20% or more, salaries alone will result in the lowest tax cost.

EXHIBIT 13-5
Income eligible for Small Business Deduction

	Individual	
	Combined federal and provincial tax bracket	
	26.0% (up to $35.6K)	46% (115.7K +)
Tax on $1,000 of salary . . . . (A)	$260	$460
Tax on $1,000 corporate income distributed as a dividend after corporate tax:		
Corporate tax @ 18.12% (i.e., 38% – 10% + 1.12%– 16% + 5% (assumed prov.)) (B)	$181	$181
Combined federal and provincial personal tax* on remainder distributed as a dividend (tax on $1,000 – $181 = $819 dividend)	61	266
(C)	$242	$447
Tax saving on dividend alternative (A) – (C)	$ 18	$ 13
Tax deferred while funds left in corporation (A) – (B)	$ 79	$279

* Includes the effect of the combined federal and provincial rates on the grossed-up dividend and dividend tax credit — e.g., at the lowest personal rate: [26% of ($/₄ × $819) – 20% of $/₄ × $819] and at the highest personal rate: [46% of ($/₄ × $819) – 20% of $/₄ × $819].

EXHIBIT 13-6
Salary vs. Dividends

A. Data

Company earns $120,000 of active business income eligible for small business deduction.

Shareholder has no other income and has federal personal tax credits of $2,000 and provincial personal tax credits of $1,250 which are allowable for both regular Part I tax and minimum tax.

B. Comparison*

	Salary	Dividend
Pre-tax corporate income	$120,000	$120,000
Salary	(120,000)	—
Taxable income of corporation	—	$120,000
Corporate tax @ 18.12%		
(i.e., 38% – 10%+ 1.12% – 16% + 5%)................	—	(21,744)
Available for payment of dividend.....................	—	$ 98,256
Personal tax on salary or dividend	$ 38,332	$ 15,065**
Add: corporate tax	—	21,744
Total tax paid....................................	$ 38,332	$ 36,809
Difference $1,513		
Savings as a percentage of $120,000 .... 1.3%		
Savings as a percentage of tax on salary 3.9%		

* Includes the corporate surtax.

** Federal minimum tax would not apply to the dividend, as shown by the following calculation of federal tax:

Greater of:

(a) regular basic federal tax under Part I on dividend of $98,256. .... $ 8,786 ⎫

⎬ $ 8,786

(b) minimum tax [16% of ($98,256 – $40,000) – $2,000] .... $ 7,321 ⎭

Example Problem 1

Ethan Corporation Limited, a Canadian-controlled private corporation carrying on business in a province with a 5% corporate tax rate on its income (i.e., a total corporate tax rate of 18.12%), has earned $36,000 in its taxation year ended December 31 before a salary has been paid to the shareholder-manager. The shareholder-manager has federal personal tax credits of $2,500 and provincial personal tax credits of $1,600.

— *REQUIRED*

(A) If the full $36,000 is to be distributed either by way of salary or dividends, which should be chosen?

(B) Is there a combination of salary and dividends that is better?

— *SOLUTION*

		Part A		Part B
Corporation:		Salary	Dividend	Combination
Income before salary........... (I)		$36,000	$36,000	$36,000
Salary		(36,000)	—	(10,990)
Taxable income...................		Nil	$36,000	$25,010
Corporate tax @ 18.12% (i.e., 38% – 10%				
+ 1.12% – 16% + 5%) .... (II)		Nil	(6,523)	(4,532)
Available for dividend		Nil	$29,477	$20,478

Shareholder:

Income from salary and/or dividend*	$36,000	$29,477	$31,468
Gross-up	—	7,369	5,120
Taxable income	$36,000	$36,846	$36,588
Federal tax	$ 5,784	$ 5,970	$ 5,913
Personal tax credits	(2,500)	(2,500)	(2,500)
Dividend tax credit	—	(4,913)	(3,413)
Basic federal tax (B.F.T.)**	$ 3,284	Nil	Nil
Provincial tax.....................	3,609	3,710	3,679
Provincial personal tax credits	(1,600)	(1,600)	(1,600)
Provincial dividend tax credit	Nil	(2,456)	(1,707)
Total tax....................(III)	$ 5,293	Nil	$ 372
Cash retained (I – (II + III))	$30,707	$29,477	$31,096

* A dividend of these amounts would not be affected by the minimum tax.

** Cannot be negative.

Note that in Part A, when the dividend is paid, there is an excess of $1,443 in federal non-refundable dividend tax credit and personal tax credits that cannot be used to offset tax on other income. Suppose salary were increased by $100. At the corporate level the following would occur since all of the income is distributed:

Increase in salary expense	$ 100.00
Decrease in corporate tax ($100 × .1812)	(18.12)
Decrease in amount available for dividend................	$ 81.88

At the shareholder-manager level the following would occur since all of the income is distributed:

Increase in salary	$ 100.00
Decrease in dividend.....................................	(81.88)
Decrease in gross-up	(20.47)
Decrease in taxable income	$ (2.35)
Decrease in federal tax @ 22% of $2.35....................	$ (.52)
Decrease in federal dividend tax credit (13$\frac{1}{3}$% of $\frac{5}{4}$ × $81.88)	13.65
Increase in basic federal tax.............................	$ 13.13

Thus, every $100 increase in salary within the 22% federal marginal tax bracket will result in an increase in federal tax of $13.13 where all the income is distributed. To eliminate $1,443 (i.e., $5,970 – 2,500 – 4,913) in excess federal dividend tax credit with additional salary, a salary of $10,990 (i.e., $1,443/.1313) should be paid.

Note that this mix of salary and dividend in Part B is better than the all-salary alternative by $389 (i.e., $31,096 – $30,707). Note also that a tax saving of $389 is the difference between the tax of $4,532 at the corporate level plus $372 at the provincial personal level resulting from a salary of only $10,990 and the tax of $5,293 at the shareholder level resulting from a salary of $36,000. Thus, where the all-dividend remuneration is not taxed in the hands of the shareholder-manager due to excess federal dividend tax credit, it is better to pay a combination of some dividends and some salary to reduce the tax at the corporate level and offset any excess federal dividend tax credit at the shareholder level. Note that the difference between the cash retained of $29,477 from the all-dividend alternative of Part A and the cash retained of $31,096 from the combination alternative of Part B is $1,619. This is exactly the difference in corporate tax plus provincial personal tax paid between the two alternatives (i.e., $6,523 – ($4,532 + 372) = $1,588).

Note that a salary was found to bring basic federal tax to nil since the federal tax rate is higher than the provincial rate.

Example Problem 2

Bryan Hill owns all of the issued shares of Hill & Associates Inc., a consulting firm he started five years ago. Bryan's only source of income is from the corporation and he has federal personal, non-refundable tax credits of $2,500 and provincial tax credits of $1,600. The corporation has a tax rate of 18.12% on its income eligible for the small business deduction.

— REQUIRED

Determine the best combination of salary and/or dividend that Bryan should take in order to minimize the total corporate and personal tax for the year, assuming that the corporation earned net income of $100,000 before owner compensation and income tax. Bryan needs a pre-tax amount of $36,000 in cash to meet his personal expenses.

— SOLUTION

	Salary	Dividend	Combination[1]
Corporation			
Income before salary (I)	$100,000	$100,000	$100,000
Salary	(36,000)	—	(6,589)
Taxable income	$ 64,000	$100,000	$ 93,411
Corporate tax @ 18.12% (i.e., 38% − 10% + 1.12% − 16% + 5%) (II)	(11,597)	(18,120)	(16,926)
Available for dividend	$ 52,403	$ 81,880	$ 76,485
Paid as dividend	—	(36,000)	(29,411)
Retained by corporation	$ 52,403	$ 45,880	$ 47,074
Shareholder			
Income from salary	$ 36,000	—	$ 6,589
Income from dividend . . .	—	$ 36,000	29,411
Gross-up	—	9,000	7,353
Taxable income	$ 36,000	$ 45,000	$ 43,353
Federal tax	$ 5,784	$ 7,764	$ 7,402
Personal tax credits	(2,500)	(2,500)	(2,500)
Dividend tax credit ($13\frac{1}{3}$% of $\frac{5}{4}$ × dividend)	—	(6,000)	(4,902)
Basic federal tax	$ 3,284	Nil	Nil
Provincial tax	3,609	4,689	4,491
Provincial personal tax credits	(1,600)	(1,600)	(1,600)
Provincial dividend tax credit	Nil	(3,000)	(2,451)
Total tax (III)	$ 5,293	$ 89	$ 440
Net cash retained initially (I − (II + III))	$ 83,110	$ 81,791	$ 82,634
Ultimate tax on dividend[2]	(9,171)	(8,029)	(8,238)
Net retained ultimately after tax . . .	$ 73,939	$ 73,762	$ 74,396

— NOTES TO SOLUTION

(1) Note that, when the remuneration is paid as a dividend, there is an excess of $736 in federal non-refundable dividend tax credit and personal tax credits that cannot be used to offset tax on other income.

In this case, the marginal analysis to use up the excess tax credits is a little different, because only part of the corporate income is being distributed. Suppose salary were increased by $100. At the corporate level, the following would occur:

Increase in salary expense	$ 100.00
Decrease in corporate tax ($100 x .1812).........................	(18.12)
Decrease in amount available for dividend	$ 81.88

This only affects the amount retained by the corporation. At the shareholder-manager level, the following would occur when $100 of dividend is traded for $100 of salary:

Increase in salary...	$ 100.00
Decrease in dividend	(100.00)
Decrease in gross-up..	(25.00)
Decrease in taxable income....................................	$ (25.00)
Decrease in federal tax @ 22% of $25.00	$ (5.50)
Decrease in federal dividend tax credit (13⅓% of ⁵⁄₄ × $100.00)	16.67
Increase in federal tax	$ 11.17

Thus, every $100 increase in salary within the 22% federal marginal tax bracket will result in an increase in tax of $11.17. To eliminate $736 in excess federal dividend tax credit with additional salary, a salary of $6,589 (i.e., $736/.1117) should be paid as part of the combination of salary and dividends of $29,411 to total the pre-tax $36,000 in cash needed.

(2) When the amount retained by the corporation is paid out as a dividend, it will attract personal tax at that time. The combined federal and provincial tax can be estimated at a rate of 17.5% (i.e., (34% – 20%) of 1.25 × dividend) of the cash dividend paid. When this amount is deducted from the net cash retained initially, the ultimate net after-tax retention is computed. Of course, the tax on the dividend paid from corporate retention has not been reduced by the time value of money, which depends on when the dividend is ultimately paid.

This situation shows that it would be best to pay a combination of salary and dividends since it results in $457 (i.e., $74,396 – $73,939) of additional after-tax cash. This result is largely due to the fact that the combined federal and provincial corporate tax rate is slightly less than 20%.

D. Distributions out of Income not Eligible for the Small Business Deduction

To this point the analysis has focused on the question of salaries vs. dividends as remuneration from income eligible for the small business deduction. Exhibit 13-7 presents the comparison for income *not* eligible for the small business deduction. Note that salaries will generally be preferable. However, where income is eligible for the manufacturing and processing profits deduction, the dividend alternative produces a tax deferral advantage for individuals in the higher tax brackets. Recognize that the amount of tax deferred can be reinvested in the corporation to, perhaps, make up the added tax cost. Thus, the added tax cost of not paying a salary may be offset by the deferral advantage of dividends if there is no immediate need for the funds. In making this comparison, it is important to consider the amount of this deferral advantage and the length of time the added tax can be deferred by delaying the payment of dividends.

EXHIBIT 13-7
Income not eligible for Small Business Deduction

		Individual	
		Combined federal and provincial tax bracket	
		26% (up to $35.6K)	46% ($115.7K +)
No M & P deduction			
Tax on $1,000 of salary	(A)	$ 260	$460
Tax on $1,000 corporate income distributed as a dividend after corporate tax: Corporate tax @ 35.62% (i.e., 38% – 10% + 1.12% – 7% +13.5%)	(B)	$ 356	$356
Combined federal and provincial per- sonal tax* on remainder distribut- ed as a dividend (tax on $1,000 – $376 = $624 dividend)		47	203
	(C)	$ 403	$559
Tax cost on dividend alternative (C) – (A) . . .		$ 143	$ 99
Tax deferral (prepayment) while funds left in corporation (A) – (B)		$ (96)	$104
M & P deduction			
Tax on $1,000 of salary	(A)	$ 260	$460
Tax on $1,000 corporate income distributed as a dividend after corporate tax: Corporate tax @ 33.12% (i.e., 38%– 10% + 1.12% – 7% + 11%)	(B)	$ 331	$331
Combined federal and provincial per- sonal tax* on remainder distribut- ed as a dividend (tax on $1,000 – $331 = $669)		50	217
	(C)	$ 381	$548
Tax cost on dividend alternative (C) – (A)		$ 121	$ 88
Tax deferral (prepayment) while funds left in corporation (A) – (B)		$ (71)	$129

* Includes the effect of the combined federal and provincial rates on the grossed-up dividend and dividend tax credit — e.g., at the lowest personal rate, with no M. & P. profits deduction: [26% of ($^5/_4$ × $624) – 20% of ($^5/_4$ × $624)] and at the highest personal rate, with no M. & P. profits deduction: [46% of ($^5/_4$ × $624) – 20% of ($^5/_4$ × $624)].

E. Summary of the Salary vs. Dividends Issue

The factors affecting a decision on whether to remunerate the shareholder-manager of a corporation by salary or by dividends include the following:

(a) the corporate tax rate, including both federal and provincial components with surtaxes, applicable to the type of income of the corporation;

(b) the personal tax rate, including both federal and provincial components with surtaxes, applicable to the shareholder as a result of income other than that from the business;

(c) the amount of the shareholder's personal tax credits and deductions; and

(d) the shareholder's participation in the Canada Pension Plan, registered pension plans and registered retirement savings plans which require income in the nature of salary rather than dividends.

The number of variables involved in a specific set of circumstances make it necessary to do a set of calculations similar to those presented in this chapter to determine the best mix of salaries and/or dividends in the particular case.

The ranking found in these computations will not be the same in all circumstances. At much lower levels of pre-tax corporate income the payment of dividends will be better. At much higher levels of pre-tax corporate income the payment of salary may be better. Generally, an optimal mixture of salary and dividends can be found where the total corporate tax rate is less than 20% as is the case, for example, where income is eligible for the small business deduction and a provincial corporate tax rate is about 7% or less.

Where the corporate rate is above 20%, it may be preferable to distribute all of the owner-manager's remuneration in the form of salary. As a result, analyses pertaining to the Canada Pension Plan and registered retirement savings plan, as shown in the supplemental notes for this chapter, become unnecessary.

Recognize that if no salary is paid, the owner-manager does not have income that will qualify him or her to make deductible Canada Pension Plan or registered retirement savings plan contributions. Each of these provides for an initial tax deduction, the sheltering of income and the deferral of the ultimate payment of tax until the receipt of benefits. Similar benefits can be achieved when funds are left in the corporation after dividends have been paid to provide the shareholder-manager with the same disposable income as a required amount of salary.

One variable that has not been analyzed in detail is the effect of a provincial payroll tax when salary is paid to the owner-manager. Several provinces use a health levy, based on a percentage of salary or wages paid by an employer, to finance health care. [This additional tax cost of paying a salary will increase under the February 26, 1991 Federal Budget proposal which would place a $10,000 annual cap on the amount of provincial payroll and capital taxes that may be deducted in computing income under Division B. The proposed additional deduction from taxable income in Division C, at 6% of taxable income, may not fully compensate for the non-deductible provincial tax in excess of the $10,000 deduction ceiling, depending on the circumstances. Implementation of this proposal has been deferred until further notice.]

III. OTHER PLANNING ASPECTS OF USING CORPORATIONS

A. Use of Holding Companies[(g)]

1. An extension of integration

Inserting a holding company between a shareholder and another company requires an extension of the concept of integration, discussed in the previous chapter, to allow income ultimately to flow through the holding company to the shareholder to be taxed in his or her hands. To put this into effect, dividends must not be taxed at the corporate shareholder's level. This occurs under Part I since intercorporate dividends between Canadian companies are deductible under Division C leaving the taxable income of the recipient unaffected. However, there is the possibility of a tax under Part IV of the Act on such dividends received by a private corporation. This tax is refundable when the recipient corporation pays a taxable dividend to its shareholders such that the recipient corporation itself is not ultimately taxable on the dividends that pass through to the individual shareholder.

[(g)] For further discussion of this topic, see Wolfe D. Goodman and Barry Naiberg, "Holding Companies: Why They're Still Attractive", *CA Magazine*, March 1983, pp. 44-49.

2. Compensation

Where there are two or more owner-managers of an operating company, the use of holding companies may give more flexibility in the salary–dividend mix decision. Where there is only one corporation, the payment of dividends must be done, under corporate law, *pro rata* according to the shareholdings. Therefore, one shareholder-manager cannot normally receive all dividends and the other shareholder-manager cannot receive all salary. By inserting a management-holding company between each of the shareholders and an operating company, the operating company can pay only dividends to the holding companies. Then each holding corporation can determine what dividends are appropriate for its shareholder(s).

For example, assume Jim and Bob each own 50% of Jimbo Inc. and each have different cash flow needs. Bob is nearing retirement and wants to defer his income while Jim has a young family and needs cash. If dividends are paid, then both Jim and Bob will receive the dividends *pro rata* even if Bob does not want them. They will each then be liable for personal income tax on these dividends. In this case, each of Jim and Bob could set up holding companies to own their shares of Jimbo Inc. as follows:

As dividends are paid from Jimbo Inc. they will be received by the holding companies without either Part I or Part IV tax. Bob can then defer his personal tax liability by leaving his dividends in Bob Inc. while Jim could take the cash he needs by paying a dividend to himself from Jim Inc.

3. Deferral of tax on dividends

The use of a holding company may be advisable in the situation of a non-controlling shareholder-employee of an operating company that is paying out more taxable dividends than necessary for the shareholder-employee's immediate needs. In such a case, the shareholder could transfer his or her shares in the operating company to a holding company which he or she controls. If the holding company owned more than 10% of the total voting shares and more than 10% of the fair market value of all the issued shares in the operating company, the two corporations are connected. The dividends then could be received by the holding company without attracting the Part IV tax as long as the holding company and the operating company which had no investment income or portfolio dividends were connected.

A much smaller deferral of tax (if any) is possible on dividends from non-connected corporations on which Part IV tax is payable. The Part IV tax is levied at a 33⅓% rate. Therefore, there will only be a deferral benefit when the personal combined rate of federal and provincial tax plus surtaxes exceeds 33⅓%.

4. Implementing an estate freeze

Another reason for the use of a holding company to own shares of an operating company would be to effect a planning device known as an estate freeze. To give a very simple example, the owner of an operating company may wish to freeze or stop the growth in his or her interest in the operating company to avoid further capital gains on these shares which would ultimately be triggered at his or her death. The owner could arrange to transfer his or her common shares in the operating company to a holding company in which the common shares were owned by the next generation in the family, the children. The owner could take back in return, perhaps, preferred shares with voting rights in the holding company. These preferred shares would not grow in value, but could pay a sufficient dividend to meet his or her personal needs and would maintain control over the operating company through the voting privileges. Dividends paid on the common shares of the operating company would flow to the holding company free of Part IV tax as long as the operating company had no investment income or portfolio dividends to trigger a dividend refund while the two companies were connected. Estate planning will be discussed in greater detail in Chapter 17.

B. Qualified Small Business Corporation Shares (QSBCS)

[ITA: 110.6; 186; IT-151R5]

The corporate entity referred to as a "small business corporation" (SBC) is widely used throughout the Act. For example, the term is used in connection with a small business development bond [sec. 15.1] and a business investment loss [par. 39(1)(c)] and an exemption from the effects of the corporate attribution rules [sec. 74.4]. Dispositions of the shares of small business corporations may qualify for the capital gains deduction.

A capital gains deduction to a maximum of $250,000 of taxable capital gains net of any portion of the capital gains deduction of previously claimed is available [ssec. 110.6(2.1)]. This amount is the equivalent of a gross capital gain of $500,000.

Since there is also an equivalent deduction for qualified farm property, these two are integrated to ensure that the maximum deduction with respect to all properties combined does not exceed $250,000 [ssec. 110.6(4)].

1. Small business corporation (SBC)

A small business corporation (SBC) is defined as a Canadian-controlled private corporation of which all or substantially all of the assets, on a fair market value basis, are used principally in an active business, carried on primarily in Canada by the corporation or a related corporation [ssec. 248(1)]. The reference to a related corporation means that assets leased or loaned to a related corporation also qualify. Alternatively, the assets meeting the "all or substantially all" test may be shares or debt in an SBC that is a connected corporation [ssec. 186(4)], or a combination of assets in direct use and securities of a connected corporation.

The CRA's interpretation of the phrase "all or substantially all", as stated in about ten different Interpretation Bulletins (for example, IT-151R5, paragraph 31), is that it means at least 90%. However, in a recent court case on another issue, but in respect of the phrase "all or substantially all", the Tax Court of Canada concluded that the CRA "might be hard pressed to refuse a claim where the percentage was 89%, maybe even 85% or 80% or lower". See *Wood v. M.N.R.*, (T.C.C.) 87 DTC 312. The court concluded, at page 313, that the "term 'substantially all' does not lend itself to a simple mathematical formula" like at least 90%. The court preferred the meaning given by "small unrelated amounts" reducing the total to arrive at substantially all. The word "primarily", while not defined in the Act, is generally considered to mean more than 50%. Elsewhere (see for example, IT-73R6, paragraph 12), the CRA states that the word "principal" is not defined in the Act but it is considered that the words "chief" and "main" are synonymous to it. While a principal or main use may be less than 50% if the use is the most of many uses, the CRA has generally interpreted the word to mean more than 50%. Exhibit 13-8 presents the definition of a small business corporation in point form.

EXHIBIT 13-8
Small Business Corporation (SBC)
[ssec. 248(1)]

A Small Business Corporation is a corporation which was at any particular time:
- a Canadian-controlled private corporation, and
- all or substantially all (90% test) of the fair market value of assets (including unrecorded assets but excluding liabilities) were
  (a) used principally in an active business carried on primarily (>50%) in Canada by
     - the particular corporation, or
     - a corporation related [sec. 251] to the particular corporation; or
  (b) shares or debt
     - of a SBC that was connected [ssec. 186(4)] with the particular corporation; or
  (c) a combination of (a) and (b).

Example Problem

Maya lives in Toronto and owns 100% of Maya's Ltd. The corporation was incorporated in 1981 in Ontario to operate a retail clothing establishment in Toronto. The following is the recent balance sheet for the corporation.

Maya's Ltd.
BALANCE SHEET
as at December 31, 2005

Assets

Current

Cash	$ 2,500
Marketable securities	200,000
Accounts receivable (net of reserve)	95,000
Inventory	270,000
Prepaid expenses	2,000
Total (equal to fair market value)	$ 569,500

Fixed

Land, at cost (F.M.V.: $225,000)	150,000
Building, at net book value (F.M.V.: $350,000)	160,000
Equipment, at net book value (F.M.V.: $100,000)	120,500
	$1,000,000

Liabilities

Current

Accounts payable	$ 265,000
Income taxes payable	5,000
Due to shareholder	80,000
	$ 350,000
Mortgage payable	275,000
	$ 625,000

Shareholder's Equity

Share capital	1,000
Retained earnings	374,000
	$1,000,000

The goodwill of the business has been valued at $250,000.

—REQUIRED

Determine whether Maya's Ltd. is a small business corporation, assuming that the marketable securities were held:

(A) as a short-term investment of surplus cash at the low-point of the corporation's inventory cycle, and

(B) as a long-term investment to produce investment income.

— SOLUTION

In this case the critical condition in the definition of a small business corporation is the 90% test. It must be determined whether all or substantially all of the fair market value of the assets, including unrecorded goodwill, was used principally in an active business carried on primarily in Canada by Maya's Ltd. Retailing is an active business and it is being carried on exclusively in Canada in this case.

(A) If the marketable securities are held for use in the business, as would be the case if they represented a short-term investment of cash surplus, pending the build-up of inventory, then it can be concluded that all of the fair market value of the assets is used principally in an active business carried on primarily in Canada. Therefore, the company meets the 90% test and is a small business corporation.

(B) If the marketable securities are not considered to be used in the active business of retailing, then their relative value must be determined as follows:

	Fair market value	%
Cash	$ 2,500	0.17
Marketable securities	200,000	13.38
Accounts receivable	95,000	6.36
Inventory	270,000	18.07
Prepaid expenses	2,000	0.13
Land	225,000	15.06
Building	350,000	23.42
Equipment	100,000	6.69
Goodwill	250,000	16.72
Total	$1,494,500	100.00%

Since the marketable securities comprise more than 10% of the fair market value of the assets, the 90% test in the definition of a small business corporation is not met. (Note that the legislation does not quantify the term "all or substantially all". The courts may not interpret this term as meaning at least 90% as used administratively by the CRA.) Note that the definition of a small business corporation applies at a particular point in time. Therefore, if some of the marketable securities can be removed from the corporation: either sold with the proceeds used to pay off liabilities or invested in assets used in the active retailing business, the 90% test can be met after the removal or reinvestment. Thus, the corporation can be "purified" to meet the 90% test. It is not enough to convert the marketable securities into cash, if the cash is not used in an active business carried on by the corporation.

---

2. Basic QSBCS rules applied to a single corporation

The rules governing the eligibility of QSBC shares for the capital gains exemption of $500,000 (a deduction of $250,000) are quite complex. However, this analysis will break down the provision into several easy-to-understand components. The first application will be to a single corporation. Next, the rules will be applied to a parent and subsidiary relationship. Application beyond two corporations becomes too complex for an introductory tax course and really requires the assistance of a tax specialist.

The term "qualified small business corporation share" of an individual is defined [ssec. 110.6(1)] as follows:

(a) a share of the capital stock of a corporation that is a small business corporation (SBC) at the time of disposition (i.e., the determination time) and is owned by the individual, by the individual's spouse or by a partnership related to the individual (related party) (for determining whether a person or partnership is related to an individual, see paragraph 110.6(14)(*d*));

(b) the share was not owned by anyone, other than the individual or a person (including a personal trust) or partnership related to the individual throughout the 24-month period preceding the disposition (without exception to the 24-month period in the case of a deemed disposition caused by death);

(c) the share was, throughout that part of the 24-month period ending immediately before the disposition that the share was owned by the individual or a person or partnership related to the individual:

(i) a share of a corporation that was a Canadian-controlled private corporation, and

(ii) more than 50% of the fair market value of the corporation's assets were used principally in an active business carried on primarily in Canada by the corporation or a related corporation.

Each of the above three parts of the definition can be considered as tests which will be referred to, respectively, as:

(a) the SBC Test,

(b) the Holding Period Test, and

(c) the Basic Asset Test (50% Test).

Exhibit 13-9 presents the foregoing tests in point form for ease of reference.

EXHIBIT 13-9
Qualified Small Business Corporation Share (QSBCS)
[ssec. 110.6(1)]
Basic Tests

A Qualified Small Business Corporation Share is:

— at any time (i.e., determination time)

• typically at time of disposition or deemed disposition;

— a share that meets the following tests:

(a) SBC Test

— an SBC at determination time

— owned by:

• the individual,

• the individual's spouse, or

• a partnership related to the individual [par. 110.6(14)(d)];

(b) Holding Period Test

— throughout the 24 months preceding the determination time

— owned by no one other than

• the individual, or

• a person or partnership related to the individual [pars. 110.6(14)(c), (d), (e), (f)] (i.e., related party);

(c) Basic Asset Test (50% Test)

— throughout that part of the 24 months preceding the determination time while owned by the individual or related party

• share of a CCPC for which more than 50% of the fair market value of its assets were used principally in an active business carried on primarily in Canada by the corporation or by a related corporation.

Graphically, the timing factor in each of the three tests could be depicted as follows:

		Determination time
		I
(a) SBC Test		
(b) Holding Period Test	⊢	24 months →⊣
(c) Basic Asset Test	⊢	24 months →⊣

Example Problem ────────────────────────────────

Reconsider the facts of the previous example problem. Assume that the problem raised by the marketable securities has been resolved by removing the marketable securities from the corporation. Also, assume that the relative proportion of assets held at December 31, 2005 has not changed in the last five years.

— *REQUIRED*

Determine whether the shares are eligible for the capital gains exemption, assuming:

(A) the shares were acquired on incorporation in 1981, and

(B) the shares were acquired from the brother of Maya in blocks of 200 shares annually for the last five years.

— *SOLUTION*

At the time of their disposition or deemed disposition, to qualify for the capital gains exemption, the shares must meet three tests. The difference between parts (A) and (B) of the Required will be seen in the application of the second test.

(1) SBC Test

The shares must be of an SBC at the time of the disposition or deemed disposition. In this case, steps have been taken to make the corporation an SBC, if it did not already qualify as such, as discussed in the previous example problem.

(2) Holding Period Test

Throughout the 24 months preceding the disposition, the shares cannot be owned by anyone other than Maya or a related party (i.e., Maya's brother).

(A) This test is met, because the shares were held for the preceding two years by Maya.

(B) Where the shares have been acquired from the related individual (i.e., Maya's brother) even within the previous 24-month period, the test is still met. If the individual from whom the shares were acquired was not related, then the shares would have to be held by the present shareholder for the full 24 months. Since the holding period test is applied to each share, a series of dispositions can be staged as the shares meet the 24-month test on a first-in, first-out basis as permitted [par. 110.6(14)(*a*)].

(3) Basic Asset Test (50% Test)

This test requires that throughout the 24 months preceding a disposition or deemed disposition, while the shares were held by a particular individual (i.e., Maya) or related party (i.e., Maya's brother), the shares were of a Canadian-controlled private corporation in which more than 50% of the fair market value of the assets were used principally in an active business carried on primarily in Canada by the corporation or by a related corporation. Since no other corporation is involved in this situation, the other parts of the test pertaining to a connected corporation do not apply. In this case, even with a 13.38% investment in marketable securities which may not be considered to have been used in the active business of the corporation, the 50% asset test is still met throughout the 24 months preceding a contemplated disposition or deemed disposition at this time, since the proportion of marketable securities has been stable throughout those 24 months. Remember that, even though the securities have been disposed of to meet the SBC test, they were still assets of the corporation during the 24 months preceding the disposition.

──

3. Modification of the asset test (stacking rule)

Even where there are a number of connected corporations, the basic rules as described above must be applied, including the 50% basic asset test in the definition paraphrased above. If the particular corporation to be sold (i.e., a parent corporation) can meet the 50% basic active business asset test with its own active business assets, its shares will meet the asset test [subpar. (c)(i) of the definition of "qualified small business corporation share" in ssec. 110.6(1)].

However, where the active business assets of the parent corporation are 50% or less, then the parent corporation may still qualify by including shares and indebtedness of corporations connected with it. However, the rules are further modified to ensure that one of the two levels of corporations (i.e., parent or connected subsidiaries) meets an all or substantially all test (90%) while the other level of corporations meets a "primarily" test (50%) of the aggregate of active business assets and debts or shares of a connected CCPC [par. (d) of the definition of "qualified small business corporation share" in ssec. 110.6(1)].

Recall, from the discussion of the Part IV tax in Chapter 12, that a connected corporation is defined in subsection 186(4). A corporation is connected with another corporation where:

(a) the other corporation controls [ssec. 186(2), (7)] the corporation or

(b) the other corporation holds more that 10% of the vote and fair market value in shares of the corporation.

Thus, if the parent meets the 90% test throughout the 24-month period before the disposition with a combination of its own active business assets and shares and debt of a connected corporation, the connected subsidiary need only meet the 50% test on its assets. Alternatively, if the parent does not meet the 90% test throughout the 24-month period before the disposition, the connected subsidiary must meet the 90% test. Thus, the 50% test must be met by both corporations at all times in the 24-month period before the disposition. Furthermore, if the parent does not meet the 90% test throughout the 24-month period before the disposition, then the connected subsidiary must meet the 90% test to have its securities considered as assets of the parent company which help the parent company to meet the 50% test. This modification of the 50% test is presented in Exhibit 13-10 in point form.

Another way of stating the conclusions on the application of these tests is as follows. Where more than 50% of the assets of a particular corporation are active business assets, the Basic Asset Test (50% Test) discussed in the previous segment is met and the type of assets held by connected corporations in the chain below the particular corporation is not relevant. The modified test need not apply. It is only when the 50% Asset Test is not met by the given corporation with its own active business assets that the 90% Modified Asset Test must be used. Where the modification applies in a two-corporation chain, the given corporation and the other connected corporation below it in the chain must meet the 50% Asset Test with their own active business assets in combination with the shares and debt of connected corporations and one of the parent or the connected corporation must meet the 90% test.

EXHIBIT 13-10
Qualified Small Business Corporation Share (QSBCS)
[ssec. 110.6(1)]
Modification of the Basic Asset Test (50% Test)

— Modification of the 50% Basic Asset Test where:

 • there is a corporation (subsidiary) connected [ssec. 186(4)] to a particular corporation (parent); the subsidiary must be connected, but not necessarily a SBC,

 • the particular corporation (parent) does not meet the 50% Test (on its own active business assets (i.e., excluding the shares and debt of a connected corporation)).

— Conclusion on modification of Asset Test:

 • throughout the 24 months ending at the determination time,

  — both the parent and the connected corporation must each meet the 50% Test with a combination of their own active business assets and shares and debt of a connected corporation;

  — one of either the parent or the connected corporation must meet the 90% Test with a combination of its own active business assets and shares and debt of a connected corporation.

— Therefore,

 • conceptually, the test is

  — 90/50 for parent/connected, or

  — 50/90 for parent/connected.

If a holding company owns more than one connected subsidiary corporation, then the modified asset test applies as follows.

1. If the holding company meets the 90% test with a combination of its own active business assets and shares or debt of a connected corporation that meets the 50% test, the modified asset test is passed.
2. If the holding company meets the 50% test with a combination of its own active business assets and shares or debt of a connected corporation that meets the 90% test, the modified asset test is passed.

Example Problem

Zeto, a resident of Canada, has owned 100% of the shares of Zeto's Manufacturing Limited (ZML), a Canadian-controlled private corporation, since its incorporation in 1985. The corporation carries on a manufacturing business in Canada. He is presently considering the sale of his shares. The fair market value of the assets of ZML is comprised as follows:

	F.M.V. at present	%	F.M.V. throughout past 24 months	%
Active business assets	$200,000	40%	$160,000	40%
Shares of 100%-owned subsidiary	250,000	50	120,000	30
Investments	50,000	10	120,000	30
	$500,000	100%	$400,000	100%

The subsidiary, Zeto Wholesale Ltd. (ZWL), was incorporated by ZML in 1987 to carry on a wholesaling business in Canada. The fair market value of its assets consists of the following:

	F.M.V. at present	%	F.M.V. throughout past 24 months	%
Active business assets	$270,000	90%	$157,500	90%
Investments	30,000	10	17,500	10
	$300,000	100%	$175,000	100%

— REQUIRED

Determine whether the shares of ZML are qualified small business corporation shares at the present time.

— SOLUTION

For the shares of ZML to be qualified small business corporation shares, the following tests must be met:

(1) SBC Test

At the time of sale the shares of ZML must be of a small business corporation (SBC). An SBC is defined to be a Canadian-controlled private corporation (CCPC) [ssec. 248(1)] which ZML is. In addition, all or substantially all (i.e., at least 90%) of the fair market value of the assets of ZML must be used, at the present time, principally in an active business carried on primarily in Canada by ZML or a related corporation or must be shares or debt of a connected SBC. This test is met by a combination of ZML's own active business assets presently comprising 40% and the shares of the wholly-owned subsidiary (ZWL) presently comprising the other 50%. The subsidiary is connected with ZML because it is controlled by ZML [ssec. 186(2) and (4)] and the subsidiary is an SBC because 90% of the present fair market value of its assets are active business assets at the time of the sale.

(2) Holding Period Test

Throughout the 24 months preceding the present time, the shares cannot have been owned by anyone other than Zeto or a related party. This test is met because only Zeto owned the shares since 1985.

(3) Basic Asset Test (50% Test)

Throughout the 24 months preceding the present time, the shares must be of a CCPC with more than 50% of the fair market value of its assets used principally in an active business carried on primarily in Canada. However, ZML does not meet the 50% Test based on its active business assets alone. Therefore, the Modified Asset Test must be applied.

(4) Modified Asset Test

This test requires, first, that both corporations, ZML and ZWL, must hold more than 50% of their assets in a combination of active business assets and shares or debt of a connected corporation throughout the 24 months preceding the present time. This condition is met by ZML with its 40% active business assets in combination with its 30% in shares of the subsidiary. The subsidiary meets the test with its 90% active business assets. Then, one of the corporations must meet the 90% test with a combination of its active business assets and shares or debt of a connected corporation throughout the preceding 24 months. This condition is met by the subsidiary with its active business assets.

Since all of the relevant tests have been met, the shares of ZML are qualified small business corporation shares.

C. Capital Gains Deduction

[ITA: 39(1)(c), (9); 48.1; 110.6]

The 1985 budget introduced a lifetime cumulative deduction for net taxable capital gains (net T.C.G.s) for individuals (other than trusts) resident in Canada. The 1992 federal Budget restricted the deduction on gains from most real property disposed of after February 1992 (referred to as non-qualifying property) and the 1994 federal Budget completely eliminated the deduction for dispositions of all property after February 22, 1994, except for shares of qualifying small business corporations (QSBC) and qualified farm property.

1. Overview

The current capital gains deduction applies to individuals (other than trusts) who are resident in Canada throughout the year. There is, however, a deeming provision (subsection 110.6(5)) which extends the definition of a resident, for purposes of this section only, to include individuals who were resident at any time in the year and who were resident in Canada throughout either the preceding or the following taxation year. This rule allows an individual who has either ended or commenced residence in Canada during a particular year to qualify for the deduction on a disposition.

The deduction applies to net taxable capital gains (the excess of taxable capital gains (T.C.G.s) over allowable capital losses (A.C.L.s)) on QSBC shares and qualified farm property. Also eligible for the deduction are capital gains reserves on dispositions of farm property or QSBC shares.

The maximum fractional capital gains deduction for qualified small business corporation shares and/or qualified farm property is $250,000 (i.e., $\frac{1}{2} \times \$500,000$). Note that in this text the term "exemption" is used to refer to the full amount of a capital gain and the term "deduction" is used to refer to the fractional amount of the capital gain that gives rise to the actual deduction from taxable income of an individual under section 110.6.

2. Computation of deduction

The amount of the deduction is discretionary and is limited by cumulative taxable capital gains net of allowable capital losses, that is, net taxable capital gains exposed to tax over an individual's lifetime, to the extent of the maximum permissible deduction. The limit on the QSBC capital gains deduction in a particular year is set at the least of three amounts.

(a) Unused lifetime deduction [par. 110.6(2.1)(a)] — This restriction limits the deduction to $250,000 ($\frac{1}{2} \times \$500,000$) *minus* all previously claimed capital gains deductions adjusted to the appropriate inclusion rate for the year in which the limit is being computed.[h]

(b) Annual gains limit [ssec. 110.6(1)] — This amount is the lesser of the net taxable capital gains (net T.C.G.) for the particular year under paragraph 3(*b*) and the amount that would be determined under paragraph 3(*b*) only taking into account dispositions of QSBC shares and qualified farm property after 1984 *minus*

    (i) net capital losses of other years deducted in the current year, and

    (ii) the allowable business investment losses (A.B.I.L.s) realized during the year whether or not they are claimed under paragraph 3(*d*).

(c) Cumulative gains limit [ssec. 110.6(1)] — This amount aggregates, without an adjustment for changing inclusion rates, *all the components* of the "annual gains limit for all years" *minus* two additional amounts:

    (i) the capital gains deductions claimed in preceding years, without an adjustment for changing inclusion rates, and

    (ii) the cumulative net investment loss (C.N.I.L.) — a limitation which is defined below.

This description of the computation is relatively conceptual, rather than technical. However, it is complicated by the allowable business investment loss (A.B.I.L.) rules and the cumulative net investment loss (C.N.I.L.).

3. Allowable business investment losses

As previously discussed in Chapter 7, allowable business investment losses are deductible from all sources of income under paragraph 3(*d*). The definition of a business investment loss [par. 39(1)(*c*)] includes capital losses arising from the disposition of shares and debts of a small business corporation (S.B.C.) [ssec. 248(1)]. Reference should be made to the material on allowable business investment losses in Chapter 7. In particular, Exhibit 7-1 should be reviewed for details on the treatment of a business investment loss.

4. Cumulative net investment loss (C.N.I.L.)

As previously indicated, there is a further restriction to the "cumulative gains limit" which reduces the potential availability of the capital gains deduction. This reduction is basically the excess of property expenses over property income. The purpose of this restriction is to remove the perceived double benefit of capital gains offset by a capital gains deduction and non-capital sources of income offset by excess investment expenses at the same time.

The cumulative net investment loss (C.N.I.L.) is defined as the excess of investment expenses (a defined term in subsection 110.6(1)) over investment income (another defined term) aggregated for all years after 1987 [ssec. 110.6(1)].

Investment expense which, generally, relates to expenses incurred to earn investment income is defined as the sum of:

[h] The following table shows the factor to use to convert a capital gains deduction claimed in a prior year to the inclusion rate in use after October 17, 2000:

Year capital gain deduction claimed	Inclusion rate in that year	Factor to convert to post–Oct. 17, 2000 period
1985–1987	$\frac{1}{2}$	no adjustments
1988–1989	$\frac{2}{3}$	$\frac{1}{2} / \frac{2}{3} = \frac{3}{4}$
1990–Feb. 27, 2000	$\frac{3}{4}$	$\frac{1}{2} / \frac{3}{4} = \frac{2}{3}$
Feb. 28, 2000–Oct. 17, 2000	$\frac{2}{3}$	$\frac{1}{2} / \frac{2}{3} = \frac{3}{4}$
After Oct. 17, 2000	$\frac{1}{2}$	

(a) all property expenses, including interest (either actually incurred or deemed to have been paid by section 80.5) and carrying charges, deducted by the taxpayer in computing property income, with certain resource property exceptions;

(b) certain specific expenses, including interest and carrying charges, deducted from the income of a partnership of which the taxpayer is a specified member (subsection 248(1) basically defines a specified member as a limited partner, as defined in subsection 96(2.4) or a member who is not actively engaged in the business or a similar business on a regular, continuous and substantial basis);

(c)(i) losses incurred in the year from a partnership of which the taxpayer is a specified member, and

(ii) limited partnership loss carryovers deducted in the year under paragraph 111(1)(e);

(d) $\frac{1}{2}$ of certain resource and exploration expenses incurred and flowed through by a corporation or incurred by a partnership of which the taxpayer is a specified member;

(e) losses from all property and, specifically, rental properties (i.e., business losses from rental properties) and capital cost allowance for a certified production deducted by the taxpayer or a partnership of which he or she was an *ordinary* member; and

(f) net capital losses carried over and deducted against certain net taxable capital gains of the carryover year that were not eligible for the capital gains deduction.

Investment income is defined as the sum of [ssec. 110.6(1)]:

(a) income from all property, including recaptured capital cost allowance that was considered to be income from property and not from a business;

(b) income from a partnership of which the taxpayer is a specified member;

(c) $\frac{1}{2}$ of certain recovered exploration and development expenses under subsection 59(3.2);

(d) income (including recapture) from rental property (including MURBs) of the taxpayer or partnership of which he or she was an ordinary member;

(e) the interest element of certain annuities included in income as the net effect of paragraph 56(1)(d) or (d.1) and paragraph 60(a); and

(f) net taxable capital gains on certain property not eligible for the capital gains deduction.

5. Other related provisions

At this stage, there are several other provisions related to the capital gains deduction worth noting.

(1) An individual must file a tax return if a taxable capital gain was realized or a disposition of capital property has occurred in the taxation year [ssec. 150(1)].

(2) An individual who is resident in Canada for only part of a taxation year is deemed to be a resident throughout the entire year if he or she is resident in Canada throughout the immediately preceding or the following taxation year [ssec. 110.6(5)].

(3) A capital gains deduction in respect of a particular transaction is denied forever where the capital gain was not reported on a filed tax return or where the tax return is not filed within a one-year grace period and where the Minister can prove the taxpayer knowingly or under circumstances amounting to gross negligence did not report the gain [ssec. 110.6(6)].

(4) A number of anti-avoidance provisions are provided to prevent abuses of the capital gains deduction [ssecs. 110.6(7) to (12)].

(5) An individual may elect to use the capital gains deduction in respect of qualified small business corporation shares when the corporation becomes a public corporation because its shares are listed on a prescribed stock exchange in Canada [sec. 48.1].

Example Problem

Lenny disposed of some shares of Underground Airways Limited, a QSBC, in January 2005 and realized a taxable capital gain of $305,000. In addition, he received $13,750 in interest and incurred a net rental loss of $2,500.

Also in 2005, Lenny realized a business investment loss (before any subsection 39(9) adjustment) of $50,000.

Prior to 2005, Lenny received cumulative interest income of $6,875 and grossed-up taxable dividends of $1,563. He also incurred a cumulative net rental loss of $12,500 and carrying charges of $12,188. In 1999, Lenny realized taxable capital gains of $25,000 on QSBCS which he fully offset with the capital gains deduction. Lenny had no previous capital transactions.

— REQUIRED

Compute Lenny's capital gains deduction for 2005 under subsection 110.6(2.1) supported by all the necessary calculations.

— SOLUTION

(A) Unused lifetime deduction in 2005:

Lifetime cumulative deduction limit		$250,000
Less: prior years' deductions:		
Capital gains deduction claimed in 1999	$25,000	
Less: adjustment to 2005 inclusion rate	8,333	16,667
Unused lifetime capital gains deduction available for 2005		$233,333

(B) Annual gains limit for 2005:

Net T.C.Gs for 2005[1] ($305,000 – $16,667)		$288,333
Minus:		
Net C.L.s deducted in 2005	Nil	
A.B.I.L.s realized in 2005[1]	$ 8,333	8,333
Annual gains limit for 2005		$280,000

(C) Cumulative gains limit for 2005:[2]

Cumulative net T.C.Gs ($25,000 + $288,333)			$313,333
Minus:			
Cumulative net capital losses deducted		Nil	
Cumulative A.B.I.L.s realized		$ 8,333	
Cumulative C.G.s deductions		25,000	
Cumulative net investment loss:			
Investment expenses:			
Cumulative interest expenses and carrying charges	$12,188		
Cumulative net rental losses ($2,500 + $12,500)	15,000		
	$27,188		
Investment income:			
Cumulative investment income ($6,875 + $1,563 + $13,750)	(22,188)	$ 5,000	$ 38,333
Cumulative gains limit for 2005			$275,000

(D) Least of (A), (B), (C) $233,333

— *NOTES TO SOLUTION*

(1) Allowable business investment loss (A.B.I.L.):

B.I.L. before ssec. 39(9) reduction		$ 50,000
Disallowed portion — Lesser of:		
(a) B.I.L.	$50,000	
(b) Adjustment factor × cumulative C.G.		
deductions of previous years		
($^4/_3$ × $25,000) $33,333		
Minus: Cumulative disallowed B.I.L.		
of prior years .... Nil	$33,333	
Lesser of (a) and (b)		(33,333)
B.I.L. after adjustment		$ 16,667
A.B.I.L. ($^1/_2$ × $16,667)		$ 8,333
Allowable capital loss (A.C.L.):		
Disallowed portion of B.I.L.		$ 33,333
A.C.L. ($^1/_2$ × $33,333)		$ 16,667
Net T.C.G. for 2005:		
T.C.G.		$305,000
Less: A.C.L.		16,667
Net T.C.G.		$288,333

(2) The components of the cumulative gains limit are not adjusted for inclusion rate changes over the period of accumulation.

D. Attribution through a Corporation

[ITA: 74.4]

Since the attribution rules for spouses and minors have been extended to apply to loans affecting such individuals, corporations have become the obvious vehicle to attempt income splitting among family members. Consider the situation where the low-income spouse incorporates a company using a nominal amount of his or her own funds. The high-income spouse then loans to the corporation a large amount of money through a non-interest bearing note. Income earned on these loans and subsequently paid out in the form of dividends is not caught by the attribution rules since these provisions deal with individuals and trusts only [ssecs. 74.1(1) and (2)]. Hence, section 74.4 contains a series of rules to attribute back to the transferor income in the form of a deemed interest receipt on property transferred or loaned to a corporation.

These rules only apply during the period in which there were "designated persons" who benefit from the transfer or loan to a corporation and the corporation was not a small business corporation (SBC) [ssec. 248(1)] as discussed above in relation to qualified small business corporation shares. A designated person is the transferor's spouse or a minor who is either not at arm's length [sec. 251] with the transferor or who is a niece or nephew of that individual [ssec. 74.5(5)]. The designated person must also be a specified shareholder defined, generally, as a person who owns at least 10% of the shares of any class of the corporation [ssec. 248(1)]. Note that a small business corporation is one that, by definition, would generate mostly active business income which, if earned on a direct transfer or loan of funds, would not be subject to attribution. Also, note how designated persons are the same individuals to whom direct transfers or loans would be subject to income attribution. If the corporation, with designated persons as shareholders, ceased to be a small business corporation at some point during the year, the imputed interest benefit would be prorated for the part of the year that the corporation was not a SBC.

Subsection 74.4(2) applies where one of the main purposes of the transfer or loan may reasonably be considered to be to reduce the income of the transferor and to benefit a designated person. If subsection 74.4(2) applies, the transferor is deemed to receive, as *interest*, the following amount:

(a) interest imputed on the outstanding amount [ssec. 74.4(3)] of the loan or transferred property at the basic prescribed rates [Reg. 4301(*c*)] in effect during the year, for the period when the corporation was not an SBC and designated persons were specified shareholders

less the sum of:

(b) interest received by the transferor in respect of the loan or transfer,

(c) ⁵⁄₄ of all taxable dividends received by the transferor on shares received as consideration for the loan or transfer of property, and

(d) where dividends are received by the designated person and these dividends can reasonably be considered to be part of the benefit sought to be conferred then the amount included in the designated person's "split income" [sec. 120.4].

The term "outstanding amount", which is the base for the deemed interest receipt, is defined to be the fair market value of property "transferred or loaned" to the corporation in excess of the fair market value of consideration, other than "excluded consideration", *received* from the corporation in return [ssec. 74.4(3)]. The term "excluded consideration" is defined to mean debt, shares of the corporation or rights to receive debt or shares of the corporation [ssec. 74.4(1)]. Note that excluded consideration does *not* reduce the base for computing the deemed interest receipt because only consideration *other than* excluded consideration reduces the outstanding amount. Consideration that reduces the outstanding amount would include, for example, cash. While debt or shares received from the corporation do not reduce the outstanding amount, interest and ⁵⁄₄ of taxable dividends paid to the transferor on the debt or shares received reduce the deemed interest receipt to the transferor, as shown by the above computational formula.

Note how the reduction of the deemed interest income is as a result of the payment by the corporation of actual income that would attract tax in the hands of the transferor or lender and, therefore, would reduce the benefits of income splitting. It should also be noted that the deemed interest income included in the individual's income is not allowed as a deduction to the corporation.

Example Problem

Fresser and Klutz are spouses. Fresser operates a construction company, Fresser Inc., which uses all of its assets (fair market value of $1.2 million) in its active business carried on in Calgary. Klutz received an inheritance of $100,000 which he invested in Fresser Inc. 7% preference shares on January 1, 2003. Fresser Inc. immediately used this cash to pay down a bank loan. On January 1, 2004, Fresser Inc. ceased operations and liquidated its assets leaving $200,000 of cash in the company until January 31, 2005, when the 7% preference shares were redeemed for $100,000. In each of 2003 and 2004, dividends of $5,000 were paid on the preference shares.

— *REQUIRED*

Determine the amount attributed to Klutz over the three years, assuming that the prescribed interest rate is a constant 9%. Ignore the effects of the leap year.

— *SOLUTION*

> 2003: Subsection 74.4(2) would not attribute any amount to Klutz since Fresser Inc. was a "small business corporation" throughout the taxation year of Klutz. Klutz's income would include only the $5,000 of dividends paid on the preference shares.

2004: Fresser Inc. was not a small business corporation throughout 2004; therefore, subsection 74.4(2) applies as follows:

Interest imputed at 9% on the outstanding amount ($100,000 × 9%)	$9,000
Less: $^5/_4$ of dividends received ($5,000 × $^5/_4$)	(6,250)
Interest received	Nil
Amount deemed to be received by Klutz as interest	$2,750

In addition, Klutz will report the $5,000 of dividends ($6,250 grossed up) received from the company.

2005: Fresser Inc. was not a small business corporation during that portion of the year when the shares were outstanding; therefore, subsection 74.4(2) applies as follows:

Interest imputed at 9% on the outstanding amount ($100,000 × 9% × $^{30}/_{365}$)	$ 740
Less: $^5/_4$ of dividends received	Nil
Interest received	Nil
Amount deemed to be received by Klutz as interest	$ 740

Remember that there is a purpose test in subsection 74.4(2). It may be possible to argue that, since the purpose of the loan was to finance an active business, these attribution rules do not apply. On the other hand, it may be argued that since the money was used in the business for such a short period (13 months) that "one of the main purposes of the transfer" must have been to reduce the income of Klutz and benefit Fresser.

E. Income-splitting Tax ["Kiddie Tax"]
[ITA: 20(1)(ww); 120.4]

A special income tax [sec. 120.4] computed at the top marginal rate is levied on specified income of an individual under 18 years of age at the end of a calendar year. This income-splitting tax was discussed in Chapter 6, as an alternative to the income attribution rules, for income of a minor from business sources that is not subject to the attribution rules.

The tax is levied, generally, on the following types of income:

- taxable dividends and other shareholder benefits derived from unlisted shares of any corporation, received either directly or indirectly through a trust or partnership; and
- income from a trust or partnership which derives income from the business of providing property or services to a business carried on by a relative of the minor or a corporation in which the relative is a specified shareholder.

Income subject to this income-splitting tax is deductible [par. 20(1)(ww)] from the Part I income of the minor, so that it is not taxed twice in the hands of the minor. Similarly, income such as the dividend income, subject to the income-splitting tax, is not subject to attribution and, therefore, not taxed additionally in the hands of the transferor of the dividend-paying shares. The only tax credits permitted in computing the income-splitting tax are the dividend tax credit and the foreign tax credit. If a parent was active in the business from which the income subject to the income-splitting tax was derived, then the parent is jointly liable for the income-splitting tax payable by the minor.

The income-splitting tax is not applicable to:

- minors who have no parent who is resident in Canada at any time in the year;
- income from property inherited by a minor from a parent; and
- income from property inherited by a minor from anyone else if, during the year in which the minor receives the income, the minor is:

- in full-time attendance at a post-secondary educational institution, or
- eligible for the disability tax credit.

To the extent that income is subject to the "kiddie tax", that same income is not subject to the regular attribution rules [ssecs. 56(5), 74.5(13)]. In addition, if taxable dividends are subject to "kiddie tax", then they may reduce the deemed interest penalty calculated for corporate attribution purposes [par. 74.4(2)(g)].

IV. GENERAL ANTI-AVOIDANCE RULE UNDER THE INCOME TAX ACT
[ITA: 245; IC 88-2]

The technical notes released on June 30, 1988 to explain section 245 when it was first introduced made the following statement:

> New section 245 of the Act is a general anti-avoidance rule which is intended to prevent abusive tax avoidance transactions or arrangements but at the same time is not intended to interfere with legitimate commercial and family transactions. Consequently, the new rule seeks to distinguish between legitimate tax planning and abusive tax avoidance and to establish a reasonable balance between the protection of the tax base and the need for certainty for taxpayers in planning their affairs.

The main statement of the general anti-avoidance rule (GAAR), or provision, is presented in subsection 245(2). In essence, it states that the tax benefit that results from an avoidance transaction will be denied. In order to determine the amount of the tax benefit that will be denied, the provision indicates that the tax consequences of the transaction to a person will be determined as is reasonable in the circumstances.

The term "avoidance transaction" is defined as any transaction that by itself or as part of a series of transactions (i.e., a "step transaction") results in a tax benefit, unless the transaction can reasonably be considered to have a *bona fide* purpose other than obtaining the tax benefit [ssec. 245(3)]. The technical notes indicate that "the vast majority of business, family or investment transactions will not be affected by proposed (as it was then) section 245 since they will have *bona fide* non-tax purposes". The notes go on to state that "a transaction will not be considered to be an avoidance transaction because, incidentally, it results in a tax benefit or because tax considerations were significant, but not the primary purpose for carrying out the transaction". On the other hand, the notes indicate that:

> Ordinarily, transitory arrangements would not be considered to have been carried out primarily for *bona fide* purposes other than the obtaining of a tax benefit. Such transitory arrangements might include an issue of shares that are immediately redeemed or the establishment of an entity, such as a corporation or a partnership, followed within a short period by its elimination.

The term "tax benefit" is defined to mean "a reduction, avoidance or deferral of tax or other amount payable under this Act or an increase in a refund of tax or other amount under this Act" [ssec. 245(1)]. According to the technical notes, "the references to 'other amount payable under this Act' and 'other amount under this Act' are intended to cover interest, penalties, the remittance of source deductions, and other amounts that do not constitute tax". The term "tax consequences" is, also, defined [ssec. 245(1)] and is necessary, as indicated previously, to determine the amount of the benefit that will be denied. The actual determination of the tax consequences is provided for in subsection 245(5) which sets out some of the methods by which a benefit will be denied.

A limitation on the application of section 245 is provided [ssec. 245(4)]. In the overview commentary on section 245, the technical notes make the following statement:

> Transactions that comply with the object and spirit of other provisions of the Act read as a whole will not be affected by the application of this general anti-avoidance rule. For example, a transaction that qualifies for a tax-free rollover under an explicit

provision of the Act, and that is carried out in accordance not only with the letter of that provision but also with the spirit of the Act read as a whole, will not be subject to new section 245. However, where the transaction is part of a series of transactions designed to avoid tax and results in a misuse or abuse of the provision that allows a tax-free rollover, the rule may apply. If, for example, a taxpayer, for the purposes of converting an income gain on a sale of property into a capital gain, transfers the property, on a rollover basis to a shell corporation in exchange for shares in a situation where new section 54.2 of the Act does not apply and subsequently sells the shares, the new section could be expected to apply.

The new rule applies as a provision of last resort after the application of the other provisions of the Act, including specific anti-avoidance measures.

The commentary on subsection 245(4) in the technical notes states that "the application of new subsection 245 [*sic*] must be determined by reference to the facts in a particular case in the context of the scheme of the Act". The notes then provide the following three examples of planning that would not be affected by section 245.

> . . . the attribution provisions of the Act set out detailed rules that seek to prevent a taxpayer from transferring property by way of a gift and thereby transferring income to a spouse or minor children. A review of the scheme of these provisions indicates that income splitting is only of concern in transfers of property involving spouses or children under 18 years of age. The attribution rules are not intended to apply to other transfers of property such as gifts to adult children. This can be discerned from a review of the scheme of the Act, its relevant provisions and permissible extrinsic aids. Thus, a straight-forward gift from a parent to his adult child will not be within the scope of section 245 either because it is made primarily for non-tax purposes or because it may reasonably be regarded as not being an abuse of the provisions of the Act. If, however, the gift is made so that the adult child acquires an investment and, through a series of transactions, disposes of it and subsequently transfers the proceeds, including any income therefrom, to the parent, proposed section 245 should apply where the purpose of the transaction is the reduction, avoidance or deferral of tax. (Note that subsection 56(4.1) deals with this type of avoidance where a *loan* is made to a related person.)

> As another example, "estate freezing" transactions whereby a taxpayer transfers future growth in the value of assets to his children or grandchildren will not ordinarily be avoidance transactions to which the proposed rules would apply despite the fact that they may result in a deferral, avoidance or reduction of tax. Apart from the fact that many of these transactions may be considered to be primarily motivated by non-tax considerations, it would be reasonable to consider that such transactions do not ordinarily result in a misuse or abuse given the scheme of the Act and the recent enactment of subsection 74.4(4) of the Act to accommodate estate freezes. (See also IC 88-2, paragraph 10.)

> Another example involves the transfer of income or deductions within a related group of corporations. There are a number of provisions in the Act that limit the claim by a taxpayer of losses, deductions and credits incurred or earned by unrelated tax-payers, particularly corporations. The loss limitation rules contained in subsections 111(4) to (5.2) of the Act that apply on a change of control of a corporation represent an important example. These rules are generally restricted to the claiming of losses, deductions and other amounts by unrelated parties. There are explicit exceptions intended to apply with respect to transactions that would allow losses, deductions or credits earned by one corporation to be claimed by related Canadian corporations. In fact, the scheme of the Act as a whole, and the expressed object and spirit of the corporate loss limitation rules, clearly permit such transactions between related corporations where these transactions are otherwise legally effective and comply with the letter and spirit of these exceptions. Therefore, even if these transactions may appear to be primarily tax-motivated, they ordinarily do not fall within the scope of section 245 since they usually do not result in a misuse or abuse. (See also IC 88-2, paragraph 8.)

Finally, it should be noted that subsections 245(6) through (8) provide rules that pertain to the administration of the legislation in section 245.

On October 21, 1988, the CRA issued IC 88-2 which is intended to provide guidance on the application of the GAAR. It contains over twenty fact situations which are interpreted by the CRA in the context of the application of the GAAR.

The GAAR applies not only to a misuse or abuse of the provisions of the *Income Tax Act*, but also to the provisions of the *Income Tax Regulations*, the *Income Tax Application Rules* or a tax treaty.

A paper,[h] which resulted from a panel discussion held at the 1989 Annual Conference of the Canadian Tax Foundation, presented a "GAAR Decision Tree" to outline the logic that can be used to determine whether the GAAR would apply. Exhibit 13-11 attempts to diagram the logic used.

EXHIBIT 13-11
The GAAR Application Logic

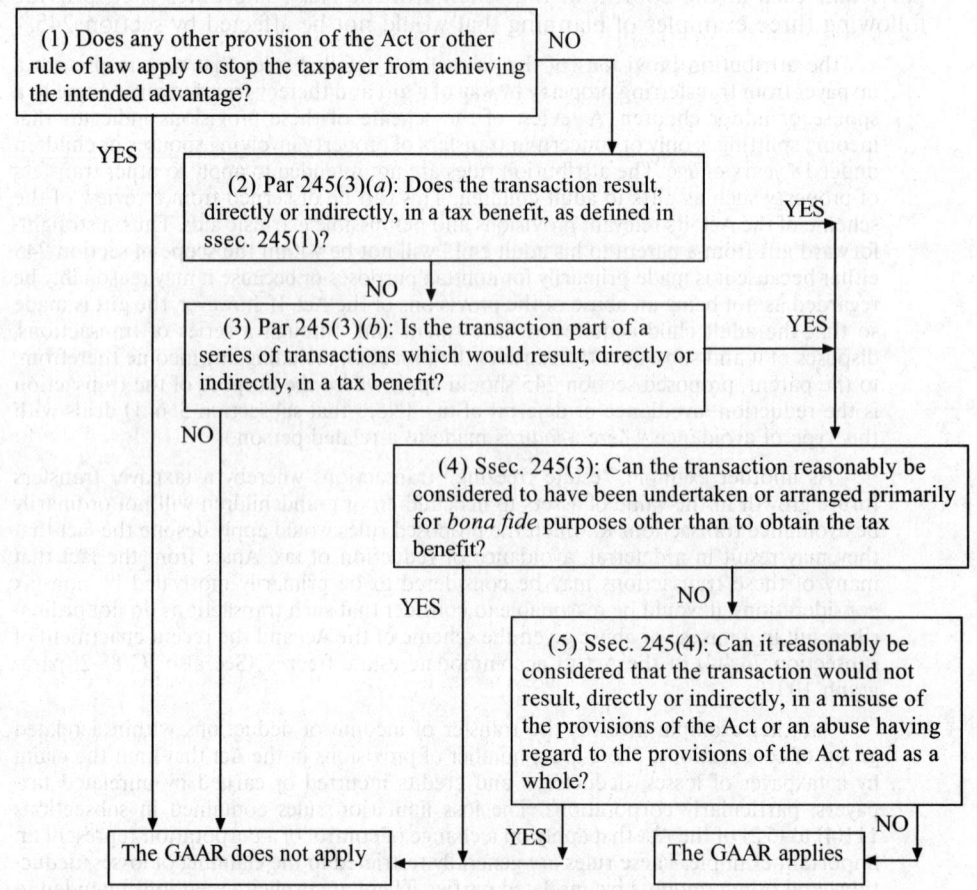

[h] Robert D. Brown, Robert Couzin, Cy M. Fien, William R. Lawlor and William J. Strain, "GAAR and Tax Practice: More Questions than Answers", *1989 Conference Report: Report of the Proceedings of the Forty-First Tax Conference*, Canadian Tax Foundation, Toronto, 1989, pp. 11:3-4.

The appeal by the taxpayer in *OSFC Holdings Ltd. v. The Queen* (FCA), 2001 DTC 5471, was the first decision of the Federal Court of Appeal on the GAAR. [(i)]After a thorough analysis of the GAAR, the court dismissed the taxpayer's appeal. It held that a series of transactions resulted in a tax benefit. The court upheld the finding of the Tax Court that the primary purpose of the transaction was to obtain a tax benefit. It also found that the transactions in question violated a clear and unambiguous general policy of the Act and, hence, concluded that the avoidance transaction resulted in an abuse of the provisions of the Act read as a whole. In June 2002, the Supreme Court of Canada refused to grant OSFC Holdings Ltd. leave to appeal.

The analytical framework used in the *OSFC* case was applied in the Crown's appeal in *The Queen v. Canadian Pacific Limited* (FCA), 2002 DTC 6742. First, the court concluded that there was a tax benefit. The court, then, upheld the Tax Court finding that the primary purpose of the transaction in question was not to minimize tax. Although the latter finding was sufficient to dismiss the Crown's appeal, the court considered the argument that there had been an abuse of the provisions of the Act read as a whole on the basis that the transaction in question contravened a policy of the Act. This argument was rejected. The court concluded that the conditions for the GAAR did not apply to the facts of this case.[(j)]

The three-step analytical framework developed by the Federal Court of Appeal in the *OSFC* case was applied in the case of *The Queen v. Imperial Oil Limited* (FCA) 2004 DTC 6044. The following summary of the three steps is quoted from the *Imperial Oil* case, at 6049–6050 and 6051 in the indicated paragraphs.

1. First, a court must determine if there is a "tax benefit" within the meaning of subsection 245(3). If there is not, GAAR will not apply and the inquiry ends [par. 34].

2. If there is a "tax benefit", a court must take the second step and determine whether there is an "avoidance transaction" under subsection 245(3). If there is no "avoidance transaction", GAAR will not apply and, again, the inquiry ends [par. 34].

3. If the transaction confers a "tax benefit" and constitutes an "avoidance transaction", a court must take the third step and determine whether the transaction is a "misuse" or an "abuse" under subsection 245(4). This inquiry involves taking two smaller steps [par. 35].

   a) First, a court must determine "if it may reasonably be considered that the transaction would not result directly or indirectly in a misuse" of the provisions of the Act. To determine if there has been a misuse, a court must identify the object, or underlying policy or policies, of the relevant provision or provisions of the Act, and decide if the avoidance transaction is contrary to those objectives or policies. If it is, the transaction constitutes a misuse and GAAR applies [par. 36].

   One must infer from the statutory language the policy, if any, on which the relevant provisions of the Act are unambiguously based. This exercise in statutory interpretation must be undertaken with the assistance of such extrinsic aids as: judicial statements, Hansard, ministerial or departmental statements, explanatory notes, bulletins, circulars, texts, periodicals and others [par. 49].

[(i)] An extensive commentary on this case by Thomas B. Akin appears in *Tax Topics*, Number 1546, CCH Canadian Limited, October 25, 2001, pp. 5-8.

[(j)] The Crown's appeals were also dismissed in the cases of *The Queen v. Produits Forestiers Donohue Inc.* (FCA), 2002 DTC 7512 and *The Queen v. Jabin Investments Ltd.* (FCA), 2003 DTC 5027. In both of these cases the OSFC framework was applied in the analysis of the applicability of the GAAR. In the latter case, the "clear and unambiguous" threshold for policy was clarified.

b) However, if there is no misuse, the second smaller step must be taken. This requires a court to decide if the transaction is an abuse, having regard to the provisions of the Act, other than those dealing with GAAR, when read as a whole. The question is whether the transaction contravenes any policy or policies underlying the provisions of the Act as a whole. If it does, the transaction may constitute an abuse for the purpose of GAAR [par. 37].

While the Act does not expressly provide that the policy must be "clear and unambiguous", this is implicit in the language of subsection 254(4), which permits the exemption for a tax avoidance scheme where "it may reasonably be considered that the transaction would not result directly or indirectly in a misuse of the provisions of this Act or an abuse having regard to the provisions of this Act ... read as a whole." [par. 39]

Thus, if the scheme may reasonably be considered not to result directly or indirectly in a misuse or an abuse, GAAR does not apply: in effect, the taxpayer is given the benefit of any doubt. Consequently, for GAAR to apply it must be clear that the provisions of the Act are being misused or the Act as a whole is being abused. It is not enough that a court might reasonably consider them to be misused or abused [par. 40].

REVIEW QUESTIONS

(1) Mr. Smith owns a small manufacturing company that has suddenly become very profitable. This year his accountant has told him to declare a bonus to himself of approximately $150,000 in order to reduce his corporate income to the business limit. His dilemma is that he also needs the money in his business in order to finance expansion. What should he do?

(2) Mr. Jones owns a manufacturing company that is earning well over $300,000 each year. He has been declaring a bonus to himself each year but is now re-thinking this strategy. What items should he consider when deciding whether to pay the bonus or leave the money in the company? Assume that the provincial corporate is 12%.

(3) What is the range of fiscal year-ends that might be chosen to allow the owner of a company to declare a bonus and be taxed on it personally in either of two calendar years?

(4) What are the five criteria for the deductibility of bonus accruals as decided in the *Totem Disposal* case?

(5) Mr. Crunchy is the sole shareholder of Chocobar Inc. His wife's brother has just come to him and asked to borrow some money in order to start up his professional accounting practice. Mr. Crunchy has decided to have Chocobar Inc. lend his wife's brother $20,000 on October 31, 2005, with interest only for the first two years and then principal payments of $10,000 per year starting in the third year. The fiscal year-end of the company is December 31. Discuss the tax implications of the loan.

(6) If your province of residence were to declare a tax holiday for all CCPCs, what impact would this have on compensation for your owner-manager clients?

(7) How much personal tax will a single individual pay on $24,000 of dividend income if that is his or her only source of income and his or her only non-refundable tax credit is his or her personal credit.

(8) Ms. Sorry owned 10% of the shares of a small business corporation that went out of business. Six months after it ceased business she sold her shares to an arm's length person, Mr. X, for $1. When she went to claim a loss on her investment she did not know how much she could write off. In order to have the loss treated as an A.B.I.L., the company needed to be a small business corporation at the time of sale and at that time it did not have any assets used in an active business. She has not used any of her capital gains exemption before. Can you clarify this situation for her?

(9) What does the phrase "all or substantially all" mean?

(10) A corporation that has had 40% of its assets invested in term deposits for the last two years, and the balance in active business assets, qualifies as a "small business corporation" but not a "qualified small business corporation". Do you agree or disagree? Explain.

(11) Mr. Smith incorporated his company 20 years ago for $100 of share capital. It has prospered since then and it now has some excess capital. He has decided to have his wife set up

an investment holding company and his company will lend her company $100,000 of cash for her to invest and thereby split income. Will the attribution rules apply?

MULTIPLE CHOICE QUESTIONS

Question 1

Stan owns 100% of the shares of S Ltd. which has a December 31 year-end. He is also an employee of S Ltd. On January 1, 2005, S Ltd. loaned Stan $200,000 interest-free to assist him in purchasing a new home. Stan signed a promissory note for the loan. Under the terms of the note, the loan is to be repaid in 5 equal annual instalments commencing January 1, 2006. Such a loan is not available to other employees. Which *one* of the following statements is *true*?

(A) Stan will have $200,000 included in his income in 2005.

(B) Stan will have $160,000 included in his income in 2006.

(C) An imputed interest benefit will be calculated for 2005 using a rate not in excess of the rate in effect at January 1, 2005, as the loan was used to purchase a home.

(D) The portion of the loan not repaid by December 31, 2006, will be included in Stan's income in 2007.

Question 2

In computing the net income on the financial statement of Fortelli Inc. for its year ended December 31, 2005, bonuses of $300,000 were accrued. On August 15, 2006, $100,000 of the bonus was paid to the owner-manager, and the remaining $200,000 of bonuses were paid to the sales staff on August 31, 2006. Which one of the following statements is *true*?

(A) If the $100,000 bonus, due to a related party, was not paid by December 31, 2006, it would be included in Fortelli Inc.'s income in the year 2008.

(B) The $100,000 bonus is not deductible in 2005, but the $200,000 bonus is deductible.

(C) An election is available to deem the bonus paid and loaned back to the corporation. This election can be used if the bonuses are not going to be paid by the appropriate deadline.

(D) The $300,000 bonus is not deductible in 2005.

Question 3

The Act contains a general anti-avoidance provision often referred to as the GAAR. Which one of the following statements concerning the GAAR is *false*?

(A) The tax benefit that results from an avoidance transaction will be denied.

(B) When the GAAR is applied, a penalty will be assessed, in addition to the tax owing plus interest.

(C) An avoidance transaction is any transaction that results in a tax benefit, unless the transaction can reasonably be considered to have a *bona fide* purpose other than obtaining the tax benefit.

(D) The GAAR does not apply to transactions that do not result in a misuse or abuse of the Act read as a whole.

Question 4

The general anti-avoidance provision, GAAR, is most likely to apply to which *one* of the following transactions?

(A) As part of an estate freeze, Bill had a trust for his adult children acquire 80% of the common shares of B Ltd. Until then, Bill had owned all the shares of B Ltd., a successful grocery retail outlet. Each year B Ltd. pays dividends to the trust which are paid to the children. The dividends are received by the children tax-free due to the dividend tax credit, since, as university students, they have no other income.

(B) Sam transferred his unincorporated Pizza business, on tax-deferred basis, to a corporation, for the sole purpose of reducing tax by claiming the small business deduction.

(C) Paul gave his son a gift of $10,000 and the son invested it in dividend-paying shares. His son does not pay tax on the dividend income as he is a 19-year old student with little other income. Paul will celebrate his 65th birthday two years after his son graduates. It is anticipated that Paul will receive a birthday gift of $10,000 from his son at that time.

(D) Mary owns all the shares of M Ltd., a CCPC which carries on an active business. For M Ltd.'s taxation year ended June 30, 2005, Mary accrued herself a bonus of $700,000 which reduced M Ltd.'s taxable income to $300,000.

Question 5

Mrs. Investor owns all the Class A common shares of a corporation which has an investment portfolio worth $500,000. The corporation has no other assets and has a December 31 year-end. On January 1 of the current year, Mr. Investor (Mrs. Investor's husband) subscribed for $1 million of Class B shares of the corporation and paid for them in cash. The purpose of this transaction was to income-split with his wife. The corporation earned $10,000 during the year and paid a $10,000 cash dividend to Mrs. Investor. Assuming the prescribed rate is 6% throughout the year, what is the minimum amount of income that Mr. Investor must report in the year in respect of his investment in the corporation?

(A) $10,000
(B) $12,500
(C) $30,000
(D) $60,000

Question 6

Ms. Prentice owns P Ltd., a Canadian-controlled private corporation with assets worth $4 million and liabilities amounting to $1 million. 60% of its assets are used in an active business carried on in Canada by the corporation and 20% are used in an active business carried on in Canada by a corporation controlled by Ms. Prentice's brother. The remaining assets (non-active business assets) earn investment income. Which of the following is the minimum amount of non-active business assets that P Co must sell in order for its shares to qualify as shares of a small business corporation? Assume that the after-tax proceeds on the sale will be used to pay off some of the corporation's liabilities.

(A) None
(B) $400,000
(C) $444,445
(D) $1,333,333

EXERCISES

Exercise 1

[ITA: 78]

Slipit Ltd. declared a bonus payable of $10,000 to Mr. Slip, its president and majority shareholder, on September 30, 2005, its fiscal year-end. If the bonus is paid it will be subject to withholding tax in the amount of $3,500.

— *REQUIRED*

(A) If the corporation is to get a deduction with no future consequences for the bonus payable, by what date must the bonus be paid?

(B) What are the consequences of not paying the bonus by this date?

(C) Assume that, instead of a bonus, the amount owing to Mr. Slip is rent, properly included on the cash basis, on the only rental property he owns and rents to the corporation:

(i) If the corporation is to get a deduction with no future consequences for the rent payable, by what date must the rent be paid?

(ii) What are the consequences of not paying the rent by this date?

(iii) How can these consequences be avoided without paying the rent?

Exercise 2

[ITA: 15(2); 80.4]

Mr. Leverage relocated his private business, Leverage-Lovers Limited, to Alberta from Ontario at the end of May 2005. As a result of the move, the corporation made the following loans on June 1, 2005 to Mr. Leverage, the president and majority shareholder:

(a) a $75,000 loan at 2% interest per year with a five-year term but amortized over a 25-year period to purchase a house in the new location;

(b) a $5,000 loan at 5% interest per year with no definite term to buy furniture for the new house; and

(c) a $10,000 loan with no interest but with a five-year term to buy previously unissued, fully paid shares from the corporation.

The corporation uses the calendar year as its fiscal year and by the end of 2006 the loans described were still outstanding. Any interest required to be paid on the loans at the indicated rates was paid in 2005. Assume that the prescribed rates applicable to shareholder loans during 2005 were: 1st quarter, 4%; 2nd quarter, 3%; 3rd quarter, 4%; and 4th quarter, 4%.

— *REQUIRED*

Discuss the tax consequences in 2005 of the loan described, if Mr. Leverage received the loans:

(A) by virtue of his employment;

(B) by virtue of his shareholdings.

Exercise 3

[ITA: 6(1)]

Consider the data provided in Exhibit 13-3 on page 709.

— *REQUIRED*

Analyze the situation if the business use of the car is 20,000 out of 30,000 km.

Exercise 4

[ITA: 82(1); 117; 121; 123–125]

Payme Now is the sole shareholder and employee of Conduit Corporation Ltd. which operates a processing business in a province with a 5% corporate rate (i.e., a total corporate rate of 18.12%) on its income. The corporation has income of $20,000 before salaries and corporate taxes which is eligible for the small business deduction. Mr. Now has no other income and has federal tax credits of $2,000 and provincial tax credits of $1,250. He requires all of the income generated by the business.

— *REQUIRED*

Consider the following three remuneration alternatives:

(A) all salary,

(B) all dividends, and

(C) $11,000 in salary and the remainder in dividends.

Compare the net cash to Mr. Now for these alternatives ignoring subsection 8(1) deductions available to an employee. Can the best of these alternatives be improved upon?

Exercise 5

[ITA: 82(1); 117; 121; 123–125]

I.M.A. Saver is a sole proprietor generating $80,000 in income before taxes from a processing business operating in a province with a 6% corporate rate (i.e., a total corporate rate of 19.12%). He requires $25,000 after taxes for living expenses and has federal personal tax credits of $2,000 and provincial tax credits of $1,250. He has no other source of income or deductions (except as assumed for (B)(iii) below). The business has a December 31 taxation year-end.

— *REQUIRED*

(A) Compute the tax that would be paid if he continues to operate the business as an unincorporated proprietorship.

(B) Compare your answer in (A) with the total tax that would be paid if he incorporates the business and remunerates himself by the following alternative methods:

(i) $29,392 in salary;

(ii) $25,000 in dividends; and

(iii) $7,432 in salary and $17,568 in dividends. (Assume that the excess federal tax credits resulting from this case can be used against tax on other income.)

Ignore deductions available to employees under subsection 8(1).

Exercise 6

[ITA: 248(1)]

Consider each of the following independent proportions of assets at fair market value. Assume the assets are owned by a Canadian-controlled private corporation. Active business assets refer to assets used principally in an active business carried on primarily in Canada.

	A	B	C	D
Active business assets	85%	50%	—	40%
Marketable securities	15	—	20%	20
Shares of a connected small business corporation	—	50	80	40
	100%	100%	100%	100%

— REQUIRED

Determine whether each of the above proportions meets the test of a small business corporation as defined in subsection 248(1).

Exercise 7

[ITA: 110.6]

Bobby Beamboy Accountant has provided you with the following information:

	2003	2004	2005
Taxable capital gains on sale of qualified small business corporation shares	$75,000	—	$300,000
Business investment loss (before ssec. 39(9) adjustment)	—	—	160,000
Interest income	—	$ 600	1,200
Grossed-up taxable dividends	—	140	—
Net rental income (loss)	—	(1,100)	(220)
Carrying charges	—	1,075	—

The 2003 taxable capital gain was fully offset by a capital gains deduction in that year.

— REQUIRED

Determine Bobby's capital gains deduction for 2005 under subsection 110.6(2.1) supported by all the necessary calculations. Assume that there were no other capital transactions before 2003.

Exercise 8

[ITA: 74.4]

Mrs. Albert owns all of the outstanding common shares of a corporation, Prince Albert Inc., which operates a small retail store in Saskatoon. Her husband owns the building with a fair market value of $200,000, in which the store is located. He is planning to transfer it to Prince Albert Inc. in exchange for $80,000 of cash, a 5% demand note for $20,000 and preference shares for $100,000. The fair market value of the business assets (which are all of the assets excluding cash used to pay for the building) in the company immediately before the transfer is $600,000. Of the total space in the building, 20% is used in the retail business. The net rental income that Mr. Albert earned in the previous year was $20,000.

— REQUIRED

Determine the tax consequences, if any, to Mr. Albert for 2005, assuming the prescribed interest rate [Reg. 4301(c)] is a constant 4% and that the sale took place on January 1, 2005. The corporation's year-end is September 30th. Dividends of $2,000 were paid on the preference shares in 2005.

Exercise 9

[ITA: 245]

Gangster Production Ltd., a Canadian-controlled private corporation, paid its share-holder-manager, Herb, a salary of $150,000 which reduced the corporation's income to $299,500 for the taxation year. The amount of the salary is considered to be reasonable.

— REQUIRED

Determine whether the general anti-avoidance rule (GAAR) would apply in this situation.

ASSIGNMENT PROBLEMS

Problem 1

[ITA: 15(1); 18(1)]

Mimi Gimmee is a vice president of Pump You Up Ltd., a private corporation she started and currently owns with three of her university colleagues. Mimi has recently signed a lease for an upscale downtown condominium which she intends to move into next month. It has been agreed that Pump You Up Ltd. will pay the $2,000 monthly rental for the condominium.

— REQUIRED

Discuss the income tax consequences of this arrangement to Mimi and to Pump You Up Ltd.

Problem 2

[ITA: 15(2); 20(1)(*j*), (*q*); 67; 78; 80.4; 80.5; 147; 147.2]

As the auditor for Skimmed Limited, a Canadian-controlled private corporation, you have discovered in your 2005 year-end audit several items that require further consideration. Mr. Skimmer is an 80% shareholder and president of the company which has a December 31 fiscal year-end.

The following items were expensed during the year:

Salary for Mr. Skimmer (assume equal to employment compensation)	$90,000
Royalty payable to Mr. Skimmer on material prepared for the corporation	54,000
Contribution to registered pension plan (money purchase plan) for Mr. Skimmer whose employee contributions are being matched by the corporation	3,000

The royalty was the only item not paid during the fiscal year. In fact, it was still unpaid at the time of the audit and Mr. Skimmer indicated to you that it could not be paid until sometime in 2007 when he anticipated that the company would have sufficient cash.

The records showed that the corporation had made several loans to Mr. Skimmer or to his son, age 30, who owns the other 20% of the shares of the corporation and is, also, an employee of the corporation. Each of the following was evidenced by a separate promissory note, duly signed and approved by the Board of Directors:

(a) a $180,000 non-interest bearing loan, dated August 1, 2005, repayable in $18,000 annual instalments, to permit Mr. Skimmer's son to purchase previously unissued, fully paid shares from the corporation at their fair market value;

(b) a $270,000 3% loan, dated June 1, 2005, repayable over 15 years in equal instalments of principal payable on the anniversary date, but with interest payable monthly, to enable Mr. Skimmer to purchase a new home, a few blocks from his old home; and

(c) a $24,000 4% loan, dated October 1, 2005, with no principal repayment arrangements, but with interest paid quarterly, to permit Mr. Skimmer to purchase a car to be used in his employment with the corporation.

Mr. Skimmer had repaid $4,800 of the car loan on May 31, 2006 and expressed the intention to repay $4,800 annually for four more years.

Any interest required to be paid on the loans at the indicated rates was paid in 2005. Assume the prescribed rates for 2005 were 4% for the first and second quarters, and 5% for the third and fourth quarters.

— REQUIRED

(A) Discuss the deductibility of expenses contained in the foregoing information (excluding the shareholder loans).

(B) Discuss the tax implications of the shareholder loans if Mr. Skimmer and his son received the loans by virtue of being:

(i) shareholders,

(ii) employees.

Support your answer with specific calculations where appropriate and provide reasons for your conclusions.

Problem 3

[ITA: 82(1); 117; 121; 123–125]

Nancy Ball presently operates a retailing proprietorship with a December 31, year-end and makes $150,000 of net income for tax purposes annually. She is thinking of incorporating her business and has asked for your advice. She lives in a province where the provincial corporate tax rate is 5% of this type of federal taxable income. She has $2,000 of federal personal tax credits, $1,250 of provincial personal tax credits, and no other income.

— REQUIRED

(A) Estimate the personal taxes that Nancy would pay currently on $150,000 of business income compared with the amount of corporate and personal taxes that would be paid if she incorporated her business and only took out a salary of $50,000? Ignore all payroll taxes (e.g., Canada Pension Plan premiums) when making your estimates.

(B) Based on your calculations in (A), estimate the amount of personal tax that Nancy defers by keeping the remaining after-tax retained earnings in her company this year? [Hint: compute the additional personal tax that she would pay on a dividend equal to the corporation's after-tax retained earnings.]

Problem 4

[ITA: 82(1); 117; 121; 123–125]

Mrs. Entrepreneur presently operates a retailing proprietorship with a December 31 fiscal year-end. She expects net income for tax purposes of $210,000 from the business. Since the business currently requires considerable amounts of working capital, she can only afford to withdraw $50,000 annually to meet her family's needs.

She lives in a province where the provincial corporate tax rate is 7% of federal taxable income. She is married and has two children (ages 18 and 19) who will start university soon. Her husband, who looks after their home, has no income and no interest in the business.

Mrs. Entrepreneur has federal personal credits of $2,200, provincial personal tax credits of $1,375 and has no other income. She is contemplating the incorporation of her business. If she does so, she has been advised that if she makes all withdrawals from the business in the form of $50,000 salary, she will end up with enough after-tax to meet her family's needs. Although she is not considering it at present, she expects to pay dividends at a time when her other taxable income is at about the same level as it is currently.

— REQUIRED

(A) Compare the total tax that Mrs. Entrepreneur would pay in 2005 on the $210,000 earned personally with the total tax that would be paid if she incorporated her business and only took out a salary of $50,000. Ignore any Canada Pension Plan premiums payable on the income.

(B) How much personal tax does Mrs. Entrepreneur defer each year by keeping the remaining after-tax retained earnings in her company? [Hint: compute the additional personal tax that she would pay on a dividend equal to the corporation's after-tax retained earnings.]

(C) Compare the total income tax incurred by using a corporation to earn income with the personal tax incurred when the income is earned directly by Mrs. Entrepreneur. Consider the corporate tax plus the personal tax on the salary and the dividend paid out of after-tax retained earnings. What is the absolute income tax cost or savings for Mrs. Entrepreneur if she incorporates?

(D) Assuming Mrs. Entrepreneur chooses the incorporated form of business, what additional tax savings could be achieved by income splitting with her family members?

Problem 5

[ITA: 82(1); 117; 121; 123-125.1]

I. M. Stressed approaches you with the following information:

(a) She resides in a province with a 5% corporate tax rate (i.e. a total tax rate of 18.12%) where she owns and operates an incorporated business which generates income in the amount of $125,000 before taxes.

(b) She has federal personal tax credits of $2,300 and provincial personal tax credits of $1,400 including, among others, the marital status tax credit.

(c) She requires $40,000 after taxes for living expenses each year. This is after she makes her CPP and RRSP contributions.

(d) She wants to maximize her Canada Pension Plan contributions each year. The CPP calculations are as follows:

Pensionable earnings (salary)	$41,100
Basic exemption	(3,500)
Maximum contributory earnings	$37,600
Employee rate	4.95%
Maximum contribution	$1,861

—REQUIRED

Determine the optimum salary/dividend combination for Ms Stressed to achieve her goals and maximize the amount remaining in the company for future dividends. [Hint — you might want to model this in a spreadsheet to compute a required dividend of $15,256.]

Problem 6

[ITA: 110.6]

Karen owns all the common shares of K Ltd. which was incorporated in 1993 to hold her 85% interest in Cyber Corp. Cyber Corp. distributes computer equipment and games to retail stores in southern Ontario. Both corporations are CCPCs. The following is a balance sheet prepared as at December 31, 2005.

Cyber Corp.
Balance Sheet
as at December 31, 2005

Assets

Cash	$ 4,500
Marketable securities (F.M.V. $700,000)	300,000
Accounts receivable (F.M.V. $780,000)	800,000
Inventory (F.M.V. $920,000)	920,000
Prepaid expenses (F.M.V. $1,000)	1,000
Fixed assets (F.M.V. $150,000)	140,000
	$2,165,500

Liabilities & Shareholders' Equity

Accounts payable and accrued liabilities	$ 600,000
Loans payable	400,000
Future income taxes	100,000
Share capital	1,000
Retained earnings	1,064,500
	$2,165,500

The relative values of Cyber Corp.'s assets have remained stable over the past three years. The marketable securities comprise Cyber Corp.'s investment portfolio which is not held as part of the corporation's business activities. The estimated value of the goodwill of the business is $200,000.

K Ltd. was recently offered $1,450,000 for the 85% interest in Cyber Corp. However, Karen has talked the prospective purchaser into buying the shares of K Ltd. instead of the shares of

Cyber Corp., as she understands that by selling the shares of K Ltd. she is able to receive a tax-free $500,000 capital gain.

K Ltd. has term deposits of $100,000 in addition to the shares of Cyber Corp.

— *REQUIRED*

(A) Advise Karen as to whether the shares of K Ltd. are qualified small business corporation (QSBC) shares.

(B) If the shares of K Ltd. are not QSBC shares, then suggest a method for purifying K Ltd. and indicate the tax consequences of your recommendations.

Problem 7

[ITA: 110.6]

Rogo Dan owns all of the common shares of Julie Inc. which in turn owns all of the shares of two other companies, Opco Inc. and RE Inc. Opco Inc. carries on an active business in Sudbury. RE Inc. owns real estate, of which 100% is used by Opco Inc. in its business. All three corporations are C.C.P.C.s. The following are further details:

Julie Inc. assets:	
Shares of Opco Inc. at F.M.V.	$850,000
Shares of RE Inc. at F.M.V.	800,000
Portfolio investments at F.M.V.	75,000
Opco Inc. assets and liabilities:	
Active business assets at F.M.V.	$900,000
Term deposits	50,000
Liabilities	100,000
RE Inc. assets and liabilities:	
Land and building at F.M.V.	$800,000
Portfolio investments at F.M.V.	200,000
Mortgage	200,000

The proportion of assets in each of the companies has been constant over the past three years. Rogo has owned the shares of Julie Inc. for the past five years.

— *REQUIRED*

(A) Determine whether Julie Inc. meets each of the three tests necessary for its shares to be qualifying small business corporation shares.

(B) If the shares of Julie Inc. are not QSBC shares, then suggest ways of purifying Julie Inc. and indicate the tax consequences of your recommendations.

Problem 8

[ITA: 110.6]

Phil Zamboni realized taxable capital gains of $12,000 in 1999. This gain was offset by a capital gains deduction of $12,000 in that year.

In 2003, Zamboni received interest income of $825 and grossed-up taxable dividends of $200. He also incurred a net rental loss of $15,000 and carrying charges totalling $1,475 in 2003.

In 2004, Zamboni earned investment income of $200. He had a rental loss that year in the amount of $13,000 and carrying charges of $2,000. He also realized a business investment loss of $20,000 in December 2004.

In 2005, Zamboni sold the shares of Maps Unlimited Ltd., a qualified small business corporation, for a capital gain of $185,000 and he realized a capital loss of $21,000 on the sale of public company shares. He also received $1,650 in interest and incurred a net rental loss of $1,000 in 2005.

Zamboni had no other previous capital transactions, investment income, or investment expenses.

— *REQUIRED*

Compute Zamboni's capital gains deduction for 2005 under subsection 110.6(2.1) supported by all the necessary calculations.

Problem 9

[ITA: 74.4]

Bob Smith incorporated Smith Inc. twenty years ago and owns all of the shares himself. Smith Inc. is a "small business corporation" which carries on an active business in Victoria, B.C. In 1993, Bob felt that he would like to involve his wife Betty in the share ownership and, on the advice of his accountant, Holdco Inc. was incorporated with Bob and Betty each owning 50 common shares which they bought for $1 each with their own funds. Bob then transferred his common shares of Smith Inc., which were worth $600,000, to Holdco Inc. on a tax-free basis. As consideration for the transfer, Bob received 6% non-cumulative preference shares with a fair market value of $600,000. On July 1, 2005, Smith Inc. sold some property that was used in the active business for net proceeds of $150,000. This amount was then paid as a dividend from Smith Inc. to Holdco Inc. on the same day. Bob and Betty plan to have the corporation invest this amount and use it as capital for their retirement. After the sale of the property and the payment of the dividend to Holdco Inc., Smith Inc. has a fair market value of $800,000 and is still a "small business corporation". Bob received $6,000 in dividends on his preferred shares of Holdco Inc.

— *REQUIRED*

Determine the tax consequences of the 2005 transactions as they relate to the corporate attribution rules. Assume that the prescribed rate [Reg. 4301(c)] for 2005 was 4%.

Problem 10

[ITA: 245]

Consider each of the following independent fact situations.

(1) Adam Aref has contributed the maximum amount to an RRSP on the first business day of each year in respect of the previous year and shortly thereafter has withdrawn the funds.

(2) Bill Loadsofmoney loaned his wife $1,000,000 in 2001 through a non-interest bearing promissory note. His wife invested the funds in GICs and earned $80,000 of interest income which was properly attributed to him, except for any compound interest. Bill gave his wife another cash amount to cover the income tax on the compound interest.

(3) Delgado Ltd. is owned 100% by Mrs. Hugejaysfan. Stieb Ltd. is owned by Mrs. Hugejaysfan's husband and minor children. Delgado Ltd. made an interest-free loan out of its taxable surplus to Stieb Ltd. such that the corporate attribution rule in subsection 74.4(2) does not apply. Stieb Ltd. used the proceeds of the loan to earn property income.

(4) Traub has $200,000 of investments and a mortgage on his personal home for a similar amount. Traub sold the investments, paid off the mortgage, and re-borrowed to acquire the investments.

(5) Guntandy made a loan to his adult child's corporation, Vancouver Hockey Puck Ltd., in order to avoid subsection 56(4.1), since the corporation used the funds to earn property income.

— *REQUIRED*

Discuss whether the general anti-avoidance rule (GAAR) applies to the above situations.

Problem 11

[ITA: 245; IC 88-2]

Consider each of the following independent fact situations:

(1) An individual transfers his or her unincorporated business to a corporation primarily to obtain the benefit of the small business deduction.

(2) An individual provides services to a corporation with which he or she does not deal at arm's length. The company does not pay a salary to the individual because payment of a salary would increase the amount of a loss that the company will incur in the year.

(3) A taxable Canadian corporation, which is profitable, has a wholly-owned taxable Canadian corporation that is sustaining losses and needs additional capital to carry on its business. The subsidiary could borrow the monies from its bank but the subsidiary could not obtain any tax saving in the current year by deducting the interest expense. Therefore, the parent corporation borrows the money from its bank and subscribes for additional common shares of the subsidiary and reduces its net income by deducting the interest from its business.

(4) Profitco and Lossco are taxable Canadian corporations. Lossco is a wholly-owned subsidiary of Profitco. Lossco has non-capital losses that would be deductible if Lossco had income. In order to generate income in Lossco from which its non-capital losses may be deducted, Profitco borrows from its bank and uses the monies to subscribe for common shares of Lossco. Lossco lends these monies to Profitco at a commercial rate of interest. Profitco repays the bank. The amount of share subscription is not in excess of the amount of monies that Lossco could reasonably be expected to be able to borrow for use in its business on the basis solely of its credit from an arm's length lender.

(5) Each of two private corporations owns less than 10% of the common shares of a payer corporation that is to pay a substantial taxable dividend. The payer corporation will not be entitled to a dividend refund on the payment of the dividend. None of the corporations is related to any of the others. The private corporations form a corporation, Newco, transfer their shares of the payer corporation to Newco in exchange for common shares of Newco, and elect under subsection 85(1) (assume that this is done correctly to avoid tax on the transfer) in respect of the transfer. Following the transfer of the payer corporation's shares to Newco, Newco will be connected with the payer corporation. The payer corporation pays the dividend to Newco, free of Part IV tax. Newco pays the same amount to the private corporations as a dividend, free of Part IV tax. The primary purpose of the transfer of the shares is to avoid the Part IV tax which would be payable if the dividend were received directly by the private corporations.

(6) The owner of land inventory has agreed to sell the property to an arm's length purchaser. The purchaser wants to buy the property for cash, but the owner does not want to have the profits recognized in the year of sale. The owner sells the land inventory to an intermediary company deferring receipt of the proceeds of disposition of the land for several years after the date of sale. In this way, a reserve can be claimed under paragraph 20(1)(n). The intermediary sells the land to the third party for cash. The owner receives interest from the intermediary in respect of the monies received by the intermediary from the third party.

— *REQUIRED*

Discuss whether the part of the general anti-avoidance rule (GAAR) that asks the question "can it reasonably be considered that the transaction would not result, directly or indirectly, in a misuse of the provisions of the Act or an abuse having regard to the provisions of the Act read as a whole" applies to the above situations.

[For more problems and solutions thereto, see the CD accompanying this book.]

SUPPLEMENTAL NOTES

(This section can be omitted without losing the continuity of the chapter. None of the review questions, multiple choice questions, exercises or assignment problems utilizes this information.)

A. Other Salary/Dividend Considerations

1. Canada Pension Plan

There can be a tax cost in paying salary from corporate income eligible for the small business deduction. To make the maximum Canada Pension Plan contribution for 2005, a salary of $41,100 must be paid. The maximum contribution is equal to 4.95% of $37,600 (i.e., $41,100 reduced by an exemption for 2005 of $3,500) or $1,861. The corporation, as employer, and the shareholder-manager, as employee, contribute equally to the Canada Pension Plan; where the maximum amount applies, each will pay $1,861 into the plan in 2005. The corporation may deduct these payments from income and the employee may claim a personal tax credit. The tax cost mentioned earlier is illustrated in the following example problem.

Example Problem

Reconsider the case of the shareholder-manager of Ethan Corporation Limited in Example Problem 1 beginning on page 713. In the case of a full distribution of the $36,000 of corporate pre-tax earnings, it was found that the optimal remuneration package involved a salary of $10,990 (see page 713).

— REQUIRED

Consider the effects in that situation of paying a salary of $34,467 and the employer's CPP contribution of $1,533 to qualify the shareholder-manager for the maximum Canada Pension Plan contribution and to fully distribute the $36,000 in corporate pre-tax earnings.

— SOLUTION

				Ex. Prob. 1 Restated for CPP
Corporation:				
Income before salary			$36,000	$36,000
Less: salary	$34,467		$10,990	
employer's contribution to CPP	1,533	36,000	371	11,361
Taxable income			Nil	$24,639
Tax @ 18.12% (i.e., 38% − 10% + 1.12% − 16% + 5%)			Nil	(4,465)
Available for dividend			Nil	$20,174
Shareholder:				
Salary			$34,467	$10,990
Dividend			Nil	20,174
Gross-up			Nil	5,044
Taxable income			$34,467	$36,208
Federal tax			$ 5,515	$ 5,830
Personal tax credits			(2,500)	(2,500)
CPP tax credit (16% of personal CPP contribution)			(245)	(59)
Dividend tax credit			Nil	(3,363)
Basic federal tax			$ 2,770	Nil
Provincial tax			3,447	3,634
Provincial personal tax credits			(1,563)	(1,563)
Provincial CPP tax credit @ 10%			(153)	(37)
Provincial dividend tax credit			Nil	(1,681)
Total tax			$ 4,501	$ 353
Net cash after tax and personal CPP			$28,433	$31,182

Net cash retained after employer and employee CPP contributions	$28,433
Net cash retained after restating Example Problem 1 to consider CPP	31,182
Incremental cost of CPP contribution	$ 2,749

This result could have been improved marginally by again modifying the salary/dividend mix to compensate for the excess of personal credits over total tax. However, this gives an indication of the complexity that can be added to the decision by simply wanting to maximize CPP.

Thus, $2,749 is the minimum total added after-tax cost of providing the additional pension from the Canada Pension Plan at retirement. This cost will increase annually as the maximum eligible for contributions and the percentage contribution rate are increased. The alternative is to invest an amount equivalent to $2,749 annually until retirement. Investing this amount annually in any of the many investment media available may accumulate a considerable sum at retirement. This accumulation can be used to purchase an annuity at retirement which could be paid in the same manner as a Canada Pension Plan pension, and the benefits from such an annuity may exceed the Canada Pension Plan benefits. The Canada Pension Plan benefits will depend on the number of years of contribution, the level of the individual's earnings subject to CPP contributions and the rate of indexing of CPP benefits for inflation. An analysis of each specific case is necessary to determine the relative advantages of such an alternative program. However, the factors to consider in that analysis would be those outlined above. It might be noted that if the optimal shareholder-manager remuneration package already consists of sufficient salary to qualify the individual for maximum Canada Pension Plan contribution, there is no incremental cost to maximum participation in the plan.

2. Registered retirement savings plan contributions

For the shareholder-manager to qualify to make deductible contributions into a registered retirement savings plan (RRSP), his or her remuneration package must contain some salary because dividends do not qualify as "earned income", [ssec.146(1)] which limits the deductible contributions that may be made into an RRSP. If the optimal remuneration package contains some salary, then a contribution to an RRSP based on that salary may result in a greater overall retention of income earned via the corporation. However, increasing the salary component of the remuneration package for 2005 to the $91,667 minimum necessary to make the 2005 maximum $16,500[k] contribution may be less than optimal. The use of an RRSP may be desirable for reasons other than the maximum retention of funds. It may be a means of saving, it shelters investment income from tax and, in the future, may provide pension income eligible for the 16% (maximum of $160) federal pension income tax credit.

These benefits must be compared with the alternative benefits of reinvestment, within the corporation, perhaps at a higher after-tax rate of return, to accumulate a retirement fund for the shareholder-manager. Although the income generated by such reinvested amounts are not sheltered from tax as in the RRSP, on retirement these

---

[k] The RRSP contribution limits are as follows:

Year	Dollar Limit	Minimum Earned Income
2003	$ 14,500	$ 80,556
2004	15,500	86,111
2005	16,500	91,667
2006	18,000	100,000
2007	19,000	105,556
2008	20,000	111,111
2009	21,000	116,667
2010	22,000	122,222

amounts can be paid out as dividends which may be taxed at lower rates than distributions from an RRSP.

Example Problem

Consider the case of the shareholder-manager of Soldier Corporation Limited. The company earns $25,000 before salary and taxes. In particular, consider a remuneration package for an after-tax cash requirement of $20,000. Ignore CPP. The individual has federal personal tax credits of $2,500 and provincial personal tax credits of $1,563. Assume that any negative federal tax due to excess tax credits can be used on other income.

— REQUIRED

(A) Consider the after-tax retention given an optimal compensation package of salary of $13,854 and dividends of $6,146.

(B) Compare the retention in the above situation with the retention that would result from the payment of salary of $16,895 from which a registered retirement savings plan contribution of 18% of $16,895 or $3,041 is made. Assume that $6,146 in dividends are paid to provide the shareholder-manager with the required after-tax funds.

(C) Compare the retention in the above situations with the retention that would result from the payment of a salary of $26,700 to allow for a registered retirement savings plan contribution of $4,806 (i.e., 18% of $26,700).

(D) Compare the retention in the above situations with the retention that would result from the payment of a salary of $21,536 to allow for a registered pension plan contribution by the corporation of $3,876 (i.e., 18% of $21,536).

— SOLUTION

	(A)	(B)	(C)	(D)
Corporation:				
Income before salary	$25,000	$25,000	$25,000	$25,000
Salary....................	(13,854)	(16,895)	(26,263)	(21,536)
RPP contribution	Nil	Nil	Nil	(3,876)
Taxable income	$11,146	$ 8,105	$(1,263)	$ (412)
Corporate tax @ 18.12%	(2,020)	(1,469)	Nil	Nil
Available for dividend.......	$ 9,126	$ 6,636	$(1,263)	$ (412)
Dividend paid	(6,146)	(6,146)	Nil	Nil
Retained by corporation (deficit)[1]	$ 2,980	$ 490	$(1,263)	$ (412)
Shareholder:				
Income from salary ..... (I)	$13,854	$16,895	$26,263	$21,536
Less: RRSP contribution .... (II)	—	(3,041)	(4,727)	Nil
Income from dividend...... ....(III)	6,146	6,146	Nil	Nil
Gross-up	1,536	1,536	Nil	Nil
Taxable income	$21,536	$21,536	$21,536	$21,536
Federal tax	$ 3,446	$ 3,446	$ 3,446	$ 3,446
Personal tax credits	(2,500)	(2,500)	(2,500)	(2,500)
Dividend tax credit.........	(1,024)	(1,024)	Nil	Nil
Basic federal tax	(78)[2]	(78)[2]	$ 946	$ 946
Provincial tax	2,154	2,154	2,153	2,153
Provincial personal tax credits	(1,563)	(1,563)	(1,563)	(1,563)
Provincial dividend tax credit	(513)	(513)	Nil	Nil
Total tax .... (IV)	Nil	Nil	$ 1,536	$ 1,536

Comparison of retention	(A) No RRSP	(B) Optimal salary	(C) Maximum RRSP	(D) RPP
Corporation retention (deficit)[1]	$ 2,980	$ 490	$ (1,263)	$ (412)
Shareholder (I – II + III – IV)	20,000	20,000	20,000	20,000
RPP	Nil	Nil	Nil	3,876
RRSP	Nil	3,041	4,727	Nil
Total	$ 22,980	$23,531	$ 23,464	$ 23,464

— NOTE TO SOLUTION

(1) The deficit in this illustration is of no consequence. It is shown only to balance total retention. If a higher corporate income figure had been chosen for the original example, there would be no deficit, given the shareholder requirement for $20,000 after taxes.

(2) Negative allowed by assumption in the facts of the problem.

Note that in this case, participating in a sheltered RRSP results in greater total retention than not participating. However, part of that retention is in the RRSP and will be taxed on withdrawal at full income rates. The corporate retention is higher when there is no participation in a registered retirement savings plan; as well, the retained amount could be paid as dividends attracting a relatively small amount of further tax at the shareholder level. Since all future taxes and the time value of money have not been accounted for in the foregoing cases, the retained amounts are not fully comparable as presented. However, the cases present some alternative remuneration plans and how they can be analyzed.

B. General Anti-avoidance Rule Under the Excise Tax Act

[ETA: 274]

The *Excise Tax Act* (ETA) contains a general anti-avoidance rule (GAAR) almost identical in nature to section 245 of the *Income Tax Act*. In its explanatory notes to the GST legislation, the Department of Finance made the following statement in regard to section 274 of the ETA:

> This section introduces a general anti-avoidance rule which, like its counterpart in section 245 of the Income Tax Act, is intended to prevent abusive tax avoidance transactions or arrangements without interfering with legitimate commercial transactions. The comments on the income tax provisions, which are found in the explanatory notes to Bill C-139 (1988, C. 55) published in June 1988, are also generally applicable in respect of this section.

These explanatory notes should be reviewed in the context of GST. The definitions and concepts in respect of the GAAR in the ETA are based on their income tax counterparts.

As with the general anti-avoidance rule under the *Income Tax Act*, the essence of the GAAR for GST purposes is that the tax benefit that results from an avoidance transaction will be denied. In order to determine the amount of the tax benefit that will be denied, the provision indicates that the tax consequences to a person will be determined as is reasonable in the circumstances. The actual determination of the tax consequences is provided for in subsection 274(5) of the ETA which sets out some of the methods by which a benefit will be denied.

The term "avoidance transaction" is defined as any transaction that by itself or as part of a series of transactions (i.e., a "step transaction") results in a tax benefit, unless the transaction can be considered to have been undertaken or arranged primarily for *bona fide* purposes other than to obtain the tax benefit [ETA: ssec. 274(3)]. Thus, if there is a primary non-tax purpose for a transaction, it is not an avoidance transaction even if a tax benefit results.

The term "tax benefit" is defined as a reduction, avoidance, or deferral of tax or other amount payable, or an increase in a refund or rebate of tax or other amount [ETA: ssec. 274(1)]. Thus, a tax benefit could arise if there is a deferral of tax or instalment payments. The term "tax consequences" is, also, defined as the amount of tax, net tax, input tax credit, rebate, or other amount payable by, or refundable to, the person under the legislation, or any other amount that is relevant for the purposes of computing that amount [ETA: ssec. 274(1)]. As indicated previously, this term is necessary to determine the amount of the benefit that will be denied.

A limitation on the application of section 274 of the ETA is provided [ETA: ssec. 274(4)]. In the explanatory notes to subsection 274(4) of the ETA, the Department of Finance makes the following statement:

> Subsection 274(4) recognizes that the provisions of Part IX are intended to apply to transactions with real economic substance, not to transactions intended to exploit, misuse or frustrate those provisions so as to avoid tax. It also recognizes, however, that tax benefits expressly provided for in the legislation should not be neutralized by this section in non-abusive situations.

Finally, subsections 274(6) through (8) of the ETA provide rules that pertain to the administration of the legislation in section 274 of the ETA.

Chapter 14

Rights and Obligations under the Income Tax Act

TOPICS DISCUSSED

	Page
OBLIGATIONS OF THE TAXPAYER	757
Returns, Penalties and Criminal Offences	757
Payments and Interest	762
Books and Records	767
POWERS AND OBLIGATIONS OF THE CRA	767
Assessments and Reassessments	767
Refunds and Interest	770
RIGHTS OF THE TAXPAYER	770
Objections and Appeals	770
Amended Returns	771
OBLIGATIONS OF PAYERS AND OTHER PERSONS	772
Employers	772
Obligations of Other Payers, Trustees, etc.	773
Deceased Taxpayers	775
OBLIGATIONS OF THE REGISTRANT UNDER THE EXCISE TAX ACT	777
Collection and Remittance of Tax	777

	Page
Disclosure of Tax	777
Returns and Reporting Periods	778
Remittance of Tax	779
Books and Records	780
POWERS AND OBLIGATIONS OF THE CRA IN RESPECT OF THE EXCISE TAX ACT	781
Assessments and Reassessments	782
Refunds and Interest	782
RIGHTS OF THE REGISTRANT	783
Objections and Appeals	783
Amended Returns and GST Adjustments	783
SIMPLIFIED METHOD AND QUICK METHOD	784
SUPPLEMENTAL NOTES	794
Penalties	794
Objections and Appeals	795
Late-filed or Amended Elections	798
Enforcement and Collections	799

Canadian income tax is based on the self-assessment system. The obligation of calculating taxable income and taxes payable and of paying taxes owing is that of the taxpayer and not the Canada Revenue Agency (CRA). The Act enumerates these obligations and also specifies the rights and powers of the CRA to enforce the system. Finally, taxpayers are given the right to appeal any actions taken by the CRA.

In the interest of efficiency and enforcement, the Act shifts some of the obligations from the taxpayer to other persons. These include employers and persons paying interest, dividends, and other payments to non-residents. The obligations of these persons to report payments and/or withhold tax and remit it to the CRA will also be discussed.

Under the Goods and Services Tax (GST), registrants are agents of the Crown and are responsible to collect tax on their taxable supplies. In addition, registrants are responsible to remit the net tax to the Receiver General and to meet certain reporting requirements.

The following chart outlines the major provisions of Part I, Division I of the *Income Tax Act*, pertaining to returns, assessments, payments and appeals discussed in this Chapter.

PART I — DIVISION I
RETURNS, ASSESSMENTS, PAYMENTS AND APPEALS

A	Liability for tax		150	Returns
B	Computation of income		150.1	Electronic filing
C	Computation of taxable income		151	Estimate of tax
			152	Assessment
D	Taxable income earned in Canada by non-residents		153-160.4	Payment of tax
			161	Interest
			161.1-161.2	Offset of Refund Interest and Arrears Interest
E	Computation of tax		161.3-161.4	Small amounts owing
E.1	Minimum tax		162-163.1	Penalties
F	Special rules		163.2	Misrepresentation of a tax matter by a third party
G	Deferred and other special income arrangements		164	Refunds
			165	Objections
H	Exemptions		166-167	General
I	Returns, Assessments, Payments, Appeals		168	Revocation of reg'n of certain org's
J	Appeals to the courts			

I. OBLIGATIONS OF THE TAXPAYER

A. Returns, Penalties and Criminal Offences

[ITA: 150; 150.1; 151; 162; 163; 163.1; 163.2; 220(3.1); 238-239; IC 73-10R3; IC 00-1R; IC 01-1]

1. Returns

The Act requires taxpayers to file returns in prescribed form and containing prescribed information, and specifies the date by which the returns must be filed as follows:

(a) Corporations — within six months after the end of the taxation year [par. 150(1)(*a*)].

(b) Individuals — on or before April 30 of the next year, unless an individual or the individual's co-habiting spouse carried on a business in the year, in which case the filing deadline is June 15 of the following year [par. 150(1)(*d*)].

(c) Deceased individuals — where an individual has died after October of a particular year and before the filing date for that year (April 30th or June 15th, as discussed above), the return for the particular year of the deceased must be filed by the legal representative by the later of:

(i) six months after the date of death, and

(ii) the usual filing date (i.e., April 30th or June 15th) following the particular year [par.150(1)(*b*)].

Where the death has occurred outside of these time limits, the normal filing dates as discussed in (b) above apply. The objective of these rules is to provide the legal representative of the deceased a minimum of six months after the date of death within which to file a return. These rules are discussed in more detail later in this chapter.

(d) Trusts or estates — within 90 days after the end of the taxation year [par. 150(1)(*c*)].

The following summarizes the filing deadlines:

Income tax return	Filing date
Corporations	6 months
Individuals	April 30 or June 15
Deceased individuals	Later of 6 months after death and the normal due date
Trusts	90 days

Note that corporations that are resident in Canada or carry on business in Canada must file for each taxation year, but individuals are only required to file if one of the following applies:

(a) a balance of tax is owing for the year [spar. 150(1.1)(*b*)(i)];

(b) a capital property has been disposed of in the year [spar. 150(1.1)(*b*)(ii)];

(c) a non-resident individual has a taxable capital gain (e.g., claimed a capital gains reserve in the previous year) [spar. 150(1.1)(*b*)(iii)];

(d) the individual's Home Buyer Plan (HBP) balance [ssec. 146.01(1)] or Lifelong Learning Plan (LLP) [ssec. 146.02(1)] is a positive amount [spar. 150(1.1)(*b*)(iv)]; or

(e) a return is demanded by the Minister [ssec. 150(2)].

Of course, individuals entitled to a refund due to over-withholding or refundable tax credits should file in any case. Low-income taxpayers should file to receive income-based benefits such as the GST credit, the Canada Child Tax Benefit and the Guaranteed Income Supplement. If they do not file a tax return, they are not eligible to receive these amounts.

Individuals can file their personal return electronically [sec. 150.1]. The primary benefit of the electronic filing program for taxpayers is that processing of a tax refund can be much faster. The primary benefit to the CRA is the elimination of data inputting errors on their computer system.

Taxpayers who electronically file their tax return are not required to submit any receipts or other supporting documentation. The CRA, however, has the right to request supporting documentation, which, in fact, may delay the processing of the return.

Alternatively, taxpayers who are issued a Web Access Code by the CRA are eligible to Netfile their personal return. Simple returns can be Telefiled where the CRA has issued a Telefile Access Code.

2. Penalties

The Act provides penalties for failure to file a tax return as and when required under subsection 150(1). The penalty is 5% of the tax unpaid at the date on which the return was due to be filed [par. 162(1)(*a*)]. In addition, a further penalty of 1% of the unpaid tax is levied for each complete month that the return was late, for up to 12 months [par. 162(1)(*b*)].

A higher penalty is imposed for a taxpayer who has already been assessed a penalty under subsection 162(1) in any of the three preceding years [ssec. 162(2)]. This penalty equals 10% of unpaid tax plus 2% per month, for up to 20 months.

A penalty of 10% of the income that a taxpayer has failed to report is imposed if there had been a previous failure to report in the preceding three years [ssec. 163(1)]. However, no penalty will apply under subsection 163(1) where the more severe penalty applies under subsection 163(2) (below) or where the previous failure was more than three years ago.

Where taxpayers knowingly or under circumstances amounting to gross negligence under-report income, the Act imposes a penalty equal to the greater of $100 and 50% of the difference in tax liability [ssec. 163(2)]. This provision is invoked frequently in cases involving omission of income on returns. The term "gross negligence" has been interpreted to include errors which amount to little more than careless omissions, if the taxpayer knew or should have known that the amount was omitted.[a] This provision would not be applied to amounts excluded because of an honest dispute as to their taxability.

The interplay between the penalties under subsection 163(1) and (2) should be noted. On the first failure to report income, subsection 163(1) would not apply, so the CRA could impose the penalty in subsection 163(2). On a repeated failure to report income within the three years specified, the CRA may have a choice between the penalty in subsection 163(1) which is based on 10% of income and the penalty in subsection 163(2) which is based on 50% of tax. For example, if no tax is payable on unreported income, due to the availability of loss carryovers, the penalty in subsection 163(1) could be used to yield 10% of the unreported income.

The Act imposes a penalty of 50% of the interest, charged under section 161, in excess of the greater of $1,000 or 25% of the interest calculated as if no instalments had been paid [sec. 163.1]. This section applies if *any* instalment for the year is late or deficient, as discussed later in this chapter.

Section 163.2 imposes civil penalties for misrepresentations by third parties in respect of another person's tax matters. The penalty is directed to tax professionals, appraisers and valuators and promoters of tax shelters and other tax minimization schemes. Two penalties are imposed.

The first penalty, referred to as the planner's penalty, is a penalty that is imposed when the third-party person makes or furnishes, or participates in the making of, or causes another person to make or furnish, a statement that the person knows, or would reasonably be expected to know but for circumstances amounting to "culpable conduct" (as defined in subsection 163.2(1)) is a false statement or omission that may be used by another person for tax purposes [ssec. 163.2(2)].

The penalty is one of two amounts [ssec. 163.2(3)]. The first amount applies where a "false statement" (as defined in subsection 163.2(1)) is made in the course of a "planning activity" or a "valuation activity" (as defined in subsection 163.2(1)). The penalty is the greater of $1,000 and the total of the person's "gross entitlement" (as defined in subsection 163.2(1)) in respect of the planning activity and the valuation activity calculated at the time at which the notice of assessment of the penalty is sent to the person. The second amount is $1,000, which applies in any other case of a false statement in a situation that falls outside of the definition of a "planning activity" or a "voluntary activity" or, perhaps, in which there is no gross entitlement.

The second penalty, referred to as the preparer's penalty, is a penalty imposed on a third-party person who makes, or participates in, assents to or acquiesces in the making of a false statement or omission statement to, or by or on behalf of, another person.

The statement must be established as one that the person knows, or would be reasonably expected to know but for circumstances amounting to "culpable conduct", is a false statement or omission that may be used for tax purposes by or on behalf of the other person [ssec. 163.2(4)]. The penalty is the greater of two amounts. The first amount is $1,000. The second amount is, generally, the amount of tax sought to be avoided, or the amount of excess refund sought to be obtained [ssec. 163.2(5)]. Additional discussion and clarification of the CRA's position on third party civil penalties is contained in IC 01-1.

---

[a] See *Cowan v. M.N.R.*, (T.A.B.) 69 DTC 553 and *Nesbitt v. The Queen*, (F.C.A.) 96 DTC 6588 for cases in this area.

The following flowchart may be helpful in applying these civil penalties.

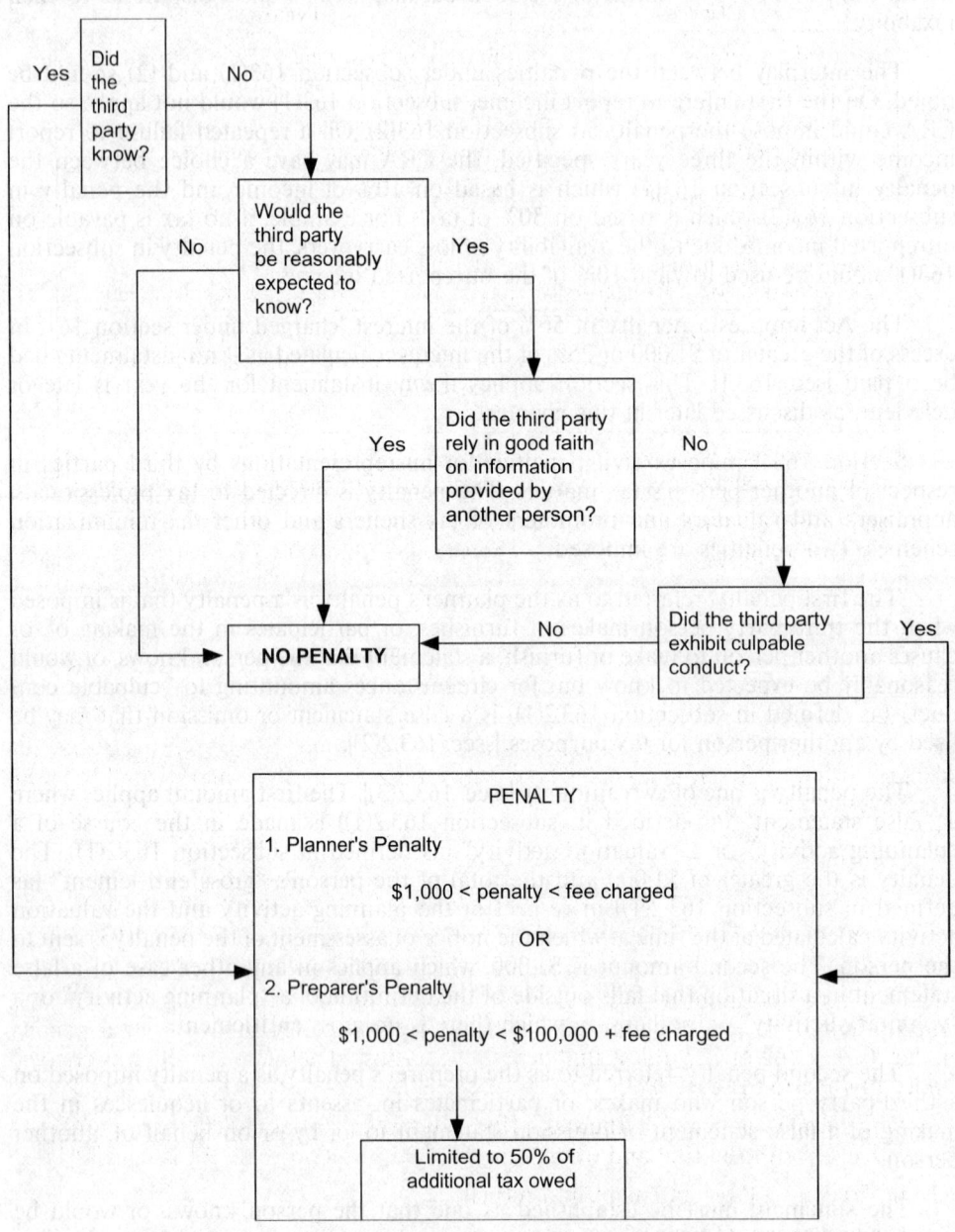

The following table summarizes the above penalties.

Offence	Penalty
Late-filed tax return	Balance of tax owing × 5% + 1% for each complete month late: Maximum = 17%
Late-filed tax return — repeat offender	Balance of tax owing × 10% + 2% for each complete month late: Maximum = 50%
Failure to report income — repeat offender	Income not reported × 10%
Under-reporting income — knowingly or gross negligence	Minimum = $100 Maximum = increased tax liability × 50%
Late or deficient instalments	[Interest charged – greater of (a) $1,000 and (b) 25% of interest that would have been charged if no instalments were made] × 50%
Third party civil penalty Planner's penalty	Minimum = $1,000 Maximum = Fee charged for the planning
Third party civil penalty Preparer's penalty	Minimum = $1,000 Maximum = $100,000 + Fee charged Limited to 50% × tax on unreported income

The CRA has the legislative authority [ssec. 220(3.1)] to waive or cancel penalties, if the taxpayer makes a voluntary disclosure. The CRA's voluntary disclosure program is outlined in IC 00-1R. Where a taxpayer makes voluntary disclosures to correct inaccurate or incomplete information or to disclose previously unreported information, the taxpayer will have to pay taxes owing plus interest, but monetary penalties and prosecution may be waived.

3. Criminal Offences

In addition to the penalties described above, the Act prescribes a number of more serious penalties that can be imposed for a variety of offences [secs. 238 and 239].

A person is liable for a fine of $1,000 to $25,000 or both the fine and imprisonment for up to 12 months on summary conviction for failing to file a return as and when required. A person convicted under this section is not liable to pay a penalty under section 162 or 227 unless that penalty was assessed before he or she was charged under this section [ssec. 238(3)].

On summary conviction, there is a fine of between 50% and 200% of tax sought to be evaded or both the fine and imprisonment for up to two years for [ssec. 239(1)]:

(a) making a false statement in a return;

(b) destroying books and records;

(c) falsifying books and records;

(d) wilfully attempting to evade compliance with the Act; and

(e) conspiring to commit any of the above four offences.

If the foregoing five offences are prosecuted by indictment at the election of the Attorney General of Canada, as indicated in the case of *The Queen v. Smythe*, (Ont. S.C.) 70 DTC 6382, a conviction can result in a fine of 100% to 200% of the tax sought to be evaded and imprisonment for up to five years [ssec. 239(2)]. Again, a person convicted under this section is not liable for the penalty under section 162, 163 or 163.2 for the same attempt to evade tax unless that penalty was assessed before charges were laid under this section [ssec. 239(3)].

B. Payments and Interest

[ITA: 156-158; 161-163; 248(7), (11); ITR 4301; 5300]

The following is a summary of the payment deadlines.

Taxpayers	Balance-due day
Individuals	April 30
Corporations	2 months after year-end
CCPC claiming Small Business Deduction with taxable income under the business limit in the previous year	3 months after year-end
Trusts	Due date for trust return

1. Individuals

Individuals whose primary sources of income are wages and salary generally do not have to pay instalments because their employers are remitting withholding tax on a monthly basis. However, if the difference between the total tax liability (federal and provincial) in either the current year or one of the two preceding years exceeds the amount of tax withheld at source by $2,000 ($1,200 if resident in Quebec [ssec. 156.1(1)]), then the Act provides that quarterly instalments must be paid [sec. 156].

These instalments must be paid by the 15th day of each calendar quarter (i.e., the 15th day of March, June, September and December), with the balance of tax due the following April 30. Each instalment is computed as the least of:

(a) one-quarter of the estimated tax payable for the current year;

(b) one-quarter of the instalment base (defined for this purpose in Regulation 5300, in essence, as tax payable excluding the effect of certain tax credits) for the immediately preceding year; and

(c) one-quarter of the instalment base for the second preceding year for the March and June instalments, and one-half of the instalment base for the preceding taxation year net of the March and June payments for the September and December instalments.

Individuals are informed by the CRA with respect to the exact amount of their instalment requirement under option (c) described previously. For example, in respect of 2005, the March and June instalments are based on one-quarter of the 2003 instalment base. The September and December instalments are equal to 50% of the excess of the individual's 2004 instalment base over 50% of the 2003 instalment base. Instalments can continue to be based on the estimated liability for the year but will be subject to interest penalties on understated amounts where an estimate is too low, as discussed below.

The Act charges interest on deficient and late instalments from the day the instalment should have been made to the day the final payment of tax is due (e.g., April 30 for individuals) [ssec. 161(2)]. An instalment interest offset is available on prepaid or overpaid instalments [ssec. 161(2.2)]. However, this credit offset can only be applied against instalment interest owing; it is not refundable and may not be applied against any other debts. Interest is calculated from the date the final payment is due until the amount is paid [ssec. 161(1)]. Interest charges on deficient instalments can be avoided by computing instalments on the preceding year's instalment base even if the current year's income is likely to be higher [ssec. 161(4.01)]. Interest on deficient instalments may be cancelled if the interest does not exceed $25 for a taxation year [sec. 161.3].

The prescribed interest rate is set quarterly in relation to the average interest rate on 90-day treasury bills during the first month of the preceding quarter. Exhibit 14-1 lists the recent prescribed rates under Part XLIII of the Regulations.

EXHIBIT 14-1
Prescribed Interest Rates under Part XLIII of Regulations

Year	Quarter	Employee or shareholder loans	CRA refunds	Unpaid tax and instalments
2003	1	3	5	7
	2	3	5	7
	3	4	6	8
	4	3	5	7
2004	1	3	5	7
	2	3	5	7
	3	2	4	6
2005	1	3	5	7
	2	3	5	7
	3	3	5	7

The lowest prescribed rate applies to imputed interest benefit calculations on employee or shareholder loans. The basic prescribed rate is increased by two percentage points for the purpose of calculating interest on amounts, such as refunds, owed by the CRA to a taxpayer. The rate applicable to late and deficient instalments and tax payments is increased by four percentage points [Reg. 4301]. Also, subject to the highest rate of interest are unpaid employee source deductions and other amounts withheld at source.

Interest paid on unpaid tax and instalments, arrears interest, is not deductible for tax purposes [par. 18(1)(t)]. However, interest received must be included in income. Refund interest accruing over a period can offset any arrears interest that accrues over the same period, to which the refund interest relates. Hence, only the excess refund interest is taxed to the individual. [sec. 161.1]

The rate of interest paid on refunds is calculated at the basic rate described above plus two percentage points. However, contra-interest [ssec. 161(2.2)], as an interest offset on overpayments of tax, contains the additional four percentage points indicated for deficient payments.

Note that all interest is compounded daily, based on the quarterly prescribed rates [ssec. 248(11)].

Example Problem

Joe is self-employed. According to the CRA Instalment Remittance form, his 2005 instalments due were $1,000 for March 15 and June 15 and $1,500 for September 15 and December 15. Due to a cash flow problem, he did not pay any instalments until September 15, 2005 when he wrote a cheque to the Receiver General for the full $5,000. On April 30, 2006, he paid the remaining balance of the tax owing. Assume that the prescribed rates, for this purpose, for 2005 are 7%, 6%, 6% and 6%, and for the first and second quarters of 2006 the prescribed interest rate is 6%.

— REQUIRED

Calculate the interest and penalty Joe will be charged on his deficient instalments. Assume that Joe pays the interest owing on April 30, 2006. Ignore the effects of the leap year.

— SOLUTION

Date	Amt. owing to CRA: opening balance[1]	Instalment due	Amt. paid	Amt. owing to RC: closing balance
Mar. 15/05 . . .	—	$1,000	—	$1,000.00
Mar. 31/05 . . .	$1,003.07	—	—	1,003.07
June 15/05 . . .	1,015.68	1,000	—	2,015.68
June 30/05 . . .	2,020.65	—	—	2,020.65
Sept. 15/05 . . .	2,046.39	1,500	$5,000.00	(1,453.61)
Dec. 15/05 . . .	(1,475.51)	1,500	—	24.49
Apr. 30/06 . . .	25.04	—	25.04	—
		$5,000	$5,025.04	

Total interest charged = $5,025.04 − $5,000 = $25.04

Penalty is nil, since $25.04 is less than $1,000 [sec. 163.1].

— NOTE TO SOLUTION

(1) Calculation of opening balances above:

$$\text{Mar. 15–Mar. 31/05 (16 days):} \quad \$1,000.00 \times (1 + \frac{.07}{365})^{16} = \$1,003.07$$

$$\text{Mar. 31–June 15/05 (76 days):} \quad \$1,003.07 \times (1 + \frac{.06}{365})^{76} = \$1,015.68$$

$$\text{June 15–June 30/05 (15 days):} \quad \$2,015.68 \times (1 + \frac{.06}{365})^{15} = \$2,020.65$$

$$\text{June 30–Sept. 15/05 (77 days):} \quad \$2,020.65 \times (1 + \frac{.06}{365})^{77} = \$2,046.39$$

$$\text{Sept. 15–Dec. 15/05 (91 days):} \quad \$1,453.61 \times (1 + \frac{.06}{365})^{91} = \$1,475.51$$

$$\text{Dec. 15–Apr. 30/06 (136 days):} \quad \$24.49 \times (1 + \frac{.06}{365})^{136} = \$\ \ \ 25.04$$

2. Corporations

Corporations must make instalment payments of their tax at the end of each month [ssec. 157(1)]. A private corporation is permitted to reduce its monthly instalments by $1/_{12}$ of the corporation's dividend refund on the payment of dividends for the year [ssec. 157(3)]. A corporation is not required to make instalments if taxes payable for the current or preceding year do not exceed $1,000 [ssec. 157(2.1)]. Corporate instalments will only be considered to have been received on time if received by the due date; i.e., postmarks will not suffice [ssec. 248(7)].

The offsetting of interest on corporate tax overpayments and underpayments is permitted [sec 161.1]. This is different from the contra interest mechanism previously discussed [ssec. 161(2.2)]. The provision is aimed at situations most commonly encountered by corporations with complex tax matters, where multiple taxation years may be reassessed concurrently to reallocate income and expenses from one taxation year to another. The provision allows a corporation to avoid paying non-deductible arrears interest for a period for which refund interest is being calculated in the corporation's favour. A written application will be required for the interest offset mechanism to be implemented [ssec. 161.1(2)]. The basis of the calculation of instalments, along with the liability for interest and penalties, is illustrated by the following problem.

Example Problem

No Flab Enterprises Limited is an incorporated company involved in the sale of muscle building and physical fitness equipment. For the fiscal year ended March 31, 2002, the company generated taxes payable of $1,864. In fiscal 2003, taxes payable were $1,904.

Mr. Flab, president and controlling shareholder of the company, planned a reduced sales effort on his part for the fiscal year ended March 31, 2004. As a result, he estimated the company's taxes payable at $1,528 for the year and paid 12 equal monthly instalments based on this amount. By March 2004, Mr. Flab had tabulated the profits and knew that the company's taxes payable would be $2,158.

Since Mr. Flab had reinvested all of the profits for fiscal 2004, he did not have the cash to pay the additional $630 in tax, so he paid nothing further. He filed the corporation's tax return on December 31, 2004 and, in order to avoid showing the further taxes payable, he did not report income for the corporation's 2004 fiscal year, thereby reducing taxes for the year by the $630. He reasoned that he would declare this income in the following year and pay the taxes on that income then.

Furthermore, instead of using the corporate tax return form readily available at his local District Tax Services Office, he filed his corporation's return on some accounting paper. As a result of filing in this way, however, his return did not contain all of the information required to be filed by the corporation.

In May 2005, the corporation's file was randomly selected for a full-scale audit during which discussions with Mr. Flab revealed the omitted taxable income. He argued with the tax auditor that the added taxable income resulted from his forgetting to record the sales of 123 units in September 2004. He was forcefully requested to pay the added tax by June 30, 2005 which he planned to do by that date. In addition to the added tax and interest, the tax auditor decided to assess the corporation for appropriate penalties, in this case, based on the evidence on hand. These were included in the notice of assessment requiring payment by June 30, 2005.

— REQUIRED

(A) Set out the basis on which the interest that the corporation must pay on June 30, 2005 would be computed, assuming it was eligible for the small business deduction under section 125.

(B) Indicate which penalties would be imposed.

— SOLUTION

(A) Interest

Corporations must make instalments on their income tax liability at the end of each month [ssec. 157(1)]. The corporation must compute the instalments on one, usually the least, of the following bases:

(i) $1/12$ of the estimated tax liability calculated at current rates on the estimated taxable income for the current year (estimated to be $1,528 in taxes payable for the year in this case);

(ii) $1/12$ of the instalment base (defined in Regulation 5301, in essence, as tax payable for this company) for the immediately preceding taxation year (amounting to $1,904 for the year in this case); or

(iii) $1/12$ of the instalment base (defined as above) for the second preceding taxation year (amounting to $1,864 for the year in this case) for the first two months, then for the next ten months 1/10 of the quantity computed as the instalment base (defined as above) for the immediately preceding taxation year minus the amount paid in instalments for the first two months.

Whichever base is used for installments, the difference between the estimate of the tax payable at the end of the fiscal period and the instalments paid must be paid two months after the end of the taxation year. However, for Canadian-controlled private corporations eligible for the small business deduction [sec. 125] in the current or preceding year and with taxable income for an associated group of corporations under the small business deduction limit of $300,000 (for the calendar year 2005) in the preceding year, the balance of tax is not due until three months after the end of the taxation year. Prudent financial management would suggest that a corporation use the base which allows it to pay the lowest amount in monthly instalments, while avoiding interest on a deficiency of installments. In periods of rising income, this will generally be the third alternative.

The monthly instalments of corporate tax and other amounts payable by corporations will be deemed for the rules relating to interest and penalties to have been remitted only when received by the Receiver General or his or her representative, not on the date of mailing [ssec. 248(7)].

Interest paid on a deficiency of instalments of a corporation is limited [ssec. 161(4.1)] to interest on the difference between the amount of instalments actually paid and an amount based on the least of the amounts referred to in subsection 157(1), i.e., the least of:

(a) the tax payable for the year (in this case $2,158);

(b) the instalment base for the immediately preceding taxation year (in this case $1,904); and

(c) the instalment base for the second preceding taxation year (in this case $1,864) and the immediately preceding taxation year (in this case $1,904).

The deficiency of instalments in this case could be set out as follows:

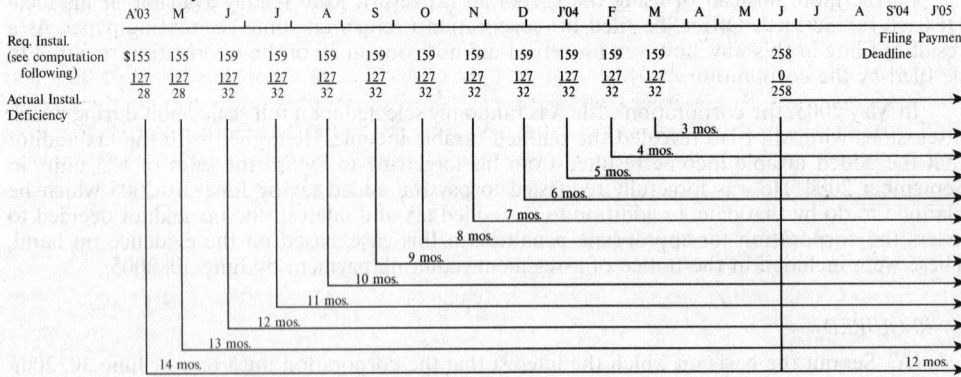

The required instalments are computed as follows:

(a) first two months: $^{1}/_{12} \times \$1,864 = \$155$

(b) next ten months: $^{1}/_{10} \times [\$1,904 - (2 \times 155)] = \$159$

(c) final instalment: $\$2,158 - [(10 \times \$159) + (\$2 \times 155)] = \$258$

Interest is imposed at prescribed rates on underpaid instalments [ssec. 161(2) and Reg. 4301]. This interest runs from the time when the instalment payment was due to either the date of payment or the date when the remainder of tax payable should be paid [par. 157(1)(*b*)], whichever is earlier, and is compounded daily. Interest is imposed on the tax *and interest* owing on June 30, 2004 from the date the remainder of tax payable and interest payable is due until it is paid on June 30, 2005 [ssec. 161(1)].

(B) Penalties

A penalty is provided for failure to file the corporate tax return on September 30, 2004 [par. 162(1)(*a*)]. The penalty is 5% of the tax unpaid at the date on which the return was due for filing. In this case, since the return was not filed on time in the prescribed form, the penalty would be 5% of the $630 in unpaid taxes or $31.50. In addition, paragraph 162(1)(*b*) levies a further penalty of 1% of the unpaid tax per complete month that the return was past due for up to 12 months. In this case, the penalty would be 1% of the unpaid taxes of $630 for three months or $18.90.

The Act imposes a penalty of $100 for failing to provide the required information on a prescribed form [ssec. 162(5)].

Where information is provided resulting in lower tax than that under proper information, the penalty is the greater of $100 and 50% of the difference in tax liability [ssec. 163(2)]. In this case, the penalty would be 50% of the $630 in reduced taxes or $315.

Interest is charged on unpaid penalties imposed under sections 162 or 163, calculated from the date the tax return was due [ssec. 161(11)].

The Act imposes a penalty of 50% of the excess interest, if any, (after any interest offsets) charged on deficient instalments of tax under section 161 minus the greater of $1,000 or 25% of the interest if no instalments had been paid [sec. 163.1].

C. Books and Records

[ITA: 230; 238; ITR: 5800; IC 78-10R3]

Taxpayers are required to keep adequate books and records [sec. 230]. This requirement is for all persons carrying on a business and persons required to pay or collect taxes, among others. While the word "adequate" is not defined or illustrated, the records (including inventory documentation) must be sufficient to support a determination of income subject to tax or of amounts to be remitted. IC 78-10R3 implies that basic transaction data, including invoices, receipts, contracts, bank statements and cancelled cheques, would be the minimum required. Electronic images of this data are acceptable as a method of keeping records [IC 78-10R3].

All such books and records must be maintained at the taxpayer's place of business or residence in Canada until the taxpayer receives written permission to dispose of these materials. A set of rules prescribes a period for keeping certain records or books together with accounts and vouchers necessary to verify them and establishes a period of six years from the end of the last taxation year to which the records and books relate for all other cases not prescribed [ssec. 230(4) and Reg. 5800]. Further subsections deal with a person who has not filed a return or a person who has a case under appeal, with a special request from the Minister and with permission to dispose of records and books before the expiration of the required period. If such materials are microfilmed to save space, guidelines for this procedure are set out in IC 78-10R3.

Failure to keep adequate books and records is a punishable offence [ssec. 238(1)]. Punishable offences will be discussed later in this chapter.

II. POWERS AND OBLIGATIONS OF THE CRA

While the Department of Finance formulates tax policy, the CRA controls, regulates, manages and supervises the income tax system. The duties of the Minister of National Revenue and the employees of his or her agency are set out in section 220. The Commissioner of the Canada Revenue Agency, the CRA's chief executive officer, is empowered to exercise all the powers and perform all of the duties of the Minister under the Act.

A. Assessments and Reassessments

[ITA: 152; IT-241; IC 75-7R3]

Having made a quick check of the return in the initial assessment process for verifying the basic information and calculations, the CRA can do a detailed review of the return, subject to the time restrictions, where applicable [ssec. 152(4)]. The CRA may assess tax, interest and penalties and, furthermore, it may reassess or make additional assessments in the following situations:

(a) at any time, if the taxpayer or person filing the return has made any misrepresentation that is attributable to neglect, carelessness or wilful default or has committed any fraud in filing the return or in supplying any information under the Act;

(b) within the normal reassessment period, which is defined [ssec. 152(3.1)] to be four years from the date of mailing a notice of assessment for all corporations, other than Canadian-controlled private corporations, and three years from the date of mailing of a notice of assessment for Canadian-controlled private corporations and all other taxpayers;

(c) within three years of the expiration of the normal reassessment period, if the taxpayer was reassessed or was eligible to be reassessed under subsection 152(6). This allows the CRA to reassess, for example, both a given year and any of the previous years to which a loss may have been carried back;

(d) at any time, if the taxpayer has filed, within the normal assessment period, a waiver of the statutory assessment period. A waiver might be used where the taxpayer wishes to be able to re-open a return for a year in which there was a very complex problem that is expected to take longer than the normal assessment period to sort out. The ability to reassess is *limited* to the matter(s) specified in the waiver, and the waiver can be revoked upon six months' notice.

The normal reassessment period can be summarized as follows.

Taxpayers	Normal reassessment period
Individuals	3 years
Trusts	3 years
CCPCs	3 years
Corporations other than CCPCs	4 years

The Act gives the Minister the discretion to reassess beyond "the normal reassessment period" where an application has been made by an individual or a testamentary trust for a reduction of taxes, interest and penalties [ssec. 152(4.2)]. Taxpayers might make such an application where they inadvertently forget to claim a deduction or tax credit. However, it should be remembered that the provision gives the Minister the discretion to either reject or accept the application. In addition, the Minister also has the discretion to waive any assessed interest and penalties [ssec. 220(3.1)]. For requests made after 2004, there is a 10-year limit on a reassessment under subsection 152(4.2) and a waiver under subsection 220(3.1).

The Minister is permitted to reassess beyond "the normal reassessment period" in situations where a reassessment within "the normal reassessment period" affects the tax liability for a year which is outside "the normal reassessment period" [ssecs. 152(4.3) and (4.4)]. However, a reassessment of this type is permitted only to the extent that it relates to the change in a particular balance of a taxpayer for a particular year [ssec. 152(4.3)]. For example, if the amount of a net capital loss is redetermined by a subsequent assessment within "the normal reassessment period" but impacts on the carryback or carryforward of taxation periods outside of "the normal reassessment period", then the Minister has the authority to reassess those statute-barred taxation years. Obviously, this provision can work either in favour of or to the disadvantage of the taxpayer.

Where fraud or misrepresentation is alleged through the issue of a reassessment after the normal assessment period, the onus is on the CRA to prove it if the taxpayer appeals the assessment. However, having proved it, the onus shifts to the taxpayer to show that the assessment of tax resulting from the fraud or misrepresentation is incorrect. In tax matters, the taxpayer always has the burden of proving that an assessment is incorrect, since it is assumed that under our self-assessment system the taxpayer has all of the basic data under his or her own control.[b]

In the case of *M.N.R. v. Taylor*, (Ex. Ct.) 61 DTC 1139, it was established that the standard of proof need only be that of the "balance of probabilities" used in civil cases

---

[b] This onus of proof was affirmed in the case of *Violi v. M.N.R.*, (T.R.B.) 80 DTC 1191.

rather than the more rigourous standard of "beyond reasonable doubt" used in criminal proceedings.

It should also be noted that misrepresentation has been interpreted to include "innocent" misrepresentation, that is, a false statement made in the honest belief that it is true, but under the current wording of the Act it may be more restricted in concept. Finally, it should be noted that where the Minister reassesses beyond the normal reassessment period, the reassessment may only be made in respect of an amount which the taxpayer failed to include in the situation under consideration either for fraud or misrepresentation or for the waiver of the normal reassessment period [ssecs. 152(4.01) and (5)].

Example Problem

Mr. Don Godfather filed a personal tax return on April 30, 2005 declaring income of $2,500 for the year ended December 31, 2004. As a result of an investigation, the CRA determined that at December 31, 2003 Mr. Godfather had total assets estimated at $125,000 and total liabilities estimated at $90,000. At December 31, 2004, the taxpayer had total assets estimated at $140,000 and total liabilities estimated at $102,500. It was also determined by the CRA that a sum of $15,500 represented personal or living expenses of the taxpayer and it was further established that the taxpayer won $1,000 from playing poker with friends during the course of the year.

— REQUIRED

(A) What legal right given by the Act does the CRA have to dispute Mr. Godfather's signed declaration of income?

(B) What will the CRA argue is the income of Mr. Godfather for 2004?

(C) What are the possible arguments available to him to substantiate a lower income figure?

— SOLUTION [See Philippe Tremblay v. M.N.R., (T.A.B.) 54 DTC 132][c]

(A) The Minister of National Revenue is not bound by a return of information supplied by or on behalf of a taxpayer, and may, notwithstanding such a return of information, assess the taxpayer [ssec. 152(7)]. It is under this provision that the Minister of National Revenue, where he or she is dissatisfied with a return, makes what are known as arbitrary assessments, in which he or she assesses the income which he or she believes the taxpayer to have had.

(B) The most common method used is the "net worth" method which involves ascertaining the taxpayer's net worth at the beginning and end of the period. The income for the period is arrived at by adding the increase in net worth to his estimated non-deductible expenditures and deducting non-taxable receipts such as gifts. In the problem at hand, the following estimate of income might be made:

(i) net worth (03)	= assets (03) – liabilities (03)	
	= $125,000 – $90,000	
	= $35,000	
(ii) net worth (04)	= assets (04) – liabilities (04)	
	= $140,000 – $102,500	
	= $37,500	
(iii) increase in net worth	= $37,500 – $35,000 = $2,500	
(iv) income	= increase in net worth + personal or living expenses – windfalls	
	= $2,500 + $15,500 – $1,000	
	= $17,000	

(C) The onus is on the taxpayer to show that this assessment is incorrect. The taxpayer might, therefore, argue using appropriate evidence that:

(i) net worth (03) was actually higher than estimated because assets (03) were higher or liabilities (03) were lower;

---

[c] For other cases involving the use of arbitrary assessments, see *George v. M.N.R.*, (T.A.B.) 64 DTC 516 and *Courtois v. The Queen*, (T.R.B.) 79 DTC 506 and (F.C.T.D.) 80 DTC 6175.

      (ii) net worth (04) was actually lower than estimated because assets (04) were lower (e.g., they belonged to a spouse) or liabilities (04) were higher;

      (iii) personal or living expenses were actually lower than estimated; or

      (iv) windfalls (e.g., inheritance, gambling winnings) were actually higher.

B. Refunds and Interest

[ITA: 152; 161; 164; ITR: 4301; IC 92-3]

The Act also requires the Minister to determine the amount of any refund owing to a taxpayer as a result of overpayment of tax [sec. 152]. The Minister *may* pay the refund upon assessment but *must* pay it upon application in writing by the taxpayer within the normal reassessment period [sec. 164]. However, the Minister is given the authority to make refunds of tax paid beyond "the normal reassessment period" [ssec. 164(1.5)]. After 2004, there is a 10-year limit on such refunds. As a practical matter, refund cheques are generally mailed out with notices of assessment. If the taxpayer has other tax liabilities, the Minister may apply the refund to that liability.

Interest, compounded daily at the prescribed rate shown in Exhibit 14-1, is paid in most cases on overpayments of tax [ssec. 164(3)] from the latest of:

(a) the day the overpayment arose;

(b) for individuals, 30 days after the balance-due day for the year, which is April 30 of the following year;

(c) for corporations, 120 days after the end of the taxation year; and

(d) where the return was filed after the filing-due date, 30 days after the date the return was filed for individuals, and the day the return was filed for corporations.

Where a refund arose from a loss carryback or other provision that changed the tax payable in a previous year, no interest is payable for the period prior to the filing of the tax return for the subsequent year in which the loss was established [ssec. 164(5)]. Similar rules are provided for other carryback provisions in the Act [ssec. 164(5.1)]. The effect of the loss carryback is also ignored in computing interest charged on deficient instalments in that carryback year [ssec. 161(7)].

Note that any refund interest received is taxable as interest income in the year received.

III. RIGHTS OF THE TAXPAYER

A. Objections and Appeals

[ITA: 165]

A taxpayer may discover that the CRA disagrees with his or her calculation of tax payable either when a CRA auditor questions particular items (more usual for large corporations which routinely undergo an audit every few years) or when a notice of assessment or reassessment is received. If matters cannot be resolved favourably through informal negotiation, the next step is to file a notice of objection, as provided under paragraph 165(1)(b), pertaining to all taxpayers except individuals, within 90 days of the mailing of the notice of assessment. The due date for the notice of objection for individuals and testamentary trusts is the later of:

(a) one year after the filing-due date of the taxpayer for the year; and

(b) 90 days after the day of mailing of the notice of assessment.

The "filing-due date" is defined [ssec. 248(1)] to be the day on or before which the taxpayer's return for the year is required to be filed, and is:

(a) for a trust, 90 days after the end of the year;

(b) for a deceased individual who died after October of one year or before June 16 of the next year, the later of six months after the day of death and the date the return would otherwise be required to be filed; and

(c) in any other case, April 30 of the following year or June 15 of the following year where an individual or a co-habiting spouse carried on a business in the year.

Deadlines for the filing of a Notice of Objection are summarized as follows.

Taxpayers	Notice of objection due date
Individuals & testamentary trusts	Later of – Mailing date on the Notice + 90 days – Tax return filing-due date + 1 year
Other taxpayers	Mailing date on the Notice + 90 days

Even if the dispute appears headed for a favourable resolution, taxpayers often file a notice of objection as protection if the 90-day period is about to expire. Limits are placed upon the right to object to assessments and determinations in respect of court decisions and specified provisions [ssecs. 165(1.1) and (1.2)].

A notice of objection can be delivered or mailed to the Chief of Appeals in a Tax Services Office or Taxation Centre of the CRA [ssec. 165(2)]. The objection may be submitted on Form T400A. The use of this form is not mandatory. The only requirement is that the notice must contain the facts and reasons for the appeal. The notice of objection is limited for individuals and trusts to assessments under Part I of the Act, individual surtax and tax on Old Age Security benefits [ssec. 165(2.1)].

B. Amended Returns

[ITA: 111; IC 75-7R3; IC 84-1]

The Act does not provide general procedures for filing an amended tax return, other than:

- subsection 49(4) relating to reassessments where options granted by a taxpayer are exercised in a subsequent year;

- subsection 152(6) which requires the Minister to amend a return if a loss or tax credit is being carried back to that year; and

- subsection 164(6) relating to amendments made by a legal representative of a deceased taxpayer.

With respect to the carryback of a loss, it should be noted that the Minister is only required to do so if the prescribed form (e.g., the T1A for individuals or T2A for corporations) or an amended return is filed by the date the tax return for the year the loss is incurred is required to be filed.

To amend other items, if the 90-day period for filing a Notice of Objection has not expired, the return may be amended by filing the Notice of Objection. Otherwise, the CRA's administrative policy, as outlined in IC 75-7R3, is that a return may only be amended if the taxpayer makes a written request for a refund within three years of the end of the year in question and:

(a) the CRA is satisfied that the previous assessment was wrong;

(b) the reassessment can be made within the normal reassessment period or the taxpayer has filed a waiver;

(c) the requested decrease in taxable income assessed is not based solely on a permissive deduction such as an increased claim for capital cost allowance where the taxpayer originally claimed less than the allowable amount; and

(d) application for a refund is not based solely on a successful appeal to the courts by another taxpayer.

Often, a previous assessment was not wrong but the taxpayer wishes to amend the discretionary deductions he or she claimed (or failed to claim) in a previous year. For example, a company in a loss position may choose not to claim capital cost allowance in the loss year because unclaimed capital cost allowance can be carried forward indefinitely whereas non-capital losses expire in seven years. Two years later, the company may find itself profitable, and may wish to claim the capital cost allowance for the previous year to increase the loss carryforward.

The CRA's position is outlined in IC 84-1. It allows such amendments to change discretionary deductions where the amendment would not alter taxes payable for that year. Where a loss is increased by claiming additional capital cost allowance, no increase in taxes payable could, of course, result.

IV. OBLIGATIONS OF PAYERS AND OTHER PERSONS

A. Employers

[ITA: 153; 227; ITR: 100–200; 205; 210; IC 75-6R]

Every person paying salary, wages, or other remuneration or any of the other amounts listed in section 153 is required to withhold prescribed amounts from the payments and remit them to the Receiver General. Where the average monthly remittances, including CPP and EI premiums, in the second preceding calendar year are between $15,000 and $50,000, tax withheld from remuneration paid in the first 15 days of a month is due on the 25th of that month, and from remuneration paid in the balance of the month on the 10th of the following month [Reg. 108(1.1)]. Where the average monthly remittances in any particular month exceed $50,000, employers are required to remit up to four times a month.

Regulation 108(1.11) relaxes these rules on an elective basis as follows:

(a) employers with average monthly remittances in the preceding calendar year of less than $15,000 are required to remit on the 15th of the month following payment; and

(b) employers with average monthly remittances between $15,000 and $50,000 for the preceding calendar year (and over $50,000 in the second preceding year) are allowed to remit on the 25th and 10th days as described above.

Small employers with average monthly withholding amounts of less than $1,000 for the second preceding calendar year and no compliance irregularities in the preceding 12 months are allowed to remit quarterly. Remittances for each quarter are due April 15, July 15, October 15 and the following January 15 [Reg. 108(1)].

The employee completes a TD1 form listing personal credits and certain other deductible amounts, and the withholding amount is based on gross salary less these amounts. The amounts of withholding on both periodic and lump-sum payments are prescribed [Regs. 100–200]. The employee can elect to increase the amount withheld if he or she so chooses.

In addition, the Act provides for a reduction in the amount withheld if the amount required to be withheld would cause "undue hardship" [ssec. 153(1.1)]. The CRA district offices will generally approve applications by employees for reduced withholding if a *pro forma* tax return indicates that a substantial refund will be forthcoming due to substantiated deductions such as RRSP contributions or support payments.

The payer is also required to file information returns as prescribed. Employers, for example, must complete forms T4 Summary and T4 Supplementary by the last day in February, and send two copies of the T4 Supplementary to the employee [Reg. 205].

Every person paying a fee, commission or other amount to a non-resident in respect of services rendered in Canada is required to withhold 15% [Reg. 105]. Non-residents exempt from paying Canadian tax by virtue of the Act or a tax treaty can apply for a waiver of this requirement.

Any person required to withhold by section 153 who fails to withhold tax is liable for a penalty of 10% of the tax that should have been withheld, together with interest [ssec. 227(8)]. A second or further occurrence of failure to withhold under section 153 will result in a penalty of 20% of the tax that should have been withheld. Withholding taxes will only be considered to have been received on time if received by the due date, i.e., postmarks will not suffice [ssec. 248(7)]. Any person who withheld tax but failed to remit it is required to pay, in addition to the tax withheld, a penalty of 10% of the amount that should have been remitted [ssec. 227(9)]. Once again, the penalty doubles to 20% of the tax withheld for second-time offenders. If a taxpayer had tax withheld at source and the withholder did not remit the amount, the CRA cannot require the taxpayer to pay the amount. See, for example, *Lalonde v. M.N.R.*, (T.R.B.) 82 DTC 1772 in which the employee was paid in cash and the employer neither remitted the tax nor provided a T4 or other documentation that tax had been withheld.

Example Problem

The *Toronto Gazette* employs a number of foreign correspondents who are often required to report from war zones. On September 30, 2005, "Ace" Johnson, a veteran reporter, is killed while reporting from Iraq. The *Gazette* decides to continue his monthly salary of $4,000 to his widow for the balance of 2005.

— REQUIRED

What are the obligations of the *Gazette* in terms of withholding tax under the Act?

— SOLUTION

The payer is required to withhold tax on a death benefit which is defined [ssec. 248(1)] as an amount received "upon or after the death of an employee in recognition of the employee's service" [par. 153(1)(*d*)]. The amount of withholding for periodic payments of remuneration is prescribed [Reg. 102(1)]. Remuneration is defined as including a death benefit [Reg. 101]. However, the definition of death benefit [ssec. 248(1)] excludes the lesser of $10,000 or the amount received as the death benefit. Thus, withholding would only be required on the amount received in excess of $10,000 (i.e., $2,000 = ($4,000 × 3) − $10,000, in this case).

The Regulations are silent on how the withholding should be spread, e.g., over all the payments or only once the total amount paid exceeds $10,000. If the widow has no other source of income for the year, the tax on the $2,000 would be less than her personal tax credits for the year and she could file a TD1 so that no withholding would be required. Otherwise, the CRA has suggested that the lump-sum withholding rate in Regulation 103(4) ($103/152$ of 10% in Ontario on amounts less than $5,000) would be satisfactory.

B. Obligations of Other Payers, Trustees, etc.

[ITA: 162(7)–(10.1); 212–217; 221; 233; 233.1–233.5; ITR: 105; 200–235; IT-393R2; IC 75-6R; IC 76-12R5; IC 77-16R4; IC 89-4]

1. Payments to residents of Canada

The Act allows the Governor in Council to make any regulations requiring "any class of person to make information returns respecting any class of information required in connection with assessment under [the] Act" [par. 221(1)(*d*)]. The provisions also require any such person to supply copies of the information to the person whose income is being reported. The Minister is allowed to demand a prescribed information return [sec. 233], and penalties for failure to make such returns are prescribed [ssec. 162(7)]. In addition, the offences on which penalties are imposed [secs. 238 and 239] apply to failure to make information returns, or giving false information on such returns.

Regulations prescribe which persons are required to make information returns, and other information such as filing dates [Regs. 200–235]. In addition to employers, these regulations affect payers of interest, dividends and royalties and persons making payments to non-residents. Other persons required to make information returns include trustees of RRSPs and other deferred income plans. Unless otherwise indicated, such returns are due the last day of February (e.g., the T5 Summary and Supplementary in respect of dividends and interest).

Promoters of tax shelters are required to file an information return in prescribed form containing information on the persons who acquired interests and the amount paid for each interest [sec. 237.1]. There are also filing requirements for partnerships [Reg. 229], and securities dealers handling sales of shares, commodities, etc. [Reg. 230], with penalties for failure to file, as discussed earlier.

2. Payments to non-residents

The Act specifies the payments on which tax must be withheld by Canadians remitting amounts to non-residents [sec. 212]. The rate of withholding specified is 25%, but this is often reduced or eliminated by the applicable tax treaty [IC 76-12R4]. Such payers are also required to file information returns (e.g., NR4 Summary and Supplementary).

Non-residents receiving rent from real property in Canada or a timber royalty in Canada can elect to file a Canadian income tax return reporting the net rental or royalty income, rather than paying the flat withholding tax (under Part XIII) on the gross rents or royalties [sec. 216]. There are no personal credits permitted on such returns, but the graduated tax rates do apply to individuals. A return must be filed within two years from the end of the year in which the rent or royalty was paid and is in addition to any other returns that may be required under Part I [sec. 216]. While withholdings must still be made by the non-resident's agent [ssec. 215(3)] on the gross rent or royalty, the election allows for a refund of excess Part XIII tax withheld, where Part I tax on the net rental or royalty income is lower.

If, in addition to the general section 216 election, the non-resident files a subsection 216(4) election on form NR6 with the CRA, committing to file a Canadian return relating to the rents or royalties, an agent for the non-resident can withhold tax on the basis of net (instead of gross) income. However, the same withholding rate applies. In this case, the tax return must be filed within six months from the end of the year that the rents or royalties are paid.

Failure to withhold, remit, or file information returns results in the same penalties imposed on persons making payments to residents in Canada.

3. Foreign reporting requirements

The Act imposes reporting requirements on Canadian corporations with respect to transactions with non-arm's length non-residents to be filed within six months from the end of the year [sec. 233.1].

Canadian taxpayers and partnerships are required to report certain information relating to foreign investments.

The Act requires a person who transfers or loans property to certain foreign trusts to file information returns [sec. 233.2]. Certain resident taxpayers and partnerships are required to file information returns relating to foreign property held, if the cost of such property exceeds $100,000 [sec. 233.3]. Resident taxpayers and partnerships are required to file information returns with respect to foreign affiliates [sec. 233.4]. Certain

Canadian entities that own a beneficial interest in a non-resident trust and are not required to file an information return under section 233.2 are required to file an information return in each year they receive a distribution from or become indebted to the trust [sec. 233.5].

Penalties for failure to file such returns and for providing false statement or omissions in these information returns are provided [ssecs. 162(7) to (10.1) and sec. 163].

Example Problem

Reconsider the previous example problem.

— REQUIRED

If the death benefit had been paid to a resident of the U.K. instead of Canada, what would the withholding tax requirement have been?

— SOLUTION

A 25% withholding tax is imposed [par. 212(1)(*j*)] on a death benefit as defined by the Act, i.e., the amount in excess of $10,000. The Canada–U.K. Tax Convention is silent on the issue of death benefits and, thus, the 25% rate would still apply.

C. Deceased Taxpayers

[ITA: 70; 104; 118.93; 150; 159; IT-210R2; IT-212R3; IT-326R3; IT-513R]

A number of special rules apply to tax returns and payment of tax for deceased taxpayers. Note that rules governing the deemed disposition of the deceased's capital property are covered in Chapter 8.

1. Tax returns

There are two provisions which govern the filing of deceased taxpayers' tax returns. Where the individual has died after October of a year and on or before the usual filing due date for the year (i.e., April 30 or June 15 of the following year), the individual's legal representative has six months or until the day the return would otherwise have to be filed, whichever is later, to file the return [par. 150(1)(*b*)]. Where the taxpayer has died outside of this time period, the normal filing deadline of April 30th (or June 15 where the deceased individual or his or her spouse carried on business in the year) is imposed [par. 150(1)(*d*)]. The key to understanding how these two provisions interact is to identify the particular tax return year to which these rules apply.

(a) *Prior Taxation Year*

Where the taxpayer has died in the period from January 1 to the usual filing due date for the prior year, the legal representative of the taxpayer has 6 months after the date of death to file a tax return for the immediately preceding year and pay the balance of tax [par. 150(1)(*b*)]. For example, for a taxpayer who died on March 1, 2005 without filing his or her 2004 tax return, the return and balance would be due September 1, 2005.

(b) *Terminal Return*

The legal representative of the taxpayer must also file a final or terminal return for the period in the year to the date of death (e.g., January 1 to March 1 in the above example). The deadline for the terminal return and the payment of any balance owing depends on the date of death. For those persons who have died between January 1 and October 31, the terminal return is due April 30 or June 15 of the following year. For those persons who have died between November 1 and December 15, the terminal return is due 6 months from the date of death, or in the case of an individual who carried on business in the year, June 15, and for deaths between December 16 and December 31, 6 months from the date of death. Therefore, in the example of a death on

March 1, 2005, the terminal return for 2005 is due April 30 or June 15, 2006. No instalments are required in respect of a terminal return.

Amounts in respect of periodic payments, such as interest, rent, salary, etc., must be accrued on a daily basis to the date of death and reported on the terminal return [ssec. 70(1)].

The full year's personal tax credits may be claimed, although the taxpayer was alive for only part of the year. Section 72 limits the reserves that may be claimed on a terminal return.

2. Rights or things

The legal representative of the taxpayer is allowed to report the income from "rights or things" of the deceased on a separate tax return [ssec. 70(2)]. The return is due on the date that is the later of one year after death and 90 days after assessment of any return for the year of death. This alternative return is generally advantageous, since personal tax credits equal to those claimed under subsections 118(1) and (2) [sec. 118.93] in the terminal return may be claimed on the rights or things return as well as on the terminal return, in addition to the benefit of lower marginal tax brackets on both returns.

Rights or things are amounts which are receivable at the date of death but have not been received such as:

- matured, uncashed bond coupons;
- declared, unpaid dividends;
- farm crops; and
- unpaid salary, commissions, vacation pay or CPP, if pertaining to pay periods *completed* before date of death.

Alternatively, the legal representative can assign, under the directions of a will, the income from "rights or things" to a particular beneficiary or beneficiaries [ssec. 70(3)]. However, the income must be distributed to the beneficiary prior to the expiry of the deadline for the subsection 70(2) election as described above. This alternative would be advantageous where the beneficiary would be taxed at a lower rate as compared to the subsection 70(2) election for a separate return of the deceased.

IT-212R3 discusses subsection 70(2) and states that where there is genuine doubt about whether the income is a periodic payment or a right or thing, its treatment is generally resolved in favour of the taxpayer.

Rights or things do not include accrued periodic amounts taxable in the terminal return under subsection 70(1). With the provision of acceptable security, tax owing under subsection 70(2) may be paid in up to 10 annual instalments [ssec. 159(5)]. Of course, interest will be charged until the balance owing is paid in full.

3. Other returns

Two other returns may be used to report income of the deceased taxpayer.

Where an individual earning business income has a transitional reserve from the 1995 conversion to a calendar year [sec. 34.2], the legal representative of the taxpayer is allowed to elect to include the reserve as income in a separate return [ssec. 150(4)]. If a separate return is filed, then a 1995 stub-period reserve [sec. 34.2] may be deducted on the terminal return and will be included in income on the separate return. As well, where the business of the deceased taxpayer has an off-calendar fiscal period, referred to as the "alternate method", and the death occurred in the year after the fiscal year-end of the business, income from the end of the last fiscal period to the date of death can be reported on a separate return, if the legal representatives so elect [ssec. 150(4)]. For example, consider the case of a proprietor, with a January 31 fiscal year-end (having elected the alternative method in 1995) for the proprietorship, who dies on

April 30. Actual income for the "stub period" of the proprietorship from February 1 to April 30 can be reported on a separate return. The election to use a separate return alleviates the hardship that otherwise would occur if the deceased individual's final return for the calendar year of death had to include the proprietorship income for the 12-month fiscal period ended January 31 (as computed with adjustments under section 34.1) and the stub period from February 1 to April 30 which would mean reporting more than 12 months of proprietorship income.

The same treatment is allowed for income from a testamentary trust [par. 104(23)(*d*)].

In both cases, personal tax credits equal to those claimed under subsections 118(1) and (2) [sec. 118.93] in the terminal return may be claimed in the returns.

These returns are due on the date that is the later of six months after the date of death and April 30 or June 15 of the year following the year of death.

4. Personal tax credits

As previously noted, the personal tax credits [ssecs. 118(1) and (2)] can be claimed on all of the four tax returns. This includes the basic personal credit, the married or equivalent-to-married credit, the infirm dependant credit and the age credit. The marital status tax credit must be reduced by the income of the surviving spouse for the full year of death in excess of the threshold for that credit [IT-513R, Appendix A — Terminology: "Income"]. For the remainder of the credits, the claim on the terminal return and the elective returns, combined, cannot exceed the credits that could have been claimed on the terminal return, if no elective returns were filed [sec. 118.93]. Some credits can only be claimed on the return on which the related income is reported (e.g., pension credit, CPP and EI credits). Note that the credit for the transfer of unused credits for a spouse [sec. 118.8] can only be deducted in the terminal return according to IT-326R3, paragraph 11.

V. OBLIGATIONS OF THE REGISTRANT UNDER THE EXCISE TAX ACT

A. Collection and Remittance of Tax

[ETA: 221(1); 222(1), (2)]

A registrant who makes a taxable supply in Canada is required, as an agent of the Crown, to collect any tax payable by the recipient in respect of the supply [ETA: ssec. 221(1)].

Any Goods and Services Tax (GST) collected by a person is deemed to be held in trust for the Crown until it is remitted [ETA: ssec. 222(1)]. Input tax credits that may be claimed by the person may be deducted from the amount held in trust when the GST return for the period is filed [ETA: ssec. 222(2)].

B. Disclosure of Tax

[ETA: 223]

Registrants are required to provide certain information regarding the GST content of taxable supplies made by them [ETA: ssec. 223(1)]. Registrants may either:

(a) indicate on the invoice or receipt issued, or on the written agreement entered into, the consideration paid or payable and the amount of GST payable in respect of that supply; or

(b) indicate on the documentation that the amount paid or payable by the recipient includes the GST payable in respect of that supply.

The Disclosure of Tax (GST/HST) Regulations (P.C. 1990-2747) prescribe a third method of fulfilling the disclosure requirements. Where a registrant includes GST in the price but does not indicate on the invoice or receipt the amount of GST payable, or that GST is included in the price, the registrant must provide a clearly visible notice at the place of supply (the business establishment) that GST is included in the price of purchases. As with the second disclosure method noted above, the purchaser is able to compute the GST content in purchases of taxable supplies by multiplying the tax-included price by 7/107ths.

This increased visibility can be contrasted with the lack of tax visibility under the former federal sales tax which was often referred to as a "hidden tax".

Subsection 223(2) of the ETA requires a registrant to provide, if requested by another registrant receiving a supply from that registrant, particulars of the transaction that may be necessary to substantiate an input tax credit claim.

C. Returns and Reporting Periods

[ETA: 123(1); 238(1); 238.1; 239(1); 243(1), (2); 244(1); 245(2); 246(1)]

Registrants are required to file returns for each reporting period by the dates specified [ETA: ssec. 238(1)]. The net tax for a reporting period must generally be remitted by the date on which the return is filed, as discussed in the next section. The reporting period of a registrant may be either the fiscal month, quarter or year. If a registrant's reporting period is the fiscal month, a return must be filed for each month. If the fiscal quarter is used as the reporting period, a return must be filed for each quarter. If the fiscal year is used as the reporting period, only one return must be filed for the year, although quarterly instalments must be filed, as discussed below. Conditions for these options are discussed below.

The "fiscal year" of a person is defined as either the person's taxation year, or the period elected to be the person's fiscal year [ETA: ssec. 123(1)]. "Taxation year" is defined in the same subsection as the person's taxation year for purposes of the *Income Tax Act*. Where the taxation year of a person is not the calendar year, the person may elect to have fiscal years that are calendar years, effective on the first day of any calendar year [ETA: ssec. 244(1)]. "Fiscal month" and "fiscal quarter" are determined in accordance with subsections 243(1) and (2), respectively, of the ETA.

In general, larger businesses that are registered for GST purposes are required to adopt monthly reporting periods, and thus must file GST returns on a monthly basis. A registrant's reporting period is automatically the fiscal month if the registrant's yearly revenues from taxable (including zero-rated) supplies exceeds $6 million [ETA: ssec. 245(2)]. Revenue in these circumstances is determined by reference to the registrant's threshold amount for the fiscal year and the fiscal quarter. The threshold amount for a fiscal year and fiscal quarter refers to taxable (including zero-rated) supplies made during the preceding fiscal year or preceding fiscal quarters ending in the current year. Thus, monthly returns are required where revenue is greater than $6 million in the preceding fiscal year or in the previous quarters ending in the current fiscal year.

Quarterly and annual reporting periods are available for smaller businesses, depending on the level of sales. Quarterly reporting is required where revenue is $6 million or less in the preceding fiscal year and in the preceding quarters ending in the current fiscal year [ETA: ssec. 245(2)]. An election for quarterly reporting is also available in certain circumstances [ETA ssec. 247(1)]. An election to file on a yearly basis rather than quarterly is available where revenue in the preceding year does not exceed $500,000 [ETA: sec. 248]. New registrants who qualify for annual reporting based on this threshold are automatically entitled to file on an annual basis (i.e., the election is not required).

The above reporting period requirements are summarized by the following.

GST/HST Returns – Reporting periods & remittances

Annual taxable sales and revenues	Reporting period	Optional reporting periods
$500,000 or less	Annual	Monthly, quarterly
$500,001 – $6,000,000	Quarterly	Monthly
$6,000,001 or more	Monthly	Nil

Returns for monthly and quarterly filers must be filed within one month following the end of the registrant's reporting period. Persons filing on an annual basis are required to file their annual return within three months following the end of their reporting period.

Any registrant can opt to file on a monthly basis if desired [ETA: ssec. 246(1)]. For example, exporters may wish to file on a monthly basis in order to obtain GST refunds on a more frequent basis (since exports are zero-rated). However, once a registrant has decided on the frequency of filing its GST return, it must proceed on that basis for the entire fiscal year.

A registrant can apply to the Minister of National Revenue to have one or more reporting periods designated for the purpose of not having to file returns [ETA: sec. 238.1]. Reporting periods eligible for designation are essentially those in which the total of the GST collected (received) or collectible (receivable) for the period (plus any other amounts that are remittable for the period) does not exceed $1,000. Input tax credits or other allowable deductions are ignored for purposes of this calculation. If more than one period is to be designated, the $1,000 threshold is determined in a cumulative basis.

Returns are generally filed on a legal-entity basis. However, where a corporation has divisions with separate accounting systems, an election can be made to file on a divisional basis [ETA: ssec. 239(1)]. In these cases, the divisions must be identifiable by virtue of their activities or locations, and separate records must be maintained.

D.　Remittance of Tax

[ETA: 225(1)–(4); 228(1)–(3); 237(1); 248]

In filing a return for a period, registrants are required to calculate "the net tax" for the period and to remit that tax [ETA: ssecs. 228(1) and (2)]. Where the net tax for a reporting period is a negative amount, a refund may be claimed [ETA: ssec. 228(3)]. Net tax is determined by adding the total amount of GST that was collected (received) or became collectible (receivable) during the period plus any amount that is required to be added for that period, and then subtracting the total amount of input tax credits claimed for the period and any amount that may be deducted for the period [ETA: ssec. 225(1)]. For example, assume $50,000 of GST has been collected, $10,000 is collectible but not yet collected, and another $5,000 must be added because a bad debt that was previously written off and deducted from net tax is recovered. Further, an input tax credit of $45,000 may be claimed and $6,000 may be deducted to reflect a refund made to a purchaser of excess GST that was previously collected. The net tax in this example is calculated as [($50,000 + $10,000 + $5,000) – ($45,000 + $6,000)] = $14,000. Where net tax is owed for a reporting period, that amount must be remitted to the Receiver General by the date on which the return is due.

In determining net tax, where an amount was previously included in calculating the amount of GST that was collected or collectible for a period, it must not be included in a return for a subsequent period [ETA: ssec. 225(2)]. Similarly, where an amount was previously claimed as an input tax credit, it may not be claimed again in a later period [ETA: ssec. 225(3)]. These two subsections are intended to prevent double-counting.

There is a four-year time limit on claiming input tax credits [ETA: ssec. 225(4)]. For most registrants, an input tax credit is not available unless it is claimed in a return filed within four years from the time the return in which the claim could have originally been made was required to be filed. For example, if a registrant who files GST returns on a monthly basis purchased goods to be used in commercial activities on February 1, 2003, an input tax credit could have been claimed in a return filed for that period (i.e., for the month of February), which is due March 31, 2003. If the input tax credit was not claimed at that time, the registrant has until March 31, 2007 to claim the credit before entitlement to the credit would be lost.

Large registrants, i.e., those with more than $6 million in annual taxable supplies, face a two-year limit for carrying input tax credits. An input tax credit for a particular reporting period is not available to these registrants unless it is claimed in a return filed for a reporting period that ends within two years after the period in which the ITC could have first been claimed.

Where annual reporting has been elected [ETA: sec. 248], quarterly instalments of tax are required [ETA: sec. 237]. The instalments are payable to the Receiver General within one month after the end of each fiscal quarter. The amount of each instalment is equal to one-quarter of the registrant's previous year's net tax.

Under the instalment base formula, a registrant is able to base instalments for the current year on an estimate of the net tax for the year, on a similar basis to income tax instalments. This is advantageous for registrants who anticipate that less tax will be payable in the current year than had been payable in the preceding year.

E. Books and Records

[ETA: 169(4), (5); 223(2); 286(1)]

Registrants are required to maintain documentation to support input tax credits, as prescribed by regulation [ETA: ssec. 169(4)]. These requirements, which are contained in the Input Tax Credit (GST/HST) Information Regulations (P.C. 1990-2755), are not restricted in terms of form or physical characteristics. Supporting documentation may include invoices, receipts, credit card receipts, debit notes, books or ledgers of account, written contracts or agreements, computer records, and other validly issued or signed documents.

Depending on the value of the purchase, the information requirements vary. The relevant information and thresholds at which requirements change are summarized below.

(1) Purchases under $30:

● the vendor's name or trading name,

● sufficient information to identify when the GST was paid or became payable, and

● the total consideration paid or payable for the supply.

(2) Purchases of $30 or more and less than $150:

- the above, plus

- the vendor's GST registration number, and

- the total amount of GST charged on the supply or, if prices are on a tax-included basis, a statement to this effect (however, if one document is used in respect of both taxable and exempt supplies, the tax status of each supply must be indicated).

(3) Purchases of $150 or more:

- the above, plus

- the purchaser's name or trading name,

- sufficient information to ascertain the terms of sale (e.g., cash or credit sale), and

- a description sufficient to identify the supply.

To a large extent, documents already being used to support expense deductions under the *Income Tax Act* may be used to support input tax credit claims. The retention period is also generally six years. Supporting documentation is not required for items such as a reasonable *per diem* reimbursements, or other cases where the Minister is satisfied that sufficient records are otherwise available [ETA: ssec. 169(5)].

Registrants are required to issue an appropriate document containing the requisite information if requested by a purchaser who is also a registrant [ETA: ssec. 223(2)].

Similar to the requirements under the *Income Tax Act*, adequate books and records must be kept. The following persons are required to maintain records and books of account for the CRA's audit purposes [ETA: ssec. 286(1)]:

- persons who carry on business or engage in a commercial activity in Canada;

- persons who are required to file a GST return; or

- persons who make an application for a refund or rebate.

The records must be adequate to determine the amount of the person's liability under the ETA or the amount of any refund or rebate to which the person is entitled. The records must be kept in either English or French at the person's place of business in Canada, unless otherwise permitted by the Minister. As under the *Income Tax Act*, the retention period is generally six years. Chapter 15.2 of the GST/HST Memoranda Series sets out the CRA's administrative policy in respect of computerized records.

VI. POWERS AND OBLIGATIONS OF THE CRA IN RESPECT OF THE EXCISE TAX ACT

While the Department of Finance has the responsibility for tax policy, the CRA is responsible for the administration and enforcement of the ETA. The duties of the Minister of National Revenue and his or her employees are set out in section 275 of the ETA. The Commissioner, the CRA's chief executive officer, is empowered to exercise all the powers and perform all of the duties of the Minister under the ETA. On imported goods, the GST is administered and enforced by the new Canada Border Services Agency (CBSA).

A.   Assessments and Reassessments

[ETA: 296–298; 322.1]

The CRA is given broad powers to assess persons for tax remittable or payable, and for interest and penalties. Reassessments and additional assessments may also be made [ETA: ssec. 296(1)]. The CRA may also assess or reassess rebate applications [ETA: ssec. 297(1)]. Assessments must be made within the following time limits [ETA: sec. 298]:

(a) at any time, if the person has committed fraud or made any misrepresentation that is attributable to the person's neglect, carelessness or wilful default;

(b) within four years after the later of the day on which the return for a period was filed or the day on which it was required to be filed; or

(c) at any time if the person has filed a waiver.

The Minister of National Revenue has authority, on an *ex parte* application to the court, to obtain judicial authorization to assess and take action to recover an amount determined by the Minister to be remittable by a registrant at the time the application is heard. This gives the Minister the power to take action to recover tax before the normal due date for the registrant's remittance. Where the court is satisfied that any delay in issuing the assessment would jeopardize the collection of GST and consequently grants the authorization, the CRA will be permitted to issue the assessment and take immediate collection action. [ETA: sec. 322.1]

B.   Refunds and Interest

[ETA: 228(3); 229(1), (2), (3); 296; 297]

If the net tax for a reporting period is a negative amount, a refund may be claimed in the return for that period [ETA: ssec. 228(3)]. The Minister is required to pay the refund with all due dispatch [ETA: sec. 229(1)]. Interest on unpaid refunds begins accruing 21 days after the tax return claiming the particular refund has been filed, provided that all required returns have been filed up to that time. Interest is payable at the prescribed rate [ETA ssecs. 229(1) and (3)]. In assessing net tax, the Minister is required to apply the amount of any net tax overpayment against any GST liability of the person for any other reporting period and refund that part of the overpayment that was not so applied [ETA: ssec. 296(3)].

Interest at the same prescribed rate used for late or deficient remittances and instalments is paid on overpayments of net tax 21 days from the later of:

(a) the day on which the return for the period was filed; and

(b) the day on which the return was required to be filed.

Interest on rebate claims is payable, provided that a rebate application has been filed; interest accrues from the 21st or 60th day after filing, depending on the nature of the rebate [ETA: sec. 297].

Interest is compounded daily. Any refund interest received is taxable under the *Income Tax Act* as interest income in the year received.

VII. RIGHTS OF THE REGISTRANT

A. Objections and Appeals

[ETA: 301; 302]

Where a person is unable to resolve a dispute with the CRA after receiving a notice of assessment, a notice of objection may be filed within 90 days of the mailing of the notice of assessment [ETA: ssec. 301(1.1)]. As noted earlier in this chapter, taxpayers often file a notice of objection as protection if the 90-day period is about to expire, even if a favourable resolution appears likely.

If, in response to the notice of objection, the Minister confirms the assessment or reassesses, the person may appeal to the Tax Court of Canada [ETA: sec. 302]. The appeal must be made within 90 days after notice is sent that the Minister has confirmed the assessment or has reassessed.

As described earlier in this chapter, a person seeking to appeal to the Tax Court of Canada may choose to have the appeal heard under the more formal general procedure or under the informal procedure. The various time limits described earlier also apply to appeals that relate to GST.

A decision of the Tax Court of Canada may be appealed to the Federal Court of Appeal and from there, possibly to the Supreme Court of Canada.

B. Amended Returns and GST Adjustments

[ETA: 232]

The legislation does not contain any provisions regarding amendments to previously filed GST returns. The CRA's administrative guidelines regarding such adjustments are set out in Policy Paper P-149R. Registrants are advised to contact their local district office, in writing, to request adjustments to previously filed GST returns. Amounts included on previously filed GST returns may be adjusted, except where a registrant is attempting to increase the amount of input tax credits or other credit adjustments without a corresponding increase in GST liability for the same reporting period.

In certain circumstances, administrative flexibility may be exercised. For example, in the case of an annual filer who would be required to wait over 12 months in order to claim a missed input tax credit, the registrant may amend the originally submitted GST return through a request for an assessment or a reassessment of the previously filed return. Resource availability and the circumstances surrounding the registrant's request will be taken into account by the CRA in deciding whether to assess or reassess the previously filed return. Flexibility may also be exercised in situations of financial hardship where delaying a net tax refund by not making an adjustment for a missed input tax credit would have a severe negative impact on the registrant's business.

The legislation outlines the procedure for refunding GST to purchasers in certain circumstances. Section 232 of the Act permits an adjustment, refund or credit of the GST in two situations. First, where an excess amount of GST has been charged or collected, and secondly, where consideration for a supply is reduced after the GST has been charged or collected and the supplier adjusts, refunds or credits the GST charged on the original consideration. Any such adjustment, refund or credit must be made within two years after the end of the supplier's reporting period in which the tax was collected or charged, or the price reduction was made. To document the tax adjustment, the supplier may issue a credit note or the recipient may issue a debit note.

VIII. SIMPLIFIED METHOD AND QUICK METHOD

[ETA: 227]

Special simplified accounting methods have been introduced to help small businesses minimize paperwork and to reduce accounting and bookkeeping costs. These simplified accounting procedures are the Quick Method and the Simplified Method. The rules for these methods are authorized in subsection 227(1) of the ETA and are contained in the Streamlined Accounting (GST/HST) Regulations (P.C. 1990-2748).

The simplified method is available to small businesses with annual taxable supplies of $500,000 or less and taxable purchases (excluding zero-rated purchases) of $2 million or less (based on the preceding fiscal year). These businesses are permitted to calculate their input tax credits by simply multiplying the total amount of their GST-taxable purchases (including GST or HST, provincial sales taxes and gratuities) by a factor of $7/107$ ($15/115$ for HST purposes). This factor also applies in the case of reimbursements for taxable expenses incurred by employees and partners.

The quick method is available to small businesses with annual taxable supplies of $200,000 or less, with some exceptions (eg. accountants, lawyers, financial consultants). Under the quick method the amount of GST/HST to remit is calculated as a percentage of taxable supplies for the period, including GST/HST, but not provincial sales tax. The percentage varies by industry and can range from 2.5% to 11.6%.

REVIEW QUESTIONS

(1) In each of the following situations indicate whether the answer is true or false and give a reference to the Act.

(a) The taxable income of Unco Inc., a corporation resident in Canada, was nil for the year. As a result, it did not have to file a corporate tax return.

(b) Mr. Lucky sold his shares in a qualified small business corporation and realized a $200,000 capital gain. The full amount of the gain was eligible for the capital gains exemption leaving his taxable income at nil. He does have to file a tax return for the year.

(c) Instalments for individuals are due on the 30th of March, June, September and December.

(2) Mr. Smith paid his first instalment on time but was unable to pay his second one on time. He paid both the second and the third instalments on September 15. Is there any way he can avoid the interest that was charged to him for the late payment on the second instalment?

(3) Badyearco Inc. has been quite profitable, but this year the corporation realized a business loss that it is going to carry back to the third preceding year. They are also hoping to collect interest from the date they filed the return for that third preceding year. What do you think?

(4) Ms Unhappy received a Notice of Reassessment from the CRA to disallow certain expenses that she had claimed. She contacted her accountant who sent a letter to the CRA outlining the basis for the deduction. Both Ms Unhappy and her accountant feel that the deduction will be allowed. Should she also file a Notice of Objection?

(5) Bad Luck Corp. has had a bad year. The corporation lost money for the first time in its history and some of its key employees have left. Because of all this confusion Bad Luck Corp. was late in getting its financial records in shape and it did not file its corporate tax returns until seven months after the end of the year. Bad Luck Corp. still needs the cash so it is waiting anxiously for the tax refund from the loss being carried back to the third preceding year. Do you think Bad Luck Corp. will be disappointed?

(6) Describe the different tax returns that can be filed for a deceased individual.

MULTIPLE CHOICE QUESTIONS

Question 1

Jane filed her tax return for the 2004 taxation year on September 15, 2005. She enclosed with the return a cheque for $10,000, the balance of tax owing. Neither Jane nor her husband carried on business in 2004. Jane will be assessed a late filing penalty of:

(A) $500

(B) $900

(C) $950

(D) $1,000

Question 2

A Canadian-controlled private corporation received a notice of assessment for its taxation year ended December 31, 2004. The date of mailing on the notice of assessment was August 15, 2005. The normal reassessment period for the corporation's 2004 taxation year ends:

(A) December 31, 2007

(B) August 15, 2008

(C) December 31, 2008

(D) August 15, 2009

Question 3

Darol disagrees with the notice of assessment he received for his 2004 tax return. The date of mailing on the notice of assessment was October 16, 2005. The tax return was filed on June 15, 2005 as Darol carried on a business in 2004. The notice of objection must be filed by:

(A) December 31, 2005

(B) January 14, 2006

(C) April 30, 2006

(D) June 15, 2006

Question 4

Bill was a lawyer with a very successful law practice. He died March 31, 2005. Which *one* of the following is the due date for his 2004 tax return?

(A) April 30, 2005

(B) June 15, 2005

(C) June 30, 2005

(D) September 30, 2005

Question 5

The controller of X Ltd., a Canadian-controlled private corporation, estimates that the company's taxes payable for its year ended December 31, 2005, will be $200,000. Taxes payable for each of the previous three years was as follows:

2002 $212,000

2003 180,000

2004 140,000 (taxable income was $600,000)

What is the minimum monthly instalment that X Ltd. must pay in the 2005 taxation year and the due date for the final balance of tax?

(A) The minimum monthly instalment is $11,667 and the due date for the final balance of tax is February 28, 2006.

(B) The minimum monthly instalment is $16,667 and the due date for the final balance of tax is February 28, 2006.

(C) The minimum monthly instalment is $16,667 and the due date for the final balance of tax is March 31, 2006.

(D) The minimum monthly instalment is $15,000 and the due date for the final balance of tax is February 28, 2006.

Question 6

Ms. Jones is a retired partner in a law firm and has taxable income of $70,000 each year from the partnership, her RRIF and her investments. She expects to pay $25,000 in tax in respect of 2005. She paid $16,400 in tax in respect of 2004 and $15,300 in respect of 2003. No tax is withheld on any of this income.

Which of the following is the minimum amount that Ms. Jones should pay for her 2005 quarterly income tax instalments, in order to avoid any unnecessary interest costs?

(A) 4 payments of $6,250

(B) 2 payments of $4,100 and 2 payments of $6,250

(C) 2 payments of $3,825 and 2 payments of $4,100

(D) 2 payments of $3,825 and 2 payments of $4,375

EXERCISES

Exercise 1

[ITA: 150(1)]

When must the tax returns for the following be filed: (a) a corporation, (b) a deceased person (under subsection 150(1) only), (c) a trust, and (d) an individual?

Exercise 2

[ITA: 152(4)]

An individual filed her 2004 tax return on April 30, 2005. The CRA responded with a notice of assessment mailed on May 27, 2005. If the CRA wishes to make an additional assessment of tax for 2004, by what date must it issue a notice of reassessment?

Exercise 3

[ITA: 153(1)]

List five payments from which the payer must withhold tax.

Exercise 4

Give two examples of a windfall that would reduce an estimate of income in a net worth assessment.

Exercise 5

[ITA: 156(1)]

In 2005, Mr. Ordinary projects his income to be $40,000 consisting of employment income of $25,000 and income from a small business, operated as a sideline, of $15,000. He expects that his tax liability will be $6,000 on the business income. During 2003 and 2004 he paid $3,000 and $4,000, respectively, in tax on the business income. Is he required to make instalments for 2005? If so, how much must he pay in instalments during 2005 so that he does not incur interest and when must each instalment be paid?

Exercise 6

[ITA: 157(1)]

A corporation uses the calendar year for its taxation year. In 2003 it paid tax of $15,840. By the end of March 2005, it had computed its tax for 2004 at $23,760. It estimates that it will have to pay $35,640 in tax for 2005. Is the corporation required to make instalments for 2005? If so, how much must it pay in instalments during 2005 and when must each be paid?

Exercise 7

[ITA: 150(1); 162(1); 238(1)]

X, Y and Z filed their tax returns on May 5, 2005, for the 2004 year. X and Y are employees and Z is a proprietorship business owner. X determined that he owed $4,700 in tax on that date and enclosed a cheque for the $4,700; Y computed a refund of $2,000; and Z included a cheque for $3,500 relating to his balance of tax. What penalties and offences might each be liable for?

Exercise 8

[ITA: 161; 164]

Compare the calculation and tax treatment of interest paid on amounts owing to the CRA and interest paid on refunds by the CRA.

Exercise 9

[ITA: 163.2; IC 01-1]

You have been engaged by Sly Coverup, a self-employed new client, to prepare an income statement and his tax return. Sly has instructed you to prepare these based on a figure for his total revenue and a list of his business expenditures, which he has provided to you. Based on your quick review of these data, you concluded that the expenditures were consistent with Sly's type of business and the amounts appeared to be reasonable. You prepared the income tax return, showing $100,000 of total revenue and $70,000 of expenses.

Subsequently, Sly's return was selected for audit. The CRA determined that many of the expenses deducted in the return could not be substantiated by adequate records. The CRA concluded that some of these expenditures may not have been made. The CRA, also, discovered that only 65% of the actual revenues of the business had been reported.

— REQUIRED

Determine whether you are at risk of being assessed under the civil penalties provisions in section 163.2 of the Act.

Exercise 10

[ITA: 165(1); 169; 172; 180]

Outline briefly the full appeal procedure indicating the time allowed between steps in the procedure.

Exercise 11

[ITA: 216; 220(3)]

A non-resident individual owns a rental property in Canada and has paid non-resident withholding tax on the gross rental revenue since 2000. He has heard that he may be able to recover some of this withholding tax if he files Canadian income tax returns for those years. What would you advise him?

Exercise 12

[ITA: 161]

Mr. Sol Proprietor's only source of income is from his dry cleaning business. In March and June of 2004, he paid instalments of $2,000 each in respect of his 2004 taxes. By September, he realized things were not going well and he would likely have a loss for the year. He, therefore, paid no further instalments.

On June 15, 2005, Sol filed his 2004 tax return claiming a loss and a refund of his $4,000 instalments. He also filed a T1A carrying the loss back to 2003. He expects a tax refund of $5,000 from the carryback.

— *REQUIRED*

What interest can Sol expect to receive on his tax refunds?

Exercise 13

[ITA: 70; 104; 111]

Sam Elder died on September 10, 2005. Discuss how the following are to be reported:

(A) $200, accrued but unpaid, interest on his bank account.

(B) $100 dividend declared on September 15, 2005 and paid on September 30 (the previous dividend was paid on March 30).

(C) CPP of $600 for August 2005, received on September 3 and $200 for the period September 1 to 10, received on October 4.

(D) Charitable donations for the period January 1 to September 10, 2005.

(E) Capital losses incurred in 2004 of $4,000, of which no amount was deducted in 2004.

(F) Income of $900 from a trust established on his wife's death, of which Sam was a beneficiary, for the year ended May 31, 2005.

(G) $50,000 in life insurance payable on Sam's death.

Exercise 14

[ITA: 70; 150]

After the 2004 personal tax season, the brother (Mr. Kaye) of one of your clients (Ms. Kaye) contacted you with respect to his sister. He indicated that his sister had passed away on May 2, 2005, at the age of 50.

Mr. Kaye indicated that his sister had the following income from January 1 to May 2, 2005:

(a) Salary — $22,000, of which $2,000 had not been paid at the time of her death.

(b) Bond interest payable of $950 which had not been received at the time of death.

(c) Interest in her savings/chequing account of $150.

(d) Interest of $140 on a 60-day GIC which matured on May 15, 2005.

(e) Dividend income of $250 on 100 Flying High shares, payable on April 30, 2005, but had not been paid at the time of her death.

(f) The fair market value of Flying High shares on May 2, 2005, was $25/share. These shares had been purchased for $10/share in 1998.

(g) Her RRSP had a value of $34,000 at the date of her death. In February 2005, Ms. Kaye made an RRSP contribution, in respect of 2005, of $9,000. Her earned income for 2004 was $80,000.

— *REQUIRED*

Discuss the tax implications and filing requirements as a consequence of Ms. Kaye's death.

ASSIGNMENT PROBLEMS

Problem 1

[ITA: 156; 156.1; 161; 163.1]

Bert Logan's daughter Amanda is an accounting student. After a brief review of Bert's previous tax returns she advised him that he would likely have to begin making income tax instalments for 2005; however, she was uncertain about how these instalments were to be calculated and the consequences of making inadequate instalments. Amanda called one of the tax specialists at her employer firm, First and Partners, for assistance.

Amanda provided the following information:

(a) 2003 actual tax liability was $8,750;

(b) 2004 actual tax liability was $7,640; and

(c) 2005 estimated tax liability is $5,520.

— REQUIRED

You are the tax specialist. Write a memo, in point form, for partner review explaining the options available to calculate instalment payments for Bert Logan and the consequences if incorrect instalments are made.

Problem 2

[ITA: 157; 162; 163; 163.1]

Ruffle Limited, a public company, specializes in the games business. For their fiscal year ended October 31, 2004, the company's tax liability was $54,024. Due to the success of the board game, Run About, the company's bottom line has increased significantly, resulting in a tax liability of $69,036 for the fiscal period ended October 31, 2005.

Ruffle Limited's climb to success came to a halt in the next fiscal year. Due to increased competition, profits are expected to decline significantly and the controller of Ruffle Limited estimates the tax payable for the fiscal period ending October 30, 2006 to be $45,000.

In addition, the controller informed you that, due to cash flow problems, the actual instalments for June, July and August 2006 were $1,050 less than the amount required. The controller also indicated that in order to compensate for this shortfall an instalment payment of $4,500 was made in October 2006 and that the remaining outstanding balance would be included in the December remittance.

— REQUIRED

The controller has asked you, his tax accountant, to provide him with the following information:

(A) The required instalments for the 2006 taxation year.

(B) Assuming that the estimated tax of $45,000 for 2006 is correct, what payment should be made on December 31, 2006 to stop further interest charges?

Assume that the prescribed interest rates on the deficient instalments are:

• last quarter of 2005: 9%

• first quarter of 2006: 8%

• second and third quarters of 2006: 7%

• last quarter of 2006: 8%.

Problem 3

[ITA: 152; 161; 162; 163.1; IC 00-1R]

On September 1, 2005, you started in your new position as manager of taxation for Malic Corporation, a large public company with a December 31 year-end. On the second day into the job, Maureen Smythe, the VP Finance, comes into your office with a folder entitled "Outstanding

Items". She tells you that the folder was found in the bottom drawer of your desk when the office was cleaned up after the previous manager of taxation left. She is concerned about the following items found in the file:

(a) Two letters from the CRA paper-clipped to the corporation's notice of assessment for the 1999 taxation year (dated September 30, 2000). One of the letters is a reassessment, dated April 30, 2005, and states that the corporation has been assessed additional tax for the 1999 taxation year in the amount of $722,500. The second letter, dated June 15, 2005, demands payment of the $722,500 within 30 days and indicates that if payment is not made, company assets will be seized.

(b) A memo to the tax files from the previous manager stating that for the 2004 taxation year minimum instalments were made for January to October, no instalment was made in November, and an instalment of $1,450,000 was made in December.

(c) A partially completed tax return for the 2004 taxation year indicating taxes payable of $10,760,000. The return had not been filed.

Ms. Smythe leaves the file with you and asks you to do the following.

— REQUIRED

(A) Determine the validity of the CRA letters and the threat of seizure.

(B) Determine if the corporation owes any additional tax and/or penalty with respect to the 2004 taxation year and, if so, the amount of the tax and/or penalty. Previous tax returns indicate the tax liabilities for the 2001 to 2003 taxation years were $7,500,000, $5,400,000, and $9,200,000, respectively.

Assume that the prescribed interest rate required by Regulation 4301, to be used for the purpose of computing imputed interest on employee and shareholder loans, is 6% for all of 2004 and 5% for all of 2005. Assume also that for the purposes of the section 163.1 penalty the amount of interest which would have been payable, if no instalments were paid is $350,000.

Problem 4

[ITA: 152(4); 163; 220(3.1); IC 00-1R]

Mr. Dishonest has approached you, on July 12, 2005, for some advice considering a reassessment notice for the 2001 year which he has received. Mr. Dishonest has misplaced the reassessment notice but assures you that it was dated June 15, 2005. In your conversation with Mr. Dishonest, he reveals that he has had considerable difficulty with the CRA in the past, and has had to pay penalties under sections 162 and 163. Mr. Dishonest is positive that he has complied with the law in this situation and wishes to dispute the assessment.

— REQUIRED

(A) Determine what additional information you require from Mr. Dishonest before discussing the relative merits of the particular disputed items.

(B) Assuming you accept the engagement, what steps would you immediately take?

(C) Explain to Mr. Dishonest the penalty under section 163.

Problem 5

[ITA: 163(2); 163.2]

Mr. Trouble visited his accountant Ms. Back Date, on March 31, 2005, to discuss the tax consequences of a large dividend received on January 10, 2005. Mr. Trouble owns 30% of the shares of Dot.com Ltd. which paid the dividend.

Ms. Back Date explained that if he had transferred his shares of Dot.com Ltd. to a holding corporation on December 31, 2005, he could have deferred tax on the dividend until they were paid out of the holding corporation.

Ms. Back Date indicated that the documentation with respect to the transfer of the shares to the holding corporation and the payment of the dividend to the holding corporation can be back-dated to achieve the result desired.

— REQUIRED

What are the tax consequences of back-dating the documentation with respect to the transfer of the securities?

Problem 6

[ITA: 163.2; IC 01-1]

Bill, an accountant, lives in an exclusive neighbourhood where house prices are in excess of $1,000,000. He has recently become friendly with a new neighbour and in March the neighbour hired Bill to prepare his personal tax return. The neighbour gave Bill a T4 reporting $60,000 of income. Thinking that the income was on the low side, Bill asked if this was all the income he had and the neighbour replied that it was. Bill did not ask any further questions but prepared the tax return. When the neighbour's tax return was audited by the CRA, it was discovered that he had in excess of $300,000 in income for the year.

— REQUIRED

Advise Bill as to whether he is at risk of being assessed under the civil penalty provisions in section 163.2 of the Act.

Problem 7

[ITA: 212(1); 215(3), (6); 216(1); IC 77-16R4]

After several years of visiting Florida, Mr. Snowbird moved from Toronto to Florida on December 31, 2004 and became a non-resident of Canada. Mr. Snowbird decided to rent his house in Canada for the next few years. Mr. Snowbird has arranged with a relocation agency, Gone-Today-Here-Tomorrow, to collect the rent, pay all expenses and remit the balance to him quarterly. During 2005, the house was rented for $1,950 for January to June, and $2,150 for July to December. Expenses amounted to $1,550 per month.

— REQUIRED

Discuss withholding tax and other tax implications concerning Mr. Snowbird's rental property.

Problem 8

[ITA: 153]

A Canadian university hires a well-known American lecturer to lecture on American history. The work will take approximately six weeks and she is to be paid $20,000.

— REQUIRED

Is there any requirement to withhold Canadian tax on the $20,000?

Problem 9

[ITA: 153; 162(1), (2); 212(1)(*d*); 233.3; ITR: 108(1.11); IC 77-16R4]

On January 10, 2006, you started your new job as controller for Bordessa Corporation, a Canadian-controlled private corporation with a December 31 year-end. On your first day, the president and owner-manager of the company has asked you to follow up on some personal and corporate tax concerns that he has.

(1) The company is the exclusive Canadian manufacturer and distributor of menswear designed by a famous U.S. designer and pays the designer a royalty equal to 10% of sales each quarter. Royalty payments are due one month after each quarter end (i.e., on April 30, July 31, October 31 and January 31). The company's financial statements show a 2005 royalty expense of $60,000. The financial statements also show the amount of royalties payable at the company's December 31, 2005 year-end to be $20,000 (the comparable number for December 31, 2004 is $10,000). According to the company's 2005 cheque register, however, only $45,000 has been paid to the menswear designer and only $5,000 has been paid to the CRA. The president wants to know how much the company should remit when it makes its January 31, 2006 payment to make up for unpaid royalties and withholding taxes it owes in respect of 2005.

(2) The company accrued a $100,000 bonus payable to the President on its financial statements. This bonus was declared by way of a director's resolution at the company's Board of Directors' last 2005 meeting. The president understands that his bonus must be paid within 180 days after the year-end in order for it to be deductible in 2005 and you have verified that this is correct [ssec. 78(3)]. This is the first time the company has accrued such a bonus and the president wants to know the deadline for the remittance of payroll deductions on the bonus. You do a quick review of payroll remittances for 2005 and 2004 and find that they amounted to about $120,000 in each year.

(3) The president tells you that he filed his 2004, 2003 and 2002 tax returns yesterday (January 9, 2006) after receiving a demand to file these returns in December 2005. He is expecting a net refund of $5,490 (see the schedule below). He wants to know whether he will be assessed any penalties for late filing and what the amount of the penalties will be. He tells you that his wife is a self-employed medical doctor.

	Balance due (Refund $)
2002	(20,500)
2003	10,000
2004	5,010
Net refund expected	(5,490)

(4) During 2005, the president of the company inherited U.S. stock from a distant relative who lived in the U.S. The value of the stock at the date of the relative's death was $120,000 Cdn. The president has asked you if he has to report this on his 2005 tax return. The stock is held in safekeeping at a stockbroker's office in Toronto.

— *REQUIRED*

Report your findings to the president.

Problem 10

[ITA: 60; 70; 118.93; IT-210R2; IT-212R3; IT-326R3]

In early March, you were preparing your client list with respect to the personal tax return preparation season. When you came across Mr. Ricky's name you realized that Mrs. Ricky had called you regarding her husband's death. Mr. Ricky had passed away March 1, 2005 at age 62.

Mr. Ricky owned and operated a Canadian-controlled private corporation, Shining Ltd., involved in reconditioning cars. Mr. Ricky's 100 shares had an adjusted cost base and paid-up capital of $55,000. The fair market value of the shares at the date of death was $750,000. Seventy-five per cent of the shares were left to his wife and the rest of the shares were left to his 25-year-old son.

Mr. Ricky earned $20,000 per month in salary. A bonus of $35,000 had been declared on February 15, 2005, but had not yet been paid at the time of his death. His February salary was due on the last day of the month, but was paid on March 10, 2005.

In addition to his shares, Mr. Ricky owned bonds which earned $5,500 of interest income in 2004 and accrued $917 of interest in 2005 to the date of his death. He owned another bond on which there was $500 in uncashed bond interest due on January 4, 2005, the anniversary date of that bond. Further, Mr. Ricky had owned two rental properties. Net rental income after capital cost allowance from January 1, 2004 to December 31, 2004 was $45,000 and net rental income before capital allowance was $4,000 for each of the months of January and February 2005.

Other Information:

(1) All assets of Shining Ltd. have been used in the active business of the corporation.

(2) The shares of Shining Ltd. have been owned by Mr. Ricky since 1988.

(3) Mr. Ricky had earned income in 2003 and 2004 of $95,000. He contributed to his RRSP the maximum amount allowed as a deduction in 2004. His RRSP was worth $295,000 at the time of his death. Mrs. Ricky is the designated beneficiary of his RRSP.

(4) Mr. Ricky had a savings/chequing account which earned $2,500 interest in 2004 and $150 during January and February 2005.

(5) Mr. Ricky had utilized $100,000 of his capital gains exemption.

(6) All of Mr. Ricky's other assets have been left to his wife, except for the two rental properties which are bequeathed to his 20 year-old daughter.

(7) The rental properties had a fair market value of $100,000 each. Both properties had the following details:

	Unit #1	Unit #2
Capital cost	$72,000	$83,000
U.C.C.	50,000	52,000

— REQUIRED

Prepare a letter, in draft form for partner review, to Mrs. Ricky explaining the tax implications and the filing requirements in respect of Mr. Ricky's death. Calculate taxable income for 2005.

Problem 11

[ETA: 169(4), (5); 223; 225(1)–(4); 228(1)–(3); 237(1); 238(1); 238.1; 239(1); 243; 244(1); 245(2); 246(1); 248; 286(1)]

Mr. E. Entrepreneur has decided to open a small car detailing company. The individual at the name registration office suggested that Mr. Entrepreneur walk down to the CRA office and pick up the information package with respect to tax filing, etc.

Mr. Entrepreneur had anticipated that the package of information obtained at the CRA office would include information on the goods and services tax (GST). Unfortunately, this information was not included in the package obtained. Mr. Entrepreneur approached his son, Sam, who is an accountant, to explain the obligations of a registrant under the *Excise Tax Act*.

— REQUIRED

As Sam, provide the appropriate explanations.

[For more problems and solutions thereto, see the CD accompanying this book.]

SUPPLEMENTAL NOTES

(This section can be omitted without losing the continuity of the chapter. None of the review questions, multiple choice questions, exercises, or assignment problems utilizes this information.)

A. Penalties

[ITA: 162(5), (6), (7), (7.1), (8), (10), (10.1); 220(3.1) – (3.7); 237.1(7.4); 163(3); IC 92-1, IC 92-2, IC 92-3]

A penalty of $100 for each failure to provide the information required on a prescribed form is imposed [ssec. 162(5)]. It should be noted, however, that section 32 of the *Interpretation Act* provides that where a form is prescribed, deviations therefrom not affecting the substance or calculated to mislead, do not invalidate the form used.

The Act imposes a penalty of $100 for each failure to provide an individual's Social Insurance Number to a person required to make an information return [ssec. 162(6)]. The penalty will not apply if the individual applies for a S.I.N. within 15 days of the request and the S.I.N. is provided to the person making an information return within 15 days after receiving it.

A penalty equal to the greater of $100 and $25 per day to a maximum of 100 days for failure to file, as and when required, certain information returns is imposed [ssecs. 162(7) and (7.1)]. Some of the more common information returns required include: partnership information returns, tax shelter information returns, transactions with related non-resident persons, and various information returns relating to foreign property.

The Act imposes a further penalty of $100 per member of the partnership for each month or part of a month, not exceeding 24 months, during which the failure continues [ssec. 162(8)]. This additional penalty only applies where a penalty under subsection 162(7.1) has been assessed, a demand for the return has been made, and a penalty under subsection 162(7.1) has already been assessed for one of the three preceding fiscal periods.

A penalty equal to the greater of $500 and 25% of any consideration received or receivable in respect of a tax shelter before correct information is provided and an identification number is obtained, for providing false or misleading information to the Minister or for selling units before an identification number is obtained is imposed [ssec. 237.1(7.4)].

The Act imposes a further penalty for each month or part of a month, not exceeding 24 months, during which the failure to file the information return of transactions with related non-resident persons continues beyond 90 days of demand [ssec. 162(10)]. The penalty applies to persons or partnerships who knowingly or under circumstances amounting to gross negligence fail to file information returns relating to certain non-arm's length foreign investments whether or not demand has been served. The amount of the penalty is $500 per month where no demand is served and $1,000 per month where a demand is served and not complied with. In addition, the Act imposes an additional penalty where a return relating to foreign investments is more than 24 months overdue [ssec. 162(10.1)].

The onus of proof changes to the Minister where any penalty has been assessed under the Act [ssec. 163(3)]. Normally, the burden of establishing the facts is initially on the taxpayer. This provision, however, reverses this initial responsibility of establishing the facts by placing that responsibility on the Minister, but only where a penalty has been assessed.

Late-filed or amended returns and certain specific elections are dealt with in a series of provisions [ssecs. 220(3.1) to (3.7)]. These provisions have the effect of waiving interest and penalties assessed by the Minister. The "Fairness Package", as these provisions are referred to, was designed to improve the fairness of the tax system. Administrative guidelines are contained in IC 92-1, IC 92-2, and IC 92-3.[d]

Example Problem

Mr. Sums, the new controller of Secret Ltd., a CCPC, is in the process of preparing the company's 2005 T2 return. He notices a section of the return asking for information about the percentage ownership of the top three shareholders of the company. Secret Ltd. is so secretive that even Mr. Sums does not know exactly how many shares the president and vice-president own. He, therefore, sends the return to Mr. Close, the president. Mr. Close writes "None of your business" in that section of the return, signs it, and returns it to Mr. Sums for filing.

Mr. Sums, worried, calls you, Secret Ltd.'s tax adviser, and asks you to speak to Mr. Close. Mr. Sums says that all tax owing for the year has been paid and that the return will be filed on time.

— REQUIRED

What would you tell Mr. Close about the risks, if any, Secret Ltd. is running by not completing the section of the T2 return?

— SOLUTION

Secret Ltd. is required to file a tax return containing prescribed information [ssec. 150(1)]. Any information asked for on a form issued by the CRA is prescribed information, since such forms are prepared and released (in theory) by order of the Minister.

The CRA could, therefore, take the position that Secret Ltd. failed to file a return "as required" and assess a penalty [ssec. 162(1)]. No amount would be payable since the penalty for a first offence is 5% plus 1% per month of unpaid tax. However, should the CRA disagree with the company's calculation of tax payable, the penalty would be based on tax unpaid per the assessment or reassessment.

In any case, Secret Ltd. would likely be assessed the $100 minimum penalty for failing to provide complete information on a prescribed form [ssec. 162(5)]. Since subsection 162(5) applies, subsection 162(7) would not likely be applied in this case.

B. Objections and Appeals

[ITA: 165(1.11); 166.1(7); 166.2]

The contents of a valid notice of objection are specified for large corporations (i.e., those corporations subject to large corporations tax) [ssec. 165(1.11)]. Such an objection must specify each issue to be decided, the relief sought (expressed as the change in the amount of a particular balance such as income taxes payable) and the facts and reasons relied on by the corporation for each issue. In addition, only those issues and the related relief set out in the notice of objection can be the subject of further objection or appeal to the courts. However, any new issues raised by the CRA on subsequent reassessments may be the subject of a separate objection.

If the response by the appeals section of the CRA does not satisfy the taxpayer, he or she can apply to the Minister who can extend the filing deadline for the notice of objection in certain situations. An extension [ssec. 166.1(7)] is possible where:

(a) the application for the extension is made within one year after the deadline for filing the notice of objection;

---

[d] For a case on the exercise of Ministerial discretion under subsection 220(3.1) and the guidelines in IC 92-2 see *Floyd Estate v. M.N.R.*, (F.C.T.D) 93 DTC 5499.

(b) the taxpayer was unable to act or to instruct another to act in his or her name; and

(c) the taxpayer had a *bona fide* intention to object to the assessment.

The taxpayer must demonstrate that:

(a) it would be just and equitable for the Minister to grant his or her application; and

(b) the application was made as soon as circumstances permitted.

The Minister's decision to refuse an application can be appealed to the Tax Court of Canada [sec. 166.2]. The appeal to the Tax Court of Canada must be made in writing by summarizing the facts and the grounds for appeal, the conditions of which are similar to those described above on an application to the Minister. This must be done:

(a) within 90 days after the day on which the notification of refusal was given; or

(b) after 90 days from the mailing of the application for extension if there has been no reply to the Notice of Objection.

Appeals are heard by one of the judges of the Tax Court of Canada and they may be heard *in camera* (i.e., closed to the public) on request. The Tax Court of Canada can, at its discretion, award costs to the taxpayer.

Section 12(1) of the *Tax Court of Canada Act* provides that the Tax Court of Canada has exclusive jurisdiction to hear appeals under the Act and certain other federal statutes. The taxpayer is given the option of an "informal procedure" or a "general procedure".

The informal procedure may be elected when the amount of federal tax and penalties at issue for one taxation year is $12,000 or less, or the amount of the loss is $24,000 or less, or the only subject matter is interest assessed under the Act. The only requirement of the informal procedure is that the appeal is submitted in writing. Court rules of evidence are flexible and, hence, the taxpayer, other than a corporation, can represent himself/herself or be represented by an agent (i.e., any individual) who need not be a lawyer. The Minister has 45 days to reply to the appeal. The court must fix a hearing for no later than 90 days following the day the Minister files a reply to the original appeal. Judgments must be rendered within 60 days of the hearing unless exceptional circumstances prevail. If the taxpayer is more than 50% successful, the court may award costs. Normally, the taxpayer cannot appeal a Tax Court decision reached using the informal procedure and the decision cannot be used as a precedent in subsequent cases. However, there may be a judicial review by the Federal Court of Appeal on errors of law or erroneous findings of fact found in a capricious manner. If the Minister appeals to the Federal Court, the taxpayer's costs must be covered by the Minister. The introduction of the informal procedure is intended to ensure that most taxpayers can have their cases resolved quickly, simply, and at a low cost.

Where the general procedure is chosen in the Tax Court of Canada, the Court will be bound by strict rules of evidence. The taxpayer can only represent himself/herself or be represented by legal counsel. Where a case has not been heard or terminated within one year after the reply to the original appeal is filed, the case may be dismissed for delay, the appeal may be allowed, or the case may be heard based on the facts filed with the appeal. If a judgment is not rendered within 75 days, the appellant may apply for a motion for judgment. Costs are in the court's discretion. In this general procedure, the taxpayer can appeal the decision of the Tax Court to the Federal Court of Appeal and the Tax Court decision can be used as a precedent in other cases.[e]

An appeal to the Federal Court of Appeal from a decision of the Tax Court of Canada can be made by either the taxpayer or the CRA. This must be done within 30 days from the date of mailing of the decision of the Tax Court of Canada [ssec. 180(1)].

The ultimate court of appeal for tax cases in Canada is the Supreme Court of Canada. An appeal can be made to the Supreme Court only if the Federal Court of Appeal decides that the issue should be referred to the Supreme Court, or if the Supreme Court authorizes the appeal, which it will do only where there is an issue of national importance. At this level, questions of legal interpretation are raised rather than questions of fact alone.

Example Problem

Wall Talk Inc., a wallpaper manufacturing company incorporated and with its head office in the U.S., sells wallpaper in Canada through a full-time employee, Mr. Zale. He lives in the U.S. and returns there on weekends and for holidays, spending his weekdays travelling throughout Canada. He signs the contracts but all merchandise is shipped from the U.S.

The Canadian operation rents a small hotel room in Toronto on a year-round basis which is empty except for the days Mr. Zale is in town. He stores some samples there and receives some voice-mail messages there. Urgent messages go to the U.S. office. In 2004, the U.S. company bought a car for $15,000 for Mr. Zale to use in Canada.

No Canadian income tax returns have ever been filed by Wall Talk Inc. However, acting on information provided by a dissatisfied customer, the CRA on May 13, 2005 mailed a notice of assessment to the Toronto office in respect of the 2004 taxation year. The $100,000 of taxable income was based on Canadian sales figures provided in the U.S. company's financial statements. In addition to Part I tax, the notice of assessment included interest, penalties and an additional 25% Part XIV tax.

Due to a combination of business in Western Canada and his annual vacation, Mr. Zale did not return to the Toronto office and, hence, did not get the notice of assessment until August 20, 2005. Wall Talk Inc.'s U.S. accountants sent it on to you on September 1, 2005.

— *REQUIRED*

What steps would you take on behalf of your client? What arguments would you put forth?

— *SOLUTION*

Although the 90 days allowed for filing a notice of objection [ssec. 165(1)] have expired, section 166.1 allows you to apply to the Minister for an order extending the time limit. The Minister cannot allow such an extension:

(a) unless the application to extend the time for objecting or appealing is made within one year after the expiration of the time otherwise limited by this Act for objecting to or appealing the assessment in respect of which the application is made; and

(b) unless the Minister is satisfied that,

(i) an objection or appeal would have been made within the time otherwise limited by the Act for so doing,

(ii) the taxpayer was unable to act or to instruct another to act in his or her name,

(iii) the application was brought as soon as circumstances permitted it to be brought, and

---

[e] Prior to proclamation of the new system, the system provided for an appeal to the Tax Court of Canada under what is essentially the "general procedure" described above. An appeal of a Tax Court of Canada decision could be made to the Federal Court–Trial Division. It was also possible to bypass the Tax Court of Canada and go directly to the Federal Court–Trial Division. Appeals from the judgments of the Trial Division were heard by the Federal Court of Appeal, under the old system.

(iv) there are reasonable grounds for objecting to or appealing the assessment.

If the Minister refuses Wall Talk Inc.'s application, it can appeal to the Tax Court of Canada.

In this case, the delay in receiving the notice of assessment would be a strong point in favour of the taxpayer.[f]

If the application was approved by the Minister, a notice of objection would be filed on the basis that Wall Talk Inc. was not subject to Canadian tax. Although it carries on business in Canada by virtue of having a full-time employee in Canada, soliciting orders and entering into contracts, the Canada–U.S. Tax Treaty prevents Canada from taxing Wall Talk Inc. unless it carries on business in Canada through a permanent establishment. You would argue that a hotel room irregularly occupied does not constitute a permanent establishment.

Furthermore, by the same treaty provision, the Part XIV "Branch Tax" cannot be imposed unless there was a permanent establishment.

You would also want to argue that even if the CRA considered there to be a permanent establishment, the income earned in Canada was less than $100,000, perhaps, because Mr. Zale's salary has not been deducted (assuming this was the case). In addition, branch tax is based on after-tax income after allowing for an investment allowance (e.g., the car purchase), rather than taxable income. Finally, branch tax is reduced to 5% by Article X of the Protocol to the Canada–U.S. Tax Treaty (1995).

C. Late-filed or Amended Elections

[ITA: 220(3.2)–(3.7); ITR: 600; IC 92-1]

Part of the Fairness Package pertains to elections under the Act or Regulations that do not specifically provide for late, amended or revoked elections [ssecs. 220(3.2) to (3.7)]. The elections which are affected by these rules are set out in Regulations [Reg. 600]. Some of the provisions which have been covered in the text so far are:

(a) capitalized interest [sec. 21];

(b) replacement properties [ssecs. 13(4), 14(6) and 44(1)]; and

(c) interspousal transfers at F.M.V. [ssec. 73(1)].

First, acceptance by the Minister of a late-filed, an amended or a revoked election is established [ssec. 220(3.2)]. For requests amde after 2004, there is a 10-year limit on requests under this provision.] For this purpose, designations made under the debt forgiveness rules [sec. 80] are considered to be elections. The taxpayer or partnership must apply for a time extension or permission to amend or revoke. IC 92-1 indicates that a request may be accepted if:

(a) the tax consequences to the taxpayer are unintended and there is evidence that the taxpayer took reasonable steps to comply with the law;

(b) the request arises out of circumstances beyond the taxpayer's control;

(c) the taxpayer acted on incorrect information provided by the Minister;

(d) the request arises from a mechanical error;

(e) the subsequent accounting of the transactions was such that the parties acted as if the election has been made; and

(f) the taxpayer was unaware of the provision and took remedial action as soon as possible.

---

[f] For other decisions on such a request, see, for example, *Kidd v. M.N.R.*, (T.C.C.) 83 DTC 639 and *Graphics Specialties v. M.N.R.*, (T.C.C.) 83 DTC 644.

A request will not be accepted if:

(a) it is reasonable to conclude that the request was made for retroactive tax planning;

(b) adequate records do not exist to verify the request; and

(c) the request is being made because the taxpayer was negligent or careless.

Two provisions have the effect of backdating or cancelling elections and requiring the Minister to reassess taking into account these changes [ssecs. 220(3.3) and (3.4)].

The Act provides for a penalty in situations where the taxpayer's application has been accepted [ssec. 220(3.5)]. The penalty is $100 for each complete month from the due date of the election to the application date to a maximum of $8,000.

Some sections of the Act have their own penalties for late-filed or amended elections. (See, for example, subsection 85(8).) Often these elections are filed late because an audit reveals that the election was inadvertently omitted. The late-filing penalty may be substantially less than the benefit from the election.

D.   Enforcement and Collections

[ITA: 222–226; 231–232]

Direct contact between the taxpayer and the CRA is generally made through one of the almost 30 District Tax Services Offices. Trained assessors and special investigators who conduct desk audits of an individual's return or field audits of business returns are located in these offices.

The Head Office in Ottawa supervises and directs the activities of the District Tax Services Offices. It serves to maintain efficiency and uniformity of treatment across Canada. In addition, a number of regional Taxation Centres are maintained to do routine operations and the initial processing of all individual income tax returns.

The sweeping powers of investigation previously available to the CRA [secs. 231 to 231.2] have been subjected to judicial safeguards as a result of amendments. Tax officials may enter the taxpayer's places of business, property, places where anything is done in connection with the business or places where records are kept. However, where the place where the records are kept is a "dwelling house", officials may not enter without either the permission of the occupant or a court-issued warrant [ssec. 231.1(2)]. The CRA may audit the books and records, examine all property and require that assistance be given and that questions be answered. Seizure of books and records for evidence must be carried out by means of a warrant, and a taxpayer may apply to the courts to have documents returned [sec. 231.3]. Finally, the Minister is allowed to demand information or documents from third parties after obtaining judicial authorization [sec. 231.2]. This would include information from the files of the taxpayer's accountant, which are not protected by the confidentiality which applies to solicitor–client communications.

The primary method of collection is based on withholding of tax at the source of payment and instalment payments. However, the Act grants the CRA further powers to collect unpaid taxes. The following is a brief outline of these powers.

(1) The CRA may obtain a judgment against a tax defaulter [sec. 223] by registering with the Federal Court a certificate showing the amount owed. If payment is not made, the judgment can be enforced by the seizure and sale of the taxpayer's property.

(2) Under the power of garnishment, the CRA may order a person who owes money to a taxpayer to make a payment on account of the taxpayer's liability for tax [sec. 224].

(3) The Act provides for the seizure and sale at public auction of certain property of the taxpayer whether or not the assessment at issue is under objection or appeal [sec. 225].

(4) The CRA may also demand immediate payment from a taxpayer whom it believes is about to leave Canada [sec. 226].

Taxpayers are required to pay all amounts owing forthwith upon mailing of a notice of assessment or reassessment [sec. 158]. However, the CRA is not permitted to exercise its collection powers [sec. 225.1]:

(a) for 90 days after the date of assessment, if no Notice of Objection is filed;

(b) for 90 days after an assessment is upheld following a Notice of Objection, if no appeal is made to the courts; or

(c) until the decision of the court is rendered.

For a "large corporation", the normal rules [ssecs. 225.1(1) to (4)] are overridden [ssec. 225.1(7)]. This provision allows the Minister of National Revenue to collect ½ of any assessed amount disputed by a "large corporation". The definition of a large corporation is discussed in Chapter 11. Generally, a large corporation is defined as a corporation which is liable for large corporation tax.

If an appeal to a higher court is undertaken, security may be posted in lieu of payment of taxes owing.

Collection action may be taken earlier (subject to judicial review) if a delay could reasonably jeopardize collection. Under more restricted circumstances, tax already paid may be refunded during the appeal process.

Chapter 15

Corporate Distributions, Windings-up and Sales

TOPICS DISCUSSED

	Page
CORPORATE SURPLUS BALANCES	803
Overview	803
Paid-up Capital of Shares	803
Capital Dividend Account	805
USE OF CORPORATE SURPLUS BALANCES	810
Taxable dividends in cash or stock	810
Dividends in kind	810
Deemed dividends	810
Capital dividend	817
WINDING-UP OF A CANADIAN CORPORATION	818

	Page
Disposition of Net Assets of the Corporation	818
Deemed Dividend on Winding-up	819
Application of the Winding-up Rules	821
SALE OF AN INCORPORATED BUSINESS	823
Assets vs. Shares	823
Analysis for the Decision	824
GST AND THE WINDING-UP OF A CANADIAN CORPORATION	832
SUPPLEMENTAL NOTES	847
GST and the Sale of an Incorporated Business	847

This chapter deals primarily with transactions between corporations and their shareholders involving the accumulated surplus of a corporation or the value of its shares. The discussion begins with distributions of corporate surplus. The chapter follows with a discussion of the winding-up of a corporation and the sale of a corporation in terms of assets or shares. All of these topics can be extremely complex. Therefore, this chapter will introduce only the general concepts and the basic calculations, rather than cover all aspects of the topics.

The following chart will help to locate the major provisions of the Act discussed in this Chapter.

PART I — DIVISION B
SUBDIVISION H
CANADIAN CORPORATIONS AND THEIR SHAREHOLDERS

DIVISION		SUBDIVISION		SECTION	
A	Liability for tax				
B	**Computation of income**		Basic rules		
C	Computation of taxable income	a	Office or employment		
D	Taxable income earned in Canada by non-residents	b	Business and property		
		c	Capital gains and losses		
E	Computation of tax	d	Other income		
E.1	Minimum tax	e	Other deductions		
F	Special rules	f	Rules relating to computation of income		
G	Deferred and other special income arrangements	g	Amounts not included in income		
H	Exemptions	h	**Cdn corporations and shareholders**	82	Taxable dividends
I	Returns, Assessments, payments, appeals			83(1)	Tax-deferred dividends
				83(2)-(5)	Capital dividends
J	Appeals to the courts	i	Shareholders of non-resident corporations	84(1)	Deemed dividend
				84(2)	Winding-up dividend
				84(3)	Redemption dividend
		j	Partnerships	84(4)	PUC reduction dividend
		k	Trusts	84.1-84.2	NAL sale of shares
				85	Transfer of property to a corporation
				85.1	Share-for-share exchange
				86	Reorg of capital
				87	Amalgamation
				88	Winding-up
				89	Definitions

I. CORPORATE SURPLUS BALANCES

A. Overview

[ITA: 82; 83(2); 84; 88; 89(1)]

The shareholders' equity section of a balance sheet has to be analyzed to arrive at the balances in the tax surplus accounts. The basic components are capital stock and retained earnings. Exhibit 15-1 is a schematic representation of a tax-basis balance sheet.

EXHIBIT 15-1
Tax-Basis Balance Sheet

ASSETS	LIABILITIES
	CAPITAL STOCK Paid-up Capital (P.U.C.)
	RETAINED EARNINGS 1. Capital Dividend Account 2. Undistributed Surplus
XXXX	XXXX

Retained earnings can be subdivided into two amounts. The capital dividend account (CDA) generally represents the non-taxed portion of net capital gains and a portion of proceeds from eligible capital property. This account provides for the integration of capital gains through a private corporation as discussed in a previous chapter. The other amount might be termed "undistributed surplus" because it has no special tax surplus designation. It consists primarily of income generated and not distributed through dividends or other means.

Corporate surplus can be distributed in a variety of ways. Paid-up capital, discussed below, can be returned as a tax-free capital receipt to shareholders under certain conditions. The capital dividend account of a private corporation can be used to pay tax-free dividends through an election [ssec. 83(2)]. Finally, most distributions of corporate surplus are made in the form of taxable dividends.

B. Paid-up Capital of Shares

[ITA: 89(1); IT-463R2]

Paid-up capital (P.U.C.) is an important tax concept as it is the amount which the corporation can return to the shareholder without it being reported as a dividend to the shareholder. The rationale for this tax-free return is that P.U.C. was contributed from the after-tax funds of the shareholder on the initial investment in corporate shares. Therefore, P.U.C. should not be taxed as a dividend on its return. However, on a *disposition* of shares by the shareholder it is the adjusted cost base, not the paid-up capital that is used to determine the gain or loss.

The definition of "paid-up capital" [ssec. 89(1)] indicates that initially the paid-up capital for tax purposes is determined in accordance with the corporate law governing the particular corporation under discussion (i.e., legal stated capital (L.S.C.)). Depending on the particular corporate law, the initial paid-up capital may refer to the stated capital of the shares, the par value of the shares or the consideration paid for the shares. However, there are a number of adjustments to the initial P.U.C. or stated capital, some of which will be examined in subsequent chapters. Therefore, P.U.C. for tax purposes and stated capital for accounting purposes may not be the same. These differences are seldom disclosed in the notes to the financial statements.

Note that paragraph (*a*) in the definition of P.U.C. in subsection 89(1) defines the paid-up capital of a share in terms of the average paid-up capital of the entire class. As a result, the paid-up capital of a particular share may not be the same amount as that paid for the share on its original issue. For example, further issues of shares from the same class at different amounts will change the paid-up capital of a particular share after such subsequent issues. Hence the paid-up capital per share is an average, over time, of issue prices of shares in a particular class.

Consider the following example for illustrative purposes.

Joe incorporated Smithco Inc. five years ago and paid $1,000 to the corporation for 1,000 common shares. His ACB of these shares is $1,000 and the PUC at the corporate level is $1,000.

This year Joe needed additional capital for expansion. Bill agreed to invest $100,000 for an additional 1,000 fully-paid common shares to be issued from Smithco Inc. After this transaction, Joe will still have an ACB on his 1,000 shares of $1,000. Bill will have an ACB on his 1,000 common shares of $100,000. At the corporate level the PUC will be $101,000. Since the PUC is allocated equally among the shares of that class it means that Joe's shares have a PUC of $50,500 and Bill's shares have a PUC of $50,500.

Most jurisdictions in Canada now permit only shares without par value. Examples of such corporate laws are the *Canada Business Corporations Act*, the *Ontario Business Corporations Act* and the *Alberta Business Corporations Act*. With respect to corporations governed by such Acts, the P.U.C. is the "stated capital" as determined by the directors of the corporation. Generally, this stated capital will be the fair market value of the consideration for which the shares were issued. However, these statutes provide that, in connection with certain non-arm's length transactions, the corporation may establish a stated capital amount which is less than the consideration for which the shares were issued. This reduced stated capital (i.e., less than the fair market value of the consideration received) will then be the initial amount of P.U.C. for tax purposes. Accordingly, a corporation may, under most jurisdictions, establish shares with a low P.U.C. and a high redemption amount (commonly referred to as "high-low shares"). In a few situations, the corporate law may not permit the creation of such shares and, in such event, it will be necessary for an alternative approach to be considered. The significance of these shares will become more evident when the topic of redemption of shares is discussed later in the chapter.

In jurisdictions which permit both par value and no par value shares to be issued, the P.U.C. with respect to the par value shares will generally be equal to the par value of the shares. When such par value shares are issued for property with a fair market value greater than the par value of the shares such surplus amount (contributed surplus in accounting terms) can be converted to paid-up capital [par. 84(1)(*c*.3)] as long as the transaction(s) was (were) not accomplished on a (tax-free) rollover basis. Amounts so converted will have been contributed to the corporation with after-tax or tax-paid property and, hence, should logically be accessible on distribution to shareholders on a tax-free basis. Generally, the P.U.C. with respect to the no par value or stated value shares will be equal to the fair market value of the property transferred to the corporation and for which the corporation issued such shares, except for certain reorganizations with non-arm's length parties, as previously mentioned.

Conceptually, the paid-up capital is computed at the corporate level (not the shareholder level) by reference to all the shares of a particular class. However, the amount of paid-up capital is relevant to any shareholder on a redemption or cancellation of the shares. These events might occur when some of the shares of the corporation are redeemed or when all of the shares are, in essence, redeemed and cancelled on the winding-up of a corporation. On the other hand, the adjusted cost base is calculated only for the shares held by a particular shareholder (i.e., at the shareholder level, not the corporate level) and is relevant only where there is a disposition or deemed disposition of the shares. However, since a redemption or cancellation of shares involves a disposition of the shares held by a shareholder, any deemed dividend arising on the redemption or cancellation (e.g., a subsection 84(2) or 84(3) deemed dividend) must be removed in calculating the resultant capital gain or loss. (Refer to the definition of proceeds of disposition in section 54.) That deemed dividend is subject to tax, as such, separately and should not be double-counted in the capital gain or loss.

As will be demonstrated, the Act is very protective about amounts that are added to P.U.C., because amounts in P.U.C. can be distributed to shareholders without creating a deemed dividend. Therefore, amounts added to P.U.C. must represent the value of property contributed to the corporation with after-tax or tax-paid funds. If an amount added to P.U.C. does not represent tax-paid funds contributed to the corporation, then, usually, a deemed taxable dividend will result, so that the amount added to P.U.C. is tax paid.

Summary	
Paid-up capital PUC	**Adjusted cost base ACB**
Calculated at the corporate level:	Calculated at the shareholder level:
• Based on capital contributed to the corporation;	• Based on amount paid for the shares;
• Averaged among all shareholders of that class based on shares held;	• Unique to each shareholder;
Can be withdrawn from the company free of deemed dividend.	Considered on the disposition of the shares.

C. Capital Dividend Account

[ITA: 14; 83(2); 89(1); IT-66R6]

The purpose of the capital dividend account is to complete integration of corporate and personal income tax on capital gains and similar receipts. When an individual realizes a capital gain of, say, $400, the individual pays income tax on $1/2$ of the capital gain or $200. The other $200 is not taxed. When a private corporation realizes the same capital gain of $400, the private corporation is taxed (including additional refundable tax and net of any dividend refund) on $200. The other $1/2$ or $200 is added to the private corporation's capital dividend account, to be distributed tax free to the corporation's shareholders. This is done to ensure that the integration concept applies to capital gains.

1. Components of the account

This post-1971 account begins to accumulate amounts only for corporations. For most corporations, the period covered would be from the date of incorporation, but this cannot be earlier than January 1, 1972.

Conceptually, for the purposes of this Chapter, this account includes five basic components:

(a) the portion of net capital gains (i.e., capital gains in excess of capital losses) not recognized in computing income for tax purposes, that is, the non-taxable portion of net capital gains, *plus*

(b) capital dividends received from another corporation, *plus*

(c) the portion of net gain not recognized in the cumulative eligible capital account, that is, the non-taxable portion of the excess of proceeds over recaptured CECA claims, on the disposition of eligible capital property, *plus*

(d) proceeds arising on death from certain life insurance policies received by the corporation net of the cost basis of the policies, *minus*

(e) capital dividends paid.

The balance of this account is computed for the entire period (refer to the next session for a discussion of "the period") as the sum of the following amounts described here in simplified terms:

(a) *the untaxed portion of net capital gains which is computed as:*

(i) the excess, if any, of all capital gains (net of capital losses), except those net gains removed by clause (a)(i)(C) of the definition, realized in this period

minus:

(ii) taxable capital gains (net of allowable capital losses) included in income during the period ($^1/_2$ for gains and losses realized before 1988, $^2/_3$ for gains and losses realized in 1988 and 1989, $^3/_4$ for gains and losses realized from 1990 to February 27, 2000, $^2/_3$ for gains and losses realized from February 28, 2000 to October 17, 2000 and $^1/_2$ thereafter);

(b) *paragraph (b) of the definition in subsection 89(1) — capital dividends received:* capital dividends [ssec. 83(2)] received from another corporation;

(c) *the untaxed portion of gains on eligible capital property:* for taxation years ending after October 17, 2000, the addition to the capital dividend account, at the end of a taxation year in which a disposition occurs, is equal to $^2/_3$ of the "gain" on the disposition of eligible capital property. The "gain" is considered to be the excess of a negative balance in the CEC pool over the cumulative CEC claims taken in prior years. This amount should be equal to the taxed portion of the negative balance. There may also be adjustments for pre-1988 deductions and exempt capital gains balances but these issues are not addressed in this book. Refer to Chapter 5 for the details of the cumulative eligible capital amount. The additions to this account in respect of eligible capital property for taxation years ended before October 18, 2000 are also not addressed.

(d) *untaxed insurance proceeds:* proceeds received, or in certain circumstances deemed to be received, as a result of death, from certain life insurance policies by the corporation in a period since it last became a private corporation, as a beneficiary of a policy, minus the adjusted cost basis of the policy;

minus (from the aggregate of the above four items)

(e) capital dividends paid or payable by the corporation.

Note that, technically, this account does not continue a balance from one year to the next with one year's opening balance being the previous year's closing balance. Each subparagraph accumulates from the beginning of "the period" to the particular time that a calculation of the balance in the account is being made. In this respect, notice that all subparagraphs except (b) require the inclusion of "the amount, *if any*, by which" the aggregate of one item exceeds another item. Thus, it is not possible to have a negative amount for these subparagraphs at a particular point in time. However, at a subsequent point in time the aggregate for one of these subparagraphs may be positive after offsetting aggregate losses or expenditures at that particular time.

2. "The period"

As indicated previously, the specific wording of the definition of the "capital dividend account" [ssec. 89(1)] must be read very carefully (not just the above summary) when actually doing the capital dividend account calculation. The major confusion relates to the various time periods referred to. The first time period is described in clause (a)(i)(A) and, as discussed above, is referred to as "the period". Since only private corporations can have a capital dividend account, this concept is important when corporations can change their characteristics (e.g., a private corporation becomes a public corporation upon the listing of its shares or acquisition of control by a public corporation or a public corporation becomes a private corporation under prescribed conditions). For private corporations, which were incorporated prior to 1972, this time period starts "on the first day of the first taxation year commencing after the corporation last became a private corporation", or January 1, 1972, the day upon which the tax legislation made a distinction between public and private corporations (see the definitions in subsection 89(1)), if that date is later. Note, however, that the subparagraphs dealing with the disposition of eligible capital property and life insurance proceeds received, use the term "the period" to refer to this time condition. Hence, the balance date for the cumulative eligible capital account "at the commencement of the period" would be January 1, 1972 for corporations incorporated prior to 1972 and, as a result, would have a nil balance. Similarly, private corporations incorporated after 1971 would have a nil balance in the cumulative eligible capital account on the first day they became private corporations. However, for public corporations which become private corporations, there may very well be a balance in the cumulative eligible capital account on this day.

3. Examples of disposition of eligible capital property

Facts: A Canadian-controlled private corporation with a fiscal year-end of December 31, had the following transactions.

Cost of eligible capital property on November 30, 2003	$12,000
Proceeds of disposition on January 15, 2005	20,000

As of January 1, 2003 the corporation had no balance in its CEC pool.

Solution:

CEC Account	
E.C.E. × ³/₄ [$12,000 × ³/₄]	$ 9,000
C.E.C.A. – 2003 [7%]	(630)
Balance December 31, 2003	$ 8,370
C.E.C.A. – 2004 [7%]	(586)
Balance December 31, 2004	$ 7,784
E.C.A. × ³/₄ [$20,000 × ³/₄]	(15,000)
Negative balance	$ (7,216)

Previous CECA   1,216
Final balance . . . . $ (6,000)

Income inclusion on December 31, 2005 [subsection 14(1)]
  Recapture of previous CECA . . . . $ 1,216
  $^2/_3$ × final balance ($6,000)   4,000
    Income* . . . . $ 5,216

Capital dividend account at December 31, 2005
  $^2/_3$ × final balance ($6,000) . . . . $ 4,000

This is equal to 50% of the economic gain on the eligible capital property i.e., 50% × [$20,000 − $12,000].

* The total of:
  (a) the lesser of:
     (i) $7,216; and
     (ii) $630 + $586 = $1,216
     the lesser is . . . . $ 1,216
  (b) $^2/_3$ × [$7,216 − $1,216]   4,000
    Income . . . . $ 5,216

Example Problem

Surplus Accumulation Ltd. provides you with the following information:

Dispositions during the fiscal year ended December 31, 2005.

	Cost	Selling costs	Proceeds
Land	$20,000	$ 1,500	$35,000
Equipment	5,000	100	500
Securities	3,000	200	2,000

Capital dividends [ssec. 83(2)] received since 1971 . . . . $10,000
Capital dividends [ssec. 83(2)] paid since 1971   5,000

In 1995, the corporation purchased goodwill for $6,000 and has deducted CECA of $2,325 to the present. In 2005, it sold an indefinite-life franchise for $19,000.

— REQUIRED

Compute the balance in the corporation's capital dividend account as at December 31, 2005.

— SOLUTION

Capital dividend account:

Par. (*a*) of the definition in subsection 89(1)
Land
  P of D . . . . $ 35,000
  A.C.B. $20,000
  Selling costs   1,500   21,500
  Capital gain . . . . $ 13,500
    $^1/_2{}^1$ thereof . . . . $ 6,750

Equipment
   (No capital loss on depreciable property) .... Nil

Securities
   P of D .... $ 2,000
   A.C.B. .... $ 3,000
   Selling costs 200   3,200
   Capital loss................................... $ (1,200)

      $\frac{1}{2}$ thereof .... (600)

Excess .... $ 6,150

Par. (*b*) of the definition in subsection 89(1)
Ssec. 83(2) dividends received 10,000

Par. (*c*) of the definition in subsection 89(1)
   CEC balance ($6,000 × $\frac{3}{4}^2$ – $2,325$) .... $ 2,175
   Proceeds × $\frac{3}{4}$ ($19,000 × $\frac{3}{4}$)..................... (14,250)
   Negative balance................................. $(12,075)
   Recaptured CECA (income) 2,325
             $ (9,750)

   Income ($\frac{2}{3}^3$ × $9,750 + $2,325$) .... $ 8,825

   Capital dividend account ($\frac{2}{3}^3$ × $9,750$) .... $ 6,500

             $22,650

Less: ssec. 83(2) dividends paid................................. (5,000)

Balance — December 31, 2005 .... $17,650

The following alternative format may be useful to keep track of the transactions, particularly when they occur in different years.

				Capital dividend account			
Year	Asset	Untaxed fraction of net cap. gains	Capital dividend received	Untaxed fraction of net gain on E.C.P.	Untaxed life ins. proceeds	Capital dividend paid	Balance
1995	Goodwill			(3,000)[4]			
2005	Land	$6,750					
	Equipment	Nil					
	Securities	(600)					
	Franchise			$9,500[4]			
	Capital dividend received		$10,000				
	Capital dividend paid.....					($5,000)	
		$6,150	$10,000	$ 6,500		$(5,000)	$17,650

—NOTES TO SOLUTION

(1) The one-half rate represents the current untaxed portion of the capital gain which is computed in paragraph (*a*) of the definition in subsection 89(1) as the full capital gain minus the taxable capital gain at the $\frac{1}{2}$ inclusion rate.

(2) Subparagraph (*c*)(vi) of the definition in subsection 89(1) deals with acquisitions before the adjustment time.

(3) Because the CEC pool uses the ³/₄ inclusion rate, the fraction used here (²/₃) brings the result to ¹/₂ (³/₄ × ²/₃ = ¹/₂). This can be roughly equated to the capital gains calculation by taking one-half of the gain into income and the other half into the capital dividend account. For example, $19,000 of proceeds – $6,000 cost = $13,000 gain.

(4) Neither the amount in respect of the cost of goodwill (in effect, ¹/₂ × $6,000 = $3,000) nor the amount in respect of the proceeds of disposition for the franchise (in effect, ¹/₂ × $19,000 = $9,500) affects the capital dividend account balance until the end of the year of the disposition, in this case, of the franchise.

II. USE OF CORPORATE SURPLUS BALANCES

A. Taxable dividends in cash or stock

[ITA: 52(3)(*a*)]

Corporate surpluses are used in the process of paying dividends. Dividends may be paid in cash, stock or kind. Where a stock dividend is paid by any corporation, it will be taxed in the same manner as a taxable dividend paid in cash. The definition of "dividend" [ssec. 248(1)] includes a stock dividend. However, the amount [ssec. 248(1)] of the dividend will be deemed to be equal to the increase in the corporation's paid-up capital as a result of the stock dividend. This amount is used regardless of the fair market value of the shares received. This same amount will be considered to be the shareholder's cost of the shares received [par. 52(3)(*a*)].

B. Dividends in kind

[ITA: 40(3.3), (3.4); 52(2)]

It is possible for a corporation to declare a dividend to be paid neither in cash nor in shares but in assets of the corporation. Such dividends are known as dividends in kind or in *specie*. The tax effect of declaring a dividend in kind is equivalent to the corporation selling the assets for fair market value and paying a cash dividend with the proceeds of disposition. Thus, as a result of paying a dividend in kind:

(a) the corporation is deemed to have disposed of the assets at their fair market value;

(b) the shareholders are deemed to have acquired the assets at their fair market value [ssec. 52(2)]; and

(c) the corporation is considered to have paid and the shareholders are considered to have received a dividend equal to the fair market value of the assets distributed.

A loss to the corporation on the transfer of the assets to a controlling shareholder is denied [ssecs. 40(3.3) and (3.4)].

C. Deemed dividends

[ITA: 40(3.6); 53(2)(*a*); 84; 251.1]

Generally, anything in a corporation's equity that is not P.U.C. or a capital dividend account balance is taxable retained earnings. The only way those retained earnings can be distributed by the corporation to a shareholder is by a taxable dividend. Therefore, any distribution made by a corporation to a shareholder in excess of P.U.C. and not elected as a capital dividend or declared as a taxable dividend will be deemed to be a dividend that will be taxable. Dividends may be deemed to have been paid in certain situations listed in section 84.

Conceptually, distributions from a corporation to a shareholder can be monitored by the following diagram of the simple equity accounts:

Simple equity		*Distribution*
P.U.C. $xxxxx	↓	Not taxable as a dividend
Capital dividend account xxxxx	↓	Not taxable by election of capital dividend
Retained Earnings xxxxx	↓	Taxable dividend (declared or deemed)

Amounts distributed from P.U.C. or the capital dividend account are not taxable to the shareholders as a dividend. Once a distribution has dipped into the retained earnings pool, the part of the distribution from retained earnings will be a taxable dividend, because the only way that these retained earnings can be distributed is by a taxable dividend.

1. Deemed Dividend on Increase in P.U.C.

A deemed dividend may occur where a corporation increases its paid-up capital without a corresponding increase in net assets [ssec. 84(1)]. This situation might arise on the sale of property to a corporation (other than on a tax-free rollover basis discussed in the next chapter). In that case, the paid-up capital of the shares issued might exceed the fair market value of the property transferred to the corporation net of the value of debt issued by the corporation. The amount of the resultant deemed dividend is added to the adjusted cost base of the shareholders' shares [par. 53(1)(b)], so that it is not taxed again as a capital gain on the disposition of the shares. The paid-up capital of a class of shares has considerable tax significance in limiting the amount that a corporation can return to its shareholders without being taxed as a dividend.[a] Thus, subsection 84(1) prevents a corporation from arbitrarily increasing this limit. The provision ensures that increases in paid-up capital represent contributions of after-tax funds or tax-paid property to the corporation. However, subsection 84(1) will not apply in the following situations, among others:

(a) where the increase in paid-up capital results from the payment of a stock dividend because other tax consequences will result as discussed previously [par. 84(1)(a)];

(b) where the paid-up capital is increased as a result of an equivalent or greater increase in net assets at fair market value as would be the case on the issue of shares for cash or other assets or on the issue of shares for existing debt [par. 84(1)(b)];

---

[a] While the return of capital represented by paid-up capital is not taxed as a dividend, there may still be a capital gain or loss as will be shown subsequently.

(c) where the paid-up capital of one class of shares is decreased and the paid-up capital of another class is increased by an amount not greater than the decrease of the first class [par. 84(1)(c)] (i.e., where there has been no net increase in the paid-up capital of the corporation);[b] and

(d) where a corporation converts its contributed surplus that arose on the issuance of shares into paid-up capital except those transactions which involve the tax-free rollover provisions as discussed in Chapters 16 and 17 [par. 84(1)(c.3)].

The following numerical examples summarize these rules for a deemed dividend under subsection 84(1), showing the conditions for the exception in paragraph 84(1)(b):

	A	B	C
Facts			
Increase in F.M.V. of net assets (cash)	$ 100	$ 90	$ 110
Increase in P.U.C. of shares issued	$ 100	$ 100	$ 100
Results			
Ssec. 84(1) deemed dividend			
Increase in paid-up capital	$ 100	$ 100	$ 100
Minus: net assets increase, if any	(100)	(90)	(110)
Excess, if any (i.e., ssec. 84(1) deemed dividend)	Nil	$ 10	Nil
Contributed surplus (which can only be distributed by a taxable dividend unless converted to P.U.C.) (see point (d) above)	Nil	Nil	$ 10

2. Deemed Dividend on Winding-up

A deemed dividend will result where a corporation distributes its assets to its shareholders on winding-up or reorganization [ssec. 84(2)]. This process will be discussed in more detail later in this chapter and will be seen to be very similar to the results of a redemption discussed next.

3. Deemed Dividend on Redemption, Acquisition or Cancellation of Shares

Where a corporation redeems, acquires or cancels its shares, there will be a deemed dividend [ssec. 84(3)] to the extent of the excess of the amount paid by the corporation on the redemption (redemption price) over the paid-up capital of the shares. The redemption price is normally the fair market value of the shares. In addition to the subsection 84(3) dividend, there may also be a capital gain or loss on the transaction. However, to remove the element of double taxation, the proceeds for capital gain (loss) purposes are reduced by the amount of the subsection 84(3) deemed dividend [par. (j) in the definition of "proceeds of disposition" in sec. 54].

Example Problem

Ms. T incorporated a company with an initial capitalization of 10 common shares @ $10 per share.

During the second year of operation, the corporation entered into a transaction which resulted in an ACB reduction under subsection 53(2) of $4 per share.

In the third year of operations, Ms. T acquired an additional 10 common shares @ $20 per share of paid-up capital equal to the fair market value.

---

[b] Under the tax-free rollover provisions discussed in Chapters 16 and 17, there is usually no subsection 84(1) deemed dividend, because the potential paid-up capital increase is offset by an equal reduction.

Two years later, Ms. T caused the corporation to redeem 5 of her shares at the then fair market value of $50.

— REQUIRED

Indicate the tax consequences of the above transactions.

— SOLUTION

First year: Ms. T's shares have an adjusted cost base and paid-up capital of $10 per share.

Second year: Ms. T's shares have an adjusted cost base of $6 per share (i.e., $10 – $4) but the paid-up capital remains the same at $10 per share.

Third year: Ms. T's shares have an adjusted cost base of $13 per share:

($10 – $4) × 10 shares =	$ 60
$20 × 10 shares =	200
20	$ 260

Ms. T's shares have a paid-up capital per share of $15:

$10 × 10 shares =	$ 100
$20 × 10 shares =	200
20	$ 300

Fifth year: Deemed dividend on redemption [ssec. 84(3)]

Redemption price ($50 × 5 shares) =	$ 250
Paid-up capital ($15 × 5 shares) =	75
Deemed dividend	$ 175

Capital gain (loss)

Proceeds of disposition (redemption amount) (5 shares @ $50)	$ 250
Less: ssec. 84(3) dividend by virtue of par. (*j*) of definition in sec. 54	175
Adjusted proceeds of disposition (equal to P.U.C.)	$ 75
Adjusted cost base ($13 × 5 shares)	65
Capital gain	$ 10

Reconciliation

Economic gain		
Actual proceeds (5 shares @ $50)		$ 250
Cost (5 shares @ $13)		65
		$ 185
Deemed dividend — ssec. 84(3)	$ 175	
Capital gain	10	$ 185

Comments

The effect of the subsection 53(2) reduction of the A.C.B. in the second year was a capital gain upon the ultimate disposition.

Assuming this redemption occurs now in a province with a provincial personal tax on income rate of 17%, and a dividend tax credit rate of 6 ⅔% of the grossed-up dividend, then the deemed dividend of $175 would bear tax at a top rate of 32.5% (see Note (1) below), whereas the capital gain of $10 would bear a tax rate of 23% (see Note (2) below). Therefore, given a choice, a taxpayer would prefer a capital gain on an outright sale rather than a deemed dividend. For example, if Ms. T wanted to sell one-half of her shares to one of her employees, then it would be to Ms. T's advantage to sell her shares to the employee directly, rather than to redeem her shares and then have the corporation sell treasury shares to the employee.

— *NOTES TO SOLUTION*

(1) $(100\% \times 1.25) \rightarrow 125\% \times [(.29 + .17) - (.1333 + .0667)] = 32.5\%$

(2) $(\frac{1}{2} \times 100\%) \rightarrow 50\% \times (.29 + .17) = 23\%$ (ignoring surtaxes)

As demonstrated in the previous example problem, on a redemption of shares, the proceeds of disposition for the calculation of the capital gain or loss will be equal to the PUC used for the calculation of the deemed dividend. This works since the adjusted proceeds for capital gains purposes is equal to the actual proceeds minus the deemed dividend which must mathematically equal the PUC. The implications of this are that where the PUC and the ACB are different there will either be a capital gain (PUC > ACB) or a capital loss (PUC < ACB).

If there is a capital loss on the redemption of shares, then subsection 40(3.6) may deny the loss. This provision applies if the shareholder and the corporation are "affiliated" [section 251.1] immediately after the redemption. For a shareholder and the redeeming corporation to be affiliated the shareholder, his or her spouse or common law partner or a corporation that they control must control the redeeming corporation. If that is the case then the capital loss will be denied and added to the ACB of any shares that the redeeming shareholder has.

Consider the following example for illustrative purposes.

Mr. A owns all 100 common shares and all 1,000 Class A shares of Aco Inc. The ACB and PUC of these shares are as follows:

	ACB	PUC
Common	$100	$100
Class A	$1,000	$100

If the Class A shares are redeemed for $2,000 then there will be a deemed dividend of $1,900 and a capital loss of $900. Since Mr. A owns all of the common shares he controls, and is, therefore, affiliated with Aco Inc., so subsection 40(3.6) would apply to deny the capital loss of $900 and add it to the ACB of Mr. A's common shares.

	ACB	PUC
Common	$1,000	$100
	($100 + $900)	

As a result, the common shares will have an ACB of $1,000 and the PUC will remain the same at $100.

Consider the following example for illustrative purposes.

Redemption of Shares

In summary, a redemption of shares involves a set of calculations that can be completed in two steps.

Step 1: Deemed dividend

Redemption amount	$xxx
Less: P.U.C. of shares redeemed...........................	xxx
Deemed dividend on redemption [ssec. 84(3)]	$xxx

In the context of the simple equity diagram introduced previously, note that the deemed dividend arises because the corporation has distributed an amount that exceeds the P.U.C. layer and, in the absence of a capital dividend account balance, dips into the retained earnings layer.

Step 2: Capital gain (loss)

Since the process of redeeming shares involves, in essence, a disposition by the shareholder [ssec. 84(9)], Step 2 computes first the adjusted proceeds of disposition and then any capital gain or loss:

Proceeds of disposition (redemption amount)	$xxx
Less: ssec. 84(3) deemed dividend — par. (*j*) of definition in sec. 54	xxx
Adjusted proceeds of disposition	$xxx
Adjusted proceeds of disposition	$xxx
Less: adjusted cost base	xxx
Capital gain (loss)	$xxx

Since a disposition includes a share redemption/cancellation, both a deemed dividend and a capital gain/loss may occur at the same time.

The deemed dividend provisions do not apply where a corporation purchases its shares on the open market in the same manner as any member of the public would purchase shares in the open market [par. 84(6)(*b*)].

In summary, the following differences between P.U.C. and A.C.B. of share capital should be noted.

P.U.C.	A.C.B.
(1) P.U.C. is utilized in determining the deemed dividend arising from a redemption and/or cancellation of a share.	(1) A.C.B. is utilized in determining the capital gain or capital loss on a disposition.
(2) P.U.C. is calculated at the corporate level and attaches itself to a particular class or series of shares, not to particular shareholders. Therefore, any increase or decrease in P.U.C. affects all shareholders equally.	(2) A.C.B. is calculated at the shareholder level and relates to a particular class or series held by a particular shareholder and may very well be a unique amount for each shareholder. For example, the price paid by each shareholder for his or her shares in an open market purchase will normally differ in each circumstance. However, the P.U.C. will be the same for each shareholder.

P.U.C. and A.C.B. have a number of separate and, in most cases, independent adjustments. P.U.C. adjustments are scattered throughout the reorganization sections of the Act and will be discussed in the next two chapters. A.C.B. adjustments are found in subsections 53(1) and (2) and may or may not affect each taxpayer on an identical basis.

4. Deemed Dividend on Reduction of P.U.C.

The fourth type of deemed dividend would occur in the occasional situation where a corporation considers it appropriate to return some of the shareholders' capital without redeeming any of the issued shares [ssec. 84(4)]. As an example of this situation, a corporation may divest itself of a major part of its business and pay the sale proceeds to its shareholders rather than reinvest those proceeds. Where such a payment is made by a private corporation and the paid-up capital of the shares is reduced by an amount equal to the payment, there will be no deemed dividend, by virtue of paragraph 84(1)(c), but the shareholders' adjusted cost base of the shares will be reduced [spar. 53(2)(a)(ii)]. A payment in excess of the paid-up capital will be a deemed dividend [ssec. 84(4)].

When a payment is made by a public corporation to reduce its paid-up capital, however, the entire payment is usually treated as a deemed dividend [ssec. 84(4.1)]. [The February 27, 2004 Revised Draft Legislation proposes to provide an exception to the deemed dividend in subsection 84(4.1) where the amount paid on a reduction of paid-up capital may reasonably be considered to be a distribution of proceeds realized by a public corporation from a transaction that occurred outside the ordinary course of the corporation's business and within the prior two-year period. The sale of a business unit of the corporation, for example, may be considered to give rise to proceeds eligible for distribution of paid-up capital. The distribution of normal earnings would not qualify, given these restrictions.]

That portion of the payment, which is deemed to be a dividend under either subsection 84(4) or (4.1), does not reduce the adjusted cost base of the shares, since the amount has already been included in income.

For example, if a private corporation makes a distribution of capital in the amount of $8 per share on shares with a paid-up capital of $10, but reduces the paid-up capital by only $7, there will be a deemed dividend of $1 [ssec. 84(4)]. Hence, if the corporation does not reduce its paid-up capital by the full amount of the distribution, the excess distribution is considered to be from taxable surplus and is taxed as a dividend. The adjusted cost base is reduced by the amount of this paid-up capital reduction, because cost has been reduced by the amount distributed as a return of paid-up capital, that is, $7 in the example.

Note that where a corporation reduces its paid-up capital (without making any payments to its shareholders in excess of the actual paid-up capital) there will be no tax consequences unless the shareholder's ACB is less than the reduction in which case there is a capital gain in the amount of the excess of the reduction over ACB. In addition, such a reduction in paid-up capital may be advantageous where share redemptions are anticipated (i.e., the smaller the P.U.C., the greater the subsection 84(3) deemed dividend) and shareholders in a low tax bracket would prefer a dividend to a capital gain.

Consider the following example for illustrative purposes.

In an earlier illustrative example two shareholders, Joe and Bill each owned 1,000 common shares of Smithco Inc. Their ACB and PUC were as follows.

	ACB	PUC
Joe	$1,000	$50,500
Bill	$100,000	$50,500

If the paid-up capital of Smithco Inc. is reduced by $101,000 there will not be a deemed dividend to either Joe or Bill since the amount of the reduction does not exceed the amount of the PUC. However, Joe will report a capital gain of $49,500 and the ACB of his 1,000 common shares will be nil. Bill will not report a capital gain, but the ACB of his 1,000 common shares will be $49,500.

Summary

To summarize the tax principles underlying the concept of a deemed dividend:

(a) a corporation may return its paid-up capital to the shareholders as a tax-free capital receipt with any excess being deemed to be a dividend; and

(b) a corporation may not increase its total paid-up capital beyond an increase in net assets without tax consequences.

D. Capital dividend

[ITA: 83; 184]

All dividends, whether actual or deemed, are taxable dividends unless some action is taken by the corporation prior to payment. The action that can be taken in the case of a private corporation in certain circumstances is to make an election to treat either an actual dividend or a deemed dividend as having been distributed from its capital dividend account [ssec. 83(2)]. Such a dividend is received tax-free by the shareholder. However, an election under subsection 83(2) in excess of the amount in the capital dividend account will result in a penalty tax under Part III of $^3/_5$ or 60% [proposed in the February 27, 2004 Revised Draft Legislation] of the excess.

There are situations envisaged by the Act in which an excess election is made inadvertently. For example, a corporation may compute the balance in its capital dividend account based on the assumption that a particular transaction resulted in a capital gain, rather than business income. On this basis, the corporation may have elected to distribute a capital dividend. Later, on reassessment, it may be determined that the gain on the transaction was business income and an amount must be removed from the capital dividend account. This could make the dividend paid in excess of the reassessed balance in the capital dividend account. Recognizing this possibility, an election which allows the corporation to avoid the 60% penalty is available [ssec. 184(3)]. This election allows the corporation to separate the dividend paid into a part that does not exceed the balance in the capital dividend account and a part that can be considered as a taxable dividend. The election must be made not later than 90 days after the day of mailing of the notice of assessment in respect of the 60% penalty.

Example Problem

Hum Along Records Ltd., a Canadian-controlled private corporation, has 5,000 outstanding preferred shares with a redemption and current fair market value of $6,000 and a paid-up capital value of $5,000 in total. The balance in its capital dividend account is $800. The company has decided to redeem the preferred shares at their fair market value and to properly elect a capital dividend on all preferred shares. As a result, a part of the deemed dividend on the redemption of the preferred shares will be a capital dividend.

— REQUIRED

What are the tax consequences to Mr. Hal Leluya who is unrelated to other shareholders and who owns 500 of the preferred shares which cost him $1.00 per share?

— SOLUTION

The following would be the results for the 10% shareholder:

Step 1: Deemed Dividend

Redemption amount paid (10% of $6,000)	$ 600
Less: P.U.C. of shares redeemed (10% of $5,000)	(500)
Deemed dividend on redemption [ssec. 84(3)]	$ 100
Capital dividend [ssec. 83(2)[1]] (10% of $800)	(80)
Taxable deemed dividend	$ 20

Step 2: Capital Gain (Loss)

Proceeds of disposition (redemption amount)	$ 600
Less: deemed dividend [ssec. 84(3)]	(100)
Adjusted proceeds of disposition [par. (j) of definition in sec. 54]	$ 500
Adjusted proceeds of disposition	$ 500
Less: adjusted cost base (500 shares × $1.00)	(500)
Capital loss	$ (nil)
Allowable capital loss	$ nil

— NOTE TO SOLUTION

(1) Since a capital dividend can only be elected on the full amount of a dividend [ssec. 83(2)], an election must be made to treat the excess of $20 as a taxable dividend [ssec. 184(3)].

III. WINDING-UP OF A CANADIAN CORPORATION

A. Disposition of Net Assets of the Corporation

[ITA: 69(5); 89(1); IT-126R2; IT-149R4; IT-463R2]

On the winding-up of a corporation, the assets could be liquidated on the open market with the net proceeds, after paying the liabilities, paid to the shareholders. Alternatively, the net assets might be distributed directly to the shareholders. If the second alternative is chosen, all property of the corporation so distributed is deemed to have been distributed at its fair market value immediately before the winding-up [ssec. 69(5)]. In either case, the disposition may result in income and losses within the corporation on the sale of current assets, such as inventory, in recapture or terminal losses on the disposition of depreciable property and in capital gains or losses on the disposition of capital property. This may result in an income tax liability and, perhaps, an increase in the refundable dividend tax on hand if the company is a private corporation. It may also result in adjustments to the "capital dividend account" [ssec. 89(1)].

B. Deemed Dividend on Winding-up

[ITA: 54; 84(2); 88(2)]

The sale of the assets of a corporation need not be followed immediately by a winding-up. The proceeds from the sale of assets can be reinvested in a new set of assets to carry on a new business or in a portfolio of securities, using the corporation as a holding company. Alternatively, the proceeds from the sale of assets can be distributed to shareholders, maintaining the corporation merely as a shell with nominal assets and shares. In this situation, distributions that did not represent a tax-free reduction of paid-up capital or a tax-free distribution from the capital dividend account will be treated as taxable dividends to the shareholders. A winding-up may not be completed for several years after the sale of the assets of a corporation, because certain clearance certificates must be issued to attest to the fact that creditors' claims, including Canada Revenue Agency (CRA), have been satisfied.

When a distribution on a winding-up does occur, subsection 84(2) establishes the portion of the amount received by the shareholders in a winding-up that is taxable in their hands. This subsection provides that any amount received in excess of the paid-up capital [ssec. 89(1)] is deemed to be a dividend. However, as indicated in the previous part of this chapter, this winding-up dividend can be broken into separate amounts under paragraph 88(2)(b) as follows:

(a) a capital dividend to the extent of the balance in the company's capital dividend account if the corporation *elects* on that amount [ssec. 83(2)];

(b) an amount *deemed not to be a dividend* to the extent of the balance in the company's "pre-1972 capital surplus on hand" account; and

(c) a taxable dividend to the extent of the balance of the deemed dividend.

In the winding-up, the shareholders dispose of their shares in return for the amounts received from the corporations. For the purpose of computing the capital gain or loss on the disposition of the shares, proceeds of disposition are deemed to be actual proceeds, or amounts received from the corporation, less the amount of the deemed dividend under subsection 84(2). [par. (j) of the definition in sec. 54]

Similar to the redemption of shares discussed earlier, the calculations for the winding-up can be completed in two steps.

Step 1: Deemed Dividend

Funds or property available for distribution to the shareholder(s)	$ xxx
Less: Paid-up capital	(xxx)
Deemed dividend on winding-up [ssec. 84(2)]	$ xxx
Less: Elected amount of capital dividend [spar. 88(2)(b)(ii)]	(xxx)
Deemed dividend taxable in hands of shareholder	$ xxx

Step 2: Capital Gain or Loss

Funds or property available for distribution to the shareholder(s)	$ xxx
Less: Deemed dividend above by par. (j) of definition in sec. 54	(xxx)
Adjusted proceeds of disposition	$ xxx
Adjusted cost base of shares	xxx
Capital gain	$ xxx

The components of the distribution can be illustrated conceptually by Exhibit 15-2.

EXHIBIT 15-2
Distribution on Winding-up

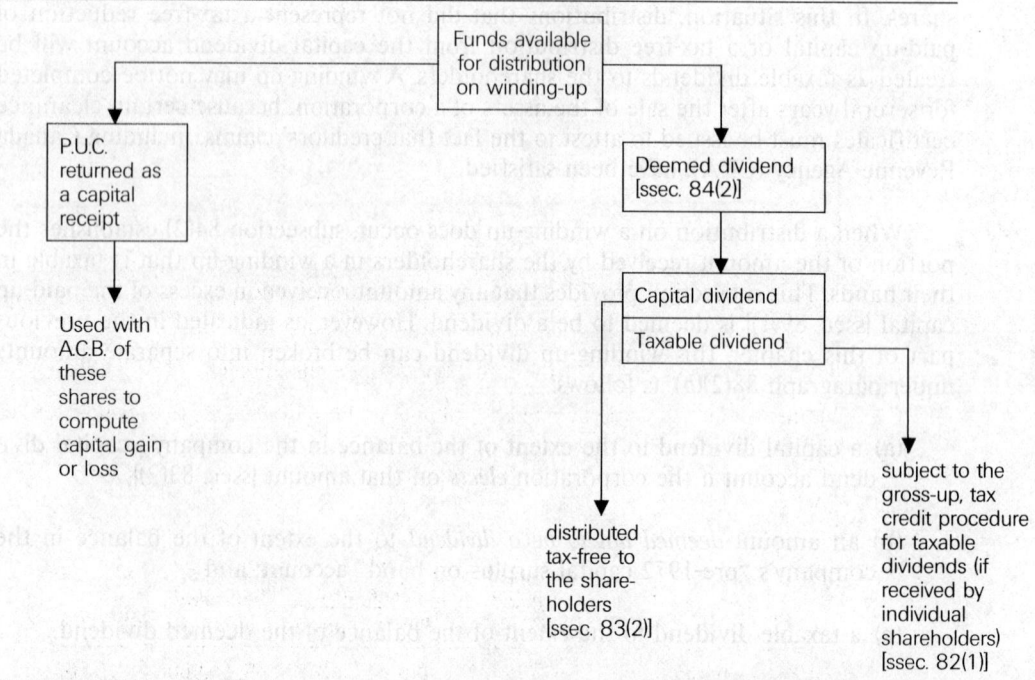

Note the similarity between the redemption/cancellation procedure under subsection 84(3) described previously in the chapter and the winding-up procedure. Both provisions have the same essential purpose on the distribution of funds from a corporation to a shareholder. The provisions must differentiate between the tax-free return of capital and a taxable distribution from retained earnings. The main difference is that a redemption usually pertains to all or part of one class of shares, while a winding-up involves the redemption or cancellation of all shares. Of course, part or all of the remaining subsection 84(2) deemed dividend can be treated as an elective non-taxable capital dividend.

C. Application of the Winding-up Rules

Example Problem

Winditup Limited is a Canadian-controlled private corporation founded in 1975 by Mr. Winditup who holds all of the shares which he purchased at that time from the company for $1,000. As of December 31, 2005 its tax balance sheet appears as follows:

Winditup Limited

BALANCE SHEET

as of December 31, 2005

Assets			*Liabilities*	
Cash	$ 5,000		Liabilities	Nil
RDTOH	5,000			
Land at cost (F.M.V. $210,000)	150,000		*Shareholders' Equity*	
			Paid-up capital	$ 1,000
Building at U.C.C. (cost $200,000;			Surplus	284,000
F.M.V. $250,000)	125,000		Total	$285,000
Total	$285,000			

The surplus accounts include $50,000 in the capital dividend account. The assets are to be liquidated and the proceeds are to be distributed to Mr. Winditup on the winding-up beginning on January 1, 2006.

— REQUIRED

(A) Compute the amount available for distribution to the shareholder assuming the company pays corporate tax at the overall rate of 20% on the first $300,000 of active business income and 40% on all other income, before the additional refundable tax of $6^2/3$%.

(B) Determine the components of the distribution to the shareholder.

(C) Compute the taxable capital gain or allowable capital loss on the disposition of Mr. Winditup's shares.

— SOLUTION

(A)

	Actual or deemed proceeds[1]	Income generated Bus.	Income generated Invest.	Capital dividend account	RDTOH
Opening balance		Nil	Nil	$ 50,000	$ 5,000
Cash	$ 5,000	Nil	Nil		
Land[2]	210,000	Nil	$30,000	30,000	
Building[3]	250,000	$75,000	25,000	25,000	
Income tax[5]	(40,667)	$75,000[4]	$55,000		14,667
RDTOH[6]	19,667				$ 19,667
	$444,000			$105,000	

(B)	Funds available for distribution to shareholder	$ 444,000
	Less: paid-up capital (return of capital)	(1,000)
	Ssec. 84(2) deemed dividend on winding-up	$ 443,000
	Less: capital dividend elected under ssec. 83(2) [spar. 88(2)(b)(i)] ...	(105,000)
	Deemed taxable dividend [spar. 88(2)(b)(iii)] (sufficient to clear RDTOH)	$ 338,000
(C)	Taxable capital gain to Mr. Winditup:	
	Actual proceeds on winding-up	$ 444,000
	Less: Ssec. 84(2) deemed dividend [par. (j) of definition in sec. 54]	(443,000)
	Proceeds of disposition	$ 1,000
	Cost	(1,000)
	Capital gain	Nil
	Taxable capital gain ($1/2 \times$ Nil)	Nil[7]

— NOTES TO SOLUTION

(1) It should be noted that in a winding-up of this nature it is possible either to sell the assets to any purchaser for proceeds equal to the fair market value of the assets or to distribute the assets to the shareholders of the corporation. If the latter alternative is taken, proceeds of disposition are deemed to be the fair market value of the assets so distributed.

(2)	Proceeds on sale of land	$210,000
	Cost	150,000
	Full increase in value	$ 60,000
	Taxable capital gain ($1/2 \times$ $60,000) (Canadian investment income)	$ 30,000
	Capital dividend account ($1/2 \times$ $60,000)	$ 30,000
(3)	Actual proceeds on sale of building	$250,000
	U.C.C	125,000
	Gain	$125,000
	Recapture ($200,000 − 125,000) (active business income)........	$ 75,000
	Capital gain ($250,000 − 200,000)	$ 50,000
	Taxable capital gain ($1/2 \times$ $50,000) (Cdn. investment income)	$ 25,000
	Capital dividend account ($1/2 \times$ $50,000)	$ 25,000

(4) The $300,000 (for calendar year 2005 and later years) business limit for the small business deduction must be prorated for the number of days in the taxation year. Since the winding-up may take some time to complete, this solution assumes that the corporation maintains its eligibility for the small business deduction in the year in which the sale of assets occurs [IT-73R6, par. 9]. In this case, there would be no need to bonus down to the business limit for the small business deduction, given active business income of $75,000. The CRA's policy of not challenging the reasonableness of bonuses paid by a CCPC to an active shareholder, resident in Canada, from the normal earnings of an active business, may not apply if a bonus is paid from the sale of assets that is not part of normal business. The CRA indicated, at the 2003 Canadian Tax Foundation Annual Conference, that it is a question of fact in a specific situation whether such a bonus from non-normal business income is reasonable.

(5)	Tax @ 20% on $75,000 of recapture	$15,000	
	Tax @ 46⅔% on $55,000 of investment income.......	25,667	$40,667
	RDTOH (spar. 129(3)(a)(i): 26⅔% of $55,000)		$14,667

(6) Assumes a minimum $59,000 (i.e., $3 \times $19,667$) is to be distributed as a taxable dividend to produce a refund [ssec. 129(1)]. Given the funds available for distribution, net of the capital dividend account, it can be seen, by inspection, that the taxable dividend resulting on the winding-up will exceed the minimum necessary to obtain the full refund.

(7) Had there been a taxable capital gain, the capital gains deduction for qualified small business corporation shares would not apply, because the shares would not meet the small business corporation test (as discussed in Chapter 13) after the assets have been sold for cash.

Summary of the Winding-up Procedure

The winding-up procedure demonstrated above can be summarized as follows:

(a) dispose of all assets at FMV and determine any resulting income or loss and adjustments to the capital dividend account;

(b) pay the liabilities including any tax liability and bonus generated;

(c) calculate the RDTOH and assume it to be fully refunded;

(d) distribute the net proceeds to the shareholder, determining a deemed dividend as the excess, if any, of such proceeds over the paid-up capital;[c]

(e) elect under subsection 83(2) on an amount not in excess of the capital dividend account. Elect under subsection 184(3) that the remainder is a taxable dividend;

(f) check to see if the taxable dividend is sufficient to generate the full dividend refund that was assumed under (c); and

(g) compute the shareholder's gain or loss on the disposition of the shares.

IV. SALE OF AN INCORPORATED BUSINESS

A. Assets vs. Shares

The sale of an incorporated business can be handled by two basic methods. One of these methods is selling the shares which entitles the buyer to control over the net assets of the corporation. This method results in a standard capital gains computation on the sale of shares.

The other method is selling the assets of the corporation. The proceeds from the sale of assets after taxes are paid would remain in the corporation after such a sale. The shareholder could then re-invest those net proceeds in the corporation or he or she could distribute them, perhaps, by winding up the corporation. This method, ultimately, results in the same procedure as the winding-up procedure demonstrated in the previous part of this chapter.

---

[c] For the purposes of corporate law, the full distribution to the shareholders (including P.U.C.) is done by way of a dividend, although only certain elements of the distribution will be taxed as a dividend.

B. Analysis for the Decision

Example Problem

Mr. Nudge owns all of the shares of Strikeout Ltd., a Canadian-controlled private corporation, whose operations have been successful, but Mr. Nudge has little time to devote to this company. As a result he is considering an offer from a Canadian public company to buy his business as at January 1, 2006. The offer is to buy the shares for $130,000. This value for the shares reflects the fact that the purchaser will not have access to tax-free dividends from the corporation's capital dividend account. Alternatively, the public company is prepared to pay $166,000 for the assets (including an investment in cash which it will need for working capital). Strikeout's fiscal year-end is December 31.

Financial information concerning Strikeout Ltd. on December 31, 2005 was as follows:

Assets	Actual cost	U.C.C.	F.M.V. at Dec. 31, 2005
Cash	$ 4,000		$ 4,000
Accounts receivable	10,000		7,000
Inventory	30,000		37,000
Land	10,000		20,000
Buildings (Class 3)	35,000	$10,000	39,000
Equipment	25,000	18,000	12,000
Goodwill	Nil		47,000
			$166,000

Liabilities	
Current liabilities	$ 20,000
Future income taxes	3,000
Depreciation claimed	22,000
Paid-up capital	10,000
Retained earnings	57,000
Reserve for doubtful accounts	2,000

The surplus accounts on December 31, 2004 before the sale were as follows:

Tax-paid retained earnings	$37,000
Capital dividend account	20,000

— *REQUIRED*

(A) Mr. Nudge requests your advice as to which option he should accept assuming that he would begin winding up the company immediately if assets are sold to the Canadian public company. You should assume that Mr. Nudge's marginal tax rate, federal and provincial, on income from this transaction is 46%. Cost of the shares in Strikeout Ltd. was $10,000. Assume that the corporation pays tax at the overall rate of 20% on active business income up to $300,000 and 40% initially on all other income, plus the additional refundable tax on investment income.

(B) What factors should the purchaser have considered in setting the offer price for the shares if the purchaser were: (a) another Canadian-controlled private corporation, (b) a Canadian public corporation, or (c) a non-resident corporation?

(C) Determine a selling price for the shares that results in the same after-tax net cash retained on the sale of assets and winding-up.

(D) Based on an offer of $166,000 for the assets, what is the maximum price the Canadian public company should be willing to pay for the shares of Strikeout Ltd.? Assume that the public company pays tax at a 40% rate, that it uses an after-tax discount rate of 8% and that it does not expect to sell the fixed assets of Strikeout Ltd. for a very long time.

— SOLUTION

Part (A): Options

Option 1 — Sale of shares for $130,000

Proceeds	$130,000
Adjusted cost base	10,000
Capital gain	$120,000
Taxable capital gain ($1/2 \times$ $120,000)	$ 60,000*
Tax thereon at 46% of $60,000	$ 27,600
Net proceeds ($130,000 − $27,600)	$102,400

* This capital gain would also be eligible for the QSBCS capital gains deduction to a maximum of $250,000 if the tests for a small business corporation are met, as discussed in Chapter 13.

Option 2 — Sale of assets and subsequent winding-up

Calculation of funds available for distribution on winding-up:

	Actual or deemed proceeds	Income generated Bus.	Income generated Invest.	Capital dividend account	RDTOH
Opening balance		Nil	Nil	$20,000	Nil
Cash	$ 4,000	Nil	Nil		
Accounts receivable[1]	7,000	$ (1,000)	Nil		
Inventory [ssec. 23(1)]	37,000	7,000	Nil		
Land[2]	20,000	Nil	$ 5,000	5,000	
Buildings[3]	39,000	25,000	2,000	2,000	
Equipment[4]	12,000	(6,000)	Nil		
Goodwill[5]	47,000	23,500	Nil	23,500	
Current liabilities[6]	(20,000)				
Income taxes[8]	(12,967)	$ 48,500[7]	$ 7,000		$ 1,867
RDTOH[9]	1,867				$ 1,867
	$134,900[10]			$50,500	

Calculation of deemed taxable dividend on the winding-up:

Funds available for distribution	$ 134,900
Less: paid-up capital	(10,000)
Deemed dividend on winding-up [ssec. 84(2)]	$ 124,900
Less: capital dividend elected under ssec. 83(2) [spar. 88(2)(b)(i)]	(50,500)
Deemed taxable dividend (sufficient to clear RDTOH)	$ 74,400

Calculation of taxable capital gain on disposition of shares in the winding-up:

Actual proceeds from distribution	$ 134,900
Less: deemed dividend [par. (j) of definition in sec. 54]	(124,900)
Proceeds of disposition (also equal to P.U.C.)	$ 10,000
Cost	(10,000)
Capital gain	Nil
Taxable capital gain	Nil

These results can be verified by the use of Exhibit 15-2.

Net cash retained after sale of assets and subsequent winding-up:

Funds distributed on wind-up...............................		134,900
Tax on incremental income from distribution:		
Deemed taxable dividend.....................	$ 74,400	
Gross-up (¼ × $74,400).....................	18,600	
Grossed-up dividend.........................	$ 93,000	
Taxable capital gain.........................	Nil	
Incremental taxable income..................	$ 93,000	
Combined federal and provincial tax @ 46%...	$ 42,780	
Less: approximate combined dividend tax credit		
((13⅓% + 6⅔%) of $93,000)............	(18,600)	(24,180)
Net cash retained...		$ 110,720
∴ Sell assets to retain net proceeds of.......................		$ 110,720

—NOTES TO PART (A) SOLUTION

(1) The reserve of $2,000 must be added to income whether or not a section 22 election is used. If a section 22 election is used the excess of face amount over proceeds of $3,000 would be a business loss such that the net effect on income in this case would be a $1,000 business loss. Under section 22, the purchaser must include the difference ($3,000) between the face amount and the amount paid in income. This inclusion permits the purchaser to deduct a reasonable reserve for doubtful debts on the receivables purchased [par. 20(1)(*l*)] and to deduct any bad debts as they occur [par. 20(1)(*p*)]. Note that one of the conditions of the section 22 election is that the seller must dispose of all or substantially all of its business assets to a purchaser who must propose to carry on the business. The following are the effects of a section 22 election made jointly between the vendor and the purchaser, as discussed in Chapter 4:

Vendor		*Purchaser*	
Reserve..............	$2,000		
Business income...........	$ 2,000		
Consideration........	$7,000	Accounts receivable...	$10,000
Business loss.........	3,000	Consideration.............	$ 7,000
Accounts receivable	10,000	Income...................	3,000

If section 22 is not used, the $3,000 loss incurred by the vendor will be a capital loss (deductible only against capital gains) and any gain or loss realized by the purchaser on collection of the receivables will be a capital gain or loss with no reserve or write-off permitted to the purchaser.

(2) Proceeds on sale of land.....................................	$20,000
Actual cost..	10,000
Full increase in value......................................	$10,000
Taxable capital gain (½ × $10,000) (investment income)......	$ 5,000
Capital dividend account (½ × $10,000)......................	$ 5,000
(3) Proceeds on sale of building.................................	$39,000
Tax value (U.C.C.)...	(10,000)
Full increase in value......................................	$29,000
Taxable capital gain (½ × ($39K − $35K)) (investment income)...	$ 2,000
Capital dividend account (½ × ($39K − $35K)).................	2,000
Recapture ($35K − $10K) (business income)....................	25,000
	$29,000

(4) Proceeds on sale of equipment $12,000
U.C.C. 18,000
Terminal loss (active business income offset) .... $ (6,000)

(5) Goodwill — increase in value $47,000
Credit to pool (sec. 14: $^3/_4$ of proceeds) ($^3/_4 \times$ $47,000) $35,250
Active business income ($^2/_3 \times$ $35,250) $23,500
Capital dividend account ($^2/_3 \times$ ($^3/_4 \times$ $47,000)) $23,500

(6) The future income tax credit is not a liability that must be paid directly. The actual income tax liability resulting from the sale of the corporation's assets is computed below.

(7) The business limit for the small business deduction ($300,000 for calendar year 2005 and later taxation years) must be prorated for the number of days in the taxation year. Since the winding-up may take some time to complete, this solution assumes that the corporation maintains its eligibility for the small business deduction in the year in which the sale of assets occurs [IT-73R6, par. 9]. In this case, there would be no need to bonus down to the business limit for the small business deduction, given active business income of $48,500.

(8) Tax @ 20% on $48,500 .... $ 9,700
Tax @ 46.67% on $7,000 3,267
Total Part I tax $12,967

(9) Refundable portion of Part I tax to RDTOH
26$^2/_3$% of investment income ($7,000) .... $ 1,867

A distribution of $5,600 (i.e., 3 × $1,867) in taxable dividends will be required to receive a dividend refund of $1,867 which clears the RDTOH account.

(10) There is no reason why Mr. Nudge could not use the net cash within the corporation to invest in securities or in another business if he wishes. In that case, the winding-up would not take place and, as a result, the RDTOH of $1,867 would not be available until dividends are paid by the corporation. On the other hand, Mr. Nudge avoids (postpones) the income taxes on the deemed dividend of $74,400. This example distributes the net proceeds in a winding-up to compare with the after-tax consequences of a sale of shares.

Part (B): Factors to be considered by the Purchaser

Theoretically, the value of a company's shares to a purchaser should be given by the present value of the expected future after-tax cash flows accruing to the purchaser when these cash flows are discounted at the purchaser's required rate of return appropriately adjusted for the risk of the situation. Tax considerations may affect the discount rate. Interest on money borrowed to acquire shares is deductible, reduces the after-tax cost of funds and, hence, it affects the discount rate used. The result of using a relatively lower discount rate is a relatively higher present value for the shares.

Tax considerations also affect the present value of the shares primarily through their effect on cash flows. The level of after-tax cash flows accruing to all purchasers will be affected by the amount of capital cost allowance that can be taken on the assets of the company whose shares have been purchased. Since, in the purchase of shares, there is no step-up in the capital cost to fair market value of the assets, the after-tax cash flows arising from capital cost allowance are not affected by the purchase of shares.

The deductibility of loss carryovers which reduce future taxes and, hence, increase future cash flows may be affected by the purchase of shares. Subsection 111(5) permits a corporation in which there has been an acquisition of control of shares to deduct non-capital losses if the business in which the losses were incurred continues to be carried on after the acquisition of control under restrictive conditions discussed in Chapter 11. However, subsection 111(4) does not permit the carryover of net capital losses when there has been an acquisition of control of the shares. If such losses cannot be carried over, the future after-tax cash flows are reduced, thereby reducing the value of the shares to the purchaser.

(a) Considerations of a Canadian-controlled Private Corporation as Purchaser

Most of the tax advantages of the small business deduction would continue if the shares of a Canadian-controlled private corporation were acquired by another Canadian-controlled private corporation as long as the corporate group had some eligibility for the small business deduction left (i.e., active business income does not exceed the business limit of $300,000 for calendar year 2005 and later taxation years). However, it should be noted that the amount of the small business deduction for a year must be allocated within a group of associated corporations resulting in a potential reduction of the deduction for a particular corporation in the group and, therefore, increased tax and lower after-tax cash flows.

(b) Considerations of a Canadian Public Corporation as Purchaser

The small business deduction would be lost to the acquired corporation on the purchase of control of its shares by a Canadian public corporation. This will reduce future after-tax cash flows and, hence, the value of the shares to the purchaser. Amounts in the acquired company's capital dividend account are no longer available for tax-free distribution after control of the company has been purchased by a Canadian public corporation. As a result, it might be advisable to elect and pay a dividend out of the capital dividend account before the purchase of control and to reduce the selling price of the shares accordingly. While ordinary dividends would still be received by the purchasing corporation without attracting tax, such dividends paid to the shareholders of the purchasing corporation may be subject to tax, thereby reducing the value of the acquiring company's shares. This may increase the cost of funds to the acquirer, thereby increasing the required return. Also, refundable taxes would be lost on the acquisition of control by a Canadian public corporation. This would clearly reduce future cash flows.

(c) Considerations of a Non-resident Corporation as Purchaser

Again, the small business deduction would be lost to the acquired corporation on the purchase of control of its shares by a non-resident corporation. This will result in additional tax that will reduce the value of the shares. Management fees, royalties, interest, dividends and capital dividend payments paid to a non-resident purchaser will be subject to withholding tax. This will result in a cash outflow earlier than might otherwise be the case, if such tax did not have to be paid immediately, resulting in a reduction of the present value of the shares. The thin capitalization rules may operate to reduce the deductibility of interest on debt, if any, held by the non-resident corporation purchaser [ssec. 18(4)]. This will reduce future cash flows. A rollover (as discussed in the next chapter) on the winding-up of a wholly-owned Canadian corporation would not be available if the purchaser is not another Canadian corporation [sec. 88]. If such a winding-up were contemplated it may result in higher taxes being paid earlier resulting in lower cash flows in early years after the acquisition and a lower value for the shares. Finally, the acquisition of shares by a non-resident corporation would be subject to government review. This would result in relatively higher expenses of acquisition and a lower value for the shares.

Part (C): Minimum Share Price Acceptable to Mr. Nudge

The calculation of the net proceeds in Part (A) above can be represented algebraically as:

$$P - .46 \left[\frac{1}{2} (P - \$10,000) \right]$$

where P = proceeds of disposition.

To equate the above expression with the net cash retained of $110,720 from the sale of assets and wind-up of the corporation, the following equation in one unknown results:

$$P - .46 \left[\frac{1}{2} (P - \$10,000) \right] = \$110,720$$

Solving for P, $\qquad$ P = $\underline{\$140,805}$

Therefore, Mr. Nudge should be willing to accept an offer of $140,805 for the shares.

A more tax-effective plan for the sale of shares would be to have Strikeout Ltd. elect to pay a tax-free dividend from its capital dividend account balance of $20,000 before the sale of the shares. This may require that the corporation borrow the cash to pay the dividend. The result would be a decrease in the value of the shares, but a saving of the tax on $20,000 which would otherwise be in the proceeds of disposition on the shares and would be taxed as a capital gain. The calculation of the net proceeds needed for the shares to equate the after-tax retention from the sale of assets would be given by the following equation:

$$\$20,000 + P - .46 \left[\frac{1}{2} (P - \$10,000) \right] = \$110,720.$$

Solving for P, $\qquad$ P = $114,831.

Part (D): Maximum Share Price Acceptable to Canadian Public Company

When shares are purchased, the purchaser, in essence, steps into the tax position of the acquired corporation. As a result, there is no step-up of cost values such as A.C.B. and U.C.C. to fair market value. Therefore, the purchaser assumes the eventual tax liability on accrued gains on the assets and loses the opportunity to benefit from the write-off of stepped-up costs. The increased write-offs on the purchase of assets can be thought of as reducing the net cost of the assets. Also, avoiding the assumption of inherent tax liabilities by the purchase of assets at fair market value and establishing their cost at that value can be thought of as decreasing the net cost of assets.

Consider the comparative effects of a purchaser of each asset in this case. On the purchase of accounts receivable, electing under section 22, income of $3,000 must be recorded, as shown. However, the purchaser can deduct a reserve in respect of those accounts receivable. If shares are purchased, the prior year's reserve of $2,000 must be included, but a new reserve can be deducted. Also, due to the acquisition of control, subsection 111(5.3) requires the deduction of the loss in value of $3,000 in the deemed taxation year resulting from the acquisition of control. The net result between a purchase of assets and a purchase of shares would be about the same in this case.

On the purchase of inventory, the cost is established at fair market value of $37,000. If shares are purchased, the purchaser assumes the liability for tax on the $7,000 of income (i.e., $37,000 – $30,000) when the inventory is sold. Since inventory is likely to be sold within the year, the tax would amount to $2,800 (i.e., 40% of $7,000). Purchasing assets avoids this tax cost.

On the purchase of the land, the A.C.B. is established at fair market value of $20,000. If shares are purchased, the purchaser assumes the inherent liability for tax on the $10,000 of capital gain accrued on the land. However, this tax is only incurred on the sale of the land by the purchaser. In this case, since the purchaser does not anticipate a sale in the foreseeable future, the present value of this future tax can be assumed to be negligible.

On the purchase of the building, the U.C.C. and the A.C.B. are established at fair market value of $39,000. If shares are purchased, the purchaser assumes the liability for tax on the $25,000 of recapture and $4,000 of capital gain, if this income is realized on the ultimate disposition of the building. Again, since the purchaser does not anticipate a sale of the building in the foreseeable future, the present value of this future tax can be assumed to be negligible.

However, on the purchase of the building, the purchaser can benefit from an increase in C.C.A. relative to a purchase of shares which will shield future income from tax. The present value of the tax shield for the purchase of the building in Class 1 in this case is given by:

$$\frac{c \times d \times t}{d + r} \left[\frac{1 + r/2}{1 + r} \right]$$

$$= \frac{\$39,000 \times .04 \times .40}{.04 + .08} \left[\frac{1 + .08/2}{1 + .08} \right]$$

$$= \$5,007$$

where c = capital cost
       d = C.C.A. rate
       t = tax rate
       r = after-tax discount rate

If shares are purchased, the corporation continues to deduct C.C.A. in Class 3 on a U.C.C. base of $10,000, providing a tax shield with a present value given by:

$$\frac{c \times d \times t}{d + r}$$

$$= \frac{\$10,000 \times .05 \times .40}{.05 + .08}$$

$$= \$1,538$$

The incremental tax saved from C.C.A. on the purchase of assets in present value terms is $3,469 (i.e., $5,007 – $1,538). This can be considered a decrease in the net cost of purchasing assets.

On the purchase of equipment at a fair market value of $12,000 (which is less than U.C.C. of $18,000), the U.C.C. base for future U.C.C. is established at $12,000. However, on the purchase of shares, there is an acquisition of control which causes the U.C.C. after the acquisition of control to be reduced to fair market value of $12,000 [ssec. 111(5.1)]. As a result, there is no difference between the effect of a purchase of the equipment and a purchase of shares in this case, except for the application of the half-year rule in the calculation of CCA on the purchase of assets.

On the purchase of goodwill at a fair market value of $47,000, the purchaser can add $35,250 (i.e., ³⁄₄ × $47,000) to its cumulative eligible capital account and it can amortize that amount at 7% on a declining balance basis. The present value of the write-off is given by:

$$\frac{c \times d \times t}{d + r}$$

$$= \frac{\$35,250 \times .07 \times .40}{.07 + .08}$$

$$= \$6,580$$

If shares are purchased, there is no balance of cumulative eligible capital to amortize. Therefore, the $6,580 is a net cost reduction on the purchase of assets.

To summarize these effects, the following is a calculation of the cost of a purchase of assets net of the cost reduction discussed above:

Cost of gross assets, per offer		$166,000
Tax savings — Present value of future CCA/CECA:		
Building	$5,007	
Goodwill	6,580	(11,587)
After-tax cost of assets		$154,413

Next, what the purchaser would pay for the shares to have an after-tax cost of the shares of $154,413 must be determined. This calculation would be as follows:

Price of shares	x =	$133,151
Liabilities assumed.................	$ 20,000	20,000
Tax savings — Present value of future CCA:		
Building	$ (1,538)	(1,538)
Tax costs — Present value of tax on accrued gains:		
Inventory	2,800	2,800
After-tax cost of shares	$154,413	$154,413

This price of $133,151 is the maximum amount that the Canadian public purchaser corporation should be willing to pay for the shares in this case.

Summary

The results of the analysis in Parts (C) and (D) can be summarized, in terms of pre-tax costs and equivalent values, as follows:

Purchaser's after-tax cost:

	Pre-tax	*After-tax*
Asset purchase.......................	$166,000 ⟶	$154,413
Share purchase	$133,151 ⟵	$154,413 ⟵

Vendor's after-tax proceeds:

	Pre-tax	*After-tax*
Asset sale	$166,000 ⟶	$110,720
Share sale..........................	$140,805 ⟵	$110,720 ⟵

This table can be further summarized by the grid as follows:

	Assets	*Shares*
Maximum that purchaser will pay	$166,000	$133,151
Minimum that vendor will accept...............	$166,000	$140,805

From this grid it can be seen that, if the value of the assets is in fact, $166,000, then the vendor should be willing to accept no less than $140,805 for the shares and the purchaser should be willing to pay no more than $133,151 for the shares. The above grid establishes that, in this particular case, there is no negotiation range within which a transaction for shares may be better than a transaction for assets. For example, at the $130,000 offered for the shares, the vendor, Mr. Nudge, will retain less in after-tax proceeds than on a sale of assets. On the other side, a purchase of shares at $130,000 results in a slightly lower net tax cost than a purchase of assets with a net after-tax cost of $133,151. If both parties agree on the value of the assets at $166,000, they will transact in assets and not shares in this particular case. The vendor will have a higher after-tax retention from the sale of assets instead of shares and the purchaser will have a lower after-tax cost.

On the other hand, if the $20,000 balance in the capital dividend account is paid to Mr. Nudge as a tax-free dividend, then he requires a minimum of only $114,831 for the shares, to be indifferent between a sale of shares and a sale of assets in terms of his after-tax retention. If the minimum that he will accept for the shares is $114,831 and the maximum that the purchaser will pay is $113,151 ($133,151 – $20,000), then there is still no negotiation range within which a transaction price will make both parties better off from the sale of shares compared with the sale of assets.

IV. GST AND THE WINDING-UP OF A CANADIAN CORPORATION

[ETA: 123(1); 165(1); 167(1)]

Where a corporation is wound up and the rules of subsection 88(2) of the *Income Tax Act* apply, the supply of property on the winding-up is subject to the general rules of the GST. GST applies to all taxable supplies made in Canada [ETA: ssec. 165(1)]. If a corporation is wound up and the corporation's property is acquired by a recipient, GST is payable by the recipient on any taxable supplies of property.

An election, however, may be available, in which case the payment of GST will generally not be required [ETA: ssec. 167(1)]. Subsection 167(1) of the ETA deals with the situation where a supplier makes a supply of a business or part thereof that was established or carried on by the supplier (or established or carried on by another person and acquired by the supplier). In that situation, the recipient must be acquiring ownership, possession or use of all or substantially all (i.e., 90% or more) of the property that can reasonably be regarded as being necessary for the recipient to be capable of carrying on the business. Where these conditions are met, the vendor and purchaser may jointly elect to have GST not apply to the sale. However, GST will still apply to the following supplies:

- a taxable supply of services to be rendered by the vendor;

- a taxable supply by way of lease, licence or similar arrangement; and

- where the purchaser is not a registrant, a taxable supply of real property by way of sale.

Reference will be made to this election repeatedly in Chapters 15 through 18, since it is an important provision in the context of various types of corporate reorganizations and other business transfers.

Subsection 167(1) applies to *all* types of property sold. Thus the election is available even when the corporation being wound up was involved in making exempt supplies. As well, the corporation does not have to be a registrant. However, if the corporation being wound up is a registrant, then the purchaser must also be a registrant.

Because businesses are entitled to claim input tax credits in respect of GST paid on purchases used in commercial activities, the use of the election under subsection 167(1) of the ETA may not result in any net GST savings. However, it may result in cash flow advantages, since GST does not have to be paid and then recovered through an input tax credit.

REVIEW QUESTIONS

(1) Assuming that you are working in a province in which only par value shares can be issued, what journal entry would you use to record the issuance of 100 common shares, which had a par value of $100 each, for $30,000?

(2) In jurisdictions without par value shares, how is the paid-up capital determined?

(3) What are "high-low" shares?

(4) What are the five basic components of the capital dividend account?

(5) Calculate the effect on the capital dividend account as a result of the sale of unrecorded goodwill this year for $100,000. The only other transaction in eligible capital property took place

three years ago when a customer list was purchased for $10,000. The balance in the CEC account is now approximately $6,000.

(6) Smith Co. has total P.U.C. of $10,000. It decided to make a distribution of capital in the amount of $9,000, but when it actually paid out the $9,000, the P.U.C. was only reduced by $8,000. What are the tax consequences?

(7) What are the three components of a distribution on the winding-up of a corporation where the only shareholder is an individual?

(8) Gone Co. is a CCPC that is in the process of being wound up under subsection 88(2). One of its assets is a building that has an accrued terminal loss. The lawyer has suggested that subsection 13(21.2) will apply to deny the terminal loss to the corporation on winding-up. What do you think?

(9) Technically, on the winding-up of a corporation under subsection 88(2), how are the proceeds of disposition of the shares calculated?

MULTIPLE CHOICE QUESTIONS

Question 1

Which one of the following statements is FALSE?

(A) A capital dividend is usually received tax-free.

(B) A corporation must elect to pay a capital dividend, not later than the day the dividend is paid.

(C) If a private corporation has had more capital gains than capital losses, it will probably have a balance in its capital dividend account.

(D) The payment of a capital dividend by a private corporation will trigger a dividend refund: one dollar refund for each three dollars of capital dividends paid.

Question 2

Mr. Andrews owned Class A special shares of Atlantis Ltd. with the following characteristics:

Fair market value	$60,000
Cost	20,000
Paid-up capital	10,000

These shares were redeemed. Which one of the following best describes the tax consequences of the redemption to Mr. Andrews?

(A) A capital gain of $40,000

(B) A dividend of $40,000

(C) A dividend of $50,000 and a capital gain of $40,000

(D) A dividend of $50,000 and a capital loss of $10,000

Question 3

X Ltd. had $40,000 available for distribution to its sole shareholder, Xavier, on winding-up. The balances in the tax accounts of X Ltd. were as follows:

Share capital (paid-up capital)	$ 2,000
RDTOH	Nil
Capital dividend account	8,000
Other surplus	30,000
	$40,000

Xavier paid $1,000 for the shares of X Ltd. when he purchased them two years ago. Which one of the following statements is TRUE?

(A) The winding-up can occur on a tax-deferred basis. Xavier will be able to defer the recognition of any income for tax purposes.

(B) Xavier will have dividend income of $30,000 which will be grossed-up to $37,500 for tax purposes. In addition, he will have a capital gain of $1,000.

(C) Xavier will have dividend income of $30,000 which will be grossed-up to $37,500 for tax purposes. In addition, he will have a capital gain of $9,000.

(D) Xavier will have a capital gain of $39,000 on the winding-up of X Ltd.

Question 4

Art, the sole shareholder of Art's Variety Inc. with a November 30 year-end, has decided to wind up the corporation, effective December 1. The balance sheet as at that date is anticipated to be as set out below.

Assets	
Cash	$ 45,000
Refundable dividend tax on hand	30,000
Land, at cost (FMV, $850,000)	250,000
Building, at UCC (FMV, $780,000; cost, $380,000)	180,000
	$505,000

Liabilities & Equity	
Liabilities	$ 20,000
Paid-up capital	5,000
Capital dividend account	10,000
Other surplus	470,000
	$505,000

Art's Variety Inc. is a Canadian-controlled private corporation. It pays tax at a combined federal and provincial rate of 18% on business income in the winding-up period and 45% including the additional refundable tax on investment income.

The amount available for distribution to Art on the windup will be:

(A) $485,000

(B) $1,394,000

(C) $1,557,333

(D) $1,838,333

Question 5

At the beginning of its first taxation year, Newco Ltd., a newly-incorporated company, issued 100 common shares to Mr. A for $10,000. On June 1 of the same year, Newco issued an additional 100 common shares to Mr. B for $15,000 (which is the fair value of the shares on that date). On December 30 of the same year, Mr. C acquired all of Mr. A's common shares for $20,000. At the end of this year (December 31), which of the following statements is true?

(A) The total paid-up capital of the common shares is $25,000, ½ of which is attributable to each of Mr. C and Mr. B.

(B) The total paid-up capital of the common shares is $35,000, ½ of which is attributable to each of Mr. C and Mr. B.

(C) The total paid-up capital of the common shares is $25,000, $10,000 of which is attributable to Mr. C and $15,000 of which is attributable to Mr. B.

(D) The total paid-up capital of the common shares is $35,000, $20,000 of which is attributable to Mr. C and $15,000 of which is attributable to Mr. B.

Question 6

C Co. is a Canadian controlled private corporation with a December 31 year-end. During the year it sold all its assets including goodwill. The goodwill was sold for fair market value: $1,000,000. The cost of the goodwill and the company's cumulative eligible capital account was Nil. Which of the following is a correct statement?

(A) C Co. will report a taxable capital gain of $500,000 and its capital dividend account will increase by $500,000.

(B) C Co. will report active business income of $500,000 and its capital dividend account will increase by $500,000.

(C) C Co. will report active business income of $750,000 and its capital dividend account will increase by $250,000.

(D) C Co. will report a taxable capital gain of $500,000 and its refundable dividend tax on hand account will increase by $133,335.

EXERCISES

Exercise 1

[ITA: 89(1)]

The following capital properties have been sold by a Canadian-controlled private corporation during the year ended December 31:

	A	B	C
Proceeds of disposition	$4,000	$1,000	$2,000
Cost	2,000	2,000	2,000
Selling expenses	400	100	200

— *REQUIRED*

Compute the effects of the disposition on the capital dividend account.

Exercise 2

[ITA: 89(1)]

Adjusted Ltd., a Canadian-controlled private corporation, sold the following two capital properties during the fiscal year ending December 31:

	Cost	Proceeds	Selling costs
Property 1	$75,000	$110,000	$11,000
Property 2	40,000	11,000	5,500

— *REQUIRED*

Compute the effects of these sales on:

(A) the net income for tax purposes, and

(B) the balance in the capital dividend account.

Exercise 3

[ITA: 83; 84]

Mr. Deemed, the sole shareholder of Dividend Limited, a Canadian-controlled private corporation, requires some cash for other personal investment transactions. Dividend Limited's share capital is composed of 100 common shares with an A.C.B. and P.U.C. of $1 per share and 1,000 6% preferred shares with an A.C.B. and P.U.C. per share of $15 and a retractable value of $75 per share. Mr. Deemed is considering the following alternatives:

(a) Mr. Deemed would cause Dividend Limited to redeem 800 preferred shares at $75 per share.

(b) Mr. Deemed would cause Dividend Limited to pay a cash dividend of $60,000 on the common shares. Dividend Limited has a capital dividend account of $75,000.

(c) Mr. Deemed would cause Dividend Limited to make a non-dividend cash distribution of $60,000 on the preferred shares.

— *REQUIRED*

Discuss the tax implication of the above transactions.

Exercise 4

[ITA: 54; 84(3); 248(1)]

A Canadian-controlled private corporation has paid a dividend this year in the form of 10 first preference shares each having a redemption value of $1,000 and a paid-up capital value of $1.00.

— *REQUIRED*

(A) What are the tax consequences of the receipt of the dividend by an individual shareholder?

(B) What are the tax consequences to the corporation?

(C) What are the tax consequences to the individual shareholder of a sale at their fair market value of the shares received?

(D) What are the tax consequences to the individual shareholder of a redemption of the shares received?

Exercise 5

[ITA: 53(1)(b), (2)(a); 84(1), (3), (4)]

The following situations deal with Canadian-controlled private corporations and their non-arm's length shareholders. However, each transaction, described below, is separate and distinct from the other transactions unless the contrary is stated.

(a) X Ltd. issued to the daughter of its only shareholder retractable special shares (preferred shares) with a P.U.C. of $150 and a redemption value of $1,000 for $100 cash.

(b) A, the sole shareholder of A Ltd., gave the corporation land with a F.M.V. of $150,000.

(c) Y, the controlling shareholder of Y Ltd., converted debt of $20,000 for preferred shares with a P.U.C. and redemption value of $2,000 plus cash of $20,000.

(d) Z, the sole common shareholder of Z Ltd., is considering causing the corporation to make a payment as a return of capital (P.U.C.). The shares have a F.M.V. of $50,000, P.U.C. of $10,000 and A.C.B. of $20,000:

(i) payment is for $5,000;

(ii) payment is for $18,000.

— *REQUIRED*

Discuss the tax consequences of the above transactions.

Exercise 6

[ITA: 54; 83(2); 84(2); 88(2); 89(1)]

Finished Limited is a Canadian-controlled private corporation, founded in 1972 by Mr. Finished who holds all of the outstanding shares. The following balance sheet reflects the position of the corporation after selling all assets and paying all liabilities:

Finished Limited

BALANCE SHEET

as at December 31, 2005

Cash	$ 950,000	Capital stock (P.U.C.)	$ 625,000
RDTOH	50,000	Capital dividend account	150,000
		Other surplus	225,000
Total assets	$1,000,000		$1,000,000

— *REQUIRED*

(A) Determine the components of the distribution to Mr. Finished.

(B) Compute the taxable capital gain or allowable capital loss on the disposition of Mr. Finished's shares on January 1, 2006, assuming that their adjusted cost base was $350,000.

Exercise 7

[ITA: 54; 83(2); 84(2); 88(2); 89(1)]

Through Ltd. has been wound up this year and its only shareholder has surrendered her shares. She received $30,000 in total from the corporation for her shares which had a cost to her equal to their paid-up capital of $2,000. The company had elected under subsection 83(2) on a dividend of $2,000.

— *REQUIRED*

What are the tax consequences to the shareholder if she will be taxed on any income from the winding-up at a combined 29% federal and 17% provincial marginal rate of 46%?

Exercise 8

[ITA: 54; 83(2); 84(2); 88(2); 89(1)]

Downandout Limited is a Canadian-controlled private corporation which will be wound up by its only shareholder, Mr. Downer, who bought the shares at their paid-up capital value of $2,000. As at December 31, 2005, its balance sheet appears as follows:

Downandout Limited

BALANCE SHEET

as at December 31, 2005

Assets			*Liabilities*	
Cash	$ 20,000		Bank loan	$ 47,000
RDTOH	10,000		Wages payable	3,000
Inventories at cost			Total	$ 50,000
(F.M.V.: $220,000) ...	200,000			
Land at cost (F.M.V.:			*Shareholder's Equity*	
$70,000)	40,000		Paid-up capital	$ 2,000
Buildings at U.C.C.			Surplus	318,000
(cost: $200,000;				
F.M.V.: $300,000)....	60,000		Total	$370,000
Equipment at U.C.C.				
(Cost: $100,000;				
F.M.V.: $80,000).....	40,000			
Total	$370,000			

The balance in the corporation's capital dividend account was nil as at the above balance sheet date. The assets are to be liquidated, the liabilities paid and the net proceeds distributed to Mr. Downer effective January 1, 2006.

— *REQUIRED*

(A) Compute the amount available for distribution to the shareholder assuming the corporation pays corporate tax at the rate of 20% on the first $250,000 of active business income and 40% initially on any other income, plus the additional refundable tax on investment income, from the winding-up.

(B) Determine the components of the distribution to the shareholder.

(C) Compute the taxable capital gain or allowable capital loss on the disposition of Mr. Downer's shares assuming that their adjusted cost base was $1,000.

(D) Discuss the GST implications on the wind-up of Downandout Limited.

ASSIGNMENT PROBLEMS

Problem 1

[ITA: 89(1)]

Surplus Accounts Limited, a Canadian-controlled private corporation, whose fiscal year-end is December 31, provides you with the following data concerning its tax accounts and capital transactions for 2005. The balance in its capital dividend account was nil on January 1, 2005.

Surplus Accounts Limited is considering winding up the corporation and wishes to determine the impact of the sale of all its capital assets on its tax surplus accounts. The following capital assets are recorded in the books of account:

Assets	Cost	U.C.C./ C.E.C.	Estimated proceeds	Estimated selling costs
Investments	$60,000		$ 22,000	$ 500
Land	40,000		200,000	10,000
Building	70,000	$ 45,000	125,000	6,000
Equipment	35,000	Nil	8,000	400
Customer lists (Note 1)	40,000	16,000	60,000	—

Additional Information

(1) The balance in the cumulative eligible capital account reflects the purchase of the customer lists in 1995 for $40,000 less the tax write-offs for 1995 to 2004, inclusive.

(2) In addition to the above assets, there is $35,000 of goodwill which will also be sold.

— *REQUIRED*

Compute the effect on income and the capital dividend account balance immediately after the above transactions.

Problem 2

[ITA: 89(1)]

You have been asked to compute the capital dividend account of Granatstein Ltd., a Canadian-controlled private corporation incorporated in 1983. You have reviewed the tax returns of the corporation for the period January 1, 1983 to December 31, 2005 and made the following notes:

1985   Disposed of bonds resulting in a capital gain of $10,000.

1987   Received taxable dividend of $2,000 and capital dividend of $5,000.

1988   Disposed of shares resulting in a capital loss of $4,000.

1990   Disposed of equipment resulting in a capital gain of $6,000 and recapture of $3,000.

1992   Eligible capital property was purchased for $40,000.

1993   Sold vacant land and reported capital gain of $100,000.

1996   1993 capital gain of sale of vacant land was reassessed by the CRA as income. Granatstein Limited did not fight the reassessment.

1999   Sold shares resulting in a capital gain of $20,000.

2001   Received life insurance proceeds of $100,000 on a life insurance policy on the life of the company president purchased in 1993. As at January 1, 2001, the policy had an adjusted cost basis of $20,000.

2002   Paid capital dividends of $50,000.

2005   Sold a customer list for $100,000. The company's cumulative eligible capital balance at the time of the sale was $25,000.

2005   Sold shares resulting in a capital gain of $37,500.

— *REQUIRED*

Compute the balance in Granatstein Ltd.'s capital dividend account at the end of the 2005 taxation year. Show *all* calculations and explain why you omitted any of the above amounts in your answer.

Problem 3

[ITA: 53(1)(b); 84]

The following situations deal with a Canadian-controlled private corporation and its shareholders. Each transaction described below is separate and distinct from the other transactions.

(a) Capital Inc. issued 135 preferred shares with P.U.C. equal to $110 each for $11,050 cash and assets with a F.M.V. of $2,800.

(b) Paid Ltd. has shares with a F.M.V. of $35,000 and a P.U.C. of $5,500. Paid Ltd. is considering making the following paid-up capital reductions on these shares. Their shareholders have an A.C.B. of $16,000 for their shares:

   (i) payment of $3,750; and

   (ii) payment of $8,750.

(c) Up Ltd. has 4,500 common shares with a P.U.C. of $22,500. In March of this year the corporation declared and distributed a 15% stock dividend in common shares with a P.U.C. of $3,375.

(d)(i) The sole shareholder of Baker Corp. Ltd. contributed assets worth $38,400 to the corporation in return for cash of $15,400 and preferred shares with a P.U.C. of $23,000 (redemption value of $23,000).

   (ii) A year later, the sole shareholder redeemed the preferred shares.

— *REQUIRED*

Discuss the tax consequences under section 84 for each of the above transactions.

Problem 4

[ITA: 54; 84(3), (6)]

Ms. Chiu owns all of the 100 Class B shares issued by Chiu Ltd., a small business corporation, which was formed by Ms. Chiu in 1972. Her son owns all the Class A shares. The current fair market value of the Class B shares is $100 per share. The paid-up capital value of the shares and their adjusted cost base to Ms. Chiu is presently $5 each. Ms. Chiu would like to know the tax consequences if (a) her shares are redeemed by Chiu Ltd. for their fair market value or, alternatively, (b) she sells her shares to her son for their fair market value.

Ms. Chiu has also sold 100 common shares of Bellco Limited, a company whose shares are listed on the CDNX Stock Exchange. She has found out Bellco Limited, itself, had purchased her shares through the exchange for $4.10 each. The paid-up capital value of the shares was $1 each and their cost to Ms. Chiu three years ago was $1.25 each.

— *REQUIRED*

Comment on the tax implication of the above transactions.

Problem 5

[ITA: 54; 83(2); 84(2), (2.1); 89(1)]

Ms. Batt owns all the common shares of Batterup Ltd., a Canadian-controlled private corporation, which started operations in 1976. Batterup Ltd. has been quite profitable since the early 1980s. As a result, Three-Strikes Ltd., a Canadian public corporation, has offered Ms. Batt $252,500 for the assets, excluding cash, as at December 31, 2005. The offer price reflects unrecorded goodwill of $47,500.

The pro forma balance sheet of Batterup Ltd. as at December 31, 2005, is as follows:

Assets	Cost	U.C.C.	F.M.V.
Cash	$ 2,500		
Accounts receivable (net)	8,750		$ 7,500
Inventory	22,250		15,500
Land	11,000	—	45,000
Building...........................	35,000	$ 7,500	95,000
Equipment	45,000	22,000	10,000
Marketable securities..................	14,250	—	32,000
	$138,750		$205,000
Liabilities			
Current liabilities	$ 54,000		
Future income taxes	5,000		
Shareholder's Equity			
Paid-up capital	10,000		
Capital dividend account	4,000		
Retained earnings....................	65,750		
Total liabilities and equity	$138,750		

Additional Information:

(1) Batterup Ltd. pays corporate tax at the overall rate of 20% on active business income eligible for the small business deduction and an initial 40% rate for investment income, plus the $6^2/_3$% additional refundable tax on investment income.

(2) The reserve for doubtful accounts at December 31, 2005, was $1,500.

(3) Batterup Ltd. and Three-Strikes Ltd. elected under section 22.

— *REQUIRED*

(A) Compute the amount available for distribution to the shareholder.

(B) Determine the components of the distribution to the shareholder.

(C) Compute the taxable capital gain or allowable capital loss on the disposition of Ms. Batt's shares on the winding-up. (Assume the adjusted cost base of Ms. Batt's common shares is $10,000.)

(D) Explain the conditions for and advantages of using a section 22 election.

Problem 6

[ITA: 54; 83(2); 84(2); 88(2); 89(1)]

You have been approached by one of your clients, Mr. Sidney Chow, for help in determining what will be the tax consequences if he sells all his assets in his corporation (at their fair market value) in 2005 to someone who will continue the business. However, Mr. Chow is not sure if he should wind up his corporation at this time. The following tax balance sheet for Chow Enterprises Ltd. has been prepared as at December 31, 2005.

Chow Enterprises Ltd.

BALANCE SHEET

as at December 31, 2005

Cash		$ 10,000
RDTOH		5,000
Accounts receivable	$30,000	
Less: reserve for doubtful debts	5,000	25,000
Land		55,000
Building (Class 3) — U.C.C		95,000
Equipment (Class 8) — U.C.C.		12,000
Shares in Bell Canada — cost		15,000
Goodwill — cumulative eligible capital balance		18,000
		$235,000
Liabilities		$ 35,000
Future income taxes		12,000
Common shares — P.U.C.		20,000
Capital dividend account		8,000
Other surplus		160,000
		$235,000

Additional Information

(1) Mr. Chow owns all the common shares of the corporation, which he acquired in 1983 for $20,000 when the business was incorporated.

(2)

Assets	Cost	F.M.V.
Accounts receivable	$30,000	$ 18,000
Land	55,000	150,000
Building — Class 3	170,000	320,000
Equipment — Class 8	30,000	3,000
Shares in Bell Canada	15,000	26,000
Goodwill	50,000	120,000

Goodwill was acquired in 1995 in connection with a similar business which was purchased that year. The fair market value reflects the goodwill for the combined businesses. The maximum amortization has been deducted for tax purposes.

(3) The corporation is taxable at a total 20% corporate tax rate for the first $300,000 of active business income and a 40% rate for any other income, plus the $6^2/_3\%$ additional refundable tax on investment income.

(4) The accounts receivable are to be sold to a factoring company.

— REQUIRED

(A) Compute the effect of the sale of the above assets on the various tax accounts in 2005, ignoring any potential normal business transactions.

(B) If Mr. Chow should decide to wind up beginning in 2006, ignoring any subsequent business transactions,

(i) determine the components of the distribution to him; and

(ii) compute the taxable capital gain or allowable capital loss on the disposition of Mr. Chow's shares.

(C) Indicate briefly the tax consequences of leaving the proceeds in the corporation and investing the money in high-yielding securities.

(D) Discuss the GST implications on the sale of assets and the subsequent winding-up.

Problem 7

[ITA: 54; 83(2); 84(2); 88(2)]

J. Tilkenhurst Limited (JTL) is a Canadian-controlled private corporation which was started in 1976 by Mr. Santosh Prasad with an initial investment in common shares of $18,000. Mr. Prasad has decided that it's time to retire and move to his retirement home in Saskatoon, Saskatchewan. Therefore, Mr. Prasad wishes to wind up JTL.

The following is a projected tax balance sheet prior to the sale and distribution of the assets as at the intended date of the winding-up:

J. Tilkenhurst Limited
BALANCE SHEET
as at December 31, 2005

Cash		$ 15,000
RDTOH		6,000
Accounts receivable	$60,000	
Less: reserve for doubtful accounts	5,000	55,000
Inventory		110,000
Marketable securities		26,000
Land		85,000
Building — U.C.C.		23,000
Equipment — U.C.C.		10,000
Customer list — CEC account balance		20,600
		$350,600
Liabilities		$ 45,000
Future income taxes		41,000
Common shares (P.U.C.)		18,000
Capital dividend account (no unabsorbed negative amounts)		12,000
Other surplus		234,600
		$350,600

Additional Information

(1) The corporation is taxable at a total 20% corporate tax rate for the first $300,000 of active business income and an initial 40% rate for all other income, plus the $6^2/3\%$ additional refundable tax on investment income.

(2)

Assets	Cost	F.M.V.
Accounts receivable....................	$ 60,000	$52,000
Inventory	110,000	127,000
Marketable securities	26,000	26,000
Land...............................	85,000	150,000
Building	66,000	97,000
Equipment..........................	30,000	6,000
Customer lists*......................	42,453	70,000

* The customer lists were acquired in 1999 from a similar business which was acquired that year. The balance in the C.E.C. account includes the maximum cumulative eligible capital amounts in each year.

(3) The books of account do not reflect unrecorded goodwill with an estimated fair market value of $60,000. This is in addition to the customer lists.

(4) The accounts receivable are to be sold to a factoring company.

— REQUIRED

Prepare an analysis of the income tax implications of the winding-up.

Problem 8

[ITA: 14; 38; 82; 83(2); 117; 121; 123; 124; 129]

Mr. Lotsaluck incorporated a company in 2005 in a province with a 20% corporate tax rate on active business income, a 40% total corporate tax rate on other income, before the $6^2/3\%$ additional refundable tax, and a 46% combined personal tax rate (including a 17% personal provincial tax on income rate), taking one share with a paid-up capital value of $1 and a note representing a loan to the company of $499,999. The company, Luck Unlimited Limited, a private corporation, purchased the assets of a business in the same year for $500,000. The purchase price was allocated to the land and building of the business in the amount of $400,000 and to goodwill in the amount of $100,000. However, before the business had commenced, the company sold the assets of the business for $700,000, including $170,000 for goodwill.

— REQUIRED

Assume that the sale of land and building was considered to result in a *capital gain*. How much of the $700,000 received in the corporation would Mr. Lotsaluck retain, if he removed all of this amount from the corporation.

Problem 9

[ITA: 54; 83(2); 84(2), (2.1); 89(1)]

Ms. Debbie, the sole shareholder of Shining Limited, a CCPC, has been considering selling her common shares to Let's-Make-a-Deal Ltd., a CCPC. However, Ms. Debbie recalls reading somewhere that one should compare a share sale with an asset sale to determine which would result in higher after-tax cash flow.

Ms. Debbie provides you with the following information:

(1) The cost of Ms. Debbie's common shares in Shining Limited was $120,000.

(2) Shining Limited pays tax at the overall rate of 20% on the first $300,000 of active business income, 33% on additional active business income, and 40% on all other income, plus the $6^2/_3$% additional refundable tax on investment income.

(3) Ms. Debbie's combined federal and provincial personal tax rate is 46%, including a personal provincial tax on income rate of 17%. The provincial dividend tax credit is $6^2/_3$% of the grossed-up dividend.

(4) Financial information concerning Shining Limited on December 31, 2005 is as follows:

Assets	Book cost	U.C.C.	F.M.V.
Cash (required as working capital)	$ 23,000		
Marketable securities (required as working capital)	58,000		$ 54,000
Inventory	41,000		50,000
Land	154,000		210,000
Building (Note)	213,700	$195,000	440,000
Goodwill.	Nil		85,000
	$489,700		$839,000

Liabilities		
Current liabilities	$ 43,000	
Future income taxes	4,800	
Paid-up capital	120,000	
Capital dividend account	48,000	
Retained earnings.	273,900	
	$489,700	

(5) Shining Limited earned active business income of $50,000 during the year.

NOTE: The original cost of the building in Class 3 was $410,000. Book cost of $213,700 is net book value after accumulated amortization.

— *REQUIRED*

(A) If Ms. Debbie sells all of the assets, except cash, to Let's-Make-a-Deal Ltd., pays the outstanding liabilities, and then winds up Shining Limited, what would be the net amount available for distribution to her? Show all computations.

(B) Determine the components of the distribution to Ms. Debbie.

(C) Determine the amount, including principal, Ms. Debbie would retain from this distribution.

(D) Determine a selling price for the Shining Limited shares that results in the same after-tax net cash retained as the net cash from sale of assets followed by a wind-up, as determined in Part (C).

(E) Based on the indicated fair market value of the net assets, what is the maximum price a Canadian-controlled private corporation should be willing to pay for the shares of Shining Limited? Assume that the CCPC pays tax at the low rate of 20% on all of its income, that it uses an after-tax discount rate of 10%, and that it does not expect to sell the fixed assets of Shining Limited for a very long time. Also, assume that if the purchaser bought the assets, it would have to invest $23,000 in cash to meet working capital requirements.

[For more problems and solutions thereto, see the CD accompanying this book.]

SUPPLEMENTAL NOTES

(This section can be omitted without losing the continuity of the chapter. None of the review questions, multiple choice questions, exercises, or assignment problems utilizes this information.)

GST and the Sale of an Incorporated Business

[ETA: 128(1); 141.1(3); 156; 167(1); 186(2); 200(3); 221(2); 228(4), (6)]

As discussed earlier in this chapter, the sale of an incorporated business can be handled by two basic methods — the sale of assets or the sale of shares. The election under subsection 167(1) of the ETA may be available on the sale of assets of an incorporated business. As noted above, subsection 167(1) of the ETA deals with the situation where a supplier sells a business (or part of a business) that it had established, carried on, or acquired. The recipient must acquire ownership, possession or use of all or substantially all of the property that is necessary to carry on that business or that is capable of being used to carry on a business.

Under the election, a supplier may retain certain assets that were used in the business and lease those assets to the recipient, without disqualifying the parties from using the election. As well, the election can apply to all property sold as part of a business, including property that was used in exempt activities.

It is important to note that under the election, the parties need not be registrants; however, if the vendor is a registrant (and therefore able to claim input tax credits), the recipient must also be a registrant.

Subsection 200(3) of the ETA provides some relief on the sale of capital personal property (see Chapter 5) under certain circumstances. Where a registrant sells capital personal property that was used primarily in an exempt activity immediately before the sale, the sale is deemed to be made otherwise than primarily in the course of a commercial activity. Consequently, GST is not payable. It is important to note that the vendor must be a registrant for this provision to apply.

A provision that may provide relief on the sale of a business (or the sale of most assets) between related parties, is found in section 156 of the ETA. Where an election is made under that provision, transfers between corporations in a "closely-related group" are deemed to be supplies for no consideration. In other words, no GST applies. Corporations making this election are treated as if they are part of the same legal entity, avoiding the requirement to initially pay GST on taxable supplies and then claim a corresponding input tax credit. This election is not available for sales of real property, or for supplies that are not to be used by the recipient exclusively (i.e., 90% or more) in a commercial activity.

The exclusion for sales of real property, however, will generally not have any negative implications. GST need not be collected by the vendor of real property if the recipient is a registrant and the real property is not a residential complex supplied to an individual [ETA: ssec. 221(2)]. When this applies, the purchaser is required to remit the GST payable on that real property directly to the Receiver General [ETA: ssec. 228(4)]. However, a mechanism allows the input tax credit being claimed by the purchaser of such real property to be offset against the GST remittable in these circumstances [ETA: ssec. 228(6)]. Consequently, no GST need be remitted on the sale of real property if it is to be used exclusively in a commercial activity.

The definition of a closely-related group [ETA: ssec. 128(1)] is quite detailed and is further complicated by the inclusion of additional rules in the Closely Related Corporations (GST/HST) Regulations. In basic terms, two corporations are closely related if they are registered for GST purposes and are members of a group of corporations resident in Canada with common ownership of 90% or greater. Special rules apply where the closely-related group includes a financial institution.

If, however, the business is transferred by way of a sale of shares, the transfer has no GST consequences, since the sale of shares is an exempt supply under the GST. A "financial service" is defined [ETA: ssec. 123(1), par. (*b*) of the definition] to include an equity security. A "financial service" is defined in the same subsection to include the transfer of ownership of a financial instrument. Part VII of Schedule V of the ETA provides that the supply of a financial service is an exempt supply.

Where a registrant that is a corporation resident in Canada is engaged in a takeover attempt in which it is acquiring or attempting to acquire all or substantially all (i.e., 90% or more) of the voting shares of another corporation, it is entitled to claim input tax credits for GST paid on any purchases of property and services attributable to that activity [ETA: ssec. 186(2)]. For this provision to apply, the target corporation must be engaged exclusively in commercial activities. Without this provision, GST paid in respect of the share purchase on legal fees and investment counsel fees, for example, would not be considered to be for use in a commercial activity. Consequently, the purchaser would not be entitled to an input tax credit.

To the extent that neither of these provisions under section 156 or subsection 186(2) of the ETA is applicable and GST is payable on taxable supplies made in the course of the sale, a full input tax credit will be available to the purchaser if the supplies are used exclusively in commercial activities. Any related costs, such as legal and accounting fees that are subject to GST, will also generate input tax credits under subsection 141.1(3), which states that to the extent a person does anything in connection with the acquisition, establishment, disposition or termination of a commercial activity, that person is deemed to have been engaged in a commercial activity.

Chapter 16

Income Deferral: Rollover on Transfers to a Corporation and Pitfalls

TOPICS DISCUSSED

	Page
TRANSFER OF PROPERTY TO A CORPORATION BY A SHAREHOLDER	850
The Basic Concepts	850
Basic Technical Rules on the Transfer	857
Application of the Basic Rules	860
The Corporation's Position	862
The Shareholder's Position	863
Paid-up Capital Reduction on Shares Issued as Consideration	864
Other Rules Applicable in the Rollover	868
Benefits Conferred on Shareholders and Related Persons	873

	Page
Summary of Rules	879
Fair Market Value	881
Section 22 Election	882
Application	884
TRANSFER OF SHARES	887
Non-arm's Length Sale of Shares: Dividend Strips	887
Sale of Shares by a Corporation to an Unrelated Person: Capital Gains Strips	900
SUPPLEMENTAL NOTES	917
GST and Section 85 Rollovers	917

The general rule for the taxation of capital gains and losses is that all dispositions of capital property result in an immediate recognition of a capital gain or loss. This rule also applies to non-arm's length dispositions [sec. 69]. However, in some circumstances, particularly in non-arm's length transactions, there is often no real change in the *economic interest* in the property. For example, where an individual transfers property to a wholly-owned corporation, there is no real change in the individual's economic interest in the property. A "rollover" may provide, in limited circumstances, a deferral of capital gains or losses, as well as other types of income. A rollover normally provides for a transfer of property at a value that will be referred to initially as its "tax value". This term is not used in the Act, but is meant to refer to adjusted cost base, undepreciated capital cost or other tax value representing cost.

In return for the property transferred, the transferor should receive a "package" of consideration, the total fair market value of which should be equal to the fair market value of the property transferred. This fair market value exchange is done to avoid important tax complications that will be discussed later in the chapter. On the ultimate disposition of the property by the recipient or transferee, the gain or loss that was deferred at the time of the previous transfer (rollover) is included in the transferee's income. This chapter will discuss the rollover provisions in the Act pertaining to the transfer of property to a corporation by a shareholder [sec. 85]. The chapter will also discuss two major pitfalls that can arise on the transfer of shares as a result of section 84.1 and subsection 55(2). The final part of this chapter discusses the GST implications of section 85 rollovers. The next chapter will complete the discussion of rollovers involving corporations and their shareholders.

Refer to the chart at the beginning of Chapter 15 for the location in the Act of the major provisions discussed in this Chapter.

I.   TRANSFER OF PROPERTY TO A CORPORATION BY A SHAREHOLDER

A.   The Basic Concepts

Fundamentally, on the transfer of assets to a corporation, there is a disposition at fair market value. An election under subsection 85(1) allows the transferor to choose the proceeds of disposition to defer some or all of the gain.

Section 85 permits a tax-free rollover of property to a corporation but only as long as the transferor accepts shares as part of the consideration for the transfer. The basic concept is that the transferor, who is now a shareholder of the transferee corporation, should be in the same economic position that he or she was in before the transfer. Therefore, the adjusted cost base of the shares that he or she receives should be exactly equal to the adjusted cost base of the asset transferred. Now, the deferred income inclusion (e.g., capital gain) will be triggered if the shares are sold in an arm's length transaction. Similarly, the corporation should retain the adjusted cost base of the transferred property. The above is the basic concept behind a pure tax-free rollover.

However, there are additional variables which add complexity to the pure concept. First, the transferor is permitted to trigger income inclusions (e.g., capital gains, recapture, etc.) if he or she so desires. Second, the consideration can be, not only shares (common and preferred), but also debt or cash.

Therefore, this part will introduce the basic principles of a section 85 transfer to a corporation through three specific situations; a fourth will be added later in the chapter. Each situation will begin with the conditions or rules for the particular situation. Subsequent situations will introduce new variables so that, by the end of the third situation, some, but not all, of the basic concepts underlying section 85 should be understood. The balance of the chapter will build upon these concepts with the technical rules which add refinements to the basic concepts.

The first three situations will introduce the concepts in the following order:

- Situation One shows the necessity to make a downward adjustment to the paid-up capital (P.U.C.) of the share consideration to equal the tax value of the asset transferred.

- Situation Two introduces the concept of a transfer price other than the tax value of the transferred asset so that income inclusions can be triggered.

- Situation Three introduces the additional complexity caused by accepting non-share consideration (e.g., debt or cash).

A fourth situation, which is introduced later in this chapter, demonstrates the concept that the F.M.V. of the property transferred must equal the F.M.V. of the consideration received, or adverse tax consequences will occur.

Note that the situations described are a conceptual introduction to section 85. The underlying technical rules are discussed later in the chapter. An understanding of these concepts will assist you in applying the complex technical rules that follow. Read these three initial situations carefully. In fact, you may find it helpful to revisit these concepts after you have attempted the technical readings, exercises and assignment problems.

1. Situation one

(a) *Conditions for Transfer*

The assets must be transferred at their tax values, i.e., adjusted cost base (A.C.B.), undepreciated capital cost (U.C.C.), etc., so that there are no tax consequences in respect of the transfer. The consideration received on the transfer in this first situation will be common shares.

(b) *Facts*

Mr. X wishes to transfer some land that is capital property to a corporation, X Ltd., which he presently controls through the ownership of all the Class A common shares. The land being transferred has an A.C.B. of $10,000 and an F.M.V. of $50,000. Mr. X will accept as consideration one Class B common share.

(c) *Results*

Since the conditions for the transfer indicate that there should be no tax consequences from the transfer, Mr. X and the corporation should be in the same economic position as if the transfer did not happen.

Land

(1) The proceeds of disposition should be the A.C.B. of the land of $10,000 so that no gain is triggered.

(2) The cost of the land to X Ltd. should also be Mr. X's A.C.B. of $10,000 so that X Ltd. is in the same economic position (i.e., there is a potential capital gain of $40,000 upon the disposition of the land by X Ltd.).

Consideration — One Class B common share

(1) The A.C.B. of the Class B common share should also be equal to Mr. X's A.C.B. of the land. He is now in the same economic position as before with a potential capital gain of $40,000 on the one Class B common share. The A.C.B. of the share represents the cost of the land which was acquired with after-tax or tax-paid funds and can be recovered on a disposition of the share.

(2) The F.M.V. of the Class B share should be $50,000 which is equal to the underlying value of the land transferred to X Ltd. The result is that Mr. X had exchanged land with a fair market value of $50,000 for shares with a fair market value of $50,000.

(3) Logically, the paid-up capital (P.U.C.) should be $10,000, the amount that can be withdrawn tax-free on a redemption of the share, since this $10,000 represents the cost of the land that could be recovered tax-free on its disposition. However, under corporate law, the stated capital (the equivalent of paid-up capital for tax purposes) would normally be equal to the fair market value of the transferred property of $50,000. Therefore, the paid-up capital must be reduced to the A.C.B. of the land of $10,000 in this particular situation. Note that this P.U.C. *reduction* (i.e., $40,000) is exactly equal to the deferred accrued capital gain on the land (i.e., $50,000 − $10,000). Further modifications of the P.U.C. reduction will be introduced later as additional conditions are added to the following situations.

In summary, the following has occurred.

Before transfer			After transfer	
Mr. X owned	*Land*		*Mr. X owns*	*Shares*
A.C.B.	$10,000		A.C.B.	$10,000
F.M.V.	50,000		P.U.C.	10,000
			F.M.V.	50,000
			Corporation owns	*Land*
			A.C.B.	$10,000
			F.M.V.	50,000

(d) *Conclusion*

This situation demonstrates that if an asset is transferred to a corporation at its tax value and only common share consideration is accepted, there will be no tax consequences to the transferor, Mr. X. His proceeds of disposition and A.C.B. of the consideration are exactly equal to the tax value of the transferred property. At the same time, the corporation assumes the tax value for the A.C.B. of its newly-acquired property. The P.U.C. of the common share must also be the tax value of the transferred asset. If this is not the case under corporate law, then the paid-up capital must be reduced for tax purposes.

2. Situation two

(a) *Conditions for Transfer*

The assets can now be transferred with proceeds chosen at any amount (referred to hereinafter as the "elected amount") between the tax value (A.C.B., etc.) and the F.M.V. of the particular asset. This range of elected amounts will permit the taxpayer to trigger the appropriate amount of taxable capital gains or other income (e.g., recapture) to offset loss carryforwards and the allowable capital losses in the transfer year. Again, the consideration received on the transfer in this situation will be common shares.

(b) *Facts*

Ms. B wishes to transfer land and a building to a corporation, B Ltd., which she presently controls through the ownership of all of the Class A common shares.

Land — A.C.B.	$ 10,000
— F.M.V.	50,000
Building — cost	95,000
— U.C.C.	75,000
— F.M.V.	110,000

Ms. B will accept as consideration for the transfer of the land and building, Class B common shares. Ms. B has a net capital loss carried forward from the preceding year ($\frac{1}{2}$ inclusion rate year) of $10,000 which she wishes to utilize on the transfer.

(c) *Results*

Since Ms. B wishes to utilize the net capital loss of $10,000 on the transfer, she must first decide on which asset she will trigger the taxable capital gain and what the elected amount will be. If she chooses the building, then at the same time she will trigger recapture as well as a capital gain. Since there is no evidence that she has a business loss for this year or non-capital losses, this course of action is not recommended. In respect of the land, she can choose an elected transfer price between $10,000 and $50,000. If she chooses an elected amount of $30,000, a taxable capital gain of $10,000 will result [i.e., ($30,000 − $10,000) × ½] which will offset the net capital loss.

Therefore, the recommended elected amounts would be:

Land	$ 30,000
Building	75,000

Land

(1) The proceeds of disposition for Ms. B will be $30,000, the elected amount as discussed above.

(2) The cost of the land to B Ltd. should also be $30,000, the elected amount, so that the remaining accrued gain of $20,000 (i.e., $50,000 − $30,000) will not be triggered on the transfer, but will be included in B Ltd.'s income on the ultimate disposition of the land.

Building

On the assumption that no additional income (i.e., recapture and/or a capital gain) should be triggered, the elected amount chosen should be the tax value or U.C.C. of $75,000.

(1) The proceeds of disposition for Ms. B, therefore, will be the elected amount of $75,000, resulting in no recapture or capital gain.

(2) The U.C.C. of the building for B Ltd. will also be the elected amount of $75,000 which was the U.C.C. for Ms. B. In addition, B Ltd. will assume Ms. B's capital cost of the building of $95,000 so that the corporation will be responsible for the potential recapture of $20,000 and capital gain of $15,000.

Consideration — Class B common shares

(1) The A.C.B. of the Class B common shares should logically be the sum of:

(a) A.C.B. of the land	$ 10,000
(b) the capital gain triggered on the land transfer	20,000
(c) U.C.C. of the building	75,000
	$105,000

Another way of looking at it would be the sum of the elected amounts:

Land	$ 30,000
Building	75,000
	$105,000

(2) The F.M.V. of the Class B shares should be $160,000, the underlying fair market values of the land and building transferred to B Ltd.

(3) As previously mentioned in Situation One, the stated value of the Class B shares for accounting and corporations law purposes would be $160,000. (Remember that the starting point for determining paid-up capital is the accounting or corporations law stated value.) However, the paid-up capital should be reduced to $105,000, which represents the A.C.B. and U.C.C. of the land and building, respectively, for B Ltd. (i.e., $10,000 and $75,000) plus the accrued capital gain recognized and included in income on the transfer of the land (i.e., $20,000). This paid-up capital reduction of $55,000 should be exactly equal to the stated value of the Class B shares ($160,000) minus the elected amount ($105,000) [i.e., F.M.V. ($160,000) minus B Ltd.'s tax values ($30,000 +

$75,000)]. The P.U.C. after the reduction should reflect the tax-paid cost values of the assets of $105,000 (i.e., ($10,000 + $20,000) + $75,000).

In summary, the following has occurred:

Before transfer				*After transfer*	
Ms. B owned	*Land*	*Building*		*Ms. B owns*	*Shares*
A.C.B./Cost	$10,000	$ 95,000		A.C.B.	$105,000
U.C.C.	n/a	75,000		P.U.C.	105,000
F.M.V.	50,000	110,000		F.M.V.	160,000

Ms. B had a net capital loss carryforward of $10,000.

Taxable capital gain of $10,000 offset by net capital losses.

Corporation owns	*Land*	*Building*
A.C.B./Cost	$30,000	$ 95,000
U.C.C.	n/a	75,000
F.M.V.	50,000	110,000

(d) *Conclusion*

As long as the transferor (Ms. B) elects an amount for the transferred asset(s) within the range between tax value (A.C.B., U.C.C., etc.) and the F.M.V., this elected amount will be:

(a) the proceeds of disposition of the transferor (Ms. B);

(b) the tax value (i.e., A.C.B., U.C.C., etc.) of the transferred asset to the transferee corporation (B Ltd.);

(c) the A.C.B. of the common share consideration received by the transferor (Ms. B); and

(d) the paid-up capital of the common shares held by the transferor (Ms. B) after the paid-up capital reduction which will be equal to the remaining deferred gain of $55,000 (i.e., $160,000 – $105,000), resulting in a P.U.C. of $105,000 (i.e., $160,000 – $55,000).

3. Situation three

(a) *Conditions for Transfer*

The asset(s) can be transferred at any amount between the tax value and F.M.V. of the particular asset. However, in this situation, the consideration can be a mixture of common shares and non-share consideration (referred to as "boot") such as cash or debt, including debt attached to the transferred property (assumed debt). The inclusion of non-share consideration, however, imposes a further limitation — namely, that the non-share consideration or boot cannot exceed the elected amount without adverse tax consequences which are discussed below.

(b) *Facts*

Mr. C wishes to transfer land to a corporation, C Ltd., which he presently controls through the ownership of all the Class A common shares.

Land — A.C.B. $10,000
       — F.M.V. 50,000

The land has an outstanding mortgage of $4,000 attached to it. Mr. C will accept as consideration for the transfer:

(a) a promissory note of $14,000 from C Ltd.;

(b) the assumption of the mortgage of $4,000 by C Ltd.; and

(c) the balance of the F.M.V. of the land in Class B common shares.

Mr. C has $6,000 of net capital losses arising in 1999 which he wishes to utilize on the transfer.

(c)   *Results*

Since Mr. C wishes to utilize the $4,000 ($6,000 × $^4/_3$ × $^1/_2$) of net capital losses, he must elect at an amount which will trigger a capital gain of $8,000, yielding a taxable capital gain of $4,000. Therefore, he should elect at $18,000 ($10,000 A.C.B. plus $8,000 capital gain). Since he has accepted, as part of his consideration, boot of $18,000 (a $14,000 note plus the assumed mortgage of $4,000) he has not violated the condition that the boot cannot exceed the elected amount (i.e., $18,000).

Land

(1) The proceeds of disposition to Mr. C is the elected amount of $18,000 which will trigger a capital gain of $8,000 to offset the net capital loss of $4,000 (i.e., $^1/_2$ × $8,000).

(2) The cost of the land to C Ltd. will be the elected amount of $18,000 so that the corporation will only be liable for the remaining capital gain of $32,000.

Consideration

(1) The A.C.B. of the Class B common shares will be the elected amount minus the F.M.V. of the boot.

Elected amount		$18,000
Boot — note	$14,000	
— mortgage	4,000	18,000
Excess		Nil

∴ A.C.B. of the shares is nil.

This result is logical since Mr. C has recovered from the corporation $18,000 of debt consideration equal to the full amount of the A.C.B. of land ($10,000) plus the realized capital gain of $8,000. When the debt is repaid by the corporation, there will be no further tax consequences since the repayment amount reflects the tax-paid cost of the land transferred after the realization of $8,000 of capital gain.

(2) The P.U.C. should logically be nil since Mr. C has recouped all of his invested cost in the land in the form of boot. If Mr. C had not accepted boot as part of the consideration package, then the P.U.C. would have been equal to the tax-paid cost of the transferred land (i.e., $18,000) as demonstrated in Situations One and Two. However, in this situation Mr. C has recovered all of the tax cost of the land (i.e., note of $14,000 and a mortgage of $4,000). Therefore, the stated value of the Class B common shares (i.e., F.M.V. of $32,000) must be reduced by $32,000 to give a paid-up capital of nil.

Another way of arriving at the P.U.C. of nil is:

Stated capital (F.M.V. of land ($50,000) – Boot ($18,000))		$32,000
Minus: elected amount	$18,000	
Less: boot	18,000	Nil
P.U.C. reduction		$32,000
∴ P.U.C. = (F.M.V. ($32,000) – P.U.C. reduction ($32,000))		Nil

Thus the P.U.C. of nil reflects the fact that all of the tax-paid cost of the land has been recovered through boot, leaving no more tax-paid cost to be recovered in the shares on their redemption.

Note how this result differs from Situation Two where only Class B common shares were accepted as consideration. The A.C.B. and the paid-up capital were not reduced to nil in Situation Two, since Ms. B had not extracted from the corporation any non-share consideration (i.e., cash or debt).

In summary, the following has occurred:

Before transfer		After transfer			
Mr. C owned	*Land*	*Mr. C owns*	*Debt*	*Corporation owns*	*Land*
A.C.B. .... $ 10,000		A.C.B. .... $ 14,000		A.C.B. .... $ 18,000	
F.M.V. 50,000		F.M.V. 14,000		F.M.V. 50,000	
Mr. C owed $4,000 on a mortgage.		*Mr. C owns*	*Shares*	*Corporation owes to:*	
		A.C.B. .... Nil		Mr. C .... $ 14,000	
Mr. C had a net capital loss carryforward of $4,000 (adjusted).		P.U.C. .... Nil		Mortgage 4,000	
		F.M.V. .... $ 32,000			
		Mr. C no longer owes $4,000 on a mortgage.			
		Taxable capital gain of $4,000 offset by net capital losses.			

(d) *Conclusion*

The elected amount of $18,000 in this situation was used to determine the following values:

(a) proceeds of disposition to Mr. C of $18,000, triggering a capital gain of $8,000;

(b) an A.C.B. of the Class B common shares of nil, since all of the elected amount was assigned to the boot of $18,000;

(c) a cost of the land to C Ltd. of $18,000 since the corporation is responsible for the remaining capital gain of $32,000; and

(d) a paid-up capital of the Class B common shares of nil since all of the elected amount has been extracted from C Ltd. through the boot consideration.

Finally, the non-share consideration or boot did not result in any adverse tax consequences, since the total boot (debt of $14,000 and the assumption of Mr. C's liability of $4,000) did not exceed the elected amount of $18,000.

(e) *Boot Consideration in Excess of Elected Amount*

If Mr. C had forgotten the assumed mortgage of $4,000 was part of the non-share/boot consideration and had taken back a promissory note of $18,000 (equal to the elected amount), the following would be the tax consequences.

(1) The elected amount would be bumped automatically by the $4,000 which is the excess boot over the elected amount (i.e., ($18,000 + $4,000) − $18,000) to arrive at a new elected amount of $22,000.

(2) The proceeds of disposition to Mr. C would be the *new* elected amount of $22,000, triggering a taxable capital gain of $6,000 ($1/2 \times$ ($22,000 − $10,000)) of which only $4,000 would have been offset by the net capital loss (as adjusted).

(3) The cost of the land to C Ltd. would be the *new* elected amount of $22,000.

(4) The A.C.B. of the Class B common shares would still be nil, computed as:

New elected amount		$22,000
Less: boot:		
(a) note...	$18,000	
(b) mortgage	4,000	22,000
A.C.B. of Class B shares		Nil

(5) The paid-up capital of the Class B common shares would still be nil since the entire elected amount of $22,000 would be recovered through boot.

P.U.C. Reduction		
Stated value of shares*		$28,000
Minus: elected amount	$22,000	
Less: boot	22,000	Nil
Reduction		$28,000
∴ P.U.C. = ($28,000 − $28,000)		Nil

* F.M.V. of land transferred of $50,000 minus the boot or non-share consideration of $22,000 ($4,000 + $18,000).

B. Basic Technical Rules on the Transfer

[ITA: 85(1), (1.1), (6); 89(1); IT-291R3; IC 76-19R3]

Section 85 provides for the transfer of "eligible" property, as defined [ssec. 85(1.1)], to a corporation by a person who, after the transfer, is a shareholder. The provision is applicable on many transfers of property to a corporation, including transfers on the incorporation of a proprietorship, a partnership, or an investment portfolio and transfers to a subsidiary. Section 85 is also applicable on the transfer by an individual of shares in one corporation to another corporation, perhaps, to effect one form of estate freeze to be discussed more fully in the next chapter. The party transferring property (i.e., the transferor) can be an individual, a trust, a corporation or a partnership (discussed in more detail in Chapter 18), either resident or non-resident in Canada.

In order for the rollover to apply, the following conditions must be met:

(a) the corporate transferee must be a taxable Canadian corporation as defined [ssec. 89(1)];

(b) the consideration received by the transferor must include shares (i.e., at least one share or a fraction of a share by virtue of IC 76-19R3, paragraph 8, although a more literal interpretation of the provision might suggest two or more shares or fractions thereof for each type or class of asset) of the corporation;

(c) the property transferred must be eligible property defined to include capital property (including both depreciable and non-depreciable capital property, but usually not real property owned in any manner by a non-resident), eligible capital property, a resource property, or inventory (other than real property, an interest therein or an option in respect thereof) [ssec. 85(1.1)]; and

(d) the taxpayer(s) and the corporation must jointly elect to have these rollover provisions apply (form T2057 for transfers from an individual, trust, or corporation or T2058 for transfers from a partnership) on or before the first time for filing a tax return of any person, who was a party to the election, for the year in which the property was transferred [ssec. 85(6)]. A late election may be filed within three years of the due date [ssec. 85(7)]. There is a penalty equal to the lesser of $1/4$ of 1% of the deferred gain and $100 for each month that the election is late to a maximum penalty of $8,000 [ssec. 85(8)]. The Minister may accept new elections or amendments to previous elections filed after the three-year deadline in cases where this would be just and equitable [ssec. 85(7.1)].

The importance of filing the election with complete and correct information is evident from the case of *Deconinck v. The Queen*, (F.C.T.D.) 88 DTC 6410 (affirmed by the Federal Court of Appeal, 90 DTC 6617), in which the taxpayer failed to refer to four of the five properties he intended to transfer in his rollover election. The Federal Court–Trial Division held that section 85 provides a significant advantage to the taxpayer, but to take advantage of that provision, the information provided must be correct. Intention of the taxpayer is not sufficient. As a result, the four properties were not subject to the rollover and were considered to be transferred at their fair market value.

The price at which property is transferred may be elected within a range set out in Exhibit 16-1. This elected transfer price is very important because it is used to solve the following four problems that arise on the transfer:

(a) proceeds of disposition to the transferor [par. 85(1)(a)];

(b) the cost of the property to the corporation [par. 85(1)(a)];

(c) the cost of the package of consideration taken by the transferor from the corporation in return for the assets transferred to the corporation [pars. 85(1)(f), (g) and (h)]; and

(d) a part of the calculation of paid-up capital for tax purposes of the share consideration received [ssec. 85(2.1)].

In order to defer the maximum capital gain or income, the elected transfer price should be the minimum in the range. To ensure that the absolute minimum is selected, it is necessary to make sure that consideration other than shares, e.g., debt, cash, etc. ("boot") taken from the corporation is no more than the lesser or least of two or three amounts at the bottom of the appropriate column in Exhibit 16-1. It should be recognized that the amount of this non-share consideration taken from the corporation is the only decision variable in establishing the limits on the elected transfer price range. The other items such as fair market value and tax value of the property transferred are fixed, although often not with great precision, at the time of the transfer and cannot be varied on the transfer.

EXHIBIT 16-1
Restrictions on Elected Transfer Price

	Inventory* or capital property other than depreciable property [par. 85(1)(c.1)]	Depreciable capital property [par. 85(1)(e)]	Eligible capital property [par. 85(1)(d)]
UPPER LIMIT	F.M.V. of property transferred [par. 85(1)(c)]	F.M.V. of property transferred [par. 85(1)(c)]	F.M.V. of property transferred [par. 85(1)(c)]
LOWER LIMIT	*Greater of:*	*Greater of:*	*Greater of:*
[par. 85(1)(e.3)]	F.M.V. of non-share consideration received [par. 85(1)(b)]	F.M.V. of non-share consideration received [par. 85(1)(b)]	F.M.V. of non-share consideration received [par. 85(1)(b)]
	and	and	and
	Lesser of [par. 85(1)(c.1)]:	*Least of [par. 85(1)(e)]:*	*Least of [par. 85(1)(d)]:*
	(1) F.M.V. of property**	(1) F.M.V. of property**	(1) F.M.V. of property**
	(2) A.C.B. of property if capital property or tax value of	(2) U.C.C. of class of property	(2) ⁴/₃ of the cumulative eligible capital balance
	property if inventory	(3) cost of property to transferor	(3) full or actual cost of property to transferor

* Other than real property (i.e., land and buildings) held as inventory.

** The fair market value of the property restriction prevents the creation of an artificial loss. Further restricted by subsection 13(21.2) for depreciable capital property, to be discussed subsequently, and by subsection 14(12) for eligible capital property.

Although it is not necessary to take non-share consideration, it will usually be beneficial to take the maximum amount of "boot" that will still permit a transfer of the property at an amount which will fully defer the accrued gains on the property. The benefits of receiving cash as "boot" without triggering tax on the accrued gains are obvious. Even if debt of the corporation is received as "boot", the debt can be redeemed for cash later without any adverse tax consequences. However, where section 84.1 applies on the transfer of shares, as discussed later, taking the maximum "boot" will not be beneficial.

One of the most common errors in the application of section 85 is to forget to include in "boot" the debts of the transferor which are assumed by the corporation. Where the maximum new debt has already been exchanged on the transfer, this omission will cause unwanted income inclusions through an automatic bump in the elected amount for the excess boot (i.e., the assumed debts).

If the fair market value of non-share consideration received ("boot"), labelled as the lower limit, is greater than the fair market value of property transferred to the corporation, labelled as the upper limit, then the transfer price will be the latter amount [par. 85(1)(c)]. This will create other problems which will subsequently be discussed in more detail.

C. Application of the Basic Rules

[ITA: 85(1), (2.1); IT-432R2]

Exhibit 16-2 presents three basic alternative combinations of the three key variables: fair market value of the property transferred, adjusted cost base or other tax value equivalent of the property transferred, and non-share consideration ("boot") received. The rules summarized in Exhibit 16-1 are applied to these three cases on the assumption that there is, at least, nominal share consideration (e.g., one cent) to meet the requirement in subsection 85(1). Other possible cases will be discussed later.

EXHIBIT 16-2
Range of Elected Amounts (nominal share consideration assumed)

	1	2	3
$100	F.M.V. (U) ⎤ Ⓣ	F.M.V. (U) ⎤ Ⓣ	A.C.B.
75	A.C.B. (L) ⎦	Boot (L) ⎦	F.M.V. Ⓣ
60	Boot	A.C.B.	Boot

U — upper limit; L — lower limit; T — transfer price; Boot — non-share consideration plus nominal share consideration.

In Case 1 of Exhibit 16-2, the range of elected amounts is between the A.C.B. (the lower limit of $75) and the F.M.V. (the upper limit of $100). Since the boot of $60 is below the A.C.B. of $75, it does not affect the lower limit. In Case 2, the range of elected amounts is still between $75 and $100. However, the boot of $75 is the lower limit in this situation and would result in a capital gain of $15 (i.e., $75 – $60). In Case 3, there is no range of elected amounts, but only one amount which is both the upper and lower limit.

In Case 1 of the Exhibit, if the objective was to fully defer the accrued gain on the property of $25 (i.e., $100 – $75) on the transfer, the elected transfer price should be $75. Taking "boot" of up to $75 as consideration would not jeopardize the lower limit on the transfer price of $75. Since "boot" is considered to be "hard" consideration like cash or debt which can be repaid in cash without tax consequences, taking the maximum of $75 in this case is most beneficial. To take less than $75 of "boot" in Case 1 will still permit a full deferral of the accrued gain on the property transferred, but it wastes an opportunity to receive consideration without tax consequences. The reason that $75 of "boot" can be received as consideration without tax consequences, is that the $75 represents the cost of the asset transferred. The cost was incurred by expending after-tax funds. Therefore, it should be recovered on a disposition of the property without tax consequences. Hence, the maximum "boot" of $75, in this case, allows a tax-free recovery of the cost of the property transferred.

In Case 2 of the Exhibit, the lower limit is the boot of $75 rather than the A.C.B. of $60, as was the situation in Case 1. This result is because the taxpayer has extracted from the corporation $75 of boot which is $15 more than the tax value of the asset transferred (i.e., $60). Since the elected amount is the proceeds of disposition to the transferor, a capital gain of $15 is triggered (i.e., $75–$60). Under the technical rules of section 85, this result is accomplished by automatically bumping the elected amount by the excess of the boot over the cost amount [par. 85(1)(c)]. In Case 3 of the Exhibit, it would have been possible to receive boot of $75, i.e., the fair market value of the asset transferred, without adverse tax consequences. Only where boot exceeds fair market value, does this problem arise.

Consider the following numerical example of the application of the rules on the transfer of capital property having an adjusted cost base of $1,000 and a fair market value of $1,500:

Consideration	Alternatives		
	A	*B*	*C*
Cash, etc..	0	$ 1,000	$ 1,300
Preferred shares (F.M.V. and legal stated capital).....	$ 1,000	300	180
Common shares (F.M.V. and legal stated capital).....	500	200	20
Total......................................	$ 1,500	$ 1,500	$ 1,500
Election range:			
high[1].....................................	$ 1,500	$ 1,500	$ 1,500
low[2]	$ 1,000	$ 1,000	$ 1,300
Election price (assumed at lowest).................	$ 1,000	$ 1,000	$ 1,300
Adjusted cost base............................	1,000	1,000	1,000
Capital gain	Nil	Nil	$ 300
Taxable capital gain at $1/2$ inclusion rate	Nil	Nil	$ 150

NOTE: (1) Fair market value of property transferred.

(2) Fair market value of consideration received other than shares, limited further in Case A by the adjusted cost base of the property transferred.

Example Problem

Mr. Sole Proprietor owns the following assets in a business that he wants to incorporate:

	Tax value*	Fair market value
Short-term investments	$ 15,000	$ 18,000
Inventory	45,000	46,000
Machinery (cost: $54,375)........................	26,250	38,500
Goodwill......................................	—	30,000
	$ 86,250	$132,500
Liabilities	10,000	10,000
	$ 76,250	$122,500

*Cost values for tax purposes used to describe the lowest limit of the elected transfer price range in Exhibit 16-1.

As fair market value consideration, he wants $70,000 in new debt, $35,000 in preferred shares and the balance in common shares to total the fair market value of the net assets transferred to the corporation. Also, the corporation will assume the existing debt of the proprietorship.

— REQUIRED

Indicate the appropriate elected amounts which should be used to defer any taxation upon the incorporation of the proprietorship.

— SOLUTION

	Tax value	Fair market value	Elected transfer price	F.M.V. of consideration[2]				
				Assumed debt[3]	New debt[3]	Preferred shares	Common shares	Income
Short-term investments[1]	$ 15,000	$ 18,000	$ 15,000	$ 10,000	$ 5,000	$ 3,000	$ —	Nil
Inventory.......	45,000	46,000	45,000	—	45,000	1,000	—	Nil
Machinery	26,250	38,500	26,250	—	20,000	6,250	12,250	Nil
Goodwill	Nil	30,000	1[4]	—	—	24,750	5,250	$0.50
	$ 86,250	$132,500	$ 86,251[5]	$ 10,000	$70,000	$35,000	$17,500	

— NOTES TO SOLUTION

(1) Short-term investments should only be transferred to the corporation if they can be considered assets used in the active business of the corporation, in this case. If they are investment assets, they may jeopardize the status of the corporation's shares as qualifying small business corporation shares (QSBCS). Here, it is assumed that the short-term investments represent the investment of temporarily surplus cash needed for active business operations.

(2) The order of the allocation of debt and share consideration, as shown in this example, is arbitrarily made in the order that the assets are listed in the facts. This particular method, while not required by the legislation, allows for a systematic allocation, first of the "boot", including assumed debt, up to the maximum, if desired, and, then, of the share consideration.

(3) Note that the debt, as non-share consideration, can be set at any level, but the amount taken affects the minimum elected transfer price. It is the only consideration that has an effect on that minimum elected transfer price and must be selected to meet the transferor's objective of, in this case, deferring any taxation on the transfer. In this situation, the maximum new debt consideration or boot (i.e., $76,251) was not taken in order to demonstrate certain effects. However, the transferor might be advised to take debt consideration, including assumed debt, to a total of $86,251 which is equal to the desired minimum elected amount. By not receiving the maximum debt consideration, where financially feasible, the transferor is wasting an opportunity to recover, at the time of the transfer to the corporation, his cost in the property transferred on a tax-free basis. The share consideration, which has no effect on the elected amount, is used to balance the fair market value of the total consideration received, including "boot" and shares, with the total fair market value of all property transferred to the corporation. Under the rollover, this balancing of fair market value is necessary to avoid the problems which will be discussed later.

Note, however, that preferred shares generally have a fixed value (i.e., redemption value or retraction value), whereas common shares have a floating value which absorbs the fair market value of the property transferred net of the other consideration (i.e., boot and preferred shares).

(4) To have a valid election the minimum elected transfer price must be a nominal amount (i.e., $1.00) [IC 76-19R3].

(5) The elected amount is used as proceeds of disposition to the transferor, as the cost of the property to the corporation and as adjusted cost base of the consideration received by the transferor from the corporation.

D. The Corporation's Position

[ITA: 85(1)(a); 85(5); ITR: 1100(2.2); 1102(14)]

As previously indicated, the elected transfer price becomes the corporation's cost of the property [par. 85(1)(a)]. For depreciable property, the Act provides that the capital cost of the property to the corporation will be deemed to equal the capital cost of the property to the transferor [par. 85(5)(a)]. The corporation will be deemed to have claimed capital cost allowances equal to the amount by which the capital cost exceeds the transfer price [par. 85(5)(b)]. In essence, the corporation steps into the transferor's tax position in all respects on transfer of the assets of the corporation at undepreciated capital cost. The corporation takes capital cost allowance from undepreciated capital cost and it is liable for recapture up to the transferor's original capital cost.

Note that the half-net-amount rule for calculating capital cost allowance in the year of acquisition of an asset does not apply in a subsection 85(1) election if two conditions apply [Reg. 1100(2.2)]:

- the transferor was not dealing at arm's length with the corporation at the time of the transfer; and

- the property was owned continuously by the transferor for the period from at least 365 days before the end of the taxation year of the corporation in which the asset was acquired to the date of the election.

Similarly non-arm's length transfers of depreciable property retain the same capital cost allowance class [Reg. 1102(14)]. For example, a Class 3 asset (building) acquired by a non-arm's length party, as would be the case where the property is transferred to a corporation controlled by the transferor or a person related to the transferor, would be placed in Class 3. In an arm's length acquisition, the asset would be placed in Class 1.

E. The Shareholder's Position

[ITA: 53(1); 54.2; 85(1)]

For the shareholder, the elected transfer price is basically allocated to become the cost of the property received (i.e., boot or shares) as consideration in exchange for the property transferred in the following order:

(a) property other than shares (i.e., boot or non-share consideration) up to the fair market value of that property as long as that fair market value does not exceed the fair market value of the assets transferred to the corporation [par. 85(1)(f)];

(b) preferred shares up to the fair market value of those shares after the transfer as long as that fair market value does not exceed the proceeds of disposition (elected amount) minus the fair market value of the non-share consideration received [par. 85(1)(g)]; and

(c) common shares to the extent that proceeds of disposition (elected amount) exceed the sum of the fair market value of the non-share consideration and the cost allocated to the preferred shares above (non-negative amounts only) [par. 85(1)(h)].

The Act defines a preferred share as a share other than a common share [ssec.248(1)]. A common share is defined as a share the holder of which is not precluded from participating in the assets of the corporation beyond the amount paid up on that share plus a fixed premium and a defined rate of dividend [ssec. 248(1)].

The shares received as consideration are deemed to be capital property of the recipient of the shares where all or substantially all of the assets transferred to the corporation were used in an active business carried on by the transferor [ssec. 54.2]. This rule ensures that where a transfer is made in contemplation of the sale of the shares received as consideration, the latter sale of shares will be treated as a capital transaction. Where the seller of the shares is an individual, the sale may qualify for the capital gains deduction for Q.S.B.C. shares.

Recall the three-alternative example on page 861, involving the transfer of the single capital property. Applying these rules, the following shows the cost of the *consideration* received under each alternative:

Consideration	Alternatives		
	A	*B*	*C*
Elected transfer price	$ 1,000	$ 1,000	$ 1,300
Cost after ssec. 85(1):			
Cash, etc.	—	$ 1,000	$ 1,300
Preferred shares	$ 1,000	Nil	Nil
Common shares	Nil	Nil	Nil
	$ 1,000	$ 1,000	$ 1,300

Example Problem ————————————————————

Reconsider the previous example problem starting on page 861.

—*REQUIRED*

Compute the cost of the consideration taken from the corporation for the net assets transferred.

—*SOLUTION*

Elected transfer price		$ 86,251
Allocation to cost of non-share consideration:		
Liabilities assumed	$10,000	
New debt	70,000	80,000
Allocation to preferred shares (up to their f.m.v.)		$ 6,251
Allocation to common shares		Nil

Note that the $86,251 of elected amount represents the tax-paid cost in the assets transferred to the corporation, that is, $86,250 of tax value and $1 elected on goodwill and included in income. The cost of the consideration received for these assets reflects that tax-paid cost. The $10,000 of liabilities are assumed without any tax consequences on the transfer or in the future. The new debt of $70,000 can be repaid without tax consequences in the future. The preferred shares have a cost of $6,251 which can be recovered tax free in the future. The common shares have a cost of nil, because all of the tax-paid cost in the assets transferred to the corporation has been recovered in the debt and preferred shares received.

F. Paid-up Capital Reduction on Shares Issued as Consideration

[ITA: 85(2.1); 257]

Recall the discussion of paid-up capital of shares in the previous chapter. Where shares have no par value or stated value under corporate law, their paid-up capital value normally reflects the fair market value of the property for which the shares were issued. In the previous example problem (on page 861) this legal stated capital (L.S.C.) was $35,000 for the preferred shares and $17,500 for the common shares, since, on the issue of the shares, the fair market value of net assets of the corporation increased by a total of $52,500 (i.e., $132,500 − ($10,000 + $70,000)). This value of $52,500 is also the fair market value of all the shares issued and reflects, in part, the accrued income on the inventory, machinery and goodwill deferred on the transfer of those assets to the corporation. Since the adjusted cost base of the preferred shares is $6,251 and that of the common shares is Nil, as determined under subsection 85(1), a capital gain would result from an arm's length sale of the shares. This capital gain may be eligible for the Q.S.B.C. share capital gains deduction while the original income deferred on the transfer would not have been. Similarly, if the shares were redeemed by the corporation for their fair market value, there would be no deemed dividend [ssec. 84(3)], because their fair market value is equal to their paid-up capital value. As a result, on the redemption there would be a capital gain which, again, may be eligible for the Q.S.B.C. share capital gains deduction. Finally, if the individual shareholder were to continue to hold indefinitely the shares received as consideration, the paid-up capital could be removed on a tax-free basis through a payment that would result in a P.U.C. reduction that would not be subject to deemed dividend rules in subsection 84(4) or (4.1).

The Q.S.B.C. share capital gains deduction has apparently necessitated an anti-avoidance rule which is provided in subsection 85(2.1). Paragraph 85(2.1)(*a*) provides for a reduction (often referred to in practice as a "grind") in the paid-up capital of a *particular* class of shares of a corporation after the disposition of property equal to:

$$(A - B) \times \frac{C}{A}$$

where A = the increase in legal stated capital of all shares of the corporation after the disposition under section 85;

B = the excess, if any, of the corporation's cost of the property determined under subsection 85(1) (i.e., the elected amount) *over* the fair market value of the non-share consideration (i.e., the "boot");

C = the increase in legal stated capital of a particular class of shares on the transfer of property to the corporation.

If the amount (A − B) is negative, section 257 deems it to be nil.

To better understand the effects of subsection 85(2.1), consider a capital asset with the following features:

Tax value...	$10,000
Fair market value	15,000

If this property is sold in an arm's length transaction, there will be either business income or a capital gain, depending on the nature of the asset, in the amount of $5,000. Hence, of the $15,000 of proceeds received, $5,000 is income subject to tax in some form and the other $10,000 is a recovery of the cost (i.e., tax value) of the asset on a tax-free basis, because the asset was purchased with after-tax funds.

Now consider a transfer of the above asset to a corporation pursuant to subsection 85(1) as follows:

Elected amount (equal to tax value)	$10,000
Fair market value of non-share consideration ("boot")	10,000
Fair market value and L.S.C. of share consideration	5,000
Adjusted cost base of share consideration [par. 85(1)(*g*) or (*h*)]	Nil

If the share consideration received from the corporation is subsequently sold in an arm's length transaction for its current fair market value, a capital gain of $5,000 would result in most circumstances. This capital gain is equal to the gain that had accrued on the asset transferred to the corporation. If the asset was a capital property that would have resulted in a capital gain on its arm's length disposition, the usual capital gain on the disposition of the share consideration would provide the equivalent treatment, that is, taxation of one-half of the gain.

However, if the asset was inventory that would have resulted in business income on its arm's length disposition, a transfer to a corporation in the manner described would potentially convert the business income into a capital gain on the ultimate sale of the share consideration. Shares accepted as consideration on a disposition to a corporation are deemed to be capital property of the transferor [sec. 54.2]. The provision requires, however, that all or substantially all of the assets, used in an active business by the transferor, must be disposed of to the corporation. Note that the definition of a business [ssec. 248(1)] specifically excludes an adventure in the nature of trade for purposes of section 54.2.

On the other hand, if the share consideration received from the corporation is subsequently redeemed by the corporation, subsection 85(2.1) will have an effect. First, subsection 85(2.1) will reduce (or grind) the paid-up capital for tax purposes of the share consideration to nil as follows:

L.S.C. of share consideration before reduction............		$5,000
Less: ssec. 85(2.1) reduction in P.U.C.		
(1) increase in L.S.C. of all shares on the transfer to the corporation.............	$5,000 (A)	
(2) elected amount..............	$10,000	
less: boot...................	10,000	
excess if any..........................	Nil (B)	
total reduction (A − B).........................		5,000*
Tax P.U.C. of share consideration after reduction.........		Nil

* This P.U.C. reduction equals the untaxed gain (i.e., the deferred gain) on the transfer of the property to the corporation.

Since only one class of shares was assumed to have been received as consideration, there is no need to apply the prorating component of the formula.

P.U.C. of New Shares Received

Note how the tax P.U.C. of the share consideration after the reduction under subsection 85(2.1) is nil. This P.U.C. value for tax purposes represents the amount of the original cost of the asset transferred (i.e., $10,000) that has not been recovered through "boot". Since the "boot" of $10,000 in this case can be thought of as a full recovery of the original cost of the asset transferred, there is no further amount of that cost to be recovered on a tax-free basis and, hence, the tax P.U.C. value should be nil. Recall that P.U.C. represents an amount that can be returned to a shareholder on a tax-free basis, because it represents a contribution to the capital of the corporation made with after-tax funds. In this case, the "funds" contributed to the corporation consisted of a property with an untaxed, accrued capital gain. This conceptual approach to determining the tax value of the P.U.C. of shares can be used to predict or to check the application of the technical formula.

Assume the shares received as consideration are now redeemed for their fair market value of $5,000. The following compares the effects of subsection 85(2.1) on the results of a redemption if subsection 85(2.1) had not been added to the legislation:

	With ssec. 85(2.1) P.U.C. reduction	*Without ssec. 85(2.1) P.U.C. reduction*
Proceeds on redemption	$5,000	$5,000
Less: P.U.C.	Nil	5,000
Deemed dividend [ssec. 84(3)]	$5,000	Nil
Proceeds on redemption	$5,000	$5,000
Less: deemed dividend [ssec. 84(3) above]	5,000	Nil
Proceeds of disposition [sec. 54]	Nil	$5,000
Less: adjusted cost base	Nil	Nil
Capital gain	Nil	$5,000

Note that a *redemption* of the shares, received as consideration under the subsection 85(1) transfer, results in a deemed dividend, rather than a capital gain that might have been eligible for the Q.S.B.C. share capital gains deduction. In other words, subsection 85(2.1) converts what would have been a taxable capital gain into a deemed dividend if the corporation is redeeming the shares.

The foregoing analysis illustrates the effects of subsection 85(2.1) as an anti-avoidance rule which prevents the conversion of an amount that might have been taxed as property income into a potentially tax-free capital gain on the *redemption* of shares received as consideration.

Example Problem

Reconsider the previous example problem on page 861.

— REQUIRED

Compute the paid-up capital for tax purposes of the preferred and common shares received from the corporation.

— SOLUTION

	Preferred shares	*Common shares*
Subsection 85(2.1) reduction in P.U.C.:		
(1) increase in L.S.C. of *all* shares on the transfer to the corporation .... $52,500 (A)		
(2) elected amount ... $ 86,251 less: non-share consideration 80,000		
excess, if any .... 6,251 (B)		
total reduction (A – B) .... $46,249[1]		
(3) increase in L.S.C. of a class of shares issued	$ 35,000 (C)	$ 17,500 (C)
Reduction in each class $[(A - B) \times \frac{C}{A}]$		
Preferred shares: $46,249 $\times \frac{\$35,000}{\$52,500}$	(30,833)	
Common shares: $46,249 $\times \frac{\$17,500}{\$52,500}$		(15,416)
P.U.C. (for tax purposes) of each class	$ 4,167	$ 2,084

This P.U.C. reduction will have no tax consequences unless and until the shares are *redeemed* by the corporation. Arm's length sales are unaffected by the P.U.C. reduction. On redemption for fair market value of the shares, the following will occur:

	Preferred shares	Common shares
Redemption amount (F.M.V.)	$ 35,000	$17,500
Less: P.U.C. (tax)	4,167	2,084
Deemed dividend [ssec. 84(3)]	$ 30,833	$15,416
Redemption amount...............................	$ 35,000	$17,500
Less: deemed dividend...........................	30,833	15,416
Proceeds of disposition [sec. 54]....................	$ 4,167	$ 2,084
Proceeds of disposition	$ 4,167	$ 2,084
Less: adjusted cost base [ssec.85(1)]	6,251	Nil
Capital gain (loss)	$ (2,084)	$ 2,084

Note that, had the P.U.C. not been reduced, there would not have been a deemed dividend, because redemption proceeds would have been equal to P.U.C. The result would have been a capital gain on the preferred shares of $28,749 (i.e., $35,000 − $6,251) and on the common shares of $17,500 (i.e., $17,500 − Nil). Therefore, subsection 85(2.1) converts, at least in part, what might have been a taxable capital gain into a taxable deemed dividend.

— NOTE TO SOLUTION

(1) Again, this P.U.C. reduction appears to be the untaxed gain (i.e., the deferred gain) on the transfer of property with a fair market value of $132,500 at an elected amount of $86,251 for a deferred gain of $46,249 (i.e., $132,500 − $86,251). The resultant P.U.C. for tax purposes of $6,251 (i.e., $4,167 + $2,084) represents the tax value or cost (that has not been eroded by a decline in fair market value below cost) that has not been recovered through debt consideration, including assumed debt. Of the $86,251 of tax value in the assets originally transferred, $80,000 (i.e., $10,000 + $70,000) has been recovered through "boot" received on the transfer. The remainder of unrecovered tax value is $6,250 (i.e., $86,250 − $80,000) which differs from the tax value of P.U.C. by the $1 included in income from the required elected amount on the goodwill.

From the foregoing example problem, it can be seen that if property is transferred to a corporation utilizing the provisions of section 85 and, in consideration, the corporation issues common shares without par value, the fair market value of the shares will reflect to some degree the fair market value of the assets transferred. The adjusted cost base of the shares will depend upon the elected transfer price and the P.U.C. will be determined as has been previously mentioned. Therefore, it can be seen that each of these three amounts, that is, the fair market value, adjusted cost base and P.U.C. can and likely will all be different as each is determined independently.

G. Other Rules Applicable in the Rollover

[ITA: 13(7)(*e*), (21.2); 14(12); 40(3.3), (3.4), (3.6); 53(1)(*f*); 85(1)(*e*.1); IT-291R3]

1. Depreciable capital property

(a) *Ordering of Dispositions within a Class*

When a transfer involves a number of items of eligible capital property or depreciable property of the same prescribed class, the taxpayer must designate the order of disposition. Otherwise the Minister will make the designation. By having separate, sequential dispositions, the undepreciated capital cost or cumulative eligible capital balance will be reduced after each separate disposition for the purpose of determining the minimum transfer price. For example, consider the following case:

	Depreciable property	
	1	*2*
Capital cost........................	$7,000	$14,000
Fair market value	9,000	12,000
U.C.C. of class	$13,000	
Possible elected amounts [par. 85(1)(*e*)]....................	7,000	12,000

Were it not for the rule in paragraph 85(1)(*e*.1), the total elected amount of $19,000 for both assets would be subtracted from the balance in the class resulting in a credit balance of $6,000 (i.e., $19,000–13,000) which would be included in income as recapture. However, using the rule in paragraph 85(1)(*e*.1), property 1 could be transferred first at its elected amount of $7,000. Proceeds of disposition would, thus, be $7,000 and this would be subtracted from the balance of $13,000 in the class to leave an undepreciated capital cost balance of $6,000. Then, property 2 would be transferred. Using the rule in paragraph 85(1)(*e*), the elected amount cannot be less than the least of: fair market value of the property transferred ($12,000), undepreciated capital cost of the class of the property transferred ($6,000), and cost of the property transferred ($14,000). Thus, the elected transfer price would be established at $6,000 which would become proceeds of disposition. When this is subtracted from the undepreciated capital cost balance of $6,000 the new balance becomes nil and no recapture results.

(b) *Terminal Losses*

A terminal loss generally occurs where there is a positive balance in a depreciable capital property class and the taxpayer no longer owns any property in that class. Although depreciable capital property can be transferred under section 85, there is no advantage in doing so in the case of an individual transferring depreciable capital property with an unrealized terminal loss and subjecting the transfer to all the conditions imposed under section 85 (i.e., taking back share consideration, etc.). Therefore, it is recommended that depreciable capital property with an unrealized terminal loss should not be transferred under section 85, but should be sold to the corporation at fair market value, taking back debt consideration.

The rules in subsection 13(21.2) deny a terminal loss on a transfer of depreciable capital property by an individual, corporation, trust or partnership to a corporation, among others, with which the transferor is affiliated, as defined [sec. 251.1]. Section 85 does not apply to the transfer in these situations. The amount of the unrealized terminal loss is held in the capital cost allowance class from which the property came and the transferor subject to these rules will be allowed to claim capital cost allowance on that class. On the occurrence of one of several specified events in the future, involving a disposition or deemed disposition of the property by the transferee corporation, the remaining U.C.C. can be written off as a terminal loss by the transferor. The recipient corporation is allowed to deduct capital cost allowance on a U.C.C. equal to the F.M.V. of the property at the time of the transfer. The recipient corporation will be liable for recapture up to the original capital cost of the property to the transferor. (A parallel set of rules applies to the transfer of eligible capital property [ssec. 14(12)].)

(c) *Limitations on Transferee's Cost Basis*

Where depreciable property with an accrued capital gain (and, perhaps, an undepreciated capital cost equal to or only slightly less than capital cost) is transferred to a corporation with which the transferor does not deal at arm's length, there may be a temptation to elect at fair market value on the transfer to trigger the accrued capital gain. The capital gain would be only $1/2$ taxable, and the corporation would be deemed to have acquired depreciable property at full fair market value which would become the base for the future undepreciated capital cost in the corporation. The prospect of such a transfer probably resulted in the introduction of paragraph 13(7)(*e*). Conceptually, paragraph 13(7)(*e*) restricts any step-up of the original capital cost, in respect of a non-arm's length transfer, to the *taxable* capital gain realized.

Consider the transfer by an individual to a corporation, which he or she controls, of a depreciable capital property, the only asset in the class, with an undepreciated capital cost of $50,000, a capital cost of $55,000 and a fair market value of $95,000. If the individual can offset all of the accrued taxable capital gain with net capital losses and he or she elects under subsection 85(1) to transfer the property at fair market value of $95,000 the following taxable income would result for the individual:

Recapture ($55,000 – $50,000)	$ 5,000
Taxable capital gain [$1/2 \times$ ($95,000 – $55,000)]	20,000
Income	$25,000

Where the cost of the property to the corporation (i.e., the elected amount of $95,000) exceeds the capital cost of the property to the transferor (i.e., $55,000), paragraph 13(7)(*e*) applies on a non-arm's length transfer of depreciable property. As a result, in this case subparagraph 13(7)(*e*)(i) deems the capital cost of the property to the corporation to be equal to the aggregate of:

(a) The capital cost of the property to the transferor		$55,000
(b) The transferor's proceeds of disposition (i.e., the elected amount)	$ 95,000	
Less: the capital cost (A.C.B.) of the property to the transferor	55,000	
Excess, if any	$ 40,000	
$1/2$ of excess		20,000
Deemed capital cost to the corporation		$75,000

This technical calculation can be summarized as follows:

Sum of:	
(a) transferor's original capital cost	$55,000
(b) taxable capital gain [$1/2 \times$ ($95,000 – $55,000)]	20,000
Deemed capital cost	$75,000

This deemed capital cost of $75,000 will be the base for future capital cost allowance for the corporation and the limit of recapture on a future disposition. Hence, only an amount that has been fully taxed to the transferor is eligible for the C.C.A. base which will give rise to fully deductible C.C.A. However, for the purposes of future capital gains, the capital cost will be the $95,000 elected amount by virtue of paragraph 85(1)(*a*) which is not affected by the rules in subparagraph 13(7)(*e*)(i) for that purpose.

2. Transfer of non-depreciable capital property with unrealized capital losses to affiliated persons

The legislation imposes restrictions on a capital loss arising from property that is transferred to certain non-arm's length persons, referred to as "affiliated persons". Some of the restrictions depend upon the type of the affiliated person (i.e., individual, corporation, etc.); others are common to all affiliated persons. These provisions are often referred to as the "stop-loss" rules.

(a) *Definition of Affiliated Persons*

Subsection 251.1(1) defines an "affiliated person". In order to understand this definition, a few additional rules should be noted at the outset. Subsection 251.1(3) states that persons are considered to be affiliated with themselves and that a person includes a partnership. Subsection 251.1(2) defines the following terms:

(a) an "affiliated group of persons" refers to a group each member of which is affiliated with every other member; and

(b) "controlled" means controlled, directly or indirectly in any manner whatever, and, hence, includes *de facto* control as defined [ssec. 256(5.1)], discussed in a previous chapter.

Paragraph 251.1(1)(*a*) provides that two individuals are considered to be affiliated only when they are spouses of each other, including common-law partner as defined [ssec. 248(1)].

Paragraph 251.1(1)(*b*) describes a corporation as being affiliated with three types of persons:

(a) a person by whom the corporation is controlled (as defined above);

(b) each member of an affiliated group (as defined above) by which the corporation is controlled; and

(c) the spouse of a person in either of the first two categories above.

Very generally, for example, a corporation affiliated with an individual transferor, as contemplated by section 85, is one which is controlled by the individual or the individual's spouse.

Consider the following example. A, an individual who is not married, controls A Ltd., A and two other individuals, B and C, own an equal number of shares and votes in ABC Ltd. B and C are married to each other.

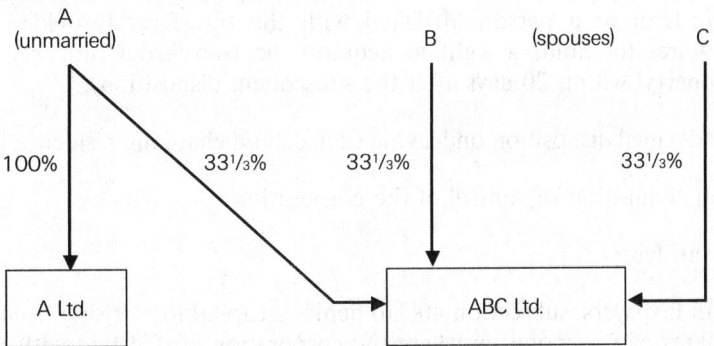

A is not affiliated with any individual, since he is not married. B and C are affiliated, because they are spouses. A Ltd. is affiliated with A since A controls it. ABC Ltd. is affiliated with both B and C, since they are members of an affiliated group that controls (i.e., owns 66²/₃% of) ABC Ltd. ABC Ltd. is not affiliated with A unless A has some form of non-voting *de facto* control.

(b) *Unrealized Capital Losses*

The "stop-loss" provisions deny the immediate recognition of the capital loss in all situations where the transferee is affiliated with the transferor. However, the subsequent treatment of the capital loss will depend upon the type of non-depreciable asset that is transferred and the type of person which is the transferor and/or transferee.

(i) Individual Transferors

For individual transferors, the denied capital loss (except for certain share transfers discussed below) is added to the adjusted cost base of the property held by the corporate transferee [par. 53(1)(f)]. For individuals, the capital loss denial is achieved through the interaction of two provisions: the definition of a "superficial loss" [sec. 54] and the superficial loss denial [par. 40(2)(g)]. The definition of a "superficial loss" includes any capital loss arising on a transfer of capital property by individuals to an affiliated person, as described in section 251.1.

For example, if Ms. X transfers to her wholly-owned corporation land which has an unrealized capital loss of $10,000 (e.g., F.M.V. of $90,000 and A.C.B. of $100,000), then the capital loss of $10,000 will be added to the F.M.V. of the land of $90,000 resulting in a $100,000 adjusted cost base of the transferred land held by the corporation. In essence, the corporation will hold the land with an A.C.B. of $100,000 and a F.M.V. of $90,000, as Ms. X did before the transfer. To accomplish the transfer, it is not necessary to elect under section 85 with its conditions. A simple sale at fair market value for consideration like debt of equal fair market value is all that is necessary in the case of an individual transferor.

(ii) Corporate, Trust and Partnership Transferors

For corporations, trusts and partnerships, the denied capital loss (except for certain share transfers, discussed below) is subject to subsections 40(3.3) and (3.4) which cause the affected capital loss to be retained by the transferor and its recognition by the transferor to be deferred until the earliest of the following events:

(a) a subsequent disposition of the transferred property to a person that is not the transferor or a person affiliated with the transferor (provided that neither acquires (or holds a right to acquire) the transferred property (or identical property) within 30 days after the subsequent disposition);

(b) a deemed disposition on leaving Canada and changing residence [sec. 128.1]; or

(c) an acquisition of control of the corporation.

(iii) All Transferors

For all taxpayers, subsection 40(3.6) denies a capital loss arising from the redemption of shares of a corporation where the corporation is affiliated with the transferor immediately after the transfer. In this situation, the denied capital loss is added to the adjusted cost base of any shares held by the transferor in the transferee corporation. For example, if the transferor transfers *all* its shares to the issuing corporation (i.e., all of the shares are redeemed) and, as a result, the transferor is no longer affiliated, then the loss is recognized because the transferor is no longer affiliated with the transferee corporation. If, however, the transferor (or another affiliated shareholder) controls the corporation after the transfer, then the loss is denied and the denied loss is added to the adjusted cost base of the remaining shares held by the transferor. However, if the transferor does not hold any shares after the transfer, but is still affiliated, the denied loss is lost.

3. Summary of stop-loss rules

The loss denial rules discussed above are often referred to as "stop-loss" rules. These rules are summarized in Exhibit 16-3.

EXHIBIT 16-3
Stop-loss Rules

Transferor is a corporation, trust or partnership	Transferor is an individual
Capital loss on transfer	**Capital loss on transfer**
● to an affiliated purchaser [sec. 251.1]	● to an affiliated purchaser [sec. 251.1]
● capital loss is denied [ssec. 40(3.4)]	● capital loss is denied as a superficial loss [sec. 54, par. 40(2)(*g*)]
● capital loss is kept with the transferor until the transferee sells the asset to a non-affiliated person	● denied loss is added to the cost of the asset to the transferee
Terminal loss	**Terminal loss**
● on transfer to an affiliated purchaser [sec. 251.1]	● same as for corporations, trusts or partnerships
● terminal loss is denied [ssec. 13(21.2)]	
● terminal loss is kept with the transferor until the transferee sells the asset to a non-affiliated person	
● transferee records the asset with a cost equal to the cost to the transferor and an addition to UCC equal to FMV [par. 13(7)(*e*)]	
Capital loss on redemption	**Capital loss on redemption**
● affiliated [sec.251.1] immediately after the redemption	● same as for corporations, trusts or partnerships
● capital loss is denied [ssec. 40(3.6)]	
● capital loss is added to the ACB of any other shares owned by the transferor; if no other shares owned, but the transferor is still affiliated, then capital loss is lost	

H. Benefits Conferred on Shareholders and Related Persons

[ITA: 15(1); 85(1)(*e*.2)]

Throughout the chapter so far, it has been emphasized over and over again that the fair market value of the consideration taken back by the transferor must equal the fair market value of the property transferred. Now the adverse tax consequences of not adhering to this rule will be examined.

The topic will be introduced, first, conceptually. Then, the technical rules will be examined in two situations:

(a) where the consideration package is valued at less than the fair market value of the property transferred; and

(b) where the consideration package is valued at greater than the fair market value of the property transferred.

1. Conceptual example

(a) *Conditions for Transfer*

The assets can be transferred at any amount between the tax value and the fair market value of the particular asset. The consideration in this situation will be preferred shares with a specific redemption value or retraction value (shares are redeemed at the option of the corporation and retracted at the option of the shareholder). Remember that common shares, as used in the previous situations, will automatically pick up the F.M.V. of the asset transferred net of any boot or non-share consideration. This is not true for preferred shares unless the retraction or redemption value is fixed exactly equal to the F.M.V. of the property transferred net of any boot. Therefore, as long as the F.M.V. of the property transferred is exactly equal to the F.M.V. of the consideration (i.e., boot plus preferred shares) there will be no negative tax consequences as demonstrated below.

(b) *Facts*

Ms. D wishes to transfer land to a corporation, D Ltd., which her daughter presently controls through the ownership of all the common shares.

Land — A.C.B.	$ 30,000
— F.M.V.	150,000

Ms. D is considering three different consideration packages:

(a) a promissory note of $30,000 plus non-voting preferred shares with a retraction and stated value of $120,000 for a total F.M.V. equal to the F.M.V. of the land;

(b) a promissory note of $10,000 and non-voting preferred shares with a retraction and stated value of $20,000 for a total F.M.V. which is less than the F.M.V. of the land; or

(c) a promissory note of $200,000 and non-voting preferred shares with a retraction and stated value of a nominal amount for a total F.M.V. which is greater than the F.M.V. of the land.

Package (a) is on-side and there are no adverse tax consequences. However, Packages (b) and (c) are off-side and result in adverse tax consequences.

Ms. D and D Ltd. are going to choose an elected amount of $30,000 equal to the A.C.B. of the land.

(c) *Results*

The *first* consideration package is on-side and will not have any adverse tax consequences since the F.M.V. of land (i.e., $150,000) equals the F.M.V. of the consideration (i.e., $30,000 of boot plus preferred shares retractable at $120,000). Note that the boot is also on-side since it does not exceed the elected amount of $30,000. The $30,000 of boot, which will be received ultimately tax-free, reflects the tax-paid cost of the land. See Situation Three where the boot is off-side.

In summary, the following has occurred:

Before transfer		After transfer			
Ms. D owned	*Land*	*Ms. D owns*	*Debt*	*Corporation owns*	*Land*
A.C.B.	$ 30,000	A.C.B.	$ 30,000	A.C.B.	$ 30,000
F.M.V.	150,000	F.M.V.	30,000	F.M.V.	150,000
		Ms. D owns	*Shares*	*Corporation owes to:*	
		A.C.B.	Nil	Ms. D	$ 30,000
		P.U.C.	Nil		
		F.M.V.	$120,000		

The *second* consideration package is off-side since Ms. D has accepted consideration which, in total, is less than the F.M.V. of the land (i.e., ($10,000 + $20,000) compared to $150,000). Ms. D is deemed to have conferred a benefit (gift) on her daughter of $120,000 (i.e., the F.M.V. of the land ($150,000) − the F.M.V. of the consideration ($10,000 + $20,000)). Since the daughter is the common shareholder, this $120,000 difference (contributed surplus in accounting terms) will increase the F.M.V. of the common shares. In essence, Ms. D has attempted to pass $120,000 of the accumulated growth in the land which should be taxed in her hands to her daughter. The tax consequences of this off-side transaction will be as follows:

(1) The original elected amount of $30,000 will be bumped by the amount of the gift (i.e., $120,000) to $150,000 which is exactly equal to the F.M.V. of the land (i.e., $150,000) and a capital gain of $120,000 will be triggered in Ms. D's hands since her proceeds of disposition are now $150,000.

(2) The A.C.B. of the land now held by D Ltd. will be the new elected amount of $150,000.

(3) Since the A.C.B. of the preferred shares cannot exceed their retraction amount of $20,000 (the fair market value), a downward adjustment must be made. The A.C.B. of the preferred shares of $20,000 is determined as the original elected amount of $30,000 (not the new elected amount of $150,000) minus the $10,000 allocated to the boot. This A.C.B. of $20,000 is now equal to the retraction amount. However, there is an inherent, but hidden penalty in the daughter's common shares, since they retain their original A.C.B. while the value has increased by $120,000 as a result of the gift. Therefore, she will realize a capital gain of $120,000 upon the ultimate disposition of her shares. This is analogous to the one-sided adjustments in section 69, discussed in Chapter 8, on non-arm's length transfers which can result in a double-counting of income.

(4) The P.U.C. of Ms. D's preferred shares, however, will be calculated with the *increased* elected amount of $150,000 as calculated below:

Stated capital*		$ 20,000
Less: elected amount (new)	$150,000	
less: boot.	10,000	140,000
P.U.C. reduction		Nil
∴ P.U.C.		$ 20,000

This $20,000 represents the remaining cost of the land transferred (i.e., $30,000) after taking out boot in the form of a promissory note (i.e., $10,000).

*Note that under the *Canada Business Corporations Act* (CBCA), normally the stated value of the share consideration must equal the fair market value of the property transferred (i.e., $150,000, the F.M.V. of the land). However, for non-arm's length transactions, the stated value can, at the discretion of the corporate directors, be set at less than the fair market value (i.e., $20,000).

In summary, the following has occurred:

Before transfer		After transfer	
Ms. D owned	*Land*	*Ms. D owns*	*Debt*
A.C.B. .... $ 30,000		A.C.B. .... $ 10,000	
F.M.V. 150,000		F.M.V. 10,000	

Corporation owns	*Land*
A.C.B. $150,000
F.M.V. 150,000

Ms. D owns	*Shares*
A.C.B. .... $ 20,000
P.U.C. 20,000
F.M.V. 20,000

Corporation owes to:
Ms. D .... $ 10,000

Ms. D has a capital gain of $120,000 to include in her income.

The value of the corporation's common shares held by the daughter has increased by $120,000 with no A.C.B. increase.

The *third* consideration package is also off-side since Ms. D has accepted consideration which, in total, is more than the F.M.V. of the land (i.e., $150,000 compared to $200,000 boot plus preferred shares with a retraction and stated value of a nominal amount). The tax consequences are as follows:

(1) The boot of $200,000 exceeds the elected amount of $30,000; hence, the elected amount is bumped to $150,000 triggering a capital gain of $120,000. Note that the elected amount can never exceed the F.M.V. of the transferred property (i.e., land with a F.M.V. of $150,000 in this case).

(2) There will be a benefit conferred on Ms. D as a shareholder [ssec. 15(1)]:

F.M.V. of consideration		
Boot	$200,000	
Retraction value of preferred shares	nominal	$200,000
Less: F.M.V. of land		150,000
Subsection 15(1) benefit		$ 50,000

This benefit of $50,000 will be added to the cost of the boot consideration received [ssec. 52(1)]. Since the elected amount of $150,000 becomes the initial cost of boot, the A.C.B. of the boot is increased to $200,000 (i.e., the $150,000 of the elected amount allocated to the boot plus the subsection 15(1) benefit of $50,000).

(3) The cost to the corporation of the land will be the *new* elected amount of $150,000.

(4) The A.C.B. of the preferred shares will be:

Elected amount (new)	$150,000
Less: boot	200,000
Excess	Nil

(5) The P.U.C. will be reduced to nil as follows:

Stated value		nominal
Less: elected amount (new)	$ 150,000	
boot	(200,000)	Nil
Reduction		nominal
∴ P.U.C. = (nominal − nominal)		Nil

All of the tax-paid cost of $200,000 is represented in the value of the boot which will be repaid without further tax cost in the future. Therefore, nothing is left to recover tax free in the P.U.C. of the shares on their redemption. In this situation, after the transfer, there is a total tax-paid cost of $200,000 derived from:

Cost of the original land..............................	$ 30,000
Capital gain triggered on the section 85 transfer (i.e., $150,000 – $30,000)..........................	120,000
Benefit [ssec. 15(1)]..................................	50,000
	$200,000

This tax-paid cost is reflected in the A.C.B. of the boot (i.e., the $200,000 demonstrated above).

In summary, the following has occurred:

Before transfer		*After transfer*			
Ms. D owned	*Land*	*Ms. D owns*	*Debt*	*Corporation owns*	*Land*
A.C.B. .... $ 30,000		A.C.B. $200,000		A.C.B. $150,000	
F.M.V. 150,000		F.M.V. 200,000		F.M.V. 150,000	
		Ms. D owns	*Shares*	*Corporation owes to:*	
		A.C.B. .... Nil		Ms. D $200,000	
		P.U.C. .... Nil			
		F.M.V. .... Nil			
		Ms. D has income from a capital gain of $120,000 and property income of $50,000.			

(d) *Conclusion*

This situation clearly demonstrates that as long as the F.M.V. of the consideration received equals the F.M.V. of the property transferred there will be no adverse tax consequences. Where these two amounts are not equal then income inclusions will be triggered.

2. Benefit conferred on a related person — Technical rules

A benefit is deemed to have been conferred on a related person:

(a) where the fair market value of the property, immediately before it is transferred to the corporation, exceeds the greater of:

(i) the fair market value immediately after the transfer of all consideration (including shares or rights to receive shares) received from the corporation, and

(ii) the elected amount; and

(b) where it is reasonable to regard any part of that excess as a benefit conferred by the taxpayer on a person related to the taxpayer (including the transferee corporation itself unless it is wholly-owned by the transferor).

The result is that the elected amount or transfer price is increased by that part of the excess that is a benefit, but there is no increase in the cost of the share consideration received [par. 85(1)(e.2)].

For example, consider a capital property that has a cost of $100 and a fair market value of $200. To defer maximum capital gains, the transfer price is elected at $100. Consideration from the corporation consists of cash in the amount of $100 and preferred shares with a fair market value of $40. In this case, an asset worth $200 is transferred to a corporation for consideration worth $140. The $60 discrepancy in fair market value would form part of taxable surplus (contributed surplus)[a] and would be taxed eventually as a dividend. The tax implications of the benefit of $60 depends upon who is the recipient of the benefit, as described below.

If the transferor owned none of the common shares of the company after the transfer and persons related to the transferor owned the common shares, it may be argued that the transferor has given the other shareholders a benefit equal to the excess of fair market value of the property transferred ($200) over the consideration received ($140). This argument is based on the principle that common shareholders own the residual equity, including contributed surplus, in a corporation. Thus, the elected amount or transfer price would be increased by $60 (i.e., $200–$140) for the purpose of determining the proceeds of disposition to the transferor and the cost of the property to the corporation.

However, as a penalty, the cost of the shares received as consideration by the transferor would remain at nil. Thus, there will be recognition of income on the transfer but no parallel increase in the cost base of the shares received as consideration. Furthermore, the fair market value of the common shares held by other shareholders will increase by $60, but there will be no offsetting increase in the adjusted cost base of the shares held by those shareholders. Therefore, the $60 capital gain will be taxed potentially in the hands of the other shareholders when they dispose of their shares. The penalty inherent in this "benefit" rule is similar to the one where there is an arm's length transfer between related individuals. In this case, paragraph 69(1)(*b*) evokes a one-sided adjustment and as a result the capital gain is taxed twice.

To avoid the pitfall of this benefit rule, the transferor should always take as consideration from the corporation a package with a total fair market value equal to the fair market value of the property transferred to the corporation.

An alternative might be to first gift $60 worth of property to the related shareholders who could then transfer the gifted property to the corporation using subsection 85(1). The other shareholder could then transfer the $140 of property to the corporation for consideration with a total fair market value of $140. However, the potential effects of the GAAR should be evaluated before making this suggestion.

In the above example, if the transferor owned 100% of the shares of the corporation, there would be no benefit, because of the exception in paragraph 85(1)(*e*.2). If the transferor owns some but not all of the common shares, then the benefit would be prorated between the transferor and the related common shareholders, with the amount allocated to the related shareholders comprising the benefit.

3. Subsection 15(1) benefit conferred on a shareholder — Technical rules

This benefit rule provides for what is, in essence, a penalty where the fair market value of the property transferred to a corporation is less than the fair market value of the non-share consideration received from the corporation. In these circumstances, the Act encourages a balancing of the fair market value of the total consideration with the fair market value of the property transferred. The excess consideration will result in a benefit conferred on a shareholder [ssec. 15(1)] which is taxed as income to the transferor.

Exhibit 16-4 presents an analysis similar to that in Exhibit 16-2. Here, three more alternative combinations of the following three key variables are used: fair market value of the property transferred, adjusted cost base (or other tax value) of the property transferred, and non-share consideration "boot" received. Note that in each case, the "boot" exceeds the fair market value of the property transferred, resulting in income under subsection 15(1).

---

[a] The right to convert this contributed surplus to paid-up capital [par. 84(1)(*c*.3)] would be denied since the amount arose under section 85. See page 803 in Chapter 15.

EXHIBIT 16-4
Range of Elected Amounts
(nominal share consideration assumed)

	1	2	3
$100	boot	boot	A.C.B
75	F.M.V.	A.C.B.	boot
60	A.C.B.	F.M.V.	F.M.V.

T — transfer price; I — income (ssec. 15(1)); boot — non-share consideration.

Now consider the following numerical example involving the transfer of a capital property having an adjusted cost base of $1,000 and a fair market value of $1,500:

Consideration

Debt	$ 1,800
Preferred shares (F.M.V. and L.S.C.)	nominal[1]
Common shares (F.M.V. and L.S.C.)	nominal[1]
Total	$ 1,800
Election range:	
high[2]	$ 1,500
low	$ 1,500
Election price (no choice; deemed by par. 85(1)(c))	$ 1,500
Adjusted cost base	1,000
Capital gain	$ 500
Taxable capital gain at $1/2$ inclusion rate	$ 250
Income inclusion [ssec. 15(1)]:	
F.M.V. of "boot"	$ 1,800
F.M.V. of shares issued	nominal[1]
	$ 1,800
F.M.V. of assets transferred	(1,500)
Ssec. 15(1) income amount[3]	$ 300

NOTE: (1) A nominal amount, in this case, could be one cent or even $1/10$ of a cent.

(2) Paragraph 85(1)(c) restricts the upper limit of the elected transfer price to the fair market value of the property transferred to the corporation.

(3) The income amount computed [ssec. 15(1)] would be added to the cost of the debt [ssec. 52(1)].

I. Summary of Rules

Exhibit 16-5 presents a schematic summary of the major rules of subsection 85(1) and their consequences for a case involving property with an accrued gain at the time of the transfer.

EXHIBIT 16-5
Schematic Summary of Subsection 85(1) Rules

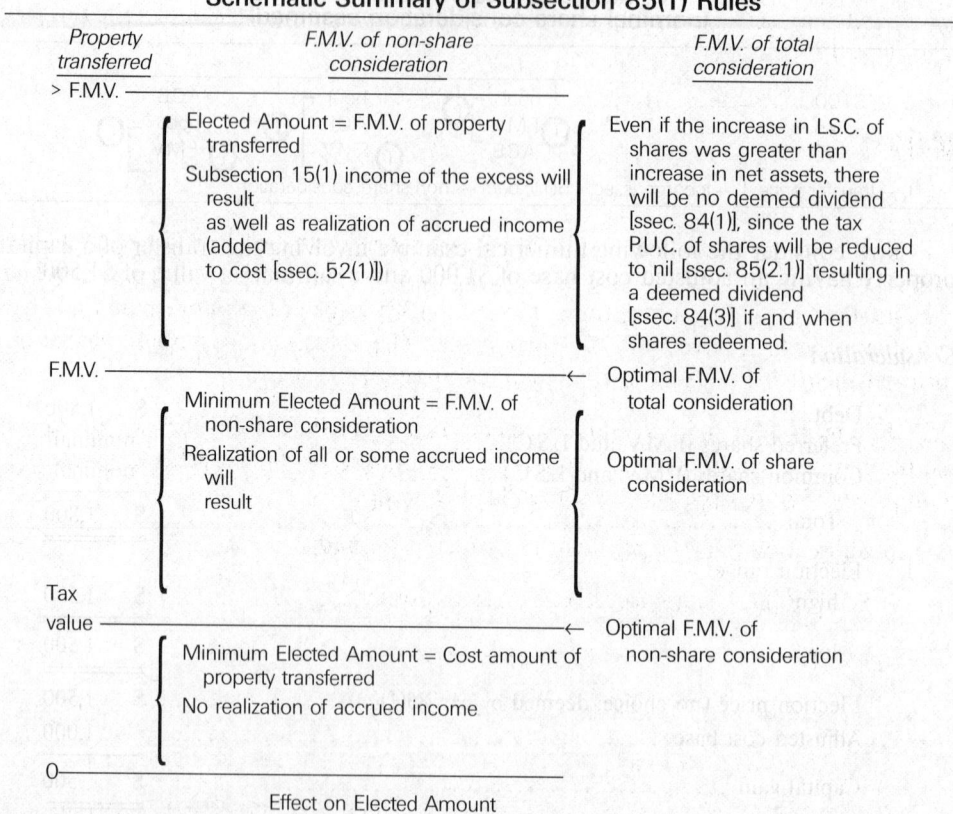

Property transferred	F.M.V. of non-share consideration	F.M.V. of total consideration
> F.M.V.	Elected Amount = F.M.V. of property transferred Subsection 15(1) income of the excess will result as well as realization of accrued income (added to cost [ssec. 52(1)])	Even if the increase in L.S.C. of shares was greater than increase in net assets, there will be no deemed dividend [ssec. 84(1)], since the tax P.U.C. of shares will be reduced to nil [ssec. 85(2.1)] resulting in a deemed dividend [ssec. 84(3)] if and when shares redeemed.
F.M.V.		← Optimal F.M.V. of total consideration
	Minimum Elected Amount = F.M.V. of non-share consideration Realization of all or some accrued income will result	Optimal F.M.V. of share consideration
Tax value		← Optimal F.M.V. of non-share consideration
	Minimum Elected Amount = Cost amount of property transferred No realization of accrued income	
0		

Effect on Elected Amount

First, consider the middle column which deals with the effect of the fair market value (F.M.V.) of non-share considerations (i.e., boot) on the elected amount. If the fair market value of the boot is less than the tax value of the asset transferred, the lower limit on the elected transfer price range will be the tax value and none of the accrued income on the property will be triggered on the transfer. If the fair market value of the boot is greater than the tax value of the property transferred, the lower limit on the elected transfer price range will be equal to the fair market value of the boot and part or all of the accrued income on the property transferred will be realized and subjected to tax. The optimal fair market value of the boot, therefore, is equal to the tax value of the property transferred. This is optimal, because it permits the maximum amount of non-share consideration with the maximum accrued income deferred. Since non-share consideration will typically involve either cash or debt of the corporation which can be repaid in cash without tax consequences, taking the maximum boot is worthwhile.

Now consider the third column dealing with the fair market value of *total* consideration. If the optimal fair market value of boot (equal to the tax value of the property transferred) is taken, then the fair market value of share consideration when added to the fair market value of boot should equal, in total, the fair market value of the property transferred. To take less share consideration may result in the benefit rule being invoked [par. 85(1)(e.2)]. To take more share consideration will result in a deemed dividend, if and when the shares are redeemed [ssec. 84(3)]. Therefore, it is usually best to take back from the corporation share consideration with a fair market value which, when added to the fair market value of boot, totals the fair market value of the property transferred to the corporation.

J. Fair Market Value

[IT-169; IC 89-3]

From the foregoing discussion, the importance of the role of fair market value should be apparent. The fair market value of property transferred to a corporation must be established in order to determine the fair market value of both non-share and share consideration to receive from the corporation. The valuation of common shares of a privately-held corporation, in particular, can present problems.

The term "fair market value" is mentioned more than 600 times in the Act. In addition to the requirements of section 85, determinations of fair market value are most commonly required pursuant to the following sections:

- Subsection 52(2) — payment of dividends in kind

- Section 69 — non-arm's length transactions

- Section 70 — deemed dispositions on death

- Subsection 104(4) — deemed disposition of trust property after 21 years

- Section 160 — certain transfers between spouses.

Historically, the Canada Revenue Agency (CRA) has provided little guidance as to what was required of taxpayers to support valuations required for these sections. Business valuations are generally not filed with the CRA as part of typical transaction documentation. In order to ensure that a subsequent review of fair market values by the CRA does not result in a one-sided adjustment causing double taxation, many taxpayers avail themselves of a price adjustment clause.

A price adjustment clause, however, can ensure that if the CRA determines that a sale price does not reflect fair market value, the price will be adjusted appropriately [IT-169]. Case law indicates that a price adjustment clause will only be recognized if the parties have reasonably, and in good faith, attempted to determine transaction prices that equal fair market values.[b]

IC 89-3 provides a detailed listing of specific factors that should be considered and analyzed in business valuations. The Circular discusses the conventional approaches to business valuations, being the assets and the earnings methods, and also deals with such sophisticated areas as options, buy–sell agreements and the concepts of family and group control.

IC 89-3 suggests that the CRA is undertaking sophisticated reviews of fair market value determinations. Undoubtedly, the income tax practitioner must be aware of these requirements in order to ensure compliance with the various sections of the Act as illustrated by section 85 where fair market value determinations are required.

---

[b] *Guilder News Co. (1963) Ltd. et al. v. M.N.R.*, (F.C.A.) 73 DTC 5048.

K. Section 22 Election

[ITA: 22; IT-188R]

Where there is a potential capital loss on the transfer of accounts receivable to a corporation by an affiliated person, subsection 85(1) should not be used. Accounts receivable are capital property, and any capital loss triggered on any transfer (not just a section 85 election) to an affiliated corporation would be denied, as discussed previously. For an individual transferor, this capital loss would be passed on to the corporation through a bump in the adjusted cost base of the accounts receivable [par. 53(1)(*f*)]. For other transferors, the recognition is deferred in a different manner, as discussed previously. The better alternative is to use an election under section 22 [form T2022] on the transfer of accounts receivable in order to qualify them for a reserve for doubtful debts and bad debt write-off in the corporation.

One of the main requirements for the deduction of a reserve or a bad debt is that the transaction that gave rise to the debt must have been included previously in the taxpayer's income [par. 20(1)(*l*) or spar. 20(1)(*p*)(ii)]. If the corporation buys the receivables and one subsequently goes bad, it cannot meet this test. Section 22 covers this situation in a case where a person has sold all or substantially all the property (including receivables) used in a business to a purchaser who proposes to continue the business. IT-188R, in paragraph 1, indicates that where 90% of the assets of the business carried on in Canada are sold, "all or substantially all" of the assets of such business will be considered sold. If the vendor and purchaser jointly execute and file an agreement in the prescribed form, a future reserve for doubtful debts and bad debt write-offs will be permitted to the purchaser.

Consider the following set of facts:

1. the accounts receivable have a face amount of $6,000;

2. they have a fair market value of $4,700; and

3. last year, the allowance for doubtful accounts was $500.

In this case the following entries would be made:

Proprietor (Vendor)			*Corporation* (Purchaser)		
Reserve........	$ 500		Accounts		
Income [(par.			receivable......	$6,000	
12(1)(*d*)]		$ 500	Considera-		
Consideration	4,700		tion		$4,700
Loss from busi-			Income		1,300
ness...........	1,300		— Can take reserve at		
Accounts			year-end.		
receivable....		6,000	— Can write off bad		
— Note that loss offsets			debts.		
income.					

If the section 22 election is not made, the vendor will still have to include last year's reserve in income ($500 in this case), but the loss in this case would be a capital loss. This loss would be denied on the transfer to the corporation by an individual under paragraph 40(2)(*g*) and would be added to the adjusted cost base of the accounts receivable in the corporation [par. 53(1)(*f*)]. The purchaser will have acquired the accounts receivable as capital property at the transferor's cost, i.e., F.M.V. plus the denied capital loss. If the corporation recovers less than adjusted cost base, it will have a capital loss. The purchaser would not be eligible to take a reserve for doubtful accounts or a bad debt write-off for tax purposes on the accounts acquired without the election under section 22.

The decision tree in Exhibit 16-6 may be useful in providing an approach to problems dealing with transfer of property to a corporation.

EXHIBIT 16-6
Subsection 85(1) Decision Tree

L. Application

[ITA: 14(1)(a); 22; 53(1)(f); 85; IC: 76-19R3]

Example Problem

Rollmeover operates an unincorporated business having the following balance sheet stated in tax values at its taxation year-end:

	Tax value	Fair market value
Cash	$ 1,000	$ 1,000
Marketable securities	11,000	15,000
Accounts receivable	5,500	4,700
Inventory	7,000	7,000
Prepaid rent	3,000	3,000
Land	42,000	31,000
Buildings (capital cost — $46,000)	28,000	50,000
Equipment (capital cost — $20,000)	8,000	3,000
Goodwill	—	47,000
Total assets	$105,500	$161,700
Liabilities		8,000
		$153,700

The marketable securities represent an investment of surplus funds held for anticipated future expansion and can be considered to pertain to the active business. The accounts receivable figure is shown net of the reserve of $500 deducted at the end of the preceding taxation year.

— REQUIRED

(A) For the above assets, indicate which can be transferred to a corporation under subsection 85(1) and the amounts of debt (to the nearest $100) and shares that can be taken as consideration to defer the maximum possible capital gain. For those assets which cannot or should not be transferred under subsection 85(1), state the reasons for this determination and, also, indicate the tax implications of another method of transfer.

(B) Compute the cost and the paid-up capital for tax purposes of the shares taken from the corporation as consideration for the transfer.

(C) (i) Compute the taxable capital gain on a subsequent sale of the shares at $73,000.

(ii) Compute the tax consequence of a redemption of the shares by the corporation for $73,000.

— SOLUTION

(A) (i) Items which cannot or should not be transferred under ssec. 85(1):

	Tax value	Fair market value	Transfer price	New debt	Income effect
Cash[1]	$ 1,000	$ 1,000	$ 1,000	$ 1,000	nil
Accounts receivable[2]	6,000	4,700	4,700	4,700	business loss allowed
Inventory[3]	7,000	7,000	7,000	7,000	nil
Prepaid rent[1]	3,000	3,000	3,000	3,000	nil
Land[4]	42,000	31,000	31,000	31,000	capital loss denied
Equipment[5]	8,000	3,000	3,000	3,000	terminal loss denied
Total	$67,000	$49,700	$49,700	$49,700	

Note that where the fair market value is less than the adjusted cost base of capital property (but not depreciable capital property) to be transferred to a corporation by an individual, the capital loss is denied [sec. 54 definition of a superficial loss and par. 40(2)(g)] for any transfer to an affiliated person [sec. 251.1]. This loss denial applies to all transfers to a corporation, not just section 85 transfers (e.g., a cash sale to the corporation). The denied loss, however, is added to the corporation's adjusted cost base of the transferred asset [par. 53(1)(f)]. This puts the corporation in exactly the same tax position as an individual transferor was in prior to the transfer. As a result, capital property with accrued losses should not be transferred to the corporation under section 85 since there is no gain to defer. For example, land, in this case, can be sold at fair market value in return for boot like any of the above assets.

(ii) Items transferred under subsection 85(1):

	Tax value	Fair market value	Elected transfer price	F.M.V. of consideration			Income Effect
				Assumed debt[9]	New debt	Shares	
Marketable securities[6]	$11,000	$ 15,000	$11,000	$8,000	$ 3,000	$ 4,000	Nil
Buildings	28,000	50,000	28,000	—	28,000	22,000	Nil
Goodwill[7]	Nil	47,000	1	—	—	47,000	$ 0.50
	$39,000	$112,000	$39,001[8]	$8,000	$31,000	$73,000	

Note that if the transferor had a net capital loss available, the securities could have been transferred at an elected amount of $15,000 to trigger the $4,000 of accrued capital gains which would not be taxed after using the net capital loss. This would allow debt consideration of $15,000 which can be repaid by the corporation later without any tax consequence. Furthermore, the corporation would be deemed to have acquired the marketable securities at an adjusted cost base of $15,000 for future capital gain purposes.

If an election is made on the building at fair market value of $50,000 to trigger the accrued capital gain of $4,000, the rules in subparagraph 13(7)(e)(i) would apply to restrict the capital cost to the corporation to only $48,000 (i.e., the original capital cost of $46,000 plus the taxable capital gain of $2,000 ($\frac{1}{2} \times$ ($50,000 – $46,000))). The transferor would also trigger recapture of $18,000 (i.e., capital cost of $46,000 minus U.C.C. of $28,000). The latter election on the building, therefore, would probably not be beneficial, unless the transferor had some non-capital losses to offset the recapture.

An election, at up to $47,000, for the goodwill would have resulted in business income, which could be offset by a non-capital loss or a current business loss (an alternative which is not available in this example). In this case, there is a potential business income of up to $23,500 (i.e., $\frac{2}{3} \times \frac{3}{4} \times$ $47,000) [spar. 14(1)(a)(v)]. This would, also, have allowed debt consideration of $47,000. The corporation would have been deemed to have made an eligible capital expenditure of a similar amount which could be written off [par. 20(1)(b)]. The actual amount that would be added to the cumulative eligible capital account would have been $23,500 (i.e., $\frac{3}{4} \times$ $47,000 – $\frac{1}{2} \times$ $23,500). Since the transfer to a controlled corporation would be a non-arm's length transaction, the usual addition of $\frac{3}{4}$ of the purchase price is reduced by $\frac{1}{2}$ of the transferor's income under paragraph 14(1)(b), as a result of amount A in the definition of cumulative eligible capital in subsection 14(5). [That reduction was proposed in the February 23, 2004 Draft Legislation. The effect of the reduction is to add, in a non-arm's length transaction, an amount to the cumulative eligible capital account that will provide a base for the deduction of amortization. The added amount is only equal to the income of the transferor that was included in income. A similar adjustment is made to undepreciated capital cost in a non-arm's length transfer of depreciable property [par. 13(7)(e).]

(B) The cost of shares would be:

Elected transfer price of assets (in total)		$ 39,001
Deduct:		
Debt issued	$31,000	
Liabilities assumed[9]	8,000	39,000
A.C.B. of the common shares		$ 1

The tax P.U.C. of the shares would be:

L.S.C. of share consideration before reduction			$ 73,000
Less: ssec. 85(2.1) reduction in P.U.C:			
(i) increase in L.S.C. of all shares on the transfer to the corporation		$73,000 (A)	
(ii) elected amount under ssec. 85(1)	$39,001		
less: non-share consideration	39,000		
excess, if any		1 (B)	
	(A – B)	$72,999	
(iii) increase in L.S.C. of a class of shares issued on the transfer		$73,000 (C)	

$$\text{Reduction: } (A - B) \times \frac{C}{A} = \$72,999 \times \frac{\$73,000}{\$73,000} \qquad \$72,999$$

Tax P.U.C. of share consideration	$ 1

(C) (i) Taxable capital gain

Proceeds of disposition	$ 73,000
A.C.B. of shares	1
Capital gain	$ 72,999
Taxable capital gain ($\frac{1}{2} \times \$72,999$)	$ 36,500

(ii) Tax consequence of redemption of all the shares

Redemption amount	$ 73,000
Less: tax P.U.C.	1
Deemed dividend [ssec. 84(3)]	$ 72,999
Redemption amount	$ 73,000
Less: deemed dividend	72,999
Proceeds of disposition [sec. 54]	$ 1
Less: adjusted cost base	1
Capital gain/loss	Nil

Note how the net economic effect of $72,999 of deemed dividend on the redemption is the same as the capital gain in (c)(i) above and is equal to the gain on the assets deferred by subsection 85(1) on their transfer to the corporation.

—NOTES TO SOLUTION

(1) Cash and prepaids (i.e., prepaid rent) are not normally capital property. Therefore, these two assets cannot be transferred under section 85. However, they can be loaned to the corporation at their F.M.V., taking back debt consideration.

(2) Accounts receivable are capital property; hence, any capital loss arising on the transfer would be denied and, for an individual transferor, as discussed in Part (A)(i) of this solution, added to the adjusted cost base of the transferred accounts receivable. If, however, Rollmeover and the corporation jointly elect under section 22, then:

(a) the loss of $1,300 (i.e., $5,500 tax value net of reserve + $500 reserve taken into income – $4,700 fair market value) is deemed to be a business loss, rather than a capital loss; and

(b) the business loss of Rollmeover must be taken into the corporation's income. This action will permit the corporation to write off any uncollectible accounts receivable and to set up a reserve in respect of doubtful accounts receivable.

(3) A transfer of the inventory under subsection 85(1) is not recommended, because there is no income to defer on the transfer and the transfer would be subject to all of the section 85 restrictions.

(4) A transfer of the land under subsection 85(1) is not recommended, because there is no gain to defer on the transfer and the transfer would be subject to all of the section 85 restrictions. The capital loss will be denied on the transfer, as noted in Part A(i) of this solution. However, the accrued loss would be preserved in the A.C.B. of $42,000 in the corporation.

(5) A transfer of the equipment under subsection 85(1) is not recommended. Although the terminal loss would not be recognized by the transferor using subsection 85(1), the transfer would be subject to all the section 85 restrictions. The simpler alternative is to sell the equipment directly to the corporation and take back debt equal to the fair market value.

(6) Shares should be taken as consideration to bring the total consideration up to the fair market value of the property transferred. Before transferring the short-term investments to the corporation, it should be ascertained that they can be considered assets used in an active business, to preserve the QSBCS status of the corporation's shares.

(7) Goodwill must be transferred at least at a nominal amount of $1.00 so that it is listed in the election under subsection 85(1). Since the courts have consistently determined that Nil is not an amount, the CRA would apply section 69 to deem the sale at the fair market value which would trigger an income inclusion under subsection 14(1) of $23,500 ($2/3 \times 3/4 \times $47,000$) [IC 76-19R3 pars. 4 and 6.] Note that it is permissible to take $1 in debt, but the instruction was to take debt only to the nearest $100.

(8) The elected transfer price becomes the proceeds of disposition for each property to the transferor, the cost of each property to the corporation and the adjusted cost base of the consideration received from the corporation by the transferor.

(9) Consider the liabilities assumed by the corporation as part of the consideration other than shares received from the corporation against part of the property transferred, thereby reducing the amount of new debt to be taken. According to the CRA, the most common error made in using subsection 85(1) is to forget that assumed liabilities are part of the "boot" received. Note that the $8,000 of liabilities could have been assumed by the corporation in return for the assets not transferred under subsection 85(1), instead of in return for the assets transferred under subsection 85(1).

II. TRANSFER OF SHARES

A. Non-arm's Length Sale of Shares: Dividend Strips

[ITA: 54; 84.1; 85; IT-489R]

1. The situation: Post-1971 QSBC shares

Consider the case of Mr. Strip. He incorporated a company Strippit Limited in 1990 having paid-up capital of $1,000. These shares, all of which are owned by Mr. Strip, currently have a fair market value of $200,000. If Mr. Strip sold the shares in an arm's length transaction, he would realize a capital gain of $199,000. Perhaps more important, Mr. Strip would receive, at least, part of the capital gain tax free by offsetting it with, say, $99,000 of available Q.S.B.C. share capital gains exemption. Actually, Mr. Strip does not want to sell his shares and give up the business, but the prospect of receiving of $99,000 of the accrued gain tax free is attractive. Alternatively, he may simply want to implement an estate freeze as discussed later in the next chapter. In either case, if Mr. Strip continues to own the shares, the only way that he can receive the surplus represented by the $200,000 value is to receive a taxable dividend of $199,000.

To achieve this objective without losing control of the corporation, Mr. Strip decides to set up a holding company, Holdit Ltd., and to transfer his shares in Strippit Ltd. to Holdit Ltd. using the provisions of section 85. He chooses to transfer his shares at an elected amount of $100,000 to realize $99,000 of capital gains on the transfer. As consideration for these shares, he can take from Holdit Ltd. up to $100,000 in debt or shares as long as he takes at least one share to qualify the transfer under section 85 and as long as the total non-share consideration does not exceed $100,000 to avoid capital gains subject to tax on the transfer. It should be easy to see that if he takes, for example, cash of $100,000 from Holdit Ltd. which borrowed these funds, he will have received $99,000 of the accrued gain on the shares of Strippit Ltd. tax free.

If, in fact, Holdit Ltd. had borrowed the funds, the loan could be repaid by having Strippit Ltd., which Holdit Ltd. now owns, pay a dividend to Holdit Ltd. which, in turn, would be used to repay the borrowed funds. This dividend would be received by Holdit Ltd. free of Part I tax and, normally, free of Part IV tax, since Strippit Ltd. is connected with Holdit Ltd. Other variations of this scheme are possible using debt or shares of Holdit Ltd. issued to Mr. Strip. The general situation can be diagrammed as shown in Exhibit 16-7.

EXHIBIT 16-7
Non-Arm's Length Sale of Shares

Recognize that if the shares of Strippit Ltd. are not sold at arm's length, the only way that Mr. Strip could realize the surplus which creates the values shown for the shares is through a dividend or a deemed dividend on redemption, both of which would be taxable. Thus, the process illustrated by Exhibit 16-7 is an attempt to convert what might otherwise have been paid out as a taxable dividend into a tax-free capital gain, without giving up control of the shares. The resultant capital gain is received tax free, because it is protected through the qualified small business corporation share (Q.S.B.C.S.) capital gains deduction. This process is often referred to as "dividend stripping" and, historically, such attempts have been popular whenever capital gains were taxed at a lower rate than taxable dividends.

One of the provisions of section 84.1 will be shown to turn capital gains derived by the process described back into taxable deemed dividends under certain conditions. It appears to be the non-arm's length nature of the sale of shares, in which the benefits of owning the shares are effectively maintained, that offends the legislation. Any other type of asset, such as land, buildings or eligible capital property, transferred to a corporation under similar conditions is not affected by the rules of section 84.1.

2. Conditions for section 84.1 to apply

The following conditions, as set out at the beginning of subsection 84.1(1), must exist in order for the rules of section 84.1 to apply:

(a) the disposition must be made by a taxpayer resident in Canada other than a corporation;

(b) the subject shares (the shares being transferred) must be shares of a corporation resident in Canada and must be capital property to the taxpayer;

(c) the disposition must be made to a corporation with which the taxpayer does not deal at arm's length within the standard meaning of the phrase under subsection 251(1);[c] and

(d) the subject corporation must be connected [ssec. 186(4)] with the purchaser corporation immediately after the disposition, i.e., the purchaser corporation must control (as defined specifically [ssec. 186(2)]) the subject corporation, or the purchaser corporation must own more than 10% of the voting shares and more than 10% of the fair market value of all of the issued shares of the subject corporation.

3. The basic rules of subsection 84.1(1) formulated

(a) *P.U.C. Reduction*

Paragraph 84.1(1)(*a*) provides for a reduction in the paid-up capital of the shares issued by a purchaser company.[d] The following formula computes a reduction in paid-up capital for all new shares of the corporation issued and, then, allocates a part of the reduction to each class of shares.

P.U.C. reduction [par. 84.1(1)(*a*)]:

(1) Increase, if any, in legal stated capital (L.S.C.) of purchaser corporation . . . . xxx (A)

Less:

(2) Greater of:

    (a) P.U.C. of shares transferred xxx

    (b) modified A.C.B. of shares transferred (based on adjusted actual cost determined without using V-Day rules for shares acquired before 1972 and ignoring any increase in the A.C.B. as a result of the capital gains exemption) xxx   xxx

Less: Fair market value of non-share consideration received ("boot") . . . . (xxx)

Excess, if any . . . . xxx (B)

Total P.U.C. reduction of all shares (A – B) xxx

P.U.C. reduction of shares of any particular class for which increase in L.S.C. was C:
$$(A - B) \times C/A$$

Note how the adjusted cost base of the shares transferred (i.e., the subject shares) is modified in paragraph 84.1(2)(*a*) which provides that where the subject shares were

---

[c] The definition of non-arm's length is extended to include groups of persons under certain circumstances [par. 84.1(2)(*b*) and ssec. 84.1(2.2)].

[d] Note that the P.U.C. reduction in subsection 85(2.1) will not apply at the same time as the P.U.C. reduction in section 84.1 (see the condition in the preamble of ssec. 85(2.1)).

acquired before 1972, the individual's adjusted cost base of the shares, or even substituted shares, is their adjusted actual arm's length cost, ignoring the effects of the Valuation Day or median rules. The adjustments to be made to cost are those found in section 53. Paragraph 84.1(2)(*a*.1) provides rules for determining the adjusted cost base for subject shares. This adjusted actual cost is referred to as modified A.C.B. here.

Adjustments to cost base are made in two possible situations.

(1) If shares were owned before 1972 by that person or a related person, then the modified ACB will be determined by ignoring the V-Day value.

(2) If the ACB of the shares includes an amount claimed as the capital gains exemption by that person or a related person, then the modified ACB will be determined by ignoring the capital gains exemption claimed.

Recognize that a reduction in paid-up capital under paragraph 84.1(1)(*a*) has no tax consequences unless and until the shares received as consideration are redeemed by the issuing corporation.

> Conceptually, the P.U.C. of the shares after the reduction will be equal to their "hard" cost (i.e., the greater of P.U.C. and modified A.C.B.) that has not been recovered by the boot received in the transfer.

(b) *Deemed Dividend*

Paragraph 84.1(1)(*b*) provides for an immediate deemed dividend to the transferor of subject shares. The following formula computes the deemed dividend.

Deemed dividend [par. 84.1(1)(*b*)]:

Sum of:

(1) Increase, if any, in L.S.C. of purchaser corporation . . . .   xxx (A)

(2) Fair market value of non-share consideration received
("boot"). . . . .   <u>xxx</u> (D)

                                                        (A + D).   xxx

Less sum of:

(3) Greater of:

    (a) P.U.C. of shares transferred . . . .   <u>xxx</u>

    (b) modified A.C.B. of shares transferred
         (based on adjusted actual cost determined without using V-day rules for shares acquired before 1972 and ignoring any increase in the ACB as a result of the capital gains exemption.) . . . .   <u>xxx</u>   xxx (E)

(4) Total P.U.C. reduction under par. 84.1(1)(*a*) . . . .   <u>xxx</u> (F)

                                   (E + F). . . . .   (xxx)

Deemed dividend . . . .   (A + D) – (E + F)   <u>xxx</u>

> Conceptually, the deemed dividend will usually be equal to the boot received in the transaction in excess of the "hard" cost of the shares (i.e., the greater of their P.U.C. and their modified A.C.B.).

---

4. Application of rules to post-1971 shares

Recall the case of Mr. Strip on page 887 with the following basic data:

Paid-up capital and cost of shares transferred (Strippit)	$ 1,000
Fair market value of shares transferred	200,000
Elected amount under ssec. 85(1)	100,000
Available Q.S.B.C. share capital gains exemption	99,000

Exhibit 16-8 shows the application of the rules in section 84.1 to this situation if Mr. Strip takes one of two consideration packages from Holdit Ltd. on the transfer of the above shares. Case A uses the "optimal" package of consideration from the point of view of using the rules in subsection 85(1) to advantage as discussed previously and Case B uses no non-share consideration.

EXHIBIT 16-8
Examples of Section 84.1 Application

Consideration received by individual on transfer of shares	*A*	*B*
Cash, notes or other non-share consideration	$100K	Nil
Common shares (L.S.C. and F.M.V.)	100K	$200K
Total F.M.V.	$200K	$200K
P.U.C. reduction [par. 84.1(1)(a)]		
(1) Increase in L.S.C. of purchaser corporation ...... (A)	$100K	$200K
Less		
(2) Greater of:		
(a) P.U.C. of shares transferred.....................	$ 1K	$ 1K
(b) Modified A.C.B. of shares transferred	1K	1K
Less: F.M.V. of non-share consideration received	100K	Nil
Excess, if any .... (B)	Nil	$ 1K
P.U.C. reduction .... (A – B)	$100K	$199K
P.U.C. after reduction	Nil	$ 1K
Deemed dividend [par. 84.1(1)(b)]		
Sum of:		
(1) Increase in L.S.C. of purchaser corporation ...... (A)	$100K	$200K
(2) F.M.V. of non-share consideration received ...... (D)	100K	Nil
(A + D)	$200K	$200K
Less sum of:		
(3) Greater of:		
(a) P.U.C. of shares transferred..................... (E)	$ 1K	$ 1K
(b) Modified A.C.B. of shares transferred	1K	1K
(4) P.U.C. reduction under par. 84.1(1)(*a*)........... (F)	100K	199K
(E + F)	$101K	$200K
Deemed dividend ....(A + D) – (E + F)	$ 99K	Nil

In Example A, note how the P.U.C. of the shares received as consideration is reduced to nil, because all of the hard cost of the old shares (i.e., $1,000) has been recovered through the receipt of boot. Note, also, how the deemed dividend of $99,000 is equal to the excess of boot of $100,000 over the $1,000 of hard cost. In Example B, since there is no boot consideration, the P.U.C. after the reduction is $1,000, exactly equal to the hard cost, and there is no deemed dividend. Hence, the rules in section 84.1 only permit the immediate tax-free recovery of hard cost in the transaction that meets the conditions for the rules to apply.

> To generalize, the deemed dividend can be avoided, as in example B, by limiting the fair market value of non-share consideration to the greater of:
>
> (a) the paid-up capital of the subject shares transferred, and
>
> (b) the modified adjusted cost base of the subject shares transferred.

In order to fully comprehend the effects of the provisions in section 84.1, it is necessary to do some further analysis beyond the rules in section 84.1. Exhibit 16-9 illustrates the effect of the deemed dividend under paragraph 84.1(1)(b) on the use of the elected amount as proceeds of disposition of the subject shares. Note how the deemed dividend resulting from paragraph 84.1(1)(b) is excluded from the proceeds of disposition of the subject shares [par. (k) of the definition of "proceeds of disposition" in section 54]. This procedure is similar to the one used in Chapter 15 in determining the proceeds of disposition for capital gains purposes on the redemption of shares where the subsection 84(3) dividend is deducted. Since the definition of "proceeds of disposition" is of general application within Subdivision c, this exclusion will occur whether or not subsection 85(1) is used for the transfer of subject shares to the purchaser corporation. The result may be a capital loss on the subject shares, as in Case A, which will be denied as a superficial loss [par. 40(2)(g)], where Mr. Strip, an affiliated person, still controls Holdit Ltd., the purchaser corporation, after the disposition of the Strippit Ltd. shares, whether or not the transfer is made pursuant to subsection 85(1). Therefore, an outright sale at fair market value of shares to a non-arm's length holding company, without a subsection 85(1) election, will have the same effect under section 84.1 as that discussed here.

EXHIBIT 16-9
Calculation of A.C.B. of Purchaser Corporation (Holdit Ltd.) Shares

	A	B
Elected amount under ssec. 85(1) (proceeds of disposition)	$ 100K	$100K
Less: sec. 54 exclusion from proceeds for sec. 84.1 deemed dividend	99K	Nil
Adjusted proceeds of disposition for transferred shares . . .	$ 1K	$100K
A.C.B. of transferred shares	1K	1K
Capital gain (capital loss may be denied by par. 40(2)(g))*	Nil	$99K
Capital gain utilized	Nil	99K
Effect on taxable income	Nil	Nil
Cost and A.C.B. of purchaser (Holdit Ltd.) shares after ssec. 85(1)**		
(a) Elected amount ($100) – Boot ($100)	Nil	
(b) Elected amount ($100) – Boot (Nil)		$100K

* Loss denial, if any, depends on whether the corporation was controlled by an affiliated person, e.g., the transferor, the transferor's spouse or corporation(s) controlled by the transferor or the spouse. If the loss is denied, it is added to the A.C.B. of the Strippit Ltd. shares held by Holdit Ltd. [par. 53(1)(f)].

** Note that for the purposes of paragraph 85(1)(h) which determines the adjusted cost base of the purchaser corporation's shares by allocating the elected amount (i.e., proceeds of disposition under subsection 85(1)), the exclusion of the deemed dividend in paragraph (k) of the definition of "proceeds of disposition" in section 54 does not apply. That exclusion applies only where the term "proceeds of disposition" is being used in Subdivision c to compute a capital gain or loss. It does not apply, therefore, to the use of the term in paragraph 85(1)(h).

In summary, in Case A, paragraph 84.1(1)(*b*) deemed the transferor to have received a taxable dividend of $99,000 on the transfer (Exhibit 16-6). Thus, the attempt to strip the $99,000 taxable surplus by converting it into an exempt capital gain, resulted in the same amount of taxable dividend as the amount of surplus that would otherwise have been converted. Note, in particular, that no capital gain resulted from the transfer of the shares to the holding company (Exhibit 16-7), although a capital gain was the objective of electing on the transfer at $100,000. In essence, the deemed dividend under section 84.1 removed the capital gain by adjusting the proceeds, leaving nothing available against which to use the Q.S.B.C. share capital gains deduction.

In Case B, where non-share consideration did not exceed $1,000, there was no deemed dividend and the A.C.B. of the holding company shares reflected the elected amount in excess of non-share consideration. This higher A.C.B. would reduce a future capital gain on the disposition of the holding company shares, thereby resulting in a benefit from utilizing the Q.S.B.C. share capital gains deduction on the original transfer and election of $100,000. Therefore, if non-share consideration is limited in this manner, section 84.1 will not prevent the "crystallization" of an individual's Q.S.B.C. share capital gains deduction through the transfer of shares to a holding company. Section 84.1 discourages the removal of non-share consideration in excess of P.U.C. or adjusted actual cost on the transaction.

To complete the analysis of the consequences of section 84.1, Exhibit 16-10 shows the results of a redemption of the purchaser corporation shares for their fair market value at the time of their issue as shown in Exhibit 16-8. Note that the amount of the "net economic effect" is equal to the gain in excess of the utilized capital gains exemption on the original subject shares. However, recognize that the components of that net economic effect are taxed differently and at different times. In both cases shown in Exhibit 16-10, the total deemed dividend is equal to the full accrued gain on the original subject shares at the time of their transfer to the purchaser corporation. The advantage of Case B over Case A is that there is no immediate taxable deemed dividend on the transfer to the purchaser corporation in Case B. The capital loss shown for Case B is equal to the accrued gain that is offset by the available capital gains exemption on the transfer of the original subject shares. Of course, to obtain the tax shield effect from that capital loss, a capital gain must be realized. Note that if the original subject shares had themselves been redeemed, there would not have been a capital loss of $99,000, only a deemed dividend of $199,000.

EXHIBIT 16-10
Hypothetical Redemption of Purchaser's (Holdit Ltd.'s)
Shares for Fair Market Value
(based on the facts and results in Exhibits 16-8 and 16-9)

	A	B
Deemed dividend on redemption		
Redemption amount	$ 100K	$ 200K
Less: P.U.C. after par. 84.1(1)(*a*)	Nil	1K
Deemed dividend [ssec. 84(3)]	$ 100K	$ 199K
Capital gain (loss) on redemption		
Redemption amount	$ 100K	$ 200K
Less: Deemed dividend [ssec. 84(3)]	100K	199K
Adjusted proceeds of disposition	Nil	$ 1K
A.C.B. (Exhibit 16-9)	Nil	100K
Capital gain (capital loss)	Nil	$ (99K)*

[*Exhibit 16-10 — continued*]

	A	B
Summary of income effects		
Sec. 84.1 deemed dividend (Exhibit 16-8)	$ 99K	Nil
Ssec. 84(3) deemed dividend (above)	100K	$ 199K
Capital gain on disposition of Strippit Ltd. shares (Exhibit 16-9)................................	Nil	99K
Capital gains exemption utilized (Exhibit 16-9)	Nil	(99K)
Capital loss on redemption of Holdit Ltd. shares	Nil	(99K)
Net economic effect..........................	$ 199K	$ 100K

* The capital loss is not denied, because Mr. Strip redeemed all of his shares in Holdit Ltd. and, therefore, he is no longer affiliated with Holdit Ltd.

As an alternative to disposing of the purchaser corporation shares by redemption, Exhibit 16-11 shows the results of an arm's length sale, if this is possible in the circumstances, for their fair market value at the time of their issue as shown in Exhibit 16-8. While the net economic effect is, again, equal to the gain on the shares in excess of the utilized capital gains exemption, part of that effect for Case A is an immediate deemed dividend that occurred on the original transfer of the subject shares. Of course, the results for Case B are the same as they would have been if the original subject shares had been sold in an arm's length transaction. Thus, Case B represents a method of avoiding the adverse consequences of section 84.1 if a non-arm's length transfer of shares is necessary, perhaps, to implement an estate freeze as will be discussed in the next chapter.

EXHIBIT 16-11
Hypothetical Sale of Purchaser's Shares for Fair Market Value
(based on the facts and results in Exhibits 16-8 and 16-9)

	A	B
Capital gain (loss) on sale		
Proceeds of disposition	$ 100K	$ 200K
A.C.B.	Nil	(100K)
Capital gain (loss)	$ 100K	$ 100K
Summary of income effects		
Sec. 84.1 deemed dividend (Exhibit 16-8)	$ 99K	Nil
Capital gain on disposition of Strippit Ltd. shares (Exhibit 16-9)................................	Nil	99K
Capital gains exemption utilized (Exhibit 16-9)	Nil	(99K)
Capital gain (loss) on sale of Holdit Ltd. shares (above)	100K	$ 100K
Net economic effect..........................	$ 199K	$ 100K

Conclusions

The results illustrated by the foregoing analysis can be summarized as follows:

(1) The paid-up capital reduction [par. 84.1(1)(*a*)] is for tax purposes only and has effect only if and when the shares of a purchaser corporation are redeemed. The amount of P.U.C. after the reduction will represent the amount of hard cost in the old shares that has not been recovered through boot.

(2) The deemed dividend which arises immediately on transfer of the subject shares [par. 84.1(1)(*b*)] and which is the penalty inherent in section 84.1 caused by receiving boot in excess of the hard cost in the old shares, can be avoided by limiting the fair market value of non-share consideration to the greater of:

(a) paid-up capital of the subject shares transferred; and

(b) modified adjusted cost base (based on actual cost with section 53 adjustments made to it) of the subject shares transferred.

(3) A subsequent redemption of the shares of the purchaser corporation will result in a deemed dividend [ssec. 84(3)] and a capital loss. On the redemption, the overall "net economic effect" is income equal to the gain in excess of the utilized capital gains exemption on the subject shares. However, this effect consists of:

(a) a possible immediate deemed dividend (which can be avoided);

(b) a deemed dividend at the time of redemption; and

(c) a capital loss at the time of redemption.

Of course, taxable dividends are taxable in one manner (through the gross-up and tax credit procedure) and capital losses can only be used to offset capital gains taxable in another manner. There are, also, time value of money consequences, since the immediate deemed dividend will not occur at the same time as the deemed dividend and capital loss on redemption. Also, capital gains to offset the capital loss may not be realized at the same time as the capital loss on redemption. If the immediate deemed dividend is avoided, the results on redemption of the purchaser corporation shares are no different than the results for a redemption of the original subject shares would have been.

(4) A subsequent disposition of the shares of the purchaser corporation by an arm's length sale, if this is possible in the circumstances, will result in the realization of the gain in excess of the utilized capital gains exemption on the subject shares, on a "net economic effect" basis. However, this gain may be taxed as:

(a) a possible immediate deemed dividend (which can be avoided); and

(b) a capital gain at the time of sale of the purchaser corporation shares.

Again, the tax consequences and their timing will differ, but if the immediate deemed dividend is avoided, the results on the arm's length sale of the purchaser corporation shares are the same as they would have been on the arm's length sale of the original subject shares.

Example Problem

Ms. Annalen owns all of the common shares of Margen Ltd. The shares have a P.U.C. and a cost of $10,000. Their current fair market value is $100,000. She transferred these shares to a holding company, Howal Ltd., receiving as consideration controlling shares of Howal Ltd. having an L.S.C. value of $75,000 and debt with a principal amount of $25,000. She elected under subsection 85(1) at $25,000 in order to use $15,000 of her available Q.S.B.C. share capital gains exemption.

— REQUIRED

(A) Indicate conceptually the immediate tax consequences of the transfer.

(B) Provide a technical explanation and computations to support your conclusions in Part (A).

(C) Assume that Ms. Annalen has $90,000 of QSBC share capital gains exemption available and that she sells her shares of Margen Ltd. to Howal Ltd., in which she already owns controlling shares, for their fair market value of $100,000, receiving as consideration $100,000 of debt from Howal Ltd. No subsection 85(1) election is made. Determine the immediate tax consequences of the sale.

(D) Assume, again, that Ms. Annalen has $90,000 of QSBC share capital gains exemption available and that she sells her shares of Margen Ltd. to Howal Ltd., which she controls, for their fair market value of $100,000, receiving as consideration $100,000 of preferred shares of Howal Ltd. No subsection 85(1) election is made. The preferred shares are subsequently redeemed for $100,000. Determine the tax consequences of the sale of Margen Ltd. shares and the ultimate redemption of the Howal Ltd. preferred shares.

— SOLUTION

Verify that all of the conditions for section 84.1 to apply are met:

(a) the share disposition was made by a taxpayer resident in Canada, Ms. Annalen, other than a corporation;

(b) the subject shares, shares of Margem Ltd., are shares of a corporation resident in Canada and are capital property to Ms. Annalen;

(c) Ms. Annalen and Howal Ltd. are not dealing at arm's length, since Ms. Annalen controls Howal Ltd. [spar. 251(2)(*c*)(i)]; and

(d) the subject corporation, Margem Ltd., is connected with the purchaser corporation, Howal Ltd., since Howal Ltd. controls Margem Ltd. [par. 186(4)(*a*)].

(A)

The following tax consequences should occur on the application of section 84.1:

(a) the P.U.C. of the Howal Ltd. shares should be nil since Ms Annalen has taken back debt ($25,000) which is greater than the P.U.C. and modified A.C.B. of the Margen Ltd. shares ($10,000);

(b) there will be a deemed dividend of $15,000 because the debt received ($25,000) exceeds the greater of the P.U.C. and modified A.C.B of the Margen Ltd. shares ($10,000); and

(c) the proceeds of disposition on the transfer of the Margen Ltd. shares will be reduced by the deemed dividend of $15,000.

(B)

P.U.C. reduction [par. 84.1(1)(*a*)]:

(1) increase in L.S.C. of Howal Ltd.		$75,000 (A)
less		
(2) greater of:		
(a) P.U.C. of Margen Ltd. shares	$10,000	
		$10,000
(b) Modified A.C.B. of Margen Ltd. shares	$10,000	
Less: F.M.V. of "boot"	25,000	
Excess, if any		Nil (B)
P.U.C. reduction (A − B)		$75,000
P.U.C. of Howal Ltd. after reduction ($75,000 − $75,000)		Nil

While this P.U.C. reduction occurs on the transfer, because all of the $10,000 hard cost of the Margen Ltd. shares was recovered in the boot received from Howal Ltd., the reduced P.U.C. has no effect unless and until the shares of Howal Ltd. are redeemed. There will also be a deemed dividend immediately, as a result of the transfer, because the $25,000 of boot received exceeds the $10,000 hard cost of the Margen Ltd. shares transferred, computed as follows:

Deemed dividend [par. 84.1(1)(*b*)]:

Sum of:		
(1) increase in L.S.C. of Howal Ltd. shares		$ 75,000 (A)
(2) F.M.V. of "boot"		25,000 (D)
(A + D)		$100,000
Less sum of:		
(3) greater of:		
(a) P.U.C. of Margen Ltd. shares	$10,000	
		$10,000 (E)
(b) Modified A.C.B. of Margen Ltd. shares	$10,000	
(4) P.U.C. reduction under par. 84.1(1)(*a*)	75,000 (F)	
(E + F)		85,000
Deemed dividend (A + D) − (E + F)		$ 15,000

This particular case involves an attempt, which is thwarted by section 84.1, to convert $15,000 of surplus in Margen Ltd., which could otherwise be realized only through a taxable dividend, into an exempt capital gain on the transfer. The result is a deemed taxable dividend of $15,000 and, as is shown below, no capital gain eligible for the QSBC share exemption. The case, also, involves an increase in P.U.C. from the $10,000 that existed in Margen Ltd. to the $75,000 of L.S.C. shares issued from Howal Ltd. However, the individual only has an entitlement to recover the $10,000 in P.U.C. on a tax-free basis, since that is all that was originally contributed on an after-tax basis. Since the $10,000 was recovered in debt from Howal Ltd. on a tax-free basis, the P.U.C. of the Howal Ltd. shares issued should be reduced to nil for tax purposes, reflecting the fact that no more of the P.U.C. of Margen Ltd. is left to be recovered on a tax-free basis.

The adjusted cost base of the Howal Ltd. shares held by Ms. Annalen would be computed as follows:

Elected amount [ssec. 85(1)]	$ 25,000
Less: non-share consideration (debt)	25,000
ACB of Howal Ltd. shares after ssec. 85(1)	Nil

The capital gain or loss on the disposition of the Margen Ltd. shares would be determined as follows:

Elected amount [ssec. 85(1)] — Proceeds of disposition of Margen Ltd. shares	$ 25,000
Less: par. (*k*) of def. in sec. 54 exclusion from proceeds for sec. 84.1 deemed dividend	15,000
Adjusted proceeds of disposition for Margen Ltd. shares	$ 10,000
A.C.B. of Margen Ltd. shares	(10,000)
Capital gain (capital loss denied by par. 40(2)(*g*))	Nil

In this case there is no denied superficial loss [par. 40(2)(*g*)] on the disposition of the transferred shares to add to the A.C.B. of the Howal Ltd. shares owned. There is, also, no capital gain on the disposition of the Margen Ltd. shares and, hence, nothing against which to use the capital gains exemption.

(C)

Note how the conditions of section 84.1 also apply to this sale of shares at their fair market value. Shares of a corporation resident in Canada (Margen Ltd.), held as capital property by an individual (Ms. Annalen), are sold to a non-arm's length corporation (Howal Ltd., controlled by Ms. Annalen). Since Howal Ltd. will control all of the shares of Margen Ltd. the corporations are connected.

Since no new shares of Howal Ltd. were issued in this transaction, there is no P.U.C. reduction. However, there will be an immediate deemed dividend, because the $100,000 of boot received exceeds the $10,000 of hard cost in the Margen Ltd. shares, computed as follows:

Deemed dividend [par. 84.1(1)(*b*)]:

Sum of:

(1) increase in L.S.C. of Howal Ltd. shares	Nil	(A)
(2) F.M.V. of "boot"	$100,000	(D)
(A + D)	$100,000	

Less sum of:

(3) greater of:

(a) P.U.C. of Margen Ltd. shares	$10,000		
		$10,000	(E)
(b) Modified A.C.B. of Margen Ltd. shares	$10,000		
(4) P.U.C. reduction under par. 84.1(1)(*a*)	Nil	(F)	
(E + F)		10,000	
Deemed dividend (A + D) − (E + F)		$ 90,000	

Proceeds of disposition for the Margen Ltd. shares will be reduced, so that there will be no capital gain against which to offset the capital gains deduction, as follows [par. (*k*) of the definition of "proceeds of disposition" in sec. 54]:

Proceeds of disposition (i.e., debt received)	$100,000
Less: par. (*k*) of def. in sec. 54 exclusion from proceeds for sec. 84.1 deemed dividend	90,000
Adjusted proceeds of disposition	$ 10,000
A.C.B. of Margen Ltd. shares	(10,000)
Capital gain	Nil

When the $100,000 of debt is repaid by Howal Ltd. there will be no further tax consequences, since all of the gain in the shares has been taxed on their sale to Howal Ltd.

(D)

Again the conditions of section 84.1 would be met by this transaction. There would be a P.U.C. reduction computed as follows:

P.U.C. reduction [par. 84.1(1)(*a*)]:

(1) increase in L.S.C. of Howal Ltd.	$100,000	(A)

less

(2) greater of:
    (a) P.U.C. of Margen Ltd. shares $10,000

                                                    $10,000

    (b) Modified A.C.B. of Margen
        Ltd. shares $10,000

Less: F.M.V. of "boot" . . . . Nil

Excess, if any. . . . . 10,000 (B)

P.U.C. reduction (A − B) . . . . $ 90,000

P.U.C. of Howal Ltd. after reduction ($100,000 − $90,000) . . . . . . $ 10,000

Note how the P.U.C. of the Howal Ltd. shares is reduced to $10,000 despite there being no boot. The $10,000 of P.U.C. of the Howal Ltd. shares reflects the $10,000 of P.U.C. of the Margen Ltd. shares transferred. The result is no increase in the P.U.C. entitlement to a tax-free recovery of hard cost.

Since no "boot" was received, there will be no deemed dividend, as shown by the following:

Deemed dividend [par. 84.1(1)(*b*)]:
Sum of:
    (1) increase in L.S.C. of Howal Ltd. shares . . . . $100,000 (A)
    (2) F.M.V. of "boot" . . . .   Nil   (D)

        (A + D) $100,000

Less sum of:
    (3) greater of:
        (a) P.U.C. of Margen Ltd.
            shares $10,000

                                        $10,000 (E)

        (b) Modified A.C.B. of
            Margen Ltd. shares $10,000

    (4) P.U.C. reduction under par. 84.1(1)(*a*) . . . . . . 90,000 (F)

        (E + F) 100,000

Deemed dividend (A + D) − (E + F) . . . . Nil

Since there is no deemed dividend, proceeds of disposition for the Margen Ltd. shares are equal to the $100,000 of preferred share consideration received from Howal Ltd. The result is the following:

Proceeds of disposition for Margen Ltd. shares $100,000
A.C.B. . . . . (10,000)

Capital gain . . . . $ 90,000

Taxable capital gain ($1/2$ × $90,000) . . . . $ 45,000
Less: QSBC share capital gains deduction 45,000

Effect on taxable income of Ms. Annalen . . . . Nil

On the ultimate redemption of all of the Howal Ltd. preferred shares, the following will result:

(1) Deemed dividend on redemption:
    Redemption proceeds . . . . $ 100,000
    Less: P.U.C. (after par. 84.1(1)(*a*) reduction) 10,000

    Deemed dividend [ssec. 84(3)] . . . . $ 90,000

(2)	Proceeds of disposition..............................	$ 100,000
	Less: Deemed dividend [ssec. 84(3)]..................	90,000
	Adjusted proceeds of disposition [sec. 54]...............	$ 10,000
	A.C.B. of Howal Ltd. shares (equal to F.M.V. of property sold for	
	preferred shares).............................	(100,000)
	Capital loss	$ (90,000)

The net economic effect of the redemption is seen to be nil, but in reality the deemed dividend of $90,000 cannot be offset by the capital loss of $90,000.

In this case, the sale of the Margen Ltd. shares for preferred shares of Howal Ltd. resulted in the successful crystallization of the $45,000 QSBC share capital gains deduction (i.e., ¹/₂ × $90,000 capital gains deduction). The crystallization effect is found in the increased A.C.B. of the Howal Ltd. shares which results in a capital loss on their redemption. That capital loss can be used to offset capital gains from other property, thereby gaining the benefit of the capital gains deduction in the future.

B. Sale of Shares by a Corporation to an Unrelated Person: Capital Gains Strips
[ITA: 55(1)–(6); 84(3)]

1. Situation addressed by section 55

Subsections 55(1) to (6) form a set of anti-avoidance provisions which prevent a Canadian-resident corporate shareholder from converting a capital gain on the disposition of shares held in another corporation into a dividend that would not be taxable under Part I due to subsection 112(1) or under Part IV due to the connected corporation exemption in subsection 186(1). This conversion is referred to as capital gains stripping and is opposite to the dividend stripping prevented by section 84.1.

A typical set of transactions which would be caught by section 55 is described below.

Facts:

(a) Corp. B is a wholly-owned subsidiary of Corp. A.

(b) Corp. A wishes to dispose of the shares of Corp. B to Corp. C but does not wish to trigger a capital gain on the sale.

(c) Corp. C is not related to Corp. A and Corp. B.

Avoidance transactions:

(a) Prior to the sale of the Corp. B shares, Corp. A causes Corp. B to declare a large dividend the funds for which are obtained by a short-term bank loan.

(b) The shares of Corp. B are sold to Corp. C.

(c) Corp. C injects enough cash into Corp. B to pay off the bank loan.

Results of the avoidance transactions:

(a) The inter-company dividend is not taxed:

(i) under Part I because of the section 112 deduction, or

(ii) under Part IV because of the connected corporation rules under subsections 186(1) and (4).

(b) The fair market value of the Corp. B shares will drop by the amount of the dividend and should, with good planning, eliminate the capital gain on the sale of the Corp. B shares.

Effects of section 55:

(a) The offensive dividend is deemed not to be a dividend but proceeds of disposition for capital gains purposes, thereby re-establishing the capital gain which Corp. A tried to avoid.

(b) However, the offensive dividend is reduced by any post-1971 income (referred to as "safe income") and/or dividends subject to Part IV tax.

Subsection 55(2) applies to any dividend received by a corporation as part of a transaction or a series of transactions[e] [ssec. 248(10)] that resulted in a disposition of any property to a person with whom the corporation was not related [par. 55(3)(a)]. It also applies if the transaction resulted in an unrelated person gaining a significant increase in ownership interest in the corporation receiving the dividend.

The term "related person" is defined generally in section 251, and related persons include brothers and sisters. However, as an exception to these general rules, paragraph 55(5)(e) deems brothers and sisters not to be related to each other such that the "not related" condition in subsection 55(2) would apply to transactions between corporations which they control. Furthermore, if an attempt is made to escape subsection 55(2) by transactions which cause two or more persons to be related, these persons shall be deemed not to be related to each other [ssec. 55(4)].

2. Illustration of the effect of section 55

Consider the case of corporation X that owns a controlling interest in the shares of corporation Y. Corporation X has an adjusted cost base on its shares of corporation Y of $1.00 each and the current fair market value of these shares is $20.00 each. Corporation X wishes to dispose of its interest in the shares of corporation Y. One method of doing so would be to sell the shares for their fair market value resulting in a capital gain of $19.00 per share (i.e., $20 − $1). In that case, of the $20 received per share, $1 would be a tax-free return of cost and the other $19 would be a capital gain of which one-half would be subject to tax.

Alternatively, since corporation X controls corporation Y, it could cause corporation Y to pay a dividend of $19 per share. If corporation Y has no refundable taxes, the dividend would be received by corporation X without tax consequences under Part I or Part IV of the Act. With the payment of a $19 dividend, the fair market value of the shares of corporation Y should fall to $1.00 each. These shares could then be sold to an unrelated purchaser for their fair market value which is now equal to their adjusted cost base of $1.00 with no tax consequences. The result of this alternative would be to convert what would have been a $19 capital gain subject to tax into a $19 dividend not subject to tax in corporation X on the disposition of its shares in corporation Y.

However, to the extent that the $19 dividend cannot reasonably be considered to be attributable to income earned or realized by corporation Y after 1971 and before the dividend was received by corporation X, it will be deemed not to be a dividend received by corporation X [par. 55(2)(a)]. Then paragraph 55(2)(b) will deem the $19 amount received in the transaction to be part of the proceeds of disposition of the shares. If that is the case, total proceeds of disposition will be $20 resulting in a capital gain of $19 (i.e., $20 − $1) which is the same outcome as the original sale of the shares for proceeds of disposition of $20. The following calculation would be made:

---

[e] For a discussion of the meaning of the phrase "part of a transaction or series of transactions or events" *see Meager Creek Holdings Limited v. the Queen* (TCC) 98 DTC 2073. For a discussion of whether a series exists at common law, see the case of *The Queen v. Canadian Utilities Limited et al.* (FCA), 2004 DTC 6475.

Dividend received		$19
Less: dividend attributable to post-1971 income (designated as a separate dividend [par. 55(5)(f)])	Nil	
dividend subject to Part IV tax	Nil	(Nil)
Deemed proceeds of disposition [par. 55(2)(b)]		$19
Add: actual proceeds of disposition		1
Total proceeds of disposition		$20
Less: adjusted cost base		(1)
Capital gain		$19

Now consider another alternative for corporation X to dispose of its shares of corporation Y. Corporation X could transfer its shares in corporation Y to a purchaser corporation, using subsection 85(1) to select an elected amount of the $1.00 adjusted cost base of the shares transferred. As consideration for this transfer, corporation X could receive shares of the purchaser corporation with a paid-up capital and redemption/retraction value of $20 which represents the fair market value of the shares of corporation Y transferred. The paid-up capital value of the shares received after the subsection 85(2.1) reduction would be $1.00. The adjusted cost base of the shares received as consideration by corporation X would be $1.00, the elected amount, since the transaction did not involve boot. If the appropriate number of shares (votes and value test) are received as consideration, corporation X may be connected with the purchaser corporation (i.e., more than 10% of the votes and value of all the outstanding shares).

The purchaser corporation could then redeem its shares held by corporation X for $20 each. This would result in a deemed dividend to the extent that the redemption price of $20 exceeds the paid-up capital of $1.00 of the shares redeemed [ssec. 84(3)]. This deemed dividend of $19 would not be taxable under Part I or Part IV of the Act. Furthermore, corporation X would be deemed to have disposed of its shares of the purchaser corporation for proceeds of disposition equal to the excess of the redemption price of $20 over the deemed dividend of $19. This would result in proceeds which are equal to the adjusted cost base of the shares of $1.00 such that there is no capital gain on the disposition of the shares.

Again, subsection 55(2) would apply in this case with the same result as that in the previous illustration. Thus, the deemed dividend of $19 would be deemed not to be a dividend and, therefore, would be part of the proceeds of disposition of the shares in corporation Y. Using the two-step redemption procedure outlined previously, the following would result:

Step 1 — Deemed dividend on redemption

Redemption amount paid		$20
Less: P.U.C.		1
Deemed dividend on redemption [ssec. 84(3)]		$19
Less: part of dividend designated as a separate dividend attributable to post-1971 income [par. 55(5)(f)]	Nil	
part of dividend subject to Part IV tax	Nil	Nil
Part of dividend deemed not to be a dividend [ssec. 55(2)]		$19

Step 2 — Capital gain or loss on disposition of shares

Redemption amount paid	$20
Less: designated part of ssec. 84(3) dividend (see above)	Nil
Proceeds of disposition	$20
Less: adjusted cost base	1
Capital gain	$19

3. Exceptions to the application of section 55

It should be emphasized that section 55 is not applicable where the entire dividend, in either of the transactions described by the foregoing illustrations, can reasonably be considered to be attributable to income, referred to as "safe income" earned or realized on a tax basis by corporation Y after the later date of acquisition of the shares and 1971 and before the dividend was received by corporation X. In this situation, the dividend is not deemed to be proceeds of disposition of the shares disposed of by corporation X. Therefore, it does not offend this legislation to pay a tax-free intercorporate dividend from "post-1971 earnings". Paragraph 55(5)(*f*) permits the separation of the total dividend resulting from the transaction into a part that would not be affected by subsection 55(2) because it was attributed to post-1971[f] realized earnings and a part that would be subject to the deemed proceeds of disposition rules of subsection 55(2). Alternatively, the same effect would be achieved by actually declaring and paying a separate dividend equal to post-1971 earnings before any other transaction is made. Note that the post-1971 income of a corporation, earned or realized *after* the transaction or series of transactions that gave rise to the dividend in question, cannot be used to reduce the tax liability under subsection 55(2).

Therefore, in the previous numerical examples, if corporation Y had post-1971 income of, for example, $15, the capital gain would have been only $4 in both cases.

If the dividend received by corporation X in the foregoing illustrations had been subject to Part IV tax either because corporation X was not connected with the corporation paying the dividend or because that payer corporation had refundable taxes, then that dividend received would also not be subject to the deemed proceeds of disposition rules of subsection 55(2). However, for this exception to apply, the Part IV tax paid cannot be refunded as a consequence of the payment of a dividend to a corporation as part of a series of transactions or events.

Finally, paragraph 55(3)(*b*) provides an exemption for *bona fide* corporate reorganizations including an estate freeze and what is known in practice as a "butterfly" transaction. The latter typically involves the breaking up of a corporation with the assets of the corporation being distributed to holding companies owned by the shareholders of the corporation being broken up. The specifics of these transactions are beyond the scope of this text.

> *Key signals:*
>
> Here are four key factors which may signal an application of section 55:
>
> (a) a dividend(s), ordinary or deemed, has occurred;
>
> (b) the dividend is a part of a transaction or a contemplated series of transactions usually involving the corporate reorganization provisions;
>
> (c) one of the main purposes was to effect a significant reduction of the potential capital gain; and
>
> (d) the dividend is followed by the disposition of shares of a corporation to an arm's length party.

---

[f] For the CRA's view on the calculation of post-1971 income, see John R. Robertson, "Capital Gain Strips: A Revenue Canada Perspective on the Provisions of Section 55", *1981 Conference Report*, Canadian Tax Foundation, pp. 88-91 and Michael A. Hiltz, "Section 55: An Update," *1984 Corporate Management Tax Conference*, Canadian Tax Foundation, pp. 45-46. For the courts' views on the calculation of "safe income", see the cases of *The Queen v. Nassau Walnut Investments Inc.* (FCC), 97 DTC 5051, *The Queen v. Kruco Inc.* (FCA), 2003 DTC 5506, *VIH Logging Ltd. v. The Queen* (TCC), 2004 DTC 2090, and *729658 Alberta Ltd. et al. v. The Queen* (TCC), 2004 DTC 2909. These cases illustrate a divergence by the courts from the CRA's administrative position.

REVIEW QUESTIONS

(1) In tax terms, what does the word "rollover" mean and how does it impact on both the transferor and the transferee?

(2) Della Inc. is a corporation that was incorporated in Delaware, U.S.A., in 1965 and has been resident in Canada since 1973 when its sole shareholder, Mr. Della, moved to Canada. During this year, Mr. Della wanted to transfer some land and a building, that was capital property to him, to Della Inc. for use in the business. He did transfer the property to the corporation and used section 85 to defer the accrued gain. Comment on whether there is any technicality that would not allow him to use section 85.

(3) When using section 85, the elected price is very important since it is used in the determination of four things that arise on the transfer. What are they?

(4) Since the tax value and the fair market value are usually fixed, what is the one decision variable that you can use that will have an effect on the limits of the elected transfer price range?

(5) When using section 85, what is the maximum amount of "boot" that should be taken in order to maximize the deferral?

(6) Ms. Smith heard at a party last night that she can avoid the "half-year rule" in Regulation 1100(2) by first purchasing the equipment personally and then selling it shortly thereafter to her corporation and electing under section 85. She thinks that the corporation will then be able to claim the full C.C.A. in the first year instead of only one half. What do you think and why?

(7) How is the cost of the consideration taken back by the transferor in a subsection 85(1) transfer determined?

(8) Bar Ltd., a CCPC, owns shares in Loser Ltd., a small business corporation, that have gone down in value. Bar Ltd.'s problem is that it cannot sell the shares because there is no market. Bar Ltd. then decides that it will sell the shares to a company owned by the wife of the sole shareholder of Bar Ltd., called Spouse Ltd., claim an A.B.I.L. and at least be able to withdraw from Spouse Ltd. the fair market value of the shares of Loser Ltd. Bar Ltd. does not own any shares in Spouse Ltd. Since there is no gain to defer, they will not elect under section 85. Comment on this strategy.

(9) Using section 85, what is the amount that determines how much the transferor can withdraw from the company on a tax-free basis?

(10) Ms. Smith has decided to transfer some portfolio shares to her wholly-owned company in exchange for more shares of the company. The shares have a cost of $5,000 and a fair market value of $8,000. She plans to elect at $8,000 and take back shares with a P.U.C. and redemption amount of $10,000. What are the tax consequences to Ms. Smith and her company?

(11) If the optimal value of the boot is equal to the tax value of the property transferred under section 85, what will the A.C.B. and P.U.C. of the shares taken back be?

(12) Given that F.M.V. is often not easily arrived at when transferring assets under section 85, what protection can you use to avoid a one-sided adjustment by the CRA if their value is different than yours?

(13) What is the purpose behind section 84.1?

(14) Mr. Big got a good deal a few years ago on the shares of a company that he just bought. He paid $10,000 for the shares even though the P.U.C. of the shares is $100,000. Today the company is worth $100,000 again thanks to his hard work. Mr. Big has never used his Q.S.B.C. share capital gains exemption. How can he get money out of the company without paying any personal tax?

MULTIPLE CHOICE QUESTIONS

Question 1

Pauline plans to sell a depreciable asset to a corporation owned by her husband. The characteristics of the assets are as follows:

FMV	$3,000
Capital cost	2,200
UCC	800

Which *one* of the following statements is *true*?

(A) The gain will be deferred due to the spousal rollover since the corporation is owned by Pauline's husband.

(B) Pauline should file a subsection 85(1) election and elect at $2,200 to defer the tax on the sale.

(C) Pauline should file a subsection 85(1) election and elect at $800 to defer the tax on the sale.

(D) If a subsection 85(1) election is not made, the capital cost and UCC of the asset to the corporation will be $3,000.

Question 2

Steve plans to sell a non-depreciable asset which has a mortgage of $15,000 to S Ltd. S Ltd. is a taxable Canadian corporation. Steve owns all the shares. Steve and S Ltd. will file an election under subsection 85(1). S Ltd. will assume the mortgage. For proceeds, Steve would like to receive a non-interest bearing note for the maximum amount possible without incurring adverse tax consequences. The balance of the consideration will be in shares of S Ltd. Steve considers any tax incurred an adverse consequence. The asset has the following characteristics:

FMV	$100,000
ACB	40,000

What is the maximum amount of the note that Steve should take?

(A) $100,000

(B) $85,000

(C) $40,000

(D) $25,000

Question 3

Susan sold a Class 1 depreciable asset to a corporation that she controls in exchange for a non-interest bearing demand loan of $100,000 and preferred shares redeemable for $80,000 in total. Susan and the corporation filed a section 85 election electing for the transfer to take place at $120,000. The characteristics of the asset were as follows:

FMV	$180,000
Capital cost	100,000
ACB	100,000
UCC	75,000

The capital cost of the asset to the corporation is:

(A) $120,000

(B) $110,000

(C) $90,000

(D) $75,000

Question 4

Sylvia is the sole shareholder of Strained Ltd., a taxable Canadian corporation. Sylvia transferred a non-depreciable capital property having an adjusted cost base of $40,000 and a fair market value of $50,000 to Strained Ltd. in exchange for the following package of consideration.

Cash	$ 3,000
Debt	2,000
Preferred shares (FMV and legal stated capital)	15,000
Common shares (FMV and legal stated capital)	30,000
	$50,000

Sylvia and Strained Ltd. made a joint election under subsection 85(1), electing a transfer price of $40,000.

The cost to Sylvia of the common shares received as consideration is:

(A) $35,000

(B) $23,000

(C) $23,333

(D) $20,000

Question 5

Which one of the following is an advantage for a vendor and purchaser using a section 22 election to transfer accounts receivable rather than electing under subsection 85(1)?

(A) The vendor will realize a loss that may be a superficial loss.

(B) The vendor will realize a loss that is a capital loss.

(C) The vendor will not be required to add the prior year's doubtful debts reserve to income.

(D) The purchaser will be able to take a doubtful debts reserve on the accounts receivable.

Question 6

Rebecca transfers land to R Co and makes a joint election with R Co under subsection 85(1) of the *Income Tax Act* in the amount of $50,000. The land has a cost of $50,000 and a fair market of $210,000. Rebecca takes back a demand promissory note of $60,000 and redeemable, retractable preference shares worth $150,000 in value. The tax consequences of this transaction are that:

(A) Rebecca is deemed to dispose of the land for proceeds of $50,000.

(B) R Co.'s cost of the land is $50,000.

(C) Rebecca's cost of the preference shares is $150,000.

(D) R Co.'s cost of the land is $60,000.

EXERCISES

Exercise 1

[ITA: 85(1), (5.1)]

Consider the following cases involving the transfer of capital assets to a corporation for consideration including both common shares and "boot".

	A	B	C	D	E	F	G
Fair market value	$120	$100	$ 80	$100	$110	$100	$ 80
Adjusted cost base	N/A	75	N/A	75	N/A	75	N/A
Capital cost	100	N/A	100	N/A	100	N/A	100
U.C.C. of class.........	200	N/A	50	N/A	150	N/A	50
F.M.V. of class.........	170	N/A	110	N/A	140	N/A	110
"Boot"	150	200	80	50	80	90	20

— *REQUIRED*

(A) Compute the minimum elected amount possible given these data.

(B) Compute the effects on income given these data.

(C) Indicate the maximum "boot" that should be taken in each case to maximize the deferral of taxation.

Exercise 2

[ITA: 85(1), (2.1)]

Dee transferred capital property to Dee Ltd. The capital property had an adjusted cost base of $5,000 and a fair market value of $10,000. Dee could receive any of the following packages of consideration:

	A	B	C
Notes at fair market value	$5,000	$2,500	$4,000
Preferred shares at fair market value and L.S.C.	4,500	7,500	—
Common shares (L.S.C.)..........	500	—	6,000

— REQUIRED

(A) Given an elected amount of $5,000, what would be the cost of each item of consideration under each possible package of consideration?

(B) What will be the P.U.C. for tax purposes under each possible package of consideration?

Exercise 3

[ITA: 13(7)(*e*); 84(3); 85(1), (2.1); 110.6]

Last year Mr. Goodroll purchased a business location including land for $150,000 and a brick building for $436,224. He operated the business as a sole proprietorship for a year taking maximum capital cost allowance on the building. On your advice, this year he incorporated the business using section 85 to transfer the land and building to the corporation without triggering any of the gain that had accrued on these assets during the year. The following is a summary of the transfer under section 85.

	Tax value	Appraised F.M.V.	Elected amount	Consideration Assumed mortgage	Consideration New debt	Consideration Common shares
Land........	$150,000	$375,000	$150,000	$150,000	—	$225,000
Building (U.C.C.)	427,500	525,000	427,500	97,500	$330,000	97,500
	$577,500	$900,000	$577,500	$247,500	$330,000	$322,500

— REQUIRED

(A) What are the tax consequences of electing a transfer price of $577,500 as indicated?

(B) (i) Compute the cost of the consideration received from the corporation.

(ii) Compute the P.U.C. for tax purposes of the common shares.

(C) (i) What are the tax consequences to Mr. Goodroll if the corporation redeemed the debt issued by the corporation for $330,000 and he sells his shares in the corporation for $425,000?

(ii) What are the tax consequences to Mr. Goodroll if the corporation redeems the common shares for $425,000?

Exercise 4

[ITA: 85(1)(*e*.2), (2.1)]

Mother owned some debt securities which she transferred to a corporation in which Daughter (age 29) owns all of the common shares. These securities cost Mother $100,000 in 1975 and had a fair market value at the time of transfer of $125,000. Section 85 was used to transfer the securities at an elected amount of $100,000. As consideration for the securities transferred, Mother received a note having a value of $100,000 and a preferred share having a fair market value and an L.S.C. of $1,000.

— REQUIRED

What are the tax consequences of this transaction and how could they have been avoided?

Exercise 5

[ITA: 85(1)(*e*.1), (2.1)]

Rancid Rollover, who owns 100% of Rollover Ltd., has come to you concerning transferring some additional assets to the corporation. The following facts relate to the transfer:

Asset #1
Capital cost	$10,000
Undepreciated capital cost	5,000
Fair market value	20,000

Asset #2

Adjusted cost base .... $ 8,000
Fair market value 14,000

Rancid wishes to take back one no par value common share and $18,000 cash.

— *REQUIRED*

Discuss the tax implications of the proposed transaction.

Exercise 6

[ITA: 22; 85]

Mrs. Designer has provided you with the following balance sheet and additional information relative to her unincorporated ladies' fashion business.

Mrs. Designer

(A Proprietorship)

BALANCE SHEET

May 31, 2005

Cash		$ 4,000	Accounts payable		$ 14,000
Short-term investments		10,000	Mortgage payable (current maturity)		6,000
Accounts receivable ...	$ 12,000				$ 20,000
Allowance for doubtful accounts	(2,000)	10,000			
Inventory ...		5,000			
Prepaid insurance ...		500			
		$ 29,500			
Building cost	$ 80,000		Mortgage payable	$ 60,000	
Accumulated depreciation	(18,000)	$ 62,000	Current portion	(6,000)	$ 54,000
Land, cost		30,000	Proprietor's equity		47,500
		$ 92,000			$101,500
		$121,500			$121,500

Additional Information

(1) Incomes for tax and financial accounting purposes have always been the same.

(2) All assets were acquired after 1971.

(3) The May 31, 2005 fair market value of various assets owned by the proprietorship are:

Short-term investments .... $ 5,000
Accounts receivable 9,000
Inventory 25,000
Prepaid insurance 400
Building.. 60,000
Land 26,500
Goodwill....................................... 44,000

Effective June 1, 2005, Mrs. Designer wants to transfer her business assets to a corporation (Hi-Fashion Co. Ltd.) in which her husband owns 100% of the common shares.

She has indicated that, provided the company assumes the business debts, she would receive the balance in debt and preferred shares (stated value $100) as full consideration.

— REQUIRED

(A) Determine which assets should not be transferred to the corporation under section 85 and those that should not be transferred at all and give reasons.

(B) Determine the amounts to be elected on the various assets to avoid any taxes.

(C) Determine the consideration to be received without any tax consequences.

(D) Determine the adjusted cost base of the consideration in part (C) above.

(E) Determine the tax P.U.C. of the preferred shares received.

(F) Determine the cost/capital cost of the transferred assets for the corporation, Hi-Fashion Co. Ltd.

Exercise 7

[ITA: 13(7)(*e*); 85(1), (2.1); 110.6]

In 2005, Ms. Kvetch transferred a depreciable capital property (the only one in its class) to a corporation which she controls. The property had an undepreciated capital cost of $27,000, a capital cost of $30,000 and a fair market value of $100,000. She elected to transfer the property under subsection 85(1) at $80,000 in order to offset the resultant taxable capital gain with a 1999 net capital loss of $37,500. As consideration for the property, she received a note for $80,000 and common shares with a stated value of $20,000.

— REQUIRED

What are the income tax implications of this transaction?

Exercise 8

[ITA: 84(3); 84.1; 85]

Mr. Nailed, a Canadian resident, owned all of the common shares with a paid-up capital value and cost of $75,000 in an operating company, Opco Ltd. He transferred these shares under section 85 to a company, Broco Ltd., owned by his brother at a time when the value of the Opco Ltd. shares was $800,000. As consideration for the shares transferred he received a note with a principal amount of $500,000 and preferred shares with a paid-up capital and fair market value of $300,000 such that an elected amount of $500,000 was possible under section 85. Mr. Nailed offset all of the resultant $425,000 of capital gain with his available Q.S.B.C. share capital gains exemption. Both Opco Ltd. and Broco Ltd. are Canadian-controlled private corporations.

— REQUIRED

(A) What are the tax consequences of the transfer to Mr. Nailed?

(B) What are the tax consequences if the preferred shares received from his brother's corporation are redeemed by that corporation for their fair market value?

(C) What are the tax consequences if the preferred shares are sold in an arm's length transaction for their fair market value?

Exercise 9

[ITA: 54; 84(3); 84.1]

Ms. Erin owns all of the common shares of Davpet Ltd. The shares have a P.U.C. and cost of $1,000. Their current fair market value is $300,000. The shares are qualified small business corporation shares and she is anxious to crystallize her capital gains exemption on the accrued gain in these shares. Her father owns all of the common shares of Lenmeag Ltd., a Canadian-controlled private corporation, and is willing to use that corporation to assist her in her plans.

— REQUIRED

(A) Determine the immediate tax consequences, if Ms. Erin sells her common shares in Davpet Ltd. to Lenmeag Ltd. for their fair market value, receiving a $300,000 note from Lenmeag Ltd. which will ultimately be repaid in cash. Her father will allow her to continue to manage Davpet Ltd. and she will ultimately inherit the shares of Lenmeag Ltd. to reacquire control of Davpet Ltd.

(B) Determine the tax consequences, alternatively, if she sells her shares of Davpet Ltd. to Lenmeag Ltd. for their fair market value of $300,000, receiving $300,000 of the common shares of Lenmeag Ltd. No subsection 85(1) election is made.

Exercise 10

[ITA: 55(1)–(6)]

Vendco Ltd. owns all of the shares of Preyco Ltd. The shares of Preyco have a total adjusted cost base of $100,000 and a fair market value of $1,000,000. Since 1971 Preyco has realized and retained $700,000 of income and has no refundable taxes.

Vendco wishes to sell its shares in Preyco to Purchco. It causes Preyco to borrow $900,000 from the bank and to pay a dividend on its shares of $900,000. This reduces the fair market value of Preyco's shares to $100,000 and Purchco buys the shares for this amount.

— *REQUIRED*

What are the tax consequences of these transactions?

ASSIGNMENT PROBLEMS

Problem 1

[ITA: 85(1)]

The following assets are to be transferred under section 85 for consideration including common shares plus "boot" as indicated below:

	Fair market value	A.C.B./ Capital cost/ E.C.E.	U.C.C./ C.E.C.	Boot
Land	$ 75,000	$60,000	—	$50,000
Marketable securities	65,000	55,000	—	60,000
Building*	95,000	85,000	$70,000	55,000
Equipment.	50,000	65,000	40,000	45,000
Furniture and fixtures	10,000	15,000	7,000	5,000
Licence**	100,000	82,500	60,000	15,000

* Only asset in class.
** Indefinite life.

— *REQUIRED*

(A) Compute the minimum possible elected amounts.

(B) Compute the effects on income.

(C) Indicate the maximum "boot" that should be taken to maximize the deferral of taxation.

Problem 2

[ITA: 85(1)]

Pete Handyman is the sole proprietor of a hardware store, The Handyman Shop. Pete has decided to incorporate the business but wishes to minimize any income inclusions on the transfer of his business to the new corporation.

The Handyman Shop has the following assets:

	Tax value	F.M.V.
Cash	$22,000	$22,000
Inventory (cost: $44,000)	39,500	39,500
Furniture and fixtures (cost: $12,000)	6,000	8,000
Building ($75,000 cost)	45,000	55,000
Land	8,000	30,000

As consideration for the transfer of the above assets, Pete would like to take back the maximum amount of debt and the balance in the form of common shares.

— *REQUIRED*

Determine the appropriate transfer price under subsection 85(1) for the assets which can and should be transferred. Determine the amount of debt and share consideration that Pete can accept without any adverse tax consequences. Compute the adjusted cost base and the P.U.C. for tax purposes of the common shares received as consideration.

Problem 3

[ITA: 84(3); 85]

Ms. Hart, a Canadian resident, has provided you with the following balance sheet and additional information concerning to her unincorporated active retail clothing business. Effective November 10, 2005, she wishes to transfer all of her business assets and liabilities to a corporation (Hart Ltd.) in which her husband owns 100% of the common shares. She wants to minimize her personal tax on the transaction and insists on receiving the following package of consideration:

(1) The maximum amount of debt (to the nearest $100); and

(2) Voting, redeemable, retractable preferred shares for the balance of the consideration with a legal stated capital equal to their fair market value.

The following financial information concerning the business as of November 10, 2005, was provided:

	Tax value	Fair market value
Shares in public companies (note 1)	$ 11,000	$ 6,000
Accounts receivable (note 2)	13,000	10,000
Inventory	8,000	9,000
Land (held as inventory)	100,000	220,000
Prepaid property insurance	600	600
Building (Class 1, cost $90,000)	70,000	50,000
Land (capital property)	140,000	160,000
Goodwill	nil	80,000

Additional Information:

1. The shares are capital property to Ms. Hart. Ms. Hart owns less than 1% of each public company.

2. The tax reserve for doubtful debts taken in the previous year was $1,000. The original cost of the accounts receivable before deducting the reserve was $14,000.

3. The unincorporated business has liabilities of $60,000 which are to be assumed by Hart Ltd..

— *REQUIRED*

(A) Prepare an analysis, with explanations as necessary, of the income tax consequences of selling the assets to Hart Ltd. without electing under subsection 85(1) or section 22. Show all calculations whether or not relevant to the final answer.

(B) Recommend a more tax-effective manner in which to achieve Ms. Hart's objectives. Explain your recommendation in detail, including the income tax implication for Hart Ltd., as well as for Ms. Hart.

(C) What are the tax consequences if Ms. Hart sells her preferred shares to a third party for their fair market value?

(D) What will be the tax consequences if Hart Ltd. redeems Ms. Hart's preferred shares for their fair market value?

Problem 4

[ITA: 85]

Joe Schmaltz has carried on a retail business since 1986. He intends to transfer the business assets and liabilities to a corporation, Schmaltz Enterprises Ltd. (SEL), in which he will own all of the voting preferred shares. His three children, all in their 20's, have already subscribed for all of the common shares in equal numbers. The balance sheet of the proprietorship and certain additional information are provided as follows:

Assets	Balance sheet, April 30, 2005	Fair market value April 30, 2005
Cash	$ 12,000	$ 12,000
Accounts receivable	120,000	102,000
Reserves for doubtful debts[1]	(10,000)	—

Inventories..........................	90,000	100,000
Shares of Supplyco Ltd.[2]	36,000	40,000
Shares of Clientco Ltd..............	1,000	100
Land	96,000	103,000
Buildings[3]	48,000	144,000
Equipment[3]......................	72,000	40,000
1987 Oldsmobile[3]	3,000	5,000
Goodwill	—	90,000
	$468,000	$636,100

Liabilities[4]

Bank loan	$ 30,000
Accounts payable	31,000
Accrued liabilities	6,000
Mortgage on land and building	84,000
	$151,000
Proprietor's equity	317,000
	$468,000

Notes to Balance Sheet

(1) The reserve for doubtful debts represents the closing reserve for the previous fiscal period.

(2) These shares represent a 2% ownership in the common shares of Supplyco Ltd. which is a small business corporation.

(3) Fixed assets are recorded at original cost less accumulated financial accounting depreciation. Tax data follow:

	Original cost	*U.C.C.*
Buildings	$ 95,000	$42,000
Equipment	110,000	57,000
1987 Oldsmobile..............	18,000	1,000

No single piece of equipment was fairly valued in excess of its cost at April 30, 2004.

(4) Liabilities are to be assumed by the corporation. In addition, Joe Schmaltz will receive as consideration for the transfer of assets under subsection 85(1) the maximum in notes payable by the corporation to permit the maximum deferral of taxation on the transfer and voting retractable preferred shares.

— *REQUIRED*

(A) Indicate which assets should not be transferred to the corporation at all.

(B) Indicate which assets should be transferred to the corporation, but cannot or should not be transferred under subsection 85(1) and explain why.

(C) Assuming that the appropriate procedure has been adopted to take advantage of the provisions of subsection 85(1) of the Act, indicate the elected amounts which should be used in order to defer any taxation upon the transfer of the business to the company and the effect of the consideration package as expressly requested by your client. He has $4,500 of net capital losses (arising in 1999) that he would like to use on the transfer.

(D) What is Joe's cost on the consideration and the P.U.C. for tax purposes of the shares he receives for the transfer of assets?

(E) Without re-doing all of the calculations, indicate the tax consequences of having the corporation issue the maximum debt, as indicated above, but only $150,000 of voting, retractable preferred shares.

(F) What are the tax consequences, if on a subsequent assessment the CRA determines that the value of the goodwill was higher than $90,000? What protection from this eventuality can be implemented?

Problem 5

[ITA: 85]

Mr. Schminkie, the sole proprietor of a small manufacturing business wishes to have his wife involved in the business on an equal basis. Mr. Schminkie's barber advised him that this is possible by incorporating a company and having Mr. and Mrs. Schminkie subscribe for all the common shares equally. Then, Mr. Schminkie could transfer all the assets of the business to the newly formed company, taking back Class A and Class B non-voting preference shares as consideration. Mr. Schminkie thought this was a wonderful idea and proceeded with incorporating the company.

The assets and liabilities of the proprietorship and certain additional information are provided as follows:

Assets	Balance sheet Dec. 31/05	Fair market value Dec. 31/05
Cash	$ 20,000	$ 20,000
Accounts receivable[1]	90,000	85,000
Inventories	86,000	86,000
Shares in Public Co.	50,000	20,000
Land — Parcel I[3]	200,000	339,000
Building[2]	15,000	75,000
Land — Parcel II[4]	20,000	45,000
Equipment[2]	35,000	5,000
Auto[2]	10,000	12,000
Goodwill	—	60,000
	$526,000	

Liabilities[5]	
Bank loan	$169,000
Accounts payable	43,000
Mortgage on building	30,000
	$242,000
Proprietor's equity	284,000
	$526,000

Notes to Balance Sheet

(1) The accounts receivable are net of a $6,000 reserve for doubtful accounts which represents the closing reserve for the previous fiscal period.

(2) Fixed assets are recorded at original cost less accumulated financial accounting depreciation. Tax data is as follows:

	Original cost	U.C.C.
Building	$60,000	$15,000
Equipment	80,000	35,000
Auto	16,000	11,000

(3) Parcel I of land is the property upon which the building used in the business is sited.

(4) Parcel II of land was acquired in 2004. Mr. Schminkie purchased it with the intention to sell as soon as the fair market value exceeded $50,000. Mr. Schminkie speculates this will occur by April 19, 2006, at which point he will sell for the quick profit.

(5) Liabilities are to be assumed by the corporation.

— REQUIRED

(A) Indicate which assets should not be transferred to the corporation at all.

(B) Indicate which assets should be transferred to the corporation, but cannot or should not be transferred under subsection 85(1) and briefly explain why.

(C) For the assets which can be transferred under subsection 85(1) to the corporation, indicate the maximum amount of debt in addition to the shares that can be taken as consideration to defer all possible capital gains, losses, other income and other available adverse tax consequences given the consideration to be taken. The corporation will issue a maximum of $200,000 Class A retractable non-voting preference shares with a dividend rate of 8% and the remainder of the share consideration will be Class B retractable, non-voting preference shares with no dividend entitlement.

(D) What is Mr. Schminkie's cost of the consideration and the P.U.C. for tax purposes of the preferred shares that he receives for the transfer of assets?

(E) Compute the tax consequences of a redemption in 2006 of the preferred shares of the corporation at their fair market value after the transfer of assets to the corporation.

(F) What could be done to avoid a benefit problem, if the Class B consideration is limited to an authorized share capital amount of only $50,000 and the Class A consideration remains the same?

Problem 6

[ITA: 84.1; 85(1)]

Mrs. Andrews, a Canadian resident, set up VonTrapp Holdings Limited (VHL) to hold all of her shares in Plummer Enterprises Inc. (Plummer) in order to crystallize her remaining $400,000 capital gains exemption for qualified small business corporation shares.

Mrs. Andrews owns 100% of the outstanding common shares of Plummer. Plummer is a small business corporation and meets all the tests for the shares to be qualified small business corporation shares. Plummer and VHL are both Canadian resident corporations. She purchased the Plummer shares in 1986 from an unrelated third party for their then fair market value of $200,000.

The fair market value of the Plummer shares today is $1,000,000. The paid-up capital of these shares is $1,000.

Mrs. Andrews will jointly elect under section 85 with VHL and will take back the following consideration:

(a) non-interest bearing note for $200,000, and

(b) 6% voting preference shares with a retractable and fair market value equal to the balance of the fair market value of the Plummer common shares.

— *REQUIRED*

Discuss the tax implications of the proposed transaction, supported by your computations.

Problem 7

[ITA: 84(3); 84.1; 85]

Mrs. Diet owns all 100 common shares of Low-Cal Caterers Inc. (Low-Cal), a Canadian-controlled private corporation with a December 31 year-end. Low-Cal was incorporated in 1982 when Mrs. Diet invested $250,000 in common shares with a paid-up capital of the same amount. The Low-Cal shares are now valued at $2,000,000.

Mrs. Diet would like to freeze the present value of Low-Cal so that any future increase in value would accrue to her 20-year old son, Slim. She proposes that Slim incorporate a new corporation, Slim Pickings Holdings Ltd. (Slim Pickings), with $100 of his own money by acquiring all the common shares of the new corporation.

Mrs. Diet would then transfer her common shares in Low-Cal to Slim Pickings using a section 85 election in order to defer the inherent gain on these shares. Mrs. Diet would like to receive as consideration a non-interest bearing note for $750,000 and the balance of the fair market value for 1,000 8% non-cumulative, voting preference shares with a retraction value, fair market value and paid-up capital of $1,250,000. Since she would also like to use all her capital gains exemption (of $500,000 for Q.S.B.C. shares), she proposes that the elected amount under subsection 85(1) be $750,000. You have determined that both Low-Cal and Slim Pickings are small business corporations at the present time and that Low-Cal meets all the conditions for Q.S.B.C. shares.

— REQUIRED

(A) Describe the tax consequences to Mrs. Diet of the proposed subsection 85(1) transfer of the Low-Cal common shares to Slim Pickings.

(B) How would you change the above proposed consideration package so that Mrs. Diet achieves her objectives as stated above?

(C) What would be the tax consequences if Mrs. Diet sold to Slim Pickings for cash or debt just enough of the 100 common shares of Low-Cal common shares to realize a capital gain of $500,000 in order to utilize her capital gains exemption as described above?

(D) Indicate the tax consequences for parts (A) and (B) if Mrs. Diet:

(i) redeems all the preference shares in Slim Pickings for their fair market value; or

(ii) sells all the preference shares in Slim Pickings to an arm's length party for their fair market value.

Problem 8

[ITA: 55(1)–(6)]

Strip Limited has received an offer from an unrelated corporation, Corporate Raider Inc., to purchase all of Strip's common shares in a wholly-owned subsidiary, Profits Galore Ltd. All three corporations are Canadian-controlled private corporations and have December 31 year-ends.

The common shares of Profits Galore Ltd. have an adjusted cost base and paid-up capital of $500,000 and a fair market value of $2,400,000. Profits Galore Ltd. has realized and retained income for tax purposes of $900,000 since 1971. All of this realized income was derived from active business assets.

Strip Limited has come to you for your comments on two acquisition alternatives proposed by Corporate Raider Inc.

Plan A would first have Profits Galore Ltd. borrow from the bank $1,900,000 and, then, immediately pay a dividend to its parent corporation, Strip Limited, for the same amount. Corporate Raider Inc. would then purchase the common shares of Profits Galore Ltd. from Strip Limited for the residual fair market value of $500,000. Then, Corporate Raider would inject $1,900,000 into Profits Galore Ltd. through a common share subscription so that the bank loan could be repaid.

Plan B would have Strip Limited transfer its common shares in Profits Galore Inc. to Corporate Raider Inc. on a tax-free basis by jointly electing under subsection 85(1) at a transfer price of $500,000. Strip Limited Inc. would accept as consideration only special shares of Corporate Raider Inc. with a paid-up capital of $500,000 and a redemption/retraction value of $2,400,000. These shares would represent 15% of all the voting rights and fair market value of Corporate Raider Inc. Strip Limited would, then, retract the special shares which it holds in Corporate Raider.

— REQUIRED

Describe the tax implications of the above acquisition alternatives supported by any relevant calculations.

[For more problems and solutions thereto, see the CD accompanying this book.]

SUPPLEMENTAL NOTES

(This section can be omitted without losing the continuity of the chapter. None of the review questions, multiple choice questions, exercises, short questions or assignment problems utilizes this information.)

A. GST and Section 85 Rollovers

[ETA: 123(1); 141.1(3); 153(1)(*b*); 156; 167(1)]

If the property that is the subject of the section 85 rollover, was used by the taxpayer in a commercial activity, the rollover will be a taxable transaction for GST purposes. For example, if a sole proprietorship or partnership transfers property on incorporation, the transfer will be subject to GST. However, an election may be available [ETA: ssec. 167(1)] to cancel any potential GST liability. As discussed in Chapter 15, the election is available where a supplier makes a supply of a business, an acquired business, or part thereof that was established or carried on by the supplier or previous owner. The recipient must acquire ownership, possession or use of all or substantially all (i.e., 90% or more) of the property that can reasonably be regarded as being necessary for the recipient to be capable of carrying on the business or part thereof as a business. If an election is made under this subsection, tax is generally not payable in respect of the supply.

On a section 85 rollover, the election for closely-related groups [ETA: sec. 156] (see Chapter 15) will only be available if the transferor and transferee are both corporations and the other criteria for the use of the election are met.

If neither of the elections [ETA: ssec. 167(1) or sec. 156] are available, the transfer of property under section 85 of the *Income Tax Act* will be subject to the general rules of the GST. To the extent the transfer of property is a taxable supply, GST will be payable on the consideration paid or payable for the property, and the elected amount under section 85 will not be relevant. The value of the consideration received will be deemed to be equal to the fair market value of the consideration at the time of transfer [ETA: par. 153(1)(*b*)]. Thus, the value of the consideration will be deemed to be equal to the fair market value of the share and non-share consideration received. If the transferred property is for use in commercial activities, the recipient may claim an input tax credit for any GST paid or payable on the transfer, to the extent the property is for use in such activities. If, on the other hand, the property will be used exclusively in making exempt supplies, an input tax credit cannot be claimed. The issuance of shares is an exempt financial service and, hence, not subject to GST.

If advisory fees such as legal and accounting fees are incurred by the transferor, subsection 141.1(3) of the ETA provides that anything done by a person in connection with the acquisition, establishment, disposition or termination of a commercial activity is deemed to be part of the commercial activity. Consequently, these fees will also generate input tax credits. The transferee is not entitled to claim input tax credits in respect of GST paid on advisory fees that relate to the making of exempt supplies, i.e., the issuance of shares. However, other fees that relate to the acquisition of property (taxable supplies) to be used in a commercial activity will qualify for an input tax credit [ETA: ssec. 141.1(3)].

Chapter 17

Income Deferral: Other Rollovers
and
Use of Rollovers in Estate Planning

TOPICS DISCUSSED

	Page
ROLLOVERS INVOLVING CORPORATIONS AND THEIR SHAREHOLDERS	920
Share for Share Exchange	920
Reorganizations	922
Statutory Amalgamations	931
Winding up a Subsidiary	935
ROLLOVERS INVOLVING SHARES OR CORPORATE SECURITIES	939
Convertible Properties	939

	Page
Inter-spousal Transfers	939
USE OF ROLLOVERS IN ESTATE FREEZING	940
Objectives	940
Holdco Freeze	941
Internal Freeze	941
Reverse or Asset Freeze	942
SUPPLEMENTAL NOTES	950
GST Consequences of Rollovers Involving Corporations and Their Securities	950

This chapter completes the discussion of rollovers which permit the deferral of income on transactions between corporations and their shareholders. The chapter also discusses the application of some of the rules presented in this and previous chapters to the planning technique known as "estate freezing". The final part of this chapter will discuss the GST consequences of the income tax rollovers presented in the chapter.

For a chart that locates the major provisions discussed in this Chapter, refer to the beginning of Chapter 15.

I. ROLLOVERS INVOLVING CORPORATIONS AND THEIR SHAREHOLDERS

A. Share for Share Exchange

[ITA: 85.1; IT-450R]

1. The concept

Subsection 85.1 permits a tax-free rollover to a shareholder of a corporation who exchanges his or her shares for shares of another corporation. The provision is most often used in a business combination or take-over situation where a shareholder of one corporation exchanges his or her shares for shares of the purchasing corporation. While the application of this provision is automatic, this deferral of the potential capital gains or losses is conditional on a set of very specific rules that must be adhered to in order to avoid immediate tax consequences.

For example, Mr. Investor owns shares of A Ltd. Another company B Ltd., wants to acquire his A Ltd. shares in exchange for shares in B Ltd. Where Mr. Investor exchanges his A Ltd. shares for new shares of B Ltd., the inherent capital gain or loss on the shares of A. Ltd. is deferred. The adjusted cost base to Mr. Investor, now holding the new shares from B Ltd., is the adjusted cost base of the original A Ltd. shares. Therefore, Mr. Investor is in the same tax position that existed prior to the exchange.

However, unlike other rollover provisions, section 85.1 deems that the cost of A Ltd. shares, now held by B Ltd., is the lesser of the fair market value and the paid-up capital of A Ltd. shares prior to the exchange. If the fair market value of the A Ltd. shares has increased above the P.U.C. of those shares, establishing their cost to B Ltd. at their P.U.C. will be disadvantageous to B. Ltd. on the future sale of the A Ltd. shares. Establishing cost to the purchaser at this lesser amount is mandatory and is independent of whether the vendor chose to defer the gain on the exchange of A Ltd. shares.

2. The conditions

The provision envisages a situation where a taxpayer, referred to as the "vendor", exchanges shares in a corporation for shares in another corporation, referred to as the "purchaser".

(1) The transferred shares of the taxpayer/vendor must be capital property [sec. 54 definition].

(2) The purchaser must be a Canadian corporation [ssec. 89(1) definition]. Subsections 85.1(5) and (6) allow for foreign share for share exchanges but this topic is beyond the scope of this book.

(3) In respect of the exchanged shares the only consideration, given by the purchaser to the taxpayer/vendor, must be previously unissued shares of any particular class [par. 85.1(2)(*d*)]. Therefore, the consideration appears to be restricted to shares of only one class.

(4) Immediately prior to the exchange, the vendor and the purchaser must be dealing with each other at arm's length [par. 85.1(2)(*a*)].

(5) Immediately after the exchange, the vendor/taxpayer, along with non-arm's length persons, must not:

(a) control the purchaser; or

(b) own more than 50% of the fair market value of all the outstanding shares [par. 85.1(2)(*b*)].

(6) The vendor and the purchaser cannot have elected under subsection 85(1) or (2) in respect of the exchanged shares [par. 85.1(2)(*c*)].

(7) The vendor cannot have recognized any portion of the potential capital gain or loss in respect of the exchanged shares through any other provision [par. 85.1(1)(*a*)].

3. The consequences

If the above conditions are met on the exchange, then the vendor is deemed to have disposed of the shares for an amount equal to their adjusted cost base and to have acquired the purchaser's shares for the same amount [par. 85.1(1)(*a*)]. The cost of the exchanged shares to the purchaser is deemed to be the lesser of fair market value and the paid-up capital of the vendor's shares immediately before the exchange [par. 85.1(1)(*b*)].

Furthermore, the P.U.C. of the exchanged shares of the purchaser, acquired by the vendor, will be limited to the amount of the P.U.C. of the vendor's shares through a P.U.C. reduction or grind mechanism [ssec. 85.1(2.1)].

4. Other issues

If any of the above conditions are not met, the vendor will not receive the benefit of a deferral of the capital gain or loss on exchange. As a result, the exchange would take place for proceeds equal to fair market value.

In situations where the paid-up capital of the vendor's shares is less than their cost, section 85 should be considered as an alternative to avoid the deemed cost restriction described above. The elected amount becomes the transferee corporation's cost and the capital gain is thereby deferred. The subsection 85(1) alternative may not be practical if the vendors hold shares in a public corporation and the transfer requires literally hundreds of section 85 elections. However, the deemed cost restriction under paragraph 85.1(1)(*b*), described above, may not be important if the purchaser is anticipating a subsequent amalgamation or wind-up under subsection 88(1), as described later in the chapter.

Finally, the condition that the consideration be only shares of any particular class of shares of the purchaser does not preclude another separate and distinct transaction which includes non-share consideration and/or shares of a different class.

Example Problem

Nat owns common shares in Nat's Trading Corporation Limited with the following values:

F.M.V.	$950,000
A.C.B.	100,000
P.U.C.	10,000

Elaine's Pubco Ltd., a widely-held Canadian public company, has acquired all of the common shares of Nat's Trading Corporation Limited owned by Nat. In exchange for these common shares, Elaine's Pubco Ltd. has issued its common shares for a total fair market value of $950,000, representing 10% of the fair market value of all of its shares.

Nat would like to defer the realization of the capital gain accrued on his shares.

—REQUIRED

What are the tax consequences of applying section 85.1 in this case?

— SOLUTION

As long as Nat (the vendor) does not include in his income any portion of the gain on the shares he has given up in the exchange, all of the conditions of the rollover appear to apply [sec. 85.1]. The tax consequences of the rollover, which applies automatically, to Nat will be as follows:

Proceeds of disposition for Nat's Trading Corporation Limited shares	$100,000
A.C.B. of Nat's Trading Corporation Limited shares	(100,000)
Capital gain	Nil
A.C.B. of Elaine's Pubco Ltd. shares acquired on exchange	$100,000

As a result, the A.C.B. of the shares given up becomes the A.C.B. of the shares acquired in the exchange and the accrued capital gain is deferred.

The A.C.B. of the Nat's Trading Corporation Limited shares to Elaine's Pubco Ltd. (the purchaser) will be equal to $10,000 being the lesser of:

F.M.V. of Nat's Trading Corporation Limited shares before exchange	$950,000
P.U.C. of Nat's Trading Corporation Limited shares before exchange	$ 10,000

The rules will apply to limit the addition to the P.U.C. of Elaine's Pubco Ltd. on the issue of its shares in the exchange to the amount of the P.U.C. of Nat's Trading Corporation Limited (i.e., $10,000) through a P.U.C. "grind" mechanism [ssec. 85.1(2.1)].

Nat may not receive non-share consideration from Elaine's Pubco Ltd. for his shares [par. 85.1(2)(*d*)]. If this restriction on the use of section 85.1 is a concern, then a subsection 85(1) election can be made, as an alternate method of accomplishing a deferral of the accrued gain in the exchange. Thus, Nat and the purchaser corporation could jointly elect to transfer Nat's shares at an elected amount of $100,000. Nat could receive as consideration boot for up to the $100,000 A.C.B. of these shares and shares of Elaine's Pubco Ltd. for the remaining $850,000 (i.e., $950,000 – $100,000) of value.

An election under section 85 may not be feasible when the exchange involves widely dispersed share holdings held by many diverse shareholders who must elect. In these cases, the automatic nature of section 85.1 is more advantageous.

B. Reorganizations

[ITA: 40(3.6); 53(1)(*f.*2); 84(1); 84(3); 86]

1. Overview

In the course of a reorganization of capital of a corporation, a class of outstanding shares may be changed into another newly-authorized class of shares[(a)] and, perhaps, there may also be non-share consideration. Such reorganization will be accomplished by way of amendment to the articles or letters patent of the corporation. Such an amending document is referred to as articles of amendment or supplementary letters patent, respectively. Of course, the governing corporate law must permit the desired changes to be effected.

Such capital reorganizations might involve the exchange of common shares for special (preferred) shares, for example, to allow for an estate freeze discussed later in this chapter or to facilitate the purchase of a business. In such a reorganization the outstanding common shares would be exchanged for newly-authorized special shares with, usually, a fixed dividend rate and a provision with respect to the redemption/retraction amount of the share. Newly-authorized common shares would be issued and these might be subscribed for by, say, trusts for the children in the case of an estate freeze or by the purchaser where the business is being sold. Other examples of capital

---

[(a)] There is no statutory definition of the phrase "in the course of a reorganization of capital"; nor have the Canadian courts addressed this issue. Conservative planning for a section 86 reorganization would require a change in the articles of incorporation to authorize completely new shares for the exchange.

reorganizations might involve an exchange of voting shares for a new class of voting shares and another new class of non-voting shares on the reorganization of control of the corporation or a reorganization of an existing class of shares into two new classes, one of which would have a lower unit value in order to facilitate an employee share purchase program.

Generally, section 86 provides for a deferral of any accrued gain on the shares held immediately prior to the reorganization as long as the sum of the fair market value of the non-share consideration (boot) and the paid-up capital of the share consideration which are received as part of the reorganization does not exceed the paid-up capital of the existing shares. The P.U.C. of the new shares will normally be equal to the P.U.C. of the old shares less any non-share consideration.

2. Conditions

In order for the rollover to apply, the following conditions must be met:

(a) the shares are capital property to the shareholder;

(b) all of the shares of a particular class owned by the shareholder are exchanged; and

(c) property receivable by the shareholder on the exchange includes other shares.

The exchange need not apply to all shareholders who hold a particular class of shares for the rollover to apply. Only one class of shares need be the subject of the exchange. A class of shares also includes a subclass or what is referred to as a "series of shares" [ssec. 248(6)].

Note that section 86 will not apply if a rollover in section 85 has been used [ssec. 86(3)].

3. A conceptual view of section 86

A section 86 reorganization is really the issuance of new shares and the redemption or cancellation of old shares. Therefore, a section 86 reorganization consists of two transactions and related calculations.

SECTION 86 — OVERVIEW

(a) Issuance of new shares

Calculate:

- PUC of the new shares; and

- ACB of the new shares.

(b) Redemption of old shares

Calculate:

- deemed dividend on the redemption of the old shares; and

- capital gain or loss on the disposition of the old shares.
Note:

- To fully defer the unrealized gain on the old shares, i.e., for a full rollover, non-share consideration (boot) exchanged for the old shares should not exceed their PUC.

- To avoid the benefit rule, balance the fair market value of the old shares with the total fair market value of the package of consideration received.

(a) *Issuance of New Shares*

Calculate:

- PUC of the new shares; and

- ACB of the new shares.

On the issuance of new shares under section 86 there is an initial downward adjustment to the paid-up capital of the new shares in order to avoid the triggering of a subsection 84(1) deemed dividend. In the end, the P.U.C. of the new shares issued should reflect the P.U.C. in the old shares that has not been recovered in non-share consideration received on the exchange.

The cost and, hence, the initial adjusted cost base of the new shares received in the exchange are computed by first allocating the adjusted cost base of the existing share to the non-share consideration received, if any, up to its fair market value [par. 86(1)(a)] and, then, allocating the remainder to the new shares. If more than one class of new shares is received, the remaining adjusted cost base allocation must be made to each class in the proportion that the fair market value of the shares of a given class received is to the fair market value of all classes of shares received [par. 86(1)(b)].

(b) *Redemption of Old Shares*

Calculate:

- deemed dividend on the redemption of the old shares (proceeds – P.U.C.); and

- capital gain or loss on the disposition of the old shares (adjusted proceeds – A.C.B.).

In Chapter 15, the redemption proceeds were only cash or debt and usually resulted in a subsection 84(3) deemed dividend plus a capital gain or loss. The mandatory inclusion of shares in the exchange transaction adds additional complexity.

The proceeds of the redemption of the old shares under section 86 will be the sum of any boot consideration plus the P.U.C. of the newly issued shares [par. 84(5)(d)]. On the other hand, the proceeds of disposition for capital gains purposes will equal the sum of the FMV of the boot consideration plus the cost of newly issued shares (see above).

In certain circumstances, the rules in section 86 may result in a capital loss being realized. If this happens, then the loss is denied and added to the adjusted cost base of any shares owned by that person immediately after the transaction [ssec. 40(3.6) and par. 53(1)(f.2)]. The capital loss will only likely occur if the P.U.C. of the old shares was less than the adjusted cost base of those shares and the boot exceeds that P.U.C.

If, during the reorganization, a benefit is conferred on a related person, then a different calculation of the capital gain or loss must be completed, as discussed later in this chapter.

Exhibit 17-1 uses a simple numerical example to summarize all of the steps in the calculation that must be done when section 86 is used. Note that a balancing of the fair market value of the shares given up with the fair market value of the total package of consideration received on the exchange is essential. Also, note from the facts that the exchange will not result in the realization of income through a subsection 84(3) deemed dividend because the total of non-share consideration plus the reduced P.U.C. of the new shares does not exceed the P.U.C. of the old shares. Therefore, the consideration in this case allows for a perfect rollover.

EXHIBIT 17-1
Summary of Calculation Procedure for Section 86

Facts:

Old shares		Package of consideration	
F.M.V.	$150	Boot — F.M.V.	$100 ⎤
A.C.B.	100		⎟ $150
P.U.C.	100	New shares — F.M.V.	50 ⎥
		— L.S.C.	50 ⎦

Calculation Procedure:

Issuance of New Shares

(1) Reduced P.U.C. [par. 86(2.1)(*a*)]:

L.S.C. increase for new shares		$ 50
Less: P.U.C. of old shares	$100	
Less: boot	100	Nil
P.U.C. reduction		$ 50
Reduced P.U.C. ($50 – $50)		Nil

(2) Cost of new shares received [par. 86(1)(*b*)]:

A.C.B. of old shares	$100
Less: F.M.V. of non-share consideration	100
Cost of new shares (allocate if more than one class)	Nil
Cost of non-share consideration (boot) received (equal to its F.M.V.) [par. 86(1)(*a*)]	$100

Redemption of Old Shares

(1) Proceeds on redemption of old shares [par. 84(5)(*d*)]:

Reduced P.U.C. of new shares	Nil
F.M.V. of non-share consideration (boot)	$100
Redemption proceeds	$100

Deemed dividend on redemption [ssec. 84(3)]:

Redemption proceeds (above)	$100
P.U.C. of old shares	(100
Deemed dividend on redemption [ssec. 84(3)]	Nil

(2) Proceeds of disposition of old shares for capital gains purposes [par. 86(1)(*c*)]:

Cost of new shares (above)	Nil	
F.M.V. of boot	$100	$100
Less: deemed dividend on redemption [ssec. 84(3)]		Nil
Proceeds of disposition of old shares		$100

Capital gain (loss) on old shares:

Proceeds of disposition	$100
A.C.B.	(100)
Capital gain (loss) (may be denied [ssec. 40(3.6)], but, if so, add to cost base of new shares [par. 53(1)(*f*.2)])	Nil

[*Exhibit 17-1 — continued*]

Net Economic Effect:

Deemed dividends on redemption [ssec. 84(3)]		Nil
Capital gain (loss) on sale of old shares		Nil
Accrued capital gain on new shares:		
Fair market value	$ 50	
A.C.B. — Cost of new shares	Nil	$ 50
Net economic effect (equal to accrued gain on old shares)		$ 50

P.U.C. of new shares will be Nil since all of the original P.U.C. of $100 has been recovered through the boot of $100 [ssec. 86(2.1)].

Example Problem 1

Trebor Maeb owns a controlling interest in Six Sixty-One Ltd. and, therefore, is not at arm's length with the corporation. His present common shares have a P.U.C. and adjusted cost base of $2,500 and a fair market value of $3,700. The corporation is in the process of reorganizing its capital structure and will exchange these shares for the following package of consideration:

Notes (at fair market value)	$1,000
New preferred shares (fair market value and legal stated capital)	2,700
Total	$3,700

— REQUIRED

Determine the tax consequences to Mr. Maeb as a result of the capital reorganization.

— SOLUTION

Calculation Procedure:

Issuance of new shares

(1) Reduced P.U.C. [par. 86(2.1)(*a*)]:

L.S.C. increase for new preferred shares		$ 2,700
Less: P.U.C. of old common shares	$2,500	
Less: boot	1,000	1,500
P.U.C. reduction		$ 1,200
Reduced P.U.C. ($2,700 − $1,200)		$ 1,500

The primary objective of this calculation is to show that the P.U.C. reduction will avoid the triggering of a subsection 84(1) deemed dividend.

(2) Cost of preferred shares received [par. 86(1)(*b*)]:

Adjusted cost base of old shares	$ 2,500
Less: fair market value of non-share consideration	1,000
Cost of preferred shares received	$ 1,500
Cost of the notes received [par. 86(1)(*a*)] (equal to their fair market value)	$ 1,000

Redemption of old shares

(1) Proceeds on redemption of old shares [par. 84(5)(*d*)]:

F.M.V. of boot	$ 1,000
Reduced P.U.C. — New preferred shares (as determined in (1) above)	1,500
Redemption proceeds	$ 2,500
Proceeds on redemption — above	$ 2,500
P.U.C. — Old common shares	2,500
Deemed dividend on redemption [ssec. 84(3)]	Nil

(2) Proceeds of disposition of old shares for capital gains purposes [par. 86(1)(*c*)]:

Cost of all new shares (as determined in (2) above)	$ 1,500

Plus: cost of all non-share considerations		$ 1,000
Proceeds of disposition of old shares		$ 2,500
Less: deemed dividend on redemption [ssec. 84(3)]		Nil
Proceeds of disposition of old shares		$ 2,500
Proceeds of disposition of old shares		$ 2,500
A.C.B. — Old shares		2,500
Capital gain/loss...		Nil

Net Economic Effect:

Deemed dividend on redemption [ssec. 84(3)]		Nil
Capital gain (loss) on sale of old shares		Nil
Accrued capital gain on new shares:		
Fair market value	$ 2,700	
A.C.B. — Cost of new shares	1,500	$ 1,200
Net economic effect (equal to accrued gain on old shares)		$ 1,200

Comments:

(1) The reduced P.U.C. of the preferred shares of $1,500 reflects the fact that only $1,000 of the original P.U.C. of $2,500 of the old common shares has been recovered through boot consideration. The receipt of boot up to $2,500 is tax free both on the exchange and in the future, if the boot is debt that is repaid later.

(2) Since the reduced P.U.C. of the preferred shares ($1,500) plus the boot ($1,000) is less than or equal to the P.U.C. of the old common shares ($2,500) there can be no subsection 84(1) deemed dividend.

(3) No deemed dividend is triggered on the redemption [ssec. 84(3)] of the old common shares since the proceeds on redemption (the reduced P.U.C. of $1,500 plus the boot of $1,000) is equal to the P.U.C. of the old common shares.

(4) There is no capital gain or loss since the proceeds of disposition for capital gains purposes (cost of the new shares of $1,500 plus the boot of $1,000) is exactly equal to the A.C.B. of the old common shares of $2,500.

(5) The final P.U.C. of $1,500 reflects the unrecovered portion of the P.U.C. of the old common shares as indicated in (1) above. The addition to final P.U.C. [par. 86(2.1)(*b*)] does not appear to have a general application to all cases.

(6) If the new preferred shares are sold immediately, there would be a capital gain of $1,200, exactly equal to the accrued capital gain on the old common shares.

New preferred shares: P. of D. ($2,700) − cost ($1,500) = $1,200

Old common shares: F.M.V. ($3,700) − A.C.B. ($2,500) = $1,200

Example Problem 2

Ms. Oasis owns some of the common shares of Capital Structure Ltd. with an adjusted cost base and paid-up capital of $1,200 and a fair market value of $3,700. In the course of a capital reorganization, Ms. Oasis exchanged all of her shares for the following package of consideration:

Cash	$ 500
Notes (at fair market value)	1,500
New preferred shares (at fair market value and L.S.C.)	1,000
New common shares (at fair market value and L.S.C.)	700
Total...	$3,700

— *REQUIRED*

Determine the tax consequences to Ms. Oasis as a result of the capital reorganization.

— SOLUTION

Calculation Procedure:

Issuance of new shares

(1) Reduced P.U.C. [par. 86(2.1)(*a*)]:

L.S.C. increase for all new shares		$ 1,700
Less: P.U.C. of old commons	$ 1,200	
Less: boot ($500 + $1,500)	2,000	Nil
P.U.C. reduction in total		$ 1,700

Proration of P.U.C. reduction:

(a) Preferred shares: $1,700 × $\dfrac{\$1,000}{\$1,700}$ = $1,000

(b) Common shares: $1,700 × $\dfrac{\$\,700}{\$1,700}$ = $700

	Preferred shares	Common shares
L.S.C. increase by class of share	$ 1,000	$ 700
Less: P.U.C. reduction by class of share	1,000	700
Reduced P.U.C.	Nil	Nil

(2) Cost of preferred and common shares received [par. 86(1)(*b*)]:

Adjusted cost base of old shares	$ 1,200
Less: fair market value of non-share consideration	2,000
Cost of preferred and common shares received	Nil

Allocation of cost of new shares:

Preferred shares:

$\dfrac{\text{F.M.V. of preferred shares}}{\text{F.M.V. of all shares}}$ × total cost of new shares

$\dfrac{\$1,000}{\$1,000 + \$700}$ × Nil .... Nil

Common shares:

$\dfrac{\text{F.M.V. of common shares}}{\text{F.M.V. of all shares}}$ × total cost of new shares

$\dfrac{\$700}{\$1,000 + \$700}$ × Nil .... Nil

Cost of the cash and notes received at F.M.V. [par. 86(1)(*a*)] .... $ 2,000

Redemption of old shares

(1) Proceeds on redemption [par. 84(5)(*d*)]:

Boot — Cash	$ 500	
— Notes	1,500	$ 2,000
Reduced P.U.C. — New preferreds	Nil	
— New commons	Nil	Nil
		$ 2,000

Deemed dividend on redemption [ssec. 84(3)]:

Proceeds on redemption	$ 2,000
P.U.C. of old common shares	1,200
Deemed dividend on redemption [ssec. 84(3)]	$ 800

(2) Proceeds of disposition:

Cost of boot	$ 2,000
Cost of shares	
— Preferred shares	Nil

— Common shares		Nil
		$ 2,000
Less: deemed dividend on redemption [ssec. 84(3)]		800
Proceeds of disposition of old shares		$ 1,200
Capital gain (loss) on old shares:		
Proceeds of disposition of old shares		$ 1,200
Less: A.C.B. of old shares		1,200
Capital gain (loss[1])		Nil

Net Economic Effect:

In the foregoing case, the "net economic effect" can be aggregated as a conceptual illustration as follows:

Deemed dividend on redemption [ssec. 84(3)]		$ 800
Accrued capital gain on new shares:		
Fair market value	$1,700	
A.C.B. (total)	Nil	1,700
Net economic effect equal to accrued gain on old common shares (i.e., $3,700 − $1,200)		$ 2,500

Comments:

The final P.U.C. of Nil for both the new common and preferred shares is logical since all of the P.U.C. of the old common shares ($1,200) has been removed in the form of boot (i.e., cash of $500 and notes of $1,500).

The subsection 84(3) deemed dividend was caused by taking back a non-share consideration package (i.e., boot comprised of cash of $500 and notes of $1,500) in excess of the P.U.C. of the old shares (i.e., $1,200). The deemed dividend could have been avoided by taking back less boot to reflect the $1,200 of P.U.C. in the old shares that can be received tax free.

— NOTE TO SOLUTION

(1) If a capital loss is triggered, the resultant tax treatment depends on whether the corporation, after the exchange, is affiliated with the shareholder. If, for example, the shareholder or the shareholder's spouse still controls the corporation and, hence, the corporation is affiliated with the shareholder, then the capital loss is denied and added to the remaining shares, including the exchanged shares owned by the shareholder after the transaction [ssec. 40(3.6) and par. 53(1)(f.2)].

4. Benefit rule

There is a benefit rule provided in subsection 86(2) (similar to the one in paragraph 85(1)(e.2)) to reduce the effect of a deferral where a reorganization is used to confer a benefit on a related person. The benefit is any part of the excess of the fair market value of the old shares over the cost of the non-share consideration received plus the fair market value of the new shares that can reasonably be regarded as a benefit conferred on a person related to the taxpayer who disposed of old shares in the reorganization.

Where there is a benefit, the proceeds of disposition of the old shares for capital gains purposes are different from subsection 86(1). Proceeds of disposition will be deemed to be the lesser of:

(a) the fair market value of the non-share consideration plus the amount of the gift determined by the excess above; and

(b) the fair market value of the old shares.

Where a capital loss is created, the loss is deemed to be nil [par. 86(2)(d)]. The cost of the new shares will be reduced by the fair market value of the non-share consideration plus the benefit.

Example Problem

Adam owns all of the Class A common shares of BJay Ltd. His son, Stieb, owns all of the Class B common shares and is active in the management of the corporation. Adam is now prepared to pass all of the future growth in the corporation to his son. To do so, Adam will give up all of his Class A common shares which have a fair market value of $500,000, an adjusted cost base of $100,000 and a paid-up capital value of $100,000. In return, he will receive $100,000 in cash and preferred shares with a fair market value of $350,000 and a legal stated capital of $350,000. Stieb will then own all of the only class of common shares outstanding and, thereby, will receive all of the future growth of BJay Ltd.

— REQUIRED

What are the income tax consequences under section 86 to Adam on the proposed transaction?

— SOLUTION

Subsection 86(2) will apply in this case, because the $500,000 fair market value of Adam's Class A common shares is greater than the sum of the $100,000 of cash and $350,000 fair market value of the preferred shares received on the reorganization. Furthermore, it is reasonable to regard the $50,000 excess as a benefit that Adam desired to have conferred on a related person, his son.

The following are the consequences of the transaction:

Issuance of new shares

(1) Reduced P.U.C. [par. 86(2.1)(a)]:

L.S.C. increase for new shares		$ 350,000
Less: P.U.C. of old shares	$100,000	
Less: boot	100,000	Nil
P.U.C. reduction		$ 350,000
Reduced P.U.C. ($350,000 − $350,000)		Nil

(2) Cost of preferred shares received [par. 86(2)(e)]:

A.C.B. of Class A shares		$ 100,000
Less: cost (equal to F.M.V.) of non-share		
consideration	$100,000	
benefit	50,000	150,000
Cost of preferred shares (excess, if any)		Nil
Cost of non-share consideration (equal to its F.M.V.)		$ 100,000

Redemption of old shares

(1) Proceeds on redemption of old shares:

Reduced P.U.C. of preferred shares	Nil
F.M.V. of non-share consideration	$ 100,000
Proceeds on redemption	$ 100,000

Deemed dividend on redemption [ssec. 84(3)]:	
Redemption proceeds	$ 100,000
P.U.C. of Class A shares	(100,000)
Deemed dividend on redemption [ssec. 84(3)]	Nil

(2) Proceeds of disposition of Class A shares [par. 86(2)(c)]:

Lesser of:		
(a) cost (equal to F.M.V.) of non-share consideration	$ 100,000	
Plus: benefit	50,000	
	$ 150,000	
(b) F.M.V. of Class A shares	$ 500,000	
Proceeds of disposition		$ 150,000

Capital gain (loss) on Class A shares:

Proceeds of disposition	$ 150,000
A.C.B.	(100,000)
Capital gain	$ 50,000

Net Economic Effect:

Deemed dividend on redemption [ssec. 84(3)]		Nil
Capital gain on sale of Class A shares		$ 50,000
Accrued gain on preferred shares:		
F.M.V.	$ 350,000	
A.C.B.	Nil	350,000
Total (equal to the accrued gain on the old shares)		$ 400,000

The final P.U.C. of the new shares reflects the fact that, of the $100,000 of the P.U.C. of the old shares, all $100,000 has been recovered in boot. Therefore, the final P.U.C. of the new shares is logically nil.

Note the total net economic effect in this case. In addition to the immediate capital gain of $50,000, there is an accrued gain on the new shares of $350,000 to be realized on ultimate disposition. This $400,000 reflects the gain that had accrued on the Class A shares (i.e., $500,000 – $100,000) before the reorganization. However, it should be recognized that Adam has given up shares with a value of $500,000 for a package of consideration worth a total of only $450,000. From another point of view, he has paid tax on $50,000 of capital gain on the Class A shares and he has received consideration with a total cost value of $100,000 in non-share consideration ($100,000, from (2) under "Issuance of New Shares" above) and preferred shares (nil, from (2) under "Issuance of New Shares" above) in return for the Class A shares which had a cost of $100,000. As a result, he has incurred a tax-paid cost that he cannot recover.

Furthermore, the fair market value of the common shares held by the son, Stieb, will increase in value by the $50,000 benefit without any offset in the cost base of the common shares. Therefore, the $50,000 of accrued gain will be taxed on the disposition of the common shares. This potential $50,000 gain to be taxed in the hands of the common shareholder, along with the lost opportunity for Adam to recover the $50,000, is the penalty inherent in subsection 86(2).

To avoid this penalty the fair market value of the total package of consideration received in the reorganization should be equal to the fair market value of the shares given up in the exchange.

C. Statutory Amalgamations
[ITA: 87; IT-474R; IC 88-2]

This rollover provision applies automatically at both the corporate level and the shareholder level in an amalgamation situation. First, it should be emphasized that a statutory amalgamation is distinct from business combination accounting. In a statutory amalgamation, two or more corporations are merged into one with the result being a single legal entity with one charter. In business combination accounting, for which consolidated financial statements are usually prepared, the original companies continue to exist as separate legal entities and are taxed separately.

Subsection 87(1) sets out several conditions for the rollover to apply:

(a) the predecessor corporations must be taxable Canadian corporations;

(b) all of the property and liabilities of the predecessor corporations, except inter-company accounts, must belong to the new corporation by virtue of the amalgamation;

(c) all shareholders of the predecessor corporations, other than predecessor corporate shareholders, must receive shares of the new corporation by virtue of the amalgamation; and

(d) the transfer of property cannot occur as the result of a normal purchase of such property or the distribution on a winding-up of a corporation.

The rollover for a statutory amalgamation deals with:

(a) the transfer of capital property from the predecessor corporation to the successor or amalgamated corporation to permit a deferral of accrued capital gains transferred at the corporate level; and

(b) the exchange of shares of a predecessor corporation by its shareholders for shares of the successor corporation to permit a deferral of capital gains at the shareholder level.

Under section 87 the amalgamated corporation is treated, for many purposes, as a continuation of the predecessor corporations. The effect would be like placing the balance sheets of two corporations side by side and adding together the similar accounts on each balance sheet based on the tax values such as adjusted cost base or undepreciated capital cost of each asset. The result would be a single balance sheet based on those tax values with no realization of capital gains or losses or recapture.

While the new corporation is considered by most Corporations Acts to be a continuation of the predecessor corporations, for tax purposes a new corporation is deemed to have been formed and the predecessor corporations are deemed to have a year-end immediately before the amalgamation.[b] Thus, any provision of the tax legislation that counts taxation years will be affected by the amalgamation. As a result, the following could occur:

- one short taxation year will be counted in respect of unpaid amounts subject to treatment under section 78;

- capital cost allowance will be claimed on a declining balance basis;

- the amount of the business limit ($300,000 for calendar 2005 and later taxation years) allocated for the small business deduction will also be prorated for a short taxation year; and

- non-capital losses carried forward by a predecessor corporation will be deductible in the short taxation year, but that taxation year will count as one of the carryforward years available. Note that for non-capital losses incurred in a taxation year that ends after March 22, 2004, the carryforward period is 10 years.

The new corporation begins its first taxation year on the date of amalgamation. It may choose any year-end it wishes, but in this first year it will be liable for instalments of tax based on the instalment bases of the predecessor corporations adjusted for a twelve-month equivalent in the case of a short taxation year.

Consider the case of Corporation A with a December 31 year-end and Corporation B with a June 30 year-end. Assume that an amalgamation took place on October 1,

---

[b] Paragraph 9 of IT-474R states that "the effective date of amalgamation is governed by corporate law and is generally the date of issuance of letters patent or the date shown or set forth in the certificate of amalgamation, as the case may be. The time of the amalgamation is the earliest moment on that date in the absence of a particular time specified in the certificate of amalgamation".

2005 and that the amalgamated corporation, Amalco, chooses a December 31 year-end. This situation can be diagrammed as follows:

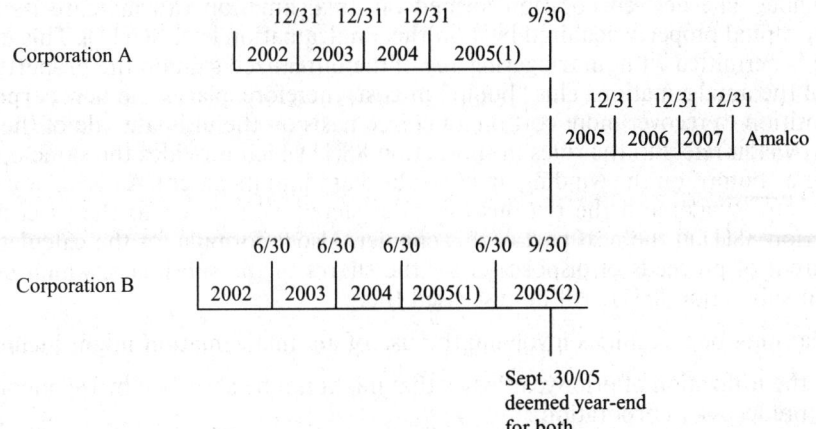

Exhibit 17-2 summarizes the effect of the major rollover provisions in section 87.

EXHIBIT 17-2
Major Rollover Provisions of Section 87

Paragraph	Item	Rollover effect
	Assets and Reserves	
Par. 87(2)(*b*)	Inventory	at cost amount
Par. 87(2)(*d*)	Depreciable capital property	at u.c.c.[1]
Par. 87(2)(*e*)	Non-depreciable capital property	at a.c.b.
Par. 87(2)(*f*)	Eligible capital property	at $^4/_3$ of c.e.c. balance[2]
Par. 87(2)(*g*)	Reserves	flowed through
	Loss Carryforwards	
Ssec. 87(2.1)	Non-capital losses	flowed through[3]
Ssec. 87(2.1)	Net capital losses	flowed through
Ssec. 87(2.1)	Restricted farm losses	flowed through
Ssec. 87(2.1)	Farm losses	flowed through
	Tax Accounts	
Par. 87(2)(*z1*)	Capital dividend account	flowed through[4]
Par. 87(2)(*aa*)	Refundable dividend tax on hand	flowed through[4]

Note: (1) The new corporation will be liable for recapture in the same manner that a predecessor corporation would have been liable for such recapture.

(2) This amount becomes an eligible capital expenditure of the amalgamated corporation, which would add ¾ of the e.c.e. to its c.e.c. balance under item A of the definition of "cumulative eligible capital" [ssec. 14(5)]. In this way, the amalgamated corporation steps into the tax position of the predecessor corporation on this property.

(3) The limitations regarding the carrying on of the loss business on a previous acquisition of control of a predecessor corporation will apply after the amalgamation to losses previously subject to those limitations in the predecessor corporation. Note that there is not necessarily an acquisition of control on amalgamation itself (e.g., the relative shareholdings have not changed from those of the predecessor corporations). The deemed year-end of a predecessor corporation on amalgamation will be counted as one of the seven years available for the carryforward of non-capital losses.

(4) These accounts which pertain only to private corporations would be lost if one of the predecessor corporations were a public corporation.

Where a parent corporation and one or more subsidiary corporations are amalgamated, in what is commonly known as a "vertical amalgamation", an added advantage is available. The new corporation formed on amalgamation can increase its cost of certain capital property acquired by it on the amalgamation [ssec. 87(11)]. This increase in cost is permitted without triggering any of the unrealized gain on the property at the time of the amalgamation. This "bump" in cost, therefore, places the new corporation in a position to recover more cost on a tax-free basis on the ultimate sale of the assets. The provision refers to the rules in subsection 88(1) which provides the same opportunity for a "bump" on the winding-up of a subsidiary into its parent. A discussion of how the "bump" works and the reasons for its existence is deferred to the discussion of subsection 88(1) in the next part of this chapter. Also, a formula for the calculation for the parent of proceeds of disposition for the shares of the subsidiary, which uses the rules in subsection 88(1), will be discussed there.

Planning opportunities involving the use of an amalgamation might include:

- the utilization of prior-year losses that might not be absorbed by the income of a predecessor corporation;

- the utilization of current-year losses in one predecessor corporation against the income of another predecessor corporation; or

- the faster utilization of capital cost allowance in a high-rate or rapid write-off class.

Other planning opportunities might involve the following:

- where a parent corporation has been amalgamated with one or more wholly-owned subsidiary corporation, i.e., a vertical amalgamation, subsequent losses by the amalgamated corporation may be carried back and applied to the income of the predecessor *parent* corporation [ssec. 87(2.11)];

- it might also be possible to effect an improvement in the manufacturing or processing tax credit through an amalgamation; and

- an amalgamation might facilitate a change in fiscal year-end which would ordinarily require the consent of the Canada Revenue Agency (CRA), although IC 88-2 (October 21, 1988) pertaining to the general anti-avoidance rule in section 245 indicates, in paragraph 21, that if an amalgamation is undertaken with a shell corporation solely to effect a year-end change, the general anti-avoidance rule (GAAR)[sec. 245] would be applied (as discussed in a previous chapter).

At the shareholder's level, the shareholder is deemed to have disposed of his or her shares for proceeds equal to their adjusted cost base and to have acquired the new shares of the amalgamated corporation at that same adjusted cost base [ssec. 87(4)]. The conditions for this rollover to apply to the shareholder's position are:

(a) that he or she receive no consideration for his or her shares other than shares of the successor corporation or its Canadian parent corporation (i.e., no "boot" can be received);

(b) that the original shares are capital property to the shareholder; and

(c) the amalgamation does not result in a deemed gift to a person related to the shareholder.

Note that the potential problem of a subsection 84(1) deemed dividend exists if the paid-up capital of the amalgamated corporation increases on the issue of shares by more than the increase in the fair market value of the net assets transferred to that corporation.

D. Winding up a Subsidiary

[ITA: 88]

This provision sets out rules for an automatic rollover where a taxable Canadian corporation of which at least 90% of each class of shares is owned by another Canadian corporation, is wound up into its parent corporation under appropriate corporate law. These rules are very similar to those for a statutory amalgamation that could take place between a parent company and its subsidiary, i.e., a "vertical amalgamation". They generally avoid the recognition of accrued capital gains on the transfer of assets from a subsidiary to its parent in a winding-up. The major difference between such a winding-up and an amalgamation arises in the area of the parent's utilization of the loss carryforwards of the subsidiary, as discussed below.

Again, there are two components to the rollover. The first deals with the transfer of property to the parent in which the subsidiary is deemed to have disposed of its assets for proceeds equal to:

(a) nil, in the case of a resource property; and

(b) the cost amount [ssec. 248(1)] to the subsidiary, in the case of any other property [par. 88(1)(*a*)].

The parent is deemed to have acquired the property at a cost equal to the deemed proceeds of the subsidiary. However, when the adjusted cost base of the subsidiary's shares held by the parent exceeds the tax values of the net assets of the subsidiary transferred on the winding-up, there is a possible increase or "bump" in the adjusted cost base of some non-depreciable capital property received from the subsidiary. The amount of the increase cannot raise the adjusted cost base of an asset above the fair market value at the time when the parent acquired control of the subsidiary.

This "bump" or "step-up" in adjusted cost base is calculated [par. 88(1)(*d*)] as follows:

Parent's adjusted cost base of the subsidiary's shares *minus* the sum of:

(a) the cost amount of the subsidiary's assets plus cash net of liabilities and certain reserves; and

(b) dividends (including both taxable and capital dividends) paid to the parent on its shares of the subsidiary.

The "bump" may be allocated to any non-depreciable capital property owned by the subsidiary continuously from the time when the parent acquired control of the subsidiary to the date of the winding-up.

Consider the case of a subsidiary with the following balance sheet immediately before the winding-up:

Cash	$ 5,000	Accounts payable	$ 5,000
Land	160,000	Paid-up capital	20,000
Depreciable property	60,000	Retained earnings	200,000
	$225,000		$225,000

Other relevant facts include the following:

Parent's adjusted cost base of the subsidiary's shares	$300,000
F.M.V. of the land when the parent acquired control of the subsidiary	200,000
Dividends paid by the subsidiary to the parent	10,000

Note that the only item of non-depreciable capital property is the land. Exhibit 17-3 illustrates the application of paragraph 88(1)(*d*) to this set of facts. The adjusted cost base of the land will be increased from $160,000 to $200,000. Although a total "bump" of $70,000 was available, there were no other non-depreciable capital assets available to absorb the remaining $30,000 which is lost.

EXHIBIT 17-3
Conceptual Application of Paragraph 88(1)(d)

BEFORE WIND-UP		*AFTER WIND-UP*	
PARENT		PARENT	
Shares of subsidiary at A.C.B.	$300,000	Cost amount of net assets of former subsidiary	$220,000
Dividends from subsidiary (recovery of cost)	(10,000)		
Net cost	$290,000	Addition to A.C.B. of former subsidiary's land	40,000*
SUBSIDIARY		Total cost amount	$260,000
Cost amount of net assets ($225K – 5K)	$220,000	* Limit of "bump" on land:	
		F.M.V. of land at time parent acquired control of subsidiary	$ 200,000
Potential "bump": $70,000 (i.e., $290,000 – $220,000)		A.C.B. of land at time of wind-up	(160,000)
		Limit	$ 40,000

Note how the shares of the subsidiary, held as assets in the parent, are replaced by the cost amounts of the subsidiary's net assets. Conceptually, the net cost of the subsidiary's shares to the parent is reduced by dividends, either taxable or capital, received from the subsidiary. However, the result is that the parent replaces assets having a net cost of $290,000 with assets having a net cost of $220,000. The "bump" is meant to help the parent recover some of the difference in cost.

The same rule applies for the same reasons, in a vertical amalgamation [par. 87(1)(a)]. While there are differences under corporate law, conceptually, a vertical amalgamation and a winding-up of a subsidiary into its parent have the same effect. Therefore, it is reasonable for the tax treatment to be the same.

In the case of depreciable property, the parent corporation is deemed to have a capital cost for the property equal to that of the subsidiary and, thus, becomes potentially liable for recapture.

On the winding-up of a subsidiary into its parent, there is no deemed year-end for either corporation, as is the case for an amalgamation. The subsidiary, simply, ceases to exist on completion of the winding-up, since it has no assets and no shares outstanding, and the parent corporation continues with its same year-end that it had been using. Consider the case of Parentco with a December 31 year-end and Subcorp with a June 30 year-end. Assume that a winding-up commences October 1, 2005, when the net assets of Subcorp are transferred to Parentco. Subcorp continues to exist until it is formally dissolved some time later. This situation can be diagrammed as follows:

When a subsidiary is wound up into its parent, the deductibility by the parent of the subsidiary's non-capital losses, restricted farm losses, farm losses, limited partnership losses and net capital losses is limited [ssecs. 88(1.1) and (1.2)] as follows:

(a) the losses that have not been deducted by the subsidiary are first deductible by the parent in its taxation year following the taxation year in which the winding-up began; and

(b) the losses are only deductible by the parent to the extent that they would have been deductible to the subsidiary in any taxation year following that in which the winding-up began (if it is assumed that the subsidiary had such a taxation year); that is, the losses could not have expired in the taxation year following that of the winding-up, if the subsidiary had a taxation year then.

When the subsidiary has a taxation year different from that of the parent, the subsidiary's losses will be deemed to have occurred in the parent's taxation year which includes the taxation year-end of the subsidiary. The following illustrates this rule schematically:

Losses of the subsidiary for its fiscal year ended	losses of the parent for its fiscal year ended	Available for deduction by parent for fiscal years ended December 31										
		2005	2006	2007	2008	2009	2010	2011	2012	2013	2014	2015*
June 30,'05	Dec. 31,'05	X	√	√	√	√	√	√	√	√	√	√
June 30,'04	Dec. 31,'04	X	√	√	√	√	√	√	√	√	√	expired
June 30,'03	Dec. 31,'03	X	√	√	√	√	√	expired				
June 30,'02	Dec. 31,'02	X	√	√	√	√	expired					
June 30,'01	Dec. 31,'01	X	√	√	√	expired						
June 30,'00	Dec. 31,'00	X	√	√	expired							
June 30,'99	Dec. 31,'99	X	√	expired								
June 30,'98	Dec. 31,'98	X	expired									

⌐→losses not available in year of wind-up

* Note that for non-capital losses incurred in a taxation year that ends after March 22, 2004, the carryforward period is 10 years.

The above assumes that the winding-up commences on October 1, 2005, such that none of the losses would be available to the parent until its 2006 taxation year. The 1998 loss of the subsidiary, which would have been deductible by the subsidiary in its 2005 taxation year if it had such a taxation year, will not be available to the parent [ssec. 88(1.1)]. This represents an application of the rule that the parent cannot use a subsidiary's losses in the winding-up year. This rule on a winding-up provides a somewhat similar effect to the rule on an amalgamation which provides for a deemed year-end which may result in a short year counting as one taxation year for loss carryforwards of the loss corporation before they become available to the new corporation.

For cases where control of a parent or subsidiary has changed, paragraph 88(1.1)(*e*) provides rules restricting the availability of non-capital losses or farm losses that are similar to the restrictions discussed in Chapter 11 [ssec. 111(5)].

The planning opportunities involving the use of a winding-up will generally include the same opportunities as those considered for an amalgamation. A winding-up will usually be preferred if the timing of loss carryforwards will result in greater deductibility of such losses. It should be recognized, however, that a winding-up is considerably more expensive and time-consuming to implement than an amalgamation.

The second component of the rollover deals with the disposition or cancellation of shares by the parent on the winding-up. The parent corporation is deemed to have disposed of the shares of the subsidiary for proceeds equal to the greater of:

(a) the lesser of:

   (i) the paid-up capital of the shares of the subsidiary, and

   (ii) the aggregate of the cost amounts of the assets of the subsidiary received, net of any liabilities, and certain tax reserves assumed; and

(b) the adjusted cost base of the shares of the subsidiary held by the parent immediately before the winding-up [par. 88(1)(*b*)].

In the foregoing example, the parent corporation would be deemed to have disposed of the subsidiary for proceeds equal to the greater of:

(a) the lesser of:

(i) the paid-up capital of the shares of the subsidiary	$ 20,000	
(ii) the cost amounts of the net assets immediately before the winding-up	$220,000	
the lesser amount		$ 20,000
(b) the adjusted cost base of the shares of the subsidiary held by the parent		$300,000

Proceeds of disposition would be established at the greater amount, i.e., $300,000. Since this amount is equal to the A.C.B., no capital gain or loss will result.

As a result of this rule, the parent may realize, in fairly rare circumstances, a gain on the liquidation of its subsidiary, but it may not realize a capital loss because the deemed proceeds of disposition of the shares of the subsidiary cannot be less than their adjusted cost base to the parent. In most situations, the parent will obtain, in effect, a rollover on the disposition of the shares in the subsidiary.

The same rule with the same formula applies in the determination of proceeds of disposition to the parent for shares of the subsidiary in a vertical amalgamation [par. 87(11)(*a*)].

II.   ROLLOVERS INVOLVING SHARES OR CORPORATE SECURITIES

A.   Convertible Properties

[ITA: 51; 51.1]

Convertible properties are commonly issued in the form of shares, bonds or notes of a corporation. These securities can be exchanged for shares of the corporation under specific conditions at the option of the holder. In essence, the securities held are given up on the conversion in return for share capital. Note how section 51 differs from section 86. Section 51 does not require newly-authorized shares whereas section 86 appears to require, in the course of a capital reorganization, new shares created by a change in authorized capital through the articles of incorporation. Section 51 conversions can be made by shares that are already authorized.

Section 51 permits a deferral of the inherent gain on the exchanged securities, but only if the following conditions are met:

(a) only shares are issued for the exchanged securities;

(b) the exchanged securities are capital property to the taxpayer; and

(c) the exchanged securities, other than shares, must have a conversion right attached to the particular security.

The provision is not elective but is automatic if the above conditions are met. However, subsection 51(4) denies the application of section 51 if section 85 or 86 has been applied to the exchange transaction.

When the holder of a convertible property exercises the conversion privilege and as a result acquires the shares of one class of the capital stock of the corporation, the exchange is deemed not to have been a disposition of property. The adjusted cost base of the shares acquired on conversion is deemed to be the adjusted cost base of the convertible security before the exchange. The effect is to defer any capital gain accrued on the convertible security prior to the exchange until such time as the new shares are sold. For example, a taxpayer purchased a $1,000 bond, the terms of which conferred upon the holder the right of conversion into five common shares. The adjusted cost base of the bond is $1,000. If the bond is converted into the five shares when those shares have a value of $225, the taxpayer will not realize the accrued gain on the bond which should have a fair market value of $1,125 (i.e., 5 × $225). Instead the $1,000 cost base of the bond will flow through to the five shares such that each share will have a cost base of $200 (i.e., $1,000/5). If shares of more than one class are received on the conversion, the adjusted cost base of the convertible security before the exchange would be allocated among the classes of shares received on the conversion in proportion to their respective fair market values after the exchange.

A penalty provision [ssec. 51(2)] applies where a benefit has been conferred on a related person and is similar in effect to subsection 86(2). Subsection 51(3), which determines the paid-up capital of the newly issued shares, has a formula which is practically identical to subsection 86(2.1) as previously discussed.

A similar provision in section 51.1 covers the case where a bondholder acquires a new bond of the same debtor in exchange for the original bond. There is a similar flow-through of the adjusted cost base of the original bond to the new bond and of any tax-free zone position on the original bond.

B.   Inter-spousal Transfers

[ITA: 70(6), (6.2); 73(1); ITR: 6500]

To defer the recognition of a capital gain or loss on the transfer of property between spouses or to a qualifying trust in favour of one spouse, an automatic rollover is available. The Act does not allow the recognition of the gain or loss unless the taxpayer elects not to have the rollover apply. This rollover applies when capital property is transferred between living spouses (*inter vivos*) either by way of sale at any price or gift. A qualifying trust is one created by the taxpayer under which the spouse is entitled to receive all the income of the trust that arises before the spouse's death and no person except the spouse may receive or obtain the use of any of the trust property before the spouse's death. Also, the spouse or trust must be resident in Canada at the time of the property transfer. The topic of spousal trusts will be discussed more fully in a subsequent chapter.

The Act provides that the property is deemed to have been sold by one spouse and acquired by the other spouse or trust for an amount equal to its adjusted cost base in the case of capital property such as shares [ssec. 73(1)]. As indicated above, subsection 73(1) allows an election to transfer such property at its fair market value.

A similar rollover applies on a transfer of the same property at death through a will [ssec. 70(6)]. This rollover, like that in subsection 73(1), is applied automatically, although an election can be made [ssec. 70(6.2)] to use the general rules applicable at death to recognize capital gains and losses. For example, a husband may bequeath shares having a cost of $100 and a fair market value at the time of death of $250. If the rollover is used, the shares will be deemed to have been transferred at their adjusted cost base of $100 such that no gain or loss is realized on the transfer [ssec. 70(6)]. However, if the election under subsection 70(6.2) is made, the transfer will take place at $250, thereby, realizing a capital gain of $150. Again, similar rules apply to depreciable property.

III. USE OF ROLLOVERS IN ESTATE FREEZING

A. Objectives

The tax planning area of estate freezing has been alluded to in previous discussions of the advantages of the use of corporations to hold sources of income from business or investments. The purpose of this section of the chapter is not to deal with the topic exhaustively, but to illustrate briefly and conceptually the application as planning tools of some of the provisions discussed in this and the previous chapters.

The primary purpose of estate freezing is to freeze all or part of the value of growing assets at their current fair market value, such that future growth in these assets accrues to the next generation of family members. The result will be that this future growth will not be taxed in the hands of the taxpayer on a disposition or at his or her death. In the process of implementing an estate freeze, some of the following secondary objectives may be addressed:

- The taxpayer contemplating an estate freeze will not likely wish to incur any immediate tax cost in implementing the freeze, but may want to establish the amount of the tax liability that will arise on his or her death.

- The taxpayer will often wish to maintain control over the assets the value of which is being frozen even though their future growth in value is being passed to the next generation. At the same time, the taxpayer may wish to retain a source of income from the assets to maintain himself or herself.

- The implementation of an estate freeze may coincide with planning to split income with low tax-rate family members, although great care must be taken to avoid the adverse tax consequences of the attribution rules and the income-splitting tax imposed on minors, discussed in previous chapters.

- In the process of implementing an estate freeze, it may be possible to realize capital gains sufficient to use up a taxpayer's capital gains deduction on the disposition of the shares of a small business corporation, as discussed in a previous chapter.

- Through their ownership of common shares, the estate freeze will have the effect of placing the beneficiaries of an estate freeze in a position to generate sufficient future capital gains on those common shares to use their own capital gains deduction.

The focus of the discussion of techniques to accomplish these objectives will be on three principal methods of exchanging growth assets for non-growth assets, which can be termed: holdco freeze, internal freeze and reverse or asset freeze. The intention is only to provide a conceptual overview without dealing with the details of implementation.

B. Holdco Freeze

This type of estate freeze uses section 85 as its primary planning device. In this case, a holding company is incorporated and the growing assets are transferred to the corporation, using section 85 to avoid incurring an immediate tax cost. Growing assets subject to the freeze may include: shares of an operating company, assets of an unincorporated business or a portfolio of securities. The estate freeze is implemented by the taxpayer's taking, as consideration from the new corporation for the growing assets transferred, debt and preferred shares. The preferred shares can have voting rights attached to them to meet the objective of maintaining control over the assets transferred. Both types of security can provide income to their holder. However, neither type of security, if properly issued with appropriate features, will grow in value as the assets of the corporation grow. In structuring the consideration received from the holding company, care must be taken to avoid the adverse tax consequences of section 84.1, as discussed previously.

The future growth in the assets of the new corporation will be reflected in the value of the common shares of the corporation. These common shares can be subscribed for by the children in the family. Of course, care must be taken not to invoke the corporate or regular attribution rules and the income-splitting tax imposed on minors, as previously discussed. This problem is of particular concern if a small business corporation [ssec. 248(1)] is not involved in the estate freeze.

The process of this type of estate freeze can be illustrated schematically by the following diagram:

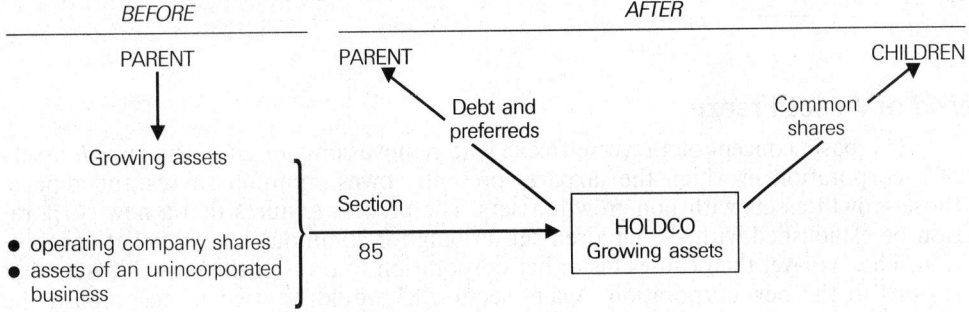

C. Internal Freeze

A capital reorganization of an existing corporation is the basis of this type of estate freeze. A taxpayer who owns common shares of a corporation may cause the corporation to undertake a capital reorganization. The taxpayer gives up the common shares in return for debt and newly-authorized preferred shares of the corporation, using section 86 to defer any accrued gains on the common shares given up. Again, the preferred shares may have voting rights to maintain control over the corporation. Both the debt and preferred shares can provide the taxpayer with a source of income. The children can subscribe for new common shares to which the future growth in the value of the corporation's assets will accrue.

This method of estate freeze has several advantages over the holdco freeze.

- First, a new company need not be incorporated, thereby avoiding the costs associated with incorporating and maintaining the additional corporation.

- Second, the rollover provision in section 86 is applied automatically without any need for an election to be made.

- Finally, the rules in section 84.1 are not applicable, thereby, avoiding a potentially serious problem. However, extreme care must be taken to structure the paid-up capital of the new shares to avoid a deemed dividend problem [ssec. 84(3)].

Note that the internal freeze or section 86 freeze cannot generate a capital gain for purposes of crystallization as demonstrated earlier in the chapter.

A final note of warning in respect of both the holdco and the internal freeze, is that careful planning is required to ensure that the corporate attribution rules are not triggered [sec. 74.4]. As long as the respective corporations are small business corporations (i.e., meet the 90% active business asset rule), then the corporate attribution rules will not apply.

The following diagram provides a conceptual illustration of an internal freeze:

D. Reverse or Asset Freeze

The basic concept of a reverse freeze is to remove some or all of the *growth* assets of a corporation in which the taxpayer presently owns common shares and replace those growth assets with non-growth assets. The process requires that a new corporation be established with the children subscribing for common shares of that corporation. The taxpayer then causes his or her corporation to transfer the growth assets that it owns to the new corporation. Again, section 85 would be used to accomplish the transfer without incurring an immediate tax cost. Since assets, other than shares of a subject corporation, are being transferred, section 84.1 will not apply. If the preferred shares taken back have voting rights, the taxpayer can maintain control over the assets transferred to the new corporation through the exercise of control over his or her corporation, which owns the voting preferred shares. His or her corporation can also earn income for his or her benefit on the debt and preferred shares it owns. However, the value of the common shares held by the taxpayer in his or her original corporation will not grow in the future if the only assets of that corporation are the non-growth debt and preferred securities of the new corporation. On the other hand, the common shares of the new corporation held by the children will grow in value as the assets transferred to that corporation grow.

One of the advantages of the reverse freeze technique is that selected growth assets can be transferred, such that the children will only participate in the future growth of the selected assets transferred. Furthermore, if different children are to participate in the future growth of different assets and each child subscribes for the common shares of a different new corporation, selected assets can be transferred to the benefit of each child as desired. Unlike the previous types of freezes, the attribution rules [ssecs. 56(4.1), 74.1, 74.2 and 74.4(2)] do not apply in the case of a reverse freeze, because the transferor or lender is not an individual.

The following diagram illustrates conceptually a basic reverse freeze:

REVIEW QUESTIONS

(1) What legal documents need to be filed in order to accomplish a reorganization under section 86?

(2) What are some of the occasions on which a section 86 reorganization of capital might be used?

(3) What adjustments are there as a result of a deemed dividend that arises on a section 86 reorganization?

(4) Legally, what happens to two corporations that are amalgamated?

(5) At the time of amalgamation there is a deemed year-end for tax purposes under paragraph 87(2)(*a*). What are some of the other tax rules that are impacted by this deemed year-end?

(6) Acme Co. is a CCPC with a January 31 year-end. The owners want to change the year-end of the company to July 31 to allow bonuses to be paid either in this year or the next. It is now July and they do not have time to receive clearance from the CRA so they incorporate another company and amalgamate it with Acme on July 31 to create a new year-end. Do you have any problems with this tactic?

(7) In order for subsection 88(1) to apply, what ownership criteria need to be met?

(8) Ms. Switch purchased 1,000 convertible preferred shares at a total cost of $10,000. These shares gave her the right to convert each preferred share into 2 common shares. She exercised her conversion right at a time when the common shares were trading at $10 each. What is the A.C.B. of her new common shares?

(9) What is the primary purpose of estate freezing?

(10) What might be some of the secondary objectives of an estate freeze?

(11) What are the three principal methods of freezing the value of growth assets?

(12) What are the basic steps involved in doing a Holdco freeze?

(13) When doing an estate freeze on the shares of a small business corporation in favour of a spouse, what is one of the biggest dangers? Assume that the freeze was done correctly.

(14) Describe when a "reverse or asset freeze" would be used and the steps you would take to accomplish it.

MULTIPLE CHOICE QUESTIONS

Question 1

P Ltd. is a profitable taxable Canadian corporation with a December 31 fiscal year-end. It has a wholly-owned subsidiary, L Ltd., with a June 30 fiscal year-end. L Ltd. has a significant 2003 non-capital loss balance. Therefore, consideration is being given to either amalgamating P Ltd. and L Ltd. or winding up L Ltd. into P Ltd. in order to utilize the loss. The amalgamation or the winding-up will take place on November 1, 2005. Which *one* of the following statements is *true*?

(A) The newly amalgamated corporation can utilize the non-capital loss in its deemed year ended October 31, 2005.

(B) The newly amalgamated corporation cannot utilize the non-capital loss until its taxation year commencing one year after the amalgamation.

(C) If a winding-up takes place, P Ltd. can utilize the non-capital loss in its taxation year commencing January 1, 2006.

(D) If a winding-up takes place, P Ltd. can utilize the non-capital loss in its taxation year ended December 31, 2005.

Question 2

On September 1, 2002, X Ltd. acquired all the shares of Y Ltd. for $500,000. At that time, Y Ltd. had land with a fair market value of $130,000 and a cost of $100,000. On September 1, 2005, a winding-up of Y Ltd. into X Ltd. took place. At the time of the winding-up, the tax values of Y Ltd.'s assets totalled $420,000. The fair market value of the land at this time was $300,000. X Ltd. received $15,000 of dividends from Y Ltd. between September 1, 2002 and September 1, 2005. The adjusted cost base of the land after the winding-up cannot exceed:

(A) $100,000

(B) $130,000

(C) $165,000

(D) $180,000

Question 3

In the course of the reorganization of the capital of A Ltd., Chris exchanged all his common shares of A Ltd. (which are capital property to him) for the package of consideration outlined below.

Cash	$ 135
Preferred shares (50 shares redeemable at $100 each)	5,000
	$5,135

At the time of the exchange, Chris' common shares had an ACB of $2,000 and a FMV of $5,135. Which one of the following best describes the tax consequences to Chris as a result of the exchange?

(A) Chris will have no capital gain on the disposition of his common shares and the ACB of his preferred shares is $2,000.

(B) Chris will have no capital gain on the disposition of his common shares and the ACB of his preferred shares is $1,865.

(C) Chris will have a capital gain of $3,135 on the disposition of his common shares and the ACB of his preferred shares is $5,135.

(D) Chris will have a capital gain of $135 on the disposition of his common shares and the ACB of his preferred shares is $2,135.

Question 4

Shelly exchanged her shares of Simpsons for shares of Hudson's Bay when Simpsons was taken over by Hudson's Bay. Her shares of Simpsons had the following characteristics:

FMV	$12,000
ACB	7,000
PUC	5,000

Section 85.1 is often used in take-over situations. Which one of the following statements with respect to section 85.1 in this case is FALSE?

(A) When there are many diverse shareholders, a section 85.1 rollover is easier to accomplish than a subsection 85(1) rollover because there is no need for each shareholder to file an election.

(B) The ACB of Shelly's shares of Hudson's Bay is $7,000.

(C) The ACB of the Simpsons' shares acquired by Hudson's Bay from Shelly is $5,000.

(D) Non-share consideration, up to the P.U.C. of the exchanged shares, $5,000, could have been received by Shelly without any adverse tax consequences to her.

Question 5

Mr. Wise owns 100% of the shares of ABC Co., a small business corporation. He would like to freeze the value of this company for tax purposes at today's value and transfer future growth to his children without giving up control over the company. He does not want to pay tax any sooner than he has to. His will currently leaves everything to his wife. Which of the following plans will achieve his objectives?

(A) His children should subscribe to common shares of a holding company and he should transfer his shares of ABC to this holding company, electing under section 85 at tax cost and taking back voting redeemable retractable preferred shares as consideration.

(B) He should change his will to leave his shares of ABC to his children rather than his wife.

(C) He should gift the ABC shares to his children during his lifetime.

(D) He should sell the ABC shares to his children at fair market value, taking back debt as consideration.

Question 6

Which of the following techniques will allow Mr. Successful to use up his $500,000 capital gains exemption on the accrued gain on shares of a qualified small business corporation? The shares were issued to him in 1983 for $1 and are worth $1 million now.

(A) A reverse asset freeze.

(B) A section 86 internal freeze.

(C) A holdco freeze, taking back boot of $1.

(D) A holdco freeze, taking back boot of $500,001.

EXERCISES

Exercise 1

[ITA: 85.1]

Magnamous Publico Ltd., a widely-held public corporation, has offered to exchange its common shares, currently trading on the CDNX Stock Exchange at $4.70 per share, for the common shares of Targetco Ltd., another widely-held public corporation. The shares of Targetco Ltd. trade currently on the CDNX Stock Exchange in the range of $2.00 to $2.25 each. Magnamous Publico Ltd. has offered to exchange one of its common shares for every two common shares tendered by shareholders of Targetco Ltd.

Mr. Sucker owns 1,000 shares of Targetco Ltd. which he bought several years ago for $1.25 each. Their paid-up capital value is $1.00 per share. On the announcement of the exchange offer their value on the market rose to $2.35. Mr. Sucker is interested in the exchange offer, but does not wish to realize any of the accrued gain on his shares of Targetco Ltd. Upon taking up the exchange offer, Mr. Sucker indicates that he will never own more than 10% of the shares of Magnamous Publico Ltd.

— REQUIRED

What are the tax consequences to Mr. Sucker and to Magnamous Publico Ltd. of taking up the exchange offer?

Exercise 2

[ITA: 86]

Abig Roller owned some Class A preferred shares of a corporation that reorganized its capital structure. He exchanged all these shares which had an adjusted cost base and paid-up capital of $2,000 and a fair market value of $3,000 for the following consideration:

Cash	$ 675
Fair market value of Class B preferred shares (L.S.C.: $1,000)	1,755
Fair market value of common shares (L.S.C.: $325)	570

— REQUIRED

What are the tax consequences to Mr. Roller as a result of this exchange?

Exercise 3

[ITA: 86(2)]

Mrs. Janna and her daughter Rayna, respectively, own 75% and 25% of the 100 common shares of Adam Ltd. The total fair market value of all the shares of the corporation is $600,000. The shares were acquired by both individuals at a total cost of $1,000 on incorporation in 1980.

Mrs. Janna is now prepared to freeze the future growth of her ownership in the corporation, so that the future growth will be passed on to her daughter. Mrs. Janna will give up all of her common shares for preferred shares of Adam Ltd. having a legal stated capital of $750 and a fair market value of $350,000. As a result, Rayna will own all of the common shares.

— REQUIRED

What are the tax consequences under section 86 to Mrs. Janna on the proposed transaction?

Exercise 4

[ITA: 87; 88(1)]

Mergem Limited owns all of the shares of Acquisition Limited. The cost of the shares to Mergem was $75,000 and they now have a fair market value of $100,000. Acquisition's only asset is land which cost it $50,000. The land had a fair market value of $90,000 when the shares of Acquisition were purchased by Mergem (at a bargain price!) and the land now has a fair market value of $100,000.

— REQUIRED

Determine the income tax consequences to Mergem Limited and Acquisition Limited of using either section 87 or subsection 88(1) to combine.

Exercise 5

[ITA: 51]

Convertit owns $10,000 of debentures of Convertibles Ltd. They were purchased several years ago at their face value and are convertible into 16 common shares of the corporation for each $100 of debentures owned at the option of the holder. When the common shares traded on the market at $100 each, Convertit exercised the conversion privilege.

— REQUIRED

What are the tax consequences of this conversion?

ASSIGNMENT PROBLEMS

Problem 1

[ITA: 85; 85.1]

Jason purchased all of the common shares of Quality Appliances Ltd., a Canadian-controlled private corporation, in 1987 for $50,000. The paid-up capital of the shares was $25,000. These shares have recently been valued at $125,000.

Big Distributors Ltd., a Canadian, arm's length corporation, has offered to buy all of Jason's shares. The following alternatives have been presented to Jason:

(a) $25,000 in cash and $100,000 of F.M.V. in common shares of Big Distributors Ltd.

(b) $125,000 of F.M.V. in Big Distributors Ltd.'s common shares.

Jason is at arm's length with Big Distributors Ltd. and, after acquiring its shares, will neither control Big Distributors Ltd. nor own more than 50% of the F.M.V. of its shares.

— REQUIRED

(A) What are the tax consequences to Jason if these transactions are conducted using the provisions of section 85.1?

(B) What are the tax consequences to Jason if these transactions are conducted using the provisions of section 85?

Problem 2

[ITA: 84(1), (3); 86]

Matt owns common shares of Maeb Inc. The adjusted cost base and paid-up capital of these shares is $300,000 and the F.M.V. is $900,000. In the course of a capital reorganization, the following two packages of consideration were offered in exchange for the shares:

(a) Cash	$ 10,000
Bond	80,000
F.M.V.* and L.S.C. of Class A preferred shares	600,000
F.M.V. and L.S.C. of Class B preferred shares	210,000
(b) Cash	$500,000
F.M.V.* and L.S.C. of Class A preferred shares	300,000
F.M.V. and L.S.C. of Class B preferred shares	100,000

* Equal to retraction and/or redemption value.

— REQUIRED

Indicate the tax consequences to Matt as a result of the above proposed reorganizations.

Problem 3

[ITA: 86(2)]

Mr. Fresser, age 67, owns 60% of the common shares of Fresser Ltd., a CCPC. The other 40% is owned by his daughter, Elana, who has worked in the business with Mr. Fresser for the past 22 years.

When the business was incorporated and capitalized in 1978, Mr. Fresser's shares had a cost and P.U.C. of $50,000. They now have a fair market value of $500,000. He proposes a capital reorganization in which he would give up his common shares in return for $90,000 in cash and $300,000 in retractable voting preferred shares with a legal stated capital of $300,000 which he could redeem at his convenience. As a result, Elana could own all of the outstanding common shares.

— REQUIRED

(A) What are the tax consequences to Mr. Fresser of section 86 on the proposed transaction?

(B) What are the tax consequences to Mr. Fresser of subsequently redeeming the preferred shares for their fair market value?

Problem 4

[ITA: 87; 88(1)]

Jonsub Ltd. is a wholly-owned subsidiary of Normpar Ltd. Normpar Ltd. plans to merge the two companies, either by amalgamating with the subsidiary under section 87 or by winding up the subsidiary under subsection 88(1). The balance sheet of Jonsub Ltd. immediately before the merger is as follows:

Assets:

Cash	$ 80,000
Marketable securities at cost (F.M.V. $950,000)	300,000
Accounts receivable (net of $30,000 reserve)	800,000
Inventory at cost (F.M.V. $920,000)	920,000
Land at cost (F.M.V. $2,000,000)	1,200,000
Building at UCC (F.M.V. $500,000)	300,000
Equipment at UCC (F.M.V. $150,000)	200,000
Total current assets	$3,800,000

Liabilities and shareholder's equity:

Accounts payable and accrued liabilities	709,000
Loans payable	1,000,000
Share capital	1,000
Retained earnings	2,090,000
	$3,800,000

Other Information

(1) Normpar Ltd. acquired all of the shares of Jonsub Ltd. for $4,000,000 in 1994. The total amount of dividends paid by Jonsub Ltd. to Normpar Ltd. during the period of ownership is $500,000.

(2) The same marketable securities were owned by Jonsub Ltd. at the time Normpar Ltd. acquired control but the marketable securities had a fair market value of only $800,000 at that time. Normpar Ltd. plans to sell the marketable securities in the next few years.

(3) The fair market value of the land and building at the time Normpar Ltd. acquired control were $1,900,000 and $400,000 respectively.

(4) The fair market value of goodwill developed by Jonsub Ltd. (i.e., not purchased) was $300,000 at the time Normpar Ltd. acquired control and $500,000 immediately before the merger.

— *REQUIRED*

What are the tax consequences to both Jonsub and Normpar on either an amalgamation under section 87 or a winding-up under subsection 88(1)?

Problem 5

[ITA: 87(2.1); 88(1.1)]

Loser Limited is a wholly-owned subsidiary of Bigbucks Limited. Loser has generated the following losses which it has not been able to absorb in a carryover year and it is not likely to generate sufficient income to absorb them in the foreseeable future.

Taxation year of loss	Non-capital loss	Net capital loss
2004	$43,000	$14,000
2003	7,000	10,000
2002	6,000	Nil
1998	4,000	5,000

Loser's fiscal year-end is December 31.

Bigbucks has a January 31 fiscal year-end and expects to generate sufficient business income and taxable capital gains to absorb any of Loser's losses that might be made available to it. As a result Bigbucks is considering either an amalgamation under section 87 or a winding-up under subsection 88(1) effective June 30, 2005. After the reorganization, the January 31 fiscal year-end will be retained.

— REQUIRED

Determine the availability to Bigbucks of the losses of its subsidiary under both alternatives being considered. Should any other factors be considered in the choice between the alternatives?

Problem 6

[ITA: 84.1; 85; 86]

Ms. Knight owns all of the common shares of Knight Manufacturing Limited (KML) that she acquired 20 years ago from an arm's length person. These shares have a paid-up capital of $100,000 and their adjusted cost base is $400,000. Their current fair market value is $1,800,000 and it is anticipated that this value will continue to grow rapidly. Ms. Knight is considering freezing the value of KML at $1,800,000 by holding non-growth debt and preferred shares and having her adult children own the common shares. Ms. Knight would like to use up her remaining (QSBC share) capital gains exemption of $400,000.

— REQUIRED

(A) One method of freezing the future growth of her KML common shares is to transfer her present common shares to a newly-formed holding company, Knight Holdings Ltd. (KHL). She would take from the holding company as consideration for the shares, debt in the amount of $800,000 and voting preferred shares with a legal stated capital and fair market value of $1,000,000. What are the tax consequences of this plan and how can the adverse tax consequences be avoided? Show all calculations.

(B) What are the tax consequences if the preferred shares in KHL received in (A) are:

(i) sold in an arm's length transaction for their fair market value?

(ii) redeemed by the corporation for their fair market value?

(C) As an alternative, Ms. Knight is considering a capital reorganization of KML under section 86 in which she would receive $800,000 in debt and $1,000,000 in voting preferred shares in return for her common shares. The $1,000,000 amount of preferred shares represents their legal stated capital, fair market value and retractable value. What are the tax consequences to Ms. Knight on the reorganization? How can the adverse tax consequences be avoided?

(D) What are the consequences if the shares received by Ms. Knight on the reorganization in (C) are:

(i) sold in an arm's length transaction for their fair market value?

(ii) redeemed by the corporation for their fair market value?

(E) Compare the alternatives in (B) and (D) in terms of their total "net economic effects":

(i) with the adverse tax consequences of the plan as outlined, and

(ii) with the tax consequences of the plan that avoids these adverse tax consequences.

[For more problems and solutions thereto, see the CD accompanying this book.]

SUPPLEMENTAL NOTES

(This section can be omitted without losing the continuity of the chapter. None of the review questions, multiple choice questions, exercises or assignment problems utilize this information.)

A.   GST Consequences of Rollovers Involving Corporations and Their Securities

Often businesses will engage in a reorganization of their affairs into separate corporations, wind up a corporation for income tax or other reasons, or undertake some other form of rollover transaction without considering the GST consequences. Under the GST, a number of these transactions trigger a liability, while other transactions involving reorganizations or rollovers have no GST consequences.

1.   Share for share exchange

[ETA: 123(1); 185(1); 186(2); Sch. V, Part VII]

Where a share for share exchange under section 85.1 of the *Income Tax Act* is undertaken, there will be no GST consequences in respect of the exchange. The definition of "financial instrument" [ETA: ssec. 123(1)] includes, among other things, an equity security. "Financial service" is defined in the same subsection to include, among other things, the issue, granting, variation or transfer of ownership of a financial instrument. Thus, the exchange of shares will qualify as a financial service, which is exempt pursuant to Part VII of Schedule V of the ETA.

Any GST that is paid in respect of services related to the share for share exchange, such as legal or investment counsel fees, will not be recoverable as an input tax credit, except to the extent allowed under sections 185 or 186. As discussed in Chapter 15, where a registrant that is a corporation resident in Canada is engaged in a takeover attempt in which it is acquiring or attempting to acquire all or substantially all (i.e., 90% or more) of the voting shares of another corporation, it is entitled to claim input tax credits for GST paid on any purchases of property and services attributable to that activity [ETA: ssec. 186(2)]. For this provision to apply to a share for share exchange, one corporation must acquire or attempt to acquire 90% or more of the shares of the other corporation. Also, where the share for share exchange is considered to be a financial service that relates to the registrant's commercial activities, the registrant is not required to apportion the inputs [ssec. 185(1)].

2.   Reorganizations

[ETA: 123(1); 185(1); 186(1); Sch. V, Part VII]

A reorganization of capital under section 86 of the *Income Tax Act* does not have GST consequences. The variation of existing shares would qualify as an exempt financial service. Any GST that is paid in respect of services related to the capital reorganization, however, will generally not be recoverable as an input tax credit.

Relief may be available in limited circumstances [ETA: ssecs. 185(1) and 186(1)]. Under subsection 186(1), where a parent corporation resident in Canada has an investment in shares of the capital stock of a related corporation, and the related corporation is engaged exclusively in commercial activities, the parent may claim an input tax credit in respect of any tax on the supply of property or services acquired by it that may reasonably be considered to relate to those shares. Thus, the parent must have acquired the services in respect of the reorganization and paid GST on those services in order to obtain relief. Also, where the reorganization of capital is considered to be an incidental financial service of the registrant, the registrant is not required to apportion the inputs [ssec. 185(1)].

3. Statutory amalgamations

[ETA: 149(2); 231; 249; 271]

Section 271 of the *Excise Tax Act* deals specifically with amalgamations. Where two or more corporations (referred to as predecessors) are merged or amalgamated to form a single corporation, the new corporation is generally treated as being a person separate from each of the predecessor corporations. No supplies are considered to have been made in respect of property transferred on the merger or amalgamation and, hence, there are no GST consequences. However, the new corporation will be deemed to be the same corporation as, and a continuation of, each predecessor for the purposes of sections 231 and 249 of the ETA, and for other prescribed purposes. Section 231 of the ETA deals with bad debts while section 249 of the ETA covers threshold amounts for purposes of the new corporation's reporting requirements (see Chapter 14). The new corporation will report the appropriate deduction from, or addition to, net tax, as the case may be, in relation to an amount owed to a predecessor that is written off as a bad debt or recovered after the amalgamation [ETA: sec. 231]. The new corporation's threshold amounts under section 249 of the ETA are calculated by reference to supplies made by the predecessor corporations. For example, if the predecessor corporations previously reported on a quarterly basis because their individual threshold amounts for the fiscal year were $4 million and $3 million, respectively, the new corporation will be required to report on a monthly basis because its threshold amount exceeds $6 million by reference to the supplies made by the two predecessors. The Amalgamations and Windings-Up Continuation (GST/HST) Regulations prescribe additional provisions of the ETA where the new corporation is deemed to be the same corporation as, and a continuation of, the predecessor corporations.

Section 271 of the ETA does not apply where the merger or amalgamation occurs as the result of the acquisition of property of one corporation by another corporation pursuant to the purchase of the property by the other corporation or as the result of the winding-up of the other corporation.

Special rules are provided for amalgamations that involve financial institutions [ETA: ssec. 149(2)].

4. Winding up a subsidiary

[ETA: 231; 249; 272]

Section 272 of the ETA deals specifically with wind-ups where 90% or more of the issued shares of each class of the capital stock of the wound-up corporation were, immediately before that time, owned by another corporation. This provision is similar to section 271 of the ETA which applies to amalgamations. On the wind-up, the transfer of assets to the parent is deemed not to be a supply.

The parent will be deemed to be the same corporation as, and a continuation of, the subsidiary for the purposes of sections 231 and 249 of the ETA, and for other prescribed purposes. As explained above in the context of amalgamations, any amount that is owed to the subsidiary that is written off as a bad debt [ETA: sec. 231] or recovered after the amalgamation is to be reported by the parent in its calculation of net tax. Similarly, in determining the parent's threshold amount for reporting purposes under section 249 of the ETA (see Chapter 14), any taxable supplies made by the subsidiary prior to the wind-up are deemed to be made by the parent. The Amalgamations and Windings-Up Continuation (GST/HST) Regulations prescribe additional provisions of the ETA where the parent corporation is deemed to be the same corporation as, and a continuation of, the subsidiary.

5. Convertible properties

[ETA: 123(1), Sch. V, Part VII]

Where section 51 of the *Income Tax Act* applies to the exchange of convertible properties for shares, the exchange will be an exempt financial service. The transfer of the convertible properties by the holder and the issuance of shares by the corporation are both exempt for GST purposes. The definition of "financial instrument" [ETA: ssec. 123(1)] includes, among other things, debt and equity securities. Thus, shares, bonds or notes of a corporation are considered to be financial instruments. "Financial service" is defined in the same subsection to include, among other things, the issue, granting, variation or transfer of ownership of a financial instrument. The exchange would qualify as a financial service, which is exempt pursuant to Part VII of Schedule V. Any GST paid on expenses incurred on the exchange will only be eligible for an input tax credit if the requirements of subsection 186(1) or (2) or subsection 185(1), as discussed above, are satisfied.

Chapter 18

Partnerships and Trusts

TOPICS DISCUSSED

	Page		Page
PARTNERSHIPS	955	Settlement of Trust	972
Nature of a Partnership	955	Computation of Income	972
Partnership Income	956	Computation of Tax	975
Partnership Interest	960		
Reorganization of Partnerships	963	SUPPLEMENTAL NOTES	987
Fiscal Period of Terminated Partnership	967	Partnerships	987
		Dispositions from Trust	991
TRUSTS	968	GST and Partnerships	993
Nature of Trust	968	GST and Trusts	996

This chapter is intended to provide only an overview of the provisions in Subdivision j of Division B in Part I of the Act dealing with partnerships. The chapter will deal, in general terms, with the computation of partnership income, the concept of a partnership interest, and some of the rollover provisions affecting partnerships. This area is quite complex. To reduce some of the complexity, the discussion will focus on partnerships commenced after 1971. However, it should be recognized that problems with respect to transitional rules for the treatment of depreciable property and for establishing the cost base of a partner's equity (called "partnership interest") must be addressed when dealing with a partnership established prior to 1972.

The chapter will also introduce some basic concepts in the taxation of trusts and illustrate some of the ways in which trusts are used in tax planning. There are two types of trusts for tax purposes: the personal trust and the commercial trust. In general, a commercial trust is any trust that is not a personal trust. A personal trust is one in which there is no consideration paid or payable by a beneficiary for an interest in the trust. Most of the rules discussed in this chapter apply to both types of trusts. There are, however, certain provisions of the Act that have been designed to deal specifically with commercial trusts. This chapter will focus, in general, on the provisions of the Act as they relate to personal trusts. Certain types of trusts which are provided for specifically in the Act, such as registered pension plans, registered retirement savings plans and deferred profit sharing plans have already been introduced. The focus of this part of the chapter relates to the taxation of trusts which are not created under any of these specific statutory provisions.

The following chart will help locate in the Act the major provisions discussed in this Chapter pertaining to trusts.

SUBDIVISION J
PARTNERSHIPS

DIVISION	
A	Liability for tax
B	Computation of income
C	Computation of taxable income
D	Taxable income earned in Canada by non-residents
E	Computation of tax
E.1	Minimum tax
F	Special rules
G	Deferred and other special income arrangements
H	Exemptions
I	Returns, Assessments, payments, appeals
J	Appeals to the courts

SUBDIVISION	
	Basic rules
a	Office or employment
b	Business or property
c	Capital gains and losses
d	Other income
e	Other deductions
f	Rules relating to computation of income
g	Amounts not included in income
h	Cdn corporations and shareholders
i	Shareholders of non-resident corporations
j	Partnerships
k	Trusts

SECTION	
96	General rules
97	Contributions to a partnership
98	Partnership ceases
98.1	Residual interests
98.2	Transfers on death
99	Fiscal periods
100	Disposition of partnership interests
101	Farmland
102	Definition of Canadian partnership
103	Agreement to share income

SECTION	
104	General rules
105	Benefits under a trust
106	Income interests
107	Capital interests
107.1-107.4	Special trusts
108	Definitions

The Supplemental Notes for the chapter contain an overview of the GST implications for partnerships and trusts.

I. PARTNERSHIPS

A. Nature of a Partnership

[IT: 90]

The term "partnership" is not defined in the Act. The Act merely outlines the tax consequences if a partnership exists. In order to determine whether a particular relationship is a partnership, reference must be made to the definitions contained in the various provincial Partnership Acts. Generally, these statutes define a partnership as a legal relationship existing between two or more persons who carry on a business in common for the purpose of profit. Partnerships can be formed by individuals, corporations or a combination of individuals and corporations. In addition, two other factors generally suggest the existence of a partnership:

(a) joint and several liability with respect to debts incurred by the partnership; and

(b) an agreement indicating the method in which profits and losses are to be shared.

The Canada Revenue Agency (CRA), has issued IT-90 which sets out the factors it considers in determining whether a partnership exists.

Partners may set out their interests in partnership property and their rights and duties in relation to the partnership by written agreement. In the absence of a written agreement, the interests of the partners may be implied from all of the surrounding circumstances. If there is no agreement, express or implied, then the Partnership Acts generally provide that all the partners are entitled to share equally in the capital, profits and losses of the partnership.

A partnership is to be distinguished from a joint venture. The tax consequences of being a partner or co-venturer (a member of a joint venture) are quite different. A partnership is a separate entity. Therefore, unless a rollover provision applies, transfers of property by the partner to the partnership take place at fair market value. On the other hand, a co-venturer generally retains title to any property used in the joint venture. If the co-venturer should contribute property to the joint venture, this is not a taxable transaction, as the contribution to a joint venture is not a disposition; there has been no change in ownership. Also, in a partnership net income is computed at the partnership level. Therefore, capital cost allowance is deducted at the partnership level. Each partner does not have the discretion to deduct capital cost allowance independently of the other partners. In a joint venture, each co-venturer computes net income separately. Therefore, each co-venturer is able to deduct capital cost allowance independently of the other co-venturers.

Whether a particular relationship is a partnership or a joint venture is a question of fact. It is not easy to determine. The fact that an agreement refers to a relationship as a partnership or a joint venture is not determinative of that relationship. The true nature of the relationship must be determined from all the facts.

A Canadian tax case, *Woodlin Developments Ltd. v. M.N.R.*, (T.C.C.) 86 DTC 1116, has stated that the following are indicators of a joint venture:

(a) joint property interest in the subject-matter of the venture;

(b) a right of mutual control and management of the enterprise; and

(c) generally, a limitation of the objective to a single undertaking or a limited number of undertakings.

B. Partnership Income

[ITA: 82(1); 96(1), (2.1), (2.2); 103(1), (1.1); 110.1(1)(*a*); 111(1); 118.1(3), (8); 121; 126; 127; 249.1; ITR: 229; IT-90]

1. General rules

A partnership is not a person, nor is it deemed to be a person for the purposes of the Act. However, the Act provides that the income of a partner under Division B of Part I of the Act is computed as if the partnership was a separate person resident in Canada [ssec. 96(1)]. So, for example, deductions such as capital cost allowance are taken at the partnership level. The taxation year of the partnership is the fiscal period of the partnership. The fiscal period of a partnership of which a member is an individual must end on December 31 [sec. 249.1].

Each taxable capital gain and allowable capital loss from the disposition of property owned by the partnership and the amount of any income or loss of the partnership from such sources as business or property will be calculated for each fiscal period of the partnership. However, this income under Division B is not taxed at the partnership level but is allocated to the partners according to the terms of the partnership agreement. The partners then include their share of the partnership income in their income for the year. If, in computing income, the partnership deducts amounts that, for purposes of the Act, are deductions either from taxable income or from taxes payable, these amounts are added back to the partnership income before they are allocated to the partners.

The income that flows through to each partner retains its original character or source, thereby enabling the partner to benefit, for example, from the dividend tax credit, the foreign tax credit and the capital gains deduction in respect of qualified farm property or qualified shares of a small business corporation. The income of the partnership will be combined on each partner's tax return with the partner's non-partnership income or losses. For example, non-partnership capital losses of an individual partner may be offset against that partner's share of partnership capital gains, since these gains are allocated to the partner. Similarly, a partner's share of rental income allocated by the partnership may be used to offset rental losses created by capital cost allowance on the partner's own rental property. Taxable income is computed by each partner, and each partner reports his or her partnership income on his or her own return and pays tax. The partnership itself does not file a tax return.

The partnership is required to provide an information return [Reg. 229] to each partner as follows:

(a) where all of the partners are corporations, five months from the end of the fiscal period;

(b) where all the partners are individuals, the last day of March in the calendar year following the calendar year in which the fiscal period of the partnership ended; and

(c) in every other case, the earlier of five months after the end of the fiscal period and the last day of March following the calendar year in which the fiscal period of the partnership ended.

Failure to file a partnership information return on time will result in penalties.

Example Problem —————————————————————————————

The following income statement was prepared for the Alpha Beta Partnership, a partnership comprised of two individuals that carries on an active business:

Alpha Beta Partnership
INCOME STATEMENT
For the year ended December 31, 2005

Gross revenue		$350,000
Less:		
Office salaries	$29,000	
Rent	42,000	
Office supplies	8,950	
Depreciation on office furniture	3,375	
Charitable donations	3,000	86,325
		$263,675
Gain on sale of securities	$50,000	
Dividends received from taxable Canadian corporations	4,000	54,000
Net income		$317,675

The partners drew a total of $67,000 in "salaries".

— REQUIRED

Compute the partnership income for the year and the income to be allocated to the partners for income tax purposes. Assume that the office furniture is included in Class 8 for capital cost allowance purposes. The capital cost allowance available in respect of the office furniture is $2,750, based on an undepreciated capital cost of $13,750.

— SOLUTION

Partnership's net income for financial accounting purposes[1]	$317,675
Deduct: Gain on sale of securities	(50,000)
Capital cost allowance	(2,750)
Add: Depreciation on office furniture	3,375
Charitable donations[2]	3,000
Taxable capital gain ($\frac{1}{2} \times \$50,000$)	25,000
Income to be allocated (Division B)	$296,300

	Partnership
Nature of income:	
Taxable capital gain ($\frac{1}{2} \times \$50,000$)	$ 25,000
Dividends	$ 4,000
Active business income	267,300
	$ 296,300

— NOTES TO SOLUTION

(1) Salaries paid by a partnership to its members do not constitute a business expense but are a method of distributing partnership income to members of the partnership.

(2) Charitable donations are not deductible in computing Division B income. Instead, they are allocated to the partners and are used as the basis for computing the charitable donations tax credit for an individual partner.

2. Limitation on deduction of partnership losses

Generally, business or property losses may be deducted by a limited partner only to the extent that the partner's investment in the partnership and share of the partnership's profit (known as the partner's "at-risk" amount [ssec. 96(2.2)]) exceeds any amount owing to the partnership by the partner and any guaranteed return in respect of the partnership interest, guaranteed buy-back of the partnership interest and so on [ssec. 96(2.1)]. To the extent that the business or property losses otherwise allocable to the limited partner are restricted in the manner described above, they are added to the limited partner's "limited partnership loss" in respect of the partnership for the year and are deductible only to the extent that the partner has an "at-risk" amount in future years in respect of the partnership that gave rise to the loss.

A limited partner is generally a partner whose only interest in the partnership is financial. If a limited partner takes part in the management of the partnership's business then, under provincial partnership law, that partner will lose status as a limited partner. Nevertheless, that partner may continue to be a limited partner for purposes of the "at-risk" rules.

Unlike a limited partner of a limited partnership, a member of limited liability partnership (LLP) can be liable for the general debts and obligations of a limited liability partnership. However, a member of a limited liability partnership is not liable for the debts of the partnership, or any member of the partnership, arising from negligent acts or omissions that another partner or an employee, agent or representative of the partnership commits in the course of the partnership business. Paragraph 96(2.4)(*a*) excludes from the "at-risk" rules members of limited liability partnerships where a partner's liability is limited by operation of a statutory provision of Canada or a province that limits the member's liability.

3. Partnership allocations: Anti-avoidance

The partnership agreement will set out how the partners have agreed to allocate any income or loss among themselves. An anti-avoidance provision applies to a situation where the partnership agreement to share income or loss is considered to result in a reduction or postponement of tax that might otherwise have been payable [ssec. 103(1)]. For example, the income allocated between partners may reflect more of a desire to split income or to allocate losses than a desire to reward each partner for his or her respective contribution. An anti-avoidance provision permits the partnership's income sharing arrangement to be set aside for tax purposes [ssec. 103(1.1)]. The amounts would then be reallocated to the partners in a manner which is reasonable in the circumstances.

Where the partners do not deal at arm's length, specific rules are provided to determine a reasonable allocation of profit [ssec. 103(1.1)]. Each partner's capital contribution and work performed, together with any other relevant factor, will be considered.

4. Computation of taxable income

Charitable gifts made by the partnership provide a deduction for partners who are corporations [par. 110.1(1)(*a*)]. A partner who is an individual includes a *pro rata* share of the donation in the partner's total charitable gifts for purposes of calculating the personal tax credit [ssec. 118.1(3)]. These donations are flowed through to a partner according to the partner's share of partnership income.

Taxable capital gains generated by a partnership retain their character as part of the net income of the partnership flowed out to the partners. As a result, these taxable capital gains may provide individual partners with eligibility for the capital gains deduction available for qualified farm property and qualified small business corporation shares and provide partners with an opportunity to utilize personal net capital losses.

Since there is no computation of taxable income at the partnership level, losses carried forward and backward are not deductible by the partnership. Losses of the partnership are allocated to the partners at the end of each fiscal period. Any losses that are not utilized by a partner in the year incurred are carried forward or backward by the partner and deducted by the partner in the computation of that partner's taxable income according to the rules provided [sec. 111]. However, as already stated, in certain circumstances the ability of a limited partner to deduct an amount may be restricted by the partner's at-risk amount.

5. Tax credits generated by the partnership

Charitable gifts made by the partnership entitle the individual partners to a tax credit [ssec. 118.1(8)]. These gifts and the corresponding credits are flowed through to a partner according to the partner's share of partnership income.

Dividend income of the partnership maintains its source characteristics when allocated to the partners. An individual who is a member of a partnership will be entitled to claim a dividend tax credit in respect of the partner's share of any taxable dividend received by the partnership from a taxable Canadian corporation during a fiscal period of a partnership [sec. 121]. When dividend income is allocated to a partner who is an individual, the dividend allocated to the partner must be grossed up by the usual rules, when it is included in the partner's income [ssec. 82(1)].

Similarly, the partner may deduct any foreign tax credits on foreign income allocated to the partner by the partnership [sec. 126]. Also, political contributions made by a partnership are allocated to each partner and, thus, provide each partner with a tax credit [ssec. 127(4.2)]. The investment tax credit is treated on a similar basis [ssec. 127(8)]. However, in certain circumstances, the ability of a limited partner to deduct an amount in respect of the investment tax credit may be restricted by the partner's at-risk amount [ssecs. 127(8.1) to (8.5)].

Example Problem

Refer to the previous example problem concerning Alpha Beta Partnership. Mrs. Alpha and Mrs. Beta share income equally.

— REQUIRED

Compute Mrs. Alpha's taxable income for 2005, assuming she has no other income.

— SOLUTION

Income to be allocated (Division B)	$296,300
Dividends ($1/2 \times \$4,000$)	$ 2,000
TCG ($1/2 \times \$25,000$)	12,500
ABI ($1/2 \times \$267,300$)	133,650
	$148,150
Dividend gross-up ($1/4 \times \$2,000$)	500
Taxable income	$148,650

— NOTE TO SOLUTION

Mrs. Alpha will be eligible for a dividend tax credit of $333 ($2/3 \times \$500$) and a charitable donation credit computed on $1/2$ of the partnership's charitable donations in computing her basic federal income tax.

C. Partnership Interest

[ITA: 40(3); 53(1)(e), (2)(c); 100(2)]

1. The concept

As indicated previously, the property of a partnership is owned by the partnership, not the individual partners. Thus, any gains or losses on the disposition of that property are included in the computation of the net income of the partnership. The property owned by the partnership must be distinguished from each partner's interest in the partnership, which is a separate property owned by each partner. A taxpayer's "partnership interest" represents his or her total rights and obligations as a partner. It may be bought and sold by the partner. In this respect, a partnership interest is analogous to the share held by a shareholder of a corporation. A person acquires a partnership interest by becoming a member of a partnership and disposes of a partnership interest when he or she withdraws from the partnership.

Generally, a partnership interest is a capital property. As a capital property, a partnership interest has an adjusted cost base. The gain or loss from the disposition of a partnership interest is calculated as the difference between the adjusted cost base of the partnership interest and the partner's proceeds of disposition. The taxable capital gain or allowable capital loss arising on the disposition of the partnership interest is included in a partner's income. The basic computation made on the disposition of a partnership interest is illustrated by Exhibit 18-1.

EXHIBIT 18-1
Gain or Loss on Disposal of a Partnership Interest

	Case 1		Case 2	
Proceeds received by partner for his or her interest		$22,750		$12,750
Less: Adjusted cost base of his or her interest	$16,000		$16,000	
Selling expenses	1,750	17,750	1,750	17,750
Partner's capital gain (loss).........		$ 5,000		$ (5,000)
Taxable capital gain (allowable capital loss)		$ 2,500		$ (2,500)

2. Adjusted cost base (ACB)

The adjusted cost base of a partner's partnership interest is basically the partner's net investment in the partnership business. Each partner's adjusted cost base is the original cost of the partnership interest with adjustments for earnings, drawings and other similar transactions between a partner and the partnership.

Generally, items which increase a partner's net investment in the partnership are added to the adjusted cost base of the partnership interest. The following are some of the more common items added to the adjusted cost base:

(a) the partner's share of income of the partnership for each fiscal period ending after 1971, except that 100% of any gains on the disposition of capital property owned by the partnership is added to the adjusted cost base, instead of the inclusion percentage [spar. 53(1)(*e*)(i)];

(b) the partner's share of any capital dividends [ssec. 83(2)] received on shares of the capital stock of a corporation which were owned by the partnership [spar. 53(1)(*e*)(ii)];

(c) the partner's share of the net proceeds on death of life insurance policies received by the partnership after 1971 [spar. 53(1)(*e*)(iii)]; and

(d) the partner's contributions of capital to the partnership after 1971 [spar. 53(1)(*e*)(iv)].

Generally, items which reduce or erode a partner's net investment in the partnership are deducted from the adjusted cost base of the partnership's interest. The following are some of the more common items deducted from the adjusted cost base:

(a) the partner's share of any loss of the partnership for each fiscal period ending after 1971 (other than limited partnership losses), except that 100% of losses on the disposition of capital property owned by the partnership is deducted from the adjusted cost base, instead of the inclusion percentage [spar. 53(2)(*c*)(i)];

(b) the partner's share of any charitable gifts or political contributions made by the partnership after 1971 [spar. 53(2)(*c*)(iii)];

(c) the partner's drawings of his or her share of partnership income or capital after 1971 [spar. 53(2)(*c*)(v)]; and

(d) the amount of any investment tax credit used by the partner in respect of expenditures made by the partnership [spar. 53(2)(c)(vi)].

Exhibit 18-2 summarizes the most common adjustments to the ACB of a partnership interest.

EXHIBIT 18-2
SUMMARY
PARTNER'S ACB IN A PARTNERSHIP

Capital

Add	Capital contributions
Deduct	Capital withdrawals

Income

Add	Partner's share of the partnership's income
Deduct	Partner's share of the partnership's losses
Add	Partner's contributions to finance partnership losses
Deduct	Partner's drawings from partnership income
Add	Untaxed portion of any capital gain (The TCG is included in income that has been added above to the ACB.)
Deduct	Untaxed portion of any capital losses
Add	Partner's share of capital dividends (These dividends are in the partnership, but not in the income, so they need to increase the ACB. Then, their withdrawal will not cause a negative ACB, since the withdrawal is of funds that should be received tax free.)

Other

Add	Partner's share of life insurance proceeds received by the partnership (These proceeds are in the partnership, but not in the income, so they need to increase the ACB. Then their withdrawal will not cause a negative ACB, since the withdrawal is of funds that should be received tax free.)
Deduct	Partner's share of charitable donations or political contributions (Since partnerships do not pay tax, it is the partners who use the charitable donations. This adjustment recognizes that the funds, while not deductible, have been paid out of the partnership.)
Deduct	Partner's share of any investment tax credit earned by the partnership.

The adjusted cost base of a partnership interest may be a negative amount. A negative adjusted cost base in respect of all other capital property other than a partnership interest is deemed to be a capital gain as soon as it arises even when there is no actual disposition of the property at the time [ssec. 40(3)]. The provision does not apply where a negative adjusted cost base arises as a result of deductions made by virtue of paragraph 53(2)(c). Therefore, as long as there is no actual disposition of his or her interest by the partner, a negative adjusted cost base will not be taxed as a capital gain. However, the subsection 40(3) treatment does apply to a negative adjusted cost base of limited and certain other passive partners [ssec. 40(3.1)]. This exception represents an extension of the at-risk rules and its implementation affects film tax shelters, in particular.

Where a taxpayer disposes of only part of his or her partnership interest, an equivalent proportion of the adjusted cost base as calculated at that particular time is deducted from the proceeds of disposition in computing the taxpayer's gain or loss.

If the adjusted cost base of the partnership interest is negative at the time of disposition, the negative amount (or, in a partial disposition, an equivalent portion of the negative amount) is added to the gain otherwise determined [ssecs. 40(1) and 100(2)]. Exhibit 18-3 illustrates this treatment.

EXHIBIT 18-3
Treatment of Negative Adjusted Cost Base

Assumptions: Partner sells a partnership interest for proceeds of disposition of $5,000. The selling expenses total $250. The partner's adjusted cost base of the partnership interest is a negative $1,250.

Proceeds of disposition received	$5,000
Deduct: selling expenses	250
Gain otherwise determined	$4,750
Add: negative adjusted cost base at date of sale	1,250
Partner's capital gain	$6,000
Taxable capital gain ($^1/_2 \times $6,000$)	$3,000

D. Reorganization of Partnerships

[ITA: 13(21.2); 40(3.3), (3.4); 85(2), (3), (4); 97(1), (2); 102; 103; 251.1]

The provisions which deal with the reorganization of partnerships parallel the tax-free corporate rollover discussed in the preceding chapters. Conceptually, the problems encountered in the partnership scenario are similar in nature to those in the context of a corporation. The major difference is that on a transfer of property to a partnership the consideration received by the transferor must include a "partnership interest" as compared to "share capital". Both types of reorganizations can include non-partnership interest consideration or "boot" and the amount of "boot" is restricted to prevent the stripping of accrued gains on the entity's assets.

1. Transfer of partnership property to a corporation

The partners of the partnership may wish to incorporate the partnership's assets. The eligible assets of the partnership can be transferred to a Canadian corporation for consideration, including shares of the corporation [ssec. 85(2)]. These shares then become the assets of the partnership. The partnership must only be a Canadian partnership if the property that is being transferred is real property that is capital property, or an interest or option in respect of real property. This rollover parallels directly the rollover available to a person transferring property to a corporation [ssec. 85(1)]. A joint election is required by the corporation and all of the members of the partnership.

It may be desirable to wind up the partnership and have the former partners hold the shares of the corporation directly. This transaction is accomplished on a tax-deferred basis [ssec. 85(3)]. In order for the rollover to apply, the only partnership assets must be cash or shares received from the corporation as consideration for the transfer of partnership property to the corporation [par. 85(3)(*c*)]. Also, the partnership must be wound up within 60 days of the transfer [par. 85(3)(*b*)]. This rollover is automatic and there are no filing requirements.

Example Problem ————————————————————————————

The partners of ABC Partnership wish to incorporate the partnership's asset. The partnership's asset is land which was purchased in 1986 for $12,000. The fair market value of the land is now $48,000 and the land is capital property. On the transfer of the land to the corporation the partnership receives the following from the corporation:

Cash	$12,000
Preferred shares (F.M.V.)	12,000
Common shares (F.M.V.)	24,000
Total	$48,000

One month after the transfer of the land to the corporation, the partnership is wound up, using the provisions in subsection 85(3).

— REQUIRED

What is the position of Mr. Aleph who received a ⅔ share of each asset distributed by the partnership on the winding-up? The adjusted cost base of his partnership interest is $12,000.

— SOLUTION

Cost of preferred shares [par. 85(3)(e)]:
Lesser of:

(a) fair market value of shares (⅔ × $12,000)	$ 8,000
(b) A.C.B. of partnership interest less F.M.V. of consideration other than shares ($12,000 − ⅔ × $12,000)	$ 4,000

Cost of common shares [par. 85(3)(f)]:

A.C.B. of partnership interest		$12,000
Less: F.M.V. of non-share consideration	$8,000	
cost of preferred shares	4,000	12,000
		Nil

Proceeds of disposition of partnership interest [par. 85(3)(g)]:

Deemed cost of preferred shares	$ 4,000
Deemed cost of common shares	Nil
Other consideration	8,000
Total proceeds	$12,000

Since the proceeds for the partnership interest equal its adjusted cost base, there is no gain or loss on the disposition of the partnership interest. As a general rule, as long as the "boot" received by the partner does not exceed his or her A.C.B. there will not be a gain.

2. Transfer of property to a partnership

Generally, when a partner transfers property to a partnership, the partner is deemed to dispose of the property for proceeds equal to its fair market value and the partnership is deemed to acquire the property for the same amount [ssec. 97(1)]. This rule may result in gains or losses where there is no actual change in economic interest in the property. To prevent this inequity, a rollover is provided where a Canadian partnership acquires property from a person who immediately after the transfer is a partner [ssec. 97(2)]. To qualify, the partnership must be a Canadian partnership immediately after the transfer, and all partners must elect to have the rollover apply. The types of property that can be transferred are limited to capital property (including depreciable capital property), eligible capital property, inventory (including land inventory) and certain resource properties [ssec. 97(2)].

A Canadian partnership is defined [sec. 102] as a partnership all the members of which are resident in Canada at the particular time.

The partners elect an agreed amount on a form which is filed with the CRA. The agreed amount is the proceeds of disposition of the property to the partner and the cost of the property to the partnership. In essence, subsection 97(2) provides the same rules for establishing the elected amount range as found in subsection 85(1) applicable to transfers of property to a corporation. At the upper limit, the agreed amount at which the property can be transferred is the fair market value of that property. At the lower limit, the agreed amount can be set at the fair market value of consideration, other than a partnership interest, received for the property transferred, if that amount is not less than the lesser of the fair market value and the tax value of the property transferred. Any excess of the agreed amount over the fair market value of the consideration other than a partnership interest received is added to the adjusted cost base of the partnership interest of the partner.

A loss-denial rule applies where the fair market value of depreciable property is less than both its cost and its undepreciated capital cost (terminal loss) and the transferor is a person (i.e., an individual, a corporation or a trust), or partnership [ssec. 13(21.2)]. Where the transferor or certain affiliated persons hold the property 30 days after the disposition, no loss is recognized on the transfer. Instead, the accrued terminal loss is retained by the transferor in the same CCA class. The recognition of the loss by the transferor will generally be deferred until such time as the depreciable property is transferred to a person who is not an affiliated person as defined [sec. 251.1].

An adjustment must be made where depreciable property is transferred to the partnership by a non-arm's length person or partnership (the transferor), and the capital cost of the property to the transferor is less than the cost of the property to the partnership [par. 13(7)(e)]. The partnership is deemed to have a capital cost equal to the cost of the property to the transferor plus the person's or partnership's taxable capital gain inclusion. The deemed capital cost is for purposes of computing capital cost allowance, not future capital gains or losses.

Where the transferor is a corporation, trust or partnership (but not an individual), a capital loss arising on the transfer of non-depreciable capital property to a partnership of which the transferor is a majority-interest partner is denied [ssecs. 40(3.3) and (3.4)]. A majority-interest partner as defined [ssec. 248(1)] is a partner who is entitled to more than one-half of the partnership's income from all sources in the immediately preceding year or would be entitled to more than one-half of the amount paid to all members of the partnership if it were wound up at the time. The loss is retained by the transferor and not recognized until the earliest of several events. Where the taxpayer is an individual who is a majority-interest partner, the superficial loss rule will apply to deny the loss [spar. 40(2)(g)(i) and sec. 54] and add it to the cost of the property in the partnership.

On the transfer of depreciable capital property, the partnership generally assumes the position of the transferor with respect to the capital cost of the property for the determination of capital gains and recapture when the partnership eventually disposes of the property.

Recognize that, as a result of the rollover [ssec. 97(2)], part of the deferred income may, in effect, be transferred to the other partners. Each partner will include his or her proportionate share of the income when the partnership disposes of the property.

Example Problem

Mr. Black and Mr. Red operate accounting practices as sole practitioners. They wish to form a partnership in which Mr. Black will hold a 60% share and Mr. Red a 40% share. The relevant financial data for the separate practices as at December 31, 2005 are as follows:

	Mr. Black		Mr. Red	
	Cost	F.M.V.	Cost	F.M.V.
Cash	$ 94,000	$ 94,000	$ 60,000	$ 60,000
Marketable securities	20,000	10,000	10,000	5,000
Land (capital property)	5,000	50,000	—	—
Accounts receivable	130,000	130,000	40,000	40,000
Furniture and fixtures	80,000	80,000	30,000	34,000
Leasehold improvements......	30,000	40,000	20,000	—
Goodwill..................	20,000	50,000	—	—
	$379,000	$454,000	$160,000	$139,000
Accounts payable		$120,000		$130,000

The tax values of the following assets are:

	Mr. Black	Mr. Red
Furniture and fixtures (U.C.C.)	$70,000	$24,000
Leasehold improvements (U.C.C.)	30,000	—
Balance of cumulative eligible capital	9,000	—

— REQUIRED

(A) Compute the values at which the assets should be transferred to defer any immediate tax consequences of the transfer assuming the accounts payable are not transferred to the partnership and no consideration other than a partnership interest is received.

(B) Compute the adjusted cost bases of the partnership interests of Mr. Black and Mr. Red.

(C) Indicate the tax effects of having the partnership assume the accounts payable of Mr. Black and Mr. Red.

(D) Indicate the tax consequences to Mr. Black and Mr. Red of having the partnership dispose of the land in 2005 for proceeds of disposition of $50,000. Assume that the land is capital property to the partnership, and that no consideration, other than a partnership interest, is received by the partners.

— SOLUTION

(A)

	Mr. Black	Mr. Red
Cash	$ 94,000	$ 60,000
Marketable securities	10,000[1]	5,000[2]
Land	5,000	—
Accounts receivable................................	130,000	40,000
Furniture and fixtures	70,000	24,000
Leasehold improvements	30,000	—
Goodwill ($4/3 \times \$9,000$)	12,000	—
	$351,000	$129,000

(B)

Adjusted cost base:

	Mr. Black	Mr. Red
Transfer value of assets	$351,000	$129,000

(C) If Mr. Black's accounts payable are transferred to the partnership, the transfer value of his net assets would be $231,000 ($351,000 − $120,000) resulting in an adjusted cost base for his partnership interest of $231,000. In Mr. Red's case there will be a gain of $1,000. This results from the requirement that the elected transfer price be no less than the non-partnership interest consideration received (which in this case would be $130,000). Since the proceeds of disposition are $130,000 and the adjusted cost base of the assets is $129,000 there would be a gain of $1,000. Since the proceeds of disposition of the property do not exceed the fair market value of the non-partnership interest consideration received the adjusted cost base of the partnership interest to Mr. Red would be nil.

(D)	Proceeds of disposition		$50,000
	Adjusted cost base...		5,000
	Capital gain		$45,000
	Taxable capital gain (½ of $45,000)		$22,500
	Income to be allocated		$22,500

	Mr. Black	Mr. Red
Share of income.................................	$ 13,500	$ 9,000
Adjusted cost base of partnership interest	$351,000	$129,000
Add: share of capital gain (i.e., income from taxable capital gain + untaxed fraction of capital gain)	27,000	18,000
	$378,000	$147,000

On the transfer of the land to the partnership, Mr. Black deferred the recognition of a $45,000 capital gain. When the partnership disposed of the land, it realized a capital gain of $45,000 and a taxable gain of $22,500. A portion of that capital gain was allocated to each partner as his share of the partnership income for the year. Because a portion of the taxable capital gain was allocated to Mr. Red, as well as Mr. Black, part of the deferred gain ($18,000) and the tax liability on that gain was essentially transferred from Mr. Black to Mr. Red. The partnership agreement could have been structured to require the full amount of this gain to be allocated to Mr. Black to avoid this inequity.

— NOTES TO SOLUTION

(1) Under the definition of "superficial loss" [sec. 54], Mr. Black will have a superficial loss, since the partnership is a person that is affiliated with him [par. 251.1(1)(*e*)]. Accordingly, the loss is deemed to be nil. The amount of the denied loss will be added to the adjusted cost base of the marketable securities to the partnership [par. 53(1)(*f*)].

(2) Since Mr. Red is not a majority interest partner he is not denied the loss.

E. Fiscal Period of Terminated Partnership

[ITA: 99; 249.1]

The fiscal period of a terminated partnership is deemed to have ended on the date the partnership ceases [sec. 99].

Where an individual is a member of a partnership, the individual may elect to have the fiscal period terminate on the date it would have normally ended had the partnership not ceased to exist. The election is only valid if the individual is resident in Canada on the date the fiscal period of the partnership normally would have ended.

The purpose of these provisions is to permit a partner to spread his or her income over two years rather than have two fiscal years' income included in the same taxation year of the individual partner.

Section 249.1, which requires a December 31 fiscal year-end for a partnership of which an individual is a member, renders this rule generally unnecessary, because the termination of a partnership cannot cause a deemed year-end in the same year as a calendar year-end. If an off-calendar year and the alternative method are used, [ssec. 249.1(4)] by the partnership, then section 99 may have some application.

II. TRUSTS

A. Nature of Trust

[ITA: 70(6); 73(1); 104(2); 108(1); IT-447]

1. General

(a) *Definition of Trust*

Before dealing with the taxation of a trust one must understand what is a trust. The law of trusts is a separate area of law just as the law relating to land and the law relating to contracts are separate areas of law.

A trust is not a contract. In a contract there are mutual covenants (or promises) where one person promises to do something in return for the other person promising to do something. It is enforceable only by the parties and is dependent upon "consideration".[a] A trust is a relationship whereby a person (who is called a trustee) is bound to deal with property over which he or she has control (which is called the trust property) for the benefit of persons (who are called the beneficiaries) any of whom may enforce the obligation.[b]

A trust is created when a person (called the settlor) transfers the title of a property to the trustee who holds it for the benefit of the income and capital beneficiaries. Therefore for a trust to exist, there must be three certainties present. There must be certainty of intention; the settler must have intended to establish a trust. There must be a certainty of subject matter; there must be a specific property given to the trustee. There must be certainty of objects; it must be clear who the income and capital beneficiaries are.

Therefore, one of the fundamental characteristics of a trust is the separation of title-holding and the management of property from its enjoyment. For example, assume that a parent wants to provide an income for a child in order to pay that child's personal living expenses. That parent may also be prepared to transfer investments which will earn that income to the child when he or she has reached a certain age. Until that time, however, the parent does not want the child to control the investments. A trust may be used to accomplish all of these objectives. The investments would be transferred to a trustee. The trust agreement would provide for the distribution of income to the child annually and the distribution of the investments to the child when the child reaches a specific age.

---

[a] J. Wardlaw, "Inter Vivos Trusts: A Base Primer," *Estates and Trusts Quarterly*, Vol. 5, 1980-81, p. 298.

[b] Underhill and Hayton, *Law Relating to Trusts and Trustees*, 14th ed., 1987, p. 3.

The following diagram illustrates the relationship among the settlor, trustees and beneficiaries.

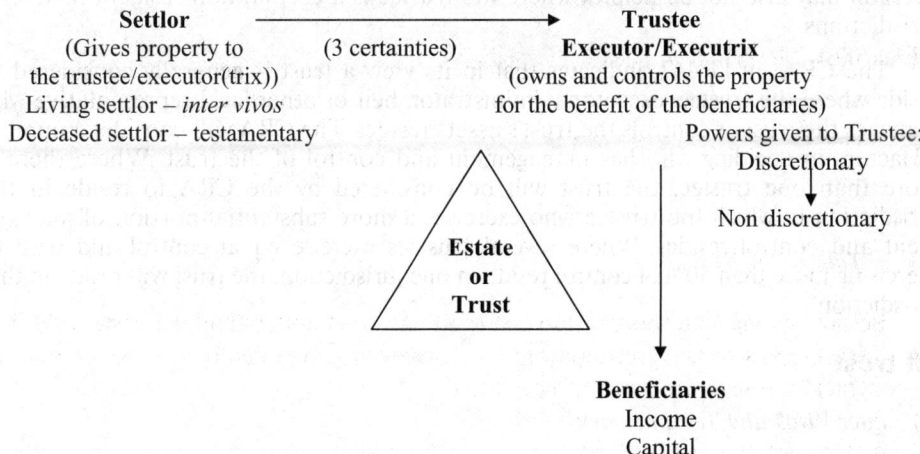

TAXATION OF TRUSTS – OVERVIEW

Trusts are particularly useful when the beneficiaries are minors. Generally, with certain limited exceptions, a minor cannot enter into a binding contract. All other contracts are voidable at the option of the minor. This means that they cannot be enforced unless ratified by the minor when he or she reaches the age of majority.

(b) *Taxation of Trusts*

A trust is considered to be a taxpayer separate and distinct from its settlor, trustees or beneficiaries. As a separate taxpayer, the trust is deemed to be an individual [ssec. 104(2)]. Therefore, the income of the trust is generally computed in the same way as is the income of any individual.

(c) *Residency of Trusts*

Determining the residency of a trust is an important tax issue. If the trust is resident in Canada, it will be taxed on its worldwide income. If it is not resident in Canada, it will be taxed in Canada as a non-resident.

There is still some uncertainty as to the rules that determine the residence of a trust. The leading Canadian case on the question of the residence of a trust is *Thibodeau Family Trust v. The Queen*, (F.C.T.D.) 78 DTC 6376. In that case, one trustee was resident in Canada. Two other trustees were residents of Bermuda. The assets and administration of the trust were in Bermuda. Under the provisions of the trust agreement, the trustees had the power to act by a majority. Evidence suggested that the trustees in Bermuda had exercised independent judgment and had at times declined to accept the suggestion of the Canadian trustee. Some of the beneficiaries were resident in the U.S. while others were resident in Canada.

The court held that the trust was solely resident in Bermuda. The decision was based on two facts: the majority of the trustees were resident in Bermuda and the trust document permitted a majority decision on all matters of trustees' discretion.

The decision provides little assistance in situations where a majority of trustees do not reside in one jurisdiction or situations where trustees must act unanimously. The decision may also not be helpful where the trustee is a corporation resident in several jurisdictions.

The CRA, in IT-447, indicates that in its view a trust is generally considered to reside where the trustee, executor, administrator, heir or other legal representative who manages the trust or controls the trust's assets resides. The CRA will consider a number of factors in deciding who has management and control of the trust. Where there is more than one trustee, the trust will be considered by the CRA to reside in the jurisdiction in which the trustee who exercises a more substantial portion of management and control resides. Where several trustees exercise equal control and trustees exercising more than 50% of control reside in one jurisdiction, the trust will reside in that jurisdiction.

2. Types of trust

(a) Inter Vivos and Testamentary

A testamentary trust, as specifically defined [ssec. 108(1)], arises as the consequence of the death of an individual. An *inter vivos* trust is created while the settlor is still alive and it is defined in the Act to be a trust other than a testamentary trust [ssec. 108(1)].

A testamentary trust can be "tainted" and, hence, no longer a testamentary trust, if property is contributed to the trust otherwise than as a result of the individual's death [par. 108(1b)]. For example, if some other individual contributes property to the trust, the trust loses its testamentary status and becomes an *inter vivos* trust. A trust can also lose its testamentary trust status if, after December 20, 2002, it borrows money from a beneficiary or someone not dealing at arm's length with a beneficiary. This borrowing restriction was put in place to prevent income splitting through this type of trust to take advantage of the graduated tax rates [Proposed in the February 27, 2004 Draft Legislation].

(b) Discretionary and Non-discretionary

Trusts may be discretionary or non-discretionary. In a discretionary trust, the trustee is given the power of choice. The trustee may be given the power to determine the date of the distribution of trust property, whether income is to be paid to a beneficiary, how much is to be paid to a beneficiary and in what proportions among a group of beneficiaries it is to be paid. For example, by using their discretionary powers trustees may, in certain circumstances, allocate income to taxpayers with a lower marginal tax rate. The trustee may also be given the discretion to decide when a trust is to be terminated. The flexibility provided by the discretionary trust has made it a useful tool in tax planning. With a non-discretionary trust, the trustee does not have the power of choice. The trust document sets out certain decisions which the trustees are obliged to implement.

(c) Personal Trust and Commercial Trust

The conditions for a personal trust are set out in subsection 248(1) of the Act. A personal trust is either a testamentary trust or an *inter vivos* trust, where no beneficial interest in the trust was acquired for consideration paid either to the trust or to a person who made a contribution to the trust. The term "commercial trust" is not defined in the Act. The term "commercial trust" is generally used to describe a trust that is not a personal trust.

(d) *Spousal Trust*

A spousal trust is one which meets certain conditions set out in the Act. The conditions for an *inter vivos* spousal trust are provided in the Act [ssec. 73(1)]. The conditions for a testamentary spousal trust are also set out in the Act [ssec. 70(6)]. In either case, under the trust:

(a) the spouse must be entitled to receive all of the income of the trust that arises before the spouse's death; and

(b) no person except the spouse may, before the spouse's death, receive or otherwise obtain the use of any of the income or capital of the trust.

In addition, for an *inter vivos* trust to qualify as a spousal trust, both the settlor and trust must be resident in Canada at the time of transfer. In the case of a testamentary trust there is a further requirement that the property must vest in the trust within 36 months after the death of a taxpayer, or a later period where a written application has been made to the Minister.

If all of the conditions for a spousal trust have been satisfied, property is transferred to the trust for proceeds equal to its tax cost. For example, non-depreciable capital property may be transferred to the trust at its adjusted cost base, while depreciable capital property may be transferred to a trust at the property's proportionate amount of undepreciated capital cost of the class. The trust is deemed to acquire the property at a cost equal to the tax cost of the property to the transferor. The tax consequences apply automatically. No election need be filed.

An election can be made not to have the rollover provisions apply [ssecs. 70(6.2), 73(1)]. If this election is made, the general rules apply and the property will be deemed to have been disposed of for proceeds of disposition equal to its fair market value.

(e) *Alter-ego Trust*

Alter-ego trusts [defined in ssec. 248(1)] allow for a rollover of property to the trust as long as the following conditions are met:

(1) the taxpayer was entitled to receive all the income for the trust that arose before the taxpayer's death;

(2) no person, except the taxpayer could, before the taxpayer's death, receive or otherwise obtain the use of any of the income or capital of the trust;

(3) the individual who establishes the trust must be 65 years of age; and

(4) the trust is created after 1999.

This type of trust does not avoid the deemed disposition on death. That event occurs at the same time that it would have happened if no trust had been established, on the death of the taxpayer that established the trust.

(f) *Joint Spousal or Common-law Partner Trust*

Joint spousal or common-law partner trusts [defined in ssec. 248(1)], referred to as joint partner trusts, allow for a rollover of property to the trust as long as the following conditions are met:

(1) the taxpayer who created the trust and/or the taxpayer's spouse or common-law partner are entitled to receive all the income of the trust that was earned prior to the later of the death of the taxpayer and the spouse or common-law partner;

(2) that taxpayer who created the trust and/or the taxpayer's spouse or a common-law partner must be the only persons able to receive income or capital of the trust prior to the later death of the taxpayer and spouse or the common-law partner;

(3) at the time of the trust's creation, the taxpayer creating the trust was alive and had attained 65 years of age; and

(4) the trust was created after 1999.

This type of trust does not avoid the deemed disposition on death either. The deemed disposition occurs at the same time it would have happened if no trust had been established, on the death of the surviving spouse or common-law partner.

B. Settlement of Trust

As a general rule, capital property is transferred to the trust at fair market value. Therefore, if a settlor transfers capital property to a trust with accrued income and gains, these amounts will be taxed in the hands of the settlor. The trust will acquire the assets at a cost equal to their fair market value. As already noted, there are exceptions to the general rule for a qualifying spousal trust.

C. Computation of Income

[ITA: 56(4.1), (5); 74.1; 74.2; 74.3; 74.4; 74.5; 104(6), (13.1), (13.2), (14), (19), (20), (21), (21.2), (21.3), (22), (24); 108(1); 120.4; IT-394R2]

1. Income of trust

As already discussed, the net income of the trust is computed in generally the same way as is the income of any individual.

2. Income payable to beneficiary

A trust is entitled to deduct in computing its net income, income that is paid or payable to a beneficiary [ssecs. 104(6), 104(24)]. In this way, the trust is not taxed on such income, but acts as a conduit for its beneficiaries. An amount is considered to be payable to a beneficiary in a taxation year if he or she is entitled in the year to enforce payment thereof.

The income deducted from the trust's net income is taxed in the hands of the beneficiary as income from property [ssec. 108(5)] unless it falls within certain categories specified in the Act. In this case, the income retains its source for the purposes of calculating the taxable income and tax payable of the beneficiary. This special treatment applies to the following sources of income:

(a) taxable dividends from a Canadian corporation (which enables the beneficiary to utilize the dividend tax credit) [ssec. 104(19)];

(b) non-taxable dividends (which are then excluded from the computation of taxable income) [ssec. 104(20)];

(c) net taxable capital gains (net capital losses do not flow through to the beneficiary) [ssec. 104(21)]; and

(d) foreign income and its related foreign tax paid (which enables the beneficiary to take full advantage of the foreign tax credit) [ssec. 104(22)].

Net taxable capital gains of a trust (within the meaning of subsection 104(21.3)) that are allocated to individual beneficiaries and designated by the trust are eligible for the capital gains deduction available in respect of qualified farm property and qualified shares of a small business corporation [ssec. 104(21.2)]. In order to qualify, the trust must be resident in Canada throughout the year.

A trust is allowed to deduct less than the amount of income paid or payable to a beneficiary in computing its income [ssec. 104(13.1)]. This provision enables a trust to utilize its loss carryforwards without having to reduce its current income distributions. Where the trust is a testamentary trust, income splitting can be achieved, thereby allowing income to be taxed at the graduated rates, notwithstanding the fact that income has been distributed to the beneficiaries. A similar rule is provided for taxable capital gains [ssec. 104(13.2)].

Example Problem

The income of a trust for the year is $6,000 of dividends from resident Canadian public corporations. The sole beneficiary of the trust is the spouse of the deceased settlor. The trustee paid $5,000 to the beneficiary.

— REQUIRED

What is the taxable income of the trust and the spouse?

— SOLUTION

(A) Trust

Income from dividends	$6,000
Deduction [ssec. 104(6)]	5,000
Net dividend income	$1,000
Gross-up	250
Taxable income	$1,250

(B) Spouse

Income (designated [ssec. 104(19)])	$5,000
Gross-up	1,250
Taxable income	$6,250

3. Attribution

As a general rule, where an individual has transferred or loaned property to a trust for the benefit of a non-arm's length person or a niece or nephew under the age of 18, or for the benefit of the spouse, the appropriate attribution rules will operate to include the income from the property in the income of the transferor. These rules are applicable only where the trust income would otherwise be taxed in the hands of a beneficiary. The attribution rules will also apply to any property substituted for the property originally loaned or transferred to the trust. The accumulating income (other than the income that is the subject of a preferred beneficiary election, discussed subsequently) will be subject to tax in the trust. It will not be attributed back to the transferor.

Taxable capital gains and allowable capital losses realized by an *inter vivos* spousal trust and allocated out of the trust to be taxed in the hands of the beneficiary spouse will be attributed to the individual who loaned or transferred the property to the spousal trust [sec. 74.2, 74.3]. For any other *inter vivos* trust, any property income earned in the trust and allocated out to "designated persons" [defined in ssec. 74.5(5)] will be subject to attribution [secs. 74.1, 74.3].

The amount to be attributed is determined by the Act [sec. 74.3]. Only the income and capital gains earned by spouses and the income earned by non-arm's length persons and nieces or nephews under 18 ("designated persons") from loaned or transferred property are subject to the attribution rules.

The amount of income of a person that is a designated person from property loaned or transferred to a trust to be attributed to the transferor is the lesser of [par. 74.3(1)(a)]:

(a) the income of that person from the trust; and

(b) the income earned by the trust from loaned or transferred funds multiplied by the fraction where the numerator is the total income of the designated person from the trust and the denominator is the aggregate income from the trust of all designated persons.

The amount of taxable capital gains of a spouse beneficiary of a trust to be attributed is the lesser of [par. 74.3(1)(b)]:

(a) the amount designated by the trust under subsection 104(21) to be a taxable capital gain of the beneficiary spouse; and

(b) the net taxable capital gains for the year from the disposition by the trust of the property.

The exceptions to the general attribution rules provided in section 74.5 as discussed in a previous chapter also apply to trusts.

Loans of property by an individual to a non-arm's length individual or indebtedness between such individuals are also subject to the attribution rules [ssec. 56(4.1)]. Income will be taxed in the hands of the transferor if it may reasonably be considered that one of the main reasons for the loan was to reduce or avoid tax by having the income taxed in the transferee's hands. This rule will also apply where the loan is made to an individual or the indebtedness arises by means of a trust.

Example Problem

Assume that this year John Smith makes a non-interest bearing loan of $1,000 to a trust. The trust acquires a $1,000 bond. The trust has four beneficiaries: Betty Smith, John's wife, and their three children, one of whom is under 18. The income of the trust for the year prior to claiming any deductions for amounts paid or payable to the beneficiaries is $240 of which $100 is interest from the bond. All income is payable to the beneficiaries.

— REQUIRED

How much income is attributed to John Smith in the year?

— SOLUTION

There are two designated beneficiaries, Betty Smith and the child who is under 18.

The income attributed to John Smith for each designated beneficiary is determined as follows:

A = income of the designated person from the trust

= ¼ × $240 = $60

B = income of all designated persons from the trust

= $120

C = income from the loaned property

= $100

$$\frac{A}{B} \times C = \frac{\$60}{\$120} \times \$100 = \$50$$

Therefore, the total income attributed to John Smith is $50 × 2 = $100.

Two aspects of the formula should be noted. First, the income of a designated beneficiary is deemed to be received first from the income derived from property acquired with the loan. Second, the amount of income attributed in respect of the spouse or minor cannot exceed the amount of that person's income from the trust.

---

4. Tax on Split Income or "Kiddie Tax"

"Kiddie tax" [sec. 120.4] was introduced to discourage income splitting with minor children. This tax is levied at the top marginal rate and is imposed on certain income of individuals age 17 or under. The types of income which are taxed in this way are:

- taxable dividends and other shareholder benefits of unlisted Canadian and foreign companies received directly or through a trust or partnership; and

- income from a partnership or trust where the income is derived by the partnership or trust from the business of providing goods or services to a business carried on by a relative of the child or in which the relative participates.

The income subject to this tax is not eligible for any deductions or credits other than the dividend tax credit and foreign tax credit. Income taxed in this way is not subject to the regular attribution rules [ssecs. 56(5), 74.5(13)]. In addition, income that is subject to kiddie tax reduces the deemed interest benefit assessed under the corporate attribution rules [par. 74.4(2)(*g*)].

5. Accumulating income and preferred beneficiary election

In certain circumstances, a trust is entitled to a deduction in computing income for accumulated income for which an election was filed in respect of a beneficiary that is a preferred beneficiary. The preferred beneficiary election is a joint election [ssec. 104(14)] made within 90 days of the trust's year-end by both the trustees and a preferred beneficiary. As a consequence of making the election, the beneficiary is required to include in income his or her share of the accumulating income of the trust. The income in the trust, having been taxed, is not subject to tax when it is actually distributed to the beneficiaries.

A preferred beneficiary [ssec. 108(1)] is a resident of Canada who is a beneficiary of the trust and who is either the settlor of the trust, spouse or common-law partner (or former spouse or common-law partner) of the settlor, or a child, grandchild or great grandchild of the settlor of the trust (or spouses thereof) and who is entitled to the tax credit for mental or physical impairment [ssec. 118(3.1)].

D. Computation of Tax

[ITA: 104(13), (23); 122(1), (1.1); 127.5; 150(1)(*c*)]

1. Fiscal years

The fiscal year-end of an *inter vivos* trust is December 31 [spar. 249.1(1)(*b*)(i.1)]. The taxation year of a testamentary trust does not have to be on a calendar year basis; however, it cannot exceed 12 months [par. 104(23)(*a*)]. The fiscal year can be based on the year for which accounts have ordinarily been made up. The first fiscal period of a testamentary trust must end no later than one year from the death of the settlor. Whatever the fiscal year of the trust, tax returns must be filed within 90 days of the end of the trust's fiscal period [par. 150(1)(c)].

A beneficiary includes in income the amount paid or payable by the trust during the year [ssec. 104(13)]. The beneficiary includes that amount in income in the calendar year in which the trust's taxation year ends.

2. Tax rate

The Act provides that trusts are to be taxed as individuals. *Inter vivos* trusts are subject to a federal rate of 29% [ssec. 122(1)].

Testamentary trusts are subject to the same marginal rates of tax as individuals.

3. Tax credits

No deduction may be made for personal credits in computing the tax payable by a trust for a taxation year under section 118 [ssec. 122(1.1)]. However, trusts are still entitled to claim other credits such as the dividend tax credit and the foreign tax credit.

4. Minimum tax

Trusts are subject to the minimum tax in respect of income that is not paid or payable to beneficiaries.

The $40,000 exemption from the minimum tax is available only to a testamentary trust. The $40,000 exemption must be shared by all trusts that arose as a consequence of contributions to the trust by the same individual.

Where income is accumulated in the trust and a preferred beneficiary election has been made, any amounts that are non-deductible for minimum tax purposes and that were deducted in computing the trust's income must be separately identified and allocated to the trust's beneficiaries.

REVIEW QUESTIONS

(1) What does the term "partnership" mean and where would you find the definition?

(2) A limited partner can deduct in full losses allocated to that partner by the partnership. True or false? Explain.

(3) An older man, Dadd, and his son, Ladd, wish to carry on a business as a partnership. Dadd is going to contribute land, building and equipment and cash while Ladd is going to contribute energy. They have agreed that they will split the profit from the business on a 50/50 basis; however, they would allocate any capital gain on the land and building fully to Dadd. In addition, any losses in the first five years are to be allocated fully to Dadd. What are your comments on the allocation of the gains and losses?

(4) Assume that you are a partner in a partnership and you are entitled to 25% of the income. How would your income allocation and adjusted cost base be affected by a $1,200 capital gain realized by the partnership?

(5) Assume that you are a partner in a partnership and you are entitled to 25% of the income. How would your income allocation and adjusted cost base be affected by a $100,000 receipt from a life insurance policy on the death of one of your partners?

(6) Ms. Jones is about to become a partner in a partnership and she wants to contribute some property on a rollover basis under subsection 97(2). There are 13 other partners involved

although one of them has just moved to the U.S. for a four-year assignment. Should Ms. Jones have any concerns about the availability of the rollover?

(7) What is a trust?

(8) Comment on this statement: "Trusts are taxed in much the same way as partnerships; they are both conduits of income and neither is liable to pay tax".

(9) How is a testamentary and an *inter vivos* trust created?

(10) What is a discretionary trust and how does it work?

(11) One method of transferring the tax liability from the trust to the beneficiary is to either pay out the income or make it payable to the beneficiaries under subsection 104(6). What types of income retain their source for purposes of calculating the taxable income and tax payable of the beneficiary?

(12) Ms. Betty is the sole beneficiary of a trust that arose on the death of her father. He died on March 15, 2004. March 15 is the year-end chosen for the trust. When does the trust file a tax return for the fiscal period ended March 15, 2005? When does Ms. Betty report the income that is allocated to her by the trust in fiscal 2005?

(13) Mr. Bill had an income interest in a trust set up on his father's death. He now finds that he needs some capital to pay off gambling debts, so he is selling his income interest to his sister for $30,000. What are the tax implications to Mr. Bill and his sister?

(14) Ms. Daisy had a capital interest in a trust set up on her father's death. She now finds that she needs some capital to pay off shopping debts, so she is selling her interest in the trust to her chauffeur for $45,000. What are the tax implications to Ms. Daisy and her chauffeur?

MULTIPLE CHOICE QUESTIONS

Question 1

Bert & Ernie
Partnership Income Statement
For the year ended December 31, 2005

Income:

Consulting fees		$300,000
Dividends received from taxable Canadian corporations		40,000
Gain of sale of shares of taxable Canadian corporations		120,000
		$460,000

Expenses:

Salaries to staff	$50,000	
Capital cost allowance on equipment	15,000	
Office rent	10,000	
Charitable donations	20,000	$ 95,000
Net income		$365,000

Bert and Ernie each took drawings of $30,000 in the year.

Bert and Ernie share income from the partnership equally. Bert has no other source of income in 2005. Bert will have taxable income in 2005 of:

(A) $182,500

(B) $187,500

(C) $167,500

(D) $162,500

Question 2

On January 1, 2005, Ann and Bob formed a partnership to provide window cleaning services. The partners each contributed $5,000 and agreed that all income and losses would be shared equally. For the fiscal period January 1 to December 31, 2005, the following information is available.

(1) The partnership earned income for tax purposes of $200,000. Included in this amount is a taxable capital gain of $40,000.

(2) The partnership made charitable donations of $12,000.

(3) Ann took draws totalling $70,000.

(4) Ann contributed additional capital of $14,000 to the partnership.

The adjusted cost base of Ann's partnership interest at January 1, 2006, is:

(A) $33,000

(B) $43,000

(C) $63,000

(D) $69,000

Question 3

Al Smith settled a trust in favour of his two children on May 1, 2005. He settled the trust with marketable securities worth $50,000. His adjusted cost base for the marketable securities was $20,000. Al, his wife, and a family friend were named as trustees. His two children are ages five and six. Which one of the following statements is FALSE?

(A) The tax return for the first year of the trust is due March 30, 2006.

(B) The trust is entitled to a deduction in computing its income for amounts paid to the children during the year.

(C) Income in the trust will be subject to a 29% federal rate of tax.

(D) Al can defer the recognition of the capital gain on the transfer of the securities to the trust.

Question 4

The James Stewart family trust was created on and as a consequence of the death of James Stewart on May 1, 2005. Which one of the following statements with respect to the trust is TRUE?

(A) The trust must have a December 31 year-end.

(B) The income in the trust will be subject to the same graduated rates of tax applicable to individuals.

(C) The trust return is due six months after the year-end of the trust.

(D) The trust is not entitled to claim a dividend tax credit for dividends received and retained in the trust.

Question 5

Which of the following types of trusts has a deemed disposition of all its assets at fair market value on the settlor's death?

(A) An *inter vivos* trust

(B) A joint partner trust

(C) An alter ego trust

(D) A discretionary trust

Question 6

Which of the following is **not** an advantage of providing for testamentary trusts in your will for each of your children with a giftover to your grandchildren on each child's death?

(A) Income-splitting using the subsections 104(13.1) and (13.2) designations.

(B) Avoiding a deemed disposition of assets at fair market value on the child's death that would result if the assets were left directly to the child.

(C) Avoiding the deemed disposition of trust assets at fair market value at the end of 21 years.

(D) Providing your children with beneficial ownership over their inheritances, but giving control over their inheritances to the trustees of each trust.

EXERCISES

Exercise 1

[ITA: 96; 110.1; 118.1; 121]

The following income statement was prepared for Bob and Stan Tax Services, a partnership of two individuals who share income equally:

Bob and Stan Tax Services

INCOME STATEMENT

for the year ended December 31, 2005

Gross revenue from operations		$400,000
Less: Depreciation on office furniture	$ 3,750	
Donations to charities	5,500	
Dues to Canadian Tax Foundation	550	
Employees' salaries	67,220	
Fringe benefits for employees	11,500	
Heat, light and water	2,400	
Interest expense	725	
Membership in fitness club	1,250	
Office rent	9,000	
Office supplies	2,250	
Repairs and maintenance	575	104,720
		$295,280
Dividends received from a taxable Canadian corporation		4,000
Capital gain		5,000
Net income		$304,280

Additional Information

(1) Maximum capital cost allowance on the furniture for the year is $4,300.

(2) The partners each took drawings of $54,000 in the year.

— *REQUIRED*

Bob is your client. He has received personal investment income consisting of $3,500 in Canadian-source dividends and $1,200 in interest income. Determine his taxable income for 2005 and analyze the nature of his income.

Income Tax

ation in Canada

Exercise 2

[ITA: 53(1)(e); 53(2)(c)]

Early in 2000 a partnership was formed between David and Katie to carry on a professional accounting practice. Both partners made an initial contribution of $50,000 at that time agreeing to make equal drawings and to share equally in the profits and losses of the practice. The following data pertain to the partnership business during the period from its inception to the present:

Income of the partnership during the period	$450,000
Losses of the partnership during the period	15,000
Net taxable capital gains included in the above income (2003)	20,000
Drawings by the partners in the period	176,000
Capital dividends received by the partnership	4,000
Charitable donations made by the partnership	27,000
In 2005, Katie will retire from the partnership and will receive in full settlement of her partnership interest	250,000

— REQUIRED

What are the tax consequences to Katie of the disposition of her partnership interest in 2005?

Exercise 3

[ITA: 104]

On January 1, 2005, Mr. Ruester settled a trust for the benefit of his two children, Rebecca and Robert, both over the age of 18, neither of whom has other income. Robert attends, for eight months a year, a university in Canada where tuition is $3,500 per year. All tuition for 2005 was paid in respect of that year. Under the terms of the trust, the trustees have complete discretion to allocate the accumulated income to the beneficiaries in any manner they wish. The trust earned income from cash transferred to the trust by Mr. Ruester. For the 2005 taxation year, the trust received the following income:

Interest	$11,500
Dividends received from a taxable Canadian corporation	9,000
Capital gain	9,000

The trustees paid the income, and made the appropriate designations as follows:

	Interest	Dividend	Capital gain
Rebecca	$5,500	$3,000	$3,000
Robert	1,500	3,000	3,000
Total paid	$7,000	$6,000	$6,000
Total income accumulated in trust	$4,500	$3,000	$3,000

The remaining income was accumulated in the trust.

— REQUIRED

Compute the taxable income and the federal taxes payable of the trust and each beneficiary.

ASSIGNMENT PROBLEMS

Problem 1

[ITA: 53(1)(*e*); 53(2)(*c*)]

The following income statement was prepared for Ludlum, Clancy, Follet & Associates, a partnership comprised of four partners who share income equally:

Ludlum, Clancy, Follet & Associates
INCOME STATEMENT
for the year ended December 31, 2005

Gross revenue		$994,250
Less:		
Professional staff employee salaries	$229,000	
Office salaries	74,000	
Rent	42,000	
Office supplies	17,000	
Client entertainment	5,075	
Capital cost allowance	16,222	
Donations to charities	250,000	633,297
		$360,953
Gain on sale of securities of public companies	$100,000	
Dividend income:		
Dividends received from taxable Canadian corporations	25,000	
Capital dividends	5,000	130,000
Net income for accounting purposes		$490,953

The adjusted cost base to Mr. Clancy of his partnership interest was $45,792 at the beginning of the year. His drawings for the year were $77,500.

— *REQUIRED*

(A) Compute the partnership income for the year, the income to be allocated to Mr. Clancy and the nature of the income.

(B) Compute Mr. Clancy's taxable income and tax payable for 2005 assuming a marginal federal tax rate of 29%. Assume a provincial tax on income rate of 17%.

(C) Compute the adjusted cost base to Mr. Clancy of his partnership interest.

Problem 2

[ITA: 53(1)(*e*); 53(2)(*c*)]

Early in 2000, Guiseppe, Cristina, Giovanni and Brunco formed a partnership to carry on a snow removal and landscape business. All the partners, except Cristina, made an initial contribution of $40,000. Cristina made an initial contribution of $80,000. Each agreed to share in the profits and losses of the practice based on their initial capital contribution. At the end of the 2005 fiscal year of the partnership, Cristina and Brunco decided to go their separate ways. Brunco received $125,000 for his partnership interest, while Cristina received $250,000. The tax records for the five years ended December 31, 2004 reflected the following cumulative amounts:

Income (before capital gains) from operations for tax purposes	$750,000
Losses	80,000
Capital gains (2000-2004)	10,000
Drawings by the partners	730,000*
Charitable donations (added back to Division B income for tax purposes)	15,000

* Cristina, $170,000; Guiseppe, $150,000; Brunco, $250,000; and Giovanni, $160,000.

Financial results for the year ended December 31, 2005, are as follows:

Net income per financial statements	$60,000
Charitable donations (deducted from accounting income)	2,000
Drawings:	
Cristina	10,000
Brunco	5,000
Guiseppe	5,000
Giovanni	4,000

Other Information

(1) Cristina is single, and has interest income of $2,500 for the year 2005.

(2) Brunco is divorced, has interest income of $6,600, and paid his former spouse $16,000 for her support in 2005. He has made an RRSP contribution in 2005 of $2,700 (his 2004 earned income was $15,000).

— REQUIRED

(A) Compute the partnership income for the year ended December 31, 2005, and the income to be allocated to the partners.

(B) What are the tax consequences to Brunco and Cristina as a result of the disposition of their partnership interests in 2005?

(C) Compute Brunco's and Cristina's taxable income and tax payable for 2005 using the hypothetical provincial tax rate table presented in Chapter 10.

Problem 3

[ITA: 22; 97(2)]

Adam and Amit formed a partnership this year to operate a retail store specializing in gag gifts. Adam, who has been in the business since 1989 as a sole proprietor, owned the following assets:

	Cost amount	Fair market value
Accounts receivable	$17,500	$ 17,000
Inventory	22,000	22,000
Store fixtures (cost: $17,500)	16,000	19,500
Leasehold improvements (cost: $37,500)	33,500	35,000
Goodwill	—	40,000
	$89,000	$133,500

Adam transferred these assets to the partnership on February 1, 2005, in exchange for a 60% partnership interest. Amit contributed $59,000 in cash and marketable securities with a fair market value of $30,000 in return for a 40% interest. The marketable securities were purchased in 1994 at a cost of $25,000.

— REQUIRED

(A) How can Adam's assets be transferred to the partnership without immediate tax consequences? What is the cost to the partnership of Adam's assets?

(B) What is the maximum non-partnership consideration that Adam can receive without adverse tax consequences?

(C) What is the adjusted cost base of his partnership interest to Adam, assuming that the only consideration received for the transferred assets is a partnership interest?

(D) What is the adjusted cost base of his partnership interest to Amit, assuming that (i) the only consideration received for the transferred assets is a partnership interest and (ii) Amit and the partnership elected jointly to have the rollover provisions of subsection 97(2) apply to the transfer?

Problem 4

Part A

[ITA: 117(2); 122; 248(1)]

Identify the federal rate of tax payable by each of the following trusts settled by Mrs. A:

(a) On June 1, 2005, Mrs. A settled a maple leaf gold coin on her daughters, B and C, in trust for her grandchildren.

(b) Mrs. A's will provides that her shares of ABC Co. are to be held in trust for her grandchildren.

(c) Same as (b) above; however, subsequent to Mrs. A's death, Mrs. A's daughter, B, transfers assets to the trust.

Part B

[ITA: 70(6)]

Mr. B died on March 15, 2005. Mr. B's will provides that the residue of his estate is to be transferred to a trust for the benefit of his wife, Mrs. B, a resident of Canada. The will provides that the income of the trust is to be paid to Mrs. B. The will also provides for a liberal power to encroach on capital for the benefit of Mrs. B. On Mrs. B's death, the trust's assets are to be distributed to the Bs' children. Mr. B's assets include shares of ABC Inc. which were purchased in 1979 for $10 and have a fair market value at his death of $1,000.

— *REQUIRED*

(A) What are the tax consequences to Mr. B arising out of the transfer of the ABC Inc. shares to the trust for Mrs. B?

(B) How would your answer to (A) be different if Mr. B's will provided the trustees with the power to encroach on capital for the benefit of the Bs' children?

Part C

[ITA: 104(13.1), (13.2); 108(1)]

Mrs. Jones died in 1999. Under the terms of her will, an investment portfolio was settled on Mr. Shrewd and Mrs. Clever, as trustees, for the benefit of her daughter, Hilary Jones. In 2005, the trust will have substantial income comprised almost exclusively of capital gains. The trust has a non-capital loss carryforward which arose three years ago.

— *REQUIRED*

Hilary's income from other sources is substantial with the result that any allocation of income from the trust to her will increase her overall tax liability. Is there any strategy that can be adopted by the trustees in order to reduce the taxes payable in respect of a distribution to Hilary?

Problem 5

[ITA: 104]

On January 1, 2003, Mr. Bucks settled a trust for his daughter Jane, who became age 17 in 2003. The trust was documented by a written agreement. There are three trustees, Mr. Bucks, Mrs. Bucks and a long-time family friend. Among other important provisions, the trust provided that the trustees had complete discretion to distribute any portion of the annual income of the trust to the beneficiary.

Mr. Bucks transferred the following assets into the trust on January 1, 2003:

(a) $250,000 cash; and

(b) 1,500 shares of Successful Retailers Ltd., a corporation that is incorporated in Canada and is listed on the CDNX Exchange. The original cost of the shares in 1982 when they were purchased by Mr. Bucks was $17 per share. At the date of transfer the fair market value was $20 per share.

The trust purchased a rental property with the $250,000 cash early in January 2003. The value of the property was allocated 55% to the land and 45% to the building. The rental income before capital cost allowance but after all other expenses is estimated to be $12,000 per annum.

The amount of dividends paid on the Successful Retailers Ltd. shares for each of 2003 and 2004 is $7,500. The estimated dividend to be paid in 2005 is $7,500.

On July 1, 2005, the trust sold the rental property for $350,000, allocating 60% to the land and 40% to the building.

In each year, the trust "accumulated" 60% of the income earned and paid out the remainder before capital cost allowance to the beneficiary to meet her financial needs.

— REQUIRED

(A) Outline the income tax consequences to Mr. Bucks of the transfer of property to the trust in 2003.

(B) Calculate the amount of net income allocable to each of Mr. Bucks, Jane and the trust in 2003, 2004 and 2005, assuming that no elections under the Act have been utilized.

(C) What steps could have been taken when the trust was established to minimize the income allocable to Mr. Bucks?

(D) Calculate the taxes payable by Jane and the trust in 2005. Use the hypothetical individual tax rate table presented in Chapter 10.

Problem 6

[ITA: 84(1); 85; 86; 104; 129(6)]

Mr. Wealthy is 55 years old. He is the President and sole shareholder of Amazing Results Inc. ("Amazing"). Amazing was incorporated in 1982. At the time of incorporation, Mr. Wealthy subscribed for 100 common shares without par value for subscription proceeds of $100. These are still the only shares that are issued and outstanding.

Amazing has been involved in the lobbying business and achieves results for its clients which are considered to be simply amazing. Amazing has just been involved in a very successful high-profile lobbying effort. Business is booming. Amazing has been a very profitable company. It is estimated that the fair market value of the shares is $1,000,000 today. Mr. Wealthy believes that the value of the shares of Amazing will increase dramatically over the next two years to about $3,000,000.

Included in Amazing's assets is land and building (the "real estate") which is located steps away from the provincial legislature. The real estate was purchased in 1985 for $200,000 and is estimated to be worth about $700,000 today. The cost and value of the real estate is allocated

50/50 between land and building. The undepreciated capital cost of the building as at today's date is $35,000. It is estimated that the property will be worth about $1,200,000 within five years.

Mr. Wealthy is divorced with three children. Wendy is 30 years old and very active in the business. Her intention is to make a career out of Amazing. Wayne, who is 25 years old, is an artist with no interest in Amazing. Winona, who is 15 years old, is a high school student with no income. She has stated her intention is to become a doctor. She attends a private school to which Mr. Wealthy pays $4,000 tuition annually.

Mr. Wealthy would like to retire from active involvement in Amazing within the next 10 years. He estimates that he will continue to require an income of $50,000 per year thereafter. He wants to take action now so that, in the event of his death, he will not be taxed on the expected growth of Amazing in the next five years.

Mr. Wealthy has decided that a plan should be implemented to ensure that Wendy will benefit from the future growth of Amazing. At the same time, Mr. Wealthy wants to be fair to Wayne and Winona by providing them with some benefits from the growth of his estate in the future. He wants to maintain sufficient control over Amazing during his life in the event that Wendy does not fulfil his expectations of her involvement in the business. Mr. Wealthy tells you that his neighbour has "frozen" everything in favour of his children as a means of saving taxes. Mr. Wealthy would like to freeze everything too. Mr. Wealthy has never claimed a capital gains exemption.

— REQUIRED

(A) Advise Mr. Wealthy of the tax consequences and merits of the following proposals to achieve his objectives:

(i) Mr. Wealthy would transfer the shares of Amazing, using section 85, to a corporation (Holdco) of which Wendy holds the common shares. Mr. Wealthy would receive as consideration preferred shares with a P.U.C. of $100 and a redemption value of $600,000.

(ii) The same as in (i); however, the consideration for the transfer would be a promissory note of Holdco for $500,000 and fixed-value preferred shares of Holdco with a redemption value and legal stated capital of $500,000.

(iii) Mr. Wealthy would exchange the shares of Amazing for a newly-created class of fixed-value preferred shares of Amazing. Mr. Wealthy has been advised that under corporate law the stated capital of the fixed-value preferred shares can be $1,000,000. He would like the paid-up capital to be $1,000,000 since he understands that paid-up capital can be returned to him tax free.

(iv) Mr. Wealthy would cause Amazing to transfer its land and building to a new corporation in exchange for preferred shares of the new corporation having a fair market value of $700,000 and then lease the real estate back from the new corporation. The common shares of the new corporation would be owned by Wayne and Winona.

(B) Suggest to Mr. Wealthy an alternative to his plans, taking into consideration his age and objectives.

Problem 7

[ITA: 74.1; 74.3; 74.5; 84.1; 85; 86; 104(6), (13.1), (13.2); 122(1), (1.1); 150(1); 249(1)(*b*)]

Cora Dusk owns 100% of the common shares of a corporation, Cee Ltd. These shares have an original cost of $1,000, a paid-up capital of $1,000 and a fair market value of $1,800,000. At the current time, the common shares are the only shares of Cee Ltd. that are issued and outstanding.

Cora is a Canadian resident, 70 years old and a recent widow. She wants to freeze the value of her common shares of Cee Ltd. in favour of a trust for her children and grandchildren. Cora has a 40 year-old daughter, Jordan, and a 35 year-old daughter, Susanne. All of Cora's grandchildren are under the age of 10. Her current will leaves these shares equally to Jordan and Susanne.

Cee Ltd. carries on a real estate rental business and has nine full-time employees throughout the year, including Cora, Jordan and Susanne. The company qualifies as a small business corporation and the shares which Cora owns meet all the tests to be qualified small business corporation (QSBC) shares.

Cora's plan is to settle one trust for her daughters and grandchildren with $100. The trust would use the $100 to subscribe and pay for 100 common shares of a holding company (Holdco Inc.) at a cost of $1 each. The trustees of the trust will be Jordan, Susanne and the family's lawyer and decisions would be made by a majority of trustees. The trust agreement would allow the trustees discretion as to the allocation of income to beneficiaries on an annual basis. The trust agreement would provide that, at the end of 21 years, the trust capital would be distributed equally to the children of Jordan and Susanne.

Cora would then sell her common shares of Cee Ltd. to Holdco Inc. Since she wants to crystallize the $400,000 remainder of her lifetime QSBC capital gains exemption when she freezes the value of her shares, she plans to make an election under section 85 of the Act in the amount of $401,000. She will receive $401,000 of debt, with the balance of the consideration being Holdco Inc. shares with a fair market value and legal stated capital of $1,399,000 from Holdco Inc. in return for her common shares of Cee Ltd.

Cora currently pays tax at the top marginal rate, but Jordan and Susanne do not because of child care expenses, RRSP contributions and other deductions and tax credits.

— *REQUIRED*

(A)(i) Determine the tax consequences of Cora transferring her common shares of Cee Ltd. to a holding company using the plan to set out above. Show all calculations.

(ii) What improvements do you recommend to the plan set out above? Briefly explain your reasons.

(B) Provide a brief explanation of an alternative way of freezing the value of Cee Ltd. that accomplishes Cora's objectives, but does not involve setting up a holding company.

[For more problems and solutions thereto, see the CD accompanying this book.]

SUPPLEMENTAL NOTES

(This section can be omitted without losing the continuity of the chapter. None of the review questions, multiple choice questions, exercises or assignment problems utilizes this information.)

A. Partnerships

[ITA: 125(1)(*a*), (6); 53(1)(*e*)(iv); 98(3), (5), (6); IT-471R]

1. Corporate partnerships

A partnership may have, as its partners, a number of corporations. At one time, corporate partnerships were used as a means of multiplying the use of the small business deduction. The Act now provides that corporate partners must share the benefit of a single annual small business deduction by allocating one annual business limit ($300,000 for calendar year 2005 and later taxation years) among them with respect to the partnership income as discussed in Chapter 12. This limitation applies whether or not the corporations are associated. However, partners, who are not associated, may have additional active business income from sources other than the partnership. This income may be added to the annual business limit allocated to them from the partnership income up to the maximum of $300,000 in total (for calendar year 2005 and later taxation years).

There are a number of anti-avoidance rules in the Act to prevent the multiplication of the small business deduction. Where a corporation or an associated corporation is a member of more than one partnership and it may reasonably be considered that one of the main reasons for the separate existence of the partnership is to increase the amount of the small business deduction of any corporation, the specified partnership income of the corporation for the year (within the meaning of paragraph 125(7)(*f*)) will be the income from the partnership with the greatest income [ssec. 125(6)]. The income of all other partnerships will be deemed to be nil for the purpose of determining that corporation's specified partnership income. For example, suppose A Co. Ltd. is a partner of ABC partnership and BCA partnership. The specified partnership income of ABC partnership is $300 and the specified partnership income of BCA partnership is $100. For purposes of this rule, the specified partnership income of A Co. Ltd. in respect of ABC partnership is $300; the specified partnership income of A Co. Ltd. in respect of BCA partnership is nil.

Where a corporation is a member of a partnership which is itself a member of a partnership, there is a look-through rule which ensures that a corporation that is a member of a partnership is deemed to be the member of the second partnership [ssec. 125(6.1)].

Example Problem ─────────────────────────────────

A partnership of two unassociated corporations A Ltd. and B Ltd. earns $400,000 of active business income in the year. In addition, A Ltd. earns $50,000 of active business income from a second business venture.

— REQUIRED

Determine how much income of A Ltd. and B. Ltd. is eligible for the small business deduction if they allocate equally their entitlement to the small business deduction on partnership income.

— SOLUTION

A Ltd. —Specified partnership income equal to the
      lesser of:
      (a) share of partnership income (50% of
          $400,000) $200,000
                                                  $150,000
      (b) share of business limit (50% of $300,000) $150,000

Income from other venture 50,000

Income entitled to small business deduction $200,000

B Ltd. —Specified partnership income as computed above $150,000

The remaining $50,000 of income of the partnership for each partner is subject to the higher corporate rates of tax discussed in previous chapters.

2. Transfer of property from a partnership

(a) *Cessation of a Partnership*

Under the general rules, if a partnership transfers property to one of the partners, there is a deemed disposition of that property at fair market value. However, in the situation where a partnership ceases to exist, there is an opportunity for a Canadian partnership to transfer the property to a partner on a tax-deferred basis [ssec. 98(3)].

The partnership is deemed to have disposed of each property at its tax cost. Each partner is deemed to acquire an undivided interest in each property equal to his or her percentage of the cost amount to the partnership of the property.

Each partner must take an undivided interest in each property distributed under the rollover. This means that each former partner will own an interest in each property of the former partnership equal to his or her interest in the partnership. This will prevent partners in a low tax bracket from taking property with high accrued income and partners in a high tax bracket from taking property with low accrued income to minimize the ultimate tax consequences of the liquidation. As a result each partner will share in the tax consequences inherent in the accrued capital gains or recapture on each property.

Each partner is deemed to have disposed of his or her partnership interest for proceeds equal to the greater of:

(a) the adjusted cost base of his or her partnership interest; or

(b) cash plus his or her share of the cost amount to the partnership of property distributed. ("Cost amount" is defined [ssec. 248(1)].)

The cost to each partner of his or her share of property distributed to him or her can be increased by the excess of (a) over (b) above [par. 98(3)(c)]. The excess can be added to non-depreciable capital property up to the fair market value of that property. If any excess remains after the allocation to non-depreciable capital property, it cannot be allocated to any other property.

The assumption of partnership liabilities by a partner prior to the cessation of the partnership is a contribution of capital to the partnership that increases the adjusted cost base to him or her of his or her partnership interest [spar. 53(1)(e)(iv)].

Example Problem ───

Debits and Credits, Chartered Accountants, is a partnership that was formed several years ago. At that time Ms. Debit contributed $60,000 cash as consideration for her $\frac{3}{4}$ partnership interest. The adjusted cost base of Ms. Debit's partnership interest is now $75,000.

The partnership is going to cease to exist with both partners taking an undivided interest in each property. The attributes of the partnership property at the date of the cessation of the partnership are the following:

Property	Cost amount	F.M.V.
Supplies inventory	$24,000	$35,000
Land	15,000	20,000
Building	33,000	40,000
	$72,000	$95,000

── *REQUIRED*

What are the tax consequences to Ms. Debit on dissolution of the partnership?

── *SOLUTION*

Proceeds of disposition of partnership interest [par. 98(3)(*a*)]
    Greater of:
        (a) partner's share of cost amount ($\frac{3}{4}$ × $72,000) $54,000
        (b) A.C.B. of partnership interest......................... 75,000

Since the proceeds of disposition ($75,000) equals the adjusted cost base to Ms. Debit of her partnership interest, there is no gain or loss to her on the cessation of the partnership. However, because the cost to Ms. Debit of her partnership interest exceeds her share of the cost amount to the partnership of the property distributed to her ($54,000), the excess ($21,000) can be added to non-depreciable capital property up to the fair market value of that property, as follows:

	Undivided interest $\frac{3}{4}$ of cost amount	Par. 98(3)(c) allocation	Increased cost
Supplies inventory	$18,000	—	$18,000
Land	11,250	$3,750	15,000
Building	24,750	—	24,750
	$54,000	$3,750	$57,750

The potential bump to the adjusted cost base of the land is limited to $\frac{3}{4}$ of the fair market value of the land (i.e., $\frac{3}{4}$ × $20,000). The excess of $17,250 (i.e., $21,000 − $3,750) cannot be allocated to any other property.

──

(b) *Sole Proprietorship*

If one of the partners continues to operate the business as a sole proprietorship within 3 months of the dissolution of the partnership (the "proprietor"), an automatic rollover is available to the proprietor [ssec. 98(5)]. This rollover applies to the partnership assets that are used by the proprietor to carry on the business. The partnership must be a Canadian partnership.

The partnership is deemed to have disposed of the partnership assets to the proprietor for proceeds of disposition equal to their cost amount. The cost to the proprietor of each property received by him or her is equal to its cost amount. The proprietor is deemed to have disposed of his or her partnership interest for proceeds of disposition equal to the greater of:

(a) the adjusted cost base of his or her partnership interest; and

(b) the cost amount to the partnership of property received by him or her used to carry on the business plus the fair market value of any property distributed to him or her but not used to carry on the business.

Note that, because the deemed proceeds of disposition are at least equal to the adjusted cost base of his or her partnership interest, the proprietor may realize a capital gain on the disposition of his or her partnership interest, but not a capital loss.

The cost to the proprietor of each property received by him or her can be increased by the excess of (a) over (b) [par. 98(5)(c)]. The excess can be added to non-depreciable capital property up to the fair market value of that property. If any excess remains after the allocation to non-depreciable capital property, it cannot be allocated to any other property.

In the event of a loss on property transferred to the partnership, the rules permit an allocation within limits of the potential loss to the assets received for the continuation of the business.

Example Problem

Schlemeel and Schlemozzle have operated a partnership for 10 years. Schlemozzle plans to retire this year while Schlemeel carries on the partnership business on his own. The following partnership property will be used in Schlemeel's business:

Property	Cost amount	F.M.V.
Inventory	$ 5,000	$ 6,000
Land	24,000	26,000
Building	40,000	46,000
	$69,000	$78,000

In addition Schlemeel is to receive other consideration having a fair market value of $5,000 for his partnership interest.

Schlemeel's partnership interest has an adjusted cost base of $80,000.

— *REQUIRED*

What are the tax consequences to Schlemeel?

— *SOLUTION*

Deemed proceeds of disposition of partnership interest [par. 98(5)(a)]

Greater of:
(a) cost amount of property plus other consideration
    ($69,000 + $5,000)..................................... $74,000
(b) A.C.B. of partnership interest......................... 80,000

Since the proceeds of disposition ($80,000) equal the cost to Schlemeel of his partnership interest, there is no gain or loss to him on the transfer of the partnership assets to the proprietorship. However, because the cost to Schlemeel of his partnership interest exceeds the cost amount of the partnership property used by him in the proprietorship and other consideration ($74,000), the excess ($6,000) can be added to non-depreciable capital property up to the fair market value of that property, as follows:

Property	Cost amount	Par. 98(5)(c) allocation	Cost
Inventory	$ 5,000	—	$ 5,000
Land	24,000	$2,000	26,000
Building	40,000	—	40,000
	$69,000	$2,000	$71,000
Other consideration			$ 5,000

Note the fair market value upper limit on the allocation of the loss for capital property. The excess ($4,000) cannot be allocated to any other property.

(c) *Continuation of Partnership*

A partner may withdraw from the partnership and the remaining partners may continue to carry on the business in a new partnership. Depending on the terms of the partnership agreement, the withdrawal of a partner may result in a dissolution of the original partnership. Under the general rules this would result in the disposition of the partnership property by the partnership and the partnership interests by the remaining partners. However, a specific rollover provision [ssec. 98(6)] allows the new partnership to be a continuation of the original partnership. Any member's partnership interest in the new partnership is deemed to be a continuation of his or her partnership interest in the original partnership. All of the property of the original partnership must be transferred to the new partnership and all of the members of the new partnership must have been members of the original partnership [ssec. 98(6)]. This provision applies only to Canadian partnerships.

The partners of the new partnership must consist only of partners who were members of the old partnership [ssec. 98(6)]. Therefore, it does not apply to the situation where one or more new partners are admitted to the new partnership. However, in such a case, the original partnership could be dissolved using the rollover provision of subsection 98(3) and the remaining partners, along with any new partners, could use the rollover rules in subsection 97(2) to transfer property to the new partnership. A similar combination of the rollovers in subsection 98(3) and subsection 97(2) would have to be used to merge two or more existing partnerships into one new partnership such that all transfers involved could be made on a tax-deferred basis. This is the subject of discussion in IT-471R. Note, however, that the provisions in subsection 97(2) and subsection 98(3) apply only to Canadian partnerships and that a joint election is required under subsection 97(2).

B. Dispositions from Trust

[ITA: 104(4); 106(2)(*a*), (*c*); 106(3); 107(1)(*a*), (2), (4.1); 108(1)]

1. Disposition of capital property

(a) *Deemed Dispositions*

All capital properties held by a trust are deemed to be disposed of 21 years after [ssec. 104(4)]:

(a) the surviving spouse's death in the case of a spousal trust;

(b) the later of the trust's inception date and January 1, 1972 for all non-spousal trusts; or

(c) the previous date of deemed disposition for all trusts.

For deemed dispositions of depreciable capital property under the 21-year rule discussed below, the trust is deemed to dispose and reacquire the depreciable property at its fair market value. However, where the capital cost prior to the disposition was greater than the deemed proceeds (i.e., the F.M.V.), then the original capital cost will still be the capital cost for capital cost allowance purposes and the difference will be deemed to be capital cost allowance subject to future potential recapture by the trust [ssec. 104(5)].

For non-depreciable property, the trust is deemed to have disposed of, and reacquired the assets at fair market value. It is then taxed upon the applicable capital gains or losses arising from the difference between the fair market value and adjusted cost base of each asset [ssec. 104(4)].

Until 1999, a trust could elect to defer the application of the 21-year deemed disposition rule until the interests of exempt beneficiaries under the trust have terminated. An exempt beneficiary would include a child, spouse or parent of the settlor. An exempt beneficiary would not include a member of any generation after the child (for example, the settlor's grandchild). Once the election was made, the trust would not be permitted to distribute the trust property on a tax-free basis except to beneficiaries that are exempt beneficiaries. Capital property, land inventory and resource property held on January 1, 2000 by a trust that made the election to defer application of the 21-year rule will be deemed to be disposed of by the trust on that day for proceeds equal to fair market value.

(b) *Actual Dispositions*

When a trust disposes of capital property through an actual transaction, it is subject to tax on the difference between the proceeds of disposition and the adjusted cost base for each property. The difference is a capital gain or a capital loss, as the case may be.

2. Disposition of income interest

A person has an income interest in a trust when he or she has a right as a beneficiary under the trust to receive all or any part of the income of the trust. A taxpayer with an income interest in a trust having income which is currently payable to him or her is currently liable to pay tax on that income.

On disposition of an income interest to a third party, the Act requires the beneficiary to include the full proceeds of disposition in income [par. 106(2)(a)]. The cost of this income interest and any income currently payable to him or her by the trust are fully deductible against the proceeds of disposition. The income interest is not a capital property.

Distributions of property by the trust to the beneficiary in satisfaction of his or her income interest are deemed to have been acquired by the beneficiary at fair market value. There are no income tax consequences to the beneficiary. The trust, however, will be deemed to dispose of the property at fair market value. This may, depending on the circumstances, trigger capital gains and recapture.

3. Disposition of capital interest

A capital interest in a personal trust is a right of the taxpayer as a beneficiary under the trust to receive all or any part of the capital of the trust. This interest is a capital property.

Disposition of a capital interest, like other capital property, may result in either a capital gain or capital loss to the beneficiary. Capital gains are computed as the excess, if any, of proceeds of disposition over the greater of [par. 107(1)(a)]:

(a) adjusted cost base of capital interest; and

(b) "cost amount" to the beneficiary.

"Cost amount" is defined as the beneficiary's proportionate interest of the tax cost of the trust's assets less its liabilities. Capital losses on disposition of a capital interest are computed by deducting the proceeds of disposition from the adjusted cost base, as for any capital property.

In general, if the beneficiary of the personal trust receives a distribution of property from the trust in satisfaction of all or part of his or her capital interest, the trust is deemed to dispose of the property for its cost amount and the beneficiary is deemed to acquire the property at its cost amount [ssec. 107(2)].

It is not possible to defer a gain by a commercial trust on a disposition of its property in satisfaction of a capital interest.

C. GST and Partnerships

[ETA: 123(1); 141.1(3); 167(1); 174; 175; 253; 272.1(1)–(7); Sch. V, Part VII]

1. Treatment of Partnerships under the Excise Tax Act

The term "partnership" is not defined in the ETA. Consequently, the problems that arise for income tax purposes in determining whether a partnership exists also arise for GST purposes. The discussion earlier in this chapter on the nature of a partnership should be reviewed in the context of GST.

Unlike the treatment of partnerships under the *Income Tax Act*, for GST purposes, partnerships are treated as if they are separate legal entities and there is no flow-through to partners. Commercial activities engaged in by the members of a partnership are deemed to be commercial activities of the partnership [ETA: sec. 272.1]. Consequently, partnerships are required to register and collect GST on taxable supplies. Individual partners are not required to register separately for GST purposes.

Generally, it is the partnership, rather than the individual partners, that is entitled to claim input tax credits for GST paid on purchases of property and services used in the commercial activities of the partnership. However, members (other than individuals) of a partnership are entitled to claim input tax credits for GST paid by them on purchases used in the commercial activities of the partnership [ETA: ssec. 272.1(2)]. This provision applies to members of a partnership that are corporations, trusts or other partnerships.

Where a partnership pays a reasonable allowance to a partner for travel and other expenses incurred in Canada on which the partner has paid GST, the partnership may claim an input tax credit equal to 7/107ths[c] of the allowance [ETA: sec. 174]. This provision was referred to in Chapter 4 in the context of employer allowances.

Similarly, where a partner incurs an expense that is reimbursed by the partnership, any GST included in the reimbursement is deemed to have been paid by the partnership [ETA: sec. 175]. As a result, the partnership may claim an input tax credit under this provision, provided that the partner has not claimed a credit [ssec. 272.1(2)].

A rebate of GST may be claimed by partners in certain circumstances [ETA: sec. 253]. This rebate is similar to the rebate available to employees, as discussed in Chapter 3. The rebate is available to individual members of a partnership who incur expenses outside the partnership that are subject to GST and that are deductible in computing the individual's income from the partnership (an individual is defined to mean a natural person [ETA: ssec. 123(1)]). This rebate is also available in respect of capital cost allowance claimed in respect of a motor vehicle, aircraft or a musical instrument, provided the purchase of the property was subject to GST. As well, the

---

[c] 15/115ths for HST purposes.

rebate is available in respect of leases of musical instruments, motor vehicles or aircraft, and in respect of an importation of any property. The rebate is calculated as 7/107ths[(d)] of the amount deducted for income tax purposes (including GST and provincial sales tax). For income tax purposes, the portion of the rebate that relates to expenses other than capital cost allowance will be added to the partner's income, while the amount in respect of capital cost allowance will reduce the capital cost under subsection 13(7.1) of the *Income Tax Act*.

As discussed in Chapter 3 in the context of employees, a partner is also not entitled to claim a GST rebate under this provision in respect of expenses for which the partner has received an allowance, unless the partnership certifies that it did not consider the allowance to be reasonable for income tax purposes at the time it was paid (the test of reasonableness is based on the assumption that the partner was an employee for the purposes of subparagraph 6(1)(*b*)(v), (vi), (vii) or (vii.1) of the *Income Tax Act*).

The amount of the rebate that may be claimed is limited to the amount that would qualify as an input tax credit if the expenses had been incurred, and GST paid thereon, by the partnership [ETA: ssec. 253(2)]. Thus, the GST rebate is not available to partners to the extent that the expense relates to an activity that is not a commercial activity. Thus, if the partnership is engaged in making exempt supplies, such as a medical or dental practice, the individual partners are not entitled to claim a rebate for GST paid personally on purchases that relate to that activity.

The application for a rebate must be filed within four years after the end of the year to which the rebate relates [ETA: ssec. 253(3)]. Generally, the rebate will be filed when the partner files his or her income tax return.

2. The partnership interest

The definition of "financial instrument" [ETA: ssec. 123(1)] includes, among other things, an interest in a partnership or any right in respect of such an interest. The definition of "financial service" in the same subsection includes, among other things, the issue or transfer of ownership of a financial instrument. Pursuant to Part VII of Schedule V, financial services are exempt supplies. Therefore, no GST will be payable on the issue or transfer of ownership of a partnership interest.

Advisory services, however, such as legal and accounting services, will be subject to GST. Input tax credits will only be available for GST paid on these fees if they are incurred in the course of the partnership's commercial activities. Anything done by a person in connection with the acquisition, establishment, disposition or termination of a commercial activity will be deemed to be part of the commercial activity [ETA: ssec. 141.1(3)]. In other words, these fees will only generate input tax credits if they are incurred in connection with the acquisition, establishment, disposition or termination of the partnership's commercial activities and not in connection with the issuance or transfer of ownership of the partnership interest.

3. Transfer of property to a partnership

Notwithstanding the rollover available under subsection 97(2) of the *Income Tax Act*, the transfer of property to a partnership will generally be subject to GST, with certain exceptions. If the partners contribute cash to the partnership, there are no GST implications since the definition of "property" [ETA: ssec. 123(1)] specifically excludes money. The transfer of debt and accounts receivable are considered to be exempt financial services and, hence, not subject to GST. Furthermore, if the partners were not previously engaged in commercial activities and the property was not used in such

---

[(d)] 15/115ths for HST purposes.

activities, GST will not be payable on the transfer. For example, GST will not be payable on the transfer of property to a medical or dental partnership, since doctors and dentists are engaged in making exempt supplies and are not engaged in commercial activities.

If the transfer of property to the partnership is subject to GST, partial relief may be available by using the election in subsection 167(1). As discussed in Chapter 15, this election is available where:

(a) a supplier makes a supply of a business or part thereof that was established or carried on by the supplier (or established or carried on by another person and acquired by the supplier); and

(b) the recipient is acquiring ownership, possession or use of all or substantially all (i.e., 90% or more) of the property that can reasonably be regarded as being necessary for the recipient to be capable of carrying on the business or part thereof as a business.

Because businesses are entitled to claim input tax credits in respect of GST paid on purchases used in commercial activities, the use of this election may not result in any net GST savings. However, it may result in cash flow advantages, since GST does not generally have to be paid and then recovered through an input tax credit.

A partner who transfers property to a partnership, will also be entitled to claim an input tax credit for GST paid on expenses related to the transfer, such as legal and accounting fees. As discussed above, the ETA states that to the extent a person does anything in connection with the acquisition, establishment [ETA: ssec. 141.1(3)], disposition or termination of a commercial activity, the person is deemed to have done that thing in the course of commercial activities. Thus, an input tax credit will be available.

4. Transfer of property from a partnership

On the cessation of a partnership, the transfer of property to the partners may be subject to GST. If the partnership was not a registrant, for example, because it was engaged in making exempt supplies, GST would not be payable on the transfer. If the partnership was a registrant and is transferring the business as a going concern, the election under subsection 167(1) of the ETA, as discussed above, may be available. If this election is not available, the general rules relating to the sale of property used in a commercial activity will apply.

Where a partnership disposes of partnership property to a partner or prospective partner, or to a person who is ceasing to be a partner, the partnership is deemed to have made a supply of the property for consideration equal to the total fair market value of the property (including the fair market value of the person's interest in the property) [ETA: ssec. 272.1(4)]. The consideration is deemed to become due at the time the property is disposed of.

5. Joint and several liability

Partners and former partners (other than a member who is a limited partner and not a general partner) are jointly and severally liable with the partnership for the payment or remittance of all GST amounts that become payable or remittable by the partnership before or during the period in which the person is a member of the partnership [ETA: ssec. 272.1(5)]. Where the person was a member of the partnership at the time the partnership was dissolved, the liability also applies to amounts that become payable or remittable after the dissolution of the partnership. However, the liability for amounts that became payable or remittable before the person became a partner is limited to the property and money of the partnership, as determined under provincial law (relating to partnerships).

In all cases, the joint liability is discharged to the extent of the payment or remittance by the partnership or by any member of an amount in respect of the liability.

Partners and former partners are also jointly and severally liable for all other obligations for which the partnership is liable, such as filing returns.

6. Continuation of partnership

Where a partnership would otherwise be regarded as having ceased to exist (i.e., because of the addition or departure of a partner), the partnership is not deemed to have ceased to exist until the registration of the partnership is cancelled [ETA: ssec. 272.1(6)].

Special rules apply to certain partnership reorganizations, such as the dissolution of a partnership into two separate partnerships. Where a majority of the members of the predecessor partnership (i.e., that together had more than a 50% interest in the capital of the predecessor partnership) comprise more than half of the members of a new partnership, and those members transferred all or substantially all of the property distributed to them in settlement of their capital interests in the predecessor partnership, the new partnership is deemed to be a continuation of the predecessor partnership [ETA: ssec. 272.1(7)]. However, this rule does not apply if the new partnership applies for registration.

D. GST and Trusts

[ETA: 123(1); 267.1(2), (3); 268; 269]

1. Treatment of trusts under the Excise Tax Act

A trust is included in the definition of "person" [ETA: ssec. 123(1)]. Consequently, a trust that is engaged in commercial activities is required to register and collect GST on taxable supplies.

The definition of "financial instrument" [ETA: ssec. 123(1)] includes, among other things, an interest in a trust or any right in respect of such an interest. The definition of "financial service" in the same subsection includes the transfer of ownership of a financial instrument. Consequently, the sale of an interest in a trust is an exempt financial service pursuant to Part VII of Schedule VII of the ETA.

The GST rules relating to trusts also apply to estates of deceased individuals.

2. Settlement of trust

For GST purposes, where property is settled through the use of an *inter vivos* trust (within the meaning of the *Income Tax Act*), the settlor and the trust are deemed to have sold and purchased the property, respectively, for consideration equal to the amount determined under the *Income Tax Act* to be the proceeds of disposition of the property [ETA: sec. 268]. Consequently, the supply is generally treated as having been made at fair market value and GST is payable on supplies that are taxable. As previously noted, the definition of property specifically excludes money [ssec. 123(1)].

3. Distributions of property

Where the trust distributes property, the distribution is deemed to be a supply of property made by the trust for consideration equal to the amount determined under the *Income Tax Act* to be the proceeds of disposition [ETA: sec. 269]. In this regard, reference should be made to the discussion earlier in this chapter on trust distributions.

4. Liability of trustees

Each trustee is liable to satisfy every obligation imposed on the trust, such as the obligation to file returns [ETA: ssec. 267.1(2)]. However, where one trustee satisfies a particular obligation, the liability of the other trustees is discharged.

Joint and several liability is imposed on trustees for the payment or remittance of all GST amounts that become payable or remittable by the trust while the trustee acts as trustee [ETA: ssec. 267.1(3)]. This liability is extended to periods before which the trustee began to act as a trustee. However, it applies only to the extent of the property and money of the trust under the control of the trustee. The payment or remittance by the trust or trustee of an amount in respect of the liability discharges the joint liability to the extent of that amount.

Chapter 19

Computer-Assisted Tax Research

TOPICS DISCUSSED

	Page
INSTALLATION OF THE RESEARCH SOFTWARE AND DATA	1000
Content Overview	1000
Minimum System Requirements	1000
Basic Installation	1000
FOLIO 4.3 SOFTWARE	1001
Content Overview	1001
Launcher Screen	1001
Advanced Query Screen	1003
Table of Contents Screen	1005
Document Screen	1008
Other Screens: Viewing and Navigating	1017
Options For Queries and Visual Presentations	1019
Part II Exercises	1027

	Page
BASIC SEARCH AND NAVIGATION COMMANDS	1027
Content Overview	1027
Major CRA Documents	1027
Basic Search Commands	1028
Errors: Query and Inputting	1037
Tagging, Printing and Saving Search Results	1039
Help Infobases	1042
Part III Exercises	1044
ADVANCED AND ALTERNATE COMMANDS	1044
Content Overview	1044
Additional Infobases	1044
Additional Search Commands	1046
Multiple Infobases	1048
Speciality Queries	1049
Part IV Exercises	1051

This Chapter is divided into several modules. The first module explains how to install the search software and some of the factors to be considered in deciding which installation is best suited for your particular needs and hardware. The second module examines some of the supportive functions of the search software such as screen layout, basic navigation tools and basic terminology. A good initial understanding of these software features and enhancements will help you become an excellent electronic researcher. The third module demonstrates some of the basic research commands and navigation tools and will enable you to do some basic research immediately. The fourth module introduces additional and more complicated search and navigational commands plus some alternative methods of doing these tasks.

Most Windows-based products have several different methods of achieving the same objective. This aspect of Windows-based products can be confusing to the novice researcher; therefore, in the first three modules, normally only one method of the alternative methods available will be demonstrated. Once you have mastered these first three modules, then you will be ready to move on to the fourth module where you can pick and choose among the various alternatives presented. In addition, the fourth module will introduce additional search commands and navigation tools.

Finally, it is strongly recommended that the reading of this chapter should be alternated with an actual application of these materials. Action reinforces the passive act of reading. Continual repetition is necessary for long-term retention and the mastery of these research tools.

However, do not expect to arrive at exactly the same number of hits as in the Exhibits in this chapter. Databases are continually changing with the insertion of new materials and the deletion of outdated materials. Your CCH TaxWorks infobases are fixed as at March 31, 2005. However, the authors were working with constantly changing infobases as they wrote these materials throughout the year. Therefore, there will be small differences in your search results and search results that are shown in the exhibits. These small differences should not impede your learning by executing the same commands on your own computer.

Note that the solutions to the Exercises of this chapter which are found in Appendix III will reflect exactly the search results from your April 2005 TaxWorks CD.

I. INSTALLATION OF THE RESEARCH SOFTWARE AND DATA

A. Content Overview

- Minimum System Requirements
- Basic Installation

The research software used by CCH is called "Folio" and is produced by Nextpage Limited (formerly known as the Folio Corp.). The version of the software that we will use is Folio 4.3 and CCH's name for their tax research product is TaxWorks.

B. Minimum System Requirements

- Minimum processor is an Intel-compatible 486 with 16MB of RAM
- A VGA or SVGA monitor
- Windows Operating System: any one of Windows 95/98/2000/XP Pro or Windows NT 4.0. Note that Windows Millennium (Me) and Windows XP Home are not supported. The authors have used both of these operating systems with Folio but there have been a few difficulties such as freezing of screens, and hence, losing data
- Minimum Hard Disk space of 20 MB
- Minimum Free Conventional Memory of at least 510 KB

C. Basic Installation

There is one CD to be installed for this student edition of TaxWorks: The Federal Tax Library and the summaries of the Dominion Tax Cases Archival (1920-2004) April 2005. The installation will begin with Federal Tax Library followed by the Summaries Archival. The actual procedure is fairly straight forward thanks to an InstallShield Wizard.

II. FOLIO 4.3 SOFTWARE

A. Content Overview

- Launcher Screen
- Advanced Query Screen
- Table of Contents Screen
- Document Screen
- Other Screens: Viewing and Navigating
- Options for Queries and Visual Presentation

B. Launcher Screen

The opening screen in TaxWorks is referred to as "the Launcher" because it launches or opens up the various income tax infobases as directed by the researcher. In Exhibit 19-1 a check mark has been placed in the little square box that precedes the line descriptive, i.e., Income Tax Act. Therefore, the Launcher will open up this infobase by clicking on the LAUNCH button near the bottom of the right-hand side of the screen.

Exhibit 19-1
Launcher Screen

The TaxWorks Income Tax infobase is composed of three separate categories of data located on the left-hand side of the Launcher:

- Canadian Tax Reports is composed of a number of separate infobases. However, the titles of these infobases and their actual content can be very deceptive. For example, the Income Tax Act infobase contains more than just the Act. It also includes the regulations, technical notes to the present legislation and regulations, proposed legislation and supporting technical notes and detailed notes on the progress of the various pieces of tax legislation in progress throughout the legislative process. The other infobases under this title are just as extensive.

- Dominion Tax Cases (DTC) infobase is composed of three sub-infobases of court cases:

  - Current DTC Cases on an accumulative basis for the current year;

  - Archival DTC Cases for preceding years (not on your disk); and

  - Archival Dominion Tax Cases Digests (short summaries).

- Tax Window Library deals with certain Canada Revenue Agency (CRA) interpretative documents:

  - Tax Window Files are responses by the CRA to technical queries by taxpayers and/or their advisors on particular fact situations.

  - Window on Canadian Tax is commentary by CCH and its advisors on the CRA's responses to the Tax Window Files.

As you can begin to see, the amount of information in TaxWorks is massive. Therefore, it is incumbent on the tax professional/student to be aware of the basic content structure of all the various tax documents contained in these infobases. This cannot be done overnight. In fact, for tax professionals, it is a life-long learning process. This chapter will introduce you to the process. At this point do not worry about unexplained documentation. Most of the basic documents will be explained in a practical context, rather than a theoretical context, as this chapter progresses by using practical examples. However, it will not be possible to teach all aspects of these very technical documents and related procedures in this very short introductory chapter on electronic tax research.

The dark buttons in the centre of the Launcher represent the major tax infobase series which are potentially available from CCH. Your CD contains only the first one, Federal Tax Library (Canadian Tax Library). The others are available only on a fee basis and will normally be available to your employer in a professional tax environment.

The date and time buttons on the right-hand side of the Launcher are aids in preparing time reports and for billing clients for tax services.

In the upper left-hand corner of the Launcher is the word, Options. Click on this word and a drop-down dialogue box will appear. The first two items will have a checkmark beside them. It is recommended that you remove these checkmarks by clicking on them and thereby deactivating these features. The first title, Display Reminder Messages, reminds you to complete your client-time report. The second title, Save Title Selections, saves your selection of infobases in the previous search session. This alternative is a matter of personal preference which you can determine after working with CCH's TaxWorks.

C. Advanced Query Screen

The Advanced Query Screen is a template found in all of the info bases that initiates searches or queries and is shown in Exhibit 19-2. There are two methods to activate the Advanced Query Screen:

- The quickest and simplest method is to press the function key, F2.

- The other method is to click on the Search tab located in the Main Menu at the top of the screen and a drop-down dialogue box will appear. Just click on the words, Advanced Query, to activate this screen.

Exhibit 19-2 demonstrates a query/search in the *Income Tax Act* info base for the word, benefit, and shows the numeric and the diagram results of this search.

Exhibit 19-2
Advanced Query Template
(a query for the word, benefit)

There are three main parts to this screen:

- The word wheel — labeled, Word;

- The results map — labeled, Records with hits;

- The search command — labeled, Query For.

As you type your query or search command in the Query For box, the Word Wheel will search a word infobase that contains all the words in the particular infobase that you are using currently. In fact, Folio will even attempt to guess the next letters that you will type in your query.

To initiate a search or query for a word (the word, benefit in our example above), slowly type that word in the Query For box. Notice that as you type each letter, the Word Wheel moves down the internal alpha dictionary. Also note how your search term is surrounded by other words in the Word Wheel with the same stem or prefix, bene. You may want to expand your query to include some of these words. For example, to expand the above query to include the plural of the word, benefit, (i.e., benefits), just add the words . . . or benefits . . . to your query as demonstrated in Exhibit 19-3.

Exhibit 19-3
Advanced Query Template
(a query for the words: benefit or benefits)

The Results Map

The area immediately below the title, Records with hits, (plus a number that represents the hits found by this query, not the occurrences) is referred to as the Results Map. The actual map below indicates the number of hits for each word and joins the two words together with a small vertical bar which represents the OR command and gives a numeric result. This example is for the purpose of demonstrating the functions of the Advanced Query Screen and not for the purpose of teaching you how to search. Searching is the function of Modules 3 and 4. The Results Map is extremely important in the search process because it explains exactly what Folio did or did not do in executing your correct or incorrect search command.

When you finish typing your query, you execute the search by clicking on the OK button at the bottom of the template. Your search is complete when there is a number beside the title, Records with hits, i.e., 5868 in Exhibit 19-9 above and it coincides with the number in the Results Map.

Clicking on the Apply To All button would result in the same number of hits since only the Income Tax Act of the Canadian Tax Report series is open. If, however, you had other infobases open (e.g., the Bulletins, Circulars & Rulings, Commentary etc.) then clicking on the Apply To All button will execute the query in all opened infobases.

Caution: Opening all of the infobases that are on the Launcher, even for Windows XP Professional, is not recommended. At some point the Folio software breaks down usually because of internal memory limitations. For Windows XP Home and Millennium (Me) only one infobase should be open at any one time.

Before proceeding any further, two terms must be explained: hits and records. A record is defined as a unit of data or information. In TaxWorks, it is most often defined for purposes of the Income Tax Act infobase as a paragraph. In other CCH infobases a record will be defined differently. For example, a record in the court infobases is most often defined as the hard copy of a page of a court decision. A hit, on the other hand, is defined as the first occurrence of a search word/words in a record. For example, a record may have 20 occurrence of the searched term or terms but only the first one signals a hit. If we apply the above definitions to Exhibit 19-9, we can say that the results were 5868 records that had at least one occurrence of either searched term: benefit or benefits.

There are three additional items on the query template that should be explained:

- The square brackets in the bottom left-hand corner are special commands for the very advanced searcher. These commands search groups or levels of information rather paragraphs; they are extremely complex. We will not be using these commands, but will rely on specially-designed templates which will overcome these complexities. These special templates will be introduced slowly throughout the chapter.

- The PREV and NEXT buttons on the right-hand side near the bottom of this template enable the researcher to recall previously executed search commands. The NEXT button permits forward movement among the queries rather than backward movement as with the PREV button. Remember that this operation only works with executed queries through the OK button or Apply To All button.

- Checked Branches box is an alternative method of restricting queries to branches of the Table of Contents and will be discussed in the next segment.

D. Table of Contents Screen

Folio-based electronic infobases provide a table of contents similar to ones you find in books. One of the major differences is that an electronic table of contents can be expanded or contracted at will depending on the needs of the user. In Folio, the Table of Contents can be expanded (or contracted) up to nine levels of subtitles and/or headings. Once a query has been completed, you should go directly to the Table of Contents to see the number of hits for each of the expandable branches so that you can hone in on the particular items of interest. For this reason, the Table of Contents Screen is one of the most important aids in effective searching.

To bring forward the Table of Contents Screen, just click on the Contents Tab which can be found on the fourth bar/line from the top of the screen and is labelled with a stacked plus-minus sign and the word, Contents.

Exhibit 19-4
Table of Contents Screen
(after a query for the word, benefit)

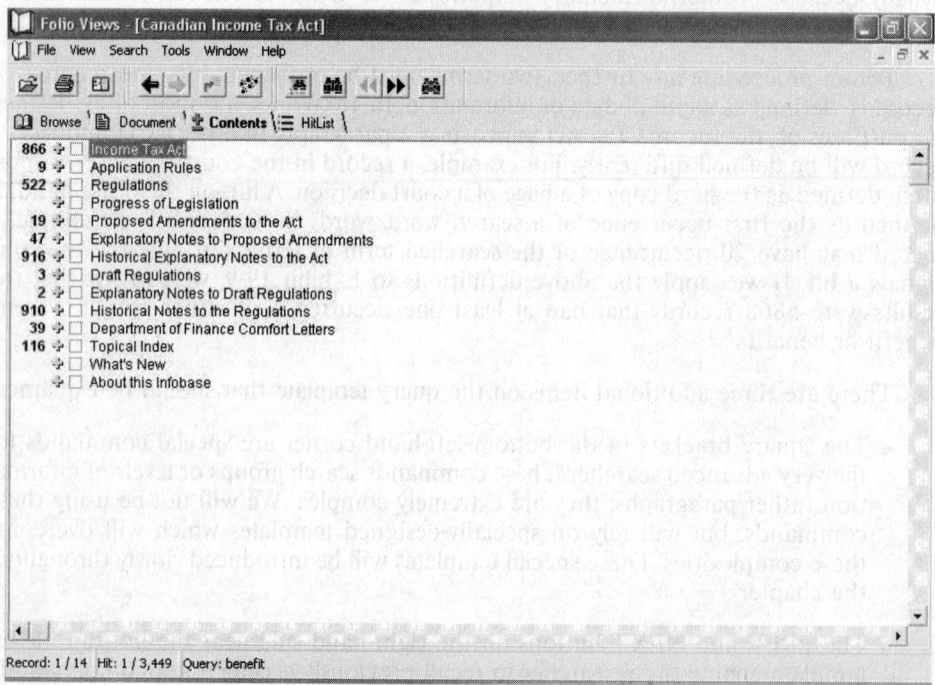

Each line of the Table of Contents begins with the number of Hits that was achieved with query for the word, benefit as shown in Exhibit 19-4. These lines are referred to as "expandable branches" that can be expanded down to nine different levels of data; however, not all nine levels are available for each branch.

To move down to the next level for a particular branch, just click on the plus sign (+). For an example, examine Exhibit 19-5.

Exhibit 19-5
An Expanded Table of Contents Screen
(after a query for the word, benefit)

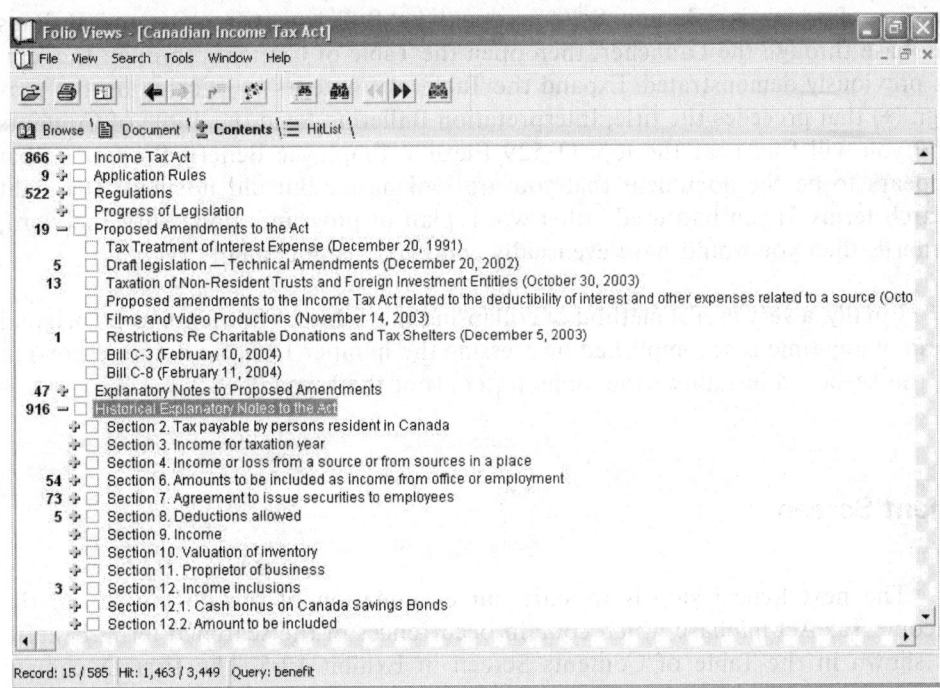

In Exhibit 19-5 above, the two branches that are expanded, are the Proposed Amendments to the Act branch and the Historical Explanatory Notes to the Act branch. Note that this method of expansion only expands/contracts the Table of Contents to the next level above or below. Now, if you examine carefully Exhibit 19-11 you can see that a minus sign now precedes those branches that were expanded. If you click on these minus signs the expanded branch will collapse to its original form, a single line.

The key-board variation of the above expansion method expands a highlighted branch with the command, SHIFT +, and contracts the expanded branch with a single minus sign, - .

Also, note that each of the expandable branches and sub-branches has a little square box preceding the line description in addition to the plus-minus signs and the number of hits. When the user clicks on one or more of these boxes (prior to the executing of a query) a checkmark is inserted that indicates that subsequent queries will be restricted to the checkmarked branch(es).

The Table of Contents Screen also assists in locating documents for which you do not have an identification number, name or title but you remember seeing it somewhere. As long as you know the document infobase/category, expanding the Table of Contents may help you find the document. For example, suppose you want to find a recent CRA Interpretation Bulletin which deals with "benefit packages". An Advanced Query search for the words, benefit and package, yields only two hits neither of which is relevant. So now open the Bulletins, Circulars and Rulings infobase through the Launcher; then open the Table of Contents through the icon as previously demonstrated. Expand the Table of Contents by clicking on the plus sign (+) that precedes the title, Interpretation Bulletins. Scan the Table of Contents and you will find near the top, IT-529 Flexible Employee Benefit Programs, that appears to be the document that you are looking for but did not have the right search terms. If you had used either word, plan or program, along with the word, benefit, then you would have eventually come to this document.

Finally, a very useful method of collapsing the Table of Contents to its original form at any time is accomplished by pressing the number 1 on the numeric portion of the keyboard just above the alpha letters (not the keypad).

E. Document Screen

The next logical step is to start our examination of the documents in the Income Tax Act infobase which contain occurrences of the searched term, benefit, as shown in the Table of Contents Screen in Exhibit 19-5. The first Document Screen of this query can be activated by clicking on the Document icon which can be found on the fourth bar of information from the top of the screen (next to the Contents icon). This icon is represented by a single page of writing with the upper right-hand corner folded down. See Exhibit 19-6 for an example of the first Document Screen after the query for the word, benefit. Note how a Popup (footnote) is overlayed on this Document Screen. Popups are used in many ways just like footnotes. In this example, the popup provides additional or supplementary material to your query results which may be relevant.

Exhibit 19-6
The Document Screen
(with a Popup)

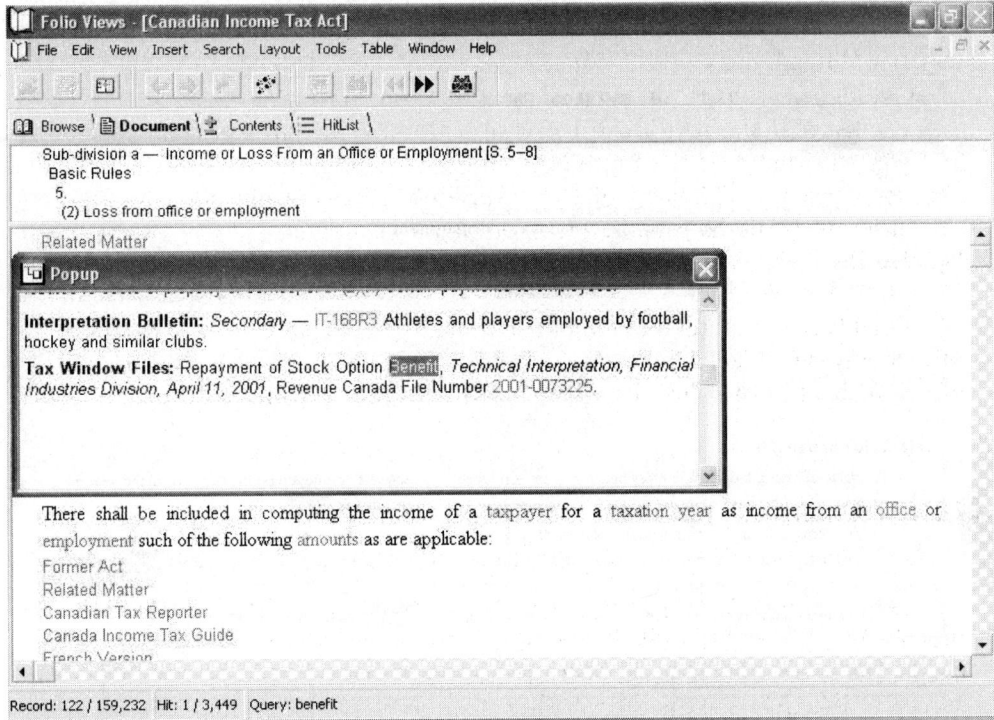

Now close out the popup and our examination of the Document Screen will start at the top of Exhibit 19-7. Note that Exhibit 19-7 may differ slightly from your equivalent screen and you may have to adjust the screen (up or down) to capture the identical information that will be discussed below.

Exhibit 19-7
The Document Screen
(after the removal of the popup)

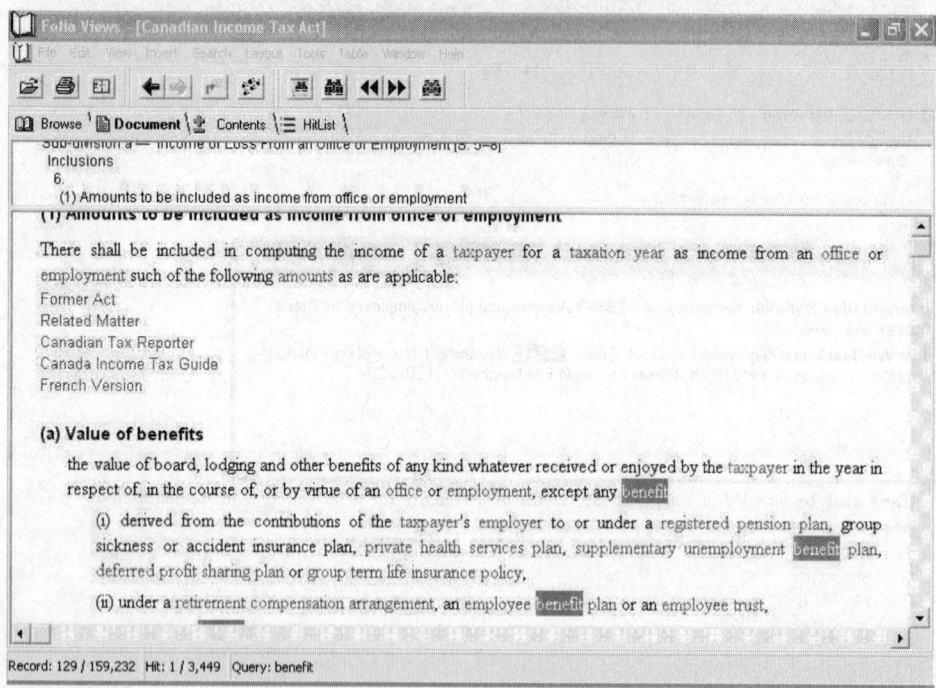

Main Menu

The first line under the title Folio Views — [Canadian Income Tax Act] is the Main Menu which contains a series of tabs each of which has a distinct function. Some of these functions are common with all Microsoft Windows products such as File, Edit, View, Layout, and Help but modified for use with Folio. Others are unique to database searching such as Search, Tools and Window. Each of these functions is supported by a drop-down dialogue box which provides a subset of commands that is related to this tab function.

For example, the View Tab has a drop-down dialogue box which contains a helpful symbol which identifies a record. See Exhibit 19-8.

Exhibit 19-8
View Dialogue Box
(activating codes for exhibit 19-7)

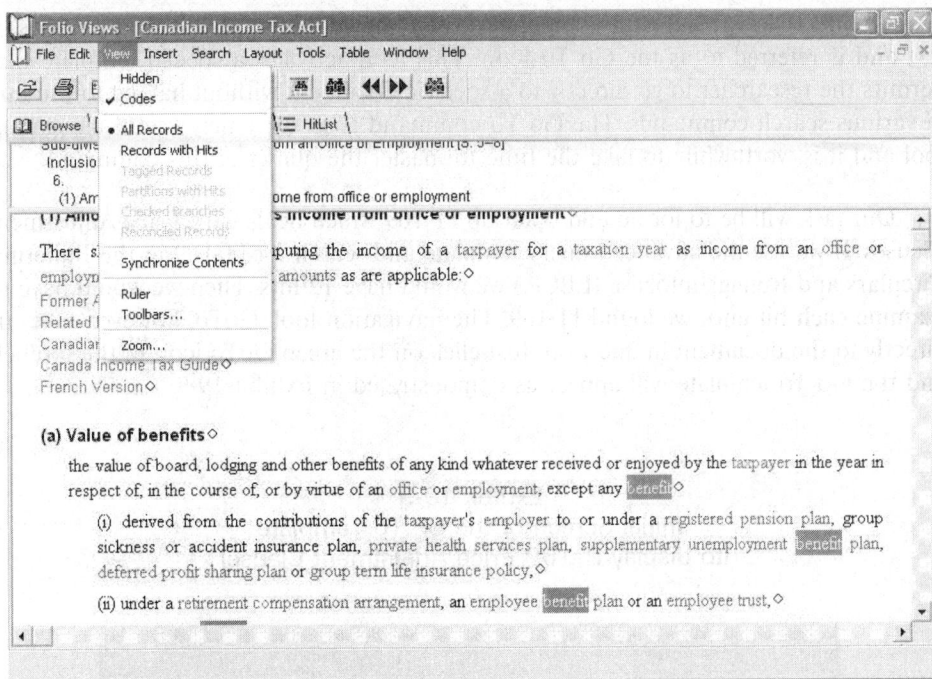

Click on the word, Codes, and a checkmark will be placed by this word. Now go back to Exhibit 19-7 and compare the two screens. Note that a diamond symbol, (♦), has been placed at the beginning/end of each record, e.g., a paragraph in this infobase. A paragraph is also defined as text which follows a blank line. Therefore, a title is a paragraph which in turn is a record. It is strongly recommended that you leave these codes on until you have mastered the characteristics of a record for each of the infobases. Note that this procedure must be done for each infobase, e.g., ITA, Commentary, etc. In the next topic, Options, features such as Codes can be turned on/off for all infobases.

Toolbar

The next line of the Document Screen, the Toolbar, is composed of three sets of icons:

- Standard icons for Windows operations — first three icons;

- Navigation icons for Folio inter-infobase and intra-infobase operations — next four icons; and

- Search/Query icons — last five icons.

Go To Icon and Other Navigation Icons

The first two Navigation icons, left and right arrows with a stem or shaft, are directional arrows within a particular infobase or between infobases. These two icons will be used in an example below.

The next Navigation icon is the green right-angled icon with some mock lines of text and is referred to as the Go To Icon. This icon activates a special template that permits the researcher to go directly to a specific document without having to use one of various search commands. The Go To command is an extremely useful navigation tool and it is worthwhile to take the time to master the quirks of this command.

Our task will be to locate and open up IT-169 which deals with Price Adjustment Clauses. If we use the advanced query template and search for IT-169 in the Bulletins, Circulars and Rulings infobase (EBCR) we would have 12 hits. Then we would have to examine each hit until we found IT-169. The navigation tool, GoTo, however, takes us directly to the document in question. Just click on the green GoTo icon in the toolbelt and the Go To template will appear as demonstrated in Exhibit 19-9.

Exhibit 19-9
Initial Screen of the Go To Template
(to display IT-169 Price Adjustment Clause)

First, remove the highlighted reference, 00-1(1), that is immediately below the title, Go To, by pressing the Backspace key. See Exhibit 19-9 above. Then type in the document identification in the space that you just cleared using the chart below, in this case, IT-169, and that is demonstrated in Exhibit 19-10.

Jump Destination Input Reference Chart for Selected Infobases

Infobase	Particular Part of Infobase	Document Identification
Income Tax Act	ITA Section Income Tax Regulation Income Tax Application Rule	ita (provision #) (e.g., ita 20(1)(c) itr (provision #) (e.g., itr 1100(1)(a) itar (provision #) (e.g., itar 26(3)
Bulletins, Circulars & Rulings	Interpretation Bulletin Information Circular Advance Tax Ruling	it-120r5 ic 93-3 atr-10

Commentary	Commentary for: ITA
	            ITR
	            ITAR
	Tax Topics
	Tax Agreements
		Same as Income Tax Act above
		Or
		CCH paragraph number date of issue: e.g., January 15 1996
		canada/france (use word wheel)

Revenue Canada Round Table	Question	1985,q4
Dominion Tax Case	either current or archive	90 dtc 6059
Window on Canadian Tax	CCH paragraph or Revenue Canada File Number	6009 9912655
Tax Window Files	Document Number	9915745

Exhibit 19-10
Completed Go To Template
(to display IT-169 Price Adjustment Clauses)

Note that the document identification must be identical to the examples that are shown in the chart above except that you can use either upper or lower case. Be careful that you put spaces in their proper position and there should be no spaces after a hyphen. Also, watch carefully as you input the document identification and follow the format of the document identification. To display the document press the OK button.

Some of the more recent versions of ITs are linked to specific numbered paragraphs within the document. Exhibit 19-10 displays the six numbered paragraphs.

To use GoTo with other infobases or sub-infobases, just type in the identification number, as shown in the above chart, after the removal of the initial highlighted entry. For the Information Circulars sub-infobase, type the letters IC, followed by a space and then the numeric identification number. For Winfiles enter the document number. For the ITA infobase enter the sub-infobase acronym (i.e., ita, itr, itar) followed by space and the provision number. For the court infobases, the reference format is the last two digits of the year, space, dtc, space, page number, e.g., 96 dtc 6265. Remember, if you forget the format just follow the examples on your screen or the Chart above.

Reference Window (Go back to Exhibit 19-7)

The first box of information is the Reference Window which gives the technical reference for the information that is contained in the Document Window which is immediately below. To be specific, it is the reference for the exact position of the bar cursor in the Document Window. The Reference Window in Exhibit 19-19 indicates that the document contained in the Document Window below was obtained from the *Income Tax Act* — Section 6 where the bar cursor is presently located.

Document Window (Go back to Exhibit 19-7)

There is a faint double line that separates the Reference and Document windows. If you place your cursor on this double line so that a small directional icon appears (four arrows) you can move the double line up or down and thereby expand or contract the Reference Window. However, the more space you provide in the Reference Window the less space there is for viewing in the Document Window. So to maximize the space in the Document Window, it is recommended that you only expose one line of information in the Reference Window and use the multi-directional arrow for expansion when a more detailed reference is needed.

The Document Window displays the information that was requested through the search or query command, in this case the word, benefit. Exhibit 19-7 displays the occurrences of the word, benefit, in a highlighted blue. All subsequent occurrences of the searched term will be shown in this manner. There are three blue highlighted words in Exhibit 19-7.

Note that some of the information is colour-coded and/or underlined. These colour-coded, underlined terms indicate that additional or complementary information can be accessed or linked by simply clicking on the highlighted terms. Now move your cursor over any of the words in red and a small-hand icon will appear. This hand verifies that your cursor is over a link or connection to other sources of information. This red link is a data link and it will take you directly to this document which is stored in a different part of the infobase. Exhibit 19-11, which is also a document mode, shows the actual linked document to the phrase, retirement compensation arrangement, found at the bottom of Exhibit 19-7. To return to the original document, just click on the arrow with a stem that is located in the toolbar (fourth icon from the left).

Exhibit 19-11
Example of a Linked Document from Exhibit 19-7
(definition of retirement compensation arrangement)

In addition to the words and phrase links, there are links to other infobases at the end of each provision of the ITA. For example in Exhibit 19-7, right after the (1) of section 6, there is list of five infobases: Former Act, Related Matter, Canadian Tax

Reporter, Canada Income Tax Guide and French Version. Click on Related Matter and a list of related materials will appear (e.g., related sections of the ITA, related ITs, court cases etc.) will appear. See Exhibit 19-12.

Exhibit 19-12
Related Matter Linked to Subsection 6(1)
(arising from Exhibit 19-7)

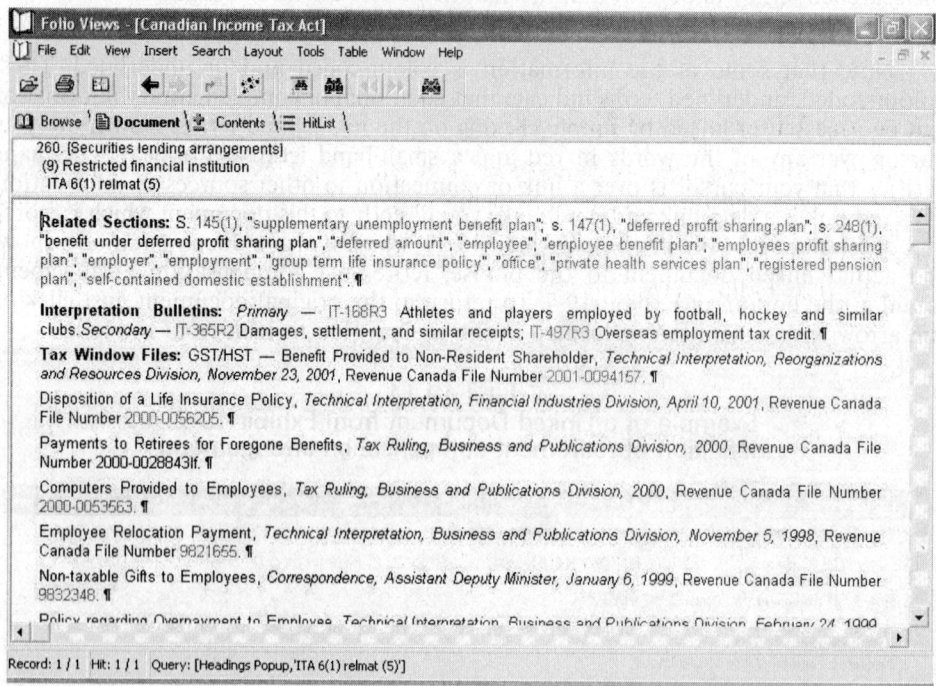

Click on Canadian Tax Reporter and CCH's interpretation for the particular section of the ITA, paragraph 6(1)(a), will appear. Use the arrow with a stem to return to the original query document.

Status Bar (Return to Exhibit 19-7)

This bottom line of the Document Screen is the Status bar which provides important information concerning the results of your query. For an example, look at the status line of Exhibit (19-7). The first box, the record box, (i.e., Record: 129 /159,232) indicates the numerical position in the database of the information displayed in the Document Window, e.g., paragraph 6(1)(a) of the *Income Tax Act* infobase. These numbers indicate that the document on the screen is the 129th record of this infobase out of a total available records of 159,232.

Remember that the length of a record can vary from infobase to infobase and even within a particular infobase. However, you can recognize the beginning and the ending of a record by the diamond symbol, ♦, accompanied by a line space. The most common type of records are paragraphs, titles, headings and subheadings but there are others.

The second box, the Hit Box, indicates the positive results (hits) arising from the execution of the search command and indicates the position in the infobase that you are viewing through the Document Window. A hit can be defined as a record (see above) which contains at least one occurrence of the searched term. Where there are multiple occurrences of the blue-highlighted term in a record you still have only one hit. Watch this Hit Box as you scroll the various highlighted occurrences. For example, the status line in Exhibit 19-7 indicates that there are 3,449 records that have at least one occurrence of the searched term, benefit, and that the blue-highlighted occurrences are in the 1st record.

The third box, the Query Box, indicates the word(s) you were searching for, i.e., benefit.

F. Other Screens: Viewing and Navigating

At this point, we have explained two of the four viewing screens: The Table of Contents Screen and the Document Screen. There are two more viewing screens that should be demonstrated: the Browse Screen and the Hit List Screen. The icons for all of these viewing screens are located on the third bar of icons/directions immediately below the title, Folio Views.

Browse Screen

As with all the viewing screens, clicking on the appropriate icon opens the particular view. The Browse Screen is a combination of the Table of Contents Screen and the Document Screen. See an example in Exhibit 19-13.

Exhibit 19-13
Browse Screen
(after a query for the word, benefit)

The size of the two screens can be altered just as we did with the Reference Window and Document Window of the Document Screen. Place your cursor over the double lines separating the two screens and when the multi-directional arrow appears, adjust the size of one of the screens to meet your needs.

Note that the two screens are synchronized initially at the first-branch level. The Table of Contents Screen is at the Income Tax Act branch/infobase and the Document Screen is at the position of the first hit, subsection 6(1). The particular branch is identified with a blue rectangle over the name of the branch/sub-infobase. See Exhibit 19-19 above.

To synchronize at the paragraph level of the ITA, click on the icon in the toolbar that also looks like an open book but with a plus/minus sign on the left-hand page (Table of Contents Screen) and mock writing on the right-hand page (Document Screen).

Hit List Screen

The Hit List Screen is a different presentation of the hits in the Document Window in the format of a single line per hit surrounded by a specified number of words plus a single reference line of the information that is found in the Reference Window. See Exhibit 19-14.

Exhibit 19-14
Hit List Screen
(after a query for the word, benefit)

To change the number of surrounding words, open the View dialogue tab at the top of the screen, click on Hit List Properties on the resultant drop-down dialogue box, and change the number of surrounding words in the input box at the bottom of this screen.

To complete the examination of the Document Screen, the last five icons on the right-hand-side of the Toolbar (the search/query icons) need some explanation. We have already dealt with the directional arrow heads (no stems) whose function is to move around the highlighted occurrences of the query terms. The only icons remaining are the query-related binocular icons. The binocular, on the left-hand side with a red number one in the lower left-hand corner, is the first of two specialized query templates for the ITA infobase. These specialized query templates are designed to modify or restrict the advanced query in some manner such as restricting the search to a specific time period. We will look at these special templates in Module 4. The last binocular, with the faint red X superimposed thereon, cancels an advanced query. The remaining binocular, (the middle one) brings forth the Advanced Query template as does the F2 function key.

G. Options For Queries and Visual Presentations

Folio 4.3 provides the user with a series of templates that enable the user to turn on/off certain visual attributes of the Folio Views such as modifying the display options for the various screen/view alternatives described previously, providing various print alternatives, etc. Some but not all of the many options or alternatives may also be turned off/on through the View tab in the main menu as previously discussed. Changes via the View tab are activated only for the particular infobase that is presently on your screen. Changes activated through the Option templates affects all of the infobases. An understanding of these options will make you a better and more efficient researcher.

To activate the Options Templates, click on the Tools tab in the main menu and then click on the word, Options, in the resultant drop-down dialogue box. See Exhibit 19-15.

Exhibit 19-15
Various Options Templates

As you can see in the above exhibit, there are eight option tabs each of which has a specific template. We will examine some of these templates starting with the General Options template. However, there are some alternatives in each of these templates that we will not or cannot use and, hence, these alternatives will not be discussed. The reasons that some of the features of the templates are not available are:

- some features are determined by and activated by the supplier, i.e., CCH;

- some features will be dictated by the purchaser (e.g., your employer) because of a need for consistency and/or server security;

- some features do not work well in some infobase environments which change constantly, e.g., shadow files in tax infobases.

1. General Options Template (see Exhibit 19-15)

This template is designed for some personal preferences of the overall display of the entire infobase. In the box labelled, Show, there are three items that are active.

Since the Status bar is so important in assessing the status of your search results this feature/option should always be on. Similarly, the option, Infobase view tabs, (various screens such as Document Screen, Table of Contents Screen etc.) should always be on; however, you have a choice of a top or bottom positioning.

The option, Recently Used Files, enables the researcher to switch between other CCH infobases such as provincial legislation or commodity tax, where available. This ability is not available on your discs.

The Infobase View Font box permits the user to change the font and its size for certain window panes e.g., the Table of Contents.

The option, Measurement Units, permits the user to change from inches to centimetres or points.

The Zoom option allows the researcher to expand or contract the size of the various panes. The default is 100 but you can expand to 500 and contract to 10.

2. The Print Options Template (See Exhibit 19-16)

Exhibit 19-16
Print Options Template

The following print options are potentially available, but only if you have a printer with the necessary capabilities, i.e., colour for highlighter attributes, link attributes and field attributes.

- Query results prints in bold the query occurrences and also underlines these occurrences. It is recommended that this feature remain on unless you are printing a document where the query occurrences are not relevant.

- Inline headings prints the contents of the reference window on a single line. This feature is very useful for identifying partial documents and will be discussed in more detail in a later module under the heading, printing/tagging.

- Highlighter, Link, and Field attributes prints these reference points in the appropriate colour. Obviously you need a colour printer. These colour attributes do not show up well on a printer with only black and white capabilities.

- Hidden text prints all the topography symbols such the diamond symbol that identifies records, right-angled arrows that identify paragraphs. This feature is very useful for the novice researcher in learning how records are defined for each infobase.

- Notes prints the embedded notes in the text as end notes on the last page of the print out. It is recommended that you leave this option on and discard the paper containing the endnotes when not necessary.

- Popup link text prints out a brief description of reference links which are embedded in the text and usually are represented by picture icons. These popup links will be printed as an endnote on the last printed page. These popup links will described in more detail in the subsequent modules.

- Inline heading font is very useful because it allows the user to print partial highlighted portions of a document with a label or inline heading. However, you are limited to only one line of information that is contained in the Reference Window. By changing the font and reducing its size you should be able to expand the information contained in the inline heading.

- When Page breaks active is ON (checkmarked), the page breaks embedded in the text of the infobase by the publisher are active. When Page breaks active has been turned off (no checkmark), then the user determines the page breaks. This option may be useful in printing documents with large blank space gaps.

- Columns prints the text in newspaper style columns up to a maximum of five columns.

3. Query Options Template (See Exhibit 19-17)

This template provides alternate methods of displaying query hits in the Document Presentation mode previously described.

Exhibit 19-17
Query Options Template Alternate Presentation of Query Hits

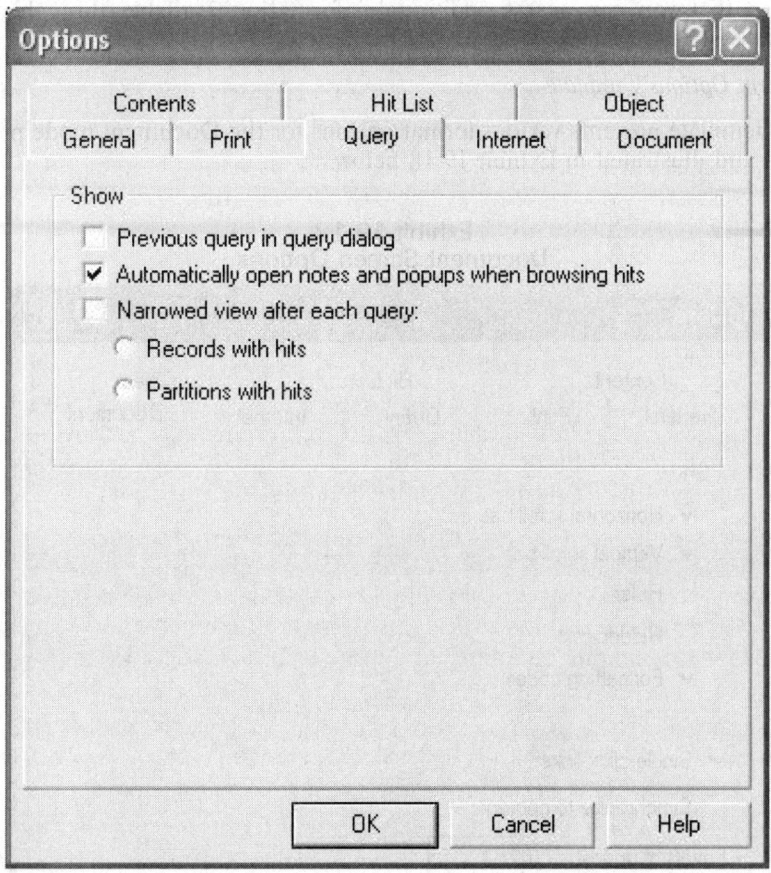

- Previous query in query dialogue, when checkmarked, automatically places the previous query in the Query For box of the Advanced query template. However, this result can be achieved more easily by using an option which is right on the Query Template, PREV and NEXT buttons which were described at the beginning of this module under the topic, the Launcher.

- Automatically opens notes and popups when browsing hits option operates exactly as described in its title. It is recommended that this option be activated at all times.

- Narrowed view after each query option changes the viewing default from occurrences in records to the first (and only the first) occurrence in a record. Remember that a hit is defined as a record which has at least one occurrence. The default procedure displays and moves from occurrence to occurrence in each record. This option, the narrowed view, moves to the first occurrence in the record and then moves on to the first occurrence in the next record and so on. This alternative is especially useful for the experienced researcher who can evaluate quickly that first occurrence and determine whether the particular record should be examined in more detail.

4. Internet Options Template (not Shown)

This template simply provides an input box for the name of your default web browser so that you can access additional information available through an URL internet link .

5. Document Options Template

This template presents various format options for the Document mode previously described and illustrated in Exhibit 19-18 below.

Exhibit 19-18
Document Screen Options

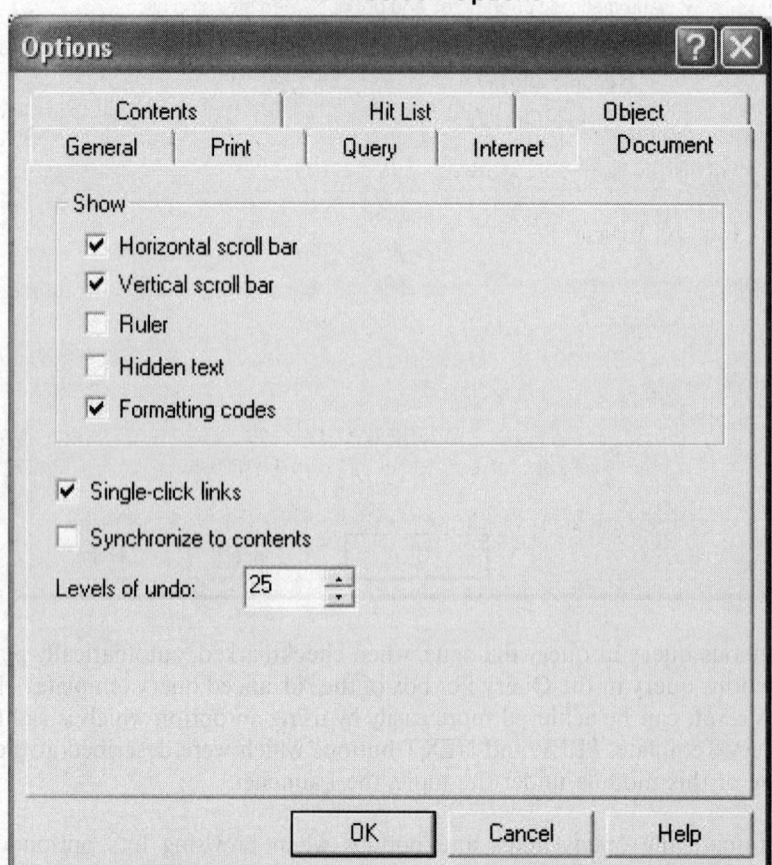

- The Scroll Bars, both Horizontal and Vertical, should be turned on all the time. The Vertical is necessary for scrolling down documents line by line using the up and down arrows (the equivalent of turning a page in a book). You can also move more than one line at a time by moving the little box on the vertical scroll bar. However, this method (little box) is extremely sensitive because of the compression of the data and you may be better off using the page-up and page-down keys. The Horizontal scroll bar is important for viewing query results that are off the computer screen such as a results map which illustrates a particularly complex query or using the Words Around Hits option.

- Ruler acts as a toggle switch which displays or hides the ruler function which should be activated only when necessary since it takes valuable screen space.

- Hidden text refers to such items as popups and links which are imbedded in the text and can only be altered by CCH. Obviously, this option should be left on or you will have removed one of the most important infobase research tools, i.e., hyper-text links.

- Formatting codes such as record identification codes (the diamond symbol) are important and should be left on.

- Single-click links, when activated, changes the default (double-click links) to single-click links.

- Synchronize to contents causes the Document window to display the opening frame of the infobase or branch that is highlighted in the Table of Contents. To examine the hits, you must first double click on the blue-highlighted line in the Table of Contents. This action changes the blue-highlighted line to a box containing the line description. You are now ready to examine the hits using the arrowhead icons in the toolbar.

6. Contents Options Template

The following options affect the Table of Contents Screen as shown in Exhibit 19-19 and as described in the text below this exhibit.

Exhibit 19-19
Table of Contents Screen Options

- Horizontal and Vertical scroll bars — See explanation for previous Exhibit 19-18).

- Expandable branches — This feature is a toggle switch that places a plus sign or a minus sign before each line of the Table of Contents so that a particular line can be expanded and/or contracted using the mouse or its equivalent.

- Checked branches — Checked branches enable the researcher to restrict queries and other operations, such as printing to a particular branch or any sub-branch below it. Therefore, the researcher has the ability to narrow the query to a particular part of the infobase, and thereby increase the search efficiency. When this feature is activated through the Options template, a small empty box is placed at the beginning of each line of the Table of Contents. When a checkmark is placed in a box (boxes) of any particular branch or sub-branch of the Table of Contents, queries will be restricted to the checkmarked branches. When none of these boxes has a check mark, then the whole infobase is searched on the execution of a query. When some of the boxes have a checkmark only those lines/branches in the Table of Contents are active, i.e., only those lines will be searched.

- Headings with hits, when active, only shows in the Table of Contents those lines (branches or sub-branches) which have hits. Please note that for novice researchers, it is recommended that this option should not be turned on until you have mastered all the contents of all the branches and the first level of the sub-branches. To remove the hits (and the query) from the Table of Contents just click on the binocular icon with the red X in the toolbar near the top of the screen.

7. Hit List Options Template

This template appears to be of limited value as applied to TaxWorks. The vertical scroll bar is useful; however, a horizontal scroll bar is also needed. Header only repeats the reference line. The numerical limitation of Words around Hits is useful if the researcher wants the same standard for all infobases. Using the View Tab for each infobase, as needed, would appear to be the better alternative.

The Apply Picture String does not seem to have any effect on the TaxWorks screen and the Display Rank Scores is not available in TaxWorks.

H. Part II Exercises

1. The following query template has certain specific areas and buttons that are identified with a capital letter in the template. For each of the four areas/buttons so identified explain their function.

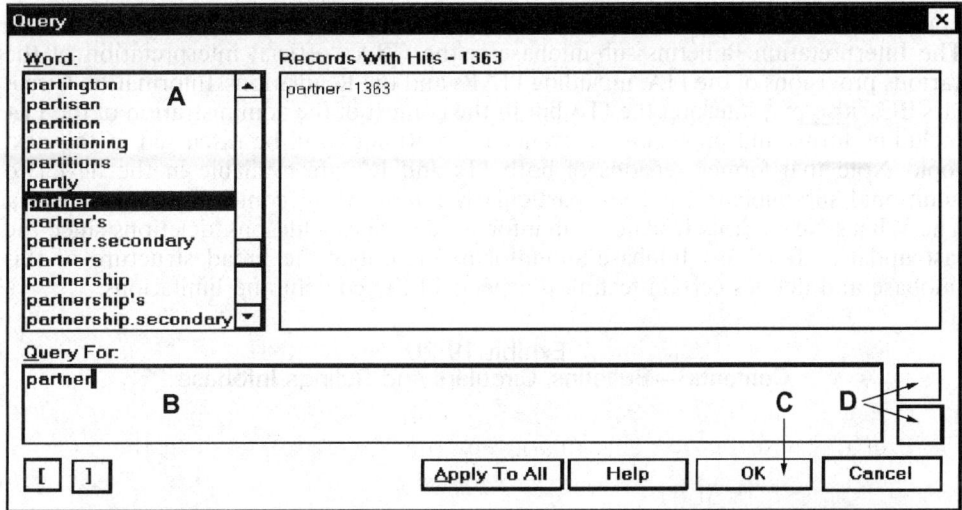

2. The Reference Window gives the technical reference for the information that is displayed in the Document Window. Explain the various ways the Reference Window can be enlarged or contracted.

3. The size of a record differs from infobase to infobase in TaxWorks. How can you determine the size of a record of the infobase that you are currently in?

4. The toolbelt screen presentation can be changed in a number of ways. Describe these various formats.

III. BASIC SEARCH AND NAVIGATION COMMANDS

A. Content Overview

- Major CRA documents — Interpretation Bulletins — Information Circulars — Technical Interpretation Letters
- Basic Search Commands
- Errors: Query and Inputting
- Tagging, Printing and Saving Search Results
- Help Infobases
- Module 3 Exercises

B. Major CRA Documents

In Module 2 — Accessing the Infobases, the *Income Tax Act* infobase was used as the basis for most of the examples and, hence, its major components were discussed.

In this module, the examples will be based on the two major CRA infobases:

- Interpretation Bulletins, Information Circulars and Advance Tax Rulings infobase which will be referred to throughout by its electronic acronym, EBCR;

- Tax Window Files.

The EBCR infobase is composed of seven sub-infobases as shown in Exhibit 19-20. The Interpretation Bulletins sub-infobase is the CRA's official interpretation of the various provisions of the ITA, including ITARs and the Regulations. Information Circulars (ICs) also may interpret the ITA but in the context of the administration of the ITA including forms and procedures. Advanced Tax Rulings will be discussed in the next topic. Note that former versions of both ITs and ICs are available in the next two additional sub-infobases and are particularly important in contesting reassessments. The What's New in this Update ? sub-infobase describes additions/deletions since the last update. About this Infobase sub-infobase describes the broad structure of this infobase and defines certain technical aspects of the content and limitations.

Exhibit 19-20
Contents — Bulletins, Circulars and Rulings Infobase

- ☐ Interpretation Bulletins
- ☐ Information Circulars
- ☐ Advance Tax Rulings
- ☐ Former Interpretation Bulletins
- ☐ Former Information Circulars
- ☐ What's New
- ☐ About this Infobase

Winfiles is a collection of CRA technical interpretations that are based on written enquires by taxpayers and/or the their representatives. These documents were obtained, at least initially, through the authority of the *Access to Information Act* and are sometimes referred to as Access Letters. Advance Tax Rulings (found in the EBCR infobase) are similar documents that preceded Winfiles and ended in 1995/96. These technical interpretations are used extensively by tax practitioners.

C. Basic Search Commands

The most common fault of novice electronic researchers (and sometimes even experienced researchers) is to refuse to do the necessary basic research (either manually or electronically) that will enable them to form well-constructed search commands using the appropriate terminology. Folio searches only for those words that the researcher indicates in his or her search command (query). The correctness or accuracy of the query is the researcher's responsibility not Folio's. The common adage, garbage-in, garbage-out, is particularly *apropos* to electronic research. Therefore, most tax research requires an initial review of the relevant provision(s) of the ITA to ensure that the correct words are being searched or, perhaps, eliminated. However, when the research is being done in infobases other than the ITA infobase (the infobase which contains the most structured and uniform language), then the researcher must include in the query potential synonyms and similar phrases.

In this part, five different search commands will be introduced. It is recommenced that after you read and comprehended each command, you practice using that command, before moving on to the next search command.

The OR Search Command

The OR operator/connector expands a query or search, because the presence of either word in a record results in a hit which is defined as, the first occurrence of the searched words. Remember a record is defined differently for different infobases. If you should forget the definition for the infobase that you are searching, go to the Table of Contents and click on the sub-infobase, About this Infobase. Usually, you can find this definition in the first section of this sub-infobase.

An example query with the OR operator in the EBCR infobase would be:

employee or employer

This query would result in 2,362 hits at the time of writing as shown in Exhibit 19-21.

Exhibit 19-21
Example of the OR Operator

Now carefully examine Exhibit 19-21.

The results map, which is just below the bolded title, Records With Hits, presents your query and the results thereof in the form of a diagram. Note that the OR operator is replaced by a symbol. The symbol that looks like a half or partial box indicates that the two words are connected or joined. The short vertical half line which follows indicates that the words are connected or joined by the OR operator. If you wish, you can use this symbol in place of the word OR in your queries. This vertical symbol is found on the key board just above the backslash and looks similar to two vertical hyphens. Your query with the OR symbol would look like this:

employee | employer.

Now, examine carefully the Word Wheel which displays all the words with the prefix or stem, employ, some of which are hidden. You may want to add some of these words to your query and, in particular, the plural form of employee and employer. The *Interpretations Act* states that in all federal statutes, except as specifically excepted in the statute at issue, singular and plural words should be read as the same.[a] Therefore, in tax research, your query would not be complete without the pluralization of these words. Note that subsequent versions of the Folio Products pluralize automatically but not Folio 4.3 which is used in the present version of Taxworks. Now add the pluralization of the initial search words (employee or employer) by modifying our original query and also add an additional word, employment. See Exhibit 19-22.

Exhibit 19-22
Example of Word Pluralization

Note in the Results Map that each subsequent word is joined to the preceding word by a partial box followed by the OR symbol. However, if you add the actual hits for

---

[a] See Section 33 of this legislation for the pluralization and gender rules for all federal legislation. The *Interpretations Act* is found in the Commentary infobase under the sub-infobase, Related Statutes. The formal name of this legislation is the *Income Tax Conventions Interpretations Act*, (ITCIA). The next module will look at the extensive and varied components of the Commentary infobase.

each single word as shown in the Results Map, their sum will not equal the final total number of hits, since multiple occurrences within a record will only count as a single hit.

The AND Search Command

The AND operator restricts a query or search because both words must be in the record at least once in order to have a hit. An example query with the AND operator in the EBCR infobase for employee and employer would be:

employee and employer

This query would result in 537 hits at the time of writing as shown in Exhibit 19-23.

Exhibit 19-23
An Example of the AND Operator

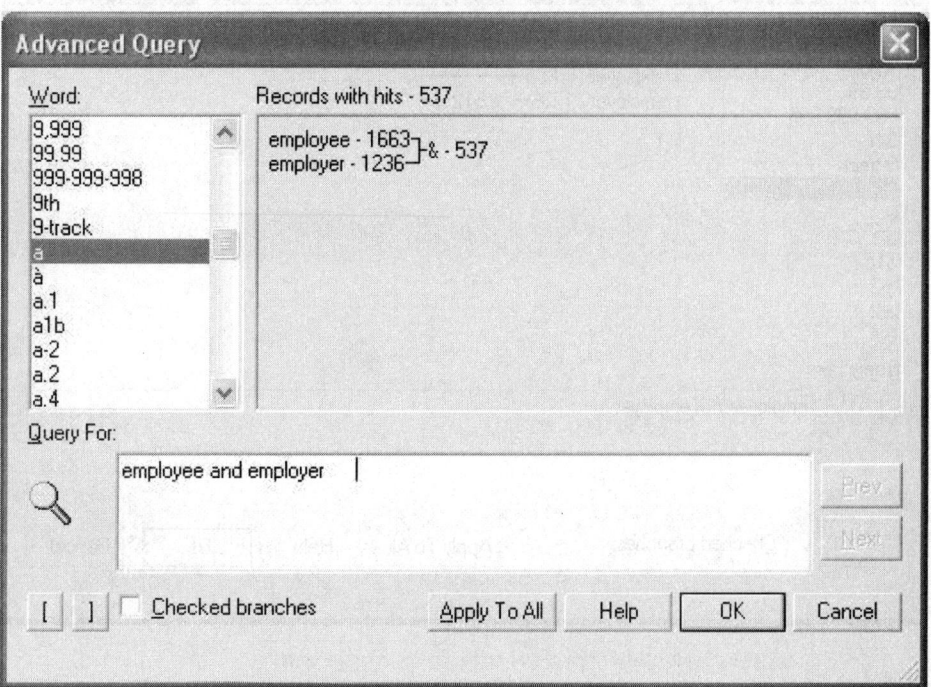

Now look at the Results Map and note how the query was executed. First, each word was searched separately and resulted in 1,663 hits for employee and 1,236 hits for employer. Then these results were combined with AND operator by its symbol &, referred to as the ampersand. The final result was Records With Hits of 537.

The AND operator can also be represented by a space between the two searched words. Therefore, a query with the AND operator can look like any of the following;

employee and employer

employee & employer

employee employer

The NOT Search Command

The NOT operator is a little more complicated since it can be used in two different ways depending upon what word, if any, precedes or follows the NOT in the query statement. The most common NOT query would have a single word before and after the NOT operator. This format finds all records that contain the first word but then eliminates those records that contain the second word (the word that follows the NOT operator). An example shown in Exhibit 19-24 would be:

employee not employer

Exhibit 19-24
An Example of the NOT Operator

The Results Map shows that there were 1,663 hits with first word, employee. For the word, employer, there were 51,258 hits but when the query is restricted by the NOT operator, this number is reduced to 1,126. The NOT operator symbol is the caret, an inverted v (i.e., ^) which is found on the keyboard above the number 6. The two results were joined together by a partial box and a software-generated ampersand (&) to present a final number of hits of 1,126.

The other application of the NOT operator is where there is no first word, i.e., the word before the NOT operator. With this query, Folio will find all the records that do not contain the word that follows the operator. An example would be:

NOT employer

With this type of NOT operator, Folio finds all the records that do not contain the word, employer.

Multiple Operators/Connectors in a Query

When more than one type of operator is used in a query, the Folio software often becomes confused as to the order of the operators. The confusion is caused by both the researcher and the software. The following is an example of the problem. The researcher is trying to structure a query that finds all the records that contain either the word, employee or employer, but not shareholder. For the sake of simplicity, the problem of pluralization will be ignored. See Exhibit 19-25.

Exhibit 19-25
An Example of a Vague Query

First of all, there is a problem with the query itself. The researcher has not indicated whether the phrase, not shareholder, modifies both words, employee or employer, or just employer. Second, the Folio software has some internal ordering rules and some application inconsistencies, which may give rise to some incorrect results. In this example, the software has automatically joined the first two words with an OR operator as shown by the diagram in the Results Map. This software-generated action leaves the next two words, not shareholder, without a preceding word which results in the alternative usage of the NOT operator as described above.

Therefore, the software finds all records that do not have the word shareholder (51,958) and combines this with the results of the OR connector above (2,362) to give a final combination of hits of 2,288. The 536 represents the number of records that contain the word, shareholder.

The solution is that the researcher should break the query into sub-queries which will leave no doubt as to his/her intention and which will override any software-generated problems. This is accomplished by surrounding each operator and the searched words with round brackets i.e., ( ). e.g., (employee or employer) not shareholder. Therefore, in the exercises in this chapter you must insert the round brackets into your queries so that your query logic can be evaluated.

Remember the brackets must be round brackets, not square brackets [ ] or squiggly brackets { }. You can use as many brackets as you like as long both brackets (left and right) are present or errors will occur. You can also have brackets within brackets; in this situation, the inside brackets will be executed first. With exception of brackets within brackets, these sub-queries are executed from left to right.

The Exclusive OR Operator

The Exclusive OR operator is represented by the command XOR or the symbol ~ which is referred to as the tilde and is usually found on the left-hand side of the keyboard on the number row above and combined with a slanted single quotation mark. This search command finds records that contain either searched word but not both words. This operator or connector is most useful in situations where the query results are compared with another similar query and the differences are recorded as hits. An example will be presented after an examination of the next search command.

Phrase Searches

A specific phrase search is executed by enclosing the phrase in double quotation marks. Single quotation marks will not work. Furthermore, you cannot include any other operators or search commands within the double quotation marks. An example would be:

associated corporations

as shown in Exhibit 19-26.

Exhibit 19-26
A Search For A Specific Phrase

The Results Map indicates that Folio first found the number of occurrences of the two words: associated 405 and corporations 1,022. Then, the double quotation marks were applied to find the two words side by side with the word, associated, preceding the word, corporation, to give us 62 hits for the phrase, associated corporations.

Let us assume that the above specific search phrase, "associated corporations", did not find the documents that we know exist. Perhaps looking at the limitations of a specific phrase search will help us construct a different query. For example we know that a specific phrase search must be constructed so that the query words are side by side, and enclosed with quotations marks. Therefore, the query would not recognize the following phrase as a hit, ...(the corporations were associated) . . . . because the words, associated and corporations, are not be side by side and the word, associated, did not precede the word, corporations.

However, we do know that the AND operator would work in this situation if we combined it with the specific phrase query but we do not want duplicate hits — only additional hits. It is in this type of situations that the XOR operator would be very useful. We will construct a double query that compares hits that contain the phrase, associated corporations, with hits that contained the two search words joined with the AND operator.

i.e., "associated corporations" xor (associated and corporations)

Now examine the Results Map in Exhibit 19-27 and you will see that the XOR operator compared the two searches and found only those records in which one search phrase or the other search phrase was present but not both, i.e, 99 hits. The end result is that XOR command identified only the hit differences between the two queries.

Exhibit 19-27
Example of the XOR Operator

Searching for Specific Provisions

Provision searching is really an exact phrase query but because of its importance in tax research it is worthy of a separate examination. Let us begin with a simple search for paragraph 6(1)(a). Folio does not recognize the brackets as brackets and assigns a blank space in its place. The reason is that round brackets represent a sub-query with an operator or connector. Without the quotation marks, i.e,. 6(1)(a) is read as one of the alternatives below;

6 and 1 and a

6 & 1 & a

6 1 a

and in the EBCR infobase you would have 901 records at the time of writing which have all three alpha/digits. If any of the above three alternatives is enclosed with double quotation marks the number of hits at the time of writing decreases to 110 records. If the provision descriptive is added, i.e., paragraph 6 1 a, the number of records decrease significantly to 86. This is because provision descriptives are not always used and often are replaced with an acronym (e.g., ita; par.; para.; s.; sec.). Therefore, provision descriptives are not generally used. However, having said that, it is recommended that certain very common section numbers (e.g., numbers 1 to 31) do need a descriptive and/or a limiting word(s) with the AND connector rather than quotation marks for reasons stated above. For example, a search in Tax Window Files for section 31 using the number alone would have 3,107 hits, at the time of writing. Adding a descriptive with the AND operator, the result is shown below:

31 and farm	86
31 and section	1,311
31 and farm and loss	32

One final comment about quotation marks in phrase searching. A phrase with double quotation marks will change the function of the operators that are contained within the enclosed phrase, AND, OR and NOT, back to ordinary words. Similarly if you enclose any of the above operators in double quotation marks, the operator reverts back to its normal usage.

Some General Comments and Helpful Hints

Remember that your search is not complete (even if you can see a search result on the Results Map) until a number is entered beside the bolded title, Records With Hits. There are several possible reasons for this discrepancy between the Results Map and its title. First, the software has not finished its processing of the query and you cannot see the word, processing, because part of the query diagram is off the screen to the right. Use the left horizontal arrow at the bottom of the screen to bring into view the whole diagram in the Results Map. Second, the query cannot be executed because you have not completed the query statement, e.g., you have forgotten to enter both quotation marks for exact phrase query or you have omitted one of the round brackets in a series of sub-queries. When this occurs there will be an error message in red type on the Results Map — see Exhibit 19-28 for an example of a query in the EBCR infobase of an error message (e.g., enter another word or enter a " to end phrase); however, the text is in black print rather than the weak electronic red.

Exhibit 19-28
Error Messages on the Results Map

After executing a query you should always examine the Results Map very carefully to verify the execution of your query. In particular, make sure that you have inserted both round brackets around all potential sub-queries and especially when you have used the NOT connector. Make sure that each line of the Results Map has a hit. No hits on a particular line usually indicate an inputting error, e.g., a spelling error.

Phrase searching is the last search command in this module. However, rest assured that you can find all potential hits with the limited search commands demonstrated so far. It is strongly recommended that you practice with these limited commands before moving on to additional commands in Module 4 because the commands that are presented in this module are really the backbone of electronic searching.

D. Errors: Query and Inputting

When you are satisfied with the structure of your query and where you have only one infobase open, press the OK button at the bottom of the Advanced Query template and one of the various screens discussed in Module 2 will appear.

For this demonstration of the basic navigation commands, a fairly complex query in the EBCR infobase will be used as shown in Exhibit 19-29. Note how the query used four sets of round brackets including brackets within brackets.

Exhibit 19-29
Multiple Brackets in a Query

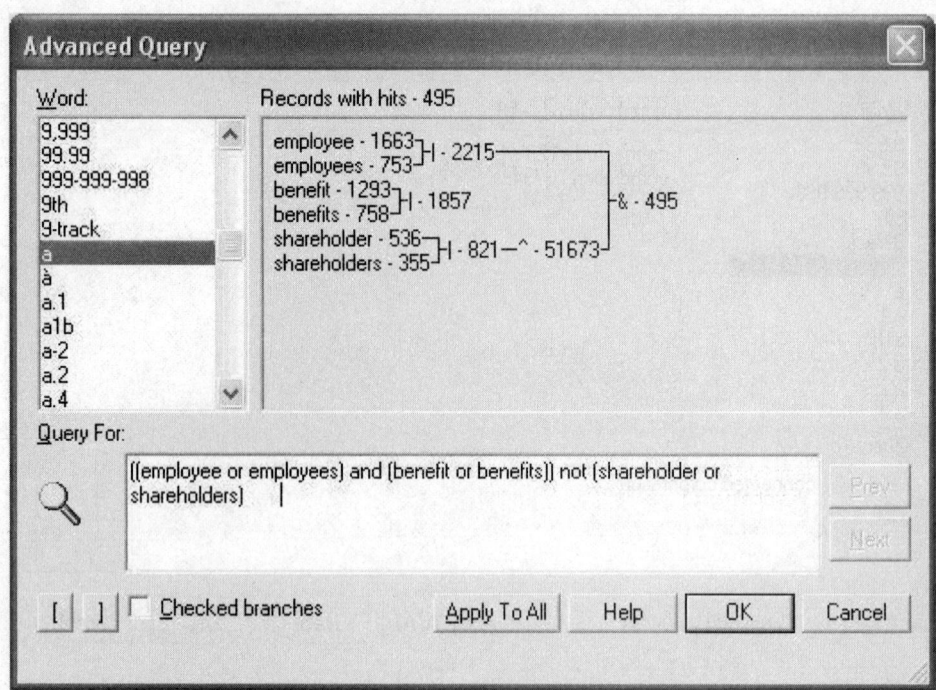

Observe in the Results Map that the two bracketed OR commands were searched first. The round brackets indicate to the software that these are sub-searches that should be executed first. This avoids the problem in Exhibit 19-25 because now there is a word/phrase substitute that completes the Not command.

Exhibit 19-30 demonstrates what may happen when one of the brackets in a query is missing. There should be two consecutive left-hand brackets at the beginning of the query, (see Exhibit 19-29 above), to complete the combined phrase. However, only one of the brackets is present. Note that the last part of the query has been dropped because of this omission resulting in a serious error and there is no red error message to warn you of this problem.

Exhibit 19-30
Missing Bracket Results in an Error

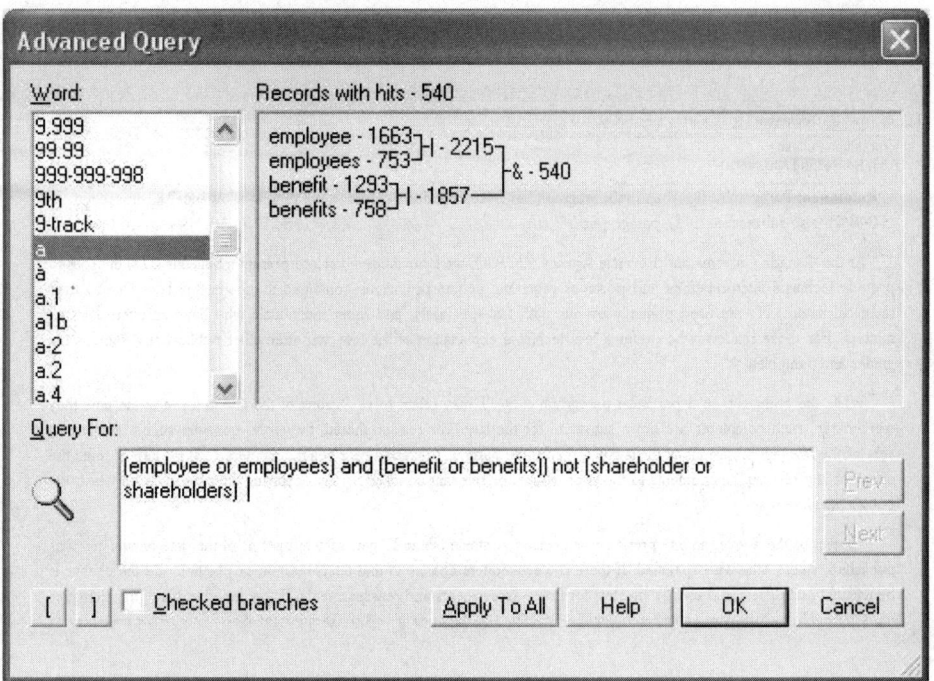

E. Tagging, Printing and Saving Search Results

Tagging is a unique method of gathering selected records rather than continuous records. Highlighting or selecting cannot be applied because the records are not continuous. The tagging function places a red line with small arrows in the left hand margin beside the record to be tagged which is identified for tagging by having the cursor on the particular record. See Exhibit 19-31 for an example of tagging.

Exhibit 19-31
Tagged Records
(Selected Paragraphs in IT-337R4)

First, click on the record that you wish to tag and then press the key combination of Ctrl + T. Alternatively, click on the particular tagging function which can be found under the Edit button on the main menu. Note, however, that clearing tags can only be accomplished through the Edit button.

Also see below for the topic, Printing, for printing tagged records.

A problem with tagging is the identification of the source of the tagged material when you are flitting among documents. The easiest method, but one which can result in a very cluttered print-out, is to change the print attributes through Print Options as previously demonstrated in Module 2 above. See Exhibit 19-22 and related text above and click on inline headings and each tagged record will be preceded by the information in the reference pane of the Document Window.

Folio has its own unique print dialogue box which differs from the various Window's print dialogue screens. This Folio Print Dialogue is shown in Exhibit 19-32.

Exhibit 19-32
Folio Print Dialogue

Note that you must identify the type of View you want to print by clicking on the appropriate tab, e.g., Print Document, Print Contents [table of] etc., because each of these alternatives has special print instructions. In Exhibit 19-32 the print alternatives for the view Print Document, are displayed. Click on the next tab, Print Contents, and a different set of alternatives would be displayed.

Print Document Alternatives

All

It is recommended that this option should not be used because of a possible execution problem. First, All refers to what data can be accessed by the computer not necessarily what you see presently on the computer screen. For example, if you open the ITA infobase and then choose print option All, the entire Income Tax Act will be printed not just what is currently on the screen. However, if you have restricted the view by any one of the other options (discussed below), the potential problem vanishes and you can use All.

Records

This option is useful when you require selected text which runs for 30 or more pages of consecutive materials. Place your cursor at the beginning of the required text and note the record number as indicated in the status line at the bottom of the screen.

Advance to the end of the selected text and again note the record number of the last selected record. Enter the first and last record number in the appropriate boxes.

Selection

Selection is the most widely used of all the printing options under Folio. This method requires that the selected text be highlighted. The quickest method but the hardest to control is the drag method. Hold down the left mouse button and drag the pointer over the selected text. However, because of the compression of the text in a database format, it is very difficult to restrict the highlighted text to specific paragraphs let alone lines and partial lines. Therefore, it is recommended that you highlight by using the Page Down (or UP) and then clean up the text at the end of selected text by using the arrow keys: up and down arrows for line additions or removal and the east-west arrows for word additions or removal.

Tagged Records

Tagged Records prints only those records that you have tagged. It is particularly useful when you do not want to print consecutive records.

Section

Section restricts the printing to a particular branch or branches of the infobase as indicated by the check-marked boxes discussed previously.

Saving

Saving is the process of storing data. The data may have been just created and is presently on the computer screen, e.g., query results. Alternatively, the data may have been already saved and resides in another document or file from which it is to be saved again to a new document or file. Copying is another form of saving whereby the data will be stored in a least two places: the original storage position and a new storage position. As with any windows-based product, there are usually a half-dozen different methods to achieve your objective. Since data can be easily misplaced during the saving process, it is recommended that you choose one saving method and stick with it.

The saving methods available are the same ones as demonstrated in the printing process: highlighting or selection, record number to record number and tagging.

Highlighting or selection is the most common method and there are two alternatives for saving highlighted information. The first alternative is the Windows Cut/Copy and the Paste procedure which you may have already used with your Windows-based word processor. If you are familiar with this procedure then it is recommend that this saving method should be your first choice. The other alternative for saving highlighted data is to use the Save As dialogue box which is found under the File option of the main menu.

F. Help Infobases

There are two different types of Help sources: text sources which are not searchable and a help infobase with several alternate ways of obtaining the requested information.

The text sources are a Quick Reference List and a User's Guide, both of which are CCH specific, rather than Folio generic. It is recommended that you print these references and leave them by your computer because both of these sources are not accessible while in TaxWorks. To access these sources go to the Windows Start button, click on Programs, and click on CCH Library. A dialogue box will appear. Note that this is the same dialogue box which contains the TaxWorks Launcher. Print these two sources by using the Selection method previously described in this module.

The infobase sources are searchable in the same manner as all CCH electronic products. The first alternative method to access the Help infobase and the easiest is to press the F1 function key which will present a screen of information pertaining to the function you are trying to perform. For example, you are presently in the Advance Query Template and you need some additional information. Then, press F1 and a series of screens will be presented on the topic of the Advance Query template.

One caution about the Help infobases. These are generic sources of Help for all users of Folio products, not just CCH users. Therefore, unique aspects of CCH's use of the Folio software are not explained. Furthermore, this infobase is designed for all users including novices, experienced users and even the suppliers of Folio products who actually reconfigure the software for their specific products. Therefore, as a novice, you may find much of the information in this infobase is not relevant.

However, the information that you seek is there. It is just difficult to find. Here are a couple of alternative methods of obtaining information from the Help infobase. Click on the word, Help, in the main menu and a drop-down dialogue box will appear see Exhibit 19-33.

Exhibit 19-33
Help Infobase Drop-down Dialogue Box

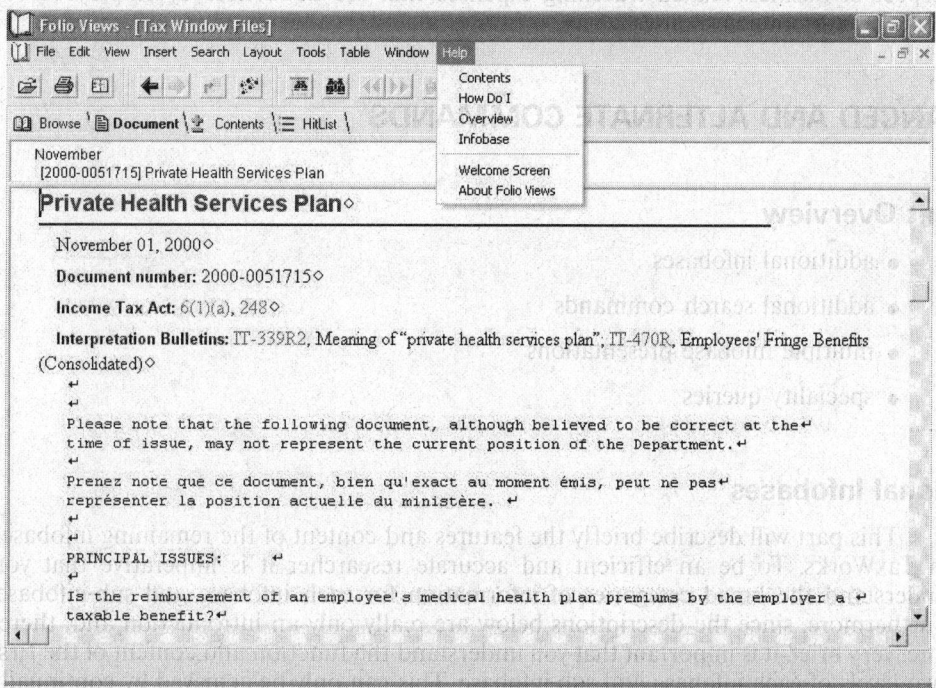

Click on the word, Contents, and list of Help topics will appear. Click on the Help topic title for detailed information. Click on the magnifying glass for an overview of the topic.

Alternatively, the How Do I infobase in the Help dialogue box provides a list of typical TaxWorks tasks. Just click on the relevant topic.

Still no luck, then do a query using the Advance Query template with subsequent modifications with the, and, operator to narrow your search.

G. Part III Exercises

1. Why would the following queries in the *Income Tax Act* which were constructed by the researcher to go directly to paragraph 6(1)(a) fail to achieve their objective?

a) "paragraph 6(1)(a)"

b) 6(1)(a)

2. What command overcomes the problem that is raised in Exercise 1 above and why is it able to do this?

3. Construct a query that will find records in the Bulletins, Circulars, Rulings (EBCR) infobase each of which contains the following words: student, university, scholarship.

4. Construct a query that will find records in the Bulletins, Circulars, Rulings (EBCR) infobase each of which will find corporations that are associated and/or connected but are not affiliated.

5. Construct a query that will find records in the Tax Window Files infobase in respect of business-related travelling expenses that are deductible by employees but exclude automobile expenses.

IV.   ADVANCED AND ALTERNATE COMMANDS

A.   Content Overview

- additional infobases
- additional search commands
- multiple infobase presentations
- speciality queries

B.   Additional Infobases

This part will describe briefly the features and content of the remaining infobases in TaxWorks. To be an efficient and accurate researcher it is imperative that you understand the broad categories of information for each infobase and sub-infobase. Furthermore, since the descriptions below are really only an introduction and, therefore, very brief, it is important that you understand the function and content of the first two levels of each infobase and sub-infobase. This can only be achieved by continually reviewing each level of the table of contents and ensuring that you understand the importance of each infobase and sub-infobase. Remember each infobase has a description of its contents and function in a sub-infobase that is usually found at the end of the Table of Contents under the title, About this Infobase. The following infobases will be discussed below:

- CCH Commentary
- Income Tax Forms and Guides
- Dominion Tax Cases: Current and Archival Summaries
- Revenue Canada Round Table
- Window on Canadian Tax

CCH Commentary Infobase

The main purpose of this infobase is to present CCH's interpretation of each provision of the ITA, ITARs and ITRs, and is referred to as CCH Commentary. In this sub-infobase, CCH has carefully analysed each provision with the assistance of a team of tax specialists: legal and accounting. Imbedded in the analysis is a series of red-highlighted links to other important documents that are related to the topic that is currently being analysed. At the beginning of each provision CCH has prepared a concise overview of the relevant section of the ITA which is particularly helpful for the novice tax researcher.

In addition to the ITA Commentary sub-infobase, there are over 20 additional sub-infobases in this infobase. The sub-infobases are summarized below:

- Federal Budgets for prior years — (note that these are budgets, not legislation or legislation-in-progress which can be found in the ITA infobase.)

- CRA Publications include the CRA's Technical News plus a number of industry-specific newsletters such as Registered Charities and SR & ED.

- Income Tax Treaties including international and Canadian conventions and all of Canada's tax treaties.

- Related Statutes contains over 25 pieces of legislation to which the ITA makes specific reference, e.g. *Canadian Pension Plan, Canada Business Corporations Act,* etc.

- Recent Case Digests is a cumulative list of all the headnotes to the court cases since 1977.

- Quick Access provides certain common tools-of the-trade of an income tax specialist, such as income tax rates, both federal and provincial, for individuals and corporations, prescribed interest rates, automobile rates and limits, CCA classes and rates, selected withholding tax rates, a tax calendar with the important filing dates, etc.

- Progress of Legislation infobase shows the status of each piece of proposed legislation as it passes through the legislative process.

- Bibliographies is a current collection of substantive Canadian income tax articles. The sources of these articles come from CCH Publications as well as law journals, the Canadian Tax Foundation, and other outside sources.

- News Releases is a compilation of tax-related news releases by year from all government sources, not just the department of Finance and the CRA.

- Tax Topics is CCH's monthly tax news letter with current relevant information for tax practitioners.

- Website links are internet connections to outside organizations' websites such as the Canadian courts, trade associations, media, educational institutions, Federal government and International tax sources.

Income Tax Forms and Guides Infobase

This infobase contains literally hundreds of income tax forms for individuals, trusts, partnerships and corporations. Remember to load in the Adobe software that is necessary for access to both the forms and guides. The guides sub-infobase contains about a dozen special situation pamphlets for individuals such as persons who are students, recently retired, disabled, going south for the winter, etc. In addition, there are over 120 detailed guides on how to deal with specific administrative and filing problem areas such as trusts, farming income, payroll deductions, benefit guides, etc. This infobase has a lot of excellent information but is often overlooked by tax researchers.

Dominion Tax Cases Infobase

This infobase is composed of two sub-infobases:

1. Current DTC Cases, which contains all the complete cases for the present year. In this sub-infobase, a record is defined as the summary/digest, as described below and each page of hard copy.

2. Archival DTC Past Cases, but in a summary format rather than the complete case. The Summary format has all the relevant information that is required for your needs at this level, e.g., references to ITA, the names of plaintiff and the defendant, a summary of the facts and the court's decision with the basic underlying reasons.

Revenue Canada Round Table Infobase

This infobase arose from one of the sessions at the Annual Conference of the Canadian Tax Foundation. The format of this session was "question and answer". Practitioners would submit questions to Revenue Canada prior to the conference and Revenue Canada would respond to those questions at the conference. The Round Table was extremely popular for about ten years and then it lost its lustre and was abandoned in 1993.

The infobase covers the time period 1979 to 1993 and still contains very valuable information that should not be overlooked. Another feature of the infobase is the insightful editorial comments of one of Canada's leading tax practitioners.

Window on Canadian Tax Infobase

This infobase is expert commentary on the validity of the CRA's response to certain specific technical interpretations as found in the Tax Window Files infobase which was discussed in Module 3. This analysis is extremely important in tax practice and should not be overlooked because of the brevity of this description.

C. Additional Search Commands

1. Unordered Proximity Connector

Recall the Phrase search command with double quotation marks that was described in Module 3. One of the examples was the query "associated corporations" and it was noted at the time that such a Phrase search would not find records that had the following phrase, the corporations were associated.

The solution is found in a new search command, an unordered proximity connector — a title that describes its uniqueness. The unordered proximity connector looks for words that are near each other (in proximity) but can be either before or after each other. Therefore, this new search command would find the exact phrase, associated corporations, and similar phrases, such as, the corporations were associated. The query would be:

"associated corporations"@4

The two words that are being connected must be enclosed by double quotation marks just as you would for a Phrase search. However, the enclosed phrase would be followed immediately by the AT symbol, @, and the number of proximity words, i.e., 4. The number of proximity words can range from 2 to 9, including the searched terms.

The following chart reflects multiple unordered proximity searches in the CCH Window on Canadian Tax infobase at the time of writing for the proximity words, associated and corporations. As you can see, each change in the @ modifier resulted in some additional hits.

"associated corporations"@2	34
"associated corporations"@3	48
"associated corporations"@4	55
"associated corporations"@5	64
"associated corporations"@6	65
"associated corporations"@7	65
"associated corporations"@8	66

To view only the additional hits, an additional query must be constructed using the XOR operator as described in Module 3. For example, to find the additional hits for query @3 as compared to query @2, the search command would be:

("associated corporations"@3) XOR ("associated corporations"@2)

Then the additional 14 hits would have to be examined to see if these hits were relevant to the search objectives.

Note that if this number of records is too high, then the query should be modified with an AND connector plus another word or, perhaps, a provision number.

2. Acronyms and Legislative Changes

In our investigation of the hits for the previous query, we would have found the extensive use of the acronyms, SR&ED and R&D. SR&ED is the acronym for the present title for section 37. R&D was the acronym for section 37 for the years prior to 1992. However, the acronym, R&D, is still used today as shown in Exhibit 19-34.

Exhibit 19-34
Use of the Acronyms R&D and SR&ED
Table of Contents — Window on Canadian Tax Infobase

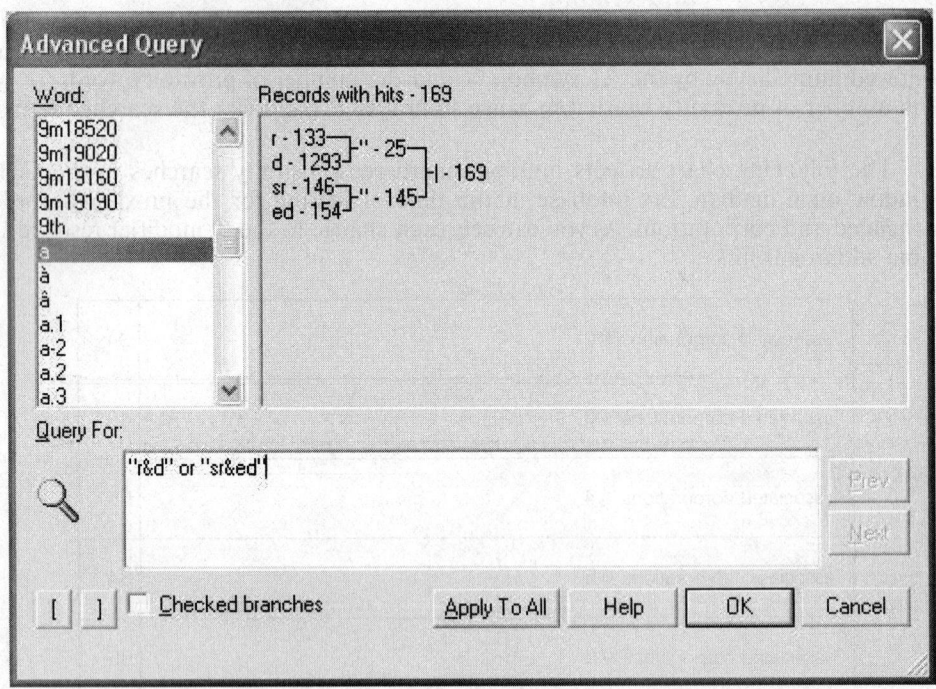

The above acronym anomaly is a good example of why some preliminary investigative research is necessary before you finalize search queries. Similarly the phrase, Research and Development, is also used today rather than the much longer but technically correct phrase, Scientific Research and Experimental Development. In some records both acronyms and phrases will be present. However, such duplication can be isolated by use of the XOR command as previously demonstrated.

D. Multiple Infobases

Up to this point, only single infobase searches have been demonstrated. Now the opening and viewing of multiple infobases will be presented. To open multiple infobases initially, you must use TaxWorks Launcher as described in the opening modules.

Before opening the multiple infobases, you must decide on the screen presentation format. There are four alternatives which can be found under the Windows tab in the main menu: new window, cascade, tile vertically and tile horizontally. The choice is yours; however, only the Cascade mode will be presented. See Exhibit 19-35.

Exhibit 19-35
Multiple Infobases in the Cascade Presentation Mode

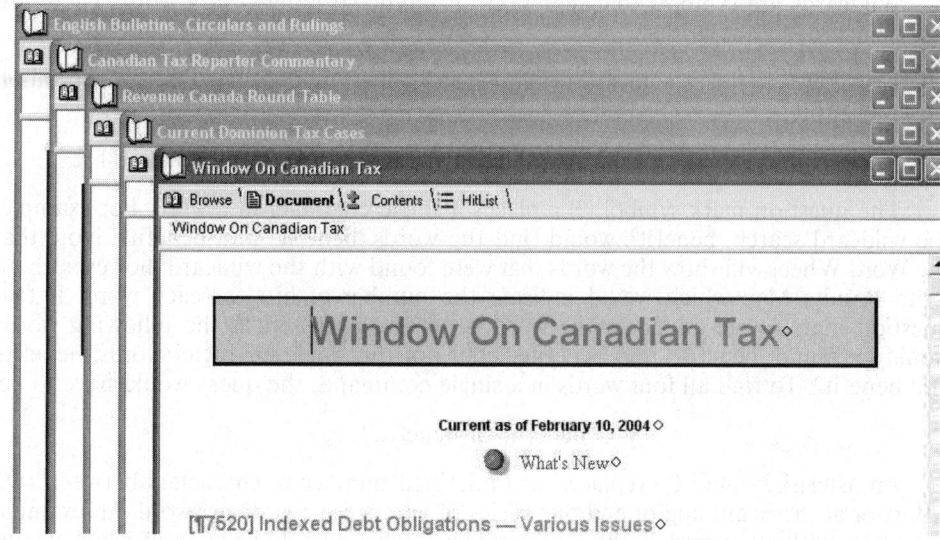

    To open an infobase folder, just click on its title and an enlarged version of the infobase will come forward in the normal manner. To open a different infobase, go back to the Windows tab in the main menu and choose a different infobase by clicking on the title at the bottom of the Windows dialogue box as shown in Exhibit 19-41 above.

E. Speciality Queries

    Speciality queries are aids in composing search commands and are part and parcel of the necessary initial work that must be done before structuring meaningful and effective search commands. The following speciality queries will be described:

- Thesaurus queries
- Wildcard queries
- Stem queries
- Serial OR queries

Thesaurus Queries

    Thesaurus queries enable the researcher to find alternative search words or synonyms. The search command is simply the word that you want to replace followed by the dollar sign ($), e.g., employ$ that would yield over 30,000 hits in the Commentary infobase. Unfortunately, thesaurus queries cannot display a Results Map; therefore, the researcher must examine a sample of the alternative words, make a list of rejected words, and eliminate the word(s) from the query with the NOT command. Thesaurus queries are especially useful in the DTC infobases where the range of potential words is very wide.

Wildcard Queries

Wildcards are symbols that represent an unknown letter(s) in a word. There are two wildcards in TaxWorks:

- a single character wildcard which is represented by the question mark, symbol, (?), and

- a multiple character wildcard which is represented by the asterisk, (*).

The question mark symbol (?) replaces a single character in a word. For example, the wildcard search, benefit?, would find the words, benefits and benefit2. Note that the Word Wheel will show the words that were found with the wildcard; however, there is no Results Map which would indicate the number of hits for each word. If two question marks were added to the word benefit, e.g., benefit??, the following words would be found, benefit's and benefited, but not the single character words, benefits and benefit2. To find all four words in a single command, the query would have to be:

benefit? or benefit??

An asterisk symbol (*) replaces an undefined number of characters between two letters or at the beginning or end of a series of letters e.g., word* or *word. An example of a query with an asterisk in the Commentary infobase would be benefit* which would yield over 110,000 hits composed of the words such as: benefit, benefit's, benefit2, benefited, benefiting, benefits, benefitted, benefitting. Note that the last two words are spelling errors that could be either the court's or the publisher's. Once again, the number of hits for each word is unknown, because there is no Results Map, which severely limits the usefulness of this command. However, we still have the ability to scan the hits and determine the usefulness of each word variation and then restrict the query with the NOT operator.

Stem Queries

Stem queries search for words with a common stem that can be simply stated as the main part of the word. If the searched-stem word is a noun, then stem query will only look for nouns unless, of course, the searched-stem word can be both a noun and a verb. Where the searched-stem word is a verb, the software will find tense variations, such as begin, began, begun. Furthermore, the meaning of the searched-stem word cannot be changed. For example, a stem search for the word, employee, would not find the words, employer(s), employment.

Stem queries have two further limitations. First, as with wildcard queries, stem searches do not produce a Results Map and the Word Wheel does not indicate specifically the words found in the stem search. In conclusion, stem searches and wildcard searches are not very efficient search tools. The solution lies in the next topic which, in fact, you may have already concluded.

Serial OR Queries

The problem with the stem and wildcard searches is that the researcher has little or no control over the search structure. For example, for a wildcard search such as employ*, the researcher cannot control which words are included. Of course, after the execution of the wildcard search, the researcher can restrict the included words by modifying the query with the NOT operator.

The better alternative involves the researcher constructing the query from scratch using his or her specialized knowledge base and experience. The tools are all there and we have used them over and over in this Chapter: the Word Wheel, the OR operator and the XOR operator, plus a little trick demonstrated below.

First, input the search word without the wild card. Then examine the Word Wheel in order to determine which variations of the search word you would like to include. Now you can input additional words without any further inputting/typing by following the next few steps. First, double click on the highlighted search word in the word list that you just inputted. This operation sets up a procedure that enables the researcher to add selected additional words by just double clicking on those words. The secret is that the researcher is selecting the search words not the software. Watch the Results Map carefully as each word is added. Then, if you wish to evaluate the effect of the addition of a particular word, do a comparison with the XOR command as previously demonstrated.

F. Part IV Exercises

1. Create a list of infobases and/or sub-infobases that you would search and examine to find the CRA's interpretation on a particular income tax issue?

2. Construct a series of separate but related queries in the Bulletins, Circulars and Rulings infobase using the following constraints:

(A) first construct a query to find all records containing the exact phrase, *Canadian-controlled private corporations*;

(B) modify the query for (A) above to include any relevant acronym;

(C) restrict the query for (B) above to include only those records that refer to stock options.

Discussion Notes for Review Questions

CHAPTER 2
Liability for Tax

(1) Canadian individuals are taxed based on residency and not their citizenship [ssec. 2(1)]. Canadian residents are taxed on their world income.

(2) Subsection 250(1) will deem him or her to be a resident only if he or she sojourned in Canada for 183 or more days during the year.

(3) You need to look at other factors to determine where they have a "continuing state of relationship", such as family and social ties and other personal property. IT-221R3 categorizes the type of facts that can be used to establish residential ties.

(4) He or she would be considered to be a non-resident of Canada throughout the year. However, since he or she carried on business in Canada during the year while a non-resident, he or she would be taxable in Canada on his or her Canadian business profits for the year [ssec. 2(3)].

(5) If he or she is establishing a "fresh start" in Canada on March 31 then he or she becomes resident on that date and is taxed in Canada on his or her world income from that date. The sojourning rules would not apply since they only apply to non-residents who are in Canada on a temporary basis.

(6) The residency of a corporation is either determined by the common law test of "central management and control", or a corporation is deemed to be a Canadian resident [ssec. 250(4)] if it is incorporated in Canada after April 26, 1965, or it meets the tests outlined in subsection 250(4) if it was incorporated before that date.

(7) Paragraph 250(4)(a) deems the corporation to be resident in Canada if it was incorporated in Canada after April 26, 1965. Reference to the tax treaty would be the next step but Canada does not have a tax treaty with Bermuda. Therefore, it would be resident in Canada and taxable in Canada on its world income.

(8) Paragraph 250(4)(c) deems any company which was incorporated in Canada before April 27, 1965 and which carried on business in Canada in any year after that date to be resident in Canada. Paragraph 253(b) provides an extended meaning of carrying on business which includes soliciting orders in Canada. The facts fit the meaning because of the continuity of the order solicitation over a period of years. Therefore, the company would be resident in Canada and taxable in Canada on its world income.

(9) Subsection 2(3) refers to "employed in Canada in the year or a previous year". Therefore, section 115 of Division D requires the income from an office or employment to be taxed in Canada [par. 115(2)(c)].

(10) While the income would be business income, it would not be income from "carrying on" business under normal circumstances, since this term implies some ongoing activity which

does not exist in this case. However, since the land was offered for sale in Canada it may fit into the extended definition of carrying on business in Canada [sec. 253], but this is unlikely since, in order to fit into this "extended" definition, he or she first has to be "carrying on business" which he or she is not. Therefore, the transaction cannot be included in the extended definition and would not be taxable in Canada.

(11) The U.S. company is soliciting orders in Canada and, therefore, is carrying on business in Canada [sec. 253]. The corporation is, thus, taxable in Canada on the profits related to these sales [ssec. 2(3) and sec. 115].

(12) Under the extended meaning of carrying on business [sec. 253], the company would be resident in Canada. However, under the Canada–U.S. tax treaty, the U.S. company would not have a permanent establishment in Canada and, therefore, would not be taxable here.

(13) Yes, a person can be a resident of more than one country since residency is determined under the laws of each country. Article IV of the Canada–U.S. tax treaty provides rules for resolving who collects the tax where a person is a resident of both the U.S. and Canada.

(14) Under Article VII of the Canada–U.S. tax treaty, it will only be subject to tax on the income attributable to that permanent establishment.

(15) Article XIV of the Canada–U.S. tax treaty will cause him to be taxed in the U.S. only if he has a "fixed base regularly available to him" in the U.S. Therefore, he will only pay tax in Canada on this income.

CHAPTER 3

Employment Income

(1) The personal tax return (T1 General) does not include RPP contributions, union and professional dues and other paragraph 8(1)(i) deductions in the calculation of employment income. These are included under the heading "Net Income" in the personal tax return. It would be misleading to use the personal tax return format for this specific purpose, because certain deductions are limited to the amount of employment income in the year, such as the home office expense deduction.

(2) An employee can only deduct those expenses that are specifically allowed under section 8 whereas a self-employed individual may deduct all expenses incurred to earn business and property income as permitted by Subdivision b. Both the employee and the self-employed individual are subject to the reasonableness test in section 67.

(3) No one test is conclusive in itself. All tests should be considered together before a conclusion is reached.

(4) The control subtest in the economic reality or entrepreneur test determines whether one person is in a position to order or require not only what is to be done but how it is to be done. Where such control, by the business over the individual, does exist, an employer–employee relationship is implied.

(5) The integration or organization test examines the degree of economic dependence of the individual on the organization. Where the individual is financially dependent on the organization, then an employer-employee relationship is implied.

(6) The specific result test looks at the expected results of the work performed. An employee–employer relationship usually contemplates the employee putting his or her personal services at the disposal of his or her employer during a given period of time without reference to a specified result and, generally, envisages the accomplishment of work on an ongoing basis. On the other hand, where a party agrees that certain specified work will be done for the other, it may be inferred that an independent contractor relationship exists.

(7) Section 5 uses the word "received" to determine the timing of the taxation of employment income. In this case, she will be considered to have received her bonus in the year she received the cheque. Just because she chose not to cash the cheque does not change the timing of when she received the payment.

(8) Section 5 uses the word "received" to determine the timing of the taxation of employment income. The voluntary deferment of an unconditional right to receive the bonus is not an acceptable method of deferring income [*Blenkarn v. M.N.R.*, (T.A.B.) 63 DTC 581].

(9) Employers cannot deduct all of the taxable benefits reported on the employee's T4. Items such as deemed interest benefits under section 80.4 and standby charges for automobiles are not deductible to the employer since they are not expenses that are incurred for the purpose of earning income.

(10) If the employer makes *any* of the premium payments then the benefit payments received will likely be taxable [par. 6(1)(f) and IT-428].

(11) The CRA follows normal commercial practice such that the first day of the contract is counted and the last day is excluded for purposes of determining the number of days of interest. In this case the number of days from June 2 to June 29 inclusive will be used to determine the benefit, that is, 28 days.

(12) A reimbursement is a payment by an employer to an employee for expenses of the employer which have been paid by the employee and which are substantiated by receipts. This is normally accomplished by submitting an expense report. An allowance is a fixed amount which is paid to an employee in excess of his or her salary without the requirement that the employee be accountable for the amount expended [IT-522R, pars. 40 and 50].

(13) The standby charge is calculated as follows:

$$\frac{20,004}{20,004} \times 2\% \times 12 \times (\$40,000 + \$3,200 + \$2,800) = \$11,040.$$

(14) The five conditions, as outlined under paragraph 8(1)(f), that a salesperson must meet in order to be able to deduct expenses are:

(a) he or she must be employed in the year in connection with the selling of property or negotiating of contracts for his or her employer;

(b) under the terms of his or her contract of employment he or she must be required to pay his or her own expenses;

(c) he or she must be ordinarily required to carry on his or her duties away from his or her employer's place of business;

(d) he or she is remunerated in whole or in part by commissions or other similar amounts fixed by reference to the volume of the sales made or the contracts negotiated; and

(e) he or she was not in receipt of a reasonable allowance for travelling expenses in respect of the taxation year that was, by virtue of subparagraph 6(1)(b)(v), not included in computing his or her income.

(15) The four conditions, as outlined under paragraph 8(1)(h), that must be met to allow an employee to deduct travelling expenses, other than car expenses, are:

(a) he or she is ordinarily required to carry on his or her duties away from his or her employer's place of business or in different places;

(b) under his or her employment contract, he or she is required to pay the travelling expenses incurred by him or her in the performance of his or her duties;

(c) he or she was not in receipt of a reasonable allowance for travelling expenses that was, by virtue of subparagraph 6(1)(b)(v), (vi) or (vii), not included in computing his or her income; and

(d) he or she did not claim any deduction under paragraph 8(1)(e), (f) or (g) for railway company employees, salespersons, or transport company employees.

(16) There is nothing in paragraph 6(1)(b) that would exclude this allowance from income. However, subsection 81(3.1) would apply to cause this receipt to be exempt from tax. In order to be exempt under this provision, the allowance must meet the following tests:

(a) he must deal at arm's length with his employer;

(b) he must have other employment or business income (not necessary in this case, since he is employed as a professor or teacher at a designated educational institution);

(c) the amount received must be reasonable and must relate only to travel to and from part-time employment; and

(d) the part-time location must be at least 80 km away from both the employee's ordinary place of residence and his principal place of employment or business.

(17) Neither word is defined in the Act. However, paragraph 2 of IT-352R2 interprets the word "principally" as more than 50%. Therefore, as long as the employment-use of the work space is its main or chief purpose, the test is met. "Exclusively" is not defined in the tax law, so reference is made to other sources. *Webster's English Dictionary* defines "exclusively" as "to the exclusion of all others" which is a much more onerous test.

(18) Subsection 153(3) deems that taxes withheld have been received at the time the bonus was paid. Therefore, even though the company still had the government's portion of the bonus, tax cannot be deferred on it. In addition, if the amount withheld in respect of the tax was not deemed to have been received by Ms. Smith, then she would not have received credit for the payment of this tax on her personal tax return.

CHAPTER 4
Income from Business: General Concepts and Rules

(1) This type of transaction is commonly referred to as an "adventure in the nature of trade" and would result in business income, if the facts of the situation indicate that it has the "badges of trade". One of the indicators that a transaction is an adventure in the nature of trade is that the taxpayer has specialized knowledge in respect of the transaction. Mr. Flip is a real estate salesperson and, hence, on the surface appears to meet this test. Since "business" is defined in subsection 248(1) to include "an adventure in the nature of trade", this transaction would be classified as business income.

(2) There is no requirement in the Act to use GAAP for tax purposes. The courts have, on occasion, rejected conformity between income for accounting and tax purposes, particularly in cases where GAAP is at variance with the court's concept of ordinary commercial trading and business principles and practices or common law principles. However, GAAP profits are usually used as the starting point for the calculation of net income for tax purposes.

(3) No. Since the performance of this contract would have been income to Opco if the customer had completed it, the damages received would also be treated as business income.

(4) The agreement was of such importance to Aco Ltd. that it would constitute a large part of the company's total business structure. As a result, the receipt may be treated as a capital transaction on the sale of eligible capital property with no cost base. Thus, 50% of the receipt is included in business income. (See Chapter 5.)

(5) No. Income from illegal activities is taxable. Subsection 9(1) does not impose conditions on how the profit is earned. See IT-256R for the CRA's position. See, also, the cases listed in the text on this issue.

(6) The subsidy is taxable as if it were an expense reduction to Opco. Refer to IT-273R2 for the CRA's position.

(7) In section 18 there are a number of limitations that restrict the deductibility of expenses even though they may have been incurred to earn income. Expenditures that are not deductible include:

- capital outlay or loss [par. 18(1)(*b*)];
- use of recreational facilities and club dues [par. 18(1)(*l*)];
- political contributions [par. 18(1)(*n*)]; and
- limitations on interest and property taxes [ssecs. 18(2) & (3.1)].

(8) Paragraph 18(1)(*t*) specifically prohibits the deduction of any amount paid or payable under the Act. As a result, the interest paid to the Receiver General will not be deductible.

(9) Not necessarily. Section 67 also places a limitation on the amount of an outlay or expense. It can only be deducted to the extent that it is "reasonable in the circumstances."

(10) If the replacement of the roof served to restore it to its original condition then the cost should be fully deductible in the year incurred. If the replacement roof was superior to the old roof, the cost could be considered capital in nature. This would result in an addition to the undepreciated capital cost pool. Then, the cost would be deductible over a number of years. IT-128R comments on the issue of income *versus* capital expenditures.

(11) No. Paragraph 67.1(4)(*a*) specifically excludes airplane, train or bus fares from the 50% limitation.

(12) The paragraph 20(1)(*m*.1) reserve is only allowed if the company is the manufacturer of the product and pays an arm's length party to take over the obligations of the warranty for the company.

(13) Yes. Paragraph 37(1)(*b*) permits the deduction of certain expenditures of a capital nature made in Canada that are in respect of scientific research and experimental development. These expenditures do not include land.

CHAPTER 5
Depreciable Capital Property and Eligible Capital Property

(1) The full amount of the capital cost is added to the CCA class. The half-net-amount rule [Reg. 1100(2)] makes a separate adjustment for purposes of calculating CCA in the year of acquisition, but this adjustment does not affect the capital cost.

(2) A terminal loss is allowed only when the asset sold is the last asset in the class [ssec. 20(16)]. Otherwise, the proceeds are credited to the UCC of the class under the definition of "undepreciated capital cost" [ssec. 13(21)] and CCA is claimed on the remaining balance.

(3) "Cost amount" reflects the tax value of an asset at a particular moment in time [ssec. 248(1)]. With respect to depreciable property, cost amount is that proportion of the UCC that the capital cost of the asset is of the capital cost of all the assets in the class. Capital cost is not defined, but as used in subsection 13(21), it means the laid-down cost which includes the actual cost plus all costs of preparing the asset for use.

(4) The "capital cost" is the amount that is added to the CCA class when the asset is first acquired [item A in the definition of "undepreciated capital cost" in ssec. 13(21)]. See (3) above for a broadly worded definition.

(5) Certain exceptions to the half-net-amount rule are found in Regulation 1100(2). However, Regulation 1100(1)(*b*) for leaseholds and Regulations 1100(1)(*t*) and (*ta*) for classes like Classes 24 and 27 provide their own version of the half-net-amount rule.

(6) The half-net-amount rule is a simple, arbitrary adjustment that is made to reflect a period of ownership during the year. It is a simpler alternative to prorating CCA for the number of days the asset is owned during the year.

(7) Normally, the statement is true. However, subsections 13(26) to (32) outline the "available-for-use" rules which do not allow CCA to be claimed until the asset is available for use by the taxpayer.

(8) Paragraphs 9 and 10 of IC 84-1 provide the CRA's position on when the CCA claim for prior years can be changed. If the change results in a lower taxable income for the year, it must be requested within the normal time limits for appeals (see Chapter 14). If the change does not result in a lower taxable income, as, for example, the case of a loss year, the change will be allowed.

(9) Regulation 1100(3) provides for this daily proration in the case of the short taxation year of a business, as might occur, for example, in the start-up year.

(10) Normally, this statement is true. However, Regulation 1100(2.5) allows a CCA claim equal to one-half the normal CCA in the year of disposition, as compensation for the inability to claim a terminal loss on the disposal of a Class 10.1 automobile. To qualify, the taxpayer must have sold an auto that was in Class 10.1 and that was owned by him or her at the end of the preceding year.

(11) Your client is correct. Subsection 13(7.1) reduces the capital cost of depreciable property for grants, subsidies, forgivable loans, deductions from tax, investment allowances or other assistance received on the acquisition of the property.

(12) There are four choices available for the legal costs of obtaining the patent:

(a) deduct them as expenses of representation [par. 20(1)(*cc*)];

(b) deduct the costs equally over 10 years [ssec. 20(9)];

(c) capitalize them in Class 14 by an election [Reg. 1103(2h)] not to include them in Class 44 and depreciate them over the life of the patent; or

(d) capitalize the costs in Class 44 and depreciate them at a 25% declining-balance rate.

Any deduction under paragraph 20(1)(*cc*) or subsection 20(9) is subject to recapture by virtue of subsection 13(12). Also refer to IT-99R5.

(13) There is only *one* CEC pool for all eligible capital expenditures for each business. Since Mrs. Smith is only carrying on one business within her corporation, the additions to the company's CEC account in the year will be 75% of $10,800.

(14) He is able to deduct the full CEC balance as a business loss in the year that he ceased to carry on business [sec. 24].

CHAPTER 6
Income from Property

(1) Paragraph 20(14)(*a*) would separate the principal from the accrued interest and cause the interest to be included in Billy's income as interest income. Paragraph 20(14)(*b*) allows the purchaser to deduct the same amount that the vendor included in income.

(2) Subsection 12(4) would include interest accrued annually to the anniversary date of the bond, requiring tax to be paid from some other source of funds, since no interest will be received on the compound interest bond. Your client may wish to invest in the type of Canada Savings Bonds that pay interest annually. Note that the annual accrual rules may not present a cash flow problem if the holder of the bond is not taxable on the accrued interest due to a low level of total income.

(3) Since Ms. Jones is a shareholder and received a loan, the rules of subsection 15(2) apply. Although Ms. Jones is an employee, the boat does not fit into one of the exceptions in paragraphs 15(2.4)(*b*) to (*d*). Therefore, Ms. Jones will have to take the $25,000 into income unless she repays it within one year from the end of the taxation year in which she received the loan [ssec. 15(2.6)]. If she has to include the principal in income then section 80.4 will not apply [par. 80.4(3)(*b*)].

(4) Subsection 74.1(1) would not appear to apply to cause any income allocated to Mrs. Soleprop to be reallocated to her husband since there is no attribution of business income. (It should be noted that, if she is not actively involved in the business, then she will not be a specified member of the partnership (as defined in subsection 248(1)) and subsection 96(1.8) will deem the income from the partnership to be income from property.)

(5) Although the corporation is carrying on a business, Mrs. Smith is not. She will be earning property income (i.e., dividends on the shares), so the exception to the attribution rules for business income does not apply. Subsection 74.5(7) deals with attribution as a result of guarantees but it would only cause the attribution rules [ssec. 74.5(1)] to apply if the loan was not at commercial rates. If the bank is charging commercial interest rates, then the attribution rules will not apply.

(6) The interest on the 10 acres would be capitalized since it is not used in business and there is no revenue from the land [ssec. 18(2)].

(7) Regulations 1100(11) to (14) do not allow CCA to be claimed to create or increase a loss on rental property. However, Regulation 1100(12) provides that those loss limitation rules do not apply to a corporation whose principal business was the leasing, rental, development or sale, or any combination thereof, of real property owned by it. In this case, Rent Co. will be able to claim CCA to create or increase a loss.

(8) No interest is deductible if Ms. Cautious is considered to realize a capital gain on the sale of the gold. Since capital gains are not income from business or property [ssec. 9(3)], she does not meet the requirements of paragraph 20(1)(*c*) and cannot deduct the interest. Also, there is no provision in section 53 that would allow her to capitalize the interest to the cost of the gold. On the other hand, if the gain on the sale of the gold is considered to be income from business or

property, the interest would be deductible. Note that paragraph 8 of IT-346R would allow her to choose income treatment for these transactions.

(9) In the *Attaie* case, the Federal Court–Trial Division (87 DTC 5411) agreed that the interest expense was deductible. However, the Federal Court of Appeal (90 DTC 6413) reversed this decision and decided that the interest was not deductible, since there was not a direct link between the borrowed funds and the income from property.

(10) Under the proposed plan, the interest would not be deductible since the money is not being used to earn income. However, if your client were to borrow from the bank the $100,000 needed to loan to the purchaser in order to complete the sale of his existing house, then at least the interest would be deductible up to 8%. The purchaser would then be in a position to pay the full purchase price for the new residence.

(11) Since the corporation that your client invested in has gone out of business, there is no longer a possibility of earning income from business or property. However, subsection 20.1(1) would deem the amount of the lost capital to continue to be borrowed for the purpose of earning income and, hence, would allow the interest in this case to continue to be deductible. Refer to IT-533, paragraph 19.

CHAPTER 7
Capital Gains: An Introduction

(1) The transaction will probably be an income receipt. The partnership appears to have been set up specifically to buy and hold the land. The partnership agreement seems to confirm that their primary intention was to make a profit, since the agreement specifically states how the income is to be split. If, after five years, they still have done nothing to develop the land to earn rental or other income, then it would appear to be a speculation gain and, therefore, income.

(2) The transaction will probably be an income receipt. Rachel has used her specialized knowledge, derived from her normal occupation, to make the large profit. This factor, combined with her trading history, would weigh heavily in favour of income treatment.

(3) Normally, stock market transactions are treated as capital gains or losses. However, his intention seems to be to make a profit in trading shares, thereby indicating an income receipt. He may elect to have these transactions treated as capital gains [ssec. 39(4)]. However, Winston should be careful that the CRA does not subsequently deem him to be a "trader" and thereby revoke his election [ssec. 39(5)].

(4) The transaction would probably be an income receipt. Her primary intention is to develop the shopping centre for sale which would be an income transaction. Therefore, the sale of the land prior to development would also be an income transaction.

(5) Capital receipt (not taxable). Doug's $15,000 net winnings should not be treated as income because his actions are more in the nature of a hobby, not making a profit. If this was his business, the profits would be taxable [IT-334R2, par. 10].

(6) Section 54 defines "proceeds of disposition" to include, in paragraph (h), the principal amount of the mortgage that is owed to the mortgage company. This transaction may trigger recaptured CCA [ssec. 13(1)] or a terminal loss [ssecs. 20(16) and 13(21.1)].

(7) Subsection 40(3) provides that whenever the adjusted cost base becomes negative there will be an immediate capital gain. The only exception to this rule is for a partnership interest in a general partnership (but not a limited partnership).

(8) Until the end of 1981 each individual could own and claim a principal residence. After that time the principal residence exemption is restricted to one residence per family by paragraph (c) of the definition of "principal residence" in section 54. The rules in paragraph 40(2)(b) provide the framework for deciding which residence should be claimed for which years in order to maximize the exemption. Mr. Confused and his wife must choose one residence or the other for the exemption.

(9) The cottage is considered to be "personal-use property" (P.U.P.) as defined in section 54. Any loss on the disposal of P.U.P. cannot be deducted [spar. 40(2)(g)(iii)]. The losses are considered to arise as a result of normal personal use over time.

(10) For the purpose of calculating the capital gain or loss on any disposal of P.U.P. the taxpayer's cost is deemed to be the greater of the adjusted cost base of the property and $1,000 [ssec. 46(1)]. Similarly, the taxpayer's proceeds of disposition are deemed to be the greater of actual proceeds and $1,000. Listed personal property (L.P.P.) is defined in section 54 to be a subset of P.U.P.; therefore, the $1,000 rule also applies to L.P.P.

(11) The dividend should be included with the gross-up in income. The amount of the dividend before the gross-up will increase the cost base of the shares [ssec. 53(2)] and effectively reduces the capital gain or increase the capital loss when the shares are sold.

(12) The result of the taxable capital gains minus the allowable capital losses cannot be negative [par. 3(b) of Div. B]. Any negative amount is then referred to subsection 111(8) to determine whether there is a "net capital loss" that can be carried back three years or forward indefinitely [par. 111(1)(b) of Division C].

(13) You would be deemed to have acquired the prize at a cost equal to its fair market value at the time you received it [ssec. 52(4)].

(14) The car has a cost base equal to the $35,000 benefit included in her income under subsection 15(1) [ssec. 52(1)].

CHAPTER 8
Capital Gains: The Finer Points

(1) The loss on foreign currency is a capital loss [par. 39(2)(b)]. However, as an individual, she must deduct $200 from the loss in arriving at her capital loss. In this case her capital loss is $2,300.

(2) One way to approach this question is to assume that the cost was allocated equally to each acre. Therefore, the cost of the three acres sold would be $^1/_2$ of the original cost of the six acres or $12,000. However, the CRA, in applying section 43, may consider that $12,000 is too high an amount to be "reasonably regarded as attributable to that part," since the lake-front portion would usually be more valuable than the non-lake-front property assuming that access is still available to both parcels. This, then, becomes a valuation issue.

(3) He has to replace the land before the end of the second taxation year after the initial year [par. 44(1)(c)]. If they finally agreed to the price in 2005 then he has until December 31, 2007 to replace the property. The preamble to subsection 44(1) states that the initial year is the year that the "amount has become receivable as proceeds of disposition." Subsection 44(2) defines that to be 2005 in this case.

(4) Yes. In order for these rules to apply the destroyed equipment must be either property that was stolen, destroyed or expropriated or a "former business property" [ssec. 248(1)]. The definition of former business property only refers to real property which has a common law definition of "land and building." Equipment is not included in that definition. However, if the property is stolen, destroyed or expropriated, it only has to meet the definition of "property." In this case the equipment meets this definition and the replacement property rules can apply. Of course, any potential recapture would be offset, by the normal rules, because the purchase of the new machine was made in the year of loss.

(5) Under the definition of "former business property" [ssec. 248(1)] the advice she received was incorrect. This building qualifies as a former business property, since it is rented to a related corporation [sec. 251] and is used in the related corporation's business.

(6) A change in use [ssecs. 13(7) and 45(1)] does not include a transfer of property from one income-producing use to another [IT-218R]. In this case the property is being transferred from earning property income to earning business income. As a result there is no income to report on July 1 of last year when zoning was applied for. However, when the property is eventually sold an assessment will need to be done at July 1 of last year since the increase in value up to that point will be a capital gain and any profit after that date will be business income from the sale of the condominiums.

(7) If Mrs. Smith did not make any structural changes to the house, then there will not be any change in use [IT-120R6, par. 30]. The house will still remain her principal residence. She will have to declare the rental income and can deduct the expenses that relate to it.

(8) Since she was moved by her employer nine years ago and was still employed by that employer when she moved back this year, section 54.1 modifies paragraph (*d*) of the definition of "principal residence" in section 54 to allow her to continue to claim her house as her principal residence for more than the 4 years generally allowed on a normal change in use under the definition. All years qualify since she was still resident in Canada, a requirement under paragraph 40(2)(*b*). She still has to make the election [ssec. 45(2)] not to have a change in use in the year they moved. As a result, on the sale of the house, she will be able to claim the full principal residence exemption.

(9) Subsection 128.1(4) causes a deemed disposition on all her property other than certain property and certain items that are subject to withholding tax. In this case the term deposits will be deemed to be disposed of, but since there is no capital gain, there would not be any tax [ssec. 128.1(4)].

(10) Mr. State will be excepted [ssec. 128.1(4)] from the deemed disposition rules on the shares of his U.S. employer since he was in Canada less than 60 months in the past 10 years.

(11) Subsection 49(1) generally treats the sale of this option as a disposition with the cost base being nil. Therefore, the capital gain will be equal to the proceeds and will be taxed in the year the option is sold.

(12) On the granting of an option there is a disposition [ssec. 49(1)] and the A.C.B. is deemed to be nil. He does not have the alternative of reducing the cost base.

(13) Ms. Sorry can elect [ssec. 50(1)] to have disposed of her note when it is established to have become uncollectible. This will result in a capital loss equal to $100,000 and the note will then have a cost equal to nil. All or some of this loss can then be carried back under Division C to be applied against the previous capital gain. If the original property disposed of was personal-use property then the debt would have been "personal-use property" [the definition of that term in sec. 54]. Then subsection 50(2) allows a capital loss only to the extent of the capital gain on the original disposition.

(14) Section 51 provides for a rollover on the exchange of the common shares for the debentures as long as the debenture had the conversion feature built into its terms and no cash was received. The shares will have a cost base of $10 each, so the accrued gain of $10 per share will be deferred until the common shares are sold.

(15) If a person sells something to someone with whom he or she does not deal at arm's length then the proceeds will be deemed to be the fair market value [sec. 69]. Related parties do not deal at arm's length, but in this case the two are not related [sec. 251]. However, it is a question of fact whether persons not related to each other are dealing at arm's length [par. 251(1)(*c*)]. In this case there is no evidence of hard bargaining and the transaction is obviously not at fair market value. Therefore, it would be unlikely that they would be considered to be dealing at arm's length and the proceeds would likely be deemed to be $100,000. Her friend will have a cost base equal to what she paid for the land of $50,000. As a result there will be double taxation.

(16) At the time of the gift, Bill will be deemed to have sold the shares at their fair market value [par. 69(1)(*b*)]. Scott will be deemed to have received the shares at a cost to him equal to the fair market value at the time of the gift [par. 69(1)(*c*)]. Since the shares were a gift, the attribution rules in subsection 56(4.1) will not apply.

CHAPTER 9
Other Sources of Income and Deductions in Computing Income

(1) The payment was made to Ms. Tired "upon or after retirement of a taxpayer from an office or employment in recognition of her long service" and as such should qualify as a retiring allowance [ssec. 248(1)] and be included in income [spar. 56(1)(*a*)(ii)]. IT-337R4, paragraph 2, states that "the cessation of employment for any reason is considered as being retirement or loss of employment." Therefore, even though she quit, this amount should still qualify as a retiring allowance.

(2) The accumulated sick days will qualify as a "retiring allowance" [ssec. 248(1)] and be taxed as such [spar. 56(1)(*a*)(ii) and IT-337R4, par. 5]. However, the unused vacation days will not

qualify under this definition, according to the Interpretation Bulletin, and will be taxed as employment income [ssec. 6(3)].

(3) Since the $3,000 per month is contained in the written agreement and the $1,200 mortgage payment is part of the "allowance," the full amount should be deductible. However, the deductibility for the mortgage payment is limited to $^1/_5$ of the original principal [ssec. 60.1(2)]. In this case, $^1/_5 \times \$120,000 = \$24,000$. After 20 months ($24,000/$1,200), Charles will no longer be able to deduct the payments related to the mortgage and Dee will no longer have to take them into income.

(4) Under this agreement, the $500 in monthly fees paid to the financial institution will qualify as an allowance since Mark does have the discretion as to where the $500 is paid. In addition, this amount is part of the monthly spousal maintenance payment specified in the agreement.

(5) The loan would have to be included in employment income when received [ssecs. 6(3) and 5(1) and IT-340R]. Such amounts are not awards and are not subject to the rules in paragraphs 56(1)(*n*) and (*o*). As a result, neither the $3,000 exemption nor research expenses are available as deductions. Any repayment of this repayable award is deductible [par. 8(1)(*n*)] provided the conditions of that paragraph are met.

(6) The OAS Supplement would fall into the category of "social assistance payments" since it is based on an income test [par. 56(1)(*u*)]. As a result, the payments are included in net income, but there is a corresponding deduction to exclude it from taxable income [par. 110(1)(*f*)]. The effect of these two provisions is to raise Mrs. Smith's income to a point that no one can claim her as a dependant, but at the same time not to make Mrs. Smith taxable on this amount.

(7) Subsection 56(2) would apply to cause the $15,000 to be taxed in Mr. Slippery's hands and not in Mrs. Slippery's hands.

(8) Defined benefit pension plans are approved by and registered with the CRA. Once the CRA has agreed to the terms of the plan, the amount that the company can deduct is determined by an actuary who certifies the amount that is necessary to fund the accruing benefits of the plan.

(9) The maximum benefit that may be provided to an individual under a defined benefit plan is 2% of the individual's average best 3 years of remuneration times the number of years (normally a maximum of 35 years) of pensionable service, with a dollar limit of $70,000 in 2005.

(10) Under a defined benefit plan, the benefit that is to be paid is defined, usually in regard to a certain percentage of an employee's earnings in the last few years of employment, regardless of the cost to the employer or the earnings experience of the plan. The benefit that is tax-assisted is limited to an annual maximum pension of $70,000. Under a money purchase plan, the contribution that is required by the employer and the employee is defined rather than the benefit. The retirement benefit of the employee is based on the amount accumulated in the plan at retirement and the annuity that this amount can buy at that time.

(11) The "18%" part of the limit for RRSP contributions was arrived at as follows:

(a) it is assumed that $9 of contributions buys $1 of annual pension income,

(b) pension income is limited to 2% of income per year up to an effective maximum of 35 years,

therefore, to get $1 of pension income in the future you will need a contribution of 18% (9 × 2%) of current income.

(12) The "$18,000" part of the RRSP limit was arrived at as follows:

(a) it is assumed that $9 of contributions buys $1 of annual pension income,

(b) pension income is limited to 2% of income per year up to an effective maximum of 35 years,

(c) the maximum pension available out of a defined benefit plan is $70,000,

(d) the maximum number of years that are eligible for the defined benefit calculation is normally 35 years at the 2% rate, this amounts to $70,000/35 years = $2,000 per year. Thus, to fund the maximum pension of $70,000, a contribution of $2,000 × 9 = $18,000 is needed.

(13) The explanation is based on the fact that the two pension systems are integrated and the integration is based on how rich your pension plan is. The richness of your pension plan is determined by the Pension Adjustment calculation. For this system to work, the pension calculation has to come first. So, your maximum pension contribution is based on your current income. Then, early in the following year your pension adjustment (PA) is calculated. Finally, your RRSP limit is determined, based on your earned income and PA, both of which relate to the prior year.

(14) Using the assumptions given in the question, the calculation would be as follows:

(a) $2,000 compounded at 10% for 15 years within the RRSP minus 46% tax on withdrawal equals $4,511.

(b) $2,000 compounded at 5.4% after tax for 15 years outside the RRSP equals $4,402.

If the rate of return was only 8% the funds would have to be left in the plan for about 18.5 years:

(a) $2,000 compounded at 8% for 18.5 years within the RRSP minus 46% tax on withdrawal equals $4,485.

(b) $2,000 compounded at 4.32% after tax for 18.5 years outside the RRSP equals $4,374.

(15) Regulations 103(4) and (6) set the withholding rates based on the amount of the withdrawal — 10% of the amount if it is $5,000 or less; 20% if the amount is between $5,000 and $15,000; and 30% if the amount exceeds $15,000. The rates are one-half of these amounts in Quebec. Based on this formula, the withholdings would be 30% of $20,000 or $6,000. Instead, if she were to withdraw four payments of $5,000, then the tax withheld would amount to only 10% of $20,000 or $2,000. In both cases the $20,000 withdrawn will have to be included in her income for the year and the same amount of ultimate tax will have to be paid. The tax will have to be funded from other sources to allow for the $20,000 to be spent for the car. Alternatively, the withdrawal will have to be increased for the amount of the tax to be paid. The necessary withdrawal would be $20,000/(1 − t), where t is her marginal tax rate.

(16) Since he left his RRSP to an adult child, the estate will have to pay tax on the basis that the full amount of the RRSP was included in income in the year of death. At a 50% tax rate, this will amount to $75,000 of tax which will come out of the residue or Jim's share of the estate. As a result, Kim will receive $150,000 of cash and Jim will receive the residue of the estate minus the $75,000 of tax and any other tax that may be payable. Mr. Mort should have calculated the division of property based on the after-tax values to the estate.

(17) The following items would show up on her personal tax return:

(a) the $40,000 would be included in income as a retiring allowance;

(b) $35,000 could be deducted under paragraph 60(j.1) as a transfer of a retiring allowance in respect of pre-'96 years of service to an RRSP; and

(c) $5,000 of the $8,000 of legal fees could be deducted under paragraph 60(o.1).

The full amount of the legal fees was deductible; however, the deduction is limited to the net of the retiring allowance less the amount transferred to the RRSP and deducted under paragraph 60(j.1). She should have only contributed $32,000 to her RRSP from the retiring allowance.

CHAPTER 10

Computation of Taxable Income and Taxes Payable for Individuals

(1) Within section 111 there is no ordering that is required to be followed when choosing among the different kinds of losses, except that the oldest losses are always applied first [par. 111(3)(b)]. Generally, the rule of thumb is that the most restricted losses are claimed first. The factors that would have to be taken into account in making this decision are as follows:

(a) Does she have the kind of income needed to offset the losses? She would need net taxable capital gains to offset net capital losses.

(b) Which losses are going to expire first? Net capital losses can be carried back 3 years and forward indefinitely and non-capital losses can be carried back 3 years and forward 10 years for taxation years ending after March 22, 2004.

(c) What is the likelihood that she will realize the type of income needed in future years to offset those losses she decides not to claim this year? If she uses up her non-capital losses this year and not her net capital losses, what is the likelihood that she will have a taxable capital gain in the future?

(2) His marginal tax rate on dividend income would be:

Cash dividend	$10,000
Gross-up	2,500
Taxable dividend	$12,500
Federal tax @ 29%	$ 3,625
Dividend tax credit	(1,667)
Basic federal tax	$ 1,958
Provincial tax @ 17% of $12,500	2,125
Provincial dividend tax credit @ 6²/₃% of $12,500	(833)
Total tax	$ 3,250

His marginal tax rate on these dividends is $3,250/$10,000 = 32.5%.

(3) His marginal tax rate on interest income would be:

Interest earned	$10,000
Federal tax @ 29%	$ 2,900
Provincial tax @ 17% of $10,000	1,700
Total tax	$ 4,600

His marginal tax rate on this interest is $4,600/$10,000 = 46%.

(4) Her marginal tax rate on capital gains would be:

Capital gain	$10,000
Taxable capital gain (¹/₂)	$ 5,000
Federal tax @ 29%	$ 1,450
Provincial tax @ 17% of $5,000	850
Total tax	$ 2,300

Her marginal tax rate on this capital gain is $2,300/$10,000 = 23%.

(5) Subsection 118.1(7) allows an artist to designate the proceeds of the piece of art that is not established to be cultural property at anywhere between the cost and the fair market value, in this case between $200 and $8,000. Looking at the two alternatives:

(a) if she designates $200 she will report no net income since her proceeds equal her cost. However, she will receive a donation receipt for $200 which is worth a federal credit of $200 × 16% = $32;

(b) if she designated $8,000 as the proceeds, she would report an additional $7,800 in income and pay an additional federal tax of $7,800 × 16% = $1,248. However, she will also receive a donation receipt for $8,000 which will generate a federal credit of $200 × 16% + $7,800 × 29% = $2,294. On a net basis she would have a net federal credit from this alternative of $2,294 − $1,248 = $1,046.

On a net basis, she would be further ahead to designate the full $8,000 as the proceeds. She would receive an incremental benefit of $1,014 (i.e., $1,046 − $32) plus the provincial tax credit.

Subsection 118.1(7.1) deems the artist to have received proceeds of disposition equal to the cost of the work of art that is a cultural gift. However, subsection 118.1(1) would entitle the artist to a credit based on the certified fair market value of the work. As a result, no income needs to be reported on the disposition and a credit based on the full value is available.

(6) Ms. Hurry will receive a personal credit of 16% times the maximum CPP contribution for the year of $1,861 [sec. 118.7]. The excess $1,861 will be refunded to her since it will be an overcontribution. She will not have any liability for CPP on her self-employed earnings since the full amount has been paid by her and the matching employer contributions.

(7) Given the short-term nature of the move, the fact that his family does not move with him, and the fact that he will be moving back to Canada within 15 months indicate that he will continue to be a resident of Canada for income tax purposes and he will be taxable in Canada on his worldwide income. However, since he is a Canadian resident, was employed by a Canadian resident corporation and was working outside Canada on a construction contract for more than 6 months, Mr. Jones will be entitled to a tax credit [sec. 122.3]. The credit for 2005 will be equal to:

the lesser of:

(a) $80,000 \times 365/365 = $80,000

(b) 80% $\times$ $120,000 = $96,000   } $80,000

divided by $120,000

times the tax otherwise payable.

As a result, he will receive a credit for $80,000/$120,000 or $66^{2}/_{3}$% of his tax otherwise payable on his personal tax return for 2005. In 2006 the same calculation would be made prorating the $80,000 for the 90-day period abroad and another credit would be claimed.

CHAPTER 11

Computation of Taxable Income and Tax after General Reductions for Corporations

(1) Charitable donations are tax credits only on personal tax returns. On corporate tax returns they are deductions under section 110.1 under Division C. Donations up to 75% of net income plus 25% of the amount of a taxable capital gain and 25% of recapture in respect of gifts of capital property with appreciated value can be deducted in the year. If the charitable donations are in excess of this amount then the excess can be carried forward for 5 years.

(2) Income can be increased in the current year by not claiming some of the optional deductions for tax purposes. For example, the deductions for the allowance for bad debts, CCA, CECA or scientific research and experimental development expenditures can be forgone in order to increase income. These deductions will be available in future years and will not be lost. Also, the CRA will allow the revision of some permissive deductions for prior years. IC 84-1 sets out their guidelines on this matter. In addition, the company could consider the sale of any redundant assets to generate income through recapture and/or capital gain.

(3) Where there has been an acquisition of control, the corporation cannot carry over its net capital losses [ssecs. 111(4) and (8)]. To the extent that the corporation has *net* taxable capital gains in the year, it may take an optional deduction of net capital losses which may in turn increase the amount of non-capital losses. Accrued capital losses are deemed to be realized in the deemed year-end immediately preceding the acquisition of control [ssec. 111(4)]. However, there may be some relief because the corporation is allowed to trigger, on an elective basis, enough unrealized accrued capital gains to use up the net losses that are going to expire [par. 111(4)(e)].

(4) The first restriction is on the type of income against which the loss carryover can be deducted, and the second restriction is on the number of years a loss can be carried over.

Net Capital Losses: Applied against taxable capital gains only; carried back 3 years and forward indefinitely.

Non-capital Losses: Applied against all sources of income; carried back 3 years and forward 10 years for taxation years ending after March 22, 2004.

Restricted Farm Losses: Applied only against farm income; carried back 3 years and forward 10 years.

Farm Losses: Applied against all sources of income; carried back 3 years and forward 10 years.

(5) The deemed year-end applies whenever there is an acquisition of control even if the company acquired is not a loss company. Mr. Magoo will not be able to claim a full year of CCA since CCA is prorated for a short fiscal year [Reg. 1100(3)].

(6) The three main objectives are:

(a) alleviate double taxation;

(b) prevent the avoidance of tax through the use of a corporation; and

(c) provide tax incentives to corporations.

See the text under the heading II.A. of Chapter 11 for details.

(7) The gross revenue from that sale will be attributed to Alberta since, even though the sale was handled from Ontario, the order was delivered to a province in which the company had a permanent establishment [Reg. 402(4)(a)].

(8) The M&P profits deduction is available on "Canadian" M&P profits which are defined to be income from an active business carried on in Canada and related to M&P in Canada [ssec. 125.1(3)]. Just because this company exports all of its products does not mean that it is carrying on business in the U.S. All of its manufacturing is carried on in Canada and, therefore, Export Inc. will qualify for the M&P profits deduction.

(9) The theory is that the country where the income is earned has the first right to tax the income. Then, in order to prevent double taxation when Canada also taxes this income, a credit is given in Canada for the foreign taxes paid.

(10) Investment income may be taxed in the foreign country even though there is no permanent establishment in that country. Canada assumes that this investment income is earned through its permanent establishment in Canada and, therefore, considers this income to be earned in a province for purposes of section 124. Foreign business income, on the other hand, is assumed to be earned in a permanent establishment in the foreign country and, therefore, is not eligible for the federal abatement.

(11) Since LossCo. does not have any net income or Canadian income tax, it cannot claim a foreign tax credit. No carryover is allowed for non-business income tax [ssec. 126(1)]. However, the corporation can deduct the foreign taxes [ssec. 20(12)] which will increase its loss for the year. This deduction will at least provide the benefit of the foreign taxes being carried forward as part of the non-capital losses.

CHAPTER 12
Integration for Business and Investment Income of the Private Corporation

(1) The purpose of integration is to avoid the double taxation of income earned through a corporation. Integration should cause the total tax paid by a corporation and its shareholders to be equal to the total tax paid by an individual who carries on the same economic activity directly and not through a corporation. The system should be neutral as to the form of organization used.

(2) Ideal integration depends on:

(a) When the corporation itself pays tax, the shareholder must include in income and pay tax on the full pre-tax income earned by the corporation and then get a full credit for all the income tax paid by the corporation.

(b) All after-tax income would have to be either paid out as dividends in the year earned or taxed in some manner at the shareholder level in that year to avoid the indefinite deferral of tax that might otherwise be available if the corporate rates were lower than individual tax rates. This would equate the position of the shareholder with the position of the proprietor, partner or owner of investments who must pay tax on income from his or her economic activity whether or not it is distributed.

(3) The gross-up is intended to add to the dividend received by the individual shareholder an amount equal to the total income tax paid by the corporation on the income that gave rise to the dividend. Thus, the grossed-up dividend is intended to represent the corporation's pre-tax income. The shareholder will pay tax on the grossed-up dividend at his or her personal rate. The tax credit is intended to give the shareholder credit for the total tax paid by the corporation on the shareholder's behalf. This procedure is intended to equalize the tax paid on the income that is flowed through the corporation to its shareholders with the tax paid on the same income that is

earned directly. When the total (i.e., federal and provincial) corporate tax rate is 20%, integration is theoretically perfect.

(4) Its purpose is to help small CCPCs retain capital in order to expand their businesses. This is accomplished by using a relatively low corporate tax rate after the small business deduction to defer tax until the income is paid out as a dividend.

(5) There is a deemed year-end on July 15 as a result of the acquisition of control and he is deemed to acquire control at the commencement of that day [ssecs. 249(4) and 256(9)]. Mr. Smith can now choose any year-end he wants and the company should qualify as a CCPC throughout the year.

(6) Paragraph 125(1)(a) deals with Division B income (net of expenses) while paragraph 125(1)(b) starts off with taxable income. Therefore, if there are Division C deductions such as donations or loss carryforwards then paragraph 125(1)(b) could be lower.

(7) The concept is that foreign income which is not taxed in Canada because of a foreign tax credit should be removed from the base amount on which the small business deduction is calculated.

A $^{10}/_3$ × factor is applied to the non-business foreign tax credit in order to estimate the foreign non-business income. This is based on the theory that the corporate rate is 30%.

A 3 × factor is applied to the business foreign tax credit in order to estimate the foreign business income. This is based on the theory that the corporate rate is 40% less the general tax reduction of 7% on foreign business income. The abatement is not applied since it is assumed that the income is attributable to a permanent establishment outside of Canada.

(8) Some advantages of incorporation are:

(a) limited liability except for personal guarantees;

(b) tax savings if the combined corporate tax rate is under 20%;

(c) tax deferral;

(d) income splitting with family members as employees or shareholders (beware of the attribution rules and the tax on split income);

(e) estate freezing;

(f) availability of registered pension plans to the owner;

(g) separation of business and personal activities;

(h) greater flexibility as to the timing of income received personally;

(i) continuity of separate legal entity;

(j) deferral of accrued capital gains on transfer of shares to a spouse;

(k) access to financing

(l) availability of capital gains exemption on QSBCS; and

(m) availability of deferral of capital gains on shares of a SBC.

(9) Some disadvantages of incorporation are:

(a) tax cost if combined corporate tax rate is over 20%;

(b) a prepayment of tax at lower levels of personal income on business income not eligible for the small business deduction;

(c) additional costs including provincial capital tax; and

(d) inability to deduct losses against personal income. This disadvantage may be offset somewhat by the availability of the A.B.I.L.

(10) He will not be able to get the M&P profits deduction on income eligible for the small business deduction [par. 125.1(1)(a)]. In addition, the question does not indicate whether this venture is incorporated. If it is not, then these deductions are not available since they are only available to incorporated businesses. Finally, the current rate for M&P is 7%.

(11) Part IV tax of 33$^1/_3$% on portfolio dividends prevents a significant deferral of tax.

(12) (a) Refundable Part I tax;

(b) Part IV tax;

(c) Dividend gross-up and tax credit;

(d) Refundable dividend tax on hand; and

(e) Dividend refund.

(13) The gross-up is intended to place the shareholder in an income position equivalent to that of the corporation before it paid corporate taxes. At an assumed corporate tax rate of 20%, the 25% gross-up represents the underlying corporate tax. This is added to the after-tax dividend to tax, theoretically, the pre-tax corporate profits in the hands of the individual shareholder.

(14) The dividend tax credit is intended to give the shareholder credit against his or her taxes for the taxes paid by the corporation on the income from which the dividend was paid. Since the gross-up theoretically takes the dividend up to the pre-tax corporate income level, the dividend tax credit is needed to reduce the individual tax by the theoretical amount of corporate tax already paid on that income. At a corporate tax rate of 20%, tax of $20 would be paid on corporate income of $100. The gross-up of 25% would take the individual's income on that dividend of $80 back up to the $100 of corporate pre-tax income level. Assuming a provincial dividend tax credit of $6^2/_3$ the total dividend tax credit would be 20% of the grossed-up dividend or $20. Thus the dividend tax credit represents the underlying corporate tax paid on the dividend.

(15) Of the $1,000 capital gain, $500 is not taxable and is allocated to the capital dividend account to be passed out to the shareholders tax-free as a capital dividend [ssec. 82(3)]. This provides for the tax-free receipt of this $500 whether the capital gain is realized in the corporation or by the individual directly.

The remaining $500 is theoretically taxed at an approximate initial rate of Part I tax of 40%. An additional refundable tax of $6^2/_3$% is also levied and added to this account. Then, $26^2/_3$% of the income is classified as refundable Part I tax and added to the refundable dividend tax on hand account. Dividend payments result in a return to the corporation of $1 for every $3 of dividends that are paid. This would leave an effective tax rate in the corporation on taxable capital gains of 20% which is the level at which integration works.

(16) Ordinarily the interest would be taxed at the full rate of 38% plus the $6^2/_3$% additional refundable tax under Part I with part of this being classified as refundable Part I tax and added to the refundable dividend tax on hand account. However, since the two companies are associated and the interest is being deducted against the active business income of Opco, subsection 129(6) will deem the interest income to be active business income and not eligible for the refundable tax treatment.

(17) While A Ltd. does not have more than 10% of the votes and value of B Ltd., A Ltd. does have control [ssec. 186(2)], since A Ltd. and the son of the only shareholder are related and do not deal at arm's length. Thus, over 50% of the voting shares belong to a person with whom A Ltd. does not deal at arm's length.

(18) The factors to be considered are:

(a) the same non-capital losses cannot be deducted under both provisions;

(b) the normal corporate tax rates under Part I are usually higher than the $33^1/_3$% Part IV tax;

(c) the Part IV tax is a refundable tax and not a permanent tax like Part I tax;

(d) the non-capital losses would otherwise expire without any value; and

(e) the corporation is not expected to pay a dividend to claim the refund until years in the future.

CHAPTER 13

Planning the Use of a Corporation and Shareholder-Manager Remuneration

(1) Mr. Smith can pay the bonus within the 179-day limit [ssec. 78(4)] and loan the net after-tax amount back to the company. If he actually does this, he should consider charging interest to the company in order to reduce payroll taxes by converting his salary into interest income. This will also protect his ability to claim a capital loss or an A.B.I.L. in the event the company was unable to repay the loan. He should also consider securing the loan.

(2) (a) If he leaves the money in the company, the income over $300,000 (in calendar year 2005 and later years) will not be eligible for the small business deduction, but it will be eligible for the manufacturing and processing profits deduction. The marginal tax rate will be 34.12% (i.e., 38% − 10% + 1.12% − 7% + 12%).

(b) If he declares and pays the bonus the personal marginal tax rate will be 46% (i.e., 29% + 17%).

(c) He can defer approximately 11.9% of tax by leaving the income in the company to be taxed.

(d) If he leaves the income in the company to be taxed, he will have to pay tax on the dividend when he eventually pays it out. The combined tax rate at that point will be approximately 55.5% which is well above the 46% personal tax cost of paying out the bonus now.

(e) Calculation:

Corporate income	$1,000
Corporate tax	(341)
After-tax income	$ 659
Dividend paid	$ 659
Gross-up	165
Taxable dividend	$ 824
Federal tax @ 29%	$ 239
Dividend tax credit	(110)
Basic federal tax	$ 129
Provincial tax @ 17%	140
Provincial dividend tax credit (6⅔% of $824)	(55)
Total personal tax	$ 214
Net cash after tax	$ 445
Total tax ($341 + $214)	$ 555

(3) If he or she chooses a fiscal year-end on or after July 6 and before December 31, then the bonus can be paid within the 179 days [ssec. 78(4)] in either this calendar year or on January 1 of the next calendar year.

(4) The following are the five criteria for the deductibility of bonus accruals as decided in the *Totem Disposal* case:

(a) reasonableness of the bonus in relation to profit and services rendered;

(b) payment for real and identifiable service;

(c) some justification for expecting a bonus over regular salary (e.g., a company policy);

(d) reasonableness of the time between determining profit and establishing the bonus; and

(e) a legal obligation to pay the accrued bonus.

(5) Mr. Crunchy is related to his brother-in-law [ssec. 251(2)]. Therefore, they are deemed not to deal with each other at arm's length and the brother-in-law is connected with Mr. Crunchy [ssec. 15(2.1)]. As a result, the conditions in subsection 15(2) are met and none of the exceptions in subsection 15(2.4) are met. Therefore, the brother-in-law will be required to take the full amount of the loan into income in 2005 since none of it was repaid by December 31, 2006. In 2007 and 2008 the brother-in-law will be able to deduct the principal repayments [par. 20(1)(*j*)]. The section 80.4 benefit included in his 2005 tax return can be removed through an amended return to eliminate the benefit [par. 80.4(3)(*b*)].

(6) This provincial tax holiday would bring the combined corporate tax rate on income eligible for the small business deduction down below 20% and would provide a tax incentive to flowing active business income through a corporation, paying corporate tax and then paying dividends. Thus, there would then be an advantage to paying dividends instead of salary to the owner due to the fact that the dividend tax credit is greater than the underlying corporate tax.

(7) With the dividend gross-up his taxable income would be $30,000. The federal tax would be $4,800 less the dividend tax credit of $4,000 and the personal credit of $1,304 (in 2005) leaving basic federal tax of nil. Provincial tax @ 10% of $30,000 would be $3,000, less the provincial dividend tax credit of $2,000 (i.e., $6^2/_3$ % of $30,000) and the provincial personal tax credit of $815 (i.e., ($1,304/.16) × .10), leaving provincial tax of $185.

(8) It is true that in order to claim an A.B.I.L. the shares need to be shares in a small business corporation. However, the definition of small business corporation allows the status as a small business corporation to continue for 12 months for purposes of paragraph 39(1)(*c*) which deals with the A.B.I.L. provisions [ssec. 248(1)]. Since she sold the shares within six months she should be able to claim the loss as an A.B.I.L.

(9) IT-151R5, paragraph 31, for example, states that the phrase means at least 90%. It should be noted that this phrase has not been specifically determined by the courts and it is unclear whether the courts would allow 85% or require 95% as the percentage necessary to meet this test. Practitioners generally use 90%.

(10) This corporation is neither, since in order to meet the definition of "small business corporation" it has to meet the 90% test at the determination time. Since the corporation does not meet this test it is neither an SBC nor a QSBC.

(11) The preamble to subsection 74.4(2) refers only to situations where "individuals have transferred or loaned property." In this case his corporation has loaned the funds to her corporation. It could not even be said that he did it indirectly since he has not loaned or transferred any money to his own corporation. Therefore, even though her corporation is not an SBC, the corporate attribution rules should not apply. However, GAAR should be considered.

CHAPTER 14
Rights and Obligations under the Income Tax Act

(1) (a) False. All corporations resident in Canada have to file tax returns within six months of the end of the year [par. 150(1)(*a*)].

(b) True. An individual is required to file a tax return if he or she "has disposed of a capital property" [ssec. 150(1)]. Even if there is no taxable income or tax liability a return must be filed. In addition, Mr. Lucky may lose his capital gains deduction in respect of this transaction, if he does not file the return [ssec. 110.6(6)].

(c) False. Instalments must be paid on the 15th of each of those months [ssec. 156(1)].

(2) An instalment interest offset is available on prepaid or overpaid instalments [ssec. 161(2.2)]. However, this credit offset can only be applied against instalment interest owing; it is not refundable and may not be applied against any other debt. To benefit, he would have to pay the December 15 instalment on September 15 which would offset the fact that the June 15 instalment was three months late. In addition, the prescribed interest rate for the last quarter would have to be equal to or greater than the prescribed interest rate for the second quarter.

(3) They will not be able to collect interest for the last three years. Interest will not be paid for the period prior to the filing of the tax return for the year in which the request is made to carry the loss back [ssec. 164(5)].

(4) Since the accountant sent a letter to the CRA, it may take some time before a reply is received. If the reply is received late and there is disagreement, it may be too late to file a Notice of Objection [ssec. 165(1)]. Therefore, it may be prudent to file the Notice of Objection in the first place unless the matter is a minor one.

(5) In order to amend the tax returns for the third preceding year the company would have had to file form T2A by the time the corporate tax returns are due for the loss year which is six months after the fiscal year-end [ssec. 152(6)]. However, Bad Luck did not meet this deadline since it did not file until seven months after the year-end. Therefore, the CRA will not have to let the corporation carry the loss back at all. However, the loss will still be available to be carried forward.

(6) The following are the four returns that can be filed:

(a) Terminal return [ssec. 70(1)] — This return reports the income for the period in the year before the date of death and includes any gain or loss on the deemed disposition on death. Full personal credits may be claimed.

(b) Rights or things [ssec. 70(2)] — "Rights or things" can be reported on a separate return to take advantage of the lower marginal tax brackets. Also, the full personal tax credits allowed [ssecs. 118(1) and (2)] can be claimed again.

(c) Proprietor or partner [ssec. 150(4)] — If there is a 1995 stub-period reserve being carried forward or if there is more than one fiscal year that ends in the year as a result of the individual's death then a separate tax return can be filed claiming the income for the deemed year-end and claiming the full personal tax credits allowed [ssecs. 118(1) and (2)] again. In addition, the lower marginal tax bracket can be used again.

(d) Trust return [par. 104(23)(*d*)] — Similar rules to those in (c) above apply to those situations that have more than one trust year-end in the same calendar year. This would only apply in the case of a testamentary trust since they are the only ones that can have an off-calendar year-end. Again, the lower marginal tax rates and the personal tax credits are available.

CHAPTER 15
Corporate Distributions, Windings-up and Sales

(1) Dr.: Cash $30,000
    Cr.: Share capital $10,000
    Cr.: Contributed surplus $20,000

(2) In these jurisdictions, the paid-up capital is the "stated capital" as determined by the directors of the corporation. Generally, this stated capital will be the fair market value of the consideration for which the shares were issued. However, these statutes provide that, in connection with certain non-arm's length transactions, the corporation may establish an amount which is less than the consideration for which the shares were issued as the stated capital and such amount as so determined will then be the amount of P.U.C. for tax purposes.

(3) In no par value jurisdictions, in certain non-arm's length situations, the stated capital (P.U.C.) can be set at less than the fair market value of the consideration received by the corporation. In these situations, the P.U.C. may be kept low to avoid certain penalty provisions of

the Act. This will result in the redemption value of the shares being high to represent the value of the assets transferred and the P.U.C. being low to avoid tax penalties or to benefit from a deemed dividend on redemption rather than a capital gain, since the tax on dividends is lower than the tax on an equal amount of capital gain. This ignores the capital gains exemption.

(4) The five basic components of the capital dividend account are:

(a) the non-taxable portion of net capital gains;

(b) capital dividends received from other corporations;

(c) the untaxed portion of the proceeds of eligible capital property;

(d) proceeds from life insurance policies net of their adjusted cost base; and

(e) capital dividends paid, which reduce the account.

(5)

CEC balance	$6,000
Proceeds ($\frac{3}{4} \times \$100,000$)	(75,000)
	$(69,000)
Previous CECA claims (($\frac{3}{4} \times \$10,000$) – $6,000)	1,500
	$(67,500)
Income (($\frac{2}{3} \times \$67,500$) + $1,500)	$46,500
Capital dividend account ($\frac{2}{3} \times \$67,500$)	$45,000

Even though the goodwill may not relate to the customer list, the two are both included in the same calculation as long as they both relate to the same business.

(6) The $8,000 reduction in capital will not cause a deemed dividend. However, the extra $1,000 of payment will be a deemed dividend [ssec. 84(4)] since it is considered to be a distribution out of taxable surplus.

(7) The three components of a distribution [ssec. 88(2)] are:

(a) paid-up capital which is returned tax-free;

(b) a capital dividend to the extent of the capital dividend account and the election under subsection 83(2); and

(c) a taxable dividend to the extent of the balance.

(8) On the winding-up of the corporation, subsection 13(21.2) does not apply [par. 69(5)(*d*)]. Therefore, the terminal loss will be allowed as a deduction to the corporation.

(9) Section 54 provides the definition of "proceeds of disposition" for purposes of the calculation of capital gain or loss. The proceeds do not include the deemed dividend under subsection 84(2). Therefore, the proceeds are calculated as the amount distributed less the deemed dividend.

CHAPTER 16

Income Deferral: Rollover on Transfers to a Corporation and Pitfalls

(1) In general, a rollover allows for a partial or complete deferral of the recognition of income on the transfer of property from one person to another. The transferor, in return for the property transferred, should receive a package of consideration, the total fair market value of which should be equal to the fair market value of the property transferred. The transferor is the one who is deferring the recognition of income. The transferee usually steps into the position of the transferor in terms of the tax value of the asset received. Therefore, on the ultimate disposition of the asset by the transferee, the income will be recognized. Examples of rollovers include subsections 73(1), 85(1), 88(1) and sections 51 and 86.

(2) In order to use section 85, the corporation must be a "taxable Canadian corporation" which is defined in subsection 89(1) to be a "Canadian corporation" that is not exempt from tax. A "Canadian corporation" is defined to include a company that is resident in Canada and was either incorporated in Canada or resident in Canada since before June 18, 1971 [ssec. 89(1)]. In

this case, Della Inc. has been resident in Canada only since 1973 and, therefore, is not a Canadian corporation and not a taxable Canadian corporation. Although the real estate is capital property to Mr. Della and, thus, it is "eligible property" [ssec. 85(1.1)], this property cannot be transferred using section 85 since the transferee is not a taxable Canadian corporation.

(3) The following are the four uses of the elected price:

(a) it is the proceeds of disposition to the transferor;

(b) it is the cost of the property to the corporation;

(c) it is used to determine the A.C.B. of the package of consideration taken by the transferor from the corporation in return for the assets transferred to the corporation; and

(d) it is used to calculate the paid-up capital of the shares taken as consideration by the transferor from the corporation.

(4) On the transfer, the only decision variable you have is the non-share consideration or boot. If the boot is higher than the lower limit for the particular asset transferred, then the lower limit is increased [par. 85(1)(b)]. The boot cannot, however, raise the upper limit above fair market value [par. 85(1)(c)].

(5) The maximum "boot" that should be taken in order to maximize the deferral is the lower limit on the election range as determined by the tax value, unless the F.M.V. is lower. This will cause a problem if the asset being transferred is shares and section 84.1 applies. This problem could occur if the shares being transferred were Q.S.B.C.S. and an amount was elected to trigger a gain equal to the available exemption. When section 84.1 applies, the maximum boot should be the greater of the P.U.C. and the arm's-length cost, not a higher elected amount.

(6) Regulation 1100(2) would still apply. She may have heard about Regulation 1100(2.2) which allows the transferee to avoid the half-year rule as long as the transferor was not dealing at arm's-length with the corporation at the time of the transfer (which is true in this situation) and the property was owned continuously by the transferor (Ms. Smith) for the period from at least 364 days before the end of the taxation year of the corporation in which the asset was acquired to the date of the election. If the taxation year of the corporation occurs at least 364 days after the purchase of the equipment, then the condition is met.

(7) The elected transfer price is equal to the total cost of the consideration taken back. This elected amount is allocated among the different types of consideration in the following manner:

First: to non-share consideration (boot) up to the F.M.V. of that property as long as that F.M.V. does not exceed the F.M.V. of the assets transferred to the corporation [par. 85(1)(f)];

Second: to preferred shares up to the F.M.V. of those shares after the transfer but only to the extent that there is a balance left after the boot has been deducted from the elected amount [par. 85(1)(g)]; and

Third: to common shares to the extent that the elected amount exceeds the F.M.V. of the boot and the cost allocated to the preferred shares [par. 85(1)(h)].

(8) Normally, the sale of shares in an SBC would allow Bar Ltd. to claim the loss as a business investment loss. However, the A.B.I.L. is denied, since it must sell to an arm's length person [par. 39(1)(c)]. Bar Ltd. and Spouse Ltd. do not deal at arm's length since they are related [sec. 251]. Therefore, the loss will be an ordinary capital loss.

However, in this case, Bar Ltd. is transferring the shares to a corporation controlled by the sole shareholder's wife, an affiliated person; therefore, paragraph 40(2)(g) will deny the superficial loss [sec. 54] to Bar Ltd. However, Spouse Ltd. can take advantage of the ability to add the loss to the cost base of the Loser Ltd. shares now owned by Spouse Ltd. [par. 53(1)(f)]. Paragraph 40(2)(g) does not require an election under subsection 85(1) in order to apply. It applies whenever a taxpayer disposes of capital property to an affiliated person, including a corporation that was controlled, directly or indirectly in any manner whatever, by the taxpayer, by the spouse of the taxpayer or by other affiliated persons.

(9) The "elected amount" determines how much can be withdrawn tax-free since this is the starting point for determining the A.C.B. and the P.U.C. of the shares. In addition, it is the amount that is used to determine how much boot to take back on the transaction to fully defer the accrued income.

(d) the short taxation year will count as one of the carryforward years available [sec. 111].

(6) The CRA has indicated in IC 88-2 that, if an amalgamation is undertaken with a shell corporation solely to effect a year-end change, section 245 (GAAR) would be applied. Therefore, this is considered to be an offensive transaction as far as the CRA is concerned.

(7) In order for subsection 88(1) to apply, not less than 90% of the issued shares of each class of the capital stock of the subsidiary need to be owned by the parent, which is a taxable Canadian corporation, and all of the shares of the subsidiary that were not owned by the parent immediately before the winding-up were owned at that time by persons with whom the parent was dealing at arm's length.

(8) Her new A.C.B. is the total A.C.B. she had on her preferred shares divided by the total number of new common shares [sec. 51]. In this case her new A.C.B. on the common shares would be $10,000 divided by 2,000 or $5 per share.

(9) The primary purpose of estate freezing is to freeze all or part of the value of growing assets at their current fair market value, such that future growth in these assets accrues to someone else, usually the next generation of family members. The result will be that this future growth will not be taxed in the hands of the taxpayer on a disposition or at his or her death.

(10) Some secondary objectives of an estate freeze would be to:

(a) defer any immediate tax cost on the freeze transaction and establish the amount of the tax liability on death;

(b) maintain control over the asset that has been frozen;

(c) maintain a source of income from the asset being frozen;

(d) split income with low tax-rate family members; and

(e) use up the QSBC share capital gains exemption on the asset being frozen (holdco freeze only).

(11) The three principal methods of freezing the value of growth assets are:

(a) holdco freeze [sec. 85];

(b) internal freeze [sec. 86]; and

(c) reverse or asset freeze between corporations [sec. 85].

Refer to the text for details of these methods.

(12) The basic steps involved in a Holdco freeze are:

(a) incorporate the holding company;

(b) transfer the shares of an operating corporation to the holding corporation using section 85 to avoid incurring an immediate tax cost; and

(c) have the transferor take back, as consideration for the growth asset, debt and preferred shares of the holding company. The preferred shares will have certain characteristics to achieve the freezor's objectives including a fixed retraction value which will freeze the value. Other features would revolve around desired voting control, income and security.

(13) One of the biggest dangers of doing an estate freeze on the shares of an SBC in favour of a spouse or minor children is that the corporation will subsequently lose its SBC status and the corporate attribution rules will apply to deem an interest benefit on the transferor [ssec. 74.4(2)]. Remember that the corporation only has to accumulate over approximately 10% of the F.M.V. of its assets in non-active business assets in order to fall offside. This may be done easily if the company is generating excess cash and invests it. Keep in mind that the rules in subsection 74.4(2) only apply if "one of the main purposes of the transfer or loan may reasonably be considered to be to reduce the income of the individual and to benefit, either directly or indirectly, by means of a trust or by any other means whatever, a person who is a designated person in respect of the individual." Thus, before subsection 74.4(2) applies, this purpose test must be met.

(14) A "reverse or asset freeze" would be used to transfer some or all of the growth assets of a corporation in which the taxpayer owns common shares to a new corporation owned by family members who will benefit from the future growth through their ownership of the new corpora-

tion's common shares. The consideration taken back on the transfer will usually consist of non-growth assets such as debt and preferred shares with a fixed retraction value. For example, an operating company owns land and building that are used in the business and the present shareholders want the increase in value of the land and building to go to their adult children.

The steps that would be taken are as follows:

(a) a new company would be incorporated with the adult children subscribing for the common shares usually for a nominal amount;

(b) the existing corporation would then transfer the growth assets to the new corporation using section 85 to defer any tax; and

(c) the transferor corporation will take back, as consideration for the growth assets, debt and preferred shares of the new corporation. The preferred shares will have certain characteristics to achieve the freezor's objectives including a fixed retraction value which will freeze the value. Other features would revolve around desired voting control, income and security.

CHAPTER 18
Partnerships & Trusts

(1) The term "partnership" is not defined in the *Income Tax Act*. The term "partnership" is defined in the provincial Partnership Acts. The Ontario *Partnership Act*, for example, provides that a "partnership is a relation that subsists between persons carrying on a business in common with a view to profit."

(2) False. The amount of losses a limited partner can deduct in computing income in respect of losses allocated by the limited partnership is limited [ssec. 96(2.1)]. The losses can only be deducted to the extent of the limited partner's "at-risk amount" as defined [ssec. 96(2.2)]. Generally, the losses may be deducted by a limited partner only to the extent that the total of his or her investment in the partnership plus his or her share of the partnership profit exceeds any amount owing to the partnership by him or her and any guaranteed return as a result of a buy-back of the partnership interest, guaranteed buy-back and so on. To the extent that limited partnership losses are restricted, they can be carried forward indefinitely and deducted under paragraph 111(1)(e), but only against income from the limited partnership that gave rise to the loss.

(3) Because Dadd and Ladd do not deal at arm's length, subsection 103(1.1) must be considered. The issue is whether the allocation is reasonable in the circumstances having regard to the capital invested in or work performed for the partnership by the members thereof, or such other factors as may be relevant. For example, the allocation of the capital gain to Dadd may be reasonable given that it was his property in the first place. Since Dadd is the only one with capital and cash invested in the partnership, any losses may be his losses, as the losses impair his capital in the partnership. Arguments can be made that the allocation is reasonable in the circumstances.

Because the decision has been made to allocate income on a 50/50 basis but to allocate all of the losses to Dadd, reference should also be made to subsection 103(1). There should be no problem with this allocation on the basis that the principal reason for the allocation cannot reasonably be considered to be the reduction or postponement of the tax otherwise payable under the Act.

(4) Income is calculated at the partnership level and then allocated to the partners. A $600 taxable capital gain would be included in the income of the partnership, of which your share is $150 (25% × $600). Your adjusted cost base will be increased by $300, being your share of the taxable capital gain of $150 and your share of the non-taxable portion of $150 [par. 53(1)(e)].

(5) Income is calculated at the partnership level and then allocated to the partners. A $100,000 receipt would not be included in the partnership's income, since life insurance proceeds are not taxable. The adjusted cost base of your partnership interest will be increased by your share or $25,000 [par. 53(1)(e)].

(6) A rollover under subsection 97(2) is available only on a transfer to a Canadian partnership. This is defined [sec. 102] to include only those partnerships where all the members are resident in Canada at the particular time. In this case, Ms. Jones will need to determine whether the partner in the U.S. is still considered a resident of Canada for purposes of the Act. If not, the rollover will not be available.

(7) A trust is a relationship whereby a person (who is called a trustee) is bound to deal with property (which is called the trust property) over which he or she has control for the benefit of persons (who are called the beneficiaries) any of whom may enforce the obligation according to the terms of the trust document. A trust is created when a person (called the settlor) transfers property to a trustee.

(8) While it is true that trusts are conduits by allowing certain types of income to flow through to the beneficiaries and retain their character for tax purposes (for example, dividends, capital gains, foreign income), the income of a trust may be subject to tax. Trusts are taxed as an individual [ssec. 104(2)] on any income that is not paid or payable to the beneficiaries [ssec. 104(6)]. The rate of tax paid depends on whether the trust is an *inter vivos* trust or a testamentary trust.

(9) A testamentary trust is created as a consequence of the death of an individual. An *inter vivos* trust is one that is created during the lifetime of an individual. An *inter vivos* trust may also be created for tax purposes where a person other than the deceased has contributed property to a testamentary trust.

(10) A discretionary trust is a trust where the trustee is given the power of choice. The trustee may be given the power to determine the date of distribution of trust property, whether income or capital is to be paid to a beneficiary, how much is to be paid to a beneficiary and in what proportions among a group of beneficiaries it is to be paid. This feature gives the trust a great deal of flexibility and is a very useful planning tool for income splitting and estate equalization purposes.

(11) The special treatment applies to the following types of income:

(a) taxable dividends from a Canadian corporation which allows the beneficiary to use the dividend gross-up and tax credit [ssec. 104(19)];

(b) net taxable capital gains which are eligible for the capital gains deduction available in respect of qualified shares of a small business corporation and qualified farm property [ssecs. 104(21), (21.1), (21.2) and (21.3)] (note that net capital losses do not flow through to the beneficiary);

(c) non-taxable dividends which are excluded from the computation of taxable income [ssec. 104(20)];

(d) foreign income and related foreign tax paid to allow the beneficiary to claim the foreign tax credit [ssec. 104(22)]; and

(e) superannuation and pension benefits [ssecs. 104(27) and (28)].

(12) The trust would file a tax return for the fiscal period ending on March 15, 2005 on or before June 13, 2005 (that is, 90 days after the end of the trust's year). She would report the income in the calendar year in which the fiscal year-end of the trust fell [ssecs. 104(13) and (14)]. For example, in 2005 Ms. Betty would report the income that is allocated to her out of the trust for the period ended March 15, 2005.

(13) An income interest in a trust is not a capital property. The sale by Mr. Bill will cause the full amount of the proceeds to be included in his income [par. 106(2)(*a*)]. His sister will have a $30,000 cost of her income interest. She will benefit from that addition to the cost when she sells this interest, or receives future income from the trust.

(14) A capital interest in a trust is a capital property. As a result, a disposition of a capital interest in a trust to a third party will give rise to a capital gain or loss. In this case she will have a capital gain [par. 107(1)(*a*)]. It will be calculated as the excess of the proceeds over the greater of:

(a) the adjusted cost base of the capital interest (in this case nil); and

(b) the "cost amount" to the beneficiary which is defined as the beneficiary's proportionate interest of the tax cost of the trust's assets less its liabilities. In this case we do not know what this "cost amount" is.

Her chauffeur will have a cost base for his capital interest in the trust equal to $45,000. This will be recognized if he were to sell the interest. However, if he were to receive a capital distribution from the trust then he would receive the assets tax-free with a potential bump (or step-up) in adjusted cost base for his cost of the interest [ssec. 107(2)].

Solutions to Multiple Choice Questions

CHAPTER 2

Liability for Tax

Question 1

(B) is correct. Since X Ltd. is not incorporated in Canada, it is not deemed to be resident in Canada under subsection 250(4). Since the directors are not resident in Canada, X Ltd. is not resident in Canada under the common law "central management and control" rule.

(A) is incorrect because X Ltd. is deemed to be resident under paragraph 250(4)(*a*).

(C) is incorrect because X Ltd. is resident under the common law "central management and control" rule.

(D) is incorrect because X Ltd. is deemed to be resident under paragraph 250(4)(*c*) and under the common law "central management and control" rule.

Question 2

(C) is correct. Generally, the CRA will consider the individual not to have severed residential ties within Canada if he has a dwelling available for occupancy [IT-221R3, par. 6].

(A) is incorrect, because taking his wife and children with him to Germany is not feasible, since the couple is legally separated and the children are not dependent on him for support [IT-221R3, par. 7].

(B) is incorrect, because giving up Canadian citizenship has little relevance in determining residency.

(D) is incorrect. Although putting all his household furniture and personal effects into storage in Canada is a residential tie [IT-221R3, par. 8], the tie is a weaker one than that cited in (C).

Question 3

(B) is correct. Only the $50,000 of employment income earned in Canada would be reported on Mr. N's Canadian personal income tax return for the year [ssec. 2(3); sec. 115].

(A) is incorrect. The $10,000 interest, earned by the non-resident, is not taxable under Part I. However, the interest would be subject to Part XIII tax withheld at source.

(C) is incorrect for the same reason as (A).

(D) is incorrect, because only residents of Canada are subject to Canadian income tax on their worldwide income [ssec. 2(1)].

Question 4

(C) is correct. Because Jerry Dykopf ceased to be a resident of Canada on April 30 of the year, only his worldwide income during the first four months of the year ($26,000 = $25,000 + $1,000) is subject to tax in Canada under Part I and would be reported on his Canadian personal income tax return for the year [ssec. 2(1); sec. 114].

(A) includes income earned while not a resident of Canada: $58,000 = $25,000 + $1,000 + $30,000 + $2,000. The $30,000 of employment income earned in Israel and the $2,000 of Canadian interest earned from May 1 to December 31 of the year are not subject to Part I tax because Jerry is not resident in Canada at that time [ssec. 2(1); sec. 114]. The $2,000 of Canadian interest is subject to tax under Part XIII, not Part I. Tax is withheld at source under Part XIII — no return is filed.

(B) includes the salary earned in Israel: $56,000 = $25,000 + $1,000 + $30,000. As in (A) above, the $30,000 of employment income earned in Israel is not subject to tax in Canada.

(D) excludes the worldwide income earned while Jerry was a resident in Canada. As discussed in (A) above, this would be reported on his Canadian personal income tax return for the year [ssec. 2(1); sec. 114].

Question 5

(B) is correct. Judy is a non-resident. She seems to have severed her residential ties to Canada (moving her belongings) and established new ties to London, England (buying a house).

(A) is incorrect. James is still a resident of Canada. There is no indication that James has severed his residential ties to Canada or established ties to London, England.

(C) is incorrect. Since ERT Limited was incorporated in Canada after April 26, 1965, it is deemed to be a resident of Canada [par. 250(4)(a)].

(D) is incorrect. Doug is deemed to be a resident of Canada because he is a member of the Canadian armed forces. [par. 250(1)(b)].

Question 6

(C) is correct.

Sales (taxable at 7%)	$250,000
Purchase of supplies from a registrant	30,000

$220,000 × 7% = $15,400.

(A) incorrectly takes a deduction for salaries which is an exempt supply: $250,000 – $30,000 – $70,000 = $150,000. $150,000 × 7% = $10,500.

(B) incorrectly takes a deduction for interest expense: $250,000 – $30,000 – $20,000 = $200,000. $200,000 × 7% = $14,000.

(D) incorrectly includes exports (which are zero-rated) and takes a deduction for interest expense (an exempt supply): $250,000 + $100,000 – $30,000 – $20,000 = $300,000. $300,000 × 7% = $21,000.

CHAPTER 3

Employment Income

Question 1

(A) is correct: $12 \times 2\% \times \$34,500 = \$8,280$ [ssec. 6(2)].

(B) and (C) are wrong because the operating cost benefit is computed as: 20 cents $\times$ 15,000 personal use km. = \$3,000 [par. 6(1)(*k*); Reg. 7305.1]. Part (B) incorrectly computes the operating cost benefit as: 15,000/20,000 $\times$ \$3,300 = \$2,475. Part (C) incorrectly computes the operating cost benefit as: 17 cents $\times$ 15,000 personal use km. = \$2,550.

(D) is wrong because he does not have more than 50% employment use [spar. 6(1)(*k*)(iv)].

Question 2

(B) is correct: \$50,000 salary + \$3,500 allowance − \$3,000 automobile expenses = \$50,500. The car allowance is taxable because it is not based solely on kilometres driven [spar. 6(1)(*b*)(x)]. Since the car allowance is taxable, the automobile expenses can be deducted [spar. 8(1)(*h*.1)(iii)]. The entertainment expenses are not deductible because she has no commission income [par. 8(1)(*f*)].

(A) incorrectly excludes a deduction for automobile expenses: \$53,500 = \$50,000 salary + \$3,500 allowance. The automobile expenses are deductible under paragraph 8(1)(*h*.1) because the allowance is included in income under paragraph 6(1)(*b*).

(C) incorrectly includes a deduction for entertainment expenses: \$49,500 = \$50,000 salary + \$3,500 allowance − \$3,000 automobile expenses − \$1,000 entertainment expenses. The entertainment expenses (50% $\times$ \$2,000) are not deductible because she has no commission income or income from negotiating contracts [par. 8(1)(*f*)].

(D) incorrectly excludes the car allowance and the deduction for automobile expenses and incorrectly includes a deduction for entertainment expenses: \$49,000 = \$50,000 salary − \$1,000 entertainment expenses.

Question 3

(A) is correct. Susanne Denholm can claim home office expenses because she is required by contract to maintain an office in her home and she works principally in her home (i.e., "most of the time") [spars. 8(1)(*i*)(iii) and 8(13)(*a*)(i)]. The \$500 correct amount of deductible home office expenses is calculated as follows:

Heat, hydro & maintenance: $\$5,000 \times 10\% = \$500$

(B) incorrectly includes a deduction for property taxes and insurance: \$1,100 = \$500 + \$200 insurance + \$400 property taxes. The insurance (10% $\times$ \$2,000) and property taxes (10% $\times$ \$4,000) are not considered to be supplies for the purposes of subparagraph 8(1)(*i*)(iii) [IT-352R2, par. 6]. However, if Susanne had commission income, 10% of her insurance and property taxes would be deductible under paragraph 8(1)(*f*).

(C) incorrectly includes deductions for insurance, property taxes and the general telephone line: \$1,400 = \$500 + \$200 insurance + \$400 property taxes + \$300 general telephone line. The insurance, property taxes and the cost of the general telephone line (50% $\times$ \$600) are not deductible under subparagraph 8(1)(*i*)(iii) [IT-352R2, pars. 6 and 10(a)]. If Susanne had commission income, the cost of the general telephone line would still not be deductible — only a special phone line and/or long distance calls would be deductible.

(D) incorrectly includes insurance, property taxes, the general telephone line and mortgage interest: \$3,800 = \$500 + \$200 insurance + \$400 property taxes + \$300 general telephone + \$2,400 mortgage interest. The insurance, property taxes, the cost of the general telephone line and mortgage interest (10% $\times$ \$24,000) are not considered to be supplies for the purposes of subparagraph 8(1)(*i*)(iii) [IT-352R2]. If Susanne had commission income, the mortgage interest would still not be deductible since paragraph 8(1)(*j*) limits interest expense to interest on automobiles and planes.

Question 4

(A) is correct. The loan qualifies as a home relocation loan. The benefit is computed using the lower of the prescribed interest rate at the time of the loan (4%) and the prescribed interest rate during the year (3%). Therefore the employment benefit is $1,000 (3% × $100,000 − 2% × $100,000 interest paid) [ssecs. 6(9), 80.4(1), (4)].

(B) incorrectly computes the employment benefit using 4%: $2,000 = 4% × $100,000 − 2% × $100,000.

(C) incorrectly ignores the 2% interest paid in the computation of the interest benefit: $3,000 = 3% × $100,000.

(D) incorrectly computes the employment benefit using 4% rather than 3%. The 2% interest paid is not deducted: 4% × $100,000.

Question 5

(D) is correct. The stock option benefit is ($40 − $30) × 1,000 shares = $10,000. She meets the conditions for deferral because the option price was greater than the fair market value at the date of grant ($19 per share) in March 2004. She can therefore defer the employee benefit until she sells the shares. The benefit is therefore $10,000 in 2005.

(A) incorrectly reports the benefit in 2004 rather than 2005 and incorrectly subtracts the paragraph 110(1)(*d*) deduction (¹/₂ × $10,000) in computing the benefit ($10,000 − $5,000). This deduction is a Division C deduction.

(B) and (C) incorrectly compute the benefit based on the sales price of $38,000 ($38,000 − $30,000 = $8,000) rather than the price of the stock at the time of purchase. The benefit is $10,000. The $2,000 subsequent decline in value of the stock is a capital loss.

Question 6

(B) is correct.

Meals and entertainment (50% × $14,000)	$ 7,000
Driving costs (90% × $10,000)	9,000
Expenses eligible under paragraph 8(1)(*f*)	$16,000

Tim can either claim a deduction for these amounts under paragraph 8(1)(f) to the extent of his commission income ($5,000) or he can claim a deduction for his automobile costs ($9,000) under paragraph 8(1)(*h*.1). The maximum deduction is therefore $9,000.

(A) is incorrect because it is the paragraph 8(1)(*f*) amount.

(C) is incorrect because it is the full meals and entertainment amount ($14,000) [sec. 67.1] and ignores the $5,000 commission limitation.

(D) is incorrect because it represents the expenses eligible under paragraph 8(1)(f) ($16,000) but ignores the $5,000 commission limitation.

CHAPTER 4
Income from Business: General Concepts and Rules

Question 1

(D) is correct. Paragraph 18(1)(*t*) denies a deduction for interest and penalties on late income tax payments.

(A) is a deductible item. Paragraph 20(1)(*aa*) allows a deduction for amounts paid for landscaping business premises.

(B) is a deductible item. Paragraph 20(1)(*c*) allows a deduction for interest on money borrowed to finance the purchase of a factory for use in its business.

(C) is a deductible item. If the beneficiary of a $100,000 term life insurance policy on an employee is the employee's family, the cost of the insurance premium is part of the cost of the employee's remuneration package. As such, it is not denied by paragraph 18(1)(*a*) as it is incurred for the purpose of earning income.

Question 2

(C) is correct. The entire $15,000 spent on three social events for all employees at a particular location is deductible as long as the number of events does not exceed six [par. 67.1(2)(*f*)].

(A) The deduction for $11,000 of accrued legal fees for a pending law suit is not allowed, because it is a contingent liability [par. 18(1)(*e*)]. There is no legal liability to pay this amount.

(B) The deduction for $4,000 of donations to registered charities is denied under paragraph 18(1)(*a*), because it is not incurred for the purpose of earning income. The donations would be deductible in the computation of taxable income [par. 110.1(1)(*a*)].

(D) The deduction of $1,500 for golf club membership dues for employees is denied by paragraph 18(1)(*l*).

Question 3

(D) is correct, because paragraph 67.1(2)(*b*) provides an exception to the 50% rule for the cost of meals and entertainment relating to a fund-raising event the primary purpose of which is to benefit a registered charity.

(A) is incorrect since donations to political parties are not deductible [par. 18(1)(*n*)]. The federal political donation would be eligible for a tax credit [ssec. 127(3)].

(B) is incorrect, because accrued bonuses are not deductible if they are unpaid 180 days after year-end [ssec. 78(4)].

(C) is incorrect, because the deduction for a financial accounting reserve for warranty expenses is denied by paragraph 18(1)(*e*).

Question 4

(A) is the correct answer. The $13,000 to be added back is computed as follows:

Legal expenses related to the purchase of an investment in shares [par. 18(1)(*b*)]	$ 5,000
Legal expenses incurred to dispute a tax assessment [par. 60(*o*)]	0
Legal expenses related to the issuance of debt [par. 20(1)(*e*)]	4,000
Accounting fees in connection with the preparation of a prospectus [par. 20(1)(*e*)]	4,000
	$13,000

(B) incorrectly adds back $4,000 (instead of $5,000) for the legal expenses related to the purchase of an investment in shares: $12,000 = $4,000 + $4,000 + $4,000.

(C) incorrectly adds back nothing for either the legal expenses related to the issuance of debt or the accounting fees in connection with the preparation of a prospectus: $9,000 = $5,000 + $4,000.

(D) incorrectly adds back only the $5,000 legal expenses related to the purchase of an investment in shares.

Question 5

(D) is correct. Most of the facts support capital gains treatment: the nature of the asset (real estate), its use and intended use (rental), the 10-year holding period and the unsolicited offer for sale. As a result, the gain on the sale of the land will likely be treated as a capital gain for income tax purposes.

(A) is incorrect. Because Sam is a real estate agent, the CRA may argue that the gain on the sale of the land is business income (not a capital gain).

(B) is incorrect. The fact that the land has been held for ten years supports capital gains treatment, not business income treatment.

(C) is incorrect. The unsolicited offer for sale supports capital gains treatment, not business income treatment.

Question 6

(A) is correct. Legal fees to defend a lawsuit brought by a customer would be deductible under paragraph 18(1)(a).

(B) and (C) are incorrect because these items (accounting losses on the sale of capital property and the principal amount of a mortgage) are on account of capital and therefore not deductible [par. 18(1)(b)].

(D) is incorrect because personal and living expenses are not deductible [par. 18(1)(h)].

CHAPTER 5
Depreciable Property and Eligible Capital Property

Question 1

(C) is correct. The maximum CCA is: $\frac{1}{2} \times 30\% \times \$30,000 = \$4,500$ [par. 13(7)(g), Reg. 7307(1)].

(A) incorrectly uses the $50,000 cost of the vehicle to compute CCA: $\frac{1}{2} \times 30\% \times \$50,000 = \$7,500$.

(B) incorrectly ignores the half-year rule: $30\% \times \$30,000 = \$9,000$.

(D) incorrectly uses the pre-2001 maximum Class 10.1 cost of $27,000: $\frac{1}{2} \times 30\% \times \$27,000 = \$4,050$.

Question 2

(A) is correct. $10,000 is the lesser of $\frac{1}{5} \times \$80,000 = \$16,000$ and $\$80,000/8 = \$10,000$ [Schedule III]. For 2005, the year the cost was incurred, the maximum CCA = 50% of $10,000 = $5,000 [Reg. 1100(1)(b)].

(B) is incorrect. It is 50% of the $16,000 amount calculated in (A).

(C) is incorrect because the $10,000 figure does not take into account the 50% rule in Regulation 1100(1)(b).

(D) is incorrect for the reasons outlined for (B) and (C) combined.

Question 3

(D) is correct. The maximum CECA claim is: $75\% \times \$100,000 \times 7\% = \$5,250$.

(A) is incorrect: $100,000/40 = $2,500. Forty years is the maximum period for amortization of goodwill for accounting purposes only.

(B) is incorrect: $\frac{1}{2} \times \$100,000 \times 7\% = \$3,500$. The $\frac{1}{2}$ rate does not apply for purposes of additions to the CEC pool.

(C) is incorrect: $7\% \times \$100,000 = \$7,000$. Only 75% of the cost is used before multiplying by 7%.

Question 4

(B) is correct because the remaining lease term in 2005 is 3 years and the first renewal period is 3 years. The maximum CCA claim is $5,000, calculated as follows:

Lesser of: (i) $1/5 \times \$60,000$ = $12,000
 (ii) $\$60,000/(3 + 3)$ = $10,000

For 2005, the year the cost was incurred, the maximum CCA is: 50% of $10,000 = $5,000 [Reg. 1100(1)(*b*)].

(A) is incorrect, because it uses the initial 5-year term of the lease in the calculation in place of the remaining lease term of 3 years: $60,000/(5 + 3) = $7,500 × 50% = $3,750.

(C) is incorrect, because the greater ($12,000), as opposed to the lesser ($10,000), of the two amounts calculated has been used: $6,000 = 50% × $12,000.

(D) is incorrect, because it uses the initial 5-year term of the lease in the calculation in place of the remaining lease term of 3 years and ignores the 50% rule in Regulation 1100(1)(*b*): $60,000/(5 + 3) = $7,500.

Question 5

(B) is correct. Under paragraph 1100(2) of the Regulations, dies and moulds and software are not excepted from the half net-amount rule, but the other Class 12 items are: linens are listed in paragraph (*g*), cutlery and dishes are listed in paragraph (*b*) and kitchen utensils costing less than $200 are listed in paragraph (*c*). ¹/₂ ($1,200 + $600) + $15,000 + $400 = $16,300.

(A) is incorrect because it uses the half net-amount rule on all Class 12 assets: ¹/₂ ($1,200 + $600 + $15,000 + $400) = $8,600.

(C) is incorrect because it ignores the half net-amount rule on the dies and moulds: $1,200 + ¹/₂ × $600 + $15,000 + $400 = $16,900.

(D) is incorrect because it ignores the half net-amount rule on the dies and moulds and software: $1,200 + $600 + $15,000 + $400 = $17,200.

Question 6

(A) is correct. The costs can be included in Class 14 or 44 or deducted in the year incurred under paragraph 20(1)(cc).

(B), (C) and (D) are incorrect because the costs are not an eligible capital expenditure because a patent has a limited life.

CHAPTER 6

Income from Property

Question 1

(B) is correct. The calculation is as follows:

Grossed up dividend ($12,000 × 1.25)	$15,000
Combined tax rate	× 46%
	$ 6,900
Dividend tax credit	(3,000)
Net tax	$ 3,900

(A) incorrectly ignores provincial tax: $15,000 × 29% – $3,000 = $1,350.

(C) incorrectly ignores the dividend tax credit:

$$\$15,000 \times 46\% = \$6,900$$

(D) incorrectly ignores the gross-up and the dividend tax credit: $12,000 × 46% = $5,520.

Question 2

(B) is the correct answer. The calculation is as follows:

	Property 1	Property 2	Property 3	Total
UCC at Jan. 1st	$100,000	$75,000	$150,000	
Rental revenue for the year	$ 58,000	$22,000	$ 20,000	
Expenses for the year	50,000	20,000	20,000	
Income before CCA	$ 8,000	$ 2,000	(Nil)	$10,000
4% × UCC	$ 4,000	$ 3,000	$ 6,000	$13,000
Maximum CCA [Reg. 1100(11)]				$10,000

(A) is incorrect. $13,000 is the CCA calculation ignoring the rental property restriction [Reg. 1100(11)].

(C) is incorrect. $7,000 is the maximum CCA calculation on the first two buildings only. This calculation ignores the fact that the CCA on the third property can be claimed against the net rental income on the first two properties.

(D) is incorrect. It is one-half of the $13,000 calculated in (A) above.

Question 3

(C) is the correct answer. Subsection 15(2) would include the principal amount of the loan in Mrs. C's income in 2005 because none of the exception tests in subsections 15(2.2), (2.3), (2.4) and (2.6) are met.

(1) The exception test in subsection 15(2.2) does not apply because Mrs. C is resident in Canada.

(2) The exception in subsection 15(2.3) does not apply since the money is not lent in the ordinary course of money lending business.

(3) None of the exceptions for employees in subsection 15(2.4) are met, because it is not reasonable to conclude that the loan is received because of employment since no other employees have received similar loans.

(4) The exception in subsection 15(2.6) does not apply since the debt was repaid on April 1, 2007, which is more than one year from the end of S Ltd.'s December 31, 2005 fiscal year.

The loan in (A) would not be included in Mrs. A's income because the exception test in subsection 15(2.6) applies: the debt is repaid on April 1, 2006, which is within one year from the end of S Ltd.'s December 31, 2005 fiscal year. Note, however, that subsection 80.4(2) would apply to compute a deemed interest benefit on the loan.

The loan in (B) would not be included in B Ltd's income because subsection 15(2) does not apply to corporate shareholders resident in Canada.

The loan in (D) would not be included in Mr. D's income because one of the exceptions for employees in subsection 15(2.4) is met: Mr. D is not a specified employee and it is reasonable to conclude that the loan is received because of employment, since the computer is for employment use and other employees currently working at home have received similar loans. Since Mr. D is not a specified employee, the loan does not have to be for any specified purpose. A specified employee is an employee who is either a specified shareholder (i.e., generally, a person who owns at least 10% of the shares of any class of the corporation) or a person who does not deal at arm's length with the corporation [ssec. 248(1)]. Since Mr. D owns only 5% of the shares of S Ltd. and deals at arm's length with the corporation, he is not a specified employee.

Question 4

(B) is the correct answer. Subsection 56(4.1) will attribute the $12,000 of dividend income to Mr. P. Mabel and Mr. P are related and it can reasonably be considered that one of the main reasons for making the loan was to reduce tax.

(A) is incorrect. The $3,000 of interest income will not be attributed. Peter is not under 18 years of age and, therefore, subsection 74.1(2) does not apply. If it had been a loan, instead of a gift, subsection 56(4.1) would apply and may attribute the income.

(C) is incorrect. Even though an interest-free loan was made to which subsection 56(4.1) would apply, there is no property income from the cottage to attribute.

(D) is incorrect. Even though a gift was made to a spouse to which subsection 74.1(1) would apply, there is no property income from the chequing account to attribute.

Question 5

(B) is correct. The premium paid on a $100,000 term life insurance policy on the taxpayer's life which is required as collateral for a $100,000 bank loan used to purchase a $100,000 investment in common shares is deductible [par. 20(1)(e.2)].

(A) is incorrect because commissions paid on the purchase of an investment in common shares are capitalized as part of the cost of the shares [par. 18(1)(b)].

(C) is incorrect because paragraph 18(11)(b) does not allow a deduction for interest expense on a loan to invest in a registered retirement savings plan.

(D) is incorrect because commissions paid on the sale of an investment in common shares are a selling cost deducted in computing the capital gain on the sale of the shares. One-half of a capital gain is a taxable capital gain which is computed under Subdivision c of Division B of Part I of the Act, whereas income from business or property is computed under Subdivision b.

Question 6

(D) is correct: $20,000 × 1.25 [ssec. 82(1)] + $8,500 + $1,500 tax withheld = $35,000.

(A) is incorrect because it ignores the gross-up on the dividend and the foreign income: $20,000.

(B) is incorrect because it ignores the gross-up on the dividend and the foreign tax withheld: $20,000 + $8,500 = $28,500.

(C) is incorrect because it ignores the gross-up on the dividend: $20,000 + $8,500 + $1,500 = $30,000.

Question 7

(D) is correct.

(A) is incorrect because the tax on split income only applies to taxpayers under age 18 throughout the year [see definition of specified individual in sec. 120.4]. Since Ron is 18, the tax on split income will not apply.

(B) is incorrect because the only exemption regarding inherited shares is for shares inherited from a parent [see definition of excluded amount in sec. 120.4]. If Ron had been under 18 at any time in the year, the tax on split income would have applied to dividends received on the shares.

(C) is incorrect because the tax on split income does not apply to capital gains [see definition of split income in sec. 120.4].

CHAPTER 7
Capital Gains: An Introduction

Question 1

(B) is correct. The gain is: $600,000 - $100,000 = $500,000. The maximum 2005 reserve is computed using the lesser of the percentage of proceeds payable after the end of the year ($510K/$600K or 85%, in this case) and four fifths ($^4/_5$) [par. 40(1)(a)]. Since the lesser amount is four fifths, the reserve is $400,000 ($^4/_5$ × $500,000) and the capital gain is therefore $100,000 ($500,000 - $400,000). The minimum taxable capital gain is therefore $50,000 ($^1/_2$).

(A) is incorrect, because the capital gain must be multiplied by $^1/_2$ to compute the taxable capital gain.

(C) is incorrect, because it uses the 85% figure to compute the reserve and does not multiply the result by $^1/_2$: $500,000 - 85% × $500,000 = $75,000.

(D) is incorrect, because it uses the 85% figure to compute the reserve: $75,000 × $^1/_2$.

Question 2

(C) is correct. The loss on the automobile is not allowed since it is personal-use property (PUP). The $1,000 rule means that the gain on the boat (which is PUP) is $500, the gain on the painting (which is listed personal property (LPP)) is $300, and the loss on the jewellery (which is LPP) is $400. Since the deductible portion of the $400 LPP loss is limited to the LPP gain in the year ($300), the capital gain is: $500 + $300 - $300 = $500. The $100 LPP loss can be carried over against LPP gains [sec. 54; ssecs. 46(1), 41(1); sec. 2].

(A) is incorrect, because it ignores the $1,000 rule and computes the gain on the boat (PUP) as $900, the gain on the painting (LPP) as $700, and the loss on the jewellery (LPP) as $1,200. The LPP gain is then offset by a portion of the LPP loss, leaving the $900 gain.

(B) is incorrect, because it does not subtract the deductible portion of the LPP loss from the LPP gain: $500 + $300 = $800.

(D) is incorrect, because it deducts the full LPP loss ($400) against all the gains: $500 + $300 - $400 = $400.

Question 3

(A) is correct since only the gift to the son will result in a taxable capital gain.

The ACB of Mike's stock is:

100 × $3.11 plus $39 commission (incl. sec. 7 benefit)	$350
100 × $4 plus $50 commission	450
$\underline{\underline{200}}$	$\underline{\underline{\$800}}$ = $4 ACB per share. [sec. 47; par. 53(1)(i)]

His taxable capital gain on the gift to his son is: $^1/_2$ ($6 - $4) × 100 = $100.

There is no taxable capital gain on the gift to his wife, because the transfer occurs at his $4 ACB since no special election was filed [ssec. 73(1)].

(B) incorrectly excluded brokerage commissions from the ACB of his shares as: $^1/_2$ ($6 - $711/200) × 100 = $122.

(C) incorrectly computes a capital gain on the gift to Mike's wife: $^1/_2$ ($6 - $4) × 200 shares = $200.

(D) is incorrect, because it incorrectly computes a capital gain on the gift to his wife and does not apply the $^1/_2$ fraction to compute the taxable portion of the gain: ($6 - $4) × 200 = $400.

Question 4

(B) is the correct answer. Since Amanda had no capital gain on her house, she must have designated it as her principal residence for all but one of the years 1996 to 2004. She therefore has 2 years to designate in respect of the cottage: one of the years not used on the house (say, 2004) plus 2005. Since she owned the cottage 8 years (1998 to 2005), the principal residence exemption for the cottage is: $^3/_8 \times \$80,000 = \$30,000$ (3 = 2 years designated + "one-plus rule"). Therefore, Amanda's taxable capital gain is $25,000 ($^1/_2 \times$ ($80K – $30K principal residence exemption)).

(A) is incorrect, because $80,000 is the capital gain before the exemption.

(C) is incorrect, because it uses $^2/_8 \times \$80,000 = \$20,000$ as the principal residence exemption: $^1/_2 \times$ ($80K – $20K) = $30,000.

(D) is incorrect, because $50,000 is the capital gain, not the taxable capital gain.

Question 5

(B) is correct. The amount of the dividend is $4, the increase in the paid-up capital, and this is also the cost of the shares (ssec. 53(3)). However, the individual's net income would increase by $5, since it is a taxable dividend: 4×1.25 gross-up = $5 [ssec. 82(1)].

(A) is incorrect because although $4 is the amount of the dividend, the amount included in net income is the grossed-up dividend ($1.25 \times \$4 = \$5$).

(C) is incorrect because the amount of the dividend is not based on the $10 fair market value of the share.

(D) is also incorrect because the amount of the dividend is not based on the $10 fair market value of the share and the amount included in income is the increase in paid-up capital grossed up by 1.25, not the fair market value grossed up by 1.25.

Question 6

(C) is correct.

Shares		$1,600
Personal-use property		700
Listed personal property	$500	
Listed personal property	(140)	
Listed personal property losses of prior year	(100)	260
Shares		(820)
Personal-use property		Nil
Capital gain		$1,740
Taxable capital gain ($^1/_2$)		$ 870

(A) is incorrect because it deducts the $1,000 personal use property loss: $^1/_2$ ($1,740 – 1,000) = $370.

(B) is incorrect because it deducts the $1,000 personal use property loss and does not multiply by the $^1/_2$ fraction: ($1,740 – $1,000) = $740.

(D) is incorrect because it does not deduct the listed personal property loss of other years: $^1/_2 \times$ ($1,740 + $100) = $920.

CHAPTER 8
Capital Gains: The Finer Points

Question 1

(D) is the correct answer. Since the expropriation is an involuntary disposition, the property must be replaced by the later of two years and 24 months from the end of the taxation year in which the disposition took place. Since the relevant taxation year was May 31, 2006, the two-year deadline is May 31, 2008 [par. 44(1)(c)].

(A) incorrectly uses the one-year deadline which is applicable for voluntary dispositions.

(B) incorrectly uses two years from the disposition date as the deadline.

(C) incorrectly uses two years from the end of the calendar year of the disposition as the deadline.

Question 2

(A) is correct [ssec. 74.1(2)].

(B) is incorrect, because capital gains or losses do not attribute on loans or gifts to minors.

(C) is incorrect, because there will be a capital gain on the gift [sec. 69].

(D) is incorrect. $100,000 is the capital gain. The taxable capital gain is:

$$\frac{1}{2} \times \$100,000 = \$50,000.$$

Question 3

(C) is correct. There is a superficial loss because Ms. Y has incurred a loss and an affiliated person (Mr. Y) acquired the shares within 30 days of the disposition [sec. 54; par. 40(2)(g)].

(A) is incorrect, because it ignores the superficial loss rule and computes the loss as $\frac{1}{2} \times$ ($800K – $900K).

(B) is not correct, because Ms. Y elected out of the subsection 73(1) rollover.

(D) is not correct. There is no attribution because she elected out of the subsection 73(1) rollover and received fair market value consideration (i.e., $800,000 cash) [sec. 74.5].

Question 4

(B) is correct, because the taxable capital gain is computed as follows: listed shares of a public corporation resident in Canada (= $\frac{1}{2} \times$ ($40,000 – $10,000) = $15,000) + painting (= $\frac{1}{2}$ ($10,000 – $6,000) = $2,000) = $17,000.

The rental real estate in Canada and the registered retirement savings plan are specifically exempted from the deemed disposition rules [ssec. 128.1(4)].

(A) incorrectly excludes the taxable capital gain on the painting.

(C) incorrectly includes $\frac{1}{2}$ of the gain on the RRSP ($10,000).

(D) incorrectly includes a $25,000 taxable capital gain on the rental real estate in Canada.

Question 5

(C) is correct. The calculation is as follows:

	Division B income
Toronto home (no capital gain; principal residence)	—
Rental property in London, Ontario	
— Land: $\frac{1}{2}$ ($100,000 – 50,000)	$25,000
— Building: recapture = $25,000 – $2,000	23,000
Taxable capital gain = $\frac{1}{2}$ ($35K – $25K)	5,000
Mutual fund units: $\frac{1}{2}$ ($60K – $12K)	24,000
Shares of a public company: $\frac{1}{2}$ ($100K – $90K)	5,000
	$82,000

(A) incorrectly ignores recapture: $82,000 – $23,000 = $59,000.

(B) incorrectly multiplies the recapture by the $\frac{1}{2}$ taxable capital gains fraction: $25,000 + $\frac{1}{2}$ $\times$ $23,000 + $5,000 + $24,000 + $5,000 = $70,500

(D) incorrectly includes a capital gain on the principal residence: $82,000 + $\frac{1}{2} \times$ ($240K – $100K) = $152,000

Question 6

(B) is correct. Because Gary made a subsection 45(2) election in respect of the property, there is deemed to be no change in use in 1999. The only disposition occurs in 2005 on the date of sale. Section 54 allows Gary to designate the property as his principal residence for up to 4 years where a subsection 45(2) election was made. The gain on the property is $200,000 ($250K –

$50K) and the total years of ownership were 18 (1988 to 2005) and the maximum number of years that can be designated is 16 (1988 to 1999 plus 4). Therefore, the principal residence exemption is $[(16 + 1)/18] \times \$200,000$ or $188,888. The capital gain is therefore $11,112 ($200K – $188,888) and the taxable capital gain is $5,556 ($\frac{1}{2} \times \$11,112$).

(A) is incorrect because there is a taxable capital gain to report in 2005 because not all years of ownership qualify as years eligible for a principal residence. Section 54.1 does not apply to extend the period to more than 4 years because Gary did not move back into the residence before it was sold.

(C) incorrectly calculates taxable capital gains of $50,000 in 1999 [$\frac{1}{2}$ ($150K – $50K)] and 2005 [$\frac{1}{2}$($250K – $150K)]. The timing is wrong because there is no deemed disposition in 1999 because of the subsection 45(2) election. The amount is also wrong because 12 years (1988 – 1999) can be designated in respect of the residence.

(D) correctly calculates the gain in 2005 as $200,000 without claiming any principal residence exemption, thus resulting in a taxable capital gain of $100,000 ($\frac{1}{2} \times \$200K$).

CHAPTER 9
Other Sources of Income and Deductions in Computing Income

Question 1

(C) is the correct answer under paragraph 60(j.1) and is calculated as follows:

21 years employed before 1996 (1975 – 1995) × $2,000	$42,000
14 years employed before 1989 when no RPP or DPSP benefits vested (1975 – 1988) × $1,500	21,000
	$63,000

(A) incorrectly ignores the $1,500 rule for pre-89 years where RPP or DPSP benefits have not vested.

(B) incorrectly excludes one of the years: $20 \times \$2,000 + 13 \times \$1,500 = \$59,500$.

(D) incorrectly counts 1996 to 2005 in the calculation: $31 \times \$2,000 + 14 \times \$1,500 = \$83,000$.

Question 2

(C) is correct. The $6,000 is calculated as follows:

The lesser of:

the 2005 RRSP dollar limit		$16,500
18% of earned income:		
Income from employment	$44,000	
RPP contributions	1,000	
Support received	3,600	
Real estate rental income	1,400	
	$50,000 × 18%	$ 9,000
The lesser amount		$ 9,000
minus 2004 PA		(4,000)
add unused deduction room		1,000
		$ 6,000

(A) incorrectly uses $44,000 as earned income: $18\% \times \$44,000 - \$4,000$ PA $+ \$1,000 = \$4,920$.

(B) incorrectly excludes the unused deduction room: $9,000 – $4,000 = $5,000.

(D) incorrectly ignores the earned income calculation: $16,500 – $4,000 + $1,000 = $13,500.

Question 3

(A) is correct. The calculations are as follows:

	Meg	James
Salary	$46,000	
Employment expenses [sec. 8]	(2,800)	
Business income	—	$18,000
Interest income	800	1,500
Net income	$44,000	$19,500
Earned income [sec. 63]	$46,000	$18,000

Since James has the lower net income ($19,500), he must claim the deduction, which is the least of:

(a) Eligible child care expenses: $15,000 + ($100 × 2 weeks) $15,200

(b) Eligible children:
$4,000 × 1 = $4,000
$7,000 × 2 = 14,000 .... $18,000

(c) ²/₃ × James' earned income: ²/₃ × $18,000 .... $12,000

Since Joanne is age 17, she is not an eligible child. The deduction for the overnight camp for Susie is restricted to $100 per week [ssec. 63(3)].

(B) is incorrect, because Meg cannot claim the deduction, since she has the higher net income.

(C) and (D) are incorrect because they are not the least amount calculated in (A) above.

Question 4

(B) is correct and is calculated as follows:

Moving van to transport household effects	$ 5,000
Travelling cost — self, spouse and two children	1,800
Legal fees — Vancouver house	900
Legal fees — Toronto house	1,100
Hotel costs while waiting for Vancouver house — $100 per day for 15 days (max.)	1,500
	$10,300

(A) incorrectly excludes the legal fees on the houses: $10,300 – $2,000 = $8,300.

(C) incorrectly includes all the hotel costs: $10,300 + 1,500 = $11,800.

(D) incorrectly includes all the hotel costs and the house hunting trip: $10,300 + $1,500 + $800 = $12,600.

Question 5

(D) is correct. The earned income that should be used to calculate her RRSP deduction for 2005 is her 2004 earned income under subsection 146(1) is:

	2003
Salary	$100,000
Taxable benefits under sections 6 and 7	8,000
Travel expenses under section 8	(3,000)
Business losses	(1,000)
Rental income (net of expenses and CCA)	3,200
Spousal support paid	(12,600)
2004 Earned income under s. 146(1)	$ 94,600

(A) and (C) are incorrect. The earned income that should be used to calculate her child care expense deduction for 2005 according to subsection 63(3) is $118,000:

	2004
Salary	$110,000
Taxable benefits under sections 6 and 7	8,000
Earned income under subsection 63(3)	$118,000

(A) incorrectly includes 2005 salary only ($110,000). (C) is the 2005 net income under Division B which includes amounts for travel expenses, RPP contributions, business losses, rental income and spousal support which are not part of the earned income calculation under subsection 63(3).

(B) is Sahar's 2005 earned income under subsection 146(1) which should be used for computing her 2006 RRSP deduction:

	2005
Salary	$110,000
Taxable benefits under sections 6 and 7	8,000
Travel expenses under s. 8	(2,000)
Business losses	(1,200)
Rental income (net of expenses and CCA)	3,600
Spousal support paid	(12,000)
Net income under Division B	$106,400

Question 6

(D) is correct. Deductible moving costs under subsection 62(3) are:

Moving van	$2,600
Travelling costs to move Natalie and family	1,200
Cost of maintaining vacant former residence (maximum amount)	5,000
Cost of changing address on legal documents	100
	$8,900

(A) which totals $26,000 incorrectly includes all expenses listed.

(B) which totals $15,900 incorrectly includes the actual cost of maintaining the former residence (an additional $4,000) plus the $3,000 house hunting trip.

(C) which totals $12,900 incorrectly includes all actual cost of maintaining the former residence (an additional $4,000).

CHAPTER 10
Computation of Taxable Income and Taxes Payable for Individuals

Question 1

(C) is correct. Since BL is a CCPC and is at arm's length with Brad, the stock option benefit will be included in Brad's income in the year of sale (along with Brad's taxable capital gain) [Sec. 7(1.1)]. The stock option benefit is $3,000 (($5 – $2) × 1,000). Brad's taxable capital gain is $1,000 ($1/2 × ($7 – $5) × 1,000). Since Brad held the shares for at least 2 years, he can claim a paragraph 110(1)(d.1) deduction of $1,500 ($1/2 × his $3,000 option benefit).

(A) incorrectly includes the section 7 benefit in 2003 and ignores the paragraph 110(1)(d.1) deduction.

(B) incorrectly includes the section 7 benefit and paragraph 110(1)(d.1) deduction in 2003 (where tax deduction was $1/4 of the $3,000 benefit).

(D) incorrectly ignores the paragraph 110(1)(d.1) deduction.

Question 2

(C) is correct and is calculated as follows:

Basic [par. 118(1)(c)]		$ 8,148
Age [ssec. 118(2)]: $3,979 – 15% × ($47,500 – $29,619)		1,297
Pension [ssec. 118(3)]		1,000
	$10,445 × 16% =	$1,671
Dividend tax credit [sec. 121]: 13.33% × $2,500		333
		$2,004

(A) incorrectly ignores the dividend tax credit under subsection 121: ($8,148 + $1,297 + $1,000) × 16% = $1,671.

(B) incorrectly ignores the pension credit under subsection 118(3): ($8,148 + $1,297) × 16% + $333 = $1,844.

(D) incorrectly ignores the income restriction on the age credit under subsection 118(2): ($8,148 + $3,979 + $1,000) × 16% + $333 = $2,433.

Question 3

(C) is correct. Shabir's net income and taxable income is calculated as follows:

Scholarship income ($1100 – $3,000)		$ Nil
Employment income		8,000
Moving expenses:		
to McGill University (limited to scholarship income)		Nil
to Toronto		(200)
		$ 7,800

Since Shabir's income is less than $8,148, his entire tuition fee and education credits can be transferred to his parent (up to a maximum of $5,000 [sec. 118.9]).

Tuition fee	$3,900
Education credit: 8 × $400	3,200
	$7,100; max. $5,000 × 16% = $800

(A) incorrectly computes the credit base on tuition only ($3,900 × 16% = $624).

(B) incorrectly includes the entire scholarship in income and claims the full moving costs to McGill: $1,100 + $8,000 – $500 – $200 = $8,400. Since this income exceeds $8,148 ($8,400 – $8,148 = $252), then $4,748 ($5,000 – $252) can be transferred resulting in a credit of $760 to a parent.

(D) incorrectly ignores the $5,000 (i.e., 800/.16) limit: $7,100 × 16% = $1,136.

Question 4

(A) is correct

Salary	$ 60,000
Cdn dividends ($20K × 1.25)	25,000
Stock option benefit	200,000
Taxable capital gain (¹/₂ × $200K)	100,000
Net income	$385,000
Stock option deduction (¹/₂ × $200K)	(100,000)
Taxable income	$285,000

Tax:

1st $115,739	$ 25,109
balance @ 29% of $169,261	49,086
Basic personal amount (8,148 × 16%)	(1,304)
Transfer of tuition and education credits (16% × $5,000 × 3)	(2,400)
Dividend tax credit ($^2/_3$ × $5,000)	(3,333)
Federal tax	$ 67,158

(B) incorrectly omits the gross-up on the dividend and the dividend tax credit: $67,158 – (29% × $5K) + $3,333 = $69,041

(C) incorrectly omits the dividend tax credit: $67,158 + $3,333 = $70,491

(D) incorrectly omits the stock option deduction: $67,158 + 29% × $100K = $96,158

Question 5

(A) is correct

Taxable income	$285,000
Add:	
30% of capital gain	60,000
$^3/_5$ of the stock option deduction	60,000
Deduct:	
Gross-up on dividends	(5,000)
Adjusted taxable income...	$400,000
Less: Basic Exemption..	(40,000)
Net	$360,000
Minimum tax before minimum tax credit ($360,000 × 16%)	$ 57,600
Basic personal amount ($8,148 × 16%)	(1,304)
	$ 56,296

(B) incorrectly deducts the $2,400 transfer of tuition and education credits: $56,296 – $2,400 = $53,896.

(C) incorrectly omits the adjustment to add back the stock option deduction: $56,296 – 16% × $60K = $46,696.

(D) incorrectly omits the adjustment to add back the tax-free portion of the capital gain and the stock option deduction: $56,296 – 16% × $120K = $37,096.

CHAPTER 11

Computation of Taxable Income and Tax after General Reductions for Corporations

Question 1

(B) is correct. Loss Co may select any date, within the 53-week period commencing February 1, 2005, as its new year-end [pars. 249(4)(*b*), (*d*)].

(A) is incorrect as paragraph 249(4)(*a*) deems the taxation year to have ended immediately before control was acquired. Since control was acquired on February 1, 2005, the year is usually deemed to have ended January 31, 2005. (Technically, it is possible to have an acquisition of control occur at a specific time, say, 10 am, on February 1, in which case, the taxation year can be deemed to have ended on February 1 at 9:59 am. Usually, a time is not specified, in which case, the taxation year is deemed to end the day before.)

(C) is incorrect because of paragraph 249(4)(*d*) which deems the corporation not to have established a fiscal period yet. This being the case, the corporation is free to select any year-end, within the 53-week limitation.

(D) is incorrect for the same reason as (C).

Question 2

(C) is correct. The ACB of the land is reduced from $200,000 to $140,000, its FMV [par. 111(4)(*c*)]. The $60,000 reduction is deemed to be a capital loss for the taxation year ended May 14, 2005 [par. 111(4)(*d*)].

(A) is incorrect as it includes the $25,000 accrued loss on the building which is depreciable property. Depreciable property is specifically excluded [par. 111(4)(*c*)].

(B) is incorrect as it includes the $20,000 accrued loss on the inventory which is not a capital property.

(D) is incorrect, because the $60,000 accrued loss on the land was reduced by the $10,000 accrued gain on the marketable securities. The recognition of the accrued gain on the marketable securities is not required. An election is available under paragraph 111(4)(*e*) to recognize the accrued gain, if it is desirable.

Question 3

(C) is correct. The UCC of the Class 10 computer equipment is reduced by $5,000, from $38,000 to $33,000. The UCC of the Class 8 office furniture and equipment is reduced by $10,000, from $58,000 to $48,000. The total of the two reductions, $15,000, is deemed to have been claimed as CCA in the year ended March 31, 2005 [ssec. 111(5.1)].

(A) is incorrect as this amount adjusts the UCC of all the classes to the FMV of the classes. This amount includes an adjustment of $8,000 to increase the UCC of the Class 10 automobiles and the Class 12 assets to the FMV of the respective classes. The $8,000 is then subtracted from the $15,000 reduction calculated in (C). This is incorrect. The subsection 111(5.1) adjustment applies only to the classes where the UCC is higher than the FMV.

(B) is incorrect as it includes only 72% of the adjustment calculated in (C).

(D) is incorrect for the same reason as (A). The difference between (A) and (D) is that in (D) the positive and negative adjustments have been totalled, whereas in (A) they have been netted.

Question 4

(D) is correct. For its year ending December 31, 2005, Loss Co will be able to deduct non-capital losses of $15,000 (maximum), provided the widget retailing business is carried on throughout the taxation year ended December 31, 2005 with a reasonable expectation of profit [par. 111(5)(*a*)].

(A) is incorrect as net capital losses incurred prior to the acquisition of control expire on the date control is acquired [par. 111(4)(*a*)].

(B) is incorrect. Non-capital losses realized prior to an acquisition of control cannot be deducted against taxable capital gains incurred after the acquisition of control. Non-capital losses are only deductible against income from the business in which the losses were incurred and income from a similar products or services [par. 111(5)(*a*)].

(C) is incorrect. The non-capital loss deduction has been limited to the income from a similar products or services net of the loss from the widget business. The netting of the widget business loss is not required [par. 111(5)(*a*)].

Question 5

(D) is correct.

Net income for tax purposes	$600,000
Canadian dividends [sec. 112]	(100,000)
Charitable donations........	(200,000)– not exceeding $450,000 (75% of net income)
	$300,000

(A) incorrectly makes no adjustments: $600,000.

(B) incorrectly omits the deduction for charitable donations: $600,000 – $100,000 = $500,000.

(C) incorrectly omits the section 112 deduction for Canadian dividends: $600,000 – $200,000 = $400,000.

Question 6

(C) is correct.

Taxable income as per the answer to Question 5.....................	$300,000
Part I tax on taxable income	
Tax @ 38% on $300,000..	$114,000
Deduct: Federal tax abatement (10% × 90% × $300,000).............	(27,000)
	$ 87,000
Add: Corporate surtax (4% × (38% – 10%) × $300,000)..............	3,360
Deduct: M & P deduction (note 1)...............................	(17,500)
Deduct: 7% rate reduction on income not eligible for the M & P deduction: 7% × [$300K – $250K]........................	(3,500)
Total federal tax..	$ 69,360

Note 1 – M & P deduction

7% of the lesser of	
(a) manufacturing and processing profits......................	$250,000
(b) taxable income..	$300,000
7% of lesser amount	$ 17,500

(A) incorrectly applies the rate reduction to all income, including that eligible for the manufacturing and processing profits deduction: $69,360 + $3,500 – 7% × $300K = $51,860

(B) incorrectly calculates the surtax as 4% × 21% × $300K rather than 4% × 28% × 300K. $69,360 − $3,360 + $2,520 = $68,520.

(D) incorrectly omits the 7% rate reduction: $69,360 + 3,500 = $72,860.

CHAPTER 12

Integration for Business and Investment Income of the Private Corporation

Question 1

(B) $18,400 is correct. It is calculated as follows:

Least of:	(a) income from an active business carried on in Canada net of loss from an active business carried on in Canada	$120,000 (0)
		$120,000
	(b) taxable income	$132,000
	(c) business limit: $300,000 − $185,000	$115,000

The least is (c): $115,000 × 16% = $18,400

(A) $16,000 is incorrect. The foreign business loss of $20,000 has been netted against the $120,000 of Canadian business income.

(C) $19,200 is incorrect. This amount is 16% of the Canadian active business income.

(D) $21,120 is incorrect. This amount is 16% of the taxable income.

Question 2

(D) is correct. M Ltd. is carrying on an active business as defined in subsection 125(7). The business is not a personal services business as the services are provided to an associated corporation. M Ltd. and ACC Ltd. are associated by paragraph 256(1)(*d*). M Ltd. is not a specified investment business as the principal purpose is not to derive income from property. Thus, by default, it is carrying on an active business.

(A) is incorrect. M Ltd. is not carrying on a personal services business for the reasons outlined above.

(B) is incorrect. M Ltd. is not carrying on a personal services business for the reasons outlined above.

(C) is incorrect. M Ltd. is not carrying on a specified investment business as the principal purpose is not to derive income from property.

Question 3

(A) $700 is correct. The amount is calculated under section 125.1 as follows:

7% × the lesser of:	(a) Cdn. M&P profits	$ 310,000
	Income subject to the SBD	(300,000)
		$ 10,000
	(b) Taxable income	$ 320,000
	Income subject to the SBD	(300,000)
		$ 20,000

7% × $10,000 = $700

(B) $1,400 is incorrect. This amount is 7% of taxable income in excess of $300,000.

(C) $18,340 is incorrect. This amount is 7% of Cdn. M&P profits in excess of the SBD of $48,000.

(D) $21,700 is incorrect. This amount is 7% x Cdn. M&P profits.

Question 4

(C) $68,000 is correct [ssecs. 186(1), (4)].

Dividend received from non-connected corporation, C Ltd.:	
$120,000 × ⅓	$40,000
70% of $40,000 dividend refund received by connected corporation, B Ltd.	28,000
	$68,000

B Ltd is connected to A Ltd., because of *de jure* control and because A Ltd. holds more than 10% of the issued share capital in both votes and value [ssecs. 186(2) and (4)].

(A) $60,000 is incorrect. This amount is 70% and 8% of the dividend refunds received by B Ltd. and C Ltd., respectively.

(B) $64,000 is incorrect. This amount applies the Part I tax rate on investment income, 26⅔%, to the total dividends received.

(D) $80,000 is incorrect. This amount is ⅓ × the dividends received and ignores the special rules for connected corporations.

Question 5

(D) is correct because (A), (B) and (C) are all correct.

(A) and (B) are correct because Joanne controls J Co. and her spouse controls D Co. Two corporations are associated under paragraph 256(1)(c), if related persons control each corporation and either person owns at least 25% of the shares of the related persons' corporation. Spouses are related by marriage [par. 251(6)(b)].

(C) is correct because if a trust for their twin daughters controls a third company, T Co., those shares are deemed to be owned by the beneficiaries [spar. 256(1.2)(f)(ii)]. In addition, because those beneficiaries are minors, their shares are deemed to be owned by each of Joanne and Doug [ssec. 256(1.3)]. Therefore, J Co. and T Co. are associated under paragraph 256(1)(a) because they are deemed to be controlled by the same person (Joanne). The same is true for D Co. and T Co. (each deemed to be controlled by Doug). Under subsection 256(2), two corporations are deemed to be associated with each other unless an election is made to deem the third corporation (T Co.) to have a business limit of nil.

Question 6

(C) is correct. X Ltd. and Y Ltd. are not associated because although X Ltd. is controlled by a person who is related to each member of the various groups of persons (i.e., an pair of the two daughters and one son or all three) who controls Y Ltd., there is no cross-ownership of at least 25%. Thus, X Ltd. and Y Ltd. are not associated under paragraph 256(1(d).

(A) is not correct. X and Y are associated under paragraph 256(1)(b). The same group (Rod and Patrick) controls both corporations. This group controls X Ltd., despite the fact that Patrick himself controls X Ltd. [spar. 256(1.2)(b)(i)]. It does not matter that the individuals are not related.

(B) is not correct because X Ltd. and Y Ltd. are associated under paragraph 256(1)(c) because they are controlled by related persons (a parent and son are related by blood under paragraph 251(6)(a)) and one of the persons owns not less than 25% of the shares of both companies.

(D) is not correct because the corporations in (A) are associated.

CHAPTER 13

Planning the Use of a Corporation and Shareholder-Manager Remuneration

Question 1

(A) is correct. The entire loan will be included in Stan's income in 2005, the year he received the loan [ssec. 15(2)]. He does not meet the criterion for exclusion in subsection 15(2.6) as the loan will not be repaid within one year after the end of the taxation year of the lender in which the loan was made. He does not meet the criteria for exclusion in subsection 15(2.4). Since such a loan is not available to other employees, it is not reasonable to conclude that he received the loan because of his employment.

(B) is incorrect. If the loan is not repaid within one year of the end of the year of S Ltd. in which the loan was made, then $200,000 must be included in the year of the loan. Repayments are deductible in the year of the repayment.

(C) is incorrect. There is no imputed interest benefit when the loan is included in income [par. 80.4(3)(*b*)]. If there was an imputed interest benefit the prescribed rate protection rule would not apply as the loan was not received because of his employment [ssecs. 80.4(4) and 80.4(1)].

(D) is incorrect. One year after the end of the calendar year in which the loan is received has no significance. Subsection 15(2) includes the loan in income in the year it is *received* unless it is repaid by one year after the end of the taxation year of the *lender* in which the loan was made, or the loan meets one of the specific exclusions.

Question 2

(D) is correct. Since the $300,000 bonus is unpaid on the 180th day after the end of the taxation year of Fortelli Inc. in which the expense was incurred, it is not deductible until 2006, the taxation year in which it is actually paid [ssec. 78(4)].

(A) is incorrect. This amount refers to the rules in subsection 78(1) for unpaid amounts due to related persons, other than pension benefits, retiring allowances, salary, wages, or other remuneration.

(B) is incorrect. Subsection 78(4) does not distinguish between amounts owed to related and unrelated persons.

(C) is incorrect for the same reason as (A).

Question 3

The correct answer is (B). There is no penalty. The tax benefit that would otherwise have been enjoyed is denied [ssec. 245(2)].

(A) is incorrect as it is true in accordance with subsection 245(2).

(C) is incorrect as it is true in accordance with subsection 245(3).

(D) is incorrect as it is true in accordance with subsection 245(4).

Question 4

(C) is correct. The purpose of the transaction seems to be the reduction or avoidance of tax on the income earned on the $10,000 gift. This transaction goes against the spirit of the Act, read as a whole, and falls within the definition of an avoidance transaction in subsection 245(3). Note that subsection 56(4.1) would apply if it was a loan instead of a gift.

(A) is incorrect. The transaction is an estate freeze which can reasonably be considered to have been undertaken for *bona fide* purposes other than to obtain the tax benefit. This transaction does not result in a misuse or abuse of the Act, read as a whole [IC 88-2, par. 10].

(B) is incorrect. The incorporation of a business and the claiming of a small business deduction by a CCPC is specifically provided for in the Act. This transaction does not result in a misuse or abuse of the Act, read as a whole [IC 88-2, par. 11].

(D) is incorrect. Section 67 will deny the deduction of the bonus to the extent it is in excess of a reasonable amount. To the extent the transaction is reasonable, it does not result in a benefit. Corporate tax will be reduced by the accrual, but Mary will pay tax on the income personally [IC 88-2, par. 18].

Question 5

(D) is correct. All the conditions of section 74.4 are met. As a result, Mr. Investor is deemed to have income of 6% × $1 million = $60,000.

(A) incorrectly attributes the cash dividend received by Mrs. Investor to Mr. Investor: $10,000.

(B) incorrectly attributes the grossed up dividend received by Mrs. Investor to Mr. Investor: $12,500.

(C) incorrectly computes the section 74.4 attributed amount to Mr. Investor based on $500,000: 6% × $500,000 = $30,000.

Question 6

(C) is correct. In order to be a small business corporation, the percentage of assets used in an active business by the corporation and the corporation controlled by Ms. Prentice's brother must be at least 90% (ssec. 248(1) definition of small business corporation). It is now 80% (60% + 20%) or $3.2 million.

Therefore total assets must be $3.2 million/90% or $3,555,555.

Therefore $444,445 ($4 million – $3,555,555) of the non-active business assets must be sold.

(A) is incorrect because the corporation does not currently meet the 90% test.

(B) incorrectly assumes that 10% of the assets must be sold: 10% × 4 million = $400,000.

(D) incorrectly ignores the assets used by the related corporation and calculates that since active business assets are $2.4 million (60% × $4M), total assets must be $2.4 million/90% or $2,666,666 to meet the 90% test. As a result, $1,333,333 ($4 million – $2,666,666) of the non-active business assets must be sold.

CHAPTER 14

Rights and Obligations under the Income Tax Act

Question 1

(B) is correct. The penalty is $900. The initial penalty rate of 5% is increased by 1% for each *complete* month after April 30, 2005 that the return was not filed to a maximum penalty of 5% + 4% = 9% [ssec. 162(1)].

(A) is incorrect as it includes only the initial penalty of 5% of the unpaid tax.

(C) is incorrect as it includes 1/2% for the half month of September. Only complete months should be counted for purposes of the penalty.

(D) is incorrect as it includes 1% for the month of September. Only complete months should be counted for purposes of the penalty.

Question 2

(B) August 15, 2008 is correct. The normal reassessment period for a CCPC ends 3 years after the day of mailing of a notice of assessment for the year [ssec. 152(3.1)].

(A) December 31, 2007, 3 years after the end of the taxation year, is incorrect. The 3-year period commences with the date of mailing of the notice of assessment, not the last day of the fiscal year.

(C) December 31, 2008, 4 years after the end of the taxation year, is incorrect.

(D) August 15, 2009, 4 years after the day of mailing of a notice of assessment for the year, is incorrect. It would be correct if the taxpayer were a corporation other than a CCPC [ssec 152(3.1)].

Question 3

(D) June 15, 2006 is correct. The notice of objection filing due date is one year after Darol's filing-due date for 2004 [ssec. 165(1)].

(A) December 31, 2005, being one year after the end of the taxation year, is incorrect.

(B) January 14, 2006, being 90 days after the date of mailing of the notice of assessment, is incorrect in this case. For an individual and a testamentary trust, the due date is the later of this date and one year after the filing-due date for the tax return.

(C) April 30, 2006, being one year after the filing-due date for 2004 for an individual *not* carrying on a business, is incorrect. Darol's filing-due date for 2004 was June 15, 2005, as he carried on business in 2004.

Question 4

The correct answer is (D) September 30, 2005, being 6 months after the date of death [par. 150(1)(*b*)].

(A) is incorrect. It is the most common due date for 2004 personal tax returns [spar. 150(1)(*a*)(i)]. This date is not correct for two reasons: first, he has income from carrying on business, and second, he died after October 2004.

(B) is incorrect. It is the date the return would have been due if he had not died [spar. 150(1)(*a*)(ii)].

(C) is incorrect as it is 6 months after the end of the year for which the return is being filed.

Question 5

(A) is correct. The minimum monthly instalment is the least of:

– $1/12$th of the estimated taxes payable: $1/12 \times \$200,000 = \$16,667$

– $1/12$th of the prior year's taxes payable: $1/12$ of $\$140,000 = \$11,667$

– $1/12$ of the second prior year's taxable payable ($1/12$ of $\$180,000 = \$15,000$) for 2 months and 10 payments of $\$11,000$ ($1/10 \times [\$140K - 2 \times \$15,000]$).

The least of these is either the prior year method or the second prior year method. Only the prior year method ($\$11,667$ per month) is listed as a choice in this question. Because X Ltd. had taxable income in the prior year of more than the small business deduction limit, it must pay its final balance due within 2 months of year end (February 28, 2006).

(B) and (C) incorrectly base the instalments on estimated taxes payable. (B) has the correct final due date. (C) incorrectly uses the balance-due day that is 3 months after the end of the year which is applicable only for Canadian-controlled private corporations that have taxable income that is less than the small business deduction limit in the prior year.

(D) incorrectly uses the amount for the first two payments of the second prior year method for all 12 payments but has the correct final due date for the balance due. (D) would have been a correct answer had it indicated that the payments for the last ten months would be $\$11,000$ per month.

Question 6

(D) is correct (2 payments of $3,825 and 2 payments of $4,375). The minimum monthly instalment is the least of:

– ¹/₄ of the estimated taxes payable: ¹/₄ × $25,000 = $6,250

– ¹/₄ of the prior year's taxes payable: ¹/₄ of $16,400 = $4,100

– ¹/₄ of the second prior year's taxable payable (¹/₄ of $15,300 = $3,825) for 2 months and 2 payments of $4,375 (¹/₂ × [$16,400 – 2 × $3,825]).

(A) is incorrect because 4 payments of $6,250 is not the minimum payment.

(B) is incorrect because 2 payments of $4,100 and 2 payments of $6,250 is not the minimum amount. Four payments of $4,100 would result in the minimum amount.

(C) is incorrect because 2 payments of $3,825 and 2 payments of $4,100 is not the minimum amount. If the first 2 payments are $3,825, the last 2 payments must be $4,375. Alternatively, 4 payments of $4,100 can be made.

CHAPTER 15
Corporate Distributions, Windings-up and Sales

Question 1

(D) is correct. Only taxable dividends paid are included in the computation of dividend refunds [ssec. 129(1)].

(A) is incorrect as it is true [par. 83(2)(*b*)].

(B) is incorrect as it is true [ssec. 83(2)].

(C) is incorrect as it is true [ssec. 89(1), par. (*a*) of def. of the capital dividend account].

Question 2

(D) is correct.

Redemption amount	$ 60,000
PUC	(10,000)
Dividend [ssec. 84(3)]	$ 50,000
Redemption amount	$ 60,000
Dividend	(50,000)
Proceeds of disposition [ssec. 54]	$ 10,000
ACB	(20,000)
Capital loss	$(10,000)

(A) is incorrect. This amount ignores the dividend under subsection 84(3).

(B) is incorrect. This amount calculates the dividend using the cost as opposed to the PUC.

(C) is incorrect. The dividend has not been subtracted from the redemption amount to arrive at the proceeds of disposition.

Question 3

(B) is correct.

Funds available for distribution	$ 40,000
PUC	(2,000)
Deemed dividend [ssec. 84(2)]	$ 38,000
Elected amount of capital dividend	(8,000)
Taxable dividend	$ 30,000
Funds available for distribution	$ 40,000
Deemed dividend	(38,000)
Proceeds of disposition [sec. 54]	$ 2,000
ACB	(1,000)
Capital gain	$ 1,000

(A) is incorrect. Only subsidiaries in which the parent company owns at least 90% of the shares can wind up on a tax-deferred basis.

(C) is incorrect. The capital dividend has not been subtracted in the calculation of the proceeds.

(D) is incorrect. The ACB has been subtracted from the funds available to arrive at a $39,000 capital gain. Subsections 88(2) and 84(2) has been ignored.

Question 4

(C) $1,557,333 is correct.

	Deemed proceeds	Business income	Investment income	CDA	RDTOH
Opening balance		Nil	Nil	$ 10,000	$ 30,000
Cash	$ 45,000				
Land	850,000		$300,000	300,000	
Building	780,000	$200,000	200,000	200,000	
	$1,675,000		$500,000	$510,000	
Liabilities	$ (20,000)	× 18%	× 45%		
Tax	(261,000)	$ 36,000	$225,000		$133,333
RDTOH	163,333				$163,333
	$1,557,333				

(A) $485,000 is incorrect. The liabilities of $20,000 have been subtracted from the asset total of $505,000 on the balance sheet.

(B) $1,394,000 is incorrect. The RDTOH has been omitted.

(D) $1,838,333 is incorrect. The liabilities and the income tax have not been deducted in the computation of the amount available for distribution.

Question 5

(A) is correct. The total paid-up capital of the common shares is $25,000, ¹/₂ of which is attributable to Mr. C and ¹/₂ is attributable to Mr. B. The total paid-up capital of the common shares is

100 common shares issued to Mr. A	$10,000
100 common shares issued to Mr. B	15,000
	$25,000

(B) and (D) are incorrect. The total paid-up capital of the common shares is not $35,000. The sale by Mr. A to Mr. C for $20,000 does not affect the paid-up capital of the shares.

(C) is incorrect because the $25,000 total paid-up capital of the common shares is split equally among the shares and is not based on the issue price of the shares.

Question 6

(B) is correct. The $^3/_4 \times$ the proceeds would be deducted from the CEC pool which would cause it to have a negative balance of $750,000. Paragraph 14(1)(*b*) states that this negative balance should be multiplied by $^2/_3$, which makes it $500,000. Paragraph 89(1)(*c*.2) requires the tax-free portion of the gain ($500,000) to be included in the capital dividend account.

(A) and (D) are incorrect because there is no taxable capital gain on the sale of goodwill. As well, the reference in (D) to the refundable dividend tax on hand account is incorrect. The account is not affected.

(C) is incorrect as it does not take into consideration paragraphs 14(1)(*b*) and 89(1)(*c*.2).

CHAPTER 16

Income Deferral: Rollover on Transfers to a Corporation and Pitfalls

Question 1

(C) is correct. Electing at $800, the UCC of the transferred asset, will defer recapture as well as the capital gain [par. 85(1)(*e*)].

(A) is incorrect. The spousal rollover in subsection 73(1) applies to transfers to a spouse or a spousal trust, but never to a corporation.

(B) is incorrect. Electing at $2,200 will defer the capital gain, but recapture of $1,400 will be incurred.

(D) is incorrect. Since the corporation will have acquired the depreciable asset from a non-arm's length individual, $2,600 (i.e., $2,200 + $^1/_2$ ($3,000 – $2,200) is the maximum amount that the capital cost could be [par. 13(7)(*e*)].

Question 2

(D) $25,000 is correct. In order to defer the gain, Steve will elect under subsection 85(1) at $40,000, the ACB of the asset. The elected amount cannot be less than the non-share consideration. Since S Ltd. assumed the mortgage of $15,000, an additional $25,000 of non-share consideration is the maximum that can be taken.

(A) $100,000 is incorrect. This amount would result in a capital gain of $60,000 as well as a subsection 15(1) benefit of $15,000.

(B) $85,000 is incorrect. This amount would result in a capital gain of $60,000.

(C) $40,000 is incorrect. This amount would result in a capital gain of $15,000.

Question 3

(B) $110,000 is correct. Since the corporation has acquired the depreciable property from a non-arm's length individual, the capital cost is limited to the transferor's capital cost, $100,000 plus the taxable capital gain on the transfer, $10,000 [par. 13(7)(*e*)]. This totals $110,000.

(A) $120,000, the elected transfer price, is incorrect for the same reason that (B) is correct.

(C) $90,000, the transferor's UCC plus the taxable capital gain on the transfer, is incorrect. The starting point is the transferor's capital cost, not UCC [par. 13(7)(*e*)].

(D) $75,000, the transferor's UCC, is incorrect for the same reason that (B) is correct.

Question 4

(D) $20,000 is correct.

Elected transfer price		$40,000
Allocated to non-share consideration:		
Cash	$3,000	
Debt	2,000	$ 5,000
Allocated to the preferred shares, up to their FMV [par. 85(1)(g)]		15,000
Allocated to the common shares, remainder [par. 85(1)(h)]		20,000
		$40,000

(A) $35,000 is incorrect. The elected amount, in excess of the non-share consideration, has all been allocated to the common shares.

(B) $23,000 is incorrect. None of the elected amount has been allocated to the cash.

(C) $23,333 is incorrect. The allocation between the preferred and common shares has been done based on proportionate values.

Question 5

(D) is correct because a section 22 election ensures that the purchaser will be able to take a doubtful debts reserve on the accounts receivable.

(A) and (B) are incorrect because a section 22 election ensures that the loss to the vendor is a business loss rather than a capital loss or superficial loss. If no section 22 election is made, the vendor will realize a loss that is a capital loss. Further, if the vendor and purchaser are affiliated persons, the loss will be denied and will be a superficial loss [ssec. 54(1)].

(C) is incorrect because the vendor is always required to add the prior year's doubtful debts reserve [par. 12(1)(d)]. It does not matter whether or not a section 22 election is made.

Question 6

(D) is correct. Because the promissory note is $60,000, the elected amount is deemed to be $60,000. The elected amount determines the proceeds of disposition to Rebecca, R Co.'s cost of the land, the cost of the consideration to Rebecca, and the paid-up capital of the shares issued as consideration after the subsection 85(2.1) paid-up capital reduction.

(A) is incorrect because the proceeds to Rebecca are deemed to be $60,000 not $50,000 as discussed above.

(B) is incorrect because R Co.'s cost of the land is deemed to be $60,000, not $50,000 as discussed above.

(C) is incorrect because Rebecca's cost of the preference shares is zero under para. 85(1)(g). It is calculated as the elected amount minus the boot ($60,000 – $60,000 demand note).

CHAPTER 17

Income Deferral: Other Rollovers and Use of Rollovers in Estate Planning

Question 1

(C) is correct. On winding-up, the losses of the subsidiary are not available to the parent, until the parent's taxation year commencing after the commencement of the winding-up [ssec. 88(1.1)]. Thus, the losses of L Ltd. would first be available to P Ltd. in its taxation year commencing January 1, 2006.

(A) is incorrect. The predecessor corporations are deemed to have a year-end immediately before the amalgamation, October 31, 2005. The amalgamated corporation first exists on November 1, 2005.

(B) is incorrect. The amalgamated corporation can utilize the losses in its first taxation year commencing November 1, 2005 [ssec. 87(2.1)].

(D) is incorrect for the reasons (C) is correct.

Question 2

(B) is correct.

X Ltd's adjusted cost base of the shares of Y Ltd.	$500,000
Less: Cost amount of Y Ltd.'s assets	(420,000)
Dividends paid to X Ltd.	(15,000)
Potential bump [par. 88(1)(d)]	$ 65,000

The ACB of the land can be bumped by $30,000, up to its FMV at the time X Ltd. acquired control of Y Ltd., $130,000 [par. 88(1)(d)].

(A) is incorrect. The bump available under paragraph 88(1)(d) on a winding-up has not been applied.

(C) is incorrect. The full amount of the bump available has been allocated to the land. The ACB of the land cannot be bumped above the FMV of the land when X Ltd. acquired control of Y Ltd. [par. 88(1)(d)].

(D) is incorrect for the same reason as (C). In addition, the potential bump has not been reduced by the dividends received from X Ltd.

Question 3

(B) is correct. Since Chris exchanged all his common shares as part of a reorganization of capital, section 86 applies automatically. The cost of the preferred shares is equal to the cost of his common shares, less the non-share consideration: $2,000 − $135 = $1,865 [par. 86(1)(b)]. For purposes of calculating the capital gain on the disposal of the common shares, paragraph 86(1)(c) defines proceeds as the cost of the new shares, plus non-share consideration received: $1,865 + $135 = $2,000. As the proceeds equal his ACB, there is no capital gain.

(A) is incorrect. The ACB of the preferred shares has not been reduced by the non-share consideration received.

(C) is incorrect. The tax deferral provisions have been ignored.

(D) is incorrect. A capital gain equal to the non-share consideration has been recognized.

Question 4

(D) is correct as it is false. Subsection 85.1(2) specifically states that subsection 85.1(1) does not apply where consideration other than shares of the particular class of the purchaser was received by the vendor. Therefore, in the absence of any other election being made, Shelly would have a capital gain of $5,000 on the exchange if she received any non-share consideration.

(A) is incorrect as it is true. Section 85.1 is automatic; no election is required.

(B) is incorrect as it is true [par. 85.1(1)(a)].

(C) is incorrect as it is true [par. 85.1(1)(b)].

Question 5

(A) is the correct answer because this plan will freeze the value of his interest in ABC for tax purposes (since preferred shares don't grow in value) and transfer future growth to his children (because common shares do grow in value) without giving up control (because the preferred shares are voting). There will be no tax on the transfer since he will be electing at tax cost.

(B) is incorrect because changing his will to leave his shares of ABC to his children does not achieve his objective of freezing the value of his interest and having no tax on the transfer.

(C) is incorrect because gifting the ABC shares to his children results in the loss of control and immediate tax on the accrued capital gain because the gift results in a deemed disposition at fair market value [sec. 69].

(D) is incorrect because, although a sale at fair market value taking back debt as consideration will defer tax somewhat because of the 10-year reserve available for such transfers [sec. 40], there will be tax on the accrued gain payable over the 10-year period and there is a loss of control.

Question 6

(C) is correct, assuming an election is made at $500,001. The boot must be limited to $1 because subsection 84.1(1) will cause any boot in excess of this amount to be a deemed dividend not a capital gain. That is why (D) is incorrect.

(A) is incorrect because a reverse asset freeze involves a transfer by a company rather than an individual. Hence, the $500,000 capital gains exemption cannot be used.

(B) is incorrect because a section 86 internal freeze involves an automatic rollover. Hence, the $500,000 capital gains exemption cannot be used.

CHAPTER 18
Partnerships and Trusts

Question 1

(C) $167,500 is correct.

Net income per financial statement		$ 365,000
Add: Donations		20,000
Sale of shares — Taxable capital gain	$ 60,000	
— Accounting gain	(120,000)	(60,000)
		$ 325,000
Bert's share		× ½
		$ 162,500
Dividend gross-up: $20,000 × ¼		5,000
Taxable income		$ 167,500

(A) $182,500 is incorrect. All of the adjustments have been ignored: donations, net accounting/tax gain, and the dividend gross-up.

(B) $187,500 is incorrect. The only adjustment that was made was for the dividend gross-up.

(D) $162,500 is incorrect. All adjustments were made except for the dividend gross-up.

Question 2

(C) $63,000 is correct.

Contributions — initial	$ 5,000
— additional	14,000
Share of profit	100,000
Share of non-taxable portion of capital gain	20,000
Share of charitable donations	(6,000)
Drawings	(70,000)
ACB	$ 63,000

(A) $33,000 is incorrect. The capital gain has been excluded completely.

(B) $43,000 is incorrect. The non-taxable portion of the capital gain has not been included.

(D) $69,000 is incorrect. The ACB has not been reduced by Ann's share of the charitable donations.

Question 3

(A) is true. The tax return is due 90 days after the year-end of the trust [par. 150(1)(*c*)]. *Inter vivos* trusts are taxed on a calendar year basis [par. 249(1)(*b*)].

(B) is true. The trust is entitled to the deduction [ssec. 104(6)].

(C) is true. The tax rate is 29% [ssec. 122(1)].

(D) is false. Al is deemed to have received proceeds equal to the fair market value of the marketable securities transferred to the trust [par. 69(1)(*b*)]. Therefore, Al is required to recognize the $30,000 capital gain.

Question 4

(B) is true. Testamentary trusts are taxed as individuals [ssec. 104(2)].

(A) is false. The taxation year of a testamentary trust does not have to be on a calendar year basis [ssec.104(23)].

(C) is false. The trust return is due 90 days after the end of the fiscal period of the trust [par. 150(1)(*c*)].

(D) is false. The trust is entitled to claim a dividend tax credit for dividends received from taxable Canadian corporations [ssec. 104(2); sec. 121].

Question 5

(C) is correct. An alter ego trust has a deemed disposition on the settlor's death [ssec. 248(1)].

(A) is incorrect. An *inter vivos* trust generally has a deemed disposition at fair market value at the end of 21 years, unless it is a joint partner trust (described in (B)), in which case the deemed disposition takes place on the partner (ie., spouse or common-law partner) beneficiary's death.

(D) is incorrect. A discretionary trust would always have a deemed disposition at fair market value at the end of 21 years, since it cannot be a joint partner trust (which, by definition, must pay the income out to the beneficiary and, therefore, cannot be discretionary).

Question 6

(C) Avoiding the 21-year rule is not an advantage. You cannot avoid it unless the trust is a joint partner trust [ssec. 104(4)].

(A) is incorrect because income-splitting using the subsections 104(13.1) and (13.2) designations is an advantage.

(B) is incorrect, because avoiding the deemed disposition on the child's death is an advantage.

(D) is incorrect, because providing your children with beneficial ownership but not control over their inheritance is an advantage.

Appendix III

Solutions to Exercises

CHAPTER 1
Introduction

Exercise 1

The following summary is discussed in more detail below:

Case	Topic	Part	Division	Subdivision	Provision
(A)	Taxable capital gain............	I	B	c	paragraph 38(*a*)
(B)	Membership dues............	I	B	a	subparagraph 8(1)(*i*)(i)
(C)	Personal injury award............	I	B	g	paragraph 81(1)(*g*.1)
(D)	Expense limit ...	I	B	f	section 67
(E)	Parent............	XVII			subsection 252(2)
(F)	*Inter vivos* trust	I	B	k	subsection 108(1)
(G)	Filing deadline	I	I		paragraph 150(1)(*b*)
(H)	Shareholder benefit............	I	B	b	subsection 15(1)
(I)	Non-arm's length	I	B	f	paragraph 69(1)(*b*)
(J)	Investment fees	I	B	b	paragraph 20(1)(*bb*)

(A) Part I, Division B, Subdivision c, paragraph 38(*a*): — Most definitions applicable to the Taxable Capital Gains and Allowable Capital Losses subdivision of Part I, Division B are found in section 54. However, this definition is set out at the beginning of Subdivision c. Definitions of terms used throughout the Act are found in subsection 248(1). If a term is not specifically defined in subsection 248(1) or in a section elsewhere in the Act, judicial precedents should be consulted for the meaning of the word.

(B) Part I, Division B, Subdivision a, subparagraph 8(1)(*i*)(i): — Employment income and deductions are set out in sections 5 to 8 of Part I, Division B, Subdivision a of the Act. All deductions from this source appear in section 8 with the major list of deductions occurring in subsection 8(1) and further explanation or restriction of these deductions appearing in subsections 8(2) to 8(11).

(C) Part I, Division B, Subdivision g, paragraph 81(1)(*g*.1): — Income from property acquired as personal injury award is one in a limited list of items found in section 81 which are not included in computing income.

(D) Part I, Division B, Subdivision f, section 67: — Inclusions and deductions in the computation of income are generally found in Part I, Division B, Subdivisions a, b, c, d or e. In this case, however, the rule is found in Subdivision f dealing with general rules relating to the computation of income from all sources.

(E) Part XVII, subsection 252(2): — The word "parent" appears throughout the Act, so the definition is most likely to be in Part XVII on "Interpretation."

(F) Part I, Division B, Subdivision k, subsection 108(1): — Trusts and their beneficiaries are dealt with in Subdivision k of Part I, Division B. The definitions section for this subdivision is section 108.

(G) Part I, Division I, paragraph 150(1)(*b*): This is a procedural matter generally handled in Division I of Part I of the Act dealing with Returns, Assessments, Payment and Appeals.

(H) Part I, Division B, Subdivision b, subsection 15(1): — A benefit received by a shareholder, if it is to be taxed, would likely be income from property which is handled in Subdivision b of Division B of Part I. Inclusions from that source are generally listed in sections 12 to 17.

(I) Part I, Division B, Subdivision f, paragraph 69(1)(*b*): — This provision can be found in the set of general rules pertaining to the computation of income in Subdivision f of Division B of Part I because it affects the computation of income from a variety of sources.

(J) Part I, Division B, Subdivision b, paragraph 20(1)(*bb*): — Investments provide income from property and deductions from such income are generally listed in subsection 20(1).

Exercise 2

DIVISION B

Par. 3(*a*)	*Subdivision a*			
	Sec. 5	Salary............................	$ 60,000	
	Par. 6(1)(*c*)	Director's fees....................	5,000	
	Ssec. 6(9)	Imputed interest..................	3,000	$ 68,000
	Less:			
	Par. 8(1)(*i*)	Professional engineering fees	$ 300	
	Par. 8(1)(*m*)	Registered pension plan contributions	4,000	4,300
				$ 63,700
	Subdivision b			
	Sec. 9	Business income — share of partnership tax profits.........	$ 10,000	
	Par. 12(1)(*c*)	Canadian bank interest.............	3,000	13,000
	Subdivision d			
	Par. 56(1)(*a*)	Retiring allowance		20,000
		Total par. 3(*a*) income		$ 96,700
Par. 3(*b*)	*Subdivision c*			
	Par. 38(*a*)	Taxable capital gain	$ 20,000	
	Par. 38(*b*)	Allowable capital loss	(2,000)	18,000
				$114,700
Par. 3(*d*)	*Subdivision b*			
	Ssec. 9(2):	Rental loss		
		Rental revenue	$ 25,000	
		Less: Expenses		
		Par. 20(1)(*c*) Mortgage interest	(23,000)	
		Par. 18(1)(*a*) Taxes and insurance....................	(4,500)	
		Par. 18(1)(*a*) Maintenance.....	(1,500)	(4,000)

Division B income		$110,700
Par. 110(1)(*j*)	Home relocation interest deduction ...... $ 1,000	
Par. 111(1)(*a*)	Non-capital loss 3,000	
Par. 111(1)(*b*)	Net capital loss 5,000	(9,000)
Taxable income		$101,700

Federal tax after credits

Tax before credits		$ 21,459
Sec. 118	Personal credits	(2,411)
Sec. 118.7	CPP contributions credit	(298)
Sec. 118.7	E.I. premium credit	(122)
Sec. 118.5	Tuition credit	(68)
Sec. 118.6	Education credit transfer	(80)
Sec. 118.1	Charitable donation credit	(550)
Basic federal tax		$ 17,930

CHAPTER 2
Liability for Tax

Exercise 1

(A) Alpha is a part-time resident of Canada until August 27 of the year when he appears to have made a "clean break" with Canada. While in Canada he would not have been sojourning, so paragraph 250(1)(*a*) would not apply.

(B) Beta has no residential ties with Canada. Citizenship is not a determining factor in establishing such ties.

(C) Gamma is a non-resident of Canada and is taxable only on employment income earned in Canada [par. 2(3)(*a*) and spar. 115(1)(*a*)(i)].

(D) Delta is either a part-time resident of Canada or a non-resident employed in Canada, depending on the facts of his stay in Canada. He is also taxable under paragraph 2(3)(*c*) because the shares are taxable Canadian property [spar. 115(1)(*b*)(iv)].

(E) Epsilon is deemed a resident of Canada [par. 250(1)(*f*)] because of his relationship to his mother [spar. 250(1)(*c*)(i)].

(F) Mu is not deemed to be a resident of Canada, because she has never been resident in Canada, although she is the spouse of a person described in paragraph 250(1)(*b*) [par. 250(1)(*e*)].

Exercise 2

[See: *MacDonald v. M.N.R.*, (T.A.B.) 68 DTC 433.]

(A) The full-time residence alternative→taxed in Canada on worldwide income for full year [ssec. 2(1)]:

Criterion: residence is a question of fact dependent on the degree of permanency in the relationship between a person and a place;

Evidence:

(i) factors indicating this relationship between the appellant and Canada,

    1. he sold his house in the United States and paid an American capital gains tax for not buying another residence,

    2. his wife, upon arriving in Canada, rented premises pending the purchase of a house,

    3. she and the children, whom the appellant was supporting to the extent of $600 per month, stayed in Canada all year-round,

    4. he stayed in Canada when he was off-duty to the extent of 166 out of 180 days in 1964,

    — full-time presence is not necessary,

5. other non-determining factors,

— joint account in Canada where pay cheques were deposited during his vacations,

— joint ownership of a car with New Brunswick registry,

— citizenship irrelevant;

(ii) factors detracting from a relationship with Canada,

1. a few rooms, without exclusive use, made available for him at his sister's house in the United States,

— not a permanent abode,

— an individual can have more than one residence,

2. U.S. citizen and previously and subsequently resided in the United States with a stated intention to return,

— but only 1964 in question on the facts,

— stated intention must be supported by behavioural facts,

— worked for a U.S. company and paid in U.S. currency,

— but not determining because a Canadian resident can be involved in such a situation, providing employment services abroad for a non-Canadian company,

— memberships and investments including bank accounts, securities and pension plan in United States,

— factors may indicate U.S. residence, but not determining and also possible for a person resident in Canada,

— no Canadian memberships or investments and no application for family allowances,

— not determining factors and also possible of a Canadian resident,

— children living in United States,

— married and apparently not dependent,

— phone in wife's name in Canada,

— a factor, but hardly determining,

— neither employed in Canada nor carrying on business in Canada,

— not necessary condition for full-time residence.

(This list of factors is longer but there is more substance for full-time residence.)

(B) The deemed residence alternative→taxed in Canada on worldwide income for full year [ssec. 2(1)]:

Criterion: the condition of sojourning an aggregate of 183 days or more [ssec. 250(1)];

Evidence: his total stay in Canada in the year was only for 166 days; therefore, the condition is not met.

(C) The part-time residence alternative→taxed in Canada on worldwide income for part of the year resident in Canada [ssec. 2(1)] with deductions applicable to the period of part-time residence [sec. 114] and non-refundable tax credits either prorated for or applicable to the period of part-time residence [sec. 118.91] (as long as not resident in Canada during some other part of the year);

Criterion: clean break or fresh start during 1964;

Evidence: neither occurred.

(D) The non-residence alternative→taxed in Canada on income earned in Canada [ssec. 2(3)]:

Criteria: employed in Canada, carried on business in Canada or disposed of taxable Canadian property in the year;

Evidence: none of these conditions occurred in the year [ssec. 2(3)].

(E) Conclusion: if the taxpayer is to be found a resident it must be as a full-time resident:

— the major factors indicate a relationship with Canada which would warrant a conclusion of such resident status.

Exercise 3

(A) Inch Incorporated is resident in Canada by virtue of the common law principle of central management and control. The corporation cannot be deemed resident in Canada because it was not incorporated in Canada [ssec. 250(4)].

(B) Foot Limited is deemed resident in Canada because it was incorporated in Canada after April 26, 1965 [par. 250(4)(*a*)].

(C) Yard Incorporated is not resident this year by virtue of the common law principle of central management and control. Furthermore, the corporation cannot be deemed resident in Canada because it was not incorporated in Canada.

(D) Mile Limited is resident in Canada. The corporation was incorporated in Canada before April 27, 1965 and after that time it was resident by virtue of the central management and control rule [par. 250(4)(*c*)].

CHAPTER 3
Employment Income

Exercise 1

[See: *Isaac v. M.N.R.*, 70 DTC 1285]

The following tests are applied to determine whether R.N. is an employee or an independent contractor.

Economic Reality or Entrepreneur Test

In applying the control subtest, the question is whether Canadian Forces Hospital, Halifax controlled not only what was done by R.N. but how it was done. In this case the Hospital exercised control over R.N. in connection with dividing up the patients to be cared for among the available nurses and imposing routine rules and regulations with regard to the administration of drugs and other medications. On the other hand, the Hospital did not exercise any control over the method in which R.N. did her work, which requires special knowledge, skill, and judgment. Accordingly, it does not appear that the Hospital exercised sufficient control to conclude that R.N. was an employee on the basis of this test alone.

However, the application of the other subtests is particularly revealing. R.N. does not run the risk of financing the equipment, supplying other assistants necessary to carry out her duties in the Hospital or seeking out clients. R.N. used the equipment and supplies furnished by the Hospital. She neither hired nor fired any of the nursing assistants who worked under her. She could only request that the Hospital hire additional staff to assist her. The clients were patients of the Hospital. R.N. was not in a position to substitute the services of another nurse if she was unable to perform her duties. All this evidence tends to establish that from an economic reality point of view R.N. was an employee, but this test may not be definitive in this case.

Integration or Organization Test

The Hospital deducted Canada Pension Plan contributions from her pay as they did with the nurses who were employed full-time by the Hospital. R.N. appeared to be economically dependent on the hospital, although she was not precluded from offering her services elsewhere. R.N. was subject to co-ordinational control of the hospital in terms of where to perform her services and when to do so. On the other hand, R.N. was not eligible for the regular benefits of a full-time nurse such as holidays, sick pay, retirement plan, etc. She was hired on a day-to-day basis at a *per diem* rate of pay. Her services could be terminated on 24 hours notice if full-time nurses became available. On the weight of the evidence it can be argued that R.N. is an employee of the Hospital based on the integration test.

Specific Result Test

On the one hand, it was R.N.'s personal services that were at the disposal of the Hospital. Her work was done on a continuous day-to-day basis without there being any limited or specified amount of work that she had, by contract, to accomplish. She could not substitute another person to perform her duties if she was unable to do so. On the other hand, R.N. was not a full-time nurse for any specified period of time. Her time was made up on a weekly basis in advance. She could be laid off on 24 hours notice. On balance, it appears that the evidence leads to the conclusion that, by applying the specific result test, R.N. was an employee. This conclusion is consistent with that for the integration or organization test.

Conclusion

The application of the control subtest of the economic reality or entrepreneur test leads to the conclusion that R.N was not an employee of the Hospital. The application of the other subtests of the economic reality test, the integration test and the specific result test leads to the inference that R.N. was an employee of the Hospital. (Your own conclusion after weighing all of these tests.)

Exercise 2

(A) Specifically exempted [par. 6(1)(a)].

(B) Taxable; only private medical plan premiums and provincial health service levies are exempted [par. 6(1)(a)].

(C) and (D) Exempted, since the premium was paid to a private medical plan [par. 6(1)(a)].

(E) Taxable [par. 6(1)(a)]. IT-470R, paragraphs 18 and 19, only exempts tuition fees where the course is primarily for the benefit of the employer.

(F) Normally, taxable [par. 6(1)(a)], but since the payment meets the conditions, namely that the Christmas gift is under $500 and is not cash or near cash, the CRA's position is that the gift is not a taxable benefit.

(G) Partly taxable [par. 6(1)(a)]: The CRA takes the position that there will be no benefit if William had reimbursed the company the actual cost ($420) [IT-470R, par. 28]. Since William did not completely reimburse the company for the actual costs, then the benefit would be calculated by taking the difference between the actual costs ($420) and the amount paid by William ($200) for a taxable benefit of $220.

(H) Taxable [par. 6(1)(a)], but the CRA takes the position that the amount would not be taxable if the membership was principally for the employer's advantage rather than the employee's [IT-470R, par. 34].

(I) Taxable [par. 6(1)(a)] unless the financial counselling was in respect of re-employment or retirement [clause 6(1)(a)(iv)(B)].

Exercise 3

The $6,000 merchandise discount is a taxable benefit. IT-470R does exempt discounts on merchandise, but they must be offered to all employees and not to just select groups. If there was an overall discount of 10% to all employees, it would seem reasonable in the circumstances to include only 25% in income; however, the Interpretation Bulletin is silent on this point [IT-470R, par. 27].

Exercise 4

The entire $5,500 is a taxable benefit [par. 6(1)(a) and sec. 6(19)]. The exclusion for an eligible housing loss [ssec. 6(20)] does not apply, because the loss was not incurred in an eligible relocation [ssec. 248(1)]. IT-470R, paragraph 35, does provide some relief in this area, but only when an employee moves because he or she:

(a) has been transferred from one establishment of the employer to another; or

(b) has accepted another position at a location other than his or her former location.

If either of the above situations had existed, there would be no taxable benefit. Note that on the sale of the house, the loss cannot be greater than the actual loss to the employee, calculated as the amount by which the cost of the house exceeds the net selling price received [IT-470R, par. 37].

Exercise 5

Premiums paid:

    (A) Provincial medical plan premiums paid by an employer are a taxable benefit [par. 6(1)(*a*)]; however, a provincial health service levy paid by an employer is not a taxable benefit.

    (B) and (C) The extended health care and dental care plans are private medical plans; hence, the premiums paid by the employer are not employment income [par. 6(1)(*a*)].

    (D) Since the income protection plan is a group plan, premiums paid by the employer are exempt from employment income [par. 6(1)(*a*)].

Conclusion:

    The following rearrangement would result in a lower tax cost:

    (A) Company should pay for 100% of the extended health care and dental plan.

    (B) Employees should pay the provincial medical plan premiums since company payments would be taxable benefits.

    (C) Employees should consider paying the income protection premium themselves.

        When an employer pays *any* portion of the premium for this type of plan, amounts that are paid out of the plan are taxable as employment income, less the employee's contribution to date [par. 6(1)(*f*)]. Conversely, if the employee pays all of the premiums, none of the amounts paid out of the plan are taxable. Since this particular plan has benefits of only 50% of the wages, the employee would be in a relatively poor cash position. The imposition of tax, even though at a lower rate, would certainly result in extreme hardship if the illness is prolonged.

Exercise 6

Subsection 6(9) benefit as calculated under section 80.4 would be the sum of:

(A) Car loan — prescribed rates

1st quarter	7% × $15,000 × 90/365	= $259
2nd quarter	6% × $15,000 × 91/365	= 224
3rd quarter	8% × $15,000 × 92/365	= 302
4th quarter	7% × $15,000 × 92/365	= 265

$ 1,050

(B) Home purchase loan[1]

The lesser of the prescribed rate at the time of the loan (i.e., 7%) and the prescribed rate per quarter.

1st	7%	× $100,000 × 90/365	= $ 1,726
2nd	6%	× $100,000 × 91/365	= 1,496
3rd	7%	× $100,000 × 92/365	= 1,764
4th	7%	× $100,000 × 92/365	= 1,764

6,750

(C) Other loan

1st	7%	× $ 10,000 × 90/365	= $ 173
2nd	6%	× $ 10,000 × 91/365	= 150
3rd	8%	× $ 10,000 × 92/365	= 202
4th	7%	× $ 10,000 × 92/365	= 176

701

$ 8,501

Less amounts paid[2]

(a) 6% × $ 15,000 × 365/365	$ 900	
(b) 4% × $100,000 × 365/365	4,000	
(c) 7% × $ 10,000 × 365/365	700	5,600

$ 2,901

    Section 80.5 would deem $150 of the car loan interest ($1,050 – $900) to be paid in the year and therefore eligible for a paragraph 8(1)(*j*) deduction, since the interest was deemed to be paid within 30 days of the year-end as required by paragraph 80.4(1)(*c*).

    IT-522R paragraph 27 indicates that the deemed interest expense must be prorated for employment use.

$$\frac{27,000 \text{ km}}{45,000 \text{ km}} \times \$150 = \$90$$

Paragraph 8(1)(*j*) would deny a prorated deduction of the $900 paid on January 15 of the following year, since it was not paid in the taxation year in question. However, this amount would be eligible for a deduction in the following taxation year to the extent of the business use.

The section 67.2 limitation restricts the interest to the lesser of (a) $90 and (b) $300 $\times\,^{365}/_{30}$ $\times$ 27,000/45,000 = $2,190.

—*NOTES TO SOLUTION*

(1) If this loan had been as a consequence of an employment relocation, paragraph 110(1)(*j*) would have provided a deduction for five years, equal to the imputed interest benefit on the first $25,000 of the "home relocation loan", as defined in subsection 248(1). As a result, in this particular case, the overall benefit on the housing loan would have been reduced by $1,688 (i.e., $25,000/$100,000 of $6,750). See Chapter 10 for a complete discussion of this provision. The "lesser of" comparison is made on a quarter-by-quarter basis.

(2) The section 80.4 benefit is calculated on an aggregate basis. Any excess interest payment on one loan effectively reduces the deemed interest benefit on the other loans.

Exercise 7

Year 1 — No tax effect.

Year 4 — No tax effect.

Year 5 — No tax effect, since the employer is a Canadian-controlled private corporation.

Year 6 — Must take into employment income under Division B (under subsection 7(1.1)) the following:

$$50,000 \text{ shares} \times (\$3 - \$1) = \underline{\underline{\$100,000}}$$

— Will have a capital gain of

$$50,000 \text{ shares} \times (\$6 - \$3) = \underline{\underline{\$150,000}}$$

— May be eligible for the capital gains deduction for qualifying small business corporation shares [ssecs. 110.6(1) and 248(1)].

— Since Katrina sold these shares within two years after the date of acquisition, she is not entitled to a deduction of one half of the subsection 7(1.1) inclusion [par. 110(1)(*d*.1)]. She is also not entitled to a general deduction since the exercise price of $1.00 was less than fair market value ($1.50) at the date the option was granted [par. 110(1)(*d*)].

Exercise 8

(a) Car benefit if business–use kilometres are 10,000

  Par. 6(1)(*e*) and ssec. 6(2) — Standby

  $\dfrac{20,004 \text{ km}^1}{20,004 \text{ km}} \times [2\% \times (\$20,000 \times 12)] =$ $4,800

  Spar. 6(1)(*k*)(v)^2 operating costs (12,000 km × $0.20)   2,400 $7,200

  Less: amount reimbursed   400

  Total car benefit if business-use kilometres are 10,000 $6,800

(b) Car benefit if business-use kilometres are 20,000

  Par. 6(1)(*e*) and ssec. 6(2) — Standby

  $\dfrac{12,000 \text{ km}^3}{20,004 \text{ km}} \times [2\% \times (\$20,000 \times 12)] =$ $2,879

  Spar. 6(1)(*k*)(v) operating costs^4 (50% × $2,879) =   1,440 $4,319

  Less: amount reimbursed   400

  Total car benefit if business-use kilometres are 20,000 $3,919

NOTES

(1) The employee does not qualify for the standby charge reduction since the car is not used more than 50% in the performance of employment duties when the business use is only 15,000

km. Therefore, in this outcome, the value of A in the formula (i.e., 12,000 km) is deemed equal to the value of B in the formula (i.e., 1,667 x 12 rounded).

(2) The subparagraph 6(1)(*k*)(iv) election method is not available to the employee, since the car is not used more than 50% for business.

(3) When the business-use kilometers is 20,000, the employee qualifies for the standby charge reduction and the numerator becomes the lesser of (a) 12,000 km, and (b) 1,667 km x 12 months.

(4) The operating benefit election at 50% of the standby charge is less than $0.20¢ × 12,000 km = $2,400. The election method is available since employment kilometres comprise more than 50% of the total.

Exercise 9

Subsection 8(13) would appear to deny any deduction in respect of Calvin's work space in the home. In order for Calvin to avoid the restrictions in subsection 8(13), one of two conditions must be met, neither of which appear to be adhered to. The first alternative condition is that the work place in the home must be where the individual principally performs the employment duties. The second alternative condition is even more stringent, namely, that the work place must be used exclusively for employment income purposes and that the work place must be used on a regular and continuous basis as a meeting place for employment-connected persons.

If Calvin had met one of the conditions of subsection 8(13), then he would be able to deduct some of the expenses indicated as long as he met the conditions of paragraph 8(1)(*i*). First Calvin must have a contract with his employer indicating that he must pay for office rent and supplies and the employer completes and signs a T2200. However, of the expenses indicated, only the maintenance expense, including fuel, electricity, light bulbs, cleaning materials and minor repairs, on a prorated basis will be permitted [IT-352R2, par. 3]. The imputed rent of $1,000 is not deductible [IT-352R2, par. 2]; this position was confirmed in the *Thompson* case by the Federal Court – Trial Division, 89 DTC 5439.

Exercise 10

Allowances and related expenses: Subparagraph 6(1)(*b*)(vii) has two conditions that must be met in order to permit the allowance to be excluded from income:

(a) the allowance must relate to travel outside of the municipality in which the employer's office is situated;

(b) the allowance must be a reasonable amount.

The $10,000 accommodation allowance is a taxable allowance [spar. 6(1)(*b*)(vii)], since the amount is an unreasonable amount on the assumption that the incurred expenses of $12,000 were reasonable. Therefore, she is entitled to a deduction [par. 8(1)(*h*)], since she meets the other conditions of this paragraph; namely, she ordinarily travels in respect of her employment duties and is required by her employment contract to pay for her own expenses.

Total accommodation expenses	$12,000
Less: disallowed meal portion [ssec. 67.1(1)] (50% × $4,500)	2,250
	$ 9,750

The car expenses are deductible under paragraph 8(1)(*h*.1)] since she meets the conditions of this paragraph which are quite similar to paragraph 8(1)(*h*), described above, to the extent of the following calculations:

Gas	$1,500
Maintenance	500
Capital cost allowance (½ × 30% × $30,000 × 1.13)	5,085
Insurance	1,200
Licences	90

Interest — lesser of:

(a) $4,000

(b) $300 × $\frac{361 \text{ days}}{30}$ = $3,610 $\underline{3,610}$

$\underline{\$11,985}$

Deductible car expenses:

$\frac{15,000 \text{ km}}{21,000 \text{ km}}$ × $11,985 = $8,561

Exercise 11

7/107 of the sum of:

(a) Deductible expenses including GST and PST but excluding exempt supplies[1]:

Accommodation and meals	$ 9,750
Gas and maintenance	1,429[2]
	$11,179
(b) Capital cost allowance	3,632[3]
	$14,811
(c) Less: any expenses for which a reasonable allowance was received	Nil
	$14,811
Rebate (7/107 of $14,811)	$ 969

Par. 6(8)(c) Employment income inclusion in year of receipt of rebate:

$\frac{\$11,179}{\$14,811}$ × $969 = $731

Par. 6(8)(d) Capital cost reduction under ssec. 13(7.1) in year of receipt:

$\frac{\$ 3,632}{\$14,811}$ × $969 = $238

— *NOTES TO SOLUTION*

(1) Exempt supplies: insurance, licences and interest in respect of car.

(2) $\frac{15,000 \text{ km}}{21,000 \text{ km}}$ × ($1,500 + $500) = $1,429

(3) $\frac{15,000 \text{ km}}{21,000 \text{ km}}$ × $5,085 = $3,632

CHAPTER 4

Income from Business: General Concepts and Rules

Exercise 1

[See *Hiwako Investments Limited v. The Queen*, (F.C.A.) 78 DTC 6281]

The intention of the taxpayer corporation in this case can only be inferred from the facts of the case. The nature of the asset involved in the transaction is of prime importance in this case. It was an income-producing asset that would have been regarded as a fixed capital asset had it been held longer. Normally, the increase in value on the sale of a capital asset is taxed as a capital gain. The gain represents an enhancement of value by realizing a security in the same sense that a growth stock may be sold for a gain that is regarded as a capital gain. Thus, the prospect of an increase in value does not, by itself, characterize the gain as income from business.

The nature of the activity surrounding the transaction could characterize it as an adventure in the nature of trade. However, it could be argued that an income-producing property was purchased as an investment and circumstances changed such that the investment had to be sold. This would not necessarily be regarded as a gain made in an operation of business in carrying out a scheme for profit-making.

The court indicated that the concept of "secondary intention" does no more than refer to a practical approach for determining certain questions that arise in connection with "trading cases". If property is acquired where there is no business or the purchaser has not considered how he or she will use it, then the sale may be regarded as an adventure in the nature of trade, supporting a secondary intention to sell at a profit. However, where the property in question is an active, profit-producing property, it may be more difficult to conceive of its having been held as a speculation in the sense of an adventure in the nature of trade.

The fact that the principal shareholder of the corporation had a long history of trading in real estate does not necessarily mean that his intention in the transaction at hand was to trade. That fact could be outweighed by the income-producing capital nature of the particular property in question.

The court held that the gain was not income from a business, based on the foregoing reasons. However, some believe that the arguments for business income are stronger in this case and that the decision in this case should be limited to its specific facts.

Exercise 2

The $225,000 would be considered a capital receipt (see *Parsons-Steiner Limited v. M.N.R.*, (Ex. Ct.) 62 DTC 1148).

Exercise 3

Since actual cost is known it must be used. Therefore, an assumption about cost is not appropriate. Market value is probably best reflected in net realization value for this inventory. The following calculation of inventory values could be used:

Item	Actual cost	Reg. 1801 Market	Ssec. 10(1) Each item at lower of cost or market
Mufflers	$1,120.00	$ 992.00	$ 992.00
Tailpipes	745.75	706.50	706.50
Exhaust system	633.75	604.50	604.50
Shock absorbers	4,979.20	5,056.00	4,979.20
Brackets	1,304.80	1,211.60	1,211.60
Clamps	1,134.90	1,396.80	1,134.90
Total		$9,967.40	$9,628.70

Either the $9,967.40 value can be used [Reg. 1801] or the $9,628.70 value can be used [ssec. 10(1)]. However, subsection 10(2.1) requires that the ending valuation method used in a particular year be the same as that used for the end of the preceding year.

Exercise 4

(A) Paragraph 18(1)(*l*) would prohibit the deduction of these costs, notwithstanding the argument that the lodge was used to produce income from client business.

(B) Paragraph 18(1)(*l*) would allow the deduction of costs if they were incurred in the ordinary course of the company's business of providing the property for rent. The facts of this case *may* fit this exception.

Exercise 5

(A) — contribution may be made within 120 days of the end of 2005,

      — an employer contribution to a defined-benefit RPP is deductible where it is made on the recommendation of an actuary in whose opinion the contribution is required so that the plan will have sufficient assets to provide benefits in accordance with its terms as registered,

            — in this case, both the current service contribution and the lump-sum amount based on an actuarial valuation would be deductible in 2005, if they are in accordance with the plan.

(B) Paragraph 20(1)(*cc*) permits a full deduction of an amount paid in the year; or a taxpayer may elect to write it off in equal amounts over the 10-year period beginning in the current year [ssec. 20(9)].

(C) Paragraph 20(1)(*ee*) permits the deduction of the full amount of utilities connection costs. Since the taxpayer does not own the gas lines but the utilities company does, the amount is not eligible for capital cost allowance.

(D) Salary of an owner-employee's spouse is an allowable deduction to a corporation as long as it is reasonable in the circumstances. While $7,000 per month for full-time secretarial work is probably not reasonable, some lesser, reasonable amount would be deductible in this case. The amount in excess of a reasonable amount will not be deductible to the corporation, but will be included in the recipient's income from employment.

Exercise 6

Paragraph 20(1)(*f*): deduct $\frac{1}{2}$ of the discount of $108.10 because the bond was issued at less than 97% even though within the $\frac{4}{3} \times 9\%$ or 12% yield range.

Given that the discount is paid effectively on maturity when the principal amount is repaid, then the $54.05 is deductible in 2005.

Exercise 7

Net income per financial statements...........................		$150,000
Add: Items deducted in financial statements but not deductible for tax purposes:		
Par. 18(1)(*e*)	Provision for income taxes — current	25,000
	— future	130,000
Par. 18(1)(*b*)	Depreciation expense......................	40,000
Par. 18(1)(*t*)	Non-deductible interest — re interest on late taxes	2,500
Par. 18(1)(*b*), (*e*)	Bond discount	7,500
Ssec. 10(1)	Inventory (closing) to FIFO basis	10,000
		$365,000
Deduct: Items not deducted in financial statements but deductible for tax purposes:		
Par. 20(1)(*aa*)	Landscaping costs $12,000	
Ssec. 10(1)	Inventory (opening) to FIFO basis 15,000	(27,000)
Net Income for tax purposes before C.C.A........................		$338,000

Exercise 8

This transaction would likely involve a receipt of income because the intention is likely to make a profit on the purchase and sale of land. This would be substantiated by the frequency of transactions in land or, at least, the indication of an adventure in the nature of trade. During the year of sale the following income would be computed:

			Reference
Revenue from the sale of land		$250,000	
Less: cost of land	$107,500		
real estate commission	12,500	120,000	
Income from the sale of land		$130,000	Sec. 9
Less: reserve for amount not due until later year*			Spar. 20(1)(*n*)(ii)
$\frac{\$130,000}{\$250,000} \times (\$250,000 - \$110,000)$		72,800	
Income after reserve		$ 57,200	

* Paragraph 20(8)(*b*) does not apply unless the sale occurred within 36 months of the end of the year in which a reserve is to be taken.

Note that the minimum two-year repayment period does not apply on the sale of land which qualifies for the reserve [spar. 20(1)(*n*)(ii)]. In the next year, the reserve of $72,800 would be taken into income [spar. 12(1)(*e*)(ii)].

Exercise 9

Since Mr. Flogger has sold substantially all of his business assets to a person who intends to carry on the business, a section 22 election is available. Note that Mr. Flogger and Mr. Sucker must elect jointly in prescribed form [T2022] to have section 22 apply. Mr. Flogger must include last year's reserve deducted under paragraph 20(1)(*l*) in income [par. 12(1)(*d*)]. Then, Mr. Flogger may deduct, as a business loss, the difference between the face value of the accounts ($45,000) and the consideration paid by Mr. Sucker which should be equal to their fair market value ($36,000). Hence, Mr. Flogger will have a deduction of $9,000 [par. 22(1)(*a*)]. Mr. Sucker must include the same $9,000 difference in his business income for the taxation year of the purchase [par. 22(1)(*b*)]. However, Mr. Sucker will now be put in a position to deduct an appropriate reserve for doubtful debts at the end of the taxation year [par. 20(1)(*l*)] or to write off any of the accounts that can be established to have become bad debts [par. 20(1)(*p*)], since an amount has been included in income in respect of these receivables [par. 22(1)(*c*)].

		Income Effect
Mr. Flogger		
Last year's reserve		$ 6,500
Loss on sale: Proceeds	$36,000	
Face amount	(45,000)	(9,000)
Net effect		($ 2,500)
Mr. Sucker		
Mr. Flogger's loss on sale included in income		$ 9,000
Face amount of receivables		$45,000

If the election in section 22 is not used, the loss of $9,000 would be a capital loss, only ½ deductible as an allowable capital loss. Furthermore, an allowable capital loss can only be offset against a taxable capital gain.

Exercise 10

Since the corporation is carrying on business, it is engaged in a commercial activity. [ETA: ssec. 123(1)] Therefore, the corporation is required to register and collect GST on its supplies, i.e., sales of goods, which are "taxable supplies." As a registrant, the corporation is entitled to a full input tax credit (ITC) in respect of GST paid or payable on goods and services that it purchases exclusively for use in its commercial activity. [ETA: sec. 169(1)] If GST collected or collectible on its sales exceeds its ITCs, the corporation must remit the difference. On the other hand, if ITCs exceed GST collected or collectible, a refund of the excess is available.

The following is the appropriate GST treatment of the items listed:

(a) Net income per financial statements would have been increased by GST charged which is included in revenue and reduced by GST paid or payable which is included in costs. GST charged net of ITCs from GST paid or payable must be remitted.

(b) There are no GST implications for the provision for income taxes.

(c) GST paid on the purchase of depreciable property provides an ITC, as discussed in Chapter 5. When the cost of the asset is subsequently written off through depreciation or capital cost allowance, there are no further GST implications.

(d) The cost of inventory contains purchases of goods on which GST is paid. This GST will give rise to an ITC.

(e) The payment of interest is not subject to GST. Therefore, no ITC is available.

(f) Bond interest paid also results from a financial service which is an exempt supply. No GST is paid and, hence, no ITC is available.

(g) Landscaping costs are incurred for goods and services which are taxable supplies. Hence, GST would be paid in respect of these costs and an ITC would be available.

CHAPTER 5
Depreciable Property and Eligible Capital Property

Exercise 1

The overpass is not eligible for capital cost allowance, since the owners have no title to the land on which the footings are placed and capital cost allowance cannot be claimed on assets that are not owned (see *Saskatoon Community Broadcasting Co. Ltd. v. M.N.R.*, (T.A.B.) 58 DTC 491). The cost of the overpass qualifies as an eligible capital expenditure.

Exercise 2

No terminal loss can be deducted for an automobile in Class 10.1 [ssec. 20(16.1)]. The special "half-year rule" to compute capital cost allowance in the year of disposition applies to Class 10.1 [Reg. 1100(2.5)].

(A)	Jan. 1/05	U.C.C. (Class 10.1)	$ 18,475
	2005	C.C.A. ($\frac{1}{2} \times .30 \times \$18,475$)	(2,771)[1]
		Proceeds of disposition	(12,000)
		Terminal loss of $3,704 denied	Nil
(B)	2005	Purchase ($36,000) (new Class 10.1) max.	$ 34,500[2]
	Dec. 31/05	U.C.C. before adjustment	$ 34,500
		One-half of net amount ($\frac{1}{2} \times \$34,500$)	(17,250)
		U.C.C. before C.C.A.	$ 17,250
		C.C.A. @ 30% of $17,250	(5,175)[3]
		Add: $\frac{1}{2}$ net amount	17,250
	Jan. 1/2006	U.C.C.	$ 29,325

—NOTES TO SOLUTION

(1) Note that 75% of $2,771 or $2,078 is the deduction based on business use.

(2) Limited to $30,000 plus PST (8%) and GST (7%) or $34,500, since it was acquired after 2000.

(3) Note that 75% of $5,175 or $3,881 is deductible, since CCA claimed [par. 8(1)(j)] is not subject to the limitation on sales/negotiating person's expenses [par. 8(1)(f)].

Exercise 3

	Cl. 1: 4%	Cl. 8: 20%	Cl. 10: 30%	Cl. 13: S.L.	Cl. 14: S.L.	Cl. 43: 30%
Jan. 1/05						
U.C.C.	$120,000	$75,000	$40,000	$42,000	$54,400	Nil
2005 Purchases:						
— mfg. equip.						$50,000
— off. equip.		10,000				
Disposals:						
— building	(100,000)[1]					
— equip.						
Dec. 31/05						
U.C.C. before adjustment	$ 20,000	$85,000	$40,000	$42,000	$54,400	$50,000
½ net-amount	Nil	(5,000)	Nil	Nil	N/A	(25,000)
U.C.C. before C.C.A.	$ 20,000	$80,000	$40,000	$42,000	$54,400	$25,000
C.C.A.	(800)	(16,000)	(12,000)	(1,250)[2]	(3,400)[3]	(7,500)
½ net-amount	Nil	5,000	Nil	Nil	N/A	25,000
Jan. 1/2006						
U.C.C.	$ 19,200	$69,000	$28,000	$40,750	$51,000	$42,500

—NOTES TO SOLUTION

(1) Capital gain on disposition of building of $50,000.

(2) Lesser of: (a) ⅕ of $50,000 .... $10,000 ⎫
$1,250
(b) $50,000/40 (max.) .... $ 1,250 ⎭
— not reduced by ½ because not first year of ownership.

(3) $\dfrac{\$68,000}{(20 \times 365)} \times 365 = \$3,400$

Exercise 4

		Cl. 3: 5%
Jan. 1, 2004	U.C.C.	$ 221,000
	Disposal[1]	
	lesser of:	
	(a) capital cost $300,000	
	(b) proceeds $295,000	(295,000)
Dec. 31, 2004	U.C.C.	$ (74,000)
	Recapture	74,000
Jan. 1, 2005	U.C.C.	Nil

Aug. 2005   File an amended return for 2004 [ssec. 13(4)] as follows:

				Cl. 3: 5%
Jan. 1, 2004	U.C.C.			$ 221,000
	Deemed proceeds [par. 13(4)(c)]			
	lesser of:			
	(a) capital cost	$300,000		
	(b) proceeds	$295,000	→ $295,000	
	reduced by lesser of:			
	(a) recapture ($295K − $221K)	$ 74,000	→ $ 74,000	
	(b) replacement cost	$400,000		$(221,000)
Dec. 31, 2004	U.C.C.			Nil
	Recapture			Nil
Jan. 1, 2005	U.C.C.			Nil

			Cl. 1: 4%[2]
2005	Purchase of new building	$400,000	
	Less: reduction above [par. 13(4)(c)]	74,000	$ 326,000
Dec. 31, 2005	U.C.C.		$ 326,000
	C.C.A. @ 4% of [$326,000 − ($\frac{1}{2}$ × $326,000)]		(6,520)
Jan. 1, 2006	U.C.C.		$ 319,480

— NOTES TO SOLUTION

(1) IT-259R3, paragraph 3, appears to require that even if a replacement property is purchased before the tax return for the year of disposition must be filed (i.e., within six months of the taxation year-end), the recapture must be reported in the year of disposition. The taxpayer can request a reassessment if and when the replacement is purchased within the specified time limits. In lieu of paying tax initially on the recapture, the Department will take acceptable security until the final determination of tax is made.

(2) Note how the rules [ssec. 13(4)] allow for a replacement with an asset of another class.

Exercise 5

The change in use rules [par. 13(7)(d)] could be applied as follows:

		Cl. 10[1]: 30%
2003	Purchase (85% of $14,600)	$12,410
Dec. 31, 2003	U.C.C.	$12,410
	C.C.A. @ 30% of [($12,410 − ($\frac{1}{2}$ × $12,410)]	(1,862)
Jan. 1, 2004	U.C.C.	$10,548
2004	Disposal (5% of $12,200)[2]	(610)
Dec. 31, 2004	U.C.C.	$ 9,938
	C.C.A. @ 30% of $9,938	(2,981)

Jan. 1, 2005	U.C.C.		$ 6,957
2005	Purchase (10% of $9,800)[3]		980
Dec. 31, 2005	U.C.C.		$ 7,937
	C.C.A. @ 30% of [$7,937 − (½ × $980)]		(2,234)
Jan. 1, 2006	U.C.C.		$ 5,703

In practice, however, the following calculation of capital cost allowance might be made:

		Cl. 10: 30%	Business deduction of C.C.A.
2003	Purchase	$14,600	
Dec. 31, 2003	U.C.C.	$14,600	
	C.C.A. @ 30% of		
	½ × $14,600 ...	(2,190)	85% of $2,190 = $1,862
Dec. 31, 2004	U.C.C.	$12,410	
	C.C.A. @ 30%	(3,723)	80% of $3,723 = $2,978
Dec. 31, 2005	U.C.C.	$ 8,687	
	C.C.A. @ 30%	(2,606)	[80% + ½ (90% − 80%)][4]
			of $2,606 = $2,215
Jan. 1, 2006	U.C.C.	$ 6,081	

— NOTES TO SOLUTION

(1) Since the automobile cost less than the limit prescribed for paragraph 13(7)(g), it is placed in Class 10.

(2) Lesser of proceeds at fair market value and capital cost.

(3) Since fair market value is less than cost, the increase in capital cost is based on fair market value.

(4) An increase in use for business represents an addition to the class which is subject to the half-net-amount rule. In practice, the CCA may be computed simply as 90% of $2,606 or $2,345.

Exercise 6

The cumulative eligible capital account would be affected as follows:

Year	Opening balance	Par. 20(1)(b) deduction[1]	Ssec. 14(1) business income inclusion	Closing balance
1993	$ 8,100	$ 567		$7,533
1994[2]	7,533	527		7,006
2004	7,006	490		6,516
2005	6,516	—	$18,684[3]	
Total		$1,584		

2005 Opening balance	$ 6,516
Sale (¾ × $45,000)	(33,750)
Negative balance	(27,234)
Minus: previous C.E.C.A. claims	1,584
Balance	($25,650)
Income inclusion:	
Previous CECA claims	$ 1,584
⅔ × $25,650	17,100
Total	$ 18,684

— NOTES TO SOLUTION

(1) 7% of the declining balance.

(2) No paragraph 20(1)(b) deductions taken in the 1995–2003 period because of business losses.

(3) The sale in 2005 would result in $18,684 of business income which is equal to the sum (rounded) of par. 20(1)(b) deductions ($1,584) plus $\frac{1}{2}$ of the gain of $34,200 ($45,000 − $10,800).

Exercise 7

Jan. 1, 1997	Purchase of goodwill ($\frac{3}{4}$ × $40,000)	$ 30,000
Dec. 31, 1997	Cumulative eligible capital amount @ 7%	(2,100)
Jan. 1, 1998	Cumulative eligible capital	$ 27,900
Dec. 31, 1998	Cumulative eligible capital amount @ 7%	(1,953)
Jan. 1, 1999	Cumulative eligible capital	$ 25,947
June 1, 1999	Purchase of license ($\frac{3}{4}$ × $50,000)	37,500
	Cumulative eligible capital	$ 63,447
Dec. 31, 1999	Cumulative eligible capital amount @ 7%	(4,441)
Jan. 1, 2000	Cumulative eligible capital	$ 59,006
Dec. 31, 2000	Cumulative eligible capital amount @ 7%	(4,130)
Jan. 1, 2001	Cumulative eligible capital	$ 54,876
Mar. 1, 2001	Purchase of trademark ($\frac{3}{4}$ × $20,000)	15,000
	Cumulative eligible capital	$ 69,876
Dec. 31, 2001	Cumulative eligible capital amount @ 7%	(4,891)
Jan. 1, 2002	Cumulative eligible capital	$ 64,985
Nov. 1, 2002	Purchase of goodwill ($\frac{3}{4}$ × $50,000)	37,500
	Cumulative eligible capital	$ 102,485
Dec. 31, 2002	Cumulative eligible capital amount @ 7%	(7,174)
Jan. 1, 2003	Cumulative eligible capital	$ 95,311
Sept. 7, 2003	Sale of goodwill ($\frac{3}{4}$ × $100,000)	(75,000)
	Cumulative eligible capital	$ 20,311
Dec. 31, 2003	Cumulative eligible capital amount @ 7%	(1,422)
Jan. 1, 2004	Cumulative eligible capital	$ 18,889
Dec. 31, 2004	Cumulative eligible capital amount @ 7%	(1,322)
Jan. 1, 2005	Cumulative eligible capital	$ 17,567
Aug. 3, 2005	Sale of license ($\frac{3}{4}$ × $150,000)	(112,500)
	Sale of trademark ($\frac{3}{4}$ × $200,000)	(150,000)
Dec. 31, 2005	Cumulative eligible capital	$(244,933)
	Business income under subsection 14(1)	172,433
	Non-taxed $\frac{1}{3}$ of "gain" [$\frac{1}{3}$ × ($244,933 − 27,433)]	72,500
Jan. 1, 2006	Cumulative eligible capital	$ Nil

The business income in 2005 is calculated as:

The total of:

(a) the lesser of:
  (i) the negative amount .... $ 244,933

  and
  (ii) the total of: ....
  all cumulative eligible capital deductions $ 27,433
  less: all recaptured deductions in prior
  years .... nil
  $ 27,433

	The lesser is	$ 27,433
and		
(b)	⅔ of negative amount less recaptured deductions above [⅔ × ($244,933 – 27,433)]	145,000*
	Business income	$172,433

* This is the same as:

Proceeds ($100,000 + $150,000 + $200,000)	$ 450,000
Cost ($40,000 + $50,000 + $20,000 + $50,000)	(160,000)
Gain	$ 290,000
½ =	$ 145,000

CHAPTER 6
Income from Property

Exercise 1

(A) In its June 30, 2005 taxation year, the corporation would be required to include in income the interest received March 31, 2005 for the period October 1, 2004 to March 31, 2005 plus interest accrued from April 1 to June 30, 2005 [ssec. 12(3)]. Accrued interest from October 1, 2004 to January 1, 2005 (the period prior to acquisition), which was purchased with the bond, would give rise to a deduction [ssec. 20(14)].

(B) Subsection 12(4) would require accrued interest from November 1, 2005 to October 31, 2006 to be included in income in 2006.

(C) The anniversary day would be December 31, 2005. Accrued interest from the date of purchase to December 31, 2005 would be included in 2005 income.

(D) The first anniversary day would occur October 31, 2006 and accrued interest would be included at that time. The CRA has, in the past, administratively allowed Canada Savings Bond interest to be accrued on a "bond year" basis [IT-396R, par. 25]. Subsection 12(4) gives legislative effect to this practice.

(E) The $80 received each year would be included in income [par. 12(1)(c)]. On November 30, 2005, there will be an anniversary day, but all of the interest accrued to that day will have been included in income as interest received in the year [par. 12(1)(c)].

Exercise 2

(A) The Department indicates that it examines the balance in the account at the end of each year of the lender considering a net increase as a loan to be included in the income of the borrower and a net decrease as a repayment to be deducted from the income of the borrower [IT-119R4 par. 34-35]. This approach would result in the following:

Lender's year end	Change from previous year	Income [ssec. 15(2.6)] or repayment [par. 20(1)(j)]
Year 2	$45,000	income
Year 3	(32,000)	repayment
Year 4	(2,000)	repayment
Year 5	12,000	income
Year 6	(14,000)	repayment

(B) If there is no series of loans and repayments, then repayments are considered to apply first to the oldest loan out-standing unless the facts clearly indicate otherwise [IT-119R4 par. 27]. Applying this approach would result in the following:

Lender's year end	Net inclusion (or deduction)	Explanation
Year 2	$25,000	— only the $20,000 borrowed in year 2 is repaid within one year of year 2; the $25,000 loan was not fully repaid within one year, so it must be taken into income in year 2
Year 3	(12,000)	— repayment of $12,000 of the $25,000 year 2 loan previously included
Year 4	(12,000)	— repayment of part of balance of year 2 loan
	Nil	— Nov. 30/year 4 loan repaid within one year of year 4
Year 5	(1,000)	— repayment of remainder of April 30/year 2 loan
	23,000	— full amount of Nov. 30/year 5 loan, since not fully repaid within one year of year 5
Year 6	(14,000)	— repayment of $14,000 of year 5 loan

Note that these methods of calculation are based on administrative practice and are not stipulated by the Act. Note that based on these methods, while total inclusions net of deductions over the period amount to $9,000 under each alternative, the time pattern of net inclusion is more favourable in this case if there is no series of loans and repayments considered.

If the loans are all part of a single running loan account, they are likely a series of loans and repayments. However, if the loans are for separate purposes, with differing repayment or other terms, and the repayments relate to specific loans, the facts might suggest there was no series of loans and repayments.

Exercise 3

Since he is a shareholder of the corporation, subsection 15(2) applies and the loan that was received by the taxpayer should be included in income. However, paragraph 15(2.4)(*d*) provides an exclusion for the $35,000 principal amount of the loan because:

— the taxpayer is an employee of the lender;

— the loan is to enable him to acquire a motor vehicle to be used by him in the performance of his employment duties;

— the taxpayer received the loan because of his employment, not because of his share-holdings, since other employees were eligible for a loan; and

— *bona fide* arrangements were made, at the time the loan was made, for repayment within a reasonable time.

Since the loan is a low-interest loan, subsection 80.4(1) applies to impute an interest benefit calculated as follows:

April 1 to June 30: $91/365 \times 4\%$ of $35,000 = ...	$ 349
July 1 to Sept. 30: $92/365 \times 5\%$ of $35,000 = ...	441
Oct. 1 to Dec. 31: $92/365 \times 6\%$ of $35,000 = ...	529
Total	$1,319
Less: interest *paid* (not payable) ($214/365 \times 3\%$ of $35,000)	616
Net interest benefit	$ 703

Section 80.5 deems the imputed interest benefit of $703 to have been paid in the year. As a result, a part of the interest will qualify as a deduction of interest *paid* under paragraph 8(1)(*j*), limited by section 67.2 as follows:

Lesser of:

(a) interest deemed paid $703
   interest *paid* ($^{214}/_{365}$ × 3% of $35,000) 616 $1,319

(b) $\dfrac{\$300}{30}$ × 214 days of interest paid $2,140

Lesser amount × 60% business usage (60% of $1,319) .... $ 791

Exercise 4

(A) (i) Subsection 74.1(1) would attribute the income on the bond to him even though she is legally entitled to receive it, since a gift is considered to be a transfer and is not a fair market value exchange which would be exempt [ssec. 74.5(1)].

(ii) Since a sale is also considered to be a transfer, subsection 74.1(1) would apply except that, in this case, paragraph 74.5(1)(*a*) would exempt the transfer because it was for fair market value consideration, as long as they elect jointly not to have the rollover apply [ssec. 73(1)].

(iii) This situation still involves a sale directly between husband and wife and is, therefore, a transfer subject to the attribution of income [ssec. 74.1(1)]. A non-interest bearing demand note would not qualify for the exception [par. 74.5(1)(*b*)] because a commercial rate of interest was not charged.

(iv) The loan of funds would result in attribution [ssec. 74.1(1)], because the exception would not apply since a commercial rate of interest was not charged on the loan [par. 74.5(2)].

(B) If the loan was to a non-arm's length minor or a niece or nephew who is also a minor, then subsection 74.1(2) would apply to transfers or loans by means of a trust to or for the benefit of a minor in the same way as subsection 74.1(1) applied in part (A) above. However, there are special rules pertaining to transfers or loans to a trust which will be discussed in Chapter 18.

(C) Attribution of income does not apply to a transfer under subsection 74.1(2) involving an individual who is 18 or older. However, subsection 56(4.1) might apply to transactions (iii) and (iv) involving loans. The key condition for this rule to apply is that one of the main reasons for the loan was to reduce or avoid tax on income from property or substituted property. A loan bearing a commercial rate of interest would be exempt from the rule in subsection 56(4.1).

Exercise 5

(i) Subsection 18(2) should not apply to limit the deductibility of carrying charges because the land is being used in the course of the hotel business.

(ii) Paragraph 18(2)(*e*) will limit the deductibility of carrying charges to 75% of their total (i.e., to the amount of the net revenues) so as not to create a loss by their deduction, unless the land is owned by a corporation whose principal purpose meets the test in paragraph 18(2)(*f*). The principal purpose of a hotel corporation is not considered to be the rental of real property (i.e., land and building) owned by it.

(iii) Subsection 18(2) may limit the deductibility of carrying charges in the same manner as in (ii) above until the property is used in the business.

Exercise 6

	Class 1: 4% Building 1	Class 1: 4% Building 2[1]	Class 8: 20%	Total
U.C.C., January 1	$148,000	—	$25,000	
Purchases	—	$137,500	—	
U.C.C., December 31	$148,000	$137,500	$25,000	
C.C.A.	5,920	2,750[2]	4,350[3]	$13,020
U.C.C., January 1	$142,080	$134,750	$20,650	

—NOTES TO SOLUTION

(1) Separate class for rental building costing $50,000 or more [Reg. 1101 (1ac)].

(2) 4% of [$137,500 – (¹/₂ × $137,500)].

(3) Net rental income before C.C.A. ($9,270 + 3,750) $13,020

C.C.A. on rental building and leasing properties (i.e., furniture and fixtures) limited to $13,020 [$13,020 – ($5,920 + $2,750) = $4,350] . . . .   (13,020)

Net income from rental properties . . . .   Nil

Note that where less than maximum capital cost allowance is taken, the less than maximum amount should be taken in classes with relatively higher C.C.A. rates, so that the U.C.C. carried forward to the following year is eligible for C.C.A. at the higher rate in that subsequent year.

Exercise 7

Ms Prudent should buy the car with her accumulated savings of $5,000 and borrow $5,000 from the stockbroker for her investments. While the pre-tax cost of the investment loan will be higher than a car loan, the 7% will be deductible resulting in an after-tax cost of 5.2% (i.e., 7% (1 – .255)) compared with the 5.9% car loan which is not tax deductible. The result is a saving of .7% which on a loan of $5,000 would be about $35 in the first year.

Exercise 8

(A)

	Property A	Property B	Total
U.C.C., January 1	$330,000	$480,000	
Disposal	(336,000)	—	
U.C.C., December 31	$ (6,000)	$480,000	
Recapture	6,000		
C.C.A. @ 5% (Class 3) — see below	—	(12,000)	
U.C.C. forward	Nil	$468,000	
Revenue	$ 13,500	$ 22,500	$36,000
Recapture	6,000	—	6,000
Expenses before C.C.A.	(11,250)	(18,750)	(30,000)
Net	$ 8,250	$ 3,750	$12,000
C.C.A. (5% of $480,000 = $24,000; limited to net above)			(12,000)
Net income from property			Nil

(B)

The provisions of subsection 13(4) apply on a voluntary disposition of a "former business property," as defined in subsection 248(1). A rental property is excluded from the definition and, hence, subsection 13(4) does not apply.

Exercise 9

Since the benefit at issue is not taxable under subsection 15(1) of the *Income Tax Act*, subsection 173(1) of the ETA does not apply. The loan and any interest on the loan are in respect of financial services, as defined in subsection 123(1) and Schedule V, Part VII of the ETA. As a result, these amounts pertain to exempt supplies and there are no further GST implications to be considered.

CHAPTER 7
Capital Gains: An Introduction

Exercise 1

Step 1: Determine gain per year of ownership

		City home		Cottage
Par. 40(2)(*b*)				
P. of D.		$ 247,000		$ 164,000
A.C.B.	$ 180,000		$ 90,000	
S.C.	12,000	(192,000)	6,000	(96,000)
Gain		$ 55,000		$ 68,000
Gain per year	$\dfrac{\$55{,}000}{16 \text{ years}} =$	$ 3,438	$\dfrac{\$68{,}000}{11 \text{ years}} =$	$ 6,182

Step 2: Assignment of no-option years

In the five taxation years 1990 to 1994, Peter owned only the city home. Therefore, there is no option in those years but to designate the city home as his principal residence.

Step 3: Gain determined under paragraph 40(2)(*b*)

The gain per year of ownership for the cottage ($6,182) exceeds that for the city home ($3,438). If all 11 years are assigned to the cottage, however, one year will be wasted. Hence, the city home should be designated for one of the years 1995 to 2005.

	City home	Cottage
Gain.	$ 55,000	$ 68,000
Exemption	(24,063)[1]	(68,000)[2]
Capital gain	$ 30,937	Nil

— *NOTES TO SOLUTION*

(1) $\dfrac{1 + 5 + 1}{16} \times \$55{,}000 = \$24{,}063$; years designated — 1990–94 and one of 1995–2005

(2) $\dfrac{1 + 10}{11} \times \$68{,}000 = \$68{,}000$; years designated — all but one of 1995–2005

Exercise 2

	Painting		Antique clock		Outboard motor		Gold coin	
P of D.		$2,000		$1,200		$1,000		$1,000
A.C.B.	$1,000		$1,000		$1,000		$1,000	
S.C	100	(1,100)	20	(1,020)	15	(1,015)	10	(1,010)
C.G. (C.L.) . . .		$ 900		$ 180		$ (15)		$ (10)

Net taxable capital gain:		
L.P.P. — Painting	$ 900	
— Gold coin	(10)[1]	
	$ 890	
— ¹⁄₂		$ 445
P.U.P. — Antique clock (¹⁄₂ × $180)		90
		$ 535

— *NOTE TO SOLUTION*

(1) Listed personal property losses, whether current or carried-over, are applied at the full capital gain (capital loss) amount.

Exercise 3

(A) P. of D. 200 shares @ $25 .... $5,000

A.C.B. 200 shares @ $33[1] $6,600

S.C. 75 (6,675)

C.L.[2] (Superficial loss of $1,675) .... Nil

(B) Adjusted cost base of shares

50 shares @ $33	=	$1,650
200 shares @ $26	=	5,200
superficial loss		1,675
		$8,525 ÷ 250 shares = $34.10

— *NOTES TO SOLUTION*

(1) 100 shares @ $30	=	$3,000
150 shares @ $35	=	5,250
		$8,250 ÷ 250 shares = $33

(2) Since Ivan acquired additional shares of Solid Investments within the 30-day period.

Exercise 4

Adjusted cost base:

1,000 shares @ $35 .... $35,000

brokerage 500

1974 — stock dividend (50 shares × $10) 500

1985 — stock dividend — 105 shares (10% × 1,050) .... Nil

2000 — stock dividend — 231 shares (20% × 1,155) × $10 2,310

$38,310

Shares (1000 + 50 + 105 + 231) = 1,386

A.C.B. per share: $38,310 ÷ 1,386 = $27.64

Exercise 5

2004: Capital gain allocated .... $ 96.37

Taxable capital gain ($1/2 × $96.37) .... $ 48.19

The taxable capital gain of $48.19 must be included in her income for 2004.

2005: P. of D. (25 units) .... $ 718.00

A.C.B. (25 units @ $27.38[1]) .... (684.50)

C.G. .... $ 33.50

T.C.G. ($1/2 × $33.50) .... $ 16.75

— *NOTE TO SOLUTION*

(1) Adjusted cost base of units:

72.788	units	$2,000.00
3.774	units @ $25.535	96.37
76.562	units	$2,096.37

Weighted average: $2,096.37 ÷ 76.562 = $27.38

Exercise 6

			2004	2005
Par. 3(a)	Income from non-capital sources (non-negative):			
	Employment income........................		$25,000	$30,000
	Property income		10,000	—
	Business income — other....................		8,000	—
			$43,000	$30,000
Par. 3(b)	Net taxable capital gains (non-negative):			
	Taxable capital gain — personal-use property ($1/2 \times \$8,000$)		$ 4,000	—
	Plus			
	Listed personal property gain	$4,000		—
	Less: LPP loss carryforward — 2001	(1,000)		
	LPP loss carryback — 2005	(1,500)		
		$1,500		
	Taxable net gain — $1/2$ thereof.................	1,750		
			$ 4,750	
	Public corporation — allowable capital loss......	(4,750)	Nil[1]	
	— taxable capital gain			$ 4,500[2]
			$43,000	$34,500
Par. 3(d)	Losses from non-capital sources:			
	Property loss		—	(4,000)
	Business loss................................		—	(9,000)
	Allowable business investment loss		(3,000)[4]	(1,000)[5]
	Division B income		$40,000	$20,500

— NOTES TO SOLUTION
(1) Of the $6,000 allowable capital loss ($1/2 \times \$12,000$), $1,250 cannot be claimed in 2004 and will be carried back or forward under Division C as a "net capital loss" to be discussed in Chapter 10.

(2) $1/2 \times \$9,000$

(3) $1/2 \times \$6,000$

(4) $1/2 \times \$2,000$

CHAPTER 8
Capital Gains: The Finer Points

Exercise 1

Sale of car

P. of D. — Canadian dollars ($10,000 ÷ .80)........................	$12,500
A.C.B. — Canadian dollars.......................................	(4,000)
C.G...	$ 8,500
T.C.G. ($1/2 \times \$8,500$)	$ 4,250

Currency

P. of D. — Canadian dollars received	$13,800
A.C.B. — Canadian dollars at time of sale	(12,500)

Gain	$ 1,300
Exempt portion	(200)
C.G.	$ 1,100
T.C.G. ($^1/_2 \times$ $1,100)	$ 550

Exercise 2

(A) During the years prior to the settling of the claim, Tax Processing Ltd. is deemed to own the destroyed asset [ssec. 44(2)]. Hence the company can continue to take capital cost allowance.

Class 10: 30%

U.C.C. before the fire		$17,150
C.C.A. — 2003	$ 5,145	
C.C.A. — 2004	3,601	(8,746)
U.C.C. before proceeds received		$ 8,404

(B) In the second year after the fire (2005) when the company received the proceeds, the company would be deemed to have sold the computer for $60,000 with the following tax consequences:

Taxable capital gain:

P. of D.	$60,000
A.C.B.	(50,000)
C.G.	$10,000
T.C.G. ($^1/_2 \times$ $10,000)	$ 5,000

Recapture:

U.C.C. before proceeds received		$ 8,404
Less the lesser of:		
(i) Capital cost	$50,000	
(ii) P. of D.	60,000	50,000
Recapture		$41,596

(C) In the year of purchase of the new computer (2007), which is within the 24-month time limit for an involuntary disposition, Tax Processing Ltd. would file an amended return for the 2005 year in which the taxable capital gain and recapture were recognized.

Taxable capital gain:

$^1/_2$ of the lesser of:

(i) capital gain (see above)		$10,000	
(ii) P. of D.	$60,000		= Nil
less replacement cost	70,000	Nil	

A.C.B. of new computer in 2007 [par. 44(1)(*f*)]: ($70,000 – $10,000) = $60,000

Recapture [ssec. 13(4)]:

Class 10: 30%

U.C.C. before proceeds received (see above calculation)			$ 8,404
Less deemed disposal [par. 13(4)(*c*)]:			
lesser of (i) cost ($50,000)			
(ii) P. of D. ($60,000)		$50,000	
Less the lesser of:			
(i) the recapture			
($8,404 – $50,000)	$41,596		
(ii) replacement cost	70,000	41,596	8,404

	Class 10: 30%
U.C.C. after proceeds received, Dec. 31, 2005	Nil

2007 addition:

Capital cost of replacement property	$70,000
Less reduction for deferred gain [par. 44(1)(*f*)]	10,000
Deemed capital cost	$60,000
Less reduction for deferred recapture [par. 13(4)(*d*)]	41,596
U.C.C. before C.C.A.	$18,404
C.C.A. (30% of ¹/₂ × $18,404)	(2,761)
U.C.C. after C.C.A.	$15,643

Exercise 3

When Howard rents his home, he is deemed to have changed the use of the home and a capital gain may be triggered [ssec. 45(1)]. However, Howard can designate the home with the appropriate number of years and should not be taxed on the gain. Under this course of action, Howard would now have a rental property from which he must declare the income less all his expenses. However, a rental loss could not be generated with capital cost allowance on the home and equipment therein [Reg. 1100(15))].

Alternatively, Howard could elect to defer the gain until he either sells the home or rescinds his election [ssec. 45(2)]. Note that IT-120R6 normally permits a retroactive election at the time of sale. In this situation, Howard would not be allowed to claim any capital cost allowance on the home or the election under subsection 45(2) would be invalid.

The subsection 45(2) election would permit Howard to designate his Vancouver home as his principal residence for at least four extra years depending upon whether he is self-employed or employed.

(A) Self-employed

Paragraph (*d*) in the definition of a "principal residence" in section 54 permits Howard to designate his Vancouver home as his principal residence for four years, while it is being rented, if he elects under subsection 45(2) according to paragraphs (*b*) and (*d*) of the definition.

Howard might consider rescinding his election after the fourth year. This course of action would enable Howard to claim capital cost allowance after the fourth year subject to the loss restrictions discussed above.

(B) Employed

Section 54.1 waives the four-year restriction discussed above if Howard (or his wife) has moved at least 40 km closer to his new work location. Howard then can designate his Vancouver home as his principal residence during all the rental years if:

   (i) Howard subsequently resumes ordinary habitation of his home while employed with the same employer; or

   (ii) Howard subsequently resumes ordinary habitation of his home within one year from the end of the year in which he terminates employment with that employer; or

   (iii) Howard dies.

Note that "ordinarily inhabited" means any time during the year [IT-120R6], but Howard cannot temporarily move back in order to qualify for this exemption.

Exercise 4

Capital property A

(A) If Mr. Emigrant departs prior to June 1, 2005, there will be no capital gain on the capital asset which he brought from the U.S. by virtue of the 60-month short-term exemption [ssec. 128.1(4)].

(B) If he departs subsequent to June 1, 2005, there will be a taxable capital gain on ¹/₂ of the excess of the proceeds of disposition ($12,000) over the fair market value at the time of entry ($5,000), namely, $3,500.

Capital property B

(A) First, it is necessary to determine whether the capital property acquired in Canada is exempt from immediate departure tax but will be taxed on its ultimate disposition [ssec. 2(3)].

(B) If the property is not exempted then the taxpayer will be taxed at the time of exit from Canada.

Exercise 5

Doctor Quick

July 1, 2004 — acquired an option (capital property) with an adjusted cost base of $5,000.

Feb. 1, 2005 — transaction resulted in a capital loss of $3,000 (i.e., $2,000 – $5,000) of which only $1,500 would be recognized since 50% of the option was for a principal residence.

Doctor Slow

Feb. 1, 2005 — acquired an option with an adjusted cost base of $2,000.

May 1, 2005 — acquired a property with an adjusted cost base and a capital cost of $102,000 ($100,000 + $2,000).

Devalued Properties Ltd.

July 1, 2004 — received business income of $5,000; not a capital gain.

May 1, 2005 — received business income of $100,000; not a capital gain. May subtract the cost of property inventory to arrive at income for tax purposes.

— note that section 49 is not applicable if the gain is not a capital gain.

Exercise 6

(A) Since they are related by marriage [pars. 251(2)(a) and (6)(b)], they are not at arm's length.

(B) Since they are not considered to be related by blood [par. 251(6)(a)], they are at arm's length.

(C) Since they are still legally married, they are not at arm's length.

(D) The facts of a situation can determine that two unrelated persons are not at arm's length [par. 251(1)(b)].

Exercise 7

	James (seller or transferor)	*Hayden* (purchaser or transferee)
(A) sale at $2,000	has proceeds of $2,000 and, hence, a capital gain of $800 (i.e., $2,000 – $1,200)	deemed [par. 69(1)(a)] to have acquired at $1,500 resulting in potential double-counting of $500 gain
(B) sale at $1,200	deemed [par. 69(1)(b)] to have proceeds of $1,500 and, hence, a capital gain of $300	acquired at $1,200 resulting in potential double-counting of $300 gain
(C) gift	deemed [par. 69(1)(b)] to have proceeds of $1,500	deemed [par. 69(1)(c)] to have acquired at $1,500

Exercise 8

(A) (i) Since a gift is a transfer, section 73 would automatically deem that Alice's proceeds of disposition are equal to her adjusted cost base ($12,000), resulting in no capital gain.

(ii) Alice would be subject to the income attribution rules [sec. 74.1] on any dividends from the shares, because a gift would not meet the exception in paragraph 74.5(1)(a), since the fair market value of the property transferred exceeded the fair market value of the consideration received and an election under subsection 73(1) was not made.

(iii) Alice would also be subject to capital gains attribution [sec. 74.2] for the same reason as discussed in part (A)(ii) above. There would be full capital gains attribution on all substituted property [IT-511R, par. 27].

(B) (i) Since Alice does elect under subsection 73(1), subparagraph 69(1)(b)(ii) with which the transaction conforms, will apply, since the cash consideration ($15,000) was equal to the fair market value of the property transferred. A capital gain of $3,000 would be triggered.

(ii) There would be no income or capital gains attribution, because Alice has conformed with the paragraph 74.5(1)(a) exception. The fair market value of the property transferred did not exceed the fair market value of the consideration received and an election under subsection 73(1) was made.

(C) (i) Unless Alice elects not to have the provisions of section 73 apply, there will be no capital gain triggered on the transfer to her husband.

(ii) Although Alice has received consideration (debt) with a face value ($15,000) equal to the fair market value of the property transferred, the interest rate must be at least equal to the prescribed rate at the time or a commercial rate [spar. 74.5(1)(b)(i)]. In addition, paragraph 74.5(1)(c) requires that Alice elect under subsection 73(1). Therefore, Alice will be subject to both income and capital gains attribution.

(D) The result would be the same as in (A) above since the shares would be considered substituted property for a transfer of cash for no consideration.

(E) The result would be the same as in (C) above since the shares would be considered substituted property.

Exercise 9

If section 22 is not used, Mr. Flogger must still include in income last year's reserve of $6,500. However, the loss of $9,000 will be regarded as a capital loss which is only fractionally deductible and can be offset only against taxable capital gains. Since Mr. Sucker has not included any amount as income in respect of these accounts receivable, he will not be allowed a deduction for a reserve or for bad debts because the conditions of paragraphs 20(1)(l) or 20(1)(p) will not be met. If Mr. Sucker collects more than the $36,000 fair market value, the excess will be a capital gain and, if he collects less than $36,000, the difference will be a capital loss.

CHAPTER 9
Other Sources of Income and Deductions in Computing Income

Exercise 1

The $200 monthly payments made for Ursalla's support prior to November 1st are income to Ursalla and deductions to Uriah as long as the agreement provides for their being considered as part of the agreement and the agreement makes a specific reference to subsection 56.1(3). The payments of $200 for November and December are income to Ursalla and deductions to Uriah [pars. 56(1)(b) and 60(b)].

The mortgage payments of $400 would qualify as income to Ursalla and deductions for Uriah since they are considered to be an allowance as referred to in paragraphs 56(1)(b) and 60(b) [ssecs. 56.1(2) and 60.1(2)], as long as the conditions of these provisions are met. Conceivably, if the payments are recognized in the agreement, then the conditions would be met.

The $700 monthly support payments for the children and the medical expense payments are neither income to Ursalla nor deductions for Uriah, since they are child support amounts [ssec. 56.1(4)].

Exercise 2

The maximum amount that Don is able to deduct in respect of a spousal RRSP is his annual contribution limit, less any contributions made to his own RRSP in respect of the year.

Don's annual contribution limit for 2005 is calculated as the lesser of 18% of his 2004 earned income (i.e., $11,916 as calculated below) and the RRSP dollar limit for 2005, which is $16,500, less the PA reported by his employer in respect of 2004 of $6,084.

Don's earned income [ssec. 146(1)] for 2004 is calculated as:

Employment income — Subdivision a	$68,400	
Add: RPP contribution	2,800	$71,200
Rental loss		(5,000)
Earned income		$66,200
18% thereof		$11,916

Therefore, Don is able to deduct $5,832 (i.e., $11,916 − $6,084) of RRSP contributions in 2005. Since he has already contributed $5,000 to a spousal RRSP, he can either contribute $832 to his own RRSP, or an additional $832 to the spousal RRSP for 2005.

Exercise 3

Mr. Retired is able to contribute $15,800 to an RRSP for 2005 [(lesser of 18% of his earned income from 2004 (i.e., 18% of $120,000) and $16,500) less his 2004 PA of $700]. He may make this annual contribution to either his own or a spousal RRSP, as long as the total of the contributions does not exceed $15,800. These contributions may be made in the year or within 60 days of December 31, 2005.

He does not have to include the lump-sum transfer from his RPP in his income nor does he get an offsetting deduction [ssec. 147.3(9)], as long as it is eligible to be transferred [ssec. 147.3(4)].

Mr. Retired is able to transfer $44,000 to his RRSPs in respect of his retiring allowance. Since all of his employer's contributions have vested, he is able to contribute $2,000 for each of the 22 pre-'96 years of employment, including the part year for 1974. Since he is able to make such a transfer in the year or within 60 days of the year under paragraph 60(j.1), he may make an additional contribution of $4,000 ($44,000 less his initial contribution of $40,000) in the first 60 days of 2006 and he will be able to deduct the full $44,000 in his 2005 return.

Mr. Retired may also make a one-time additional $2,000 contribution to his RRSP for 2005 without incurring penalties. He will not receive a deduction for this additional contribution, but as long as he has enough earned income in 2006 to deduct at least $2,000 in respect of 2007, the year prior to the year in which he must remove the funds from the plan (i.e., at the end of the year in which he turns 69, which is 2008), he will not be double-taxed on the funds when they are withdrawn from the plan. This will be the case if, instead of making a $2,000 contribution in 2007, he uses the carryforward rules to deduct the $2,000. It may also be worthwhile for Mr. Retired to contribute the additional $2,000 in 2005 if he expects to have enough earned income in 2007 to make a $2,000 contribution in 2008. Although he is not able to make a contribution to his RRSP in 2009, since his RRSP matured at the end of 2008, he is able to take an RRSP deduction in 2008 using the carryforward rules.

Exercise 4

Allowable moving expense deduction

(A) 2004		
Par. 62(3)(a)	Travelling cost — air fare	$ 1,300
Par. 62(3)(b)	Household effects — transporting	1,000
Par. 62(3)(e)	Selling costs of Vancouver residence	
	— legal fees	500
	— real estate commission	10,000
Par. 62(3)(f)	Allowable purchase cost of Montreal residence	
	— legal fees	1,000
	— Quebec transfer tax	300
Total potential deductions		$14,100

		Less		
	Par. 62(1)(*c*)	Amount paid by the employer not included income	$ 5,000	
			$ 9,100	

Par. 62(1)(*f*)	Deduction restricted to income from new work location — 2005 .... $ 7,000

(B) 2005

Ssec. 62(1)	Balance deductible from income from the new location only in 2006	2,100
		$ 9,100

Exercise 5

This problem situation does not appear to be affected by subsection 63(2.2). This situation does not involve a single parent attending a qualifying education program or both parents attending a qualifying education program at the same time, as the legislation requires. Therefore, the limits in subsection 63(2.3) are not applicable.

Cathy Childcare's maximum deduction under section 63 is the lesser of:

(A) the least of:
 (i) amount paid in the year
 ($200 × 52) $10,400

 (ii) 1 × $4,000 = $ 4,000

 2 × $7,000 = $14,000 ....
 ....$18,000

 (iii) $2/3$ × earned income
 ($2/3$ × ($47,000
 + $4,000)) $34,000

 least amount................... $10,400

(B) the sum of:
 (i) $175 × 2 = $350

 (ii) $100 × 1 = 100 × 30
 $450 weeks = $13,500

 Lesser amount $10,400

Charles Childcare's maximum deduction under section 63 is the least of:

 (a) $200 × 52 weeks = $10,400
 (b) 1 child × $4,000 = $ 4,000
 2 children × $7,000 = $14,000 $18,000 $10,400
 (c) $2/3$ × earned income ($24,450)[1] = $16,300

 minus amount deducted by Cathy 10,400
 Nil

—NOTE TO SOLUTION

 (1) Earned income
 Gross salary................. $23,000
 Taxable benefits 850
 Scholarship ($3,600 – $3,000) 600
 $24,450

Note that earned income under subsection 63(3) is defined differently than earned income under subsection 146(1) for a registered retirement savings plan.

CHAPTER 10
Computation of Taxable Income and Taxes Payable for Individuals

Exercise 1

(A)		2003	2004	2005
Par. 3(*a*): Income from non-capital sources (≥0):				
Property income		$ 1,000	Nil	$ 2,000
Par. 3(*b*): Net taxable capital gains (≥0).				
Taxable capital gains				
(see Schedule 1, Part (A) below)		$18,750	$25,000	$ 5,625
Allowable capital losses		(7,500)	Nil	(11,250)
		$11,250	$25,000	Nil
Par. 3(*c*): Par. 3(*a*) + par. 3(*b*)		$12,250	$25,000	$ 2,000
Par. 3(*d*): Losses from non-capital source and A.B.I.L.:				
Property loss		Nil	$(7,000)	Nil
A.B.I.L..........................		Nil	(15,000)	Nil
Division B income		$12,250	$ 3,000	$ 2,000
(B) Deduct: Net capital losses (see Schedule 1, Part (B) below for maximum)		(4,102)	(Nil)	Nil
Non-capital losses		Nil	Nil	Nil
Taxable income (max. equal to personal tax credit base)		$ 8,148	$ 3,000	$ 2,000

SCHEDULE 1

	2003	2004	2005
(A) Net taxable capital gains — Net T.C.G. (Net allowable capital losses — Net A.C.L.)			
Taxable capital gains (T.C.G.)	$18,750	$ 25,000	$ 5,625
Allowable capital losses (A.C.L.) ...	(7,500)	—	(11,250)
	$11,250	$ 25,000	$ (5,625)

(B) Net capital losses [pars. 111(1)(*b*), (1.1)(*a*) and (8)(*a*)].

	2003	2004	2005
Lesser of:			
(i) Net T.C.G.s for the year...	$11,250	$25,000	Nil
(ii) Total of adjusted net C.L.s	$ 7,500	$ 8,287	$8,287
Lesser amount	$7,500	$8,287	Nil

(C) Loss continuity schedule

	2001	2005	Total
Net C.L	$ 7,500	$5,625	$13,125
Utilized in 2003	(4,102)	N/A	(4,102)
Available in 2006	$ 3,398	$5,625	$ 9,023

Exercise 2

(A) Personal tax credits [sec. 118]

Par. 118(1)(*a*)	Basic personal tax credit base	$ 8,148
	Dolly's tax credit base: $6,919 – ($3,000 – $692)	4,611
Par. 118(1)(*d*)	Don[1]: over 18 years old and not infirm	Nil
Par. 118(1)(*d*)	Dave's tax credit base[2]: $3,848 – ($3,200 – $5,460)	3,848
Par. 118(1)(*d*)	Mother's tax credit base[3]: $3,848 – ($6,000 – $5,460): claim	Nil
Par. 118(1)(c.1)	Alternative caregiver credit[3]	3,848
	Total tax credit base[4]	$20,455
	Total personal tax credits @ 16%	$ 3,273

—NOTES TO SOLUTION

(1) Don's father may claim the transferred tuition fee and education tax credit, since Don's income tax will be completely offset by his basic personal tax credit [ssec. 118.9(1)].

(2) The alternative caregiver tax credit of $616 would have the same base of $3,848 (i.e., $616/.16).

(3) The alternative caregiver tax credit of $616 would have a higher base of $3,848 which would not be reduced, since the mother's income is under $13,141.

(4) An impairment tax credit of $1,055 ($6,596 × 16%) is also available in respect of the mother and son Dave, if their impairment is certified by a medical doctor [ssec. 118.3(1)].

Exercise 3

(A) Optimum personal tax credit:

Jack's tax credit base:

Par. 118(1)(*a*) — Jack		$ 8,148
— Jill: $6,919 – ($9,600 – $692)		Nil[1]
Par. 118(1)(*b*)		Nil[2]
		$ 8,148
Jack's tax credit @ 16%		$ 1,304

Jill's tax credit base:

Spar. 118(1)(*b*)(i) — Jill		$ 8,148
Spar. 118(1)(*b*)(ii) — one of Jill's children[3]		6,919
		$15,067
Jill's tax credits @ 16%		$ 2,411

(B) In 2006, Jack and Jill could each claim a basic personal tax credit. Neither is eligible for the equivalent-to-married tax credit.

— NOTES TO SOLUTION

(1) All income of a spouse during the year of marriage is used in determining a spousal tax credit [spar. 118(1)(a)(ii)].

(2) Jack does not have the option of claiming either of the children under paragraph 118(1)(b) since they were not related to nor living with him at the time during the year that he was single.

(3) Jill has the option of claiming either Jack under paragraph 118(1)(a) (however, his income is too high in this fact situation) or one of her children under paragraph 118(1)(b) since she falls into both paragraphs [IT-513R par. 27]. It would appear that Jack and Jill cannot both claim each other at the same time according to a court decision which determined that spouses cannot simultaneously support each other. (See *The Queen v. Robichaud*, (F.C.T.D.) 83 DTC 5265.)

Exercise 4

Par. 8(1)(m)	$300 contribution is an employment deduction.
Par. 56(1)(a)	$800 is pension income.
Ssecs. 118(3), (7)	Nil since the amount is not from a life annuity, as required in the definition of "qualified pension income" [ssec. 118(7)].

Exercise 5

(A) Division B and taxable income.................................	$5,000
Federal tax @ 16% of $5,000.....................................	$ 800
Less: basic personal tax credit..................................	1,282
Federal tax payable	Nil
Credits available for transfer:	
Tuition fee tax credit (16% of $1,800)......................	$ 288
Education tax credit (16% of $400 × 8)......................	512
Total...	$ 800
Amount deductible by qualified transferee:	
Lesser of:	
(a) $800	
(b) student's tuition fee and education tax credit	$ 800
Less: amount of tax credit required to reduce student's tax payable to nil	Nil
Net amount deductible by transferee	$ 800

Note that the Employment Insurance premium and CPP contribution tax credits cannot be transferred.

(B) If Sammy was married, his wife could deduct the $800 in tuition fee and education tax credit, since Sammy's federal tax, after his personal tax credit, is nil [sec. 118.7]. Sammy's parent or grandparent can deduct all or some part of the $800 as a tax credit, if Sammy so designates.

Exercise 6

Tax payable by Tina:		
Division B income and taxable income		$ 9,005
Federal tax 16% of $9,005		$ 1,441
Less: basic personal tax credit.......................	$1,304	
other tax credits (age, pension)	709	2,013
Federal tax payable..		Nil

Transferable tax credits available:

Age credit (16% of $3,979)	$ 637
Pension credit (16% of $450)	72
Total credits available to Tina's husband	$ 709
Less: federal tax payable net of basic personal tax credit ($1,441 − $1,304)	137
	$ 572

Exercise 7

Income increased by grossed-up dividend		**$1,125**
Increase in federal tax @ 29% of $1,125		$ 326
Less increase in tax credits:		
Married credit with subsection 82(3) election [16% of ($6,919 − (excess, if any, of nil − $692))]	$ 1,107	
Married credit without election [16% of ($6,919 − ($1,125 − $692))]	(1,038) $ 69	
Dividend tax credit (13⅓% of $1,125)	150	219
Net federal tax cost		$ 107

Therefore, the subsection 82(3) election should not be made in this case.

Exercise 8

Federal foreign tax credit

lesser of:

(i) $225

(ii) $\dfrac{\$1,500}{\$156,800 - \$6,000} \times (\$34,000 + \$50^*) = \underline{\$339}$ $\Big\}$ $225

* The dividend tax credit is equal to 13⅓% of the grossed-up dividend of $375 (i.e., ⁵⁄₄ × $300).

Exercise 9

	Regular Part I Tax		Minimum Tax	
(A) $100 interest	($100 × .29) =	$29	($100 × .16) =	$16
(B) $100 cash dividend ($125 grossed up)	$125 × .29 = $36		($100 × .16)=	$16
	DTC (17)	$19		
(C) $100 capital gains ($50 taxable capital gains)	($50 × .29)	$15	($50 + $30) × .16	$13

Exercise 10

Taxable income	$100,000
Add: C.C.A. loss on resource property shelter	97,500
	$197,500
Less: gross-up of dividends	(7,500)
Adjusted taxable income	$190,000
Less: basic exemption	(40,000)
	$150,000

Minimum tax before minimum tax credit (16% of $150,000)		$ 24,000
Less basic minimum tax credits:		
Basic personal (16% × $8,148)	$1,304	
Employment Insurance premiums........................	122	
CPP contributions	298	1,724
Minimum amount		$ 22,276

Betty Bucks' Part I tax will be her minimum amount of $22,276 and $7,983 ($22,276 − $14,293) can be carried forward and applied to reduce tax payable in a subsequent year.

CHAPTER 11
Computation of Taxable Income and Tax after General Reductions for Corporations

Exercise 1

		2003		2004		2005	
Income under Division B.......		$(7,350)		$22,050		$14,700	
Deduct: charitable donations limited by 75% of income above							
— carried forward	Nil			$ 2,625		Nil	
— current	Nil	Nil		4,700	(7,325)	$11,025[1]	(11,025)
unlimited charitable donation							
— carried forward	Nil			—		$ 3,675	
— current	Nil	Nil		$14,725[2]	(14,725)	—	(3,675)[3]
non-capital loss from 2003[4]		Nil		Nil		Nil	
Taxable income		Nil		Nil		Nil	

— *NOTES TO SOLUTION*

(1) $975 is available to carry forward to 2006 and an additional four years to 2010.

(2) If the donation of the land gave rise to a capital gain, the taxable portion would be included in the amount of income under Division B.

(3) $1,300 is available to carry forward to 2006 to 2009.

(4) $7,350 is available to carry forward from 2004 to 2010 [10 years for taxation years ending after March 22, 2004.]

Exercise 2

	2003	2004	2005
Alternative A: Claiming maximum charitable donations			
Income before C.C.A.......................	$ 100,000	$115,000	$132,250
C.C.A...................................	(200,000)	(101,667)[1]	(116,917)
Income (loss) under Division B	$(100,000)	$ 13,333	$ 15,333
Charitable donations:			
— Carried forward...................	Nil	(10,000)[1]	(11,500)[1]
— Current	Nil	Nil	Nil
Non-capital loss carried forward from 2003	n/a	(3,333)	(3,833)[2]
Taxable income	Nil	Nil	Nil
Alternative B: Non-capital loss utilization			
Income before C.C.A.......................	$100,000	$115,000	$132,250
C.C.A.	(107,167)[3]	(86,333)	(132,250)

	2003	2004	2005
Income (loss) under Division B.............	$ (7,167)	$ 28,667	Nil
Charitable donations:			
— carried forward...................	Nil	(21,500)	Nil
— current	Nil	Nil	Nil
Non-capital loss carried forward from 2003	n/a	(7,167)[3]	Nil
Taxable income......................	Nil	Nil	Nil

Alternative C: Maximum donation and non-capital loss utilization

	2003	2004	2005
Income before C.C.A.....................	$100,000	$115,000	$132,250
C.C.A.	(107,166)	(101,667)	(116,917)
Income (loss) under Division B.............	$ (7,166)	$ 13,333	$ 15,333
Charitable donations:			
— Carried forward	Nil	(10,000)[4]	(11,500)[4]
— Current.........................	Nil	Nil	Nil
Non-capital loss carried forward from 2003	n/a	(3,333)	(3,833)
Taxable income..........................	Nil	Nil	Nil

- **Summary**

	Alternatives		
	A	B	C
Total donations claimed	$ 21,500	$ 21,500	$ 21,500
Total C.C.A. claimed	418,584	325,750	325,750
Unclaimed non-capital loss	92,834	Nil	Nil

—NOTES TO SOLUTION

(1) C.C.A. amount selected to provide sufficient Division B income for a deduction of charitable donations (maximum of 75% of Division B income for 2003 and subsequent years). The 1999 charitable donations would, otherwise, expire after 2004.

(2) $92,834 of non-capital loss from 2003 remains.

(3) Determined by looking forward to 2004 and creating the maximum non-capital loss in 2003 that can be fully utilized in 2004.

(4) Uses the five-year carryforward of charitable donations to the maximum — i.e., the $11,500 donations of 2000 may be carried forward to 2005, as in Alternative A.

Exercise 3

Sum of: loss from business.......................................	$129,000
allowable business investment loss	8,000
dividends deductible under sec. 112	10,750
net capital loss deducted [$1/2 \times$ ($46,400 – $12,000)]	17,200[1]
	$164,950
Less: income from property $32,250	
net taxable capital gains [$1/2 \times$ ($46,400 – $12,000)] ...... 17,200[1]	(49,450)
Non-capital loss for the year	$115,500

—NOTE TO SOLUTION

(1) The corporation may deduct the net capital loss from income even though it has no impact on the taxable income. However, the deduction is restricted to the net taxable capital gain for the year. Once deducted, the net capital loss can be included in the non-capital loss computation.

Exercise 4

Allowable capital loss (excluding A.B.I.L.)	$ 51,750
Less: taxable capital gain	(4,700)
Net	$ 47,050
Add: unutilized allowable business investment loss in respect of which the carryover period expires in the year (i.e., the 10th carryforward year)	Nil
Net capital loss for the year	$ 47,050

Exercise 5

	Alternative A[1]	Alternative B[1]
Income from business	$55,500	$55,500
Taxable capital gains	37,000	37,000
Income under Division B	$92,500	$92,500
Less: net capital losses	(37,000)[2]	(10,000)[2]
non-capital losses	(55,500)	(82,500)
Taxable income	Nil	Nil

Summary:

Unutilized non-capital losses	$27,000	Nil
Unutilized net capital losses	3,000[2]	$30,000[2]

— *NOTES TO SOLUTION*

(1) In Alternative A, maximum net capital losses are claimed before non-capital losses. In Alternative B, maximum non-capital losses are claimed before net capital losses.

	Alternative A	Alternative B
1999 Net capital losses available	$60,000	$60,000
Adjusted to 2005 ($60,000 × ½ / ¾)	40,000	40,000
Utilized in 2005 (limited to t.c.g.)	(37,000)	(10,000)
Available to carryforward	$ 3,000	$30,000

Exercise 6

Part (a)

Because of the acquisition of control by Holdco Ltd., Loser Ltd. is deemed to have a taxation year-end on March 9, 2005 [ssecs. 249(4) and 256(9)]. This taxation year will be only 69 days long, having commenced on January 1, 2005. The paragraph 249(4)(c) exception does not apply, since the date of the acquisition of control is more than seven days after the last year-end.

Loser Ltd. will be required to make certain adjustments as of March 9, 2005. The adjustments will increase the company's business losses of $3,000 to $48,000, as follows:

Business losses	$ 3,000
Excess of U.C.C. ($70,000) over fair market value ($40,000) of assets in Class 8 [ssec. 111(5.1)]	30,000
Accrued inventory losses	Nil
Doubtful accounts receivable deemed to be actual bad debts [ssec. 111(5.3)]	15,000
Losses from non-capital sources (all from business)	$48,000

The balance in the C.E.C. account is not affected by the acquisition of control, because there was no unrealized loss at the time of the acquisition of control (i.e., $^3/_4$ of the fair market value of $68,000 = $51,000 which is greater than the $50,000 C.E.C. account balance).

Division B income for the deemed taxation year ended March 9, 2005 would be computed as follows:

Par. 3(a):	Income from non-capital sources..............		Nil
Par. 3(b):	Net taxable capital gains:		
	Election under par. 111(4)(e) on land ($^1/_2$ × $56,000)...................................	$28,000	
	Allowable capital losses	Nil	$28,000
Par. 3(c):	Par. 3(a) + par. 3(b).....................................		$28,000
Par. 3(d):	Losses from non-capital sources (above)		(48,000)
	Division B income and taxable income		Nil

Since the net capital losses of $30,000 will expire on March 10, 2005, if nothing is done, the corporation should deduct the net capital losses of $30,000. Although the taxable income will be unaffected, the non-capital losses can be increased by this amount.

The non-capital loss for the deemed year ending March 10, 2005, would be:

Losses from business sources..	$48,000
Add: net capital losses deducted at $^1/_2$ inclusion rate ($30,000 × $^4/_3$ × $^1/_2$)	20,000
	$68,000
Less: par. 3(c) income determined above............................	28,000
Non-capital loss for deemed year	$40,000

The adjusted cost base of the land will be increased by the amount of the gain elected under paragraph 111(4)(e) to $256,000 (i.e., $200,000 + $56,000) on March 10, 2005.

The undepreciated capital cost in Loser's Class 8 will be reduced from $70,000 to $40,000 as at March 10, 2005 [ssec. 111(5.1)]. Loser Ltd. will be deemed to have deducted the $30,000 as capital cost allowance for taxation years ending before March 10, 2005; thereby, making Loser Ltd. liable for recapture on that amount if the assets are subsequently sold.

Similarly, the corporation will be deemed to have made a claim for bad debts totalling $15,000 under paragraph 20(1)(p) [ssec. 111(5.3)]. Accordingly, Loser Ltd.'s accounts receivable will be $225,000 as at March 10, 2005, the start of its next taxation year.

Subsection 111(5) will permit the deduction by Loser Limited of the 2004 $600,000 non-capital losses in any year up to 2010 including the short deemed taxation year (if the corporation reverts to a December 31 year-end) after which they will expire. However, in order to be deducted, the widget manufacturing business must be carried on by Loser Ltd. for profit or with a reasonable expectation of profit throughout each of those taxation years. Similarly, the $40,000 non-capital losses of the March 9, 2005 taxation year will be eligible for carryforward 10 years, under the same conditions, to December 31, 2014 if the company reverts to a December 31 year-end. It appears that this condition will be met, since Holdco Ltd. will provide capital and management to turn Loser's business around. The non-capital losses may be deducted in a carryforward year from the incomes of the widget manufacturing business and a business with similar products in that year.

Part (b)

Loser Limited would still have business losses of $3,000 plus the deemed business loss on the Class 8 assets of $30,000 and the loss on the accounts receivable of $15,000, which gives a total of $48,000 of losses from business sources. In addition, Loser Limited has a property loss of $10,000.

The 1999 net capital loss of $30,000 is $20,000 when converted from a $^3/_4$ to a $^1/_2$ inclusion rate.

The minimum designated proceeds or deemed proceeds would be as follows [par. 111(4)(e)]:

Deemed proceeds = 2 × ($20,000 net capital losses plus $10,000 property losses)
plus A.C.B. of the land of $200,000
= $260,000

Now, the Division B and taxable income for the deemed taxation year ended March 9, 2005 would be:

Par. 3(a)	Income from non-capital sources		Nil
Par. 3(b)	Net taxable capital gains:		
	Election under par. 111(4)(e) —		
	($260,000 – $200,000) × ½	$30,000	
	Less allowable capital losses	Nil	$30,000
Par. 3(c)	....		$30,000
Par. 3(d)	Losses from non-capital sources:		
	Business losses	$48,000	
	Property losses	10,000	(58,000)
Division B income...............................			Nil
Division C deductions:			
Net capital losses.........................			$20,000
Taxable income			Nil

Note how just enough paragraph 3(c) income was created (i.e., $30,000) to offset the property loss of $10,000 plus the net capital loss of $20,000, both of which are about to expire.

The non-capital loss balance for the deemed year ended March 9, 2005 would be:

Par. 3(d) losses	$58,000
Add: net capital losses deducted............................	20,000
	$78,000
Less: par. 3(c) income	(30,000)
Total non-capital loss for the year ended March 9, 2005	$48,000

The non-capital loss of $48,000 for the year ended March 9, 2005 would be added to the 2004 non-capital loss balance to give a total of $648,000 to be deducted in the future. If Loser Limited reverts to a December 31 year-end, these could be deducted in any year that the loss business is carried on against income of the business that generated the loss or against business income from the sale of similar products up to:

2004 non-capital loss 2013
March 2005 non-capital loss 2014

The adjusted cost base of the land will now be increased to $260,000.

Exercise 7

	2004	2005
Net income (loss) per financial accounting statements......................	$ (53,000)	$126,000
Add total of items not deductible for tax purposes.........................	127,700	240,700
	$ 74,700	$366,700
Less C.C.A. ($7,900 less in 2004)	51,700	51,670
Income for tax purposes..................	$ 23,000	$315,030
Inter-company dividends $23,000		$23,000

	2004	2005	
Charitable donations (max. 75% of income):			
Carried over	—	15,000	
Current	Nil	15,000	
Non-capital loss carryover	—	23,000	18,000	71,000
Taxable income	Nil	$244,030	
Taxable income originally computed....	Nil	$245,610	

Conclusion:

This calculation produces better results. All of the inter-company dividends are fully deductible in 2004 with the reduction of the capital cost allowance by $7,900. Both alternatives allowed, in total, an equal amount of non-capital losses and donations to be claimed over the two-year period. Although the original calculation enabled $6,320 (i.e., $59,600 + $50,090 – $51,700 – $51,670) more capital cost allowance to be claimed in total over the two years, the original calculation could not utilize $7,900 of the potential dividend deduction. This alternative increases the future C.C.A. write-offs by $6,320 as shown below.

Capital cost allowances were computed as follows:	Building Class 1: 4%	Equipment Class 8: 20%
2005: U.C.C., January 1, 2005	$ 356,250	$ 187,100*
C.C.A. (total deduction: $51,670)	(14,250)	(37,420)
2006: U.C.C., January 1, 2006	$ 342,000	$ 149,680
U.C.C. originally computed	$ 342,000	$ 143,360

* $179,200 + $7,900.

Exercise 8

Division B income..	$116,850
Less: charitable donations limited to 75% of $116,850 or $87,638	
— carried forward	$10,250
— current	77,388[1]	(87,638)
dividends from taxable Canadian corporations	(12,300)
subtotal	$ 16,912
non-capital losses[2]	(16,912)
net capital losses[2] (not to exceed the taxable capital gains for the year)	(Nil)[4]
Taxable income	Nil

— *NOTES TO SOLUTION*

(1) The balance of $2,612 in current charitable donations may be carried forward to the next five years.

(2) These carried-over losses may be claimed in a different sequence and in different amounts from that shown. For example, if there is little prospect of future capital gains, the corporation might make the following deductions:

subtotal	$16,912
net capital losses ($41,000 × 1/2 / 3/4)[4]	(27,333)
non-capital losses	Nil
taxable income	Nil

(3) The balance of the net capital losses may be carried forward indefinitely.

(4) Net capital losses claimed are added to the non-capital loss balance carried forward.

Exercise 9

Capital:

Capital stock [par. 181.2(3)(a)]	$360,000,000
Bonds payable [par. 181.2(3)(d)]	350,000,000
Accounts payable [par. 181.2(3)(f)]	5,000,000
Deferred revenue	10,000,000[1]
Deficit [par. 181.2(3)(i)]	(100,000,000)
Taxable capital	$625,000,000[2]

Investment allowance:

Shares in Canadian and U.S. companies [par. 181.2(4)(a)]	$425,000,000
Demand loan [par. 181.2(4)(b)]	75,000,000
Total investment allowance	$500,000,000[3]
Taxable capital ($625,000,000 − $500,000,000)	$125,000,000
Taxable capital employed in Canada (92%[4] of $125,000,000)	$115,000,000
Capital deduction	50,000,000
Amount subject to Part I.3 tax	$ 65,000,000
Part I.3 tax at 0.175%	$ 113,750 (A)
Surtax for the year (4% of 28% of $20,000,000)	$ 224,000
Canadian surtax payable (92%[4] of $224,000)	$ 206,080 (B)
Part I.3 tax liability: (A) − (B) ($113,750 − $206,080)	Nil

—*NOTES TO SOLUTION*

(1) Reserves are required to be included in capital to the extent that they are not deductible for income tax purposes [par. 181.2(3)(b)]. A reserve for prepaid rent is allowed [spar. 20(1)(m)(iii)]. However, a reserve for guarantee fees is specifically denied [ssec. 20(7)].

(2) Since paragraph 20(1)(l) allows a reserve in respect of doubtful debts, the $1,000,000 allowance need not be included in capital (assuming that the paragraph 20(1)(l) reserve was actually claimed for tax purposes).

(3) The three-year term deposits do not qualify for the investment allowance [par. 181.2(4)(d)] by virtue of the definition of "long-term debt" [ssec. 181(1)].

(4) A full 10% abatement would have amounted to $2,000,000 (i.e., 10% of $20,000,000). Since the abatement was $1,840,000, 92% (i.e., $1,840,000 / $2,000,000) of the income must have been earned in a province.

Exercise 10

$$MC = \text{lesser of: (a) } \frac{100}{85} \times \$543,750 = \underline{\$639,706}$$

$$\left.\begin{array}{l} \\ \\ \end{array}\right\} \$639,706$$

$$\text{(b) } \$750,000$$

$$ML = \text{lesser of: (a) } \frac{100}{75} \times \$2,855,000 = \underline{\$3,806,667}$$

$$\left.\begin{array}{l} \\ \\ \end{array}\right\} \$3,750,000$$

$$\text{(b) } \$3,750,000$$

$$MP = \frac{MC + ML}{C + L} \times ADJUBI$$

$$= \frac{\$639,706 + \$3,750,000}{\$750,000 + 3,750,000} \times \$375,000 = \$365,809$$

Manufacturing and processing profits deduction:
7% of lesser of:

(a) M&P profits		$365,809
(b) Taxable income ($500,000 – 250,000)	$250,000	
Less: 3 × foreign business tax credit		
(3 × $15,000)......................	(45,000)	$205,000

7% of $205,000 = $14,350

Exercise 11

Income from Japan in Canadian dollars (61,318,408 yen × .01206)		$ 739,500
Total income under Division B ($2,500,000 + $739,500)		$3,239,500
Less: Dividends deductible under sec. 112	$100,000	
Net capital losses carried forward (adjusted to current year inclusion rate)	25,000	125,000
Taxable income		$3,114,500
Tax @ 38%		$1,183,510
Less: general tax reduction @ 7% of 3,114,500...................		218,015
Net tax		$ 965,495

Foreign Business Tax Deduction

Least of: (a) amount paid (24,527,363 yen × .01206).............		$ 295,800

$$\text{(b)} \quad \frac{\text{income from Japan}}{\begin{array}{c}\text{Div. B income minus s. 112 ded.}\\ \text{and net capital loss ded.}\end{array}} \times \begin{array}{c}\text{tax otherwise}\\ \text{payable before}\\ \text{abatement plus surtax}\end{array}$$

$$= \frac{\$739,500}{\$3,239,500 - (\$100,000 + 25,000)} \times \begin{array}{c}(\$965,495 +\\ \$34,882^*) =\end{array} \quad \$\ 237,527$$

(c) Part I tax otherwise payable plus surtax minus foreign non-business tax credit ($965,495 + $34,882 – nil) $1,000,377

Therefore, the foreign tax deduction is $237,527.

* 4% of [$1,183,510 – (10% of $3,114,500)], or 4% of 28% of $3,114,500.

Exercise 12

Income under Division B		$2,645,000
Less: Charitable donations	$ 69,000	
Taxable dividends deductible under sec. 112	517,500	
Non-capital losses	127,600	714,100
Taxable income		$1,930,900
Tax @ 38%		$ 733,742
Less: Federal tax abatement (10% of 86% of $1,930,900).........		166,057
		$ 567,685
Add: Surtax[1]		21,626
Total		$ 589,311

Less: Non-business foreign tax credit (see Schedule 1)	$ 25,875	
Business foreign tax credit (see Schedule 2)	36,800	
Manufacturing and processing profits deduction (see Schedule 3)	104,650	
Tax reduction (see Schedule 4)	30,513	
Federal political contributions tax credit (max.)	650	198,488
Part I tax payable		$ 390,823

Schedule 1: Non-business foreign tax credit

Lesser of: (a) amount paid .... $ 25,875

(b) $\dfrac{\text{foreign non-business income}}{\text{Div. B income minus s. 112 ded. and net capital loss ded.}} \times$ tax otherwise payable after abatement plus surtax minus general tax reduction

$= \dfrac{\$172,500}{\$2,645,000 - (\$517,500 + 0)} \times \$558,798^2 ....$ $ 45,308

Schedule 2: Business foreign tax credit

Least of: (a) amount paid .... $ 36,800

(b) $\dfrac{\text{foreign business income}}{\text{Div. B income minus s. 112 ded. and net capital loss ded.}} \times$ tax otherwise payable before deductions plus surtax minus general tax reduction

$= \dfrac{\$115,000}{\$2,645,000 - (\$517,500 + 0)} \times \dfrac{(\$733,742 + \$21,626}{- 30,513)}$ $ 39,181

(c) $733,742 + $21,626 − $30,513 − $25,875 .... $698,980

Schedule 3: Manufacturing and processing profits deduction

7% of lesser of: (a) manufacturing and processing profits		$1,495,000
(b) taxable income	$1,930,900	
less: 3 × for. bus. tax credit (see Schedule 2)	110,400	$1,820,500

7% of $1,495,000 = $104,650

Schedule 4: Tax reduction

Taxable income	$1,930,900
Less 100/7 M&P profits deduction (100/7 × $104,650)	1,495,000
Net	$ 435,900
7% of $435,900	$ 30,513

—NOTES TO SOLUTION

(1) 4% of [$733,742 − (10% of $1,930,900)], or 4% of 28% of $1,930,900.

(2) $733,742 − $166,057 + $21,626. − $30,513 (Schedule 4)

Exercise 13

The total investment tax credit is 10% of $900,000 = $90,000.

Taxable income before c.c.a. on eligible property		$300,000
Less: c.c.a. on qualified property ($\frac{1}{2} \times$ 4% of $900,000)		18,000
Taxable income		$282,000
Net federal tax: @ 22.12% of $282,000		$ 62,378
Less: fed. pol. contributions tax credit	$ 500	
investment tax credit (limited to ($62,378 − $500))	61,878	$ (62,378)
Part I tax payable		Nil

Note that the $61,878 of investment tax credit will reduce the balance of U.C.C. in Class 1 in the following year. The remainder of $28,122 (i.e., $90,000 − $61,878) of ITC may be carried back three taxation years and forward 10 taxation years. Any amount used to reduce tax in a particular carryover year will reduce the U.C.C. in the year following the year of use or the year following the purchase, whichever is later.

Exercise 14

Earned investment tax credit of 10% of $3,500,000 = $350,000

Income under Division B before c.c.a. on eligible property		$2,645,000
Less: c.c.a. on eligible property ($\frac{1}{2} \times$ .30 $\times$ $3,500,000)		525,000
Income under Division B		$2,120,000
Less: charitable donations	$ 69,000	
taxable dividends deductible under sec. 112	517,500	
non-capital losses	127,600	714,100
Taxable income		$1,405,900
Tax @ 38%		$ 534,242
Less: federal tax abatement (10% of 86% of $1,405,900)		120,907
		$ 413,335
Add: surtax[1]		15,746
Total		$ 429,081
Less: manufacturing and processing profits deduction (see Schedule 1)	$67,900	
non-business foreign tax credit (see Schedule 2)	25,875	
business foreign tax credit (see Schedule 3)	36,800	
Tax reduction (see Schedule 4)	30,513	
federal political contribution tax credit	500	161,588
Part I tax payable before investment tax credit		$ 267,493
Investment tax credit		(267,493)
Part I tax payable		Nil

The remaining investment tax credit of $82,507 (i.e., $350,000 − $267,493) can be carried forward ten years.

The U.C.C. balance in Class 43 will be reduced by $267,493 in the following year and by the amount of the $82,507 remainder in subsequent years, if that amount is deducted.

Schedule 1: Manufacturing and processing profits deduction

7% of lesser of:

(a)	manufacturing and processing profits before c.c.a. on eligible property	$1,495,000
	less: c.c.a on eligible property ($\frac{1}{2} \times .30 \times \$3,500,000$)	525,000
	manufacturing and processing profits	$ 970,000
(b)	taxable income	$1,405,900
	less: $3 \times$ foreign business tax credit (see Schedule 3)	110,400
	net	$1,295,500
	7% of $970,000	$ 67,900

Schedule 2: Non-business foreign tax credit

Lesser of:

(a)	amount paid	$25,875
(b)	$\dfrac{\$172,500}{\$2,120,000 - \$517,500} \times \$398,568^2$	$42,904

Schedule 3: Business foreign tax credit

Least of:

(a)	amount paid	$ 36,800
(b)	$\dfrac{\$115,000}{\$2,120,000 - \$517,500} \times (\$534,242 + \$15,746^1 - 30,513)$	$37,279
(c)	$\$534,242 + \$15,746^1 - \$30,513 - \$25,875$	$493,600

Schedule 4: Tax reduction

Taxable income	$1,405,900
Less 100/7 M&P profits deduction ($100/7 \times \$67,900$)	970,000
Net	$ 435,900
7% of $435,900	$ 30,513

— *NOTES TO SOLUTION*

(1) 4% of [$534,242 – (10% of $1,405,900)], or 4% of 28% of $1,405,900.

(2) $534,242 – $120,907 + $15,746 – $30,513.

CHAPTER 12
Integration for Business and Investment Income of the Private Corporation

Exercise 1

[Note: The facts of this case are those of *The Queen v. Rochmore Investments Ltd.*, 76 DTC 6156. However, the legislation under which the case was decided did not contain a definition of "active business" or "specified investment business".]

Under the current legislation, "active business" is defined [ssecs. 125(7) and 248(1)] to exclude "a specified investment business" in such a way that if a business is not a specified investment business [ssec. 125(7)] (and is not a personal service business [ssec. 125(7)]), it is an active business. Note that the definition under subsection 125(7) includes an adventure in the nature of trade and is only applicable in respect of section 125.

In this particular case, the facts indicate that it is carrying on a specified investment business. It would appear that the principal purpose of the corporation's business is to derive income from interest on mortgage loans. It does not appear to be carrying on the business of a credit union and it is not in the business of leasing movable property. If it did, the corporation would be considered to be carrying on an active business. Since the corporation had no full-time employees, it cannot escape the definition of a specified investment business, to be treated as an active business, through paragraph (*a*) of the definition in subsection 125(7) which requires more than five full-time employees.

The only possibility for escape is in paragraph (*b*) of the definition of "specified investment business" in subsection 125(7). If the taxpayer company did not have more than five full-time employees because another corporation associated with it provided the services to the taxpayer corporation that would otherwise be performed by its own full-time employees, then the taxpayer corporation could be considered as carrying on an active business. In this case, the two principal operators of the taxpayer corporation own and manage a number of other companies. Further facts are required to determine if any of these other corporations are associated with the taxpayer corporation and if such an associated corporation provides services that would otherwise be provided by more than five full-time employees of the taxpayer corporation. This seems unlikely given the facts outlined in the case.

The taxpayer corporation, therefore, is likely carrying on a specified investment business. It is not carrying on a personal services business because it is not likely that the principals of the taxpayer corporation would reasonably be regarded as employees of the persons to whom the mortgage loans were made.

Exercise 2

(A) (i)   Mr. Beta is at arm's length with the corporation because his 25% ownership does not give him control [par. 251(2)(*b*)]. However, paragraph 251(1)(*b*) could always apply if the facts indicate that the non-related persons are not dealing at arm's length at a particular moment in time.

(ii) Mr. Beta and his brother are not at arm's length with the corporation [spar. 251(2)(*b*)(ii)]. Mr Beta and his brother form a related group; since they are siblings, each is related by blood [par. 251(6)(*a*)].

(iii) Mr. Delta is not at arm's length with the corporation [spar. 251(5)(*b*)(i)] because of the share purchase option. This provision deems Mr. Delta to control Alpha Corp. unless the exceptions in this subparagraph are met.

(iv) Mr. Epsilon is at arm's length with the corporation because of the exception, which is contingent on the death of Mr. Beta [spar. 251(5)(*b*)(i)], unless paragraph 251(1)(*b*) applies, as described in (i) above.

(B) (i)   The corporations are not at arm's length [spar. 251(2)(*c*)(iii)]. This subparagraph applies where Lambda Corp. is controlled by a person (i.e., A) and Tau Corp. is controlled by a related group (i.e., A and B). A is related to himself for purposes of share ownership [par. 251(5)(*c*)] and to his brother [par. 251(6)(*a*)].

(ii) The corporations are at arm's length because subparagraph 251(2)(*c*)(iv) does not apply where there is an unrelated group of persons controlling one corporation, unless the person controlling the other corporation is related to each member of the unrelated group. For example, if two first cousins control one corporation and their grandfather controls the other, the two corporations would be related. Of course, factual non-arm's length can always apply as described in (A)(i) above.

(iii) The corporations are related and, hence, they are not at arm's length [ssec. 251(3)]. This provision deems two corporations to be related where each corporation is related to another common corporation.

Exercise 3

(A) Jay-one Ltd. and Jay-two Ltd. are associated, both being controlled by the same person [par. 256(1)(*b*)]. Jay-one Ltd. and Jay-three Ltd., are associated [par. 256(1)(*a*)]. Since Janna has voting control of Jay-one Ltd. and Jay-one Ltd. in turn has voting control of Jay-three Ltd., then

Janna controls Jay-three Ltd. Therefore, all three corporations are controlled by the same person [par. 251(1)(b)]. As a result of this application of the association rule in paragraph 256(1)(b), the election under subsection 256(2) is not available to Jay-one Ltd., because Jay-three Ltd. and Jay-two Ltd. are associated without subsection 256(2).

(B) Famco Ltd. and Rayco Ltd. are associated [par. 256(1)(c)]. Famco Ltd. is controlled by Rayna's mother and Rayco Ltd. is controlled by Rayna. Rayna and her mother are related [par. 251(6)(a)]. Rayna owns at least 25% of the shares, which are not of a specified class, of both corporations.

(C) Adamco Ltd. and Kidco Ltd. are associated [par. 256(1)(d)]. Adamco Ltd. is controlled by Adam. Kidco Ltd. is controlled by the group consisting of Adam, his daughter and his son-in-law. Adam is related to himself [ssec. 256(1.5)], to his daughter [par. 251(6)(a)] and to his son-in-law [pars. 251(6)(a) and 252(1)(e) or par. 251(6)(b)]. Adam owns at least 25% of the shares which are not of a specified class of Kidco Ltd.

(D) Since both corporations are controlled by a group, paragraph 256(1)(e) is the only possibility for association. However, while Sisco Ltd. is controlled by a related group of sisters [par. 251(6)(a)], Cousco Ltd. is not controlled by a related group. The two sisters as a group do not control Cousco Ltd. One sister and her daughter do not control the company. Finally, cousins and aunts and nieces are not related by the rules in section 251 or 252. Therefore, the condition in paragraph 256(1)(e) fails and the two corporations are not associated unless subsection 256(5.1) can be used with the argument that control in fact is exercised by Sister One and Sister Two through direct or indirect influence on their daughters or unless subsection 256(2.1) is invoked on the basis that one of the main reasons for the separate existence of the two corporations is to reduce taxes.

Exercise 4

Taxit and Sibling are associated [par. 256(1)(c)]:

— each corporation is controlled by one person;

— the person who controlled one was related to the person who controlled the other;

— one of these persons owned not less than 25% of the shares which are not of a specified class of each corporation.

Since the two corporations are associated, they must share the small business deduction on a maximum of $250,000 of active business income for calendar year 2004. Subsection 125(3) requires that the corporations file an agreement, in prescribed form, allocating the $250,000 business limit. If an agreement is not filed within the time period indicated in subsection 125(4), that subsection empowers the Minister to make an allocation.

They could each gain their eligibility for the small business deduction on a full $250,000 by having Beta reduce her holdings in Taxit to below 25% or by having Beta convert her holdings in Taxit to shares of a specified class (i.e., in essence, non-voting preferred shares). However, this strategy would work only as long as there are no factors present of the kind that would enable the deeming provisions in subsection 256(2.1) to apply.

Exercise 5

Since neither corporation is controlled by one person, and both corporations are not controlled by the same group of persons, the only provision in subsection 256(1) that can potentially apply is paragraph 256(1)(e). That paragraph sets out three conditions, each of which must be met by the facts of the case for association.

(1) Each corporation must be controlled by a related group. — The group of brothers controlling Chutzpah Enterprises Limited is related [pars. 251(2)(a) and (6)(a)]. The group consisting of Bett and Dalled Chutzpah controlling Shlock Sales Limited are related by paragraph 251(6)(b) as brother-in-law and sister-in-law or by paragraph 251(6)(a) and paragraphs 252(2)(b) and (c). Therefore, the condition is met.

(2) Each of the members of one of the related groups was related to all of the members of the other related group. — Consider the group consisting of Aleph and Bett Chutzpah which is a related group controlling Chutzpah Enterprises Limited and the group Bett and Dalled Chutzpah which is a related group controlling Shlock Sales Limited. Aleph is related to his brother Bett, as discussed above, and to Dalled [pars. 251(2)(a) and (6)(a)]. Bett is related to himself [ssec. 256(1.5)] and his sister-in-law, Dalled, as discussed above. Therefore, the condition is met.

(3) One or more members of both related groups must own, either alone or together, not less than 25% of the issued shares of any class, other than a specified class, of shares of the capital stock of the other corporation. — Bett, who is a member of both related groups, owns alone the minimum 25% of the shares necessary to meet this condition. Common shares are not shares of a specified class [ssec. 256(1.1)].

Exercise 6

Part I tax payable

Part I Tax on Taxable Income

Taxable income	$ 79,700
Tax @ 38% on $79,700	$ 30,286
Deduct: Federal tax abatement (10% of $79,700)	7,970
Net	$ 22,316
Federal surtax @ 4% of ($30,286 − 10% of $79,700) (or 4% of 28% of $79,700)	893

Additional refundable tax (ART) — $6^2/_3$% × lesser of:

(a) AII	$ 7,000	
(b) TI − SBD amount (Schedule 1)	$ 3,500	
$\quad$ $6^2/_3$% of $3,500		233
Total		$ 23,442

Deduct: Non-business foreign tax credit (assumed)	$ 1,050	
$\quad$ Small business deduction (see Schedule 1)	12,192	
$\quad$ Manufacturing and processing profits deduction (see Schedule 2)	Nil	
$\quad$ General reduction (see Schedule 3)	Nil	13,242
Part I federal tax payable		$ 10,200
Provincial tax @ 12% of $79,700		9,564
Total tax payable		$ 19,764

Schedule 1: *Small Business Deduction*

16% of the least of:

Income from an active business		$110,000(I)
Taxable income...............................	$79,700	
Less: $^{10}/_3$ × foreign non-business tax credit (see above) ($^{10}/_3$ × $1,050)	3,500	$ 76,200(II)
Business limit		$300,000(III)
Small business deduction — 16% of $76,200 = $12,192		

Schedule 2: *Manufacturing and Processing Profits Deduction*

Canadian manufacturing and processing profits		$84,000(I)	
Deduct: income eligible for small business deduction		76,200(II)	$ 7,800(III)
Taxable income..................................		$79,700	
Deduct: income eligible for small business deduction	$76,200		
foreign investment income	7,000	83,200	Nil (IV)
7% of lesser of amounts (III) and (IV) — 7% of Nil.........		Nil	

Schedule 3: *General Reduction*

taxable income.....................................		$ 79,700	
less: $^{100}/_7$ of the M & P profits deduction	$ Nil		
$^{100}/_{16}$ of the small business deduction..........	76,200		
AII	7,000	(83,200)	
net		Nil	
7% of Nil			Nil
Total			$ Nil

Exercise 7

Paragraph 186(1)(*b*) requires that Part IV tax be calculated as follows:

$$\frac{\$90,000}{\$120,000} \times \$18,000 = \$13,500$$

Exercise 8

(A) *Computation of Taxable Income*

Net income for income tax purposes		$186,250
Deduct: taxable dividends............................	$18,750	
non-capital losses............................	37,500	
net capital losses ($68,750 × $^1/_2$ / $^3/_4$; limited to t.c.g.)	37,500	93,750
Taxable income		$ 92,500
Part I Tax on Taxable Income		
Tax @ 38% of $92,500		$ 35,150
Deduct: federal tax abatement (10% of $92,500)		9,250
Net..		$ 25,900
Add: surtax @ 4% of ($35,150 − 10% of $92,500) (or 4% of 28% of $92,500)		1,036

Additional refundable tax (ART) — 6²/₃% of lesser of:

    (a) AII ($37,500 + $45,000 + $18,750 − $37,500 − $18,750) = $45,000

    (b) TI − SBD amount ($92,500 − $85,000) = $7,500   500

                                                      $ 27,436

Deduct: small business deduction (see Schedule 1)....... $13,600

                General reduction .... Nil $ 13,600

Part I tax payable (federal) .... $ 13,836

Provincial tax @ 12% of $92,500 11,100

Total tax payable... $ 24,936

Schedule 1: *Small Business Deduction*

Income from active business .... $ 85,000(I)

Taxable income (no foreign tax credits) .... $ 92,500(II)

Business limit... $300,000(III)

16% of the least of amounts (I), (II) and (III)................. $ 13,600

(B) *Refundable Portion of Part I Tax*

    Least of:

    (a) 26²/₃% × aggregate investment income (26²/₃% × ($45,000 + $37,500 + $18,750 − $37,500 − $18,750)) ...... $ 12,000

    (b) Taxable income .... $ 92,500

         Less: Amount eligible for the SBD .... (85,000)

                                       26²/₃% × $7,500 = $ 2,000

    (c) Part I tax − surtax ($13,836 − $1,036) .... $ 12,800

Refundable portion of Part I tax — the least amount .... $ 2,000

Part IV Tax on Taxable Dividends Received

Taxable dividends subject to Part IV tax × ¹/₃ ($18,750 × ¹/₃) .... $ 6,250

Deduct: non-capital loss claimed for Part IV × ¹/₃ (all claimed under Part I)... Nil

Tax .... $ 6,250

Refundable Dividend Tax on Hand

Refundable dividend tax on hand at end of last year ..... Nil

Deduct: dividend refund for last year................... Nil

                                         Nil

Add: refundable portion of Part I tax .... $ 2,000

      Part IV tax .... 6,250 $ 8,250

Dividend Refund

Taxable dividends paid in the taxation year ($112,500 × ¹/₃)...... $ 37,500(VI)

Refundable dividend tax on hand................................ $ 8,250(VII)

Dividend refund — lesser of (VI) and (VII) .... $ 8,250

Exercise 9

(A) *Part I Tax on Taxable Income*

Tax @ 38% of $130,000	$ 49,400
Deduct: federal tax abatement (10% of 95% of $130,000)	12,350
Net	$ 37,050
Add: surtax @ 4% of ($49,400 − 10% of $130,000) (or 4% of 28% of $130,000)	1,456

Additional refundable tax (ART) — $6\frac{2}{3}$% of lesser of:

(a) AII ($50K + $30K + $20K + $50K − $20K − $50K) = $80,000

(b) TI − SBD amount ($130K − $90K) = $40,000   2,667

Total		$ 41,173
Deduct: non-business foreign tax credit (given)	$ 4,000	
business foreign tax credit (given)	1,000	
small business deduction (see Schedule 1)	14,400	
General reduction	Nil	19,400
Part I tax payable (federal)		$ 21,773
Provincial tax @ 9% of 95% of $130,000		11,115
Total tax		$ 32,888

Schedule 1: *Small Business Deduction*

16% of least of:

Income from active business			$ 90,000(I)
Taxable income		$130,000	
Deduct: non-business foreign tax credit × $\frac{10}{3}$	$13,333		
business foreign tax credit × 3	3,000	16,333	$113,667(II)
Business limit			$300,000(III)
Small business deduction — 16% of $90,000			$ 14,400

(B) *Refundable Portion of Part I Tax*

Least of:

(a) $26\frac{2}{3}$% × aggregate investment income ($26\frac{2}{3}$% × $80,000)			$ 21,333
Less: non-business foreign tax credit	$4,000		
minus: $9\frac{1}{3}$% × foreign investment income ($9\frac{1}{3}$% × $30,000)	(2,800)	(1,200)	$ 20,133
(b) Taxable income		$130,000	
Less: amount eligible for SBD		(90,000)	
$\frac{25}{9}$ × non-business FTC ($4,000)		(11,111)	
3 × business FTC ($1,000)		(3,000)	
		$26\frac{2}{3}$% × $25,889 =	$ 6,904
(c) Part I tax − surtax ($21,773 − $1,456)			$ 20,317
Refundable portion of Part I tax — The least			$ 6,904

Part IV Tax on Taxable Dividends Received

Taxable dividends subject to Part IV tax:

Non-connected corporations × ⅓ ($30,000 × ⅓)	$ 10,000
Connected corporations to the extent of share of dividend refund to payer	4,000
Total Part IV tax payable	$ 14,000

Refundable Dividend Tax on Hand

R.D.T.O.H. at end of last year		Nil
Deduct: Dividend refund for last year	Nil	Nil
Add: Refundable portion of Part I tax		$ 6,904
Part IV tax		14,000
R.D.T.O.H. at end of year		$ 20,904

Dividend Refund

Taxable dividends paid in year ($70,000 × ¹/₃)	$ 23,333(VI)
R.D.T.O.H. at end of year	$ 20,904(VII)
Dividend refund — lesser of (VI) and (VII)	$ 20,904

Exercise 10

(A) Splitinc Limited and Husband Ltd. are associated [par. 256(1)(*d*)]. Husband Ltd. is controlled by one person, Mr. Split. He is related to each member of the group, Husband Ltd. and Wife Ltd. that controls Splitinc Limited, because he is related to Husband Ltd. which he controls [spar. 251(2)(*b*)(i)] and he is related to Wife Ltd., which is controlled by his wife [spar. 251(2)(*b*)(iii)]. Also, he owns not less than 25% of the shares of Splitinc Limited through his ownership of shares in Husband Ltd. [par. 256(1.2)(*d*)]. These shares are not specified shares. By a similar analysis, Splitinc Limited and Wife Ltd. are associated.

Since the rental income would be deductible as an expense from the income of an active business of an associated payer, it will not be income from property of the recipient [spar. 129(6)(*a*)(i)]. It will be deemed to be income from an active business of the recipient, Husband Ltd. [spar. 129(6)(*b*)(i)]. Since Husband Ltd. has only dividend income it will be eligible for the small business deduction [ssec. 125(1)] in respect of the rental income as long as it is allocated a part of the business limit of the associated corporations.

(B) Since Splitinc is connected with both holding companies there will be no Part IV tax liability unless Splitinc gets a dividend refund as a result of the dividends it pays. However, Splitinc earns only active business income which is not subject to refundable taxes and dividend refunds.

Exercise 11

(A) Rent from RCSL:

(i) RCSL is associated with JML [par. 256(1)(*b*)];

(ii) RCSL deducts the rent from its active business.

Therefore, the rent is deemed to be income of JML from an active business [spar. 129(6)(*b*)(i)], eligible for the small business deduction [ssec. 125(1)].

(B) Services fee from Dr. Adam:

(i) JML's income from providing services would be considered income from an active business unless further facts indicate that it is carrying on a personal services business;

(ii) the business of providing services would be a personal services business if one or both of the shareholders of JML, who are specified shareholders (because they own at least 10% of the shares of JML), performed the services and would be regarded as an employee of the professional practice of Dr. Adam.

Therefore, if the services fee is considered income from an active business, it would qualify for the small business deduction.

Exercise 12

Interest income		$ 7,000
Dividends grossed up ($5/4 \times \$15,000$)		18,750
Taxable capital gains ($1/2 \times \$6,000$)		3,000
Incremental taxable income		$28,750
Federal tax on total taxable income of $48,750		
(i.e., $28,750 incremental + $20,000 other income):		
Tax on first $35,595	$ 5,695	
Tax on next $13,155 @ 22%	2,894	$ 8,589
Less: dividend tax credit (13¹/₃% of $18,750)	$ 2,500	
other personal tax credits	1,300	3,800
Basic federal tax		$ 4,789
Provincial tax		
Tax on first $35,595	$ 3,560	
Tax on next 13,155 @ 12%	1,579	
		$ 5,139
Less: dividend tax credit (6²/₃% of $18,750)	$ 1,250	
other personal tax credits	813	(2,063)
Total tax on taxable income of $48,750		$ 7,865

Taxation of Income from Investment Portfolio through a Corporation

Corporation		Available cash
Interest income	$ 7,000	
Dividends	15,000	
Taxable capital gains	3,000	
Income	$25,000	$25,000[1]
Less: dividends [sec. 112]	15,000	
Taxable income	$10,000	
Tax under Part I @ 44.62% (38% − 10% + 1.12% + 15.5%)	$ 4,462	
Additional refundable tax at 6²/₃% of $10,000 ($7K + $15K + $3K − $15K)	667	
Tax under Part IV @ 33¹/₃% of $15,000	5,000	10,129
Retained in corporation[1]		$14,871
Refundable tax:		
Part I (26²/₃% of ($7K + $15K + $3K − $15K))	$ 2,667	
Part IV (33¹/₃% × $15,000)	5,000	7,667
Available for distribution to shareholders as taxable dividend		$22,538[2]

Shareholder		*Available cash*
Taxable dividend (per requirements)...........................		$15,000
Gross-up (¼ × $15,000)		3,750
Incremental taxable income		$18,750

Federal tax on total taxable income of $38,750
(i.e., $18,750 incremental + $20,000 other income):

Tax on first $35,595	$ 5,695	
Tax on next $3,155 @ 22%	694	$ 6,389
Less: dividend tax credit (13⅓% of $18,750)...................	$2,500	
other personal tax credits	1,300	(3,800)
Basic federal tax		$2,589
Provincial tax		
Tax on first $35,595	$3,560	
Tax on next 3,155 @ 12%	379	
	3,939	
Less: dividend tax credit (6⅔ of $18,750)............ $1,250		
other personal tax credits 813	2,063	1,876
Total tax on taxable income of $38,750		$4,465

Total Taxes Paid
Through corporation:

Corporation after refund on $15,000 of dividends paid		
($10,129 – ⅓ × $15,000)		$ 5,129
Shareholder		4,465
Total[3]		$ 9,594
Received directly...		$ 7,865

—NOTES TO SOLUTION

(1) Ignores the non-taxable portion of capital gain which can be distributed tax free.

(2) Note that a dividend of $22,538 will result in a dividend refund of only $7,513 (i.e., $22,538 × ⅓), not the $7,667 that was added to the RDTOH for the year. This deficiency results from imperfections in the tax rates. A larger dividend of $23,000 (i.e., 3 × $7,667) would have to be paid, using other sources of funds, to clear the RDTOH. Alternatively, the maximum dividend that can be paid in this case is $22,307, determined algebraically, as follows:

$$R = \tfrac{1}{3} D$$
$$D = N - T + R \qquad \text{where:} \quad R = \text{dividend refund}$$
$$= N - T + \tfrac{1}{3} D \qquad\qquad D = \text{dividend}$$
$$= (N - T) \times \tfrac{3}{2} \qquad\qquad N = \text{Division B net income}$$
$$= (\$25,000 - \$10,129) \times \tfrac{3}{2} \qquad T = \text{total tax}$$
$$= \$22,307$$
$$R = \$7,436$$

Note that if the combined federal and provincial corporate tax rate had been 40%, before the additional refundable tax and the dividend refund, the amount available for dividends would be sufficient to clear the RDTOH.

(3) This amount is higher because not all of the corporate tax has been refunded as yet, and because the provincial corporate tax is 5.5% higher than the theoretical rate of 10%.

CHAPTER 13

Planning the Use of a Corporation and Shareholder-Manager Remuneration

Exercise 1

(A) The bonus must be paid on or before 179 days from the end of the year in which it was deducted. In this case, it must be paid on or before March 28, 2006. (Administrative practice, reflected in IT-109R2, par. 10, would allow payment on the 180th day).

(B) If the bonus is not paid on or before March 28, 2006, the corporation may not deduct the bonus in its 2005 taxation year. The bonus may only be deducted when it is paid.

(C) (i) The rent must be paid within two years from the end of the year in which it was deducted. In this case, it must be paid by September 30, 2007.

(ii) If the rent is not paid by September 30, 2007, the corporation must add the $10,000 to its income for its 2008 taxation year beginning October 1, 2007. This does not cancel the payable, such that if the rent is ever paid, the shareholder will declare the rental income, but there will be no deduction for the corporation.

(iii) An election can be filed before the date on which the corporation must file its tax return for 2008 [par. 78(1)(*b*)]. In this case, that date is March 31, 2009. If such an election is filed, Mr. Slip will be deemed to have income of $10,000 and to have loaned that amount back to the corporation on October 1, 2007. When the loan is repaid to Mr. Slip, there are no tax consequences since the amount of the loan has already been taxed. The election can be filed late [ssec. 78(3)]. However, $2,500 (effectively, a late-filing penalty) will be added back to the income of the corporation for its 2008 fiscal year. Mr. Slip's tax position is not affected by this late-filed election.

Exercise 2

(A) *Employee*

Principal-Amount

— Note that subsection 15(2) applies in this case because he is a shareholder.

(a) House Loan

Paragraph 15(2.4)(*b*) would exempt the principal amount of this loan from income since Mr. Leverage received the loan in his capacity as an employee (i.e., by virtue of his employment), the purpose of the loan was to purchase a house and *bona fide* arrangements were made for repayment of the loan within a reasonable time;

     — however, section 80.4 would include an interest benefit on a "home purchase loan" as shown in the calculation below.

(b) Furniture Loan

There is no exemption from income for this loan in subsections 15(2.3) and (2.4) and it is not exempt by subsection 15(2.6) because it was not repaid within one year of the 2005 taxation year of the corporation;

     — since the loan is included in income in 2005 under subsection 15(2), it is an exception for the purposes of paragraph 80.4(3)(*b*) and, hence, there is no interest benefit.

(c) Share Purchase Loan

This loan is exempt from income [par. 15(2.4)(*c*)] because Mr. Leverage received the loan in his capacity as an employee and *bona fide* arrangements were made to repay the loan within a reasonable time;

     — since this type of loan is not an exception to the rules of section 80.4, there is an interest benefit as shown in the calculation below.

Interest Benefit

     (a) interest on "home purchase loan" made to an officer or employee computed [par. 80.4(1)(*a*) and ssec. 80.4(4)], at lesser of: (i) the prescribed rate in effect during the period in the year that the loan was outstanding, and (ii) the prescribed rate in effect at the time the loan was made. This "lesser of" choice can be made on a quarter-by-quarter comparison of tax rates. In this case, the 3% prescribed rate in June 2005, when the loan

Exercise 4

	Remuneration alternatives		
Corporation	Salary	Dividends	Combination
Income before salary and taxes	$ 20,000	$20,000	$ 20,000
Salary	(20,000)	—	(11,000)
Income for tax purposes and taxable income	Nil	$20,000	$ 9,000
Tax @ 18.12% (i.e., 38% − 10% + 1.12% − 16% + 5%)	—	(3,624)	(1,631)
Available for dividends	Nil	$16,376	$ 7,369
Shareholder			
Employment income (ssec. 8(1) deductions not considered)	$ 20,000	—	$ 11,000
Grossed-up dividends ($^5/_4$ × dividend)	—	$20,470	9,211
Taxable income	$ 20,000	$20,470	$ 20,211
Federal tax before dividend tax credit	$ 3,200	$ 3,275	$ 3,234
Dividend tax credit ($13^1/_3$% of grossed-up dividend)............	—	(2,729)	(1,228)
Personal tax credits	(2,000)	(2,000)	(2,000)
Basic federal tax*	$ 1,200	$ Nil	$ 6
Provincial tax	2,000	2,047	2,021
Provincial dividend tax credit ($6^2/_3$% of grossed-up dividend).............	—	(1,365)	(614)
Provincial personal tax credits	(1,250)	(1,250)	(1,250)
Total tax*	$ 1,950	Nil	$ 163
Summary			
Income before salary and taxes	$ 20,000	$20,000	$ 20,000
Less: tax paid by corporation	Nil	(3,624)	(1,631)
tax paid by shareholder..........	(1,950)	Nil	(163)
Net cash to shareholder	$ 18,050	$16,376	$ 18,206
Excess federal dividend and personal tax credits ($3,275 − $2,729 − $2,000)		$ 1,454	

* Cannot be negative.

Effect of additional $100 of salary on all-dividend alternative at the corporate level when all of the income is distributed:

Increase in salary expense	$ 100.00
Decrease in corporate tax @ 18.12%.........................	(18.12)
Decrease in amount available for dividend	$ 81.88

Effect of additional $100 in salary on all-dividend alternative at shareholder level:

Increase in salary	$ 100.00
Decrease in dividend	(81.88)
Decrease in gross-up...	(20.47)
Decrease in taxable income	$ (2.35)

Decrease in federal tax @ 16% of $2.35 .... $ (.38)
Decrease in federal dividend tax credit (13⅓% of ⁵⁄₄ × $81.88)   (13.65)

Increase in tax .... $ 13.27

Additional salary to eliminate $1,454 in excess tax credit
($1,454/.1327) .... $ 10,957

Corporation:
Income before salary .... $ 20,000
Salary .... (10,957)

Taxable income .... $ 9,043
Corporate tax @ 18.12% .... (1,639)

Available for dividend .... $ 7,404

Shareholder:
Income from salary .... $ 10,957
Income from dividend 7,404
Gross-up 1,851

Taxable income .... $ 20,212

Federal tax .... $ 3,234
Dividend tax credit (13⅓% of ⁵⁄₄ × $7,404) .... (1,234)
Personal tax credits .... (2,000)

Net federal tax (cannot be negative) .... Nil
Provincial tax 2,021
Provincial dividend tax credit .... (617)
Provincial personal tax credits .... (1,250)

Total tax .... $ 154

Net cash to shareholder ($20,000 − $1,639 − $154) .... $ 18,207

Improvement ($18,207 − $18,206) .... $ 1

Exercise 5

(A)   *Taxation of Income from Sole Proprietorship*

Income from business and taxable income $80,000

Federal tax
    Tax on first $71,190 .... $13,526
    Tax on next $8,810 @ 26% 2,291 $15,817

Personal tax credits .... (2,000)

Basic federal tax $13,817
Provincial tax (15% of ($80,000 − $71,190) + $7,831)) 9,153
Provincial personal tax credits .... (1,250)

Total tax paid $21,720

(B)

Taxation of Income through a Corporation

	Remuneration alternatives		
	All salary	All dividends	Combination
Corporation			
Income before salary and taxes	$ 80,000	$ 80,000	$ 80,000
Salary	(29,392)	—	(7,432)[3]
Taxable income	$ 50,608	$ 80,000	$ 72,568
Tax @19.12% (i.e., 38% – 10% + 1.12% – 16% + 6%)	(9,676)	(15,296)	(13,875)
Available for dividend	$ 40,932	$ 64,704	$ 58,693
Shareholder			
Salary[1] ....(A)	$ 29,392	—	$ 7,432
Dividend ....(B)	—	$ 25,000	17,568
Gross-up @ ¼ of dividend	—	6,250	4,392
Income	$ 29,392	$ 31,250	$ 29,392
Federal tax	$ 4,703	$ 5,000	$ 4,703
Dividend tax credit (13⅓% of grossed-up dividend).............	—	(4,167)	(2,928)
Personal tax credits.................	(2,000)	(2,000)	(2,000)
Basic federal tax....................	$ 2,703	Nil	(225)[4]
Provincial tax	2,939	3,125	2,939
Provincial dividend tax credit	Nil	(2,083)	(1,464)
Provincial personal tax credits	(1,250)	(1,250)	(1,250)
Total tax ....(C)	$ 4,392	Nil	Nil
Disposable income (A + B – C)	$ 25,000	$ 25,000	$ 25,000
Total Taxes paid			
Through corporation:			
Corporation	$ 9,676	$ 15,296	$ 13,875
Shareholder...................	4,392	Nil	Nil
Total	$ 14,068	$ 15,296	$ 13,875
Paid directly by proprietor	$ 21,850	$ 21,850	$ 21,850
Tax Saving (maximum[2])	$ 7,782	$ 6,554	$ 7,975

—*NOTES TO SOLUTION*

(1) Assumes no deductions available under subsection 8(1).

(2) Assumes amount retained in the corporation can be distributed as taxable dividends in amounts that will not attract tax after personal tax credits.

(3) Note that the marginal analysis used in Example Problem 2 on page 715 of the book can be used to derive this amount. The excess tax credits in the all-dividend alternative amount to $1,375 (i.e., $5,000 – $4,167 – $2,000 + $3,125 – $2,083 – $1,250), assuming that all excess federal credits can be used on other income, as required in this problem. Since only part of the corporate income is being distributed, the focus is on the shareholder-manager. If salary is increased by $100, the following would occur:

Increase in salary	$100.00
Decrease in dividend	(100.00)
Decrease in gross-up	(25.00)
Decrease in taxable income	$ (25.00)
Decrease in tax @ 26% (i.e., 16% federal and 10% provincial) of $25.00	$ (6.50)
Decrease in dividend tax credit (20% of 5/4 × $100.00)	25.00
Increase in tax	$ 18.50
Increase in salary to eliminate $1,375 of excess tax credits ($1,375/.1850)	$ 7,432

(4) Negative allowed only due to assumption in the required.

Exercise 6

In each of the cases, the test to be applied to the facts is whether all or substantially all (i.e., at least 90%) of the fair market value of the assets are:

(a) used principally in an active business carried on primarily in Canada by the corporation (or a related corporation);

(b) shares or debt of a connected SBC; or

(c) a combination of (a) and (b).

(A) This situation depends on whether the marketable securities are used in the active business or are passive investments not necessary to the active business. If the marketable securities are used in the active business, then the 90% test is met. This would be the case, for example, if the marketable securities represented a short-term investment of cash surpluses, awaiting the purchase of inventory for the next season.

(B) In this situation, the 90% test is met with a combination of active business assets and shares in a connected SBC.

(C) In this case, the marketable securities cannot be considered to be used in an active business, because the corporation has no other active business assets to carry on such a business. Since the shares of a connected SBC represent only 80% of the total fair market value of the corporation's assets, the 90% test is not met.

(D) Again, this case fits the definition of an SBC if the marketable securities are considered to be used in an active business. If the facts of this case so indicate, then the 90% test is met by a combination of active business assets (including the marketable securities) and the shares of a connected SBC.

Exercise 7

(A) Unused lifetime deduction in 2005:

Lifetime cumulative deduction limit	$ 250,000
Less: prior years' deductions:	
Capital gains deduction claimed in 2003	75,000
Capital gains deduction available for 2005	$ 175,000

(B) Annual gains limit for 2005:

Net taxable capital gains for 2005[1]	$ 225,000
Minus:	
Net capital losses deducted in 2005	Nil
A.B.I.L.s realized in 2005[1]	5,000 5,000
Annual gains limit for 2005	$ 220,000

(C) Cumulative gains limit for 2005:

Cumulative net taxable capital gains ($75,000 + $225,000)			$ 300,000
Minus:			
Cumulative net capital losses deducted		Nil	
Cumulative A.B.I.L.s realized	$ 5,000		
Cumulative capital gains deductions	75,000		
Cumulative net investment loss:			
Investment expenses —			
Cumulative carrying charges	$ 1,075		
Cumulative net rental losses			
($1,100 + $220)	1,320		
		$ 2,395	
Investment income —			
Cumulative interest income			
($600 + $1,200)	(1,800)		
Cumulative grossed-up dividends	(140)	455	80,455
Cumulative gains limit for 2005			$ 219,545

(D) Least of (A), (B), (C) . . . . $ 175,000

— NOTE TO SOLUTION

(1) Allowable business investment loss (A.B.I.L.):

B.I.L. before ssec. 39(9) reduction			$ 160,000
Disallowed portion — Lesser of:			
(a) B.I.L.		$ 160,000	
(b) Adjustment factor ×			
cumulative C.G. deduc-			
tions of previous years			
(2 × $75,000)	$150,000		
Minus: Cumulative dis-			
allowed B.I.L. of prior			
years	Nil	$ 150,000	
Lesser of (a) and (b)			(150,000)
B.I.L. after adjustment			$ 10,000
A.B.I.L. (¹⁄₂ × $10,000)			$ 5,000

Allowable capital loss (A.C.L.):	
Disallowed portion of B.I.L.	$ 150,000
A.C.L. (¹⁄₂ × $150,000)	$ 75,000

Net T.C.G. for 2004:	
T.C.G.	$ 300,000
Less: A.C.L.	75,000
Net T.C.G.	$ 225,000

Exercise 8

The disposition of the real estate is a transfer for tax purposes in 2005. The facts do not provide enough details on the cost base to determine the tax effect of the disposition.

In this case it can likely be established that one of the main purposes of the transfer of the building may reasonably be considered to be to reduce the income of Mr. Albert and to benefit

Mrs. Albert who is a designated person and a specified shareholder. Had Mr. Albert kept the building himself he would have earned $20,000 of rental income on which he would have been taxable. Instead, he will receive $1,000 of interest and $2,000 of dividends. Mrs. Albert benefited from the rental income since this will accrue to the common shares of the corporation. Therefore, it may be argued that the purpose test will have been met.

Furthermore, the corporation will no longer be a "small business corporation" [ssec. 248(1)], since the fair market value of the assets of the corporation will be as follows:

Retail assets, 75%..	$600,000
Building, 25%	200,000
Total	$800,000

Even if 20% of the building (F.M.V. $40,000) is classified as an active business asset, the corporation will still not be a small business corporation since all or substantially all of the fair market value of the assets are not used principally in an active business carried on primarily in Canada.

Mr. Albert's attributed amount

F.M.V. of the building transferred	$200,000
Less: cash received	(80,000)
Outstanding amount...	$120,000
Interest imputed at 4%	$4,800
Less: interest received (5% of $20,000)	(1,000)
$^5/_4$ of dividends received	(2,500)
Attributed amount...	$1,300

Mr. Albert would also have

Interest income	1,000
Taxable dividends ($2,000 × 1.25)................................	2,500
Total income	$4,800

Exercise 9

The following comments are based on the application of the logic presented in Exhibit 13-11 to the facts of this situation.

(1) Does any other provision of the Act or other rule of law apply to stop the taxpayer from achieving the intended advantage? No, the amount paid is considered to be reasonable and, hence, is not prohibited by section 67. Remuneration is considered to be an expense incurred to produce income from business and, thus, is not prohibited by paragraph 18(1)(*a*).

(2) Does the transaction result, directly or indirectly, in a tax benefit, i.e., a reduction, avoidance or deferral of tax or an increase in a refund [ssec. 245(1)]? On the one hand, corporate tax is reduced, but on the other hand the individual receives income subject to tax at approximately the same rate. However, the reduction of income to the corporation reduces the potential for double taxation on income taxed at more than a 20% rate in the corporation which may be considered to be a tax benefit. If it is concluded that there is no tax benefit, GAAR should not apply.

(3) Is the transaction part of a series of transactions, which would result, directly or indirectly, in a tax benefit? If the answer to question 2 is yes, then proceed directly to question 4.

(4) Can the transaction reasonably be considered to have been undertaken or arranged primarily for *bona fide* purposes other than to obtain the tax benefit? No, a tax reduction for the corporation was probably the primary purpose. On the other hand, it might be argued that, since the amount paid was reasonable, it is necessary remuneration.

(5) Can it reasonably be considered that the transaction would not result directly or indirectly in a misuse of the provisions of the Act or an abuse having regard to the provisions of the

Act read as a whole? Yes, as indicated in IC 88-2 at paragraph 18, "the Act recognizes the deductibility of reasonable business expenses."

CHAPTER 14
Rights and Obligations under the Income Tax Act

Exercise 1

Subsection 150(1):

(a) corporations — within 6 months from the end of the taxation year;

(b) deceased persons — for a tax return of a given year where the individual died after October 31 of the given year and before the normal filing due date for that year, on or before the later of 6 months after the day of death and the day the return would otherwise be due; in all other cases by April 30 (or June 15, if the deceased individual or his or her spouse carried on a business in the year of death) following the year of death (i.e., if the death occurs in the first 10 months of a year, the return is due by April 30 or June 15 of the next year);

(c) trust — within 90 days from the end of the taxation year;

(d) individual — on or before April 30 of the next calendar year unless the individual or his or her spouse carried on a business, in which case the deadline is June 15 of the next year.

Exercise 2

Subsection 152(4):

— No limit if fraud or misrepresentation in the 2004 return can be established or on a matter for which the taxpayer has filed a waiver of the limit by May 27, 2008;

— Otherwise, the reassessment must be made within 3 years of May 27, 2005.

Exercise 3

Subsection 153(1):

(a) salary or wages or other remuneration from employment;

(b) a superannuation or pension benefit;

(c) a retiring allowance;

(d) a death benefit for long service from an employer;

(e) an Employment Insurance benefit;

(f) a benefit under a supplementary unemployment benefit plan;

(g) an annuity payment;

(h) a benefit from a deferred profit sharing plan;

(i) fees, commissions and other amounts for services;

(j) a payment under a registered retirement savings plan;

(k) certain amounts resulting from an income averaging annuity;

(l) a payment from a registered retirement income fund.

Exercise 4

Inheritance, gambling winnings, lottery prize, etc.

Exercise 5

As his net tax owing in the current year and one of the two preceding years is in excess of $2,000, he is required to make instalments.

Instalments of $750 ($^1/_4$ × $3,000) must be paid by March 15th and June 15th and instalments of $1,250 (i.e., ($4,000 − 2 × $750) × $^1/_2$) must be paid by September 15th and December 15th. The balance of the tax liability must be remitted by the balance-due date of April 30, 2006.

Exercise 6

As the corporation's estimated taxes payable for the current year and the taxes paid for the preceding year exceed $1,000, instalments are required.

Subparagraph 157(1)(*a*)(iii) would allow the following:

January 31 and February 29, 2005 — $^1/_{12}$ of $15,840 or $1,320;

Last day of March to December 2005 — $^1/_{10}$ of ($23,760 − 2 × $1,320) or $2,112;

Balance on the last day of March 2006, where a small business deduction was taken by virtue of section 125 in the current or preceding year and the corporation and associated corporations' aggregate taxable incomes for the preceding year did not exceed the small business deduction limit of $300,000 (for the calendar year 2005), or the last day of February 2006 in any other case.

Exercise 7

Subsection 150(1):

Y and Z will incur no penalties; furthermore, Y is not required to file since no tax is payable, unless he disposed of capital property.

Subsection 162(1):

Failure to file when required — 5% of unpaid tax plus 1% of unpaid tax per complete month past due for a first offence:

X — 5% of $4,700 or $235 plus 1% of $4,700 × nil = $235.

Y — 5% of nil or nil.

Z — no penalty as the return is not due until June 15. Interest charges on the unpaid tax from April 30 will, however, apply.

Subsection 238(1):

Failure to file as or when required — liable on summary conviction to a fine of $1,000 to $25,000 or a fine and imprisonment for up to 12 months;

— Y could be fined if there has been a demand to file under subsection 150(2).

Exercise 8

Section 161 computes interest at a basic prescribed rate plus 4% on amounts owing to the CRA from the earliest date the amount was due until the date it was paid;

— the interest is not tax deductible.

Interest is computed at the same basic prescribed rate plus 2% on refunds by the CRA [ssec. 164(3)];

— the interest is taxable;

— if the interest relates to instalments, an interest offset is computed using the 4% addition, against interest owing on late instalments for interest earned on early instalments [ssec. 161(2.2)].

Both interest calculations are based on daily compounding.

Interest on the overpayment of taxes for individuals will start to accrue 30 days after the later of the balance due day for the return (i.e., April 30, 2006 for 2005 returns) or the date the return is filed.

An individual's refund interest accruing over a period can be offset by any arrears interest that accrues over the same period, to which the refund interest relates. Hence, only the excess refund interest is taxed to the individual.

Exercise 9

The following comment on this situation is provided by the CRA in IC 01-1:

There was nothing in the income statement that would have made the accountant question the validity of the information provided to him. Therefore, he could rely on the good faith defense and would not be subject to the preparer penalty.

Use of the flowchart presented in the chapter may be helpful in analyzing this situation and reaching this conclusion.

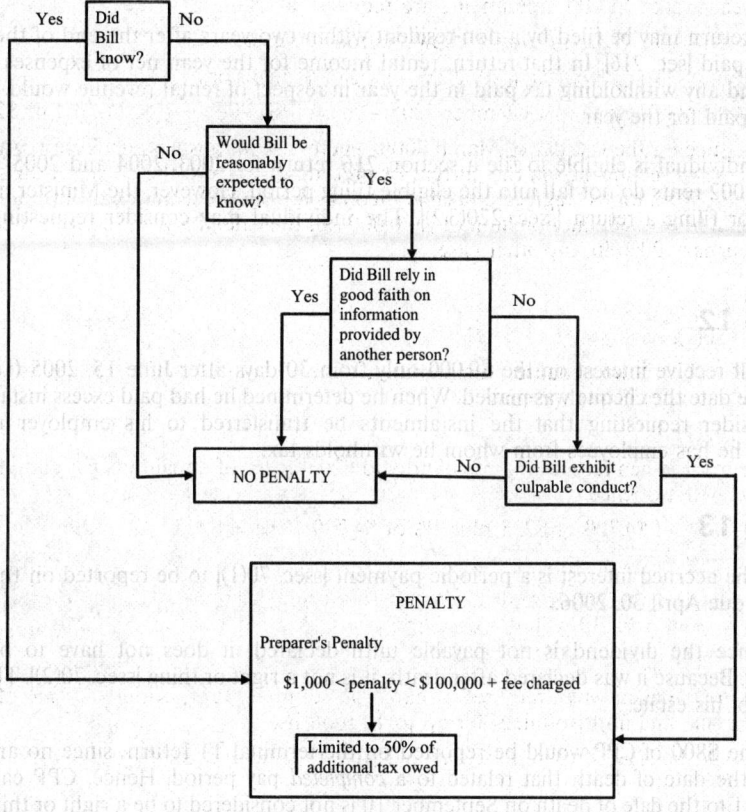

Exercise 10

(a) Notice of objection [ssec. 165(1)]:

— to be filed by *individual* taxpayers by the later of:

(i) one year after the filing-due date [ssec. 248(1)] which is normally April 30 or June 15 except for trusts and deceased persons, and

(ii) the 90th day after the mailing date of the notice of assessment;

— to be filed within 90 days of mailing of notice of assessment for all other taxpayers;

— a prescribed form is not required.

(b) Appeal to the Tax Court of Canada [sec. 169]:

— after 90 days of date of decision on notice of objection or 90 days after the mailing of the notice of objection if there has been no response to it;

— may be able to elect informal procedure under subsection 18(1) of the *Tax Court of Canada Act*.

(c) Appeal to the Federal Court of Appeal (section 17.6 of the *Tax Court of Canada Act*):

— within 30 days from date of mailing of decision of the Tax Court of Canada only if that taxpayer chose the general procedure in the Tax Court of Canada.

(d) Appeal to Supreme Court of Canada:

— on recommendation of Federal Court of Appeal;

— with permission of Supreme Court of Canada.

Exercise 11

Section 216

A tax return may be filed by a non-resident within two years after the end of the year that rents were paid [sec. 216]. In that return, rental income for the year, net of expenses, would be reported and any withholding tax paid in the year in respect of rental revenue would be considered taxes paid for the year.

This individual is eligible to file a section 216 return for 2003, 2004 and 2005. The 2000, 2001 and 2002 rents do not fall into the eligible filing period. However, the Minister may extend the time for filing a return [ssec. 220(3.2)]. The individual may consider requesting such an extension.

Exercise 12

Sol will receive interest on the $9,000 only from 30 days after June 15, 2005 (i.e., July 15, 2005) to the date the cheque was mailed. When he determined he had paid excess instalments, he could consider requesting that the instalments be transferred to his employer remittance account, if he has employees from whom he withholds tax.

Exercise 13

(A) The accrued interest is a periodic payment [ssec. 70(1)] to be reported on the terminal T1 return, due April 30, 2006.

(B) Since the dividend is not payable until declared, it does not have to be accrued [ssec. 70(1)]. Because it was declared after death, it is not a right or thing [ssec. 70(2)]. Therefore, it is income of his estate.

(C) The $800 of CPP would be reported on the terminal T1 return, since no amount was unpaid at the date of death that related to a *completed* pay period. Hence, CPP earned from September 1 to the date of death on September 10 is not considered to be a right or thing, since it is not legally receivable for a completed pay period on the date of death.

(D) The donations are creditable, to the extent of 100% of net income reported, on all the year of death returns combined or in the preceding year's return. Only personal tax credits, allowed under subsections 118(1) and (2), may be deducted on each of the separate returns for the year of death [sec. 118.93].

(E) Net capital losses are deductible from any source of income in the year of death and the preceding year [ssec. 111(2)].

(F) Trust income of $900 for the year ended May 31, 2005 must be reported on the terminal return. An election is permitted to report the trust income payable to Sam for the stub period, June 1, 2005 to September 10, 2005 on a separate return, also due April 30, 2006 [par. 104(23)(*d*)]. The personal tax credits [ssecs. 118(1) and (2)] can be deducted on this return.

(G) Life insurance proceeds received on death are not taxable.

Exercise 14

Ms. Kaye's 2005 terminal personal tax return is required to be filed by April 30, 2006 [par. 150(1)(*d*)]. In Ms. Kaye's 2005 return all accrued income earned on a periodic basis during the period January 1 to May 1, 2005 should be included [ssec. 70(1)]. In addition, all capital property (such as her Flying High shares) is deemed to have been disposed of at the fair market value [ssec. 70(5)]. A claim for the full personal tax credits can be made on the terminal return even though Ms. Kaye died on May 2, 2005. The RRSP contribution of $9,000 is deductible on her 2005 terminal return, since it is less than the maximum amount (i.e., lesser of $16,500 and 18% of $80,000).

Ms. Kaye's 2005 terminal return will include the following:

Salary	$22,000
Bond interest	950
Savings account interest	150
GIC interest	140
Dividend income	250
Taxable capital gain [¹/₂ ($25–$10)×100]	750
RRSP accumulation	34,000
RRSP contribution	(9,000)
Taxable income	$49,240

Ms. Kaye's legal representative can report amounts which were receivable but not received at the date of death, on a separate tax return, called a "rights or things" return, instead of on the terminal return [ssec. 70(2)].

The unpaid salary of $2,000, interest payable of $950 and $250 of dividend income would qualify as income from "rights or things." Personal tax credits equal to the amounts claimed in the terminal return may be claimed again on the "rights or things" return. This return is due on the date that is the later of one year after death and 90 days after assessment of any return for the year of death.

Alternatively, the legal representative can assign the income from "rights or things" to a particular beneficiary [ssec. 70(3)].

CHAPTER 15
Corporate Distributions, Windings-up and Sales

Exercise 1

	A	B	C
Proceeds of disposition	$ 4,000	$ 1,000	$ 2,000
Less: adjusted cost base	(2,000)	(2,000)	(2,000)
selling expenses	(400)	(100)	(200)
Capital gain (loss)	$ 1,600	$ (1,100)	$ (200)
Adjustment to C.D.A. (¹/₂ × capital gain (loss))	$ 800	$ (550)	$ (100)

Exercise 2

(A) Net income for tax purposes	Property 1		Property 2	
Proceeds of disposition		$110,000		$ 11,000
Less: A.C.B.	$75,000		$40,000	
selling costs	11,000	86,000	5,500	45,500
Capital gain (loss)		$ 24,000		$ (34,500)
Taxable capital gain (allowable capital loss)		$ 12,000		$ (17,250)
(B) Adjustment to C.D.A. (¹/₂ × capital gain (loss))		$ 12,000		$ (17,250)

Exercise 3

(A) Where Dividend Limited redeems the preferred shares, Mr. Deemed will have a deemed dividend [ssec. 84(3)] equal to:

Redemption amount	$60,000
Less: P.U.C. (800 × $15)	12,000
Deemed dividend [ssec. 84(3)]	$48,000

Mr. Deemed will not have a capital gain on the transactions because the adjusted proceeds of disposition equals the A.C.B. of shares as demonstrated below:

Proceeds of disposition	$60,000
Deemed dividend [ssec. 84(3)]	48,000
Adjusted proceeds of disposition [par. (*j*) of def. "proceeds of disposition" in sec. 54]	$12,000
Less: A.C.B. (800 shares × $15)	12,000
Capital gain	Nil

(B) The dividend payment of $60,000 will be a taxable dividend unless Dividend Limited makes an election to treat the cash dividend as a distribution from the capital dividend account [ssec. 83(2)]. Where this election is made, the dividend will be tax-free to Mr. Dividend.

(C) A non-dividend distribution to Mr. Deemed in excess of the P.U.C. of the preferred shares will result in a deemed dividend of $45,000 [ssec. 84(4)] (i.e., $60,000 – $15,000). The A.C.B. of the shares will be reduced by the non-taxed portion of the payment of $15,000 [spar. 53(2)(*a*)(ii)]. The P.U.C. of the shares must be reduced by the $15,000 in this case to reflect the tax-free distribution of P.U.C. If P.U.C. is not reduced by $15,000 in this transaction, an additional $15,000 will be treated as a deemed dividend [par. 84(4)(*a*)].

Exercise 4

(A) The amount of the stock dividend is $1.00 per share and must be grossed up and included in income of the shareholder. Thus, income would total $12.50 ($5/4 \times 1.00×10 shares). The dividend tax credit would be available on the $1.00 amount of the stock dividend or about $.25 total (including provincial tax effect) per share. The adjusted cost base of the shares on the acquisition date would be $10.00 in total (i.e., $1.00 per share).

(B) The corporation will be deemed to have paid a dividend of $10.00 for determining its dividend refund and other amounts dependent on dividends paid.

(C)	P. of D. (10 shares @ $1,000 F.M.V.)		$10,000
	A.C.B. (see (A) above)		(10)
	Capital gain		$ 9,990
	Taxable capital gain (eligible for capital gains deduction)		$ 4,995
(D)	(i)	Redemption amount (10 shares @ $1,000)	$10,000
		P.U.C. (10 shares @ $1.00)	(10)
		Deemed dividend on redemption [ssec. 84(3)]	$ 9,990
	(ii)	Proceeds of disposition (above)	$10,000
		Less: deemed dividend [par. (*j*) of def. "proceeds of disposition" in sec. 54]	(9,990)
		Adjusted proceeds of disposition	$ 10
		A.C.B.	(10)
		Capital gain	Nil

Exercise 5

(a) This transaction would cause an immediate deemed dividend of $50 [ssec. 84(1)] since the daughter could immediately retract the shares and receive $150 tax free whereas the price paid for the shares was only $100.

Ssec. 84(1) deemed dividend

P.U.C. increase	$150
P.U.C. decrease	(Nil)
	$150
Increase in net assets	(100)
Ssec. 84(1) deemed dividend	$ 50

This $50 deemed dividend would be added to the A.C.B. of the preferred shares acquired by the daughter.

In addition, there would be a subsection 84(3) deemed dividend on the ultimate redemption of the preferred shares as calculated below:

Redemption of shares

Redemption amount		$1,000
P.U.C. — Special share		(150)
Deemed dividend on redemption [ssec. 84(3)]		$ 850
Proceeds of disposition		$1,000
Less: Ssec. 84(3) deemed dividend [par. (*j*) of def. "proceeds of disposition" in sec. 54]		850
Adjusted P. of D.		$ 150
A.C.B.		
— original cost	$100	
— ssec. 84(1) deemed dividend [par. 53(1)(*b*)]	50	(150)
Capital gain		Nil

Economic consequences

Redemption amount	$1,000
Actual price paid	(100)
Economic gain on redemption	$ 900

Tax results:

Ssec. 84(1) deemed dividend	$ 50
Ssec. 84(3) deemed dividend	850
Total gain taxed ($1,000 − $100)	$ 900

(b) As long as there is no capital gain or loss triggered on the transfer, the gift of land to the corporation should have no other immediate tax consequences. The accounting and tax records would show an increased balance in the contributed surplus account. However, the withdrawal of this contributed surplus can only be in the form of taxable dividend subject to the gross-up and tax credit mechanism. However, paragraph 84(1)(*c*.3) permits the capitalization of the contributed surplus into P.U.C. as long as the amount did not arise under one of the corporate tax-free rollover provisions, discussed in the next few chapters.

(c) Y has received $2,000 more in consideration than the cancelled debt (i.e., $2,000 + $20,000 versus $20,000); therefore, Y will have an income inclusion of:

P.U.C. increase	$2,000
Net asset increase ($20,000 − $20,000)	Nil
Ssec. 84(1) deemed dividend	$2,000

The cost of the shares is nil since the $20,000 cash cancelled the debt; however, there will be an increase in A.C.B. [par. 53(1)(*b*)] equal to the deemed dividend of $2,000.

(d) (i) Since the payment of $5,000 is less than the P.U.C. of the outstanding share(s) (i.e., $10,000), there are no immediate tax consequences because this payment is a return of the original investment in the corporation with tax-paid funds. However, the adjusted cost base of the shares is reduced to $15,000 (i.e., $20,000 – $5,000) by the amount of the return of capital [spar. 53(2)(*a*)(ii)] which would result in a potential higher capital gain on the ultimate disposition of the shares.

Ssec. 84(1) deemed dividend

P.U.C. before distribution	$10,000
P.U.C. after distribution	(5,000)
P.U.C. decrease (not an increase)	$ 5,000

Adjusted cost base

A.C.B. prior to distribution	$20,000
Distribution amount	(5,000)
New A.C.B.	$15,000

(ii) Since the payment of $18,000 exceeds the P.U.C. of the outstanding share(s), there will be a deemed dividend of $8,000 [ssec. 84(4)]. However, the A.C.B. of the share(s) will only be reduced by the non-taxed portion of the payment to $10,000.

Exercise 6

(A)	Funds available for distribution to shareholder	$1,000,000
	Less: paid-up capital	(625,000)
	Deemed dividend on winding-up [ssec. 84(2)]	$ 375,000
	Less: capital dividend elected under ssec. 83(2) [spar. 88(2)(*b*)(i)]	(150,000)
	Taxable dividend (sufficient to clear RDTOH)	$ 225,000
(B)	Taxable capital gain (allowable capital loss) to Mr. Finished:	
	Proceeds on winding-up	$1,000,000
	Less: deemed dividend [par. (*j*) of def. "proceeds of disposition" in sec. 54]	(375,000)
	Proceeds of disposition	$ 625,000
	A.C.B.	350,000
	Capital gain	$ 275,000
	Taxable capital gain (½)	$ 137,500

Exercise 7

Funds available for distribution	$30,000
Less: paid-up capital	(2,000)
Deemed dividend or winding-up [ssec. 84(2)]	$28,000
Less: capital dividend elected under ssec. 83(2) [spar. 88(2)(*b*)(i)]	(2,000)
Deemed taxable dividend	$26,000
Capital gain or loss on disposition of shares:	
Actual proceeds from distribution	$30,000
Less: deemed dividend [par. (*j*) of def. "proceeds of disposition" in sec. 54]	(28,000)
Proceeds of disposition	$ 2,000
Cost	(2,000)
Capital gain (loss)	Nil
Taxable capital gain	Nil

Net cash retained:

Funds distributed		$30,000
Tax on incremental income from distribution:		
Deemed taxable dividend	$26,000	
Gross-up ($1/4 \times \$26,000$)	6,500	
Taxable capital gain	Nil	
Incremental taxable income	$32,500	
Combined federal and provincial tax @ 46%	$14,950	
Less: combined dividend tax credit in province @		
$(6^2/_3\% + 13^1/_3) \times {}^5/_4 \times \$26,000$	(6,500)	8,450
Net cash retained		$21,550

Exercise 8

(A)

	Proceeds	Income		C.D. a/c	RDTOH
		Bus.	*Invest.*		
Opening balances ...		Nil	Nil	Nil	$ 10,000
Cash	$ 20,000	Nil	Nil		
Inventories	220,000	$ 20,000	Nil		
Land[1]	70,000	Nil	$ 15,000	$15,000	
Buildings[2]	300,000	140,000	50,000	50,000	
Equipment[3]	80,000	40,000	Nil		
Liabilities	(50,000)				
Income taxes[5]	(70,333)	$200,000[4]	$ 65,000		17,333
RDTOH[6]	27,333				$ 27,333
	$597,000			$65,000	

(B)

Funds available for distribution to shareholder	$597,000
Less: paid-up capital	2,000
Deemed dividend on winding-up [ssec. 84(2)]	$595,000
Less: capital dividend elected [ssec. 83(2)]	65,000
Deemed taxable dividend (clears RDTOH)	$530,000

(C) Taxable capital gain to Mr. Downer

Actual proceeds on winding-up	$597,000
Less: deemed dividend	595,000
Proceeds of disposition	$ 2,000
Cost	(1,000)
Capital gain	$ 1,000
Taxable capital gain ($1/2 \times \$1,000$)	$ 500

(D)

Where a corporation is wound up and the rules of subsection 88(2) of the Act apply, the supply of property on the wind-up is subject to GST. GST is payable on any taxable supplies of property. However, an election may be available, in which case the payment of GST is not required. In order to qualify, a registrant must have sold or transferred all or substantially all of the assets used in a commercial activity that is part of a business carried on [ETA: ssec. 167(1)]. Since Downandout Ltd. is being wound up by Mr. Downer it would qualify for this election.

—*NOTES TO SOLUTION*

(1) Proceeds on sale of land	$ 70,000
Cost	40,000
Capital gain	$ 30,000
Taxable capital gain ($1/2 \times \$30K$) (investment income)	$ 15,000
Capital dividend account ($1/2 \times \$30K$)	$ 15,000

(2) Actual proceeds on sale of building $300,000
    U.C.C. 60,000

Gain $240,000

Recapture ($200K – $60K) (business income) $140,000

Taxable capital gain ($1/2 \times$ ($300K – $200K)) (investment income) .... $ 50,000

Capital dividend account ($1/2 \times$ ($300K – $200K)) .... $ 50,000

(3) Actual proceeds on sale of equipment .... $ 80,000
    U.C.C. 40,000

Gain .... $ 40,000

Recapture ($80K – $40K) — fully accounts for gain
    (business income) .... $ 40,000

(4) The $300,000 business limit for the small business deduction (for calendar year 2005 and later taxation years) must be prorated for the number of days in the taxation year. Since the winding-up may take some time to complete, this solution assumes that the corporation maintains its eligibility for the small business deduction in the year in which the sale of assets occurs [IT-73R6, par. 9]. In this case, there would be no need to bonus down to the business limit for the small business deduction, given active business income of $200,000.

(5) Income taxes
    20% $\times$ A.B.I. ($200,000) $40,000
    $46^2/_3$% $\times$ investment income ($65,000) .... 30,333 $ 70,333

RDTOH ($26^2/_3$% of $65,000) .... $ 17,333

(6) Assumes a minimum $81,999 (i.e. 3 $\times$ $27,333) is to be distributed as a taxable dividend to produce a refund of the full RDTOH.

CHAPTER 16
Income Deferral: Rollover on Transfers to a Corporation and Pitfalls

Exercise 1

		A	B	C	D	E	F	G
(A)	Minimum elected amount or deemed proceeds	$120	$100	$ 80	$ 75	$100	$ 90	$ 50
(B)	Proceeds	$120	$100	$ 80	$ 75	$100	$ 90	$ 50
	Cost	100	75	100	75	100	75	100
	Capital gain	$ 20	$ 25	Nil*	Nil	Nil	$ 15	Nil
	Taxable capital gain ($1/2$)	$ 10	$ 13	Nil	Nil	Nil	$ 8	Nil
	Lesser of cost or proceeds	$100		$ 80		$100		$ 50
	U.C.C. of class	200		50		150		50
	Recapture	Nil		$ 30		Nil		Nil
	Income [ssec. 15(1)]	$ 30	$100	Nil	Nil	Nil	Nil	Nil
(C)	Maximum "boot"	$100	$ 75	$ 50	$ 75	$100	$ 75	$ 50

* No capital loss on depreciable property.

Exercise 2

(A) Cost of consideration received:

	A	B	C
Elected transfer price.....................	$5,000	$5,000	$5,000
Allocated to note up to f.m.v.	5,000	2,500	4,000
Allocated to preferred up to f.m.v.	Nil	$2,500	Nil
Allocated to common shares	Nil	Nil	$1,000

(B)

		A		B		C
L.S.C. before reduction		$5,000		$7,500		$6,000
Subsection 85(2.1) reduction in P.U.C.						
(a) Increase in L.S.C. of all shares.......		$5,000 (A)		$7,500 (A)		$6,000 (A)
(b) Elected amount	$5,000		$5,000		$5,000	
Less: boot	5,000		2,500		4,000	
Excess, if any......		Nil (B)		$2,500 (B)		$1,000 (B)
Total reduction in P.U.C. (A – B)...		$5,000		$5,000		$5,000

(c) Allocation of reduction to different classes:

Preferred shares

$$\$5,000 \times \frac{\$4,500}{\$5,000} = \$4,500$$

Common shares

$$\$5,000 \times \frac{\$500}{\$5,000} = \$500$$

Tax P.U.C.

Preferred shares	Nil	$2,500	
Common shares	Nil		$1,000

Note how the P.U.C. after reduction is equal to the amount of the $5,000 A.C.B. of the original capital property that has not been recovered through the notes received as consideration.

Exercise 3

(A) The elected amount becomes the proceeds of disposition of the assets transferred by Mr. Goodroll. Since his adjusted cost base on the land and his undepreciated capital cost on the building are equal to these proceeds, there will be no capital gain on that land and no recapture on the building. The corporation is deemed to acquire these assets at a cost equal to the elected amount. On the building, the corporation is deemed to have a capital cost of $436,224 and to have taken capital cost allowance of $8,724 making it liable for future recapture and for a potential future capital gain if ultimate proceeds exceed $436,224. This places the corporation in the same position as Mr. Goodroll was in with respect to the building prior to the transfer.

(B) (i) The cost of the debt and shares taken as consideration would be computed as follows:

Elected transfer price		$577,500
Allocated to debt:		
— mortgage assumed....................	$247,500	
— new debt issued	330,000	577,500
Allocated to shares		Nil

    (ii) L.S.C. before reduction $322,500

        Subsection 85(2.1) reduction in P.U.C.

          (1) Increase in L.S.C. of all shares .... $322,500 (A)

          (2) Elected amount $577,500

              less: boot ($247,500 +

                 $330,000) 577,500

          Excess, if any .... Nil   (B)

              Total P.U.C. reduction (A − B) .... (322,500)

        Tax P.U.C. after reduction .... Nil

(C) (i) If the new debt is redeemed for $330,000, given its adjusted cost base in Mr. Good-roll's hands of $330,000, there would be no gain or loss. However, on the disposition of the shares, the following would result:

        Proceeds of disposition $425,000

        Adjusted cost base .... Nil

        Capital gain $425,000

        Taxable capital gain $212,500

  (ii) Redemption amount $425,000

        Less: P.U.C. .... Nil

        Deemed dividend [ssec. 84(3)] $425,000

        Redemption amount $425,000

        Less: deemed dividend 425,000

        Proceeds of disposition [par. (j) of def. in sec. 54] .... Nil

        Less: adjusted cost base .... Nil

        Capital gain .... Nil

Exercise 4

The benefit rule [par. 85(1)(e.2)] would apply. The amount of the benefit would be equal to:

Fair market value of property transferred $125,000

Less greater of:

    (a) fair market value of all consideration received .... $101,000 ⎤ 101,000

    (b) elected amount .... $100,000 ⎦

Benefit .... $ 24,000

The proceeds of disposition of the securities to Mother would be increased by the amount of the benefit, $24,000, to $124,000 resulting in a capital gain of $24,000 on the transfer. The cost of the property to the corporation would also be increased by $24,000 to $124,000. However, the cost of the consideration received would be as follows:

Elected amount $100,000

Allocated to note (up to f.m.v.) 100,000

Allocated to preferred share .... Nil

Thus, the cost of the consideration received or of the shares owned by Daughter, which would increase in value by $24,000, is not increased by the amount of the benefit resulting in potential double taxation.

The $1,000 L.S.C. of the preferred share would not be reduced and would equal tax P.U.C.

Subsection 85(2.1) reduction in P.U.C.

(a)	Increase in L.S.C.		$ 1,000 (A)
(b)	Elected amount (as increased by benefit)	$124,000	
	Less: boot	100,000	
	Excess, if any		24,000 (B)
	Total P.U.C. reduction (A – B) [sec. 257]		Nil

To avoid the problem of the $24,000 benefit being potentially taxed twice, Mother should have taken more share consideration in the amount of $24,000 such that the fair market value of all consideration received was equal to the fair market value of the property transferred. The P.U.C. of these shares will be reduced to nil by the above formula for subsection 85(2.1), but this will not have any immediate tax consequences.

Exercise 5

Elected amount	*Range*
Asset #1	$5,000 — $20,000
Asset #2	$8,000 — $14,000

However, paragraph 85(1)(*b*) forces the minimum elected amount to be $18,000 because of the non-share consideration taken in that amount.

Assign the elected amount as follows:

Asset #1	$ 5,000
Asset #2	13,000
	$18,000

Note that the minimum amount is assigned to the depreciable asset to avoid recapture being fully taxed.

Income

Asset #1	P. of D.	$ 5,000
	A.C.B.	10,000
	C.L.	Nil
Asset #2	P. of D.	$13,000
	A.C.B.	8,000
	C.G.	$ 5,000
	T.C.G.	$ 2,500

Under corporate law[1], the paid-up capital of the one common share would be equal to the net fair market value of the assets transferred to the corporation. In this case, the P.U.C. would be $16,000 (i.e., $20,000 + $14,000 – $18,000). However, subsection 85(2.1) will reduce the P.U.C. as follows:

(a)	Increase in legal P.U.C. of all shares on the transfer to the corporation		$16,000 (I)
(b)	Elected amount	$18,000	
	Less: non-share consideration ("boot")	18,000	
	Excess, if any		Nil (II)
	Total P.U.C. reduction (I – II)		$16,000

Since there is only one class of shares issued, there is no prorating of this reduction. As a result, the P.U.C. of the share will be reduced to nil (i.e., $16,000 – $16,000) for tax purposes. The P.U.C. is reduced to nil, because all of the tax-paid cost in U.C.C. of $5,000 and A.C.B. of $8,000 has been recovered through cash.

—NOTE TO SOLUTION

(1) Where the transferor and the corporation do not deal at arm's length, the legal stated capital (the initial P.U.C.) can be less than the fair market value of the transferred assets at the discretion of the corporate directors.

Exercise 6

(A) Items not transferred under subsection 85(1):

Cash	$ 4,000	(not capital property)
Short-term investments	5,000	(superficial loss denied)
Accounts receivable	9,000	(use section 22[1])
Prepaid insurance	400	(business loss of $100)
Building..............	60,000	(terminal loss of $2,000 denied)
Land	26,500	(superficial loss denied)
Total	$104,900	(assume proprietorship debt of $74,000 and take back new debt for the balance of $30,900.)

The building may be transferred using the rules in subsection 85(1), but there is no advantage to doing so, because of the unrealized terminal loss. Subsection 13(21.2) applies to deny the loss. The corporation will acquire the building with a U.C.C. of $60,000 which is equal to its fair market value and the amount paid by the corporation.

If the short-term investments can be considered assets used in the active business of the corporation, they can be transferred to the corporation. However, the capital loss will be considered to be a superficial loss [sec. 54] because the corporation is affiliated with the transferor, Mrs. Designer. Therefore, paragraph 40(2)(g) will deny the loss to Mrs. Designer. The amount of the loss will be added to the cost of the investments to the corporation, such that the corporation's A.C.B. of the investments will be $10,000 [par. 53(1)(f)].

Section 85 need not be used when there is no accrued income to defer. If the short-term investments cannot be considered as assets used in an active business, then they should not be transferred to the corporation, because it will seriously jeopardize the qualification of the shares of the corporation as QSBCS.

The land need not be transferred under section 85 for the same reasons as the short-term investments, because of the accrued capital loss. While the loss will be denied to Mrs. Designer, the corporation will acquire the land for $26,500 of consideration, but hold it with an A.C.B. of $30,000 which was Mrs. Designer's tax position in the land before the transfer.

(B) and (C) Items transferred under subsection 85(1) and consideration:

	Tax value	F.M.V.	Elected amount	Assumed debt[2]	New debt	Pref. shs.	Income
Inventory ...	$ 5,000	$25,000	$ 5,000	Nil	$ 5,000	$20,000	Nil
Goodwill ...	Nil	44,000	1	Nil	Nil	44,000	$0.50
	$ 5,000	$69,000	$ 5,001	Nil	$ 5,000	$64,000	

Since the corporation will qualify as a small business corporation [ssec. 248(1)], section 74.4 will not apply to attribute income or capital gains back to Mrs. Designer.

(D) Elected transfer price			$ 5,001
Allocated to debt consideration:			
debt assumed		nil	
new debt		5,000	5,000
Allocated to A.C.B. of preferred shares			$ 1

(E) L.S.C. before reduction $64,000

Subsection 85(2.1) reduction in P.U.C.

    (i) Increase in L.S.C. of all shares . . . . $64,000 (A)

    (ii) Elected amount . . . . $ 5,001

        Less: boot 5,000

        Excess, if any . . . . 1 (B)

        Total P.U.C. reduction (A − B) . . . . (63,999)

Tax P.U.C. after reduction . . . . $ 1

The $1 of P.U.C. after the reduction represents the amount of tax-paid cost that has not been recovered through boot received from the corporation. The $1 of income resulting from the transfer of the goodwill is a tax-paid cost. A total of $5,000 of total tax-paid cost was recovered through boot.

(F) For those assets *not* transferred under subsection 85(1) and not subject to the specific provisions discussed below, the cost for tax purposes to the corporation would be equal to the fair market value of the consideration:

Cash . . . . $ 4,000

Prepaid insurance 400

Building 60,000

$64,400 = debt consideration

Under section 22, the purchaser, Hi-Fashion, would record the accounts receivable at their face value of $12,000 which would be their adjusted cost base for tax purposes. Under the conditions of section 22, the corporation must include in its income the business loss of $3,000 recognized by the transferor (i.e., difference between the face value ($12,000) and the fair market value ($9,000)). Hi-Fashion is now entitled to set up a reserve to offset any potential doubtful debts (i.e., $3,000), plus an amount equal to any further decline in value. In addition, the corporation is now eligible to write off any realized bad debts since it has included an amount in income in respect of these receivables.

The A.C.B. of the short-term investments and the land to the corporation will be their fair market value plus the denied superficial loss. Therefore, the A.C.B. of the short-term investments will be $10,000 ($5,000 F.M.V. + $5,000 denied loss) and that of the land will be $30,000 ($26,500 F.M.V. + $3,500 denied loss). This puts the corporation in the same tax position on these assets as Mrs. Designer was in before the transfer.

The capital cost and, therefore, the ACB of the building in the corporation is $80,000.

For the inventory that has been transferred under subsection 85(1), the cost base would be the elected amount (i.e., inventory — $5,000). The goodwill, which is eligible capital property, would have a cost base of 75 cents (i.e., $\frac{3}{4} \times \$1.00$).

— *NOTES TO SOLUTION*

(1) Reserve of $2,000 from last year must be brought into income this year. There will be a full business loss of $3,000 (i.e., face value of $12,000 less fair market value of $9,000) using section 22.

(2) The $104,900 of debt consideration for the assets not transferred under subsection 85(1) could include all assumed liabilities of $74,000, leaving none to be assumed in the subsection 85(1) transfer.

Exercise 7

The subsection 85(1) election with an elected transfer price of $80,000 will result in the following:

Recapture ($27,000 – $30,000)	$ 3,000
Taxable capital gain [½ ($80,000 – $30,000)]	25,000
Income	$28,000
Less: 1999 net capital loss ($37,500 × ½ / ¾ to adjust to 2004	25,000
Incremental taxable income	$ 3,000

A.C.B. of consideration received:

Note	$80,000
Common shares	Nil

P.U.C. of common shares [ssec. 85(2.1)]:

L.S.C. of shares issued		$20,000
Less: ssec. 85(2.1) P.U.C. reduction		
(a) increase in L.S.C.	$20,000 (A)	
(b) elected amount	$80,000	
boot	80,000	
excess, if any	Nil (B)	
(A – B)		$20,000
P.U.C. for tax purposes		Nil

Capital cost of transferred property to corporation for C.C.A. and recapture purposes is equal to the aggregate of:

(a) capital cost to transferor		$30,000
(b) proceeds of disposition to transferor	$80,000	
less: capital cost of property transferred	30,000	
excess, if any	$50,000	
½ of excess		25,000
Deemed capital cost to corporation [spar. 13(7)(*e*)(i)]		$55,000

The capital cost used for future C.C.A. write-offs, which shield business income from full tax, will be increased by the taxable capital gain triggered, but not, in effect, the untaxed portion of the capital gain.

Capital cost of the depreciable property for future *capital gains* purposes (equal to elected amount) is $80,000.

Exercise 8

Part (A)

Section 84.1 applies because Mr. Nailed is a Canadian resident and is not at arm's length with his brother who controls the corporation to which the Opco shares were transferred. Therefore, Mr. Nailed is not at arm's length with the corporation [spar. 251(2)(*b*)(iii)]. In addition, Opco Ltd. is connected with Broco Ltd., since Broco owns all of its outstanding common shares [ssec. 186(2)].

P.U.C. reduction [par. 84.1(1)(a)]:

(a) Increase in L.S.C. of brother's corporation	$ 300,000	(A)
Less:		
(b) Greater of:		
(i) P.U.C. of operating company shares $75,000		
(ii) Modified A.C.B.* of operating company shares $75,000	$ 75,000	
Less: f.m.v. of boot	500,000	
Excess, if any	Nil	(B)
P.U.C. reduction (A – B)	$ 300,000	
P.U.C. after reduction	Nil	

The P.U.C. after reduction is nil because all of the $75,000 hard cost in the operating company shares has been recovered in boot from the brother's corporation.

Deemed dividend [par. 84.1(1)(b)]:

Sum of:		
(a) Increase in L.S.C. of brother's corporation	$ 300,000	(A)
(b) F.M.V. of boot	500,000	(D)
(A + D)	$ 800,000	
Less sum of:		
(c) Greater of:		
(i) P.U.C. of operating company shares $ 75,000		
(ii) Modified A.C.B.* of operating company shares $ 75,000	$ 75,000	(E)
(d) P.U.C. reduction [par. 84.1(1)(a)]	300,000	(F)
(E + F)	375,000	
Deemed dividend (A + D) – (E + F)	$ 425,000	

* Adjusted actual cost.

This deemed dividend is equal to the excess of the $500,000 in boot received from the brother's corporation over the $75,000 of hard cost in the operating company shares transferred.

Capital gain or loss on disposition of Opco Ltd. shares:

Elected amount and proceeds of disposition for operating company shares [ssec. 85(1)]	$ 500,000
Less: par. (k) in def. "proceeds of disposition" in sec. 54 exclusion for par. 84.1(1)(b) deemed dividend	425,000
Adjusted proceeds of disposition for operating company shares	$ 75,000
Less: A.C.B. of operating company shares	75,000
Capital gain (loss) if any, (not denied by par. 40(2)(g)*)	Nil

A.C.B. of Broco Ltd. shares received:

Cost of shares of Broco Ltd. after par. 85(1)(g) allocation of $500,000 elected amount to "boot"	Nil

* He is not affiliated with Broco Ltd. by the definition of "affiliated person" in section 251.1, since he does not control, directly or indirectly, Broco Ltd.

Part (B)

Ultimate redemption of shares of brother's corporation	
Redemption amount	$ 300,000
Less: P.U.C.	Nil
Deemed dividend on redemption [ssec. 84(3)]	$ 300,000
Proceeds of disposition	$ 300,000
Less: deemed dividend on redemption [ssec. 84(3)]	300,000
Adjusted proceeds of disposition [par. (j) in def. "proceeds of disposition" in sec. 54]	Nil
Less: adjusted cost base	Nil
Capital gain (loss)	Nil
Summary of income effects:	
Sec. 84.1 deemed dividend	$ 425,000
Ssec. 84(3) deemed dividend	300,000
Capital gain (loss) on ssec. 85(1) transfer	Nil
Capital gain (loss) on redemption	Nil
Net economic effect	$ 725,000

Note that $725,000 represents the accrued gain on the Opco Ltd. shares at the time of the transfer.

Part (C)

Ultimate arm's length sale of shares of brother's corporation	
Proceeds of disposition	$ 300,000
Less: adjusted cost base	Nil
Capital gain	$ 300,000
Summary of income effects:	
Sec. 84.1 deemed dividend	$ 425,000
Capital loss on ssec. 85(1) transfer	Nil
Capital gain on arm's length sale	300,000
Net economic effect	725,000

Again, the $725,000 represents the accrued gain in the Opco Ltd. shares at the time of transfer.

Exercise 9

For either alternative involving the sale of the Davpet Ltd. shares, the conditions of section 84.1 are met. Davpet Ltd. is a corporation resident in Canada and its shares are held as capital property by Ms. Erin, a Canadian resident. These shares are sold to a non-arm's length corporation, Lenmeag Ltd., since Ms. Erin is related to her father who controls Lenmeag Ltd. The two corporations are connected, since all of the shares of Davpet Ltd. are owned by Lenmeag Ltd. after the sale.

(A) Since no new shares of Lenmeag Ltd. were issued in this alternative, there is no P.U.C. reduction. However, there will be an immediate deemed dividend computed as follows:

Deemed dividend [par. 84.1(1)(b)]:

Sum of:

(a) Increase in L.S.C. of Lenmeag Ltd. shares	Nil	(A)
(b) F.M.V. of "boot"	$300,000	(D)
(A + D)	$300,000	

Less sum of:

(c) Greater of:

(i) P.U.C. of Davpet Ltd.
shares $1,000

$1,000 (E)

(ii) Modified A.C.B. of
Davpet Ltd. shares $1,000

(d) P.U.C. reduction [par. 84.1(1)(*a*)] ...... Nil (F)

(E + F) 1,000

Deemed dividend (A + D) – (E + F) $299,000

This deemed dividend represents the excess of the $300,000 in boot received from Lenmeag Ltd. over the $1,000 in P.U.C. of the Davpet Ltd. shares.

Proceeds of disposition for the Davpet Ltd. shares will be reduced [par. (*k*) of the definition in sec. 54] so that there will be no capital gain against which to offset the QSBC share capital gains deduction, as follows:

Consideration in debt received on sale....................................	$300,000
Less: par. (*k*) in def. "proceeds of disposition" in sec. 54 exclusion from proceeds for sec. 84.1 deemed dividend	299,000
Adjusted proceeds of disposition	$ 1,000
A.C.B. of Davpet Ltd. shares	(1,000)
Capital gain..	Nil

When the $300,000 debt is repaid by Lenmeag Ltd., there will be no further tax consequences. However, the plan is ineffective, because Ms. Erin will have to pay tax on a deemed dividend of $299,000 at the time of the sale of her shares instead of the intended capital gains.

(B) In this alternative, there will be a P.U.C. reduction, computed as follows:

P.U.C. reduction [par. 84.1(1)(*a*)]:

(a) Increase in L.S.C. of Lenmeag Ltd. .... $300,000 (A)

Less:

(b) Greater of:

(i) P.U.C. of Davpet Ltd. shares $1,000

$ 1,000

(ii) Modified A.C.B. of Davpet Ltd. shares $1,000

Less: F.M.V. of "boot" .... Nil

Excess, if any .... 1,000 (B)

P.U.C. reduction (A – B) $299,000

P.U.C. of new Lenmeag Ltd. shares after reduction
($300,000 – $299,000) .... $ 1,000

The P.U.C. of $1,000 after reduction represents the $1,000 of hard cost in the Davpet Ltd. shares transferred. None of that $1,000 of cost was recovered through boot on this transfer.

Since no "boot" was received, there will be no deemed dividend. As a result, proceeds of disposition for the Davpet Ltd. shares are equal to the $300,000 common share consideration received from Lenmeag Ltd. The result is the following:

Proceeds of disposition for Davpet Ltd. shares	$300,000
A.C.B.	1,000
Capital gain	$299,000
Taxable capital gain ($\frac{1}{2} \times$ $299,000)	$149,500
Less: Capital gains deduction for QSBCS	149,500
Effect on taxable income of Ms. Erin	Nil

The A.C.B. of the Lenmeag Ltd. shares acquired by Ms. Erin will be equal to the $300,000 fair market value of the shares in Davpet Ltd. given up. As a result, when the shares of Lenmeag Ltd. are either sold or redeemed the $300,000 A.C.B. of the shares will shield an equal amount from being taxed as a capital gain and the objective of crystallizing the QSBC share capital gains exemption will be accomplished without an immediate capital gain or deemed dividend on the sale of the Davpet Ltd. shares.

Exercise 10

Of the $900,000 dividend received by Vendco, $700,000 can be attributed to post-1971 earnings of Preyco and, therefore, can be received by Vendco without tax consequences under Part I and Part IV of the Act. The other $200,000 of the total dividend received will be deemed not to be a dividend received and will be deemed to be part of the proceeds of disposition of the shares sold to Purchco. As a result, the following capital gain on the disposition of the shares would be computed:

Actual proceeds on the disposition of the shares to Purchco	$100,000
Deemed proceeds of disposition [par. 55(2)(*b*)] ($900,000 – $700,000)	200,000
Total proceeds of disposition	$300,000
A.C.B.	100,000
Capital gain	$200,000

These results are equivalent to Vendco's receiving a dividend from Preyco, of $700,000 without tax consequences and then selling the shares of Preyco to Purchco for their fair market value of $300,000 (i.e., $1,000,000 – $700,000). With an adjusted cost base of $100,000 for the shares, a capital gain of $200,000 would result.

CHAPTER 17

Income Deferral: Other Rollovers and Use of Rollovers in Estate Planning

Exercise 1

Section 85.1 applies because shares of a Canadian corporation (Magnanimous, the purchaser) are being issued to a taxpayer (Mr. Sucker, the vendor) in exchange for capital property (shares of Targetco) of Mr. Sucker. Since Mr. Sucker wishes to fully defer the accrued gains in his shares he should not include any amount in his income on the disposition of his Targetco shares as a result of the exchange. Mr. Sucker and Magnanimous are at arm's length before the exchange. Furthermore, Mr. Sucker will neither control nor own more than 50% of the fair market value of all of the outstanding shares of Magnanimous after the exchange.

The tax consequences to Mr. Sucker will be as follows:

Proceeds of disposition for Targetco shares ($1.25 $\times$ 1,000)	$1,250
A.C.B. of Targetco shares	(1,250)
Capital gain	Nil
A.C.B. of Magnanimous shares received by Mr. Sucker in exchange	$1,250

As a result, the A.C.B. of the 1,000 shares of Targetco given up by Mr. Sucker becomes the A.C.B. of the 500 shares acquired in the exchange and the accrued capital gain on the Targetco shares is deferred. The A.C.B. per share of the Magnanimous shares held by Mr. Sucker will be $2.50 (i.e., $1,250/500).

Magnanimous will have acquired the 1,000 Targetco shares from Mr. Sucker at an A.C.B. equal to the lesser of:

F.M.V. of Targetco shares before exchange (1,000 × $2.35) $2,350

P.U.C. of Targetco shares before exchange (1,000 × $1.00)................. $1,000

Subsection 85.1(2.1) will apply to limit the addition to the P.U.C. of Magnanimous shares on their issue in exchange to the amount of the P.U.C. of the Targetco shares received (i.e., $1.00 per share).

Exercise 2

There is no deemed dividend, because the redemption amount paid, consisting of cash for $675 and total reduced P.U.C. of the new shares for $1,325, does not exceed the P.U.C. of the old shares of $2,000 [ssec. 84(3)]. (See calculations (4) and (5) below.)

Issuance of New Shares

(1) Reduced P.U.C. [par. 86(2.1)(a)]:

L.S.C. increase for all new shares................................		$1,325
Less: P.U.C. of old class A preferred shares	$2,000	
Less: boot..	675	1,325
P.U.C. reduction...............................		Nil
Total reduced P.U.C. (class B preferreds, $1,000; commons, $325)...		$1,325

(2) Cost of class B preferred and common shares received:

Adjusted cost base of old shares	$2,000
Less: fair market value of non-share consideration	675
Cost of Class B preferred and common shares received.............	$1,325
Cost of non-share consideration (boot) received (equal to F.M.V.) [par. 86(1)(c)]..	$ 675

Allocation of cost of new shares:

Class B preferred shares:

$$\frac{\text{F.M.V. of class B preferred shares}}{\text{F.M.V. of all shares}} \times \text{cost of new shares}$$

$$= \frac{\$1,755}{\$1,755 + \$570} \times \$1,325 = \$1,000$$

Common shares:

$$\frac{\text{F.M.V. of common shares}}{\text{F.M.V. of all shares}} \times \text{cost of new shares}$$

$$= \frac{\$570}{\$1,755 + \$570} \times \$1,325 = \underline{\underline{\$325}}$$

Redemption of Old Shares

(1) Proceeds on redemption of old shares [par. 84(5)(*d*)]:

Boot or non-share consideration	$ 675
Reduced P.U.C. of the new shares [par. 84(5)(*d*)] — see above	1,325
Redemption proceeds	$2,000

Deemed dividend on redemption [ssec. 84(3)]:

Redemption proceeds	$2,000
Less: P.U.C. of old shares	2,000
Deemed dividend on redemption [ssec. 84(3)]	Nil

(2) Proceeds of disposition of old shares [par. 86(1)(*d*)]:

Cost of all new shares (above)	$1,325	
Plus: cost of all non-share consideration (equal to F.M.V.)	675	$2,000
Less: ssec. 84(3) deemed dividend		Nil
Proceeds of disposition of old shares		$2,000

Capital gain or loss on disposition of old shares:

Proceeds of disposition of old shares	$2,000
Adjusted cost base of old shares	2,000
Capital gain (loss)[1]	Nil

Net economic effect:

Deemed dividends on redemption [ssec. 84(3)]		Nil
Capital gain (loss) on disposition of old shares		Nil
Accrued capital gain on new shares:		
F.M.V. ($1,755 + $570)	$2,325	
A.C.B.	(1,325)	$1,000
Net economic effect		$1,000

This $1,000 reflects the accrued gain (i.e., $3,000 – $2,000) on the old shares before the reorganization.

— NOTE TO SOLUTION

(1) Capital losses on a redemption are denied where the corporation is still affiliated with the shareholder (e.g., where the shareholder or the shareholder's spouse still controls the corporation after the exchange) [ssec. 40(3.6)].

Exercise 3

Subsection 86(2) will apply in this case because the F.M.V. of Mrs. Janna's common shares ($450,000, i.e., 75% of $600,000) is greater than the F.M.V. of the preferred shares received on the reorganization ($350,000) and it is reasonable to regard the $100,000 excess as a benefit that Mrs. Janna desired to have conferred on a related person, her daughter.

There is no deemed dividend [ssec. 84(3)], as shown by the following:

Issuance of New Shares

(1) Reduced P.U.C. [par. 86(2.1)(a)]:

L.S.C. increase for new preferred shares		$750
Less: P.U.C. of old common shares	$750	
Less: boot	Nil	750
P.U.C. reduction		Nil
Reduced P.U.C. ($750 – Nil)		$750

(2) The cost of the preferred shares received will be equal to [par. 86(2)(e)]:

A.C.B. of common shares		$ 750
Less: cost of non-share consideration	Nil	
benefit	$100,000	100,000
Cost of preferred shares		Nil

Since no boot was taken back on the exchange the final P.U.C. of the preferred shares will be $750.

Redemption of Old Shares

(1) Redemption amount:

Non-share consideration		Nil
P.U.C. of preferred shares received	$ 750	$ 750
Less: P.U.C. of common shares given up		(750)
Deemed dividend on redemption [ssec. 84(3)]		Nil

(2) The deemed proceeds of disposition of Mrs. Janna's common shares will be equal to the lesser of [par. 86(2)(c)]:

(a)	Cost (equal to F.M.V.) of non-share consideration	Nil
	Plus: benefit	$100,000
		$100,000
(b)	F.M.V. of common shares given up	$450,000

There will be a capital gain on the disposition by Mrs. Janna of her common shares equal to:

Deemed proceeds of disposition (lesser of (a) and (b) above)	$100,000
A.C.B. of common shares (75% of $1,000)	(750)
Capital gain	$ 99,250

The following net economic effect can be aggregated from the foregoing:

Deemed dividend on redemption [ssec. 84(3)]		Nil
Capital gain on disposition of common shares		$ 99,250
Accrued capital gain on preferred shares:		
F.M.V.	$350,000	
A.C.B.	Nil	350,000
Net economic effect		$449,250

This $449,250 reflects the accrued gain (i.e., 75% of ($600,000 – $1,000)) on the common shares held by Mrs. Janna, before the reorganization. Note how $99,250 is realized immediately on the reorganization and the remainder will be realized on the disposition of the preferred shares.

Furthermore, Mrs. Janna has lost the ability to recover $100,000 in tax-paid cost, because the cost of the preferred shares is nil, having been reduced by the benefit. The $100,000 is tax-paid cost because it reflects the $750 of cost in the common shares, plus $99,250 of capital gain realized on the disposition of those shares and included in income. At the same time, Rayna has had the benefit of a $100,000 increase in the value of her shares without any increase in their adjusted cost base. Therefore, the $100,000 of gain will be taxable in her hands on the disposition of her common shares.

Exercise 4

If either section 87 or subsection 88(1) is used:

(A) Acquisition Limited will be deemed to have proceeds of disposition on the land of $50,000, so the capital gain will be deferred.

(B) Mergem will be able to "bump" the cost base of the land on its books

— the "bump" would be computed [par. 88(1)(d)] as follows:

Mergem's A.C.B. of Acquisition's shares		$75,000
Less the sum of:		
(I) cost amount of Acquisition's assets	$50,000	
(II) dividends paid by Acquisition to Mergem	Nil	50,000
Increase in A.C.B. of land		$25,000

— this "bump" cannot exceed:

fair market value of the land at the time control was acquired	$90,000
less: A.C.B. of the land	50,000
maximum "bump"	$40,000

— therefore, the A.C.B. of the land to Mergem will be $75,000 after a "bump" of $25,000.

Exercise 5

Adjusted cost base of common shares equal to adjusted cost base of the debentures at the time of conversion	$10,000

Adjusted cost base of each common share:

Number of shares received on conversion ($\frac{\$10,000}{\$100} \times 16$)	1,600
A.C.B. of each share ($10,000/1,600)......................	$ 6.25

CHAPTER 18
Partnerships and Trusts

Exercise 1

Partnership's net income for financial accounting purposes		$304,280
Deduct: Capital gain		5,000
		$299,280
Add: Depreciation on office furniture...................	$ 3,750	
Donations.......................................	5,500	
Membership in fitness club	1,250	
Taxable capital gain ($\frac{1}{2} \times \$5,000$)	2,500	13,000
		$312,280
Deduct: Capital cost allowance		4,300
Income to be allocated (Division B)		$307,980
Bob's share of income from partnership		$153,990
Add: Gross-up of Bob's share of partnership dividends ($\frac{1}{4} \times \$4,000 \times \frac{1}{2}$).....................	$ 500	
Grossed-up personal dividends	4,375	
Personal interest income.......................	1,200	6,075
Bob's net income (Division B) and taxable income		$160,065

Analysis of Bob's income:

	Personal	Partnership	Total
Grossed-up dividends.....................	$4,375	$ 2,500	$ 6,875
Interest	1,200	—	1,200
Taxable capital gains	—	1,250	1,250
Business income		150,740	150,740
Total.....................................	$5,575	$154,490*	$160,065

* $153,990 + $500 gross-up

Notes:

(1) Drawings taken by the members of a partnership do not constitute a business expense but are a method of distributing partnership income to members of the partnership.

(2) Charitable donations are not deductions in computing the income of a partnership but are used as the basis for computing the charitable donations tax credit for an individual partner.

(3) Fees paid to a fitness club are non-deductible expenses [par. 18(1)(*l*)].

(4) Bob will be eligible for the following federal dividend tax credit:
— on share of partnership dividends ($13^1/_3$% of $^5/_4 \times ^1/_2 \times$
   $4,000$) .... $ \$ \quad 333 $
— on personal dividends ($13^1/_3$% of $^5/_4 \times \$3,500$) .... $ 583 $

Total .... $ \underline{\$ \quad 916} $

Exercise 2

Adjusted cost base of Katie's partnership interest:

Contributions			$ \$ 50,000 $
Add:	Share of profits excluding taxable capital gain ($^1/_2 \times (\$450,000 - \$20,000)$)	$215,000	
	Share of full capital gain ($^1/_2 \times \$20,000 \times ^2/_1$)	20,000	
	Share of capital dividends ($^1/_2 \times \$4,000$)	2,000	237,000
			$287,000
Deduct:	Share of losses ($^1/_2 \times \$15,000$)	$ 7,500	
	Drawings ($^1/_2 \times \$176,000$)	88,000	
	Share of donations ($^1/_2 \times \$27,000$)	13,500	109,000
A.C.B. of partnership interest			$178,000

Capital gain on disposition of partnership interest:

Proceeds of disposition		$250,000
A.C.B.		178,000
Capital gain		$ 72,000
Taxable capital gain ($^1/_2$ of $72,000$)		$ 36,000

Exercise 3

	Trust	Rebecca	Robert
Income			
Interest	$4,500	$ 5,500	$ 1,500
Taxable capital gain	1,500	1,500	1,500
Taxable dividends	3,750	3,750	3,750
Net income/taxable income	$9,750	$10,750	$ 6,750
Federal tax (@29% for trust and 16% for individuals)................................	$2,828	$ 1,720	$ 1,080
Personal tax credit @ 16% of $8,148	—	(1,304)	(1,304)
Tuition credit and education credit............	—	—	Nil
Dividend tax credit @ $13^1/_3$% of $3,750	(500)	(500)	—
Total tax	$2,328	$ Nil	Nil

Note: None of the tuition and education tax credits were claimed by Robert. Federal tuition and education tax credits of $800[1] are transferable to a parent [ssec. 118.9(1)], or the unused amount of $1,072 less any amount transferred to a supporting person may be carried forward [sec. 118.61]. The definition of tax payable [sec. 118.81] and the ordering rules [sec. 118.92] require that the personal, tuition and education tax credits be deducted before the dividend tax credit which is lost in this case.

— NOTE TO SOLUTION

(1) Lesser of:
    (a) $800 (federal) =$800

    (b) (16% × $3,500) + (16% of ($400 × 8)) = $1,072 $ 800

    Minus ($1,080 − $1,282) . . . .   Nil

    Net amount transferred to parent . . . . $ 800

CHAPTER 19
Computer-Assisted Tax Research

Part II Folio 4.3 Software

Exercise 1

(A) The area that is labelled (A) and has the title, Word, is the Word Wheel which contains all the words (including misspellings) of the particular infobase that you are presently searching. As you input your query the Word Wheel will constantly change as each alpha-numeric symbol is inputted. Furthermore, the Word Wheel will anticipate your next few letters and so indicate this expectation in the Query For box. The Word Wheel is an important aid in structuring search commands because it presents variations of your search terms, i.e., words with same root or prefix.

(B) The area that is labelled (B) and has the title, Query For, is where search commands or queries are entered and operates in the same manner as a word processor.

(C) The button that is labelled OK executes queries. If the search commands are not executed then these queries cannot be recalled with the button with vertical arrows.

(D) The buttons with the vertical directional arrows that are labelled (D) recall previously executed queries so that the researcher can make alterations to these search commands without re-entering the entire query.

Exercise 2

The Reference Window can be enlarged or contracted in the following ways:

(A) Under the View tab in the main menu the Reference Window can be opened or closed (hidden) but only for the infobase that you are presently in.

(B) Under the Preferences Template, the Reference Window can be permanently opened or closed for all infobases.

(C) Under the Preferences Template, the Reference Window can be expanded or contracted for all infobases by specifying the number of lines of information that will be exposed.

(D) Using the multi-directional arrow that appears when the cursor is placed over the bottom line of this window the Reference Window can be expanded or contracted.

Exercise 3

There are two ways you can determine the size of a record for the infobase that you are presently in. The first method uses the sub-infobase, About this Infobase. You can find this sub-infobase on the Table of Contents near the end or in the What's New section of the first screen of the infobase. Just scan quickly the first few frames of the this sub-infobase using the page-down key and you will find a description of a record. Alternatively, you can determine the size of a record by looking for the diamond codes which signify the beginning and/or the end of a record. Of course you must activate these codes through the Preferences Template. It is recommended that these codes be left on all the time.

Exercise 4

The presentation format of the toolbelt can be changed in the following ways:

(A) The various tools can be identified by a brief word description, a symbol representing the action of the particular tool or both the symbol and a word description.

(B) The toolbelt can be oriented vertically on the left-hand side of the screen or horizontally near the top of the screen.

(C) The tools in the toolbelt can be changed to suit the needs of the researcher by transferring particular tools in the Available Tools list to Current Tools list through the horizontal arrows and vice versa.

(D) The order of presentation of the tools in the toolbelt can also be changed by highlighting the particular tool in the available list and moving it up or down using the vertical arrows.

Part III Basic Search and Navigation

Exercise 1

The basic problem is that the researcher has assumed that these phrases will be in a single record. This is not the case in the ITA because a record is defined as a paragraph, which would include titles and headings. Turn to 6(1)(a) in a print version of the ITA and you will see that the six, the bracketed one and the bracketed small *a* are on different lines with a space either preceding or following. Therefore, each alpha/numeric symbol is in a different record. This can be seen more clearly in TaxWorks when the Formatting Codes feature of the Document Options is turned on, resulting in a diamond symbol at the beginning and end of each record. Remember that records are defined differently for the various infobases.

Note also that word, paragraph, is not present in this section either in the print or electronic version because the visual presentation provides this information. However, the presence of the word, paragraph, would find cross-references to 6(1)(a) in other records in the ITA but not internally in section 6.

Exercise 2

The command that overcomes the problems that are described in Exercise 1 is Go To Template which is represented by a green right-angled symbol in the toolbar. When you click on this icon, special templates (see Exhibits 19-15 and 19-16 in Chapter 19) appear. These templates do not search records but specific locations (destinations). For example, using paragraph 6(1)(a), the software first looks for the record where the first word in a record is the word, *paragraph*, followed by a space and then a number(s), i.e., 6. Then it looks for a subsequent record where the first word is the number one ignoring the brackets since brackets are query commands that separate multiple query phrases. Then the software looks for a subsequent record where the first word is a letter(s), again ignoring the brackets. However, the word paragraph is not present in 6(1)(*a*) of the ITA.

For this template to operate correctly, the researcher must input the command exactly as demonstrated in the chart on page 1014. Otherwise, the researcher would be describing a different location or destination. In our example, the command would be:

ita 6(1)(a)

Exercise 3

The correct query would be:

(student or students) and (university or universities) and (scholarship or scholarships)

Since the subsection 33(2) of the Interpretations Act states that words in the singular include the plural and *vice versa*, then commentary on the Income Tax Act, e.g. ITs, are subject to the same rules. The *Interpretations Act* can be found in the Commentary Infobase under the heading related statutes.

A record in the EBCR infobase is normally a paragraph except for charts and tables and a blank line creates the beginning of a new record and the end of the previous record. This information is in the sub-infobase, About this Infobase, which can be found on the first screen of the EBCR infobase or on the Table of Contents of the EBCR infobase.

This query would result in the following hits:

3 - Interpretation Bulletins

2 - Information Circulars

8 - Former Interpretation Bulletins

1 - Former Information Circular

Exercise 4

A correct query to the specific instructions that were given would be:

((corporation or corporations) and (associated or connected)) not affiliated

Note the use of brackets. The outside brackets connect the two queries with internal brackets so that the phrase, *not affiliated*, applies to the two internal queries.

This command resulted in 302 hits which, in most situations, would be too many records and should be restricted by adding another parameter. For example, the query might be restricted by adding a descriptive as to the type of corporation (e.g., private).

Exercise 5

This search exercise is more difficult than the preceding ones which were very directed. In this exercise, you would have to consider alternate terminology.

First, a record in the Tax Window Files infobase is each individual letter/document as described in the About this Infobase sub-infobase found in the Table of Contents. This means that such a query would have fewer hits in this infobase, compared to an infobase that has records defined as paragraphs such as the ITA and EBCR sub-infobases.

The simplest query for the facts in this exercise would be the alpha/numeric reference to the ITA, i.e. "8(1)(h)" which would yield 128 hits. If you forgot to place the quotation marks around the 8(1)(h) then you would have 1161 hits because brackets are search commands and ignored unless they are enclosed with quotation marks which convert them back to their normal function.

Another approach would be to use word queries using words selected from the fact situation. Unfortunately, all of the possible words are very commonplace, and would result in a very large number of hits, unless our query was very carefully crafted. However, in many situations, this alternative may be our only possibility. It might be useful at the outset to determine the extent of the problem by finding the number of occurrences in the infobase at hand.

business	12561	— too many; would not use this word
"business-related"	43	— hyphens not recognized; use brackets — 20 hits
travelling	261	— needed as a modifier
expenses	4117	— too many; would not use
automobile	596	— too many; needs some modifier
automobile expenses	160	— good but add car
"automobile expenses"	44	— too restrictive
car	494	— too many; needs some modifier

A possible query could be:

((employee or employees) and travelling and expenses) not (automobile or car)

This query results in 100 hits.

Comments:

- the plural of expense is more common than the singular when modifying a noun;
- "automobile expenses" is too restrictive because it would not find such phrases as "car expenses"; "expenses including automobile" etc.;
- similarly, travelling expenses should not be put in quotes but each word should be separate but joined by an *and*;
- always insert the sub-query brackets so that your query logic can be followed.

Part IV Advanced and Alternative Commands

Exercise 1

The following infobases/sub-infobases should be searched and examined:

- Interpretation Bulletins found in the EBCR infobase;
- Technical interpretation letters prepared by the CRA and found in the Tax Window Files infobase;
- Press releases prepared by the CRA and found in the New Releases sub-infobase of the Commentary infobase along with other relevant press releases;
- Current technical announcements prepared by the CRA and found in the Technical News sub-infobase of the Commentary infobase;
- Commentary on the validity of the CRA's interpretation letters referred to above and found in the Window on Canadian Tax infobase;
- Guides and pamphlets prepared by the CRA and found in the Income Tax Forms and Guides infobase;
- Questions and Answers in the Revenue Canada Round Table infobase.

Exercise 2

(A) The query would be:

"canadian-controlled private corporation" or "canadian-controlled private corporations"

　　OR

"canadian-controlled private" and (corporation or corporations)

Comments:

Both queries resulted in 148 hits. This is not surprising since a record in this infobase is defined as a paragraph. In other infobases such as the court infobases, where the records are much longer, (e.g., a page), there would be more non-relevant hits with the second query but not so significant so as to reject it as a possible alternative.

Without the double quotation marks around the phrase or parts thereof, this would have been a series of an automatic, *and*, connectors.

In addition, the quotation marks enable the Folio software to recognize the hyphenated word, *canadian-controlled*. Normally, hyphenated words are not recognized by Folio since hyphens are part of special screen-formatting commands. The quotation marks revert the hyphen back to its normal usage.

(B) The following changes should be added to the query commands in (A):

To the first query in Part (A), add the relevant acronyms joined by or connectors:

"canadian-controlled private corporation" or "canadian-controlled private corporations" or ccpc or ccpcs

To the second query in part A, add brackets to the that query in order to distinguish it from the following addition of the relevant acronyms.

("canadian-controlled private" and (corporation or corporations)) or ccpc or ccpcs

Both modified queries would result in 267 hits.

(C) Finally, the above queries should be restricted by the following phrase:

and "stock options"

The final queries would be:

("canadian-controlled private corporation" or "canadian-controlled private corporations" or ccpc or ccpcs) and "stock options"

   OR

(("canadian-controlled private" and (corporation or corporations)) or ccpc or ccpcs) and "stock options"

and would result in five hits.

To the second query in part A, add brackets to the final query in order to distinguish it from the full array addition of the relevant acronyms.

"canadian-controlled private" and (corporation or corporations) or cepc or cepcs

Both modified queries would result in 267 hits

(2) Finally, the above queries should be restricted by the following phrase:

... and stock options ...

The final queries would be:

"canadian-controlled private corporation" or "canadian-controlled private corporation" or (cepc or cepcs) and "stock options"

OR

(("canadian-controlled private" and (corporation or corporations)) or cepc or cepcs) and "stock options"

and would result in five hits

Topical Index

A

	Page
Abatement of federal tax	
. income earned in a province	575
Accident and sickness insurance	
. shareholder-manager benefits	708
Accountants	
. role in tax matters	25
Accounting	
. depreciation compared with CCA	227
. generally accepted accounting principles	15
. . income computation	16
. . interpretation of Income Tax Act	6
Accounts receivable	
. accrued or unrealized losses on	
. . acquisition of control	555
. ceasing to carry on business	190
Active business	
. common law background	695
. defined	627
. income	
. . eligible for small business deduction	644
. . ineligible for small business and	
. . . manufacturing and processing profits	
. . . deductions	64
. . ineligible for small business deduction	
. . . but eligible for manufacturing and	
. . . processing profits deduction	644
. . small business deduction	624
Additional refundable tax	
. aggregate investment income	653
. avoiding circular calculation	654
Adjusted cost base	
. adjustments to	324
. assets owned on Dec. 31, 1971	411
. capital gains and losses	320
. capital property	322
. convertible properties	389
. defined	322
. depreciable property	336
. gifts between spouses	394
. grants and subsidies	325
. interest on land	325
. negative	325
. non-depreciable capital property	411
. partnership interest	960
. . negative	962
. pre-1972 assets	411
. stock options	332
Administration and enforcement of Act	
. appeals	26
. CCRA's role	27
. onus of proof	26
Advance Tax Rulings	
. interpretation of Income Tax Act	10

	Page
Adventures in the nature of trade	
. business	151
. GST application	194
Affiliated persons	
. capital loss on property transferred	870
. defined	871
After-tax financing	
. concept	541
Age	
. tax credit	493
Agency agreement	
. cancellation damages	158
Aircraft	
. cost and expenses	115
. input tax credit	246
Alimony — see Support payments	
Allowances	
. meaning	89
. motor vehicles	112
. . conditions	113
. . unreasonable	113
. travelling expenses	
. . other employees	90
. . sales/negotiating persons	89
Amalgamations	
. rollover provisions of sec. 87	931
. statutory	
. . GST applications	951
. . rollover provisions	931
Amounts receivable	
. included in business income	164
Annuities	
. capital portion, deduction	430
. income	424
Anti-avoidance rules	
. attribution	281
. capital gains	321
. Part IV tax	658
. partnership allocation	958
Appeals	
. assessment or reassessment of taxes	782
. Federal Court of Appeal	27
. GST	783
. informal	26
. notice of objection	26
. onus of proof	26
. Supreme Court of Canada	27
. Tax Court of Canada	26
Assessments	
. GST	782
. objections and appeals	783
. tax returns	778
Assets	
. lease-option agreements	258

1207

Page

Assets — continued
. sale of incorporated business................818
.. analysis for decision........................818
.. GST implications...........................847

Associated corporations
. allocation of business limit................629
. association rules............................631
. association with third corporation.........637
. basic rules..................................631
. control......................................634
.. extended meaning...........................635
. controlled by group.........................635
. corporate partnerships......................638
. deemed association..........................638
. deeming of income...........................657
. ownership of shares.........................636
. provisions for determining association.....629
. related persons.............................629
. small business deduction....................629

Attendant care expenses
. deductions..................................455
. residents absent from Canada...............456

Attribution
. anti-avoidance rule.........................281
. avoidance of................................280
. income from property........................278
. loans.......................................278
.. non-arm's length persons..................282
. reasons for rules...........................278
. related persons.............................279
. rules — see Attribution rules
. transactions subject to.....................278
. type of income subject to..................282

Attribution rules
. capital gains on spousal transfers.........394
. income......................................278
. loans.......................................394
.. through corporation........................731
. non-arm's length transfers.................392
. trust.......................................973

Automobiles
. allowances..................................112
.. conditions.................................112
.. input tax credit...........................198
.. unreasonable...............................113
. capital cost allowance......................221
.. Class 10...............................221, 227
.. Class 10.1.............................221, 226
. costs and expenses..........................113
. employee-owned, operating expense
.. benefit....................................95
. expenses....................................113
.. deduction prohibited.......................167
.. employee deduction provisions
... compared.................................114
.. imputed interest..........................116
. input tax credit
.. vehicle owned by individuals or
... partnerships.............................246
.. vehicle owned by registrant other than
... individuals or partnerships..............246
. leasing costs, restrictions.................117

Page

Automobiles — continued
. operating cost benefit
.. alternative calculations...................92
.. calculation...............................91
.. income....................................89
. operating cost paid by employer, GST
.. application..............................196
. passenger vehicles
.. input tax credit.........................246
.. interest on money borrowed...............116
. shareholder-manager benefits...............701
. standby charge.............................91

Available-for-use rule
. capital cost allowance.................221, 223

B

Bad debts
. ceasing to carry on business...............190
. GST remitted but not collected,
.. adjustment...............................198
. proceeds of disposition....................389
. reserves...................................176

Beneficiaries
. accumulated trust income...................975
. preferred, election by trust...............975
. trust income payable to....................972

Benefits
. comparison between shareholders and
.. employees................................704
. employee stock options.....................473
. employer-paid GST..........................96
. income inclusion...........................421
. preferred beneficiary election.............975
. related person on transfer of property....877
. reorganization conferring benefit on
.. related person...........................929
. shareholders..............................704
. shareholders on transfer of property......878
.. fair market value........................881
.. received from corporation................272
.. schematic summary........................880
. transfer of property, conceptual example...874

Betting and gambling
. profits....................................159

Board and lodging
. value as income............................81

Bonds and debentures
. payments, non-deductible expenses..........166
. payments on discounted, not deductible.....166
. rollover provisions........................939

Bonuses
. shareholder-manager........................701
.. accrued..................................702

Books and records
. GST..780
. liability to keep..........................780

Borrowing expenses
. deductibility..........................173, 174

Branch tax
. non-resident carrying on business in Canada...616

	Page
Buildings and structures	
. allocation of proceeds of disposition, land	
vs. building	376
Business	
. adventures in the nature of trade	151, 195
. carrying on, GST application	194
. ceasing to carry on	190
.. sale of accounts receivable	190
.. sale of inventory	190
. contracts, damages for non-	
performance	158
. expenses — see Business expenses	
. income — see Business income	
. incorporated, sale	818
.. GST	847
. investment losses — see Business	
investment losses	
. liability for GST	57
. personal services, defined	628
. specified investment, defined	627
Business expenses	
. capital nature	166
. ceasing business	190
. deductibility	165
.. reasonable expectation of profit, checklist	171
. deductions permitted	174
.. cancellation of lease	180
.. convention expenses	181
.. disability-related modifications and	
equipment	180
.. discount on debt obligations	175
.. employer's contributions to DPSP	179
.. employer's contributions to RPP	179
.. expenses of borrowing money	175
.. expenses of issuing shares	175
.. interest	174
.. investigation of site	180
.. landscaping expenses	180
.. lease cancellation expenses	180
.. premiums on life insurance used as	
collateral	175
.. representation expenses	180
.. reserves specifically allowed	176
.. rules for deduction	181
.. utilities service connection	180
.. write-offs of capital expenditures	174
. deductions prohibited	166
.. accrued expenses	167
.. automobile expenses	167
.. investing in sheltered plans	167
.. payments on discounted bonds	166
.. payments on income bonds	166
.. payments under the Act	167
.. political contributions	167
.. prepaid expenses	167
.. provincial capital and payroll taxes	167
.. recreational facilities and club dues	166
.. reserves	169
.. unpaid amounts	169
.. unpaid remuneration	169
.. work space in home	167
. limitations on deductible amounts	173
. rules for deduction	181
. sales/negotiating persons	185

	Page
Business expenses — continued	
. unregistered employee compensation	
plans contributions	217
. warranties	414
Business income	
. active — see Active business	
. adjusted, manufacturing and processing	
industry	585
. amounts received or receivable	164
. automobile allowances, input tax credit	198
. automobile operating cost paid by	
employer, GST application	196
. basic rules	151
. capital receipts, vs	153
.. analytical framework	156
. concept	151
. damages	
.. cancellation of Agency agreements	158
.. loss of property	158
.. non-performance of contracts	158
. deductions	165
. distinction from property income	328
. factors determining	150
. foreign tax credits	636
. forgiven debt	159
. inclusions	164
. incorporation	644
.. tax cost and deferral	647
. integration	644
. integration with investment income	621
.. holding companies used for	775
.. major tools in Act	621
.. objectives	621
.. problems addressed by	621
. profits from illegal business	158
. reserves	166
. sole proprietorship	163
. subsidies	159
Business investment losses	
. allowable	340
.. accrued on acquisition of control	555
.. deduction	727
.. defined	340
.. treatment	545
. deductions allowed	340
. deductions disallowed	340
. tax treatment	341
Business or Property	
. Subdiv. b chart	150

C

	Page
Canada Education Savings Grant	
. registered education savings plans	425
Canada Pension Plan	
. contributions, tax credit	508
. premiums paid for assistant	109
. shareholder-manager remuneration	750
Canada – U.S. Tax Convention	
. application to corporations	55
. application to individuals	46
Canadian-controlled private corporations	
. dividend refund	660
. employee stock options	473

Page

Canadian-controlled private corporations —
continued
. investment tax credit.................................640
. . rate..640
. . refundable...641
. small business deductions........................625
. . not available to large corporations............626
. stock options to employees.......................99

Capital
. comparison with income............................16
. receipts compared with business income.....153
. . analytical framework..............................156

Capital cost
. capital gains and losses............................321
. depreciable property, reduced by
    assistance received................................239
. passenger vehicles, limitations..................117
. pre-1972 depreciable property...................411

Capital cost allowance
. automobile...226
. available-for-use rule...............................225
. basic rules...221
. . applied to prescribed classes..................222
. capital cost reduced by assistance
    received..239
. change in use of property..........................235
. . change in proportion..............................237
. . income-producing to other purposes.........235
. . non-income-producing to income-
        producing.......................................236
. . property acquired for multiple purposes.....237
. classes...221
. computer equipment acquired after
    March 22, 2004.....................................229
. declining balance method
. . exception to...228
. . leasehold improvements.........................228
. depreciation compared with......................227
. disposition of property.............................226
. electronic office equipment.......................228
. franchise...239
. half-net-amount rule.........................223, 236
. . change in use of property........................236
. half-year rule..223
. . common property not affected by..............223
. insurance proceeds on depreciable
    property..231
. involuntary dispositions............................232
. leasehold improvements...........................230
. lease-option agreements...........................258
. leasing property......................................260
. limited-life intangible properties.................231
. ownership of property...............................226
. part disposition of property........................235
. patents..239
. permissive deduction...............................225
. prescribed classes of assets......................223
. proceeds of disposition............................231
. recapture..228
. . involuntary disposition of depreciable
        property...232
. . voluntary disposition of depreciable
        property...233
. rental property..318

Page

Capital cost allowance — continued
. replacement property...............................232
. separate class rule..................................228
. similarities with deductions on eligible
    capital expenditures..............................241
. straight-line base....................................239
. taxation year less than 12 months..............225
. voluntary dispositions..............................228

Capital dividend account
. components..805
. eligible capital property
. . disposition...807
. "period" in sec. 89(1)(*b*).........................807

Capital gains
. adjusted cost base...................................322
. anti-avoidance provisions.........................321
. assets owned on Dec. 31, 1971.................354
. attribution rules......................................394
. . spousal transfers...................................394
. Canadian securities, election re disposition...321
. capital receipts vs. income receipts............318
. computation...321
. . adjusted cost base.................................322
. convertible property.................................389
. death of taxpayer....................................398
. deductions — see Capital gains
        deductions
. deferral...390
. depreciable 1351
. determining factors..................................318
. eligible for refundable tax, flow-through of....665
. exchange of property...............................368
. exempt, balance.....................................413
. foreign exchange....................................367
. history of taxation....................................317
. identical property, post-1971.....................319
. leaving and entering Canada.....................385
. listed personal property............................329
. options..386
. part disposition of property........................367
. personal-use property..............................328
. pre-1972 assets......................................411
. primary intention.....................................317
. principal residence............................325, 380
. . change of use.......................................380
. . disposition...325
. . employment transfer..............................382
. . exemption..325
. . exemption, change in use.......................378
. . joint-ownership.....................................385
. . land used in farming business..................361
. . owned after Dec. 31, 1981......................354
. . single-ownership...................................383
. . transfer between spouses........................383
. . 1-plus rule..325
. property with more than one use................378
. reconciliation with book gains....................399
. reserves..323
. secondary intention.................................318
. taxable, computation...............................321
. terminology..319
. Valuation day value.................................355

Page

Capital gains deductions
. allowable business investment losses.......... 340, 728
. computation.. 727
. cumulative net investment loss...................... 728
. elimination.. 481
. exempt capital gains balance........................ 413
. history.. 317
. lifetime... 481
. qualified small business corporation shares......... 720

Capital losses
. allowable
. . business investment loss.................... 339, 545
. . computation.. 340
. computation... 321
. . adjusted cost base..................................... 322
. foreign exchange.. 367
. listed personal property................................. 329
. median rule.. 354
. personal-use property.................................... 328
. terminology.. 319
. Valuation day value...................................... 355
. warranty.. 414

Capital personal property
. input tax credit... 245
. . primary-use test.. 261

Capital property
. adjustments to cost base............................... 336
. cost.. 335
. depreciable — see Depreciable property
. disposition by trust....................................... 991
. eligible — see Eligible capital property
. non-depreciable
. . adjusted cost base...................................... 411
. . losses on acquisition of control.................... 553
. personal — see Capital personal property
. real — see Capital real property
. shares deemed as.. 370

Capital real property
. GST application
. . change of use rules..................................... 417
. . dispositions... 417
. . input tax credit... 416

Caregiver
. tax credit... 492

Carrying charges
. land, deduction.. 285

Carryovers — see Loss carryovers

Cars — see Automobiles

Charitable donations — see also Gifts
. deductions by corporations............................ 542
. tax credits... 496
. . carryforward.. 496
. . income limit.. 496

Child
. care expenses
. . deductions... 452
. . residents absent from Canada...................... 456
. support amount, tax treatment....................... 422
. tax benefits.. 517
. . eligibility... 517

Page

Clubs
. memberships, input tax credit........................ 197

Commercial activity
. defined... 59, 194
. excluded activities.. 195
. exclusions from.. 60

Competent authority
. international tax conventions........................... 47

Computation of income — see Income computation

Connected corporations
. concept illustrated.. 659
. defined... 658
. Part IV tax... 659

Control
. concept... 634
. corporations.. 629
. . by group... 629
. . extended meaning...................................... 635

Convention
. expenses... 181

Convertible property — see Securities

Corporate distributions
. capital dividend.. 805
. capital dividend account................................ 805
. convertible properties.................................... 939
. disposition of eligible capital property............. 807
. dividends
. . cash or stock... 810
. . deemed.. 810
. . deemed, on increase in P.U.C...................... 811
. . deemed, on redemption or acquisition
. . of shares... 812
. . deemed, on reduction of P.U.C..................... 816
. . deemed, on winding-up................................ 812
. . in kind... 810
. paid-up capital of shares............................... 803
. sale of incorporated business......................... 818
. . analysis for decision.................................... 818
. . GST and Winding-up.................................... 847
. surplus.. 803
. surplus balances... 810
. . special taxes.. 911

Corporate partnership — see Partnerships

Corporations
. acquisition of control
. . losses... 555
. . losses, deemed year-end.............................. 553
. amalgamations — see Amalgamations
. associated — see Associated corporations
. attribution rules
. . designated persons..................................... 731
. . loans or transfers....................................... 731
. basic computation of tax............................... 573
. capital dividend account................................ 805
. capital reorganization.................................... 922
. . benefit rule.. 929
. . calculation procedure for sec. 86.................. 923
. . conceptual view of sec. 86........................... 923
. . conditions... 1003
. computation of tax — see Tax
. computation, corporations

Page

Corporations — continued
. computation of taxable income........................... 539
. connected — see Connected corporations
. controlled by group...629
. deduction of taxable dividends............................539
.. after-tax financing..541
. deemed dividend, distribution............................810
. distribution — see Corporate distributions
. dividends from
.. income...265
.. untaxed income...541
. dividends paid on shares sold for loss................542
. double taxation prevented...................................540
. elective capital gains on capital property............557
. elective recapture on capital property..................557
. federal tax abatement...575
. general rates of tax...574
. holding companies — see Holding
    companies
. income earned in a province, allocation...............578
. international tax treaties application......................55
. large — see Large corporations
. liability for GST..57
. liability for tax...53
.. charging provisions..53
. non-arm's length sale of shares..........................887
.. application of rules to post-1971 shares............891
.. basic rules of ssec. 84.1(1).................................889
.. conditions for section 84.1.................................889
. non-resident carrying on business, branch tax......616
. partnership..987
. provincial tax abatement.....................................575
. residence...54
.. common law concept..54
.. comprehensive considerations............................56
.. deemed...56
. rollovers, GST applications..................................950
. sale...823
.. analysis for decision...818
.. assets v. shares..823
.. GST and Winding-up...832
. sale of shares to unrelated person
.. capital gains strips...900
.. effects of sec. 55...900
.. exceptions to sec. 55 rule...................................903
.. situation addressed by ss. 55.............................900
. sec. 85 rollovers, GST application.......................917
. share for share exchange....................................920
.. conditions...920
.. consequences..921
. statutory amalgamations.....................................932
. tax credits...588
. tax rates per income types..................................672
. taxable income..571
. transfer of property by shareholders....................850
.. basic rules...857
.. benefits, conceptual example.............................874
.. benefits on related person..................................873
.. benefits on shareholder......................................873
.. corporation's position..862
.. depreciable capital property...............................868
.. fair market value..881
.. GST application..917

Page

Corporations
. transfer of property by shareholders — continued
.. paid-up capital reduction on shares
      issued as consideration...................................864
.. restrictions on elected price................................859
.. rollover applications...888
.. schematic summary..880
.. sec. 22 election..882
.. shareholder's position...963
.. specific situations..851
. using for shareholder-manager
      remuneration..698
. windings-up...801
. disposition of net assets......................................818
. GST..832
. winding-up of subsidiary
.. GST application..951
.. rollover provisions..939

Cost
. capital properties...335
. dividends in kind...335
. lottery prizes...335
. stock dividends..335

Cost base
. adjusted — see Adjusted cost base
. adjustments to..336
. identical property...333

Courts
. interpretation of Income Tax Act.............................9

CRA
. administration and enforcement of Act.................26
. powers and obligations..767
.. GST..781
. publications re Income Tax Act.............................10

Crown gifts
. tax credit...497

Cultural gifts
. tax credit...497

Cumulative net investment losses
. defined..728

D

Damages
. cancellation of agency agreements......................158
. income or capital...158
. loss of property..158
. non-performance of contracts...............................158

Debts
. doubtful
.. ceasing to carry on business...............................190
. forgiven, business income....................................159
. obligations
.. discount...175

Deceased persons
. capital gains..398
. deemed disposition of property............................399
. personal tax credits...777
. rights or things..776
. tax returns...775
.. filing-due dates..757
.. other returns..776
.. prior taxation years..775

Deceased persons
. tax returns — continued
. . terminal returns...775

Deductions from income
. aircraft cost and expenses...............................115
. allowable business investment losses...........340, 545
. annuities, capital element of.............................430
. attendant care expenses....................................455
. automobile allowances and expenses...............112
. automobile costs and expenses........................115
. . employee deduction provisions
        compared..114
. borrowing expenses...175
. business investment loss, allowable................545
. carrying charges on land....................................285
. child care expenses..452
. child support amounts.......................................422
. computational rules..339
. corporations...539
. . charitable donations.......................................542
. . net capital losses..546
. CPP and EI premiums paid for assistant..............109
. deduction of net capital losses to
        preserve non-capital losses.........................549
. dues and other expenses...................................108
. employee stock options.....................................473
. employment expenses.......................................104
. expenses of issuing shares................................175
. foreign tax credits...588
. GST rebate on employee deductions..................122
. home relocation loan..476
. interest expense...293
. . current legislation..290
. . draft legislation..291
. . loss of source of income..................................295
. interest on money borrowed for
        passenger vehicle...116
. investment tax credits...595
. legal expenses...108
. loss carryovers...478
. . corporations..543
. . ordering of deductions....................................548
. . restrictions on deductions...............................548
. losses on acquisition of control.........................553
. manufacturing and processing industries..............583
. mortgage interest...297
. moving expenses...450
. net capital losses...479
. non-capital losses..478
. ordering of Division C deductions......................482
. ordering rules for individuals.............................19
. overpayments to pension plans.........................449
. partnership losses, limitations...........................958
. passenger vehicle
. . capital cost...116
. . leasing cost..117
. personal loan interest expense.........................293
. premiums on life insurance used as
        collateral..175
. restricted farm losses...481
. restrictions on reserves......................................176
. RPP contributions...109
. . post-1989 service..111
. sales/negotiating person's expenses............104, 185

Deductions from income — continued
. scientific research and experimental
        development expenditures.............................191
. support payments...422
. Supreme Court Decisons....................................294
. taxable dividends..539
. travelling expenses...105
. . limitations..107
. work space in home..109

Deferred profit sharing plans
. employer's contributions.....................................179
. features...432
. income from...424
. integration of limits...433
. pension adjustment...437
. transfer provisions..447

Defined benefit pension plans
. defined...431
. integration of limits...433
. pension adjustment...437
. . net past service..470
. . reversals...470
. tax-assisted benefits...431

Department of Finance
. technical notes..10

Dependants
. defined...492
. personal tax credits...492

Depreciable property
. adjustments to cost base.....................................332
. capital cost
. . pre-1972..411
. . reduction...240
. . reduction by assistance received......................240
. capital cost allowance...221
. capital gains
. . computation..411
. . pre-1972..411
. change in use..235
. . change in proportion...237
. . income-producing to other purposes................235
. . non-income-producing to income-
        producing..236
. . property acquired for multiple purposes...........237
. damaged, insurance proceeds expended on........231
. elective capital gains and recapture on
        deemed disposition.......................................557
. losses on acquisition of control..........................553
. non-arm's length transfer...................................239
. part disposition...235
. proceeds of disposition......................................231
. . involuntary..232
. . voluntary...233
. replacement property..232
. transfer from partnership to corporation..............963
. transfer to corporation by shareholder................850
. . limitations on transferee's cost base................850
. transfer to partnership...964

Depreciation
. comparison with capital cost allowance..............227

Director's fees
. income...91

Disability

Page
. expenses for modifications and equipment...........180

Discretionary trusts — see Trusts

Dividends
. assessable...658
. cash or stock, distribution.......................810
. deemed
. . distribution as surplus........................810
. . increase in P.U.C...............................811
. . redemption or acquisition of shares.........812
. . reduction of P.U.C.............................816
. . winding-up.......................................819
. gross-up..269
. GST exemption....................................298
. inter-corporate deduction......................539
. . after-tax financing............................541
. not subject to Part IV tax, flow-through......665
. paid from untaxed income......................541
. portfolio..658
. . flow-through, subject to Part IV tax.........665
. . integration......................................665
. . refund...660
. shareholder-manager
. . amounts allowed tax-free......................711
. . deferral of tax..................................719
. . paid as salary...................................710
. spousal election..................................269
. stock, cost...335
. stripping, non-arm's length sale of shares.....887
. subject to Part IV tax, flow-through............665
. tax credit.....................................269, 511
. . election..511
. . investment income.............................668
. taxable Canadian corporation's................269
. taxation to individuals..........................622

Donations — see Charitable donations, Gifts

Dues
. employee's, deduction...........................108

E

Ecological gifts
. tax credit..498

Education
. assistance payments............................426
. tax credit..506
. . carryforward....................................506
. . transfer to parent or grandparent............506
. tax-free RRSP withdrawals......................442

Election
. accounts receivable on sale of business......190
. convertible property transfer to corporation...939
. corporation re capital gains and recapture...557
. exchange of property............................368
. preferred beneficiary of trust..................975
. property disposition, additional deferral......373
. transfer of property
. . between spouses...............................397
. . sec. 22 application..............................882
. . shareholder to corporation...................850
. . to partnership..................................963

Electronic office equipment
. capital cost allowance..........................228

Eligible capital property

Page
. amortization of costs.............................241
. . similarity with capital cost allowance system......241
. capital dividend account
. . cumulative account............................805
. . disposition......................................805
. . cumulative eligible capital account..........242
. eligible capital expenditures...................240
. franchise...239
. goodwill..239
. losses on acquisition of control...............553

Employee benefit plans
. contributions and benefits......................217
. deferral of tax....................................217
. unregistered compensation plans.............217

Employee stock options — see also Stock options
. benefits as income...............................473
. offsetting deductions............................473

Employees
. automobile, capital cost allowance............226
. benefit plans — see Employee benefit plans
. CPP and EI premiums paid for assistant.......109
. dues and other expenses.......................108
. expenses re work space at home..............109
. goods and services tax
. . employer-paid, on benefits....................96
. . rebate...122
. legal expense deduction........................108
. loan
. . forgiveness......................................89
. . fringe benefits..................................84
. part-time, travelling expenses.................107
. payments by employer...........................97
. principal residence, when transferred........380
. restrictive covenants.............................99
. tax withheld by employer........................772
. tests to determine.................................77

Employers
. automobile allowances, input tax credit.......198
. automobile operating cost paid by, GST
. . application.......................................196
. payments to employee...........................97
. payments to non-residents.....................774
. withholding tax, obligations....................772

Employment
. expense, deduction..............................104
. outside Canada, tax credit.....................519
. retiring allowance.................................421
. termination payments............................421

Employment income
. allowances...89
. amounts received..................................81
. application of Subdiv. a rules...................125
. automobile provided by employer...............91
. . alternative benefit calculations................92
. benefits from employer-paid GST................96
. board and lodging values........................81
. concept...75
. deductions — see Deductions from income
. director's fees......................................91
. employed vs. self-employed......................77

Employment income — continued
. employee loans..86
. . forgiveness..89
. expense deduction..104
. fringe benefits..82
. . administrative practice...................................84
. gratuities...80
. insurance benefits...96
. payments by employer to employee.................97
. remunerations...80
. salary, wages, etc..80
. sales/negotiating persons.................................185
. shareholder-managers......................................698
. specific inclusions...81
. stock options..99

Employment Insurance
. payments...426
. premiums
. . tax credit...508

Entertainment expenses
. GST application..199

Estate freeze
. holdco freeze..941
. . rollover provisions...940
. internal freeze...941
. objectives..940
. reverse freeze...942
. rollovers..940

Excise Tax Act
. general anti-avoidance rule................................753
. organization...28
. schedules...31
. structure..29
. treatment of partnership...................................993
. treatment of trusts...996

Exempt capital gains balance
. flow-through entity...413

Exemption from income — see Deductions from income

Expenses
. attendant care...455
. business, capital nature.....................................166
. . write-offs, deductible......................................174
. child care...452
. motor vehicles..111
. prepaid, deduction prohibited............................167
. sales/negotiating persons..................................185
. travelling...105
. . limitations..107

Expropriation
. involuntary dispositions....................................232

F

Fair market value
. benefits on transfer of property..........................881
. inventory valuation...154
. property transferred to corporation by
   shareholders..878
. related person's benefits on transfer of
   property..877
. shareholder's benefits on transfer of
   property..878

Farming
. shareholder's benefits on transfer of
   property
. . carryback rules..560
. . deductions...559
. . same or similar business..................................560

Federal Court of Appeal
. appeals..27

Fees
. directors...91

Financial services
. GST exemption...298

Fiscal period
. terminated partnership......................................967

Fiscal year
. trusts..975

Flow-through entity
. exempt capital gains balance.............................413

Foreign exchange
. capital gains and losses....................................367

Foreign income
. tax credit...519

Foreign tax credits
. business income..519, 591
. corporations...519, 588
. income earned outside of Canada......................519
. non-business income...................................519, 589
. purpose and approach......................................519

Forms
. prescribed under Act..10

Franchises
. capital cost allowance......................................239
. eligible capital property....................................240

Fringe benefits
. employee loans..86
. . forgiveness...89
. housing loss and costs......................................86
. income..820
. shareho;der-managers......................................708
. . life insurance premiums..................................708
. . registered pension plans.................................708
. . retirement benefits...708
. . sickness or accident insurance.........................708

G

Gambling
. profits...159

General anti-avoidance rule
. Excise Tax Act...753
. Income Tax Act...734

Generally accepted accounting principles
. income computation...16
. interpretation of Income Tax Act........................11

Gifts
. non-arm's length transaction.............................392
. publicly traded securities..................................497
. tax credit...496
. . carryforward...496
. . charitable..497
. . Crown...497

Page

Gifts
. tax credit — continued
. . cultural..497
. . ecological..498
. . income limit...496

Goods and services tax
. adventures or concerns in the nature of trade......195
. application of rules......................................199
. application to partnership.............................993
. . continuation of partnership.........................996
. . joint and several liability.............................995
. . property transfer from partnership.................995
. . property transfer to partnership....................994
. application to partnership interest..................994
. application to trusts....................................996
. . distribution of property..............................997
. . liability of trustees....................................997
. . settlement of trust....................................996
. assessment..782
. automobile allowances, input tax credit.............198
. automobile operating cost paid by
    employer..196
. bad debts where tax remitted but not
    collected..198
. basic concepts..32
. books and records.......................................780
. capital property defined................................245
. capital real property
. . acquisition..416
. . change of use rules...................................417
. . dispositions...417
. capital reorganization..................................950
. carrying on business....................................194
. collection...777
. commercial activity.................................59, 194
. . exclusions from...60
. convertible properties..................................952
. disclosure..777
. employee benefits..96
. entertainment expenses................................199
. exempt services and income...........................298
. financial instruments exemption......................298
. food and beverages expenses.........................199
. harmonization with provincial sales tax...............35
. harmonized sales tax.....................................35
. impact on business activity............................199
. imports..62
. input tax credits — see Input tax credits
. interest on overpayment................................782
. legislation..29
. . structure..29
. liability..57
. non-resident defined......................................61
. objections and appeals.................................783
. payments based on production or use................313
. personal-use real property disposition................361
. price reduction adjustment.............................198
. property income..313
. property transfers.......................................917
. purchases — see "supplies" below
. reassessment..782
. rebate on employee deductions.......................122
. recapture on passeng57
. refundable tax credits...................................515

Page

Goods and services tax — continued
. refunds..782
. registration...59
. . exceptions..60
. registration of non-residents...........................61
. . mandatory..61
. . voluntary..61
. remittance..779
. rental property...313
. reporting period..778
. residential property disposition.......................361
. returns...778
. . amended..783
. rollovers
. . commercial property...................................917
. . corporate securities...................................950
. . sec. 85 rollovers.......................................917
. services re capital reorganization....................950
. share for share exchange..............................950
. shareholder benefits....................................298
. simplified accounting...................................784
. soft costs...299
. supplies
. . concept...32
. . exempt..33
. . in Canada..58
. . zero-rated...33
. trade-ins..363
. used goods disposition.................................363
. used residential property disposition.................361
. value of consideration received.......................195
. when payable..195
. winding-up of subsidiary...............................951

Goodwill
. eligible capital property................................240

Grants and subsidies — see also Scholarships
. adjusted cost bases.....................................325

Gratuities
. income inclusion...80

H

Half-net-amount rule
. capital cost allowance..................................223
. . change in use of property............................237

Half-year rule
. capital cost allowance..................................223
. . common property not affected.......................224

Harmonized sales tax
. provincial harmonization of GST........................35

Holding companies
. deferral of tax on dividends...........................719
. estate freeze......................................719, 940
. extension of integration................................718
. shareholder-manager's compensation................719

Home
. office expenses, input tax credit......................197
. relocation loan, special deduction....................476
. work space
. . deductions allowed....................................109
. . expenses, deduction..................................168

Home Buyers' Plan
. tax-free withdrawals from RRSP.......................441

	Page
I	
Identical properties	
. cost base	333
. pooling of assets after 1971	329
. post-1971 assets, capital gains	329
Impairment	
. mental or physical, tax credits	504
. transfer	504
Imports	
. GST application	62
Income	
. adult training allowances	426
. amounts not included as	429
. annuity payments	424
. attribution — see Attribution	
. business — see Business income	
. business and property, difference	298
. capital receipts vs. income receipts	318
. child support amounts	423
. comparison with capital	16
. computation — see Income computation	
. constructive receipt	15
. corporations, tax rates per income types	672
. deductions — see Deductions from income	
. deferral on transfers of assets by	
. shareholders	849
. definition	14
. . economist's perspective	15
. determination	18
. DPSP payments	431
. employment — see Employment income	
. indirect payments	427
. interest — see Interest income	
. investment — see Investment income	
. minors	281
. non-business, foreign tax credit	589
. not earned in a province	515
. partnership	956
. property — see Property income	
. reconciliation with book gains	399
. RESP payments	425
. retiring allowances	421
. RRIF payments	444
. RRSP payments	434
. scholarship and bursaries	426
. sole proprietorship	163
. splitting through minors	281
. splitting through spouses	708
. support payments	422
. taxable — see Taxable income	
Income computation	
. aggregation formula	16
. allowances	89
. amounts excluded	429
. annuity payments	424
. automobile	
. . operating cost benefit	91
. . operating cost benefit, alternative	
. calculations	91
. . operating expense benefit	95
. . standby charge	91
. benefits from employer-paid GST	96
. board and lodging values	81

	Page
Income computation — continued	
. bursaries	426
. business income	151
. . deductions	165
. . inclusions	164
. capital gains	413
. child support amount	423
. computational rules	339
. deductions	430
. director's fees	91
. DPSP payments	431
. employee loans	86
. . forgiveness	115
. Employment Insurance benefits	96
. employment termination payments	421
. exempt income	429
. flow chart, under sec. 3	17
. fringe benefits	82
. generally accepted accounting principles	15
. gratuities	80
. income from other sources	421
. indirect payments	427
. interest income	265
. . accrual basis	266
. . accrued to transfer date	266
. . methods of reporting	265
. non-capital sources	421
. non-refundable tax credits, ordering rules	19
. ordering rules of deductions for	
. individuals	19
. partnership's taxable income	959
. payments by employers to employees	97
. pensions	421
. property income	263
. provisions of the Act	11
. remunerations	80
. research grants	426
. RESP payments	425
. retiring allowances	421
. RRIF payments	444
. RRSP payments	430
. salary and wages	30
. scholarships	426
. sourcing and tracing of income	18
. stock options	99
. support payments	422
. travelling allowances	
. . other employees	90
. . sales/negotiating persons	89
. trusts income	972
Income Tax Act	
. administration	14
. Advance Tax Rulings for interpretation	10
. CCRA releases	10
. divisions	11
. draft legislation	8
. forms	10
. general anti-avoidance rule	734
. generally accepted accounting principles	11
. history	2
. interpretation	14
. . tax legislation	22
. interpretive sources	9
. judicial decisions	9

Income Tax Act — continued   **Page**
. organization.. 6
. Parts dealing with special transactions................... 13
. pending amendments....................................... 8
. provisions dealing with income
    computation... 12
. provisions dealing with minimum tax................... 12
. provisions dealing with non-residents.................... 14
. provisions dealing with tax computation............... 11
. provisions dealing with tax liability...................... 11
. provisions for computation of taxable income........ 12
. provisions for large corporations......................... 12
. provisions for Old Age Security benefits................ 12
. regulations — see Income Tax Regulations
. rights and obligations..................................... 755
. structure... 6, 11
. tax conventions and treaties............................... 8
. technical notes issued by Department of
    Finance.. 10

Income Tax Application Rules, 1971
. transitional rules for Act.................................. 8

Income tax liability
. corporations.. 53
. . common law concept..................................... 54
. full-time residents
. . common law concept..................................... 42
. . deemed... 42
. . departmental practice.................................... 43
. individuals.. 41
. international tax treaties................................... 46
. non-resident corporations................................. 56
. non-residents.. 45
. part-time residence... 44
. residents.. 41

Income Tax Regulations
. administration and enforcement of Act.................. 9
. allocation of income to province......................... 576

Income Tax Technical News
. CRA's comments on tax issues............................. 10

Individuals
. international tax treaties................................... 46
. liability for tax — see Income tax liability
. personal tax credits.. 489
. residence
. . analysis of factual situation............................. 51
. . Comprehensive Consideration.......................... 50
. . non-tax factors.. 53
. . Summary... 48
. tax returns, filing due dates.............................. 757
. taxable income, computation............................. 473
. taxes payable, computation.............................. 487

Inducement payments
. acquisition of assets....................................... 164

Information Circulars
. administrative and procedural matters of
    Income Tax Act.................................... 10

Information returns
. foreign investments.. 774
. non-residents.. 774
. payments to residents...................................... 773
. required of payers.. 757
. trustee's obligation... 773

Input tax credits   **Page**
. aircraft.. 246
. automobile allowances..................................... 198
. capital personal property
. . basic rules.. 245
. . primary-use test... 261
. club memberships... 197
. concept.. 32
. general rules... 196
. home office expenses....................................... 197
. passenger vehicles.. 246
. . owned by registered individuals or
      partnerships...................................... 246
. . owned by registrant other than
      individuals or partnerships..................... 246
. personal or living expenses............................... 197
. reasonableness.. 198
. restrictions... 197

Instalment payment of tax
. corporations.. 764
. GST... 780
. individuals.. 762

Insurance
. benefits as income.. 96
. proceeds on depreciable property....................... 232

Interest
. capitalization... 293
. deductible business expenses............................. 174
. deduction limitation... 293
. eligible for refundable tax, flow-through............... 665
. expenses
. . current legislation... 290
. . deductibility... 293
. . deductibility, personal loan............................. 293
. . draft legislation... 291
. GST exemption... 298
. imputed, shareholder loans............................... 274
. income — see Interest income
. income-producing borrowings............................ 291
. land.. 285
. . adjusted cost base.. 324
. loss of source of income.................................. 291
. money borrowed for passenger vehicle................. 116
. mortgage.. 297
. overpaid tax.. 764
. prescribed rates... 763
. shareholder loans, imputed............................... 750
. unpaid tax instalments
. . corporations.. 764
. . individuals.. 762

Interest income
. accrual basis... 266
. accrued to transfer date................................... 267
. defined.. 265
. methods of reporting....................................... 265
. prescribed debt obligations............................... 311
. property income... 265

International tax conventions
. application to corporations................................ 55
. application to individuals.................................. 46
. competent authority.. 47
. permanent establishment.................................. 48
. relationship to Income Tax Act........................... 8

Page

Interpretation Bulletins
. interpretation of Income Tax Act................................10

Inventory
. allocation of depreciation and
    obsolescence...162
. ceasing business..190
. losses on acquisition of control....................553
. valuation...160
. . cost..160
. . depreciation and obsolescence.................162
. . fair market value..161
. . FIFO and LIFO..160
. . replacement cost..160

Investment
. business, specified.......................................627
. contract, interest..265
. mortgage..297
. sheltered plans, expenses...........................167

Investment income
. additional refundable tax..............................654
. . circular calculation.....................................654
. aggregate investment income defined..........654
. calculation, deeming rules...........................657
. Canadian
. . defined...649
. . refundable taxes..655
. dividend tax credit..667
. effective tax rate...650
. foreign..654
. incorporation, advantages and
    disadvantages..671
. integration with business income........621, 649
. . conceptual illustration of integration.........652
. . holding companies used for......................718
. . imperfections...665
. . major tools in Act.......................................621
. . objectives...621
. . permanent tax savings...............................668
. . portfolio dividends.....................................652
. . problems addressed by..............................621
. . tax deferral at higher tax rate.....................665
. special refundable taxes...............................653
. tax biases, corporations and individuals......649
. . portfolio dividends.....................................652

**Investment losses — see Business investment
    losses**

Investment tax credits
. availability...595
. Canadian-controlled private corporations......640
. computation...595
. qualified property..596
. rates...596, 640
. refundable...641
. scientific research expenditures....................597
. . capital expenditures...................................643
. . prescribed proxy amount............................642

L

Land
. carrying charges..285
. interest and taxes adjusted to cost base........324
. soft costs re ownership..................................299

Page

Landscaping
. expenses...180

Large corporations
. provisions dealing with....................................11
. small business deductions, not available.......626
. taxation...580

Lease
. cancellation expenses...................................180
. cost deduction for automobiles.....................117

Leasehold improvements
. capital cost allowance...................................230

Lease-option agreements
. capital cost allowance...................................258
. distinctions between sale and lease..............258

Legal expenses
. deductions..108

Licences
. capital cost allowance...................................239

Life insurance
. premiums, used as collateral.........................175
. shareholder-manager benefits.......................763

Listed personal property
. capital gains and losses................................329
. defined..329

Loans
. attribution rules...278
. . non-arm's length persons..........................282
. attribution through corporation......................731
. employees
. . forgiveness...89
. . fringe benefit..84
. interest expenses..297
. personal, interest expense............................293
. shareholder — see Shareholder loans
. students, tax credit for interest......................508

Loss carryovers
. corporations..543
. . allowable business investment losses........545
. . net capital losses.......................................479
. . non-capital losses......................................478
. . ordering of deductions...............................482
. . restrictions on deductions..........................482
. deductions..478
. farm losses..481
. restricted farm losses....................................481

Losses
. accrued
. . accounts receivable....................................555
. . depreciable capital property.......................555
. . eligible capital property...............................556
. . inventory...555
. . non-depreciable capital property.................556
. acquisition of corporation
. . deemed year-end..553
. . utilization strategies....................................554
. allowable business investment......................340
. allowable business investment losses...........728
. business investment — see Business
    investment losses
. capital — see Capital losses
. carryovers — see Loss carryovers

Losses — continued   **Page**

. cumulative net investment losses.............................728

. net capital — see Net capital losses

. non-capital — see Non-capital losses

. partnerships, deduction limitation............................958

. rental property...287

. restricted farm — see Restricted farm losses

. terminal — see Terminal losses

. unrealized

. . accounts receivable...555

. . depreciable capital property.....................................555

. . eligible capital property..556

. . inventory..555

. . . non-depreciable capital property............................556

. warranties..414

M

Maintenance — see Support payments

Manufacturing and processing profits deduction

. adjusted business income..585

. calculation formula...638

. computation

. . application of rules..586

. . cost of capital...585

. . cost of labour..585

. . cost of manufacturing and
       processing labour..586

. . cost of manufacturing and
       processing capital..585

. . formula...585

. reduced rate of tax...583

. small business deductions...639

. tax credits, eligibility..583

. tax rates applicable..583

Married persons — see also Spouses

. dividend election...269

. income attribution...278

. income splitting...708

. tax credits...490

Median rule

. assets owned on Dec. 31, 1971.................................354

Medical expenses

. defined..499

. tax credit

. . notch provision...502

. . supplemental..517

Minimum tax

. adjusted taxable income...524

. basic credits..525

. basic exemption..525

. provisions dealing with...12

. trusts...976

Minister

. powers re reassessment...767

Money

. borrowing expenses..175

Money purchase pension plans

. integration of limits...433

. pension adjustment...437

. . net past service..470

. . reversals...470

Mortgage

. interest deductibility..297

. investing in own..297

Motor vehicles — see Automobiles

Moving expenses   **Page**

. deductions...450

. residents absent from Canada...................................451

. students..490

N

Negotiating persons

. business income..185

. expenses..104, 185

. travelling allowances...89

Net capital losses

. carryovers...479

. corporations

. . acquisition of control...553

. . carryovers...546

. . deducted to preserve non-capital losses.................549

. . deemed year-end...553

. deductions...479

. defined..479

Non-arm's length transactions

. consideration...392

. defined..392

. gifts..392

Non-capital losses

. allowable business investment losses........................559

. carryback rules..561

. carryovers...478

. corporations

. . carryovers...543

. . net capital losses deducted to preserve.................549

. deductions...478

. defined..478

. . corporations...543

. same or similar business..560

Non-depreciable capital property

. capital loss on transfer to affiliated
     persons...870

. elective capital gains on deemed
     disposition..557

Non-residents

. carrying on business

. . liability for tax...45

. corporations, tax liability...55

. defined for GST purposes..61

. GST registration requirements.....................................61

. . mandatory..61

. . voluntary..62

. liability for tax..45

. payments by Canadian employers.............................774

. provisions dealing with...14

. supplies for GST purposes...59

. tax credits...513

. taxable income..486

Nothings

. defined..240

Notice of objection — see also Appeals

. appeal procedure...26

. assessment or reassessment of taxes......................782

. GST..783

O

Old Age Security benefits

. provisions dealing with...12

. taxation...520

Onus of proof

. administration and enforcement of Act........................26

                                                                    Page
Options
. capital gain...386
. Capital Property..386

                              P

Paid-up capital
. adjustments...803
. concept...803
. no par value shares.....................................803
. par value shares...803
. reduction, shares issued as consideration
. . on rollovers...864
. stated capital...803

Part IV tax
. anti-avoidance rule.....................................660
. assessable dividends..................................658
. conditions summarized................................661
. connected corporations...............................658
. dividend refund...660
. flow-through of dividends.............................665
. portfolio dividends......................................658
. private corporations....................................658
. reduced by non-capital losses.....................662
. subject corporations....................................658

Partnerships
. allocations, anti-avoidance..........................958
. Canadian, defined.......................................964
. cessation..988
. computation of taxable income....................959
. continuation..991
. corporate..987
. . associated corporation rules......................637
. . small business deductions.........................637
. defined...955
. depreciable capital property transfer............965
. distinguished from joint venture...................955
. GST application...993
. . continuation of partnership........................996
. . joint and several liability............................995
. . partnership interest...................................994
. . property transfer to partners......................994
. . transfer of assets......................................994
. income...956
. information return to partners......................956
. interest...960
. . adjusted cost base....................................961
. . defined...961
. . gains or losses on disposition...................961
. . negative adjusted cost base......................962
. loss deduction limitation..............................958
. reorganization...963
. . transfer of property to corporation.............963
. . transfer of property to partnership.............964
. tax credits..959
. taxable income...959
. terminated, fiscal period..............................967
. transfer of assets to proprietorship..............988
. treatment under Excise Tax Act...................993

Passenger vehicles — see Automobiles

Payments
. indirect, income..427
. retroactive lump sum...................................521

Penalties
. failure to file return.....................................758
. gross negligence on returns.........................758
. incomplete returns......................................758
. late filing of returns....................................758

                                                                    Page
Penalties — continued
. RRSP excess contributions..........................437

Pension adjustment
. calculation..437
. deferred profit sharing plans........................437
. defined benefit pension plans.......................437
. money purchase pension plans....................437
. net past service..470
. reversals...470

Pensions — see also Registered pension plans
. income, transfer to registered plans.............447
. income inclusion..421
. tax credit, age requirement..........................494

Permanent establishment
. allocation of taxable income.........................576
. cases re meaning of....................................576
. defined...576
. international tax convention............................46

Personal property — see Capital personal
             property, Listed personal property

Personal services business
. defined...628

Personal tax credits
. categories and computation..........................489

Personal-use property
. capital gains and losses..............................328
. deemed cost and proceeds..........................328
. listed personal property...............................329
. real property, GST application......................361

Political contributions
. non-deductible business expenses...............167
. tax credits..520

Portfolio dividends — see Dividends

Prescribed proxy amount
. scientific research expenditures....................642

Principal residence
. capital gain...325, 380
. . disposition..325
. . exemption...325
. . exemption, change in use..........................380
. . land used in farming business...................361
. . residences owned after Dec. 31, 1981......355
. . residences owned on Dec. 31, 1981.........325
. . 1-plus rule..325
. change of use...382
. defined...360
. designation...325
. employees transferred.................................382
. joint-ownership..385
. options...381
. ordinarily inhabited......................................386
. single-ownership...383
. transfer between spouses............................383

Private corporations
. capital dividend account..............................805
. dividend refund...660
. integration of business and
      investment income..................................619
. . major tools in Act.....................................621
. . objectives...621
. . problems addressed by.............................621
. . taxation of dividends to individuals............622
. Part IV tax on portfolio and other
      dividends..658

Page

Private corporations — continued
. small business deductions — see Small
   business deductions

Prizes
. lottery, cost..335

Proceeds of disposition
. defined...322

Profit sharing plans
. employer's contributions............................179

Profits
. betting and gambling...................................187
. determination, generally accepted
   accounting principles...................................15
. illegal business...158

Property
. benefits to shareholders..............................271
. capital — see Capital property
. change in use..235
. . change in proportion...................................237
. . income-producing to other purposes..........236
. . non-income-producing to income-
      producing..236
. . property acquired for multiple purposes......237
. contribution to RRSP....................................430
. convertible
. . GST applications..950
. . rollover provisions......................................933
. damages on loss..158
. depreciable — see Depreciable property
. disposition — see Property disposition
. exchange, capital gains................................367
. identical — see Identical properties
. income — see Property income
. leasing, capital cost allowance.....................260
. limited-life intangible, capital cost
   allowance...231
. more than one use, capital gains..................378
. owned on Dec. 31, 1971, adjusted cost base.....411
. personal use — see Personal-use property
. pre-1972, capital gains.................................411
. real — see Real property
. replacement...232
. soft costs..299
. taxes on land...299

Property disposition
. additional deferral, election..........................373
. change in use..235
. debts established to be bad..........................389
. deemed
. . change of use...378
. . death of taxpayer..398
. . leaving and entering Canada.......................385
. defined...226
. election for additional deferral......................373
. involuntary...232
. land and building sold together.....................373
. part disposition
. . capital gains...367
. . depreciable property...................................232
. proceeds — see Property disposition
   proceeds
. transfer to spouse
. . attribution rules..394
. . avoidance of recapture................................396
. voluntary...233

Page

Property disposition proceeds
. capital cost allowance..................................231
. change in use..235
. debts established to be bad..........................389
. deemed
. . death of taxpayer..398
. . exchange of property...................................368
. . leaving and entering Canada.......................385
. depreciable property....................................232
. . expropriation proceeds...............................232
. . involuntary...232
. . pre-1972 assets...411
. . voluntary...233
. non-arm's length transactions......................392
. options...386
. part dispositions..367

Property income
. attribution...278
. . conceptual summary...................................283
. comparison with business income.........263, 297
. deductions..285
. dividends..269
. GST application..313
. inclusions...265
. interest...265
. shareholder benefits or loans.......................271

Property transfers — see also Rollovers
. affiliated persons, capital losses...................870
. cessation of partnership...............................988
. GST applications..950
. . commercial property...................................917
. income attribution..278
. partner to partnership..................................967
. . depreciable capital property.......................965
. . fair market value..964
. . GST application..993
. . majority interest partner.............................965
. partnership to partners.................................988
. . cessation of partnership.............................988
. . GST application..993
. partnership to sole proprietorship.................989
. shareholder to corporation...........................926
. . schematic summary....................................880
. . shareholders position.................................863
. shares of small business corporations...........939

Province
. income not earned in....................................515

Provincial tax
. corporations
. . allocation of taxable income........................578
. . federal abatement.......................................577
. . permanent establishment............................576
. non-deductible business expenses................199

Purchases — see Supplies and purchases

R

Rate Reduction
. CCPC..626

Real property — see also Capital real property
. personal-use, GST application.......................361

Reassessments
. GST..782
. objections and appeals................................770
. onus of proof...767
. tax returns..767
. waiver of time limit......................................767

	Page
Recapture	
. capital cost allowances claimed	228, 258
Refundable dividend tax on hand	
. defined	655
. investment income, special taxes	655
. principal components	655
Refundable taxes	
. capital gains eligible for, flow-through	666
. deeming rules	656
. incorporating investment income eligible for	669
Refunds	
. overpayment of GST	782
. overpayment of income tax	770
Registered education savings plans	
. Canada Education Savings Grant	425
. income from	425
Registered pension plans	
. contribution deductions	109
. . post-1989 service	111
. employer's contributions	179
Registered Pension Plans	
. pre-1990 deductions while a contributor	148
. pre-1990 deductions while not a contributor	147
Registered pension plans	
. shareholder-manager benefits	704
. transfer provisions	447
Registered retirement income fund	
. income from	421
. rules applicable	447
. transfers on death	445
Registered retirement savings plans	
. contributions	
. . additional	437
. . excess, penalty	437
. . limits	434
. . maximum annual limits	434
. . property contributed for	438
. . room carried forward	437
. features	432
. financial institution plans	432
. income from	424
. integration of limits	433
. life insurance company plans	432
. overpayments of receipts, deductions	439
. retirement options	443
. . fixed-term and life annuities	444
. rules applicable	430
. self-administered plans	433
. shareholder-manager's contributions	751
. spousal	
. . attribution on	441
. . contributions to	440
. tax-free withdrawals for learning	442
. threshold amount for excess contributions	438
. transfer provisions	447
. . direct transfers	447
. . on death	445
. . retiring allowance	447
. types	432
. withdrawals before retirement	441
. withdrawals under Home Buyers' Plan	441
Reimbursement	
. deductible expenses	164
. meaning	89

	Page
Related persons	
. associated corporations	631
. benefit on transfer of property	873
. . conceptual example	871
. defined	392
. income attribution	279
Remunerations — see also Salary and wages	
. income	80
. shareholder-managers — see Shareholder-managers	
. unpaid, non-deductible business expenses	166
Rental property	
. capital cost allowance	287
. GST application	313
. losses	287
. separate classes	287
Representation	
. expenses	180
Research Software	
. advanced comands	1044
. . CCH comentary infobase	1045
. . dominion tax cases	1046
. . income tax forms and guides	1046
. . window on Canadian tax	1046
. advanced query	1003
. . results map	1004
. document screen	1008
. . go to template	1014
. . main menu	1010
. . navigation	1012
. . status bar	1016
. . toolbar	1011
. errors	1037
. Folio 4.3 software	
. . content overview	1001
. . launcher screen	1001
. . options	1002
. help infobases	1042
. installation	1000
. . content overview	1000
. . minimum system requirements	1000
. multiple infobases	1048
. printing	1039
. . print document alternatives	1041
. queries and visual presentations	1019
. . contents options	1025
. . general options	1020
. . hit list options	1026
. . internet options	1024
. . print options	1021
. saving	1039
. search and navigation	1027
. . acronyms	1047
. . AND search comand	1031
. . helpful hints	1036
. . legislative changes	1047
. . OR search command	1029
. . phrase searches	1034
. . specific provisions	1036
. . unordered proximity connector	1046
. speciality queries	1049
. . serial queries	1050
. . stem queries	1050
. . thesaurus queries	1049
. . wildcard queries	1050
. table of contents screen	1005
. . expanded table of contents screen	1007

Page

Research Software — continued
. viewing and navigating......................................1017
.. hit list..1018
. tagging..1039

Residence — see also Principal residence
. corporations..54
.. common law concept...54
.. comprehensive considerations.............................56
.. deemed...54
. full-time, tax liability
.. common law concept...42
.. deemed...42
.. departmental practice..43
. individuals
.. analysis of fact situation.......................................51
.. Checklist of Facts..49
.. Comprehensive Consideration.............................50
.. non-tax factors...53
.. Summary...48
. part-time, tax liability..44

Residential property
. GST application rules...361

Residents
. absent from Canada
.. moving, child care and attendant care
    expenses..456
. GST registration, requirements.............................59
. tax liability..41

Restricted farm losses
. carryover...481
. limitations on deduction...481

Retirement
. options re RRSPs..443
.. fixed-term and life annuities.................................443
. shareholder-manager benefits..............................704
. withdrawal from RRSP before...............................441

Retirement compensation arrangement
. contributions, refundable tax.................................218

Retirement pension plans
. earned income, defined..436
. integration of limits...433
. objectives of pension reform.................................430
. types of tax-assisted plans....................................431

Retiring allowances
. income inclusion...421
. transfer provisions...447

Returns
. amended..771
. assessment..767
. deceased person's...775
.. prior taxation years...775
. failure to file...758
. false statements or omissions...............................758
. filing due dates...757
. GST...777
.. amended...783
. incomplete...758
. late filing...758
. penalties...758
. terminal...776

Rights or things
. deceased person's...775

Rollovers — see also Property transfers
. amalgamations
.. provisions of section 87..931

Page

Rollovers
. amalgamations — continued
.. statutory...931
. asset freeze..942
. capital reorganizations..922
.. benefit rule...929
.. calculation procedure for sec. 86.......................923
.. conceptual view of sec. 86...................................923
.. conditions...923
. commercial property, GST application..................917
. continuation of partnership....................................996
. convertible properties..939
. corporate securities...939
. depreciable capital property..................................868
.. limitations on transferee's cost base..................869
.. terminal losses..869
. estate freeze...940
. exchange of property, capital gains......................368
. internal freeze...942
. inter-spousal transfers...939
. partnership property to partners...........................994
. partnership property to sole proprietorship.........995
. reverse freeze..942
. sec. 85..920
. share for share exchange......................................924
.. conditions...920
.. consequences...921
. shareholder to corporation....................................850
.. basic rules..857
.. benefits, conceptual example..............................874
.. benefits on related persons.................................873
.. benefits on shareholders......................................873
.. corporation's position...862
.. depreciable capital property.................................868
.. election...857
.. fair market value...881
.. paid-up capital reduction on shares
    issued as consideration....................................864
.. restrictions on elected price.................................859
.. schematic summary...880
.. sec. 22 election...882
.. shareholders' position...863
.. specific situations...850
.. summary of rules...880
.. shares..939
. winding-up of subsidiary..935

S

Salary and wages — see also Remunerations
. income computation..80
. shareholder-managers...701
.. salary versus dividends..710

Salespersons
. business income...185
. expenses...185
.. deductions...104
. travelling allowances...89

Scholarships — see also Grants and subsidies
. income inclusion...426

**Scientific research and experimental
    development**
. deduction of expenditures......................................191
. election to determine deduction............................193
. investment tax credit..595
.. capital expenditures..643
.. prescribed proxy amount......................................642
. meaning...191

Page

Securities — see also Shares
. Canadian, election re disposition............................321
. capital gains...392
. rollover...939
. . GST applications...950

Self-employed persons
. tests to determine..77

Shareholder loans
. application of rules...276
. capacity (*qua*) issue.......................................704
. deduction of repayment.......................................273
. exceptions to rules..272
. home purchase..274
. imputed interest..274, 707
. principal..272
. tax treatment..705

Shareholder-managers
. company car benefits...709
. CPP contributions..750
. distributions out of
. . income not eligible for small business
. . . deduction..716
. . income taxed at small business rate.......................711
. fringe benefits..708
. income splitting between spouses............................708
. life insurance benefits.....................................709
. remunerations...701
. . accrued bonuses...702
. . bonus...701
. . bonus versus dividends...............................698, 717
. . deferral of tax on dividends.............................719
. . dividends as...710
. . employment remuneration..................................698
. . income splitting between spouses.........................708
. . salary and bonus...701
. . use of holding company...................................718
. . using corporation..697
. retiring allowances...708
. RPP benefits..708
. RRSP contributions..751
. salary versus dividends.....................................710
. summary...717
. sickness or accident insurance benefits....................708

Shareholders
. benefits
. . capacity (*qua*) issue....................................704
. . GST application...298
. benefits and loans..704
. benefits on transfer of property...........................878
. . schematic summary...880
. benefits received from corporation..........................271
. loans — see Shareholder loans
. sec. 85 rollovers, GST application..........................917
. transfer of property to corporations.......................850
. . basic rules...857
. . benefits, conceptual example..............................874
. . benefits on related persons...............................877
. . benefits on shareholders..................................873
. . corporation's position....................................862
. . depreciable capital property..............................868
. . fair market value...881
. . GST application...917
. . paid-up capital reduction on shares
. . . issued as consideration.................................864
. . restrictions on elected price.............................858
. . rollover application.......................................857
. . schematic summary...880

Page

Shareholders
. transfer of property to corporations — continued
. . sec. 22 election..882
. . shareholder's position....................................863
. . specific situations.......................................851

Shares — see also Securities
. collateralized preferred....................................911
. deemed capital property.....................................392
. for share exchange
. . GST application...950
. . rollovers...920
. . rollovers, conditions.....................................920
. . rollovers, consequences...................................921
. issuing expenses..175
. non-arm's length sale
. . basic rules of ssec. 84.1(1)..............................889
. . conditions for sec. 84.1 to apply.........................889
. . dividend strips...887
. . paid-up capital...803
. . reduction on shares issued as
. . . consideration...864
. reorganization of capital...................................922
. . benefit rule...929
. . calculation procedure for sec. 86........................923
. . conceptual view of sec. 86...............................923
. . conditions...923
. rollover provisions..939
. . GST applications...950
. sale of incorporated business..............................818
. . analysis for decision.....................................818
. sale to unrelated person
. . capital gains strips......................................900
. . effects of sec. 55..900
. . exceptions to ssec. 55 rule...............................903
. . situations addressed by sec. 55..........................900

Site
. investigation expenses......................................180

Small business corporations
. allowable business investment losses.......................340
. defined...720
. qualified shares..720
. . basic asset test...724
. . basic asset test, modification...........................724
. . basic rules of application...............................722
. . holding period test......................................724
. . SBC test...724

Small business deductions
. active business...624
. . defined..627
. calculation, basic limits...................................625
. Canadian-controlled private corporation,
. . basic limits...625
. corporate partnership.......................................638
. distributions out of
. . income eligible for......................................711
. . income not eligible for..................................716
. distributions to shareholder-managers, tax
. . cost or saving...711
. investment tax credit.......................................640
. large CCPCs not eligible....................................626
. manufacturing and processing business......................638
. tax rates on eligible income...............................624

Soft costs
. construction of buildings...................................287
. GST application...299
. land ownership...287

Software — see Research Software

Page

Sole proprietorship
. business income.................................... 163
. fiscal period....................................... 163
. partnership property transfer to.............. 989

Specified financial institutions — see Financial institutions

Specified investment business
. defined.. 627

Split Income
. Taxes.. 975

Spouses — see also Married persons
. attribution of capital gains on transfers........ 394
. . recapture avoidance............................ 396
. attribution of trust income....................... 973
. child care expense deductions.................. 452
. income attribution................................. 279
. income splitting.................................... 708
. . attribution through corporation............... 731
. principal residence, transfer between........... 383
. RRSP
. . attribution on................................... 441
. . contribution to................................. 441
. support payments
. . deduction....................................... 442
. . income inclusion............................... 424
. unused tax credits, transfer to................ 508

Stock dividends
. cost... 335

Stock options — see also Employee stock options
. adjusted cost base................................ 336
. employment income................................ 99

Stop-loss Rules
. Summary.. 873

Students
. education tax credit............................... 505
. . carryforward.................................... 506
. . transfer to parent or grandparent............ 506
. loans, tax credit for interest.................... 508
. tuition tax credit................................. 505
. . carryforward.................................... 506
. . transfer to parent or grandparent............ 506

Subsidiaries
. winding-up, rollover provisions.................. 1015

Supplies and purchases
. GST application..................................... 57
. . concept.. 32
. . exempt... 33
. . non-residents.................................... 61
. . zero-rated....................................... 33
. input tax credits.................................. 34

Support payments
. deduction... 422
. income inclusion................................... 422

Supreme Court of Canada
. appeals... 27

T

Tax
. abatement re income earned in a
    province... 575
. avoidance — see Tax avoidance
. characteristics...................................... 4
. classification....................................... 3

Page

Tax — continued
. computation
. . corporations — see Tax computation,
        corporations
. . individuals — see Tax computation,
        individuals
. . provisions of the Act........................... 11
. trusts — see Tax computation, trusts
. credits — see Tax credits
. constitutional basis............................... 3
. evasion, different from avoidance,
        planning.. 27
. GST, remittance.................................... 777
. interest on overpayments......................... 770
. liability.. 11
. payment — see Tax payment
. planning — see Tax planning
. rates — see Tax rates
. refunds... 829
. shelters, depreciation-based..................... 289

Tax avoidance
. capital gains....................................... 321
. distinction from evasion, planning.............. 27
. general anti-avoidance rule
. . Excise Tax Act.................................. 753
. . Income Tax Act................................. 734

Tax computation, corporations
. basic... 573
. classification for tax purposes.................. 573
. federal tax abatement............................ 575
. foreign tax credits................................ 588
. investment tax credit............................. 595
. large corporations................................ 580
. rates, general federal............................ 574
. taxable income earned in a province........... 578

Tax computation, individuals
. age credits... 493
. alternative minimum tax.......................... 524
. . adjusted taxable income....................... 524
. . basic credits.................................... 525
. . basic exemption................................ 525
. . carryforward.................................... 525
. . impact of....................................... 525
. . minimum amount............................... 524
. annual indexing adjustments..................... 487
. application of rules............................... 522
. basic... 487
. caregiver tax credit............................... 492
. charitable donations tax credits................ 496
. CPP contributions tax credits................... 508
. dependants... 492
. dividend tax credits.............................. 511
. education tax credits............................. 505
. . carryforward.................................... 506
. . transfer to parents............................ 506
. EI premiums tax credits.......................... 508
. employment outside Canada, tax credits...... 515
. equivalent-to-married status..................... 490
. GST credits.. 515
. married status..................................... 490
. medical expense tax credits..................... 498
. . notch provision................................. 502
. . supplemental.................................... 517
. mental or physical impairment tax credits..... 504
. . transfer... 508
. Old Age Security benefits........................ 520
. ordering of credits................................ 514

	Page
Tax computation, individuals — continued	
. pension credits	494
. personal amounts	492
. political contributions tax credits	520
. single status	492
. summary	487
. tax calculation	487
. tax credits	489
. . application of rules	522
. . transfer to spouse	508
. . types	488
. tax credits for interest on student loans	508
. tax rates	487
. tuition fees tax credits	505
. . carryforward	506
. . transfer to parents	506
. wholly dependent persons	490
Tax computation, trusts	
. fiscal years	975
. minimum tax	976
. tax credit	976
. tax rate	976
Tax Court of Canada	
. appeals	26
Tax credits	
. adoption expense	510
. age credit	493
. annual indexing adjustment	487
. basic alternative minimum tax credits for individual	525
. Canada Pension Plan contributions	508
. caregiver	492
. caregiver and infirm dependant	492
. charitable donations	496
. computation, application of rules	522
. dependants	492
. dividends	511
. . election	511
. education	506
. . carryforward	506
. . transfer to parent or grandparent	506
. Employment Insurance premiums	508
. employment outside Canada	515
. equivalent-to-married status	490
. foreign — see Foreign tax credits	
. individuals	487
. input — see Input tax credits	
. interest on student loans	508
. investment — see Investment tax credits	
. manufacturing and processing	
. . eligibility	583
. . industries	583
. . rates applicable	583
. married status	490
. medical expenses	498
. . notch provision	502
. . supplemental	517
. mental or physical impairment	504
. . transfer	504
. non-refundable	489
. . ordering rules	19
. non-residents	515
. ordering of	514
. partnerships	987
. part-time residents	513
. pension	494
. personal amounts	492

	Page
Tax credits — continued	
. political contributions	520
. single status	492
. transfer to spouse	508
. tuition fees	505
. . carryforward	506
. . transfer to parent or grandparent	506
. wholly dependent persons	489
Tax payment	
. corporations	764
. deceased person	775
. employer's obligation	772
. individuals	762
. obligations under Excise Tax Act	777
. trustees obligation	773
Tax planning	
. . different from avoidance, evasion	27
Tax rates	
. corporations	574
. individuals	487
. trusts	976
Tax reform	
. guidelines	5
Tax treaties — see International tax conventions	
Taxable income	
. computation	
. . corporations	539
. . individuals	473
. . partnerships	959
. determination	18
. provisions of the Act	11
Taxable income, corporations	
. after-tax financing	541
. allowable business investment losses	545
. deduction of net capital losses to preserve non-capital losses	549
. deductions available	539
. . charitable donations	542
. general rates	574
. loss carryovers	543
. . ordering of deductions	548
. . restrictions on deductions	548
. net capital losses	546
. . carryovers	546
. non-capital losses	543
. taxable dividends deduction	539
Taxable income, individuals	
. business investment losses	340
. capital gains deduction	481
. employee stock options	473
. farm losses	481
. home relocation loan deduction	476
. loss carryovers	478
. miscellaneous receipts	476
. net-capital loss	479
. non-capital loss	478
. non-residents	486
. restricted farm losses	481
Taxable preferred shares — see Shares	
Taxation year	
. corporation's year-end, acquisition of control	553
. deceased taxpayer	775
. less than 12 months	225

	Page
Taxpayers	
. books and records	767
. . GST	777
. deceased — see Deceased persons	
. obligations under Excise Tax Act	777
. rights and obligations under Income Tax Act	770
Term preferred shares — see Shares	
Terminal losses	
. buildings sold with land	376
. role in CCA system	228
. transfer of depreciable property to partnership	964
Testamentary trusts — see Trusts	
Trade-ins	
. GST application	363
Transfers — see Property transfers	
Travelling expenses	
. allowances, exception	90
. deduction	104
. . conditions	106
. . limitations	107
. . part-time employee's	107
Trusts	
. attribution rules	973
. capital interest, disposition	992
. capital property, disposition	991
. commercial	970
. computation of tax	975
. . minimum tax	976
. defined	968
. discretionary	970
. . accumulation of income	975
. fiscal year	975
. GST application	993
. . distribution of property	997
. . liability of trustees	997
. income	
. . computation	972
. . payable to beneficiary	972
. income interest, disposition	972
. *inter vivos*	970
. non-discretionary	970
. personal	970
. residency	969
. settlement	972
. . GST application	996

	Page
Trusts — continued	
. spousal	971
. tax credits	976
. tax rates	976
. tax returns, filing due dates	757
. testamentary	970
. treatment under Excise Tax Act	996
. types	970
Tuition fees	
. tax credit	505
. . carryforward	506
. . transfer to parent or grandparent	506
U	
Used goods	
. GST application rules on sales	363
Utilities	
. service connection expenses	180
V	
Valuation Day value	
. assets owned on Dec. 31, 1971	354
W	
Warranties	
. business expense	414
Winding-up	
. Canadian corporation	
. . application of rules	821
. . deemed dividends	810
. . disposition of net assets	818
. . GST	832
. . procedure summarized	823
. components of distribution, illustration	820
. deemed dividends	880
. GST applications	951
. subsidiaries, rollover provisions	935
Withholding tax	
. obligation	773
. payments to non-residents	774
Work in progress	
. professional business	191
Work space in home	
. deductions allowed	109
. expenses, deduction prohibited	168